The **Rough Guide** to

Cuba

written and researched by

Fiona McAuslan and Matt Norman

NEW YORK • LONDON • DELHI

www.roughguides.com

Contents

Coastal Cuba colour
section following p.312

**Cuban music and
dance** colour section
following p.536

◄◄ Varadero beach ◄ El Morro, Habana del Este

Introduction to
Cuba

**Long known for its isolation from the Western world
and its precarious relationship with the United States
in particular, the last decade has seen Cuba emerge as
one of the top tourist destinations in the Caribbean, as
well as the leading political light in leftist Latin America.
Communist credentials notwithstanding, this is a nation
that well understands the commercial power of rebranding
and has reinvented itself as the home of sun, *salsa* and
rum with a unique blend of chutzpah and casual manner
that's intrinsic to the Cuban character.**

Shaped by one of the twentieth century's
longest-surviving revolutions, Cuba's image
was inextricably bound up with its politics
until relatively recently. Even five decades
after Fidel Castro and the rebels seized power,
Cuba's long satiny beaches, offshore cays and
jungle-covered peaks – the defining attractions
of neighbouring islands – played almost no part in the popular international
perception of this communist state in the Caribbean. Now, having opened the
floodgates to global tourism, the country is characterized as much as anything
by a frenetic sense of transition as it shifts from socialist stronghold to one of
the Caribbean's major tourist destinations, running on capitalist money.

At the same time, visitors may think that nothing has changed for decades,
even centuries. Cut off from the capitalist world until the end of the
Cold War, and hit hard by the economic crisis that followed the collapse
of the Soviet Union (which provided hefty subsidies to this communist
outpost that thumbed its nose at nearby America), the face of modern-day
Cuba is in many respects frozen in the past – the classic American cars,
mustachioed cigar-smoking farmers, horse-drawn carriages and colonial
Spanish architecture, all apparently unaffected by the breakneck pace
of modernization. At the same time, you will see many newly opened
department stores and shopping malls, state-of-the-art hotels and entire
resorts created from scratch, an improbable combination of transformation

Fact file

• Cuba lies at the mouth of the Gulf of Mexico and is bound on the south by the Caribbean Sea and on the north and east by the Atlantic Ocean. It is the largest island in the Caribbean and covers 110,861 sq km.

• Cuba has a 95.7% literacy rate, the highest in all of Latin America. Life expectancy at birth is 76 years, also the highest in Latin America.

• Ethnically, the population is predominantly of mixed African and European ancestry, as the indigenous Taíno who inhabited Cuba before Columbus's arrival were almost entirely wiped out by Spanish invasion and European diseases. The population is currently 51 percent mixed race, 37 percent white, 11 percent black and 1 percent Asian.

• Cuba is a republic with a centralized socialist government. Political power rests with the Popular Power National Assembly, which nominates the Council of Ministers, the highest executive body. The Communist Party is enshrined in the constitution as the only legal political party.

• Tourism is the country's main industry, while sugar is the second. It's estimated that some 3% of the economy is constituted by remittances sent to family members here by Cuban-Americans.

and stasis that's symbolic of this contradiction-riddled country. Besides being sharply split between modern and traditional, Cuba is a country which, in a sense, has become divided by tourism. Foreign visitors are the surest way of bringing in hard currency, which has led to the development of a two-tier economic system whereby anybody with the means to make money out of tourists is automatically better off than just about everyone else. In a place where taxi drivers earn more than doctors, and where capitalist reforms are seen as the answer to preserving socialist ideals, understanding Cuba is a compelling but never-ending task.

Despite the hard-to-swallow favourable treatment of tourists and the crippling US trade embargo, there is surprisingly little resentment directed at foreign visitors, and your overwhelming impression is likely to be that Cubans are outgoing, sociable and hospitable, notwithstanding the queues, food rationing, free-speech restrictions and the government's reliance on foreign investment and tourism. What's more, in most of Cuba it's difficult not to

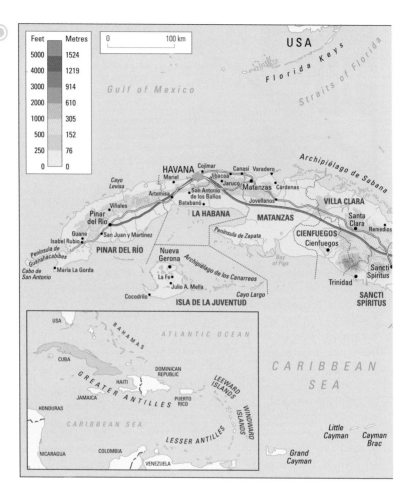

come into contact with local people: the common practices of renting out rooms (*casas particulares*) and opening restaurants in homes (*paladares*) allow visitors stronger impressions of the country than they might have thought possible in a short visit. The much-vaunted Cuban capacity for a good time is best expressed through music and dance, both vital facets of

Understanding Cuba is a compelling but never-ending task

the island's culture. As originators of the most influential Latin music styles, such as *bolero*, *rumba* and *son*, thereby spawning the most famous of them all – *salsa* – people in Cuba seem always ready to party.

Surging forward into its second decade, there is much more to Cuba's tourism industry than the central tenets of music, revolution and rum.

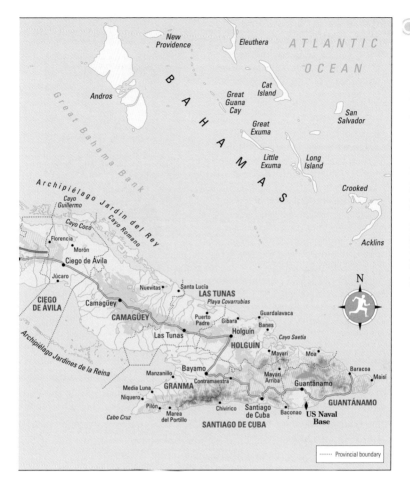

For those seeking a more cultural visit, there is plenty of pre-Revolution opulence illustrated by Art Deco architecture and decadent interiors, as well as a vibrant arts scene and Cuba's legendary musicians.

You are bound to come across occasional reminders that Cuba is a centralized, highly bureaucratic one-party state, which can give a holiday here an unfamiliar twist, especially if and when things go wrong. Going to the police, finding your hotel room double-booked or simply needing to make an urgent phone call can prove to be unnecessarily and frustratingly complicated. These are the times when you discover Cuba has its own special logic and that common sense doesn't count for much here. This is not to say you're more likely to experience mishaps in Cuba than anywhere else – not only are all the major resorts well equipped, but

Street art

As with much of Cuban culture, some of the most captivating **artwork** can be found not within the walls of institutions, but on the streets. Calligraphic eulogies to José Martí and the bons mots of Che and Fidel unfurl along city walls, while drab apartment blocks are enlivened with bold murals in bright colours. In recent years urban graffiti has become more prevalent, with foreign and homegrown artists leaving their mark. Keen-eyed visitors will spot iconic images by British graffitist Banksy, particularly in Habana Vieja, while French graffiti collaborative Mosko et Associes have sown a menagerie of animals throughout Cuba. Perhaps the most arresting mural is in Regla (a suburb of Havana), where a collaboration between Cuban artists and the Brazilian graffitists Os Gemeos has created a dreamy fairyland near the main square. Catch it while you can – street art is a beautiful but transitory pleasure in Cuba, as the sea air is very corrosive.

violent crime is remarkably absent from Cuban cities. On the other hand, a certain determination and a laid-back attitude are essential requirements for exploring less-visited parts of the country, where a paucity of facilities and reliable public transport can make travelling hard work. Although the tourist infrastructure has been slowly and steadily improving over the years, a recent slight downturn in travel here, coupled with hurricane damage, could potentially slow these improvements.

The perception that Cuba sees tourists as little more than deep pockets is pervasive, but there are still ways to make the most of a trip without breaking the bank. Compared to some areas of Latin America, Cuba can seem expensive, but simply choosing to stay in a *casa particular* instead of a hotel, buying produce in the markets and visiting less commercial resorts are all ways to spend less while simultaneously enriching your trip with authentic experience. For the foreign visitor, things are becoming easier all the time, though, with the introduction of more efficient bus services, simplified currency systems and a wider variety of consumer goods. Ironically, these improvements also mark an irreversible move away from what makes Cuba unique. Inevitably you'll need to scratch harder at the surface these days to uncover something most visitors haven't. Virgin beaches, untouched diving and fishing areas, quaint, unaffected villages and hidden *paladares* are fewer and further between. Though the nation's unique culture and resourceful character will always ensure that Cuba is more than just another island paradise, the determination to sell the country to a worldwide market means the time to go is now rather than later.

Where to go

No trip to Cuba would be complete without a visit to the potent capital, **Havana**. A unique and personable mini-metropolis characterized by a small-town atmosphere, its time-warped colonial core, Habana Vieja, is crammed with architectural splendours, some laced with Moorish traces and dating as far back as the sixteenth century. Elsewhere in the city there are handsome streets unspoilt by tawdry multinational chain stores and restaurants: urban development here has been undertaken sensitively, with the city retaining many of its colonial mansions and numerous 1950s hallmarks.

The provinces to the immediate east and west of Havana, together with the capital itself, are where tourist attractions are most densely concentrated. Visited frequently by day-trippers from Havana, **Pinar del Río**, the centre of nature tourism in Cuba, offers more than enough to sustain a longer stay.

The most accessible resorts here are **Las Terrazas** and **Soroa**, focused around the subtropical, smooth-topped mountain ranges of the Sierra del Rosario and Sierra de los Organos, but it's the peculiar *mogote* hills of the prehistoric **Viñales Valley** that attract most attention. Beyond, on a gnarled rod of land pointing out towards Mexico, there's unparalleled seclusion and outstanding scuba diving at **María la Gorda**.

There are **beach resorts** the length and breadth of the country but none is more complete than **Varadero**, the country's long-time

▼ Iglesia de la Caridad del Cobre

Micro-capitalism

Private enterprise in Cuba, with all the strict rules and regulations that govern it, expresses itself in some pretty novel ways. Small-scale businesses, whose impact on state control of the economy is all but insignificant, have flourished in the jamboree of street-side vendors found in neighbourhoods across the land. The most common are the front-room caterers, the Cuban answer to the local candy store or mobile café, banging out everything from cakes and peanut bars to pizzas and sandwiches. Understanding the need to extend the life of seemingly replaceable items, enterprising businesspeople have developed roaring trades in cigarette lighter refuelling, watch mending, and bike-tyre repair. And tourism creates a market for another line of production that Cubans can supply, namely old books or handmade arts and crafts, often both sold in hallway shops and front-room galleries.

premier holiday destination, two hours' drive east from Havana, in **Matanzas province**. Based on a highway of dazzling white sand that stretches almost the entire length of the 25-kilometre **Península de Hicacos**, this is where most tourists come for the classic package-holiday experience. For the tried-and-tested combination of disco-nightlife, watersports, sunbathing and relaxing in all-inclusive hotels, there is nowhere better in Cuba. On the opposite side of the province, the **Península de Zapata**, with its diversity of wildlife, organized excursions and mixture of hotels, offers a melange of different possibilities. The grittier towns of **Cárdenas** and the provincial capital **Matanzas** contrast with Varadero's made-to-measure appeal, but it's the nearby natural attractions of the **Bellamar caves** and the verdant splendour of the **Yumurí Valley** that provide the focus for most day-trips.

Across the eastern border from Matanzas in **Cienfuegos province**, tourist attractions are harder to come by. Travelling east of here, either on the *autopista* or the island-long Carretera Central, public transport links become weaker and picturesque, but worn-out towns take over from brochure-friendly hot spots. There is, however, a concentration of activity around the historically precious **Trinidad**, a small colonial

Revolutionary icons

There is no getting away from Cuba's long history of rebellions or its cast of characters. In every village, town and city, the same names crop up time and again, in the titles of museums, squares, hospitals, schools and streets. José Martí, Antonio Maceo and Máximo Gómez, all heroes of the nineteenth-century Wars of Independence, as well as Camilo Cienfuegos and Che Guevara, who both fought in the Revolutionary War of the 1950s, have all become almost mythical in status. The State never misses an opportunity to remind its citizens of the ideals they should aspire to emulate: rare is the town that doesn't have a Parque Martí or an Avenida Camilo Cienfuegos, while busts and statues, particularly of Martí and Maceo, are everywhere you look.

city brimming with symbols of Cuba's past, which attracts group tours and backpackers in equal numbers. If you're intending to spend more than a few days in the island's centre, this is by far the best base, within short taxi rides of a small but well-equipped beach resort, the **Península de Ancón**, and the **Topes de Collantes** hiking centre in the **Sierra del Escambray**. Slightly further afield from Trinidad are a few larger cities: sociable **Santa Clara** with its convivial main square and thronging crowds of students is the liveliest of the lot, while laid-back **Cienfuegos**, next to the placid waters of a sweeping bay, is sprinkled with colourful architecture, including a splendid nineteenth-century theatre. Further east, the workaday cities of **Sancti Spíritus** and **Ciego de Ávila**, both capitals of their namesake provinces, provide excellent stopoffs on a journey along the Carretera Central. Two of the most popular destinations in this part of the country,

> The much-vaunted Cuban capacity for a good time is best expressed through music and dance

the luxurious resorts of **Cayo Coco** and **Cayo Guillermo**, are off the north coast of Ciego de Ávila province, featuring wide swathes of creamy white beaches and tranquil countryside.

Continuing eastwards into **Camagüey province**, the smaller, rather remote resort of **Santa Lucía** is a much promoted though less well-equipped option for sun-seekers, while there's an excellent alternative north of here in tiny **Cayo Sabinal**, with long empty beaches and romantically rustic facilities. Back on the Carretera Central, the romantic and ramshackle city of **Camagüey**, the most populous city in the central part of the island, is a sightseer's delight, with numerous intriguing buildings and a lively nightlife,

▲ A café in Havana

while the amiable city of **Holguín** is the threshold to the province of the same name containing the biggest concentration of pre-Columbian sites in the country. **Guardalavaca**, on the northern coast of Holguín province, is one of the country's liveliest and most attractive resorts, spread along a long and shady beach with ample opportunities for watersports.

While **Guantánamo province**, forming the far eastern tip of the island, is best known for its infamous US naval base (and an odd tourist attraction in itself), it is the jaunty seaside town of **Baracoa** that is the region's most enchanting spot. Isolated from the rest of the country by a high rib of mountains, the quirky town is freckled with colonial houses and populated by friendly and hospitable locals, making it an unrivalled retreat popular with long-term travellers.

Santiago de Cuba province, on the island's southeast coast, could make a holiday in itself, with a sparkling coastline fretted with golden-sand beaches such as **Chivirico**, the undulating emerald mountains of the **Sierra Maestra**, made for trekking, and **Santiago**, the country's most vibrant and energetic city after Havana. Host to the country's most exuberant **carnival** every July, when a deluge of loud, sweet and passionate sounds surges through the streets, the city's musical heritage is testified to by the fact that you can hear some of the best Cuban musicians here all year round. Trekkers and Revolution enthusiasts will want to follow the Sierra Maestra as it snakes west of here along the south coast into **Granma** province, offering various revolutionary landmarks and nature trails.

Lying off the southwest coast of Havana province, the **Isla de la Juventud** is often overlooked, despite its immense though low-key charms. Easily explored over a weekend, the island promises leisurely walks, some of the best diving in the country and a personable capital town in Nueva Gerona. In the same archipelago is luxurious and anodyne **Cayo Largo**, the only sizeable beach resort off the southern coastline of Cuba.

When to go

Cuba has a hot and sunny tropical climate with an average yearly temperature of 24°C, but in the winter months of January and February temperatures can drop as low as 15°C, and even lower at night. This is during the **dry season**, which runs roughly from November to April, when if you intend to go into the mountains it's advisable to pack something warmer than a T-shirt. If you visit Cuba in the summer, and more broadly between May and October, considered the **wet season**, expect it to rain on at least a couple of days over a fortnight. Don't let this put you off, though: although it comes down hard and fast, rain rarely stays for very long in Cuba, and the clouds soon break to allow sunshine through to dry everything out. Eastern Cuba tends to be hotter and more humid during this part of the year, while the temperature in the area around Trinidad and Sancti Spíritus also creeps above the national average. September and October are the most threatening months of the annual **hurricane** season that runs from June to November. Compared to other Caribbean islands and some Central American countries, however, Cuba holds up relatively well even in the fiercest of hurricanes, though rural areas are more vulnerable.

What happens after Fidel?

Cuba watchers have been asking the big question for three decades now, but since July 2006, when Fidel Castro underwent serious intestinal surgery, the answer to the big question has gathered urgency. Following the surgery, Fidel ceded his powers as head of Cuba's Communist party to his brother Raúl and divided up other responsibilities amongst six senior members of the party. Raúl's leadership is likely to be less charismatic than his older brother's, but he's expected to address the inefficiency of state-run enterprises and, it is rumoured, to move away somewhat from a centralized economy. Impassioned, dogmatic and obsessive, Fidel has very much created post-Revolution Cuba in his own image. Though less commanding than Fidel, Raúl may very well bring the country fresh direction and renewed vitality, although some pundits suggest that without Fidel at the helm, long-suppressed factions will open up within the party. One thing is sure, however: Cuba's ability to confound the expectations of critics and admirers alike has been consistently astonishing for nearly fifty years.

The **peak tourist season** in Cuba runs roughly from mid-December to mid-March and all of July and August. Prices are highest and crowds thickest in high summer when the holiday season for Cubans gets under way. As much of the atmosphere of the smaller resorts is generated by tourists, Cuban and foreign, out of season they can seem somewhat dull – although you'll benefit from lower prices. Compared to the all-out celebrations in other countries, **Christmas** in Cuba is a low-key affair. For a long time it was banned on anti-religious grounds and even now the festivities are confined predominantly to the hotels. **New Year's Eve**, also the eve of the anniversary of the Revolution, is much more fervently celebrated. The cities, however, particularly Havana and Santiago, are always buzzing and offer good value for money all year round. For festivals, July and August are the best times to be in Havana and Santiago, while the capital is also enlivened in November by the Latin American International Film Festival.

Average temperatures and rainfall in Havana

	Jan	Feb	Mar	Apr	May	Jun	July	Aug	Sept	Oct	Nov	Dec
Havana												
Temp (°C)	25	25	27	29	29	30	32	32	30	29	27	25
Temp (°F)	78	78	80	84	84	87	89	89	87	84	80	78
Rainfall (mm)	71	46	46	58	119	165	125	135	150	173	79	58
Rainfall (inches)	2.8	1.8	1.8	2.3	4.7	6.5	4.9	5.3	5.9	6.8	3.1	2.3

things not to miss

It's not possible to see everything that Cuba has to offer in one visit, and we don't suggest you try. What follows is a selective taste of the country's highlights, from lively festivals and delicious local cuisine to natural wonders and stunning architecture, arranged in five colour-coded categories. All highlights have a page reference to take you straight into the text, where you can find out more.

01 **Varadero beach** Page **260** • Spend time lazing about the most archetypal Caribbean destination in Cuba, its golden sand backed by palm trees and fronted by unruffled blue-and-green waters.

02 **Baracoa's countryside** Page **481** ● Jewel of the eastern coast, tiny Baracoa makes an ideal base for exploring the verdant rainforest, mountain peaks and tranquil rivers dotted about the eastern coastal region.

03 **Mojitos** Page **62** ● Just the ticket after a hard day on the beach, Cuba's quintessential cocktail, a refreshing concoction of rum, limes and mint, is always welcome.

04 **Necrópolis de Colón** Page **166** ● Wander through the quiet splendour of this extensive cemetery in Havana's Vedado district to simply admire the grandiose mausoleums of the dead.

06 **Edificio Bacardí** Page **112** •
The Bacardí family's pre-Revolution headquarters – a dazzling piece of Art Deco architecture in Habana Vieja – is a fitting place to enjoy a *Cuba Libre*.

05 **Habana Vieja** Page **127** •
Visit one of the most well-preserved colonial centres in the Americas, with postcard-perfect buildings dotted throughout its narrow streets and historic plazas.

08 **Small-town street parties** Page **74** • Attend a weekly street party, where music, barbecues and beer stalls create an ideal opportunity to rub shoulders with locals.

07 **Vintage American car ride** Page **39** • You won't soon forget your first drive in a seemingly frozen-in-time vintage car. The tenacity and longevity of these vehicles are a tribute to both US engineering and Cuban ingenuity.

09 **Baseball** Page **77** • Watch a well-played game of Cuba's national sport alongside an exuberant crowd.

10 **Santiago in July** Page **496** • This is the best time to visit Cuba's second city, when its vibrant music scene boils over and carnival drenches the town in fabulous costumes, excitement and song.

11 **Diving** Pages **316**, **385** & *Coastal Cuba* **colour section** • With some of the most unspoilt coral reefs and other dive sites in the world, Cuba is one of the best places in the Caribbean to go scuba diving.

12 Viñales Page 236 • Particularly enchanting in the morning when mist rises from the valley floor, Viñales is unforgettable.

13 Taking a salsa lesson Page 31 •Learn to dance the Cuban way through private lessons or as part of a packaged *salsa* holiday.

14 Fábrica de Tobaco Partagas Page **145** • Tour the famous Havana cigar factory, for a fascinating look into cigar-making and some idiosyncratic Cuban working practices, too.

15 Staying in a casa particular Page **56** • Rent a room in a Cuban household to get an inside look at daily local living.

17 **Museo Emilio Bacardí Moreau** Page **511** • Take in all manner of art here, from colonial antiquities and Egyptian artefacts to an excellent assortment of contemporary works.

16 **Hershey train** Page **290** • Take a trip on this toy-like electric train that slowly winds through the best of the gentle countryside from Havana province to Matanzas.

18 **Valle de los Ingenios** Page **386** • In the heart of the oceans of sugar cane that make up the Valle de los Ingenios, a colonial estate comes complete with museum and watchtower from which you can take it all in.

19 **Long-distance truck ride** Page 50 • Catching a truck from the side of the motorway is a quintessentially Cuban form of transportation.

20 **Che memorial** Page 346 • Revolutionary devotees should make the pilgrimage to the provincial town of Santa Clara, where the rebel is lovingly commemorated and his remains now lie.

21 **Downtown Trinidad** Page 375 • This sixteenth-century town is brimful of colonial mansions and churches, threaded together by cobbled streets and compact plazas.

22 **Yumurí Valley, Matanzas** Page **300** • This lush, overgrown valley looks spectacular from the hillsides which form its borders. A trip down into its verdant depths reveals a splendidly unspoilt landscape, mottled with tiny villages.

23 **Birdwatching on the Península de Zapata** Page **306** • Venture around the peninsula's virtually undisturbed tracts of swamp and forest to gawk at flocks of flamingoes and other birds above.

24 **La Guarida restaurant** Page **177** • Dine in style in Havana's most atmospheric *paladar*, where the excellent food is matched by Baroque surroundings, guttering candlelight and the aura of a bygone era of romance.

25 **The Tropicana** Page **184** • Be ready to be dazzled, as frills, feathers and sequins are the order of the day at the world's most lavish and sensual cabaret.

27 **Hotel Nacional** Page **126** • Perhaps the finest way to sink into the stately bygone glamour of 1930s Havana's showcase hotel is with a cooling cocktail on one of its elegant terraces.

26 **Museo de Presidio Modelo** Page **564** • Tour the eerie and isolated prison on the Isla de la Juventud to get a vivid feel for the incarceration of Fidel Castro and his cohorts following their 1953 attack on the Moncada Barracks in Santiago.

Basics

Basics

Getting there

Although Cuba is becoming more firmly established on the Caribbean tourist circuit, there are still not as many direct flights as one might expect. It's easier to get to Cuba from Europe or Canada than, say, the US, from where passage is fraught with problems and best avoided. That said, there are several airlines flying to Cuba, and with forward planning you should have little problem picking up a flight to suit your budget.

Airfares always depend on the season, with the highest being around mid-December to mid-March and all of July and August, when the weather is best. You'll get the best prices during the low season, mid-March to mid-April and mid-November to mid-December. You can often cut costs by going through a **specialist flight agent** – either a consolidator, who buys up blocks of tickets from the airlines and sells them at a discount, or a discount agent, who in addition to dealing with discounted flights may also offer special student and youth fares and a range of other travel-related services such as car rentals, tours and the like. Some agents specialize in **charter flights**, which may be cheaper than anything available on a scheduled flight, but departure dates are typically fixed and withdrawal penalties are high.

While the majority of flights to Cuba still involve a change somewhere in Europe, the Virgin routes from the UK to Havana are a direct connection. It's certainly worth comparing prices, and the best place to start is with one of the **flight agents** listed on p.32 or online. Though Cuba now regularly features in the brochures of all high-street travel agents, the experience of the smaller agents, particularly those specializing in Latin American destinations, such as Journey Latin America and South American Experience, gives them an edge over their better-known rivals. More familiar with the details specific to Cuba, such as airport departure tax and tourist cards, they can also usually find the cheapest flights. Other good sources of information include the classified section of London's *Time Out* magazine and *Evening Standard* daily newspaper, the travel supplements in the weekend travel pages of many

newspapers including the *Independent*, the *Daily Mail*, the *Observer*, Teletext and Ceefax.

Flights from the US, Canada, Mexico and the Caribbean

Since the United States continues to maintain a Cold War-era **embargo** on trade with Cuba, US citizens are not allowed by their government to travel there freely. The basic idea behind the prohibition is to keep the Cuban economy from benefiting from US tourist dollars. That said, it is actually possible for US citizens to go to Cuba, and something like 150,000 of them do so every year.

Canadians are as free to travel to Cuba as to any other country, and there are regular flights from Toronto and Montréal to Havana on Cubana, as well as on a number of charter carriers. Travelling via Canada is one of the obvious alternatives for US citizens; nationals of other countries can also travel from Canada without a problem.

From the US

The majority of US visitors to Cuba go legally by obtaining a **"licence"** from the US Treasury Department. Who qualifies for one of these and under what circumstances tends to change quite often due to the ongoing tug-of-war between the US government's conservative and liberal factions about the provisions and enforcement of the embargo (for more details, see p.28).

If you do succeed in obtaining a licence to travel to Cuba, you can call **Marazul Tours** in New Jersey or Miami (see p.37) about booking a place on one of their permitted direct charter flights to Havana from JFK

Airport in New York or from Miami. If you don't have a licence, don't bother calling them, as they (and all other agencies) are prohibited by law from advising you on getting around the restrictions. Marazul Tours runs flights from Miami for US$300 and from New York for US$625. Note that non-US citizens cannot use these routes if they are travelling as tourists or without government approval.

For everyone else who wants to visit Cuba for reasons less acceptable to the US government, like tourism, a degree of ingenuity is required. Usually this means doing little more than **travelling via a third country**, and there are a number of well-established routes to choose from should you decide to do this, including Canada, Mexico and other Caribbean islands. In addition, the Cuban authorities make it easier for US citizens to get around the travel ban by agreeing to requests not to stamp the passports of American tourists entering or leaving Cuba (stamping their tourist cards instead).

If you are a US national, it's important to understand that you will be operating outside the law by going to Cuba without a licence. It is probably a good idea to find out exactly what the restrictions are, and the possible consequences to you for ignoring them, before you decide to make the trip.

From Canada, Mexico and the Caribbean

Regardless of how you travel or where you buy your ticket, fares to Cuba will vary depending on the season. In the low season it is possible to get **APEX fares** from Montréal or Toronto to Havana on Cubana for as little as US$350, though the average fare is about US$550. While Cubana is the only airline with

regularly scheduled flights to Cuba from Canada, there are a number of **charter companies** flying the route, so there are alternatives to check out. Since the charter operators are not allowed to deal directly with the public, to find out about these flights you must go through a travel agent.

The following are sample fares for round-trip travel from Mexican and Caribbean cities to Havana: Mexico City (US$400); Cancún (US$275); Kingston or Montego Bay (US$225); Nassau (US$175). Flights to Nassau in the Bahamas are the most direct route from the US for blockade-busting Americans or non-US citizens who want to move on to Cuba from the States. From there it is a simple step to make your own connection to one of the daily Cubana flights to Havana.

Although flights from Canada, Mexico and the Caribbean are frequent and quite reasonably priced, and it is surprisingly easy to explore Cuba independently, you might well be tempted by the comfort and convenience of a **vacation package**. Many of the Canadian tours are geared toward lying on a beach for a week or two, but if this is not your idea of a trip to Cuba, there are alternatives. A few specialist operators offer thematically designed trips, with special-interest itineraries. This is particularly so with US tour operators, as those groups who do organize trips have to be, by definition, engaged in one of the specific activities, like study tours, permitted by the US government; the definition of "studying" Cuba on one of these tours can be quite broad, however.

By sea

Out of deference to, or fear of, the US blockade, very few **cruise ships** stop at

---

Obtaining permission to travel to Cuba

If you're an American citizen and think you have a case for being granted permission to travel to Cuba, perhaps as a journalist, student or on some sort of humanitarian mission, contact the **Licensing Division**, Office of Foreign Assets Control, US Department of the Treasury, 1500 Pennsylvania Ave NW, Washington DC 20220 ☏202/622-2480, ⊕www.treas.gov/ofac. You can also get information from the Cuban government at the **Cuban Interests Section** at 2630 16th St NW, Washington DC 20009 ☏202/797-8518; or the **Cuban Consulate Office** at 2639 16th St NW, Washington DC 20009 ☏202/797-8609. Most of the specialist tour operators in the US should also be able to assist you in getting your licence.

Cuban ports – ships which do stop are then prohibited from docking in the States for six months.

With a history of confrontation at sea between Florida-based Cuban exile groups and the Cuban maritime authorities, and the rocky relationship between Cuba and the States in general, sailing into Cuban waters can be problematic. Normal **visa requirements** apply, and you should make sure you have these before you embark on your trip. While it is not currently a legal requirement to notify the Cuban authorities of your arrival, it is common maritime courtesy to do so. You should radio ahead where possible – frequencies of the most commonly used ports are listed below. By law you can only be cleared at a port of entry which also has a marine facility, so check the box carefully. Most visiting yachts aim to enter at the Hemingway Marina in Havana Province; it's worth bearing in mind that facilities for repairing vessels are fairly limited in Cuba.

The possibilities for sailing from the States took a turn for the worse in February 2004, when President Bush passed legislation decreeing that all sailors must apply for a **"sojourn license"** from the Commerce Department. However, as these are not issued to pleasure trips, sailing vacations to Cuba for US citizens are effectively outlawed for now. A good source for gathering detailed information

about this subject is *The Cruising Guide to Cuba*, by Simon Charles (US$24.95). Another useful resource is ⓦwww.noonsite.com.

In Cuba, the best organization to contact for information on entry requirement updates is **Federación Nautical de Cuba**, INDER, Via Blanca y Boyeros ⓣ7/57-7146, ⓕ7/33-3459.

Fllights from the UK and Ireland

Cuba has been the fastest-growing **tourist destination** in the Caribbean in recent years, and for anyone in Britain and Ireland there's a wide choice of ways to get there. With a healthy stock of travel agents, tour operators and airlines offering anything from flight-only to all-inclusive accommodation and travel packages, it pays to shop around.

From Britain

Three airlines have direct scheduled flights to Cuba from Britain. **Cubana**, the national Cuban carrier, has one weekly flight departing from London Gatwick for Havana on Saturdays. Though Cubana tends to offer the least expensive flights on the market, they have, in the past, had a reputation for unreliability. Their record has improved over recent years, but Cubana does not have a good customer service record overall, and

---

Ports with marinas

Marina Hemingway 5ta Ave y 248 Santa Fe, Havana ⓣ7/209-7270, ⓕ/204-5280, ⓔrpublicas@prto.mh.cyt.cu (VHF Channel 16, 72). The biggest and most impressive marina in the country; has a good range of services (see p.173), and boats can be hauled out by crane and stored ashore. The GPS coordinates of the sea buoy are reported as 23°05.3'N, 82°30.6'W.

Marina Internacional Puerto de Vita Gaviota, Carretera de Guardalavaca, Km 38, Holguín ⓣ24/3-0475, ⓕ24/3-0446, ⓔcomercial@marinavita.co.cu (VHF Channel 13 or 16). Well positioned for those sailing in from the Bahamas. Has 38 slips with water, electricity, fuel, restaurant, email, laundry, car hire and a water taxi service. Vita Bay offers protection from hurricanes and also has repair facilities. Latitude 21°05'N, Longitude 75°57'W.

Marina Puertosol Cayo Largo del Sur Cayo Largo del Sur, Archipelago de los Canarreos, Isla de la Juventud ⓣ45/4-8213, ⓕ45/4-8212, ⓔgcom@margca.cls .tur.cu (VHF Channel 06 and 16). Coordinates: 21°37'N, 81°34'W.

Marina Puertosol Cienfuegos Calle 35 s/n, e/. 6 y 8, Punta Gorda, Cienfuegos ⓣ432/55-1241, ⓕ432/55-1275, ⓔmpsolcfg@ip.etecsa.cu (VHF Channel 16). Water, electricity and fuel are available. 22°18'N, 80°28'W.

getting compensation can be a struggle. Return fares start at as little as £450 in low season and average out at about £550 in high season. **Air Jamaica**, which flies from London to Havana, has direct flights on Mondays – note that the return trip includes a two-hour stop over in Kingston, Jamaica. Prices range from £440 in low season to £600 in high season.

If **non-direct flights** aren't a problem for you, then Air France is the most versatile option, with two flights daily from London Heathrow or London City Airport to Paris, where another plane takes you on to Havana. Their prices are competitive, ranging from £500 to £600 for most of the year, with the glaring exception being in late December, when a ticket is likely to cost £800 or more.

Iberia flies daily from London Heathrow and Manchester with a change of plane in Madrid; return fares are between £500 and £600, with similar late-December price rises.

Air France also flies from regional airports in Britain, namely Birmingham, Glasgow, Manchester, Newcastle, Edinburgh, Southampton, Teesside and Humberside. Iberia and British Airways offer excellent-value connections from Aberdeen, Edinburgh and Glasgow, amongst other places.

There are a number of **charter operators and airlines** as well, such as Airtours (℡01706/240033) and Monarch (℡01582/400 000), flying from Britain predominantly to Varadero or Holguín as part of an inclusive accommodation package, but sometimes also offering flight-only fares in

Fly less – stay longer! Travel and climate change

Climate change is a serious threat to the ecosystems that humans rely upon, and air travel is among the fastest-growing contributors to the problem. Rough Guides regard travel, overall, as a global benefit, and feel strongly that the advantages to developing economies are important, as is the opportunity of greater contact and awareness among peoples. But we all have a responsibility to limit our personal impact on global warming, and that means giving thought to how often we fly, and what we can do to redress the harm that our trips create.

Flying and climate change
Pretty much every form of motorized travel generates CO_2 – the main cause of human-induced climate change – but planes also generate climate-warming contrails and cirrus clouds and emit oxides of nitrogen, which create ozone (another greenhouse gas) at flight levels. Furthermore, flying simply allows us to travel much further than we otherwise would do. The figures are frightening: one person taking a return flight between Europe and California produces the equivalent impact of 2.5 tonnes of CO_2 – similar to the yearly output of the average UK car.

Fuel-cell and other less harmful types of plane may emerge eventually. But until then, there are really just two options for concerned travellers: to reduce the amount we travel by air (take fewer trips – stay for longer!), and to make the trips we do take "climate neutral" via a carbon offset scheme.

Carbon offset schemes
Offset schemes run by ⓦclimatecare.org, ⓦcarbonneutral.com and others allow you to make up for some or all of the greenhouse gases that you are responsible for releasing. To do this, they provide "carbon calculators" for working out the global-warming contribution of a specific flight (or even your entire existence), and then let you contribute an appropriate amount of money to fund offsetting measures. These include rainforest reforestation and initiatives to reduce future energy demand – often run in conjunction with sustainable development schemes.

Rough Guides, together with Lonely Planet and other concerned partners in the travel industry, are supporting a **carbon offset scheme** run by climatecare.org. Please take the time to view our website and see how you can help to make your trip climate neutral.

ⓦ**www.roughguidescom/climatechange**

order to fill seats. These are usually cheaper, if you can get them, but offer very little flexibility in terms of return dates.

From Ireland

No airline flies nonstop **from Ireland** to Cuba, and you'll usually change planes in London, Paris or Madrid. Iberia flies from Dublin to Havana via Madrid for £550, while Air France offers similar fares for its flights via Paris. The British Airways equivalent is somewhat more expensive, with standard prices at around £580.

The Cuban authorities supply agents with **tourist cards** only if the travel agent can meet their minimum number requirements,

and until now only **Cubatravel** in Dublin (see p.34) has been able to do that. Other agents can nonetheless still sell you the flight and in some cases obtain a tourist card for you, either through Cubatravel or through the Cuban authorities themselves; otherwise you will have to visit the **Cuban Embassy** yourself.

Flights from Australia, New Zealand and South Africa

Cuba is hardly a bargain destination from Australasia. There are no direct flights from Australia or New Zealand, so you'll have to take a flight to Canada, the Caribbean,

Packages and tours

A high proportion of visitors to Cuba **from Britain and Ireland** are on **package holidays**, a hassle-free and relatively inexpensive alternative to paying separately for your flight, accommodation and transfers. Packages work best for anyone happy to stay at the same resort for the entire two weeks, the timescale on which most deals are based, but some include day-trips to locations around the island. They range from **all-inclusives** – where one price covers everything (theoretically, at least – see p.55) from meals and unlimited drinks to hotel nightlife and entertainment – to **self-catering** options. In Varadero, the package-holiday capital of Cuba, most of the four- and five-star hotels operate on an all-inclusive basis, while the self-catering apartments tend to be at the less sophisticated end of the market. Increasingly popular are two-week packages which offer a seven-day tour of the country, staying overnight in hotels around the island, followed by a second week relaxing by the pool at your chosen resort.

For a two-week all-inclusive package in July or August, expect to pay upwards of £850 per person, while room-only prices start at around £450. Winter months are cheaper – starting at £620 from October through early December and rising to £800 around Christmas and up to £950 in January and February. Self-catering deals, which are much harder to come by, cost between £400 and £500. All of these options include a return flight and transfer to and from the airport.

People looking for a more adventurous stay, or those with specific requirements and preferences, might prefer to arrange a trip through a **specialist tour operator**, many of which offer trips that combine hikes with town visits and avoid the main tourist resorts. Alternatively, there are trips that focus on a particular activity, such as diving or cycling, put together by operators with years of experience and the kind of in-depth knowledge necessary to make the most of your time in the country.

Package holidays **from Australia and New Zealand** to Cuba are few and far between, although some operators can arrange worthwhile deals. For example, Adventure World has three-day holidays in Santiago de Cuba for Aus$280/NZ$350 excluding airfare, or twelve-day holidays taking in Havana, Santiago de Cuba, Camagüey, Trinidad and Matanzas costing upwards of Aus$2000/NZ$2600 (based on per person three-star accommodation and low-season airfares from Australia). Another operator, Caribbean Destinations, also has reasonable deals, including a high-end airfare and accommodation package at around Aus$3500/NZ$4500 for seven nights in Havana.

Central or South America, Europe, or the US (but only if you have permission from the US government to travel to Cuba; see p.28), and pick up onward connections from there. The least expensive and most straightforward route is **via Tokyo to Mexico City**, from where there are frequent flights to Havana.

If you're planning to see Cuba as part of a longer trip, **round-the-world (RTW) tickets** are worth considering, and are generally better value than a simple return flight. Whatever kind of ticket you're after, your first call should be a **specialist travel agent** (see opposite). If you're a student or under 26, you may be able to undercut some of the prices given here; STA is a good place to start.

RTW flights

If Cuba is only one stop on a longer journey, you might want to consider buying a **round-the-world (RTW) ticket**. Some travel agents can sell you an "off-the-shelf" RTW ticket that will have you touching down in about half a dozen cities; others will have to assemble one for you, which can be tailored to your needs but is apt to be more expensive. Bear in mind, though, that you will not be able to fly from the US to Cuba, or vice versa, meaning you'll most likely have to include another country in the Caribbean or Latin America.

Fares and air passes

The **fares** quoted below are for travel during low season, and exclude airport taxes; flying at peak times (primarily Dec to mid-Jan) can add substantially to these prices.
From Australia, Qantas Airlines has flights from Melbourne and Sydney to Tokyo (where you stay overnight), then on to Mexico City and Havana for Aus$2399. From New Zealand, Air New Zealand flies from Auckland to Mexico City, with connections on to Havana, starting at around NZ$2700. Lan Chile in conjunction with Qantas also has flights from Auckland to Papeete and Santiago and on to Havana for NZ$3800.

Airlines, agents and operators

Online booking

ⓦ www.cheapflights.com (in UK and Ireland)
ⓦ www.expedia.co.uk (in US), ⓦ www.expedia.com (in US), ⓦ www.expedia.ca (in Canada)
ⓦ www.lastminute.com (in UK)
ⓦ www.opodo.co.uk (in UK)
ⓦ www.priceline.com (in US)
ⓦ www.orbitz.com (in US)
ⓦ www.travelocity.co.uk (in UK), ⓦ www.travelocity.com (in US), ⓦ www.travelocity.ca (in Canada)
ⓦ www.zuji.com.au (in Australia), ⓦ www.zuji.co.nz (in New Zealand)

Airlines

Aer Lingus US and Canada ☎ 1-800/IRISH-AIR, UK ☎ 0870/876 5000, Republic of Ireland ☎ 0818/365 000, ⓦ www.aerlingus.com.
Aeroflot US ☎ 1-888/686-4949, Canada ☎ 416/642-1653, Australia ☎ 02/9262 2233, UK ☎ 020/7355 2233, ⓦ www.aeroflot.com.
Air France US ☎ 1-800/237-2747, Canada ☎ 1-800/667-2747, UK ☎ 0870/142 4343, Australia ☎ 1300/390 190, ⓦ www.airfrance.com.

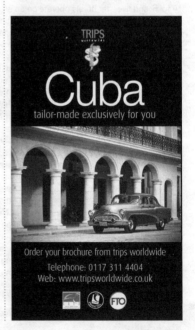

Air Jamaica US ☎1-800/523-5585, UK
☎020/8570 7999, ⓦwww.airjamaica.com.
Air New Zealand Australia ☎13 24 76; New
Zealand ☎0800/737 000, ⓦwww.airnz.com.
Bahamasair US ☎1-800/222-4262,
ⓦwww.bahamasair.com.
British Midland Republic of Ireland ☎01/283
8833; Northern Ireland ☎0345/554 554,
ⓦwww.flybmi.com.
Cubana Canada ☎416/967-2822, UK ☎020/7537
7909, ⓦwww.cubana.co.cu.
Iberia US ☎1-800/772-4642, UK ☎0870 609
0500, Republic of Ireland ☎0810/462 000,
ⓦwww.iberia.com.
(JAL) Japan Air Lines US and Canada
☎1-800/525-3663, UK ☎0845/774 7700, Ireland
☎01/408 3757, Australia ☎02/9272 1111, New
Zealand ☎09/379 9906, ⓦwww.jal.com or
ⓦwww.japanair.com
LanChile US and Canada ☎1-866/435-9526,
UK ☎0800/917 0572, Australia ☎1300/361 400
or 02/9244 2333, New Zealand ☎09/977 2233,
ⓦwww.lan.com.
Mexicana US ☎1-800/531-7921, Canada
☎1-866/281-3094, UK ☎020/8492 0000,
Australia ☎03/9699 9355, New Zealand ☎09/914
2573, SA ☎011784-0985, ⓦwww.mexicana.com.
Qantas Airways US and Canada ☎1-800/227-
4500, UK ☎0845/774 7767, Republic of Ireland
☎01/407 3278, Australia ☎13 13 13, New Zealand
☎0800/808 767 or 09/357 8900,
ⓦwww.qantas.com.
Virgin Atlantic US ☎1-800/821-5438, UK
☎0870/380-2007, Australia ☎1300/727 340,
ⓦwww.virgin-atlantic.com.

Agents and operators

Adventure World Australia ☎02/8913 0755,
ⓦwww.adventureworld.com.au; New Zealand
☎09/524 5118, ⓦwww.adventureworld.co.nz.
Agents for a vast array of international adventure
travel companies that operate trips to every continent.
Apex Travel Republic of Ireland ☎01/671
5933. Specialists in worldwide airfares with some
reasonable deals to Cuba.
AS Tours Mexico ☎52/5-575-9814. Spanish-
speaking agency with flights and packages.
Baha Tours Bahamas ☎242/328-7985. Books space
on the daily Cubana service from Nassau to Havana.
Bel Air Travel US ☎1-877/675-7707; Canada
☎1-888/723-5247 or 416/699-8833, ⓦwww
.belairtravel.com. Specializes in travel to Cuba; flights
only or package tours.
Blazing Saddles Travels 76 Hindes Rd, Harrow,
London HA1 1SL ☎020/8424 0483,

www.blazingsaddles.net. The only tour company dedicated solely to cycling trips. Organizes one- and two-week tours to a variety of locations around the island, including Santiago de Cuba to Baracoa and Trinidad to Matanzas, as well as the easier-going Havana to Pinar del Río route.

Budget Travel New Zealand ☏ 0800/808 480, www.budgettravel.co.nz.

Canadian-Cuban Friendship Association ☏ 416/742-6931, www.ccfatoronto.ca. A non-profit volunteer organization setting up exchanges in areas such as health, education and culture, as well as material aid to Cuba.

Captivating Cuba Fraser House, 15 London Rd, Twickenham, Middlesex TW1 3ST ☏ 020/8891 2222. Specialist branch of Travelcoast Ltd, offering mostly resort-based packages but also tailor-made tours and a seven-day tour of Havana and Pinar del Río.

Caribbean Destinations Australia ☏ 03/9614 7144 or 1800/354 104, www.caribbeanislands .com.au. Specializes in festivals and hotel accommodation in Jamaica, Cuba, Antigua and the rest of the Caribbean.

Caribic Air Services Jamaica ☏ 876/953-2600. Arranges trips from Jamaica to Cuba.

Center for Cuban Studies US ☏ 212/242-0559, www.cubaupdate.org. An excellent information resource; sends expeditions to Cuba on humanitarian missions, such as administering eye tests and distributing eyeglasses, and arranges trips for various professionals, including lawyers, artists, architects and filmmakers (who can attend the international film festival). Prices from US$3300.

Co-op Travel Care UK ☏ 0870/112 0085, www .travelcareonline.com. Flights and holidays around the world from the UK's largest independent travel agent. Non-partisan and informed advice.

Cubatravel Republic of Ireland ☏ 01/671 3422. The most experienced agent in Ireland for holidays and flight deals to and in Cuba. The emphasis is on flexibility and independent travel, though they do offer resort-based packages, with a variety of interests catered for including scuba diving. This is also the only agent in Ireland able to issue tourist cards on the spot.

Destinations Unlimited Level 7, FAI Building, 220 Queen St, Auckland ☏ 09/373 4033.

ebookers UK ☏ 0800/082 3000, Republic of Ireland ☏ 01/488 3507, www.ebookers.com. Low fares on an extensive selection of scheduled flights and package deals.

Exodus UK ☏ 020/8675 5550, Republic of Ireland ☏ 01/677 1029, www.exodus.co.uk. Active and adventure holidays. Highlights include the two-week biking trips covering the best of Cuba's eastern regions, including some strenuous biking in the Sierra Maestra.

Explore Worldwide UK ☏ 01252/760 000, www.explore.co.uk. Big range of small-group tours, treks and expeditions centred on hiking, birdwatching and visiting nature reserves.

Flightcentre UK ☏ 0870/890 8099, www .flightcentre.co.uk. Rock-bottom fares worldwide.

Flights4Less UK ☏ 0871/222 3423, www .flights4less.co.uk. Good discount airfares. Part of Lastminute.com.

Flynow UK ☏ 0870/444 0045, www.flynow .com. Large range of discounted tickets; official South African Airways agent.

Gane & Marshall 98 Crescent Rd, New Barnet, Herts EN4 9RJ ☏ 020/8441 9592, www .ganeandmarshall.co.uk. Organized tours and tailor-made itineraries starting at £750 from this specialist in travel to Cuba, Ecuador and Venezuela. Can arrange cycling, trekking and cultural or historical tours.

Global Exchange US ☏ 415/255-7296, www .globalexchange.org. A non-profit organization that leads "reality tours" to countries like Cuba, Ecuador and Guatemala. "Travel seminars" explore local culture, music, health, religion or agriculture; you can also take a class on Cuban rhythms or the Spanish language, or book a place on a bicycle tour. Prices start at around US$1950.

Greyhound US ☏ 1/800-231-2222, Canada ☏ 1/416-367-8747, www.greyhound.com.

Green Tortoise US and Canada ☎1/800-867-8647, ⓦwww.greentortoise.com.

Hayes & Jarvis UK ☎0870/898 9890, ⓦwww.hayes-jarvis.com. Some of the package options are a little pedestrian but very strong on destination diving.

Hola Sun Holidays Canada ☎905/882-9445, ⓦwww.holasunholidays.com. Handles bookings through travel agents only for eight destinations in Cuba.

Holidays4Less UK ☎0871/222 3423, ⓦwww.holidays4less.co.uk. Discounted package deals worldwide. Part of Lastminute.com.

The Holiday Place 1–3 Drakes Court Yard, London, NW6 7JR ☎020/7644 1770, ⓦwww.theholidayplace.co.uk. Escorted fourteen-day tours taking in an impressive range of the island's major attractions, plus shorter, four-night tours and a wide selection of all-inclusive resort holidays.

Interchange UK ☎020/8681 3612, ⓦwww.interchange.uk.com. Specialist in multi-hotel holidays and tailor-made itineraries, with a catalogue of over two dozen hotels across the island.

Intrepid Travel UK ☎020/8960 6333, ⓦwww.intrepidtravel.com. Small-group tours with the emphasis on cross-cultural contact and low-impact tourism.

Journey Latin America UK ☎020/8747 8315 (London) or ☎0161/832 1441 (Manchester), ⓦwww.journeylatinamerica.co.uk. Well versed

in the various flight deals to Cuba and usually able to dig out some of the best-value flights on the market. Offers reliable and well-planned escorted group tours and individual itineraries.

Lee Travel Republic of Ireland ☎ 021/427 7111,
🕸 www.leetravel.ie. Flights and holidays worldwide.
The London Flight Centre UK ☎ 020/7244
6411, 020/7727 4290 or 020/8748 6777. Long-
established agent dealing in discount flights.
Madre US ☎ 212/627-0444, 🕸 www.madre.org. An
international women's human rights organization which
offers legal trips to Cuba twice a year. The emphasis
is on socio-economics and includes visits to hospitals,
schools and liaisons with the Federation of Cuban
Women (see p.87).
Marazul Tours US ☎ 201/319-9670 or 305/644-
0255, 🕸 www.marazulcharters.com. Books tickets
on charter flights, for the officially sanctioned, to
Havana from Miami or New York, and can arrange
hotel accommodation as well.
McCarthys Travel Republic of Ireland ☎ 021/427
0127, 🕸 www.mccarthystravel.ie. Established Irish
travel agent featuring flights, short breaks, pilgrimages
and group holidays.
Mexicana de Aviacion Mexico ☎ 52/5-448-0990,
🕸 www.mexicana.com. Airline that also arranges
tours and packages.
New Frontiers/Nouvelles Frontières Canada
☎ 514/871-3060, 🕸 www.nouvelles-frontieres
.com. French discount travel firm, with branches in
Montréal and Québec.
North South Travel UK ☎ 01245/608 291,
🕸 www.northsouthtravel.co.uk. Friendly, competitive
travel agency, offering discounted fares worldwide.
Profits are used to support projects in the developing
world, especially the promotion of sustainable
tourism.
Northern Gateway Australia ☎ 1800/174 800,
🕸 www.northerngateway.com.au.
Peter Pan US ☎ 1/800-237-8747 or 1/413-781-
2900, 🕸 www.peterpanbus.com.
Premier Travel UK ☎ 028/7126 3333, 🕸 www
.premiertravel.uk.com. Discount flight specialists.
Progressive Tours 12 Porchester Place, Marble
Arch, London W2 2BS ☎ 020/7262 1676. The
emphasis is on grassroots visits, including study
tours designed to provide close contact with Cuban
people. Also arranges more traditional but very
reasonably priced one- or two-week hotel-based
holidays.
Regaldive 58 Lancaster Way, Ely, Cambs, CB6
3NW ☎ 0870 2201 777, 🕸 www.regal-diving.co.uk.
Accomplished scuba diving specialists operating in an
excellent choice of locations, including remote María
La Gorda in western Pinar del Río, Cayo Largo, and
the Península de Ancón near Trinidad.
Regent Holidays UK ☎ 0117/921 1711, 🕸 www
.regent-holidays.co.uk. Cycling holidays and coach
tours including a nature-based tour of the Sierra
Maestra.

Rosetta Travel UK ☏ 028/9064 4996, ⓦ www .rosettatravel.com. Flight and holiday agent, specializing in deals direct from Belfast.

Silke's Travel Australia ☏ 1800/807 860 or 02/8347 2000, ⓦ www.silkes.com.au. Gay and lesbian specialist travel agent.

South American Experience UK ☏ 020/7976 5511, ⓦ www.sax.mcmail.com. Experts in travel all over Latin America who can arrange internal Cuban flights as well as the transatlantic crossing.

STA Travel US ☏ 1-800/781-4040, Canada ☏ 1-888/427-5639, UK ☏ 0870/1630 026, Australia ☏ 1300/733 035, New Zealand ☏ 0508/782 872, ⓦ www.statravel.com. Worldwide specialists in independent travel; also student IDs,

travel insurance, car rental, rail passes, and more. Good discounts for students and under-26s.

Student Uni Travel Australia ☏ 02/9232 8444; New Zealand ☏ 09/300 8266, ⓔ sydney@sut .com.au.

Sun Holidays Canada ☏ 416/789-1010 or 1-800/387-0571, ⓦ www.sunholidays.com. Specializes in travel to Cuba, flights only or packages.

Tip's Travel Mexico ☏ 52/5-584-1557, ⓔ ttravel @netservice.com.mx. Mexico City-based company arranging flights and packages.

Trailfinders UK ☏ 0845/058 5858, Republic of Ireland ☏ 01/677 7888, Australia ☏ 1300/780 212, ⓦ www.trailfinders.com. One of the best-informed and most efficient agents for independent travellers.

Cuban tour operators and travel agents

Cubamar Viajes Calle 3 e/ 12 y Malecón, Vedado, Havana ☏ 7/832-1116 & 831-0008, ⓦ www.cubamarviajes.cu. Though it can't compete with the big guns for variety, Cubamar, a smaller operator responsible for running most of the country's *campismos*, does have some of its own off-the-beaten-track day-trips.

Cubanacán Calle 17A e/ 174 y 190, Siboney, Playa, Havana ☏ 7/208-8666, ⓦ www .cubanacan.cu. Among the largest tourism entities in the country, Cubanacán has its fingers in almost every aspect of the tourist industry and has a suitably impressive portfolio of organized excursions.

Cubatur Main agency branch is at Calle 23 esq. L, Vedado, Havana ☏ 7/833-3142 & 833-4135. Head office is at Calle F no.157 e/ Calzada y Novena, Vedado, Havana ☏ 7/835-4155 to 60, ⓦ www.cubatur.cu. One of the most comprehensive programmes of excursions with offices and *buros de turismo* all over the country.

Gaviota Tours Head office is at Ave. del Puerto, Edif. La Marina 3er piso, Habana Vieja, Havana ☏ 7/866-9668 & 866-6777. Main agency branch is at Calle 47 no. 2833 e/ 28 y 34, Rpto Kohly, Havana ☏ 7/204-5708 & 204-7526, ⓦ www .gaviota-grupo.com. With their jeep and truck safaris in Matanzas province, or their helicopter trip from Havana to Cayo Levisa, Gaviota can provide something a little different as well as the more run-of-the-mill day-trips.

Havanatur Edificio Sierra Maestra, Calle 1ra e/ 0 y 2, Miramar, Havana ☏ 7/203-9815 & 203-9510, ⓦ www.havanatur.cu. Featuring offices all over Latin America, Europe and Canada, Havanatur is the only national Cuban travel agent that comes with an international reputation. Their range and choice of excursions from Havana, Santiago and Varadero is unbeatable, but they stand out also for their multi-destination packages around the Caribbean.

Paradiso Calle 19 no.560 esq. C, Vedado, Havana ☏ 7/832-9538 & 832-9539, ⓦ www .paradiso.cu. Specialists in "*turismo cultural*" with offices in only five provinces. In addition to historically and culturally oriented excursions they provide music and dance classes and courses and stage special events such as music festivals.

San Cristóbal Calle Oficios no.110 e/ Lamparilla y Amargura, Plaza de San Francisco, Habana Vieja, Havana ☏ 7/861-9171, 861-9172 & 866-4102, ⓦ www .viajessancristobal.cu. Operating exclusively from the capital, this small agency belongs to the Oficina del Historiador de Ciudad de la Habana, the organization responsible for rebuilding and preserving Habana Vieja, and therefore tends to offer tours with an historic slant. There is a variety of themes through which you can tour Havana, such as visiting all the Ernest Hemingway-connected locations or seeing the old city from a horse and carriage.

Travel Bag UK ℡0870/890 1456, 🖥www
.travelbag.co.uk. Discount deals worldwide.
The Travel Bug UK ℡0870/890 1456.
Travel Cuts UK ℡020/7255 2082, Canada
℡1-800/667-2887 or 416/979-2406, 🖥www
.travelcuts.co.uk or 🖥www.travelcuts.com. Budget,
student and youth travel and round-the-world tickets,
with offices in London and abroad.
Top Deck UK ℡020/7244 8000, 🖥www
.topdecktravel.co.uk. Long-established agent dealing
in discount flights and tours.
Trips Worldwide UK ℡0117/311 4400, 🖥www
.tripsworldwide.co.uk. Good-value tailor-made
trips around the island. Their speciality is fly-drives
starting in Havana. Two main routes are offered, one
heading west to Pinar del Río, the other covering the
overland route east down towards Baracoa, with all
accommodation arranged along the way.
USIT Northern Ireland ℡028/9032 7111, 🖥www
.usitnow.com; Republic of Ireland ℡0818/200 020,
🖥www.usit.ie. Specialists in student, youth and
independent travel – flights, trains, study tours, TEFL,
visas and more.

Usit Campus UK ℡0870/240 1010, 🖥www
.usitcampus.co.uk. Student/youth travel specialists,
with branches all over Britain, some of them in YHA
shops and on university campuses.
Walshes World Australia ℡02/9318 1044, New
Zealand ℡09/379 3708.
World Expeditions UK ℡020/8870 2600,
🖥www.worldexpeditions.co.uk. Australian-
owned adventure company offering more than just
Antipodean expeditions. Their Cuba programme offers
a two-week cycling and walking tour.
World of Vacations Canada ℡416/620-8687 or
1-800/661-8881, 🖥www.worldofvacations.com.
Offers packages to beach resorts only.
World Travel Centre Republic of Ireland ℡01/416
7007, 🖥www.worldtravel.ie. Excellent fares to
Europe and worldwide.
Worldwide Quest Nature Tours Canada
℡416/633-5666 or 1-800/387-1483, 🖥www
.worldwidequest.com. Mountain resort and lodge
stays for hiking or cycling tours with ecotourist
agendas.

Getting around

Mastering the different ways to get around Cuba can be a fascinating, if
sometimes frustrating, experience – just understanding the nuances of hitching a
lift and catching a private taxi can take years. Although public transport conditions have been improving, the system is still characterized for Cubans by waiting
lists, endless queues and uncomfortable conditions. Things are much easier for
convertible peso-carrying travellers, who can bypass many of the problems that
national peso-paying Cubans have in getting around, what with access to a better
bus service, plenty of car-rental agencies and state-run taxis.

If you're willing to pay a little extra, you can
get around fairly quickly and efficiently. On
the other hand, in Cuba the journey is all part
of the fun, especially when it's a 200-
kilometre taxi ride in one of the thousands of
classic American cars from the 1940s and
50s that have survived since the 1959
Revolution, some beautifully maintained,
others no more than rolling scrapheaps.

By air

Given the relatively slow road and rail routes
in Cuba, **domestic flights** offer a temptingly

quick way of getting around. However, the
significant number of accidents involving
Cuban airlines over the last couple of
decades might be enough to negate this
advantage for some people. In addition, the
vast majority of domestic flights are on old
twelve-seater, single-engine Russian
biplanes, and flying in them is no more
reassuring than you would expect.

The national airline, **Cubana** (℡7/834-4446
& 204-9647, 🖥www.cubana.cu), which has
offices all around the country, operates regular
flights from Havana's José Martí Airport

(☎7/649-7777) to most of the much smaller airports around the island. There are daily flights from the capital to Camagüey ($80CUC), Holguín ($90CUC) and Guantánamo ($110CUC), two daily to Santiago ($100CUC) and three daily to the Isla de la Juventud ($32CUC). The other airports have just once- or twice-weekly scheduled Cubana flights connecting them with Havana, while only Varadero, Holguín and Santiago have direct regular links with one another. The other national airlines with scheduled domestic flights are Aerocaribbean (☎7/879-75-25, ⓦwww.aero-caribbean.com) and Aerogaviota (☎7/203-0686 & 203-0668, ⓦwww.aerogaviota.com. Fares are almost identical to those of Cubana, but they both offer connections between Havana and smaller provincial airports that Cubana does not, such as Cayo Coco in Ciego de Ávila (Aerocaribbean) and Cayo Santa María in Villa Clara (Aerogaviota). All three airlines also operate **chartered flights**.

Main domestic airports

Baracoa ☎21/4-2580 or 4-2216.
Camagüey ☎32/6-1862 & 6-1000.
Cayo Largo ☎45/24-8141.
Ciego de Ávila ☎33/22-5717.
Cienfuegos ☎43/45-1328.
Granma ☎23/42-3695 & 42-4501.
Guantánamo ☎21/3-4816.
Havana ☎7/649-5777.
Holguín ☎24/46-2512, 46-2534 & 42-5707.
Manzanillo ☎23/5-4984.
Nueva Gerona ☎61/32-2690 & 32-2184.
Santiago de Cuba ☎22/69-1014.
Trinidad ☎41/99-6393.
Las Tunas ☎31/4-2702, 4-2484 & 4-2900.
Varadero ☎45/61-3016.

By rail

At present, Cuba is the only country in the Caribbean with a functioning **rail system**, and although trains are slow they neverthe-less provide a good way of getting a feel for the landscape as you travel about. You'll need your passport to **buy a ticket**, which you should do at least an hour before departure, direct from the train station. (If you show up less than an hour beforehand, the ticket office will refuse to sell you a ticket.) Strictly speaking, all foreign travellers must

pay for tickets in convertible pesos, but on some of the less-travelled routes you may get away with a peso ticket.

The **main line**, which links Havana with Santiago, is generally reliable and the trains operating on it are surprisingly comfortable, given, or perhaps as a result of, their apparent age. Most of Cuba's major cities are served by this route, and while there are branch lines to other towns and cities and a few completely separate lines, any train not running directly between Havana and Santiago will be subject to more delays and even slower trains.

The quickest of the two main services, known as the **Servicio Especial**, leaves Havana twice a week and calls at just five stops on the 12-hour journey to Santiago, most significantly at Matanzas, Santa Clara and Camagüey. The slightly slower **Servicio Regular** leaves Havana for Santiago daily at around 7.30pm, stopping at the following stations in between: Matanzas, Santa Clara, Guayos (around 20km from the centre of Sancti Spíritus), Ciego de Ávila, Camagüey, Las Tunas, Cacocum (around 20km from the centre of Holguín) and San Luis (around 30km from Santiago). Conditions on these fast trains are comfortable, with air condi-tioning and on-board refreshments. Servicio Especial fares from Havana start at $10CUC for Matanzas and increase by about $4CUC per stop up to $43CUC, which takes you all the way to Santiago for $43CUC; there are discounted fares for children.

The two most obvious routes beside the main line are the **Havana–Pinar del Río line**, one of the slowest in the country, and the **Hershey line**, an electric train service running between Havana and Matanzas. Some of the trains on these and other lesser routes are no more than a single carriage and, like the buses, only sometimes run in accordance with their timetables.

By bus

With a relatively low percentage of car owners on the island, **buses** are at the heart of everyday Cuban life and by far the most commonly used form of transport both within the cities and for long-distance journeys. Though improvements have been made in recent years, the system is still characterized by long queues and overcrowding for national peso-paying travellers which, coupled with the complicated system of timetables and buying tickets, can make using them a nightmare.

Interprovincial bus routes

There are two separate services for **interprovincial routes**, one operated by Astro, the other by Víazul. Víazul (☎7/881-1413 & 881-5652, ⊛www.viazul.cu) is used predominantly by tourists, as the convertible-peso-only fares are economically out of reach for most of the population. This efficient service allows anyone who can afford it to bypass the confusion and delays of the Astro system, and enjoy its buses, which are equipped with air conditioning, toilets and, in some cases, TV sets. The buses can get very cold, so remember to take a sweater on board with you.

The number of routes for Víazul buses is limited, with only seventeen towns, cities and resorts forming the entire network (see box, p.42). It is, however, still the quickest, most reliable and most hassle-free way to get about the country independently. The current small size of Víazul's fleet means that there are no more than four departure times for any destination in any one day, and along some routes there is only one bus per day. Tickets, which are usually one-way, can be booked in advance at the offices of one of the three major Cuban travel agents – Cubanacán, Cubatur and Havanatur – found in most provincial capital cities. You'll be given a voucher, which you'll need to exchange for the actual ticket when you get to the station. You can also buy tickets at the bus station itself, but these don't go on sale until an hour before the departure time; turning up more than an hour in advance will therefore usually give you no advantage, though your name may be taken down on a waiting list. Costs for the most frequently made journeys range from $10CUC for between Havana and Varadero to $51CUC for between Havana and Santiago.

If you don't have enough time to wait for the next Víazul bus, one possible solution is to book a seat on a tour bus, paying for only the journey portion of an organized excursion. Known as a **transfer**, this can be arranged through most of the main travel agents, but there is no guarantee there will be spare seats and it's a relatively expensive way to travel; a one-way transfer with Cubatur from Havana to Viñales, for example, costs over twice as much as it would with Víazul.

Though most foreign visitors find the Víazul service reaches all the destinations they need, there are many more routes served exclusively by Astro (☎7/870-3397), and if you intend to travel off the beaten track then the chances are you will make a journey in one of its vehicles. Even if going to a destination covered by Víazul, you may decide that the Astro fare, usually between half and two-thirds of the price of a Víazul ticket, justifies the slightly longer journeys and added waiting time.

Foreign passport-holders on Astro buses are obliged to pay for their ticket in convertible pesos, but by doing so they forgo the rigmarole of queuing to get into another queue, joining waiting lists and all the other confusing rituals which dominate the public transport system. Most bus stations in cities or larger towns have a separate office where convertible peso tickets are sold. The buses used for the most popular routes have two or more seats specifically reserved for these higher-rate customers, and though this means you will usually get a seat there is no guarantee that a bus will not already have met its convertible peso quota, in which case you'll usually have to wait for the next bus unless there are spare national peso seats, but this is unlikely.

Astro staff, like their Víazul equivalents, usually advise customers to arrive at the bus station at least an hour before departure. Before you do that, however, you should ring to check whether the bus is actually leaving, particularly if you are catching it in a non-tourist area. Chalkboard timetables can be found on the walls of most bus stations, but they should be taken with a giant pinch of salt. There are occasions when buses don't leave simply because there's not enough petrol to go around, with those running the most heavily used routes naturally given priority. It's also worth bearing in mind that buses going to the same place don't always take the same route. Check beforehand whether the bus is going via the *autopista* (the motorway) or the slower Carretera Central (the most common variation), as this will significantly affect the journey time.

In Havana there are separate bus stations for Víazul and Astro services, but anywhere else both depart from either the local Terminal de Omnibus Nacionales or Interprovinciales. This is not to be confused with the intermunicipal station, which may look very similar but in most towns is in a different location and serves only those towns within the provincial borders.

Local bus services

While foreign travellers have become a familiar sight on long-distance buses, catch a **local town bus** and you're bound to attract a few stares. The lack of timetables, information-less bus stops and overcrowding are more than enough to persuade most people unfamiliar with the workings of the

local bus system to stay well away. However, as most journeys cost less than half a national peso, you may be tempted to try your luck.

The only written information you will find at a bus stop is the numbers of the buses that stop there. The front of the bus will tell you its final destination, but for any more detail you'll have to ask. Once you know which one you want, you need to mark your place in the queue, which may not appear to even exist. The unwritten rule is to ask aloud who the last person is; so, for example, to queue for bus #232 you should shout *"¿Ultima persona para la 232?"*. When the bus finally pulls up, make sure you have, within a peso, the right change – there's a flat fee of 40c.

Other than the familiar-looking single-deck buses, many of them imported from Europe and called *gua-guas*, there are *camellos*, the converted juggernauts employed throughout

The Víazul bus network

Most of the Viazul departure times from Havana are between 7 and 9am. The cheapest fares start at $6CUC, with the most expensive being $51CUC for the full length of the Havana–Santiago de Cuba route. Given below are the nine Víazul routes with all the destinations which they serve (destinations besides the beginning and end of the route are inside parentheses) and the daily frequency of departures. In all cases there is the same number of departures in either direction. For timetable updates check ⓦ www.viazul.cu.

Havana–Guardalavaca	3 weekly	$44CUC
Havana–Playas del Este	2 daily	$6CUC
Havana–Santiago de Cuba (Jagüey Grande, Santa Clara, Sancti Spíritus, Ciego de Ávila, Camagüey, Las Tunas, Holguín, Bayamo)	3 daily	$51CUC
Havana–Trinidad (Cienfuegos, Jagüey Grande)	2 daily	$25CUC
Havana–Varadero (Matanzas)	3 daily	$10CUC
Havana–Viñales (Pinar del Río)	1 daily	$12CUC
Santiago de Cuba–Baracoa (El Cristo, La Maya, Guantánamo, San Antonio, Imías)	1 daily	$15CUC
Trinidad–Santiago de Cuba (Sancti Spíritus, Jatibonico, Ciego de Ávila, Florida, Camagüey, Sibanicú, Guáimaro, Las Tunas, Holguín, Bayamo, Palma Soriano)	1 daily	$33CUC
Varadero–Trinidad (Santa Clara, Sancti Spíritus, Cienfuegos)	1 daily	$20CUC

Cuba but especially in Havana. Almost always heaving with passengers, they tend to cover the longer city journeys but actually charge less, usually just 20c.

By car

Given that so much of Cuba is not properly served by public transport, the most convenient (though relatively expensive) way to get around the island is in your own rental car. On the positive side, traffic jams are almost unheard of and, away from the cities, many roads, including the *autopista* (motorway), are almost empty. In addition, driving a car opens up the possibility of visiting the numerous places that still have no formal public transport links at all with major urban centres. Even resort areas such as Topes de Collantes near Trinidad or the Sierra del Rosario in Pinar del Río are pretty much unreachable for the non-package traveller without a car.

All this said, driving on Cuban roads is a bit of an anarchic experience. Many drivers show scant regard for the rarely enforced highway code, while on trips out of the cities there can be any number of obstacles set up to get in your way (see "Driving in Cuba", p.44). In general, it pays to be prepared and have your wits about you, as they are often the only guide you'll have when travelling around a rudimentary road system with little in the way of guidelines and safety features.

Renting a car

Given that they are all state-run firms, Cuba has a surprising proliferation of different car-rental agencies; internationally recognized companies like Avis and Hertz do not exist in Cuba. Apart from prices – which are rarely less than $35CUC a day and usually between $50CUC and $70CUC – the essential difference between rental locations is the type, condition and make of cars available, which can range from shiny chauffeur-driven limousines to rusty two-door hatchbacks. The classic American cars that you'll see so often on the road can only be rented out with a driver, effectively as taxis (see p.47).

Havanautos and Cubacar have the most branches throughout the island, as well as the widest range of vehicles, and in general their prices do not differ a great deal from one branch to the next. However, it is still worth shopping around even between these two, as demand usually far outweighs supply, meaning agencies can often only offer for rent one or two of the cars in their fleet. For the same reason it is often difficult, if not impossible, to book a car in advance, especially in Havana, with most agencies only able to suggest you turn up on a certain day and hope something is available. You do, however, have a better chance of booking in advance if you choose one of the more expensive models of car or one of the pricier agencies, such as Rex. These pricier options are also worth considering because the cheapest cars (especially the ones from Havanautos, Cubacar and Micar) are often pretty battered and more liable to break down.

All agencies require you to have held a driving licence from your home country or an international driving licence for at least a year and that you be 21 or older.

Most agencies offer numerous **packages** which are usually split into two groups: those which allow unlimited distance and those which set a daily maximum, usually 100km, with a charge for every kilometre above that limit. Unless you intend to stay within the limits of a city, the latter option is likely to be unnecessarily expensive. The average prices for the most basic unlimited-distance deals are around $50CUC a day, with an extra $10–15CUC a day for insurance and a deposit of $200CUC or $250CUC. Costs go down by about $5CUC a day if you rent the car for a week or more. Be prepared for extra charges, legitimate or otherwise, which won't appear in the agency brochure (see box, p.44).

Car-rental agencies

Cubacar ☎7/835-0000 & 273-2277, ⊛www .transtur.cu. Offices all over the island, many of them based in hotels; standard prices.

Gran Car ☎7/33-5647 & 41-7980, ⊛www.cuba .cu/turismo/panatrans/grancar. Classic American cars; operates predominantly in Havana.

Havanautos ☎7/203-9805, 203-8925 & 203-9833, ⊛www.havanautos.cu. Offices all over the island, with a fleet ranging from beach buggies to jeeps, hatchbacks and saloons.

Micar ☏7/204-8888, ⊛www.micarrenta.cu.
The cheapest agency, with the most flexible price
packages but a fairly limited number of offices and a
relatively small choice of cars.
Palcocar ☏7/208-8888. Operating almost
exclusively from Havana, and aimed at business
travellers. Reasonable rates but strictly limited choice
of cars. Chauffeur-driven vehicles can also be rented.
Panautos ☏7/55-3255 & 55-3286, ⊛www
.panatrans.cu. The most expensive of the island-wide
agents, specializing in Citroëns and luxury jeeps.
Rex ☏7/33-9160, ⊛www.rex-rentacar.com. One
of the most professionally run services, offering luxury
Volvos at extremely high prices. Branches in Havana
only; minimum age requirement is 25.

Driving in Cuba

The first thing to be aware of when driving in
Cuba is that **road markings** are almost
nonexistent. Most of the major roads in large
cities have white lines on them, but these are
completely absent on side roads and
backstreets. Logically this is cause for extra
care at junctions, where you should keep a
keen lookout for traffic lights since, where
they do exist, there is often only one
suspended high above the road. Nor are
there any road markings to be seen on the
motorways, where traffic lanes are
determined by no more than the width of the
road. The quality of the road surface isn't
much better and you should expect
potholes wherever you go; even some of
the main streets in Havana are dotted with
them, though they are thankfully largely
absent from the *autopista*. The quality of
minor roads in the provinces varies
enormously, with some, particularly in Pinar
del Río province and parts of Santiago de
Cuba, in a dire state. Take extreme care on
mountain roads, many of which have killer
bends and few crash barriers. See p.652 in
"Language" for a brief glossary of driving
terms.

To add to the confusion, away from the
most touristy areas there is a marked **lack of
road signs** which, coupled with the absence
of detailed road maps, makes getting lost a
distinct possibility. On journeys around
provincial roads you will almost certainly have
to stop and ask for directions, but even on
the motorways the junctions and exits are
completely unmarked. One of the few signs
you do have a good chance of seeing is the
large X, known as a *crucero* in Spanish,
announcing a **railroad crossing**. Be
especially vigilant for these, as there are no
barriers before any crossings in Cuba. The

Rental-car scams and hazards

The most common hidden cost when renting a car in Cuba is a charge for the cost
of the petrol already in the vehicle; if you are charged for this, however, then logically
you should be able to return it with an empty tank. In general, it pays to be
absolutely clear from the start about what you are being charged for to avoid any
nasty surprises on returning the car.

Tampering with the petrol gauge is another popular trick – it's sometimes a good
idea to take the car to a petrol station as soon as you've rented it and make sure the
tank really is full before setting off on a long journey. By the same token, if you want
your deposit back you should check the car over thoroughly before setting off to
make sure every little scratch is recorded in the log-book by the agent.

You may find that if you pay by credit card – widely accepted in all rental
agencies – the agent will ask you to pay for a small part of the overall cost, usually
the insurance or petrol in the tank, in cash, as this will be the only way they can
cream anything off. (Note that this "scam" won't necessarily cost you anything
extra.) You should also be aware that all rental cars come with easy-to-spot tourist
number plates, so there is no hiding on your travels from *jineteros* and street
entrepreneurs. However, this makes it far less likely that anyone will steal your car,
as Cubans driving tourist cars are likely to attract the immediate attention of the
police. The plates are less of a deterrent, though, to people stealing your wheels or
anything you have left inside the car, the most common form of car crime in Cuba,
so be particularly careful where you park (see box, opposite).

accepted practice is to slow down, listen for train horns and whistles and look both ways down the tracks before driving across.

There is a high proportion of **cyclists** on the road in Cuba, their apparent lack of concern for their own safety making them generally unpredictable. But your driving skills need to be at their best on the **autopista**, which has a whole road culture of its own. First off, you should be aware that large groups of **hitchhikers** sometimes congregate at the side of the road, usually at junctions, under flyovers, and occasionally spilling onto the road itself. The other kind of *autopista* pedestrian is the **salesman**, with farmers appearing along many of the most travelled routes, selling all sorts of produce to passing motorists. Complicating matters further is the fact that *autopista* traffic includes an array of **horse-drawn transport** and even the occasional cow.

If all this weren't enough to contend with during the day, the **absence of street**

Traffic lights

A permanently flashing yellow light at a junction, either on a standard traffic light or a single light on its own, means you have right of way. A flashing red light at a junction means you must give way.

lighting on all but the busiest city streets means driving at night can become a real nightmare. The majority of roads, including the *autopista*, have no cat's eyes either, and therefore your car headlights are often the only guide to where the edge of the road is. Remember also that **push-bikes** in Cuba rarely have any lights and can therefore appear from nowhere. In short, driving anywhere outside the cities at night is dangerous, and to mountain resorts like Viñales or Topes de Collantes is positively suicidal.

Parking

Car parks with meters are nonexistent in Cuba, and car parks themselves, outside of Havana, are few and far between. Even in the capital you could easily pass a car park without realizing it, as they are often makeshift affairs, sometimes in the ruins of old buildings and almost always the product of local enterprise. Don't expect to see many parking signs either, though you may see "*parqueo*" scribbled on a wall or posted up on a piece of cardboard. Most of the large and luxurious hotels have their own car parks, but if you are staying in a *casa particular* or a smaller hotel the chances are you will need to ask someone where you can and should leave your vehicle. Leaving your car on the street is of course an option, but bear in mind that few if any car rental firms in Cuba offer insurance covering the cost of your wheels if they are stolen – a distinct possibility if you leave your car unattended overnight. Furthermore, the police have a tendency to look less favourably on any theft or damage to a vehicle if it is left anywhere other than a garage or a car park. At the very least you should look for someone who will watch your car for a fee; in most places even remotely touristy there will usually be someone willing (and sometimes looking) to do just that. In fact, even if you do leave your car unattended there is a decent chance that by the time you come back to it someone will be watching over it and maybe will have washed it – they will of course be expecting you to tip them.

If you can find a car park, however, there are still several things to be aware of. There will almost always be an attendant and you will need to establish whether to pay in advance or when you return. If you are leaving your car overnight, the chances are you will have to cough up in advance, as there will be someone else on guard by the time you go to pick it up and they will expect a payment also. A couple of convertible pesos are usually more than enough to cover a nightshift, but logically it makes sense to establish a price beforehand and to find out when the attendant's shift ends. If the car park is particularly crowded you may be asked to leave your keys in the event that your car needs to be moved to allow another driver out.

Wherever and whenever you drive, expect to be beeped at quite frequently, though not necessarily because you're doing anything wrong. Cuban drivers often use their horn when overtaking and when approaching crossroads in town centres.

Petrol stations are few and far between (you can drive for up to 150km on the *autopista* without passing one), and with so few cars on the *autopista* and no emergency telephones by the side of the road it's a good idea to keep a canister of petrol in the boot, or at the very least make sure you have a full tank before any long journeys. Officially, **tourist cars** can only fill up at convertible-peso petrol stations, identifiable by the names Cupet-Cimex and Oro Negro, the two chains responsible for running them. They are rarely if ever self-service, and tipping is not unheard of. The cost of petrol is 95¢ per litre for *especial* (which some rented cars require by law), 75¢ for regular and 45¢ for diesel, still used in one or two models. Black-market prices hover around 50¢ per litre for *especial*, but getting hold of it can be tricky unless you have a trusted contact.

Roads

Strictly speaking, there are two **motorways** in the whole of Cuba: the A4 between Havana and the provincial capital of Pinar del Río and the A1 between Havana and the eastern edge of Sancti Spíritus province. However, both are referred to simply as *el autopista*, literally "the motorway", and are

Road trip essentials

With petrol stations and roadside services so scarce, it pays to be prepared when making long-distance journeys in Cuba. Below are a few suggestions for items to take out on the road with you, some of which could prove invaluable.

- Toilet paper
- Torch/flashlight
- Soap
- Water bottle
- Canister of petrol
- Medical kit (see p.52)
- Guía de Carreteras

sometimes considered one and the same given that they form the sole motorway links to either side of the capital. Supposedly, *el autopista* fluctuates between six and eight lanes wide but road markings are almost nonexistent, a fact that, combined with the 100km/hr speed limit, would undoubtedly lead to accidents were there more traffic. As it stands, the *autopista* is amongst the most deserted major roads in Cuba, and there is as much chance of colliding with a cow as with another vehicle.

Though, as is the case all over Cuba, there is a desperate lack of road signs along the *autopista*, there is one way to know roughly where you are: down the middle are **small plaques** marking the distance from Havana in kilometres. This system is also used as a form of giving directions and addresses in Cuban maps and travel literature. Thus, the turn-off for a town may be given as being at Km 50, or fifty kilometres along the motorway from Havana. We use this same system in this book. In some provinces, such as Matanzas, these plaques appear sporadically, while in others, such as Pinar del Río, they line almost the entire length of the route.

The main alternative route for most long-distance journeys is the two-lane **Carretera Central** (sometimes marked as CC on maps), an older, more congested road running the entire length of the island with an 80km/hr speed limit. This tends to be a more scenic option, which is just as well, as you can spend hours on it stuck behind slow-moving tractors, trucks and horse-drawn carriages. It is also the only major road linking up the eastern half of the island, and on a drive from Havana to Santiago de Cuba it becomes the nearest thing to a motorway from the eastern side of Sancti Spíritus province onwards.

There are more options for alternative routes in the western half of Cuba, where there are two other principal roads: the **Circuito Norte** (CN), the quickest route between some of the towns along the northern coast, and the **Circuito Sur** (CS), linking up parts of the southern coast. The Circuito Norte runs between Havana and Morón in Ciego de Ávila and is the best road link between the capital and Varadero, a stretch better known as the **Vía Blanca**.

Taxis

Taxis are one of the most popular expressions of private enterprise in Cuba. There are essentially four different kinds of automotive taxi service, although it often seems that merely owning a car qualifies a person as a taxi driver.

Metered state taxis

The official metered state taxis, often referred to as **tourist taxis** (or *turistaxis*), are usually modern cars, commonly Nissans, Peugeots and Mercedes. Though older Russian models like Ladas are also used by some state-run taxi services, these are rarely referred to as tourist taxis. Most towns with a convertible-peso hotel have a tourist taxi service, often run from the hotels themselves, and getting hold of one by telephone isn't usually a problem. Fares are always charged in convertible pesos; Panataxi tend to work out marginally cheaper than most of the other firms, while Gaviota taxis are amongst the most expensive.

The size and style of the car determine the cost of your ride more than anything else; that said, some agencies, Transtur for example, operate three or four different tariffs for the same car. Which tariff you are charged will depend on a number of murky factors including high or low season and the state of business in general, but it can come down to the whim of the man setting the rates at HQ, which could change on a daily basis. For the smallest hatchback taxi in a provincial town you will be charged just 30¢/km, while in Havana a large car can cost as much as 90¢/km, with luxury taxis a grade above that. On the whole, though, in most cities and resorts, expect to pay around 55¢/km.

Private taxis

Just as common as the newer, metered state taxi vehicles are the privately owned cars, predominantly 1950s American classics or Ladas, which have been converted into taxis by their owners. The local name for these is *máquinas* or *taxis particulares*, but those that carry tourists are referred to throughout this guide as **private taxis**.

There is no way of telling from outward appearances which currency the taxi is licensed to accept – national pesos or convertible pesos. It is assumed that as a foreigner you will be paying in convertible pesos, and, as illegality is not enough to deter most drivers, the suspicious behaviour and strange routes which characterize many a private taxi ride more likely means the driver is national-peso-licensed and trying to avoid the police rather than trying to rip you off.

The least expensive metered state taxis invariably work out cheaper than many private drivers' rates. Most journeys within a city will cost between $2CUC and $5CUC, but **negotiation** is part of the whole unofficial system, and if you don't haggle the chances are you'll end up paying double what a cheap state taxi would have cost. For example, most drivers in Havana would accept $4CUC for the journey from the Parque Central in Habana Vieja to the Plaza de la Revolución. The essential thing is that you **establish a price** before you begin your journey. In general, you're better off hailing a cheap state taxi wherever possible, but outside of Havana and the major resorts you may not have much choice. Be aware also that private taxi drivers may pick up another passenger en route, effectively but unofficially becoming what is known as a *taxi colectivo*.

Taxis colectivos

Taxis colectivos are usually national-peso-charging taxis and similar to a bus service. These can be either state-run or privately owned vehicles, but the key thing to remember is that they tend to work **specific routes** and only local knowledge will inform you as to what these routes actually are. It's difficult to distinguish a *taxi colectivo* from a private taxi, but if you see an old American car packed with people, it's most likely a *colectivo*.

A *colectivo* driver will pack as many people into his car as will fit, replacing anyone who gets out as quickly as possible, and it is usual for a driver to seek to fill his car with the maximum number of passengers before he sets off, shouting out his destination in the hope of finding more customers. You may find it hard to flag down a *colectivo* because it's unusual for tourists to use these taxis, so many drivers assume you're expecting a normal taxi service. Although *colectivos* primarily operate inside cities or towns, drivers are often willing to take you long distances and there is usually a specific area of a town, invariably next door to a bus station, where taxis waiting for long-distance passengers congregate.

It is generally accepted in Havana that a trip in a *colectivo* anywhere within the city will cost $10CUP; the rest of the country follows along similar lines. Don't expect, though, to necessarily be charged the same fare as Cubans: understandably, few drivers will let pass the opportunity to charge in convertible pesos and at tourist taxi rates, but again **negotiation** is part of the process. The universally accepted but nonetheless unofficial fare for interprovincial routes is $20CUP, but those filling their cars with tourists will charge in convertible pesos. As a rough indicator, a driver will be looking for between $20CUC and $30CUC per 100km, but this depends heavily upon whether the car is a gas-guzzling antique, in which case you should expect to pay more, or something more efficient like a Lada, the usual alternative.

State-run long-distance taxis

Though still underused, there are a growing number of **state-run long-distance taxi services**. These are actually a more realistic way of getting around the country than you might expect, given the kinds of fares you would be likely to clock up travelling the same distances by cab in other countries. You will only find official state-run long-distance taxis in the main tourist areas, but even in these the service is little known and rarely advertised. The easiest place to fix up a trip is Havana, also the only place where you can shop around and have a choice of the kind of car you travel in. For riding in style, Gran Car (☎7/33-5647) has a small fleet of near-perfect mid-twentieth-century American originals, which it also uses for shorter trips and tours around the city. Getting around the country in a '57 Chevy or Mercury doesn't come cheap: the return trip to Trinidad, for example, costs $350CUC, much more expensive than flying. Better value still is the transfer service available through Havanatur (☎7/203-9815 & 203-9510, ⓦwww.havanatur.cu), who run timetabled taxis between Havana and

destinations in Pinar del Río for about $12CUC per journey, while links to other destinations can be negotiated.

Bicitaxis and cocotaxis

Bicitaxis (also known as *ciclotaxis*) are three-wheeled bicycles with enough room for two passengers, sometimes three at a squeeze. In use all over the island, there are legions of these in Havana, where you won't have to wait long before one crosses your path. Fares are not all that different from tourist taxis, but again, negotiation is part of the deal. Around $1CUC per kilometre should usually be more than enough.

Less common **cocotaxis**, sometimes called *mototaxis* are aimed strictly at the tourist market and offer the novel experience of a ride around town semi-encased in a giant yellow bowling ball, dragged along by a small scooter. Fares in Havana have become standardized at 50¢ per kilometre, but there will always be drivers looking to charge unsuspecting tourists a higher rate.

Cycling

Cycling is one of the best ways of getting around Cuba, assuming you have the stamina for the heat. However, though bicycles are a common transportation alternative, cycling for recreation is less popular, and there are only limited opportunities for visitors not on a prepackaged cycling tour – only a few hotels, mostly beach resorts, rent out bicycles, and there are just a few cycling shops on the whole island and only one specialist Cuban-run rental firm, El Orbe in Havana (see p.194). This gap in the market has been partially filled by a couple of Canadian firms who have set up bicycle workshops in Havana (see opposite).

The national travel agents Havanatur (ⓦwww.havanatur.cu) and Cubamar (ⓦwww.cubamarviajes.cu) offer *cicloturismo* packages, usually week-long cycle tours which need a minimum number of people, usually six. Both operate along similar lines, with routes based on journeys in between well-known tourist poles and each night spent in a hotel at the day's destination. Rates start at between $850CUC and $1000CUC per person for groups of ten or less but the price goes down for bigger groups, as low as $600CUC per person for groups of thirty or more. The Canadian-based company MacQueen's Island Tours (®www.wowcuba.com), which also offers cycling tours around the island, is one of the few institutions in Cuba providing a professional bike rental service, though this is only available to people who have booked their holiday accommodation through the same company. From their office (☎7/95-1010 ext. 154, ©wowcuba@enet.cu) in the *Hotel Panamericano* in Havana's Cojímar district, you can rent out hybrid and mountain bikes starting at $100CUC for three days.

The best place to go if you want to rent out bikes individually and independently without having to book in advance is Bicicletas Cruzando Fronteras (☎7/860-8532 & 862-7065), a non-profit organization which has set up a bicycle workshop at San Juan de Dios esq. Aguacate in Habana Vieja. They have by far the widest selection of bikes for rent anywhere in the country, including mountain bikes, racers and various other models, and offer very reasonable rates and will do repairs, too. Travellers from the UK

might prefer to contact Blazing Saddles, a small, independent company based in London which will deliver bicycles for rent to wherever you are staying once on the island (see p.33).

If you get a puncture or your brake cable snaps, you won't have to travel far before coming across a *ponchera*. These places are usually run from a front room or roadside shelter, where for a few national pesos you can get your puncture repaired or replace anything they have spare parts for, which often isn't that much.

If you do intend to cycle in Cuba it's worth bringing your own padlock, as they are rarely supplied with rental bikes and are difficult to find for sale. Most Cubans use the commonplace *parqueos de ciclos*, privately run bike-parks, often down the side of houses or actually inside them, where the owner will look after your bike for a peso or two until you get back.

By ferry

There are very few ferry services linking the mainland of Cuba with the numerous cays

Addresses

Most addresses are written as being located between one street, or *calle* in Spanish, and another, with the Spanish word for between, *entre*, abbreviated to *e/*. Thus the address of a hotel located on street L between street 23 and street 25 would normally be written as Calle L e/ 23 y 25. If a building is on a corner, then the abbreviation *esq.*, short for *esquina*, is used. So the address of a house on the corner of San Lázaro and the Avenida de Italia would appear as San Lázaro esq. Ave. de Italia. You may also see this written as San Lázaro esq. a Ave. de Italia or even San Lázaro y Ave. de Italia. Ordinal numbers also appear in addresses in abbreviated form, so that Avenida Primera is written Ave. 1era or 1ra with the following sequence for the numbers from 2 to 9: 2da, 3era or 3ra, 4ta, 5ta, 6ta, 7ma, 8va and 9na. You should also look out for the use of the words *altos* and *bajos*, which indicate top-floor and ground-floor flats, respectively. When an address incorporates the *autopista* or the Carretera Central, it may often include its distance from Havana. Thus the address Autopista Nacional km 142, Matanzas is 142km down the *autopista* from Havana. These distances are often marked by signs appearing every kilometre at the roadside.

Following the 1959 Revolution, streets in towns and cities throughout Cuba were renamed after people, places and events held in high esteem by the new regime. The old names, however, continued to be used and today most locals still refer to them. Where a name appears on a street sign it will almost always be the new name. Wherever addresses are written down they tend to also use the new name, though some tourist literature has now returned to using the old names. Where an address incorporating a renamed street appears in this book the new name will be used with the old name in brackets.

Hitching a lift is as common in Cuba as catching a bus, with some people getting around exclusively this way. The petrol shortages following the collapse of trade with the former Soviet Union meant every available vehicle had to be utilized by the state effectively as public transport. Thus a system was adopted whereby any private vehicle, from cars to tractors, was obliged to pick up anyone hitching a lift. The yellow-suited workers employed by the government to hail down vehicles at bus stops and junctions on the *autopista* can still be seen today, though their numbers have decreased somewhat. Nevertheless, the culture of hitching, or *coger botella* as it is known in Cuba, remains, though drivers often ask for a few pesos these days. Crowds of people still wait by bridges and junctions along the major roads for trucks or anything else to stop. Tourists, though they are likely to attract a few puzzled stares, are welcome to join in. That said, it's always important to consider the risks involved with hitchhiking.

off both its north and south coasts. The only established, regular ferry service goes to the Isla de la Juventud from the Terminal Marítima de Batabanó (☎62/58-8240) on the southern coast of Havana province. In the same group of islands, Cayo Largo remains out of reach by anything other than aeroplane.

Health

Providing you take common-sense precautions, visiting Cuba poses no particular health risks. In fact, some of the most impressive advances made by the revolutionary government since 1959 have been in the field of medicine and the free health service provided to all Cuban citizens. Since 1959, vaccination programmes have eliminated malaria, polio and tetanus, while advances in medical science have attracted patients from around the world who come for unique treatments developed for a variety of conditions such as night blindness, psoriasis and radiation sickness.

No **vaccinations** are legally required in order to visit Cuba, unless you're arriving from a country where yellow fever and cholera are endemic, in which case you'll need a vaccination certificate. It is still advisable, however, to get inoculations for hepatitis A, tetanus and typhoid. For anyone intending to make frequent visits to Cuba, it is worth bearing in mind that a booster dose of the hepatitis A vaccination within six to twelve months of the first dose will provide immunity for approximately ten years.

It is essential to bring your own medical kit (see box, p.52), painkillers and any other medical supplies you think you might need, as they are difficult to buy on the island and choice is extremely limited.

Food and water

Drinking tap water is never a good idea in Cuba, even in the swankiest hotels. Whenever you are offered water, whether in a restaurant, *paladar* or private house, it's a good idea to check if it has been boiled – in most cases it will have been. **Bottled water** is available in convertible-peso shops and most tourist bars and restaurants, but there are a number of ways that you can purify water yourself. If you **boil your water**, make sure that once it reaches boiling point (100°C) you allow it to stay bubbling for a full two minutes. The two main alternatives to boiling are **filters** and **purification tablets**, neither of which is widely available in Cuba. To be extra safe, you can combine the last two methods, but if you do so make sure you filter first, as this can remove some of the active chemicals in the tablets.

Although reports of **food poisoning** are few and far between, there are good reasons for exercising caution when eating in Cuba. Food bought on the street is in the highest risk category and you should be aware that there is no official regulatory system ensuring acceptable levels of hygiene. Self-regulation does seem to be enough in most cases, but you should still take extra care when buying pizzas, meat-based snacks or ice cream from street-sellers. National peso restaurants can be equally suspect, particularly those in out-of-the-way places, where the near-absence of both tourists and competition means neither nonchalance nor negligence has any repercussions. The food is often very basic and, even when properly cooked, can be quite a shock to the untrained stomach. Convertible peso restaurants and *paladares*, on the other hand, tend to be much more reliable, although the state-run fast-food places are sometimes poorly maintained.

The most common food-related illness for travellers is diarrhoea, sometimes accompanied by vomiting or a mild fever. Try to avoid taking antibiotics unless prescribed by a doctor, and stick to the basic principles of rest and rehydration, drinking plenty of liquid (preferably bottled water, not alcohol or sugary drinks) and trying to replace lost salts. Eat plain foods like rice or bread and avoid fruit, fatty foods and dairy products. If symptoms persist for more than a few days, then salt solutions containing a small amount of sugar are recommended. If you haven't brought rehydration sachets, you can prepare your own solution by adding eight level teaspoons of sugar and half a teaspoon of salt to one litre of water.

Pests, bites and stings

Despite Cuba's colourful variety of fauna, there are no dangerously **venomous animals** on the island, the occasional scorpion being about as scary as it gets,

Heat-related problems

Cuba has a **hot and humid** climate, which can be hard to adjust to. The temperature remains relatively high even at night and so the body sweats more. Generally speaking, this means you will need an increased intake of salt and water, a lack of which can lead to heat exhaustion. Fatigue, headaches and nausea are all symptoms of **dehydration** and should be treated with rest and plenty of water, preferably with added salt. If sweating diminishes and the body temperature rises, this could be a sign of heatstroke, also known as **sunstroke** and potentially fatal, in which case immediate professional treatment is essential.

A common skin disorder caused by hot climates is **prickly heat** – symptoms consist mainly of rashes and sore skin – which can be guarded against by taking frequent showers, keeping yourself clean and dry and wearing loose cotton clothing. It can be treated with calamine lotion and you should avoid applying sunscreen or moisturiser to affected areas.

All the usual common-sense precautions should be taken when exposing yourself to the sun; most importantly, you should take care not to stay out in it for too long and don't use a **sunscreen** with a protection factor of less than 15. You may find sunscreen difficult to come by away from the hotels and the convertible peso shops, so be sure to pack some before taking any trips into less-visited areas. If you do burn, apply calamine lotion to the affected areas or, in more severe cases, a mild antiseptic.

A traveller's first-aid kit

Following are some of the items you might want to carry with you – especially if you're planning to go hiking (see p.74).

- Antihistamines
- Antiseptic cream
- Insect repellent
- Plasters/Band-aids
- Imodium (Lomotil) for emergency diarrhoea treatment
- Lint and sealed bandages
- Paracetamol/aspirin
- Multivitamin and mineral tablets
- Rehydration sachets
- Calamine lotion
- Hypodermic needles and sterilized skin wipes
- Thrush and cystitis remedies.

while the chances of contracting diseases from bites and stings are extremely slim. There are a number of insects whose bites are potentially very irritating but rarely if ever lethal.

Mosquitoes are the biggest pests, found throughout the island but particularly prevalent in Viñales, the Península de Zapata and the Isla de la Juventud, and although Cuba is not malarial there are occasional outbreaks of **dengue fever**, the most recent one in late 2006 when there were a number of fatalities as a result of the disease. There is no vaccine for this viral infection, most common during the rainy summer season, but, in general, serious cases are rare. Symptoms develop rapidly following infection and include extreme aches and pains in the bones and joints, severe headaches, dizziness, fever and vomiting. Rest is the best treatment, but, as with all disease, prevention is better than cure. Long sleeves and trousers significantly reduce the chances of being bitten, as do lotion, cream and spray repellents that contain DEET (diethyltoluamide). It's a good idea to pack **repellents** and **mosquito coils**, two of the most effective easy-to-carry insect-busters, before you leave for Cuba, as they are impossible to get hold of in quite a few areas. Air conditioning and fans also act as deterrents. If you do get bitten, try to resist scratching, which can encourage infection and will increase irritation. Instead, apply antihistamine cream or calamine lotion to the

affected areas or take antihistamine tablets.

In some areas **ticks** are also a problem, burrowing into the skin of any mammal they can get hold of and therefore more widespread wherever there is livestock. They lie in the grass waiting for passing victims, making walking barefoot a risky business. Repellent is ineffective against these creatures so your best form of defence is to wear trousers, which you should tuck into your socks. It is possible to remove ticks from your skin with tweezers but make sure that the head, which can easily get left behind, is plucked out along with the body. Smearing them first with Vaseline or even strong alcohol leaves less of a margin for error. Minuscule **sand flies** can make their presence felt on beaches at dusk by inflicting bites which cause prolonged itchiness.

AIDS and HIV

Cuba has a very low incidence of **HIV** positive citizens, but it has achieved this using controversial prevention techniques – though criticism has come from outside rather than from within the country. Between 1986 and 1989 the government compulsorily tested 75 percent of the adult population, and those people who tested positive were quarantined in residential parks, the most infamous being Finca Los Cocos in Havana. The approach to preventing and handling the disease has changed considerably since then, with AIDS sufferers' liberty no longer being restricted and Cuba still retaining one of the lowest HIV infection rates in the world.

The influx of foreign tourists – and the resultant expansion of the sex trade – threatens state control of the disease, but for now at least the risk of contracting AIDS in Cuba remains very low. All the usual common-sense precautions of course still apply, while the poor quality of Cuban condoms means it's worth bringing your own supply. Note that anyone planning on staying in Cuba longer than 90 days is required upon entry to show proof of their HIV-negative status.

Hospitals, clinics and pharmacies

Don't visit Cuba assuming that the country's world-famous free **health service** extends to foreign visitors – far from it. In fact, the government has used the advances made in medicines and medical treatments to earn extra revenue for the regime, through a system of health tourism. Each year, thousands of foreigners come to Cuba for everything from surgery (especially a night blindness operation unique to the island) to relaxation at a network of anti-stress clinics, such as the one at Topes de Collantes, offering massage and various other therapies. Such services don't come cheap, entailing some pretty unhealthy medical fees for visitors who spend time in Cuban hospitals, effectively subsidizing health care for the country's citizens.

Even with all the government investment in the medical sector, Cuba's health service has been hit hard by the US trade embargo. The worst affected area is the supply of medicines, and some hospitals now simply cannot treat patients through lack of resources.

Hospitals and clinics

There are specific **hospitals** which accept foreign patients and one or two that are exclusively for non-nationals, most of them run by Cubanacán (Ⓦwww.cubanacan.cu /espanol/turismo/salud) and its subsidiary Servimed (Ⓦwww.servimedcuba.com), an organization set up in 1994 to deal

exclusively with health tourism. The only general hospital for foreigners, as compared to the various institutions set up for specific ailments and conditions, is the Clínica Central Cira García (☎7/204-2811 to 14, Ⓦwww.cirag.cu) at Calle 20 no.4101 esq. 41 in the capital's Miramar district. There are, however, dotted around the island, various **medical centres** set up specifically for tourists, known as *Clínicas Internacionales*. Some hospitals, such as Havana's Hospital Hermanos Ameijeiras, considered the best of its kind in Cuba, have designated sections for convertible-peso-paying patients. In these, unlike in the Cuban sections, patients are not expected to supply their own towels, soap, toilet paper and even their own food.

If you do wind up in hospital in Cuba, one of the first things you or someone you know should do is contact **Asistur** (Ⓦwww.asistur .cu; see p.66 for office addresses), who usually deal with insurance claims on behalf of the hospital, as well as offering various kinds of assistance, from supplying ambulances and wheelchairs to obtaining and sending medical reports. However, for minor complaints you shouldn't have to go further than the hotel doctor, who will give you a consultation. If you're staying in a *casa particular*, things are slightly more complicated. Your best bet, if you feel ill, is to inform your hosts, who should be able to call the family doctor, the *médico de la familia*, and arrange a house-call. This is common practice in Cuba where, with one doctor for every 169 inhabitants, it's possible for them to personally visit all their patients.

Pharmacies

There are two types of **pharmacy** in Cuba: tourist pharmacies operating in convertible pesos, and national peso pharmacies for the population at large. Tourists are permitted to use the antiquated peso establishments but will rarely find anything of use in them besides aspirin, as they primarily deal in prescription-only drugs. You may have to ask to be directed to the convertible-peso equivalents, which only exist in some of the largest towns, as detailed throughout the guide. Most of the tourist pharmacies are run by Servimed (☎07/204-0141 to 42, Ⓦwww .servimedcuba.com) and you should ask for the nearest *Clínica Internacional* within which they are normally located. Even in these there is not the range of medicines that you might expect, and if you have a preferred brand or type of painkiller, or any other everyday drug, you should bring it with you. A small number of hotels, such as the *Hotel Nacional* in Havana, have their own pharmacies, while some tourist hospitals have a counter generally selling only non-prescription drugs.

Medical resources for travellers

US and Canada

CDC ⓦ www.cdc.gov/travel. Official US government travel health site.
International Society for Travel Medicine ⓦ www.istm.org. Has a full list of travel health clinics.
Canadian Society for International Health ⓦ www.csih.org. Extensive list of travel health centres.

Australia, New Zealand and South Africa

Travellers' medical and Vaccination Centre ⓦ www.tmvc.com.au, ☎ 1300/658 844. Lists travel clinics in Australia, New Zealand and South Africa.

UK and Ireland

British Airways Travel Clinics ☎ 012776/685-040 or ⓦ www.britishairways.com/travel /healthclinintro/public/en_gb for nearest clinic.
Hospital for Tropical Diseases Travel Clinic ☎ 020/7387-5000 or 0845/155-5000, ⓦ www .thehtd.org.
MASTA (Medical Advisory Service for Travellers Abroad) ⓦ www.masta.org or ☎ 0113/238-7575 for the nearest clinic.
Travel Medicine Services ☎ 028/9031 5220.
Tropical Medical Bureau ☎ 1850/487 674, ⓦ www.tmb.ie.

Accommodation

Broadly speaking, accommodation in Cuba falls into two types, state and private. All hotels in Cuba are either fully or partially state-owned, and you'll find at least one in every large town for which you should budget at least $25–30CUC per night. Private accommodation, in *casas particulares*, works out cheaper at between $15CUC and $30CUC. Only in major tourist areas like Havana, Varadero and Guardalavaca will you need to pay more.

State hotels

The major downside of staying in a **state hotel** is that your contact with Cubans will be more limited than if staying in a *casa particular*. Although the rigorous restraints of the late 1990s have been relaxed, you are unlikely to be able to entertain Cuban friends in your room unless they have a foreign passport. While rooms in most state hotels, even the ones at the cheaper end of the scale, are generally a decent size and often have a balcony, there are a few things worth mentioning. In all but the top-end hotels the air-conditioning unit is likely to be large, leaky and noisy. There is little point complaining to the management about this: all the rooms are equally equipped. Earplugs are really the only option for a peaceful night's sleep. Also, take a sink plug with you, as these are often missing in the rooms.

Check-out time in state hotels is usually noon but is relatively flexible, particularly in the less expensive hotels; make sure to tell the front desk if you plan to be significantly later. Also, most hotels have a luggage room

Accommodation price codes

All accommodation listed in this guide has been graded according to the following price categories.

- ❶ less than $20CUC
- ❷ $20–30CUC
- ❸ $30–40CUC
- ❹ $40–50CUC
- ❺ $50–60CUC
- ❻ $60–80CUC
- ❼ $80–120CUC
- ❽ $120–180CUC
- ❾ $180CUC or above

Rates are for the cheapest available double or twin room during high season – usually mid-December to mid-March and all of July and August. During low season, some hotels lower their prices by roughly 10–25 percent.

where you can store your bags once you have checked out of your room.

Luxury hotels

Gran Caribe owns the majority of classic hotels in Havana like the *Hotel Nacional* and the *Hotel Inglaterra*, as well as many of the all-inclusives. Rooms are on a par with those in international luxury hotels, with all mod cons including minibars, television, hot water and a full complement of miniature bath products. These hotels generally have several restaurants (often serving some of the best food Cuba has to offer), huge pools, and an array of other services.

The remaining luxury hotels are owned by Cuban and foreign hotel companies, including the **Sol Meliá** chain (®www .solmelia.com). If smooth service of an international standard is your priority, you'll want to stay at hotels co-owned by international companies. The joint ownership has a visible impact on the quality of service and amenities, with extras such as gyms, tennis courts, wireless Internet connection in lobbies and decent restaurants on offer. Be prepared to pay accordingly – prices for a double room can be as high as $150–250CUC a night. However, it is always worth trying to negotiate an off-peak rate, as several of these hotels are prepared to

offer reduced-rate rooms when not fully booked. It's better to arrange this by speaking directly to the hotel manager, as opposed to going through a tour operator. You should ensure that you get confirmation of any arrangement made, by fax where possible. At the very least, take the name and number of the person with whom you made the arrangement.

Hostales

These state-owned hotels are similar to Western boutique hotels in that they are usually smaller than the big corporate hotels and are invariably more stylish. Competitively priced when compared with standard state hotels, they are still a more expensive option than staying in a *casa particular*. The chief attributes of **hostales** are style and location. Carved out of existing beautiful buildings, some of which were pre-Revolution hotels, *hostales* are generally quaint and attractive places to stay, though service is likely to fall short of unadulterated luxury. They offer all the facilities you would expect to find in a good-quality hotel, including decent restaurants, concierge services and shops.

All-inclusives

The first fact to grasp about **all-inclusives** in Cuba is that many aren't inclusive of

Several of the larger hotels in Cuba have been temporarily converted into hospitals or accommodation for overseas visitors awaiting operations in accordance with Misión Milagro, an international aid programme in which people from Venezuela and other countries are given free medical care in Cuba (see p.604). Any hotels converted at the time of writing have been removed from the text. Those converted tend to be the larger state hotels often located at the edge of provincial towns.

everything at all. Although billed as a complete package of room, meals, drinks, watersports and entertainment, sometimes this will mean only nationally produced drinks and extra charges for motorized watersports, so you should check the conditions at each hotel carefully. Prices are generally upwards of $70CUC a night, with cheaper deals for those on package tours. All-inclusives can still be excellent value if you are looking for a sun-sea-sand holiday with minimum hassle, and they're often your only accommodation option at the country's better beaches. However, as many of the prime resorts, like Santa Lucía, Guardalavaca and Cayo Coco, tend to revolve around a deserted beach, they can be rather remote, with no real infrastructure to support them. In effect, resorts like these really consist of a series of all-inclusive hotels and a few purpose-built tourist restaurants and attractions, which consequently can make them feel a little contrived. A two-week stay in an all-inclusive here – while nice and often competitively priced against similar resort packages in other Caribbean countries – certainly won't give you a real impression of Cuba.

Peso state hotels

The cheapest accommodation in Cuba is a **peso state hotel**, most commonly found in less cosmopolitan towns away from the tourist centres. Although their nightly rates are sometimes the equivalent of a couple of convertible pesos, you get your money's worth, as these are often extremely dilapidated properties, with bare-bones facilities including basically only a very poor bathroom and ripped sheets. Peso state hotels are intended to be exclusively for Cubans, and the state does not promote them for visitor use; they are listed in the guide only where other options do not exist. If you go to one you may well be told that all rooms are full, whether they actually are or not. Despite this, if you're looking for an absolute budget option it's always worth asking, as admission often depends on the whim of the person on reception – a donation to whoever is in charge sometimes helps.

Casas particulares

For many visitors, staying in *casas particulares* – literally "private houses" – is an ideal way to gain an insight into the country and its people. They are becoming more common throughout Cuba, and today are found in all major towns and many smaller ones. They'll often as not find you, with touts (called *jineteros* or *intermediarios*) waiting in many towns to meet potential customers off the bus. Their services don't come free, though; if you're brought to the *casa particular* by a tout, you can expect an additional cost of roughly $5CUC per night. *Casas particulares* are identifiable by blue or green insignia (shaped like a capital I or sideways H) usually displayed near the front door. (Houses displaying insignia in red or yellow rent in pesos and to Cubans only).

As the trade has burgeoned over the past few years, a number of *casas particulares* in the larger towns have become increasingly professional, moving away from the homely room in a family house which was once the industry standard and offering as many facilities as possible, such as (noisy) air conditioning and private bathrooms with hot water. Many places in popular visitor enclaves like Trinidad and Baracoa offer several rooms (between three and seven) and are run much more like a boarding house or *pension*, with a central eating area, lounges and sometimes the use of a patio or terrace. However, since a larger number of rooms have been sliced out of existing spaces, they often have no natural light, making them a little dingy. Recent legislation (see box, opposite) theoretically prohibits owners from renting more than two rooms, but this rule is often bent in the interests of free enterprise. While they may be subject to penalization if caught, you are not breaking the law by staying in such a property.

It's a good idea to phone ahead where possible and book. This is, however, not always a guarantee that you will secure a room in the house of your choice. Many *casas particulares* will not tell you when they are full; instead they will allow you to turn up, and then they will escort you to another *casa particular* from which they will collect a commission. There is little you can do to circumvent this, but you can mention when

Casas particulares and the law

The laws governing *casas particulares* change in a frequent and often bizarre-seeming fashion. Basically, this is done so that the government can maintain control of the income that Cubans make from private enterprise – though the party line is that it's to ensure that quality of life is not supplanted by private enterprise. For example, at the time of writing, recent changes to the law have decreed that families may now only let "spare" rooms not otherwise being used as family living quarters. This effectively puts out of business a lot of smaller *casas particulares* which otherwise might have cleared out a family bedroom for the duration of a guest's stay.

Of the host of other, new and seemingly minor legal caveats, the ones most likely to affect you say that proprietors can only rent a maximum of two rooms and can no longer rent a whole apartment or house unless it has a connecting door to the owners' living quarters. Also, guests cannot have more than two people per room unless they're parents with children under the age of 16.

you book that you would prefer not to be referred elsewhere.

Casas particulares all have business cards that they give out to travellers who have stayed with them. It is an excellent idea to ask other travellers for cards and recommendations, as presenting this on arrival will often secure a reduction in rate and allow you again to avoid the touts. Some places also have email accounts, allowing you to book well in advance. Other useful resources include ⓦwww.casahavana.co.uk, ⓦwww.casaparticular.info, ⓦwww.cubacasas.net and ⓦwww.lahabana.com, which allow you to book online.

Prices vary according to area and level of taxation, but all are reasonably priced and as a rule $25–30CUC is the most you will ever pay. You can also negotiate a lower rate for a longer stay. The law requires proprietors to register the names and passport numbers of all guests, and you are expected to enter your details into an official yellow book as soon as you arrive. You usually settle up in cash at the end of your stay, as traveller's cheques are not accepted.

Most *casas particulares* offer breakfast and an evening meal for an extra cost, which can be anything between $1CUC and $10CUC, with $5CUC the average. Make sure that you are clear about the cost of meals and agree to the rate at the start of your stay. Drinks will also be added to your bill: if you are drinking beer with your evening meal this will also be charged to your bill, with most houses charging around $2CUC a bottle.

Remember you'll be charged for any bottled water you drink, too.

In addition to registered *casas particulares*, there are many that operate illegally without paying taxes. You are not breaking the law by staying in one, and they can be as viable an option as their registered counterparts, if usually no cheaper. If you do stay in this type of accommodation and encounter a problem, however, you will get little sympathy from the authorities.

Campismos

Often overlooked by visitors to Cuba, **campismos**, quasi-campsites, are an excellent countryside accommodation option. Although not prolific, all provinces have at least one, often set in sweeping countryside near a sparkling ribbon of river or small stretch of beach, making them perfect for a relaxing break. While a number of *campismos* have an area where you can pitch a tent, they are not campsites in the conventional sense, essentially offering basic accommodation in rudimentary concrete cabins. Some have barbecue areas, while others have a canteen restaurant. They are all very reasonably priced, usually around $5–10CUC a night per cabin, though expect to pay more like $20CUC in more tourist-oriented areas. Although foreigners are welcome, this is one accommodation choice where Cubans actually have priority, and *campismos* are sometimes block-booked in June and July for workers' annual holidays. For more details contact Cubamar, Ave. Paseo no.306 e/ 13

Avoiding the accommodation touts

The biggest drawback of staying in *casas particulares* is that you might have to run the gauntlet of the touts, also known as *jineteros* or *intermediarios*. Ostensibly, these are locals who work as brokers for a number of houses and try to collect as many clients as possible. In return they collect a commission, usually $5CUC, which gets added to your nightly bill. Be aware that they will often demand their commission from any *casa particular* to which they have taken customers – even when they have done little more than given directions to you. There is no way to avoid the attention of these people outright when you arrive in a town and it can be incredibly frustrating when you feel besieged by people hassling you at every turn. There are, though, several ways to avoid falling prey to touts and thus having your accommodation bill increased unnecessarily:

If you are approached, state that you have already organized accommodation, but don't disclose where. Often touts will arrive at your chosen house first and tell the owners that they have sent you themselves.

Always book ahead. When you arrive in town phone the *casa particular* and ask the owners to come and meet you to escort you to the house. They are usually happy to do this, particularly as it ensures you are not spirited away by other touts.

One of the best ways of finding a *casa particular* in another town is by referral. Most *casas particulares* owners have a network of houses in other towns which they will recommend, and will often even phone and make a reservation for you, or at the very least give you that house's card.

If possible, avoid searching for the *casa particular* of your choice while loaded with your bags. If you are not travelling alone, one person should stay with the bags while the others go and look.

If you need to ask for directions, ask for the street by name rather than the house you want to get to. Another trick to watch for is that *intermediarios* will pretend to direct you to the house of your choice but will actually take you to a totally different house where their commission is better.

---

y 15, Vedado, Havana (℡7/66-2523 to 24, ⓦwww.cubamarviajes.cu).

Youth hostel associations

US and Canada

Hostelling International-American Youth Hostels ℡301/495-1240, ⓦwww.hiayh.org.
Hostelling International Canada ℡1-800/663-5777, ⓦwww.hihostels.ca.

UK and Ireland

Youth Hostel Association (YHA) England and Wales ℡0870/770 8868, ⓦwww.yha.org.uk.

Scottish Youth Hostel Association ℡01786/891 400, ⓦwww.syha.org.uk.
Irish Youth Hostel Association ℡01/830 4555, ⓦwww.irelandyha.org.
Hostelling International Northern Ireland ℡028/9032 4733, ⓦwww.hini.org.uk.

Australia, New Zealand and South Africa

Australia Youth Hostels Association ℡02/9565 1699, ⓦwww.yha.com.au.
Youth Hostelling Association New Zealand ℡0800/278 299 or 03/379 9970, ⓦwww.yha.co.nz.

Food and drink

While you'll often be able to feast well on simply prepared, good food in Cuba, mealtimes here are certainly not the gastronomic delight enjoyed on other Caribbean islands. With the exception of garlic and onion, spices are not really used in cooking, and most Cubans have a distaste for hot, spicy food altogether. The main culinary aspiration is North American, with fast food popular and readily available, to which the fried chicken and hybrid pizza outlets you'll find in all major towns and some smaller places bear witness. The quality is likely to be poorer than you are used to, though, even by fast-food standards; fried chicken is often either cooked to a frazzle or still alarmingly pink within, while pizzas are little more than a doughy base spread with sauce.

In some ways Cuba is still suffering from the aftershock of the severe food shortages of the Special Period in the 1990s. While everyone now has enough to eat, choice is still rather limited – you'll find the same platters cropping up time and again, and it is rare that you will find a restaurant can actually serve all that the menu boasts. The rather indifferent answer "no hay" (there isn't any) will be an oft-repeated refrain.

Whatever people may tell you, however, Cuba's culinary blandness is not all due to the Revolution. There is a general lack of creativity and few ingredients are combined to make original dishes. That said, all ingredients used are usually fresh and often **organic** and so less prone to the health scares common to the Western world's food chain. There is no factory farming in Cuba, and the food is not pumped full of hormones and artificial fertilizers – partly due to the constraints of the Special Period, Cuba was a pioneer in the use of ecologically sound farming, all of which means that the ingredients do tend to be full of flavour.

One of the worst problems you will encounter when eating out is **overcharging**, which is so widespread that it's unlikely you will make it through your trip without experiencing it. Fail-safe troubleshooting methods include asking for the menu with your bill and tallying your own bill accordingly. Point out the discrepancy calmly – you'll gain nothing by having a paddy – and it will usually be amended without comment (or apology).

As a general rule, always carry enough money to pay for your meal in **cash**. Although some of the top-end restaurants take credit cards, using this form of payment results in problems (real or created) so often that it's best avoided entirely.

State restaurants and paladares

Restaurants in Cuba are divided into two categories: state restaurants and cafés, and privately run *paladares*. Covering both convertible-peso establishments and national peso eateries, **state restaurants** differ greatly in quality – ranging from tasty meals in congenial settings to simply diabolical. As a visitor you are more likely to stick to the convertible-peso establishments which, particularly in the large cities and tourist areas, tend to have better-quality food and and a wider range of options, including some international cuisine like Chinese and Italian; they also tend to be cleaner and generally more pleasant. (The other viable option for decent meals is the restaurants in the **tourist hotels**, although the food dished up in these is quite removed from Cuban cuisine – with pizza and pasta dishes figuring heavily.) There are also various **state café chains**, Rumbos and El Rápido being the two most common, serving cheap fried chicken, fries, hot dogs and occasionally burgers.

Peso restaurants, mostly located outside tourist areas, cater essentially to Cubans. While undeniably lower in quality than convertible peso restaurants, these are still worth checking out, as you can occasionally get a decent meal very cheaply. You should not have to pay more than locals do, so make sure your menu has prices listed in pesos. In contrast, state-run roadside **peso cafés** are as a rule unhygienic and poorly run, and should be avoided wherever possible.

Service in many state establishments, particularly at the cheaper end, is at best leisurely, at worst infuriatingly slow. It's not uncommon to see staff chat on relentlessly, their backs to the restaurant while customers wait. It's pointless to get worked up about this: instead, just don't plan to hurry over your meals.

Privately run, usually from a spare room in the proprietor's house, **paladares** – a 1990s Cuban phenomenon – are a godsend. Introduced by the state in response to Cubans wanting to earn money through private enterprise, they offer visitors a chance to sample good Cuban home cooking in an informal atmosphere. Tight restrictions are imposed on what food they can serve: beef and seafood are always prohibited (although you may be offered them anyway), and lamb and mutton are banned in some provinces. Chicken and pork, however, are always on the menu, generously dished up in well-cooked, usually fried, meals. Although the menu will have few, if any, set vegetarian options, *paladares* are more accommodating than state restaurants to off-menu ordering, making them a good choice for non-meat-eaters.

Technically, *paladares* are allowed to seat no more than twelve people, but several, notably the smartest establishments in Havana, have considerably more. (Theories abound as to why this is.) *Paladares* are plentiful in Havana, and while most large towns have at least one, some smaller towns don't have any. *Paladar* owners in certain towns, such as Matanzas and Santa Clara, have even tighter restrictions to contend with (eg, they can't providing any seating to customers). As a result, you may come across standing-room-only *paladares*, sometimes with a bar to lean against but generally intended as takeaway places.

Prices are usually uniform, with a main meal costing $5–12CUC, but always check your bill carefully to avoid overcharging – some also include a service charge – and make sure it's itemized. Also, make sure that the menu has the prices written on it; every *paladar* has one, so request to see it. Be aware that if you're seen pulling up to a *paladar* in a state taxi, this usually pushes the prices up, so try to get dropped off a short distance away. Another thing to watch out for is touts (see box, p.58) – they can increase the price of a meal if they lead you to the *paladar*.

Street stalls

Also privately run, but usually from front gardens and driveways, the peso **street stalls** dotted around cities and towns are invariably the cheapest places to eat and an excellent choice for snacks and impromptu lunches, usually freshly home-made and very tasty. Dishes to look out for include corn fritters, cold pasta salad, pizza, sweet coconut or guava pies, sweets made from shredded coconut and copious amounts of sugar, and *torticas* – shortbread-style biscuits that are particularly good. It's wise to avoid the soft drinks, or at least ask if they have been prepared with boiled water (*agua hervida*) before sampling.

Cuban cuisine

Whether you eat in a restaurant, a *paladar*, or enjoy a meal cooked by friends, you will find that there is essentially little variety in **Cuban cuisine**, which revolves around a basic diet of pork or chicken dishes accompanied by rice and beans, generally known as **comida criolla**. Check meat carefully before you eat it, as pork sometimes comes undercooked. Cubans don't tend to eat as many fruit and vegetables as Westerners do, but these are plentiful and available in the markets.

While it's unlikely you'll be regularly sending fulsome compliments to the chef, there are a couple of **national dishes** worth trying. The majority of *paladares* serve variants on *ropa vieja*, an agreeable meat stew (either lamb or beef) prepared over a slow heat with green peppers, tomatoes, onions and garlic. Most often found on street stalls, *tamales* are prepared from cornmeal, peppers and onions, then wrapped in the outer leaves of the corn plant and steamed until soft. The somewhat bland taste is enlivened with a piquant red pepper sauce served on the side. One particularly divine delicacy is Lechón suckling pig, commonly marinated in garlic, onions and herbs before being spit- or oven-roasted.

Invariably accompanying any Cuban meal are the ubiquitous **rice and beans** (black or kidney), which come in two main guises: *congrís*, where the rice and beans are served mixed (also known as *moros y cristianos*), and *arroz con frijoles*, where white rice is served with a separate bowl of beans, cooked into a delicious soupy stew, to pour over it. Other traditional accompaniments are fried plantain; mashed, boiled or fried green bananas, which have a buttery, almost nutty taste; cassava, a starchy carbohydrate; and a simple salad of tomatoes, cucumber and avocado.

Breakfast and lunch

Breakfast in Cuba tends to be light, consisting of toast or, more commonly, a bread roll eaten with fried, boiled or scrambled eggs. The better hotels do buffet breakfasts that cover cooked eggs and meats, cold meat cuts and cheeses, and cereals; even if you're not a guest, these are the best places to head if you're hungry in the morning. It goes without saying you can expect to find *café con leche* – made with warm milk – on every breakfast table too.

Lunch also tends to be light, and although all restaurants serve main meals at lunchtime, the best bet is to follow the locals' lead and snack on maize fritters, *pan con pasta* – bread with a garlic mayonnaise filling – or cold pasta salad from the peso street stalls. Widely available and cheap, at between six and ten pesos, a pizza is a good basic option, but can differ wildly in quality, making it a good idea to look at what's being served before ordering.

Dinner

Cubans eat their main meal in the evening. The basis for a **typical dinner** is fried chicken or a pork chop or cutlet fried in garlic and onions, although some restaurants and *paladares* also serve goat, mutton and lamb. Although there is not as much fresh fish and seafood as you may expect, what you can get is excellent, particularly the lobster, prawns and fresh tuna. As a rule of thumb, the simpler the dish the better it will be. Grilled or pan-fried fish is usually a safe bet, but a more complex dish like risotto will most often disappoint.

Vegetarians

Vegetarianism is still in its infancy in Cuba, where the idea is basically the more meat there is on a plate, the better. Fussy eaters are seen as self-indulgent, especially since the Special Period, when all food was scarce. As a vegetarian your staple diet will be rice and beans, eggs, fried plantain, salads and pizzas. Cubans often class *jamonada* (Spam) as not really meat and will often mix pieces into vegetarian dishes, so always remember to specify that you want something without meat (*sin carne*) and ham (*sin jamón*).

Vegans will find that they will be extremely limited in what they can eat in Cuba and should take special care not to miss out on any vital nutrients. A good way to combat this is by taking along several bags of snacks like nuts and dried fruit. However, in recent years the government has begun a public health programme to promote the benefits of vegetables. A welcome result of this campaign is a new, small chain of vegetarian peso restaurants in Havana (confusingly, although the chain is called Vergel, each restaurant has its own name) which vary in quality, the best being quite impressively inventive. All the Vergel restaurants feature a wide range of salads (mainly shredded vegetables like carrots, cabbage and lettuce in vinaigrette) as well as various fried rice dishes and tofu-style soya confections (hamburgers, lasagne and croquettes) alongside delicately prepared vegetable dishes like baked aubergine and tomato and okra ratatouille.

Snacks

Convertible peso stores and supermarkets stock **snack foods** of varying quality; in the better ones you can get decent Western potato chips, unimaginative cookies, olives, canned fish for sandwich fillers and some fruit in addition to UHT long-life milk and breakfast cereal. Most of these items are fairly expensive – you can run up a grocery bill of $10–15CUC for just a handful of simple ingredients, but after a few days of Cuban fare you may consider it a small price to pay.

As you might expect from a sugar-producing country, there are several delicious **sweets** and desserts which you are more likely to find on a street stall than served up in a restaurant. Huge slabs of sponge cake coated in meringues are so popular at parties that the state actually supplies them for children's birthdays to make sure no one goes without. Also good are *torticas*, small round shortcake biscuits; *cocos*, immensely sweet confections of shredded coconut and brown sugar; and thick, jelly-like *guayaba* pasta that is often eaten with cheese.

Although **fruit** is plentiful in Cuba, much is for export and the top end of the tourist market. The best places to buy some are the *agromercados*, where you can load up cheaply with whatever is in season. Particularly good are the various types of mangoes, juicy oranges and sweet pineapples, while delicious lesser-known fruits include the prickly green soursop, with its unique sweet but tart taste, and the mamey, the thick, sweet red flesh of which is made into an excellent milkshake.

Drink

If you like *ron* or **rum** you'll be well-off in Cuba – the national drink is available every-where in several manifestations and is generally the most inexpensive tipple available – you can pick up a bottle for as little as $3CUC in supermarkets and hotels, while cocktails in bars only cost around $2–4CUC. Havana Club reigns supreme as the best brand, but also look out for Caribbean Club and Siboney. White rum is the cheapest form, generally used in cocktails, while the darker, older rums are best appreciated neat. As well as the authorized stuff sold bottled in hotels and convertible peso shops, there is

also a particularly lethal bootleg white rum, usually just called street rum (*ron de la calle*), which is guaranteed to leave you with a fearful hangover and probably partial memory loss. Thick and lined with oily swirls, it is usually sold in most neighbourhoods in the bigger cities; *jineteros* will certainly know where to go, but don't let yourself be charged more than a couple of convertible pesos a litre if you're brave enough to try the stuff.

Apart from rum itself, Cuba's most famous export is probably its **cocktails**, including the ubiquitous *Cuba Libre*. Made from white rum, Coke and a twist of lime, it's second only in popularity to the *mojito*, a refreshing combination of white rum, sugar, sparkling water and mint. A recent introduction to the drinks list is *alcopops*, made with a rum base and resembling Bacardi Breezers. Spirits other than rum are also available and are generally reasonably priced in all bars and restaurants, other than those in the prime tourist areas. The bottles on sale in many convertible-peso shops usually work out cheaper than in Europe.

Lager-type beer (*cerveza*) is plentiful in Cuba and there are some excellent national brands, particularly Cristal and Bucanero. These are usually both sold in cans and, less commonly, in bottles, even when served in bars and restaurants. Beer on draught is less common in Cuba, although you can find it in some bars, all-inclusive resorts and *moneda nacional* establishments.

When drinking **water** in Cuba, it's a good idea to stick to the bottled kind, which is readily available from all convertible-peso shops and hotels – or follow the lead of prudent locals and boil any tap water you plan to drink (see p.51).

Canned **soft drinks** are readily available from all convertible-peso shops, and in addition to Coke and Pepsi you can sample Cuba's own brands of lemonade (Cachito), cola (Tropicola, refreshingly less sugary than other cola drinks) and orangeade (the alarm-ingly Day-Glo Najita). Malta, a fizzy malt drink, is more of an acquired taste. Peso food stalls always serve non-carbonated soft drinks made from powdered packet mix – these cost just a couple of pesos, though you should be cautious about hygiene and the water supply. With the same caveats, try *granizado* (slush), served in a paper twist from portable street wagons; *guarapo*, a super-sweet frothy drink made from pressed sugar cane and mostly found at *agromercados*; and, a speciality in eastern Cuba, Prú, a refreshing drink fermented from sweet spices that tastes a little like spiced ginger beer. If you are in a bar, fresh lemonade (*limonada*) is rarely advertised but almost always available.

Coffee, served most often as pre-sweetened espresso, is the beverage of choice for many Cubans and is served in all restaurants and bars and at numerous peso

coffee stands dotted around town centres. Cubans tend to add sugar into the pot when making it, so there is little chance of getting it unsweetened other than in hotels and tourist restaurants. Aromatic packets of Cuban ground coffee and beans are sold throughout the country, and it's well worth buying a few packets to take home.

Tea is less common but still available in the more expensive hotels and better restaurants as an often unsuccessful marriage of lukewarm water and limp tea bag or a very stewed brew.

Money

Cuba's national unit of currency is the Cuban peso (CUP), or *peso cubano* in Spanish; it's referred to also as the national peso, and it's divided into 100 centavos. Banknotes are issued in denominations of 50, 20, 10, 5, 3 and 1. The lowest-value coin is the worthless 1c, followed by the 5c, 20c, 1-peso and 3-peso coins, this last adorned with the face of Che Guevara. Though virtually obsolete, you may still also see the 2c and 40c coins.

Whilst Cuban citizens are paid in national pesos, the currency used by the vast majority of foreign visitors is the **convertible peso** (CUC), or in Spanish the *peso convertible*, divided into centavos and, like the national peso, completely worthless outside of Cuba. Introduced in 1995, this unit of currency was previously interchangeable with the US dollar until, in late 2004, the Cuban Government declared that the dollar was no longer a valid currency on the island and whacked a hefty 10 percent tax on exchanging US dollars to convertible pesos. The colour and images on convertible peso banknotes are distinct from those on regular pesos and the notes clearly feature the words "*pesos convertibles*." The banknote denominations are 100, 50, 25, 10, 5 and 1, while there are 50c, 25c, 10c and 5c coins. At the time of writing 1 convertible peso ($1CUC) is worth 24 national pesos ($24CUP) and worth £1.80GDP or €1.25EUR or $0.92USD.

This confusing dual-currency system has its own vocabulary, consisting of a collection of widely used terms and slang words (see

box, opposite). The first thing to learn when trying to make sense of it all is that both national pesos and convertible pesos are represented with the dollar sign ($). Sometimes common sense is the only indicator you will have to determine which of the two currencies a price is given in, but the most commonly used qualifiers are *divisas*

Cuban currency glossary

baro (slang): convertible pesos/dollars

divisas: convertible pesos/hard currency

fula (slang): convertible pesos/dollars

kilos (slang): cents or centavos

un medio: five cents or centavos

moneda efectivo: convertible pesos

moneda nacional: national currency, ie national pesos

una peseta: twenty cents or centavos

for convertible pesos and *moneda nacional* for Cuban pesos. Thus one national peso is sometimes written $1MN. However, many Cubans refer to either currency as pesos, in which case you may have to ask if they mean *pesos cubanos*. Some tourists are told that a dollar sign with one slash running through it represents peso currency while those with two represent dollar prices, but there is no truth in this whatsoever.

Traveller's cheques, credit cards and ATMs

Hard currency is king in Cuba, and although you'll generally be OK using credit cards in the major tourist areas and big hotels, when dealing with any kind of private enterprise, from *paladares* to puncture repairs, anything other than cash isn't worth a *centavo*. Wherever you are it pays to always have at least some money in **cash**, particularly given the fact that power cuts are common in Cuba and sometimes render credit cards unusable.

Keep in mind that it is virtually impossible at weekends, when most banks are closed, to obtain money outside of the major cities and resorts, and even in these it's still quite a chore.

Traveller's cheques

Although **traveller's cheques** are easily exchangeable for cash in many banks and bureaux de change, known as *cambios* in Spanish, subject to a small commission (2.5–4 percent), a significant number of shops and restaurants refuse to accept them, and US-dollar traveller's cheques will be subject to an additional 10 percent tax. A further complication is that most banks and *cambios* require a receipt as proof of purchase when cashing traveller's cheques. Also, make sure that your signature is identical to the one on the original on the cheque submitted: cashiers have been known to refuse to cash cheques with seemingly minor discrepancies like, for example, an "I" dotted in a different place.

Convertible or national pesos?

Official tourist-oriented facilities, including all state-run hotels, most state-run restaurants and virtually all shop products, are charged in **convertible pesos**, though in six of the major resorts, namely Varadero, Cayo Largo, Jardínes del Rey, Santa Lucía, Playa Covarrubias and Holguín, you can use **euros** to pay for official goods and services. You'll be expected to pay for a room in a *casa particular*, *paladares* meals and most private taxis in convertible pesos, though there is some flexibility. Entrance to most cinemas and sports arenas, rides on local buses, snacks bought on the street and food from *agromercados* are all paid for with national pesos. There are also goods and services, such as stamps, and, most notably, long-distance transport, that can be paid for with either currency. Sometimes this means the peso charge applies only to Cubans, while non-Cubans pay the equivalent in convertible pesos, as is the case with tollgates on roads and museum entrance fees. However, in some instances tourists are merely advised rather than obliged to pay in convertible pesos, and by doing so occasionally enjoy some kind of benefit, such as being able to bypass a waiting list for a bus or getting a guaranteed seat. It should be noted, however, that it is perfectly legal for a non-Cuban to pay for meals and private taxis with national pesos, despite the funny looks or contrary advice you might well receive.

The general rule for the visitor is to assume that everything will be paid for with convertible pesos, but should you ever pay for anything with national pesos – which will usually be in situations where you are the only non-Cuban – expect it to only cost you the equivalent of a few cents or less.

It's best to carry convertible pesos in low denominations, as many shops and restaurants simply won't have enough change. Be particularly wary of this at bus and train stations or you may find yourself unable to buy a ticket. If you do end up having to use a $50CUC or $100CUC note, you will usually be asked to show your passport for security.

Credit cards

Credit cards – Visa and MasterCard in particular, but Eurocard and Diners Club to a lesser extent – are more widely accepted than traveller's cheques, especially around the large tourist resorts, but in most small to medium-sized towns plastic is absolutely useless as a method of payment. For most Cubans, credit cards remain an unfamiliar alternative to cash, and even in the largest cities you should be careful not to rely exclusively on your credit card as a form of payment. All credit card transactions are converted from convertible pesos to US dollars and then, if your bank is outside the US, from US dollars into the respective currency. You will also incur an extra 11% charge on top of your card issuer's charges.

No cards issued by a US bank are accepted in Cuba, nor is American Express, regardless of the country of issue. Credit cards are more useful for obtaining cash advances, which are charged to your bank back home in US dollars and converted to convertible pesos at the bank in Cuba. So if you withdraw $100CUC this will appear on your receipt and bank statement as $108USD. For most cash advances you'll need to deal with a bank clerk, as a majority of banks still don't have ATMs and you'll need to show your passport. There is a minimum withdrawal when dealing with a bank clerk, currently set at $100CUC, and a maximum limit of $500CUC.

ATMs

The number of **ATMs** in Cuba is slowly increasing but there are still relatively few and most of them only accept cards issued by Cuban banks. Among those that do accept foreign credit and debit cards, very few take anything other than Visa, and again none accept cards issued by American banks. Most ATMs display stickers stating clearly the cards they accept. Those that take foreign cards are generally found in top-class hotels or branches of the Banco Financiero Internacional or the Banco de Crédito y Comercio. Though finding an ATM in Havana is now fairly easy, they are still all but nonexistent outside of the largest cities and Varadero.

As with all transactions involving a foreign credit card in Cuba, the amount you withdraw in convertible pesos will be converted into US dollars and, when using ATMs, there will also be a commission charge, details of which should appear on the withdrawal slip issued with your cash.

In Cuba, ATM machines return your card at the end of the transaction. Remember to collect your card before you leave.

Banks and exchange

Banking hours in Cuba are generally Monday to Friday 8am to 3pm, but in the larger tourist resorts, particularly Varadero, some banks stay open until 6 or 7pm and a tiny minority are open Saturday mornings. As a general rule, make sure you have any money you'll need for the weekend by Friday.

The Banco Financiero Internacional is the most efficient and experienced at dealing with foreign currency transactions, with a branch in each of the major cities. Also generally reliable is the Banco de Crédito y Comercio, which has a larger number and wider spread of branches. Be warned that some banks are only equipped to deal with national pesos, and are therefore useless as far as foreign visitors are concerned. Whether withdrawing money with a credit card or cashing traveller's cheques, you'll need to show your passport for any transaction at a bank.

Most of the larger hotels have *cambios* where you can exchange money, with more flexible hours than the banks – the *cambio* at the *Hotel Nacional* in Havana (daily 8am–noon & 1–11pm) is one of the few places in the country where you can withdraw or exchange money on a Sunday. Commission for changing foreign cash to convertible pesos ranges from 2 to 4 percent.

For changing convertible pesos into national pesos, the government body CADECA runs its own *casas de cambio*, often in the shape of white kiosks at the side of the road. There is no minimum or maximum quantity restriction and you can use a credit card. Conversion rates are only given for convertible pesos; all transactions at *casas de cambio* involve convertible pesos and national pesos only, no other currency. Opening hours are generally Monday to Saturday 9am to 6pm and often Sunday 8.30am to 12.30pm, though in Havana some are open much later. No commission is charged for buying national pesos. You can change traveller's cheques at *casas de cambio* but the 4 percent commission means it's often cheaper to change them elsewhere.

Black market salesmen often hang around outside *casas de cambio* and may offer a favourable exchange rate or, sometimes more tempting, the opportunity of buying pesos without having to queue. Although dealing with a black market salesman is unlikely to get you into any trouble, it could result in a prison sentence for the Cuban. You may also be approached by people on the street offering to exchange your money, sometimes at an exceptionally good rate. This is almost always a con.

Emergency cash

For any kind of money problems, most people are directed to **Asistur** (🖎 www .asistur.cu), set up specifically to provide assistance to tourists with financial difficulties, as well as offering advice on a number of other matters, legal and otherwise. Asistur can arrange to have money sent to you from abroad as well as providing loans or cash advances. There are branches in a few of the big cities and resorts (see below). The firm to contact if you have problems with your credit or debit cards is FINCIMEX, which has offices in at least ten Cuban cities and can provide records of recent card transactions and shed light on problems such as a credit card being declined in a shop.

One of the most efficient ways of getting hold of **emergency cash** is to have money from your home bank account or that of a friend or family member sent by wire transfer to a bank in Cuba, but note that only branches of the Banco Financiero Internacional, and the Banco Internacional de Comercio in Havana, can handle money transfers from abroad. The person sending you the money will need to know your address in Cuba, whether at a hotel or in a *casa particular*, and your passport number. Be aware that the bank from which the money is sent will charge a hefty commission fee. The Havana International Bank in London, the National Australia Bank in Melbourne and the Canadian Imperial Bank of Commerce in Toronto all have links with the Banco Internacional de Comercio and may prove to be better prepared than others for this kind of transaction. Money transfers can also be made through Western Union and Transcard, both represented in Cuba.

Asistur offices

Cienfuegos Calle 25 no.5405 e/ 54 y 56 ☎/🖷 43/51-3265.

Havana Avenida del Prado no.208 esq. Trocadero, Habana Vieja, ☎ 7/866-4499; or in emergencies the 24hr numbers ☎ 866-8527 or 866-8339, 🖷 866-8087, 🖎 asistur@asistur.cu.

Holguín *Hotel Atlántico*, Playa Guardalavaca ☎/🖷 24/3-0148.

Santiago de Cuba *Hotel Casa Granda*, Calle Heredia no.201 e/ San Pedro y San Félix ☎/🖷 22/68-6128, 🖎 asisturstago@enet.cu.

Varadero Calle 31 no.101 e/ 1era y 3era ☎/🖷 45/66-7277, 🖎 asisturvaradero@enet.cu.

Phones

Over the last ten years or so, Cuba has undergone the complicated switch from the antiquated analogue telephone system to digital. This has meant a constant change of telephone codes and numbers, and, increasingly, numbers contain six digits and provincial codes consist of two digits. However, there are still plenty of four- and five-digit numbers and in sparsely populated areas there are two- and even single-digit numbers, while in Havana some numbers now have seven digits. Frustratingly, there is often a whole series of different numbers for the same place and no way to determine which one is most likely to get you connected. Thus you may see a number written as "48-7711 al 18", meaning that when dialling the final two digits you may have to try all the numbers in between and including 11 and 18 before you get through.

Payphones

There are increasing numbers of **payphones** all over the island, and they are relatively easy to find in the major cities and resorts. There are, however, three distinct kinds, all operated by the only national telecommunications network operator, ETECSA, but each with very different characteristics. The most common payphones are coloured blue and don't accept coins, only Chip **prepaid phone cards** (see box, p.69). Most of these convertible peso phones are located in call centres, of which there are two kinds: glass-walled phone booths called Minipuntos and the larger Telepuntos, which are in buildings and also usually house Internet facilities (see p.88).

The oldest, rustiest kind of payphones, which only accept 5 national-peso centavo coins, are useless for international calls and have a slim chance of working at all. They are, however, still the only kind of public phone in many smaller Cuban towns and villages, though they are increasingly rare in the larger cities and resort areas. There are now, at last, newer national peso payphones appearing around the country and these are just as reliable as their blue, convertible-peso-charging counterparts. They are grey and, unlike the older centavo-charging type, have a digital display. Most are coin-operated and accept 5 centavo, 20 centavo and 1 peso coins, but some accept prepaid phone cards, charged in pesos and available

in 3, 5 and 7 peso versions, though these national peso phone cards are rarely sold in hotels and other places where the majority of customers are not Cuban. The grey national peso phones are sometimes found in the Telepuntos but most commonly found in places where tourists are unlikely to see them, especially public buildings like hospitals and *bodegas*. It should be noted that international calls on any kind of national peso phone are impossible.

National rates for payphones are reasonable, starting at 5¢/min for calls within the same province (see opposite for international rates).

Making a call

To **make a call** within the same province but to a different municipality, or *localidad*, you will not need to dial the area code of the place you are calling but instead you may need the **exit code** for the place from where you are making the call. The exit code,

Useful numbers

Directory enquiries ☎113.
Operator ☎00 from most places, including major towns, cities and resort areas. The most common alternative is ☎110.
International dialling code for calls to Cuba ☎53

available either through the operator or from the telephone directory, can itself depend upon where you are calling to. However, if calling from a prepaid card phone (which you most likely will be) simply dial ☏0 followed by the area code and number and this will put you through directly to the number you are calling.

For interprovincial calls you will need to dial first the appropriate **national grid prefix**, or *prefijo de teleselcción nacional* (usually ☏0 or 01 but there are a number of variations depending on where you are in the country, all of these available through the Telephone Directories available in all call centres), wait a couple of seconds, then dial the area code, followed finally by the number. Finding the right **area code** can be a task in itself since although several provinces are covered by one single area code most contain at least one or two towns, cities or municipalities with random variations, usually consisting of an extra digit. So, for example, the interprovincial

---

Numbers needed to make a telephone call

Dial the listed numbers from these towns to have an international operator connect your call.

In Baracoa ☏0323798
In Bayamo ☏182
In Camagüey ☏ 90
In Cayo Coco ☏180
In Cayo Largo ☏180
In Ciego de Ávila ☏180
In Cienfuegos ☏180
In Guantánamo ☏111
In Guardalavaca ☏12
In Havana ☏09
In Holguín ☏180
In Las Tunas ☏06

In Matanzas ☏180
In Morón ☏180
In Nueva Gerona ☏08
In Pinar del Río ☏030
In Península de Zapata ☏180
In Sancti Spíritus ☏
In Santa Clara ☏180
In Santa Lucía ☏0290
In Santiago de Cuba ☏180
In Trinidad ☏180
In Varadero ☏180

Interprovincial area codes

When dialling, each code is preceded by the appropriate *prefijo de teleselección nacional*, which is either ☏0 or 01 depending on where in the country the call is made from.

Baracoa ☏21
Bayamo ☏24
Camagüey ☏32
Cayo Coco ☏33
Cayo Largo ☏45
Ciego de Ávila ☏33
Cienfuegos ☏43
Guantánamo ☏21
Guardalavaca ☏24
Havana (city) ☏7
Havana (province) ☏47
Holguín ☏24
Las Tunas ☏31

Matanzas ☏45
Morón ☏33
Nueva Gerona ☏61
Pinar del Río ☏48
Península de Zapata ☏45
Sancti Spíritus ☏41
Santa Clara ☏42
Santa Lucía ☏32
Santiago de Cuba ☏22
Trinidad ☏41
Varadero ☏45
Viñales ☏8

Dialing international numbers from public phones

To the UK dial ☏119, then 44 then the area code (without the first zero) and number.

To the US and Canada dial ☏119, then 1, then the area code and number.

To Australia dial ☏119, then 61, then the area code and number.

To New Zealand dial ☏119, then 64.

area code for Pinar del Río is ☏48, but for Viñales, which is in the same province, it's ☏8. Although area codes have been included throughout the guide, some inter-provincial calls are only possible through the operator. If you're consistently failing to get through on a direct line, dial ☏00 or 110.

Calling abroad

International calls made from Cuba are charged at exorbitant rates. The cheapest method is to call from a payphone, as opposed to calling from a hotel – often up to 50 percent more expensive – or a private phone, which can be both confusing and expensive.

Currently, a payphone call to the US or Canada costs $2CUC/min; to Central America and the Caribbean it costs $2CUC/min; to South America it costs $3.40CUC/min and to the rest of the world it costs $4CUC/min. However, calling the US from Cuba is subject to a US-based tax, an extra cost of 24.5¢/min not included in the officially listed call rates. A call connected via the international operator from a payphone incurs even higher call rates, roughly between $1.50CUC and $2CUC more expensive than the standard rate, though a call to Europe and Australia made in this way is charged at a wallet-emptying $8.75CUC per minute.

For international calls without operator assistance, possible from the newer convertible peso payphones but only on a relatively small proportion of private phones, dial the international call prefix, which is ☏119, then the country code, the area code and the number.

Making an overseas phone call from a private phone in a house has its own special procedure and can be quite confusing – use a payphone if at all possible. If you are staying at a *casa particular* and ask to ring abroad, be aware that a direct call will probably not be possible and that you will be obliged to reverse the charges (call collect). However, there are only a limited number of countries to which a reverse charge call is even permitted. These include the US, Canada, the UK, France and Spain but exclude, for example, Australia, New Zealand and Germany. Ideally, you should get the person you are trying to contact to ring you, as it could cost them up to ten

Prepaid phone cards

There are three kinds of **prepaid phone cards** in Cuba: convertible peso cards (sometimes known as Chip), national peso cards (sometimes known as Banda Magnética) and Propia. Tourists are more likely to use Chip cards, which only work in the newer blue payphones often found in hotels and other tourist installations. They are available in denominations of $5CUC, $10CUC and $20CUC, and are straightforward phone cards which, once the credit has expired, are useless and can be thrown away. Chip cards are available from post offices, hotels, national travel agents, some banks, Minipuntos and Telepuntos (the ETECSA call centres). The national peso equivalent works in the same way but must be used in a national peso prepay payphone, which are usually grey and foreign visitors are most likely to encounter them in Telepuntos. These cannot be used for international calls but make the cost of local or national calls over twenty times cheaper. They are available in $3CUP, $5CUP and $7CUP denominations.

Propia cards are compatible with all phones besides the Chip-compatible ones and are therefore used much more widely by Cubans, and rarely by tourists. They are rechargeable and reusable cards, effectively phone credit accounts with unique account codes to be entered every time the user makes a call. Propia credit is sold in both national pesos, usually in $5CUP or $10CUP credits, and convertible pesos, usually in $10CUC or $25CUC credits, but as a foreigner you will be expected to pay convertible pesos. If you're in an area where the cards will work, they're a better deal as Propia, unlike the other prepaid cards, has off-peak rates for international calls made between 6pm and 6am that are on average 40¢/min cheaper.

Main Cubacel offices

Camagüey *Gran Hotel*, Maceo no.67
e/ Ignacio Agramonte y General
Gómez ☏32/25-9222.

Havana Calle 28 no.510 e/ 5ta y
7ma, Miramar ☏7/880-2222. Salón
de Tráfico de Cubana de Aviación,
Calle 23 no.64, La Rampa, Vedado
☏7/885-0200. Miramar Trade Center,
Edificio Jerusalén, bajos, Havana
☏7/880-0200.

Santiago Meliá Santiago de Cuba,
Ave. de las Américas esq. M
☏22/68-7199.

Varadero Edificio Marbella, apto. 2,
Ave. 1era e/ 42 y 43.

times more to receive a reverse-charge call
from Cuba. What's more, calls are charged
by the minute and not the second, so that a
ten-second call at the rate of $10CUC a
minute will cost $10CUC.

If you do make an international call from a
Cuban household, then you should first ring
the international operator, the number for
which differs from place to place (see box,
p.99). The operator will ask for the name and
number of the person you are calling, the
number you are calling from and your name,
usually in that order.

Cellphones

Cubacel is the sole **cellphone service
provider** in Cuba (🌐www.cubacel.com), and
if you intend to bring your own handset to
Cuba you should check first whether or not
your service provider has a "roaming"
agreement with them. Many of the major
European, Australasian and Canadian
operators now have such agreements.

Renting or buying a cellphone

The alternative to bringing your own
handset is to rent or buy one in Cuba,
which Cubacel will be happy to do at
inflated costs. They offer temporary as well
as permanent contracts to visitors and
residents alike, but you are more likely to
use the pay-as-you-go deals using prepaid
cards. The prepaid service costs a daily rate
of $3CUC for line rental and call rates for
calls within Cuba are between 40¢ and 60¢
per minute depending on whether you call
another cellphone or a landline and the time
of day. You will also be charged to receive
calls, though at slightly lower rates. International call rates are currently $2.45CUC to
Canada, $2.70CUC to the US and
$5.85CUC to Europe, Australia and New
Zealand. Prepaid cards are not widely
available so make sure you stock up at the
provider's office.

Calling home from abroad

Note that the initial zero is omitted from the area code when dialling the UK, Ireland,
Australia and New Zealand from abroad.

US and Canada international access code + 1 + area code.
Australia international access code + 61 + city code.
New Zealand international access code + 64 + city code.
UK international access code + 44 + city code.
Republic of Ireland international access code + 353 + city code.
South Africa international access code + 27 + city code.

The media

All types of media in Cuba are tightly censored and closely controlled by the state. While this means that the range of information and opinion is severely restricted and biased, it has also produced media geared to producing (what the government deems to be) socially valuable content, refreshingly free of any significant concern for high ratings and commercial success.

Newspapers and magazines

There may be some significance in the fact that *Granma*, Cuba's main national **newspaper** (Tues–Sun; ⓦwww.granma.cu), works out considerably cheaper than buying toilet paper, and certainly there are sections of the population who feel this is the only positive thing that can be said of it. Such a judgement, though harsh, reflects the disillusionment many Cubans feel with the role of the press in Cuba as a propaganda tool for the state. The government does little to hide this fact; the front page of *Granma* openly declares it the official mouthpiece of the Cuban Communist Party. The stories in its eight tabloid-size pages are almost exclusively of a political or economic nature, usually publicizing meetings with foreign heads of state, denouncing US policy towards Cuba, or announcing developments within some sector of industry or commerce.

Castro's speeches are often published in their entirety, while international news takes a firm back seat. The occasional article challenging the official party line does appear, but these are usually short pieces on the inside pages, directed at specific events and policies rather than overall ideologies.

There are two other national papers: *Trabajadores*, representing the workers' unions, and *Juventud Rebelde*, claiming to be the newspaper of the Cuban youth. These are effectively repackaged versions of *Granma*, although *Juventud Rebelde*, in its Thursday edition, features a weekly set of listings for cultural events and things to do.

Hotels are more likely to stock the weekly *Granma Internacional* ($0.50CUC), twice as thick as its daily counterpart and tailored to a foreign readership. Printed in Spanish, English, French, German, Italian, Turkish and Portuguese editions, it offers a roundup of the week's stories but sometimes comes off like a political brochure, extolling the

Listings

Finding out about forthcoming events is a somewhat hit-and-miss business in Cuba. Although the free monthly **listings** booklets *Bienvenidos* and *Cartelera* – only available in Havana and sporadically available in the larger hotels and at branches of Infotur – carry information on a variety of Havanan goings-on, it is far from comprehensive and many local events, particularly those organized principally by and for Cubans, don't get a mention. The national newspaper, *Granma*, has details of baseball games and is one of the only sources of television programming schedules, whilst *Juventud Rebelde* publishes cultural listings in its Thursday edition. Radio Taíno often broadcasts details of major shows and concerts as well as advertisements for the tourist in-spots. For less mainstream events the principal method of advertising is word of mouth, with posters and flyers seldom if ever seen. Your best bet for up-to-the-minute information is to consult hotel staff, or, better still, *casa particular* owners, while in Havana there is the luxury of the Infotur offices where the staff are usually very well informed.

virtues of the Cuban state to its supposedly impressionable foreign audience. Although there is a disproportionate number of articles based on tourism, to its credit the paper usually carries a couple of pages of culture-oriented reporting.

Cuba has its own **sports** weekly newspaper, *Jit*, consisting of just four pages (50 *centavos*). It's concerned predominantly with national sporting events and is only available in Spanish. There are two weekly **business papers**, *Opciones* ($1CUC) and *Negocios en Cuba* ($1CUC), which are unlikely to catch your attention unless you're interested in trading with the government, although *Opciones* does have a listings page geared to tourists.

There are very few **international newspapers** available in Cuba, a couple of Spanish and Italian dailies being the only ones that appear with any regularity. Away from the more sophisticated hotels you're unlikely to find even these, and certainly tracking down an English-language newspaper of any description is an arduous, usually unrewarding task. The *Hotel Nacional* and the *Meliá Habana* hotels in Havana are two of the best places in the whole country for picking up what foreign press can be found. There is also a growing number of **bookshops**, mostly in the capital, stocking non-Cuban newspapers and magazines, though editions are often months, even years, out of date.

Presenting a rather more diverse picture of Cuban society than the newspapers are its **magazines**. Amongst the most cultured of them is *Bohemia* (Ⓦwww.bohemia.cu), Cuba's oldest surviving periodical, whose relatively broad focus offers a mix of current affairs, historical essays and regular spotlights on art, sport and technology. The best of the more specialized publications are the bimonthly *Revolución y Cultura*, concentrating on the arts and literature, and the tri-monthly *Artecubano*, a magazine of book-like proportions tracking the visual arts. There are a number of other worthy magazines, such as *La Gaceta de Cuba*, covering all forms of art, from music and painting to radio and television; *Temas*, whose scope includes political theory and contemporary society; and *Clave*, which focuses on music. The most common

English-language magazines are *Time*, *Newsweek*, *Rolling Stone*, *Sports Illustrated* and *Cosmopolitan*.

Radio

There are eight national **radio** stations in Cuba, but tuning into them isn't always easy, as signal strength varies considerably from place to place. You're most likely to hear broadcasts from Radio Taíno (Ⓦwww.891fm.cu), the official tourist station to which most sets in public places are tuned, and the only one on which any English is spoken, albeit sporadically. Playing predominantly mainstream pop and Cuban music, the station is also a useful source of up-to-date tourist information such as the latest nightspots, forthcoming events and places to eat. Tune in between 4 and 5pm on Saturday or Sunday for *La Gran Jugada*, a show carrying the results of sporting events from around the globe, including European football, NBA and MLB.

Musically speaking, other than the ever-popular sounds of Cuban *salsa*, stations rarely stray away from safe-bet US, Latin and European pop and rock. The predominantly classical music content of Radio Musical Nacional is about as specialist as it gets.

Of the remaining stations there is little to distinguish one from the other. The exception is Radio Reloj, a 24-hour news station with humourless reports read out to the ceaseless sound of a ticking clock in the background as the exact time is announced every minute on the minute.

On the northern coast of Cuba, particularly in and between Havana and Varadero, it is quite possible to tune into stations broadcasting from southern Florida, a fact which has not escaped the attention of the exile community in Miami who set up Radio Martí specifically for that purpose. Established in 1985, the station is a provocative attempt to supply the Cuban population with allegedly impartial perspectives on news and current affairs as an alternative to the government-controlled Cuban media. Even though a more balanced point of view would fall somewhere between these two poles of opinion, the station nevertheless represents a significant voice in the wider Cuban community, providing a platform for ex-political prisoners and the

Cuban immigrant population in general. Tuning in can be quite hit-and-miss as the Cuban government does its best to scramble the signal, which is broadcast on a large number of frequencies that differ according to the time of day. The best way to know where to turn to on your dial is to consult their website (@www .martinoticias.com/radio).

National Cuban radio stations and frequencies

Radio Arte (FM)
Dramas and documentaries.
Radio Enciclopedia (1260MW/94.1FM) Strictly instrumental music drawn from various genres.
Radio Habana Cuba (106.9FM) News and chat in a number of languages.
Radio Musical Nacional (590MW/99.1FM) Internationally renowned classical music.
Radio Progreso (640MW/90.3FM) Music and drama broadcast daily 3–6pm.
Radio Rebelde (670 and 710MW/96.7FM) Sport, current affairs and music.
Radio Reloj (950MW/101.5FM) National and international news 24hr a day.
Radio Taíno (1290MW/93.2–93.4FM) Tourist station playing popular Cuban and international music.

Florida radio stations heard in northwestern Cuba

Radio Martí (AM)
WAIL (99.5FM) Classic rock.

WCTH (100.3) Country and easy listening.
WEOW (92.5FM) Pop and R&B chart hits.
WKWF (1600AM) Sports results and commentary.

Television

There are four national **television** channels in Cuba: Cubavisión, Telerebelde, Canal Educativo and Canal Educativo 2, all commercial-free but littered instead with public service broadcasts, revolutionary slogans and daily short slots commemorating historical events and figures. None of them broadcasts 24 hours and sometimes, particularly on Sundays, do not begin transmitting until late in the day, though usually they are up and running by 9am.

Surprisingly, given the sour relationship between Cuba and the US, **Hollywood films** are a staple on television here, sometimes preceded by a discussion of the film's value and its central issues. Many of these are impressively recent, the result of pirating from US satellite channels, while the frequent use of Spanish subtitles, as opposed to dubbing films into Spanish, makes them watchable for non-Spanish speakers. Cubavisión shows most of the films, and for years has broadcast two of them, usually well-known blockbusters, on Saturday nights starting around 10pm. Other than this, however, North American culture has penetrated very little into programming schedules.

Cinema

Cinemas are widespread, ranging from huge auditoriums to tiny fleapits. In all venues the film is screened continuously: Cubans enter at any point and leave again when the film has come full circle. The atmosphere is often riotous, especially when there is a popular film showing, and raucous catcalls, loud cheers and appreciative clapping are all the norm. Although there are some heavyweight Cuban films like *Memorias de Subdesarrollo*, the most popular ones tend to be the burlesques typified by *Guantanamera* and *La Muerte de un Burócrata* by director Tomás Gutiérrez Alea. Dubbed and subtitled North American and European films also show regularly, usually reaching the Cuban screens about twelve to eighteen months after their domestic release. You can catch more recent films in the ubiquitous Salas de Video, literally "video rooms", although as a rule viewing quality leaves much to be desired. Tickets cost 1 or 2 pesos, although as a foreigner in Havana you may be charged the equivalent in dollars.

If you're particularly keen to see some home-grown Cuban cinema, visit in December during Havana's film festival, when new work is featured, offering up-to-date insights into the heart of Cuban culture, in addition to the current arthouse films from all over the world.

Cubavisión also hosts another long-standing Cuban television tradition, the staggeringly popular **telenovelas**, usually Brazilian or Colombian soap operas, going out on Mondays, Wednesdays and Fridays at around 9.30pm. Their melodramatic characters and outlandish plots are offset by the consistently more sober, home-grown soaps shown on Tuesdays and Thursdays. There are several weekly music programmes showcasing the best of contemporary Cuban music as well as popular international artists. Saturday evenings are the best time to catch live-broadcast performances from the cream of the national *salsa* scene.

Telerebelde is the best channel for **sports**, with live national-league baseball games shown almost daily throughout the season, and basketball, volleyball and boxing making up the bulk of the rest. As the names suggest, both Canal Educativo channels are full of educational programmes, including courses in languages, cookery and various academic disciplines.

Officially, **satellite television** is the exclusive domain of the hotels, which are also the recipients of Cubavisión Internacional, the tourist channel showing a mixture of films, documentaries and music programmes. Although most hotel rooms in Varadero, Havana and the other major resort areas come with a broad range of satellite channels, many hotels in the rest of the country still have only two or three, ESPN and CNN amongst the most common. The government has ensured that TV Martí, set up for the same purpose as its radio namesake, rarely if ever gets through, by jamming the signal.

The best places to look for **programme times** are in the pages of *Granma* and, for Cubavisión Internacional, *Opciones*. The plusher hotels usually carry a television schedule magazine for the satellite channels.

Festivals

Cultural festivals like the International Theatre Festival and world-celebrated International Festival of New Latin American Film have won Havana global applause, though there are plenty of lesser-known festivals celebrating Afro-Cuban dance, literature, ballet and other arts, and a whole host of smaller but worthwhile events in other provinces. Catching one of these can make all the difference to a visit to a less-than-dynamic town.

Cuba's main **carnival** takes place in Santiago de Cuba in July and is an altogether unmissable experience. As well as numerous parades featuring dramatically costumed carnival queens waving from floats, and more down-to-earth neighbourhood percussion bands, several stage areas are set up around the town where live *salsa* bands play nightly. Perhaps the most enjoyable aspect of carnival, though, is the *conga* parades, unique to Santiago de Cuba. Signalling the unofficial start to carnival, the *conga* usually takes place on the first evening, and locals and visitors alike can join in. Each neighbourhood forms its own parade, led by its own percussion band. Amid a mad cacophony of sound, with musicians blowing shrill Chinese horns, beating drums and general uproar, men and women flood from their houses (children borne aloft) to form an unruly parade that weaves around the town. Also worth checking out are the smaller carnivals held in Havana and Camagüey, which feature parades and boisterous street parties as well. The excellent Egrem website, Ⓦwww.egrem.com.cu, and Ⓦwww.canalcubano.com both have information about forthcoming events.

Calendar of events

January

Cubadanza Gran Teatro, Habana Vieja ☎7/31-1357, ℮paradis@turcult.get.cma
.net. Cuban contemporary dance festival featuring performers from around the
country.

Winter Cuballet Gran Teatro, Habana Vieja ☎7/20-8610, ℮paradis@turcult.get
.cma.net. The national ballet's winter season.

February

Havana Carnival ☎7/62-3883, ℮rosalla@cimex.com.cu. The first and smaller of
two carnivals held annually in Havana (see July, below). Festivities in Havana get
under way in the second week of February, with parades and street parties around
the city centre for about three weeks.

March

Ciego de Ávila International Carnival Ciego de Ávila ☎33/23-3335. A more
tourist-oriented version of the traditional carnival.

Festival de Música Electroacústica "Primavera en La Habana" Habana Vieja.
Festival of electro-acoustic music held every even-numbered year in the bars,
museums and cafés around Habana Vieja.

April

Dia de los Niños Countrywide. The 4th of April is children's day, with events and
attractions taking place around the city.

May

Primero de Mayo Countrywide. May 1st is International Workers' Day, and there are
speeches and parades in every major town, usually around the Plaza de la
Revolución. The Havana display is worth catching, with a crowd of around 20,000
loyal party faithful waving painted banners, and marching past dignitaries in front of
the José Martí memorial. Quintessentially Cuban.

Romería de Mayo San Isidoro de Holguín. A pilgrimage held every May 3, when a
Mass at the summit of La Loma de la Cruz hill is followed by a three-day celebration
down in town.

Feria Internacional del Disco "Cubadisco" Havana. A week-long annual event in
which Cuban musicians from every genre who have released albums in the
preceding 12 months compete for the title of best album of the year. As well as
celebrating current releases, homage is paid to classics. Concerts take place in
many of the city's major venues, with the grand finale held at the Pabexpo in
Cubanacán, west of Miramar.

July

Fiesta of Fire Festival Santiago de Cuba ☎22/62-3569, ℮upec@mail.infocom
.etecsa.cu. Santiago's week-long celebration of Caribbean music and dance culture
takes place at the beginning of July.

Santiago Carnival Santiago de Cuba ☎22/62-3302, ℮burostgo@binanet.lib.cult
.cu. Cuba's most exuberant carnival holds Santiago in its thrall for the last two
weeks of July, with costumed parades and *congas, salsa* bands and late-night
parties. Official dates are 18–27 but the week-long run-up is often just as lively.

Camagüey Carnival Camagüey. Smaller than Santiago's version but exciting
nonetheless.

Carnival de La Habana Havana. Held over the last two weekends of July and the
first two weekends of August, carnival in Havana is a jubilant affair, with many of
the country's top bands playing to packed crowds along the Malecón and
throughout the city. On the final weekend a huge parade winds its way down the

Malecón from Habana Vieja, an energetic display of costume and song. Although the Santiago Carnival is undeniably a higher-quality affair, this is an excellent second choice.

August

Cubadanza Gran Teatro, Habana Vieja ☏7/31-1357, ©paradis@turcult.get.cma.net. The summer season of the Cuban contemporary dance festival, which draws performers from all over the country to Havana.

Summer Cuballet Gran Teatro, Habana Vieja ☏7/20-8610, ©paradis@turcult.get .cma.net. The national ballet's summer season.

Festival de rap Cubano Asociación Hermanos Saíz, Havana ☏7/832-3511. Taking place in late August, this is an excellent chance to see Cuba's emergent hip-hop scene in full action. The event attracts international stars and is well worth the trip to the outskirts suburb Alamar, where the main events take place; other events are held at venues around the city.

September

Havana International Theatre Festival Havana ☏7/31-1357, ©paradis@turcult .get.cma.net. Excellent ten-day theatre festival showcasing classics and contemporary Cuban works at various theatres around the city.

El Wemilere African Roots Festival Havana. An annual festival celebrating Afro-Cuban culture which takes place in Guanabacoa. Activities include art exhibitions, dance shows and theatre productions, but the real draw is the live Afro-Cuban music.

October

Festival de Matamoro Son Santiago
This three-day festival, drawing music stars from around the country, takes place towards the end of the month in venues near the city centre. While the focus is on *son*, expect to see many other traditional styles of music, including *salsa*.

December

International Festival of New Latin American Film Havana ☏7/55-2854, ©rosalla@cimex.com.cu, ⌨www.habanafilmfestival.com. One of Cuba's top events, this ten-day film festival combines the newest Cuban, Latin American and Western arthouse films with the finest classics, as well as providing a networking opportunity for leading independent film directors. You can find information in *Hotel Nacional*, from where the event is run.

Havana Jazz Festival Teatro Nacional, Havana ☏7/79-6011. Held every even-numbered year. See the best of Cuban jazz, including the legendary Irakere with Chu Chu Valdés, play around the town at a range of different venues, including *El Zorro y El Cuervo*, Teatro Nacional and *Jazz Café*. International guest stars also feature.

Sports and outdoor activities

In terms of participatory sports and outdoor pursuits in Cuba, most of it, like golf and hiking, is still in the development stages. Watersports are the exception, with diving sites and centres all over the island near some of the richest and most unspoilt waters in the world. Live spectator sports cost next to nothing, and you can't beat a Havana versus Santiago match-up, whether in baseball or basketball.

Spectator sports

Like *salsa*, **baseball** is in the blood for most Cubans, and, with a tradition going back to 1874, when the first game was played on the island, there are few better places outside of the US to appreciate this most American of pastimes. Games in the national league, the Serie Nacional de Béisbol, take place between sixteen teams over a ninety-game regular season, which usually begins in October or November and runs through the play-offs and finals, usually in April. Every provincial capital has a baseball stadium and, during the season, teams play five times a week (Tues, Wed, Thurs & Sat 8pm or 9pm; Sun 3pm). Due to the frequency of games, there are rarely capacity crowds (except occasionally during the play-offs and finals) and the atmosphere is unintimidating and friendly. Historically the best team has been Indus-triales, one of the two Havana teams, but Pinar del Río, Villa Clara and Santiago de Cuba have fielded teams in recent years that have been at least as strong, and the battle for the title is never a foregone conclusion.

The other league which generates enough excitement to make a live game worth catching is the Liga Superior de Baloncesto, the national **basketball** league. Though everything is on a smaller scale compared to baseball, from the number of teams to the size of the crowds, the smaller arenas and the faster pace of the game itself often give live basketball an edge over the national sport. There are only six teams in the league, with Havana's Capitalinos and Santiago's Orientales usually the strongest title contenders. The best places to see a game are both in Havana, either at the Sala Polivalente Ramón Fonst, near the Plaza de la Revolución, or the Ciudad Deportiva, on the way to the airport. The basketball season usually takes place between November and January.

Sports listings and information

Finding out in advance about sporting events in Cuba is notoriously difficult. Most locals rely on word of mouth or are in-the-know fans, but for the foreign visitor there are very few publications carrying any useful **information**. The daily newspapers *Granma* and *Juventud Rebelde* usually have a page dedicated to sport, and you can sometimes garner information on forthcoming events from these. However, your best bet is to go online. The web-based sports publication *Jit* (⊛www.jit.cu) is the official mouthpiece of INDER (National Institute of Sport, Physcial Education and Recreation) and covers all Cuban plus some international sports. There is a calendar of sporting events on the Cubadeportes website (⊛www.cubadeportes.cu), and the sport section of the Radio Coco website (⊛www.radiococo.cu) is a useful resource as well. There is also a specialist Cuban baseball site published by the Federación Cubana de Béisbol Aficionado (⊛www.beisbolcubano.cu), which covers baseball in fantastic detail and carries a calendar of games.

There is a national football (soccer) league as well, with its season running from October to February, followed by play-offs and finals finishing up in March. Pinar del Río and Villa Clara are the two strongest teams at the moment. The national team qualified for the World Cup in 1938 but has since failed to make it past the preliminary qualifying rounds and, partly as a result of this, very few meaningful international games are played on Cuban soil. There are very few custom-built football stadiums, with many games taking place in baseball stadiums or on scrappy pitches with very little enclosure.

Amateur **boxing** bouts are held in cities all over Cuba throughout the year, with the main international fights usually held at the Ciudad Deportiva, or in the Sala Polivalente Kid Chocolate, one of the country's oldest sporting arenas, opposite the Capitolio building in Habana Vieja. One of the most prestigious annual competitions, the Giraldo Córdova Cardín Tournament, usually takes place in April and has been held in Villa Clara for the last few years. Boxing has been one of Cuba's most successful Olympic sports, but the government's strictly non-professional policy has kept Cuban names out of the international limelight. Two of the most respected Cuban boxers of late, and still names to look out for, are the bantamweight Guillermo Rigondeaux and heavyweight Odlanier Solis Fonte.

A new sports competition, the **Olimpiada del Deporte Cubano**, was inaugurated in 2003. This national event involves all the modern Olympic sports and, after a lukewarm reception with the public, it's slowly beginning to stir the public imagination.

Scuba diving and other watersports

Cuba is a **scuba diving** paradise. Diving here is worthwhile in any season but winter is the best time to get a chance of seeing whale sharks, arguably the highlight of any diving trip to the island, while in the spring the fish are in greater abundance. On the other hand, from late April to late May there is an increased chance of swimming into what Cubans call el caribé, invisible jellyfish with a severe sting, found predominantly off the southern coast of the island. To counter this you can either wear a full wetsuit or simply make sure you do your diving off the northern coastline at this time of year.

Most of the major beach resorts, including Varadero, Santa Lucía and Guardalavaca, have at least one well-equipped **diving centre** while Havana has two: the Aguja Dive Centre at the Marina Hemingway in the western suburb of Miramar and the Tarará-Mégano Dive Centre at the Marina Tarará in the east of the city. Varadero is one of the most suitable places for novice divers, with three marinas and two diving clubs. For a more secluded expedition, head for María La Gorda in western Pinar del Río, where you'll find what many consider the most spectacular dive sites in the country. Along with Punta Frances on the western tip of the Isla de la Juventud, and the Jardines de la Reina off the southern coastlines of Ciego de Avila, María La Gorda has been declared a National Marine Park by the Cuban government and as a result is protected from man-made abuses, particularly commercial fishing. All three of these areas are widely regarded as offering some of the best diving in the Caribbean, with fish in impressive sizes and quantities, but the Jardines de la Reina, a coral reef stretching out over 75 miles, is the most highly lauded amongst professionals. With over sixty dive sites and fish in phenomenal abundance, it has an almost endless variety of possible sights, scenes and experiences for divers, from schools of silky sharks to 180kg goliath groupers and ten-metre-high coral formations.

The principal **dive operator** in Cuba is Marlin (@www.nauticamarlin.com), running most of the centres in the country. The only other real players in this market are Gaviota (@www.gaviota.cu), Havanatur (@www.havanatur.cu) and Cubanacán (@www.cubanacan.cu), which runs diving clubs from some of its hotels. Some diving centres are run as joint ventures with foreign companies and offer the internationally recognized PADI and ACUC courses. There are countless opportunities for all levels of diving, from absolute beginners to hardened professionals, but the best place to start is in a hotel-based diving resort where you can take your first lesson in the safety of a swimming pool. Typically, a beginners' course involving some theory, a pool lesson and an open-water dive costs between $60CUC and $80CUC, while a week-long ACUC course costs in the region of $375CUC. For one single-tank dive expect to pay $30CUC to $35CUC, but bear in mind that there is usually an extra charge for rental of equipment which will add between $5CUC and $10CUC per day.

Other watersports

Facilities for sports like **water-skiing** and **kayaking** are available at the major resorts so this isn't really the place for surfboard but generally there is less chance of finding motorized equipment at resorts totalling just two or three hotels, like the Península de Ancón. Cuba does not usually experience much surf, out at to.

Fishing

Cuba is an angler's paradise, mostly free from the voracious appetite of the huge US **fishing** market and relatively underused by Europeans. Cuba's lakes, reservoirs and coastal areas offer all kinds of excellent opportunities and there are numerous possibilities for organized fresh- and saltwater fishing trips.

Bass and trout are particularly abundant inland, especially at Lake Hanabanilla in Villa Clara (legendary for its bass), the Zaza Reservoir in Sancti Spíritus and the several artificial lakes in Camagüey province. The best opportunities for saltwater fish are off the northern coast, where blue marlin, sail fish, white marlin, barracuda and tuna are among the most dramatic potential catches.

Another great area for saltwater fishing lies south of the Ciego de Avila and Camagüey coastlines around the Jardines de la Reina archipelago. This southern group of some 250 uninhabited islands about eighty kilometres offshore is regarded by some experts as the finest light-tackle fishing to be found anywhere in the Caribbean. With commercial fishing illegal here, other than around the outer extremities, since 1996, there are virtually untapped sources of bonefish and tarpon as well as an abundance of groupers and snappers. To get a look-in at the Jardines de la Reina archipelago, you will most likely have to go through one of the Canadian or Italian outfits (see below) which have attained exclusive rights to regulate and organize the fishing here, in conjunction with the Cuban authorities.

There is no bad time for fishing around Cuba, but for the biggest blue marlin, July, August and September are the most rewarding months, while April, May and June attract greater numbers of white marlin and sail fish. The best bass catches usually occur during the winter months, when the average water temperature drops to 22°C.

The hotels and marinas will be your main points of contact when organizing a fishing trip, many of them working in conjunction with one another. The hotel chain Islazul

Cuban fishing tournaments

For more details on any of these fishing tournaments contact Havanatur (⊛www .havanatur.cu).

Torneo Internacional de la Pesca de la Aguja "Ernest Hemingway".

The International Garfish Fishing Tournament usually takes place in June and runs from the Marina Hemingway in Havana.

Torneo Internacional de la Pesca del Castero "Blue Marlin".

The annual Blue Marlin Fishing Tournament takes place in September and also runs from the Marina Hemingway in Havana.

Torneo Internacional de la Pesca del "Wahoo".

Takes place in November from the Marina Hemingway.

Calendar of sporting events and activities

January
National Basketball League Play-offs and Finals

February
Vuelta a Cuba ©cpd@inder.get.cma.net. The annual cycling race around the island.

March
International Trout Fishing Tournament Moron, Ciego de Ávila ℡335/45-63.

Trans-Caribbean Yachting Regatta Marina Hemingway, Havana ℡7/204-6653 or 204-6689.

Black Bass Fishing All Star Open Tournament Lake Hanabanilla, Villa Clara ℡7/204-7520.

National League Baseball Finals

April
Giraldo Cordova Cardin Tournament (held in a different city every year) ©cpd@inder.get.cma.net. Prestigious national boxing tournament.

Marathon in the Sea Tournament Varadero ℡7/57-7078. Long-distance swim.

May
Havana Cup International Yachting Regatta Marina Hemingway, Havana ℡7/204-6653 or 204-6689.

Copa Varadero Marina Dársena, Varadero ℡45/66-7550. Sailing regatta around Varadero.

International Triathlon Week Cayo Coco and Cayo Guillermo, Ciego de Ávila ℡33/2-3335.

Tournament Barrientos Estadio Panamericano, Havana ℡7/97-2101.

Morro Castle Yachting Regatta, Marina Hemingway, Havana ℡7/204-6653 or 204-6689.

International Ernest Hemingway Marlin Fishing Tournament Marina Hemingway, Havana ℡7/204-6653 or 204-6689.

June
Gregorio Fuentes Marlin Fishing Tournament Marina Dársena, Varadero ℡45/66-7550.

July
Big Island Boating Grand Prix and International Formula T1 Boats Championship Cienfuegos ℡7/33-7883.

The Old Man and the Sea International Marlin Fishing Tournament Marina Tarará, Havana ℡7/204-5923 to 26.

August
Festival Náutico "Regata Guardalavaca-Bariay" Guardalavaca, ©esp.mar@gaviota.gav.tur.cu. Sailing festival.

September
International Blue Marlin Fishing Tournament Marina Hemingway, Havana ℡7/204-6653, ©yachtclub@cnih.mh.cyt.cu.

November
Marabana Marathon Havana ℡7/54-5022.

December
International Trout Fishing Tournament Lake Hanabanilla, Villa Clara ℡42/20-2126.

(☎7/832-0570 to 79, ⓦwww.islazul.cu) is better prepared than most and operates three hotels designed specifically for fresh-water fishing holidays: additionally, there's the *Hotel Hanabanilla* in Villa Clara (see p.362), the *Hotel Morón* in Ciego de Ávila (see p.412), and the *Hotel Zaza* in Sancti Spíritus (see p.399). Before you start, you will need a **fishing licence**, which costs $20CUC, while a three- to four-hour fishing session typically costs $40CUC, rising to $70CUC for six to eight hours. There are several international fishing festivals of some repute that take place annually in Cuba (see box).

For saltwater fishing excursions, usually on motorized yachts, the two chains operating the most extensive network of marinas and fishing day-trips are Marlin (see p.78) and Cubanacán Nautica (see p.78) The cost of a day-trip, typically with four to six hours of fishing, starts at around $200CUC for four people and can go up to as much as $350CUC. The marinas always supply a boat crew and any necessary equipment.

Equipment for fishing, particularly fly fishing, is low on the ground in Cuba, and what does exist is almost exclusively the property of the tour operators. Buying anything connected to fishing is all but impossible, so it makes sense to bring as much of your own equipment as you can get in your baggage.

Foreign fishing operators in Cuba

Avalon Corso Peschiera, 249 Torino, Italy 10141 ☎335/814 9111, ⓕ222 1631, ⓦwww.avalons .net. Runs two live-aboard boats at the Jardines de la Reina.

Fly Fishing Caribe & Patagonia Paraguay 647 8° "31", (1431) Buenos Aires, Argentina ☎11/4311 1222. Offers fishing packages to the Jardines de la Reina, the Península de Zapata and in the River Agabama near Trinidad.

Reco Global Inc. Cuba Bass Adventures 113 Tall Forest Drive, Ottawa, Ontario K0A 1L0, Canada ☎613/839-5206, ⓕ839-5282. Operates a fleet of fishing barges and boats on Lake Hanabanilla.

For information on cycling, see p.48 in "Getting Around".

Golf

Its associations with the pre-1959 ruling classes made **golf** something of a frowned-upon sport in Cuba once Castro and his supporters took over the country. The advent of mass tourism, however, has brought it back, and though currently there are only two courses on the island there are plans for more. The biggest, best equipped and more expensive is the eighteen-hole course run by the Varadero Golf Club (☎45/66-7388, ⓦwww.varaderogolfclub.com), established in 1998. Less taxing are the nine holes of the Club de Golf Habana (☎7/649-8918), just outside the capital. Green fees range from $20CUC to $60CUC, while a caddy and equipment rental together will cost you around $15CUC. Both clubs offer 30- to 45-minute golf classes costing $10CUC in Havana and twice as much in Varadero.

Hiking

All three mountain ranges in Cuba feature resorts set up as bases for **hiking**, and these mostly unspoilt routes are certainly a wonderful way to enjoy some of the most breathtaking of Cuban landscapes. Desig-nated hikes tend to be quite short, rarely more than 5km, and trails are often unmarked and difficult to follow without a guide. Furthermore, orienteering maps are all but nonexistent. This may be all part of the appeal for some people, but it is generally recommended that you hire a guide, especially in adverse weather condi-tions. In the Cordillera de Guaniguanico in Pinar del Río the place to head for is Las Terrazas, where there is a series of gentle hikes organized mostly for groups. The Topes de Collantes resort in the Escambray Mountains offers a similar programme, while serious hikers should head for the Gran Parque Nacional Sierra Maestra, host to the tallest peak in Cuba, Pico Turquino.

Culture and etiquette

There are a few cultural idiosyncrasies in Cuba worth bearing in mind. Cubans tend to be fairly conventional in their appearance, and view some Western fashions, especially traveller garb, with circumspection, mainly because Cubans in similar dress (and there are a number around, particularly in Havana) are seen as anti-establishment. Anyone with piercings, dreadlocks or tattoos may find themselves checked rigorously at customs and occasionally asked to show their passport to the police.

Many **shops** restrict entrance to a few people at a time, and although as a tourist you may bypass the queue, you'll win more friends if you ask "*¿el ultimo?*" (who's last?) and take your turn. Avoid asking questions which include a possible answer, as people often give the response they think you are looking for, thus "What time does the bus leave?" is better than "Does the bus leave at noon?"

Service charges between 10–12 percent are becoming increasingly common in state restaurants and in smarter *paladares*, most notably in Havana. It is mandatory to pay this, which can be frustrating if you feel you have not received good service, and it is wise to check whether it will be included before ordering, as it is not always stated on the bill. In state restaurants where it is not included you should tip at your discretion; in *paladares* tips aren't expected but always welcome. There's no need to tip when you've negotiated a fare for a taxi, but you should normally tip when you use a state-run taxi. And it's worth knowing that a tip of a convertible peso or two can sometimes open previously closed doors – getting you into a museum without the minimum-size group, for example.

Public toilets are few and far between in Cuba, and even fast-food joints often don't have a washroom. The best places for public toilets are hotels and petrol stations, but even in these you should not necessarily expect there to be toilet paper – carry your own supply. Train and bus stations usually have toilets, but conditions are often appalling, leaving you wondering whether the attendants waiting on the doors have ever gone inside. No plumbing system, be it in a *casa particular* or hotel, can cope with waste paper, so in order to avoid blockages remember to dispose of your paper in the bins provided.

Shopping

Cigars, rum, music and arts and crafts remain the really worthwhile purchases in Cuba, and though the range of consumer products available in the shops is constantly expanding, the quality and choice are still generally poor. The late 1990s saw the first modern shopping malls emerge, predominantly in Havana, but outside of these and a few of the grandest hotels, shopping comes with none of the convenience and choice you're probably used to. Almost all shops actually carrying any stock now operate in convertible pesos, but a pocketful of national pesos allows you the slim chance of picking up a bargain.

In any convertible peso shop where the locals outnumber the tourists you should be prepared for some idiosyncratic security measures, as hilarious as they are infuriating. Don't be surprised to be asked to wait at the door until another customer leaves, and don't expect to be able to enter carrying any kind of bag – you'll have to leave it at a *guardabolso*, with some identification, to be collected afterwards. These *guardabolsos* are similar to left-luggage offices and are usually located at the entrance to the building, but sometimes you'll have to search them out. If you purchase anything, make sure you pick up your receipt at the cash till, as your shopping will be checked against it at the exit. It's also possible that your carrier bag will be sealed with tape at the till only to be ripped open when you get to the door so that the contents can be checked – ripping it open yourself will leave not only your bag but the whole precious system in tatters.

The best shopping itinerary for the Western visitor to Cuba is one featuring only those items that are, in some sense, home-grown. Don't come to the country hoping to pick up bargain-priced sneakers or cut-price electrical goods – nine times out of ten anything readily available at home will cost more in Cuba and won't come with the same kind of guarantees. A final point to bear in mind is that there are no refunds or exchanges on any goods purchased anywhere, so be sure you've chosen what you need before you buy.

Where to shop

A shopping expedition will run out of decent options very fast anywhere other than Havana – with by far the widest choice – Varadero or Santiago, but any town with a tourist hotel will usually have a couple of shops worth checking out. Most of the largest towns have an indoor craft market, at least a couple of bookshops and somewhere to buy CDs and cassettes, but more common are the single-floor **department stores** run by Tiendas Panamericanas, stocking household goods, groceries and poor-quality clothing.

The best spots for a selection of good shops in one place are the hotels and **shopping malls** in Havana and Varadero. The hotels *Habana Libre*, *Meliá Cohiba* and *Comodoro* have the best choice, especially of name-brand clothing, which is still scarce in Cuba. The biggest two malls in Havana are the Plaza de Carlos Tercero in Centro Habana and the Galerías de Paseo in Vedado.

Though you will rarely find anything of value, it is sometimes worth taking a look inside the few national peso shops still open. Poorly lit and badly maintained, some understandably won't allow foreign customers, giving priority to the national-peso-earning public. Though they are often half empty, it is still possible to unearth the odd antique camera or a long-since deleted record. The best of these are in Centro Habana; Variedades on the Avenida de Italia is a classic of its kind. Also worth looking out for are the **casas de comisiones**, the nearest thing Cuba has to a pawnbrokers. These can be delightful places to poke around, frequently full of 1950s paraphernalia ranging from pocket watches to transistor radios.

Cigars

With the price of the world's finest tobacco at half what you would pay for it outside of Cuba, it's crazy not to consider buying some *habanos* (the frequently used term for **Cuban cigars**) while on the island. There are at least five top-class cigar emporiums in Havana and numerous others around the island, with most half-decent hotels stocking at least a few boxes. The industry standard is for cigars to be sold in boxes of 25, for which prices vary enormously according to brand, strength, length and circumference. For anything less than $50CUC a box, the quality is probably questionable, while prices go as high as $300CUC and beyond for the top brands.

The most coveted brand is Cohiba – unusual in that it was established after the Revolution of 1959 – a long-time black-market favourite and top of many a connoisseur's list. However, if you're buying cigars as souvenirs or for a novelty smoke, you'd do just as well with such world-famous names as Monte Cristo, Romeo y Julieta, Punch or Hoyo de Monterrey, all classics but more affordable than Cohiba. First-time smokers should start with a light smoke for their initiation ceremony and take it from there; good beginners' cigars include most of the H. Upmann range, while for a fuller but still manageable flavour try a Churchill from the Romeo y Julieta brand. Bear in mind that without receipts you are permitted to take only 23 cigars out of the country – with receipts the limit is a total value of $2000CUC. This will be of particular relevance if you have bought your cigars on the black market (see box, p.86).

Theoretically, should you wish to leave the country with more than 23 cigars they must be declared at customs, and you must show your receipts for all cigars on request (although usually you are not checked leaving) or risk having them confiscated.

Rum and coffee

Along with cigars, **rum** is one of the longest established Cuban exports and comes with a worldwide reputation. Although there are a few specialist rum shops around the island, you can pick up most of the recognized brands in any large supermarket without fear of paying over the odds. Rum is available in several different strengths, according to how long it was distilled; the most renowned name is Havana Club, while the least expensive is the pleasantly smooth Añejo Blanco, which will set you back about $3CUC to $5CUC depending on where you shop. The other types increase in strength in the following order: Añejo 3 Años, Añejo Especial, Añejo Reserva, Añejo 7 Años, Cuban Barrel Proof and the potent Máximo Extra Añejo. The maximum number of bottles permitted by customs is six.

Spotting fake cigars

What makes a Cuban cigar a **fake** and what makes it **genuine** can be fairly academic, and some fakes are so well made that even once they are lit it is difficult to tell the difference. If you intend to sell them rather than smoke them, however, it may be more important to be certain whether or not you have been sold a bunch of duds. No method is foolproof, but if your cigars pass the following checks you'll know that at the worst you have some well-made copies.

• All the cigars in a box should be the same colour and shade.
• When the cigar is rolled between the fingers, no loose tobacco should drop out.
• All the cigars in a box should have the same strength of smell.
• There should only be extremely slight variations in the length of cigars, no more than a few millimetres.
• Genuine boxes should be sealed with three labels: a banknote-style label at the front, a smaller label reading *Habanos* in the corner and a holographic sticker.
• The bottom of the box should be stamped: *Habanos SA, Hecho en Cuba* and *Totalmente a mano*.
• A factory code and date should be ink-stamped on the base of the box.

Coffee

Coffee, first introduced to the island by French plantation owners fleeing the 1798 Haitian revolution, is one of Cuba's lesser-known traditional products. It's easy to find, and supermarkets are as good as anywhere, but for one of the few specialist shops head for the Plaza de Armas in Habana Vieja. Just off the square, on the corner of Baratillo, La Casa del Café has a modest selection of different coffees, including Cubita, the top name, but nevertheless a greater choice than anywhere else.

Books and music

Political writing is the speciality in Cuban **bookshops**. From the prolific works of the nineteenth-century independence-fighter José Martí to the speeches of Fidel Castro, there are endless lists of titles, all unwavering in their support of the Revolution. Perhaps more universally appealing, are the coffee-table books of photography covering all aspects of life in one of the most photogenic countries in the world.

Havana has some fantastic **book markets**. The best is on the Plaza de Armas, where amongst the revolutionary pamphlets you can find vintage copies of rarely seen early twentieth-century Cuban books and even colonial-era literature. These markets are the places to uncover written material, such as US-printed tourist brochures reflecting life before Castro, which have no place on the shelves of the official state-run stores.

English-language books are few and far between, but two or three bookshops in Havana and at least one in Varadero have a foreign-language literature section, usually consisting of crime novels and pulp fiction.

As with books, there is not necessarily a better choice of Cuban **music** inside the country than what you could find in London, New York or Montréal. There are, however, all sorts of titles that are unavailable elsewhere, with Cuba the best place to shop for the most up-to-date, fresh-out-of-the-studio *salsa*. Some of the most comprehensive catalogues of CDs and tapes are found in Artex stores, the chain responsible for promoting culture-based

Shopping online

The explosion of Cuban websites in recent years has inevitably brought with it a number of e-commerce companies offering products and services aimed predominantly at the foreign market, as most Cubans still have no Internet access. There are also, of course, plenty of websites based in other countries selling Cuban and Cuba-themed merchandise, some of them offering better-quality products and a greater variety than it is possible to find on the island itself. Below is a list of some of the better ones from Cuba and abroad.

Ⓦ **www.bazar-virtual.com** A reasonable choice of Cuban-published books and maps, with the strongest showing in the fiction and social science texts sections. Trades from Cuba, Canada and Spain.

Ⓦ **www.cubaconnect.co.uk** Cuba Connect bills itself as "a fair-trading company working with the Cuban people to help develop trade and solidarity". The website offers deals on posters, T-shirts, CDs, books, postcards and even coffee – all made in or themed on Cuba.

Ⓦ **www.cubanartspace.net** A US-based online gallery of work by Cuban artists including paintings, photographs and posters.

Ⓦ **www.discuba.com** A superb source of Cuban music with an impressively large list of musical styles from which to choose. Most tastes are catered for, whether jazz, pop and rock or the more traditional *rumba*, *son* and *salsa*, with *danzón*, *nueva trova* and *bolero* all garnering their own sections; a great stop for the serious collector.

Ⓦ **www.soycubano.com** Cuban Artex shops' website, offering cultural products like books, magazines, videos, CDs, original paintings and reproductions.

Cuban products. Most provincial capitals now have a branch, and in Havana there are several with sizeable stocks – though the quantity is still less than most foreigners are used to from their record stores. Look out also for Egrem stores, run by one of the country's most prolific record labels and sometimes stocking titles hard to find elsewhere. Other than these, in Havana, the record stores in the hotel *Habana Libre* and Longina on Obispo are well stocked with everything from Cuban jazz to obscure *rumba* outfits to remastered 1950s recordings by Beny Moré.

Arts and crafts

One of the most rewarding shopping experiences to be had in Cuba is looking around the outdoor markets in Havana, where the full range of local **arts and crafts**, generally referred to as *artesanía*, is on sale. The country has its own selection of tacky tailored-to-tourism items, but if you want something a bit more highbrow there are plenty of alternatives, like expressive African-style wood carvings, a wide choice of jewellery, handmade shoes and everything else from ceramics to textiles. Haggling is

par for the course and often pays dividends, but shopping around won't reveal any significant differences in price or product.

The three main **craft markets** in Havana are on Tacón, just outside the Plaza de la Catedral, La Rampa and the Malecón, a few blocks east of the *Meliá Cohiba* hotel. In the island's other tourist towns as well as all over Havana, look out for the BfC logo, a seal of above-average quality and the trademark of the Fondos Cubanos de Bienes Culturales, shops selling the work of officially recognized local artisans. Artex shops also make a good port of call for crafts, though they tend to have more mass-produced items.

Clothing

Cuba has a thriving **T-shirt** market which caters to just about every taste. Although the obvious choice is a Che T-shirt, of which you can find hundreds of different kinds, there are plenty of more original alternatives and it's worth shopping around. You'll be hard-put to find a better selection than the ones in the Palacio de la Artesanía or the T-shirt shop outside the entrance to the *Habana Libre* hotel.

The bolsa negra

The **black market**, or the *bolsa negra*, is an integral part of life for most Cubans, who rely on it to supply them with the long list of products put out of their reach both by shortages and high prices. From paint to pillowcases, the hotels, where so many of the available resources are found, are the inadvertent suppliers of much of what changes hands under the state table. The attraction of a job connected in any way with tourism, whether it be as a shop assistant, waiter, construction worker or anything else, is, for many Cubans, inextricably linked with the opportunities it will throw up for illicit dealings. Theft from the workplace is common and not surprising, given that a few towels or a map of Havana will sell for a week's typical wages.

Black market cigars

The biggest business on the black market is in the **selling of cigars** to foreign visitors, the average price of a box representing at least as much as the average monthly wage. If you spend any time at all in a Cuban town or city you will inevitably be offered a box of cigars on the street. You can find boxes for as little as $10CUC, but no self-respecting salesman is likely to sell the genuine article at that price and they will almost certainly be fakes (see box, p.84). Realistically, you should expect to pay between $20CUC and $40CUC, depending on the brand and type, for the real thing. Ideally you should ask someone you know, even just the owner of a *casa particular*; even if they don't have a direct contact, chances are they will be able to help you out – everyone knows someone who can get hold of a box of Cohibas or Monte Cristos.

Clothing and shoe sizes

Women's dresses and skirts

American	4	6	8	10	12	14	16	18
British	8	10	12	14	16	18	20	22
Continental	38	40	42	44	46	48	50	52

Women's blouses and sweaters

American	6	8	10	12	14	16	18
British	30	32	34	36	38	40	42
Continental	40	42	44	46	48	50	52

Women's shoes

American	5	6	7	8	9	10	11
British	3	4	5	6	7	8	9
Continental	36	37	38	39	40	41	42

Men's suits

American	34	36	38	40	42	44	46	48
British	34	36	38	40	42	44	46	48
Continental	44	46	48	50	52	54	56	58

Men's shirts

American	14	15	15.5	16	16.5	17	17.5	18
British	14	15	15.5	16	16.5	17	17.5	18
Continental	36	38	39	41	42	43	44	45

Men's shoes

American	7	7.5	8	8.5	9.5	10	10.5	11	11.5
British	6	7	7.5	8	9	9.5	10	11	12
Continental	39	40	41	42	43	44	44	45	46

The most archetypal item of Cuban clothing is the **guayabera**, a lightweight shirt usually characterized by four pockets and worn in all walks of life. It makes a good souvenir and is sold in tourist shops and, less expensively, in department stores such as La Epoca in Centro Habana.

If you're looking for name-brand or **designer clothing** then you'll do best to get it at the airport before you leave. An increasing number of recognizable names are creeping into Cuban shops, particularly those located inside hotels, but you're still more likely to see poor-quality, amusingly named fakes such as *Dodios*, the Cuban answer to Adidas, than a reasonably priced foreign brand.

Travelling with children

Beach and placid waters aside, Cuba is not a country with an ample stock of entertainment for children. However, what the country lacks in amenities it makes up for in enthusiasm. By and large, Cubans love children and welcome them everywhere, and having a kid or two in tow is often a passport to seeing a side of Cuban social life that would otherwise be closed to you.

When travelling around Cuba with children, it's important to remember you'll often be dealing with long lines and sporadic schedules. Long bus journeys can be particularly exhausting and uncomfortable. If you plan on renting a car, bring your own **child or baby seat**, as rental companies never supply them and there are none in Cuba.

Make sure your **first-aid kit** has child-strength fever reducers, diarrhoea medicine, cold remedies, plasters and other medicines. These are available throughout the country but not always readily so and tend to be more expensive than at home.

Similarly, you're best off packing your **nappies and baby wipes** – you can search around successfully for these particularly in Havana, but the quality might not be what you're accustomed to.

Plenty of child-friendly **sunscreen** is essential; the Caribbean sun is very hot, particularly between May and October. Remember also to bring lots of loose cotton clothing, plus a few long-sleeved tops and trousers to combat the brutal air conditioning in restaurants and buses. It's also a good idea to pack a raincoat and appropriate footwear, as sudden downpours are common even outside of the May–October rainy season. Bear in mind that with limited **laundry facilities** you may be hand washing many garments, so take items that are easy to launder and dry.

Health issues

The **heat** in Cuba can be debilitating; it's a good idea to plan excursions in the morning and factor in some downtime in the afternoons. Make sure everyone has enough to drink. Children should stick to **bottled water** or water that has been boiled as there are parasites in some areas of the country. Avoid eating uncooked food or food sold on street stalls. You should also apply the same principle to ice cream sold on the street, as water quality cannot be guaranteed.

Accommodation

Children under 12 years can stay for half-price in many **hotel rooms** but if no extra bed is required they may be able to stay for free. Staying in a **casa particular** is a great way to give children a taste of authentic Cuban life, and many households have child-friendly attractions like pets and courtyards.

Tourist information

There is a disabling shortage of printed travel literature in Cuba and getting hold of any kind of tourist information, particularly outside of the major resorts, can be difficult. You should do as much research as you can before leaving for Cuba, as printed information is often more readily available abroad. The Internet is a good place to start, the state-run sites, like Cubaweb and Cubatravel, offering more information than anything you will find on paper inside Cuba.

Be aware that all information outlets and travel agents in Cuba, like everything else, are run by the state and are unlikely to offer impartial advice on, for example, accommodation deals or places to eat. A trustworthy map is also a scarcity in Cuba, with street maps for anywhere other than each province's largest town being unavailable.

Before you leave home, it's worth contacting the nearest branch of the **Cuban Tourist Board** (see below), which has maps and information on the country. Less specialist but also a useful source of information – especially for holidaymakers and package tourists – is the Caribbean Tourism Organization (Ⓦwww.doitcaribbean.com or Ⓦwww.caribbean.co.uk), based in Barbados with branches in Britain, the US and Canada, which can help with general enquiries about travel to and inside Cuba.

Currently there is no independent nationwide **tourist board** in Cuba, so getting hold of both impartial and detailed tourist information can be difficult, particularly away from the heavily visited areas. The only tourist information network is **Infotur** (Ⓦwww.infotur .cu), which still only has a handful of branches, all in Havana – the best equipped are at Obispo e/ Bernaza y Villegas in Habana Vieja (daily 9am–7pm; ☎7/866-3333 & 862-4586) and at Ave. 5ta y 112 in Playa (☎7/204-7036); it also has desks in many hotels and at the José Martí International Airport. Concentrating on booking organized excursions, hotel room reservations and car rental, Infotur has very little information on public transport, other than the Víazul bus service (see p.41), nor can it officially supply information on *paladares* or *casas particulares*, though the staff are often willing

to help with their own recommendations. Despite these limitations, however, Infotur remains the best place to go for practical information, and the friendly staff are generally willing to try and help with all sorts of different queries, though they do try to steer visitors towards the state-run tourist apparatus.

There are also **state-run tourist travel agents**, principally Cubanacán, Cubatur and Havanatur, which effectively double up as information offices, particularly in most provincial capitals where they are the only official source of assistance to foreign visitors. Though their principal aim is to sell you their own packages and organized excursions (see p.38), the staff are usually quite willing and accustomed to supplying any kind of tourist information, including advice on eating and entertainment options, local transport and car rental as well as information on nearby attractions. They can also book hotel rooms and are usually the most convenient place to book Víazul bus tickets (see p.41). You will find the office of at least one of them in most of the major resorts and largest towns and cities, while they also have desks in most hotel lobbies. Though each has its own set of excursions and tours, the basic packages and prices differ very little between them.

Tourist offices and government sites

Australian Department of Foreign Affairs
Ⓦwww.dfat.gov.au, Ⓦwww.smartraveller.gov.au.
British Foreign & Commonwealth Office
Ⓦwww.fco.gov.uk.
Canadian Department of Foreign Affairs
Ⓦwww.dfait-maeci.gc.ca.
Irish Department of Foreign Affairs
Ⓦwww.foreignaffairs.gov.ie.

New Zealand Ministry of Foreign Affairs ⓦ www.mft.govt.nz.
US State Department ⓦ www.travel.state.gov.

Cuban tourist board offices abroad

Canada 440 Blvd Rene Levesque, Suite 1105, Montréal H2Z 1V7 ☎ 514/875-8004, ⓕ 875-8006, ⓔ montreal@gocuba.ca; 1200 Bay St, Suite 305, Toronto M5R 2A5 ☎ 416/362-0700, ⓕ 362-6799, ⓦ www.gocuba.ca.
Germany Cubanisches Fremdenverkehrsamt, An der Hauptwachb 7, 60313 Frankfurt ☎ 69/288322 or 23, ⓦ www.cubainfo.de.
Mexico Goethe 16, 3er piso, Colonia Anzures, ☎ 5/2555866, ⓔ otcumex@mail.internet.com.mx.
Spain Paseo de La Habana no.27 28036, Madrid ☎ 91/4113097 & 5625757, ⓔ otcuba@otcubaesp.com.
UK 154 Shaftesbury Ave, London WC2H 8JT ☎ 020/7240 6655, ⓕ 7836 9265, ⓔ tourism@cubasi.info (Mon–Fri 10am–7pm).

Caribbean Tourism Organization

Britain 42 Westminster Palace Gardens, Artillery Row, London SW1P 1RR ☎ 020/7222 4335.

Canada Taurus House, 512 Duplex Ave, Toronto, Ontario M4R 2E3 ☎ 416/485-8724.
US 80 Broad St, 32nd Floor, New York, NY 10004 ☎ 212/635-9530.

Useful government websites

Unless stated otherwise, the websites listed below are Spanish-language only. ⓦ www .cuba.cu Seemingly every aspect of Cuban life – from sport, art and science to business, politics and education – is covered here. Provides very useful links to the official websites of most of the country's provinces, via the Portales provinciales window on the homepage.

ⓦ www.cubaliteraria.cu Services and information on all things related to Cuban writing and writers. As well as an impressive dictionary of authors and books, short biographies, interviews and insights into literary movements and institutions, you can access publications online and read work ranging from Cuban classics to the latest names in fiction.

ⓦ www.cubatravel.cu The official website for the Cuban Ministry of Tourism contains practical information and advice on everything from customs

---

Recommended independent websites

All the websites listed below are English-language.

ⓦ **www.afrocubaweb.com** Fantastically detailed site covering absolutely anything even remotely connected to Afro-Cuban issues, from history and politics to music and dance. Also features global touring news for Cuban musical outfits.

ⓦ **www.cuba.com** Claims to be "The official website to Cuba" and is designed for US citizens who want in-depth and impartial information in English about the island from a visitor's point of view.

ⓦ **www.cubanet.org** Run from Florida, CubaNet bills itself as a champion of free press and provides a platform for Cubans, particularly journalists, to report stories and express ideas and opinions which never make it past the censors within Cuba. This website is an insightful forum for the political opposition to the Cuban government so conspicuous by its absence on the island itself. Available in Spanish, English, German and French.

ⓦ **www.cubaupdate.org** An excellent source of information for US citizens, detailing tours organized by the Center for Cuban Studies, offering advice about how to plan a trip to Cuba and providing the latest information on the state of play on the embargo, its enforcement and attempts to have it relaxed or lifted.

ⓦ **www.globalexchange.org/campaigns/cuba** A voice in the campaign to end the US blockade of Cuba, with information on the history between the two countries, the latest US-Cuba relations news and help for anyone thinking of getting involved. Also a source of information on study tours, as well as information about the legality of travelling to Cuba during the embargo.

regulations to accommodation and transport as well as some bits and pieces on Cuban cooking and music. Available in English.

ⓦ**www.cubaweb.cu** Another very comprehensive state website, slightly more commercial than ⓦ www.cuba.cu but similar in scope. Includes news reports from the Cuban press, plus information on travel, investment, trade, aid and many other subjects. Available in English.

ⓦ**www.dtcuba.com** This well-laid-out site is primarily a kind of yellow pages for tourists in Cuba but also has up-to-date news of the latest goings-on in Cuban sport, culture, health and business.

ⓦ**www.granma.cu** The national Cuban newspaper in digital format, giving the government line on international and domestic affairs. With editions in English, French, German, Italian and Portuguese.

ⓦ**www.islagrande.cu** Effectively a search engine designed specifically for people looking for Cuban or Cuba-based websites, grouped by topic. The homepage also includes up-to-the-minute news items from Cuba and a wide range of extras.

ⓦ**www.transnet.cu** Another search-engine-style site with links to anything and everything related to transport to, from and inside Cuba, including practical tourist information on taxis, car rental, marinas and flights.

Living in Cuba

Working in Cuba as a foreign national is more complicated than in most countries, and anyone thinking of picking up a casual job on the island can pretty much forget it. All wages in Cuba are paid by the state in national pesos, so if the bureaucracy doesn't stop you the hourly rates probably will. The majority of foreign workers here are either diplomats or in big business, and the only realistic chance most people have of working is to join one of the voluntary brigades. Studying here is easier, with Spanish classes not only offered at universities, but also representing a significant niche in the private enterprise market. There is, of course, no better place to learn to dance *salsa*, but be prepared to marry your instructor.

Work

Getting a visa for more than three months in Cuba, quite apart from actually being allowed to work while you're there, is not easy (see p.91). Your first port of call should be the Cuban embassy in your home country, where you can apply for a **work visa** for which there is a $15CUC fee plus an extra $75CUC charge. The principal point of contact in Cuba is the Cámara de Comercio de la República de Cuba at Calle 21 no.661 esq. A, Vedado, Havana (☏7/55-1452 & 55-1931, ⓦwww.camaracuba.cu), which processes work permit and visa applications. Work permits are usually issued for a one-year period, after which time they are renewable.

Normally, you'll need to have a sponsor before the authorities even consider giving you permission to do any kind of work. In fact, there are very few positions open to non-citizens at all, as work permits are given to foreign workers only if it can be shown that no Cuban national is available to fill the position.

Working for a foreign employer, as most journalists visiting the island do, or as a freelancer, allows only marginally more possibilities than government work and still involves a series of checks. These begin at the Cuban embassy in the home country, followed by an assessment of each application at the Centro de Prensa Internacional (☏7/832-0526 & 832-7491) at Calle 23 no. 152 esq. O in the Vedado district of Havana. There will sometimes be a further consultation of the case by the Ministerio del Turismo (Ministry of Tourism), based at Calle 19 no.

710 e/ Paseo y A in Vedado, Havana (℡7/833-4325 & 833-4319).

Other than a foreign firm there are basically two possible kinds of employer for the foreign national: the Cuban government or, the more likely, a joint venture company working in partnership with a Cuban firm, which will itself be state-run. To do any kind of salaried work you'll need to obtain a **temporary residence** from the Ministerio del Comercio Exterior (Ministry of Foreign Trade), located at Infanta no.16 esq. Calle 23, Vedado, Havana (℡7/55-0396 & 55-0354), and a **work permit** from the Ministerio del Trabajo y Seguridad Social (Ministry of Labour), at Calle 23 esq. P, Vedado, Havana (℡7/55-0008 & 55-0024).

The simplest and one of the more common ways to expend a bit of elbow grease in Cuba is to visit the country on a **working holiday**. These trips are organized in the US by the National Network on Cuba (ⓦwww.cubasolidarity.com), in Canada by the Canadian Network on Cuba (ⓦwww.canadiannetworkoncuba.ca) and in the UK by the Cuba Solidarity Campaign (ⓦwww.cuba-solidarity.org.uk). Known as brigades, these organized volunteer groups usually spend three weeks working alongside Cubans in construction or agriculture, living on purpose-built camps. Obviously there is a strong pro-government, propagandist slant to the experience – which also involves visits to schools, hospitals and trade unions – but the opportunity to witness working conditions and gain a sense of the Revolution in action is nevertheless unique. The cost of a trip from the UK is currently around £800, and interested parties should contact the Cuba Solidarity Campaign either online or at The Red Rose Club, 129 Seven Sisters Rd, London N7 7QG (℡020/7263 6452).

Study

There is an array of organizations and institutions that send people to Cuba to **study**, mostly to learn Spanish. You can, however, take Spanish classes independently without too much hassle. The most obvious place to go is the University of Havana, where the Faculty of Modern Languages has for many years been running several different courses aimed specifically at foreign students and

visitors. The most basic Spanish course is an intensive one-week affair, with two-week, three-week and month-long options, too. You can also combine Spanish studies with courses in dance or Cuban culture or even just study Cuban culture on its own. There are four-month and six-month courses for this combined option. The university provides full-board on-campus accommodation for two weeks, including the cost of lessons. Courses start throughout the year on the first Monday of every month.

For more information, costs and details on how to apply, contact the university's Postgraduate Department through Heidi Villalón at Dirección Posgrado, Calle J no. 556 e/ 25 y 27, Vedado, Havana (℡7/832-4245 & 833-4163, ℻833-5774, ⓔdpg@comuh.uh.cu), or the specialist travel agent CubanTravels.com, based in Havana in the Edificio Bacardí at Monserrate no.261, suite 502 e/ San Juan de Dios y Empedrado, Habana Vieja (℡7/866-4490 or 91, ℻866-4489, ⓦwww.cubantravels.com). Similar courses are run at just about every principal university in the country, most of them found in the provincial capital cities.

The disproportionate number of private Spanish tutors in Cuba, particularly in Havana, is testament more to the spirit of local enterprise than an excess of qualified language teachers. Many *casa particular* owners can usually find someone eager to trot out a few verb tables to anyone willing to pay in convertible pesos and you should be careful about who you take classes from. On the other hand, with state wages unable to compete with the hourly rates most foreign visitors are happy to pay for tuition, there are plenty of properly trained teachers who have sacrificed their day jobs or supplemented their wages by teaching Spanish classes in their own homes.

The best way to arrange a proper course of Spanish classes in Cuba is through professional organizations based outside the country. One of the finest is the Scotland-based Caledonia (℡0131/621 7721, ℻621 7723, ⓦwww.caledonialanguages.co.uk), whose one- and two-week courses run in Havana and Santiago de Cuba are highly recommended. For extra, they can also arrange accommodation, usually in a *casa particular*, starting at £125 for a single room for a week. Dance and percussion classes are also available.

For US and Canadian travellers wanting to study Spanish in Cuba it makes more sense to get in touch with Cactus Language (US & Canada ☎1-888-270-3949, UK ☎0845/130 4775, ⊛www.cactuslanguage.com), which has offices on both sides of the Atlantic. Classes take place at locations in Havana, Trinidad or Santiago de Cuba. Currently one of the cheapest courses lasts just one week, while for considerably more you get two weeks of classes and accommodation in a classy hotel in Havana's Miramar neighbourhood. Again, you can combine your Spanish-learning with dance classes, while there is also a course which offers a mixture of Spanish classes and scuba diving.

Study and work programmes

AFS Intercultural Programs US ☎1-800/AFS-INFO, Canada ☎1-800/361-7248 or 514/288-3282, UK ☎0113/242 6136, Australia ☎1300/131736 or ☎02/9215-0077, NZ ☎0800/600 300 or 04/494 6020, international enquiries ☎+1-212/807-8686, ⊛www.afs.org. Global UN-recognized organization running summer programmes to foster international understanding.

From the US and Canada

American Institute for Foreign Study ☎1-866/906-2437, ⊛www.aifs.com. Language study and cultural immersion, as well as au pair and Camp America programmes.
BUNAC USA (British Universities North America Club) ☎1-800/GO-BUNAC, ⊛www.bunac.org. Offers students the chance to work in Australia, New Zealand, Ireland or Britain.
Council on International Educational Exchange (CIEE) ☎1-800/40-STUDY or ☎1/207-533-7600, ⊛www.ciee.org. Leading NGO offering study programmes and volunteer projects around the world.
Earthwatch Institute ☎1-800/776-0188 or 978/461-0081, ⊛www.earthwatch.org. International non-profit organisation that does research projects in over 50 countries all over the world.

From the UK and Ireland

BTCV (British Trust for Conservation Volunteers) ☎01302/572 244, ⊛www.btcv.org.uk. One of the largest environmental charities in Britain, with a programme of national and international working holidays (as a paying volunteer).
BUNAC (British Universities North America Club) ☎020/7251 3472, ⊛www.bunac.co.uk. Organizes working holidays in the US and other destinations for students.
Camp America Camp America ☎020/7581 7373, ⊛www.campamerica.co.uk.
Council Exchange ☎020/8939 9057, ⊛www.councilexchanges.org.uk. International study and work programmes for students and recent graduates.
Earthwatch Institute ☎01865/318 838, ⊛www.uk.earthwatch.org. Long-established international charity with environmental and archeological research projects worldwide.

From Australia and New Zealand

AFS Intercultural Programs Australia ☎1300/131 736 or ☎02/9215 0088, NZ

Working and student visas

Anyone planning to work in Cuba must have the relevant **visas** organized before they arrive. You will need to have ready the name of the organization that will be sponsoring and be answerable for you ready to fill in on your form.

Journalists need to apply for a special **journalist visa**. The Cuban authorities advise you to apply at the consulate in your country of departure, and indeed, broadcast journalists have no choice but to do so as it is prohibited to enter Cuba with unauthorized professional camera equipment. Print journalists may find it easier to enter the country on a tourist card and then apply to the International Press Centre in Havana (Calle 23 esq. 0 ☎7/832-7491) to change their status, though this is not without its own problems. Similarly, students must have a **student visa** (though this can be avoided if you are attending the short courses at the University of Havana) entitling them to stay in the country for longer than a month; these can be arranged through the Cuban consulate, though sometimes language schools can assist you with this.

☎0800/600 300 or 04/494 6020, ⊛www.afs.org
.au, ⊛www.afsnzl.org.nz. Runs summer
experiential programmes aimed at fostering
international understanding for teenagers and adults.

From South Africa

AFS Intercultural Programs ☎27/11-339-2741.
Non-profit, self-funded and volunteer-based NGO
organization. wwww.afs.org/southafrica.

Travel essentials

Costs

Cuba is not a particularly cheap place to visit,
and for the package tourist the costs of eating
in restaurants and staying in hotel rooms will
generally require a budget only slightly lower
than you'd need back home. However, it is
possible to survive on relatively little, given the
availability of fresh food sold for national
pesos and the relatively inexpensive private-
room market. The existence of two currencies
can make things confusing, but on the whole
visitors stick to using convertible pesos.

You're unlikely to find a hotel room for less
than $25CUC, though some of the older,
more basic hotels that cater to both Cubans
and foreign visitors offer much lower rates.
Private rooms in a *casa particular* generally
cost between $15CUC and $35CUC
depending on where in the country you are
staying, though for long stays, of at least a
few weeks, you may be able to negotiate the
price below $15CUC in some places outside
the capital.

Discounting accommodation, your daily
budget can vary quite considerably. If you're
content with eating street vendor fare, or
buying supplies from food markets, and are
prepared to muck in with the locals for night-
time entertainment, then you can get away
with a daily budget of just $5–10CUC or
about 100–200 national pesos. In the more
likely event that you will want to eat out at
restaurants and *paladares*, you should allow
$10–25CUC a day for food and at least
another $5CUC if you want to attend a live
performance or go to a club. A daily budget
of $50CUC is relatively high-rolling, but still
easy to spend in Havana or the major resorts.

If you travel by Víazul or another tourist bus
service (the most comfortable and efficient
way to get around), then expect to pay
upwards of $15CUC for most journeys (for
example, the 335-kilometre journey from
Havana to Trinidad is $25CUC). Private taxis
can sometimes work out cheaper than
buses if you share them with three or four
other hard-currency-paying travellers, with a
100-kilometre trip costing as little as
$5–10CUC each (see p.47).

Though museum entrance costs are
generally low, often only a convertible peso
or two, most places charge a larger sum,
commonly between $2–5CUC, for the right
to take photos, and as much as $25CUC to
enter with a video camera.

Crime and personal safety

Cuba is one of the safest destinations in the
Caribbean and Latin America, and the
majority of visitors will experience a trouble-
free stay. The worst you're likely to
experience is incessant and irritating
attention from *jineteros*, *jineteras* and
hustlers. However, following a few simple
precautions will help ensure that you don't
fall prey to any petty crime.

Police

The emergency number for the
Cuban police differs from place to
place, and there is no 911 or 999
equivalent; see the listings in the
respective chapters.

Things to take with you

Most things are easy to find in Cuba, but here is a miscellaneous list of items you might consider taking from home:

- Envelopes
- A supply of rolling papers and tobacco if you like to roll your own, as these products are totally unavailable
- Toilet paper – you can buy it in Cuba but it's rarely there when you need it
- A small flashlight
- A multi-purpose penknife (remembering to pack it in your hold luggage)
- A selection of herbs and spices, if you intend to do any self-catering
- A supply of disposable nappies as required
- Some basic medication (see p.52)
- A waterproof overcoat
- Candles
- A plug – if you think you might want a bath in one of Cuba's numerous plugless hotel rooms
- Soap – if you intend to stay in *campismos* or peso hotels
- Pens and pencils – along with soap, these are often appreciated as gifts
- Water bottle or flask – invaluable, since drinks are usually sold in returnable containers
- A padlock – if you intend to use bikes
- Tampons
- Condoms

The most common assault upon tourists is **bag-snatching** or **pickpocketing** (particularly in Habana Vieja), so always make sure you sling bags across your body rather than letting them dangle from one shoulder, keep cameras concealed whenever possible, don't carry valuables in easy-to-reach pockets and always carry only the minimum amount of cash. A common trick is for thieves on bicycles to ride past and snatch at bags, hats and sunglasses, so wear these at your discretion. Needless to say, don't leave bags and possessions unattended anywhere, but be especially vigilant on beaches, where it can take a skilful thief a mere moment to be off with your possessions. While there's no need to be suspicious of everyone who tries to strike up a conversation with you (and many people will), a measure of caution is still advisable.

Other than this, the biggest crime you are likely to experience are **scams** from wily street operators. Never accept the offer of moneychangers on the street, as some will take your money and run – literally – or give you a roll of notes that on closer inspection proves to be just rolled-up paper. You should also avoid using unregistered taxis and never take a ride in a cab where "a friend" is accompanying the driver. Although you're unlikely in this scenario to suffer a violent attack, you may well find yourself pickpocketed. This is a particularly common trick on arrival at the airport, where you should be extra vigilant. Even if you are on a tight budget, it's well worth getting a registered cab into the centre when you are loaded with all your valuables and possessions.

Some **hotels** are not entirely secure, so be sure to put any valuables in the hotel security box, if there is one, or at least stash them out of sight. Registered *casas particulares* are, as a rule, safe, but you stay in an unregistered one at your peril. If you have a **rental car**, be aware that these can sometimes be seen as easy pickings. Take all the usual sensible precautions: leave nothing visible in your car – including items you may consider worthless like maps, snacks or cassettes – even if you're only away from it for a short period of time. Furthermore, thieves are not just interested in your personal possessions but will break into and damage cars to take the radios, break off wing mirrors and wrench off spare parts. To avoid this, always park your car in a car park, guarded compound or other secure place. Car rental agencies will be able to advise you on those nearest to you, or, failing that, ask at a large hotel. *Casas particulares* owners will also be able to tell you where to park safely.

If the worst happens and you suffer a **break-in**, call the rental company first as they should have supplied you with an emergency number. They can advise you how to proceed from there and will either inform the police themselves or direct you to the correct police station. You must report the crime to be able to get a replacement car and for your own insurance purposes.

There is little **violent crime** in Cuba, but should you be mugged, do not resist, just comply with your attackers' demands. As in most places, avoid walking down poorly lit alleys or deserted streets, particularly at night.

You should always carry a photocopy of your **passport** (or the passport itself), as the police sometimes ask to inspect them.

Emergencies

Should you be unfortunate enough to be robbed and want to make an insurance claim,

---

Jineterismo, or the escort industry

Everywhere you go in Cuba, you'll see Western men – or, less commonly, women – laden down with shopping bags and with a dazzling, dolled-up young Cuban hanging off his arm. There is no single issue in Cuba today as complex or contentious as **jineterismo**, or the escort and hustler culture, widely perceived as the re-emergence of prostitution in Cuba. Immediately after assuming power, Castro's regime banned prostitution – a way of life for some poorer, less educated Cubans prior to the Revolution – and, officially at least, wiped it off the streets, with prostitutes and pimps rehabilitated into society.

The resurgence of the tourist industry has seen prostitution slink back into business since the mid-1990s; however, the heavy hand of law enforcement has resulted in a rather hazily defined exchange of services. As a general definition, the pejorative term *jinetero* refers to a male hustler, or someone who will find girls, cigars, taxis or accommodation for a visitor and then take a cut for the service. He – though more commonly this is the preserve of his female counterpart, a *jinetera* – is often also the sexual partner to a foreigner, usually for material gain. In the eyes of Cubans, being a *jinetero* or *jinetera* can mean anything from prostitute to paid escort, opportunist to simply a Cuban boyfriend or girlfriend.

As an obvious foreign face in Cuba, most noticeably in Havana and Santiago de Cuba, you will often be pursued by persistent *jineteros* and *jineteras*. Given that there are times when you may well find yourself using their services – at least to get a taxi – it's better to be polite even when the hustling reaches fever pitch. Many Cubans are quite simply desperate to leave the country and see marrying a foreigner as the best way out, while others simply want to live the good life and are more than happy to spend a few days (or hours) pampering the egos of middle-aged Western swingers in order to go to the best clubs and restaurants and be bought the latest fashions. Given this fact, single foreign men may find that the ceaseless attention of sometimes stunning Cuban women may well be the defining experience of their trip – although they'd be best to remember what lies behind all the fuss being made over them.

A law passed in February 1999 increased police powers of arrest and resulted in large numbers of women going to prison for associating with foreigners. Not surprisingly, that caused many former *jineteros* to throw in the towel, leaving the path clear for the more hard-nosed and professional to continue with less competition. In Havana in particular, it is sadly not uncommon to see women and their pimps openly touting for trade on the Malecón. Legislation introduced in 2003 has given police the right to stop tourists' cars and question Cuban passengers they suspect to be *jineteros*, and *casas particulares* must register all Cuban guests accompanying foreigners; (foreigners themselves are not penalized in any way).

Foreign consulates and embassies in Cuba

There are no consulates or embassies in Cuba for Australia or New Zealand; citizens are advised to go to either the Canadian or UK embassies.

Canada Embassy, Calle 30 no.518, Miramar, Havana ☏7/204-2516, ⓕ204-2044.

UK Embassy, Calle 34 no.702–704, Miramar, Havana ☏7/204-1771, ⓕ204-8104.

US Special Interests Section, Calle Calzada y L, Vedado, Havana ☏7/33-3531, ⓕ33-3700, ⓦhttp://usembassy.state.gov/posts/cu1

you *must* report the crime to the **police** and get a statement. Be aware, though, that the **police** in Cuba are generally indifferent to crimes against tourists – and may even try to blame you for not being more vigilant. Don't expect them to take your plight seriously: at best you will spend several hours waiting to be seen and at worst they will attempt to withhold your copy of your statement, assuring you they will send the details on to you when you return home. You must insist upon getting the statement there and then, as there is little chance of receiving anything from them at a later date. Unfortunately, the chance of your possessions being recovered is equally remote.

After seeing the police, you may find it more useful to contact **Asistur** (☏7/33-8527 or 33-8920), the 24-hour assistance agency, based in Havana and Santiago, which can arrange replacement travel documents, help with financial difficulties and recover lost luggage. In the case of a serious emergency, you should notify your foreign consul (see above).

Drugs

Drugs, specifically marijuana and cocaine, are increasingly common in Cuba and you may find that you are frequently offered them, especially in Havana and the main tourist areas. If you are not interested, a firm "no" should suffice. Should you be tempted to indulge, be aware that, the authorities take a very dim view of drug abuse – one of the Revolution's triumphs was to rid the country of dealers and users – and prison sentences are often meted out for possession of small amounts of marijuana alone. The majority of foreigners held in Cuban prisons are there for drug-related crimes.

Disabled travellers

Most of the upmarket hotels are well equipped for **disabled travellers**, each with at least one specially designed room and all the necessary lifts and ramps. However, away from the resorts there are very few amenities or services provided for disabled people, and in fact, you rarely see anyone in a wheelchair in the street in Cuba.

Electricity

The **electricity** supply is generally 110V 60Hz, but always check, as in some hotels it is 220V. Some hotels also have adaptors which guests may borrow. Private houses are often prey to scheduled power cuts for both electricity and gas, an energy-saving device introduced during the Special Period to help conserve limited fuel resources. If you stay in a tourist hotel you are unlikely to be affected by this.

Entry requirements

Citizens of most Western countries must have a ten-year **passport**, valid for at least six months after your departure from Cuba, plus a **tourist card** (*tarjeta de turista*), essentially a visa, to enter Cuba. Tourist cards are valid for a standard thirty days and must be used within six months of issue. In addition to the completed application form, you'll need a photocopy of a valid passport and photocopy of your return ticket or travel agent voucher for a pre-paid package tour. Tourist cards are usually issued within one day. Although you can buy one from the Cuban consulate, your tour operator or travel agent will sell you one when you purchase your flight. The charge in the UK is £15–20, in Australia A$35, in New Zealand NZ$44.

Once in Cuba, you can renew a tourist card for another thirty days (bringing the total stay allowed to sixty days) for a fee of $25CUC. Because the terms and conditions of extended stays change regularly and without warning, you are strongly advised to check with the Cuban consulate or embassy in your country of departure before planning a long trip. The Cuban tourist board may also be able to give up-to-date information. Immigration offices in various provinces are listed throughout the guide, but you will find it far easier to renew your card in Havana, where the immigration office Control de Extranjeros in Nuevo Veddo Calle Factor esq. Final, TulipEan e/ 3 y 5 (Mon–Fri 8.30am–3pm) will process it – arrive early and expect delays. The best approach is to state that you will be travelling around the island and staying in state hotels. Avoid mentioning *casas particulares*, even if this is where you are planning to stay, as it provokes more detailed questioning. You must pay your $25CUC fee in special stamps, which you can buy from Banco Metropiolitano, either at the branch on La Rampa or in Habana Vieja. You need to buy the exact amount or your visa will not be processed. When renewing your visa you will need details (perhaps including a receipt) of where you are staying.

Should you wish to stay longer than sixty days as a tourist you will have to leave Cuban territory and return with a **new tourist card**. Many people do this by island-hopping to other Caribbean destinations or Mexico and getting another tourist card from the Cuban consulate there.

Incidentally, the **passport number** listed on your tourist card must correspond to the number on the passport you bring with you to Cuba. So if you get a new passport for some reason, be sure to get a new tourist card as well. Note that people of Cuban origin who are nationals of other countries must travel with a Cuban passport if they left Cuba after 1970.

On arrival, you must fill out on the **tourist form** the address of where you first intend to stay in Cuba. Again, although you can put the name of a registered *casa particular*, you will pass through customs much more smoothly if you enter the name of a state hotel. Putting the address of a friend is similarly likely to cause you – and them – problems. Be aware that if you don't have any address you may be forced to pay on the spot for three nights' accommodation in a hotel of the state's choosing. You must also be able to show an onward **airline ticket** when you enter the country.

Cuban consulates and embassies abroad

Australia Consulate-General, 18 Mainwaring Ave, Sydney ☎02/9311 4611, ⓕ9311 1255.

Hustle and hassle on the street

If you look obviously non-Cuban you can expect plenty of attention and hassle on the street, especially in major towns and popular visitor destinations such as Trinidad, Santiago and Baracoa. There will be times when you feel as though you are doing nothing else but rejecting offers of women, cigars, drugs, the best lobster in town and the cheapest and most comfortable bed for the night.

In addition, you can also expect plenty of attention from locals trying to befriend you or beg from you. While very often these people are simply hoping to squeeze a few drinks or some money from you with a well-rehearsed sob story, many others are genuinely interested in getting to know you and hearing a bit about where you're from. Cubans are generally gregarious and often interested in knowing about other countries to which they have not had the opportunity to travel.

All this is incredibly tiresome, to be sure, and hardly makes for a totally stress-free trip, but there is little risk of any trouble beyond this as for the most part you are dealing with people trying to make a living. The only way to completely avoid this kind of attention is to stay away from the major tourist towns and cities, including Havana, and pay for an all-inclusive resort like Guardalavaca or one of the quieter, non-touristy destinations like Las Tunas, Bayamo and Manzanillo.

Canada Embassy, 388 Main St, Ottawa, Ontario K1S 1E3 ☏613/563-0141.
Consulate-General, 5353 Dundas St West, Toronto, Ontario M9B 6H8 ☏416/234-8181.
Consulate-General, 1415 Pine Ave West, Montréal, Québec H3B 1B2 ☏514/843-8897.
Mexico Embassy, Presidente Masarik 554, Colonia Polanco, 11560 Mexico, DF ☏52/5-280-8039.
UK Embassy, 167 High Holborn, London WC1

☏020/7420 3100; 24hr visa and information service ☏0891/880 820.
US Cuban Interests Section, 2630 16th St NW, Washington DC 20009 ☏202/797-8518.
Consulate Office, 2639 16th St NW, Washington DC 20009 ☏202/797-8609.

Departure tax

The airport departure tax is $25CUC.

US citizens

The letter of US law does not actually prohibit US citizens from being in Cuba, just from spending money there. In practical terms, of course, this amounts to a ban on travel – for all except those approved and "licensed" by the US government. In 1996 the decades-long embargo was actually tightened, thanks to the power exerted by wealthy Cuban exiles in the US combined with that of old Cold Warriors in Congress like Senator Jesse Helms. The **Helms-Burton Act** of 1996 allows for fines of up to US$50,000 and the confiscation of property of US citizens who visit Cuba without permission and at their own expense. This is in addition to the already standing threats contained in the **Trading with the Enemy Act**, which make fines of up to US$250,000 and prison terms of up to ten years theoretically possible. This is why it is more than a good idea for American citizens to get their hands on the most up-to-date information about the embargo and its enforcement before deciding to ignore it.

American citizens can purchase tourist cards in Canada, Mexico or other countries, and the Cuban authorities will, on request, stamp the card instead of your passport upon entering and leaving Cuba. Most US citizens who travel to Cuba illegally do not bring the stamped tourist card back to the US with them, as this in itself can serve as proof of having been to Cuba – as, of course, can airline tickets, souvenirs, cigars and photos of yourself at recognizable monuments. The kitsch value of any of these objects may pale in comparison to their meaning to zealous US immigration officers. Strangely enough, non-US citizens can get tourist cards quite easily in the US, from the Cuban Consulate Office in Washington DC (see p.28).

Things change quite often, depending on the direction of the prevailing political winds in the US. President Clinton's administration, for instance, actually took a number of steps to make it easier for Americans to visit Cuba legally, and also to send money or humanitarian aid to the country. There has been no similar rapprochement under the Bush administration, however. By the end of 2003, the Bush administration had reversed all initiatives introduced by the previous administration, eliminating approval for all individual educational trips and most academic trips. A rather bamboozling piece of legislation now decrees that individuals travelling under a "general license" for professional research may still travel to Cuba, though even these licenses are being granted less generously than before.

For the lowdown on the current situation, check out the update offered on the website of the **Center for Cuban Studies** (🌐www.cubaupdate.org) or talk to one of the groups organizing legal tours to the island. The exact terms of the sanctions against Cuba are available from the **US Treasury Department, Office of Foreign Assets Control**, in Washington DC (☏202/622-2480, 🌐www.treas .gov/ofac). Another detailed US government website, dedicated as much to defending as to explaining the regulations governing travel to Cuba, is at 🌐www.travel.state.gov/travel/cuba.html.

Gay and lesbian travellers

Cubans in general are not particularly accommodating towards **gays and lesbians**. Open displays of affection between same-sex couples are likely to earn you at the least a few sniggers from passers-by and at worst demands from the police to produce identification.

Women travellers

Though violent sexual attacks against female tourists are virtually unheard of, women travelling in Cuba should brace themselves for a quite remarkable level of attention. Casual sex is a staple of Cuban life and **unaccompanied women** are generally assumed to be on holiday for exactly that reason, with protestations to the contrary generally greeted with sheer disbelief. The nonstop attention can be unnerving, but in general, Cuban men manage to combine a courtly romanticism with wit and charm, meaning the persistent come-ons will probably leave you irritated rather than threatened. It's worth knowing, too, that many of your would-be suitors, particularly in larger towns and cities, are likely to be *jineteros*.

If you are not interested, there's no surefire way to stop the flow of comments and approaches, but decisively saying "no", not wearing skimpy clothing and avoiding eye contact with men you don't know will lessen the flow of attention a little. You could also

Women's organizations

The main **women's organization** in Cuba is the Federación de Mujeres de Cuba (FMC), which has a branch in each province and promotes the interests of women within the Revolution. If you want to make contact with or get information on specific groups, this is the place to start. The Havana office is at Paseo no.260, Vedado ⊤ 7/55-2771.

resort to wearing a wedding ring. However, it's as well to remember that even a few hours of friendship with a Cuban man can lead to pledges of eternal love. Flattering though such a pledge may be, it's most likely nothing to do with your personal charms but because **marriage to a foreigner** is a tried-and-tested method of emigrating.

For this reason, if you do spark up a relationship in Cuba, you may well find events moving along at an alarming rate, and before you know it you could be introduced to family and friends as the fiancée (as well as finding yourself paying for everything). Establish your position at the outset – in so far as you can – and don't allow yourself to be bullied into any course of action you'd rather not follow through.

Aside from this, women travelling in Cuba are treated with a great deal of courtesy

Cuban bureaucracy

Cuba is a quagmire of **bureaucracy**. It is characterized by endless waiting, lost paperwork, low levels of competence and high levels of indifference, so dealing with any aspect of the Cuban government can feel like an unprecedented nightmare. Every aspect of life in Cuba is governed by state laws and directives, which can be extremely disadvantageous when you step outside the role assigned to you as a visitor in Cuba. Though you probably won't be affected during the course of a straightforward, trouble-free holiday, you are likely to encounter problems if you have to report a theft, renew a visa outside of Havana, change your visa status anywhere in the country, or visit areas not specifically designated as tourist regions.

Should you encounter problems, the first rule is to keep your cool. Getting cross will not impress anyone – Cubans have been coping with this situation for years and, understandably, don't see why you should get any special treatment. The second rule is always to make sure you leave at least double the time suggested by Cuban authorities to resolve a matter. Do both these things and you'll make life much easier for yourself.

and respect. The country is remarkably safe and you are able to move around freely, particularly at night, with more ease than in many Western cities and you should encounter few problems.

Insurance

Cuba's world-famous health service may be free for Cuban citizens, but it's funded at least partly by the growing number of foreigners who come here solely to take advantage of Cuban medical expertise. If you'd rather not pay through the nose for treatment that may be unavoidable, an **insurance policy** is pretty much essential.

Before paying for a new policy, however, it's worth checking whether you are already covered: some all-risks home insurance policies may cover your possessions when overseas, and many private medical schemes include coverage when abroad.

After checking with your own insurance programme, you might want to contact a **specialist travel insurance company**, or consider the travel insurance deal we offer (see box, below). A typical travel insurance policy usually provides coverage for the loss of baggage, tickets and – up to a certain limit – cash or cheques, as well as cancellation or curtailment of your journey. Most of them exclude so-called dangerous sports unless an extra premium is paid. Many policies can be chopped and changed to exclude coverage you don't need – for example, sickness and accident benefits can often be excluded or included at will. If you do take medical coverage, ascertain whether benefits will be paid as treatment proceeds or only after return home, and whether there

is a 24-hour medical emergency number. When securing baggage cover, make sure that the per-article limit – typically under £500 – will cover your most valuable possessions. If you need to make a claim, you should keep **receipts** for medicines and medical treatment, and in the event you have anything stolen, you must obtain an official statement from the police.

Internet

With printed literature of any kind still very limited on the island, **Cuban websites** are by far the best source of up-to-date tourist information. They are, of course, all state-run sites, and although this inevitably affects the sites' impartiality they are often the easiest-to-find and the only up-to-date sources of knowledge on all kinds of specialized subjects, such as Cuban cinema and art. The vast majority of foreign websites on Cuba operate from the US, many of them politically orientated (meaning: pro- or anti-Castro) and making for stimulating reading; some of the best ones are listed below. The best places for **tourist information** on just about anything run by the Cuban state, from car rental to specialized tours, are the official government sites, ⓦwww.cubaweb.cu and, more specifically aimed at tourists, ⓦwww .cubatravel.cu.

Getting access to the Internet in the major Cuban cities and resorts is pretty straightforward, with cybercafés relatively commonplace, but finding somewhere with a reliable, fast connection to the web is another matter. ETECSA, who run the national telephone network, operate two types of offices where the public can get

---

Rough Guides travel insurance

Rough Guides has teamed up with Columbus Direct to offer you **travel insurance** that can be tailored to suit your needs. Products include a low-cost **backpacker** option for long stays; a **short break** option for city getaways; a typical **holiday package** option; and others. There are also annual **multi-trip** policies for those who travel regularly. Different sports and activities (trekking, skiing, etc) can be usually be covered if required.

See our website (ⓦwww.roughguides.com/website/shop) for eligibility and purchasing options. Alternatively, UK residents should call ☎0870/033-9988; US citizens should call ☎1-800/749-4922; Australians should call ☎1300/669 999. All other nationalities should call ☎+44 870/890 2843.

online, Telepuntos and Minipuntos, both of them usually only found in provincial capitals and tourist resorts. Minipuntos are glass-walled walk-in phone booths with a couple of computer terminals offering email and Internet access via prepaid cards. Telepuntos centres are much larger and contain anywhere from three to ten Internet terminals, and offer a number of other services, including fax facilities, prepaid phone cards and telephone cabins. Some of their services are offered in national pesos, but foreign visitors are likely to be charged in convertible pesos and may be required to show a passport for Internet access. Internet connections in these ETECSA establishments are often painstakingly slow and, particularly in Havana, you're sometimes better off finding a hotel with an Internet café, where the connection will invariably be quicker and more reliable. Currently, charges in Telepuntos and Minipuntos are 10¢/min with a minimum charge of $6CUC, giving you an hour online. Hotel rates are sometimes exorbitant, and the upmarket hotels commonly charge between $6CUC and $10CUC an hour.

Having always been keen to control the flow of information to the Cuban public, the government has, unsurprisingly, restricted its citizens' access to the Internet. However, though private home Internet connections are illegal, Cubans can now use the Internet in Telepuntos and Minipuntos, something they were restricted from doing in the recent past. They also have access to Cuban-based email accounts, and there is an increasing number of Cuban homes using email, mostly in the larger towns and cities.

Email

While the vast majority of the population is still without computer access, let alone email facilities, there are a growing number of households with online addresses, though the majority of these are in the towns and cities most visited by tourists. Most private homes with email are *casas particulares*, who acquired it in response to the growing competition for customers. The number of businesses, especially hotels, with email addresses, is increasing at a much faster rate.

Laundry

There are few public laundry services in Cuba and only Havana has a laundry delivery service. Most people do their own or rely on the hotel service, although if you are staying in a *casa particular* your landlady is likely to offer to do yours for you for a small extra charge.

Mail

There's a good chance you'll get back home from Cuba before your postcards do. Don't expect **airmail** to reach Europe or North America in less than two weeks, while it is not unknown for **letters** to arrive a month or more after they have been sent. Inland mail is equally slow, with a letter from Havana to Santiago likely to take a couple weeks to get there. Pilfering is so widespread within the postal system that if you send anything other than a letter, either inland or overseas, there's a significant chance that it won't arrive at all. You should also be aware that letters and packages coming into Cuba are sometimes opened as a matter of government policy.

Stamps are sold in both convertible and national pesos at post offices, from white-and-blue kiosks marked Correos de Cuba and (for convertible pesos only) in many hotels. Convertible peso rates are reasonable at 65¢ for postcards to all countries whilst letters to the US or Canada, cost 65¢, 75¢ to Europe 85¢ to the rest of the world. However, if you request national peso stamps, which you are entitled to do, at between 40 centavos and 75 centavos for postcards and marginally more for letters to the same countries, it can work out at over fifteen times cheaper to pay for stamps with the national currency.

All large towns and cities have a **post office**, normally open Monday to Saturday from 8am to 6pm. Most provincial capitals, as well as Varadero and Cayo Largo, have a branch with DHL courier services (⊛www .dhl.com) and sometimes the cheaper Cuban equivalent, EMS. At a few select branches, such as the one at Paseo del Prado esq. San Martín in Havana, there are poste restante facilities – letters or packages should be marked *lista de correos* and will be held for about a month; you'll need your passport for collection. A more reliable alternative is to have mail sent to a hotel, which you need not necessarily be staying in, marked *esperar*, followed by the name of the addressee. They will usually hold mail for at least a week, often longer, even for non-guests. Some of the larger hotels offer a full range of postal services, including DHL and EMS, usually at the desk marked Telecorreos. What post offices there are in smaller towns and villages offer services in national pesos only and are more likely to be closed at the weekend.

An alternative to DHL or EMS, and less likely to be affected by pilfering than the latter though all of the courier services are more secure than standard mail, is the national and international courier service run by Cubanacán (ⓦwww.cubanacan.cu /ingles/express), one of the country's major tourist operators in Cuba. They will ship consignments of up to 32kg to destinations all over the world and to anywhere in Cuba. Contact them in Havana at Calle 31 esq. 72, Playa (ⓣ7/204-7848 & 204-7960, ⓔcubex@courier.cha.cyt.cu).

Maps

We've provided **maps** of all the major towns and cities and various other regions. In general, maps of Cuba are infrequently updated and there are large sections of the country for which there are no detailed maps at all. The exceptions to this are the detailed, rip-proof, waterproof, 1:850,000 **Rough Guide Map to Cuba** and the national road map *Guía de Carreteras*, which also carries basic street maps for Havana and Varadero – invaluable if you plan to make any long-distance journeys around the island. That said, some minor roads are not marked on this or any other map and there is still a gap in the market for a fully comprehensive national road map or street atlas. Geographical and orienteering maps have been published for Topes de Collantes but are otherwise also nonexistent.

Unless you plan on driving deep into Cuba's rural regions, the maps in this guide should be all you need. If you do decide, however, to purchase a locally produced version, the best map shop in the country is El Navegante at Mercaderes no.115, e/ Obispo y Obrapía in Habana Vieja (ⓣ7/861-3625 and 57-1038). Make sure you buy a map, if you want one, before leaving Havana,

as it can be a frustrating and often fruitless business trying to find one in the provinces.

Opening hours and public holidays

Cuban offices are normally open for business between Monday to Friday, 9am and 5pm, with many of them closing for a one-hour lunch break anywhere between noon and 2pm. Shops are generally open 9am to 6pm Monday to Saturday, sometimes closing for lunch, while the shopping malls and department stores in Havana stay open as late as 8pm. Sunday trading is increasingly common, with most places open until noon or 1pm, longer in the major resorts. Hotel shops stay open all day. Banks generally operate Monday to Friday 8am to 3pm, but this varies – see p.65 for more details.

Museum opening hours are not an exact science, you may arrive at one during its posted hours to find it shut for some reason, the person with the keys having failed to turn up, for instance. Theoretically, museums are usually open six days a week (Mon–Sat or more usually Tues–Sun) from 9am to between 5 and 7pm, with an hour (or two) for lunch. Those open on Sunday generally close in the afternoon. Museum opening hours, especially in Havana, vary according to season. Expect places to stay open for an hour later in July and August and for some places to open on Sunday that, for the rest of the year, would be closed that day.

National holidays

Jan 1 Liberation Day. Anniversary of the triumph of the Revolution.
May 1 International Workers' Day.
July 25–27 Celebration of the day of national rebellion.
Oct 10 Anniversary of the start of the Wars of Independence.
Dec 25 Christmas Day.

Photography

Cuba is an immensely photogenic country and keen snappers will have a field day. Don't try to photograph anything military, and remember as always that some people prefer not to be photographed, so always ask first. Kodak, Fuji and Agfa standard films are widely available (although as yet there are no APS films), but always check the expiry date on the box before buying. You can get film developed in Cuba but it may not turn out as well as it might back home.

Time

Cuba is on Eastern Standard Time in winter and Eastern Daylight Time in summer. It is five hours behind London, fifteen hours behind Sydney and on the same time as New York.

Guide

Guide

1

Havana and around

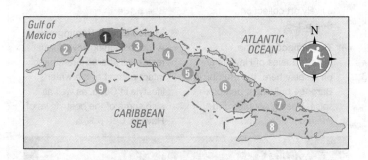

CHAPTER 1 # Highlights

* **Hotel Nacional** This luxurious, twin-towered flagship hotel, built in the 1930s, still embodies the glamour of that bygone age. See p.126

* **Fábrica de Tobacos Partagás** See the time, skill and effort that go into the production of Cuban cigars at this illustrious factory. See p.145

* **Museo Nacional de Bellas Artes** One of the few international-calibre museums in Cuba, where two buildings – sights in themselves – house a lively art collection. See p.146

* **The Malecón** All the idiosyncrasies of Havana are on display here: the crumbling Baroque buildings, beatbox *salsa*, kissing couples and *jineteros*. See p.155

* **Che Memorial** Head for the Plaza de la Revolución to pose for the ultimate Cuban photo opportunity. See p.166

* **La Guarida** This unmissable *paladar*, with its out-of-the-ordinary menu, film-set heritage and fantastic food, has no equal in Cuba. See p.177

* **Tropicana** Max out on glittery kitsch at the country's most lavish cabaret, an open-air venue with a hint of pre-Revolution hedonism. See p.184

* **Museo Ernest Hemingway** A trip to Hemingway's former residence affords a remarkably intact portrait of the writer's lifestyle in Cuba, as well as also some of the best views of Havana. See p.202

△ Giant mural along Mercaderes

Havana and around

With five times as many inhabitants as the country's next biggest city, Santiago de Cuba, **Havana** is in a class by itself. Nowhere else are the contradictions which have come to characterize Cuba – particularly since the advent of mass tourism and the introduction of a dual currency system – as pronounced as they are in the capital. The emerging middle class, most of whom have made their money through the latest wave of tourism, drift around the brand-new shopping malls, while just down the road long queues of people clutching ration books form outside the local bodega. Restoration projects have returned some of the finest colonial architecture in the Caribbean to its original splendour, even as overcrowded and dirty neighbourhoods wait for their first coat of paint since the early 1990s. There is a sense that Havana is on the move, with tourist money pouring in, new nightspots appearing regularly and an increasing variety of products in shops that not long ago either didn't exist or stood empty. Yet on the other hand, time stands still, or even goes backwards, in a city where 1950s Chevrolets, Buicks and Oldsmobiles ply the roads, locals fish from tyres floating near the ageing seawall and many people seem to spend most of the day in the street or on their crumbling nineteenth-century doorsteps.

Havana doesn't jump out at you with all-night parties or flashing lights – instead, it works its magic slowly and subtly. One of the city's most striking characteristics is the fact that the main tourist areas are residential neighbourhoods, which allows an unusually close, though often quite tiring, contact not just with the buildings and monuments but with the people. Life unfolds openly and unselfconsciously in Havana; from domino players sitting at tables on the kerb, kids playing ball games in the road, conversations shouted across balconies and street-side barber shops with their doors open, an infectious vitality pervades every neighbourhood. The less appealing side to this restless vigour is the high level of **jineterismo** in the city, making it the capital of hustle and hassle in Cuba.

Though the tourist industry is infiltrating every level of life in the capital, the city is far from a slave to tourism. Cuban **culture** is at its most exuberant here, with an abundance of theatres, cinemas, concert venues and art galleries. Along with Santiago, Havana is host to the country's most diverse **music scene**, where world-famous *salsa* and *bolero* orchestras and bands ply their trade even as the newer rock and hip-hop subcultures, almost nonexistent elsewhere on the island, are gaining momentum. Music is an ever-present accompaniment to daily life, spilling out into the streets, smoothing off some of the capital's rougher edges and injecting an irresistible sense of celebration.

The city's **suburbs** stretch out for miles and bleed gently into the province of Havana, known simply as **La Habana**, offering a range of possible

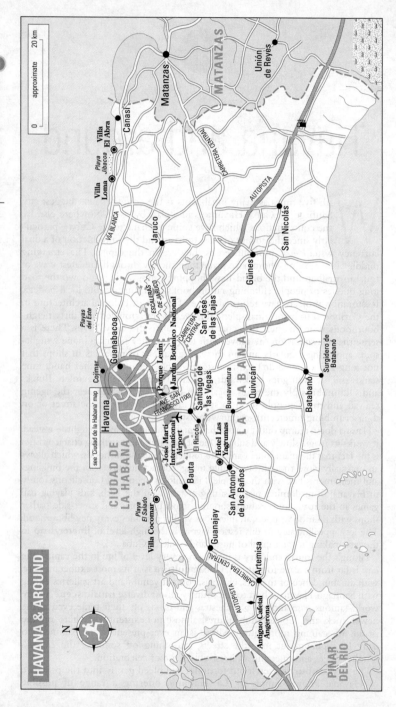

HAVANA & AROUND

N

0   approximate   20 km

MATANZAS

PINAR
DEL RÍO

CIUDAD
DE LA HABANA

LA HABANA

Matanzas

Unión
de Reyes

Canasí

Villa
El Abra

*Playa
Jibacoa*

Villa
Loma

VÍA BLANCA

Jaruco

San Nicolás

Güines

CARRETERA CENTRAL

AUTOPISTA

*Playas
del Este*

ESCALERAS
DE JARUCO

Guanabacoa

Cojímar

San José
de las Lajas

CARRETERA CENTRAL

Surgidero de
Batabanó

Batabanó

Quivicán

Buenaventura

Parque Lenin

Jardín Botánico Nacional

Santiago de
las Vegas

AVE. SAN
FRANCISCO (100)

Havana

see 'Ciudad de la Habana' map

José Martí
International
Airport

El Rincón

Hotel Las
Yagrumas

Bauta

San Antonio
de los Baños

*Playa
El Salado*

Villa Cocomar

Guanajay

Artemisa

CARRETERA CENTRAL

AUTOPISTA

Antiguo Cafetal
Angerona

day-trips. Though many of them are technically within the city's political boundaries, they feel far removed, a sense that's reinforced by the extremely poor public transport links. The province's best beaches, including the top-notch **Playas del Este**, the more subdued **Playa Jibacoa** and the even lower-key **Canasí**, are **east** of the city, past the uncomplicated provincial-style towns of **Cojímar** and **Guanabacoa**. The wild and mysterious **Escaleras de Jaruco** hills, classic Indiana Jones territory, are the only non-beach draw on this side of the province.

The neatly packaged **Museo Ernest Hemingway**, the writer's long-time Cuban residence, lies **south** of the city, while slightly further west the landscaped expanse of **Parque Lenin** and the impressive **Jardín Botánico Nacional** offer some of the city's most picturesque scenery. In the same area are the **Parque Zoológico Nacional** and **ExpoCuba**, a cross between an industrial estate, a museum and a theme park, where the Revolution's achievements are displayed in exhaustive (and exhausting) detail. The **Santuario de San Lázaro** and nearby town of **Santiago de las Vegas** won't occupy a whole day but are worth making a short journey for, while the town of **San Antonio de los Baños**, on the other hand, is one of the only places in Havana province worth staying the night in.

Most people travelling **west** from Havana are making their way to Pinar del Río and its attractions, like Las Terrazas and Soroa, wisely passing through a region whose small towns, such as **Guanajay**, serve best as stopping-off points or components of a wider tour rather than the sole reason for a day-trip.

Havana

HAVANA is a stunning city, its glorious diversity of architecture and neighbourhood design littered with reminders of this heterogeneous nation's history. Founded on the western banks of a fabulous natural harbour, it was, by the end of the seventeenth century, a fortified urban port, protected by the water on one side and a ten-metre city wall on the other. Today, what was once contained within the city walls now forms the most captivating section of **Habana Vieja**, the old city and the capital's tourist centre, a UNESCO-declared World Heritage Site of crumbling magnificence and restored beauty. This is the only part of Havana where you can wander aimlessly and still always stumble upon a notable sight or attraction of some sort. Any sightseeing you do will start here, among the fine museums, immaculately renovated colonial buildings, elegant plazas, sweeping boulevards and narrow, atmospheric streets bristling with life.

Many visitors restrict themselves to Habana Vieja and, to a lesser extent, Vedado, which together make up two of the three most central *municipios* (boroughs) running the length of the classic oceanfront promenade, the **Malecón**. In between Habana Vieja and Vedado, the predominantly residential **Centro Habana** is often bypassed by those on their way to more tourist-friendly parts of town. This, however, is a mistake, for though Centro Habana is low on specific attractions, it pulsates with energy, and wandering its busy nineteenth-century streets reveals an intrinsically Cuban side to the city.

Vedado, the heart of the *municipio* known locally as Plaza, is the city's centre, a postmodern jumble of differing architectural styles. Many of the magnificent post-colonial mansions that jostle for attention here amongst the tower blocks have been converted into public works or ministry offices and a few are museums. The area is compact enough to negotiate on foot – and in fact that's the best way to appreciate the quiet suburban streets. From here you could walk the couple of kilometres to the vast and famous **Plaza de la Revolución**, where giant monuments to the two most famous icons of the Cuban struggle for independence, Che Guevara and José Martí, present archetypal photo opportunities.

Beyond Vedado to the west, on the other side of the Río Almendares, **Miramar** ushers in yet another change in the urban landscape. Modelled on mid-twentieth-century Miami, this is a fairly anonymous part of the city but an ideal escape from the more frenzied atmosphere of Habana Vieja. A commercial district has emerged on its western fringes, accompanied by a number of luxury hotels, while some of Havana's most sophisticated restaurants are scattered around Miramar's leafy streets. South of the seafront districts, the city appears to merge into one giant residential neighbourhood, almost entirely void of hotels and restaurants, the different *municipios* blurring together.

East of the bay, the city per se soon merges into a large, sparsely populated area that's part of Havana only due to the arbitrary shifting of political boundaries. However, immediately over the other side of the channel connecting the bay to the sea, and visible from Habana Vieja, is **Habana del Este** and Cuba's most extensive network of colonial military fortifications, known collectively as the **Parque Morro-Cabaña**, forming an integral part of the capital and its history.

Havana views

Since Havana is set on relatively flat land, you have to go to the southern outskirts of the city or over to the eastern side of the bay for hills high enough to afford a decent view. There are, however, numerous tall buildings open to the public right in the heart of the capital, with fabulous vistas across its starkly contrasting neighbourhoods. Most of these buildings are worth visiting for their own sake as well as for the views they provide. Some of the most worthwhile include:

Cámara Oscura Plaza Vieja. You can catch a view of Havana from the roof terrace and experience the guided tour of parts of the city through a telescopic lens. See p.140.

Edificio Bacardi Ave. de las Misiones e/ San Juan de Dios y Empedrado, Habana Vieja. Ask in the foyer of this famous office building to be escorted to the tower at the top. The unofficial charge is usually $1CUC, making this one of the cheapest ways of seeing the city from on high.

Edificio Focsa Calle 17 no.55 e/ M y N, Vedado. There's no better combination of food and breathtaking views than from the restaurant at the top of this building, the city's second-tallest. See p.178.

Habana Libre. You'll have to eat at the restaurant or pay the nightclub's entrance fee to get up to the top of this famous Havana hotel – either way, it's worth it. See p.125.

Iglesia de San Francisco de Asís Plaza de San Francisco, Habana Vieja. Climb the wooden staircase to the top of the bell tower at this church near the edge of the bay and enjoy a great perspective of the old city. See p.136.

Memorial José Martí Plaza de la Revolución, Vedado. An obligatory part of the tourist circuit and the best vantage point for bird's-eye views of Havana, reaching as far as the western suburbs. See p.165.

Of the city's highlights, the tours around the **Fábrica de Tobacos Partagás** cigar factory are as stimulating as they are revealing, while the imposing **Capitolio** displays a phenomenal variety of architectural styles. Near both of these is the recently renovated **Museo Nacional de Bellas Artes**, arguably Havana's top museum, filled with quality works of art exhibited with surprising detail and care. Don't miss out on a visit to the fantastic and luxurious **Hotel Nacional** as well, with its beguiling gardens caressed by the sound of waves crashing against the Malecón down below. As in most Cuban cities, Havana's **hotels** play a prominent role in its social life and are a focal point for visitors. With many of the best restaurants, shops, bars, nightlife and pretty much all of the usable swimming pools located within hotel grounds, there's a strong chance you'll spend some time in or around them, even if you're not staying in one.

It's worth noting that while Havana puts the hotels, restaurants, shops and clubs of all the other Cuban cities to shame, hanging around outside most of these places, and patrolling the streets in between them, are legions of street hustlers, opportunists and *jineteros*. The government now takes the high levels of **tourist harassment** here very seriously, posting a policeman on every corner in Habana Vieja and the streets around the *Habana Libre* hotel, areas where *jineterismo* has traditionally been most concentrated. Even so, many foreign visitors are still surprised by what can seem like an inescapable onslaught of touts peddling anything from cigars and taxi rides to a place to stay (and a young woman to stay with).

Some history

Havana's success and riches were founded on the strength and position of the **harbour** – the largest natural port in the Caribbean – spotted by Sebastián de Ocampo in 1509 when he took advantage of its deep and sheltered waters to make repairs during his circumnavigation of Cuba. The original **San Cristóbal de La Habana** settlement was established on July 25, 1515, St Christopher's Day, on the south coast at Batabanó, 50km from where the city now stands. This first *villa* was an unmitigated disaster zone of swampland rife with mosquitoes and tropical diseases, with a flat coastline and shallow port that left ships unable to drop anchor close to shore. The settlement limped along under these testing conditions before finally relocating in 1519 to the north coast, at the mouth of the freshwater Río Chorrera (now the Almendares), until rising seas and the lack of a sheltered harbour forced another move less than a year later. On November 25, 1519, the city shifted a few kilometres east to the banks of the large deep-water bay, backed by heavy forests, now known as the **Bahía de la Habana**.

The *villa* began to ripple out into what is now Habana Vieja, with the first streets established down on the seafront between the present-day Plaza de Armas and Plaza de San Francisco. However, it was with the discovery of a deep, navigable channel through the treacherous shallow waters between Cuba and the Bahamas – a major step in the establishment of **trade routes** between Spain and the New World – that Havana really took off, becoming known as *Llave del Nuevo Mundo y Antemural de las Indias Occidentales* (*Key to the New World and Bulwark of the West Indies*). Helped by the city's marvellous harbour, Cuba quickly rose in global importance throughout the sixteenth and seventeenth centuries.

As the Spanish conquistadors plundered the Americas, gathering fairy-tale cargoes of gold, emeralds, pearls, indigo, and even parrots, Havana became a convenient **port of call**, with captains of the Spanish fleet steering their galleons in to have sails stitched and hulls remade, and sailors allowed to let rip one last time before setting off for Seville. An infrastucture of brothels, inns and gambling houses sprang up to cater for the seamen, and prostitution and syphilis were rife. With ships disgorging new sailors and merchants daily, **pirates** drawn by tales of wealth were able to wander anonymously through the crowded town, planning their attacks with admirable precision. Inadequately armed and with few resources, Habaneros were often forced to hand over town riches under threat of having their mud-and-thatch homes razed to the ground, as was the case when French pirate Jacques de Sores sacked and burned Havana in July 1555.

Although Spain was understandably keen to safeguard her money-spinning colony, it was still another two years before serious steps were taken to defend its capital. In 1558, after consolidating shipping operations by making Havana the only Cuban port authorized to engage in commerce, Spain started a long period of fortification with the construction of the first stone fort in the Americas, the impressive **Castillo de la Real Fuerza**, which still stands by the harbour mouth. Work started on the Castillo de San Salvador de la Punta and the formidable Castillo de Los Tres Reyes del Morro in 1589 and was finally completed in 1630. And in 1663, after more than a hundred years of discussion, a protective wall began to be built around the city, and was completed in 1740.

Attacks, however, persisted, and in 1762 the **British** made a successful two-pronged assault on the city. While part of the fleet sailed up the Río Almendares to lure Spanish forces there as a decoy, the rest of the fleet landed to the east of El Morro castle at Cojímar and attacked. This cunning tactic paid off, and after a six-week siege Havana fell to the British. The free trade that the port enjoyed during its brief eleven months of occupation – the British swapped Havana for Florida – kickstarted the island's **sugar trade**; previously restricted to supplying Spain, it was now open to the rest of the world. Spain wisely kept British trade policies intact and the consequential influx of wealthy Spanish sugar families propelled Havana into a new age of affluence.

The **nineteenth century** was a period of growth, when some of the most beautiful buildings around Habana Vieja were constructed and the city enjoyed a new-found elegance. At the same time, prostitution, crime and political corruption were reaching new heights, causing many of the new bourgeoisie to abandon the old city to the poor and to start colonizing what is now the district of Vedado. By the 1860s the framework of the new suburbs stretching west and south was in place.

In 1902, after the Wars of Independence, North American influence and money flowed into the city, and the first half of the twentieth century saw tower blocks, magnificent hotels and glorious Art Deco palaces like the Bacardí building being thrown up to serve the booming tourist industry. Gambling flourished, run by American gangsters like Meyer Lansky who aimed to turn Havana into a more glamorous Sin City than Las Vegas.

The **Revolution** put an abrupt end to all this, and throughout the 1960s the new regime cleaned the streets of crime, prostitution and general debauchery, laying out the basis of a socialist capital. Fine houses, abandoned by owners fleeing to the States, were left in the hands of erstwhile servants, and previously exclusive neighbourhoods changed face overnight. With the emphasis on improving conditions in the countryside, city development was haphazard and the **post-Revolution years** saw many fine buildings crumble while residential overcrowding increased, prompting Fidel Castro himself to eventually admit that action had to be taken. Happily, the last few years have seen slow but steady improvements, with redevelopment work now much in evidence, especially in the worst-affected areas of Habana Vieja.

Tourism, and the badly needed money it brings, has been an incentive to improve many of the city's most visited areas, with certain streets like Obispo in Habana Vieja now unrecognizable as the tumbledown areas of the mid-90s. But even though money for continued civic development is still coming in from foreign investment and the tourist trade, the economy is still shaky and tourism has actually dropped off somewhat in the last couple of years. The combination of Havana's enormous potential and the uncertain state of the economy make it very difficult, to determine, what the near future holds in store for the city.

Arrival and information

All international flights land at **José Martí International Airport** (switchboard ℡7/649-5777 & 266-4644), about 15km south of the city centre. The vast majority of international passengers are deposited at Terminal Three (℡7/649-0410) where most airport services are concentrated, including a few shops, a restaurant and a bureau de change, while there are **car rental desks** in each of the three terminals. Since there is no public transportation linking the rest of Havana directly with the airport, the chances are you'll be forced to pay for a **taxi**; the half-hour journey into Havana shouldn't cost more than $15–20CUC.

Arriving by **bus**, depending on which service you've used you'll be dropped off at either the **Víazul terminal** (℡7/881-1413 or 881-5652), on Avenida 26 across from the city zoo, or the Astro-operated **Terminal de Omnibus** (switchboard ℡7/870-9401; convertible-peso ticket office ℡870-3397; information ℡879-2456), at Avenida Independencia esq. 19 de Mayo, near the Plaza de la Revolución. Both stations are a $3CUC to $6CUC taxi ride from most of the central hotels, and there's a car rental desk at the Víazul terminal.

Trains pull in at the **Estación Central de Ferrocarriles** (℡7/860-9448 & 862-1920) in southern Habana Vieja, where picking up a taxi is slightly problematic and you'll probably have to find yourself a private cab or one of Havana's army of *bicitaxis*. There is a separate, smaller part of the station called Terminal La Coubre a couple of hundred metres down the road for trains to and from Cienfuegos.

In the less likely event that you arrive on one of the two or three **cruise ships** that dock in Havana every week, you will disembark at the splendid **Terminal Sierra Maestra** (℡7/866-6524 & 862-1925), facing the Plaza de San Francisco in Habana Vieja. Here there's a souvenir shop and car rental services.

Information

There is no independent tourist board in Havana, but state-run Infotur (Ⓦwww.infotur.cu) operates several **information centres**, the most useful of which are at Obispo no.521 e/ Bernaza y Villegas in Habana Vieja (daily 9am–7pm; ℡7/866-3333 & 862-4586, Ⓔobispodir@cubacel.net), and in Playa (the western suburbs) at Ave. 5ta y 112 (daily 9am–6pm; ℡7/204-7036, Ⓔmiramardir@cubacel.net). Both sell a few maps and basic guides but are generally low on free literature or any kind of written information, especially regarding accommodation. You can, however, book rooms, excursions and Víazul bus tickets through them. For a better choice of **maps and guides**, head for El Navegante, Mercaderes no.115 e/ Obispo y Obrapía, Habana Vieja (Mon–Fri 8.30am–5pm, Sat 8.30am–noon; ℡7/831-3625). As with the rest of the country, the national travel agents in Havana double up as useful centres for information (see p.195). Unique to Habana Vieja is the San Cristóbal agency at Oficios no.110 e/ Lamparilla y Amargura, Plaza de San Francisco (Mon–Fri 8.30am–5.30pm, Sat 8.30am–2pm & Sun 9am–12.30pm; ℡7/861-9171 & 861-9172), specializing in history- and culture-oriented tours of the old town.

The free monthly **listings guides** *Bienvenidos* and *Cartelera* make it easiest to find out what's going on in Havana than anywhere else in Cuba. In theory you can pick up these guides at Infotur branches and in some of the four- and five-star hotels, but their availability is sporadic at best. Given the paucity and scarcity of printed literature in general, it's a good idea to get used to using the Internet whilst in Havana. The online version of *Bienvenidos* is at ⓦwww .bienvenidoscuba.com; *La Jiribilla*, a cultural magazine, is on the Web at ⓦwww.lajiribilla.cu (click on the Cartelera icon for listings), and *San Cristóbal de la Habana* is at ⓦwww.sancristobal.cult.cu (click on Programación Cultural). For weekly listings of live music at some of the best venues in town, go to ⓦwww.egrem.com.cu and follow the links to "La Habana de Noche". Readily available and worthwhile print publications include the national newspaper *Juventud Rebelde*, which prints a weekly calendar of cultural events in its Friday edition, and *Prisma*, a monthly tourist magazine that carries articles on sights and events in Havana; the latter is published in parallel Spanish/English text.

Orientation and city transport

The best and simplest place for orienting yourself in Havana is the **Malecón**, the seafront road and promenade that links the three most central and visited *municipios*: Habana Vieja, Centro Habana and Vedado. The border between Habana Vieja and Centro Habana (the two oldest *municipios*) starts at the eastern end of the Malecón and runs more or less due south along the **Paseo del Prado**, marked on some maps as the Paseo de Martí. The Paseo del Prado cuts through the Parque Central and past the front of the nearby Capitolio building,

Havana's new and old street names

New name	Old name
Agramonte	Zulueta
Aponte	Someruelos
Avenida Antonio Maceo	Malecón
Avenida de Bélgica (northern half)	Monserrate
Avenida de Bélgica (southern half)	Egido
Avenida Carlos Manuel de Céspedes	Avenida del Puerto
Avenida de España	Vives
Avenida de la Independencia	Avenida de Rancho Boyeros
Avenida de Italia	Galiano
Avenida Salvador Allende	Carlos III
Avenida Simón Bolívar	Reina
Brasil	Teniente Rey
Capdevila	Cárcel
Leonor Pérez	Paula
Máximo Gómez	Monte
Padre Varela	Belascoaín
Paseo de Martí	Paseo del Prado
San Martín	San José

two convenient, central landmarks defining the edge of Habana Vieja, the most touristy part of the city. Most of these central sections of Havana are laid out on a **grid system**, so finding your way around is relatively simple. Vedado is particularly easy, as the vast majority of streets are numbered or lettered. Parallel with most of the Vedado section of the Malecón are the odd-numbered streets – 1ra (Primera), 3ra (Tercera), 5ta (Quinta), 7ma (Septima, but better known as **Calzada**) and then **Linea**, after which they are known as Calle 11, Calle 13 and so on. Bisecting these, running roughly north to south, is **Paseo**, one of Vedado's other principal streets. To the east of Paseo the calles are known by letters from A to P, and to the west of Paseo they are known by even numbers. Habana Vieja and Centro Habana are a little more complicated, not least because their streets are narrower and more densely packed, but they too are divided into grids and therefore shouldn't cause too much confusion. It is, however, in these two *municipios* that the problem of post-Revolutionary and pre-Revolutionary street names, prevalent throughout Cuba, is most acute. Locals normally refer to the old names, while street signs give only the new names. The box on opposite lists the most important of these distinctions.

Taxis

Getting around the city – outside Habana Vieja, which is best experienced on foot – will almost inevitably involve a taxi ride of some kind, unless you are prepared to join the huge queues at the information-less bus stops and squeeze onto overcrowded vehicles (see p.42). There are plenty of official **metered state taxis**, some known as **tourist taxis**, that will take you across the city for around $5CUC. Among the galaxy of different Havanan taxis, these are distinguishable as the new, modern cars and are your best bet if you don't want to negotiate your fare. It shouldn't take long to flag one down in the main hotel districts and particularly along the Malecón, but to be certain head for the *Hotel Nacional* in Vedado or the Parque Central in Habana Vieja. For a 24-hour pick-up service, ring Taxis OK (☎7/877-6666) or Panataxi (☎7/55-5555), two of the cheaper metered services.

As with the rest of Cuba, Havana is full of privately owned **taxis colectivos** – mostly huge, classic cars from the 1950s, such as Chevrolets, Oldsmobiles and Buicks, which operate like buses (see p.47). There are some all-but-official routes and roads along which the cars run; the three main arteries, linking Habana Vieja to Vedado via Centro Habana, are Neptuno, Calle L and Linea. If you wait anywhere along these roads, it shouldn't be a problem to flag a car down, especially during daylight hours. Be prepared to negotiate a fare, experience numerous delays and to pick up and drop off other passengers en route to your destination. The plus side to travelling this way is that, if you're not in a rush, this quintessentially Cuban manner of getting around town is good fun. *Colectivos*, some of which are far from roadworthy, gather around the Parque de la Fraternidad and opposite the face of the Capitolio building, where they form a huge, jumbled taxi rank. Drivers here, as is the Cuban way, often seek to fill their car with the maximum number of passengers before they set off, so be prepared to wait, or simply offer more money if you want to leave straight away.

Most of the **state-operated** vintage car taxis, the majority in fantastic condition, are run by **Gran Car** (☎7/891-0652). You can either call for a pick-up or just look opposite the *Hotel Plaza* on the Parque Central in Habana Vieja, where there are usually a few waiting. These are the most expensive taxis but fares are still not extortionate, with the standard charge from the Parque Central

Orientation and city transport

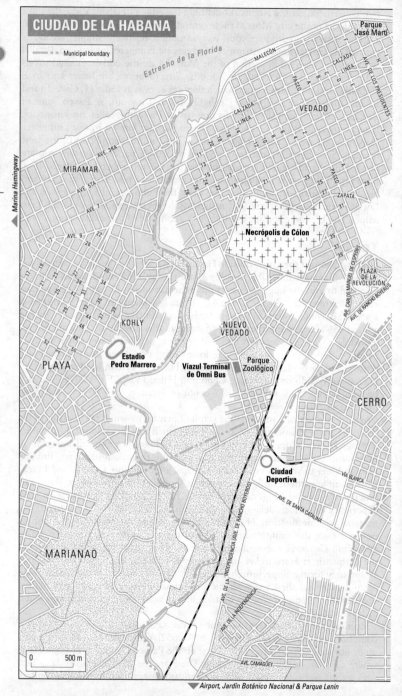

CIUDAD DE LA HABANA

Municipal boundary

Estrecho de la Florida

MALECÓN

Parque
José Martí

VEDADO

CALZADA

LINEA

AVE. DE LOS PRESIDENTES

PASEO

H

G

F

E

D

C

B

A

PASEO

ZAPATA

Marina Hemingway

MIRAMAR

AVE. 3RA

AVE. 5TA

AVE. 7

AVE. 9

Necrópolis de Cólon

PLAZA DE LA REVOLUCIÓN

AVE. CARLOS MANUEL DE CÉSPEDES

AVE. DE RANCHO BOYEROS

KOHLY

NUEVO
VEDADO

PLAYA

Estadio
Pedro Marrero

Víazul Terminal
de Omni Bus

Parque
Zoológico

CERRO

Ciudad
Deportiva

VÍA BLANCA

AVE. DE SANTA CATALINA

MARIANAO

AVE. DE LA INDEPENDENCIA (AVE. DE RANCHO BOYEROS)

AVE. DE LA INDEPENDENCIA

AVE. CAMAGÜEY

0   500 m

▼ Airport, Jardín Botánico Nacional & Parque Lenín

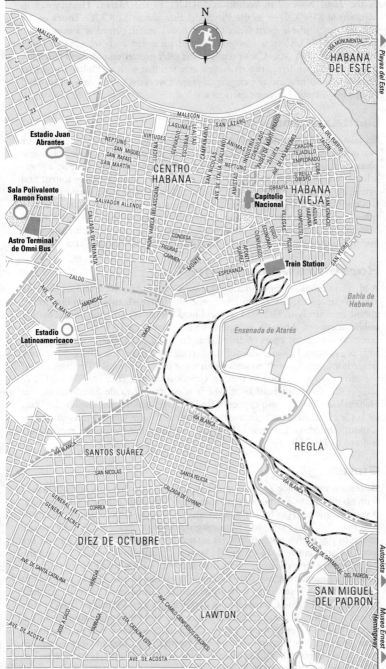

Playas del Este

HABANA DEL ESTE

MALECÓN
21
23

MALECÓN
LAGUNAS
VIRTUDES
SAN LÁZARO

Estadio Juan Abrantes

NEPTUNO
SAN MIGUEL
SAN RAFAEL
SAN MARTÍN

GERVASIO
ESCOBAR
CAMPANARIO
ÁNIMAS
NEPTUNO

SAN NICOLAS
AMISTAD
INDUSTRIA
CONSULADO
ZULUETA
AVE DE LAS MISIONES
CHACON
TEJADILLO
EMPEDRADO
CUBA
TACÓN
AVE DEL PUERTO

CENTRO HABANA

LUCENA

AVE DE ITALIA (GALIANO)
PASEO DE MARTÍ (PRADO)
O'REILLY OBISPO

HABANA VIEJA

Sala Polivalente Ramon Fonst

SALVADOR ALLENDE

PADRE VARELA BELASCOAIN

Capítolio Nacional

OBRAPIA

AGUIAR
HABANA
COMPOSTELA
SAN IGNACIO

Astro Terminal de Omni Bus

CALZADA DE INFANTA

CONDESA
FIGURAS
CARMEN

MONTE

GIRO
ECONOMIA
CIENFUEGOS

VILLEGAS
PICOTA

SAN PEDRO

ZALDO

ESPERANZA

APONTE
SUÁREZ

Train Station

AVE 20 DE MAYO

AMENIDAD

Bahía de Habana

Estadio Latinoamericaco

OMOA

Ensenada de Atarés

VÍA BLANCA

REGLA

SANTOS SUÁREZ

SAN NICOLAS

SANTA FELICIA

CALZADA DE LUYANO

VÍA BLANCA

GENERAL LEE
GENERAL LACRES
CORREA

CALZADA DE SAN MIGUEL

Autopista

DIEZ DE OCTUBRE

AVE DE SANTA CATALINA

REGLITA

JOSE A SACO

AVE DE ACOSTA

AVE CAMILO CIENFUEGOS (DOLORES)

STA CATALINA ESTE

LAWTON

DEL PADRON

SAN MIGUEL DEL PADRON

Museo Ernest Hemingway

PATRIGA

AVE DE ACOSTA

to the *Hotel Nacional* in Vedado at $4CUC, to the Marina Hemingway in Miramar at $15CUC or to the Playas del Este also at $20CUC. **Tours** of the city are also available from Gran Car, an hour's worth priced at a good-value $15CUC ($18CUC in a convertible), and there are even set fares to other provinces. Though Gran Car's polished fleet offer greater comfort and reliability than their independently run rivals, you may feel that with no Cuban passengers sharing the journey and the engine in perfect working order, some of the soul of an idiosyncratic Havana experience is lost.

Bicitaxis and cocotaxis

To take in your surroundings at a slower pace, **bicitaxis**, the three-wheeled, two-seater bicycle cabs found all over Havana, are ideal, and considerably more pleasant than a car. They are not, however, necessarily any cheaper; a two-kilometre ride is likely to cost $3CUC to $5CUC, though unlike tourist taxi prices, *bicitaxi* fares are negotiable. Swelling Havana's taxi ranks even further are the **cocotaxis**, three-wheeled novelty motorscooters encased in large yellow spheres, usually found waiting outside the *Hotel Inglaterra* and the *Hotel Nacional*. You pay no extra for their comedy value, with fares currently officially set at 50¢ per kilometre, considerably cheaper than many normal state taxis.

Horse-drawn carriages

A Havanan mode of transportation that goes even further back in time than the vintage American cars is the less numerous **horse-drawn carriage**, found almost exclusively in Habana Vieja and used these days for tours rather than as public transport. Though in many Cuban towns and cities this mode of transport is as much a part of daily life as the buses, it is a strictly tourist activity in faster-moving Havana. Most of the carriages are open-top affairs drawn by a single horse, usually with enough room for at least four people. The majority of the carriages are operated by the San Cristóbal travel agency (☏7/861-9171 & 861-9172), the main branch of which is on the Plaza de San Francisco in Habana Vieja. You can also expect to find carriages waiting just outside the Plaza de la Catedral, on the side facing the bay, at the Parque Central and outside the Capitolio building. The cost is $15CUC per hour, but for two or more hours it drops to $10CUC per hour.

Buses

Buses are usually not a good option, being overcrowded and infrequent and with no information at bus stops to indicate which route each bus takes, though if you brave it (and get lucky) your journey will cost no more than 40 centavos (less than 3¢). Make sure you have roughly the right change and don't bother trying to pay with a note unless you intend to buy tickets for everyone on the bus. The large, converted juggernauts known as **camellos** are used to cover the longer routes, many leading right out of town, usually stopping short of the provincial boundary. Most of them converge on the Parque de la Fraternidad in Habana Vieja, where, along with some of the normal buses, they begin their journeys. To be honest, unless you're desperately short on cash or fancy a taste of real Habanero life, it's difficult to justify the hassle of public transport in the capital. You have as much chance of walking to wherever you are going in the same time that you'll spend waiting at a bus stop. The most obvious exception is the seven-kilometre journey from Habana Vieja to Miramar, best made on bus #232 from the Parque de la Fraternidad.

Cars, scooters and bikes

Generally speaking, if you stay put in Havana, **car rental** is a relatively expensive way of getting around. But if you intend to make regular trips to the beach, or you are staying in one of the Miramar hotels, it could work out cheaper than the taxi rides which you'll almost certainly otherwise have to take. There is a particular concentration of rental agencies on or within a few blocks of the Malecón, between the *Hotel Nacional* and the Cupet-Cimex Tángana petrol station at the start of Linea in Vedado. The same agencies have desks in the lobbies of most of the four- and five-star hotels. Be warned though, booking a car in advance is often difficult as demand frequently outweighs supply. See p.194 for addresses.

There are surprisingly few **scooter rental** outlets in the city and most are located within hotel complexes either in the western suburbs or right outside the city at the Playas del Este. There is a Cubanacán Motoclub branch at the Dos Gardenias commercial complex, Ave. 7ma esq. 26, in Miramar and further west at the *Hotel Comodoro*, Ave. 3era esq. 84. Though the wide spread of Havana's main tourist districts means travelling by **bicycle** can be quite tiring, it is a fantastic way to see the city and there are special lanes for cyclists on many of the main roads. Despite the huge number of bicycles in the city, specialist bicycle shops or rental agencies are practically nonexistent. Thankfully, a non-profit organization called Bicicletas Cruzando Fronteras (☎7/860-8532 or 862-7065) have set up a workshop at San Juan de Dios esq. Aguacate in Habana Vieja where you can rent out mountain bikes, racers and all sorts of other bikes for very reasonable rates; repairs are done here too. Alternatively, El Orbe, one of the only well-stocked state-run bike shops, is at Ave. de Bélgica no.304 e/ Neptuno y San Rafael (☎7/860-2617).

Accommodation

Accommodation in Havana is abundant, though it's likely to be your biggest daily expense; in most of the main areas room cost anywhere from $25CUC to over $200CUC. You can usually find a hotel room on spec, but you'd do well to make a **reservation**, particularly in high season (roughly Dec to March and throughout July and Aug), when the town is chock-full.

Many visitors choose to stay in the state hotels in **Habana Vieja**, handy for a number of the key sights and well served by restaurants and bars. The massive restoration project affecting the whole of Habana Vieja tossed up new hotels here at a phenomenal rate, with at least fifteen built or restored in this relatively small city district since the late 1990s. Many of the more established state hotels are charismatic colonial-era properties, overflowing with history and patronized in the 1950s by the likes of Ernest Hemingway and Graham Greene. This is also the place to find the increasingly popular **hostales** (not to be confused with hostels), which make up the majority of the newer establishments. Essentially small hotels, *hostales* usually have ten to twenty rooms, though they're not necessarily cheaper than larger hotels. The vast majority of newly built hotels in Habana Vieja are operated by the Cuban Habaguanex chain (🌐 www.habaguanex.com).

Quieter, leafy **Vedado** is a more relaxed place to stay, although you'll need transport to make the trip to Habana Vieja. Though usually the preserve of visiting businesspeople, the slick, towering hotels in **Miramar** are a defining part of that neighbourhood's landscape. It's a bit inconvenient for sightseeing, but if money is no object and Western-style luxury a priority, this is the best the city has to offer.

Casas particulares

Unsurprisingly, Havana boasts the broadest range of **casas particulares** in the country, from houses run more like tiny hotels to a significant number of illegal places. With so great a bounty of decent, legal houses, though, there is no real need to stay in an illegal one. It can be difficult to find even the legitimate *casas particulares*, though, as they are spread throughout the city and the use of display boards advertising their existence is still rare – though touts willing to take you to one are not. Legal *casas particulares* should have a sticker of a green or blue icon (a little like a capital I) on their front door.

The three central *municipios* boast the heaviest concentration of rooms to rent, with prices steepest in Habana Vieja and Vedado ($25–30CUC). Things are cheaper in Centro Habana, where the tax on each room is roughly halved, while many places in the outer boroughs are unregistered and so often relatively inexpensive ($20–25CUC). Miramar's *casas particulares* are in a league of their own, with several offering independent apartments complete with dining areas and living space and, in some cases, swimming pools. You can expect to pay around $5–10CUC on top of the usual rates for the privilege though. Prices are negotiable in all areas, depending on how long you intend to stay and how hard you are prepared to bargain – it's wise to agree on the price at the start of your stay. The majority of places will provide breakfast for an extra $3–5CUC a day.

Habana Vieja

Hotels

Ambos Mundos Obispo no.153 esq. Mercaderes ⊤7/860-9530, ℮comercial @habaguanexhamundos.co.cu. Once home to Ernest Hemingway, this stylishly artistic 1920s hotel, bang in the heart of the most visited part of Habana Vieja, features an original metal cage lift and a fantastic rooftop terrace. Rooms are well equipped and comfortable. ❻

Armadores de Santander Luz esq. San Pedro ⊤7/862-8000, ℮comercial@santander.co.cu. A splendid hotel, tucked away in a secluded pocket of Habana Vieja. Housed in a majestic Neoclassical building that faces the harbour on the port road, with several of the rooms spread around the delightful second-floor terrace. There's a saloon bar, a pool-table room and a first-floor restaurant with views of the bay through its floor-to-ceiling windows. ❽

Beltrán de Santa Cruz San Ignacio no.411 e/ Muralla y Sol ⊤7/860-8330, ℮reserva @bsantacruz.co.cu. Located in the heart of the old city without being in the thick of the tourist circuit, this handsomely converted noble family town house has a nicely relaxed vibe. ❽

Caribbean Paseo del Prado no.164 e/ Colón y Refugio ⊤7/860-8233 & 860-8210, ℉860-9479, ℮reserva@lidocaribbean.hor.tur.cu. One of several cheaper options on or around the Habana Vieja-Centro Habana border, within easy walking distance of the Parque Central. The rooms are a bit poky, though, and many have no windows. ❻

Casa del Científico Paseo del Prado no.212 esq. Trocadero ⊤7/862-1604 & 862-1607, ℮hcientif @ceniai.inf.cu. Unlike most of Havana's remodelled colonial buildings, the opulent columned interior of this three-floor aristocratic residence has barely been touched, leaving it with all kinds of original pieces of furniture and decoration and a more rough-and-ready finish. Rooms are sufficiently well equipped, though some share bathrooms, and there's a spacious rooftop terrace. ❸

Convento de Santa Clara de Asís Cuba e/ Sol y Luz ⊤7/861-3335, ℮reaca@cencrem.cult.cu. A convent-turned-hotel suited more for backpackers than holidaymakers, with three of the nine basic but cheerful rooms holding six beds each, though there are better-equipped smaller double rooms. The rooms are located in the less leafy of the two accessible cloisters and there are fans instead of a/c. The current charge, whichever room you stay in, is $25CUC per person. ❹

Florida Obispo no.252 esq. Cuba ⊤7/862-4127 & 861-5621, ℮reservas @habaguanexhflorida.co.cu. The restoration of this building to its original aristocratic splendour has been impressively detailed and complete. There's a perfect blend of modern luxury and colonial elegance with marble floors, iron chandeliers, birds singing in the airy stone-columned central patio and potted plants throughout. ⑧

Hostal Conde de Villanueva Mercaderes esq. Lamparilla ⑦7/862-9293 to 94, ⓦwww.hostalcondevillanueva.cu. Also known as the *Hostal del Habano*, this is a cigar smoker's paradise with its own cigar shop, relaxing smokers' lounge and the freedom to smoke anywhere you want on the premises. Despite its relatively small size this place packs in a host of charming communal spaces, including a fantastic cellar-style restaurant, a delectable courtyard as well as the smokers' lounge and bar. ⑧

Hostal El Comendador Obrapía no.55 e/ Oficios y Baratillo ⑦7/867-1037, ⓔreserva @habaguanexhvalencia.co.cu. Agreeable sister *hostal* of the *Valencia*, this restored colonial building has less of the polished elegance characteristic of hotels in Habana Vieja and more of a countrified feel, with stone floors, ferns lining the wooden-railed balconies and an attractive little garden out the back. ⑧

Hostal Los Frailes Brasil (Teniente Rey) no.8 e/ Mercaderes y Oficios ⑦7/862-9383 & 862-9293, ⓔcomercial@habaguanexhfrailes.co.cu. Unique in character, this moody little place is themed on a monastery, with staff dressed as monks. The low-ceiling staircase, narrow central patio and dim lighting work well together to create a serene and restful atmosphere, while the rooms are very comfortable. ⑦

Hostal Valencia Oficios no.53 esq. Obrapía ⑦7/867-1037, ⓔcomercial@habaguanexhvalencia .co.cu. Plain but pleasant rooms in a beautiful building that feels more like a large country house than a small city hotel. Attractions include a cobbled-floor courtyard with hanging vines. Shares its facilities with *El Comendador*, located next door. ⑦

Hotel del Tejadillo Tejadillo no.12 esq. San Ignacio ⑦7/863-7283 & 863-6895, ⓔcomercial @habaguanexhtejadillo.co.cu. Just a block and a half from the cathedral, this smart, stylish place is one of the more hotel-like *hostales*, with over thirty rooms, a comfy reception area and a delectable central courtyard heaving with potted plants. ⑧

Hotel San Miguel Cuba esq. Peña Pobre ⑦7/862-7656 & 863-4029, ⓔcomercial@sanmiguel.co.cu. The only hotel in Habana Vieja with views of both the bay and the sea, best enjoyed from the rooftop terrace café. The buiding itself is rather plain, but the touches, like lavishly framed mirrors, are amongst its ostentatious touches. ⑧

Inglaterra Paseo del Prado no.416 esq. San Rafael, Parque Central ⑦7/860-8594 to 97, ⓦwww.hotelinglaterra.com. This classic nineteenth-century hotel in a superb location on the lively Parque Central has become rather complacent and could do with a little inspiration. However, the atmospheric, if slightly gloomy, interior is full of genuine colonial hallmarks and the rooms are of a high standard. ⑦

El Mesón de la Flota Mercaderes e/ Amargura y Brasil (Teniente Rey) ⑦7/863-3838, ⓔreservas @mflota.co.cu. Similar in size and character to a traditional inn, there are just five rooms at this *hostal*, all of them spacious and attractively and simply furnished. The whole ground floor is a rustic Spanish restaurant (see p.175), and this is one of the few hotels in Habana Vieja with double rooms for under $100CUC in high season. Within a block of Plaza Vieja. ⑦

Park View Colón esq. Morro ⑦7/861-3293, ⓦwww.hotelparkview.cu. Unusual in Havana Vieja, this is a relatively regular high-rise town hotel though more sophisticated than its equivalents in Centro Habana. There are great views across the city from its seventh-floor restaurant. ⑦

Parque Central Neptuno e/ Paseo del Prado y Agramonte, Parque Central ⑦7/860-6627, ⓦwww.nh-hotels.cu. Unbeatable in the old city for its range of facilities, this five-storey luxury hotel is aimed predominantly at business travellers. The sophisticated but inconsistent interior features a graceful glass-ceiling lobby, two restaurants – one aristocratic, the other 1950s retro – and a swimming pool on the roof. ⑨

Plaza Agramonte no.167 esq. Neptuno ⑦7/860-8583 to 89, ⓔreserva@plaza.gca.tur.cu. With more colonial space and charm than neighbouring hotels on the Parque Central, the *Plaza* has a bar in the colourful lobby area, complete with fountain, mosaic floor and detailed ceilings, making for a great place to hang out. There's an equally stylish restaurant and the rooms are well equipped. ⑧

Raquel Amargura esq. San Ignacio ⑦7/860-8280, ⓔreservas@hotelraquel.co.cu. Handsome and sleek with Art Deco touches, this is an unexpectedly upmarket hotel given its low-key street-side location. A cage lift, metal chandeliers and a glass ceiling revealing the first floor contribute to the sophisticated finish. ⑨

Santa Isabel Baratillo no.9 e/ Obispo y Narciso López, Plaza de Armas ⑦7/860-8201, ⓔcomercial@habaguanexhsisabel.co.cu. One of the more formal and exclusive of Habana Vieja's hotels, this impressively restored, graceful eighteenth-century building features colonial-style furnishings in all the rooms and a fountain in the idyllic, arched courtyard. ❾

Saratoga Paseo del Prado no.603 esq. Dragones ☎7/868-1000, ⓦwww .hotel-saratoga.com. This super-plush hotel is the latest Habana Vieja classic to be brought back from the dead, having gained fame in the 1930s. Dripping with lavishness and old-world style, the interior feels like a Humphrey Bogart movie set, with sleek bars and ritzy lounge areas. There's an impressive set of modern facilities, however, including a rooftop pool, a gym and a solarium. Rooms feature pseudo-antique furnishings and have DVD players and Internet connections whilst free WiFi is available throughout the hotel. ❾

Sevilla Trocadero no.55 e/ Paseo del Prado y Agramonte ☎7/860-8560, ⓦwww .hotelsevillacuba.com. Large hotel with an eclectic mix of architecture, one of Havana's most spectacular rooftop restaurants, the *Roof Garden*, and an air of refinement. Rooms are spacious, well equipped and comfortable. ❾

Telégrafo Paseo del Prado no.408, esq. Neptuno ☎7/861-1010, ⒺÌreserva@telegrafo.co.cu. The newest hotel on the Parque Central is elegant and sleek, and includes an atmospheric café where the building's original nineteenth-century structure has been cleverly blended into the new chic look. The rooms are exquisitely furnished and the restaurant serves good salads. ❽

Casas particulares

Los Balcones San Ignacio no.454 e/ Sol y Santa Clara ☎7/862-9877. A plush first-floor apartment that could pass for a colonial art museum with its antiquated furniture and decor. There are two bedrooms and two bathrooms, though neither is en suite. ❷

Casa de Daniel Carrasco Guillén Cristo no.16, 2do piso e/ Brasil y Muralla ☎7/866-2106, Ⓔcarrascohousing@yahoo.com. There are two large double bedrooms for rent in this grand old cavernous apartment. Arched doorways, a sculpted ceiling in the living room and balcony views of the Plaza del Cristo all add to the colonial appeal. There is also a modern, neat and self-contained apartment for rent with two double en-suite rooms, custom-built on the roof terrace, priced at $5CUC per night extra. ❷

Casa de Eugenio Barral García San Ignacio no.656 e/ Jesús María y Merced ☎7/862-9877, Ⓔfabio.quintana@infomed.sld.cu. Deep in southern Habana Vieja, this exceptional *casa particular* is spotlessly clean and beautifully furnished with antiques. It's a large apartment with a sensational garden roof terrace that's a terrific

spot for lounging. The two hotel-standard double bedrooms have a/c and a fridge, and the landlords are very hospitable. ❷

Casa de Fefita y Luís Aguacate no.509, apto.403, e/ Sol y Muralla ☎7/867-6433, Ⓔfefitaluis @yahoo.es. Situated on the fourth floor of a modern building in the heart of the old city, this small, comfy, self-contained unit provides fantastic views over Habana Vieja. The two double bedrooms are equipped with a/c, and both have stunning views to the north, taking in the Capitolio, while there are equally great views of the bay to the south from the kitchen area. Ringing ahead is essential as there is no doorbell on the street. ❷

Casa de Migdalia Caraballé Martín Santa Clara no.164, apto. F, e/ Cuba y San Ignacio ☎7/861-7352, Ⓔcasamigdalia@yahoo.es. Opposite the Convento de Santa Clara, this large, airy apartment contains two double rooms and another with three single beds, all benefiting from plenty of natural light thanks to the large, shuttered, street-side window. It's very popular, so reservations are recommended. ❷

Chez Nous Brasil no.115 e/ Cuba y San Ignacio ☎7/862-6287, Ⓔcheznous@ceniai .inf.cu. This magnificent *casa particular* is a real knockout. Majestic from the outside, it is no less impressive inside, dignified by perfectly preserved nineteenth-century furnishings and eye-catching features, such as the Romanesque bathroom. Two superb, well-equipped, balconied rooms are on the first floor, while from the central patio a spiral staircase leads up to the fabulous roof terrace where there's another very comfortable, contrastingly modern room with en-suite bathroom and its own porch. ❷

Centro Habana

Hotels

Deauville Ave. de Italia esq. Malecón ☎7/833-8812, Ⓔreservas@hdeauville.gca.tur.cu. The only seafront hotel in Centro Habana, this plain high-rise offers rooms with great views and is one of the few places around here with a swimming pool, albeit a very small one. ❼

Lido Consulado no.210 e/ Animas y Trocadero ☎7/867-1102 to 06, Ⓔreserva@lidocaribbean.hor .tur.cu. Located on a run-down street in a lively local neighbourhood, this hotel has dark rooms and rickety furniture, but is a good, inexpensive option, especially considering how close it is to Habana Vieja. ❻

Lincoln Virtudes no.164 esq. Ave. de Italia ☎7/862-8061, Ⓔalojamiento@lincoln.co.cu. One of the more characterful budget hotels, with reasonably equipped though unsophisticated rooms and good views over some of the grittier parts of the city. ④

Casas particulares

Casa de Ana Morales Aranda Neptuno no.519, apto. 3 e/ Campanario y Lealtad ⓣ 7/867-9899, Ⓔ ana.morales@infomed.sld.cu. A comfortable, dignified, second-floor flat where the huge, stylish bedroom comes with a street-side balcony. The owners are friendly and speak English. ②

Casa de Armando R Menéndez Castiñeiras Neptuno no.519, apto. 4, e/ Campanario y Lealtad ⓣ 7/862-8400. This quiet flat, tucked away at the back of an apartment building, is furnished with a consistency and artistic style rarely seen in Cuban homes. Much of the well-preserved Art Deco furniture has been here since the 1940s. A likeable, laid-back option. ②

Casa de Candida y Pedro San Rafael no.403, bajos, e/ Manrique y Campanario ⓣ 7/867-8902, Ⓔ candidacobas@yahoo.es. Two double rooms in a down-to-earth, small ground-floor flat with a dinky hidey-hole patio near the back of the house. Notable for its very informal, family atmosphere. ②

Casa de Dayami de Cervantes San Martín (San José) no.618, e/ Escobar y Gervasio ⓣ 7/873-3640, Ⓔ lchavao@infomed.sld.cu. Guests are given the run of the upstairs floor, which features a roof terrace at either end and two neat and cosy bedrooms, in this homely and orderly two-level apartment. The owners are a friendly family, one of whom speaks English. ②

Casa de Ernesto García Lealtad no.159 e/ Animas y Virtudes ⓣ 7/861-2753, Ⓔ garciaruiz @yahoo.es. There are two excellent rooms here, one effectively an apartment within an apartment, made up of a smartly equipped lounge, bedroom with TV, a/c and safety deposit box, and bathroom but no kitchen. The separate entrance offers complete independence, while the option of sharing the rest of this lovely ground-floor family residence with the affable owners also exists. ②

Casa de Luis Bermúdez San Lázaro no.880 e/ Soledad y Marina ⓣ 7/879-1304. This well-looked-after ground-floor apartment on the Vedado side of Centro Habana offers one room with a double bed and another with two singles. The plastic roof over the central patio casts a soothing light in the sun and complements the grace with which the place has been arranged and decorated by its friendly owners. ②

Casa de Ma. del Carmen Villafaña Rodríguez Malecón no.51 esq. Cárcel, piso 3 ⓣ 7/861-8125. There are two large, cool rooms for rent in this spacious seafront home, one of the most relaxing places to stay in this area, sealed off from the noise of Centro Habana in an Art Deco apartment block. The slanting windows taking up almost an entire wall in the huge front room allow great views along the Malecón and make the place feel like the viewing deck of a ship. Really stands out from the Havana norm. ②

Casa de Miriam y Sinaí Neptuno no.521 e/ Campanario y Lealtad ⓣ 7/878-4456, Ⓔ sinaisole@infomed.sld.cu. A smartly furnished first-floor balcony apartment with a fantastic central, open-air patio filled with rocking chairs. Two comfortable double bedrooms, both with hotel-standard en-suite bathroom and one with a balcony, run by one of the friendliest, hardest-working landladies in the city and her sociable English-, Italian- and German-speaking daughter. ②

Casa de Paula Montero Montero San Rafael no.313 e/ Rayo y San Nicolás ⓣ 7/862-7452. Two simple and clean, if slightly dark, double rooms with their own bathrooms in a ground-floor apartment where the owners have combined with neighbouring *casas particulares* to offer excursions to other provinces. ②

Casa de Ricardo Morales Campanario no.363, apto. 3 e/ San Miguel y San Rafael ⓣ 7/866-8363, Ⓔ moralesfundora@yahoo.es. Ideal for anyone looking for privacy and security, as the owner of this thoughtfully decorated, first-floor apartment (fitted with an alarm), is happy to give guests the run of the place. Has a spacious, well-equipped kitchen, one comfy double bedroom and a homely lounge-diner with a TV, large sofa, balcony and decorative items from Mexico. ②

Casa de Roberto Ferreiro y Marta Fernández San Martín no.253 e/ Ave. de Italia y Aguila ⓣ 7/860-9199. One of the best options if you're looking to rent a whole private apartment for two, this cushy little pad features three pristine rooms, including a compact kitchen, and a bathroom, all neatly painted, freshly tiled and well fitted-out. The pleasant owners live downstairs and have their own separate front door. ②

Las Delicias de Consulado Consulado no.309, apto. B e/ Neptuno y Virtudes ⓣ 7/863-7722. The big selling point at this former *paladar*, located just a block and a half from the Parque Central, is the excellent food served up in the balconied dining room. One of the two rooms for rent is surprisingly large, given the slightly cramped apartment, and well fitted-out, with TV, fridge, two beds and a small walk-in wardrobe. ②

Vedado

Hotels

Habana Libre Calle 23 esq. L ⓣ 7/33-4011, ⓕ 33-3141. Large, slick city hotel with lots of shops, a terrace pool, three restaurants, numerous bars and a cabaret, making it a solid, if somewhat anonymous, choice. **7**

🏃 **Hotel Nacional** Calle O esq. 21 ☎7/33-3564, Ⓔreserva@gnacio.gma.cma.net. The choice of visiting celebrities for decades, this handsome hotel looks like an Arabian palace and is deservedly recognized as one of Havana's best hotels. Beautiful rooms, smooth service and excellent facilities. **8**

Meliá Cohiba Calle Paseo e/ 1ra y 3ra ☎7/33-3636, Ⓕ33-4555. This good-looking, modern hotel close to the Malecón caters predominantly for the business visitor, with uniformed bellhops, indoor fountains and a mini-mall. The tasteful but unimaginative rooms are full of mod cons. **9**

Presidente Clazada no.110 esq. Ave. de los Presidentes ☎7/55-1801, Ⓔcomerc@hpdte.gcatur.cu. The *Presidente* is Vedado's most charismatic hotel. Many of the original features from the hotel's inauguration in 1928 remain, and the small lobby is a delight with marble flooring, enormous teardrop chandeliers and nineteenth-century Japanese porcelain vases. The rooms' decor complements the general feel with antique furniture, views over the city and marble bathrooms. **8**

Riviera Paseo y Malecón ☎7/33-4051, Ⓔreserves@gcrivie.gca.cma.net. Built by the Mafia in the 1950s as a casino hotel, the *Riviera* retains much of that era's cool style. Many original features, like its long, sculpture-filled lobby, rooms boasting original furniture and fittings and Copa Room cabaret, capture the retro vibe. **8**

St John's Calle O no.206 e/23 y 25 ☎7/833-3740, Ⓕ7/ 833-3561, Ⓔjrecepci@stjohns.gca.tur.cu. A pleasant mid-range hotel with an attractive lobby and friendly staff. Facilities include a 24-hour lobby-bar and rooftop pool. **6**

Victoria Calle 19 esq. M ☎7/33-3510. Small and extremely friendly, with only 28 rooms and attentive service, the *Victoria* feels like a private hotel, and features a small swimming pool. **7**

Casas particulares

Calle 21 no.4 e/ N y O. There are 13 apartments running *casas particulares* in this fabulous 1930s apartment block. Many of the apartments are good quality and excellent value, and the building, with an impressive Rococo atrium and a cranky lift, is a sumptuous bonus. Also, it's just opposite the *Hotel Nacional*, so you couldn't wish for a better Vedado location. Some of the best include: *Casa de Conchita García*, Apto. 74 (☎7/832-6187; **2**) with two very clean and modern rooms; *Casa de Lenin Rafael González y Carolina Rodríguez*, Apto 61 (☎7/832-4422, Ⓔsandelis@hotmail.com; **2**), which has

three rooms – two en suite – in an airy apartment; *Casa de Mario Zorrilla y Dora Cobas*, Apto 62 (☎7/835-5555; **2**), a kitsch apartment with one room for rent and English spoken; and *Casa de Teresa Llagun Fernandez*, Apto 54 (☎7/832-0777; **2**), featuring one a/c room with bathroom and fridge in a large apartment. If these are full they can refer you to their neighbours. It's imperative to phone ahead, as the doorman has a tendency to guide you only to the flats that pay him commission.

Casa de Acelo Hernández Méndez Calle 17 no.1105 e/14 y 16 ☎7/831-1377. This mint-green mansion on a quiet side street has two rooms, each with a bathroom, a/c and fridge. The splendid grounds include a sundeck and a beautiful patio with a barbecue oven. Breakfast and dinner are available for a few convertible pesos extra and English, French and Italian are spoken by the very accommodating owners. Parking available. **2**

Casa de Aurora Ampudia Calle 15 no.58 altos e/ M y N ☎7/832-1843. Two double rooms in a friendly household on the first floor of a beautiful mock-colonial house within a stone's throw of the Malecón, with very helpful owners and two expansive balconies tailor-made for chilling out. **3**

Casa de Dulce Maria Lopez Alcaron & Jesus Cardona Calle E no.654 e/ 27 y 29 ☎7/832-1633 Ⓔjcardona@correodecuba.cu. This clean and pleasant house has two rooms with private bath. One of the rooms doesn't have a/c and is $5CUC cheaper. The very friendly and hospitable couple also offer breakfast. **2**

Casa de Enrique Oramas Calle J no.512 e/ 23 y 25 ☎7/833-5913. Well positioned on an appealingly quiet street in Central Vedado, this house offers a self-contained room with its own entrance, private bathroom with electric shower and off-road parking. **3**

Casa de Idania Lazo Rodríguez Calle 25 no.1061 e/ 4 y 6 ☎7/830-9760, Ⓔdnsid@ccme .com.cu. Two bedrooms on a beautiful tree-lined Vedado street. Twin beds with a fridge make one room ideal for those sharing, while the second has a double bed. Each has its own bathroom and there's an ample shared patio. **2**

🏃 **Casa de Mélida Jordán** Calle 25 no.1102 e/ 6 y 8 ☎7/83-35219, Ⓔmelida@girazul .com A big, stylish house set back from the road and surrounded by a marble veranda overlooking an expansive garden. Both of the rooms for rent are beautifully furnished and have a private bath. The largest room has twin beds and the other has a double, although an extra bed can be added. English is spoken by the helpful and friendly owners and there are various extra services available. A superb choice. **3**

Miramar and the western suburbs

Hotels

Comodoro Avendia 3ra esq. 84 ☎7/204-5551, ✉reserves@comodor.cha.cyt.cu. With a selection of well-designed and comfortably equipped rooms and bungalows, sea views and a shopping mall, the *Comodoro* would be great if not for its sluggish service. Don't be deceived by brochure claims to a beach: it's artificial and basically a large sandpit. ❼

Meliá Habana Calle 3ra e/ 76 y 80, Miramar ☎7/204-8500, ☏204-8505. Very professional hotel in the heart of the business district. The impressive marble reception area (with fountain), well-stocked international restaurants, smoking room and huge pool make this excellent, stress-free lodging for visiting VIPs. ❾

Novotel Avenida 5ta e/ 72 y 76, Miramar ☎7/204-5384, ✉reserva@miramar.gav.tur.cu. Despite its uninspiring exterior, the sleek interior and smooth, professional service make the *Novotel* an excellent choice. Facilities abound, with a business centre, an excellent gym, squash and tennis courts and huge pool. Rooms have all mod cons including Internet data ports, and there's a choice of three restaurants. The only drawback is the distance from town, although a free bus service to the centre, leaving four times a day, goes some way towards compensating. ❽

Oasis Panorama Calle 7ta Av 3ra, Miramar ☎7/204 0100, ☏204-4969, ⊕www.globalia-hotels.com. A cosmopolitan and stylish hotel with an expansive marble lobby decked with greenery that hangs down from its balconies. A fitness centre, pre-pay WiFi in the lobby and rooms, a piano bar and a huge pool with swim-up bar make for a stress-free stay. ❼

Casas particulares

Casa de Alberto Prieto Calle 4 no.103 ☎7/203-5111 ✉a.prieto@laposte.net. A smart, self-contained apartment with space for three couples. Comes with a kitchen, a dining room and two bathrooms, there's a fantastic roof terrace and the owner speaks English and Italian. Prices depend on how many rooms are rented. ❸–❺

Casa de Maurisio Alonso Calle A no.312 apto. 9 e/ 3ra y 5ta ☎7/203-7581, ✉masexto@infomed.sld.cu. The major selling point of this stylish retro penthouse apartment is its view over the ocean and Havana. One of the three well-appointed and spacious rooms has its own bathroom, while the other two share one. Fresh orange juice every morning, and city tours are just some of the services offered by the very friendly English-speaking owner. ❸

Casa de Marta y Jose Calle 6 no.108 apto 6 e/ 1ra y 3ra. ☎7/209-5632. A friendly place with two rooms, each with their own bath. A balcony with a sea view and fantastic home-cooked meals make this a fine choice. ❸

Casa de Ulises Calle 8 no.503 e/ 5ta y 31 ☎7/203-7468. Two self-contained apartments set amid mansions on a lovely street. A sundeck and a tranquil garden with rockers add to the appeal. ❸

Habana Vieja

By far the richest and most densely packed sightseeing area in the city, **Habana Vieja** – or Old Havana – is fair to bursting with centuries-old buildings and a palpable sense of the past. Its narrow streets, refined colonial mansions, countless churches, cobblestone plazas and sixteenth-century fortresses make it one of the most complete colonial urban centres in the Americas. Not surprisingly, then, for many people it's the old city as a whole, rather than the individual attractions within it, that leaves the most penetrating impression.

Yet there is much more to Habana Vieja than its unforgettable physical make-up. Unlike many of the world's major cities, Havana's tourist centre is also home to a large proportion of the city's residents. Some of the capital's poorest families live right next door to the district's hotels and museums, crammed into the very buildings that tourists stare up at, instilling the vibrant, sometimes hectic atmosphere that brings the area to life. This is by far the best place in Havana to just wander, with something worth seeing or doing, both for and in spite of visitors, just around almost every corner.

Prior to the Cuban **tourism boom** of the 1990s, this was a fast-decaying part of town: as trade with the Soviet Union collapsed, so too did the oldest, most

HABANA VIEJA

Municipal boundary

0   250 m

N

Castillo de los Tres Reyes del Morro

Castillo de San Salvador de la Punta

Canal de Entrada

Fortaleza de San Carlos de la Cabaña

Caleta de San Lázaro

Parque de los Mártires

Monumento a Máximo Gómez

See inset opposite

MALECÓN

CÁRCEL

GENIOS

SAN LÁZARO

AGUILA

REFUGIO

TROCADERO

COLÓN

MORRO

PEÑA POBRE

Museo Nacional de la Música

AVE. CARLOS M. DE CÉSPEDES (AVE. DEL PUERTO)

CUARTELES

LEÓN

CHACÓN

Iglesia del Santo Angelo Custodio

CENTRO

BLANCO

CRESPO

SAN CRESPO

INDUSTRIA

CONSULADO

PRADO

BERNAL

Museo de la Revolución

TEJADILLO

PLAZA DE LA CATEDRAL

N. LÓPEZ

PLAZA DE ARMAS

JUSTIZ

HABANA

ANIMAS

VIRTUDES

PASEO DE MARTÍ (PRADO)

ZULUETA

Palacio de Bellas Artes

EMPEDRADO

AGUIAR

Palacio de los Matrimonios

CONCORDIA

NEPTUNO

Cine Actualidades

Centro Asturiano

Edificio Bacardí

PROGRESO (SAN JUAN DE DIOS)

O'REILLY

CUBA

SAN IGNACIO

Museo del Numismatico

OBISPO

HABANA

OBRAPIA

PLAZA DE SIMÓN BOLÍVAR

Terminal Sierra Maestra (cruiser terminal)

SAN MIGUEL

SAN RAFAEL

Parque Central

Gran Teatro (SAN JOSÉ)

MONSERRATE

Iglesia del Santo Cristo del Buen Viaje

LAMPARILLA

AMARGURA

MERCADERES

OFICIOS

PLAZA DE SAN FRANCISCO

BARATILLO

SAN MARTÍN

BARCELONA

Cine Payret

AVE DE BÉLGICA

BERNAZA

CRISTO

VILLEGAS

BRASIL (TENIENTE REY)

COMPOSTELA

Museo de la Farmacia Habanera

PLAZA VIEJA

CHURRUCA

Museo del Ron Havana Club

Fábrica de Tobaco Partagas

DRAGONES

Sala Polivalente Kid Chocolate

AGRAMONTE

ZANJA/ESPADA

PLAZA DEL CRISTO

MURALLA

Convento de Santa Clara de Asís

Casa de los Condes de Jaruco

SANTA CLARA

INQUISIDOR

SAN PEDRO

Capitólio Nacional

Museo de los Orishas

SOL

PORVENIR

Iglesia y Convento de Belén

LUZ

DAMAS

MÁXIMO GÓMEZ (MONTE)

AVE. SIMÓN BOLÍVAR (REINA)

Parque de la Fraternidad

Mercado Agropecuario Egido

PICOTA

ACOSTA

JESÚS MARÍA

Iglesia de Nuestra Señora de la Merced

CORRALES

APODACA

GLORIA

MISIÓN

FACTORÍA

CÁRDENAS

CIENFUEGOS

REVILLAGIGEDO

CARMEN

ECONOMÍA

ARSENAL

AGRAMONTE

CURAZAO

MERCED

CONDE

BAYONA

LEONOR PÉREZ (PAULA)

Iglesia de San Francisco de Paula

ANGELES

INDIO

FLORIDA

AGUILA

ESPERANZA

AVE DE ESPAÑA (VIVES)

SUÁREZ

MISIÓN

Casa Natal de José Martí

SAN ISIDRO

SAN NICOLA

ALAMBIQUE

PUERTA CERRADA

ANTON RECIO

TALLA PIEDRA

DIARIA

Train Station

DESAMPARADO

Terminal La Coubre

AVENIDA DEL PUERTO

Ensenada de Atarés

SEE 'CENTRO HABANA' MAP FOR DETAIL WESTWARD

fragile sections of the city. Today the streets teem with foreign visitors whose money has brought a new sense of vigour to the area. A massive restoration project has seen some of the most impressive buildings converted into hotels, and classic streets like Obispo and Mercaderes now throng with shoppers and sightseers thanks to the numerous museums and shops installed there in recent years.

With so many sights to choose from, tackling the old city can seem a daunting task. However, it's relatively easy to prioritize your options, and in fact trying to see everything can be counter-productive. If you intend to do all your sightseeing in one chunk, restrict yourself to three or four museums, as the half-hearted displays and incoherent collections which occupy many of them can become disheartening. On the other hand, since many of them are relatively small, a visit is often over sooner than expected. Also worth bearing in mind is that the majority of museums are closed on Mondays.

The **Plaza de Armas** and the nearby **Plaza de la Catedral** are both good starting points for touring the district, with numerous options in all directions (we start from the latter). For the other unmissable sights head up **Obispo**, Habana Vieja's busiest street, to the **Parque Central**. Bordered by some of the finest hotels in the city and just a few paces away from the awesome Capitolio building, this is the easiest, though not the quickest, route to the **Museo de la Revolución**, the country's most comprehensive celebration of the Revolution, as well as the **Museo Nacional de Bellas Artes**, the best and biggest art collection in the country.

The wide streets and grand buildings on this western edge of

Habana Vieja, different in feel from the rest of the old town, date predominantly from the first thirty years or so of the twentieth century. These early decades of reconstruction in Havana were heavily influenced by the United States and saw many colonial buildings demolished and replaced with flamboyant palaces and imposing Neoclassical block buildings, in tune with the ambition and growing confidence of the emerging superpower. The southern half of Habana Vieja is mostly untouched by restoration projects and still displays a more potent dose of the battered charm that gives this district so much of its unique character.

A word of warning: Habana Vieja is the **bag-snatching** centre of the city, with an increasing number of petty thieves working the streets, so take the usual precautions. Even at night, however, there is very rarely any violent crime.

Plaza de la Catedral and around

The **Plaza de la Catedral**, in northeastern Habana Vieja, is one of the most historically and architecturally consistent squares in the old city. Perfectly restored and pleasantly compact, it's enclosed on three sides by a set of symmetrical eighteenth-century aristocratic residences. The first houses were built on the site – which was swampland when the Spanish found it – around the turn of the sixteenth century. It wasn't until 1788 that the Plaza de la Ciénaga, or Swamp Square, as it was then known, was renamed the Plaza de la Catedral, after the Jesuit church on its north face was consecrated as a cathedral and subsequently remodelled into its current elaborate shape.

The striking yet relatively small **Catedral de la Habana**, hailed as the consummate example of the Cuban Baroque style, dominates the plaza with its swirling detail, curved edges and cluster of columns. Curiously, however, the perfect symmetry of the detailed exterior was abandoned in the design of the two towers, the right one noticeably and unaccountably wider than the left. The less spectacular cathedral interior (Mon–Fri 10.30am–3pm, Sat 10.30am–2pm; free) bears an endearing resemblance to a local church. It features a set of lavishly framed portraits by French painter Jean Baptiste Vermay (copies of originals by artists such as Rubens and Murillo) commissioned by Bishop José Díaz de Espada in the early nineteenth century to replace anything in the newly consecrated cathedral which he considered to be in bad taste. Other than these and an unspectacular altar, featuring imported silverwork and sculptures completed in 1820 by the Italian artist Bianchini, the three naves are relatively empty. This is due in part to the removal of one of the cathedral's principal heirlooms, a funeral monument to Christopher Columbus said to have contained his ashes which now stands in the cathedral in Seville, where it was taken when the Spanish were expelled from Cuba in 1898. For $1CUC you can climb the spiral stone staircase to the top of the **bell tower**, where the views take in the Capitolio and the other side of the bay.

Opposite the cathedral, the Casa de los Condes de Casa Bayona, built in 1720, houses the **Museo de Arte Colonial** (daily 9am–7pm, doors close at 6.30pm; $2CUC, guided tour $1CUC extra, $2CUC to take photos). Its comprehensive collection of well-preserved, mostly nineteenth-century furniture and ornaments offers more insight into aristocratic living conditions during the later years of Spanish rule in Cuba than any other building on the plaza, particularly because many of the rooms have been laid out as if they were still lived in. The predominantly European-made artefacts have been collected from colonial residences around the city and include elaborately engraved mahogany dressers and a petite antique piano. One room is full of colourful *vajillas*, plates engraved with the family coat of arms of counts and marquises from Cuba. It was customary in colonial aristocratic circles to give one of these *vajillas* to your hosts whenever visiting the house of fellow nobility. The museum also features some fine examples of the brightly coloured stained-glass arches, known as *vitrales*, a classic of colonial Cuban design used to crown doorways and windows.

Sharing the northwestern corner with the cathedral, and thoroughly deserving of a visit, is the **Casa del Marques de Aguas Claras**, the most sophisticated of the plaza's colonial mansions. Its serene fountain-centred courtyard, encompassed by pillar-propped arcs and simple coloured-glass portals, is actually part of the delightful *El Patio* restaurant (see p.176), so you'll need to eat there to see it. The popularity of the restaurant, whose tables spread right out into the centre of the square, along with the music provided by any one of a

△ El Patio

number of bands that regularly play here, inject the square with life. Next door, occupying the other half of the west side of the plaza, is the Galería Victor Manuel, a well-stocked arts and crafts shop. Across from here, the **Casa de Lombillo** (Mon–Fri 9am–5pm & Sat 9am–1pm) dates from 1741 and was originally home and office to a sugar factory owner. Much of it is closed to the public, but via the door on Empedrado you can pop inside and take a peak at the patio and scale the broad staircase.

At the end of Callejón del Chorro, a short cul-de-sac on the southwestern corner of the plaza, is the low-key **Taller Experimental de Gráfica** (Mon–Fri 9am–4pm; free), where a small selection of artwork, more innovative than most of what's on offer around this area, is exhibited in front of the large workshop where it is produced. The **Centro de Arte Contemporáneo Wifredo Lam** (Mon–Sat 10am–5pm; $2CUC), at San Ignacio esq. Empedrado, in the shadow of the cathedral, has a much larger, though often quite bare, gallery showing equally off-centre contemporary art, including photography, painting and sculpture. All exhibitions are temporary; previous shows have included huge, bizarre-looking amalgamations of modern household objects.

East to Plaza de Armas

From the Plaza de la Catedral it's a two-minute walk along either San Ignacio, Mercaderes or, a short block away, Tacón, to O'Reilly, which leads directly into the Plaza de Armas. On the way, depending on which street you take, you'll pass one of two simple distractions. Along Mercaderes you will pass a giant **mural** portraying 67 figures from the history of the arts and politics in Cuba. Pictured as a group standing outside and on the balconies of a classic colonial Cuban building, they include Carlos Manuel de Céspedes (nineteenth-century revolutionary), José de la Luz y Caballero (nineteenth-century philosopher), Jean Baptiste Vermay (French painter whose work appears in the cathedral and in El Templete on the Plaza de Armas) and José Antonio Echeverria (1950s student leader and revolutionary).

On Tacón, between O'Reilly and Empedrado, is the **Gabinete de Arqueologia** (Tues–Sat 9am–5pm, Sun 9am–1pm; $1CUC), where archeology enthusiasts will find more than enough pieces to justify the small entrance fee, although the depth and range of exhibits is slightly disappointing and the highlights unlikely to change the unconverted. The ground floor is the showcase for colonial pieces found in churches and old houses around the capital, and not very deserving of a place in a museum claiming to showcase ancient historical artefacts. There are various ceramic pieces, some seventeenth- and eighteenth-century doors and two huge sugar cauldrons as used in the old refineries, but overall this floor contains very little that you can't see better examples of in other Havana museums. The museum really earns its name, though, in the upstairs rooms where archeological finds from Cuba and Latin America include five-thousand-year-old ceramic figurines from Ecuador and a skull from the Siboney culture, the oldest peoples to have inhabited Cuba.

Around the corner on O'Reilly, a splendid colonial building is being transformed into a future must-see sight, the **Museo del Habano**. This is set to become a comprehensive showcase for Cuba's world-famous cigar industry which, amazingly, up until now has been represented in the diminutive and disappointing Casa del Tabaco on nearby Mercaderes (see p.137).

Plaza de Armas

Less than a block west from the Gabinete de Arqueologia is the **Plaza de Armas**, the oldest and most animated of Habana Vieja's squares, and also where Havana established itself as a city in the second half of the sixteenth century. Based around an attractive landscaped leafy core, the plaza is often seething with tourists as live music wafts from *La Mina* restaurant in the corner. The three brick streets and, uniquely, the single wooden one, which make up the outer border are dominated every day (save Sunday) by Havana's biggest and best secondhand **book market**. Shelves and tables full of well-worn books line the street all the way around the square, the pavement cluttered with boxes full of backup stock, much of it the same standard-issue texts to be found in households all over Cuba. This is the place to find publications of Fidel Castro's speeches or Che Guevara's theories, as well as collectable pre-revolutionary and even some colonial-era literature.

For most of the nineteenth century, the Plaza de Armas was the political heart of Havana and boasted distinguished examples of colonial architecture. Today, several of these historic buildings house museums, most notably the Museo de la Ciudad.

Museo de la Ciudad

The robust yet refined **Palacio de los Capitanes Generales** on the western, wooden-street side of the plaza was the seat of the Spanish government from the time of its inauguration in 1791 to the end of the Spanish-American War in 1898. It's now occupied by one of Havana's best museums, the **Museo de la Ciudad** (daily 9am–6.30pm; $3CUC, $4CUC with guided tour), which celebrates the original building itself as well as the city's colonial heritage in general. Highlights on the ground floor include a fantastic nineteenth-century fire engine and a collection of horse-drawn carriages. Upstairs, amongst rooms that have been restored to their original splendour, is the magnificent Salón de los Espejos (Hall of Mirrors), lined with glorious gilt-looking mirrors, ornate golden candlestick holders and three huge, ostentatious crystal chandeliers. Next door is the slightly less striking Salón Verde, also known as the Salón Dorado (Golden Hall), where the governor would receive guests amidst golden furniture and precious porcelain. Completing the triumvirate of the building's most impressive rooms is the sumptuous Salón del Trono (Throne Room), which, with its dark-red, satin-lined walls, was intended for royal visits, though no Spanish king or queen ever visited colonial Cuba.

Palacio del Segundo Cabo

In a corner of the plaza, at Tacón and O'Reilly, is the **Palacio del Segundo Cabo**, dating from the same period as the Palacio de los Capitanes Generales and similarly characterized by elegant, stern-faced architecture. It served its original purpose as the Royal Post Office for only a few years, and has been used by a host of institutions since, including the Tax Inspectorate, the Supreme Court of Justice and the Cuban Geographical Society; currently the building acts as the headquarters of the **Instituto Cubano del Libro** (Cuban Book Institute). The least accessible of the plaza's buildings, there is nevertheless usually someone on hand to accompany you into the courtyard for a gander at the august Baroque architecture, where the ageing stone archways shoulder an iron-girdered wraparound balcony complete with wooden shutters and colourful portals. You can also wander beyond the entrance if you pay to visit the discreet, single-room **art gallery**, the **Sala Galería Raúl Martínez** (Mon–Sat 9am–6pm; $1CUC), which holds temporary exhibitions, usually of modern art. Many of the artists whose work is hung here have illustrated books published by the Instituto Cubano del Libro. In the entrance hall are posted details of readings, workshops and conferences that periodically take place inside. There's also a relatively well-stocked **bookshop** featuring predominantly Spanish and Cuban titles (daily 8am–5pm).

The rest of the plaza

There's more to see around the rest of the square, such as the **Museo Nacional de Historia Natural** (Tues 10am–4pm, Wed–Sun 10.30am–6pm; $3CUC, $4CUC with guide), on the corner of Obispo and Oficios. On an international scale this is an unremarkable and rather diminutive natural history museum, but it is nevertheless the biggest and best of its kind in the country, and one of the only museums in Habana Vieja suitable for children. There are models and video displays around the first section of the ground floor, charting a brief history of life on earth. In the rooms beyond, light-and-sound effects bring the mammals of the five continents to a semblance of life, but the lack of any background scenery makes the cluttered displays feel a bit flat. There's even less life up on the first floor where Cuban fauna is the dominant theme, though you can at least have a look at some of the lesser known animals that inhabit these shores. The most unusual of them all is the prehistoric *manjuarí* fish, but there are also examples of the *jutía carabalí* (a large indigenous tree rat), iguanas, bats and various birds.

A few doors along on Obispo, just beyond what are technically the confines of the square on the other side of Oficios, is the **Museo de la Orfebrería** (Tues–Sun 9am–6.30pm; $1CUC), worth a twenty-minute scoot round. This building was a colonial-era workshop for the city's prominent gold- and silver-smiths and now displays some of their work, as well as interesting gold and silver pieces from around the world. There are all kinds of objects on display, from pocket watches and walking sticks to ceremonial swords and vases. Look out in particular for the fantastic, ostentatious old clocks and, upstairs, silver roosters from Peru. A jewellery shop is also located in the same building (see p.190).

In the square's northeastern corner, the incongruous classical Greek architecture of **El Templete**, a curious, scaled-down version of the Parthenon in Athens, marks the exact spot of the foundation of Havana and the city's first mass in 1519. The building itself was established in 1828 and the large *ceiba* tree which now stands within its small gated grounds is the last survivor of the three that were planted here on that inaugural date. Inside the tiny interior (daily 9am–6.30pm; $1CUC), two large paintings depict these two historic ceremonies, both by nineteenth-century French artist Jean Baptiste Vermay, whose work can also be seen inside the Catedral de la Habana.

Castillo de la Real Fuerza

Due north of the plaza, just across O'Reilly, the **Castillo de la Real Fuerza** is a heavy-set sixteenth-century fortress surrounded by a moat. Built to replace a more primitive fort that stood on the same site but was destroyed by French pirates in 1555, this more impressive building never really got into its role as protector of the city. Set well back from the mouth of the bay, it proved useless against the English who, in 1762, took control of Havana without ever coming into the firing range of the fortress's cannon. Having undergone recent renovations, it is expected to soon house the maritime museum which was previously located in the Castillo de San Salvador de La Punta.

Obispo

Shooting west from the Plaza de Armas, linking it with the Parque Central, is the tightly packed, thronging shopping street of **Obispo**, scene of some of the most intense recent redevelopment in Habana Vieja. Crowded with foreign visitors, and one of the city's most animated thoroughfares, Obispo is a lively mix of convertible-peso shops, street vendors, open-front bars, secondhand bookstalls, hotels, restaurants, and numerous private front-room art galleries and workshops. Away from the new shopping malls hereabouts, this is the best place in Havana for browsing in a number of great stores, including Longina, one of the better places for Cuban music, situated between Compostela and Habana.

Near the Plaza de Armas end of Obispo is a small concentration of quick-stop distractions. On the corner of Aguiar, the **Droguería Johnson**, a 1950s pharmacy that's now in reconstruction, should, once it's finished, contrast nicely with the older **Farmacia Taquechel** (daily 9.30am–6.30pm) a couple of blocks further down, between San Ignacio and Mercaderes. Founded in 1898 and perfectly restored in 1996, this fully functioning but clearly tourist-focused pharmacy specializes in natural medicines while attracting a constant stream of visitors with its admirable attention to period detail – from the shelves of porcelain medicine jars down to the cash register, there isn't a piece out of place. Next door is the hotel **Ambos Mundos** (see p.122), **Ernest Hemingway**'s base in Cuba for ten years from 1932 and allegedly where he began writing *For Whom the Bell Tolls*. The hotel's rooftop garden is one of the best places for a **drink** in the old city and is open to non-guests. While riding up in the original 1920s cage-lift, stop off on the fifth floor and visit Room 511 (daily 9am–5pm; $2CUC), where Hemingway invariably stayed. The original furniture and even his typewriter have been preserved, and there's usually a guide on hand to answer any questions.

Further west towards the Parque Central, at no.305 between Habana and Aguiar, is the recently rehoused **Museo del Numismatico** (Tues–Sat 9.15am–4.45pm & Sun 9am–1pm; $1CUC). It is much improved since it moved from its prior location on Oficios, thanks in part to the pillar-fronted, marble-walled grandeur of the building but more to the fascinating background information, all of it in Spanish, posted alongside the cabinets of coins and banknotes. There are coins, such as the silver Spanish Reales, dating back to the fifteenth century, and a collection of late nineteenth-century notes issued by the Banco Español de la Habana (including an enormous one-thousand peso example). It's the stories behind the exhibits, however, that bring the collection to life. One set of peso notes on view was issued by the República de Cuba en Armas, forced into circulation in the "liberated territories" by Cuban independence-fighters during the Ten Years' War.

Along Oficios to Plaza de San Francisco

The oldest street in the city, **Oficios**, heads south from the Plaza de Armas and is lined with colonial residences, several of which now house small museums. At no.16 is the **Casa de los Arabes** (Tues–Sat 9am–5pm, Sun 9am–1pm; free or donation), a former religious school. The building, constructed in the seventeenth century, is one of the most striking single examples of the Moorish influence on Spanish – and therefore Cuban – architectural styles; it tends to outshine the sketchy collection of Arabian furniture and costumes found in its corridor-room, which is set up like a Marrakesh market and features fabrics and rugs hanging from the walls and ceilings.

Across the street, and of wider appeal, is the **Museo del Automóvil** (Tues–Sat 9am–5pm, Sun 9am–1pm; $1CUC) where, amongst the two dozen or so cars parked inside, dating mostly from the first half of the twentieth century, the 1902 Cadillac is one of the most attention-grabbing. The 1981 Chevrolet donated to the museum by the Peruvian ambassador, 1920s Fords and a number of other models deliver a rather succinct history of the automobile, which one still can't help feeling should be more comprehensive given the number of old cars still on the streets in Cuba.

Two blocks beyond the car museum, Oficios opens out onto the **Plaza de San Francisco**, opposite the colourful **Terminal Sierra Maestra** where the two or three luxury cruisers that include Cuba in their Caribbean tour come to dock. With the main port road running the length of its west side and two of its main buildings given over to offices, the square is the most open and functional of Habana Vieja's main plazas and attracts fewer sightseers than its nearby counterparts. The surrounding architecture, however, exercises a commanding presence, particularly the impressive five-storey **Lonja del Comercio** on the north side. This corpulent construction, clasped by rows of columns and stone-arched window frames, looks like a classical Roman theatre but was in fact built in 1909. It originally served as the Chamber of Representatives but now houses the Brazilian Embassy and a variety of commercial companies in its spankingly refurbished interior, an office complex better suited to Wall Street than Habana Vieja. Across the port road, the yellow-painted, vaguely Japanese-looking Terminal Sierra Maestra, with its pointed brick-coloured tiled roof, still manages to appear homely despite its large size.

Taking up the entire southern side of the square is the **Iglesia y Convento de San Francisco de Asís**, built in 1739 on the site of an older structure, which from 1579 was one of the most prestigious religious centres in Havana, a kind of missionary school for Franciscan friars who set off from here to convert the ignorant masses throughout Spanish America. Wonderfully restored in the early 1990s, the monastery now contains the neatly condensed **Museo de Arte Religioso** (daily 9am–6pm; $2CUC, or $3CUC with English-speaking guide, $2CUC extra to take photos), featuring wooden and ceramic figurines of the saints, church furniture and pottery found on the site. The real pleasure, however, comes from wandering around the beautifully simple interior, admiring the solid curves of the north cloister, and climbing the wooden staircase up the forty-six-metre-tall bell tower for magnificent **views** across the bay and over most of Habana Vieja.

At Oficios no.162, opposite the entrance to the church, is the **Casa de la Pintora Venezolana Carmen Montilla Tinoco** (Mon–Sat 9.30am–5pm; free), a delightful colonial town house restored in the mid-1990s from scratch by Tinoco, a Venezuelan artist and friend of Fidel Castro. Used for exhibitions of Cuban and overseas artists alike, Tinoco's own surreal and sometimes morbid paintings hang on the interior balcony. Outside, on the far wall of the patio garden, is a huge ceramic mural by renowned Cuban artist Alfredo Sosabravo, made up of hundreds of leafy and mollusc-like shapes to represent Cuban flora and fauna.

Museo del Ron Havana Club

A couple of blocks south from the Plaza de San Francisco along the port road is one of Havana's flashiest museums, the **Museo del Ron Havana Club** (Mon–Thurs 9am–5pm, Fri & Sat 9am–4pm, Sun 10am–4pm; $5CUC), a showpiece for the country's sizeable rum industry. Tracing the history and production methods behind the national drink, the lively tour – English-, French-, German- and Italian-speaking guides are on hand – offers one of the city's few modern museum experiences, with interactive exhibits, slick presentation and visitor-friendly staff. Passing through darkened atmospheric rooms, the tour is designed to follow the rum-making process in sequential order, with insights into each step of the transformation of sugar cane into the potent alcoholic beverage. In one of the first rooms a five-minute film, with a pidgin-English translation, provides an overview of rum's role in Cuban culture and history. The following rooms display various pieces of historical and contemporary machinery, including a *trapiche*, used in the colonial era to press sugar cane. There's a great model of a sugar mill factory, complete with a train chugging around the outside, which you can admire from an overhead gangway. Further on, you can smell the odours from bubbling tanks full of fermenting molasses, witness distillation and filtration apparatus and step inside the moody, ageing, barrel-lined cellars. The tour finishes up in a fully functioning replica of a 1930s **bar** where you are given a sip of the brew itself. The house special, Guarabana, is a refreshing mix of freshly squeezed orange, sugar cane juice and crushed ice. There is also a shop selling cigars and all sorts of rums plus, slightly unexpectedly, a pleasant little art gallery exhibiting the work of contemporary Cuban artists. In the same building is *Bar Havana Club* (see p.181), a more sociable, atmospheric option to the museum bar, which also serves food and has its own entrance, meaning you can come here outside of museum hours.

Along Mercaderes from Obispo to Plaza Vieja

South of Obispo towards the Plaza Vieja on Mercaderes at no.114 is the **Maqueta de la Habana Vieja** (daily 9am–6pm; $1CUC), an enthrallingly detailed model of the old city, including the bay and Habana del Este. Made up of some 3500 miniature buildings, the cityscape took three years to construct and occupies the larger part of the single room that constitutes a visit here. Having to view the whole thing from behind a rope makes it a little frustrating, but you should be able to pinpoint a few hotels, the main squares and the largest buildings, like the Capitolio. Each scheduled viewing is accompanied by a lighting sequence meant to replicate a day in the life of Habana Vieja and comes complete with the sounds of birdsongs and car horns; if you listen carefully enough you should be able to make out the voice of someone offering to sell you a box of cigars.

A few doors along, at no.120, is the disappointing **Casa del Tabaco** (Tues–Sat 9am–4.45pm & Sun 9am–12.45pm; free or donation), a surprisingly patchwork collection of smoking memorabilia given Cuba's heritage and reputation in this industry. Stretched over four small rooms are modest collections of ashtrays, pipes, snuff boxes and litographs as well as a novel set of lighters and various *humidores*, the most memorable of which is a scale model of the house where Fidel Castro was born. Sure to outshine this disappointing collection when it opens will be the Museo del Habano on O'Reilly (see p.132).

Across the street, at no.111, is another museum, the **Casa de Asia** (Tues–Sat 9am–4.30pm & Sun 9am–1pm; free or donation). Its long narrow rooms hold a hotchpotch of items from numerous countries, with many pieces donated by their respective embassy in Cuba. The diversity of what's on display means that most visitors will find at least one thing to catch their eye, whether it's the samurai-style sword from tenth-century Laos, the model boats from Bangladesh or the metal statuette of the Hindu deity Shiva Nataraja. Japan and China are well represented, the latter thanks in part to immigrant Chinese families in Cuba, whose contributions include a set of furniture and a striking image of The Seven Gods of Good Luck, their smiling faces piled up on top of one another in a boat.

Plaza de Simón Bolívar and around

One block from Obispo along Mercaderes, a mixed group of museums and galleries huddles around the **Plaza de Simón Bolívar**, a cosy little square backed up against the walls of the surrounding buildings. The most exceptional of these is the **Casa de Africa**, at Obrapía no.157 e/ Mercaderes y San Ignacio (Tues–Sat 9am–5pm, Sun 9am–1pm; $2CUC), with displays relating to African and Afro-Cuban arts, crafts and religion. Currently in the middle of a five-year renovation project that's expected to finish in late 2008, only a small part of the collection is on display. A big appeal here is that all the tribal weapons, engraved elephant tusks, sculptures and other exhibits on the first floor once belonged to Fidel Castro, most of them given to him by leaders of the African countries he has visited.

Opposite the Casa de Africa, and distinguished by its ornately framed front entrance, is the more eclectic **Museo Casa de la Obra Pía** (Tues–Sat 9am–4.30pm, Sun 9.30am–12.30pm; free or donation). Effectively two museums under one roof, the ground floor is mostly devoted to Alejo Carpentier (1904–80), Cuba's most famous novelist; displays include the Volkswagen Beetle he used when he lived in France. If you can't read Spanish you'll get more out of the exhibition upstairs, where the house itself, a prestigious seventeenth-century mansion, becomes the point of interest. The Rococo- and Renaissance-style furniture in the fantastic master bedroom include an impressively grand bed and a cot designed to resemble an old

Simón Bolívar and Latin American independence

One of the few men in history to have had a country named after him, and honoured throughout Latin America for the prominent role he played in the independence struggles of the early nineteenth century, the bicentenary of Simón Bolívar's birth in 1983 confirmed him as one of the region's most enduring icons, revered in Cuba as much as anywhere.

Born into an aristocratic family on July 24, 1783, in Caracas, Venezuela, Bolívar was orphaned by the age of nine, his father having died when he was only three and his mother six years later. At the age of sixteen he was sent to Europe, where he saw out the final years of his formal education. He returned to Venezuela a married man, but his wife, the daughter of a Spanish nobleman, died of yellow fever within a year of the wedding. Grief-stricken, he returned to Europe and immersed himself in the writings of Montesquieu, Jean Jacques Rousseau and other European philosophers. It was under such influences in Paris and Rome that Bolívar developed a passion for the idea of American independence.

He returned once again to Venezuela in 1807, in time to witness the effects of the Napoleonic invasion of Spain the following year. Suffering enormous domestic problems, Spain was forced to loosen its grip on the colonies, providing independence movements all over Spanish America with the perfect opportunity for an insurrection. Over the next twenty years, all mainland South American countries broke free of their colonial shackles and declared themselves independent, leaving the Spanish clinging onto Cuba and Puerto Rico as the last vestiges of a once-vast empire.

Bolívar was to be the single most influential man during these wars of independence, involved personally in the liberation of Venezuela, Colombia, Ecuador, Peru and Bolivia. His military career began in 1811 when he enrolled himself in the army of the recently declared independent Venezuela. The Spanish were soon to claim back their lost territory and during the ensuing war Bolívar fought hard in six battles to regain control of the capital in 1813, where he assumed the political leadership of the separatist movement. The fighting was far from over, however, and it wasn't until 1821, following numerous military manoeuvres, exile in Jamaica and Haiti and the expansion of his ambitions to incorporate the freeing of the whole northern section of Spanish South America, that Bolívar was to see his vision of a truly independent Venezuela a reality.

Perhaps the most important and heroic of all the military campaigns that he waged during these eight years was the taking of New Granada (modern-day Colombia). Against all the odds he led an army of some 2500 men through the Andes, enduring icy winds and assailing the seemingly unnegotiable pass of Pisba. When Bolívar and his men descended into New Granada the colonial army was completely unprepared, and on August 10, 1819, after victory at the battle of Boyacá, they marched triumphantly into Bogotá.

Despite his prominent role in leading five South American countries to independence, Bolívar never achieved his goal of creating a federation of South American nations, and the high esteem he is held in today contrasts with how tarnished his reputation was when he died, due to the unpopularity of his attempts to establish strong central governments in those same five nations.

boat. Another room full of Chinese furniture features some particularly elaborate chairs, while the dining-room walls are lined with *vajillas*. Many of the rooms are impressively complete, as is the record of its occupants, represented by a huge family tree going back as far as the early sixteenth century. Up another flight of stairs, on the roof, are the old slave quarters, set along an outdoor corridor in distinctly low-ceiling rooms. The only room you can go inside up here contains photos of the house before and during its restoration in the 1970s, alongside a few plates, bowls and other colonial household artefacts found on site during the pre-restoration excavations.

Around the corner, facing the plaza at Mercaderes no.156, the **Casa de Simón Bolívar** (Tues–Sat 9am–4.30pm, Sun 9am–12.30pm; free or donation) informatively and originally details the life and times of the Venezuelan known throughout Latin America as *El Libertador de las Américas* (see box, opposite). The museum depicts the life of Bolívar through a series of often comically cartoonish clay models, each representing a significant or symbolic event, such as his birth, baptism and first sexual experience. He is also shown in battle and dancing with a black general in a symbolic act of solidarity. Display screens in a separate room go into greater depth with useful written explanations in English, and there are also prints of some great paintings from the period that provide a lively visual context. You can also take a look around the excellent gallery upstairs, which includes some impressionistic paintings relating to Bolívar as well as a reproduction of Picasso's *Guernica* made from coloured fabric.

Facing the plaza from the Obrapía side is the eminently missable **Casa de Benito Juárez** (Tues–Sat 9.30am–4.30pm, Sun 9am–12.30pm; free or donation), also known as the Casa de México. There are some paintings and a few pre-Columbian artefacts from various regions of Mexico, but it all occupies just one room of this relatively large building; the rest of the place is quite empty and not set up to receive visitors. The **Fundación Guayasimín**, on the same block at Obrapía no.111 (Tues–Sat 9.30am–4.45pm, Sun 9am–12.45pm; free or donation), feels only slightly less bare but can claim a more palpable subject matter. Established in 1992, the house used to double up as a studio and gallery for the Ecuadorian painter Oswaldo Guayasimín, a friend of Fidel Castro who died in 1999. Upstairs are a bedroom and a dining room that were set up for Guayasimín but never actually used by him. Examples of the artist's work are found throughout the place, including a portrait he made of Castro for his seventieth birthday.

A few more steps along Mercaderes towards the Plaza Vieja is what looks like a shop, with the original 1950s sign outside. As the sign indicates, this was once an *armeria*, or gun store, but is now the **Museo 9 de Abril**, a small **firearms museum** (Mon–Sat 9am–6pm; free) lined with display cabinets full of pistols, machetes, rifles, knives and various other weapons. It is more renowned, though, as a monument to what happened here on April 9, 1958 when, following calls for a general strike led by Fidel Castro, four rebels were killed trying to raid the store. There are photos of those killed as well as a few documents and newspaper articles from the time of the killings.

Plaza Vieja and around

Despite its name, **Plaza Vieja**, three blocks south of the Plaza de Simón Bolívar, is not the oldest square in the city (Plaza de Armas is). It became the "Old Square" when the nearby Plaza del Cristo was built around 1640, by which time Plaza Vieja had firmly established itself as a centre for urban activity, variously used as marketplace and festival site. Today, more than any of the other main old town squares, it reflects its original purpose as a focus for the local community, not yet completely overrun by tourism, with some of the two- and three-storey buildings around its colourful borders still home to local residents and one of them housing a primary school. However, with hotels now on the surrounding streets, cafés and restaurants on or just off three of its four corners and a central fountain (installed in the late 1990s), the square is attracting more foreign visitors than ever before, as well as being improved for its residents.

The most diverting activity on offer around the square is the **Cámara Oscura** (daily 9am–5.30pm; $2CUC), a ten-minute tour of Habana Vieja and the bay through a 360-degree rotating telescopic lens. At the top of the seven-storey Gómez Vila building (built in 1933 and one of only two post-colonial edifices on the square), this impressive piece of kit can pick out sights and scenes from all over the old city in entertaining detail. On the same side of the square, at Mercaderes no.307, is the **Fototeca de Cuba** (Tues–Sat 10am–5pm; free), an undersized Cuban photography showcase where the two rooms of temporary exhibitions take second-billing to the excellent little front-room shop (Mon–Sat 10am–5pm); this is perhaps the best place in the whole country for photographs of life in Cuba – from landscapes and street scenes to portraits and social commentary, with everything done by Cuban photographers. Prices for framed and mounted works start at $25CUC and go up to $1000CUC.

There are further tourist stops along Muralla on the south side, including a clothes boutique and, in an eighteenth-century aristocratic mansion on the corner of San Ignacio, a commercial art gallery-cum-shopping arcade called **La Casona**. The pictures and paintings hung here are on the pricey side but there are also rooms full of cheaper, but less unique, arts and crafts for sale. This arch-laden building is the **Casa de los Condes de Jaruco**, originally built in the seventeenth century, remodelled in 1737 and said to be one of the most important examples of eighteenth-century Cuban residential architecture, with its numerous stained-glass *vitrales* and interior friezes. In this corner of the square you'll also find the best place for a **drink** around here, the *Taberna de la Muralla* (see p.182), which serves food as well.

About half a block east of the square, on Brasil between Oficios and Mercaderes, is the tiny Habana Vieja **Aquarium** (Thurs–Sat 9am–5pm, Sun 9am–1pm; $1CUC). Its dimly lit interior contains eight rather unspectacular fish tanks, each teeming with fish from all over the world. The rarest fish here, given its own tank, and certainly the strangest in appearance, is the prehistoric *manjuarí*, looking every bit the living fossil that it is, with its elongated body and protruding jaws lined with three sets of teeth.

Museo Histórico de las Ciencias Carlos J Finlay

Heading in the opposite direction along Brasil from the other side of the Plaza Vieja, a block and a half away, around the corner on Cuba, is the **Museo Histórico de las Ciencias Carlos J Finlay** (Mon–Fri 8.30am–5pm, Sat 9am–3pm; $2CUC, $5CUC with camera). As much a monument as a museum, this has been the home of the Academia de Ciencias Médicas, Físicas y Naturales de la Habana, a science academy, since its foundation in 1863. Named after the Cuban discoverer of the vaccine for yellow fever, the simple museum commemorates the man himself, his fellow medical scientists and the history of the academy. There are busts and paintings scattered about, but it's the rooms themselves that are of interest here. The Salón Paraninfo upstairs is a splendidly ceremonious-looking chamber, garbed with shiny marble columns and artistically masoned walls and home to busts of the three founders of the academy. Downstairs is the Sala Trelles, the building's most enthralling room, lined with glass-fronted wooden cabinets stacked full of books, and pervaded by an air of seriousness and importance. You can also visit the academy's **library**, still in use today.

Museo de la Farmacia Habanera

In between Plaza Vieja and the diminutive Plaza del Cristo is the **Museo de la Farmacia Habanera** (daily 9am–6.30pm; free), at Brasil (Teniente Rey) e/ Compostela y Habana. This is the old Farmacia La Unión, a huge pharmacy established in 1853 that stayed in business until the Revolution in 1959. Recently restored to the impressive splendour of its heyday, it features an extravagantly adorned ceiling and walls lined with finely carved wooden cabinets brimming with hundreds of porcelain jars which would once have contained the medicinal mixtures sold here. Some of the nineteenth-century laboratory apparatus used to make these mixtures is exhibited to the rear of the building. Amongst the more mundane medicine bottles, pestles and mortars are some fascinating mad-scientist contraptions, such as the *champione*, used to treat skin inflammations via steam. There are still concoctions for sale here (mostly natural medicines, all made in Cuba), and some spices too.

Southern Habana Vieja and the Casa Natal de José Martí

Immediately south of plazas Vieja and del Cristo, Habana Vieja becomes much more residential, thick with churches and other religious buildings, and is home to only one museum of note. A wander around this as yet undeveloped part of town offers an undiluted taste of old Havana.

There is no particular route more or less interesting than any other; the narrow, crowded streets are all equally enchanting. Amongst all the old churches and convents you'll inevitably come across, however, there is only one properly set up to receive visitors, the **Convento de Santa Clara de Asís** (T 7/861-2877; Mon–Fri 8.30am–5pm; $2CUC). From the street, the plain high exterior walls belie the attractive interior, full of plant-filled patios and wooden balconies. Occupying two entire blocks, its entrance is on Cuba between Sol and Luz; only limited sections of the building are open to the public and there is an air of desertion about the place. Founded in 1643 as the first convent in Havana, it operated as such right up until 1922 when the nuns moved to the southern suburb of Luyanó. Today it functions principally as the offices and workshops of the Centro Nacional de Conservación, Restauración y Museología, which works to restore historical artefacts and buildings. You can visit two of the three cloisters but don't expect to see any real evidence that this place functioned as a convent for nearly three hundred years.

A series of locked doors and private rooms limits visitors mostly to the convent's outdoor areas, though the occasionally available non-English-speaking guides can extend these boundaries a little further. Most enticing is the unexpectedly leafy courtyard of the main cloister, an oasis of green in the middle of the concrete-filled part of town. Crisscrossed with paths, this miniature forest contains an old well and an occasionally functioning snack hut in the middle. There are some historic relics, however, in the cavernous hall on the left just inside the main entrance, where sometimes there are also small art exhibitions. A hatch in the hall's floor reveals steps leading a short way down into a tiny **crypt** where, in small boxes, lie burial remains first found under-neath the convent chapel in excavations made in the early 1980s. The smaller second cloister has undergone considerable reparations in recent years, with particular attention paid to the accommodation located in this part of the convent, available to tourists as a kind of hostel (see p.122).

While in southern Habana Vieja, a visit to the lively and colourful fruit and vegetable **street market** on Compostela, in between Luz and Acosta, is also worthwhile, either for some fresh groceries or simply to get a taste of shopping for food Cuban-style in a place that's a far cry from the under-stocked and overpriced supermarkets you are more likely to come across. The market runs alongside the shabby **Iglesia y Convento de Belén**, though a couple of blocks further south sits the surprisingly grand **Iglesia de Nuestra Señora de la Merced**, slotted into the local neighbourhood on the corner of Merced and Cuba. If you're lucky enough to arrive when this faded orange

José Martí

It doesn't take long for most people who spend any time touring round Cuba to start wondering, if they don't already know, who José Martí is. Almost every town, large or small, has a bust or a statue of him somewhere, usually at the centre of the main square. Born José Julián Martí y Pérez to Spanish parents on January 28, 1853, this diminutive man, with his bushy moustache and trademark black bow tie and suit, came to embody the Cuban desire for self-rule and was a figurehead for justice and independence, particularly from the extending arm of the US, throughout Latin America.

An outstanding pupil at the San Anacleto and San Pablo schools in Havana, and then at the Instituto de Segunda Enseñaza de la Habana, Martí was equally a man of action, who didn't take long to become directly involved in the separatist struggle against colonial Spain. Still a schoolboy when the first Cuban War of Independence broke out in 1868, by the start of the following year he had founded his first newspaper, *Patria Libre*, contesting Spanish rule of Cuba. His damning editorials swiftly had him pegged as a dissident, and he was arrested a few months later on the trivial charge of having written a letter to a friend denouncing him for joining the Cuerpo de Voluntarios, the Spanish volunteer corps. Only sixteen years old, Martí was sentenced to six years' hard labour in the San Lázaro stone quarry in Havana. Thanks to the influence of his father, a Havanan policeman, the sentence was mitigated and the now-ailing teenager was exiled to the Isla de la Juventud, then known as the Isla de Pinos and, finally, exiled to Spain in 1871.

Martí wasted no time in Spain, studying law and philosophy at the universities in Madrid and Zaragoza, all the while honing his literary skills and writing poetry, his prolific output evidenced today in the countless compendiums and reprints available in bookshops around Cuba. By 1875 he was back on the other side of the Atlantic and reunited with his family in Mexico. Settling down, however, was never an option for the tireless Martí, who, wherever he was, rarely rested from his writing or his agitation for an independent Cuba. Returning to Havana in 1877 under a false name, he began a series of moves that was to take him to Guatemala, back again to Havana, back to Spain for a second period of exile, Paris, Caracas and New York, where he managed to stay for the best part of a decade. His years in New York were to prove pivotal. Initially swept away by what he perceived to be the true spirit of freedom and democracy, he soon came to regard the US with intense suspicion, seeing it as a threat to the independence of all Latin American countries.

The final phase of Martí's life began with his founding of the Cuban Revolutionary Party in 1892. He spent the following three years drumming up support for Cuban independence from around Latin America, raising money, training for combat, gathering together an arsenal of weapons and planning a military campaign to defeat the Spanish. In April 1895, with the appointed general of the revolutionary army, Máximo Gómez, and just four other freedom fighters, he landed at Playitas on Cuba's south coast. Disappearing into the mountains of the Sierra Maestra, just as Fidel Castro and his rebels were to do almost sixty years later, they were soon joined by hundreds of supporters. On May 19, 1895, Martí went into battle for the first time and was shot dead almost immediately. Perhaps the strongest testament to José Martí's legacy is the esteem in which he is held by Cubans on both sides of the Florida Straits, his ideas authenticating their vision of a free Cuba and his dedication to the cause an inspiration to all.

church is open (it keeps unpredictable hours), don't miss the opportunity to marvel at its magnificently decorated interior with frescoed ceilings and tapestried arches looming tall between the three naves, once a choice location for lavish society weddings.

A couple of blocks to the southeast, stranded in the middle of the port road on the southern extremity of Habana Vieja, is another interesting, though less grand, church, the **Iglesia de San Francisco de Paula**. Again, the chances are that it'll be closed but its unusual squat shape warrants a quick skirt around the outside. Only the face of the church and its octagonal dome display any uniformity, while the rest of the building looks somewhat cobbled together, with stone walls protruding from the side or seemingly tacked on. This design-less look may be partly explained by the building's history. The church was once the chapel of a hospital for poor and homeless women, first established in 1664 but then completely rebuilt after being damaged by a hurricane in 1730. In 1946, by which time the place had passed into private ownership, the hospital was demolished, leaving the ungainly structure left standing today.

Casa Natal de José Martí

The most tangible and best-kept tourist attraction in this part of town is the **Casa Natal de José Martí** (daily 9am–6.30pm; $1CUC), a few blocks west from the Iglesia de San Francisco de Paula at Leonor Pérez no.314. This modest two-storey house was the birthplace of Cuba's most widely revered intellectual and freedom fighter, though he only lived here for the first three years of his life. Though dotted with the odd bit of original furniture, the rooms of this compact and perfectly preserved little blue-and-yellow house don't strive to re-create domestic tableaux, but instead exhibit photographs, documents, some of his personal effects and other items relating to Martí's dramatic life (see box, opposite). The eclectic set of Martí memorabilia includes a plait of his hair, his bureau and a watch chain given to him by pupils of a Guatemalan school where he taught. There are images of his arrest, imprisonment and exile on the Isla de Pinos (now the Isla de la Juventud), and details of his trips to New York, Caracas and around Spain. In tune with the endearing simplicity of the house, it will take no more than fifteen minutes to see everything here.

Parque Central and Paseo del Prado

From the Casa Natal de José Martí it's a five- to ten-minute walk north on busy Avenida de Bélgica to the grandest square in Habana Vieja. Flanked by some of the old city's most prestigious hotels, and mostly shrouded in shade, the **Parque Central** straddles the border between Habana Vieja and Centro Habana and lies within shouting distance of one of Havana's most memorable landmarks, the Capitolio Nacional. Though the traffic humming past on all sides is a minus, the grandeur of the surrounding buildings, characteristic of the celebratory early twentieth-century architecture in this section of town, lends the square a stateliness quite distinct from the residential feel which pervades elsewhere in Habana Vieja. The attention-grabber is undoubtedly the **Gran Teatro**, between San Martín and San Rafael, an explosion of balustraded balconies, colonnaded cornices and sculpted stone figures striking classical poses. There's been a theatre on this spot since 1838, though the building standing today actually dates from 1915. For a proper look inside, you'll have to attend a performance, which usually take place at weekends (see p.185 for details). Next door is the renowned **Hotel Inglaterra**, the oldest hotel in the country, founded in 1856 (see p.123); past guests include Antonio Maceo, widely considered the bravest general in

Cuban history, who lodged here in 1890 during a five-month stay in Havana. The pavement café out front belonging to the hotel, *La Acera de Louvre*, is one of the few places around the park where you can sit and take it all in.

Cutting through the park's western edge is the **Paseo del Prado**, one of the prettiest main streets in the old town. Also known as the Paseo de Martí, but more often simply as El Prado, its reputation comes from the boulevard section north of the park, beginning at the *Hotel Parque Central* and marching down to the seafront. A wide walkway lined with trees and stone benches bisects the road, while on either side are the hundreds of columns, arches and balconies of the mostly residential neocolonial buildings, some recently restored and some quite shabby, but all painted in a whole host of colours. Look out for the illustrious **Palacio de los Matrimonios** on Animas – showered in sculpted stone detail, it looks ready to receive royal guests but is in fact one of the city's many wedding ceremony buildings, the popular Cuban alternative to a church. Encouragingly, despite its position in the city's touristic centre, El Prado still belongs to the locals and is usually overrun with newspaper sellers and children playing ball games.

△ Paseo del Prado

Capitolio Nacional

Just beyond the southwestern corner of the Parque Central, and visible above the sublime detail of the Gran Teatro on the same corner, looms the familiar-looking dome of the **Capitolio Nacional** (daily 9am–7pm; $3CUC, $4CUC with guided tours, $2CUC for photos). Bearing a striking resemblance to the Capitol Building in Washington DC (though little is made of this in Cuban publications), its solid, proudly columned front gloriously dominates the local landscape. It is arguably the most architecturally complex and varied building in the country, and any doubters will be silenced once inside, where the classical style of the exterior is replaced with flourishes of extravagant detail and a selection of plushly decorated rooms. Built in just three years by several thousand workers, it was opened in 1929 amidst huge celebrations. Since 1960 the building has functioned as the headquarters of the Ministry for Science, Technology and the Environment but is today principally a tourist attraction. The sheer size of the magnificent, polished entrance hall, known as the **Salón de los Pasos Perdidos** (The Room of Lost Steps), leaves a lasting impression, but it's the two resplendent, theatrical main chambers with their breathtaking gold-and-bronze Rococo-style detail, the seat of the House of Representatives and the Senate prior to the Revolution, that make up the centrepieces for visitors. There are a number of other captivating rooms, such as the ornate Italian Renaissance-style Salón Baire, the Biblioteca Martí (supposedly a replica of the Vatican library) and, following this, a corridor full of interesting photos portraying the history of the building, including its construction and inauguration. Only one floor of this huge building is open to the public and tours are surprisingly short, but there's an excellent, albeit slightly incongruous arts and crafts shop, full of ceramics, photography, paintings, silverware and wooden sculptures, to keep you occupied a little longer.

Fábrica de Tobacos Partagás

Behind the Capitolio stands the **Fábrica de Tobacos Partagás** (tours every 30min; Mon–Fri 9am–2.30pm; every other Sat (9am–2.30pm; $10CUC), one of the country's oldest and largest cigar factories, employing some 750 workers. Founded in 1845, the factory churns out twelve brands of *habanos*, including such famous names as Cohiba, Monte Cristo, Romeo y Julieta, Bolívar and Partagás itself. Though steeply priced compared to most museum entrance fees, the 45-minute tours here are easily among the most fascinating things to do in the city, with English-speaking guides taking you through the various stages of production – drying, sorting, rolling and boxing – all performed in separate rooms over four floors. The second floor is used as a cigar-making school, from where, after a nine-month course, those who graduate will move upstairs and join the 250 expert workers making some of the finest cigars in the world. It's on this top floor that visitors' most lasting images are formed, where the sea of specialist rollers, 60 percent of them women, are expected to produce on average over 100 cigars a day, depending on the brand and style of cigar they are working on. During their eight-hour shifts they are read to, from a newspaper in the mornings and from a book in the afternoons. There's a very genuine sense here of watching an uncontrived, everyday operation, with most of the workers almost oblivious to the stares of tourists and the tour guide's commentary. The factory also has an excellent shop where you can pick up all the brands made here.

Museo de los Orishas

Doubling as a museum and a place of worship for the capital's Santería community is the **Museo de los Orishas** (Mon–Sat 9am–5pm; $10CUC for one person, $6CUC per person if there's more than one, free for children under twelve), also spelt Orichas, meaning gods (see box overleaf). Located between Monte and Dragones, at the southern extreme of the Paseo del Prado, beyond the Capitolio, this quirky set of exhibits brings to life Afro-Cuban deities with 31 full-size terracotta statues, each one set in its own representative scene. While the pantheon of Afro-Cuban gods is made up of some 401 *orishas*, only the best known amongst them are represented here. With the assistance of the on-hand English-speaking guide, this is both a straightforward and fascinating insight into the main deities, as well as some of the practices, which form the basis of this earthy, colourful faith.

Each model in the museum is full of personality, but amongst the most memorable are Naná Burukú, a squat old lady with a shark-fin haircut, holding a baby; powerful and muscular Changó, god of war, fire and thunder, holding an axe above his head against a dramatic red sky; and buxom Yemayá, goddess of the sea and of motherhood, standing proudly against a backdrop of painted waves. At the foot of each model is a vase, a basket, a fan or some other object

Santería and Catholicism

Walking the streets of Havana you may notice people dressed head-to-foot in white, a bead necklace providing the only colour in their costume. These are practitioners of Santería, the most popular of Afro-Cuban religions, and the beads represent their appointed *orisha*, the gods and goddesses at the heart of their worship.

With its roots in the religious beliefs of the Yoruba people of West Africa, Santería spread in Cuba with the importation of slaves from that region. Forbidden by the Spanish to practise their faith, the slaves found ways of hiding images of their gods behind those of the Catholic saints to whom they were forced to pay homage. From this developed the syncretism of African *orishas* with their Catholic counterparts – thus, for example, the Virgen de la Caridad del Cobre, the patron saint of Cuba, embodies the *orisha* known as Oshún, the goddess of femininity, in part because both are believed to provide protection during birth. Similarly, Yemayá, goddess of water and queen of the sea – considered the mother of all *orishas* – is the equivalent of the Virgen de Regla, whom Spanish Catholics believed protected sailors. Other pairings include San Lázaro, patron saint of the sick, with Babalu-Ayé, Santa Bárbara with Changó, and San Cristóbal with Aggayú.

used to worship that particular deity. Most of these objects were collected in West Africa where Antonio Castañeda, the director and founder of this private collection, lived for ten years. Castañeda is himself a Cuban *babalao*, a high priest of Santería and amongst those who conduct religious ceremonies here outside of museum opening hours. These ceremonies are strictly private affairs but there are other activities – classes, conferences, dance performances – open to the public, most of them organized by the Asociación Cultural Yoruba de Cuba (℡7/63-5953, @asyoruba@cubarte.cult.cu); details can be found on the notice board in the entrance hall. There's also a restaurant-cum-*cafétería* called *Ojeun*, serving a mix of African and Cuban food.

Museo Nacional de Bellas Artes

Divided between two buildings, the **Museo Nacional de Bellas Artes** (Tues–Sat 10am–6pm, Sun 10am–2pm; $5CUC for one building, $8CUC for both, $2CUC for guided tour, under-15s free) is the most impressive and spectacular of Havana's museums and by far the largest collection of art in the country. The museum stands head and shoulders above the vast majority of its city rivals, presented and put together with a degree of professionalism still quite rare for this kind of attraction in Cuba. The large and rather plain-looking Art Deco **Palacio de Bellas Artes** on Trocadero, a two-minute walk north along Agramonte from the Parque Central, is where the entire collection had been housed since 1954 but is now the showcase for exclusively Cuban art. This is a detailed examination of the history of Cuban painting and sculpture, including everything from portraits by Spanish colonists to Revolution-inspired work, though pre-Columbian art is notably absent. Artists from the rest of the world are represented in the **Centro Asturiano** (see p.148), on the east border of the Parque Central, with an impressive breadth and depth of different kinds and styles of art, including ancient Roman ceramics and nineteenth-century Japanese paintings.

No English translations have been provided for any of the titles in either building, which can prove a hindrance to fully appreciating some of the works on display, particularly in the ancient art section where it is not always clear what you are actually looking at. Both buildings have **bookshops** where you can buy good-quality, Spanish-only guides to their collections ($12CUC each), invaluable if you have an interest in the context and background of the paintings, neither of which is illuminated by the painting plaques. There are also a few books dedicated to individual artists, but again there are as yet no English versions. These shops are, however, the best source of literature on Cuban art and artists that you are likely to find anywhere in the country. Poster prints and other souvenirs are also available.

Palacio de Bellas Artes

No other collection of **Cuban art**, of any sort, comes close to the range and volume of works on display in the Palacio de Bellas Artes, beautifully lit and, refreshingly, air-conditioned. Although spanning five centuries, its collection has a far higher proportion of twentieth-century art, though given the dearth of colonial-era painting around the island the museum can still claim to best represent the country's artistic heritage.

The best way to tackle the three-floor, chronologically ordered collection is to take the lifts up to the top floor and walk around clockwise. Hall One is dedicated to colonial-era painters; its abundance of relatively ordinary, and frankly not particularly skilful, portraits of Cuban nobility and formulaic religious pictures makes this area less engaging than others. Hall One's monotony, though, is broken up by some moody Cuban landscapes and a few insightful depictions of nineteenth-century everyday Cuban life, particularly of black Cubans, as in the paintings of **Víctor Patricio Landaluze** (1830–89). An attention-grabber is *Embarque de Colón por Bobadilla* (*Deportation of Columbus by Bobadilla*) by **Armando García Menocal** (1863–1941), straddling Halls One and Two and striking for its large size and sharp colours; the painting depicts the moment when Christopher Columbus is being sent from the island of Hispaniola by order of the new viceroy of the Spanish colonies, Francisco de Bobadilla. Portraits and harmonious rural Cuban landscapes by the same early twentieth-century artist fill most of the neighbouring section of Hall Two. Typical of these is *La Carreta* (*The Cart*), a subdued and idyllic scene in which a couple have taken shade under a tree while the cow driving their cart grazes nearby. For the most historic works, check the gantry that runs most of the length of Halls One and Two. Along with cigar label designs and sixteenth-century maps of the island, there's also **Dominique Serres**'s animated drawing of the 1763 English capture of the capital, including the strange sight of the Union Jack flying from the ramparts of El Morro.

Halls Three and Four, taking up the rest of the top floor, leap straight into modern art from the twentieth century. The first thing you'll see upon entering Hall Three is the most famous of the paintings by **Victor Manuel García** (1897–1969), *Gitana tropical* (*Tropical gypsy*), an evocative yet simplistic portrait of a young Native American woman that has become a national treasure. Manuel García has been attributed as one of the first Cuban exponents of modern art, influenced by the early twentieth-century developments in art in Europe, following two stays in Paris in the 1920s. Here you can also find the distinctive work of **Fidelo Ponce de León** (1895–1949), whose morbid, sometimes sinister, imagery and style most graphically mark the noticeable change in tone to be found in these rooms. Hard to miss and as striking as anything else in this section is *El Tercer Mundo* (*The Third World*) by one of the Cuban greats, **Wifredo Lam** (1902–82); the provocative and disturbing image exemplifys the influence of Picasso on the artist.

Walking counterclockwise from the lift on the second floor takes you through Halls Five to Eight and the last fifty years of Cuban art. Halls Five, Six and Seven cover the 1950s, 60s and 70s respectively, while Hall Eight incorporates all works produced since 1979. It's in Hall Eight where pop art meets the Cuban Revolution in the work of **Raúl Martínez** (1927–95), whose José Martí heads mimic Andy Warhol's Marilyn Monroes. Styles become increasingly diverse as the paintings become more recent: in the bewildering *Esta es la Historia* (*This is History*) by **Gilberto de la Nuez** (1913–93), the history of Cuba is told all in one image. This painting, just over a metre high and over a metre and a half in length, takes some studied unravelling. From the arrival of the Spanish at the top of the picture to the triumph of the Revolution in the bottom left corner, what at first appears to be a kind of painted street plan full of little figures turns out to contain innumerable separate scenes, each of them to be puzzled through and somehow connected. Hall Eight also exhibits the collection's most dynamic holdings, where its modern sculptures and works of physical art may push the boundaries of what passes for art a little too far for some, especially with pieces like **José Manuel Fors**' (1956–) twenty transparent boxes of leaves.

It's worth having a drink at the **cafétería** on the ground floor just to sit beside the pleasant open courtyard, where there are a few modern sculptures dotted about. Before leaving, check the notice board in the entrance hall for upcoming events being held in the museum, often in its 248-seat theatre.

Centro Asturiano

In contrast to the plain exterior of the Palacio de Bellas Artes, and its own simple modern interior, the Centro Asturiano, across Agramonte from the Parque Central, is a marvel to look at in itself. Stately and grandiose, plastered with balcony-supported columns and punctuated with wisps of carved stone detail, the building's foyer is its most captivating feature. Thick pillars and a wide marble staircase announce the entrance to the museum, while looming above are spacious balustraded corridor balconies from which you can best admire the stunning colour and jaw-dropping detail of the **stained-glass ceiling**.

With the least interesting items on the lowest level, it's best to start your tour from the top floor and work your way down. The exhibits are divided up by country of origin, with the largest collections, namely the Italian, French and Spanish, unsurprisingly containing the widest variety of pieces. Restricting yourself to these three countries, on the fifth, fourth and third floors respectively, is a good way to map out a short visit.

Up on the fifth floor, the rather mundane **British** rooms are home mainly to eighteenth- and nineteenth- century portraits. Among the better-known artists here are George Romney, Joshua Reynolds, Thomas Gainsborough and John Constable, whose Malvern Hall is a pleasant, typically idyllic depiction of the English countryside. On the same side of the fifth floor, the **Italian** collection is more interesting and historically more impressive. Bassano's sixteenth-century portrayal of San Cristóbal, one of Cuba's most popular saints, shows the weary old man with stick in hand carrying an angel on his shoulders. There's an unusually dramatic depiction of Christ on the Cross, by an unknown artist, featuring an agitated-looking crowd under dark clouds. In a noticeably older style than the rest is *La recepción de un legado* (*Receiving a bequest*) by Vittore Carpaccio (1455–1525), one of the oldest paintings in the entire building.

Considerably smaller are the **German**, **Dutch** and **Flemish** collections, much of which date from the 1600s, hung around the spacious balcony overhanging the fourth floor. In amongst the run-of-the-mill portraits and landscapes are a few eye-catchers, including the classic dramatized stable scene, *La adoración de los pastores* (*The shepherds' adoration*), by Erasmus Quellinus

(1607–78). There's a small triptych by Lucas Cranach (the elder), who, along with Jan Brueghel (the younger), is one of the few internationally famous artists in this section. Brueghel's *Kermesse* is a highlight, depicting a peasant scene with all sorts of debauchery going on, a focus typical of his work.

Most of the fourth floor is dedicated to the **ancient art** of Rome, Etruria, Egypt and Greece, including plenty of vases, amphoras and busts. The Egyptian section is the most interesting, ranging from hieroglyphic-inscribed papyrus and numerous religious figurines to the coffin from a three-thousand-year-old tomb and a Pharaoh's sculpted head. On the same floor is the relatively engaging **French** collection spanning the seventeenth to nineteenth centuries, with battle scenes, harbour landscapes, portraits and religious paintings by the likes of Jules Breton (1827–1906), Eugene Boudin (1824–98) and Jean Charles Cazin (1841–1901).

On the third floor, the **Asian** collection is a small room of exclusively nineteenth-century Japanese paintings. The most comprehensive single collection is the nearby **Spanish** one, though there is not so much that stands out. Amongst the portraits, José de Ribera's (1591–1652) dark and serious *Retrato de un filósofo* (*Portrait of a philosopher*) carries more weight than most. There's a high proportion of religious painting, particularly from the seventeenth-century Murillo school, along with paintings by Eugenio Lucas Velázquez (1817–70), with·his penchant for the melodramatic encompassing bullfights and street scenes. The more light-hearted works of Joaquín Sorolla Bastida (1863–1923) include attractive garden scenes and aristocratic ladies in a boat.

Down on what is referred to in museum maps as the ground floor (though its entrance is halfway up the main staircase) are the more haphazard **Latin American** and **US** collections. Paintings from Mexico predominate in the Latin American section, as do religious imagery and themes, where much of the mostly eighteenth-century work on display remains anonymous. Amongst the small assortment of US imports are a portrait of George Washington and some splendid pictures of the North American great outdoors.

Museo de la Revolución

Facing the Palacio de Bellas Artes from the north, with the entrance a couple of blocks further down on Refugio between Agramonte (Zulueta) and the Avenida de las Misiones, next to a small piece of the old city wall, is Havana's most famous museum, the **Museo de la Revolución** (daily 10am–5pm; $5CUC, $2CUC extra for guided tour). Triumphantly housed in the sumptuous presidential palace of the 1950s dictator General Fulgencio Batista, the museum manages to be both unmissable and overrated at the same time. The events leading up to the triumph of the Revolution in 1959 are covered in unparalleled detail, but overall the museum lacks a clear narrative and your attention span is unlikely to last the full three storeys. Visitors work their way down from the top floor, which is the densest part of the museum. Rooms are grouped chronologically into historical stages, or *etapas*, from *Etapa Colonial* to *Etapa de la Revolución*, though the layout is a bit higgedly-piggedly in places, making it unclear in some rooms at what point in the timeline you have reached. The Revolutionary War and the urban insurgency movements during the 1950s were surprisingly well documented photographically and it's at this stage of the story that the exhibits are at their most engaging. Some of the classic photos of the campaign waged by Castro and his followers in the Sierra Maestra might look familiar, but even serious students of Cuban history may overdose on models of battles and exhibits of vaguely relevant topics such as miscellaneous firearms. It comes as a relief, then, to find the monotony of exhibits broken by the sensationalist **Memorial Camilo-Che**, a life-sized wax model of revolutionary heroes Camilo Cienfuegos and Che Guevara, portrayed in guerrilla uniform striding out over some rocks from a bushy thicket.

Much of the second floor is given over to tiresome depictions of battle plans and the "construction of Socialism", bringing the story up to the present. Instead, it's the interior of the building itself, built between 1913 and 1917 during the much-maligned "pseudo-republic" era, that is most captivating on this floor. There's the gold-encrusted Salón Dorado, the lavish dining room of the old palace when it was occupied by General Batista, the dignified furnishings of the Presidential Office, used by all the presidents of Cuba from 1920 to 1965, and the wonderfully colourful **mural** on the ceiling of the Salón de los Espejos. The mural is a mesmerizingly dramatic celebration of the republic, with an angel at its centre carrying the Cuban flag amidst a fanfare of heavenly and worldly onlookers.

Joined to the building but located outside to the rear of the museum in the fenced-in gardens of the palace is the **Granma Memorial**, where the boat which took Castro and his merry men from Mexico to Cuba to begin the Revolution is preserved in its entirety within a giant glass case. Also here are military vehicles, whole or in bits depending on which side they belonged to, used during the 1961 Bay of Pigs invasion. These include a US B-26 bomber shot down during the attack and a Soviet T-34 tank from which Fidel Castro opened fire on the advancing counter-revolutionary brigade.

Facing the opposite side of the museum, on the corner of Avenida de las Misiones and Cuarteles, is the nineteenth-century neo-Gothic **Iglesia del Santo Angel Custodio** (Mon, Wed & Sat 3–6pm, Tues, Thurs & Fri 9am–noon). Distinctive for its rampart-like set of spires, the church boasts a well-kept, if unremarkable, interior and some gorgeously colourful stained-glass windows.

La Punta and around

La Punta, the paved corner of land at the entrance to the bay, capping one end of the official border between Habana Vieja and Centro Habana, can be considered the outer limit for sightseeing tours in this part of town. Just above the junction of the busy Malecón and the Avenida Carlos Manuel de Céspedes, its position is less than enchanting, though it still attracts groups of chattering locals and youngsters who gather to throw themselves off the Malecón into the rocky pools that jut out from the sea wall here.

The landmark attraction at La Punta is the **Castillo de San Salvador de la Punta** (daily 10am–6pm; $2CUC), a sixteenth-century fortress occupying most of this space and one of the oldest military fortifications in the city. Construction of the fort began in 1589 at the same time as that of El Morro, and together they formed the first and most important line of defence of the city. Having undergone years of excavations and renovations, the fort finally reopened in 2002 but there is little sense inside the place that you are viewing the results of a massive project. The restorations are impressively immaculate but the simplicity of the original design means exploring the place is over too soon. The fortress consists of little more than several rectangular rooms around a desolate central courtyard, all sealed in by the ramparts from where there are modest views along the Malecón and over to El Morro, but which are empty save for a few cannon.

The maritime **museum** which was once installed here has been removed due to storm damage and will reappear within the grounds of the less exposed Castillo de la Real Fuerza (see p.134).

Monumento a Máximo Gómez and around

The wide-open space between La Punta and the rest of Habana Vieja is dominated by heavy traffic on the road that encircles the Neoclassical **Monumento a Máximo Gómez**, before winding down into the tunnel that joins the two sides of the bay. Although one of the grandest memorials in Havana, due to its traffic-island location, the statue is relegated to no more than a fleeting curiosity for most visitors, although you can cross the road for a closer look. Dedicated to the venerated leader of the Liberation Army in the nineteenth-century Cuban Wars of Independence, the statue has the general sitting on a horse held aloft by marble figures representing the People.

The aristocratic mansion facing the monument to the southeast houses the **Museo Nacional de la Música** (Mon–Sat 10am–5.30pm; $2CUC, $1CUC for guided tour in Spanish, $3CUC to take photos), a showcase for the surprising variety of musical instruments used over the last two hundred years. The most coherent single collection is in the Sala Fernando Ortíz, where several dozen Afro-Cuban drums – mostly nineteenth-century instruments from Africa, Haiti and Cuba – have been gathered together by the country's most renowned scholar of Afro-Cuban culture. Although the displays in other rooms are more disjointed, there are still some eye-catching exhibits, such as the strange-looking violin from China or the boat-shaped xylophones from Laos. There's also a beautiful little plant-lined courtyard upstairs where you can sit down, and a shop on the ground floor selling CDs and sheet music.

To the southwest, sandwiched between the El Prade and the road encircling the monument, is the pretty little **Parque de los Mártires**, marking the spot where the notorious prison, the Cárcel de Tacón, built in 1838, once held such political prisoners as José Martí. It was mostly demolished in 1939, and all that remains are two of the cells and the chapel in what is little more than a large concrete box.

Habana del Este

While many people omit the sights in **Habana del Este**, across the bay from Habana Vieja, from their itinerary, erroneously believing them to be inconveniently located, those visitors who do make it this far are rewarded by uncrowded sights that are a telling link in the city's history. The ordered surrounds of the military Parque Morro-Cabana provide a particularly fascinating insight into Havana's fortified past, while a climb up to the gargantuan statue of Christ denotes the city's latter-day religious devotion.

The easiest way to **get to** Habana del Este is to take a metered taxi ($5CUC) or a private one ($4CUC) from Habana Vieja. It's also possible to take a bus (40¢) from the stop near the Monumento a Máximo Gómez – get off at the first stop after the tunnel. Once in Habana del Este, it's a brisk half-hour walk east from the fortifications to the Cristo de La Habana. If you're heading directly to the statue from Habana Vieja, consider taking the pleasant foot-and-bicycle **ferry** (1 peso) that leaves every thirty minutes from Avenida del Puerto e/ Sol y Luz, ten minutes' walk south from Plaza San Francisco and the main Sierra Maestra Terminal.

Parque Morro-Cabaña

Even if you don't make it as far as the Cristo de La Habana, a visit to the sprawling complex of castles and fortifications that collectively make up the

Parque Morro-Cabaña is definitely worth your time. A stalwart part of the Havana skyline, they dominate the view across the harbour, and, along with the fortifications in Habana Vieja, comprise the city's oldest defence system. Crowning the rocky cliffs directly across from La Punta is the imposing **Castillo de los Tres Reyes Magos del Morro** (daily 8am–8.30pm; $3CUC, $5CUC with camera, $2CUC for lighthouse), more commonly known as El Morro. This castle was built between 1589 and 1630 to form an impeding crossfire with the Castillo de San Salvador de la Punta on the opposite side of the bay, a ploy that failed spectacularly when the English invaded overland in 1762 and occupied the city for six months. Today the castle has an eerie, just-abandoned feel, its cavernous billet rooms and cannon stores empty but in near-perfect condition. Particularly fine are the high parade grounds studded with rusted cannons and the circular Moorish bartizans in the corners, from which you could easily spend an hour or so surveying the bay. A highlight of a visit here is watching the sun set over the sea from the summit of the **lighthouse** that was built on the cliff's edge in 1844.

Roughly 250m to the southeast, the **Fortaleza San Carlos de la Cabaña** (daily 10am–10pm; $4CUC before 6pm, $6CUC after 6pm, guide $1CUC extra) needs a half day to do it justice, and, despite being the more interesting of the two sights, it's the less visited and therefore more relaxing. Built to be the most complex and expensive defence system in the Americas, the fortress was started in 1763 as soon as the Spanish traded the city back from the English. However, its defensive worth has never been proved, as takeover attempts by other European powers had largely died down by the time it was finished in 1774. You can see why it took so long to finish after touring the extensive grounds, complete with impeccable cobbled streets lined with houses where soldiers and officers were originally billeted – now a miscellany of workshops, artisanal boutiques and restaurants – lawns, private gardens and even a chapel. The Ceremonia del Cañonazo ceremony, in which soldiers in nineteen-century uniforms fire the cannon at 9pm every evening, is entertaining enough to stick around for.

Cristo de La Habana

Further east, on the hill above the picturesque village of Casablanca, is the **Cristo de La Habana** ($1CUC, free if you have visited Parque Morro-Cabaña and retained your ticket). Marta Batista, wife of the dictator, commissioned this seventeen-metre-high Christ figure – sculpted from Italian marble by Jilma Madera in 1958 – in one of the couple's last contributions to the city before departing. Although impressive close up, where you can ponder the massive scale of the sandalled feet and the perfectly sculpted hands, said to weigh a ton each, there's precious little to do on the hillside other than admire the view over Habana Vieja. This is one sight that's actually best experienced from Habana Vieja in the evening, when you can gaze across the bay and enjoy the statue's floodlit grandeur.

The only other attention-drawer in Casablanca is the **Hershey train** terminus, one end of Cuba's only electric train service (the other end is in Matanzas; see p.290). This is not an official tourist attraction and is regularly used by Cubans travelling in between the six stations which make up the line. The classic, lovable little mid-twentieth-century trains, however, are a great way to take a slow, relaxing ride through picturesque landscape to Canasí (see p.201), Jibacoa (see p.200) or all the way to Matanzas, which takes about three hours and costs just under $3CUC.

Centro Habana

For many visitors the crumbling buildings and bustling streets of **Centro Habana**, crammed between the hotel districts of Habana Vieja and Vedado, are glimpsed only through a taxi window en route to the city's more tourist-friendly areas. Yet this no-frills quarter has a character all of its own, as illuminating and fascinating as anywhere in the capital. Overwhelmingly residential, its late eighteenth- and nineteenth-century neighbourhoods nevertheless throb with life, particularly **El Barrio Chino**, Havana's Chinatown, and there's no better place to really savour the essence of the city, particularly because here it's not on display but up to you to discover.

That said, this part of town is for the most part not that attractive on the surface. Full of broken sewage systems, potholed roads and piles of rubbish, Centro Habana has not yet enjoyed the degree of investment and rejuvenation that Habana Vieja has, save for the **Malecón**, where there are at last visible signs of part of the famous seafront promenade returning to its former glory, several

of its buildings having enjoyed facelifts in recent years. For now, the most impressive sight in Centro Habana is the **Iglesia del Sagrado Corazón**, a glorious neo-Gothic church rarely visited by tourists. Another worthwhile stop, closer to the Vedado border, is the **Callejón de Hamel**, a unique backstreet dedicated to Santería.

As an alternative to the Malecón for a route between Habana Vieja and Vedado, consider taking a wander through the neighbourhood immediately east of the Avenida de Italia. This patchwork grid of virtually traffic-less streets – bordered by San Lázaro, Zanja, Padre Varela and the Malecón – is full of kids playing in the road, laundry drying on nineteenth-century balconies, makeshift bicycle repair shops and the occasional farmers' market, all set to the soundtrack of locals chatting in open doorways.

El Barrio Chino

About a block inside Centre Habana from Habana Vieja's western border, the grand entrance to **El Barrio Chino**, Havana's version of Chinatown, is likely to confuse most visitors, as it's placed three blocks from any visibly ethnic change in the neighbourhood. The entrance, a rectangular concrete arch with a pagoda-inspired roof, is south of the Capitolio Nacional, on the intersection of Amistad and Dragones, and marks the beginning of the ten or so square blocks which, at the start of the twentieth century, were home to some ten thousand Chinese immigrants. Today only a tiny proportion of El Barrio Chino, principally the small triangle of busy streets comprising Cuchillo, Zanja and San Nicolás – collectively known as the **Cuchillo de Zanja** – three blocks west of the arched entrance, is discernibly any more Chinese than the rest of Havana. Indeed, the first thing you are likely to notice about El Barrio Chino is a distinct absence of Chinese people, the once significant immigrant population having long since dissolved into the racial melting pot. The Cuchillo de Zanja itself does, however, feature its own tightly packed little backstreet **food market** composed mostly of simple fruit and vegetable stalls and is lined with eccentric-looking restaurants,

△ El Barrio Chino

many still charging in pesos, where the curious and unique mixture of tastes and styles is as much Cuban as Asian. For some of the best Chinatown restaurants you'll need to look elsewhere in the neighbourhood, particularly on Dragones where you'll find, amongst others, *Los Dos Dragones* (see p.177), offering some of the biggest and cheapest portions in the city.

Iglesia Nuestra Señora Caridad del Cobre and Iglesia del Sagrado Corazón

Three blocks southwest of the Cuchillo de Zanja, occupying the length of the block between Manrique and Campanario, is the simple though appealing **Iglesia Nuestra Señora Caridad del Cobre** (Tues–Sun 7am–6pm). Construction of the church began in 1802 and involved the joining of two existing churches, but its restoration in the 1950s has given it a distinctly modern feel, with the soft light and dusty-coloured stone walls engendering an atmosphere of soothing tranquillity. Circular portholes with stained-glass windows featuring star-shaped designs line the walls and are clearly relatively recent additions. Perched on top of the golden altar is the Cuban national badge, an unusually secular touch somehow in keeping with the overall originality of this characterful city church.

A block south on Manrique and five blocks west on Simón Bolívar sits the **Iglesia del Sagrado Corazón** (daily 8am–noon & 3–5pm, mass daily at 8am & 4.30pm), shooting out from a block of worn-out neocolonial apartment buildings. Built between 1914 and 1923, this is arguably the most magnificent church in the country. Its unlikely location in the grime of Centro Habana, with heavy traffic passing by outside, contrasts effectively with its neo-Gothic splendour and makes a wander through its imposing entrance irresistible. Inside, a second surprise awaits, as the church's interior is infinitely more impressive than that of the much more heavily visited cathedral in Habana Vieja: the cavernous vaulted roof of the three naves is supported by colossal columns and the huge central altar incorporates a dazzling array of detail. Wherever you look, something catches the eye, from the skilfully sculpted scenes etched into the central pillars to the stained-glass windows at different levels on the outer walls.

The Malecón and around

The most picturesque way to reach Vedado from Centro Habana or Habana Vieja is to stroll down the **Malecón**, the city's famous sea wall, which snakes west along the coastline from La Punta for about 4km. It's the city's defining image, and ambling along its length, drinking in the panoramic views, is an essential part of the Havana experience. But don't expect to stroll in solitude: the Malecón is the capital's front room and you won't be on it for long before someone strikes up a conversation. People head here for free entertainment, particularly at night when it fills up with guitar-strumming musicians, vendors offering cones of fresh-roasted warm nuts, and star-gazing couples, young and old alike. In recent years it's grown in popularity for the city's expanding clique of gays and transvestites who put its sinuous length to good effect as a nightly catwalk and meeting place, especially the area close to the *Hotel Nacional*. In the daytime it's crowded with schoolchildren (intent on hurling themselves into the churning Atlantic), wide-eyed tourists and wrinkled anglers.

The Centro Habana section, referred to on street signs as the *Malecón tradicional*, has been undergoing tortoise-paced renovations for over a decade now. Lined with colourful neocolonial buildings, it's the oldest, most distinct and characterful section in the city, though – potholed and sea-beaten – it looks much older than its hundred or so years. Construction began in 1901, after nearly a decade of planning, and each decade saw another chunk of wall erected until, in 1950, it finally reached the Río Almendares. Today there are a few places worth stopping in for their enjoyable sea views. The best of these is *Café Neruda* at no.353–357, *Taberna El Galeón* (see p.182) and the *Lava Día* tapas bar at no.405. In addition, there are some soulless roadside *caféterias* every few blocks.

Parque Antonio Maceo and the Convento de la Inmaculada Concepción

A few blocks from Vedado the Malecón passes in front of the **Parque Antonio Maceo**, often referred to simply as the Parque Maceo, an open concrete park marked in the centre by a statue of Antonio Maceo, the Cuban general and hero of the Wars of Independence. The only other monument of any sort in the park is the **Torreon de San Lázaro**, a lonely little solitary turret, little more than a curiosity but dating all the way back to 1665, making it 250 years older than the park itself. Once part of the city's defence system, it's now stuck in the corner of the park where Marina intersects with the Malecón. There's a small playground here and the park attracts scores of screaming kids and chattering adults every evening, the best time to visit one of the most attractive public spaces in Centro Habana.

Just south of the park across San Lázaro and next door to the best hospital in the country, the towering Hospital Hermanos Ameijeiras, is the **Convento de la Inmaculada Concepción**, which warrants at least a quick peek inside. The chapel usually has its doors open to the street and is in fine condition, made all the more appealing by the number of Cubans putting it to use. This is very much a working building, its location by the side of the hospital ensuring a relatively frequent line of people coming in to say prayers. There's a resplendent blue-and-gold central altar and marble pillars topped with bronze sculpted detail lining the walls, all bathed in the calming light shining through the stained-glass windows and reflecting off the beige and white paintwork throughout.

Callejón de Hamel

Four blocks west on San Lázaro from the Parque Maceo, a wide alleyway known as the **Callejón de Hamel** has been converted into an intriguing and cultish monument to Afro-Cuban culture. Often featured in Cuban music videos, this bizarre backstreet is full of shrines, cut into the walls and erected along the sides, brimming with colour and a mishmash of decorative and symbolic images. The backdrop is an abstract **mural** painted by Salvador González in 1990, when it was decided that it was high time for a public space dedicated to Afro-Cuba. A few chairs and tables make up a tiny café at one end and the alley also features a small studio workshop selling smaller pieces of art done by González. The best time to visit is on a Sunday from around 11am when it becomes a venue for **Santería ceremonies**. The participants of these mini street festivals dance passionately to the rhythm of *rumba* in a frenetic atmosphere, accentuated by chants invoking the spirits of the *orishas*. The alley's popularity unfortunately means it has become slightly contrived, but this is still an excellent chance to experience one of the most engaging expressions of Santería.

Vedado

The cultural heart of the city, graceful **Vedado** draws the crowds with its palatial hotels – the backbone of so much of Havana's social scene – contemporary art galleries, exciting (and sometimes incomprehensible) theatre productions and live music concerts, not to mention its glut of restaurants, bars and nightspots. Loosely defined as the area running west of Calzada de Infanta up to the Río Almendares, Vedado is less ramshackle than other parts of the city and more intimate – after a couple of trips you'll start to notice the same faces. Tall 1950s buildings and battered hot rods parked outside ultramodern stores lend the district a strongly North American air, contrasted with the classical ambience of nineteenth-century mansions; the general impression is of an incompletely sealed time capsule where the decades and centuries all run together. There are plenty of crowds, but look closely and you'll see that many people are actually part of a bus queue, waiting their turn to enter the massive ice-cream parlour, **Coppelia**, or *jineteros* keeping watch for the next buck.

Vedado is fairly easy to negotiate, divided by four main thoroughfares: the broad and handsome boulevards Avenida de Los Presidentes (also known as Calle G) and Paseo, running north to south, and the more prosaic Linea and Calle 23 running east to west. The most prominent sector is modern **La Rampa** – the name given to Calle 23 immediately west from Malecón, as well as the streets just to the north and south – which races with gunning Ladas and battered Buicks and is landscaped with high-rise 1950s hotels and blocky utilitarian buildings. Presenting a rather bland uniformity that's absent from the rest of Vedado, it's a relatively small space, trailing along the eastern part of the Malecón and spanning just a couple of streets inland. Still, La Rampa dominates your immediate impression of Vedado, first because the skyscrapers – even these fifty-year-old, peeling-paint tower blocks – are such a rarity in Cuba, and second because you'll end up spending a fair amount of time here, confirming or booking flights in the airline offices, changing money in the urbane hotels, souvenir-shopping in the homespun street markets and *divisa* shops or eating at the restaurants. It's an area for doing rather than seeing, though you will find some worthy sights, such as the grand and glitzy **Hotel Nacional**, situated at the head of La Rampa and providing a perfectly encapsulated glimpse of pre-Revolution Havana. A little to the south of La Rampa proper are the **Museo Napoleónico**, a treasure trove of extravagant artefacts relating to the erstwhile French emperor, and, nearby, the elegant **Universidad de La Habana**, attended by orderly students who personify the virtues of post-Revolution education.

Southwest of the university is the **Plaza de la Revolución** with its immense monuments to twin heroes José Martí and Ernesto "Che" Guevara. Although generally considered part of Vedado, this area is actually a municipality in its own right, and with its huge utilitarian buildings has a flavour quite distinct from the other parts of Vedado. The uncompromisingly urban landscape of the plaza itself – a huge sweep of concrete – is a complete contrast to the area's other key attraction, the atmospheric **Necrópolis de Cólon**, a truly massive cemetery. Close by in Nuevo Vedado – as the name suggests, a younger extension to the established suburb – is the **Parque Zoologico**. Although less ecologically minded than many Western zoos, several indigenous species provide a point of interest.

In the part of Vedado north of Calle 23 up to the Malecón, west to the Río Almendares and east roughly as far as Avenida de los Presidentes, the backstreets are narrow and avenues are overhung with leaves from the trees planted here in

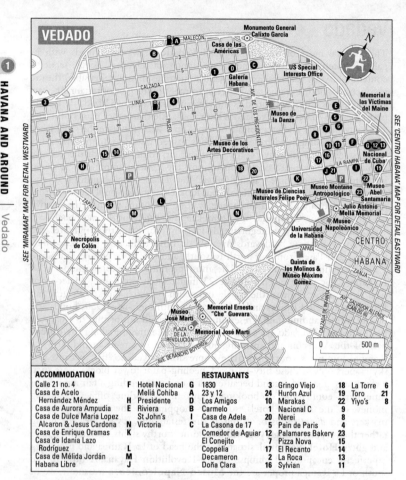

VEDADO

N

Monumento General
Calixto García

Casa de las
Américas

US Special
Interests Office

Galería
Habana

Memorial a
las Victimas
del Maine

Museo de
la Danza

Museo de los
Artes Decorativos

Nacional
de Cuba

Museo de Ciencias
Naturales Felipe Poey

Museo Montane
Antropologico

Museo
Abel
Santamaria

Julio Antonio
Mella Memorial

Museo
Napoleónico

Universidad
de la Habana

CENTRO

Necrópolis
de Colón

HABANA

Quinta de
los Molinos &
Museo Máximo
Gómez

Memorial Ernesto
"Che" Guevara

Museo
José Marti

PLAZA
DE LA
REVOLUCIÓN

Memorial José Marti

0   500 m

ACCOMMODATION

Calle 21 no. 4	F
Casa de Acelo Hernández Méndez	H
Casa de Aurora Ampudia	E
Casa de Dulce Maria Lopez Alcaron & Jesus Cordona	N
Casa de Enrique Oramas	K
Casa de Idania Lazo Rodríguez	
Casa de Mélida Jordán	M
Habana Libre	J
Hotel Nacional	G
Meliá Cohiba	A
Presidente	D
Riviera	B
St John's	I
Victoria	C

RESTAURANTS

1830	3	Gringo Viejo	18	La Torre	6
23 y 12	24	Hurón Azul	19	Toro	21
Los Amigos	10	Marakas	22	Yiyo's	8
Carmelo	1	Nacional C	9		
Casa de Adela	20	Nerei	5		
La Casona de 17		Pain de Paris	4		
Comedor de Aguiar	12	Palamares Bakery	23		
El Conejito	7	Pizza Nova	15		
Coppelia	17	El Recanto	14		
Decameron	2	La Roca	13		
Doña Clara	16	Sylvian	11		

the mid-nineteenth century to create a cool retreat from the blistering tropical sun. The small parks dotted throughout the area are also welcome oases, and some, like the **Parque John Lennon**, add quirky points of interest. Many of the magnificent late- and post-colonial buildings that line these streets – built in a mad medley of Rococo, Baroque and classical styles – have been converted into state offices and museums. Particularly noteworthy is the **Museo de los Artes Decorativos**, an exhausting collection of fine furniture and *objets d'art*. Other beautiful mansions retain their role as lavish but stricken homes, peeking through the leaves like ruined ghosts, and many now house more than one family: properties abandoned by wealthy owners during the Revolution in the 1960s were subsequently converted into multiple housing units, and in some cases the servants of the fleeing families moved in. Further west from the Malecón, dotted around Linea, Paseo and Avenida de los Presidentes, are several excellent galleries and cultural centres. Not to be missed is the **Casa de las Américas**, a slim and stylish Art Deco building that was set up to celebrate Pan

Americanism, which displays quality artworks from all over Latin America and hosts regular musical events.

Another attraction here – and of Vedado as a whole – is the threadbare but immensely personable and endearingly old-fashioned **cinemas** dotted throughout the area, with the names of the latest North American (and occasionally Cuban) films picked out in wonky and incomplete peg letters on billboards above the entrance.

La Rampa and around

Halfway along the Malecón's length is the twin-towered *Hotel Nacional* – near an artificial waterfall that doubles as a paddling pool for Havana juniors – marking the start of **La Rampa** (The Slope), the road into the centre of Vedado. Once the seedy pre-revolutionary home of Chinese theatres, casinos and pay-by-the-hour knocking shops, La Rampa is now lined with airline offices and official headquarters, its seamy side long gone (or at least well hidden).

Set on a precipice above the Taganana cave (see box, overleaf) and with a magnificent view of the ocean, the world-famous landmark **Hotel Nacional** is home to a princely tiled lobby and an elegant and airy colonnaded veranda looking out to sea across an expanse of well-tended lawn commandeered by tame guinea fowls. The perfect cinematic backdrop for a *mojito* cocktail, it was built in 1930 and quickly became a favourite with visiting luminaries – amongst them Ava Gardner, Winston Churchill, Josephine Baker and John Wayne – and since its refit in 1992 has added the likes of Naomi Campbell and Jack Nicholson to its clientele (see p.126 for accommodation details). The hotel is also famous for having played host to infamous US gangster Meyer Lansky, who ran a casino here in the 1950s, at the invitation of Batista himself.

Memorial a las víctimas del Maine

Just to the north of the *Hotel Nacional* stands the striking **Memorial a las víctimas del Maine**. It was erected by the US government in memory of 260 crew members of the US battleship *The Maine* which was blown up in Havana harbour on February 15, 1898, and so is studiously ignored by Cuban maps and guidebooks. *The Maine* had been despatched to Cuba in December 1897 to protect US interests during Cuba's war of independence with Spain. The incident did nothing to improve the relationship between the US and Spain, with both sides quick to assign blame to the other. The North American press used the opportunity to whip up jingoistic feeling against Spain, and a hastily concocted US enquiry pointed the finger at "unknown conspirators", leading ultimately to the Spanish–American War.

Modern interpretation has it that the US, keen to tighten control over Cuba's destiny, sabotaged its own ship as an excuse to enter the war, and indeed, navy officials have since admitted the explosion took place on board. Following the Revolution, crowds attacked the monument, toppling and destroying the heavy iron eagle that once perched on the top (the pieces are displayed in the Museo de la Ciudad). What remains is still impressive: above two marble Corinthian columns, great rusted cannons clad in iron chains are flanked by a dolorous, despairing mourner and solemn female figures standing almost to attention in star-spangled dresses, with stylized Art Deco griffins and sea monsters carved into the base. The present government has stamped its presence with the terse inscription: "To the victims of *The Maine* who were sacrificed by imperialist voraciousness in its zeal to seize the island of Cuba from February 1898 to 15 February 1961".

Taganana cave

You can enter the Taganana cave (Mon–Sat 9am–5pm; free) through the *Hotel Nacional* grounds, where a small display charts the history of the cave and its rocky outcrop. The cave was named after a character created by novelist Cirilo Villaverde whose story placed the fictional Indian Taganana there after seeking refuge from pursuing conquistadors. The natural cave and its vantage point overlooking the seafront were capitalized upon by the Spanish who built the Bateria de Santa Clara battery here in 1797 and then in 1895 positioned two cannons here for use during the Wars of Independence. Following the war, the battery was expanded and converted into military barracks, which remained until the 1930s when the area was earmarked for a showcase hotel. A final moment of glory for the cave came during the Missile Crisis in 1962 when Che Guevara and Castro decamped here with suitable military artillery in preparation for an air defence of the capital.

Museo Abel Santamaría

Tucked away just east of La Rampa on the corner of unassumingly residential Calle O and 25 is one of Havana's smallest but no less intriguing museums, the **Museo Abel Santamaría** (Mon–Fri 10am–5pm, Sat 10am–1.30pm; free). It was here in 1952 that Abel Santamaría, his sister Haydee Santamaría, Fidel Castro and others planned the attack on the Moncada barracks. Following the unsuccessful attack, Abel was captured and tortured to death upon Batista's orders. In tribute to him his apartment has been preserved as it was on his final days living there. The simply decorated living room and sparse kitchen have little to associate them with the ill-fated revolutionary, but the 1950s furnishings and fittings have an intrinsic interest, not least because they serve to illustrate to anyone familiar with current Cuban interiors how little advance in interior design there has been since this era.

Coppelia

In the middle of a vast park spanning a whole block of Calles 21 and 23 is Havana's mighty ice-cream emporium **Coppelia** (Tues–Sun 11am–11pm,

△ Coppelia

closed Mon), the flagship branch of this national chain. Looking like a giant space pod, with a circular white chamber atop a podium, the multi-chamber restaurant was built during the Revolution as an egalitarian eating place with prices within the reach of every Cuban. Serving over a thousand customers a day, it's hugely popular with Cubans, who consider the ice cream the equal of the finest Italian confections, regularly waiting in line for over an hour – though, contrary to its ethics, there is now a separate parlour to the left of the main entrance catering for those paying in hard currency. Cuban film buffs will recognize the park from the opening scenes of Tomás Gutiérrez Alea's seminal 1993 film, *Fresa y Chocolate*, which takes its name from the most popular and available flavours. To really appreciate Coppelia's space-age architecture go up to *La Torre* restaurant (see p.178) for a panoramic view.

Universidad de la Habana

Regal and magnificent, the **Universidad de la Habana** sits on the brow of the Aróstegui (or Pirotecnia) Hill, three blocks or so south of La Rampa, overlooking Centro Habana. Founded in 1728 by Dominican monks, the university originally educated Havana's white elite; blacks, Jews, Muslims and mixed-race peoples were all banned, though by an oversight surprising for the time, women weren't, and by 1899 one-seventh of its students were female. It counts among its alumni many of the country's famous political figures, including Cuban liberator José Martí, independence fighter Ignacio Agramonte, and Fidel Castro, who studied law here. Originally based in a convent in Habana Vieja, it was secularized in 1842 but did not move to its present site, a former Spanish army barracks, until 1902, spreading out across the grounds over the next forty years. Today, the university is an awesome collection of buildings, and home to some of the city's most unusual **museums**.

The rubbly pile of oversized grey and whitewashed concrete blocks near the foot of a sweeping stone staircase capped by twin observation points is actually the **Memorial a Julio Antonio Mella**, a modern tribute to this former student, political agitator and early member of the Communist Party, thought to have been murdered for his beliefs (see box, overleaf). Off to one side, a bust captures his likeness while the words on the main column are his: "To fight for social revolution in the Americas is not a utopia for fanatics and madmen. It is the next step in the advance of history." More conventional is the serene, Junoesque figure halfway up the stairs. Sculpted in bronze by Czechoslovak artist Mario Korbel, this symbol of wisdom presides over the steps with outspread arms upturned to the sky, while the bronze-panelled stone base features more studious and berobed women bearing symbolic globes and feathered quills. At the top of the stairs, beyond the lofty entrance chamber, lavishly feted with Corinthian columns, lies the Ignacio Agramonte courtyard, with a central lawn scattered with marble benches and bordered on four sides by grandiose faculty buildings.

The scene of countless student protests, including one led by Julio Antonio Mella in 1922, the university was long seen as a hotbed of youthful radicalism. Guns were stashed here during the Batista administration, when it was the only site where political meetings could take place unhindered. The present administration, however, keeps the university on a firm rein and firebrand protests are a thing of the past, though its politicized past is evoked in some quirky details scattered throughout the grounds. These include the original American tank captured during the civil war in 1958 and placed here by the Union of Young Communists as a tribute to youth lost during the struggle, and, opposite, an

Julio Antonio Mella, the student hero

Born in 1905 to an Irish mother and a Dominican father, charismatic, handsome Julio Antonio Mella was a leading light in the Cuban student movement. After a comfortable middle-class childhood, he enrolled in the Universidad de la Habana at the age of sixteen, and soon became one of the organizing forces behind the formation of the University Students' Federation (FEU), his rousing speeches stirring a generation of students to protest university corruption. His campaign against the appointment of incompetent and unqualified professors to well-paid posts through nepotism and political favours paid off, and in 1923 over a hundred hapless professors were dismissed. After graduation, his influence spread further and he became something of a national figure, famed for roaming Havana and giving lectures on Marxism to workers. In 1927, fearful that his outspoken diatribes against Machado's government had earned him serious enemies, he fled to Mexico to live in exile. His fears proved correct on January 10, 1929, when he was shot in the street in Mexico City while with his girlfriend, Italian photographer Tina Modotti. Although never proved, it was widely assumed that Machado was responsible.

"owl of wisdom" made of bits of shrapnel gleaned from various battle sites. Still a respected seat of learning, the university today has a rather serious air: earnest students sit on the lawn and steps in front of faculty buildings locked in quiet discussion, while inside a library-like hush reigns. With few leisure facilities available, student hipsters go elsewhere to relax, leaving the grounds to their geekier counterparts and to sightseers.

Museo de Ciencias Naturales Felipe Poey and Museo Montane Antropológico

To the left of the main entrance is the **Museo de Ciencias Naturales Felipe Poey** (Mon–Fri 9am–noon & 1–4pm; $1CUC), the most bewitching of all the university buildings, with a beautiful central atrium from which rises, as though from a marble swamp, a towering palm twisted with vines. Named after an eminent nineteenth-century naturalist, and with the musty atmosphere of a zoologist's laboratory, the dimly lit room holds an assortment of stuffed, preserved and pickled animals, its walls lined with the remains of sharks and reptiles, while a whale dangles from the ceiling. The highlight is the collection of Polymita snails' shells, delicately ringed in bands of egg-yolk yellow, black and white, while other notables are a (deceased) whistling duck, a stuffed armadillo and Felipe Poey's death mask, incongruously presented along with some of his personal papers. Parents and their offspring may wish to check out the children's corner and pet the stuffed duck, squirrel and iguana.

Those unmoved by the charms of taxidermy can press on up the right-hand staircase along the cloistered balcony to the **Museo Montane Antropológico** (Mon–Fri 9am–noon & 1–4pm; $1CUC), home to an extensive collection of pre-Columbian pottery and idols from Cuba and elsewhere. Though padded out with apparently indiscriminately selected pieces of earthenware bowls, the collection contains some excellently preserved artefacts, like the Peruvian Aztec pots adorned with alligator heads and the fierce stone figurine of the Maya god Quetzalcoatl, the plumed serpent, tightly wrapped in a distinctive clay coil design. Star attractions include a lignum vitae **Taíno tobacco idol** from Maisí in Guantánamo; roughly 60cm tall, the elongated, grimacing, drum-shaped idol with shell eyes is believed to have been a ceremonial mortar used to pulverize tobacco leaves. Also fascinating is the delicate reproduction of a Haitian two-pronged wooden **inhaler** carved with the face of a bird, which the Taíno high priest would use to snort hallucinogenic powder in the *Cohoba* ceremony, a religious ritual for communicating with the dead. These priests would also cure illness, possibly with the aid of a **vomiting stick**, such as the one on display made from manatee ribs, by inserting it into the throats of the afflicted to make them vomit up impurities of the soul. Although from different countries, the inhaler and vomiting stick correspond in shape and design and are thought to come from similar cultures. Finally, check out the stone axe found in Banes, Holguín, which is engraved with the stylized figure of Guabancex, a female deity governing the uncontrollable forces of nature, her long twisted arms wrapped around a small child.

Museo Napoleónico

Just behind the university on San Miguel no.1159, the **Museo Napoleónico** (T7/879-1460 Mon–Sat 9am–4.30pm, Sun 9am–12noon; $3CUC, $5CUC with guide) boasts an eclectic array of ephemera on the French emperor, spread over four storeys of a handsome nineteenth-century house. The collection was gathered at auction by Orestes Ferrara, an Italian ex-anarchist who became a colonel in the rebel army of 1898 and subsequently a politician in Cuba. Ranging from state portraits, *objets d'art* and exquisite furniture to military paraphernalia and sculpture, it should appeal to anyone with even a passing interest in the era.

Although crowded with eighteenth-century sketches of Voltaire, Rousseau and Diderot, the most fascinating item on the narrow staircase up to the **first floor** is Marie Antoinette's plaintive farewell note to her children, written in a shaky hand and marked with the date of her execution. The expansive first-floor chamber is awash with heavily engraved ornamental swords and bronze sabres, many belonging to Napoleon himself, and lined with stately oil portraits and large canvases depicting the Battle of Waterloo, the victory in Egypt and Napoleon's nemesis, the Duke of Wellington. The room is also filled with opulent furniture: a marble-topped sideboard with swan-shaped drawer handles laden with Sèvres china competes for attention with a hideous imperial carriage clock adorned with two golden Europeans borne along by bronze slaves. The best piece is a grandiose *guéridon* table designed after Napoleon's Egyptian campaign. Made of bronze, it's inlaid with fourteen Sèvres china miniatures of the general along with a larger picture of an ermine-clad Napoleon perched on a throne clutching a staff.

On the **second floor** there's more Sèvres china from the Napoleonic family treasure chest, along with portraits of his first wife Josephine and his fashionably attired daughters, and an extremely pompous, self-serving portrait by Pierre Alexander Tardieu, which has the little man dressed up as a Roman emperor. The best painting here is a large work by Jean-Georges Vibert which depicts Napoleon and entourage discussing his forthcoming coronation ceremony and using a set of miniature mannequins to represent the guests, with Napoleon sweeping aside the figures of the cardinals he no longer wishes to attend.

The **third floor** consists of re-creations of Napoleon's study and bedroom, with a sombre painting of his death above a bed laid with his personal bedspread; on a table sits his surprisingly smooth and wrinkle-free death mask. It's worth continuing on up to the fourth floor, less for the collection of books about the French Revolution, but more to step out on the **terraces**: the back one has a good view over Centro Habana's Capitolio and Calzada de Infanta, while the front one is simply gorgeous, with richly tiled walls and a floor decorated with shields.

Quinta de los Molinos and Museo Máximo Gómez

Heading south from the Museo Napoleónico, past the university stadium, the east side of Calle Zapata flanks the romantic remains of the **Quinta de los Molinos** tobacco mill estate (Tues–Sat 9am–5pm, Sun 9am–noon; $1 CUC). Although more could have been done with this once magnificent country house set in ramshackle overgrown grounds, it still abounds with faded charm and makes a pleasant, though low-key, diversion. The part of the villa open to the public is beautiful, with central doors opening into an airy, austere entrance room with graceful stained-glass *vitral* windows shedding slices of coloured light onto an unpolished stone floor, while leafy vines clamber out of terracotta pots and up the slender pillared arches. Built in 1836 to be the Spanish governor Capitán General Miguel de Tacón's summer residence, the elegant villa takes its name from the royal snuff mills, or *molinos*, which operated here in 1791. It is also celebrated as the site of the city's first aqueduct, the Zanja Real built in 1592, the remnants of which you can see behind the villa.

To the rear of the building is the somewhat superfluous **Museo Máximo Gómez** (no extra charge), dedicated to General Máximo Gómez, leader of the Liberation Army in the nineteenth-century Wars of Independence who moved here in 1899 after the first War of Independence. A motley collection of bric-a-brac spread around a pair of rooms includes photographs of the general himself, an old rug he once owned, plus a map of his campaigns and not much else of interest. The 1.5 square kilometres of **grounds** surrounding the house are altogether more rewarding to explore than the museum, full of faded charm with ponds brimming with lily pads, and, looming between the palm trees, stone statues with features melted by time. Benches are dotted around near the unruly wood of palms and ceiba trees to the left of the drive if you want to linger and listen to the musicians from a nearby school who rehearse in the grounds.

Plaza de la Revolución

At the southwest corner of the Quinta de los Molinos grounds, Avenida de Ranchos Boyeros starts at the intersection of Avenida Salvador Allende (also known as Carlos Tercero) and continues south for a kilometre to the **Plaza de la Revolución**. The plaza comes as a bit of a let-down at most times, revealing itself to be just a prosaic expanse of concrete bordered by policed government buildings and the headquarters of the Cuban Communist Party. It's much better to visit on May Day and other annual parade days, when legions of loyal Cubans, ferried in on state-organized buses from the *reparto* apartment blocks on the city outskirts, come to wave flags and listen to speeches at the foot of the Martí memorial. Tourists still flock here throughout the year to see the plaza's twin attractions: the Memorial Ernesto "Che" Guevara and the Memorial José Martí tower.

Memorial and Museo José Martí

Although widely seen as a symbol of the Revolution, the sleek, star-shaped **Memorial José Martí** had been in the pipeline since 1926 and was completed a year before the Revolution began. Its 139-metre marble super-steeple is even more impressive when you glance up to the seemingly tiny crown-like turret, constantly circled by a dark swirl of birds. Near the base sits a gigantic seventeen-metre sculpture of José Martí, the eloquent journalist, poet and independence fighter who missed his chance to be Cuba's first populist president by dying in his first ever battle against the Spanish on April 11, 1895. Carved from elephantine cubes of white marble, the immense monument captures Martí hunched forward in reflective pose.

Behind the statue, the stately ground floor of the tower houses the exhaustive **Museo José Martí** (Tues–Sat 10am–6pm; $3CUC, lookout $2CUC), which charts Martí's career mainly through letters and photographs, with an additional room dedicated to the achievements of the Revolution. The lavish entrance hall, its walls bedecked with green and gold mosaic interspersed with Martí's most evocative quotes, certainly befits a national hero and is the most impressive aspect of a museum that tends to stray off the point at times.

As many of Martí's more substantial artefacts are housed in his birthplace in Habana Vieja, much of what's on display in the first room is photographic, with several sepia prints of Martí at various stages of youth, curiously always wearing the same pensive, unsmiling expression. One of the most interesting exhibits is a reproduction of a Mexican mural, *Sueño de una tarde dominical en la Alameda Central* (*Dream of a Sunday Afternoon in Alameda Park*), by the Mexican artist Diego Rivera. It shows Martí standing in the Mexico City park next to Frida Kahlo, Rivera's soulmate and fellow artist, with the artist himself in front of them depicted as a boy; Martí's inclusion reflects Rivera's interest in Marxism and Pan-Americanism.

In the second room hang photographs of Martí in Spain, Mexico and North America along with an assortment of artillery, most notably Martí's six-shooter Colt revolver engraved with his name, and the Winchester he took with him into his only battle. The collection begins to falter in the third room, cluttered with numerous pre-construction plans of the tower and a large commemorative coin collection. But wade through these and the eminently missable video re-enactment of Martí's death and you'll be rewarded with plenty of atmospheric photos, including a vintage shot of the core revolutionary band, including Raul Castro, Haydee Santermaría and Celia Sánchez, standing beside a bust of Martí at the peak of Pico Turquino.

Never slow to trumpet the achievements of the Revolution, the state has pulled out the stops in the fourth, and arguably most interesting, part of the museum. Here a gallery of photographs and exhibits charts breakthroughs in Cuban medical research – such as for meningitis; the country's high standards in education, with a particular emphasis on schools in the most rural parts of the country; and achievements in the arts, including prima ballerina Alicia Alonso's frayed ballet shoes, worn to pieces when she danced *Giselle* at the Gran Teatro in 1962. Also on show are **Fidel Castro**'s most memorable photos: standing with the pope, embracing Nelson Mandela, and, famously, leaping to the ground from a tank at the Bay of Pigs. The most impressive photo captures one of Castro's myth-making moments: upon his triumphant arrival in Havana in the early days of the Revolution, he stood before the excited Habaneros to make his first speech when two doves released into the crowd circled and spontaneously landed upon his shoulders, endowing him with the universal symbols of peace and unity.

When you've finished in the museum, a lift here leads to the top floor to the highest **lookout point** in Havana – on a clear day you can see the low hills in the east and out as far as Miramar in the west. The room is divided into segments corresponding to the five spines of its star shape, so you can move around to take in five separate views, while a mosaic compass on the ground with distances from several capital cities lets you know how far you are from home.

Memorial Ernesto "Che" Guevara

Back on the ground, on the opposite side of the square to the north, the ultimate Cuban photo opportunity is presented by the **Memorial Ernesto "Che" Guevara**, a stylized steel frieze replica of Alberto "Korda" Gutierrez' famous photo of Guevara – the most widely recognized image of Guevara in existence. Taken during a speech on Calle 23 in 1960, the photo, with Guevara's messianic gaze fixed on some distant horizon and hair flowing out from beneath his army beret, embodies the unwavering, zealous spirit of the Revolution. It was only in 1967 after his capture and execution in Bolivia (for more on Guevara, see p.347), though, that the photo passed into iconography, immortalized on T-shirts and posters throughout the 1970s as an enduring symbol of rebellion. The sculpture that you see now was forged in 1993 from steel donated by the French government.

Over the past decade this image of Che has become the height of postmodern chic once again, appearing on bottles of beer and even modelled by Kate Moss in British *Vogue* in 1999. Though Che disapproved of the cult of personality, Cubans themselves (the government included) have not been slow to put him to good capitalist use, with street vendors and shops throughout Cuba making a quick buck from flogging Che T-shirts, keyrings, cartoon figurines, black berets and even CDs of soulful memorial ballads. The original photograph can be seen, along with many others, at the Museo Memorial al Che, in Santa Clara (see p.346).

Necrópolis de Colón

Five blocks northwest from Plaza de la Revolución along tree-lined Paseo, there's a worthwhile detour to the left at the Calle Zapata junction: the **Necrópolis de Colón** (daily 8am–5pm; $1CUC), one of the largest cemeteries in the Americas. With moribund foresight the necropolis was designed in 1868 to have space for well over a hundred years' worth of corpses, and its neatly numbered "streets", lined with grandiose tombstones and mausoleums and shaded by large trees, stretch out over five square kilometres. A tranquil refuge from the noise of the city, it is a fascinating place to visit – you can spend hours here seeking out the graves of the famous, including the parents of José Martí (he is buried in Santiago), celebrated novelist Alejo Carpentier and a host of revolutionary martyrs.

Originally a farm, the land was bought by the church and construction began in 1871, according to the design by Calixto Aureliano de Loira y Cardoso, a Spanish architect who won the job in a competition. He had little time to celebrate, however, having been struck by illness shortly after completing the project and dying at 33, a premature inhabitant of his own creation. His most magnificent achievement is the neo-Gothic entrance portal: a vision of overwrought piety, it comprises three arched gateways representing the Trinity, an excessive marble sculpture depicting Faith, Hope and Charity, and a plaque high above the central arch showing the Crucifixion.

The main avenue sweeps into the cemetery past tall Italian marble tombstones draped in lachrymose Madonnas and maidens, including a copy of Michelangelo's *Pietà*. Particularly noteworthy is the mausoleum, just behind the main avenue on Calle 1 y Calle D; draped with marble maidens depicting justice and innocence, it holds the remains of a group of medical students executed in 1871 on the charge of desecrating the tomb of a Spanish journalist. Also outstanding is the firemen's mausoleum on the main avenue, dedicated to those who died in a city fire in 1890. Encrusted with shields, garlands, flags and a finely worked cameo of each man who died, it features life-sized allegorical figures, including a pelican which symbolizes the self-sacrifice (the pelican traditionally fed its young from its own breast) of those who perished.

In the centre of the necropolis is the fanciful, Romanesque **octagonal chapel**, opened in 1886, which consists of three tiers, each iced in a frill of contrasting curlicues and crowned with a delicate cupola. Masses are held every day at 8am but the chapel is also open at varying times during the day. You should seize the chance to peek inside and admire the beautiful, luminous, German stained-glass windows and, towering above the altar, Cuban artist Miguel Melero's fresco *The Last Judgement*, which has Christ presiding over winged devils and other reprobates as they plummet to their peril.

Close to hand, at Calle 1 e/ F y G, always engulfed by a cornucopia of flowers and guarded by an attendant, the **tomb of Amelia Goyri de la Hoz** and her child is an arresting sight. A Havanan society woman, Goyri de la Hoz died in childbirth on May 3, 1901, and was buried with her child, who survived her by only a few minutes, placed at her feet. During a routine exhumation the following year, she was supposedly found to be cradling the child in her arms. The story spread immediately, Goyri de la Hoz was dubbed "La Milagrosa" (The Miracle Worker), and the event was attributed to the power of a mother's love working beyond the grave. Soon La Milagrosa was attributed with universal healing powers, and to this day supplicants queue round the block to have their wishes granted. A strict etiquette controls the ritual: to stand a chance of success you must first knock on the tombstone three times with the brass handles to alert the saint within, then cover the tomb with flowers before mentioning the wish and, finally, leave without turning your back.

In the southern half of the cemetery, marked by large plots of as yet unused land, veterans of the Revolution, including luminary figures Celia Sánchez, Fidel Castro's companion, and poet Nicolás Guillén, lie in an extensive and faintly austere pantheon house just off the main avenue. A little way behind this, those who accompanied Fidel Castro on the yacht *Granma* and were slain in the first revolutionary battle at Alegría de Pío repose in slightly more ornate style.

Parque Zoologico

Directly opposite the Víazul bus station on Avenida de la Independencia, about half a kilometre from the cemetery's southernmost corner, lies the **Parque Zoologico** (Tues–Sun 9.30am–5.30pm; $2CUC). Although recently renovated, the town zoo is still no sanctuary for animal lovers, with many beasts penned into inadequately small spaces. Allowed to roam free on an island surrounded by an artificial lake just inside the entrance, the zoo's three or four chimpanzees are amongst those few animals who enjoy a relatively high standard of living here. Climbing palm trees and gobbling bananas thrown into the pen at regular intervals by the keepers, they appear very happy. Similarly, a flock of flamingos with delicate black-tipped wings has plenty of space, as does a corral of crocodiles. However, a hyena and a dingo penned into a dirty, cramped space fare less well and they make a pitiful sight endlessly pacing the bare cage, while elsewhere a gibbon sits sullenly in a space that is little more than a concrete box. An assortment of other animals includes emus, kangaroos, rhinos and various rodents, none of whose habitats appears to be well maintained. An additional problem is that the paucity of signposts makes it difficult to know what species many of the huddled, furry shapes belong to. All that said, the ample walkways and tall mango, rubber and palm trees make it a pleasant enough place for a stroll – though not for the soft-hearted.

The rest of Vedado

North of the Necrópolis de Colón lies the rest of Vedado, quieter than the boisterous La Rampa area and more scenic than Plaza de la Revolución. To walk through these silent, suburban streets, once the exclusive reserve of the wealthy, is one of the richest pleasures Havana holds, the air scented with sweet mint bush and jasmine, and, at night, the stars, untainted by street lamps, forming an eerie ceiling above the swirl of ruined balconies and inky trees. No less attractive in the daytime, with few hustlers it is also one of the safest areas to stroll, and the added attraction of several museums will give extra purpose to a visit.

Parque John Lennon

Heading northeast from Necrópolis de Colón, take a short detour past the **Parque John Lennon** on the corner of Calle 17 y 6, so named for the sculpture, created in 2000, of the eponymous musician seated on one of the park benches. It's a pretty good likeness and more or less life-sized. Although Lennon never came to Cuba, the Beatles have always been wildly popular here, so much so that it's not uncommon to hear people claiming to have learnt English through listening to their songs. Perhaps proving his popularity, Lennon's trademark circular glasses have been prised off by souvenir hunters several times and now the sculpture is protected at night by an armed guard. That the state has sanctioned a rock musician in this manner is a sharp public departure from its position in the 1970s and 1980s when Western rock music was banned as it was seen as a corrupting influence. The government's new, more tolerant position was exemplified later in 2000 when the Manic Street Preachers became the first Western band to play in Cuba since the Revolution. Every year on December 8 – the anniversary of Lennon's death – there is a combination vigil and jamming session.

Museo de los Artes Decorativos

Housed in a mansion at no.502 Calle 17, a ten-minute walk east from Parque John Lennon, the beautifully maintained **Museo de los Artes Decorativos** (Tues–Sat 11am–7pm; $2CUC; $3CUC with guide, $3CUC extra with camera) contains one of the most dazzling collections of pre-revolutionary decorative arts in Cuba. Built towards the end of the 1920s, the house was the private estate of the Count and Countess of Revilia de Camargo, who fled Cuba in 1961, whereupon it was appropriated by the state as the ideal showcase for the nation's cultural treasures. With its regal marble staircase, glittering mirrors and high ceilings, it is a perfect backdrop for the sumptuous, if overwrought, collection of Meissen and Sèvres china, Chinese vases and *objets d'art*, and fine furniture – a tantalizing glimpse of Vedado's past grandeur. The rooms are divided according to period and style and each is crammed with such a dizzying display of exhibits that it becomes quite hard to appreciate each individual piece. Guides are knowledgeable and friendly but tend to bombard you with information, and with such a massive collection in so small a space you may feel more comfortable setting your own agenda and seeing the rooms unattended.

To the left of the grand entrance hall paved in marble, the Principal Salon, richly panelled in gold and cream, is full of expensive Rococo knick-knacks, like the pair of stylishly ugly eighteenth-century German dog-lions, while in the Chinese Room next door, exquisite silkscreens and porcelain compete for your attention with a lacquered table inlaid with mother-of-pearl branches and mandarin ducks. In the Neoclassical Room, an eighteenth-century mantelclock by Jean André Lepaufe, swarming with golden cherubs, takes over-the-top interior design to new heights, as do the faintly unnerving bronze male and female French candelabra by Claudio Michel Clodión. The Sèvres Room is more restrained, with a small but splendid display of rich royal-blue porcelain finely painted with pastoral scenes. Equally delicate is the Salon Boudoir with a battery of intricately painted fans, a prime tool in the flirting tactics of nineteenth-century ladies. Finally, the subtlety of the English Room's Wedgwood china and eighteenth-century Chippendale chairs goes somewhat unappreciated amongst the crowd of showier pieces, but it's still worth taking the time to examine these and the half-moon sideboard by Robert Adam, which boasts unusual painted panels.

Museo de la Danza

A block further east on Linea towards the Malecón will take you to the **Museo de la Danza** (Tues–Sat 11am–6.30pm; $2CUC). Charting the history of the ballet in Cuba, the Museum of Dance crams an immense amount of exhibits into a small colonial house. An encyclopedic effort has been made to include references to every famous ballerina regardless of any Cuban connection, with an embroidered cape worn by Anna Pavlova having a touch more excuse for inclusion than the Isadora Duncan memento – a single thread from the shawl she was wearing at the time of her fatal car accident. Some of the best exhibits are displayed in the museum's third room with some carefully executed preliminary sketches for costumes: look out for the ornate blue-and-gold designs for *La Belle Durmiente del Bosque* (*Sleeping Beauty*). The final rooms are devoted to Cuba's most famous prima ballerina, **Alicia Alonso**, and include elegant photographs of her on stage and a multitude of reverential portraits by Cuban artists. Her prettiest artefacts are kept until last, with the necklace and red tiara, various feathery stage costumes and the pointed diamante crown that she wore in *Swan Lake*, which will thrill anyone who's ever harboured balletic aspirations.

Casa de las Américas and around

Two blocks west on Linea, the road joins regal Avenida de Los Presidentes where, at the junction with Calle 3ra, you'll find the **Casa de las Américas**, housed in a slender, dove-grey Art Deco building inlaid with panes of deep blue glass. Previously a private university, it was established as a cultural institute – with its own publishing house, one of the first in the country – in 1959 by the revolutionary heroine Haydee Santermaría to promote the arts, history and politics of the Americas. Since then, its promotion and funding of visual artists, authors and musicians has been successful

△ Casa de las Américas

enough to command respect throughout the continent and to attract endorsement from such international literary figures as Gabriel García Márquez. Today it hosts regular conferences, concerts and talks and boasts two worthwhile galleries: the **Sala Contemporánea** (Mon–Fri 10am–5pm; free), showing modern Cuban pieces, and the **Galería Latinoamericana** (Mon–Thurs 10am–5pm, Fri 10am–noon; $2CUC), showing high-quality temporary exhibitions, usually of painting, from other Latin American countries.

Within view of Casa de las Américas on the Malecón is the aristocratic **Monumento General Calixto García**. Set in a walled podium, it's an elaborate tribute to the War of Independence general who led the campaign in Oriente, and shows him dynamically reining in his horse surrounded by friezes depicting his greatest escapades, and would warrant closer inspection were it not widely used as a public toilet.

US Special Interests Office and Plaza Anti-Imperialista

A few blocks back to the east down the Malecón is the **US Special Interests Office**, Calle Calzada y L (☎7/33-3531, ⓕ33-3700), the organization that has acted in lieu of a US embassy since diplomatic relations between Cuba and the US ended in 1961. Around the side of the building there are usually queues of hopeful Cubans waiting to apply for a US visa.

Almost obscuring the building is the **Plaza Anti-Imperialista**, a huge sweeping space under a series of metal suspension arches like the ribs of a giant carcass. Many of the supports are covered in plaques bearing the names and quotes of Cubans and non-Cubans who have supported the country's struggle for self-determination and independence over the last century or so. Also known as Plaza de la Dignidad, this open-air auditorium was hurriedly constructed in 2000 as a forum for Fidel's protestations and invective during the furore surrounding the flight to the US (and eventual return) of schoolboy Elián Gonzáles. Activity in the square continues to reflect the ongoing antipathy between Cuba and the US. In January 2006 North American diplomats began displaying messages about human rights on an electronic ticker tape on the side of the building facing the plaza. What the US termed an attempt to break Cuba's "information blockade" Fidel Castro denounced as a "gross provocation". Later that year the Cuban authorities retorted by erecting 138 black flags, each decorated with a white star facing the ticker tape. They are said to symbolize Cubans who have died as a result of violent acts against the country by unsympathetic regimes since the Revolution began in 1959. The flags, which are sometimes replaced with the national flag, are an impresively sombre sight – which also conveniently mask the messages from view.

Facing the Malecón, on the opposite side of the road to the west of the plaza, is a large billboard with a colourful, much-photographed cartoon depicting a Cuban revolutionary shouting across the ocean at an enraged Uncle Sam, "Mr Imperialists, we have absolutely no fear of you!" It's a long-standing poster campaign, which has more recently been joined by photomontage billboards condemning US foreign policy and the plight of the **Miami Five**, five Cuban nationals imprisoned in the US since 1998 on charges of espionage.

Miramar and the western suburbs

Larger than life, and replete with super-sleek, ice-white, Miami-style residences, flash new business developments, spanking new hotels and curvy Japanese cars streaking along wide avenues, **Miramar and the western suburbs** are

Havana's alter ego. Among the last suburbs to be developed before the Revolution, this is where the wealth was then concentrated, and it's slowly trickling back, with Miramar, at least, home to the city's growing clique of foreign investors and ambassadors.

Though the wonderful houses and embassies are good for a gawp, most visitors who venture over the river do so for the **entertainment**, particularly the famous *Tropicana* cabaret (see p.184) in Marianao on the borders of Almendares, and the area's swanky international **restaurants**, a welcome respite from pork, rice and beans. West of Miramar, the **Marina Hemingway** pulls in scores of yachties, and a couple of minor sights will help you spin out a pleasant day.

The area is divided into four main suburbs: oceanfront **Miramar**, reached from the Malecón via the tunnel under the Río Almendares; **La Sierra** to its immediate south; **Kohly** tucked underneath; and **Almendares** to the west; but you'll often hear the whole area referred to as **Playa**, and sometimes addresses are listed as such.

Museo del Ministerio del Interior

Roughly 4km from the mouth of the tunnel on Avendia 5ta is the **Museo del Ministerio del Interior** (Tues–Sat 9am–4pm; $2CUC, $3CUC with guide), the museum of the Cuban secret services. Housed in an airy Miramar mansion, much of the museum is devoted to charting the conflict between the secret services and alleged US attempts to undermine the Revolution. Many of the exhibits comprise billboards closely written in Spanish, so non-Spanish speakers will find considerably less of interest, though there is still enough here to warrant a quick spin around, should you be in the area.

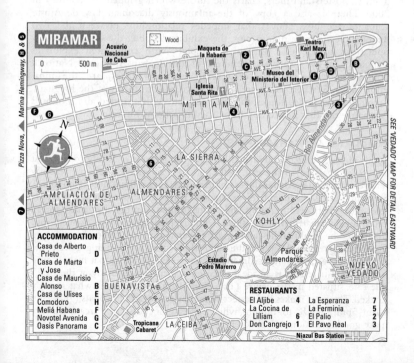

El Ley de Adjuste Cubano

Introduced in 1966, the Ley de Adjuste Cubano (or Cuban Adjustment Act) has been criticized as an unfair piece of US immigration policy. Making a different case for Cubans than for any other illegal immigrants attempting to gain entry to the US, the law states that any Cuban who reaches US soil is eligible to apply for permanent residency after they have been physically present in the country for more than one year. For many Cubans, crossing the Florida Straits on a makeshift boat is seen as an infinitely easier route to securing US citizenship than making a conventional application for one of the limited numbers of permanent residencies granted to Cubans each year.

During the Clinton administration, and as a somewhat tardy response to the events of the Mariel Boatlift in the 1980s, some of the more contentious parts of the law were addressed. The administration announced that Cubans interdicted at sea would not be brought to the US but to the base at Guantánamo instead. This became known as the "wet foot, dry foot" policy, whereby those Cubans who made it onto US soil were accepted into the country, while those who didn't were returned to Cuba. Though there has not been another exodus matching the size of Mariel, each year a significant number of Cubans do take this route to the States.

The first room, an assortment of guns and bloodstained shirts, is mostly devoted to charting the pre-1959 Revolution struggle. More illuminating, however, is the somewhat incongruous display devoted to **Elián Gonzáles** which, through information on public demonstrations and examples of T-shirts, posters and fliers, charts the furore which gripped the country in 2000. There is also a copy of the infamously draconian Ley de Ajuste Cubano (see box, above) that impedes relationships between the two nations. Of the remaining rooms, the exhibits detailing the ongoing covert operations of the CIA in Cuba, complete with confiscated explosives smuggled in by suspected members of the Cuban-American National Foundation and evidence of several terrorist attacks, are the most informative. Further rooms are less emotive with histories of the lifeguard, firefighter and police forces, the last complete with a stuffed and mounted Alsatian – the first police dog to be used in a homicide case.

Parque Almendares

South of 5ta Avenida, sandwiched between the suburbs of Kohly to the west and Nuevo Vedado to the east, is the city's largest green space, the recently renovated **Parque Almendares**, or Almond Park (Tues–Sun 10am–6pm). Straddling the Río Almendares, its tangle of palms, giant weeping figs and pine trees, along with wishing wells and white-painted iron benches, make for an exceptionally charmed space filled with dappled light. It's a popular spot frequented by local families, and *salsa* reverberates through the park emanating from speakers arrayed around the car park. As well as providing a welcome expanse of greenery, Parque Almendares has several activities that make it well worth a day-trip. This is an ideal place for a picnic, particularly as the park's sole café, situated in the centre (Tues–Sun 10am–6pm), is somewhat sparsely stocked. The river makes the perfect venue for *pedalos* and rowboats (Tues–Sun 10am–5pm, $5CUC for 30min), while a crazy-golf course, play area and aviary make good attractions for children.

Maqueta de la Habana and the Acuario Nacional de Cuba

Near to Avenida 5ta on Calle 28 e/ 1ra y 3ra in Miramar, the **Maqueta de la Habana** (Tues–Sat 9.30am–5.30pm; $3CUC) is a scale model of the whole of Havana, with tiny, Monopoly-house-sized replicas of every single building. Built as an aid to the offices of city planning and development, the city's various eras of construction are colour-coded: colonial buildings are brown, twentieth-century pre-revolutionary structures are ochre, post-revolutionary ones are cream. Some of the white buildings are monuments, while others represent buildings in the pipeline. With a scale of 1:1000 it is colossal, and much of the detail in the centre is difficult to see, although the unwieldy telescopes available for public use in the viewing gallery above do remedy this a little. You can see a similar model, the Maqueta de la Habana Vieja, in Habana Vieja (see p.136), although this one tends to draw smaller crowds, making viewing easier.

A good bet for a fun half-day is the recently refurbished **Acuario Nacional de Cuba**, a fifteen-minute walk west on Avenida 1ra (Tues–Sun 10am–6pm, $5CUC adults, $4CUC children; ☎7/202-5872 ⓦwww.acuarionacional.cu), featuring sea life indigenous to Cuban waters in tanks organized into categories of sea depth. In contrast to the Parque Zoologico, the aquarium is largely well maintained, with family favourites on display, including crocodiles, dolphins and sharks. Shows are laid on throughout the day with trained sea lions, dolphins and moray eels performing various stunts.

Marina Hemingway

Further west around 9km back along the coastal road, just beyond the small suburb of Jaimantias, is the **Marina Hemingway**, Avenida 5ta y Calle 248 Santa Fe (☎7/33-1149), which has little connection with Ernest Hemingway, despite the name. Several restaurants and a shopping centre make it a draw for visitors looking for a deluxe spot to relax, while yacht owners can dock in one of the four parallel canals, each 1km long, 15m deep and 6m wide. If you are docking you should notify your arrival through VHF channel 16 or 7462 SSB. As well as hosting annual billfish and marlin fishing tournaments, the marina is one of the only places in Havana to offer any diving, with a **dive centre** (☎7/33-1149) and two dive sites offshore. A recent addition is a huge, child-friendly pool. If interested in heading out here, the marina is about a fifteen-minute, $10–15CUC taxi ride from Vedado.

Eating

Although not a city particularly famed for its cuisine, Havana offers the most varied eating scene in Cuba, with a reasonable supply of well-priced international and local **restaurants**, although their settings are often more notable than the food: dining in a high-rise tower restaurant with panoramic city views or in one of the quirky charismatic eateries typical to the city often compensates for the somewhat staid and repetitive menus. Foodwise, the best restaurants tend to be in Miramar and the western suburbs, where you'll find imaginative, fairly sophisticated menus as well as attentive service. Numerous *paladares*, mostly concentrated around Habana Vieja and Vedado, dish up good-value portions of *comida criolla* – and the competition between them ensures good quality. As

Breakfast venues

Cafeteria La Rampa *Hotel Habana Libre*, Calle 23 esq. L, Vedado. A good choice of breakfast platters in this US-style diner, from traditional Cuban, featuring pork and rice, to the full American breakfast for $10CUC. Breakfast served all day.

Restaurante Prado *Hotel Park View*, Colón esq. Morro, Habana Vieja. Breakfast with views all the way over to Vedado from this seventh-floor hotel restaurant. When there are a sufficient number of hotel guests a breakfast buffet is laid on here, available to non-guests for $5CUC per person. Breakfast served 7–10am.

La Veranda *Hotel Nacional*, Calle O esq. 21, Vedado. The buffet breakfast in the basement of this fabulous hotel is unbeatable for sheer scale and choice, with everything you would hope to see in a classic English or American breakfast plus loads of extras including cereal, fruit, sweets and bread. All-you-can-eat for $13CUC. Breakfast served 7–10am.

Los Vitrales *Casa del Científico*, Paseo del Prado no.212 esq. Trocadero, Habana Vieja. Basic, well-priced breakfasts served 7–10am on a balcony room overlooking the Prado.

might be expected, Havana's *paladares* are the best in the country, their inventive menus, professional service and congenial surrounds meaning they often outstrip even the best state restaurants in offering value for money.

There are numerous **ethnic** restaurants in Havana; the most common are Chinese, Italian and Spanish, though you'll also find Turkish and French cuisine represented. Of these, Italian tends to be the most authentically reproduced, particularly in some of the plushest hotels in Miramar. Every major hotel usually has at least two quality restaurants, and although most are much the same, they offer dependably edible meals.

Vegetarians will find decent but predictable choices (pizza and omelettes featuring heavily) at most places, although the city is now benefiting from several well-equipped vegetarian restaurants. Vegans, however, should resign themselves largely to a diet of salad and fries. On the whole, it's best to stick to the hotels or your *casa particular* for **breakfast**, as elsewhere the choice is a bit patchy; some are of course better than others and more used to receiving non-hotel guests (see box, above). The best option for **lunch** is to grab a snack from one of the **street stalls** dotted around Centro Habana and Vedado, which sell tasty fritters and pizza slices for just a few pesos. Otherwise, most state restaurants and *paladares* operate from about noon to midnight (though a few are open only in the evening), with those in the main tourist centres offering meals from about $5–8CUC. Bear in mind that both, particularly *paladares*, take a fairly relaxed stance on opening hours and it's not unusual to find them closed for an impromptu reason.

Unfortunately, **overcharging** is rife, so to avoid this, always ask to see a menu that has prices listed alongside the dishes. *Paladares*, in particular, are prone to adjusting their prices according to how much proprietors think you can afford, although it's not an unheard-of practice in state restaurants as well. Additionally, watch out for touts who will try to guide you to a restaurant and then collar a commission from the owners, which will be passed on to your bill.

Habana Vieja and Habana del Este

State restaurants

Al Medina Oficios no.12 e/ Obispo y Obrapía ☎7/867-1041. The only Lebanese restaurant in the city, though main dishes such as Pollo Musukán and Samac Libanés sound more Middle Eastern than they taste. More unique are the mixed meze combinations ($10CUC and $15CUC), which include falafel, fatoush, tabbouleh and less-than-authentic hummus.

You can dine inside, where there's a wooden-beam ceiling, brick archways and glass lanterns, or in a canopied courtyard. Daily noon–midnight.

El Baturro Ave. de Bélgica e/ Merced y Jesús María ☎7/860-9078. A tavern restaurant near the train station, with a Spanish look and Cuban food. Doubtless you will be offered the three-course set meals of beef, chicken, shrimp or lobster with drinks and side dishes; while these are recommended and reasonable value ($15–23CUC), they cost more than a meal from the standard menu, which you may be told doesn't exist. This is the best place for lunch and escaping the heat on a tour of southern Habana Vieja.

La Bodeguita del Medio Empedrado e/ San Ignacio y Cuba ☎7/867-1374 & 866-8857. With its Ernest Hemingway associations, this restaurant is as touristy as they come. However, the labyrinthine network of rooms and cubbyholes, vibrant atmosphere and walls caked in scribbled messages and photos of the restaurant's rich and famous past customers make it a must-visit. The food comes in a distinct second but it isn't bad and it's better value than the bar selection (see p.181), with typical creole pork, beef and seafood dishes and one or two less typical offerings, like swordfish, all for between $9CUC and $16CUC.

Cabaña Cuba no.12 esq. Peña Pobre ☎7/860-5670. One of the few restaurants anywhere near La Punta, at the northern tip of Habana Vieja, this is a sightseeing pitstop offering simple $5CUC set-meals of grilled pork and chicken in its cheaper upstairs section where a window seat affords pleasant views over to the fortifications on the other side of the bay.

Café del Oriente Oficios no.112 esq. Amargura, Plaza de San Francisco ☎7/860-6686. A ritzy, high-class restaurant where the bow-tied waiters serve delicacies like deep-fried frog's legs, calf's brain and thermidor lobster for up to $30CUC a main dish. The lunchtime menu has cheaper, more familiar dishes like pasta and chicken, but the Orient Express-style decor, live piano and 1930s aristocratic ambience make this place ideal for a late-night dinner.

Café Taberna Mercaderes esq. Brasil (Teniente Rey) ☎7/861-1637. Traditional Cuban food featuring set-meals (such as a mixed seafood grill with a drink, salad, side orders and dessert) for between $12CUC and $20CUC. A seven-piece in-house band plays their trademark 1950s Beny Moré numbers, making this one of the best and loudest venues for music while you eat.

Café El Mercurio Plaza de San Francisco ☎7/860-6188. The comfy sofa-style seats at some of the tables and the rich tasting specials make this a good option for the tired and hungry. There's

beefsteak in mushroom and chocolate sauce or lobster and salmon in cream, but also more familiar seafood dishes like the seafood paella. Falls short of the formal restaurant it would seemingly like to be, partly due to the office-building location, and works better in the daytime.

Castillo de Farnés Ave. de Bélgica esq. Obrapía ☎7/867-1030. Low-priced, humble Cuban-Spanish restaurant tucked away behind a busy bar offering Cuban standards, all for between $3.50CUC and $7.50CUC. There's also paella, chorizo and Chateaubriand for $12CUC and lobster for $14CUC.

La Dominica O'Reilly esq. Mercaderes ☎7/860-2918. The quality and selection of pasta dishes is better here than at most other Italian restaurants in the area. The pizzas are generously topped and there's a number of reasonable squid and shrimp choices – all reflected in the higher-than-average prices. Eat in the polished, chandeliered interior or out on the informal pavement café where the lively in-house band *salsa* it up.

El Floridita Ave. de Bélgica (Monserrate) esq. Obispo ☎7/867-1300 & 867-1301. Expensive seafood is served in one of the old city's most formal and exclusive restaurants, a Hemingway heritage site. A velvet-curtain doorway leads in from the equally famous bar (see p.181) to an elegant circular dining area with two majestic central marble pillars.

Hanoi Brasil esq. Bernaza ☎7/867-1029. Dishes don't come much cheaper around here, with fish and meat set-meals for $3CUC, half a roast chicken for $4CUC, lobster for $12CUC and side orders all priced in cents. The supposed Vietnamese theme starts and ends with the restaurant's name, however. Daily noon–11pm.

Jardín del Eden *Hotel Raquel*, Amargura esq. San Ignacio ☎7/860-8280. Not all of the Jewish cuisine tastes authentic, but this restaurant, in an opulent hotel lobby, is still a welcome break from the regular local fare. Starters include beetroot soup, amateurish hummus and Milanese eggplant, while Hungarian goulash, fried fish in matzah breadcrumbs and shashliks feature among the main dishes, which average around $12CUC. The comfy seating is set under a sculpted ceiling and surrounded by Romanesque marble columns.

El Mesón de la Flota Mercaderes e/ Amargura y Brasil (Teniente Rey) ☎7/863-3838. Spanish-Cuban cuisine in a tavern-type restaurant where a flamenco group performs nightly on a central stage. There's a tasty selection of cheap tapas, including tortilla, fried chickpeas and squid, which double up as starters for the mostly seafood and kebab main dishes.

La Paella *Hostal Valencia*, Oficios no.53 esq. Obrapía ⏀ 7/867-1037. It's hard to believe that the house special here has won a string of international awards, even if it was a few years ago, but the paella is nonetheless about as tasty and authentic as it gets in Cuba. The colourful, farmhouse-influenced, picture- and plate-covered dining room has lots of character and is a large part of the draw. Main dishes cost between $8CUC and $28CUC.

El Patio Plaza de la Catedral ⏀ 7/867-1034. The serenity of the setting, in a courtyard of a leafy eighteenth-century mansion, goes a long way to justifying the above-average prices, as does the excellent selection of main dishes, with an emphasis on seafood, set vegetarian meals and plenty of extras.

Roof Garden Torre del Oro *Hotel Sevilla*, Trocadero no.55 e/ Paseo del Prado y Agramonte ⏀ 7/860-8560. The emphasis here is high-class dining, but the pseudo-French cooking, though well above average, takes a back seat to the setting: a cavernous, split-level, balustraded hall with marble floors, an intricately painted, coffered ceiling and towering windows offering superb views across the city. Dishes includes lobster stewed in rum, sirloin steak, rabbit and some fine fish dishes. Daily 7–10am & 7–10pm.

Santo Angel Brasil esq. San Ignacio, Plaza Vieja ⏀ 7/861-1626. This upmarket yet welcoming restaurant strays from the norm by adding spices, sauces and trimmings to dishes, serving curried shrimp, pork *tostadas* in citrus fruit juices and tuna salad with raisin and ginger vinaigrette. Has both formal dining rooms and leisurely outdoor areas. Main dishes are $8CUC and above.

El Templete Ave. Carlos Manuel de Céspedes (Ave. del Puerto) no.12–14 esq. Narciso López ⏀ 7/860-8280. The gourmet seafood at this roadside, harbourfront restaurant is the finest and tastiest in Habana Vieja, thanks in large part to the Basque head chef. From delicious salads and starters like octopus *a la gallega* and chard-filled crepes, to mouth-watering mains like eel *a la vasca* and red snapper in green sauce and sumptuous desserts like brownies with caramelized bananas and profiteroles in hot chocolate sauce, almost everything on the menu stands out and delivers. Main dishes start at $8CUC.

Agromercados, supermarkets and food shops

Farmers who have supplied their government quota are allowed to sell their surplus produce in *agromercados* (farmers' markets), where everything is fresh and you generally find more variety than you do in hotels and restaurants. The agros all sell in pesos and so are fantastically cheap – a pound of tomatoes will only set you back around 6 pesos, while oranges go for 2 pesos each. All the large agros have a Cadeca on hand where you can change convertible pesos into national currency. Make sure you take a plastic bag in which to carry your goodies as these are never provided – though you may find someone selling them for a peso each. Below are some of the more notable Havana markets not detailed elsewhere as well as the best supermarkets and shops for food:

Calle 19 y A. Vedado. Closed Monday. The prettiest of Havana's agros, this picturesque market sells meat, flowers, honey and dry goods like rice and beans alongside heaps of fresh fruit and vegetables.

J y 21. Vedado. Small daily market selling fruit and vegetables. There's not a huge choice, but basics like salad ingredients, squash and potatoes are always available.

Mercado Agropecuario Egido Av de Bélgica, e/ Corrales y Apodaca, Habana Vieja. Daily. This is the daddy of markets – a huge indoor space selling fruit and vegetables, spices, honey, rice, beans and meat as well as a few household goods like soap and razor blades.

Mercado Betania Amargura esq. San Ignacio, Habana Vieja. One of the city's only health-food shops keeps a threadbare stock of cereals, lentils, beans, coffee, tea and preservative-free jams.

Supermaercado 70 Ave. 3ra e/ 66 y 70, Miramar. The biggest supermarket in Havana but still surprisingly low on variety. There's a fresh meat counter and a better-than-average selection of dairy products.

Tulipán Ave. Tulipán y Ave de la Independencia. Large, daily open-air market selling mountains of fresh fruit and vegetables as well as other staples like rice and beans.

La Torre de Marfil Mercaderes e/ Obispo y Obrapía ☎ 7/867-1038. The only Chinese restaurant of note in Habana Vieja, with an indoor pagoda and Chinese lanterns throughout. The inexpensive menu is heavy on large portions of chow mein and chop suey, but there are also soups, wonton, and Cuban-influenced meat dishes.

La Zaragozana Ave. de Bélgica no.352 e/ Obispo y Obrapía ☎ 7/867-1040. Havana's oldest restaurant, established in 1830, was completely renovated in 2007. The mix of Spanish and Cuban cuisines here is above average in both quality and price.

Paladares

Doña Blanquita Paseo del Prado no.158 e/ Colón y Refugio. Pricey *paladar* in a roomy first-floor apartment with characterful interior arches and a wide selection of *comida criolla* dishes, particularly pork and chicken.

La Julia O'Reilly no.506a e/ Bernaza y Villegas ☎ 7/862-7438. Top-quality cooking and flavourful *comida criolla* are the main attractions of this homely little place, which has been here for years and has pork dishes down to an art. Main courses are between $8CUC and $10CUC.

La Moneda Cubana San Ignacio no.77 e/ O'Reilly y Empedrado ☎ 7/867-3852. This tiny spot near the cathedral, so narrow it almost spills onto the street, offers four set meals, each around the $10CUC mark and all with congrí, salad, fried bananas and bread. Choose from ham, pork steak, omelette or fish while you admire the walls plastered with banknotes and coins from around the world.

La Mulata del Sabor Sol no.153 e/ Cuba y San Ignacio. The decent set meals offered here, all classic Cuban combinations, include ham or liver as the main dish and, unusually, there's a vegetarian option and a wide range of egg-based courses. The bizarre and eclectic selection of ornaments and pictures reflects the effusive character of the sociable owner.

Centro Habana

State restaurants

A Prado y Neptuno Paseo de Martí (El Prado) esq. Neptuno ☎ 7/860-9636. This happening joint is always buzzing with punters and is where to come for some of the best, most bona fide pizzas in the city. There's a good selection on the menu with plenty of pasta and seafood, but the pizzas are the sensible choice here. Well suited to large, noisy groups.

Casa de Castilla Neptuno no.519 e/ Camapanario y Lealtad ☎ 7/862-5482. Set well back from the entrance, what looks like a private club is in fact one of the cheapest places worth eating at in Centro Habana. This is way off the tourist circuit in terms of both character and location. but with fresh and well-prepared *comida criolla* main dishes starting at $1.70CUC, it's worth seeking out. Tues–Sun noon–10.30pm.

Chan Li Po Campanario e/ San Martín (San José) y Zanja. The wonderfully cheap food here, in what appears to be a Chinese restaurant, is a bizarre mix of Italian and Cuban cuisine with a few chop suey dishes thrown in. Huge pizzas for $4CUC or less, Cuban-style pork, chicken and shrimp dishes for no more than $5CUC and lobster for only $7.50CUC. Usually buzzing with locals, the service is almost deliberately frantic.

Los Dos Dragones Dragones no.311 altos e/ Rayo y San Nicolás, Barrio Chino ☎ 7/862-0909. The best restaurant in Chinatown, fantastically cheap and popular with Cubans. The food is on the heavy side, the meat-ladened fried rice a meal in itself and the Tin Pan Chicken enough to feed a small family. To find *Los Dos Dragones*, look for the Sociedad Chung Shan sign hanging above the easy-to-miss street entrance, leading up a staircase to a dressed-up yet workaday eating hall.

Paladares

Amistad de Lanzarote Amistad no.211 e/ Neptuno y San Miguel ☎ 7/863-6172. Jumbo helpings of *comida criolla* where all the main dishes come with fried banana, *arroz moro* and salad and the chef has a penchant for covering things in breadcrumbs. The decoration is simple and has an unusually subtle feel.

Asahi Lealtad no.364 e/ San Miguel y San Rafael ☎ 7/878-7194. Buried in the thick of Centro Habana this simple, off-the-beaten-track, reliable front-room *paladar* has a thick photo-album menu full of all sorts of chicken, pork, fish and beef dishes, many of them covered in breadcrumbs, and all served up with healthy portions of *congrí* and enough *tostones* to double your weight. Attracts a local neighbourhood crowd as well as tourists staying at nearby *casas particulares*.

La Guarida Concordia no.418 e/ Gervasio y Escobar ☎ 7/862-4940 or 866-9047. This unbeatable *paladar* is the only one in the city with an international reputation and worth every penny of its considerably higher prices. The meat and fish menu breaks with all the national norms, and the dishes – like rabbit lasagna, salmon in a spring onion sauce with bacon and sugar-cane tuna glazed with coconut – brim with flavour and originality. Set in the aged apartment building where the acclaimed *Fresa y Chocolate* was filmed, the decor is eye-catchingly eclectic and the moody ambience in the three characterful rooms perfect for a long-drawn-out meal. Reservations are essential and a meal here unmissable.

Torreson Malecón no.27 e/ Prado y Cárcel, Centro Habana ℡7/861-7476. Chicken, pork and fish dishes for average prices in a basic balcony spot overlooking the seafront with a good view of El Morro.

Vedado

State restaurants and cafés

1830 Malecón no.1252 esqCalle 20 ℡7/55-3090. A sumptuous colonial house complete with antique furniture, chandeliers and an expansive patio. The food lives up to the surrounds with well-prepared choices including duck in orange sauce, chicken breast with honey and lemon sauce. Cuban dishes like *ropa vieja* are also superb and at between $7CUC and $12CUC well worth the splurge. If the service were not so lamentable, this would be one of Havana's finest. Open daily noon–midnight.

23 y 12 Calle 23 esq. 12. Peso restaurant with mostly decent Cuban fare. A good, cheap option for food, it's actually better for the bar scene, and the open-air seating at the front makes a good place to people-watch. The bar is purportedly 24hr.

Carmelo Calzada e/ D y E ℡7/832-4495. You can choose among a range of well-prepared dishes at this excellent vegetarian restaurant, including soya lasagna, croquettas, pilaf and various salads. Dishes like steamed okra and fried aubergine make a welcome change from run-of-the-mill tomato and cucumber salad. Brightly lit and very clean, the only drawback here is the habitual overcharging. Dishes are priced individually and a meal for two with three or four dishes should come to around $7CUC. Open daily noon–10pm.

La Casona de 17 Calle 17 no.60 e/ M y N. Although this restaurant serves fairly average food at rather high prices, dishes like barbecued beef and fries ($9CUC), as well as their house specialty, a substantial paella, are dependable options. A worthier option is the grill and snack bar built alongside.

Comedor de Aguiar *Hotel Nacional*, Calle O esq. 21. Regal à la carte restaurant serving suitably toothsome dishes, including lobster ($35CUC) and fresh fish ($15CUC), and mouthwatering desserts like profiteroles. One of two restaurants in the hotel (see below for the other, *Nacional*).

El Conejito Calle 17 esq. M ℡7/832-4671. Quirky, moderately priced restaurant with mock-Tudor panelling, staff inexplicably costumed in Teutonic regalia, live piano music and a house speciality of

rabbit (a supposed favourite of Fidel), prepared in several ways. Rabbit in burgundy wine is particularly good. Mon–Sun 12noon–11pm.

Coppelia Calle 23 esq. L. Havana's massive ice-cream emporium contains several peso-paying cafés and a convertible-peso open-air area, serving rich and creamy sundaes in a constantly changing menu of exotic flavours like coconut, mango and guava. Closed Mon.

Marakas Calle O e/ 23 y 25 ℡7/ 833-3740. Clean and friendly pizza parlour, close to La Rampa, with shiny floors and pistachio-coloured chairs. Large pizzas for around $6CUC make this good value.

Nacional *Hotel Nacional*, Calle O esq. 21. The all-you-can-eat buffet restaurant in the hotel basement is one of Havana's best feeds, with an extensive range of fish and meat and a welcome array of green vegetables.

Pain de Paris Linea e/Paseo y A. Heavenly cakes, ice cream and bread, plus buttery croissants, put this little café top of the list for snacks and breakfast. Plus it's open 24hr.

Palamares Bakery Calle 25 e/ O y Infanta. Just the place for tea and cakes, with a small seating area and a large and tempting selection of pastries and savoury breads, most for less than $1CUC.

El Rincón del Cine *Hotel Nacional*, Calle O esq. 21. Handy snack bar in the hotel basement serving excellent meaty hamburgers and creamy, thick milkshakes. It's also a good place for breakfast. Open 24hr.

La Roca Calle 21 esq. M ℡7/33-4501. This smart though over-air-conditioned restaurant is a popular spot for Cubans splashing out on Sun dinner of mediocre pasta and fish dishes. The video screen ensures a fairly boisterous atmosphere. Daily noon–midnight.

Sylvian Calle 21 e/ M y N. An excellent bakery with a plentiful supply of custard-filled éclairs – a snip at 20¢ – *senoritas*, biscuits as well as packets of crackers.

La Torre Calle 17 no.55 Edificio Focsa piso 36. Mesmerizing views from the city's second-tallest building are matched by the excellent French menu at this stylish restaurant. Definitely worth splashing out $40CUC or so to dine on foie gras, fillet of beef with rosemary, shrimps caramelized in honey, and profiteroles.

Paladares

Los Amigos Calle M no.253 e/19 y 21 ℡7/830-0880. Tasty lunchtime choices include rice and beans or *ajaco* stew and possibly the best home-made chips in Havana. The two dining rooms here are always busy so reservations are recommended (though you can wait on the patio outside if you prefer).

Casa de Adela Calle F no.503 e/ 23 y 21 ☎7/832-3776. Filled with plants, cooing birds, ethnic artefacts and the strains of Edith Piaf, this gem of a restaurant has a throwback bohemian feel. There's no menu here – instead, you pay $25CUC per person for a large selection of taster dishes, including delicious *chorizo* with coconut, meatballs, and *malanga* fritters with peanuts. Reservations essential. Open 6pm–midnight; closed Sun.

Decameron Linea, no.753 e/ Paseo y Calle 2 ☎7/832-2444. Decor and ambience are inspired and low-key, with pendulum clocks lining the walls, soft lighting, cane-backed chairs and starched linen. A mix of Italian, Cuban and European food contributes to the cosmopolitan air. The giant pizzas are possibly the largest in town, the pasta is nicely al dente and there's a decent attempt at tuna *nicoise*. Strong and sweet *mojitos*, plus attentive service, gild the lily. Open daily noon–midnight.

Doña Clara Calle 21 no.107 e/ L y N. One of the city's best stalls for lunch snacks at rock-bottom prices. Ice-cold soft drinks, *papas rellenas* and *guava* pies all available.

Gringo Viejo Calle 21 no.454 e/ E y F ☎7/831-1946. A bar area to wait at, walls lined with bottles and glasses plus a tiled floor all combine to give this place the feel of a small bistro. This professionally run establishment serves some French and Spanish dishes with a Cuban twist including *chorizo*, chicken casserole cooked with red wine and bacon, and *pollo aceitunado* (chicken with olives). The *ropa vieja* stew is also tasty. Open daily noon–midnight.

Hurón Azul Humbolt no.153 esq. P ☎7/879-1691. An intimate spot with perhaps the best food in Vedado. Starters include perfectly cooked *escovitch* fish, *maiz* fritters and pâté, while mains range from lamb with mushrooms to *cerdo gruñon* pork with plantains and cheese sauce, the house speciality. Excellent service and a good wine list complete the picture. Open daily noon–midnight daily.

Nerei Calle 19 esq. L ☎7/832-7860. Elegant mid-range spot where you can dine alfresco on pork cooked in garlic, grilled fish or fried chicken, all served with yucca, fried banana and salad. Prices are higher than usual at this *paladar* (dinner for two costs around $35CUC); watch for overcharging. Open daily 1pm–midnight.

El Recanto Calle 17 no.957 e/ 8 y 10 ☎7/30-43-96. Part of a Cuban experience that is fast disappearing, this is secret Cuba at its surreal best.

Gaining access feels like being admitted to a 1920s American speakeasy. Climb the crumbling stairs, then take the long gloomy corridor through the house and then out onto a courtyard where a canopied dining area is festooned with empty rum bottles swaying in the breeze. The food is tasty with a rich selection of pork and chicken dishes accompanied by yucca, salad and fried green bananas all served by the surliest maître d' possible. Closed Wed.

Miramar and the western suburbs

State restaurants

El Aljibe Ave 7ma e/24 y 26 Miramar ☎7/24-1583. In common with many of the Miramar restaurants, *El Aljibe* is a place to head for a touch of luxury. The food pulls no surprises, but it is well prepared and tasty. House specialities include the beef *brocheta* or kebab and chicken, and there's plenty of it. All this and an ambient open-air setting make it a must.

Don Cangrejo Ave 1ra e/16 y 18 Miramar ☎7/204-4169. Owned by the Fisheries Ministry, this plush seafood restaurant is every bit as good as it promises to be. Start with the crab bisque or grilled shrimp before choosing a fresh lobster from the pit in the terrace, crab claws or filet mignon. A bar well stocked with imported liquor and a wine store with a decent selection, two private dining rooms and a humidor add to the general air of luxury.

La Ferminia 5ta Ave. no.18207 esq. 184, Miramar ☎7/33-6555. One of Havana's swankiest restaurants, with a strict dress code and serving Cuban and international food, like well-prepared spaghetti bolognese and juicy steaks, for suitably inflated prices.

El Pavo Real Calle 7ma no.205 esq. 2, Miramar. Elegant, upmarket restaurant in an Asian-themed folly serving tasty, well-cooked Chinese food, including excellent vegetable chop suey and honeyed shrimp.

Pizza Nova Marina Hemingway ☎7/204-6969. A good place to satisfy a craving for well-prepared thin-crust pizza. The view across the marina is a bonus.

Paladares

La Cocina de Lilliam Calle 48 no.11311 e/ 13 y 15 ☎7/209-5514. Ex-pats and ex-presidents (check out Jimmy Carter's thank you letter in the menu) patronize this discreet and luxurious restaurant where tables set in a beautiful garden are hidden behind high electronic gates. The food is very good, with the *malanga* fritters, chicken crepes and *ropa vieja* particular standouts. Expect to pay around $70CUC for dinner for two. Open noon–3pm, 7–10pm; closed Sat.

La Esperanza Calle no.105 e/ 1ra y 3ra ☎7/202-4361.The owner of this fabulous restaurant has created a 1930s homage to the house's previous owner, the eponymous Esperanza. The creative menu is expertly prepared and offers dishes like chicken in soy and ginger sauce, fresh fish and smoothly prepared cocktails. Prices are around $30CUC a head. Open 7–11pm; closed Sun. Reservations essential.

La Fontana Calle 46 no.305 esq. 3ra ☎7/202-8337. A lively restaurant with a serenading trio of musicians; equally popular with the Cuban bohemian set and foreigners. The food is almost as good as the atmosphere, with large portions of grilled marlin and steak on the menu. Open daily noon–midnight.

El Palio Ave 1ra esq. 21, Miramar. Extremely pleasant open-air *paladar* offering some unusual dishes cooked to a fairly high standard. Steer clear of the pasta and choose from *pescado Walesca*, fish simmered with herbs, *pescado Florida*, fish in orange sauce, or, best of all, the flavoursome chargrilled pork.

Drinking, nightlife and entertainment

A typical **night out** in Havana is a giddy whirl of thumping *salsa* or soulful *boleros*, well oiled with rum and often a chunky bill attached for you and all your newly acquired Cuban friends. What Cuba does best is **live music**, so you should definitely try to catch at least one of the excellent *salsa*, jazz or *son* groups like Paulo FG, Azucar Negra and La Barriada which regularly do the rounds of the best-known clubs. You can pick up information on their gig dates at the *Hotel Nacional*'s information desk or in the free monthly listings booklet *Bienvenidos*, which also lists the latest goings-on at night-time venues around the city. It's worth keeping an eye on the big Vedado hotels, which have their own cabaret shows and sometimes host big-name Cuban stars. Outside of the hotels, the hot spots change unusually frequently, especially those that attract predominantly Cuban crowds. The local hip-hop and rock scenes in particular depend upon backstreet venues, sometimes in disused buildings and often open-air locations. **Discos** are okay for a giggle but are generally best avoided unless you're desperate to dance to blaring reggaeton in a pitch-black environment. Those cafés that are particularly good for nightlife as opposed to eating are listed below. Cafés and bars tend to open in the morning between 8–10am and stay open to anywhere from 1 to 3am. Discos and clubs open around 8pm and, although they don't close until 1 to 3am, rarely get going before 10 or 11pm.

A more spontaneous night out is a bit difficult, as there's no single area with a concentrated buzz. A secondary problem is that prohibitively expensive prices in tourist areas means a lack of Cuban patronage, with some of the most famous bars little more than photo opportunities. **Bar crawls** will involve a lot of walking, although the Plaza de la Catedral district is usually quite lively at night with most of the attention focused on *El Patio* bar and restaurant. Again, hotels feature prominently on any drinker's itinerary – the *Habana Libre* being central Vedado's best starting point for evening drinking, with the *Riviera* another good option. La Rampa in Vedado has a good clutch of bars and clubs and heats up after 11pm. For sheer *joie de vivre* action, though, you can't beat taking some beers or a bottle of rum down to the **Malecón** and mingling with the crowds beneath the stars or wandering between the brace of bars on the other side of the road.

A downside of Havana's nightlife is that you'll almost certainly encounter **jineteros** and **jineteras** in many of the city's nightspots, with the greatest concentration in the bars of Habana Vieja, the discos throughout the town and particularly along the Malecón after dark. If the attention is unwelcome, the best way to deal with it is to be firm but polite, and in the process try not to write off those locals who *are* just being friendly.

Bars and cafés

Habana Vieja

Bar Bilbao O'Reilly esq. Aguiar. An archetypal local's bar, with just enough room for a couple of tables and the whole place bedecked in Bilbao colours, with flags and posters of the football team. Expect cheap rum and plenty of stares.

Bar Dos Hermanos San Pedro no.304 esq. Sol. A cool saloon bar opposite the more run-down section of the Terminal Sierra Maestra, attracting at least as many Cubans as tourists with its distinguished yet workman-like character.

Bar Havana Club San Pedro e/ Sol y Muralla. Attached to the rum museum, there is a wide selection of excellent cocktails here, and it's a good place for some light food as well.

Bar Monserrate Ave. de Bélgica esq. Obrapía. A traditional bar that, though on the tourist circuit, feels more like a local drinkers' haunt than many of the nearby alternatives. There is also a full and cheap *comida criolla* menu, but food definitely comes second to drink here.

La Bodeguita del Medio Empedrado e/ San Ignacio y Mercaderes. Ernest Hemingway was a regular member of the literary and bohemian crowd that drank here, and his usual tipple, a *mojito*, has become the house speciality. One of the few places in town where you'll have to fight to get to the bar; the overcrowding makes it lively and atmospheric, but at $4CUC for a mediocre *mojito* and $5CUC for other cocktails, this is definitely a tourist trap.

Café de Paris San Ignacio esq. Obispo. Always packed with an even mix of tourists and locals, this little bar has a worn simplicity that belies the party atmosphere stirred up each night by a live band.

Café Habano Mercaderes esq. Amargura. A popular café-bar fuelling the caffeine cravings of a mostly Cuban clientele. Light snacks are served in the airy seating area and although the drinks list consists entirely of cappuccino and soda, at less than a peso a throw they won't get too many complaints. Open 10am–9pm.

Café La Barrita Edificio Bacardi, Ave. de las Misiones e/ San Juan de Dios y Empedrado. Hidden away on the mezzanine level behind the foyer of the Bacardi building is this stylish Art Deco café, a comfortable and congenial little hideout and a great spot to take a break. Good-value snacks here, too.

Café O'Reilly O'Reilly no.203 e/ San Ignacio y Cuba. Sandwiches, fried chicken and burgers accompany the drinks menu in this informal, rustic café with ceiling fans and open doors. Escape up the spiral staircase away from the bustle of Habana Vieja to the narrow balcony and enjoy the streetlife from a laid-back vantage point.

Cafetería Prado y Animas Paseo de Martí (El Prado) esq. Animas. There are no gimmicks at this dependable bar, one of the very few straight-up no-nonsense drinking venues aimed at the convertible peso market.

La Casa del Café Baratillo esq. Obispo. A shop-cum-coffee bar that's an inviting place for a quiet chat over a coffee cocktail – try the *Daiquiri de Café.*

El Floridita Monserrate esq. Obispo. Home of the Cuban *daiquiri*, this was another of Hemingway's favourite hangouts. A completely different experience to *La Bodeguita del Medio*, the comfy chairs, flowery wallpaper and velvet curtains make it feel like a posh living room, albeit one crammed with people trying to look cool while sampling an expensive range of fifty-odd cocktails, including fifteen types of *daiquiri.*

Lluvia de Oro Obispo esq. Habana. One of the liveliest and most reliably busy bars in Habana Vieja, but it depends heavily on a live band for atmosphere.

El Louvre *Hotel Inglaterra*, Paseo del Prado no.416 esq. San Rafael, Parque Central. A classic stopoff for visitors to the Parque Central, this café on the hotel's colonnaded patio porch is at the centre of the hustle and bustle revolving around this side of the park. You can eat here too.

Museo del Chocolate Mercaderes esq. Amargura. Despite the name this is more a café than a museum, and one where they serve only chocolate drinks and sweets, all made from Cuban cocoa. Order a deliciously thick hot chocolate whilst you watch the sweets being made at the back.

Puerto de Sagua Ave. de Bélgica (Egido) esq. Acosta. This classy 1930s-style bar could easily be a set for a Hollywood gangster movie. The sleek black bar is a fantastic throwback and the excellent selection of drinks, including plenty of cocktails, is surprisingly reasonably priced. Attached is a restaurant with nothing like the same character.

Roof Garden *Hotel Ambos Mundos*, Obispo no.153 esq. Mercaderes. This fabulous rooftop patio-bar gives a great perspective on the Plaza de Armas and the surrounding neighbourhood. Lolling on the tasteful garden furniture amongst the potted plants is as relaxing an option as you could wish for in Habana Vieja. There's a restaurant up here too.

Taberna de la Muralla San Ignacio esq. Muralla, Plaza Vieja. The smoothest, best beer in Havana, Cerveza Plaza Vieja, is not only uniquely on tap here but is brewed on the premises by the Austrian company that set the place up. Benches and tables fill two large halls and a corner of the plaza outside where the buzz created by this place looks unlikely to die down soon. You can order food, such as burgers, chorizo and fish, from the outdoor grill.

Taberna del Galeon Baratillo no.53 e/ Obispo y Jústiz. Just off the Plaza de Armas and a good place to avoid the sometimes frenzied atmosphere of the Obispo bars and the plaza itself, in an attic-like upstairs balcony above a rum and cigar shop. Open 10am–5pm.

Telégrafo Café *Hotel Telégrafo*, Parque Central. A distinctly soothing sense of space and light pervades this enchanting café, one of the best chill-out spots in Habana Vieja. Open 24hr.

Centro Habana

Alondra San Rafael e/ Aguila y Ave. de Italia (Galiano). This branch of the ice cream specialist, with its chain of *caféterias*, is no different from any other but, like all of them, is one of the few places you can get more than a couple of flavours of ice cream, a good selection of sundaes and all for very reasonable prices.

Bar Nautilius San Rafael e/ Consulado y Paseo del Prado. This dark and shady-looking local hangout based on a submarine theme is refreshingly and surprisingly untouristy, given that it's right next to the swanky *Inglaterra* hotel (see p.123). There's a limited selection of drinks, though and this is hustler headquarters.

Plaza de las Columnas Ave. de Italia (Galiano) esq. Zanja. This simple outdoor *caféteria* on the edge of Chinatown, suitable for a daytime break, is one of the few leafy spots in Centro Habana.

Taberna El Galeón Malecón e/ Manrique y Campanario. The only real bar on the Malecón's best stretch, as well as the best place for a light meal or snack, you can sit out front on a colon-naded porch or huddle into the tightly packed, understated interior.

Vedado

Aire Mar *Hotel Nacional*, Calle O esq. 21. Seasoned visitors swear a cooling daily *mojito* on the palatial terrace bar of this hotel is the way to beat the languid afternoon heat. The Salón de la Fama bar just inside is a bit tackier, but intriguing

for all the photos of the hotel's famous guests.

Fresa y Chocolate Calle 23 e/ 10 y 12. This unassuming bar, with a glass, arched roof and an entrance overgrown with greenery, is the hangout of choice for Cuban soap stars and musicians. Live bands play in the evening and attract an arty crowd.

Gato Tuerto Calle O e/ 17 y 19, ☏ 7/55-26-96. The pre-Revolution, beatnik jazz bar, whose name translates as "One-eyed Cat", has kept its cool edge despite a complete renovation. Excellent live Feelin' (*trova* jazz fusion) is played nightly from midnight to 4am, making it one of the best nights out in the area, though for a slightly older crowd. Entry is free but subject to a $5CUC consumption minimum. There's a stylish eating area upstairs.

Habana Café *Meliá Cohiba*, Paseo y Malecón ☏ 7/33-3636. Expensive retro cabaret-café filled with Cubamericana: classic Chevrolets and photos of Cuba at its Vegas best. Very Planet Hollywood, with an overpriced burger-and-fries menu. A brash, flashy variety show entertains the largely tourist clientele. Free entry with a $5CUC surcharge on your first drink.

Opus Bar Teatro Amadeo Roldan Calzada esq. D. A good-looking, long bar with the air of a glam VIP departure lounge, all big squashy easy chairs and sultry lighting. The available liquors include the 15-year Gran Reserva Havana Club and there's a good range of cocktails. While it gets busier between 8pm and 1am, it's not the place for a thumping night out but rather a sophisticated hide-out for those in search of a laid-back drink.

El Relicario *Meliá Cohiba*, Calle Paseo e/ 1ra y 3ra. With its wide selection of luxurious cigars and liquors, this stylish little bar feels like a gentleman's drinking club, perfect for an expensive post-prandial Cohiba and scotch.

Cabarets, nightclubs and live music

Habana Vieja

Basilica Menor de San Francisco de Asis Plaza San Francisco ☏ 7/862-9683. Classical orchestras and sometimes solo vocalists perform in the main cloister of this church, on average three times a week. Entrance is usually $10CUC.

Cabaret Nacional San Rafael esq. Paseo del Prado. This seedy basement cabaret and disco below the Gran Teatro is more than just a pick-up joint, though it is certainly that, too. Less glamorous and much cheaper than the average cabaret, its show follows the usual routines, but the place has a strong character, the low ceiling and abundance of dark red lending it a clandestine flavour. The show starts around 11pm and the disco usually gets going at about 1am. Entrance is between $5CUC and $10CUC.

Casa de la Cultura Aguiar no.509 e/ Amargura y Brasil, Habana Vieja ☎7/863-4860. In the converted Convento de San Francisco, this centre for local talent runs a full programme of evening performances ranging from folk music to hip-hop. Entrance is usually between two and five Cuban pesos.

Chico O'Farrill Snack Bar *Hotel Palacio O'Farrill*, Cuba no.102–108 esq. Chacón ☎7/860-5080. This classy and cosy little lounge-bar in an elegant hotel doubles up as a live music venue at weekends, visited by groups playing jazz, *son* and other traditional Cuban musical styles.

Disco Galicia Agramonte no.658 e/ Apodaca y Gloria. Inauspicious disco-bar at the top of a battered neocolonial building. Plenty of local flavour and a laid-back crowd. Entrance $5CUC.

Centro Habana

70s Café *Hotel Deauville*, Ave. de Italia esq. Malecón. A misleadingly named nightclub in the moody basement den of this high-rise hotel. Most nights there is a show of some sort, from pseudo cabaret to magic, followed by a DJ, as likely to play Euro-techno as 70s classics. The cover charge is $3CUC. Open Wed–Mon 10pm–2.30am.

Casa de la Música Ave. de Italia (Galiano) ☎7/862-4165. This is the biggest, snazziest and one of the newest and hippest club and live music venues on this side of the city. All the hottest names in Cuban *salsa* play here, where you can enjoy the music from a table or on the sizeable dance floor. Afternoon performances start at 4pm and at night the club is open 10pm–4.30am. Entrance $10–25CUC, depending on who's playing.

Palermo San Miguel esq. Amistad. The nightly shows put on in this untouristy, no-frills venue vary from cabaret to live music and usually include a disco whilst modern R&B and hip-hop feature also. Doors open around 10.30pm and the entrance fee varies but shouldn't be more than $3CUC or $4CUC.

Vedado

Cabaret Turquino *Habana Libre*, Calle L e/ 23 y 25. On the top floor of the *Habana Libre*, one of two nightspots in the hotel, this expansive disco/cabaret ($15–25CUC depending on who is playing) boasts a roll-back roof that reveals the stars, but even so, it still manages to look like a student bar with rather ordinary black chairs and tables. However, it puts on a cracking show, with live *salsa* on Mon, Tues, Thurs and Sat.

Café Amor Calle 23 e/ N y O ☎7/832-6757. Small but busy a/c bar with a variety of live music including *boleros*. The $3CUC entrance fee includes a drink. Open daily 10pm–4am.

Café Cantante Mi Habana Teatro Nacional de Cuba, Paseo y 39 Plaza de la Revolución ☎7/33-5713. The best club to show off your *salsa* and *merengue* moves to all the latest tunes. Top artists like Paulito F. G. and Los Van Van sometimes headline here; prices depend on who's playing but are upwards of $10CUC, with a cheaper Thurs matinee. Arrive early at weekends when the small basement gets jam-packed and the queue can be enormous.

Casa de la Amistad Paseo no.406 esq. 17 ☎7/30-3114. Resident troubadour groups gently perform well-executed *salsa*, *son* and *boleros* in the majestic grounds of a Rococo building that was once a private house. Sat are livelier with old-school *salsa* ($7CUC). Tues–Fri 11am–midnight, Sat 11–2am, Sun 11am–6pm. Closed Mon.

Casa de la Cultura Calzada 909 esq 8. ☎8/31-2023. There is no end to the activities on offer at this off-the-beaten-track culture house, be it theatre and poetry readings as well as every type of music Havana offers. Every week there's a choice of *bolero*, hip-hop, *rumba* and Feelin'. With Flamenco evenings, dance and art classes, this is a wonderful venue for those looking to immerse themselves in community-based culture. Closed Mon.

Casa de las Américas Esq. Calle 3ra y Ave. de los Presidentes ☎7/55-2706. This cultural institution regularly hosts bands in its large first-floor function room, playing anything from rap, *salsa* or rock.

Club Imagénes Calzada esq. C ☎7/333-3606. Round tables massed on the red carpet give this suave little club some movie-set glamour. Performances of *bolero* and Feelin', as well as singers, karaoke and comedy and a late-night disco draw a lively crowd of youngish Cubans and a smattering of foreigners. Open untill 3am at weekends, making for a good late-night drop-in.

Club Scheherazada Calle M e/ 19 y 17 ☎7/832-3042. This dark and noisy disco has a matinee session that starts at 4pm and is popular with locals. Open 4–8pm & 10pm–2am.

Delirio Habanero Piano Bar Teatro Nacional de Cuba, Paseo y 39, Plaza de la Revolución ☎7/33-5713. This sultry and atmospheric late-night jazz hangout is popular with Cuban sophisticates and visitors alike, with low-key piano music and live jazz bands like Sintesis nightly. Limited table space makes reservations essential at weekends. Bands play between 10.30pm and 3am, though the place stays open to 6am when it's busy.

Hurón Azul UNEAC (Unión de Escritores y Artistas de Cuba) Calle 17 no.351 e/ Ave. de los Presidentes y H. It's always worth checking out the programme posted outside this beautiful Vedado mansion, home to the Writers and Artists Union. Regular events include *bolero* (Sat 9pm–2am), *nueva trova* alternated with *rumba* (Wed from 5pm) and *son* or *rumba* (Sun from 5pm). In addition, throughout the week there are various art exhibitions, fashion shows and festivals on the grounds, and you can sometimes catch such luminaries as Pablo Milanes in concert. Entrance $5CUC.

Jazz Café Galerias del Paseo, Paseo esq. 1ra. The top floor of a shopping mall (see p.188) may seem an unlikely venue, but this laid-back café is a must for jazz aficionados. The best Cuban jazz bands, including jazz giants Irakere, often play here between 8pm and 2am, followed by a disco. Food is served, so arrive early to bag a table. Entrance $10CUC.

Karachi Calle K e/15 y 17. The action often spills out of this sweatbox disco onto the street outside where an eclectic mix of foreigners, transvestites, *roqueros* (rockers) and straights mingles to gossip and eye each other up. Music is equally diverse from reggaeton to rap and techno, and nights here are always good for a laugh. Entrance $3CUC.

La Madriguera Quinta de los Molinos, just off Calzada de Infanta at the end of Jesus Peregrino. ☎7/879-6247. Although off the beaten track for locals, let alone tourists, this place is currently among the ever-changing venues to hear Cuban and US hip-hop and R&B in the capital; held on irregular weekend nights in the backyard of a community building. Entrance 20 pesos in national money.

Pabellón Cuba Calle N no.266 esq. 23. Don't be put off by the monolithic appearance of this architectural monstrosity lurking at the foot of La Rampa. Run by the UJC (Union of Young Communists) you can catch a variety of live concerts in the large courtyard ranging from rap, rock and reggae as well as the ubiquitous *salsa*. Popular with a younger Cuban crowd. Entrance $1CUC.

El Pico Blanco Hotel St John's, Calle O no.206 e/ 23 y 25 ☎7/33-3740. Entertainment here is twofold, with the early part of the evening commanded by excellent live Feelin' and *bolero* between 11pm and 1am. Arrive early to catch relaxed tunes complemented by panoramic views over the Malecón. Later is less laid-back when the place turns into a disco. Entrance $5CUC.

Salon de los Embajadores Habana Libre, Calle L e/ 23 y 25. Cuba's finest music stars, including Chucho Valdés, Los Van Van and a host of hot *salsa* acts, play in this regal reception room, one of two salons in the hotel (see *Cabaret Turquino*, p.183). Well worth the costly price tag ($15–20CUC). Ask at reception for details of performances.

Sofía Calle 23 esq O ☎7/832-0640. A lively, brightly lit spot on a busy Vedado corner. Excellent bands play between 10pm and midnight to a mixed crowd of locals and tourists. There's no cover and a shot of rum costs $2.50CUC.

La Zorra y el Cuervo Calle 23 no.155 e/ N y O ☎7/55-2696. A cool and stylish basement venue, with contemporary decor and a European feel, which puts on superior live Latin jazz shows each night. Doors open at 9pm but it doesn't heat up till the band starts at 11pm. Entrance $10CUC.

Miramar, the western suburbs and the rest of the city

Casa de la Música de Miramar Calle 20 esq 35, Playa ☎7/202-6147. It's worth the trip out to Miramar to visit this *casa de la música*. The mansion itself is beautiful and the bands, which include Paulo FG, Elito Reve and Sur Caribe, are top-notch.

La Maison Calle 16 no 701 esq. 7ma, Miramar ☎7/204-1543. An elegant mansion containing shops, a piano bar and restaurant. The $30CUC fee covers a meal and entrance to the nightly fashion and music shows. A popular spot for wedding receptions, it's generally considered to be the height of elegance by Cubans.

Tropicana Calle 72 no.504 Marianao. Possibly the oldest and most lavish cabaret in the world, Cuba's unmissable, much-hyped open-air venue hosts a pricey extravaganza in which class acts, such as Pablo Milanes, and a ceaseless flow of dancing girls, (under)clad in sequins, feathers and frills, regularly pull in a full house. Starts at 8.30pm with the show from 10 to 11pm. You can arrange all-inclusive bus trips from $65CUC from most hotels, otherwise entrance is $75–90CUC. Closed Mon.

Villa Diana Calle 49 e/ 28A–47, Reparto Kohly. A classy establishment that makes the most of the elegant mansion in which it is set. Quality live music includes classic Cuban *son*, *boleros* and *danzón*.

Cinemas and theatres

Costing just a few pesos, **cinema** is a popular form of entertainment with Cubans, and there are plenty of atmospheric fleapits dotted around Havana, particularly in Vedado. Although as a visitor you may be charged in convertible pesos ($2–3CUC), it is still well worth the experience. Havana's cinemas usually screen a selection of Cuban, North American and European films, with the English-speaking ones generally subtitled in Spanish or, if you are unlucky, badly dubbed.

Havana also has the cream of the country's live **theatres**, where, especially during the international festival in September (see p.76), you can catch excellent avant-garde and more traditional performances.

Cinemas

Cine Actualidades Ave. de Bélgica no.362 e/ Animas y Virtudes, Habana Vieja ☎7/861-5193. Cinema offering one of the more varied monthly programmes, with performance times for the whole month usually posted in the front window.

Cine Chaplin Calle 23 e/ 10 y 12, Vedado ☎7/831-1101. An appealing arthouse with a repertoire of vintage Cuban and incomprehensible Russian films.

Cine la Rampa Calle 23 esq. O, Vedado ☎7/878-6146. A rather run-down place that shows predominantly North American films.

Cine Payret Paseo del Prado esq. San José, Habana Vieja ☎7/863-3163. The best spot in Habana Vieja to see Cuban films and the occasional

Hollywood blockbuster. One of the main venues for the Havana Film Festival.

Cine Riviera Calle 23 e/ G y H, Vedado ☎7/830-9564. A stylish cinema painted cobalt blue that shows a range of films from North American and English to Cuban and Spanish.

Cine Yara Calle L esq. 23, Vedado ☎7/867-1374. A large, old-fashioned, lofty auditorium showing the latest Spanish and Cuban releases, and a small video room showing special-interest films.

Theatres

Gran Teatro Paseo del Prado esq. San Rafael, Habana Vieja ☎7/861-3096. This outstandingly ornate building on the Parque Central is the home of the Ballet Nacional de Cuba but also hosts

Twenty-four-hour Havana

There is a common expectation amongst first-time visitors to Havana that the city is a 24-hour nonstop party. This couldn't be further from the truth, with most of the city disarmingly quiet after about 2am. Equally scarce are all-night shops and eateries. There are, however, various exceptions to these general rules. Listed below are some of the 24-hour venues worth knowing about.

Cabaña Cuba no.12 esq. Peña Pobre, Habana Vieja. A restaurant and bar but better as the latter.

Café del Oriente Plaza de San Francisco, Habana Vieja. One of the poshest-looking restaurants in Havana keeps its bar open all night. See p.175

Cafeteria La Rampa Hotel Habana Libre, Calle 23 esq. L, Vedado. An American-style diner, great for a bite to eat after a night on the tiles.

Lobby Bar Quinta Avenida Hotel Melia Habana, Calle 3ra e/ 76 y 80, Miramar. A comfortable, sociable place for winding down with a drink.

La Luz Obispo no.165 e/ San Ignacio y Mercaderes. A simple restaurant where the bar, which attracts a good mix of locals and tourists, is open all night.

Pain de Paris Calle 25 e/ Espada y Hospital, Vedado. One of the city's best bakeries, just off the Calzada de Infanta, with better-than-average quality sweets and cakes.

Pan.com Ave. 7ma e/ 24 y 26, Miramar. This branch of one of the better Cuban fast-food chains sometimes closes for a few hours but is usually open until early morning.

Panadería San José Obispo no.167 e/ San Ignacio y Mercaderes, Habana Vieja. A 24-hour bakery in the heart of Habana Vieja.

Telégrafo Cyber Café Hotel Telégrafo, Paseo del Prado no.408, esq. Neptuno. This is a delightfully subdued café and perfect for a late-night chinwag; the fact that you can pretty much get online anytime you want without waiting is just a bonus.

Drinking, nightlife and entertainment

operas and contemporary dance pieces. The biannual Festival Internacional de Ballet de la Habana takes place here in October, while every August the theatre plays host to a season of Spanish ballet. There are performances most weeks, usually from Fri to Sun, most starting around 8pm but usually a few hours earlier on Sun. Entrance is usually $10CUC.

Teatro Amadeo Roldan Calzada esq. D, Vedado ☎7/832-4521. Recently renovated, this is the home of the National Symphony Orchestra and accordingly one of the best places to hear classical music in Havana. The orchestra always plays at weekends (9pm on Fri, 5pm on Sat, and Sun at 4pm). There are opera, choral, soloists and some jazz programmes most weeknights between 6 and 8pm, but you should check in advance. $5–10CUC.

Teatro América Ave. de Italia no.253 e/ Concordia y Neptuno, Centro Habana ☎7/862-5416. Smaller

than its more renowned counterparts, this humble but happening theatre lends itself well to the comedy shows, live jazz and traditional music performances which are its mainstays.

Teatro Hubert de Blanck Calzada e/ A y B, Vedado ☎7/3-5960. This very small theatre has a good repertoire of contemporary Spanish and Cuban theatre. Entrance is a snip at $3–5CUC.

Teatro Karl Marx Calle 1ra e/ 8 y 10, Miramar ☎7/830-0720. Impressively ugly 1960s building hosting all kinds of music and dramatic arts events, including rock concerts and classical theatre. Definitely worth checking what's on.

Teatro Nacional de Cuba Calle Paseo y 39, Plaza de la Revolución ☎7/879-6011. Havana's biggest theatre puts on some of the city's best events all year round, from ballet to guitar and jazz. Spanish-speakers should check out the avant-garde drama, especially during the February theatre festival.

Shopping

Havana is no shoppers' paradise, and most visitors are happy enough to just buy bottles of rum, a handful of cigars and a souvenir T-shirt or two: a demand met by all the large hotels and the **Artex** state chain stores found all over the city. Those intent on shopping will find that **Obispo**, in Habana Vieja, offers the widest choice of shops in the most congenial setting and a handful of the jack-of-all-trades-master-of-none convenience stores that Cuba has made its own.

Elsewhere, while new **shopping malls** and **boutiques** are mushrooming steadily around the city, the general standard of merchandise is still low, with dime-store items like doe-eyed ceramic animals featuring heavily. That said, the goods available are well priced and you can often pick up inexpensive shoes and clothes in the large malls, though these won't necessarily win you many admiring glances back home. Some of the hotels sell better-quality goods, and are also where you'll have the best chance of finding name-brand clothing.

As far as basics like **toiletries** go, things have moved on since the Special Period and you can pick up most things easily enough so long as you're equipped with convertible pesos. It's worthwhile checking out the big-name perfumes available from hotels like *Cohiba* and *Habana Libre*, as they are often cheaper than back home.

As is the case all over Cuba, there are still shops in Havana selling products in **pesos**, mostly half-empty and stocking poor-quality goods. There are, however, a few novelty peso shops where you can pick up some absolute bargains, while others are worth a peek just for the twilight-zone feel to their time-warped interiors. It's particularly worth wandering up Centro Habana's **Avenida de Italia**, one of the classic shopping streets of pre-revolutionary Havana, when it was known as Galiano, and where the fading signs and barely stocked old-style stores stand as testament to a bygone era.

For supermarkets, see p.176.

Arts and crafts shops

La Casona Muralla esq. San Ignacio, Plaza Vieja, Habana Vieja. One of the less tacky selections of handcrafted souvenirs and there's a small gallery exhibiting modern Cuban art, all in the surroundings of an attractive eighteenth-century mansion.

Fototeca de Cuba Mercaderes no.307, Plaza Vieja, Habana Vieja. An excellent little gallery shop with original and artistic photographs of Havana and the rest of Cuba that cover a diverse range of subjects and avoid the usual clichéd shots.

Galería Habana Linea no.460 e/ E y F, Vedado. This place always has an impressive collection of contemporary art on display and for sale.

Galería Manos Obispo no.411 e/ Aguacate y Compostela, Habana Vieja. Run by the Asociación Cubana de Artesanos Artistas (a seal of good quality), there's an eclectic mix of items for sale here including cigar boxes (*humidores*), bags, shoes, woodcarvings, ceramics and jewellery. There's also a small patio and bar at the back.

Galería Victor Manuel San Ignacio no.56, Plaza de la Catedral, Habana Vieja. Offers a good range of *artesanía*, as well as paintings.

Palacio de la Artesania see p.189.

Venezia Tacón e/ O'Reilly y Empedrado, Habana Vieja. One of the city's few half-decent stockists of art supplies, including sketchbooks, oil paints, pastels and paintbrushes.

Bookshops

Secondhand **bookstalls** are very popular in Cuba, and proliferate in Havana, with plenty around the central tourist areas selling books in Spanish, English and sometimes French and German, some of which pre-date the Revolution. The best place for these is the daily market at the Plaza de Armas (see p.132). **Bookshops** themselves are generally disappointing, the shortages of paper during the Special Period partly explaining their relatively restricted range of titles. Most of them also double up as stationers.

La Internacional Obispo no.526 e/ Bernaza y Villegas, Habana Vieja. Amongst the better bookshops in the city, and there's a reasonably good travel section.

Librería Bella Habana Palacio del Segundo Cabo, Plaza de Armas, Habana Vieja. A good place to find collectors' editions and rarities, particularly from the 1950s and 1960s, such as the 25-volume *Complete Works of José Martí.*

Librería Centenario del Apóstol Calle 25 no.166 e/ O y Infanta, Vedado. Alongside the academic books and works on Marxismo there are old Cuban magazines and a few tatty English-language paperbacks in this tightly packed little secondhand national-peso bookstore.

Librería Fernando Ortiz Calle L esq. 27, Vedado. One of the widest selections of history and politics titles in English and Spanish, as well as a decent selection of novels.

Librería Grijalbo Mondadori Palacio del Segundo Cabo, Plaza de Armas, Habana Vieja. The official bookshop of the Instituto Cubano del Libro and

effectively two shops, one in convertible pesos and the other in national pesos. This is the city's best source for fiction, all in Spanish, and there's a section full of cultural periodicals and magazines as well as some English-language fiction.

La Moderna Poesia Obispo esq. Bernaza, Habana Vieja. The most comprehensive selection of new books in the capital and the best place for foreign-language dictionaries and publications of interest to travellers, such as specialist guides to Cuban architecture, as well as maps. Also has one of the better selections of magazines and all the Cuban newspapers.

El Navegante Mercaderes no.115 e/ Obispo y Obrapía, Habana Vieja. Dedicated to travel litera-ture, including nautical charts, and the best source of maps in the city.

Publicaciones de la Oficina del Historiador Mercaderes esq. Obispo. The best selection of books and pamphlets on the history and recon-struction of Havana.

Cigars and rum

The **Casa del Habano** chain of stores accounts for most of the cigars sold in Cuba and is well represented all over the city. Many of the top-class hotels have their own **cigar shops**, four of the best in the *Meliá Cohiba, Habana Libre, Parque*

Central and the *Nacional*, the latter one of the best places to buy individual cigars (as opposed to a *humidore*). Outside of the hotels, Habana Vieja has the largest number of cigar shops, some of which also sell rum, while specialist rum shops are much less common.

Casa del Habano Mercaderes no.202 e/ Obispo y Obrapía, Habana Vieja. A dinky little store right next to the cigar museum in the heart of Habana Vieja, but the poor selection doesn't quite match the prime location.

Casa del Habano Ave. 5ta. no.1407 esq. Calle 16, Miramar. The most impressive of Havana's cigar shops. Carrying an extensive range of brands, there are all kinds of smoking accessories, not least cutters and lighters, a conference room where you can test your smokes, a bar and a restaurant.

Casa del Habano *Hostal Conde de Villanueva*, Mercaderes esq. Lamparilla, Habana Vieja. One for the connoisseurs, this place will also appeal to anyone attracted by the stereotypical cigar smoker's image and lifestyle, with its moody smokers' lounge, low ceilings and private club atmosphere. The range of stock is above average.

Casa del Habano Partagás Fábrica de Tobacos Partagás, Industria e/ Dragones y Barcelona, Centro Habana. A busy, extremely well-stocked cigar emporium and a Mecca for cigar aficionados.

Casa del Ron y del Tobaco Cubano Obispo e/ Bernaza y Ave. de Bélgica, Habana Vieja. One of the best selections of rum under one roof, and a decent range of havanas, too.

Department stores, shopping malls and commercial complexes

Though the poor cousins of their US counterparts, Havana's modern **shopping malls** are where you'll find some of the best-quality merchandise outside of the hotel shops. Most of the more upmarket complexes are found in Miramar and Vedado, while Centro Habana and Habana Vieja are host to some of the city's best-known **department stores**. Other than the familiar large multi-floor versions, in Havana many of these are more distinctly Cuban, being much smaller in size, often set in an old mansion divided into five or six units, sometimes all part of the same chain but more often separate businesses. The other common location for commercial centres is in the larger high-end hotels, like the *Habana Libre* and *Meliá Cohiba*.

Arte Habana San Rafael no.110 esq. Industria, Centro Habana. A recently established and relatively slick commercial complex with products representing various aspects of Cuban culture – music, literature, art, clothing, etc. The quality is generally quite high.

D' Primera Primera y B, Vedado. A smart collection of mainly sportswear shops selling brands like New Balance, Merrrell, K Swiss and OP.

Dos Gardenias Ave. 7ma esq. 26, Miramar. This is a good place to combine a bit of shopping with a meal. As well as a cigar shop and a good wine and alcohol specialist, there are three restaurants here and nightime entertainment, too.

La Epoca Ave. de Italia esq. Neptuno, Centro Habana. Just about the best department store in town and certainly the biggest, with a supermarket in the basement, brand-name sports clothing on the ground floor and several more floors stocking electrical goods, home furnishings and another, cheaper, clothing department.

Galería Comercial Comodoro Ave. 3ra e/ 80 y 84, Miramar. Havana's largest and most upmarket shopping mall is also the most pleasant to shop in, surrounded by lawns and flanked by pavement cafés and outdoor eateries. There are around thirty stores here, many of them clothes shops, with outlets for Adidas, Lacoste, Mango and Ted Lapidus, as well as specialists in jewellery, watches, perfume and cigars.

Galerías Amazonas Calle 12 e/ 23 y 25, Vedado. The best thing about this shopping precinct is the delicatessen selling olives and other delicacies and an array of fancy chocolates. Other shops worth a mention include a florist and a fairly good shoe shop, Peletería Claudia.

Galerías de Paseo Paseo esq. Calle 1ra, Vedado. A classy North American-style mall, located just over the road from one of the capital's most expensive hotels. The shops themselves are more run-of-the-mill and number far fewer than you might expect from the size of the place. The excellent *Jazz Café* (see p.184) is amongst the highlights here.

Harris Brothers Monserrate e/ O'Reilly y San Juan

de Dios, Habana Vieja. One of Havana's classic department stores, generally stocking marginally better-quality products, particularly clothing-wise, than its main rival, La Epoca.

La Maison Calle 16 no.701 e/ Ave. 7ma y Ave. 9na, Miramar. A typically Cuban shopping complex, housed in a graceful colonial mansion and more upmarket than the larger department stores in the older parts of the city. Most notable for the choice of watches, jewellery, cosmetics, shoes and clothing, as well as the fashion shows which are frequently held here.

Palacio de la Artesanía Cuba no.64 e/ Cuarteles y Peña Pobre, Habana Vieja. A pleasant place to look around with several floors of shops gathered around a central courtyard. You'll find a good selection of T-shirts as well as units selling books,

perfume, music, shoes, sports gear, toys and the usual Cuban craftwork.

Plaza de Carlos Tercero Ave. Salvador Allende (Carlos Tercero) e/ Arbol Seco y Retiro, Centro Habana (Mon–Sat 10am–6pm, Sun 10am–2pm). This four-floor complex is one of the biggest malls in the city and usually swarming with customers. There's a food court on the ground floor and a number of clothes shops scattered around, but other than in the cigar shop the stuff on sale here is cheap and generally second-rate.

La Puntilla Calle A esq. 1ra, Miramar. The supermarket in this large and comprehensive mall is among the best, with a good range of pricey snack foods and Western cereals and imported liquor. Other shops sell electronics, mid-range clothes and a panorama of toiletries.

Markets

When shopping around the street **markets** in Havana be prepared to wade through the same Che Guevara-themed memorabilia, bright and simple paintings of old American cars, black coral jewellery and wooden mantelpiece-sculptures over and over again. However, if you are prepared to put in the hours you can find the occasional sculpture, piece of jewellery or handmade clothing that stands out from the rest. Markets tend to close on a Sunday or a Monday, but rarely both, and generally trade between 9am and 6pm.

Feria de Arte Obispo Obispo e/ Compostela y Aguacate, Habana Vieja. Around 15 stalls in the ruins of an old building on the main shopping street in the old town. Ornamental gifts, clothing, jewellery and ceramics.

Mercado de la Catedral Tacón, outside the Plaza de la Catedral, Habana Vieja. The largest market in the city, with over 200 stalls and the widest choice of souvenirs, from all the usual clichéd Che Guevara- and cigar-themed stuff to a fantastic range of paintings and prints and every type of handmade craft imaginable. Closed Mon.

Mercado de La Rampa La Rampa e/ M y N,

Vedado. A small craft market, its miscellaneous merchandise including inflated and lacquered puffer fish, highly suspect fat-black-mama sculptures, pumpkin seed necklaces and handmade leather items. Closed Mon.

Mercado de libros Plaza de Armas, Habana Vieja. This market features loads of stalls full of fascinating old books, a few dating back to the nineteenth century, with some asking prices going past the $100CUC mark. There are newer titles as well and, as always, numerous revolutionary publications such as transcripts of Fidel Castro's speeches. Closed Mon.

Music

Fans of Cuban **music** will be delighted by the expansive range of CDs and tapes in Havana's shops, with a wider choice of *salsa*, *son* or *bolero* than the rest of the country and all sorts of releases you are unlikely ever to see for sale outside of Cuba. Non-Cuban music, on the other hand, is rare and of dubious quality, leaving you unlikely to find anything you can't get down at the local garage/petrol station back home.

Annet Ave. de Italia no.412 e/ San Martín y San Rafael, Centro Habana. A small range of Cuban music on cassette and dusty-looking shelves full of orchestral, classical and traditional Cuban sheet music, all sold in pesos.

Egrem Ave. de Italia e/ Concordia y Neptuno, Centro Habana. Maybe not the largest but definitely one of the most varied selections of CDs in Havana, as well as having unusually good listening facilities.

Habana Sí Calle L esq. 23, Vedado. This store has one of the widest range of CDs in town as well as books and a decent collection of Cuban films on video and DVD.

Longina Obispo no.360 e/ Habana y Compostela, Habana Vieja. A good variety of Cuban music on CD, as well as musical instruments.

Seriosha's Shop Neptuno no.408 e/ San Nicolás y Manrique, Centro Habana. A little crate-diggers'

paradise for collectors of Latin and easy listening music on vinyl. At the back of a larger shop and everything is in pesos.

Tienda Artex L y 23 Calle L esq. 23, Vedado. Has one of the widest range of CDs in town, helpfully divided into classic and contemporary browsing areas.

Clothing, jewellery and accessories

The quality of Cuban-made **clothing** is generally very poor, though the numerous T-shirt specialists, most of them found in hotels such as the *Habana Libre*, tend to offer a better cut of cloth. For reliable quality you'll have to seek out the foreign brand names, only a few of which have their own stores in Havana. Well-made, good-quality **jewellery** tends to be easier to find, whilst there are several one-off shops, particularly on Obispo in Habana Vieja, like the bag-seller Novator, that offer high-grade merchandise.

Adidas Neptuno no.460–462 e/ Campanario y Manrique, Centro Habana. Two floors of sports clothing and accessories, including official merchandise from this long-time supplier of kit to the national Cuban baseball team.

Benetton Oficios no.152 esq. Amargura, Plaza de San Francisco, Habana Vieja. The usual racks of pastel-coloured clothing at one of the only dedicated name-brand stores in the city.

Galería Amelia Peláez *Hotel Habana Libre*, Calle 23 esq. L, Vedado. One of the best selections of tack-free jewellery, with some surprisingly afford-able pieces given the five-star location.

Guayabera Habanera Tacón no.20 e/ O'Reilly y Empedrado. The place to come for an authentic *guayabera*, the classic Cuban shirt with four pockets and two rows of pleats.

Novator Obispo no.365 e/ Compostela y Habana, Habana Vieja. Semi-formal little handbag specialist, also with headgear for both men and women.

Optica El Almendares Obispo no.364 e/ Compos-tela y Habana. This touristy opticians is the best place in Havana to look for sunglasses.

Paul & Shark Muralla no.103, Plaza Vieja. Upmarket clothing boutique specializing in golf-course togs and smart casual wear for men and women.

Peletería La Habana Obispo no.415 esq. Aguacate. Good-quality men's and women's shoes, some of them quite chic.

San Eloy Obispo no.115 e/ Mercaderes y Oficios. The five cabinets here contain the city's best selection of gold and silver jewellery, from $10CUC silver bracelets to $3000CUC gold rings.

Vía Uno Oficios esq. Obrapía. This shoe shop has one of the better selections of women's footwear, from formal shoes to trainers.

Specialist and novelty shops

Shops dedicated to just one thing are surprisingly uncommon in Havana, with most places specializing in the art of selling nothing in particular: enter what might look like a hi-fi shop and you're as likely to find spare parts for your car as you are to find a stereo. It is therefore worth seeking out those places that do lay a realistic claim to specialization.

Casa del Abanico Obrapía no.107 e/ Oficios y Mercaderes. Artistically embroidered hand-held fans, with made-to-order designs on offer, too.

Casa del Café Obispo esq. Baratillo, Plaza de Armas, Habana Vieja. Specialist coffeeshop, though there are cigars and rum for sale here, too.

El Clip Obispo no.501 e/ Villegas y Bernaza, Habana Vieja. Watch shop selling mostly Cuban brands.

Colección Habana O'Reilly esq. Mercaderes, Habana Vieja. Great for browsing, this unique place specializes in a wide variety of pricey products based on high-class colonial-era designs. From

chairs and dinner sets to ornaments, jewellery, bags and poster prints, you are unlikely to find many of the items here for sale anywhere else.
Fotovideo Ave. 5ta e/ 40 y 42, Miramar. Photographic equipment and supplies as well as videotaping accessories.
Galería Juan David Cine Yara, Calle L esq. 23, Vedado. Tiny commercial outlet for the Cuban film industry selling videos, film-poster art and similarly decorated souvenirs like umbrellas.

 Habana 1791 Mercaderes no.156 e/ Obrapia y Lamparilla, Habana Vieja. This unique shop sells what it bills as "aromas coloniales de la Isla de Cuba": handmade perfumes like those used during the eighteenth and nineteenth centuries in Cuba. Made from flowers and plant oils, they are sold in ceramic or glass bottles and prices range from around the $5CUC mark to $20CUC.

 ICAIC Centro Cultural Cinematográfico Calle 23 no.1155 e/10 y 12 Vedado. An excellent source of cool screen-printed film posters, the Cuban Film Institute also sells cult films on video, including many by Tomás Gutiérrez Alea, and some specialist film publications mainly in Spanish. Closed Sun.
Papelería de O'Reilly Tacón esq. O'Reilly, Habana Vieja. One of the only dedicated stationery and art supplies shops in the capital, and probably the best.
Variedades Obispo esq. Habana. The appeal here is the shopping experience rather than what you can actually buy. Usually crammed full of locals, the products on sale are of a kind usually sold in convertible but here they are in national pesos. Sparse displays in glass cabinets form a crisscross of corridors that you'll have to fight your way through, while down one side is a 1950s-style diner bar selling light refreshments. Items on sale include clothing, sun cream, towels, kitchen utensils and Tupperware.

Sports

You only need to spend a few hours wandering the streets of any part of the capital to appreciate the prominent role that **sport** plays in the lives of Habaneros. Fierce arguments strike off every evening on basketball courts all over the city and rarely will you see an open space, at any time of the day, not hosting a game of baseball. The virtually traffic-less streets of much of Centro Habana are constantly witness to local neighbourhood clashes – using rope for volleyball nets and hands for baseball bats, nothing stops the locals coming out to compete.

Spectator sports

On a professional level, Havana is the finest place for live sport in Cuba, with the best stadia in the country and several big-league teams. Entrance to most sports arenas is only one peso and booking in advance is unnecessary and rarely possible. The city has two major **baseball teams**, both of which play at the **Estadio Latinoamericano** (☏7/870-6526 & 870-6576) on Pedro Pérez in Cerro, the *municipio* south of Centro Habana and Vedado. Industriales, traditionally the most successful team in Havana, attract the biggest crowds, especially when they play their archrivals Santiago de Cuba. Expect five games a week during the regular season, usually October to March; if Industriales are playing away, Metropolitanos, the capital's second team, are playing at home. There is always plenty of banter in the crowd and a relaxed, feel-good vibe, but with so many games the stadium is often half-empty, the crowds only coming out for the big games. Check the back pages of the national newspaper *Granma* for details of forthcoming games.

Basketball, Cuba's other big spectator sport, is harder to find out about, but the smaller arenas it's played in means there's often more of a buzz. Capitalinos, the local team, spend the winter months in weekly combat with the national league's other three teams. The **Sala Polivalente Ramon Fonst**, on the

△ Estadio Panamericano

Avenida de Rancho Boyeros near the Plaza de la Revolución (☎7/881-1011 & 881-0781), is the only purpose-built basketball arena and hosts most games, though some are played at the **Ciudad Deportiva** arena (☎7/648-5000), part of a huge sports complex used predominantly by students of physical education, just off the roundabout where the airport road meets the Vía Blanca in Cerro; note that foreign visitors are not always allowed inside. Also occasional host to a basketball game is the **Sala Polivalente Kid Chocolate** (☎7/862-8634, 861-1548 & 861-1547), opposite the Capitolio Nacional on the Paseo del Prado between Brasil and San Martín, but this rickety old sports hall is more often used for **boxing** matches. A number of international tournaments have been held here in recent years but there are no regularly scheduled bouts; it's worth noting, however, that the annual interprovincial tournament, the Torneo Nacional de Boxeo, takes place from September to November and matches are often staged here.

The home of soccer in Havana is the **Estadio Pedro Marrero** (☎7/209-5428 & 203-4698) at Ave. 41 no.4409 in Marianao in the western suburbs, and this is also where the national team play their matches. The national league is slowly gaining more recognition from the public and government but still comes way behind basketball and baseball in both popularity and quality of play, making attending a game really suitable only for avid fans. Matches usually take place on Wednesdays and Saturdays at 3pm.

The other huge sports complex, also not always open to foreign visitors, is the **Complejo Panamericano** in Habana del Este, surrounding the Vía Monumental just before you reach Cojímar, originally built to host the 1991 Pan American Games. There are tennis courts, a velodrome (☎7/95-3776), an Olympic-sized swimming pool and diving pools and the centrepiece, the **Estadio Panamericano** (☎7/95-4140), an athletics stadium. Much of the time these facilities are used only for training purposes by the national teams of the respective sports, but occasionally they host competitions on view to the public.

Participatory sports

There are no public sports centres as such in Havana; instead, the best places for **participatory sports** are the local neighbourhood courts and pitches where all comers are usually welcome. The most reliable place for a game of soccer is the university stadium, the **Estadio Juan Abrantes**, which has several games going on almost every evening. One of the best places to pick up a game of basketball is the **Parque José Martí**, within sight of the Malecón next to the Avenida de los Presidentes in Vedado.

At the other end of the spectrum is the exclusive **Club Habana**, 5ta Ave. e/ 188 y 192, Reparto Flores, Miramar (daily 7.30am–9pm; ☎7/204-5700), a cross between a business centre and a sports club, which includes a luxury clubhouse, restaurant, beach, spa, gym, pool, golf driving range, diving centre and tennis courts. Actually a private members' club used predominantly by diplomats and foreign businessmen, non-guests can pay an admission fee of $20CUC during the week and $30CUC at weekends to use its facilities. Also in Miramar at Ave. 5ta e/ Calle 248 y Santa Fe is the **Marina Hemingway** (☎7/209-7270 & 209-7928), the best place in the city for watersports, with its own dive centre and regularly playing host to fishing tournaments. The other marina in Havana, the Marina Tarará (☎7/96-0242) is in Habana del Este, off the Vía Blanca.

One of the other very few participatory sports installations easily accessible to foreign visitors is the **Club de Golf Habana** (daily 8am–9pm; ☎7/649-8918), just off the Avenida de la Independencia on the way to the airport. Currently a nine-hole course, there have been plans for over five years now to add another nine, and it's anyone's guess if and when these plans will ever be realized. The complex also features a bowling alley, an Italian restaurant and a pool. The green fee is $20CUC for nine holes, you can rent a caddy for $5CUC and club hire is $10CUC.

Listings

Airlines Aerocaribbean, Calle 23 no.64 e/ Infanta y P, Vedado ☎7/879-7524 to 25, 832-7584 & 836-5936; Aeroflot, Miramar Trade Center, 5ta Ave. e/ 70 y 80, Miramar ☎7/204-3200; Aerogaviota, Ave. 47 no.2814, e/ 28 y 34, Reparto Kohly, Playa ☎7/204-5603, 203-3066 & 203-0686; Aerotaxi, Calle 27 no.102 e/ M y N, Vedado ☎7/836-4064; Air Europa, Miramar Trade Center, 5ta Ave. e/ 70 y 80, Miramar ☎7/204-6904; Air France, Calle 23 no.64 e/ Infanta y P, Vedado ☎7/833-2642 to 44; Air Jamaica, Calle 23 no.64 e/ Infanta y P, Vedado ☎7/833-2448 & 833-4011; Copa Airlines, Miramar Trade Center, 5ta Ave. e/ 70 y 80, Miramar ☎7/204-1111, 833-1758 & 833-3657; Cubana, Calle 23 no.64, Vedado ☎7/834-4446 to 49 & 836-4950 & Miramar Trade Center, 5ta Ave. e/ 70 y 80, Miramar ☎7/204-6679 & 204-9647; Iberia, Miramar Trade Center, 5ta Ave. e/ 70 y 80, Miramar ☎7/204-3444 & 833-5041; LTU, Calle 23 no.64, e/ Infanta y P, Vedado ☎7/833-3524 to 25; Martinair Holland, Calle 23 no.64, e/ Infanta y P, Vedado ☎7/833-3730 & 833-3531; Mexicana, Calle 23 no.64, e/ Infanta y P, Vedado ☎7/833-3228 & 833-3130; Virgin Atlantic, Miramar Trade Center, 5ta Ave. e/ 70 y 80, Miramar ☎7/204-0747.

Airport Ring the José Martí International Airport switchboard (☎7/266-4644 & 649-5777) and ask for information. You can call information direct (☎7/266-4133) but it tends to be harder to get through.

ATMs Machines accepting foreign credit and debit cards can be found in Habana Vieja at Cadeca Casa de Cambio, Obispo no.257 e/ Aguiar y Cuba; in Centro Habana at Banco de Crédito y Comercio, Padre Varela (Belascoaín) esq. Zanja; in Vedado in a small room in the *Hotel Nacional*, hidden away on the first floor; and in Miramar at the *Meliá Habana* hotel. If you have a problem with your credit card or if it gets stolen go to the Centro de Tarjetas Internacional at Calle 23 e/ L y M (☎7/33-4466), underneath the *Habana Libre*, where they can cancel cards and access details of recent card transactions.

Banks and exchange Of all the places where you can withdraw money with a foreign credit card and cash traveller's cheques, the Casa de Cambio in the *Hotel Nacional* has the longest opening hours (daily 8am–noon & 1–11pm). Along with the *casa de cambio* in the *Hotel Sevilla* (daily 9am–6pm) in Habana Vieja, it is also one of the very few places you can use the same services on a Sun. The Banco Internacional de Comercio (Mon–Fri 8.30am–3pm), at Empedrado esq. Aguiar, is the best bank in the old city for foreign currency transactions, while for basically the same services in Centro Habana the Banco de Crédito y Comercio is centrally located at Zanja esq. Padre Varela (Mon–Fri 8.30am–3pm); in Vedado the Banco Financiero Internacional, at Linea no.1 esq. Calle O (Mon–Fri 8am–3pm), is within walking distance of at least four hotels. For purchasing pesos there are Cadeca *casas de cambio* all over the city, including one at Obispo no.257 e/ Aguiar y Cuba, Habana Vieja (daily 8am–10pm) and at Calle 23 esq. L, Vedado (daily 8am–10pm).

Bike rental Bike parts, tools and accessories as well as all sorts of bikes for rent are available at El Orbe, Ave. de Bélgica no.304 e/ Neptuno y San Rafael ☎7/860-2617 (Mon–Sat 9am–4.30pm). Rental costs are $2CUC for an hour, $20CUC for two days and $60CUC for a week.

Bus station Víazul terminal, Ave. 26 y Zoológico, Nuevo Vedado ☎7/881-1413 & 881-5652, ⓦwww .viazul.com; open 24hr; Astro terminal, Ave. Independencia esq. 19 de Mayo, switchboard ☎7/870-9401, information ☎7/879-2456. To book Viazul tickets, see "Travel agents" (opposite) and Infotour offices.

Business facilities There are business centres (*centros de negocios*) offering PC rental, Internet hookups for laptops, photocopying, printing and faxing services and more at *Hotel Saratoga* and *Parque Central* in Habana Vieja, the *Meliá Cohiba* in Vedado and the *Meliá Habana* in Miramar.

Car parks There is an official state-run car park at Ave. de Italia esq. Ave. Simón Bolívar in Centro Habana, near the Habana Vieja border.

Car rental Micar offers the cheapest deals and has an office in the Galerias de Paseo shopping mall at Paseo esq. 1ra in Vedado and at other locations including Ave. 3ra esq. 70, Miramar (☎7/204-8888). Alternatives include Havanautos at Calle 23 esq. M, Vedado (☎7/833-3484) and Ave. 5ta esq. 112, Miramar (☎7/204-3203); Cubacar in the Terminal Sierra Maestra opposite the Plaza de San Francisco, Habana Vieja and Miramar Trade Center, 5ta Ave. e/ 70 y 80, Miramar (☎7/204-9081); Vía at Ave. 47 esq. 28a, Kohly, Playa (☎7/204-3606); and Rex, who offer the most reliable but most expensive cars with their most

central office at Malecón esq. Linea, Vedado (☎7/835-6830). Most hotels have car rental desks in their lobbies and most car rental companies also have desks in Terminal 3 of Havana airport.

Cell phone For all matters concerning cell phones, including rental of handsets, go to Cubacel, Miramar Trade Center, Ave. 3ra esq. 78, Miramar.

Embassies The vast majority of embassies and consulates are based in Miramar. They include the British Embassy, Calle 34 no.702/704 (☎7/204-1771, ☎204-8104); and the Canadian Embassy, Calle 30 no.518 (☎7/204-2516 & 204-2382, ☎204-2044). The German Embassy is in Vedado at Calle B no.652 esq. 13 (☎7/833-2569 & 833-2460, ☎833-1586); and the Spanish Embassy is in Habana Vieja at Cárcel no.51 esq. Zulueta (☎7/866-8025, 866-8026 & 866-8029, ☎866-8006. The United States is represented by the Special Interests Section, at Calle Calzada esq. Calle L, Vedado (☎7/833-3551 to 59, ☎833-3700).

Hairdressers and barbers Salón Correo, Brasil (Teniente Rey) e/ Mercaderes y Oficios; *Hotel Habana Libre*, Calle 23 esq. L, Vedado.

Immigration and legal Asistur, Paseo del Prado no.208–212 esq. Trocadero (☎7/866-8920, 866-8339 & 866-8527, ☎866-8087) deals with insurance claims, financial emergencies and can advise on renewing and extending tourist card visas; open 24hr. Otherwise, try the Consultoria Juridica Internacional in Miramar at Calle 16 no.314 e/ 3ra y 5ta (☎7/204-2490 & 204-2697; Mon–Fri 8.30am–noon & 1.30–5.30pm).

Internet and email Cybercafe Capitolio, just inside the main entrance hall of the Capitolio building offers one of the cheapest rates; daily 8am–5pm; $5CUC for an hour; printing available at 20c per page (☎7/862-0485 & 861-0560 ext. 109). There are five terminals in the Internet café in the *Hotel Inglaterra*, which is one of the few places where it's cheaper to be online for under an hour ($2CUC for 15min, $3CUC for 30min, $6CUC for 1hr). There are ETECSA Telepuntos at Aguila no.565 esq. Dragones in Centro Habana (daily 8am–9.30pm) and at Obispo esq. Habana in Habana Vieja (daily 8am–9.30pm). The *Hotel Telégrafo* cybercafé is open 24hr. You can also get online at the Centro de Negocios in the *Hotel Nacional* in Vedado. Most hotels charge between $7CUC and $10CUC an hour.

Laundry Uni Max, a launderette and dry cleaner, is located at Galeria Comercial Comodoro, Ave. 3ra e/ 80 y 84, Miramar.

Library The Biblioteca Nacional José Martí is amongst the largest in the country and is located at Ave. de la Independencia esq. 20 de Mayo, Plaza de la Revolución (Mon–Fri 8am–9pm & Sat 8am–6pm; ☎7/881-8876). Much smaller but more pleasant and well maintained is the Biblioteca Rubén Martínez Villena on the Plaza de Armas (Mon–Fri 8am–9pm & Sat 9am–4pm). It has a foreign literature section on the second floor but non-residents are not permitted to take books outside the building.

Medical There is no single emergency number for ringing an ambulance, but you can call ☎7/55-1185 & 838-2185 to get one. You can also contact Asistur, the tourist assistance agency, on their emrergency number (☎7/866-8339). One of the best hospitals, run predominantly for foreigners, is the Clínica Internacional Cira García in Miramar at Calle 20 no.4101 esq. Ave. 41 (☎7/204-2880 & 204-2811 50 13). The switchboard number for the Hospital Hermanos Ameijeiras at San Lázaro no.701 e/ Padre Varela y Marqués González in Centro Habana, with two floors reserved for foreign patients, is ☎7/876-1000.

Money transfer There's a Western Union office in the post office at Oficios no.104 esq. Lamparilla, Habana Vieja, and in the Plaza Carlos III shopping mall at Ave. Salvador Allende e/ Retiro y Arbol Seco in Centro Habana. For general information call ☎7/204-1399.

Newspapers and magazines Foreign newspapers and magazines are extremely difficult to find but your best bets are the *Hotel Nacional* and the *Meliá Cohiba* in Vedado or the *Meliá Habana* in Miramar. For Cuban press either look for a street seller or go to La Moderna Poesia, Obispo esq. Bernaza in Habana Vieja, or any other bookshop.

Pharmacies Farmacia Internacional, at Ave. 41 no.1814, esq. 20, in Miramar (☎7/204-4359 & 204-5051), is one of the best stocked in Havana. In Habana Vieja the best options are either in the *Hotel Plaza* or Farmacia Taquechel at Obispo no.155 e/ Mercaderes y San Ignacio, which stocks basic pain-relief tablets including aspirin but specializes in natural medicines. In Vedado, there are small pharmacies in hotels *Nacional* and *Habana Libre*, equipped with most of the essentials.

Photography Foto Habana at Tacón no.22 e/ Plaza de Armas y Empedrado in Habana Vieja is one of the best shops for photographic equipment and supplies. Trimagen is at Neptuno esq. Industria, Centro Habana.

Police Habana Vieja's police headquarters are in the mock-colonial fort at Tacón e/ San Ignacio y Cuba. The main station in Centro Habana is at Dragones e/ Lealtad y Escobar (☎7/862-4412). In an emergency ring ☎106.

Post offices The branch at Ave. Salvador Allende esq. Padre Varela, Centro Habana (Mon–Sat 8am–6pm) offers peso services only. The branch in the Gran Teatro building at Paseo del Prado esq. San Martín offers fax and telegram services as well as poste restante facilities (daily 8am–7pm).

Public toilets There is one at Mercaderes no.269 e/ Brasil y Amargura in Habana Vieja. Your best bet in Vedado is the washrooms on the ground floor of the *Habana Libre*.

Taxis Habanataxi (☎7/53-9086); Panataxi (☎7/55-5555); Transtur (☎7/208-6666); Taxis OK (☎7/204-0000 & 877-6666); Transgaviota (☎7/267-1626). There are taxi ranks on the Parque Central and outside the Capitolio Nacional. To call a *cocotaxi*, the novelty three-wheel scooter taxis, ring Cocotaxis (☎7/873-1411). For a ride in a 1950s American classic, ring Gran Car (☎7/33-5647 or 41-7980).

Telephone The largest banks of public telephones are in the ETECSA Telepunto centre (see "Internet and email" above). Smaller ETECSA telephone cabins are located at Tacón esq. Chacón in Habana Vieja, at Ave. de Italia esq. Ave. Simón Bolívar in Centro Habana, and at La Rampa e/ O y Malecón in Vedado.

Train station Ave. de Bélgica esq. Arsenal, Habana Vieja (☎7/860-9448 & 862-1920).

Travel agents Cubanacán, Calle 17A e/ 176 y 190, Siboney, Playa (☎7/204-3761 & 204-5009); Cubatur, Calle 23 e/ L y M, Vedado (☎7/833-3569); Havanatur, Calle 23 esq Calle M, Vedado (☎7/55-4884); San Cristóbal, Oficios no.110 e/ Lamparilla y Amargura, Plaza de San Francisco, Habana Vieja (☎7/861-9171 & 861-9172). For information on *campismos* throughout the country contact Cubamar at Calle 15 esq. Paseo, Vedado (☎7/66-2523 to 24).

East of Havana

Taking the tunnel in Habana Vieja under the bay and heading east on the Vía Monumental, past El Morro and parallel to the coast, leads you straight to

Cojímar, a fishing village famed for its Hemingway connection. Past here the road dips inland to become the Vía Blanca and runs south towards **Guanabacoa**, a quiet provincial town with numerous attractive churches and a fascinating religious history. For many, the big attraction east of Havana will be the boisterous **Playas del Este**, the nearest beaches to the city 18km away, where clean sands and a lively scene draw in the crowds. In contrast, **Playa Jibacoa**, 32km further east, offers a quieter, less glitzy beach resort, while the inland hills of the **Escalera de Jaruco** present a scenic diversion. The hippie retreat at **Canasí**, tucked away on the cliffs overlooking the ocean, is perfect for a back-to-basics camping experience and represents the province's final outpost before the border with Matanzas.

The scarcity and unreliability of **public transport** becomes even more pronounced once outside the city proper, and you'll need a car to see many of these sights.

Cojímar

Just 6km east of Havana the tiny fishing village of **COJÍMAR** is a world apart from the bustling city – tailor-made for enjoying such simple pleasures as watching fishing boats bob about in the calm, hoop-shaped bay, or wandering the tidy, bougainvillea-fringed streets.

Cojímar's sole claim to fame revolves around one of its late residents, Gregorio Fuentes, the old man upon whom Ernest Hemingway based Santiago, the protagonist of his Pulitzer- and Nobel Prize-winning novel *The Old Man and the Sea*. Fuentes was actually only in his forties when Hemingway, who used to berth his fishing boat *The Pilar* here, started writing the tale in 1951. Up until the late 1990s Fuentes could be seen sitting outside his house or in *La Terraza de Cojímar* restaurant, charging $10CUC for a consultation with fans eager for Hemingway stories. When Fuentes died in 2002, aged 104, it marked the end of an era and one of the last personal links with a man so important to the country's cultural history.

The village pays homage to Hemingway's memory in the **Monumento a Hemingway**, a weatherbeaten construction close to the small *malecón*, which looks a bit like a dwarf Acropolis, with a ring of six classic columns on a stately plinth, crowned with an entablature like a big open hoop. In the middle is Hemingway himself, represented by a rather meagre bust on top of a block, looking rather comical in contrast to the august surroundings. The whole thing has the air of a misplaced garden ornament and manages to invest the nearby **Torreón de Cojímar** with a similarly spurious air. Overhanging the water's edge, the fort, built between 1639 and 1643 as part of the Spanish colonial fortification, is so small it looks rather like a well-crafted toy. A squat and sturdy building, with sharp, clean angles and Moorish sentry boxes, it was designed by the engineer Juan Bautista Antonelli – who also designed the not-dissimilar El Morro castle – as an early-warning system for attacks on Havana harbour, and only needed to accommodate a couple of sentries rather than a whole battalion. Even so, it was usually left unmanned, a defensive weakness fully exploited by the British in 1762, who bombarded it with cannon-fire, routed the peasants' and slaves' attempts at retaliation and romped off to capture the city. The fort is still in military use, so there's no access to the building, although you are free to examine the outside.

Practicalities

Cojímar is served by the #58 **bus** from Prado, by the mouth of the tunnel in Habana Vieja, while a taxi will cost around $10CUC. There's no state-sanctioned accommodation at present, though you may be able to find an unlicensed *casa particular*. Cojímar's flagship **restaurant**, *La Terraza de Cojímar*, on the east side of the village in Calle Real (☎7/65-3471), is airy, pleasant and full of black-and-white photos of Hemingway and Fuentes, although the food isn't all it could be: go for the simple dishes and avoid the soggy paella and over-salted lobster thermidor. The house cocktail, Don Gregorio, made with dark rum and orange juice, is named for Hemingway's good friend. Reservations are recommended as the place is sometimes booked out by bus tours. Seafood is much better – and cheaper – at the *paladar La Terracita* a few streets up the slight hill on Calle 3c no.9606. Otherwise, there's a *Rumbos* café on the *malecón* serving chicken and chips, and *El Golfito* on the east side of the river that runs through the town, offering basic eats for Cuban pesos.

Guanabacoa

Less than 2km inland from the Vía Monumental turn-off to Cojímar is **GUANABACOA**, a little town officially within the city limits but with a distinctly provincial feel. The site of a pre-Columbian community and later one of the island's first Spanish settlements, it is historically important, though its disproportionately large number of churches and the strong tradition of Afro-Cuban religion hold the most appeal for visitors. The town's most coherent and impressive attraction is the **Museo Histórico de Guanabacoa**, Martí no.108 e/ Quintin Bandera y E.V. Valenzuela (Mon–Sat 9.30am–4.30pm, closed Tues; ☎7/97-9510; $2CUC), two blocks from the understated main square, Parque Martí. The museum gets its edge from the collection of cultish objects relating to the practices of Santería, Palo Monte and the Abakuá Secret Society. One room is moodily set up to reflect the mystic environment in which the *babalao*, the Santería equivalent of a priest, would perform divination rituals, surrounded by altars and African deities in the form of Catholic saints. Equally poignant are the representations of Elegguá, one of the most powerful Afro-Cuban *orishas*, with their almost threatening stares. There are also some interesting bits and pieces, including furniture and ceramics, relating to the town's history. It's worth ringing in advance to check opening hours, as the museum has undergone long periods of closure over recent years, supposedly for restorations.

The town's five churches make up the remainder of its sights, and though none has reliable opening times there's usually a staff member on hand willing to let you take a wander inside. The most accessible and intact are the run-down **Iglesia Parroquial Mayor** on Parque Martí, with its magnificent, though age-worn, wooden gilted main altar; the eighteenth-century **Iglesia de Santo Domingo** and adjoining monastery, on the corner of Lebredo and Santo Domingo, with a lovely leafy courtyard; and the huge monastery, now a school, attached to the still-functioning **Iglesia de San Francisco**, a block south of Martí on Quintin Bandera. Otherwise, once you've checked out the Afro-Cuban-style knick-knacks in the Bazar de Reproducciones Artísticas, two blocks down from the museum at Martí no.175, and eaten at *El Palenque*, the basic outdoor restaurant next door, you've done the town justice.

Playas del Este

Fifteen kilometres east of Cojímar, the Vía Blanca reaches Havana's nearest beaches – Playa Santa María del Mar, Playa Boca Ciega and Playa Guanabo, collectively known as the **Playas del Este**. Hugging the Atlantic coast, these three fine-sand beaches form a long, twisting ochre ribbon which vanishes in the summer beneath the crush of weekending Habaneros and tourists. There's

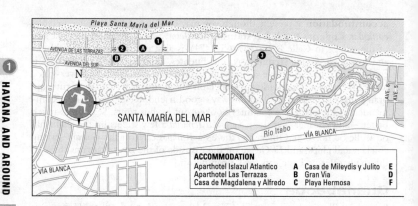

ACCOMMODATION

Aparthotel Islazul Atlantico	A	Casa de Mileydis y Julito	E
Aparthotel Las Terrazas	B	Gran Via	D
Casa de Magdalena y Alfredo	C	Playa Hermosa	F

not a whole lot to distinguish between the beaches, geographically, although as a general rule the sand is better towards the western end.

If you're based in Havana for most of your time in Cuba, the excellent self-catering and hotel accommodation here makes this area a good choice for a mini-break. Those craving creature comforts should head for the big hotels in Santa María, while budget travellers will find the best value in the inexpensive hotels and *casas particulares* in Guanabo. Other than the forbidding all-inclusive *Club Blau Arenal* (☎7/97-1272; ➐), there's nowhere to stay in Playa Boca Ciega. Although a number of restaurants serve cheap meals, these all tend to be much the same, and your best bet is to eat at the *paladar* in Guanabo; otherwise, see if one of the *casas particulares* can recommend somewhere.

In terms of **transportation** costs, a metered taxi from the centre of Havana to Guanabo will cost around $15–20CUC. Alternatively, the #295 bus runs to here from Calle 23 and G. The Víazul buses depart Havana for Playas del Este three times daily from their station in Nuevo Vedado, with additional pick-ups at the *Colina* and *Plaza* hotels, dropping off on Avenida de la Terrazas in front of the cluster of hotels. A one-way ticket costs $4CUC.

Playa Santa María del Mar

Due to its proximity to Havana, **Playa Santa María del Mar**, usually just called Santa María, is the busiest and trendiest of the eastern beaches, with boombox reggaeton, watersports and beautiful bodies on sunloungers. It extends for about 4km from the foot of Santa María Loma, a hill to the south of the Río Itabo, with the bulk of hotels dotted around the main **Avenida de las Terrazas**, just behind the beach. Arguably the most beautiful of the three beaches, golden sands backed by grasslands and a few palm trees, it's also the most touristy and can feel a bit artificial. Studded with palm-thatch sunshades and sunloungers ($2CUC a day), and patrolled by eager beach masseurs (roughly $5–7CUC for 30min), Santa María is the best bet for **beach activities** and you can play volleyball or rent a catamaran ($8CUC for 30min) or snorkelling equipment ($3CUC per hour) – though sadly you'll see more empty beer cans than fish. With thatch-hut beach bars at intervals along the beach and roving vendors selling rum-laced coconuts, there's no shortage of **refreshment**. A big convertible-peso shop on Avenida de las Terrazas sells the makings of a picnic, although the prices are higher than goods in Havana so you'd do well to bring what you need with you.

RESTAURANTS
La Caleta **2** Costarena **1** Mi Cayito **3**
Coppelia **5** Cuanda **7** Parriada **6**
                          Tropinini **4**

HAVANA AND AROUND | East of Havana

Accommodation

Aparthotel Islazul Atlantico Ave. de las Terrazas e/ 11 y 13 ☏ 7/97-1203. Spotless, spacious and airy self-catering one- two- and three-bed apartments ($5CUC extra for a cooker and fridge) in a complex of slick, ice-cream-coloured buildings with views over the beach. Good value for groups. There's a Transtur moped rental here as well. ⑤

Aparthotel Las Terrazas Ave. de las Terrazas e/10 y Rotunda ☏ 7/97-1344, ⓕ 80-2396. Despite a holiday camp vibe that's emphasized by the huge, busy swimming pool, this is a good option, with decent two- and three-bed apartments featuring kitchen, sitting room and minibar. ⑥

Eating

El Brocal Calle 5ta C Avenida esq. 500. Almost on the town's eastern limits, this fresh and bright open-air state restaurant, with tables on a wooden veranda, has the feel of a *paladar*. It's pricier than its rivals, with even basic meals costing between $6CUC and $10CUC, but worth it, with a good range of seafood and meat dishes, plus the occasional catch of the day. All meals come with cassava, salad and fried green banana.

La Caleta Ave. de las Terrazas s/n. Central to the beach, this open-air restaurant has a thatched palm roof, music at weekends and a lively air. The decent menu includes lobster *brochette* for $8 CUC, pork dishes for $5CUC and steak for $6.50CUC.

Costarena Villa Los Pinos, Santa María ☏ 7/97-1361. An average restaurant with beach views, mediocre service and decent paella.

Playa Boca Ciega

A bridge across the Río Itabo connects Santa María to Playa Boca Ciega, also known as Playa Mi Cayito. A paucity of public facilities and just one rather grubby café, *Mi Cayito*, make this the least user-friendly of all the beaches However, the beautiful sherbet-yellow beach is open to all, and the waters around the estuary mouth are usually quite busy and cheerful, with kids and adults paddling and wading in the river currents. Further west, towards Santa María, the beach is popular with the gay community.

Playa Guanabo

Far more pleasant than Playa Boca Ciega is laid-back **Playa Guanabo**, roughly 2.5km further east, where the sun-faded wooden houses and jaunty seaside atmosphere go a long way to compensate for the slightly poor brownish-sand beach. With fewer crowds and no big hotels, it feels much more authentic than Santa María, especially towards the east end of town where tourism has hardly penetrated at all. While not idyllic, it still has its charms; palm trees offer welcome shade on the generous stretch of beach, and if you're not bothered about the odd bit of seaweed clouding the sea, this is a refreshingly unaffected spot to hang out.

199

As most tourists stay on the better beaches further west, Guanabo is pretty much left to the Cubans, with many residents commuting daily from here to Havana for work. Avenida 5ta, the appealing main street, has a clutch of cafés and shops, including a convertible-peso shopping precinct selling sweets, toys and sportswear, while around the side streets and near the beach are a couple of excellent *paladares*. Other than the *Playa Hermosa* hotel all accommodation is in *casas particulares*, giving the area a pleasant homespun feel.

Accommodation

Playa Hermosa 5ta Avenida e/472 y 474 ☏7/96-2774. Basic but pleasant hotel with simple rooms, a swimming pool and daily cabaret. ❷

Casas Particulares

Bernardo y Adelina Calle 478 no.306 e/ 3ra y 5ta Guanabo ☏7/96-3609. One a/c room with a private bathroom, an adjoining sitting room, a dining area, and a kitchen area with a fridge. ❷
Casa de Magdalena y Alfredo Calle 468 no.508 e/ 5ta y 7ma, Guanabo ☏7/96-4192. Huge, airy apartment with a modern bathroom complete with bathtub and plants. The big kitchen has a fridge, and you can use the family terrace and beautiful gardens. ❸
Casa de Mileydis y Julito Calle 468 no.512 e/ 5ta y 7ma, Guanabo ☏7/96-0100. One a/c apartment, close to the beach, with a TV and a small bathroom. Has a pretty garden and a porch where you can relax. ❷

Eating

Coppelia Calle 5ta Avenida e. 478 y 480. Guanabo's small and dainty branch of the ice-cream parlour chain also offers snack meals, with chicken and chips. A firm locals' favourite. Open 24hr.
Cuanda 472 esq. 5ta D. A basic restaurant dishing up reasonable meals on the pork, salad, rice and beans theme. At $3.50CUC for a main meal, it's good value.
Parriada Calle 5ta Avenida e/ 472 y 474. Very ordinary hamburger and fried chicken-type snacks served in an open-air dining area. A meal costs about $2CUC.
Tropinini Calle 5ta Avenida no.49213 e/ 492 y 494. Excellent *paladar* open to 2am. Breakfast is a wholesome combination of eggs, toast and fruit juice, while lunch and dinner consist of well-prepared pork, chicken or spaghetti served with fried green bananas and salad for $5–6CUC. Easily the best choice in the area.

Playa Jibacoa

Forty kilometres east from the Playas del Este, tucked behind a barricade of white cliffs, is **Playa Jibacoa**, a stretch of coastline basking in the relative anonymity it enjoys as a neighbour of the more popular, more developed beaches closer to Havana. Approaching from Havana on the Vía Blanca road, the first turning after the bridge over the Río Jibacoa leads down onto the coastal road that runs the length of this laid-back resort area. Predominantly the domain of Cuban holidaymakers, the beach here is mostly small and unspectacular but pleasantly protected by swathes of twisting trees and bushes, with an appealing sense of privacy cemented by the cliffs that enclose this narrow strip of land. There are modest **coral reefs** offshore and basic snorkelling equipment can be rented at the *campismos* (see below).

For better diving opportunities, though, as well as boat trips and fishing facilities, you're better off heading 12km further east along the Vía Blanca to the nautical centre at **Puerto Escondido**, just a few kilometres short of the Havana-Matanzas border. The Centro de Buceo Puerto Escondido (☏7/866-2524), operated by Cubamar, is a relatively small outfit but it does run a ten-man dive boat used to visit the five coral reefs that provide all the centre's dive sites. Prices can be negotiated, especially if you intend several dives, but a single dive usually costs $30CUC, two for $40CUC.

There's only one fully developed, international-standard hotel in these parts, the *Superclub Breezes Jibacoa* (☏47/29-5153; 9x), an attractive, well-equipped all-inclusive on a private patch of coastline, predominantly reserved for tourists on pre-booked packages; kids under fourteen aren't allowed. More suitable for the casual visitor are the *campismo* sites along the shoreline – while several are used to accepting foreign guests, many are quite scrappy, some are for Cubans only, and closed throughout the winter months. Among the bunch, *Villa Loma* (☏47/8-3316 & 8-5316; ❸) sits up on a small hill at the Havana end of this stretch of coastline, overlooking one of the widest sections of beach, at the mouth of the river and within sight of the bridge. Peering over the water's edge, this twelve-house site is simple, rather than basic, with a charming little restaurant, a pool and a fantastic bar in a stone watchtower. Another decent, good-value option is *Villa Los Cocos* (☏47/29-5231; ❷), a relatively new complex with a pool, video room, small library and above average accommodation for a *campismo*, made up of pleasant-looking bungalows with air conditioner, TV and kitchenettes.

Canasí

Around 10km east of Playa Jibacoa, high upon a cliff-like precipice overlooking the narrow Arroyo Bermejo estuary, the tiny hamlet of **CANASÍ** doubles as the informal weekend campsite for a hippie-chic crowd of young Habaneros. In the summer, scores of revellers descend every Friday to set up camp in the tranquil woodland around the cliff's edge, spending the weekend swimming and snorkelling in the clear Atlantic waters, exploring the woods and nearby caves, singing folk songs and generally communing with nature. It's a refreshingly uncontrived experience with a peace-festival kind of atmosphere. There are no facilities, so you'll have to bring everything you need, most importantly fresh water, but don't worry too much if you don't have a tent, as the summer nights are warm enough to bed down beneath the stars.

Regular visitors take the late-night **Hershey train** ($3CUC) from Casablanca to Canasí on Friday night; this is not the most reliable form of transport, though, and you might be better off driving. The road down to the water's edge is badly signposted but look for a left turn off the Vía Blanca (a 5min walk from the station) and take the dirt track to the estuary mouth, where the fishermen who live in the waterside cottages will row you across the shallow waters to the site for about $2CUC a head, though the hardy can wade.

Escaleras de Jaruco

Around 20km inland, the **Escaleras de Jaruco**, a small crop of hills south of Playas del Este and west of **Jaruco**, the nearest town of any significant size, make a stimulating detour on the way to or from the beaches, though only feasible with your own transport. The best way to find these rarely visited hills is to first head for humble Jaruco, roughly a twenty-five kilometre drive from the Vía Blanca. There are lonely roads from any of the beach resorts east of Havana to this tiny outpost of a town, but the most straightforward route is to leave the Vía Blanca at the small coastal town of Santa Cruz del Norte, which the Vía Blanca passes through around 30km east of the Playas del Este. From Santa Cruz del Norte, the only road leading inland will take you through several small towns en route, first La Sierra, then Camilo Cienfuegos and San Antonio de Río Blanco, each only several kilometres apart, before arriving at the sloping roads of Jaruco, a fairly nondescript town of several thousand people, 25km by road from Santa Cruz del Norte. Alternatively, if you're prepared to do a lot of walking, you can catch the Hershey train from Casablanca in Habana del Este (see p.152) and jump off at Jibacoa station.

To get to the Escaleras de Jaruco, take the Carretera Tapaste, a lonely, worn-out road, west from Jaruco. Once out of town, the landscape changes surprisingly and dramatically fast, as the Escaleras de Jaruco erupt from the surrounding flatlands, this steep-sided mini-mountain range covered in a kind of subtropical rainforest. The Carretera Tapaste cuts through this area like a mountain pass, leading directly up to the second surprise, a **restaurant**, *El Arabe* (no phone), here in the middle of nowhere. In its pre-Revolution heyday, it was undoubtedly a classic, with its splendid Arabic-style interior, balcony terrace with views to the coastline and domed tower, but is now as low on food as it is on staff, and there's no guarantee it will even be open when you turn up. Nonetheless, *El Arabe* provides a focus of sorts for the area, and is still worth a brief stop.

Two minutes' drive up the road past the restaurant, at about the hills' highest point, is the *Hotel Escaleras de Jaruco* (☎ 64/3-1925 & 3-2925; ❸), run-down and low on facilities but home to a reasonably sized pool. More used to accommodating Cubans than foreign tourists, you may find your arrival raises a few eyebrows or even that you are refused a room on the grounds that the hotel is for Cubans only, though this is not strictly true. As with the restaurant, the location makes all the difference, and in the unlikely event you spend the night here, waking up to the magnificent views will more than compensate for the dull and poorly equipped rooms.

South of Havana

Heading south of Havana, the city fades in fits and starts, the buildings dying out only to reappear again almost immediately amongst the trees and green fields which bind this area together. Numerous satellite towns dot the semi-urban, semi-rural landscape, distinctly provincial in character yet so close to Havana as to be served by municipal bus routes. The best of what there is south of the city is all within a thirty-kilometre drive of the city centre.

The airport road, the **Avenida de Rancho Boyeros**, is the easiest route to most of the day-trip destinations on this side of the capital. It makes sense to visit at least a couple of these on the same day, as seeing each one on its own is unlikely to last more than a few hours. A near-perfect preservation of the great writer's home in Havana, the **Museo Ernest Hemingway**, nearer the Vía Blanca than the road to the airport, is the most concrete option and one of the few that stands up well by itself; the views across Havana alone are enough to justify the trip. The relative proximity of **Parque Lenin** – an immense park next door to the **zoo** – to the sprawling **Jardín Botánico**, over the road from **ExpoCuba**, makes these a convenient combination for anyone looking for a reasonable variety of experience. A few kilometres further south, beyond the airport, the town of **Santiago de las Vegas** and the nearby **Santuario de San Lázaro** make good stopping-off points on the way to **San Antonio de los Baños**, 15km further south, which, with its unique Museo de Humor, is the most worthwhile town to visit in the province, its picturesquely located hotel making it worth spending more than a day there.

Museo Ernest Hemingway

Eleven kilometres southeast of Habana Vieja, in the suburb of San Francisco de Paula, is Finca La Vigía, an attractive little estate centred on the whitewashed nineteenth-century villa where Ernest Hemingway lived for twenty years until 1960. Now the **Museo Ernest Hemingway** (Mon–Sat 9am–4.30pm, Sun 9am–noon, closed Tues; ⊕7/91-0809; $3CUC), it makes a simple but enjoyable excursion from the city. On top of a hill and with splendid views over Havana, this single-storey colonial residence, where Hemingway wrote a number of his most famous novels, has been preserved almost exactly as he left it – with drinks and magazines strewn about the place and the dining-room table set for guests. Brimming with character, it's a remarkable insight into the writer's lifestyle and personality, from the numerous stuffed animal heads on the walls to the thousands of books lining the shelves in most of the rooms, including the bathroom. The small room where his typewriter is still stationed was where Hemingway did much of his work, often in the mornings and usually standing up. Frustratingly, you can't actually walk into the rooms but must view everything through the open windows and doors; by walking around the encircling veranda, however, you can get good views of most rooms. In the well-kept gardens, which you can walk round, Hemingway's fishing boat is suspended inside a wooden pavilion and you can visit the graves of four of his dogs, located next to the swimming pool.

The museum closes when it rains, to protect the interior from the damp and to preserve the well-groomed grounds, so try to visit on sunny days. To **get there**, take the Vía Blanca through the southern part of the city and turn off at the Carretera Central, which cuts through San Francisco de Paula. Alternatively, you can brave the #M-7 *camello* from the Parque de la Fraternidad and walk from the bus stop.

Parque Lenin

Roughly a twenty-minute drive south of the city, about 3km west of the José Martí airport, are the immense grounds of **Parque Lenin** (Tues–Sun 10am–5pm; free; ⊕7/44-3026 to 29), a cross between a landscaped urban park and a rolling tract of untouched wooded countryside. Founded in 1972, this was once a popular escape for city residents who came here to picnic, ride horseback and unwind through simple pleasures, like boating and fairground rides, in beautifully kept surroundings. However, the deterioration in public transport since the early 1990s led to a sharp drop in visitors, and today a pervasive air of abandon blows around the park and for better or worse it remains a distinctly untouristy attraction. Nonetheless, its sheer size, almost eight square kilometres, and scenic landscape make Parque Lenin a great place for a picnic or just a breath of fresh air.

To visit the park, currently only reachable **by car**, head towards the airport on Avenida Rancho Boyeros, and look for the signposted left turn onto Avenida San Francisco, which, within 5km, leads to the park's main entrance, marked by a large billboard. You can drive right into and around the park, though the main through-road leads straight over to the far side where the park boundaries are less clearly marked and it's easy to drive out without knowing you've left. A more exciting way to explore is on horseback; the **Centro Ecuestre** is signposted, along with a number of the park's other attractions, at the first right-hand turn as you enter from the city side. Here you can rent out horses for $3CUC an hour, though it's not guaranteed they'll have anything available or even be open. This uncertainty has been seized upon by locals who often hang around the makeshift car park offering rides on their own horses, but be prepared for plenty of haggling if you choose this option.

Nearby to the Centro Ecuestre is the **Parque de Diversiones**, an outdated kids' theme park, with carousels, a small roller coaster and number of other rides, some functioning, others rusting away after years of neglect. The sweeping, dried-out lawns and abundant trees in this section, which sink into what effectively becomes open countryside but still within the park confines, make it a good option for a wander about. For a more concrete **tour** there is an old steam **train** running a 45-minute circuit around the park several times a day during peak season, but at other times it may not run at all ($2CUC).

For the rest of the park's more tangible activities, head back to the main through-road and head towards the southern part of the park, the best of it just over the other side of the reservoir near the park's centre. Here you can take a boat out on the large man-made lake; peruse the paintings, predominantly the work of the Cuban Amelia Peláez (1896–1968), at the **Galería de Arte** (10am–4pm; $1CUC); visit the freshwater fish, turtles and crocodiles at the **aquarium** (10am–4pm; $1CUC); or just admire the park's most famous monument, the nine-metre marble bust of Lenin.

For the time being, reliable **eating options** are limited to ramshackle *El Dragón*, a patio eatery just off the main road, and *Las Ruinas* (☎7/57-8286; Tues–Sun noon–11pm), a hulk of a restaurant beyond the reservoir, built amongst some ruined, moss-covered walls overlooking a tree-lined lawn. It specializes in expensive seafood, though also serves more reasonably priced spaghetti, pizza and *comida criolla*, and is more refined than you might expect from the ramshackle outside. There's also a piano bar downstairs.

Parque Zoológico Nacional

Just over a kilometre west, though technically part of Parque Lenin, is the **Parque Zoológico Nacional** (July & Aug Wed–Sun 9am–4.30pm; Sept–June Wed–Sun 9am–3.15pm; ☎7/881-8915 & 881-8215; $3CUC adults, $2CUC children, $5CUC car, including passengers), a perpetually half-finished safari park. The spacious three-and-a-half-square-kilometre site, which includes a small lake, has a suitably natural feel and the two enclosures that have been completed do allow good views of the animals. Herbivores of the African savannah, including elephants, rhinos, giraffes and zebras, roam about in the **Pradera Africana** enclosure, while the **Foso de Leones**, a huge grass- and tree-lined pit, allows excitingly close contact with the park's twenty or so lions. However, the majority of the animals, mostly big cats and apes, are kept in cramped conditions in the so-called Area de Reproducción. The park suffered severe setbacks as a result of Cuba's economic crisis in the early 1990s and is still slowly clawing its way back to respectability. If you don't want to walk or drive about the park, you can ride one of the **buses** that leave from just inside the main entrance every thirty minutes or so on tours of the park; they include guides, but don't count on an English speaker.

Jardín Botánico Nacional and ExpoCuba

Three kilometres south of the entrance to Parque Lenin, along the Carretera del Rocío, is the entrance to the **Jardín Botánico Nacional** (Wed–Sun 9am–4pm; ☎7/54-9170 & 54-7278; $1CUC, $3CUC for guided tour with own vehicle, $4CUC for train tour), a sweeping expanse of parkland that's a showcase for a massive variety of plants, particularly trees from around the world.

Laid out as a savannah rather than a forest, the grounds are split into sections according to continent, with the different zones blending almost seamlessly into one another. Highlights include the collection of 162 surprisingly varied species of **palm**, and the **Japanese Garden**, donated by the Japanese government on the thirtieth anniversary of the Revolution in 1989 – a compact, colourful and meticulously landscaped area built around a beautiful little lake and backing onto rocky terraced waterfalls and fountains. The Japanese Garden also has the best place to stop for **lunch**, at *El Bambú* (℡7/54-7278; 1–3.30pm), with a tasty $12CUC vegetarian buffet. It's worth reserving a place at the restaurant in advance or when you arrive, at the ticket booth at the entrance, especially if the park is very busy or very empty. Near the main entrance are the captivating indoor **Pabellones de Exposiciones**, two large greenhouse-style buildings with raised viewing platforms and twisting pathways, one housing a fantastic collection of cacti, the other a landscaped jungle of tropical plants and flowers.

Though you can explore the park yourself, a lack of printed literature and plaques means you'll learn far more by booking an organized excursion or taking the **guided tour**, whether in the trackless train or having a guide in your own car. The guides are impressively knowledgeable and make the whole experience interactive; besides teaching about the origins of the various species and their various medicinal uses, they let you stop within reaching distance of trees to pick and eat cherries or smell leaves. There's usually at least one English-speaking guide available, but it's worth noting that the tractor-bus tours, which generally last from one to two hours, do not necessarily cover the whole park. Tours leave every hour or so from just inside the main entrance, near the useful **information office**. There's also a small shop selling ornamental plants; at weekends a bus takes passengers from here directly to the Japanese Garden (every 30min; $1CUC).

ExpoCuba

On the other side of the Carretera del Rocío, directly opposite the gardens, what looks like a well-kept industrial estate is in fact **ExpoCuba** (Wed–Sun 9am–5pm, closed Sept–Dec, except for special events; $1CUC), a permanent exhibition of the island's endeavours in industry, science, technology and commerce since the Revolution. A series of huge pavilions, each showcasing a different area of achievement, it's impressively wide-ranging – with exhibits ranging from an entire aeroplane to a bottle of brake liquid – but only really manageable if you don't try to see everything. If you've come with a specific interest in, say, the Cuban health system or the sugar industry, you'll find plenty to occupy you in those areas alone. Despite its impressive scope, though, displays are a little dry and the hordes of children here on school trips tend to be more interested in running about the place, riding on the mini-roller coaster (50¢) and boating on the small lake ($1CUC). There's a seafood **restaurant** by the lake and various *cafeterias*, including the *Bar Mirador*, a circular revolving café balanced on top of two giant concrete stilts from where you get an excellent perspective on the layout of ExpoCuba and views across to the Jardín Botánico.

For one week every year, usually the first week in November, ExpoCuba hosts the **Feria Internacional de la Habana** (℡7/21-0758), an international trade fair. This is by far the best time to visit, as commercial enterprises from around the world come to exhibit their products and promote their services, usually with the objective of establishing export or import links with Cuban companies and the Cuban state in general, creating a livelier atmosphere and a more exciting range of exhibits. In recent years companies from over forty countries have attended the fair, representing all kinds of industries, from tourism to agriculture, with an eclectic range of products on display, from farm equipment to toothpaste including numerous US brand names, albeit brought over from other countries, such as Mexican-made Kellogg's Corn Flakes, and

Canadian-manufactured Ford trucks. There are fashion shows, concerts and all kinds of goods on display, as well as a pitch for many of the capital's most famous restaurants.

Santiago de las Vegas and the Santuario de San Lázaro

It's well worth calling in at **SANTIAGO DE LAS VEGAS**, 2km south of José Martí airport, especially if you're on your way to the popular pilgrimage point of El Rincón (see below). Half provincial town, half city suburb, Santiago de las Vegas doesn't offer a lot to do besides wander aimlessly around the dusty streets and attractive central square, but it's nevertheless a pleasantly relaxing place to get a feel for Cuba beyond the big city, entirely untouched by tourism. Avenida 409, leading off the square, is full of peso snack-sellers, and with a *casa de cambio* on the same street there's no excuse for not testing the local fast-food. The #M-2 *camello* from the Parque de la Fraternidad in Habana Vieja drops you off on the square. El Rincón is a couple of kilometres further south of the town on the Carretera Santiago de las Vegas, the main road running through it.

Ten kilometres south of central Havana, the **Santuario de San Lázaro** (daily 7am–6pm), on the edge of the tiny village of **EL RINCÓN**, is the final destination of a pilgrimage made by thousands of Cubans every December. Amidst scenes of intense religious fervour, pilgrims come to this gleaming, lovingly maintained church to ask favours of San Lázaro, whose image appears inside, in exchange for sacrifices (see box below). Whatever the month, though, people come here to cut deals with the saint and lay down flowers or make a donation, and the road through the village is always lined with people selling flowers and statuettes.

Sitting peacefully in the grounds of an old hospital, the church itself is striking only for its immaculate simplicity, though there are several fine altars inside, and the open doors and shutters let in the birds and sunlight.

San Antonio de los Baños

Of all the small towns in Havana province, **SAN ANTONIO DE LOS BAÑOS**, about 20km due south of Playa and a 45-minute drive from Habana Vieja, is the only one with the right ingredients to make more than a fleeting visit rewarding. This is due in no small part to the appeal of *Las Yagrumas* (☎47/38-4460 to 64, ✉reservas@yagrumas.co.cu; ❸), a beautifully set, family-oriented hotel just north of the town. Refreshingly, there are always large numbers of Cubans staying here, most of them on the reward schemes offered

---

El Día de San Lázaro

On December 17, the road between Santiago de las Vegas and El Rincón is closed as hordes of people from all over Cuba come to ask favours of San Lázaro in exchange for a sacrifice, or to keep promises they have already made to the saint. Some have walked for days, timing their pilgrimage so that they arrive on the 17th, but the common starting point is Santiago de las Vegas, 2km down the road. The most fervent of believers make their journey as arduous as possible, determined that in order to earn the favour they have asked for they must first prove their own willingness to suffer. In the past people have tied rocks to their limbs and dragged themselves along the concrete road to the church, others have walked barefoot from much further afield, while others bring material sacrifices, often money, as their part of the bargain.

to state employees. Based around a large pool, the palm-fringed grounds slope down to a bend in the Río Ariguanabo where you can rent rowing boats ($1CUC an hour), motor boats ($3CUC an hour) and *pedalos* ($1CUC an hour). Other activities include organized excursions, nature trails and a full programme of evening entertainment.

The town itself, only a minute's drive from the hotel, has the undisturbed, nonchalant feel that characterizes so much of Cuba's interior. Unlike most places of this size, however, San Antonio de los Baños boasts a novel little museum, almost unique in not being a formulaic, Spanish-only plod through local history. Based in a colonial home at Calle 60 e/ 41 y 45, the excellent, seven-room **Museo de Humor** (Tues–Sun 10am–6pm; $2CUC), founded in 1979, has a small permanent exhibition charting the history of graphic humour in Cuba. The museum also illuminates the tradition of political satire in Cuban newspaper art, with a couple of old anti-Spanish cartoons, anti-imperialist drawings and some *Punch*-style creations; unfortunately, though, none of it is presented with much context. The museum also hosts a number of international competitions of comic art, easily the best time to visit. The most prestigious of these, the Evento de Humor y Sátira and the Bienal Internacional del Humor, take place in alternate years every March or April. Both follow similar lines, with entries drawn from a large number of countries, falling under categories such as political humour, caricatures, photography and comic strips. The standard is usually very high, and the best entries are displayed throughout the museum for the weeks surrounding the competitions. Also worth catching is the Evento de Caricatura Personal Juan David every September, a national competition attracting the best caricaturists in the country.

A few blocks away is the modest **Museo de Historia**, at Calle 66 e/ 41 y 45 (Tues–Sat 10am–6pm, Sun 9am–1pm; $1CUC), whose relatively diverse collection includes some great photographs of local bands from the 1920s and 1930s as well as a room of colonial furniture. For **refreshment** there's a branch of the fast-food chain *El Rápido* on Calle 68, but for a more atmospheric setting follow Calle 68 uphill to its conclusion on the edge of town, where a right turn leads to *La Quintica*, a simple peso restaurant leaning over a river, serving standard *comida criolla*. The tree-lined banks of the river lend this spot a delightfully relaxing ambience, occasionally shattered by music blaring out from the restaurant itself.

West of Havana

Driving west through Miramar and the western suburbs is one of the easiest and most pleasant drives in the whole city and reason in itself to come out this way. Once out of the city, however, there's not much to see here with the exception of the beach resort of Playa El Salado, and most people head straight on to the province of Pinar del Río.

Playa El Salado

Fifteen kilometres west of the capital, straight along Avenida 5ta from Miramar, is the only coastal resort of any significance on this side of the province, **Playa**

El Salado, where you are unlikely to want to stay for more than a night. Just five minutes' drive beyond the lazy seafront hamlet of Baracoa, it's an unspectacular place with a rocky beach and an eyesore of a gutted restaurant. The only attraction here of any note is the 1.2-kilometre **go-cart track** (Mon–Sat 9am–5pm; $5CUC for 10min, $25CUC for an hour; 16 and older only), a rare recreational facility so near to the city.

A gently flowing river divides the go-cart track from *Villa Cocomar* (☎47/37-8293; ❶), a spacious if slightly exposed cabin complex on the shore, currently closed and undergoing major renovations.

West along the Carretera Central

Most people travelling through this western half of Havana province are on their way to the more dramatic scenery of Pinar del Río. The buses speed along the four-lane *autopista*, but for a closer look at rural provincial Cuba at a more relaxed pace head along the **Carretera Central**. The going is mostly flat, cutting through sugar cane territory and pleasant croplands with occasional glimpses of the south coast. The small towns along this animated route, principally Bauta, Guanajay and Artemisa, are all quite similar, with barely enough of interest in each to keep you occupied for a fifteen-minute leg-stretching break.

The one detour worth making before crossing the provincial border is to the **Antiguo Cafetal Angerona**, 6km west of Artemisa, a nineteenth-century coffee plantation where 750,000 coffee plants once grew. Here you'll find the ruins of the Neoclassical mansion where the owners lived alongside the slave quarters, and a ten-metre-high watchtower. Occasionally a tour group will stop by for a look, but you're more likely to be the only visitor wandering about.

Travel details

There are no Astro or Víazul buses from Havana to any of the worthwhile destinations around the outskirts of the city or in Havana province, so getting about without your own transport or a taxi involves either hitching lifts or chancing it with the local buses. The local buses listed below do not follow any regular timetables and are particularly susceptible to delay, cancellation, route changes and desperate overcrowding. The Hershey train running from Casablanca to Matanzas stops at some dead-end places on the way and can take you within a few kilometres of Playa Jibacoa, but generally speaking trains leaving Havana don't stop until they reach one of the neighbouring provinces.

Local buses

Havana to: Cojímar (every 20min; 40min); Guanabacoa (every 40min; 50min); Habana del Este (every 20min; 10min); Playas del Este (4 daily; 1hr); San Antonio de los Baños (2 daily; 1hr 30min); San Francisco de Paula (every 40mn; 1hr 30min); Santiago de las Vegas (every 40min; 1hr).

Víazul buses

Havana to: Bayamo (3 daily; 13hr); Camagüey (6 daily; 8hr 15min); Ciego de Ávila (4 daily; 7hr); Cienfuegos (2 daily; 4hr); Holguín (3 daily; 11hr 30min); Las Tunas (4 daily; 10hr); Matanzas (3 daily; 2hr 10min); Pinar del Río (2 daily; 3hr); Playas del Este (3 daily; 30min); Sancti Spíritus (4 daily; 6hr); Santa Clara (4 daily; 4hr 30min); Santiago de Cuba (4 daily; 15hr 30min); Trinidad (2 daily; 5hr 30min); Varadero (3 daily; 3hr); Viñales (2 daily; 3hr 30min).

Astro buses

Havana to: Baracoa (1 daily; 17hr); Cienfuegos (5 daily; 5hr); Pinar del Río (4 daily; 4hr); Santa Clara (3 daily; 5hr); Santiago (2 daily; 16hr); Trinidad (daily; 7hr 30min); Varadero (1 daily; 3hr; the Varadero bus is currently for Cubans only).

Trains

Havana to: Camagüey (daily; 9hr); Cienfuegos
(2 daily; 10hr); Ciego de Avila (3 daily; 8hr); Holguín
(daily; 14hr 30min); Matanzas (8 daily; 3hr); Pinar
del Río (daily; 5hr 30min); Sancti Spíritus (daily;
8hr); Santa Clara (4 daily; 6hr); Santiago de Cuba
(2 daily; 14hr).

Hershey trains

Havana to: Canasí (4 daily; 2hr 20min); Guanabo
(4 daily; 40min); Hershey (4 daily; 1hr); Jibacoa
(4 daily; 2hr); Matanzas (4 daily; 3hr); San
Antonio (4 daily; 2hr 45min).

Ferry

Havana to: Casablanca (every 30min; 10min).

Domestic flights

Havana to: Baracoa (2 weekly; 3hr 45min);
Bayamo (2 weekly; 2hr); Camagüey (daily; 1hr
30min); Cayo Coco (2 daily; 1hr 15min); Cayo Largo
(2 daily; 40min); Cayo Santa María (2 weekly;
55min); Ciego de Avila (1 weekly; 1hr 25min);
Guantánamo (5 weekly; 2hr 25min); Holguín
(2 daily; 1hr 30min–2hr 50min); Nueva Gerona
(2 daily; 40min); Santiago de Cuba (2 daily; 1hr
35min–2hr 30min).

Pinar del Río

CHAPTER 2 # Highlights

✳ **Hiking at Las Terrazas** The best way to delve into the sierra is along the hillside routes of the guided hikes at Las Terrazas. See p.216

✳ **Baños de San Juan** Perfect for picnics and great for a midday bathe, this delightful river haven in the hills also has a unique set of tree houses on stilts where you can stay the night. See p.221

✳ **Cabaret Rumayor** This kitschy cabaret, set against a natural backdrop on the edge of the provincial capital, is a sight to behold. See p.234

✳ **Viñales** Almost otherworldly in nature, the valley is like nowhere else in Cuba, from the *mogote* hills and prehistoric caves to the laid-back rural village on the valley floor. See p.236

✳ **Gran Caverna de Santo Tomás** The most complex cave system in Cuba, plunging into a hillside on eight different levels, is surprisingly easy to visit. See p.245

✳ **Cayo Jutías** The reputation of this virtually untouched islet is growing, so catch it at its natural best while you still can. See p.246

✳ **María La Gorda** The western tip of Cuba may seem like a long way to go for a beach and some woods, but the serenity and world-class diving make it a worthwhile journey. See p.252

△ María La Gorda

Pinar del Río

D espite its relative proximity to Havana, life in the province of **PINAR DEL RÍO** is a far cry from the noise, pollution and hustle of the capital. This is a distinctly rural region where the lazy towns and even the capital city, also named **Pinar del Río**, are characterized by a markedly provincial feel. The major attractions are well away from the population centres, the majority situated in and around the green slopes of the **Cordillera de Guaniguanico**, the low mountain range that runs like a backbone down the length of the landscape. Famous for the world's finest tobacco (that most time-consuming of crops), stereotyped as a province populated by backward country folk, and butt of a string of national jokes, life here unfolds at a subdued pace, and its hillside and seaside resorts are well suited to unfettered escapism.

Hidden within the **Sierra del Rosario**, the relatively compact eastern section of the *cordillera*, the peaceful, self-contained mountain retreats of **Las Terrazas** and **Soroa**, billed slightly inaccurately as **ecotourism** centres, provide perfect opportunities to explore the tree-clad hillsides and valleys.

Heading west along the *autopista*, which runs parallel with the mountain range along the length of the province, there are a few low-key attractions to the north but it's unlikely you'll want to make much more than a fleeting visit to any one of them. That is, unless you are in search of the healing qualities of the spa at **San Diego de los Baños**, a small village straddling the border between the Sierra del Rosario and the western section of the *cordillera*, the **Sierra de los Organos**. Although the area is host to a large park and a set of caves of both geological and historical interest, their considerable potential is mostly untapped due to neglect and isolation.

Most visitors instead head straight for Pinar del Río's undoubted highlight, the **Viñales valley**, where the flat-topped mountains or *mogotes*, provide the landscape with a unique, prehistoric look and feel. While heavily visited, Viñales remains unspoilt and the village at its centre, full of simple houses renting rooms to tourists, has an uncontrived air about it. Easily visited on a day-trip from Havana, there is enough to see away from Viñales's official sights for a longer, more adventurous stay. Conveniently close to the valley is the secluded little beach on serene **Cayo Jutías**, while on the same northern coastline is the more substantial but even more remote **Cayo Levisa**, better suited for a longer visit and for diving.

You'll need to be pretty determined in order to get to the country's western-most locations, which are beyond the provincial capital, where the *autopista* ends, and more or less out of reach unless you rent a car or book an official excursion. If you make it, you'll find the serene and scenic patchwork landscape

PINAR DEL RÍO

▲ Havana

LA HABANA

Cafetal Buenavista

Las Terrazas

SIERRA DEL ROSARIO

Hacienda Unión

A Soroa

Candelaria

San Cristóbal

Baños de Bayate

Bahía Honda

Las Pozas

Palma Rubia

La Palma

San Diego de los Baños

Cueva de los Portales

Los Palacios

Paso Real de San Diego

Maspotón

Cayo Levisa

Villa Cayo Levisa

Puerto Esperanza

San Andrés

E PARQUE D LA GÜIRA

Entronque de Herradura

SIERRA DE LOS ÓRGANOS

GUANIGUANICO

La Juventud Reservoir

PINAR DEL RÍO

ISLA DE LA JUVENTUD

Isla de la Juventud

Nueva Gerona

Golfo de Batabanó

Consolación del Sur

Aguas Claras

Alejandro Robaina tobacco Plantation

Las Canas

La Coloma

San Luis

Cayo Jutías

Santa Lucía

Minas de Matahambre

Pons

Gran Caverna de Santo Tomás

Viñales

Sumidero

Pinar del Río

San Juan y Martínez

Boca de Galafre

Playa Bailén

Sábalo

Guane

Manuel Lazo

Ensenada de Cortés

Isabel Rubio

Sandino

La Fé

Mantua

Laguna Grande

Villa Laguna Grande

La Bajada

María la Gorda

Villa María La Gorda

Bahía de Corrientes

Golfo de Guanahacabibes

Cabo de San Antonio

Villa Cabo de San Antonio

Las Tumbas

Faro Roncali

Gulf of Mexico

N

0   20 km

of the Vuelta Abajo region, said to produce the finest tobacco leaves in the world and home to some internationally renowned tobacco plantations, including the **Alejandro Robaina plantation,** which is one of the few you can easily visit. The modest **beaches** of **Playa Bailén** and **Boca de Galafre** and the small tourist site at **Laguna Grande** provide quick detours if you want to break up the journey to **María La Gorda**, whose fine sandy shores, crystal-clear waters, outstanding scuba diving and fantastic sense of out-of-reach tranquillity are the real justification for coming all this way..

Getting around

As with much of Cuba, relying on **public transport** in Pinar del Río is a hazardous, patience-testing business. Much of the province is quite simply out of range of any of the public services, which, where they do exist, are more often than not extremely unreliable. Víazul provide a daily **bus service** from Havana to the provincial capital and then north to Viñales, and there are daily Astro buses following the same route. Very few visitors ever take the **train** into Pinar del Río, as it is notoriously slow and doesn't make any useful stops except for the provincial capital itself; the other towns which it stops in are at least a few kilometres from anywhere worth visiting.

For any kind of independence travelling in and around the Sierra del Rosario or the eastern half of the Sierra de los Organos, you'll need your own car, which you will have to rent in Havana, Viñales or the provincial capital. Most drivers speed their way through the province on the **autopista**, which comes to an end at the city of Pinar del Río. Running roughly parallel is the **Carretera Central**, a slower option, which takes you closer to the mountains and gives better views of the surrounding landscape, whilst the most scenic, slowest and least travelled route of all is along the northern coastline. Once past the provincial capital, the Carretera Central is the only major road.

Sierra del Rosario

Heading west out of Havana on the *autopista*, the first attractions you'll come to, just inside the provincial border, are the isolated mountain valley resorts at **Las Terrazas** and **Soroa**. By far the best bases from which to explore the densely packed forest slopes of the protected **Sierra del Rosario**, both resorts are slightly misleadingly billed as **ecotourism** centres, designed to coexist harmoniously with their surroundings, which they undoubtedly do, but only Las Terrazas can lay any real claim to connecting tourism with conservation and the local community. Considerably smaller but no less popular than Las Terrazas, Soroa's compact layout makes it more accessible to day-trippers from Havana. The sierra was declared a Biosphere Reserve by UNESCO in 1985, acknowledgement in part for the success of the reforestation project of the 1970s (see p.218), and visitors are encouraged to explore their surroundings using official **hiking routes**: there's a comprehensive programme of guided hikes at Las Terrazas and some gentler but still rewarding walks around Soroa. Though sometimes referred to as such, the peaks of the Sierra del Rosario don't quite qualify for mountain status, the highest point reaching just under 700m, and although there is some fantastic scenery, it's rarely, if ever, breathtaking.

A mixture of semitropical rainforest and evergreen forest, the sierra is home to a rich variety of **birdlife**, fifty percent of which, according to local tourist literature, is endemic to this region, though this figure seems somewhat

Rancho Curujey and hiking at Las Terrazas

There is a set of official **hiking routes** and **nature trails** around Las Terrazas, of varying lengths and difficulty, and each characterized by a different destination of historical or ecological interest (detailed below). There is no better or more accessible way to experience the diversity and beauty of the Sierra del Rosario than along these routes, which collectively offer the most comprehensive insight available into the region's topography, history, flora and fauna. All hiking here must be arranged through the Oficinas de Reservaciones y Coordinación at **Rancho Curujey** (☏82/57-8555 or 57-8700, ✉reserva@terraz.co.cu), the reserve's visitor and information centre, which includes a Cuban cuisine-serving rustic restaurant; you can also get a map and help with almost any activity around Las Terrazas here. To reach Rancho Curujey arriving from Havana and the west, take the signposted right-hand turn off the main through-road just before the left turn that leads to the village and hotel. The centre can supply you with a guide, without which you are not permitted to make use of any of the trails through this protected area, and tailor a programme or just a day of walking to your requirements. For groups of six people or more, guides usually cost around $10CUC per person on a prebooked excursion, though prices vary depending on the size of the group and your specific wants and needs and can reach $30–40CUC. You may be able to join another visiting group if you call a day in advance, or if you arrive on or before 9am. The *Hotel Moka* works closely with Rancho Curujey and can arrange hiking packages for guests.

Hiking routes and nature trails

Cascada del San Claudio (20km) The longest hike offered here lasts a whole day, or around eight to ten hours, and is a gruelling affair scaling the hills looming over to the northwest of the complex and down the other side to the San Claudio River.

El Contento (8km) This pleasant, easy-going hike descends into the valley between two of the local peaks and joins the Río San Juan. It passes the La Victoria ruins, another of the area's old coffee plantations, as well as fresh and sulphurous water springs, and reaches its limit at the Baños de San Juan, a beautiful little set of pools and cascades where you can bathe.

Loma del Taburete (7km) One of the tougher hikes this route climbs some relatively steep inclines on the way up a 453-metre-high hill from the peak of which there are views all the way over to the coast, and slopes down to the Baños de San Juan on the other side where the hike concludes.

Sendero Las Delicias (3km) This trail finishes up at the Cafetal Buenavista and takes in a mirador at the summit of the Loma Las Delicias, where there are some magnificently panoramic views.

Sendero La Serafina (4km) A nature trail ideal for birdwatching, leading uphill through rich and varied forest, guides are able to point out some of the more notable of the 73 bird species that inhabit the sierra, such as the red, white and blue tocororo, the endemic catacuba and the enchanting Cuban nightingale.

Valle del Bayate (7km) On the road to Soroa, 6km from Las Terrazas, a dirt track next to the bridge over Río Bayate follows the river into the dense forest. Passing first the dilapidated San Pedro coffee plantation, this undemanding trail arrives at the Santa Catalina plantation ruins, a peaceful spot where you can take a dip in the natural pools.

exaggerated. Nevertheless, among the more notable of the seventy-or-so species here are the bright-green Cuban tody, the tuneful Cuban solitaire and the bluish-green, white and red Cuban trogon, Cuba's national bird; the rarer Fernandina's woodpecker and the Cuban grassquit, the latter known in Spanish as the *tomeguín del Pinar*, as well as more common species such as the Cuban bullfinch, red-legged honey-creeper and the olive-capped warbler. Not surprisingly, birdwatching features among the activities on offer at both Soroa and, more comprehensively, Las Terrazas.

△ Las Terrazas

Las Terrazas

Eight kilometres beyond the signposted turn-off at Km 51 of the *autopista*, **LAS TERRAZAS** (ⓦwww.lasterrazas.cu) is a wonderfully harmonious resort and small working community forming the premier ecotourism site in the province and one of the most important in the country. The turn-off road takes you into a thickly wooded landscape and up to a junction where, a few metres after a left turn, you'll reach a **tollbooth** marking the beginning of the main through-road for Las Terrazas. There's a charge of $4CUC per person to pass this checkpoint, though guests of the resort's solitary hotel are exempt. It's here, just a few metres past the checkpoint, where you'll turn for the **Cafetal Buenavista**, a hilltop colonial coffee plantation accessible by car or as a hike destination (see p.221), where you can also enjoy great views and a restaurant.

About 2km beyond the tollbooth there are right- and left-hand side roads in quick succession. The right-hand turn leads to Rancho Curujey, a visitor centre for both tour groups and independent travellers (see box, p.216), whilst the left-hand turn leads several hundred metres down to the **village**, a well-spaced complex of red-tile-roofed bungalows and apartment blocks, beautifully woven into the grassy slopes of a valley, at the foot of which is a man-made lake. The housing is perched on terraced slopes that dip steeply down into the centre of the community, forming a smaller, more compact, trench-like valley within the valley-settlement itself. Though the cabins look as if they're meant for visitors, they belong to the resident population of around a thousand, who have lived here since the community's foundation in 1971. These residents were encouraged to play an active role in the preservation and care of the local environment and they formed the backbone of the workforce whose first task was a massive government-funded **reforestation project** covering some 50 square kilometres of the Sierra del Rosario. As well as building the village itself, this project entailed the planting of trees along terraces dug into the hillside, thus guarding against erosion and giving the place its name. This was all part of a grander scheme by the government to promote self-sufficiency and education

△ Hotel Moka

in rural areas, one of the promises of the revolution. Today a large proportion of the community work in tourism, some as employees at the hotel and others as owners of the small businesses that have been set up in response to the growing numbers of foreign visitors.

Set back from the road between the tollbooth and the resort, the spirit of conservation persists at the **Centro de Investigaciones Ecológicas**, with research into the area's ecosystems, studies of animal habitat and related projects. Guided tours of the centre can sometimes be arranged either at the Rancho Curujey visitor centre or through the hotel, but there is no timetable for them and visits are usually confined to tour groups.

Beyond the village, a few kilometres further west along the main (and only) through-road are a couple of simple little retreats, ideal for a daytime break. The **Casa del Campesino** offers restaurant meals from a delightfully tranquil vantage point just a few paces away from Hacienda Unión, the remains of one of the area's numerous colonial-era coffee plantations. You can escape the main road again at the turning for **Baños de Bayate** where, deeper into the thick mountain vegetation, there's a natural swimming spot that's a great place to cool off and stop for lunch. South of the village, a small road leads to the **Baños de San Juan**, another set of natural pools and a beautiful riverside hangout.

The hotel and village

The best way to start a tour of the village at Las Terrazas is to drive up the winding road which begins behind the city-style apartment blocks, up to the ⚲ *Hotel Moka* (☎ 82/57-8600 to 03, ✉ reservas@commoka.get.tur.cu; ➐). This peaceful hillside hideaway is well worth a visit whether or not you intend to stay the night, as non-guests can not only admire the building itself but can make use of the restaurant and pool here. Looking over the community from the wooded slopes that form one of its borders, the hotel is hidden from view behind trees in the shadow of the Loma del Salón, one of the highest peaks hereabouts. The main building – its terracotta-tiled roof and white-pillared verandas a graceful combination of modern and colonial styles – has been sculpted into the landscape, hugging the surrounding trees, which in some places actually penetrate the floor and ceiling of the building itself. There's an adjoining **bar** and moderately priced **restaurant** serving mostly a variety of Cuban-style meat dishes, while the swimming pool and tennis court area, set further back, provide the only open spaces within the complex. The pool, with another bar and a grill sitting alongside it, costs $3CUC for day visitors. If you prefer to be among the locals and don't mind having to walk a bit further to use the hotel's facilities, you can also stay in one of the five *villas comunitarias*, also known as the *Villas Moka*, available down by the lake. These are effectively *casas particulares* run by the hotel, and are the only way you can stay in a family home here.

Several sets of steps lead from the hotel back down the slopes into the village, where some small, low-key **workshops** are set up inside some of the apartment-block buildings there. From these workshops local artists churn out pottery, silkscreen prints, paintings and other crafts and artwork, which you can buy or simply watch being produced (though a tad contrived, the latter is still quite engaging).

The two best **restaurants** at Las Terrazas are in the village, both on the hotel side of the complex and both with lovely views out across the community. In an apartment building near the steps leading down from the hotel is ⚲ *El Romero* (daily 9am–9pm), billing itself as an eco-restaurant. The unique menu consists of organic, predominantly vegetarian dishes such as a creamy cold

Outdoor activities

There's more to do around the village than might at first appear to be the case given the lazy, laid-back feel of the place. The most exciting and novel activity on offer is the **Canopy Tour** (daily 9am–6pm; $25CUC), a thrilling aerial tour of the village on one-man seats suspended from steel cables 25 metres above the ground. The tour takes off from a platform in the woodlands around the hotel and extends for 800 metres all the way down to the boating house, the Casa de Botes, on the edge of the lake, stopping at several other platforms along the way. Bookings are taken at the hotel or the Casa de Botes.

For a less adrenalin-fuelled time there is **horse riding**, which should be arranged through the hotel. There are a number of set rides, lasting between an hour and four hours and generally costing $5CUC an hour. There are two-hour rides to the *Casa del Campesino* (see opposite) and the Baños de San Juan (see opposite), a three-hour ride to the Cafetal Buenavista and a couple of four-hour, $20CUC rides, including one which scales the nearby Loma de Taburete.

If you want an even more subdued pastime, you can rent out rowing **boats** on the lake for $3CUC an hour. The Casa de Botes, where boats are moored, is just off the main road through the village and easy to find.

---

pumpkin and onion soup, bean-filled crepes and chickpea burgers, along with more traditional fare, all meticulously presented. Everything is served in small, medium or large portions, but a small main dish – though cheap at only $3CUC to $5CUC – will barely register in your stomach; it's worth paying the $9CUC to $14CUC for the large portions. Heartier meals are served a few buildings along, at the open-air ⚑ *Fonda de Mercedes* (9am–9pm daily), a restaurant-cum-*paladar* on a roof-covered balcony platform. The top-notch Cuban cuisine on offer here has a real home-cooked flavour and is great value with prices between $5CUC and $8CUC for main dishes (cheaper than those in the hotel). The house special is a traditional recipe from Camagüey province called Aporreado de Ternera, a veal stew made with aromatic herbs and spices. In between the two restaurants is the *Café de María*, a lovely little spot for a **drink**, on a balcony with pleasant views.

On the other side of the gaping trench that separates the two halves of the village is the **Plaza Comunal**, with benches, trees and modest views of the lake and valley. It's a focal point for local residents, and gets quite sociable in the evening. In the three-storey building on the side of the plaza facing the hotel is the small but concise **Museo Comunitario** (daily except Wed 8am–1pm, often closed Mon; $1CUC), where photographs and documents offer further insights into Las Terrazas' simple but interesting history, including the pre-Columbian and colonial eras. If you're planning to do some hiking, a small selection of **picnic** supplies can be found in the small Tienda Panamericana supermarket in the same building.

Down on the edge of the lake, a signposted right-hand turn on the road into the village, is a small museum called the **Peña de Las Terrazas Polo Montañez** (9am–5pm daily; $2CUC). In a cabin indistinguishable from all the others from the outside, this was where one of Cuba's most heralded musicians of recent times, Polo Montañez, lived and gave impromptu concerts before he was killed in a car accident in November 2002. It's a simple little four-room place exhibiting some of Montañez's personal effects, including his guitars, while his bedroom has been left as it was when he lived here. Some of his CDs are on sale too.

Cafetal Buenavista

Immediately inside the checkpoint at the Havana end of the resort is the turning for the **Cafetal Buenavista** (daily 9am–4pm; free), an excellent restoration of a nineteenth-century coffee plantation. French immigrants who had fled Haiti following the 1791 revolution established over fifty coffee plantations across the sierra, but this is the only one that has been almost fully reconstructed. The superbly restored stone house, with its high-beamed ceiling, now shelters a restaurant, while the food is cooked in the original kitchen building behind it. The terraces on which the coffee was dried have also been accurately restored and the remains of the slaves' quarters are complete enough to give you an idea of the incredibly cramped sleeping conditions that the plantation's 126 slaves would have experienced. You can drive here quite easily and directly by taking the side road at the tollbooth; this is also the final destination for some of the official hikes in the area (see box, p.216).

Baños de San Juan

From the south side of the village, at the junction where the road to the hotel begins, another road leads off in the opposite direction for the **Baños de San Juan**, a delightfully pleasant spot featuring natural pools, riverside picnic tables, a simple restaurant and some even simpler cabins providing rudimentary accommodation. If you have a receipt from the tollgate at the entrance to the reserve, you'll need to show it at the car park at the end of the road, about three kilometres from the village, to avoid another charge. From here it's a hop and a skip down to the river where a footbridge takes you over the water to the paths zigzagging both ways along the river's edge, mingling with tiny tributaries branching off from the main river, creating a network of walkways. There are several hundred metres of tree-covered paths, punctuated by paved clearings where you can stop and sit under matted roofs. Following the route downstream leads to the focal point here, a small set of clear, natural pools fed by dinky waterfalls and ideal for a bit of midday bathing. On the riverbank looking over them is *El Bambú* (daily 9am–7pm) a rustic **restaurant-caféteria** serving simple Cuban food. Set back from the river, at the foot of some grassy slopes breaking up the woodlands here, are five rooms (known as *cabañas rusticas*) for rent. They're no more than roof-covered platforms on stilts, aimed squarely at the backpacker set, with no furniture and about enough space to lay a couple of sleeping bags down. Rooms cost $10CUC a night and can be booked through *Hotel Moka*.

Casa del Campesino, Hacienda Unión and Baños de Bayate

Two kilometres down the main road from the checkpoint, beyond the left-hand turn for the hotel and village, a roadside sign indicates the way down a short dirt track to **Casa del Campesino**, a lazy, secluded little woodland ranch housing a **restaurant** (daily 8am–9pm). Concealed from the main road and melting into the surrounding forest, the simple wooden-panelled bungalow and adjoining terrace eating area sit on the edge of a pleasant overlook. This rural retreat, complete with chickens darting about, is a great place to spend a couple of hours unwinding, so long as you have some bug repellent, as the mosquitoes can be fierce. You can just have a drink or choose from the wholesome *comida criolla* menu, though you may have to wait a little while for the latter, especially if you arrive before one o'clock, when there are unlikely to have been any other visitors.

From the restaurant you can see, through the trees, the neighbouring **Hacienda Unión**, one of the area's partly reconstructed nineteenth-century coffee plantations. A stone path leads down the slope and onto the right-hand fork of the same dirt track that branches off from the main road. There is nothing to restrict you from wandering down and taking a look around the broken stone walls of the plantation, which has at least kept enough of its structure to be recognizable for what it once was two centuries ago. The circular grinding mill, with its cone-shaped roof and stone base, is the most intact section and the easiest to spot. The majority of the space here has been given over to the cultivation of various flowers and plants, divided up into small, rock-lined plots forming an attractively laid out if somewhat rudimentary **garden**.

Back on the main road, 3km past the turning for the *Casa del Campesino*, another dirt track, this one more of a bone rattler than the last, winds down about a kilometre to a section of a forest-shrouded river known as the **Baños de Bayate**. The depth and clearness of the water at this delightful spot provide a perfect opportunity to cool off from the jungle's humidity, although its tranquillity is sometimes broken by the screams and shouts of young swimmers leaping into the river. Stone paths run 50m or so along one side of the mostly very shallow river, linking the several rustic barbecue grills built on the water's edge. There's also an outdoor **restaurant** here, perfect for a post-swim plate of grilled pork or chicken.

The final stretch of the main road leads up to the other **tollbooth** (where you won't get charged if you already paid at the other end) on the western border of the resort, immediately after which a left turn will take you on the road to Soroa and back to the *autopista*.

Soroa and around

Sixteen kilometres southwest from Las Terrazas, the tiny village of **SOROA** nestles in a long narrow valley. The turning from the *autopista* is marked by the first gas station en route to Pinar del Río from Havana, but you can also get there direct from Las Terrazas without returning to the motorway. Although a cosy spot, access into the hills is limited and the list of attractions brief, meaning the resort is best suited for a shorter break rather than a prolonged visit. If you do decide to stay, the place to do so is **Villa Soroa** (☎85/52-3534, 52-3556 or 52-3512, ⓔrecepcion@hvs.co.cu; ❹), a well-kept complex encircling a swimming pool, whose comfortable, modern-looking cabins seem slightly out of tune with the area's ecotourist slant.

El Salto and the overlooks

Most of what you'll want to see is within ten minutes' walk, but if you've driven up from the *autopista*, the first place you'll get to, 100m or so from the hotel, is the car park for **El Salto** (daylight hours; $3CUC), a twenty-metre waterfall. Even though El Salto is perhaps Soroa's most publicized attraction, you'll be disappointed upon reaching the unspectacular cascade, especially after the long, winding walk through the woods. It's still worth visiting for a dip in the water, particularly refreshing if you've just walked from one of the two nearby scenic overlooks.

The first of the overlooks, known simply as **El Mirador**, is signposted back at the car park. Following the sign over a small bridge up towards the overlook, you'll first pass the **Baños Romanos**, located in an unassuming stone cabin, where massages, sulphurous baths and other treatments can be arranged through the hotel (daily 9am–4pm; prices from $5CUC). As the more challenging of the two easily climbable hills in the area, you may want to save the massage for after the thirty-minute hike up, which scales an increasingly steep and narrow dirt track. It's mercifully shady, though, and steps have been installed for the final stretch. While there are a number of possible wrong turns on the way up, you can avoid getting lost by simply following the track with the horse dung – if you'd rather ride up, horses can be arranged at *Villa Soroa* for $3CUC per person. At the summit you'll find vultures circling the rocky, uneven platform and the most impressive views to be had around Soroa.

El Castillo de las Nubes is the more developed of Soroa's two hilltop viewpoints and the only one you can drive to. The road up to its summit, which you'll have to follow even if you're walking up as there are no obvious trails through the woods, is between the car park for El Salto and the hotel. It shouldn't take more than twenty minutes on foot to reach the hilltop **restaurant**, housed in a building resembling a toy fortress with a single turret (the *castillo* – or castle – of the overlook's name). It's rarely open but worth stopping for a meal, as the views from the window-side tables are fantastic. Alternatively, head to the perfect picnic spot located beyond the restaurant by the deserted stone house at the end of the road – from here you can see all the way to the province's southern coastline. At the foot of the road up to the *castillo* is the **Orquideario** (daily 9am–4pm, ☎85/57-2558; $3CUC), a well-maintained botanical garden specializing in orchids and spreading across 35,000 square metres. Currently being used by the University of Pinar del Río, it was constructed by a wealthy lawyer and botanist from the Canary Islands named Tomás Felipe Camacho. Work on the gardens began when he and his wife took up permanent residence at their country house here, having abandoned their Havana business following the death of their daughter in 1943. What began as a homage to their child became something of an obsession for Camacho when, soon after the move, his wife also died. Until his own death in 1960, he dedicated his time to the expansion and glorification of the *orquideario*, travelling the world in search of different species. The obligatory tours are a little rushed, but you get to see flowers, plants, shrubs and trees from around the globe, including some 700 species of orchid, in grounds radiating out from a central villa, where Camacho lived.

If the short hikes up to El Castillo de las Nubes and El Mirador aren't enough, there are less well-trodden routes into the hills, though it's generally a case of guesswork as to where to start and you should be careful not to trample the sometimes inconspicuous crops. If interested, *Villa Soroa* offers three- to six-hour **guided treks** starting at $6CUC per person.

Practicalities

The only other **accommodation** option in the area besides *Villa Soroa* is the run-down *El Campismo La Caridad* (no phone; ❶), 1km north of the tourist complex. It's very basic, with cabins containing just a narrow single bed and a bunkbed, and no running water, meaning that you might have to flush the toilet with a bucket. There's no soap or toilet paper, though fans can be rented for $1.50CUC a night. To compensate for the lack of comfort, there's a friendly farmyard atmosphere as horses, pigs and goats roam freely about and the helpful staff can advise on some of the lesser-known sights and hikes around Soroa. There are also some muddy trails leading into the hills at the back of the cabins. Simple but substantial home-cooked **meals** are available at *Merendero El Mango* (look out for the home-made sign, just before the turning to the cabins), basically just a room with a table, run by the family of one of the *campismo* staff.

San Diego de los Baños, Parque La Güira and around

Further west from Soroa along the *autopista* towards the provincial capital there are a number of relatively entertaining detours, all within a forty-minute drive of the main road. If you are driving – which is the best option, given that no bus routes currently operate to this area from Havana or Pinar del Río city – it's easy to cover all the highlights in a single day. The place you are most likely to spend a night, or at least stop for a meal, is the sleepy town of **San Diego de los Baños**, famous for its health spa, which is said to be the best in the country, though there are now several more modern, upmarket hotel-spas on the island offering better facilities (minus the same range of therapies). From here it's only a short drive to the area's other two attractions: **Parque La Güira**, a pleasant place to stop and stretch your legs, and, slightly further north, the **Cueva de los Portales**, a modestly impressive cave that cuts a dramatic hole straight through the Loma de los Arcos, and one-time military headquarters of Che Guevara and his army. The Maspotón hunting reserve and its hunting club south of the *autopista* from here are now abandoned but get some occasional use from duck shooters on day-trips.

San Diego de los Baños

Forty kilometres west of Soroa on the *autopista*, at Km 100, a right-hand turn heads for the laid-back little village of **SAN DIEGO DE LOS BAÑOS**, on the borders of both the Sierra de los Organos and the Sierra del Rosario. Follow the turn-off from the *autopista* to its conclusion and then take the right turn signposted to San Cristóbal; 12km down this road takes you right up to the draw for most visitors, the **Balneario San Diego** (Mon–Sat 8am–5pm, Sun 8am–noon; ☎82/73-7880 or 81, ℮tsalud@sermed.cha.cyt .cu). Perched above the river that cuts along the edge of town and in need of some modernization, the *balneario*'s reputation for medicinal powers dates back to 1632, when a slave, forced into isolation because of ill health, took an afternoon dip in the natural springs here and was supposedly instantly cured. Word rapidly spread and the country's infirm began to flock here to be healed. By 1844 a town had been established to provide for the visitors, and eventually a health spa was built to house the healing waters, though this didn't take its current shape until after the revolution. Nowadays most visitors are tourists, or Cubans on a prescribed course of treatment for everything from skin disorders and rheumatic diseases to stress and even bone fractures, as well as for beauty therapy. The cost of using the baths is between $4CUC and $6CUC for the maximum allowed time of 15 minutes. Medical consultations are $25CUC, while mud therapy and Swedish massages are $20CUC and $25CUC, respectively.

The box-like exterior of the spa contrasts strikingly with the flourishing forests on the other side of the river and the graceful *Hotel Mirador* (☎82/77-8338, ℮carpeta@mirador.sandiego.co.cu; ❹) just over the road. Beautifully set in small-scale landscaped gardens, its pleasantly furnished rooms and overall tranquillity make it the perfect place to stay while visiting the spa; in fact, many of its guests are here on a treatment-plus-accommodation package deal. Qualified medical specialists based in the hotel work with staff across the road and can arrange consultations and courses of treatment. When you've had your fill of the waters, it's possible at the hotel to rent out bikes and motorbikes or arrange hiking and fishing trips into the hundred square kilometres of protected **woodlands** just a leisurely stroll away.

The only other things worth seeing in town are a couple of elegant, neocolonial Cuban-only hotels within a stone's throw of the *balneario*. The *Saratoga* is in slight disrepair, though the *Libertad* is well preserved and would make a great place for tourists to stay if they were allowed.

There's not much else to do in San Diego de los Baños, though you could happily spend a few hours in the **cinema**, next door to the *Hotel Mirador*. A quick wander around the village reveals a leafy little square with creaking see-saws and swings and the local church, plus threadbare *La Ceiba*, billing itself as a restaurant-bar-*caféteria* but whose sole realistic claim is as the exclusive local provider of peso rum. The only place you can rely on for a **meal** is the *Hotel Mirador* restaurant, offering a selection of fish, meat and basic spaghetti dishes, though you should try your luck at the unadorned and frequently closed front-yard *paladar*, *La Sorpresa*, opposite the *Hotel Libertad*, which serves wholesome, good-value *comida criolla*.

Parque La Güira

Originally a colonial estate known as Hacienda Cortina, **Parque La Güira** lies 4km west of San Diego de los Baños (daylight hours; free). Local legend has it that in 1908 the estate's wealthy owner hired a lawyer, José Manuel Cortina, to sue his wife, and gave him the property as payment. Once in his hands, Cortina imported truckloads of rock from the nearby mountains to create the kind of large landscaped **park** usually found in big cities. The medieval-style fortifications marking the entrance are promisingly grand, but the grounds show signs of the neglect suffered over the last couple of decades. Regardless, the park's former beauty is still obvious, with all the hallmarks of a once picture-perfect scene: intricately landscaped gardens, artistic sculptures with limbs missing, winding paths that no longer lead anywhere, a varied plant life starting to think

△ Parque La Güira

for itself, and the remains of an elegant fortress-like mansion somewhere near the centre. The park is still far from overgrown, and its nostalgic, lonely charm makes it ideal for a quiet picnic or contemplative wander. Technically, the park extends beyond the landscaped gardens into remoter parts rich in wildlife, but there are no marked routes and unless you're feeling reckless there's nothing much to entice you any further.

If you're coming directly from Havana, follow the road that leads up to San Diego de los Baños, where, at the petrol station marking the edge of the village, you should take the left-hand fork and follow that road for 4km. Once through the entrance, take the first left turn into the car park. Here, the dismal *Motel Dos Palmas* (no phone; ❷) is the only place to **stay** should you want to spend more time exploring the outer reaches of the park. It has a bar, a cheap but poor-quality and only occasionally functioning restaurant and nine dark, air-conditioned rooms, most of them housed in a long redbrick bungalow thankfully surrounded by greenery. There is sometimes a **disco** here at weekends, but don't expect to have to queue to get in. The far more attractive *Villa La Güira* on the far side of the park is for military personnel only and is located near the park's biggest eyesore: the oversized *Restaurant Mirflores*, an ugly semicircular building reminiscent of a school dining hall. Don't rely on the opening times posted outside the doorway leading into the restaurant, which is low on both stock and quality. A quick drink at the empty **bar** is the most you're likely to get out of the place, whose clumsy size is testament to La Güira's long-departed heyday.

Cueva de los Portales

About 10km north of Parque La Güira along a heavily potholed road, marked by a sign to the now abandoned *Cabaña Los Pinos*, is the historically significant **Cueva de los Portales**. This gaping hillside corridor, hidden beyond a recently renovated holiday cabin site, was the suitably remote **former headquarters** of Che Guevara and his army during the Cuban Missile Crisis of October 1962. It was declared a national monument in 1987, though this status slightly outweighs its capacity to impress and there are more affecting, complex and accessible cave systems elsewhere in the province. Nevertheless, anyone can drive up and wander in free of charge, and, when you're in the area, its historical significance alone makes it well worth thirty minutes of your time. If you're lucky, there'll be a guide about to offer a free tour of the complex, though undoubtedly a tip would be appreciated.

The solitary road from Parque La Güira leads all the way to the turning for the cave, a right turn as you are heading north from the park. Then, from a clearing in the woods a stone path leads into and through a wide-open tunnel, the full length of which is visible from outside the high arching entrance. Through the arch, running parallel with the path, is the **Río Caiguanabo**, a tributary of the Río San Diego. Off to the side is the headquarters cave itself, a giant chamber adorned with imposing stalactites and stalagmites. Inside there are some intriguing remnants of Guevara's occupation – the stone table where he worked and played chess, an unfinished little breeze-block hut which acted as his office and some stone staircases and paths hewn out of the rock.

Though the eleven spick-and-span cabins of the renovated *Campismo Los Portales* (☎8/49-7347; ❶) are primarily for Cubans, they are sometimes rented out to tourists, as long as there's space. Conditions are above average for this kind of accommodation in Cuba, and though the cabins are equipped with only the bare minimum of comfort requirements, everything is in good nick. Amongst the fittingly simple facilities are a four-table restaurant and a games room with a ping-pong table, where you can work up a sweat before taking a dip in the natural pool down at the river.

Pinar del Río city

Stranded out on the far side of the westernmost province in Cuba at the end of the *autopista*, **PINAR DEL RÍO** is, quite simply, a backwater of a city. Close to some more alluring destinations, particularly Viñales, just 25km to the north, but also María La Gorda and the beaches Boca de Galafre and Playa Bailén to the south, the city works best as a base or a stepping stone for exploring this half of the province. Nonetheless, this attractive-looking town is not without its own charms, adorned with palm trees and pines, and with a beautiful mountainous backdrop that's tantalizingly visible from some parts of the city. Despite its 125,000-strong population, Pinar del Río city has the feel of a much smaller place, its central streets more reminiscent of a residential neighbourhood than a town centre.

This could not, however, be described as a tranquil city, due to the increasingly aggressive nature and disproportionately large number of **jineteros** who thrive here, away from the attentions of the state, which generally focus on Havana and the more popular tourist locations. As a result, levels of pestering and prostitution are surprisingly high. Foreign visitors, particularly those in rental cars or on Víazul buses, are often surrounded by touts within minutes of arrival and are likely to attract what can become a tiring level of persistent attention throughout their time in the city.

As the capital of the province, Pinar del Río is comparatively undeveloped for tourism: none of the international or upmarket hotel chains is represented here, there are limited nightlife and dining options and the museums could do with a rethink. There are, on the other hand, countless *casas particulares* spread all over the city. You'll need no more than a couple of days to get to know the place inside out, and in fact very few of the city's visitors spend even that long here. The highlight is the **Fábrica de Tabacos Francisco Donatién**, a diminutive cigar factory offering illuminating tours. Also, try to catch the *Cabaret Rumayor*, a taste of classic Cuban entertainment whose extravagance feels somewhat out of place in this less-than-cosmopolitan town.

Arrival, orientation and information

Arriving in Pinar del Río by **car** is a breeze, as the *autopista* leads straight into the middle of town. You should, though, be particularly mindful of your speed when entering the city, as sometimes one or two of the waiting touts that line the main road are willing to stand in the middle of the street and flag you down with false urgency; drive on by, as they rarely have anything useful to tell you. (Note that shaking them off can often take a while, as the license plates on rental cars make you a conspicuous target.)

Arriving by **bus**, whether Astro or Víazul, you'll be dropped at the Terminal de Omnibus on Adela Azcuy (℡48/75-2572), one block from the city's main street, José Martí, always referred to simply as Martí. The station is within walking distance of most of the hotels and a good number of *casas particulares*; although there are usually plenty of private taxis outside the station, they are usually looking to fill their cars for long-distance journeys. In the unlikely

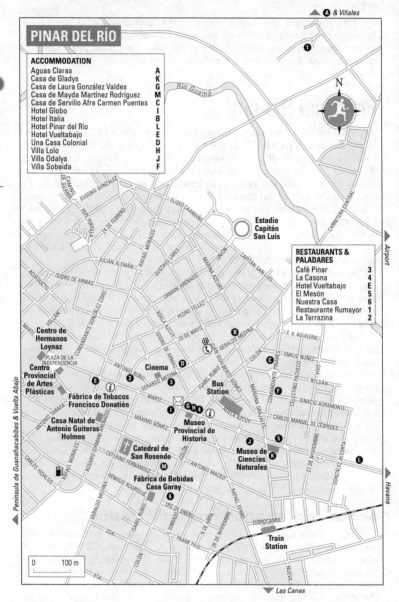

PINAR DEL RÍO

ACCOMMODATION

Aguas Claras	A
Casa de Gladys	K
Casa de Laura González Valdes	G
Casa de Mayda Martínez Rodríguez	M
Casa de Servilio Afre Carmen Puentes	C
Hotel Globo	I
Hotel Italia	B
Hotel Pinar del Río	L
Hotel Vueltabajo	E
Una Casa Colonial	D
Villa Lolo	H
Villa Odalys	J
Villa Sobeida	F

RESTAURANTS & PALADARES

Café Pinar	3
La Casona	4
Hotel Vueltabajo	E
El Mesón	5
Nuestra Casa	6
Restaurante Rumayor	1
La Terrazina	2

event that you arrive by **train**, be prepared for a walk from the small **station** (☎48/75-2272), which is four blocks south of Martí, as there are rarely any taxis there.

Orientating yourself is simple; the centre itself is manageable on foot and it's unlikely you'll stray more than three or four blocks either side of Martí, which serves as a handy north–south division.

Information

The city's three **information offices** are all on Martí. Havanatur (Mon–Fri 8am–noon & 1.30–5pm, Sat 8am–noon & 1–4pm; ☎48/79-8494, ⓔ millo@cimex.com.cu) is in the bookshop at Martí esq. Colón, and Cubanacán (Mon–Sat 8am–12pm & 1–5pm; ☎48/75-0178) is next door. Services offered by both include hotel reservations, car rental, Víazul bus tickets, guided city tours and excursions to many of the province's highlights. A similar set of services is available in Cubatur (Mon–Fri 8am–noon & 1–5pm, Sat 8am–noon; ☎48/77-8405), less than a block from the main street on Rosario e/ Martí y Máximo Gómez, who also have maps and glossy but uninformative guides to the province. The information office of the hotel chain Islazul, at Martí 127 e/ Rafael Morales y Plaza de la Independencia (Mon–Fri 9am–5pm; ☎48/75-5662), is useful only for enquiries about the city's *Hotel Pinar del Río, Vueltabajo* and *Restaurante Cabaret Rumayor*, plus the *Villa Laguna Grande* (see p.251), the other hotel it operates within the province.

Accommodation

There are five hotels in town, but three of them are officially the exclusive domain of Cuban nationals. That said, if you are willing to negotiate with the receptionist for either a room or reduced rate, it's worth at least trying the *Hotel Globo* (☎48/75-4268), at Martí esq. Isabel Rubio, or the *Hotel Italia* (☎48/75-3049), at Gerardo Medina no.215, the two least run-down of the three. There is, however, a plethora of **casas particulares** on offer, several of which are within walking distance of the train station along Comandante Pinares. There are equal numbers of *jineteros*, some of whom have adopted particularly aggressive and audacious techniques, going as far as following you to the door of a house and claiming that no one lives there or that it's full, just as the owner approaches to let you in. With this in mind, be careful if asking directions, particularly from young men who take you to the address. Many house owners have complained of touts demanding commission even when the guests have actually arrived independently. The most important thing is to make it clear to the house owner that you did not get the address from a tout, and it can also help to let the tout know you will be doing this. Rooms in *casas particulares* here are generally between $15CUC and $20CUC but go up to $25CUC in peak season in some of the more popular houses.

Hotels

Aguas Claras Carretera de Viñales, 7.5km from Pinar del Río ☎48/77-8426 to 27. By far the most attractive place to stay in or near the city (though only worth it if you have your own car), this leafy, landscaped cabin complex tucked into the trees is out of walking distance from anything other than open countryside but offers a higher class of comfort than anywhere else. There's a pool, a decent restaurant and organized excursions to all the provincial highlights. ❸

Hotel Pinar del Río end of Martí just before the *autopista* ☎48/75-5070 or 75-5077, ⓦ www .islazul.cu. Though it's the biggest hotel in the city, the *Hotel Pinar del Río* is a tad worn out and has little style and limited comfort. It is, however, cheap, plus it has plenty of facilities, all of which are available to non-guests. There's a swimming pool, two restaurants, four bars, a pizzeria, car rental, shops and the best disco in town. ❸

Hotel Vueltabajo Martí no.103, esq. Rafael Morales ☎48/75-9381, 75-9382 and 75-9383, ⓦ www.islazul.cu. Without doubt the prettiest hotel in town, this delightful little place is also the most comfortable option in the centre by a long way. The stylish colonial facade, with its dinky balaustraded, canopy-covered balconies, is complimented by a handsome, simple interior full of polished wood, shining floors and reasonably well-appointed rooms. ❻

Casas particulares

Una Casa Colonial Gerardo Medina no.67 e/ Isidro de Armas y Adela Azcuy ☎48/75-3173. The

Organized excursions from Pinar del Río

One of the best reasons to stay in Pinar del Río is to use it as a base for entertaining **excursions** into the nearby countryside. The national travel agents Havanatur, Cubanacán and Cubatur offer a number of day-trips, along with some one- and two-night stays, to the province's main tourist spots as well as a selection of hard-to-get-to attractions. As public transport is particularly poor within Pinar del Río province, an organized excursion is often the only, and certainly the easiest, way to get to these destinations if you don't have your own vehicle. Even if you do have a car, the poor roads, lack of maps and road signs and basic remoteness involved in a journey to many parts of the province mean the various excursions offered here are all the more useful. What follows is a small selection of packages currently offered by Havanatur and Cubanacán. Prices shown are generally for three people or less; there are price reductions for more than three people.

Cayo Levisa One of the area's most popular one-day excursions is to the small resort on this offshore cay. Cubanacán offers a list of different packages, starting at $29CUC per person, which includes a welcome cocktail.

Gran Caverna de Santo Tomás An organized tour of the extensive cave systems near Viñales valley; $18CUC per person, two-person minimum.

María La Gorda Amongst the one-night and two-night stays offered by Havanatur to the end-of-the-line María La Gorda beach resort is a programme which starts with visits to the cigar and rum factories in Pinar del Río and then heads west to Laguna Grande for the night. The following day is spent at María La Gorda, where fishing, snorkelling and diving are the order of the day; $190CUC per person, two person minimum. A transfer-only deal is also available, priced at $20CUC for a return ticket.

Tobacco Tour A day-trip to the nearby Vuelta Abajo region (see p.248) taking in a visit to a tobacco farm, a UBPC (farming co-operative) and the cigar factory back in the city; $30CUC per person.

Viñales Tour The basic tour does not include lunch but does offer visits to all the main sights In Viñales valley, such as the Mural de la Prehistoria and the Cueva del Indio; $40CUC per person with Cubanacán.

---

nearest thing to a privately run hotel in Pinar del Río, there are officially just two rooms for rent here but there are several more in case the legal limit is changed again. The rooms, many with en-suite bathrooms, are gathered around a lovely patio garden where, enclosed by vines, a tiny restaurant area has been set up and there's an impressive outdoor jacuzzi. There is also space for three cars in the garage. ❶

🏃 **Casa de Gladys** Ave. Comandante Pinares no.15 e/ Martí y Máximo Gómez ☎ 48/77-9698. Both the rooms for rent in this huge house have double beds and en-suite bathroom, and there are some memorable furnishings, like the matching colonial-style wardrobe, bed and dresser in one room. There's also secure parking for two cars and a fantastic backyard complete with fountain. ❶

🏃 **Casa de Laura González Valdes** Martí no.51 altos e/ Colón e Isabel Rubio ☎ 48/75-2264, ✉ ppoliva@cubarte.cult.cu. This

extraordinary, large, first-floor *casa particular*, bang in the centre of the city, stands out for its amazing library of some 15,000 books and magazines, with pieces coming from around the world and dating back to the 1950s and earlier. Each of the two double rooms for rent has its own balcony, while the communal areas include a stately dining room and a spiral staircase leading to a huge roof terrace. ❶

Casa de Mayda Martínez Rodríguez Isabel Rubio no.125 e/ Antonio Maceo y Ceferino Fernández ☎ 48/75-2110, ✉ mayda16@princesa .pri.sld.cu. An orderly, well-maintained mini-apartment with a spacious roof terrace all set atop the friendly owners' house. It's well suited to a romantic couple, with more privacy than most other places and plenty of comfort. There's a garage and the owners' son speaks English. ❶

Casa de Servilio Afre Carmen Puentes Ave. Comandante Pinares no.157 e/ Roldán y Emilio

Núñez ☎ 48/75-2309, ✉ servilios@yahoo.com. Both rooms available here have a/c, and one has a brand new en-suite bathroom and an own balcony overlooking the beautiful shady garden. Meals, offered for between $3CUC and $6CUC, are served on the garden patio. Other pluses include hot water and contacts with local taxi drivers. ❶

Villa Lolo Martí no.57 e/ Isabel Rubio y Colón ☎ 48/75-1709. A large en-suite, bedsit on the street side of this heart-of-the-city house, which dates from 1927. It's a little rough around the edges, but the lovely hosts add plenty of warmth, plus there's a towering spiral staircase leading all the way from the ground up to one of the highest domestic roof terraces in the city. ❶

Villa Odalys Martí 158 e/ Ave. Comandante Pinares y Calle Nueva ☎ 48/75-5212. A large room at the back of the house with en-suite bathroom, hot water, a/c, fridge and black-and-white TV. Ideal for those seeking privacy, while also very sociable (if that's your preference), with three people living in the house and plenty of young people always about. ❶

Villa Sobeida Ave. Comandante Pinares no.102 esq. Agramonte ☎ 48/75-5866. This down-to-earth family house with a slight Mediterranean feel offers a sufficiently equipped double-room apartment with two balconies. The owner is usually willing to drop the price below the average as long as no touts are involved. ❶

The Town

All of Pinar del Río's sights can be covered in a single day if so desired, but it's a good idea to select just three or four in order to avoid what can become a slightly monotonous tour. To be frank, your time here is probably best spent seeking out a *paladar* or *casa particular* to suit your taste and retreating to one of these, or lounging around the pool and grounds of the *Hotel Pinar del Río*, away from the attentions of the *jineteros*. That said, if you tour the city in the right order you can start with the best sights and keep going until you get bored.

With this in mind, a good starting point is at the top of town near the summit of the small hill which leads up into west suburban Pinar del Río. Here, on the pint-sized square known as the **Plaza de la Independencia**, is the small **Centro Provincial de Artes Plásticas** and the unprepossessing **Centro de Hermanos Loynaz**. Just a block and a half south of here is the **Fábrica de Tobacos Francisco Donatién**, the town's cigar factory and the focal point for all coach trips to the city. The **Fábrica de Bebidas Casa Garay**, several blocks southeast, is also worth a visit for a look at the making of Pinar del Río's renowned Guayabita rum. If you make it out of the rum factory still in the mood for sightseeing, there's always the pair of extremely unexceptional museums on Martí: the **Museo Provincial de Historia** and, at the eastern end, the **Museo de Ciencias Naturales**.

Plaza de la Independencia

On the western tip of Martí is **Plaza de la Independencia**, a small square at the highest part of town that would make for a relaxing spot were it not surrounded by roads. As it stands, the drooping branches of the resident trees dousing this concrete patch in shade and the turquoise-trim concrete bandstand don't manage to elevate the square to social-centre status.

The street forming the plaza's eastern side, Antonio Guiteras, is the location for the **Centro Provincial de Artes Plásticas** (Mon–Sat 8am–noon & 1–5pm; $0.50CUC), which, during the rare times it's actually open, houses temporary exhibitions (of varying quality and content) featuring sculptures, drawings and paintings by local artists.

With equally unreliable opening times, over on the opposite side of the plaza, is the **Centro de Hermanos Loynaz** (Mon–Sat 8.30am–4.30pm; free), a lovingly run four-room museum and study centre dedicated to the literary Loynaz siblings. All four wrote poetry and fiction in the early twentieth century and have recently become more well known. Their poetry appears frequently in newspapers and magazines, and the most famous of them, Dulce Maria Loynaz, author of three novels (the best known is *Jardín*), has received numerous awards, including the prestigious Premio Cervantes de Literatura in 1992. She died in 1997 at the age of 94, and was until her death the last of the Loynaz brothers and sisters. A rather amateurish portrait of her, painted in 1986, hangs in the museum, along with display cabinets full of her prizes, a photograph of her giving a public reading and photos of the rest of the family. More engaging than the two exhibit rooms is the crowded and cosy library in the two front rooms, crammed with publications from the 1830s to the present, including some English literature; you can browse at your leisure. One of the gems is an ornate edition of *Alice's Adventures in Wonderland*.

Fábrica de Tobacos Francisco Donatién

Two blocks southeast of the plaza on Antonio Maceo you'll find the **Fábrica de Tobacos Francisco Donatién** (Mon–Fri 9am–4pm, Sat 9am–midday; $5CUC), the city's premier attraction and home of Vegueros cigars, a lesser-known brand but one that's well respected amongst connoisseurs. Compared to the Partagas factory in Havana, this place is tiny and the tour much less illuminating, but it's still the most interesting spot to visit in the city. The imposing, high-arched 1859 building, with its balaustraded rooftop and unadorned queue of supporting columns, has housed the cigar factory since its inauguration in 1961. The exterior, though, belies the relaxed atmosphere of the intimate, non-mechanized workshop inside, and the brief guided tour (available in English or French) offers a genuine insight into the care and skill involved in producing some of the world's finest cigars. The *tabaqueros* sit at wooden desks dexterously rolling and cutting the tobacco into shape while sometimes a *compañero* reads out articles from the national newspaper, *Granma*. The cigars are then passed on to be approved by some of the more experienced workers before being banded and boxed. A selection of brands is sold in the factory shop, but for a wider choice cross over the road to the Casa del Habano, Maceo no.162 e/ Plaza de la Independencia y Rafael Morales, an excellent **cigar shop** with all the best Cuban brands on sale and a smart little smokers' lounge as well as a café out the back.

Casa Natal de Antonio Guiteras Holmes and Catedral de San Rosendo

Further down the hill on Antonio Maceo, on the corner with Ormani Arenado, the **Casa Natal de Antonio Guiteras Holmes** (Mon–Fri 9am–4.30pm, Sat 9am–noon; free) is only just worth the price of admission. Inside, a few exhibits have been scraped together in a half-hearted attempt to detail the life of this 1930s rebel activist. There is no explanation of who Holmes actually was and very little attention paid to the displays, which consist of little more than a few firearms and some old photographs. His brief tenure as Secretary of the Interior in Grau San Martín's left-leaning govern-ment of 1933 followed an active political life, particularly as a student in his native Pinar del Río. The only attention-grabber is the dramatic and quite graphic photograph of the dead bodies of Guiteras and the Venezuelan Carlos Aponte after they'd been shot by government forces in May 1935. This reversal of government attitude towards Guiteras came after Grau allowed the future dictator Fulgencio Batista a prominent place in the running of the country and Guiteras subsequently resigned.

Two blocks down Antonio Maceo at Gerardo Medina is the relatively ordinary **Catedral de San Rosendo**, built in 1883. The unsophisticated facade, with two bell towers and four pillars providing just a hint of grandeur, has to be viewed from behind a set of iron railings, and you can only see the interior if you happen to arrive during public opening times (ostensibly between 3pm and 6pm, but don't count on it).

Fábrica de Bebidas Casa Garay

Not far from the cathedral, four blocks south of Martí on Isabel Rubio, is the **Fábrica de Bebidas Casa Garay** (Mon–Fri 9am–4pm, Sat 9am–1pm; $1CUC), a rum factory, founded in 1891, where the popular Guayabita del Pinar brand is produced. The entrance charge includes a ten-minute guided tour of the three rooms and courtyard that make up the compact factory, beginning in the back room where barrels of fermenting molasses create a potent smell and finishing in the claustrophobic bottling and labelling room. Unsurprisingly, bottles of Guayabita are on sale, and you get a free sample of both the dry and sweet versions to help you make your decision.

Museo Provincial de Historia and Museo de Ciencias Naturales

The more central of the two museums on Martí is the **Museo Provincial de Historia** (Mon–Fri 8.30am–4.30pm, Sat 9pm–1pm; $1CUC), situated between Isabel Rubio and Colón. It contains some interesting bits and pieces – including pre-Columbian tools and bones and displays on the history of tobacco, coffee and slavery in the province – but overall is too disparate to present any kind of coherent narrative about the region. As with all history museums in Cuba, there is quite a bit of overemphasis placed on the Revolution.

Down at the quieter, eastern end of Martí, at the corner with Comandante Pinares, the Palacio de Guach contains the city's **Museo de Ciencias Naturales** (Tues–Sat 9am–4.30pm, Sun 8–11.30am; $1CUC). This eclectic building is the most architecturally striking in the city, its arches adorned with dragons and other monstrous figures and the whole place riddled with elaborate chiselled detail. Inside, each room has a specific theme, and although the ocean and plant rooms seem to be made up of whatever the museum could get its hands on, like bottled fruits and some miscellaneous dried leaves, there are more complete collections of butterflies, moths, exotic insects, shells and birds. Kids will enjoy the convincing giant stone tyrannosaurus and stegosaurus in the courtyard, where there's also a mural depicting other prehistoric creatures. The attraction is admittedly limited, however, and some of the stuffed animals on display in the mammal and reptile sections look as bored as visitors might start to feel after fifteen minutes here.

Eating

Not very good to start with, the options for eating out in Pinar del Río have actually managed to worsen in both quantity and quality over the last few years. The state-run **restaurants** lack both variety and ambience, with a concentration of particularly poor ones right in the centre on Martí. Only two legal *paladares* have managed to stay in business, and though nothing special they are certainly the places to head for in and around the centre. In the light of all this it's worth paying the extra to have meals included if you are staying at a *casa particular*.

Good-value **ice cream** is served during the day at *Coppelia*, Gerardo Medina e/ Antonio Rubio y Isidro de Armas, and, more expensively, in the *Alondra Heladería*, at Martí esq. Rafael Morales. The fast-food chain *El Rápido* is represented at Martí 65 e/ Isabel Rubio y Colón.

Café Pinar Gerardo Medina e/ Antonio Rubio y Isidro de Armas ☏ 48/77-8199. Main dishes at this convertible-peso restaurant and nightspot cost as little as $2CUC, but to pay more for the super-market-standard pizza, pork or chicken platters would be asking too much. Late at night it may be the only option, but otherwise eat elsewhere.

La Casona Martí no.77 e/ Isabel Rubio y Colón ☏ 48/77-8263. Speciality chicken dishes, like *tacos de pollo napolitano*, are the main event here alongside a few basic but cheap pizzas and spaghettis. The colonial theme of this sometimes lively spot is half-hearted, but the high ceiling, wooden rafters and iron railings across the large window frames do give the place some character.

Hotel Vueltabajo Martí no.103 esq. Rafael Morales ☏ 48/75-9381. The canteenish restaurant here (the best hotel in town) falls way short of the decent standard set by the hotel itself, but it's very cheap and as reliable an option as any. Basic pizzas and pastas, for less than $2CUC, and a few fancier, slightly pricier (yet dodgier) meat dishes, such as *pollo a la gordon blue*, make up the bitty menu.

El Mesón Martí e/ Comandante Pinares y Celestino Pacheco. This unatmospheric *paladar* at the quieter end of Martí is nevertheless the best place to eat out in the centre of the city given the rival-beating quailty and variety of its chicken,

pork, fish and salad dishes. The decor is dominated by a massive, simplistic mural, the service is better than elsewhere and prices are between $5CUC and $10CUC. Open noon–10pm Mon–Sat.

Nuestra Casa Colón no.161 e/ Ceferino Fernández y 1ero de Enero. Surrounded by the branches of a mature tree, the novel setting of this rooftop-cum-treehouse *paladar* (reached via a stepladder) is the main talking point here. The spoken menu is limited to simple but filling fish, pork or chicken dishes; expect to pay $8CUC for a main meal. Closed Sun.

Restaurante Rumayor Carretera Viñales Km 1 ☏ 48/76-3007. The city's biggest and best restaurant, next door to the cabaret of the same name, boasts a large, rustic dining hall adorned with African tribal imagery and a spacious shady garden. Popular with locals, the sensibly priced Cuban cuisine, although in short supply includes the recommended *pollo ahumado a la Rumayor* (wood-smoked chicken). Reservations are essential.

La Terrazina Antonio Rubio esq. 20 de Mayo. Arguably the best of the poor crop of local state-run peso restaurants. A charming terrace compensates for an uninspired interior, while the Italian cuisine, suitable for those on the tightest of budgets, is palatable. Limited opening hours, usually Mon–Sat 6–10pm.

Drinking, nightlife and entertainment

Tiny *Bar Rojo* on the third floor in the hotel *Globo* on Martí is one of the few places in Pinar del Río worthy of the **bar** label. It's a proper drinkers' corner, suitably rough around the edges, with an all-knowing barman and views across the rooftops to the south side of the city. The remaining spots are rather lacklustre, and include the shadowy little bar in the *Italia* hotel on Gerardo Medina and *Bar El Patio*, on Colón between Martí and Adela Azcuy, a simple watering hole on an enclosed patio, suitable for a break during a daytime tour of the city. *Café Pinar*, on Gerardo Medina between Antonio Rubio and Isidro de Armas, is a better spot for a drink than a meal, whilst there are a few tables and chairs inside the Doñaneli Dulcería, the local sweet and cake shop, which also stocks beers and soda, on Gerardo Medina between Martí and Máximo Gómez.

Don't expect much **nightlife** until the weekend, when the main streets buzz with young people. *Café Pinar*, Gerardo Medina e/ Antonio Rubio y Isidro de Armas, is the exception. The music here, often played live, doesn't get going until 11pm or so, by which time the place is typically bumping with dressed-up locals. The only real nightclub in town is at the *Pinar del Río* (Tues–Sun 10pm–late; $5CUC per couple), which though small has the slickest decor of all the nightspots, while the discos at the *Italia* and *Globo* amount to little more than loud music and dim lights in the bar. For traditional **live music** your best bet, other than *Café Pinar*, is the *Casa de la Música* (☏ 48/75-4794), again on Gerardo Medina, an open-air enclosure packed with uncomfortable chairs. The pleasantly entertaining, unpretentious shows cater to an undemanding audience and usually start at 9pm. Check also the noticeboard inside the entrance of the *Casa de Cultura* (℡48/75-2324), Martí no.65 e/ Rafael Morales y Roasrio, where *bolero* and *danzón* nights are amongst the fixture list, as is a *peña campesina*, a traditional rural Cuban song and dance, every Sunday at 2pm. Entrance here is usually free.

The town's most spectacular night out is the *Cabaret Rumayor*, Carretera Viñales Km 1 (Tues–Sun 10pm–late; ℡48/76-3051, 76-3052 and 76-3007; $5CUC, includes one drink), where one of the best **cabaret** shows outside Havana and Santiago draws crowds of tourists and raucous locals – who seem to know the show backwards. Like most cabarets in Cuba, the show is drenched in gaudy 1970s-style glamour, with frilly shirts, shiny loafers, stilettos, gel-drenched hairdos and neon colours in abundance. Desperately romantic, mostly ageing songsters take turns strutting out onto the open-air stage, backed up by their equally glitzy, scantily clad, all-smiling dancers. A seemingly endless sequence of song-and-dance routines takes you into the early hours of the morning, switching back and forth from tearful ballads to button-busting showtime numbers.

During the day, the **pools** at the hotels *Pinar del Río* and the out-of-town *Aguas Claras* are available to non-guests for a couple of convertible pesos. For **cinema**, there's Cine Praga, at Gerardo Medina e/ Antonio Rubio y Isidro de Armas (℡48/75-3271), and the **sala de video** run by UNEAC at Antonio Maceo 178 e/ Comandante Pinares y Rafael Ferro (℡48/75-4572); details of what's showing at both are displayed in the window of Cine Praga. Pinar del Río has one of the most successful **baseball** teams in the national league, with games played in the 14,000-capacity Estadio Capitán San Luis (℡48/75-4290 or 75-3890) near the road to Viñales, usually on a Tuesday, Wednesday, Thursday or weekend. Games start at around 7.30pm on weekdays and Saturdays, while Sunday games are held at 4pm. The nineteenth-century **Teatro Milanés** on Martí has been closed for years.

Listings

Banks and money The best bank for foreign currency transactions and credit-card withdrawals is the Banco Financiero Internacional at Gerardo Medina no.44 e/ Isidro de Armas y Martí (Mon–Fri 8am–3pm). There is also the Banco de Crédito y Comercio at Martí no.32 e/ Isabel Rubio y Gerardo Medina (Mon–Fri 8am–midday & 1.30–3pm). There's another branch at Martí e/ Rosario (Ormani Arenado) y Rafael Morales. Pesos can be purchased at the Cadeca *casas de cambio* on Gerardo Medina e/ Antonio Rubio y Isidro de Armas and Martí no.46 e/ Isabel Rubio y Gerardo Medina (Mon–Sat 8.30am–5.30pm, Sun 8.30am–12.30pm).

Books La Internacional at Martí esq. Colón has a small selection of books that may be of interest to foreign visitors, including some specialist guide books, coffee-table photography books and some English–Spanish dictionaries. There is also the library, the Biblioteca Provincial Ramón González Coro (Mon–Sat 8am–5pm), at Colón e/ Martí y Máximo Gómez, whose small foreign-fiction section includes about twenty books in English.

Car and scooter rental Most of the city's car rental agencies operate from the *Pinar del Río* hotel. Cubacar has a desk at the hotel (daily 8am–6pm; ℡48/77-8278) and can be contacted on a call-out number too (℡48/77-8278). Havanautos (daily 8am–6pm; ℡48/77-8015 or 77-3078), which also rents out scooters, and Micar (℡48/77-1454) have offices in the car park. Outside of office hours you should be able to contact a Havanautos representative by asking at the hotel desk.

Internet The local ETECSA Telepunto at Gerardo Medina no.127 esq. Juan Gualberto Gómez (daily 8.30am–6.30pm) has several Internet terminals and six phone booths.

Medical Hospital Abel Santamaria, Carretera Central Km 3 ℡48/76-2046. Ring ℡48/76-2317 for an ambulance.

Pharmacy The only pharmacy for tourists is in the *Pinar del Río* hotel.

Photography There is a branch of Photoservice at Isabel Rubio e/ Martí y Máximo Gómez.

Police Dial ☎ 48/75-2525, or ☎ 116 in case of emergency.
Post office The main branch is at Martí esq. Isabel Rubio where you can send and receive faxes and make photocopies. DHL and Cuban equivalent EMS services are also available.
Public toilet At *Bar El Patio* on Colón e/ Martí y Adela Azcuy.
Shopping There's a good selection of Cuban music CDs and cassettes in the Caracol shop at Maceo esq. Antonio Tarafa and a smaller selection, along

with some poster prints, at Bazar Pinareño at Martí no.28 e/ Gerardo Medina y Isabel Rubio. For arts and crafts, the best place, once it is rebuilt following storm damage, is the Fondo de Bienes Culturales, Martí esq. Gerardo Medina. All the supermarkets are on Martí.
Taxis The only taxi rank in town is outside the *Pinar del Río* hotel. You can call for a Turistaxi via the hotel on ☎ 48/75-5071, or directly on ☎ 48/76-3481. Alternatively, try Transtur on ☎ 48/77-8078.
Telephone See Internet.

The Viñales valley

The jewel in Pinar del Río's crown is the valley of **Viñales**, an official **National Park** and by far the most visited location in the province. With two fantastically located hotels, striking landscapes and an atmosphere of complete serenity, Viñales is an essential stop if you're in the province or anywhere near it. Though only 25km north from the city of Pinar del Río, the valley feels far more remote than this, with a lost-world kind of quality, almost entirely due to the unique *mogotes*, the boulder-like hills which look like they've dropped from the sky onto the valley floor. These bizarre limestone hillocks were formed by erosion during the Jurassic period, some 160 million years ago. Rainfall slowly ate away at the dissolvable limestone and flattened much of the landscape, leaving a few survivors behind, their lumpy surface today coated in a bushy layer of vegetation. Accentuated by the flatness of the valley floor, the virtually vertical sides of the *mogotes* seem to erupt from the ground, creating a striking sense of enclosure across the valley. Easily the most photographed examples are the **Mogote Dos Hermanas** or "twin sisters", two huge cliffy mounds hulking next to one another on the west side of the valley, with acres of flat fields laid out before them serving to emphasize the abruptness of these strange explosions of rock. The rich soils and regular rainfall, especially during the summer months, make Viñales a very productive area, and much of the valley floor between the *mogotes* is carpeted with crops, most notably tobacco. For the archetypal **view** of the valley, head for the viewing platform at the *Hotel Jazmines*, a few hundred metres' detour off the main road from Pinar del Río, just before it slopes down to the valley floor. This is usually the first port of call for coach trips and a perfect place to get a broader perspective of Viñales before you head down the hill to see it all up close.

Despite the influx of visitors, the region hasn't suffered from all the traffic. The tourist centres and hotels are kept in isolated pockets of the valley, often hidden away behind the *mogotes*, and driving through it's sometimes easy to think that the locals are the only people around. Most of the population lives in the small **village** of Viñales, which you'll enter first if you arrive from the provincial capital or Havana, and where there are plenty of *casas particulares*. From the village it's a short drive to all the official attractions, most of which are set up for tour groups, but it's still worth doing the circuit just to get a feel of the valley and a close look at the *mogotes*. If time is limited, concentrate your visit on the **San Vicente** region, a valley within the valley and home to the **Cueva del Indio**, the most comprehensive accessible cave system in Viñales. Also in San Vicente are the **Cueva de San Miguel** and **El Palenque de los Cimarrones**, a much smaller cave leading through the rock to a rustic encampment where runaway slaves once hid, but now set up to provide lunchtime entertainment for coach parties. Difficult-to-explore and little-visited **Valle Ancón** lies on the northern border of this part of the valley. On the other side of the village, the **Mural de la Prehistoria** is by far the most contrived of the valley's attractions. There are a number of places in Viñales difficult to find or impossible to access if you're not on an **organized excursion** but, conversely, a stay in any of the *casas particulares* often yields information otherwise unavailable to tourists.

There are two ready-made, worthwhile **day-trips** from the valley, well suited to a stay of a couple of nights or more in this area, both of which can be as easily done independently as on an organized excursion (see box, p.238). The closest is the Gran Caverna de Santo Tomás, an impressive and complicated set of caves set in the limestone rock of a hulking *mogote*. The nearest beach is at Cayo Jutías, further afield but easily reachable by car and still relatively undisturbed.

The valley supports its own **microclimate**, and from roughly June to October it rains most afternoons, making it a good idea to get your sightseeing done in the mornings. Mosquitoes are also more prevalent at this time of year and insect repellent is a definite must for any visit.

Arrival, information and getting around

All **buses** pull up opposite the main square outside the **Víazul ticket office** (℡8/79-3195) at Salvador Cisnero no.63a. From here all the *casas particulares* in the village are within walking distance, but to get to any of the hotels you'll need to catch a taxi or the local tourist bus (see below for more details).

Viñales's visitor centre, the **Centro de Visitantes** (Mon–Fri 9am–5.30pm, Sat & Sun 9am–noon; no phone, ℮direccion@pnvinales.co.cu), is at Carretera a Viñales Km 23, on the road into the village from Pinar del Río. Opened in July 2006, the centre is very slowly building up its set of services, which are due to include hiking, climbing and cycling excursions, but for now its resources are limited to a few informative displays and recommendations from the guides. Until the centre is fully operational, the best places for practical help remain the travel agents in the village, and to a lesser extent the *buros de turismo* in the hotels. The biggest national travel agent, Havanatur (daily 8am–10pm; ℡8/79-6262 or 79-6161, ℮vinales@cimex.com.cu), has a branch in the Sergio Dopico bookshop at Salvador Cisnero no.65, over the road from the main square. They sell a number of one-day visits to locations around Viñales and beyond (see box, p.238) and operate a useful long-distance taxi service (see p.238). You can also book Víazul bus tickets here. At Salvador Cisnero no.63c is the office of another travel agent, Cubanacán (daily 8.30am–12.30pm & 1.30–9pm; ℡8/79-6393), which offers a similar set of services. Both offices tend to close earlier in low season, usually between September and October and in April and May. Another tourist organization, Paradiso (℡8/79-6164), has set up shop in Viñales, offering access to various cultural activities and excursions, as well as horseback riding trips and dance classes (see p.244).

Viñales village can easily be handled on foot, but the rest of the sights in the valley are beyond walking distance for most. The easiest way of **getting around** is on the hop-on, hop-off **Viñales Bus Tour**, an extremely conven-ient minibus service with stops at all the tourist attractions and hotels. The service runs daily from 10am (or 9am in high season) to 7pm and begins at the bus stop just outside the main square on Salvador Cisnero. Tickets cost $5CUC, can be bought on the bus itself and are valid for a whole day. For

Organized excursions from and around Viñales

All the travel agents in the village offer very similar and similarly priced excursions, day-trips and transfers around Viñales and the rest of the province. Though there are sometimes slight variations depending on whether you opt for Havanatur, Paradiso or Cubanacán, the packages listed here are available at all three. The staff at the Museo Adela Azcuy in the village (see p.240) organize one- to four-hour walking tours setting off daily at 9am and 3pm at a cost of $8CUC per person. (All prices below are also per person.)

Cayo Jutías A trip out to this subdued offshore cay, which is actually so easy to get to that if you have your own car you're better off visiting independently. Transfer only is $14CUC; with lunch included $23CUC to $28CUC.

Cayo Levisa This daily excursion is an uncomplicated way of getting over to the more developed but less accessible of the two visitor-friendly cays in the province. The cheapest option includes transportation only. $23CUC to $50CUC.

Pinar del Río A day-trip to the provincial capital, including a visit to the cigar factory (see p.232). $20CUC to $25CUC.

Recorrido por Viñales A tour of the valley that takes in all the major attractions, with lunch included. Particularly worthwhile if you fancy eating outside the village or hotels, as many of the restaurants around the valley tailor their meal times to suit visiting tour groups. The pricier option is done on horseback. $17CUC to $20CUC.

Sendero por el valle This hike from the village into the valley is a great way to explore beyond the roads which most visitors stick to, visiting a tobacco plantation along the way. $8CUC.

independent travel, you can rent **scooters** and **mountain bikes** from Cubasol, which currently has no fixed office but sets up shop just outside Cubanacan, or Palmares (a motorclub), which operates from a table outside the *Casa de Don Tomás* restaurant.

From Viñales you can take advantage of a **transfer service**, run via minibuses, which offers an appealingly hassle-free way to get to the capital and beyond. Bookings can be made through any of the travel agents in the village, or through the Víazul ticket office on Salvador Cisnero. The only set fares are to Havana – direct, for $15CUC per person, or along of the scenic routes via Soroa or the north coast for $20CUC – and to Cienfuegos and Trinidad at $35CUC and $40CUC respectively.

Accommodation

There's an even spread of good **places to stay** in the Viñales valley, with options to suit most tastes and budgets – though there are no luxury choices amongst the hotels; the most you're likely to pay for a double room here is $80CUC. Furthermore, amongst the choices are two of the best-situated and attractive hotels in Cuba, *Los Jazmines* and *La Ermita*, as well as a surprising abundance of rooms for rent in houses. Finding the latter shouldn't be a problem, as most have signs outside and the buses that drop tourists in the valley's tiny village are usually met by a crowd of locals equipped with business cards. The rates range between $15CUC and $25CUC, depending on the season, but the houses themselves vary relatively little, the village made up almost entirely of simple concrete bungalows. If you do decide to stay in a *casa particular* in the village, however, make sure you book it during the day as, despite the large number of rooms, demand often far outweighs supply and the whole village is sometimes full to capacity by 7pm. Mosquito repellent is a must if you're going to stay in one of the places on the valley floor.

Hotels and campismos

Campismo Dos Hermanas on the road to the Mural de la Prehistoria ☎82/79-3223. Hidden away within the jagged borders of the surrounding *mogotes*, this is better equipped than most *campismos*, despite having no a/c or fans in its neat, well-kept white cabins. On the spacious site are a TV room, games room, bar and restaurant, swimming pool and a regional museum. There's also a nightly disco. The cheapest of the state-run options, this is the place to come if you want to share your stay with Cuban holidaymakers, but be prepared for the constant blare of music in peak season. ❶

La Ermita Carretera de Ermita Km 2 ☎8/79-6071, 79-6072 & 79-6100, ⓔreserva@vinales.hor.tur.cu. Gorgeous open-plan hotel in immaculate grounds high above the valley floor providing fantastic, panoramic views of the San Vicente valley and out beyond the *mogotes*. The tidy complex features three dignified apartment blocks with columned balconies, a central pool, a tennis court, a wonderful balcony restaurant and a comprehensive programme of optional activities and excursions including horse riding, trekking and birdwatching. Rooms are tasteful and reasonably well equipped. ❻

Los Jazmines Carretera a Viñales Km 25 ☎8/79-6205 & 79-6210, ⓔreserva@vinales.hor.tur.cu. This is the first hotel along the winding road into Viñales. There are stunning views of the most photographed section of the valley from virtually every part of the complex, including the elegant colonial-style main building and its balconied restaurant, almost any of the 78 rooms and the pool and terrace. The rooms themselves (some in a separate, more modern block and a few in red-roofed cabins) could do with a makeover, the restaurant food is very poor and the whole place is past its prime, but the unbeatable hillside location does enough to make up for it all. ❻

Las Magnolias over the road from the Cueva del Indio ☎8/79-6062. Three rooms in a single bungalow with communal living room and dining room where meals are served. Simple, clean and good value. ❷

Rancho San Vicente opposite the abandoned *Hotel Ranchón* on the way out of San Vicente towards the Valle Ancón ☎8/79-6201 or 79-6221, ⓔreserva@vinales.hor.tur.cu. Twenty attractive and comfortable a/c cabins spread out around the site's gentle, wooded slopes. There's a swimming pool and a bathhouse offering massage and mud therapy. ❺

Casas particulares in Viñales village

Casa Dago Salvador Cisnero no.100 ☎8/79-31-73. This place used to be a respected *paladar*, a fact reflected in the high quality of food still on offer here. Run in a relatively businesslike fashion, it has a reception room with a tiny bar where the innumerable photos of people laughing and smiling testify to the renowned entertainment skills of the singing, guitar-strumming and piano-playing owner. There is one clean, well-kept room with two double beds, a/c and a modernized bathroom. ❷

Casa de Doña Hilda casa no.4, Carretera a Pinar del Río ☎8/79-6053. There are two rooms for rent in this mini-home complex, the biggest in its own small bungalow next to the main house with en-suite bathroom and a fridge, and the other in the house next door. A large dirt courtyard joins it all together and there is a drive where you can safely park your car. ❷

Casa de Teresa Martínez Hernández Camilo Cienfuegos no.10 e/ Adela Azcuy y Seferino Fernández ☎8/79-3267. Though there is only one room to rent in this attractive and compact *casa particular*, it has a capacity for up to four people, which can make it a bargain for the price. ❷

Hostel Inesita Salvador Cisnero no.40, Viñales village ☎8/79-6012. The two rooms (one with a/c) for rent in this *casa particular* in the heart of the village are in a separate apartment taking up the entire top floor of the house and accessed via an outside set of steps. A wide balcony running around three sides of the apartment helps make this one of the best places to stay in the village. ❷

Villa El Isleño Carretera a Pinar del Río ☎8/79-3107. Right on the edge of the village and one of the first houses you'll come to if you've driven from the provincial capital, this handsome place offers two excellent double rooms; one of them – in a separate block out the back with its own terrace and an en-suite bathroom – is amongst the best rooms in the village. The backyard shares a border with a tobacco field and there are views of the Mogote Dos Hermanas. ❷

Villa La Cubana Rafael Trejo no.92, no phone but ring Esther, a neighbour, on ☎8/79-3138.

This is one of the few two-floor houses in the village and, accordingly, is less confined than many of its neighbours. Guests are given the run of the whole ground floor, which has one bedroom with two single beds. Out the back is a nicely kept garden. ❷
Villa La Esquinita Rafael Trejo no.18 e/ Mariana Grajales y Joaquín Pérez ☎ 8/79-6303. The a/c room for rent in one of the more spruced-up houses in Viñales has three beds – two double and one single – while outside is a bountiful fruit and vegetable plot. The owners will help you out by doing everything from drawing maps to organizing trips. ❷
Villa Magdalena Rafael Trejo no.41 esq. Ceferino Fernández ☎ 8/79-6029. One of the only colonial houses in the village backstreets, with a grand-looking, pillar-lined porch. Both double rooms have a/c and en-suite bathrooms, and one has a walk-in closet. A large, friendly family lives here. ❷

Viñales village

Surprisingly, considering the number of tourists who pass through it, the conveniently located village of **VIÑALES** has not been particularly developed for tourism, with only one official state restaurant, no hotels in the village itself (though several close by) and very few amenities in general. Nestled on the valley floor, simple tiled-roof bungalows with sunburnt paintwork and unkempt gardens huddle around the pine-lined streets, only the occasional car or tour bus disturbing the laid-back atmosphere as they ply their way up and down Salvador Cisnero, the main street which slopes gently down either side of a small square. Despite the village's diminutive size, there's no shortage of people offering you a place to stay or a taxi, though this doesn't constitute any kind of hassle. There's a genuine charm to the village, but there's actually little here to hold your attention for very long. All but one of the town's noteworthy buildings are on the lazy little main square, including the proud **Casa de la Cultura** (daily 10am–9pm except Mon 4–9pm & Fri 2–9pm; free), which dates from 1832 and houses a small, sporadically active theatre on the second floor. You're free to take a quick peek upstairs, where there's still some old colonial-style furniture. Next door, the diminutive **Galería de Arte** (daily 8am–11pm; free) displays small collections of paintings by local artists.

The most intriguing of the village's attractions, a five-minute walk north from the plaza, is the densely packed garden referred to as the **Jardín Botánico de Caridad**. Just past the end of Salvador Cisnero on C. P. Esperanza, a gate adorned with pieces of real fruit marks the easily missable entrance of these almost fairy-tale grounds, the property of two sisters whose small brick cottage sits in the middle. The compact shady garden is a botanist's dream, squeezing in all kinds of trees, shrubs and plants – papaya, begonias, orchids, a mango tree, a starfruit tree and many others. One of the sisters is usually around to help you pick your way through, explaining and identifying all the plants and noting many of their medicinal qualities, making it clear that there is order amongst this seeming chaos.

Heading the other way down Salvador Cisnero from the plaza is the lightweight though relatively engaging municipal museum, the **Museo Adela Azcuy** (Tues–Sat 9am–10pm & Sun 8am–noon; $1CUC), at no.115. Its four small rooms present an eclectic picture of local history, geology and culture, as well as bits and pieces of tourist information. Exhibits include a mock-up of the wall of a *mogote* and a short corridor dressed up to resemble a cave chamber, complete with stalactites. There is also a scant set of objects relating to the one-time occupant of the house, Adela Azcuy herself, one of the few women to be hailed in Cuba as a heroine of the nineteenth-century Wars of Independence.

La Palma & Palma Rubio ▲

SIERRA SAN VICENTE

Jardín Botánico de Caridad

Casa de la Cultura

Galería de Arte

JOAQUÍN
CEFERINO FERNÁNDEZ
SALVADOR CISNERO
DE RAFAEL TRIJO
CAMILO CIENFUEGOS

ADELA AZCUY
CDAD MARAÑÓ

0   500 m

H

2

I ⌂ Cuevo del Indio

▶ La Palma

SIERRA LA GUASASA

Valle de Ancón

3 Cuevas de San Miguel

CARRETERA A PUERTO ESPERANZA

SIERRA DE VIÑALES

Valle de la Guesasa

Mogote la Esmeralda

Río Palmarito

Río Esmeralda

N

4
J
Mural de la Prehistoria

Mogote del Valle

Mogote dos Hermanas

SIERRA DE VIÑALES

Viñales

see inset

K

CARRETERA A MONCADA

Valle de Viñales

L

- - - - Seasonal river

0   1 km

M ✳ (i)

CARRETERA A VIÑALES

5

Caverna de Santo Tomás & Cayo Jutías ◀

ACCOMMODATION

Campismo Dos Hermanas	J
Casa Dago	C
Casa de Doña Hilda	G
Casa de Teresa Martínez Hernández	F
La Ermita	K
Hostel Inesita	A
Los Jazmines	M
Las Magnolias	I
Rancho San Vicente	H
Villa El Isleño	L
Villa La Cubana	E
Villa La Esquinita	B
Villa Magdalena	D

RESTAURANTS

Casa de Don Tomás	1
Casa del Veguero	5
Jurásico	4
Las Magnolias	I
Restaurante Cueva del Indio	2
Restaurante El Palenque de los Cimarrones Valle	3
La Terraza	K

VIÑALES

241

▼ Pinar del Río

Mogote Dos Hermanas and the Mural de la Prehistoria

Less than a kilometre to the west of the village, the valley floor's flat surface is abruptly interrupted by the magnificent hulking mass of the **Mogote Dos Hermanas**. It plays host to the somewhat misleadingly named **Mural de la Prehistoria** (daily 8am–7pm; $2CUC), hidden away from the main road down a narrow side turning. Rather than the prehistoric cave paintings that you might be expecting, the huge painted mural, measuring 120m by 180m and desecrating the face of one side of the *mogote*, is in fact a modern depiction of evolution on the island, from molluscs to man. It's impressive only for its size, with garish colours and lifeless images completely out of tune with this otherwise humble yet captivating valley. The mural was commissioned by Fidel Castro and painted in the early 1960s. The bar, restaurant and souvenir shop just off to the side of the mural do nothing to alleviate the place's contrived nature, although it's not an unpleasant spot to have a drink and a bite to eat. The speciality at the **restaurant** (daily 9am–5pm; ℡8/79-6260) is pork cooked "Viñales style", roasted and charcoal-smoked, the highlight on an otherwise limited menu which also features a number of egg dishes.

The Cueva de San Miguel and El Palenque de los Cimarrones

By taking the left-hand fork at the petrol station at the northeastern end of the village, you can head out of Viñales through the heavily cultivated landscape to the narrower, arena-like San Vicente valley, around 2km away. Just beyond the *mogotes* that stand sentry-like at the entrance to the valley is the **Cueva de San Miguel** (daily 9am–4pm), also called the Cueva de Viñales. Unmissable from the road, the cave's gaping mouth promises drama and adventure, but it's disappointingly prosaic, with unnecessarily loud music blaring from a **bar** just inside the entrance which, though a bit tacky, does provide a welcome break from the sun.

You can pay $1CUC to investigate past the bar and venture down a corridor that disappears into the rock, emerging after just 50m or so at **El Palenque de los Cimarrones**. This reconstruction of a runaway slave (*cimarrón*) settlement provides limited insight into the living conditions of the African slaves who, having escaped from the plantations, would have sought refuge in a hideout (*palenque*) such as the one on display here. There's little more here than some cooking implements and a few contraptions made of sticks and stones, though there are some original pieces used by the slaves. You're left to guess what each piece was used for, and, although there is a small plaque declaring its authenticity, it's not even made clear whether this was actually the site of an original *palenque*.

Back in the daylight, right next to the reconstructed settlement and cut off on three sides by cliffs, is a large **restaurant** (see p.244) set under round *bohío* roofs. If you prefer not to explore the cave, you can instead get to the restaurant by driving or walking around the outside, down the bumpy road: it's not as much fun but does afford a wider perspective of the looming obelisks of rock towering over the huts. It's a pleasantly secluded spot for lunch, but becomes considerably less private in the afternoons when the tour parties arrive, though coinciding with group visits does bring the added bonus of being entertained by the Afro-Cuban folklore show put on for them.

The Cueva del Indio and the Valle Ancón

From the Cueva de San Miguel it's a two-minute drive or a twenty-minute walk north to San Vicente's most captivating attraction, the **Cueva del Indio** (daily 9am–5pm; $5CUC), 6km north of the village. Rediscovered in 1920, this whole network of caves is believed to have been used by the Guanahatabey Amerindians, both as a temporary refuge from the Spanish colonists and, judging by the human remains found here, as a burial site. On the path leading up to the caves' entrance you'll pass the *Restaurante Cueva del Indio* (see p.244), which resembles a small school dining hall.

Well lit enough not to seem ominous, the cool caves nevertheless inspire a sense of escape from the humid and bright world outside. There are no visible signs of Indian occupation; indeed the caves are almost certainly too damp to have been used as a permanent dwelling. Instead of paintings the walls are marked with natural wave patterns, testimony to the flooding that took place during the caves' formation millions of years ago. Only the first 300m of the large jagged tunnel's damp interior can be explored on foot before a slippery set of steps leads down to a subterranean river. It's well worth paying the extra peso for the **boat ride** here, where a guide steers you for ten minutes through the remaining 400m of explorable cave (there exists at least another kilometre of unlit tunnels which haven't yet been secured for visitors), pointing out images – mostly indiscernible, but supposedly resembling everything from crocodiles to champagne bottles – that have formed naturally on the rock. The boat drops you off out in the open, next to some souvenir stalls and a car park around the corner from where you started. From here a small footbridge leads across the river to *El Ranchón* (daily noon–4pm, ☏82/79-3200), a restaurant hidden behind the trees where the set meal, featuring grilled pork, costs $11CUC. The restaurant is part of a small farm, the **Finca San Vicente**, usually accessible only to tour groups, consisting mostly of orchards and coffee crops and host to the occasional cockfight.

A few hundred metres further up the road, just past an isolated **post office**, is the *Rancho San Vicente* cabin complex (see p.239). About 500m further, a left turn leads to the last stop in Viñales, the **Valle Ancón**. Mostly untouched by tourism, this least-visited and unspoilt of the valleys in Viñales is also the most complicated to explore and can become uncomfortably muddy in the rain. There's a small village of the same name, plenty of coffee plantations and a number of hard-to-find caves and rivers, but the rewards are usually outweighed by the effort needed to get there.

Eating

When it comes to **eating** in Viñales, your decision should be based predominantly on *where* rather than *what* to eat, as almost all places offer the same kind of basic Cuban cuisine. Another factor will be *when* you eat: the restaurants dotted around the valley floor are all daytime joints, in keeping with the opening hours of the nearby tourist attractions. The only places you can eat after 6pm or so are the hotels and the solitary restaurant in the village. There are also one or two snack bars and *caféterias*, such as *El Viñalero* and threadbare *Las Brisas*, both on Salvador Cisnero, within a few blocks of the village's main square, or the *Polo Montañez Centro Cultural* on the square itself, serving sandwiches and basic pizzas. None of these places serve good-quality or substantial meals, however. Because there are no longer any *paladares* in Viñales, the *casas particulares* are the only places where you can get any home-cooking here – reason enough to stay in one.

Casa de Don Tomás Salvador Cisnero no.140 ☎8/79-6300 & 79-3114. The only real restaurant in the village, set back from the road in a tree-shaded and garden-encircled ranch house. Dining on the front or back porch is the enjoyable way to appreciate the setting, and with a resident band providing the soundtrack there is no shortage of atmosphere. The house speciality is the paella-esque *Delicias de Don Tomás*, a slightly stodgy meat feast for $10CUC. Safer bets include grilled fish, fried pork and chicken dishes, starting at $4.50CUC.

Casa del Veguero Carretera a Viñales Km 25 ☎8/79-6080 Set meals of *comida criolla* are banged out for $10CUC amid the CDs, T-shirts and cigars also sold here. Next door to a tobacco-drying house just outside the village on the road to Pinar del Río.

Jurásico *Campismo Dos Hermanas*, Mural de la Prehistoria ☎8/79-3223. Decent *comida criolla*, including a tasty roast chicken special, is served in an intimate white-walled dining room in a pleasant looking tiled-roof lodge with a dinky patio out front where you can also eat.

Las Magnolias Carretera a Puerto Esperanza ☎8/79-6062. This modest restaurant (also known as the *Casa del Marisco*) over the road from the Cueva del Indio is the only place in the valley specializing in seafood. Known for dependable fish and lobster dishes.

Restaurante Cueva del Indio Cueva del Indio ☎8/79-6280. There is a slight Indocuban-slant to the creole cooking in this canteen, offering *tortas de yuca*, a form of cassava bread, and *ajiaco*, a traditional native Cuban stew, alongside the usual roast chicken and fried pork. In the building marking the entrance for tours of the cave.

Restaurante El Palenque de los Cimarrones Valle de San Vicente ☎8/79-6290. Catering predominantly to lunchtime tour groups, the food here is better than you might expect – the good, traditional Cuban dishes are cooked in appetizing seasonings, particularly the roast chicken and pork dishes. Open-air dining, under matted *bohío* roofs in the shadow of a *mogote*, is usually accompanied by live Afro-Cuban song and dance.

La Terraza *Hotel La Ermita* ☎8/79-6071. There is no finer location for a meal anywhere in Viñales than this restaurant on a balcony terrace offering sweeping views of the valley. Main dishes cost between $5CUC and $12CUC and include, in addition to the customary *comida criolla*, roasted and grilled beef platters, mussels and, for around $30CUC, several different lobster meals.

Drinking, nightlife and activities

Drinking options are mostly limited to the restaurants, with a handful of exceptions: the village nightspots, the bar at the mouth of the Cueva de San Miguel and an open-air, street-corner *cafétería* in the *Complejo Recreativo* at Adela Azcuy esq. Rafael Trejo. **Nightlife** is generally straightforward too, with the only regular after-dark action taking place in the village. The biggest, best and newest spot for live music is the *Polo Montañez Centro Cultural*, a semi-covered outdoor venue tucked away in a corner of the central square. Nightly shows of mostly traditional Cuban music begin at 9pm and are followed by recorded *salsa* and disco until the place closes down, usually no later than 2am and often earlier. Entrance is $1CUC. The only other reliable nightspots are the two bars over the road from one another on Salvador Cisnero, a block away from the square. There is often live traditional music in *El Viñalero* once they stop serving food, but for more of a show in a slightly classier setting head to the *Patio del Decimista*, where the stage, open roof and hanging plants provide a bit more fanfare. For nightlife on the valley floor, your only real option is a show and cheesy disco at the Cueva de San Miguel (☎8/79-3203), theoretically run five nights a week from 10pm to 12.30am, though lack of demand, especially in low season, means it's worth checking in advance; ring or enquire with one of the travel agents for details. There is also a disco at *Los Jazmines*, but it opens sporadically at best. For a more subdued night out there is a **cinema** and a *sala de video* at Ceferino Fernández esq. Rafael Trejo.

Though **rock climbing** has become increasingly popular in Viñales over the last ten years, it is still illegal here. There are plans to establish specific climbing routes, so check with the Centro de Visitantes (see p.237) for the latest information. **Dance classes** and **percussion lessons** can be arranged through Paradiso, the tourism agency operating from a desk outside the Casa de la Cultura on the square. In both cases, classes are $5CUC per hour with a two-hour minimum. Paradiso also organize **horseback riding** around the valley, as do Havanatur (see p.237) and the hotels, again at a cost of $5CUC per hour, but with a three-hour minimum. There are plenty of local residents who, for a fee, can fix you up with an unofficial tour through the valley by horse (you won't have to ask around for long before someone obliges, assuming the price is right). For details on organized excursions and hikes, see the box on p.238.

Listings

Banks and exchange Banco de Crédito y Comercio, Salvador Cisnero no.58 (Mon–Fri 8am–midday & 1.30–3pm, Sat 8–11am). This bank can handle credit-card transactions and cash traveller's cheques; to purchase pesos go to the *casa de cambio* at Salvador Cisnero no.92 (Mon–Fri 8am–6pm).

Bike rental Cubanacán at Salvador Cisnero no. 63c rent out bikes for just $1CUC for an hour or $5CUC for a whole day.

Car rental Micar (☎8/79-6330) on Salvador Cisnero, half a block from the petrol station in Viñales village, or Havanautos (☎8/79-6390), at the petrol station itself. There's also Cubacar (☎8/79-6060), in the Cubanacán office on Salvador Cisnero opposite the square.

Internet See Telephone.

Police station Salvador Cisnero no.69.

Post office Ceferino Fernández e/ Salvador Cisnero y Rafael Trejo.

Scooter rental The best place for scooter rental is next to the *Casa de Don Tomás* restaurant on Salvador Cisnero, where the Palmares Motoclub (daily 8.30am–8pm) set out their table and do business. Their charges start at $12CUC for 2 hours and $23CUC for a day. You can also try Havanautos at the petrol station on Salvador Cisnero, and Cubanacán at Salvador Cisnero no. 63c. Charges start at $10CUC/hr and $15CUC/3hr.

Swimming pool The pool at *La Ermita* is open to the public, $3CUC/person.

Taxi Transtur ☎8/79-6060.

Telephone ETECSA office, Ceferino Fernández no. 3 e/ Salvador Cisnero y Rafael Trejo, Viñales village.

Gran Caverna de Santo Tomás

Seventeen kilometres along the road west from Viñales village is the clearly marked turn-off for **El Moncada**, a scattering of houses that shares a sheltered valley with the magnificent **Gran Caverna de Santo Tomás**. The most extensive cave system in Cuba – and supposedly the third biggest in Latin America – the Gran Caverna de Santo Tomás attracts serious speleologists and small tour groups alike, but happily it has not yet become overrun with visitors.

A specialist school here, the Escuela Nacional de Espeleologia Antonio Núñez Jiménez (daily 8.30am–5pm; no phone), doubles as a **visitor centre** and includes a tiny museum. It also provides accommodation in a four-room, beige cement-walled bungalow. Rooms are basic and feature little more than a lamp, fan and radio, but for $20CUC per person, breakfast and dinner are included. From the turn-off a pine-lined road leads down into the valley and the first right-hand turn off this leads through El Moncada village and up to the centre's reception building. Though they're more accustomed to receiving pre-booked visits, it's possible to just turn up and pay for one of the obligatory **guides** on the spot, though you may have to wait awhile as there are only two. To book a visit to the caves ring Fran Vegerano in Viñales village (☎8/79-3145) or, alternatively, Havanatur or Cubanacán (see p.237), both of which sell day-trips from the village for around $20CUC. For anyone arriving independently the cost of the hour-and-a-half tour is $8CUC per person, including a lamp and helmet, and the guides can speak English.

Not all of the Gran Caverna de Santo Tomás's incredible 46km of caves, occupying eight different levels and with ten separate entrances, are accessible to the public. Most people, unless they are experienced spelunkers, are taken into either level six or seven, the mouths of which are semi-hidden up a rocky, forested slope from where there are fabulous views of the valley. Highlights of the walk – which covers a kilometre of chambers and passageways, quite narrow in places – include surprising cave winds, bats flying about and underground pools. There is an array of stalagmites and stalactites in all kinds of shapes and sizes, as well as all manner of contortions in the rock face which prevent the walk-through from getting monotonous. The knowledgeable guides point out a fascinating array of things along the way, such as easy-to-miss plants, deposits of guano, the significance of the markings and colourings on the walls and ceilings and, on level six, a replica of a mural found in a less accessible part of the system. The mural is part of the evidence, as is the 3400-year-old skeleton found here, that these caves were once the refuge of the Guanahatabeys, the original inhabitants of Cuba.

Cayo Jutías

Just off the north coast of this part of the province (a sixty-kilometre drive north and west from Viñales) is **Cayo Jutías**, a secluded island hideout that's relatively untouched compared to most of the other tourist magnets in the region. Though it is now firmly on the organized excursion circuit, this little cay is one of the least commercialized beach resorts in western Cuba. Besides the road ploughing through the middle of the low-lying thicket covering most of the cay, the only signs of construction are a wooden restaurant at the start of the 3km of **beach** on the north side and an old metal lighthouse built in 1902. The beach itself is admittedly a little scrappy in places and rarely more than 3m wide, but this does nothing to spoil the place's edge-of-the-world appeal. And while this may be the best spot in Cuba to lie back and do absolutely nothing, you can engage in a few **watersports** while here. Amongst the items available for rent from a hut by the restaurant are snorkelling equipment ($2.50CUC/hr or $5CUC/day) and small kayaks ($1CUC/hr for a single, $2CUC for a double), as well as sunloungers and sunshades ($1CUC each). At a cost of $5CUC per person you can explore the local coral reef in an outboard-motorboat or stay on land and play volleyball or football on the sandy pitches set up for these free activities. Eating at the **restaurant**, which is usually closed by 6pm, is more expensive compared to the options in Viñales, but the simple fish, shrimp, lobster and chicken main platters are still good value. The only way to spend a night on the cay – though very rarely does anyone do this – is to **camp**. Be sure to bring plenty of insect repellent if you do intend to do this, as the mosquitoes come out in force in the evening.

Getting there from Viñales, where most of the cay's visitors set out from, is surprisingly easy as the route is well marked. You will, however, need your own transport unless you pay for an organized excursion – Havanatur runs trips from Viñales (☎8/79-6262) for $23CUC per person, which includes lunch. When driving, follow the signposted road out of Viñales village to the Mogote Dos Hermanas until you reach the tiny village of Pons. After the posted right-hand turn here the road surface deteriorates as you twist and turn onto another village, Minas de Matahambre. From here head for Santa Lucía, following the signs to Cayo Jutías all the way, until you reach the causeway linking the cay to the mainland where, at a tollbooth, there is a $5CUC charge for foreign visitors, 5 pesos for Cubans.

Cayo Levisa

On the same stretch of north coast as Cayo Jutías, 50km northeast of Viñales, the lonely military outpost of Palma Rubia is the jumping-off point for **Cayo Levisa**, more developed for tourism but still relatively unspoilt. This three-kilometre-wide, densely wooded islet boasts some of the finest white sands and clearest waters in Pinar del Río, and unless you take advantage of its **diving centre**, there's blissfully little to do here. Don't expect any wild nights out – Cayo Levisa specializes in peace and quiet with more than enough beach for everyone to have their own private patch, even if the resort is full to its lowly twenty-cabin capacity.

To get to Palma Rubia from Viñales, follow the valley road north, past the turning for the Valle Ancón, and follow it to the small town of La Palma, just under 30km from Viñales village. From La Palma take the road heading roughly north, towards the coast, and stay on it for 17km until you reach a left turn which heads directly to Palma Rubia. The only regular **boat** to the island leaves at around 11am every day from Palma Rubia, where you can safely leave your car. If you're staying at the cabins on the island there's no charge for the twenty-minute crossing, otherwise it's a hefty $10CUC each way or a straight $25CUC return, which includes a usually seafood-based lunch at the island's restaurant. The return journey is at 5pm, which makes a day-trip fairly pointless unless you're going diving, and even then it's a little rushed.

The boat moors on a rickety wooden jetty, a two-minute walk from the forty grey-brick and newer wooden **cabins** of the *Villa Cayo Levisa* (℡082/77-3015, Ⓔ cayolevisa@cubanacan.co.cu; Ⓞ), the only accommodation on the island, sprawled untidily along the gleaming white beach. As the phone line to the cay can be unreliable you should contact the Cubanacán head office If you're booking a room here from Havana (℡7/833-4090, Ⓦ www.hotelescubanacan .com). The cabins are well equipped and furnished, with spacious interiors and large porches. Behind the beach, thick woodland reaches across the island to the opposite shore, forming a natural screen that encourages an appetizing sense of escape and privacy. Most of the coastline on this uninhabited cay is completely untouched, and although the beach is narrower and the washed-up seaweed more plentiful away from the resort area, the tranquillity is unparalleled.

The hotel has kayaks ($4–5.50CUC per hour) and catamarans ($16CUC per hour) for rent, and there's a separate **dive centre** within the small complex offering equipment rental, courses and dives around the nearby coral reef, a short boat trip away. Snorkel rental is $5CUC per hour and diving gear is $8CUC per hour. Diving charges depend on the number of times you dive: for four dives or less it's $28CUC per immersion; between five and nine dives cost $26CUC per immersion and if you intend to dive more than 20 times it will cost you $22CUC per immersion. Diving courses are offered too: a basic two-immersion course is $60CUC whilst a full course lasting for a week or more will set you back $365CUC. There are also fishing trips ($40–55CUC per person) and a day-trip is offered to nearby **Cayo Paraíso** ($20CUC per person), a similarly unspoilt islet once favoured by Ernest Hemingway, where you can dive or snorkel.

Southwest to the Península de Guanahacabibes

Heading southwest from Pinar del Río city on the Carretera Central, the only main road through this part of the region, the towns become more isolated and the tourist centres less developed. Getting around here without your own transport can be a real problem, though the unreliable and very slow train service and the occasional bus from the provincial capital do at least provide the possibility of getting to some of the beaches here on public transport. Even with a car the going can be tough, as the Carretera Central features very few signs, becomes increasingly potholed and hands over to minor roads just before the **Península de Guanahacabibes**, the highlight of this area. The snoozy towns along the route are likeable little places but hold scant reward for even the most enthusiastic explorer, and twenty minutes in any one of them should suffice for the whole lot. The one place that demands a longer visit in the region between Pinar del Río city and the peninsula is the **Alejandro Robaina tobacco plantation**, just under 25km from the centre of the provincial capital. Of the numerous *vegas* (tobacco farms) in the area, this is the one best prepared for visitors and the most renowned.

After the small town of Isabel Rubio, 60km from the provincial capital, the landscape becomes increasingly monotonous and doesn't improve until the dense forest and crystalline waters of the peninsula move into view, well beyond the end of the Carretera Central at the fishing village of **La Fe**. There are a couple of **beaches** out this way, around the wide-open bay of Ensenada de Cortés, although the appeal lies more in their proximity to the provincial capital and their popularity with locals than in their negligible beauty. The large, featureless lake at **Laguna Grande**, site of one of the region's three hotels, does not warrant a trip for its own sake. It is, though, fairly well placed if you want to break up what is bound to have been a reasonably long journey, especially if you're heading to or from **María La Gorda** in Cuba's virtually untouched western tip, one of the best scuba diving locations in the country.

Alejandro Robaina tobacco plantation

As the Carretera Central heads southwest from the provincial capital, it cuts through the famed **Vuelta Abajo** region, one of the most fertile areas in the whole country and the source of the finest **tobacco** in the world. There are countless *vegas* (tobacco plantations) in this zone, but one, the **Alejandro Robaina**, has an edge over the rest. While most plantations produce tobacco for one or more of the state-owned cigar brands, such as Cohiba, Monte Cristo and so on, this is the only one to farm the crop exclusively for its own brand, named after the grandson of the original founder who bought the plantation in 1845. The brand was established in 1997, then only the third brand to have been created since the Revolution in 1959. The owners have gone further than any other *vega* in their efforts to attract tourists, offering engaging guided tours of the plantation, product sampling opportunities and even the chance to meet Alejandro himself, now in his late 80s. Visits here remain an unofficial tourist attraction, with the enterprising owners, not the state, running the short tours. Though this adds to the sense of authenticity, it also means the plantation is difficult to find, with no street signs pointing the way nor any mention of the place in tourist literature or on maps.

To **get there**, you'll need to take a left turn, marked by a small collection of huts and a solitary bungalow, off the Carretera Central 18km from Pinar del

Río. Follow this almost ruler-straight side road for 4km until you reach another left turn, just before a concrete roadside plaque that reads "CCS Viet-Nam Heróico". This turn takes you onto a dusty track which leads right into the heart of the plantation where the owners live.

Although Carlos Forteza, the English- French- and Italian-speaking guide, is usually on hand to take visitors around the centre of the plantation on fairly well-structured **tours**, it's still a good idea to ring in advance (℡8/79-7470); impromptu visits between 10am and 5pm on any day but Sunday can usually be accommodated. The best time to visit is between October and January, the tobacco season, when the charge is $5CUC per person; for the rest of the year, when there is a little less to see, it's $3CUC. The tour takes in the various stages of tobacco production, starting with a visit to plots of land covered by cheese-cloth under which the seeds are planted. Next you are taken to one of the *casas de secado*, the drying barns, where the leaves are strung up in bundles and the fermentation process takes place, the strong smell here testament to that. Finally, in a smaller barn, you get to see a cigar being rolled. This last part is the only slightly contrived aspect of the visit, with magazine articles on Robaina laid out on a table and the person rolling the cigar clearly there for the benefit of tourists; however, it detracts little from the enjoyment of seeing the skill with which cigars are made.

For an even broader perspective on the tobacco industry it's worth attending the annual **Festival del Habano**, usually held around February or March, which takes place principally in Havana and the Vuelta Abajo region. For this week-long event various national and international commercial entities are invited to attend seminars and exhibitions at the university in Pinar del Río in a kind of trade fair where the machinery and tools used for the cultivation and production of the crop are laid bare. The more tourist-friendly side to the festival features organized tours around the region, taking in tobacco planta-tions, the cigar factory in the provincial capital and contact with some of the local *vegueros*. Contact Cubatur (℡7/833-4121, 833-3142 or 206-9803, ⓔeventos@cbtevent.cbt.tur.cu) in Havana for details.

Boca de Galafre and Playa Bailén

There's very little to choose from when it comes to the **beaches** on Pinar del Río's southern coastline, and the two around the **Ensenada de Cortés** are really just the best of a bad bunch. Fifteen kilometres beyond San Juan y Martínez on the Carretera Central, there's a clearly signposted turn-off for **Boca de Galafre**, the smaller of the two beaches. The sand and sea leave a lot to be desired – the former full of seaweed, the latter murky and unappealing – but this doesn't deter locals and Cuban holidaymakers who make the beach sociable if nothing else, the seaside equivalent of a city backstreet. A few people live in simple concrete cabins along the beachfront, while home-made **snacks and drinks** are sold from a couple of makeshift kiosks. Between September and June, sixteen of the **cabins** facing the shore can be rented for fifteen Cuban pesos a day. The only public transport to Boca de Galafre is the Sábalo **train** from Pinar del Río city (twice daily; 1hr 30min), which will leave you 2km north of the beach, and the bus to Cortés (daily; 1hr 15min), a nondescript little hamlet further southwest. The Boca de Galafre train station is halfway between the Carretera Central and the beach on the only road linking them together.

Five kilometres past the turning for Boca de Galafre, a side road leads down 8km to a more substantial beach, **Playa Bailén**, the most popular seaside resort

Tobacco

Tobacco is one of the most intrinsic elements of Cuban culture. Not as vital to the economy as sugar (Cuba's most widely grown crop), tobacco farming and cigar smoking are nonetheless more closely linked with the history and spirit of this Caribbean country. When Columbus arrived, the indigenous islanders had long been cultivating tobacco and smoking it in pipes that they would inhale through their nostrils rather than their mouth. When the leaf was first taken back to Europe it received a lukewarm reaction, but by the nineteenth century it had become popular enough to list as one of the most profitable Spanish exports from its Caribbean territories. However, it was as early as the sixteenth century that Cuban peasants became tobacco farmers, known as *vegueros*, during an era in which sugar and cattle-ranching were the dominant forces in the economy. As it became more profitable to grow tobacco, so the big landowners, most of them involved in the sugar industry, began to squeeze the *vegueros* off the land, forcing them either out of business altogether or into tenant farming. Many took their trade to the most remote parts of the country, out of reach of big business, and established small settlements from which many communities in places like Pinar del Río and northern Oriente now trace their roots. There nevertheless remained a conflict of interest which, to some extent, came to represent not just sugar versus tobacco but *criollos* versus *peninsulares*. The tensions which would eventually lead to the Cuban Wars of Independence first emerged between *criollo*, or Cuban-born, tobacco growers and the Spanish ruling elite, the *peninsulares*, who sought to control the industry through trade restrictions and price laws. Thus the tobacco trade has long been associated in Cuba with political activism. Today, when you visit a cigar factory and see the workers being read to from a newspaper or novel, you're witnessing the continuation of a tradition which began in the nineteenth century as a way of keeping the workers politically informed and aware.

along the southern coastline. The holidaymakers here are still Cuban rather than international, allowing for a real feel of what Cuban resorts were like before the better-known ones were transformed by foreign investment. The beach is wide and sandy, bordered by a beachfront path lined with shady *uva caleta* – or sea-grape – trees, and the light breezes characteristic of this stretch of coastline make gentle waves on the warm but murky water. During the summer the resort teems with families and is a good place to meet people, but for much of the rest of the year it can be rather empty and a bit depressing. Look out for men pushing carts along the beachfront path selling cold meals and rapidly melting ice cream from their unrefrigerated trolleys. If you're keen to **stay**, try the poorly equipped but affable *Villa Bailén* (no phone; ❶), which has cabins of all shapes and sizes stretched along 2km of beach. The cabin complex is split into three zones, with only Zone One, where visitors first arrive, available to convertible peso-paying foreign guests. There's a basketball court, a very basic children's playground and a number of poorly stocked *caféterias* and restaurants, each offering the same basic Cuban cuisine – you're better off bringing your own **supplies**.

Laguna Grande

Continuing westward down the Carretera Central, 10km beyond the town of Isabel Rubio and opposite a military base, you'll see the turn-off to Laguna Grande, an artificial fishing lake and modest resort. The road cuts through acres of citrus orchards that spruce up an otherwise unremarkable flat landscape until, at a crossroads, a left turn leads directly to the resort. Hidden away in a small wood,

Villa Laguna Grande (☎84/3453; ❷) is wonderfully isolated. The facilities are basic but as comprehensive as it gets in this part of the province, comprising a snack and souvenir shop, a cheap restaurant, bicycle rental for only 50¢ an hour and horses to rent. The twelve pink and blue cabins, only four of which have air conditioning, are reasonably comfortable. The off-the-beaten-track appeal of this resort is complemented by its unkempt appearance, with scruffy lawns and a few farmyard shacks dotted about the place. Laguna Grande itself is right next to the complex, hidden from sight behind a grassy bank. Large, round and bereft of features, the reservoir is not much to look at, but if you like, you can go fishing for trout, swimming and even rent small rowing boats ($1CUC per hour).

Península de Guanahacabibes

Only the most determined make their own way down to Cuba's westernmost tip, the forest-covered **Península de Guanahacabibes**, but it has become a popular organized excursion destination and in this respect is easier than ever to get to. The journey is certainly not without its rewards, especially for scuba divers, who can enjoy what are arguably the best **dive sites** in Cuba. One of the largest national forest-parks in the country, the **Parque Nacional Guanahacabibes** covers most of the peninsula, the whole of which was declared a UNESCO Biosphere Reserve in 1987. Some of Cuba's most beautiful and unspoilt coastline can be found here around the **Bahía de Corrientes**, the bay nestling inside this hook of land. It was on the peninsula that the Cuban Amerindians sought their last refuge, having been driven from the rest of the island by the Spanish colonists. Virgin beaches and water clear enough to compete with Cuba's most famous have been relatively untouched by tourism and the only two hotel resorts on or anywhere near the peninsula are the low-key **María La Gorda** and **Villa Cabo San Antonio**. This is also an important area for wildlife and is said to contain 16 species of amphibians, 35 reptiles, 18 mammals and 192 species of birds. Birdlife is particularly rich between November and March, during the migration season, whilst May to September is the best time for seeing turtles. Amongst the larger reptiles found here are crocodiles, though you are unlikely to see any as they inhabit the inaccessible northern coastal section.

Make sure you bring enough cash to cover all your costs on a trip to this area – you cannot withdraw money or use credit cards here. The only way into the peninsula is along a potholed road through a thick forest that begins where the Carretera Central ends, at the tiny fishing village of **La Fe**, 15km beyond the turning for Laguna Grande.

La Bajada

The road from La Fe twists and turns south and then west through the dense vegetation of the national park for some 30km until it reaches the broad, open bay, the Bahía de Corrientes, around which most of the peninsula's main tourist installations are based. The first of these, **La Bajada**, is a scrappy clearing on the edge of the forest just a few metres before the road hits the bay. The scattered buildings occupying this plot of land are linked only by their proximity. The biggest and most obvious installation is the twenty-three-metre-high sphere-topped tower of the meteorological station (☎82/75-1007), which holds scant appeal for visitors, though for $1CUC you can scale the tower's metal spiral staircase and enjoy 360-degree **views** across the treetops and over to the bay. It's unlikely you will want to stay the night at La Bajada, though four basic rooms with air conditioning at the station do provide the peninsula's cheapest accommodation, for $9CUC per person. You can also camp for free at the foot of the

Tours and trails around Parque Nacional Guanahacabibes

Among the small cluster of buildings at La Bajada is the **Estación Ecológica Guana-hacabibes** (☎82/75-0366, ✉aylen04@yahoo.es), the small lodge over the road from the meteorological station, from where any exploration of the peninsula is organized. There are currently three organized tours on offer, two along official **trails** (Cueva Las Perlas and Del Bosque al Mar) and one that takes in the entire area by car or jeep. Access to the trails and indeed to any part of the peninsula beyond the road and resorts is forbidden without a guide. The centre employs six guides, two of whom speak English and all of who are experts on the local flora and fauna. With no fixed days or times for excursions (the guides work on an ad hoc basis) it's vital to ring in advance to make arrangements. To get the most out of any of the three excursions, the staff at the centre generally advise that start times be between 8.30am and 10am, when you are likely to see more birdlife and the day is not at its hottest. The tour along the shortest trail, Del Bosque al Mar, usually runs a couple of hours and takes in both coastline and forested areas, beginning about 1500 metres from the Estación Ecológica. The trail skirts small lagoons where aquatic birds can be observed, while its specialty, amongst the various observable plants and trees, is orchids. Parts of the trail were flooded and destroyed by Hurricane Ivan in 2004 and the entire thing remained closed in 2007, but there are plans to re-instate it as soon as possible. The other trail, known as Cueva Las Perlas, is a 1.5-kilometre, three-hour trek through the semi-deciduous forest, offering chances to observe local birdlife such as the Cuban tody, the bee hummingbird and the red-legged thrush. At the end of the trail is the Cueva Las Perlas itself, an explorable cave sinking back over half a kilometre with various galleries and chambers and shafts of light pouring through holes in the roof. The most expensive and comprehensive offer at the centre is the so-called "safari tour" to the Cabo de San Antonio (see opposite), at the far western reaches of the peninsula. You will need your own car to take advantage of this five-hour tour, as the centre has no transport of its own. The branch of Vía (☎82/75-7693) at María La Gorda rents out jeeps for $55CUC a day, but won't rent out regular cars for this purpose as the going can be a little rough. The tour follows over 50km of road along the coast, with stops to observe wildlife and the changes in the landscape – from rocky-floored, semi-deciduous forest to marshy jungle and palm-fringed beaches, to jagged seaside cliffs. Animals you might see include iguanas, deer, hutias and boars.

The centre is happy to tailor day-trips to your own specifications and is willing to make them as long or as short as you like. **Costs** are equally unfixed, but if you stick to the basic offers expect to pay between $4CUC and $10CUC per person. You'll need to present your passport or some form of ID before you can embark on any of the excursions here. Long sleeves and insect repellent are always a good idea, particularly in May and June when the mosquitoes are out in force.

---

tower if you have your own tent, or rent a tent for $10CUC per night. There is talk of curtailing the public use of these facilities, so it's worth ringing the meteorological station in advance if you intend to shack up here. You can eat here too, at *Restaurant La Bajada*, which is actually more a roadside **snack bar** than a restaurant, dishing out sandwiches and fried chicken on an open-air terrace.

La Bajada is also host to the **Estación Ecológica Guanahacabibes** from where exploration and tours of the peninsula are organized (see box).

María La Gorda

Turn left after La Bajada to get to the peninsula's most popular spot, **María La Gorda**, where there is an international dive centre and a small hotel complex. The relaxing drive here follows the shoreline of the bay, with dense forest on one side and an open expanse of brilliant, usually perfectly placid blue-green water on the other. Along the way are a few slightly scrappy but likeable little beaches, which you can make your own if you want complete privacy, but it's best to wait, as there's usually plenty of room on the much larger beach belonging to the resort at the end of the road. There's a $5CUC charge per person to enter the resort and use its beach for anyone not renting a room at the hotel here.

You have the choice of two distinct sets of accommodation at *Villa María La Gorda* (☎82/77-8131, 77-3072 and 77-3067, ✉comercial@mlagorda.co.cu; ●), which is used as a base camp for divers as much as a hotel for beach bums; the cost of the room includes a buffet breakfast and dinner. Lined up along the top of the beach, no more than 30m from the water's edge, are wood-panelled bungalows and two-storey concrete apartment blocks, all facing out to sea. There are also newer, characterful log cabins, hidden away from the beach in their own little wooden gangway-linked complex on the edge of the forest thicket that covers most of the peninsula. The fine white-sand beach here is interrupted at its centre by the wharf where the dive centre (see box, on p.254) moors its yachts and is cut short by a fence to the south. The beach stretches north around the cape into the distance, back towards La Bajada, providing plenty of opportunity to escape the hotel area, though it becomes significantly narrower and rockier.

María La Gorda has two **restaurants**. The buffet *Las Gorgonias* (daily 8–10am, 1–3pm & 7–10pm), located at the top of the beach with serene views out to sea, serves $5CUC breakfasts and $15CUC dinners – each meal a good-quality, all-you-can-eat feed; at *El Carajuelo* (daily noon–3pm & 7.30–10pm), with its wooden-walled interior and shady front porch, you can get decent pizzas for around $6CUC and a number of pricier chicken and seafood platters. Given that there is only a tiny grocery store here and the nearest supermarket is at least 50km away, it's worth bringing some of your own supplies if you intend to stay longer than one night. You should also bring enough cash to cover all your costs here, as there are no banks, ATMs or places to change money, and the restaurants don't accept credit cards (though the little shop does).

For **activities**, there's a small soccer pitch and a sandy volleyball court which you can use for free, excepting the $1CUC charge for renting a ball. Other options include renting board games ($2CUC) and snorkelling; masks, snorkels and fins are available at the dive centre for $7CUC. **Cars** and **scooters** can be rented from the Vía office (☎82/75-7693) near the dive centre.

The easiest way to visit María La Gorda is to book a **transfer** with one of the national travel agents based in Pinar del Río city or Viñales village. Havanatur, for example, charge $20CUC for a return trip from their offices in Pinar del Río (☎48/79-8494) and $25CUC for the trip from the Viñales branch (☎8/79-6262).

Cabo de San Antonio

Back at La Bajada, heading off in the opposite direction to María La Gorda, is the recently improved but far from perfect road to the **Cabo de San Antonio**, the cape at the westernmost tip of the peninsula. There are several pleasant little beaches along the way, and at the extreme tip of the cape is a lighthouse, the **Faro Roncali**, built in 1849 (not open to visitors). Several kilometres beyond the lighthouse, past some more beautifully secluded beaches, are the last two stops on this 60-kilometre-stretch of coastal road, **Las Tumbas** and neighbouring **Los Morros de Piedra**. At the latter, an eight-cabin, sixteen-room resort, the **Villa Cabo de San Antonio** (☎82/75-0118, ☏82/75-0119; ●), and a simple, reconstructed marina have finally been completed after years of slow progress. Built with complete respect for the local environment, the neatly

Diving and boat trips at María La Gorda

The virgin waters around María La Gorda are widely regarded as among the best for **diving** in the whole of Cuba, protected by the bay and spectacularly calm and clear, averaging 25m in depth. Diving here is enhanced by a quick drop in water depth, with a large number of the fifty-or-so dive sites only ten to twenty minutes by boat from the shore, while the spectacular variety of fish life here includes barracuda, moray eels, several species of rays, lobsters, whale sharks and more. Amongst the specific **dive sites** of note are Ancla del Pirata, featuring an eighteenth-century two-ton anchor covered in coral; colourful Paraiso Perdito, which reaches depths of 33m and is particularly abundant in coral and fish life; and Yemayá, a two-metre-high cave at 32m deep, which ascends almost 20m through a long, gently curving, mysterious tunnel.

The three yachts belonging to the resort's diving club, **Centro Internacional de Buceo María La Gorda** (daily 8.30am–5.30pm; ring *Villa María La Gorda* and ask for the Centro de Buceo), depart every day at 8.30am, 11am and 3.30pm. You need to be at the club at least thirty minutes before departure time to arrange equipment and pay for your diving. A single dive costs $35CUC but there are a number of more economical packages, starting with five dives for $135CUC all the way up to twenty dives for $400CUC; you will need to add an extra $7.50 for equipment rental, unless you bring your own. The club caters to both first-timers and advanced divers, with a short initiation **course** involving some theory and a single immersion ($45CUC) four- to five-day ACUC Open Water courses ($365CUC) and a number of other specialist courses such as "Stress and Rescue" ($200CUC).

Several **boat trips** are offered at the marina as well. You can opt for an all-day excursion (four-person minimum) which includes a visit to a beach, two dives, snorkelling and lunch on board, all for $68CUC, or the Romantic Sunset cruise, which lasts three hours and is aimed at couples, with an on-board dinner included in the $24CUC per-person price. The club also runs **fishing trips**, starting at $50CUC per person for one hour for a minimum of four people.

---

constructed, comfortable wooden cabins, located about 80 metres from the shore, have solar-powered air conditioning, and nothing has been built above the height of the trees. A modest but well-kept *cafétería* facing the marina is the only source of food hereabouts; for a proper meal you'll have to travel the 77 kilometres to María La Gorda. The Estación Ecológica Guanahacabibes at La Bajada offers their "safari tour" of this area (see box p.252).

Travel details

Víazul buses

Pinar del Río to: Havana (twice daily; 3hr); Viñales (twice daily; 40min).
Viñales to: Havana (twice daily; 4hr 30min); Pinar del Río (twice daily; 40min).

Astro buses

Pinar del Río to: Cortés – for Boca de Galafre and

Playa Bailén (daily; 2hr 30min); Havana (7 daily; 3hr 30min); Viñales (daily; 40min).
Viñales to: Havana (daily; 5hr); Pinar del Río (daily; 40min).

Trains

Pinar del Río to: Boca de Galafre (daily; 1hr 30min); Havana (daily; 5hr); Playa Bailén (daily; 1hr 45min); San Cristóbal (daily; 3hr).

3

Varadero and Matanzas

CHAPTER 3   # Highlights

❋ **Varadero beach** Deservedly the most famous beach in Cuba, where you can walk for miles on golden sand or swim in turquoise water practically on the doorstep of your hotel. See p.260

❋ **Meliá Las Américas and Meliá Varadero** A spectacular pair of hotels, featuring the most eye-catching architecture and design in Varadero, which warrant a visit whether or not you are staying in them. See p.269

❋ **Yumurí Valley** Go to the Ermita de Monserrate in Matanzas or the Puente Bacunayagua on the Vía Blanca for views of the valley's plantlife, then head down to the valley floor to explore its lush landscape. See p.300

❋ **Tropicana** The province's biggest and best spot for classic Cuban cabaret. See p.301

❋ **Loma de Jacán** Climb a hillside staircase from just outside the village retreat of San Miguel de los Baños to the highest peak in the province to admire the settlement and the fir-covered private valley in which it nestles. See p.304

❋ **Río Hatiguanico boat trip** An excursion down the Río Hatiguanico takes you into the thick of some of the Península de Zapata's most untouched areas. See p.314

❋ **Caleta Buena** A relaxing, end-of-the-line coastal refuge, whose ruggedly rocky shoreline also makes it perfect for snorkelling. See p.317

△ A marina in Varadero

3

Varadero and
Matanzas

The beach resort of **Varadero** is Cuban tourism at its most developed. It's located on the **Península de Hicacos**, which reaches out from the northern coastline of the western **province of Matanzas** into the warm currents of the Atlantic, where the ocean merges with the Gulf of Mexico. A fingertip of land in the country's second largest province, Varadero's 25-kilometre stretch of fine white sand beaches and turquoise waters, within ten minutes' walk wherever you are on the peninsula, is enough to fulfil even the most jaded sunworshipper's expectations. Varadero is not, however, the complete package. Even though the beach has international renown and its increasing number of four- and five-star hotels provide optimum luxury accommodation, the poor nightlife, entertainment and restaurant options outside of the hotels keeps Varadero from being a truly world-class holiday resort.

Roughly 25km west along the coastline from the peninsula is the provincial capital, also named **Matanzas**, while somewhat closer to the east is the bayside town of **Cárdenas**. These once grand colonial towns now live largely in Varadero's shadow, and have lost some of their character since being relegated to day-trip destinations for Varadero holidaymakers. This is particularly true of Matanzas, where many of the historical buildings are in a disappointingly bad state of repair. These days, the true delights of the area around Varadero lie just outside Matanzas in the paradisiacal **Yumurí Valley** and the cave network of the **Cuevas de Bellamar**.

The centre of the province is a bit of a void from the visitor's point of view, no more than a through-route on the Carretera Central or, further south, on the *autopista*. Endless acres of sugar-cane fields and citrus orchards dominate the landscape hereabouts, Matanzas being Cuba's largest producer of agricultural goods and traditionally the thumping heart of the country's sugar industry, which has been central to the economy since colonial times. The few places worth checking out are all along the Carretera Central, the more scenic route through the province (compared to the *autopista*) and one of the most attractive ways to get to Villa Clara and the provinces beyond it. Worthy of a prolonged stopoff is **San Miguel de los Baños**, one of Matanzas's hidden treasures. **Colón** is less picturesque but still a classic example of a provincial colonial town and worth a look.

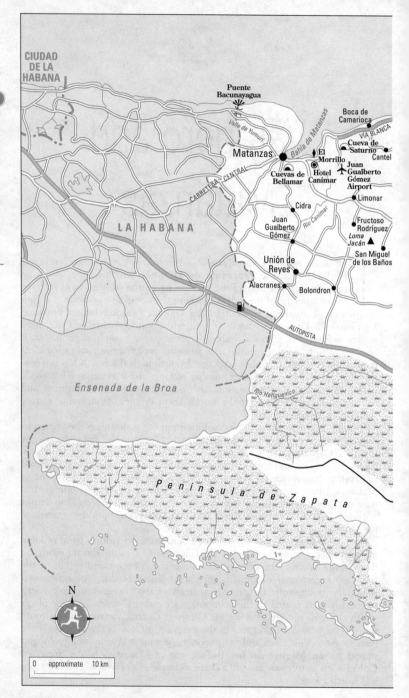

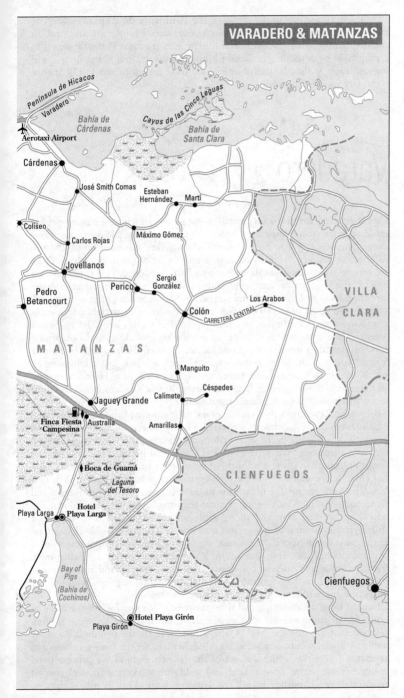

VARADERO & MATANZAS

Península de Hicacos

Varadero

Aerotaxi Airport

Bahía de Cárdenas

Cayos de las Cinco Leguas

Bahía de Santa Clara

Cárdenas

José Smith Comas

Esteban Hernández

Martí

Coliseo

Carlos Rojas

Máximo Gómez

Jovellanos

Sergio González

Perico

Los Arabos

Pedro Betancourt

Colón

CARRETERA CENTRAL

VILLA CLARA

M A T A N Z A S

Manguito

Jaguey Grande

Calimete

Céspedes

Finca Fiesta Campesina

Australia

Amarillas

Boca de Guamá

Laguna del Tesoro

C I E N F U E G O S

Hotel Playa Larga

Playa Larga

Bay of Pigs

(Bahía de Cochinos)

Cienfuegos

Hotel Playa Girón

Playa Girón

On the opposite side of the province, the **Península de Zapata**'s sweeping tracts of unspoiled coastal marshlands and wooded interior are easy to explore, thanks to an efficiently run tourist infrastructure. Perfectly suited to a multitude of activities, including hiking, birdwatching, scuba diving and sunbathing, it is also the site of one of the most infamous acts in US history – the Bay of Pigs invasion.

Varadero

Expectations of **Varadero** vary wildly: some people anticipate a picture-perfect seaside paradise; some hope for a hedonistic party resort; while others dismiss it altogether, assuming it to be a synthetic, characterless place devoid of Cubans. All three of these perceptions are considerably wide of the mark, though there are reasons why such ideas about Varadero have developed. This is *the* package holiday resort in Cuba, and large chunks of land have been taken over by sprawling four- and five-star hotel complexes. Shooting out from the mainland, virtually the entire northern coastline of this slender, ruler-straight peninsula is a brilliant white-sand beach, generally regarded as Cuba's best. The blues and greens of the calm waters washing up on the beach fade in and out of one another, creating a stunning turquoise barrier between the land and the Florida Straits. To cap it off, because the peninsula rarely exceeds half a kilometre in width, the beach is never more than a ten-minute walk away. However, despite all these natural assets and its large number of hotels, Varadero is still trying to recover its pre-1959 international reputation.

Before the Revolution, this was one of the most renowned and highly esteemed beach resorts in the Caribbean, attracting wealthy Americans and considered to be a thoroughly modern and hedonistic vacationland. Standards slipped, however, after power was seized by Fidel Castro and his rebels, who tended to frown on tourism. It wasn't until the government's attitude on this issue came full circle in the early 1990s that serious investment began to pour back into Varadero. A decade on, the improvements have been impressive, but there is still far to go. In recent years, developments in the town area have slowed down, the odd shop opening here and there, while several restaurants have enjoyed a makeover but nothing of any greater significance. The most visible changes are in the eastern section of the peninsula, where the all-inclusive mega-resorts now occupy most of the land, and where all of the new hotels are being built. Varadero continues to rely too heavily on these bigger and newer hotels, situated away from the population centres, for its nightlife options, with no new clubs opening in the town area over the last few years.

Isolated from the mainland and thinly populated, Varadero is not the place to come for an authentic taste of Cuban culture, but that's not to say, as is often claimed, that this isn't the "real" Cuba. While locals on the peninsula do enjoy a slightly higher standard of living, it's not difficult to see the same shortages and restrictions here that afflict the rest of the country. Behind the pristine hotel complexes are scraps of grassland and unlit streets skirting around modest residential neighbourhoods full of barking dogs. This is no shrine to

Varadero: tourist apartheid?

If you listened to the claims that there are no Cubans in Varadero, you might arrive expecting to find not a single local in sight. The notion that Cubans are **banned from Varadero** has arisen with good reason, but it is not entirely true – indeed, anyone spending a weekend here in the off season, when Cubans often outnumber foreigners on the beach, would find things to be otherwise. Officially nationals have as much right to use the beaches as foreign visitors, and there is a resident population here of approximately 10,000. However, Cubans are not permitted in most of the upmarket hotel complexes and, despite the party line that there are no private or exclusive beaches in Cuba, the reality is that Cubans are sometimes obliged by the police in Varadero to move on. Unsurprisingly, this is done so discreetly that you are unlikely to notice it. More obviously, Cubans entering the resort on one of the local buses from nearby Cárdenas are likely to have their bags checked before being allowed over the bridge to the mainland. Rules and regulations aside, almost all prices in Varadero are in convertible pesos, which is the single biggest thing keeping Cuban-peso-earning holidaymakers from coming here.

consumerism, and anyone hoping for a polished Disney-style resort will be disappointed: there are enough faded, paint-chipped walls and patchwork-repaired house-fronts to remind you which side of the Florida Straits you are on. With hotels, shops and nightclubs spread out across the peninsula, Varadero also lacks the buzz you might expect from the major holiday resort on the largest Caribbean island. This patchiness can detract from the holiday atmosphere, though for some people it brings a welcome lack of hustle and bustle – visit in the off season, in fact, and it can seem quite dead.

None of this detracts from what most people come to Varadero for: the **beach**, a seemingly endless runway of uninterrupted blinding white sand. This is also the best place in Cuba for **watersports**, with three marinas on the peninsula, and several diving clubs (see box, p.281). Each marina runs its own programme of fishing trips (see box, p.273) and boat trips (see box, p.274). There are over thirty rewarding **dive sites** around Varadero – including a 40-metre-long boat sunk during World War II that now provides shelter for a variety of different fish – mostly amongst the islets scattered to the northwest about an hour's boat ride away. About 5km in the opposite direction from Varadero, heading southwest along the Matanzas coastline, is a two-kilometre stretch of coral reef inhabited by a busy population of parrotfish, trumpetfish and basslets amongst many others.

A tight border control at the Varadero bridge means that the state is able to keep an even closer eye than usual on the local population, thus the level of hassle from *jineteros* here is lower than you might expect, especially if you've come from Havana. You will inevitably be approached by cigar-merchants on the beach or offered a room at some point, but on the whole tourists here blend into the local surroundings with greater ease than in most of the rest of Cuba.

Arrival and information

All international and most national flights arrive at the **Juan Gualberto Gómez Airport** (☏45/24-7015 & 25-3614), 25km west of Varadero. The single terminal of this modern but modest airport has a bureau de change and

Varadero's three principal travel agents (see opposite) can all sell you more or less the same **excursions** at very similar prices. Many of these can also be booked from the *buros de turismo* found in most hotel lobbies. There are also a couple of smaller, more specialist agents offering their own tour programmes: Gaviota Tours at Calle 56 y Playa (daily 9am–6pm; ☎45/66-7864 & 61-1844) or through its desk in the hotel *Coral* (☎45/66-7864); and Ecotur at Calle 26 no.214 e/ Ave. 2da y Ave. 3ra (☎45/61-4884 & 66-8612), which specializes in trips to areas of natural beauty, including a jeep tour of the Yumurí Valley.

The most popular trips leave on a daily basis, though during off-peak periods this can change and will depend upon a minimum number of people booking the excursion. With some of the less requested tours there is a minimum number requirement regardless of the time of year. Below is a list of the most popular and worthwhile excursions, the format which they generally follow, the operators that offer them and the average per-adult price; in many cases there are reduced rates for children under 12. All-day tours usually include lunch at a restaurant. The easiest places to visit independently from Varadero are Havana, Matanzas and Trinidad, all linked directly to the beach resort by the Víazul bus service.

Cuevas de Bellamar (Cubatur, Havanatur, Cubanacán; $25CUC). One of the easier-going excursions, lasting about half a day, focused on the network of underground caves just outside the city of Matanzas (see p.299).

Discover Tour (Cubanacán, Cubatur; $73CUC). This so-called "jeep and boat safari", one of the most animated day-trips, packs in a host of activities. After exploring the local countryside in a jeep, you'll then move on to a speedboat and travel up the Río Canímar (see p.300). The trip takes in a visit to Matanzas, horse riding and exploring a cave as well.

Havana (Cubatur, Cubanacán and Havanatur; $67CUC). A packed tour of the capital lasting a whole day and concentrated mostly in Habana Vieja. Includes visits to most of the major sites (see Chapter 1), and there's actually a bit too much covered to take in during only one day. Tiring but worth it if you're not going to visit Havana independently.

Península de Zapata (Cubatur, Havanatur, Cubanacán; $60CUC). A varied and interesting one-day tour of the major attractions within the national park occupying the whole of southern Matanzas (see p.306). One of the better excursions for kids.

Pinar del Río (Cubanacán, Cubatur; $140CUC). Fly to the capital of the westernmost province, the tobacco capital of Cuba, and then travel by bus to the unforgettable Viñales valley, unique in Cuba for its distinctive flat-top *mogote* hills. After all this you'll fly home the same day.

Trinidad (Cubatur, Havanatur; $70CUC). This one-day tour of one of Cuba's first cities leaves early in the morning to allow just enough time to take in the stunning concentration of colonial architecture and other highlights.

Yumurí Jeep Safari (Gaviota Tours; $70CUC). Off-roading through rivers and dirt tracks around the Yumurí Valley (see p.300) as well as visits to a made-to-measure ranch where horseback riding and boating are included. On the way back there is a stopoff in Matanzas.

credit card withdrawal facilities, an information centre and several **car rental** offices outside in the car park. There is no public bus service, although many hotels have buses waiting to pick up guests with reservations, and it may be worth talking to the driver or tour guide to see if there are any spare seats. There are always plenty of **taxis**, which will take you to the centre of Varadero for $25CUC ($85CUC to Havana).

The road you'll need to take when **driving** to Varadero, either from the airport or Havana, is the Vía Blanca, 6km north of the airport, which leads right to the bridge that's the only road link between the peninsula and the mainland. There's a $2CUC charge at a tollgate a few kilometres before the bridge.

All interprovincial **buses**, whether Víazul (☎45/61-4886) or Astro (☎45/61-2626), arrive at the small Terminal de Omnibus on Calle 36 and Autopista del Sur. There are five hotels within ten blocks of the terminal, some less than five minutes' walk away, though most are just beyond the sweat barrier for travellers with heavy baggage. There are often two or three taxis waiting out front, but if not, your best bet is to ring Taxi OK (☎45/61-4444 & 61-1616). At least half of central Varadero's hotels are within a $5CUC ride.

Information

The three most prominent national tourist travel agencies are represented in the lobbies of most hotels, and they each also have their own offices here which double up as **information** centres. All offer very similar services, including excursions, boat trips, hotel bookings and advice on almost anything in Varadero. Cubatur, at Calle 33 esq. 1ra (daily 8.30am–8.30pm; ☎45/66-7216 & 66-7217), is very helpful and always has a few leaflets, while the travel agent for Havanatur, Tour y Travel, has the largest number of outlets on the peninsula, with the two most central offices at Calle 31 e/ 1ra y Ave. Playa (daily 9am–6pm; ☎45/66-7154) and Ave. 3ra e/ 33 y 34 (daily 9am–6pm; ☎45/66-7027 & 66-7589). Cubanacán has its main office at Calle 24 e/ Ave. 1ra y playa (Mon–Sat 9am–6pm; ☎45/66-7061); while it's open to the public, it's also less accustomed to receiving visitors. Office times tend to differ during the low season when these agencies close an hour or two earlier. A tiny **map** shop, the Casa del Mapa, at Ave. 1ra e/ 42 y 43, which stocks maps of Varadero and other cities in Cuba as well as basic road maps.

Orientation and getting around

Varadero is divided into three distinct sections, though all are united by the same stretch of beach. The bridge from the mainland takes you right into the main **town** area (Maps A and B), where all the Cubans live. This is also where nightlife, eating and entertainment options are most densely concentrated, and if your hotel is here you may never find cause to go anywhere else. The streets here are in blocks, with short calles numbering 1 to 64 running the width of the peninsula; dissecting them all is **Avenida Primera**, the only street running the whole five-kilometre length of the town and shown on street signs and in addresses as Ave. 1ra.

Most of the upmarket accommodation is located on either side of the centre. The two-kilometre section of the peninsula west of the town, separated from the mainland by the Laguna de Paso Malo, is the **Reparto Kawama** (Map A), the narrowest section of the peninsula and the least worth visiting: the beach is generally disappointing and, besides three or four restaurants, it's mostly the exclusive domain of hotel guests. Though technically still Avenida Primera, the street running the length of this section is also known as Avenida Kawama.

The all-inclusive luxury hotels lie mostly **east** of the town (Map C), on the part of the peninsula wholly dedicated to tourism. Following directly on from the eastern edge of the town area and linking up with the end of Avenida 1ra is the **Avenida de las Américas**, a strip of road joining a line of ten hotels

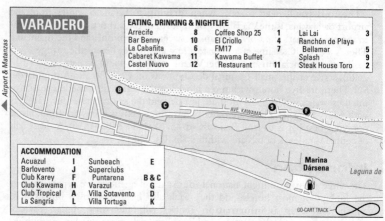

VARADERO

EATING, DRINKING & NIGHTLIFE

Arrecife	8	Coffee Shop 25	1	Lai Lai	3
Bar Benny	10	El Criollo	4	Ranchón de Playa	
La Cabañita	6	FM17	7	Bellamar	5
Cabaret Kawama	11	Kawama Buffet		Splash	9
Castel Nuovo	12	Restaurant	11	Steak House Toro	2

ACCOMMODATION

Acuazul	I	Sunbeach	E
Barlovento	J	Superclubs	
Club Karey	F	Puntarena	B & C
Club Kawama	H	Varazul	G
Club Tropical	A	Villa Sotavento	D
La Sangría	L	Villa Tortuga	K

GO-CART TRACK

CONTINUED ON MAP A

EATING, DRINKING & NIGHTLIFE

Albacora	19	Casa de la Cultura		Dante	33	Piano Bar	40
Antiguedades	27	Los Corales	21	Esquina Cuba	22	Pizzería Capri	17
Bar Terraza	25	Casa de la Música		El Galeón	23	La Red	34
La Barbacoa	24	Casa del Habano	31	La Gruta del Vino	35	El Retiro	32
El Bodegón Criollo	15	La Casa del Queso Cubano	30	El Kastillito	37	Snack Bar Calle 62	29
La Campana	39	Chong Kwok	26	Mallorca	28	La Vega	14
Cabaret Eco Disco	20	La Comparsita	36	El Mesón de Quijote	38	La Vicaria	18

CONTINUED ON MAP B

ACCOMMODATION

Mansión Xanadú	ee
Meliá Las Américas	ff
Meliá Varadero	dd
Paradisus Varadero	aa
Península Varadero	cc
Royal Hicacos	bb
Sol Palmeras	gg

EATING, DRINKING & NIGHTLIFE

La Arcada	44
La Bamba	47
Las Américas	43
Cueva del Pirata	42
Habana Café	48
Mambo Club	41
Palacio de la Rumba	46
Pizza Nova	45

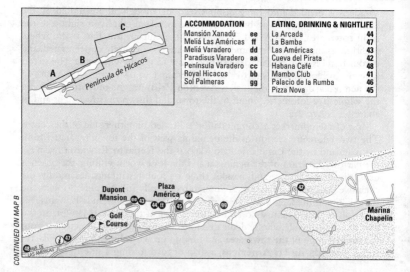

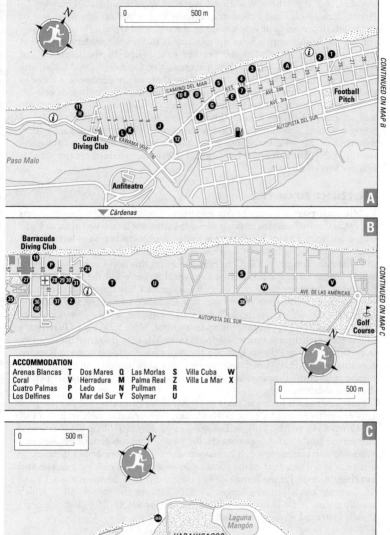

CONTINUED ON MAP B

CONTINUED ON MAP C

A

N

0 ⎯ 500 m

Paso Malo

Coral Diving Club

Anfiteatro

▼ Cárdenas

CAMINO DEL MAR

AVE. KAWAMA (AVE. 1ra)

AVE. 2da

AVE. 3ra

AUTOPISTA DEL SUR

Football Pitch

B

Barracuda Diving Club

AVE. DE LAS AMÉRICAS

AUTOPISTA DEL SUR

Golf Course

N

0 ⎯ 500 m

ACCOMMODATION

Arenas Blancas	**T**	Dos Mares	**Q**	Las Morlas	**S**	Villa Cuba	**W**
Coral	**V**	Herradura	**M**	Palma Real	**Z**	Villa La Mar	**X**
Cuatro Palmas	**P**	Ledo	**N**	Pullman	**R**		
Los Delfines	**O**	Mar del Sur	**Y**	Solymar	**U**		

C

0 ⎯ 500 m

N

Laguna Mangón

VARAHICACOS ECOLOGICAL RESERVE

Cueva Ambrosio

Visitor Centre

CARRETERA LAS MORLAS

Delfinarium

Marina Gaviota

Bahía de Cárdenas

together and also where you'll find three of Varadero's best nightclubs: *La Bamba*, *Habana Café* and *Palacio de la Rumba*. Unless you are staying at one of the hotels or are on your way to one of the nightclubs, the only other reason you are likely to want to head up this way is to visit the solitary non-hotel restaurant, *El Mesón de Quijote*. Further east, linked to the town by the **Autopista del Sur**, which then becomes the Carretera Las Morlas, the highway running the length of the southern shore of the peninsula, is the area undergoing the most changes. This is where most of the newest hotels are found and is also home to the mega-complexes and ultra all-inclusives, the highest grade of luxury hotel, with new sites still appearing along its developing coastline. The hotels and one or two worthwhile attractions are widely dispersed in this area, including, at the far eastern end of the peninsula, the unremarkable **Varahicacos Ecological Reserve**, where there are one or two pockets of interest.

Getting around

Public transport is scarcer in Varadero than elsewhere in Cuba, though if you can catch bus #47 anywhere along Avenida Primera it'll take you as far as Calle 64 for less than a peso. Easier to spot is the double-decker **Varadero Beach Tour bus**, operating between 9am and 8pm and the best way of getting around the peninsula. You pay $5CUC to ride all day on this hop-on, hop-off service which goes as far as the Varahicacos Ecological Reserve and the few hotels just beyond it. There are forty-five officially designated bus stops, and at most of these there is a timetable posted up; you shouldn't take these schedules too seriously, although it's worth checking for an estimate, as buses are infrequent and you could end up waiting for up to an hour. More leisurely is **Turitren**, a theme park-style tourist bus, which looks more like a toy train, making frequent stops along Avenida Primera between the *Superclubs Puntarena* hotel in Reparto Kawama and the Plaza América shopping mall east of the town and also making regular stops at the Parque Josone. The minimum fare is $2CUC and it operates during the daytime only.

There's a constant stream of **taxis** along Avenida Primera, as well as a taxi rank between calles 54 and 55, next to the Cubana office. Alternatively, ring Taxi OK (℡45/61-4444 or 61-1616), or Transgaviota (℡45/61-9761 or 62). Varadero is also served by the novelty **cocotaxis**, the two-seater scooter-taxis encased in a yellow sphere commonly seen in Havana and costing more or less the same as a normal taxi. For a tour of the town or beyond you can pick up a **horse and carriage** outside Parque Josone or opposite the market between calles 15 and 16, amongst other places. Charges are $10CUC for the "whole city", which usually means as far as the *Meliá Varadero* hotel, or $5CUC for "half the city", usually restricted to the town area.

Accommodation

As Cuba's tourism capital, Varadero has no shortage of **places to stay**, but there isn't the variety you might expect, except at the more expensive end of the market. Budget options are in short supply and you are unlikely to find a double room in a hotel for less than $50CUC during the high season. All the cheaper hotels are located in the town, including the one or two Cubans-only places such as *Villa Caleta* and *Villa Caribe*. If you're looking for somewhere within easy walking distance of shops, restaurants and things to do, the best area is between calles 50 and 64, where there's a small cluster of hotels and activity in the town is most concentrated. A large number of hotels in Varadero are large, indistinguishable apartment block-style buildings, most of which feature nonstop entertainment around the pool area throughout the day, usually involving an MC, recorded music and a few unfortunate holidaymakers.

Almost all the hotels east of the town are **all-inclusives**, and the further east you stay the more restricted you become to your hotel grounds. That said, pretty much every all-inclusive has on-site moped and car rental, with some also offering shuttle services into town and beyond. If you are determined to **eat** well while in Varadero your best bet is to stay in one of these all-inclusives, most of which not only have several restaurants but have also commandeered most of the best chefs. Alternatively, you can buy a **day-pass** to many of the all-inclusives (usually $30–50CUC), which allows you to use their facilities, including the restaurants. The food in most of the cheaper hotels in the town area is usually pretty poor, and you're better off eating out if you're staying in one of them.

It's best to book all-inclusive stays ahead of time, preferably via a package tour, otherwise you'll be charged what they call *turismo libre*, the cost per night for the non-package visitor, sometimes as high as $500CUC. Another point worth bearing in mind is the tendency that some hotels have, particularly in their own brochures, to include the operator's name in the title, so that the *Hotel Taínos* becomes the *Iberostar Taínos* and the *Península Varadero* becomes the *Tryp Península Varadero*. In the listings below, the operators' names have been left out unless integral to the name of the hotel. Although **casas particulares** are officially banned in Varadero, a few locals do a booming business in renting rooms illegally, usually for around $25–30CUC per room. Touts offering to take you to a *casa particular* are far less prevalent than elsewhere in Cuba but if you wander aimlessly with a suitcase you are bound to attract one or two, though the bus station is as good a place as anywhere to find them. There is no **camping** on the peninsula.

Reparto Kawama

Club Karey Ave. Kawama ☎45/66-7296, ℗66-7334, ℮reserva@karey.gca.tur.cu. This three-star all-inclusive establishment is the poorest but cheapest of the hotels in Reparto Kawama. Stretching for over 1500 metres along the narrowest part of the peninsula, you are never more than about 10 metres from the beach. Its showpiece is the restaurant *La Casa de Al*, a refined stone mansion and the former bootlegging headquarters of the Varadero branch of Al Capone's empire; the quality of food is below average, however, and the service could be better. All accommodations are in beachside villas, divided into smaller apartments with slightly dated interiors and communal living rooms. ❼

Kawama ☎45/61-4416 to 19, ℮reserva @kawama.gca.tur.cu. Large, landscaped, all-inclusive complex, bordered by 300m of beach, which loses some character away from the main building, a stylish neocolonial terraced structure built in 1930 as a gentlemen's club. Choose from private or shared houses or homely modern

apartments. There's a fantastically chic restaurant and cosy basement cabaret. ❾

Superclubs Puntarena Ave. Kawama y Final ☎45/66-7125, 66-7667 & 66-7129, ℮reservas@puntarena.gca.tur.cu. At the western tip of the peninsula, a long walk from the action, this all-inclusive features two identical high-rise accommodation blocks, an exclusive diving club and two swimming pools. It's located on one of the largest and most private sections of the beach. ❽

Villa Tortuga Calle 7 y Ave. Kawama ☎45/61-4747, ℮reservas@villatortuga.tur.cu. One of the cheaper all-inclusives outside of the town area, *Villa Tortuga* is an attractive complex, more enclosed than the others in Reparto Kawama, with pastel-coloured modern villas and two-storey apartment blocks, all set on a good patch of beach. Amenities include two restaurants, a pool, a gym, tennis courts and volleyball. ❽

The Town

Acuazul Ave. 1ra y 13 ☎45/66-7132 to 34, ℗66-7229, ⊕www.hotelacuazul.com. Inexpensive in low season but overpriced in high, when the cost of a double goes up by over $20CUC, this characterless apartment block has a poky pool area but spacious and inoffensive rooms, all with small balconies and many with great views. ⑥

Arenas Blancas Calle 64 e/ Ave. 1ra y Autopista del Sur ⓉΤ45/61-4450 & 61-4492 to 99, ℯrva@arblcas.gca.tur.cu. This all-inclusive is one of the newest, largest and most upmarket hotels in the town area, with a large, sinuous pool and grassy grounds bordering the beach. If you want to be in the centre of things without sacrificing any luxury, this is a good choice. ⑨

Barlovento Ave. 1ra e/ 10 y 12 ⓉΤ45/66-7140, ℯreserva@ibero.gca.tur.cu. A stylish and sophisticated complex with over 200 double rooms. Despite its size, the *Barlovento* retains a harmonious atmosphere, featuring a superb lobby with a fountain and a captivating pool area enveloped by palm trees. Tennis and basketball courts on-site. ⑧

Club Tropical Ave. 1ra e/ 21 y 22 ⓉΤ45/61-3915, ⒻΦ61-4676, ℯreservas@tropical.hor.tur.cu. This all-inclusive is more expensive but better value and easier on the eye than the nearby high-rise hotels. It's on the beach and has a pool and a shady, cosily penned-in terrace area. Rooms are on the small side. ⑦

Cuatro Palmas Ave. 1ra e/ 60 y 62 ⓉΤ45/66-7040 & 66-8101 to 09, ℯreserva@gcpalho.gca.tur.cu. An artistically and thoughtfully designed complex in the heart of Varadero's shopping and eating centre, featuring a variety of accommodation buildings and slightly cheaper rooms overlooking the Parque Josone. There's a good choice of restaurants, a nice pool and watersports facilities. ⑦

Los Delfines Ave. 1ra e/ 38 y 39 ⓉΤ45/66-7720 to 21, ℯh.delfines@horizontes.hor.tur.cu. This is the most tasteful and attractive of the smaller landscaped-garden hotels in the town area, incorporating several accommodation blocks, linked together by outdoor corridors cutting across grassy lawns leading right down to the beach from the main street. ⑦

Dos Mares Calle 53 esq. Ave. 1ra ⓉΤ45/66-7510, ℯrecepcion@dmares.hor.tur.cu. Atypically for Varadero, this agreeable little hotel feels more like those found in provincial colonial towns. What it lacks in facilities it makes up for with plenty of character and a pleasant intimacy. ⑤

Herradura Ave. Playa e/ 35 y 36 ⓉΤ45/61-3703, ℯdirector@herrad.hor.tur.cu. This likeable, medium-sized hotel with a sea-view terrace and waves practically lapping on its walls is the cheapest beachfront option. Rooms are grouped in pairs, and each twosome enjoys a shared lounge and sea-facing balcony. Appealingly

simple and straightforward, but the food is below par. ⑥

Ledo Ave. Playa e/ 43 y 44 ⓉΤ45/61-3206. A tiny, slightly cramped but likeable hotel over the road from the beach. It has only the bare minimum of facilities, but it's one of the cheapest spots in Varadero and a good choice if you want to avoid the larger, uglier, dated hotels in the same price category. ⑤

Mar del Sur Ave. 3ra y 30 ⓉΤ45/61-2246, ⒻΦ66-7881, ℯcomercial@mardelsur.hor.tur.cu. Large, slightly run-down family complex with basic rooms, spread along both sides of the road; it's made up of uninspired box-shaped buildings, but pleasant gardens soften the edges. Has a children's playground, a basketball court and a pool. ⑥

Palma Real Ave. 2da esq. 64 ⓉΤ45/61-4555 & 66-7500, ℯjrecep.palmareal@hotetur.com. A bright, modernized hotel inside an imposing, ugly Art Deco shell. With colour splashed all over the main building, pristine lawns clasping the sides and an entirely new extension featuring a bright columned restaurant, this is one of the best places in the town for families, complete with a decent-sized pool and an active programme of kid-friendly entertainment. ⑧

Pullman Ave. 1ra e/ 49 y 50 ⓉΤ45/66-7510, ℯrecepcion@dmares.hor.tur.cu. One of the smallest and most pleasant hotels in Varadero, whose main building is based around a castle-like turret. Has a very relaxing atmosphere and is ideal if you want to avoid the hullabaloo laid on as entertainment at most of the other hotels on the peninsula. ⑤

Sunbeach Calle 17 e/ Ave. 1ra y Ave. 3ra ⓉΤ45/66-7490, ⒻΦ61-4994, ℯreservas@sunbeach.hor.tur.cu. Though it comprises two huge, unsightly high-rise blocks, *Sunbeach* is one of the better-equipped hotels in this part of town, with a buffet restaurant, a pizzeria, several bars, a games room, a rooftop disco, a terraced pool and decent size rooms. ⑦

Varazul Ave. 1ra e/ 14 y 15 ⓉΤ45/66-7132 to 34, Ⓦ www.hotelacuazul.com. One of the only self-catering options in Varadero (there's a grocery shop on the ground floor), with tired-looking but roomy apartments featuring kitchen, living room, bathroom and bedrooms with clunky, outdated furniture. The exterior is in the same uninspired vein as its neighbour and partner *Acuazul*, whose pool, restaurants and reception it shares. ⑥

Villa La Mar Ave. 3ra e/ 29 y 30 ⓉΤ45/61-4515 to 24 & 61-2508. This dated concrete complex, popular with Cubans, is sociable but unsophisticated – though it's also the cheapest hotel in Varadero. It's on the wrong side of the peninsula and backs onto the main road, but has a pool and large gardens. ④

Villa Sotavento Ave. 1ra y 13 ☏45/66-7132 to 34, ⓦwww.hotelacuazul.com. These charming, mock-colonial, story-book-style houses are divided into apartments with dining rooms but no kitchens. The reception desk is in *Acuazul*, just over the other side of Avenida 1ra, whose facilities are also available to guests. ⑥

Avenida de las Américas

Las Morlas Ave. de las Américas Km 2 e/ A y B ☏45/66-7230 to 34, ⓔcomercia@morlas.gca.tur .cu. Deceivingly characterless from the roadside, this is the most compact and intimate of the all-inclusive options hereabouts. Considerably more subdued than some of its counterparts, the rooms are quite dark but well equipped and most look down onto the leafy and private pool area. There's an on-site tennis court and gym as well. ⑨

Sol Sirenas-Coral Ave. de las Américas e/ H y K ☏45/66-8070 & 66-7240, ⓦwww.solmeliacuba .com. A vast complex that combines two previously separate hotels, its interiors are tasteful and well polished in some buildings and plain and uninspired in others. It features the largest landscaped swimming pool in Varadero and consists of two main four-storey buildings, linked together by verdant, spacious, shady grounds which are a little scrappy in places but fun to explore. Facilities include six restaurants, tennis courts, a pool room, a beauty parlour and watersports. ⑨

Solymar Ave. de las Américas Km 1 ☏45/61-4499, ⓦwww.barcelosolymar.com. The most boldly decorated all-inclusive in Varadero: the main apartment block is aflame with glaring yellow, blue and red, while the poolside villas are painted pink and green. The whole resort looks like a giant toy town, but it has a good selection of restaurants and is located on one of the peninsula's widest sections of beach. ⑨

Villa Cuba Ave. de las Américas Km 3 e/ C y D ☏45/66-8280, ⓔreservas@vcuba.gca.tur.cu. The main building features an exciting multi-level layout with staircases and gangways zigzagging through a network of different floors and platforms. Spread out around the open-plan complex, which stretches down to the beach, there are various smaller residences, some with their own swimming pool. This impressive all-inclusive includes a sauna, gym, beauty parlour, disco, diving initiation courses and a large swimming pool. ⑨

Eastern Varadero

🎿 **Mansión Xanadú** Autopista del Sur Km 7 ☏45/66-7388, 66-8482 & 66-7750,

☏66-8481. Housed in the splendidly opulent Dupont Mansión, this unique hotel is one of the truly special places to stay in Varadero. The half-dozen refined rooms, which all face the sea, have been individually furnished – two with colonial American originals – and the hotel has a delightful wine cellar and one of the peninsula's best restaurants. There are special golfing packages for the Varadero Golf Course, whose clubhouse is next door. ⑨

🎿 **Meliá Las Américas** Autopista del Sur Km 7 ☏45/66-7600, ⓦwww.solmeliacuba .com. Next door to the *Mansión Xanadú*, this has one of the most imaginatively designed set of grounds on the peninsula, with paths weaving their way down through the intricately landscaped gardens to a secluded part of the beach. Even the pool drops down a level while it twists itself around the pathways and pond. Rooms are tastefully furnished, and there are several restaurants, a piano and lobby bar and a hair salon. ⑨

Meliá Varadero Autopista del Sur Km 7 ☏45/66-7013, ⓦwww.solmeliacuba.com. Sophisticated, star-shaped all-inclusive whose seven tentacles meet spectacularly around an indoor rainforest where ivy cascades down the circular walls from high above. There's a swimming pool with a bar in the centre, and the small collection of varied restaurants and bars includes a large thatched-roof hall looking over the sea from a low cliff. Well equipped for business travellers, with a series of convention halls and meeting rooms. ⑨

Paradisus Varadero Punta Rincón Francés ☏45/66-8700, ⓦwww.solmeliacuba.com. The design of this mind-blowing five-star "ultra all-inclusive", hidden away behind the nature reserve and right on the shore, is both striking and sophisticated. The symmetry of the enormous yet graceful lobby and its grid of garden pools blends seamlessly with the artistically landscaped plant-covered giant-pool area. All of the large, well-equipped and colourful rooms have a balcony or terrace, while the wide range of facilities includes four restaurants, two pools, a gym and tennis courts. ⑨

Península Varadero Varahicacos Ecological Reserve ☏45/66-8800 or 66-8783, ⓦwww.solmeliacuba.com. Highlights at this remote all-inclusive hotel, located on the far side of the Laguna de Mangón, include a restaurant on the lagoon's edge – positioned so that it faces the setting sun – an amphitheatre for night-time entertainment, views of offshore cays (which you can sail to on the hotel's catamarans) and fantastic kids' facilities, including an adventure playground in a separate area specifically for guests with children. ⑨

🏃 **Royal Hicacos** Carretera de las Morlas Km 15 ☎ 45/66-8844, ⓦ www .sandalshicacos.com. The rooms here, all of them suites, are a cut above what you'll find at most of the other luxury hotels, with split-level designs, living-room areas, king-size beds and all the amenities you could want. Highlights include a two-man cave built into the side of the stunning

pool, a fully equipped spa, a squash court and some great dining areas with waterways weaved around them. Over-18s only. ⑨

Sol Palmeras Autopista del Sur ☎ 45/66-7009, ⓦ www.solmeliacuba.com. Enormous luxury all-inclusive resort aimed at families, spread out over tree-swept grounds. Facilities include a basketball court, a playground, two floodlit tennis courts, a volleyball court, mini-golf, six bars and five restaurants. ⑨

The Town

Varadero has few sites of cultural or historic interest, and those that do exist won't hold your attention for long. Don't expect to see any classic works of architecture on the peninsula, other than some of the more luxurious hotels. The immaculate but modest **Iglesia de Santa Elvira**, built in 1938 on the corner of Avenida Primera and Calle 47, is about as close as buildings get to being historic this side of the Varadero bridge. **Central Varadero**, specifically the area between calles 56 and 64, has the highest proportion of sights, as well as the greatest concentration of shops and restaurants. Between calles 44 and 46 is the **Parque Central**, a large open space with a few trees spread sparsely around it. The **Parque de las 8000 Taquillas** over the road, a more enclosed space with a denser population of trees and a more likeable character, was previously the site of Varadero's biggest **arts and crafts market**, but this has now moved to a streetside location between calles 15 and 16 (see p.282) and the park is currently being redeveloped.

Museo Varadero

Detailing the history of Varadero, with rooms on sport and wildlife thrown in as well, the **Museo Varadero** (daily 10am–7pm; $1CUC), housed in a wooden 1920s Varadero residence at the beach end of Calle 57, contains a small collection of disparately connected exhibits of varying degrees of interest. Downstairs, the history display features one room full of antique furniture and another packed with unrelated odds and ends, including some Amerindian burial site remains, a model depicting "important historical places in Varadero", such as the Mansión Xanadú, and a cauldron used by rebel troops in Cárdenas during the Second War of Independence. Upstairs is a poorly presented set of stuffed animals, representing a small cross-section of Cuba's fauna. Next door to this are photographs and memorabilia of some of Cuba's sporting greats and a few early twentieth-century photographs of the straight-faced aristocratic members of the local sailing club, El Club Náutico de Varadero. The most memorable photo is a panoramic shot of the Varadero beachfront taken in 1929, the magnificent old mansions lining the shore testament to an era of bygone opulence. The upstairs balcony affords an attractive view of the beachfront.

Parque Josone

Across Avenida Primera from the Museo Varadero is the entrance to **Parque Josone**, sometimes referred to as Retiro Josone (daily noon–midnight; free), the most tranquil and picturesque spot in central Varadero. The landscaping is simple, with no intricately designed gardens, just sweeping, well-kept lawns

△ Parque Josone

dotted with trees and a small lake with its own palm tree-studded island. There are rowboats ($0.50CUC per person per hour) and pedal boats ($5CUC per boat per hour) for rent, a couple of outdoor *cafeterias*, four restaurants (see p.276), and a crazy-golf course to help you prolong what would otherwise probably be a short visit. At the southern edge of the park, where it borders the Autopista del Sur, a swimming pool (10am–6pm; $2CUC) with an adjacent bar offers further recreation. Official tourist literature claims the park is a protected reserve for local flora and fauna, but the only local animals being preserved here are a handful of ducks, geese, peacocks and chickens. You can also see, stranded on the island, a few distinctly non-native ostriches.

Reparto Kawama

Reparto Kawama, a slender strip of land at the western end of the peninsula, no more than 30m wide in places, is an essentially one-dimensional area, linked together by a single road, the Avenida Kawama. A visit here, if you're not staying at one of the four or five hotels that occupy almost all of the space, should focus exclusively on one of several restaurants or the single nightspot, *Cabaret Kawama* (see p.279) found in this section of Varadero. The only building in this neighbourhood likely to catch your eye is **La Casa de Al**, the former holiday home of Al Capone and now a restaurant within the *Club Karey* hotel complex (the building is visible from the road). The spacious grey-stone villa-residence with its arched doorways and terracotta-tile roof is one of the few remaining hallmarks of Varadero's pre-1959 exclusivity, and its style and opulence certainly stands out amongst the neighbouring hotel villas and apartment blocks.

Sandwiched in between the southern shoreline of Reparto Kawama and the mainland is the **Laguna de Paso Malo**, also known as the Varadero canal. A couple of **boat trips** (see p.274) leave from the small wharf at the far end of Avenida Kawama and squeeze through the canal's narrowest section which connects it with the Atlantic Ocean at the extreme western tip of the peninsula. On the southern side of the canal, accessible from the mainland, is the **Marina Dársena** (see box, opposite), but otherwise there is very little life in or on this short stretch of water.

Eastern Varadero

A visit to the relatively secluded eastern reaches of the peninsula should ideally focus on one of the area's few tangible attractions; wandering about is not really an option, as the landscape is dominated by either exclusive luxury hotels or inaccessible scrub. Some people make it no further than **Plaza América**, where the shopping mall, restaurants and beach provide enough for a short day-trip.

The only road along this stretch is the **Autopista del Sur**, which skirts alongside the giant hotel complexes and the unruffled green of the Varadero golf course before ending in a scrub-covered, dusty landscape that can seem quite deserted; the far eastern end of this road is known as the Carretera de las Morlas. The only interesting parts of this landscape form the **Varahicacos Ecological Reserve**, the trumped-up name for what is really just a tract of land, flanked by huge hotels, whose highlights are a large cactus, a cave and a lagoon.

Mansión Xanadú

The first attraction east of town, about 2km from central Varadero, is the **Mansión Xanadú**, located next door to the *Meliá Las Américas* hotel and now a small hotel itself. Sometimes referred to as the Mansión Dupont, it was built in 1926 by the American millionaire Irenée Dupont at a cost of over $600,000. At the same time, Dupont bought up large tracts of land on the peninsula for hotel development and effectively kick-started Varadero becoming a major holiday destination. The mansion has hardly changed since the Dupont family fled the island in 1959, and stands testament to the wealth and decadence of the pre-revolutionary years in Varadero. To appreciate the building's splendidly furnished interior these days, you either have to be a hotel guest, eat at the *Las Américas* restaurant (daily 7–10.30pm; see p.277) or sip a cocktail in the dignified bar (daily 10am–11.45pm), which boasts views along the surrounding coastline and of the golf course on the other side.

Dolphinarium

Two and a half kilometres east of the mansion, just past the Marina Chapelin, is an outdoor **dolphinarium** (☏ 45/66-8031; daily 9am–5pm) with several shows daily ($10CUC; photography $5CUC extra; $60CUC to swim with dolphins after the show). The verdant setting of the Laguna Los Taínos, a small natural pool surrounded by trees and bushes a few metres from the southern shoreline here, makes a novel change from the usual swimming pool-style design of these kinds of arenas. If you don't have your own car, the best way to get here is to book at one of the information centres, where they'll charge you $12CUC, including transport.

Fishing trips and the marinas

There are better places around Cuba to go **saltwater fishing** than off the coast of Varadero. You have to get well away from the beach to have even a chance of a half-decent catch, which could be wahoo, barracuda, grouper, snapper or tuna amongst others, and in fact you would be better off on the other side of the province, off the Península de Zapata. Nevertheless, it couldn't be easier to charter a boat here, and sailing out to the surrounding cays is a great way for the casual enthusiast to combine a spot of fishing with a relaxing day-trip. Tailor-made excursions and diving or fishing packages are available at the following marinas, and the *buros de turismo* in most hotel lobbies can usually also help with arrangements. Marina Chapelin and Marina Gaviota are the best equipped, but all three will supply any necessary equipment on fishing expeditions. The marinas are also where most of the boat trips listed in the box on p.274 leave from. For information on land-based excursions see the box on p.262, and for scuba diving see the box on p.281.

Marina Chapelin

Autopista Sur Km 12 ℡45/66-7550 & 66-7565, ℱ66-7093. Marina Chapelin's most exclusive offer is the Boat Adventure, conducted on two-man vessels. This is also the best marina for fishing trips, with packages costing $290CUC for a five-and-a-half-hour day-trip for one to four people and $30CUC for non-fishing passengers, including an on-board open bar. There's an information kiosk specifically for this marina at Ave. 1era y 59.

Marina Dársena

Vía Blanca, 1km from the Varadero bridge ℡45/66-8060 ext. 661, ℰpuerto@marlinv .var.cyt.cu. This marina is not used for boat trips and is predominantly a docking station. However, they run fishing trips around northern Varadero, which can be comparatively good value, with prices per boat for a day trip starting at $240CUC; boats take up to four passengers.

Marina Gaviota Varadero

At the eastern end of Autopista Sur, Punta Hicacos ℡45/66-7755 & 66-7756. The most remote of Varadero's three marinas. Fishing trips usually last from 9am to 3pm, with four hours of fishing at a total cost of $270CUC for up to four people, and $25CUC per extra person. There are two smart motorized yachts, both with an open bar on board. For another $15CUC they'll include a lobster lunch and an extra hour and a half's fishing. The marina also features a simple dockside restaurant, *El Galeon*, where you can choose your main seafood dish while it's still alive.

Varahicacos Ecological Reserve

Just down the road from the dolphinarium, at the eastern extreme of the peninsula, is the three-square-kilometre **Varahicacos Ecological Reserve**, also called the Parque Natural Hicacos. Billed as "the other Varadero", this is the only part of the peninsula where you can experience relatively unspoilt (if undramatic) landscapes, view the flora and fauna up close and learn some of the area's history. As the last few plots of unprotected land in Varadero are cordoned off and developed for tourism, however, the reserve is becoming increasingly surrounded by enormous hotel complexes.

The **visitor centre** (daily 8am–5pm) is by the side of the road, at a turn-off from the Carretera de las Morlas about a kilometre past the Marina Chapelin. From there you can follow one of three routes, each featuring one or more of the reserve's ecological or archeological features. Shortest is the

Boat trips

With entertainment options so thin on the ground in Varadero, it's no surprise that **boat trips** around the peninsula are so numerous and popular. Making the most of the surrounding islets, reefs and local wildlife, both above and below the water, there is a whole host of different destinations and themes, so it's well worth checking out everything that's available. The family of cays beyond the eastern tip of the peninsula – Cayo Blanco, Cayo Piedras and Cayo Romero, among others – make up most of the stopping-off points. These are where you'll get the best opportunities to snorkel, as, unlike at Varadero beach itself, there are small coral reefs bordering many of these outlying cays. Most of the boat trips leave from one of the three marinas around Varadero (see box, p.273), except for a couple based at the Laguna de Paso Malo jetty at Ave. Kawama e/ 2 y 3, and most can be booked through any one of three principal travel agents (see p.263).

If you're daunted at the thought of scuba diving, then an easy way to see what you're missing is to take a trip on one of the **glass-bottomed boats**. Almost all pre-booked excursions include transfer from your hotel to the point of departure in the price, and in most cases children under 12 are charged half-price rates.

Boat Adventure A two-hour excursion on double-seater ski-bikes or two-man speedboats which stops off at a cay where crocodiles, iguanas and other creatures can be observed. There are a number of departures from Marina Chapelin every day between 9am and 4pm; the cost is $39CUC per person.

Caribbean Cruise This is the flattering name given to the seven- to eight-hour excursion to Cayo Blanco out of Marina Gaviota. It includes a snack, cocktail, time at the beach and lunch at Cayo Blanco as well as snorkelling (gear supplied). There's a minimum requirement of six people and a cost of $85CUC per person. Book at the marina or through the *Coral* hotel.

Nautilus This glass-bottomed boat leaves from the Marina Gaviota and explores the coral reef around Cayo Blanco. The comprehensive trip around Varadero lasts five hours and includes the dolphin show at Rancho Cangrejo; the cost is $30CUC per person. Contact any of the hotels in the Gaviota Group, such as the *Coral* or *Villa Caleta*, to book for the *Nautilus*, or ring the marina direct.

Seafari a Cayo Blanco You'll need to book in advance for this tour, which leaves Marina Chapelin on a daily basis. Prices are $75CUC for adults and $38CUC for children, but can also be booked for private parties at a minimum total cost of $350CUC. Most of the day is spent on a sailing yacht, and there's an open bar and lunch at Cayo Blanco in addition to musical entertainment, snorkelling opportunities and a dolphin show.

Seafari Crucero del Sol One of the best offers available at the Marina Gaviota. It combines all of the best aspects of the other two cruises, but is on a fantastic catamaran and includes a ten-minute swim with dolphins. The cost is $85CUC per person.

Seafari Exclusivo Especial Out of Marina Gaviota, this is a similar excursion to Caribbean Cruise with the same minimum number requirement but with the added bonus of a dolphin show at Rancho Cangrejo. It's $65CUC per person, or $75CUC with an open bar.

Varasub This glass-bottomed boat leaves from the Laguna de Paso Malo and heads out to the coral reef near Boca de Guamarioca west of Varadero, where you'll generally get 30–40 minutes' viewing time of the reef. The whole trip costs $35CUC for adults, $20CUC for children. Book through any of the information centres.

half-hour-long visit to the **Cueva de Ambrosio**, where a large number of Ciboney cave paintings have been discovered. Some of the pictographs are easily deciphered but there are plenty more obscure images to exercise the imagination. The **Cueva de Musulmanes**, a smaller cave where human bones over 2500 years old were found, is included on a trail which also offers insights into the local wildlife and plantlife. The third and longest route, the **Sendero a la Laguna**, takes in an impressive 500-year-old cactus, then circles round the Laguna de Mangón and finishes at the ruins of a colonial salt storehouse and site of the first salt mine in Latin America. It's a bit of a lacklustre trail and the nearby presence of the luxury hotel *Península Varadero* makes the place feel distinctly unwild. The cactus is actually the highlight on this route, and you can see it on your own by simply following the turn-off road and taking the right-hand fork that cuts down through the trees towards the shore, at the end of which is an entrance booth that charges for parking here ($3CUC).

On any of the three routes you will be accompanied by a specialist guide, which you can pay for at the visitor centre, but to guarantee an English-speaking one you should arrange to go with a tour group through one of the information centres or *buros de turismo*. It costs $3–3.50CUC per person to be guided around any of the three set routes, but you can also arrange tailor-made excursions to suit your preferences.

Eating

For such a large international holiday resort, the quality and variety of food in Varadero's **restaurants** are remarkably mediocre. Most places play it safe with almost identical *comida criolla* menus, while foreign-food restaurants often leave you questioning the chef's geography. Nevertheless, there are more culinary choices here than anywhere else outside Havana, and you should, if you choose wisely, be able to eat out every night for a week before having to start ordering the same dishes again. It's well worth trying some of the restaurants in the deluxe hotels, as the quality of their food is often higher, thanks to their more direct access to foreign markets – though to do this in the all-inclusives you will usually have to fork out for a day-pass (see p.267). Head for the top of town between Parque Josone and Calle 64 if you fancy checking a few places out before making your decision; this is the only area where there is a concentration of better-than-average options, the Parque Josone itself counting four within its grounds. *Paladares* are illegal in Varadero, but you may still be offered a meal at someone's house by touts.

If you're looking for a quick bite to eat, there are **fast-food outlets** all over town, with the hot dog and pizza chain *El Rápido* best represented. Quick-stop open-air snack bars line the length of Avenida Primera, selling soft drinks, beer, rum and unadventurous menus of pork, rice, fried chicken and pizza. Most of these are no more than tables and chairs by the roadside, and while none stand out for atmosphere there are one or two which do offer something slightly different to the rest. Complejo Boulevard on Calle 43 e/ Ave. 1ra y Ave. Playa has a cake shop, pizzeria and various other junk food options; if you're craving ice cream, *Bim Bom*, Ave. 1ra esq. 24, or the *Casa de la Miel*, Ave. 1ra e/ 26 y 27, should be able to satisfy.

The best **supermarket** is in the Plaza América (see p.283), with a fresh meat counter selling salamis and sausages plus pots and pans for sale.

Reparto Kawama

Kawama Buffet Restaurant *Hotel Kawama*
⊕45/66-7156. Fantastically atmospheric hotel
restaurant in a 1930s mock-colonial building with a
terrace overlooking the beach. The expensive international menu changes on a regular basis and can
include anything from pizza to rump steak. Daily
7.30–10.30pm.

The Town

Albacora Calle 59 at the beach ⊕45/61-3650.
One of the best beachside restaurants, where you
can enjoy good simple fresh food. Pricey lobster
and shrimp or pork, chicken and beef dishes for as
little as $3.50CUC, under a protective canopy of
low, twisting branches on a large terrace over the
beach. Very laid-back, unless there's a group
playing music on the built-in stage.

Antiguedades Ave. 1ra e/ 58 y 59
⊕45/66-7329. The most characterful
restaurant in town justifies its slightly above-
average prices with appetizing Cuban cooking
and notably good-quality side orders served in a
highly original Aladdin's Cave-style interior. A
fantastically eclectic collection of statues, plants,
plates, helmets, pictures of all kinds and even a
wicker chair hung upside down adorn the walls,
floor and ceiling.

Arrecife Camino del Mar y 13 ⊕45/66-8563.
This quiet street-corner restaurant with a
veranda offers a good variety of moderately
priced seafood. Set meals are between $3CUC
and $10CUC.

La Barbacoa Ave. 1ra y 64 ⊕45/66-7795. A
steakhouse and barbecue grill tucked into the top
corner of town, shielded from the road by a screen
of trees. Topping the menu are the expensive and
satisfactory sirloin, T-bone and club steaks, but
there's also 10-peso lobster and the usual chicken,
pork and fish dishes.

El Bodegón Criollo Ave. Playa esq. 40
⊕45/66-7784. Varadero's version of Havana's
famous *Bodeguita del Medio* has a similarly
bohemian look and vibe, its walls covered in
handwriting and signatures; it's also one of the
best-known purveyors of Cuban cooking in the
area, and most main dishes are priced around
$10CUC or less (some go as high as $25CUC).

La Cabañita Camino del Mar y 10 ⊕45/61-3787.
This basic beachfront bungalow with a brick-
columned patio has a menu of dirt-cheap chicken
and pork dishes. It's somewhat neglected (hidden
away, out of sight from the town), but very
peaceful. Daily 9am–9pm.

La Campana Parque Josone ⊕45/66-7228. A
rustic stone-and-wood lodge with a large fireplace

in its cosy interior, plus outdoor dining on its
veranda. Expect to pay between $10CUC and
$20CUC for a traditional Cuban meal.

La Casa del Queso Cubano Ave. 1ra y 62
⊕45/66-7747. French-Swiss food – mostly
cheese fondue-based dishes – as well as tasty
tortillas and an impressive selection of
international wines, in a quaint homely decor.
Main dishes $5–15CUC.

Castel Nuovo Ave 1ra no.503 esq. Calle 11
⊕45/66-7786. Reasonable Italian cuisine and a
good selection of seafood. Popular despite being
low on charm, thanks in part to its affordable
prices, which start at $2.50CUC or even $1CUC if
you eat outside on the terrace.

Chong Kwok Ave. 1ra y 55. Cheap and very Cuban
Cantonese cuisine, while low tables and cushions
for seats make this one of the few novel
restaurants in Varadero.

El Criollo Ave. 1ra esq. 18 ⊕45/66-7793. Classic
Cuban cooking, with huge beef platters served
alongside fried or roasted chicken and pork options
(as well as a couple of lighter alternatives), all
cooked in the *criollo* style. You can eat your fill
here, on a quaint patio next to the road, for less
than $5CUC.

Dante Parque Josone ⊕45/66-7738. The hit-
and-miss Italian cuisine here demands careful
attention while selecting. Avoid the garlic bread
and be prepared for very unsubtle pasta sauces
– some rich and tasty, like the bolognese, some
odd-tasting, like the carbonara. The pizzas are
safer but only average. Better in daylight
hours, when you can enjoy the placid views
across the lake and the pleasant veranda
jutting out over the water. Main dishes
$5–12CUC.

Esquina Cuba Ave. 1ra y 36 ⊕45/61-4019. This
reasonably priced restaurant offers an unlimited
buffet of *comida criolla* for $12CUC. Tables are
set on a wide open veranda, all under a thatched
roof, where the bordering plants obscure the
view of the road, and with a vague 1950s theme
centred around a prominently displayed white-
and-pink Oldsmobile.

Lai Lai Ave. 1ra y 18 ⊕45/66-7793. There is a
good selection of seafood and some familiar dishes
at this Chinese restaurant. Less exclusive than its
grand exterior suggests, inside it suffers from
lacklustre decor. It's worth booking one of the two
private, cosier rooms upstairs if you're in a group
of four or more.

Mallorca Ave. 1ra y 62 ⊕45/66-7646. One of
the few Spanish restaurants in Varadero,
specializing in paella and $7CUC set meals. The
five varieties of paella start at $3.50CUC, but it's

worth paying the extra for the house special, as the cheaper versions are a little one-dimensional. Eat in the sombre and smart interior or out on the terrace.

Pizzería Capri Ave. Playa esq. 43 ☎45/61-2117. Low in quality and choices, but the prices (starting at 80c) are very cheap. One of the few places more popular with locals than tourists.

Ranchón de Playa Bellamar Ave. 1ra e/ 15 y 16 ☎45/66-7490. A pleasant country-ranch-style joint with views of the sea and a menu of traditionally prepared fish and meat dishes. The surrounding lawns go some way to softening the roadside location. Main courses $2.25–16.90CUC.

El Retiro Parque Josone ☎45/66-7316. This lobster specialist is Parque Josone's option for highbrow dining, with decor that's restrained rather than refined in this characterful manor house. Seven varieties of lobster, priced between $15CUC and $30CUC, but the other main dishes, including fish, shrimp and chicken, are as cheap as $5CUC.

Steak House Toro Ave. 1ra esq. 25 ☎45/66-7145. This place, sunk just below street level, is a real meat-fest, with six- to twenty-four-ounce steaks as well as spicy sausages, burgers and skewered chicken, plus some seafood. The decor follows internationally observed steakhouse norms, with a bull's head, wagon wheel and beer barrel all featured. Eating here is about as Cuban as apple pie, but its familiarity also makes it reliable.

La Vega Ave. Playa y 31 ☎45/61-1430. Hearty portions of paella are the highlights at this reasonably priced seafood restaurant on the backyard porch of a replica tobacco plantation ranch building. Giant wooden tobacco leaves droop over this pleasant beachside spot.

La Vicaria Ave. 1ra esq. 38 ☎45/61-4721. Shredded beef and ten-peso lobster stand out on the mostly meat Cuban menu at this casual open-air restaurant. Right next to the road, this is more a daytime venue, where you can lunch under your own *bohio* parasol. There is no skimping on portions despite the very cheap prices – most main dishes are around the $3CUC mark.

East of town

🏃 **Las Américas** *Mansión Xanadú*, Autopista Sur Km 7 ☎45/66-7750. One of the classiest and most expensive restaurants on the peninsula, with seating in the library, out on the terrace and down in the wine cellar. Though the international-style menu won't win any awards, it is a cut above the average; the selection of cocktails and wines is outstanding.

La Arcada *Meliá Las Américas*, Autopista del Sur Km 7 ☎45/66-7600 ext. 629. Despite the gentlemen's club image of this swanky place in a top-notch hotel, main dishes actually start at only around $15, making this an affordable way to lord it up. More in line with the club's appearance are pricey specialities like lobster and chateaubriand. Daily 7pm–midnight.

El Mesón de Quijote Ave. de las Américas ☎45/66-7796. They claim to serve "Cuban-style Spanish food", but Spanish-style Cuban food better describes the moderately priced lobster, shrimp, chicken and lamb dishes. Perched atop a small hill, the interior is rustic, with potted plants and vases making up most of the simple decoration and the views doing the rest.

Pizza Nova Plaza América, Autopista del Sur Km 7 ☎45/66-8585. The best selection and quality of pizzas in Varadero, along with mediocre pasta dishes, at the local branch of one of the better Cuban restaurant chains. The best seats are on a balcony that looks down to the sea.

Bars and cafés

Finding a straightforward **bar** in Varadero is much harder than it should be. There is no one area where you can easily bar-hop your way through the night: bars are in isolated pockets around the town and most of the best ones are in the hotels, many of these not easily accessible to non-guests. One or two of the smaller hotels in the town have bars with more character than most of the alternatives. Only a tiny percentage of places are designed simply for drinking and socializing, a formula abandoned all too often for karaoke or, in the hotels, live PA entertainment. **Cafés** are equally sparse and are found almost exclusively along Avenida Primera, though some of the places calling themselves bars could also pass as cafés, given that most of them serve snacks and a few offer table service.

El Anzuelo on the beach e/ 59 y 60. Serves cocktails like *mojitos*, daiquiris and piña coladas for $2CUC a pop.

Bar Benny Camino del Mar e/ 12 y 13. This beachside bar sometimes hosts live music on the front patio, while the tiny cellar-style interior boasts a set of photos of Cuban musician Benny Moré.

Bar Mirador Mansión Xanadú, Autopista Sur Km 7. A sophisticated shining bar with an ornate wooden ceiling supported by black pillars, located at the top of this splendid mansion and featuring views along the coastline.

Bar Terraza Complejo Mediterráneo, Ave. 1ra esq. Calle 54. Unpolished pseudo-50s-style diner bar with about as much local flavour as you can realistically expect in Varadero.

Casa del Habano Ave. 1ra e/ 63 y 64. Upstairs at this excellent cigar shop is a dinky, stylish, balconied bar which makes a good place for a quiet drink. Closes by 10pm.

Coffee Shop 25 Ave. 1ra esq. 25. A 24hr café with a shady patio that's one of the only places in Varadero specializing in hot drinks (albeit a small selection).

El Galeón *Hotel Dos Mares*, Calle 53 esq. Ave. 1ra. One of the most characterful bars in the town, set just below street level with a stylish varnished-wood finish and a slight Mediterranean feel. A good place to come if you want to avoid the trappings of most hotel bars – this is just a straight-up, laid-back place to get a drink.

La Gruta del Vino Parque Josone. This novel little restaurant has a wide selection of wine and actually works better as a bar, sinking back into a tiny cave on the far side of the lake in Parque Josone. There is a patio out front where you can sip your drinks right at the water's edge.

La Sangría Ave. Kawama esq. 5. Food is served at this spot overlooking Laguna de Paso Malo, but the real appeal is the relatively late closing time, theoretically til as late as 2am.

Piano Bar Centro Cultural Artex, Calle 60 e/ Ave. 2da y Ave. 3ra. A sleek little bar, suited to something more refined than the karaoke that it hosts most nights of the week. Avoid the singing by leaving before 11pm.

Varadero 1920 Parque Josone. An open-air bar propped above the banks of the park lake, and one of the most laid-back spots for a drink in Varadero.

Nightlife and entertainment

Nightlife in Varadero falls way short of the standards you would expect for such a large holiday resort. Venues that are even halfway decent are few and far between and there is no obvious area to head for if you just want to hop from one club to the other. Indeed, the scene is almost entirely restricted to the hotels, most of which offer something more akin to a school disco than a fully equipped nightclub. Most of these are open to non-guests, but the music policy is more or less the same wherever you go: Latin- and Euro-pop, reggaeton and watered-down house and techno. The only factors to take into account are the location and the size of the place: the two largest clubs, *La Bamba* and the *Palacio de la Rumba*, are at the Mansión Xanadú end of Avenida de las Américas, a taxi ride away for most people. There is also an extraordinary number of venues whose main billing is **karaoke**. These tend to operate as a bar beforehand and a disco once the caterwauling has finished. It should be noted that some clubs do not allow shorts or sleeveless tops to be worn.

The most popular alternative to a night sweated out on the dancefloor is the **cabarets**, which again are almost all run by the hotels. There are considerable differences in ambience created by the various settings, but the shows themselves are basically the same displays of kitsch glamour, over-sentimental crooners and semi-naked dancers wherever you go. The most famous Havanan cabaret, the *Tropicana*, has a branch just a short drive away in Matanzas, near the Río Canímar (see p.301), which knocks the socks off anything on the peninsula for sheer scale.

There are surprisingly few places to go for **live music** and not many venues outside of the hotels where live Cuban music is a regular feature.

Clubs, discos and karaoke venues

La Bamba *Hotel Tuxpán*, Ave. de las Américas. There's less buzz here than at *La Rumba* up the road, but in the slow-moving world of Varadero nightlife it's still one of the hotspots. The $10CUC entrance charge entitles you to free drinks and there are reduced rates for anyone staying at any hotel in Varadero. Daily 10pm–3am.

Habana Café next to the *Sol Club Las Sirenas* hotel, Ave. de las Américas ☎ 45/66-8070. Like its counterpart in Havana, this touristy venue is littered with 1950s Cuban and American artefacts, from a full-size Oldsmobile parked inside the door to gas pumps, barbers' chairs and Coca-Cola signs. Combines the classic holiday disco with cabaret-style entertainment. Entrance is free but there is a $12 minimum consumption charge for a table. Daily 10pm–late.

Havana Club Calle 62 y Ave. 2da. The biggest nightclub in the town area is a popular pick-up joint and often the last place in this neighbourhood to close at night. The $10CUC cover includes a free bar all night. Daily 10.30pm–3am.

El Kastillito Ave. Playa y 49. This simple disco is popular with local teenagers and so can be pretty lifeless on a school night. When it's quiet, punters sit on the beachfront terrace drinking at plastic tables. $1CUC. Daily 10pm–2am.

Palacio de la Rumba end of Ave. de las Américas just beyond the *Bella Costa* ☎ 45/66-8210. Often referred to simply as *La Rumba* and as lively a night as anywhere in Varadero, this is also one of the area's biggest and best-designed venues. After paying the $10CUC cover, there's an open bar and therefore a guaranteed night of lost inhibitions. Daily 10pm–5am.

Piano Bar Centro Cultural Artex, Calle 60 e/ Ave. 2da y Ave. 3ra. A compact and classy bar hosting a nightly karaoke from 11.30pm, with a short live music show on the tiny stage at weekends. No cover charge.

La Red Ave. 3ra e/ 29 y 30. There's a good mix of Cubans and foreigners at this popular and friendly club which packs out at weekends. Cover $3CUC. Daily 10pm–4am.

Cabarets and live shows

Cabaret Eco Disco Complejo Mediterráneo, Calle 54 e/ Ave. 1ra y Ave. Playa. Although this is one of Varadero's least glamorous and glitzy cabarets, set in the courtyard of a modest restaurant and bar complex, the songs and routines are performed with as much gusto as you could hope for. Shows

are usually followed by a disco. $5–10. Open daily 8pm–3am.

Cabaret Kawama *Hotel Kawama*. One of the more stylish cabarets, set in a cosy underground jazz-style nightclub. Cover $5 for non-guests. Mon–Sat 11pm–late.

Casa de la Cultura Los Corales Ave. 1era e/ 34 y 35 ☎ 45/61-2562. The nearest thing to a local community venue, with a main performance area resembling a town hall, the live music here ranges from rap to traditional Cuban styles. There are dance shows as well, a programme for the month is usually posted in the front window. Free–$5CUC. Open daily 2–10pm.

Casa de la Música Ave. Playa no.4206 e/ 42 y 43 ☎ 45/66-7568. High-quality live music is offered every night at this converted cinema, the newest and best live-music venue in Varadero. Covers a broad variety of mostly Cuban styles, from jazz to *son* and *salsa*.

La Comparsita Centro Cultural Artex, Calle 60 e/ Ave. 2da y Ave. 3ra T45/. This relatively professional stage venue attracts a lively mix of locals and tourists. Though performances are often in the cabaret spirit they don't always get the full treatment, so some nights you might get the wailing vocalist but without the dancing girls and other nights something more subdued altogether. Live music and dance are, however a mainstay. $10CUC. Open bar. Daily 10pm–2am.

Continental *Hotel Internacional*, Ave. de las Américas ☎ 45/66-7038. Varadero's best and most famous cabaret, exceeded in reputation only by the *Tropicana*. All the exaggerated costumes and heartfelt renditions of cheesy love songs make this show, which has travelled internationally, a classic. There's a disco afterwards, with a second show following the main event between Thurs and Sun. $40CUC. Tues–Sun 8pm–3.30am.

Cueva del Pirata Ave. del Sur, next to the entrance to *Bahia Principe* ☎ 45/66-7751 & 61-3829. The show and the disco that follows take place in a cave, which makes for a different atmosphere. The performers dress as pirates for a slight twist on the usual dress code. $10CUC. Mon–Sat 9pm–2.30am.

FM17 Ave. 1era esq. 17. A good range of live music, from traditional Cuban styles to modern *salsa* anthems, is played on a regular basis at this popular but slightly slipshod outdoor *cafétéria*.

Mambo Club Carretera Las Morlas, attached to the *Club Amigo* hotel beyond the Marina Chapelín ☎ 45/66-8565. As good a place as any in Varadero to appreciate musicians playing classic 1950s Cuban styles such as *cha-cha-cha*, *merengue* and, in particular, *mambo*. A DJ spins *salsa* and international hits after the show, and also during a short intermission, but this place is all about the live music, which goes on until 2am. Entrance is $10CUC with a free bar all night and there's a pool table, too.

Snack Bar Calle 62 Ave. 1ra esq. 62. This lively but soulless roadside bar hosts a weekly entertainment programme, usually live bands, on its small stage.

Sport and outdoor pursuits

With some thirty dive sites around the Varadero waters and several clubs hiring out equipment, **scuba diving** is naturally one of the most heavily promoted and popular activities in the resort (see box, opposite). **Fishing**, also on offer at all the marinas, is less renowned in these parts than elsewhere around the country, but is still an integral part of seabound experiences on the peninsula (see box, p.273). Back on land, most of the luxury hotels have at least one **tennis court** and a **swimming pool**, some of which, such as the one at *Arenas Blancas*, are accessible to non-guests for a few convertible pesos or with an all-day pass.

There are no regular spectator sports in Varadero – the nearest sports stadium is in the city of Matanzas – but there are one or two places for participatory activities. Most notable of these is the **Varadero Golf Club** (T 45/66-7788, W www.varaderogolfclub.com), whose 18-hole, par 72 course occupies a narrow 3.5-kilometre strip alongside the Autopista del Sur, with the caddy house and golf shop – where you should head first to pay and park your car, should you need to – right next to the Dupont Mansión. Greens fees are $48CUC for 9 holes or $77CUC for all 18 (discounts are available if you book more than five rounds in one go), to go with compulsory golf-cart rental ($30CUC); you can rent a set of clubs for $30CUC. There are classes offered and a driving range on site as well. On a smaller scale there's **mini-golf** at the town at El Golfito, Ave. 1ra e/ 41 y 42, for just $1CUC, and in Parque Josone.

You can organize your own **soccer** games on the pitch with full-size goalposts that runs alongside Calle 24 between Ave. 3ra and Autopista Sur, or take on the locals who usually play in the evening on a patch of grass at the corner of Calle 20 and Ave. 2da. Alternatively, challenge the cream of Varadero's budding tennis enthusiasts at La Raqueta Dorada (daily 9am–noon & 2–6pm) at Ave. 1ra e/ 37 y 38. It's an outdoor synthetic surface court which costs nothing to use, but you need to bring your own racquet and balls.

Unusually for Cuba, the town has two small **leisure complexes**. At Todo en Uno (24hr), Calle 54 esq. Autopista del Sur, there is a small amusement park (Mon–Thurs 11am–11pm, Fri–Sun 11am–11.30pm; $1CUC per ride) featuring bumper cars, a carousel and a diminutive roller coaster as well as a small video games arcade, pool tables ($4CUC per hour), numerous fast-food outlets and a four-lane 24-hour bowling alley. Complejo Recreativo Record (daily noon–8pm) at Ave. Playa esq. 46 has a **pool hall**, *cafétería* and another bowling alley.

For a considerably bigger thrill, the Centro Internacional de Paracaidismo (T 45/66-7256, E skygators@cubairsports.itgo.com), on the Vía Blanca a few hundred metres from the Varadero bridge, offers **skydiving** for $150CUC, which includes the transfer, a class, and the drop itself, usually in tandem with the instructor. Bookings are taken directly or through Cubanacán (see p.263).

There are far superior dive sites around Cuba than the ones off the coast of Varadero, but with several diving **clubs** and watersports **centres** on the peninsula (listed below) this is one of the best-equipped areas for such activities. The clubs can supply you with all the necessary diving equipment and instruction and also arrange excursions to elsewhere in Cuba, commonly to the Península de Zapata and the Bay of Pigs in southern Matanzas. Most of the local dive sites are on the coral reefs around the offshore cays, such as Cayo Blanco and Cayo Piedras, and at Playa Coral, along the coast towards Matanzas, just 30 metres or so from the shore. As well as the standard coral reef visits, clubs usually offer night dives and cave dives, the latter usually taking place in the Cueva de Saturno to the west of Varadero, not far off the Vía Blanca (see p.288). Many hotels, especially those on the beach, have their own watersports clubs and most offer beginners' diving classes. **Snorkelling** equipment is readily available from hotels and diving clubs but not really worth using near the beach where there isn't much to see on the seabed. The best snorkelling opportunities are on the local boat trips out to the nearby cays (see p.274).

Acuasports Camino del Mar e/ 9 y 10 ☏45/66-7166 & 61-4792 (daily 9am–6pm). This watersports club is more of a recreation centre and beachside hangout than the more professionally run diving clubs elsewhere. Of all the clubs, it's the most accessible from the beach and the best place to go if you just want to bum around. There's a good selection of equipment for rent, including jet skis ($1CUC per min), surfboards ($4CUC per 30min), kayaks ($3CUC per 30min), catamarans ($10CUC per person for 30min) and good old-fashioned deck chairs ($1CUC per day). There's a *cafétería* in the club and a few games such as air hockey.

Centro Internacional de Buceo Barracuda Ave. 1ra e/ 58 y 59 ☏45/66-7072 & 61-3481, ©comercial@barracuda.var.cyt.cu; daily 8am–7pm. Diving and watersports club and the best equipped in terms of on-site facilities, including a restaurant, bar and private rooms. Offers the most comprehensive programme of diving including internationally recognized ACUC courses for advanced divers and instructors. The basic packages are $50CUC for a single-tank dive or $70CUC with two tanks, though these prices are reduced slightly if you supply your own equipment. Also the best organized for first-time divers, with beginners' classes starting at $70CUC for a theory class, a lesson in a swimming pool and then a sea dive. Packages on offer include three dives for $92CUC, six for $174CUC and ten for $258CUC. The club can also supply equipment for almost any watersport including jet skis ($1CUC per minute), windsurfing boards ($10CUC per hour), pedal boats ($5CUC for two people per hour) and snorkelling equipment ($3CUC per hour).

Centro Internacional de Buceo Coral Ave. Kawama no. 201 e/ 2 y 3 ☏45/66-8063; daily 8am–5pm. The only diving club offering dives with nitrox: a single dive with nitrox costs $55CUC, while with two tanks it runs up to $75CUC. There are basic nitrox courses for $240CUC and a variety of ACUC-approved courses. This is also the best place for organizing cave dives; their basic one costs $60CUC. For basic daytime, prices are the same as those at Barracuda (see above)

Centro de Buceo Marina Chapelín Autopista Sur Km 12 ☏45/66-8871; daily 9am–4pm. The basic prices and packages here are the same as at the Barracuda and Coral clubs; the fundamental difference is that all dives are done from boats and, unlike with those other clubs, none are done from the shore. The dive trips here are for experienced, certified divers only, and average dive depths are 25 to 30 metres and as far down as 40 metres.

Centro de Buceo Marina Gaviota Varadero at the end of Autopista Sur, Punta Hicacos ☏45/66-7755 & 66-7756. Has on-site diving facilities and offers competitive prices as well as complimentary transfers from your hotel to the marina if you are staying in a Gaviota-run hotel.

Shopping, galleries and workshops

On the whole, **shops** in Varadero are few and far between and most are generally worth a quick browse only if you're passing. The highest concentration of shops is at the top of the town in between calles 56 and 64, where you'll find two of Varadero's three shopping complexes, the Centro Comercial Caimán and the Galería de Tiendas Palma Real, each of which is actually just several stores clustered together. In fact, only Plaza América, Varadero's solitary shopping mall, can boast more than the usual four or five stores, sometimes less, which make up the other *centros comerciales*.

There's a broad selection of **arts and crafts** on sale all around the town, much of it in the two proper markets and smaller selections in the Artex shops dotted about. The markets are open daily during high season, usually between about 9am and 8pm, but in low season tend to close an hour or two earlier, as well as sometimes closing all day Sunday. Just as good for shopping expeditions, however, are the hotel gift shops, which usually stock a few CDs, T-shirts and all sorts of souvenirs, and can also be a good source for groceries and cigars. Given that there are no big supermarkets in the town or any fresh food markets on the peninsula, your best bet for groceries is the supermarket at Plaza América, which has a fresh meat counter and the best selection of alcohol in Varadero, or Grocery Varazul at Calle 15 e/ Ave. 1ra y Ave. 2da.

Arts and crafts

Arte Cubano Ave. 1ra esq. Calle 12. Smaller version of the Fondo de Bienes Culturales, where artistic Afro-Cuban wood carvings and tacky Che Guevara place mats sit side by side.

Arte Sol y Mar Ave. 1ra e/ 34 y 35. Small but usually pleasing exhibitions of paintings and photographs by artists from all over Cuba. Everything is for sale and there's usually enough soulful work amongst the unimaginative landscapes to balance things out. There's often a small craft market out front.

La Casa Ave. 1ra esq. 59. The upstairs floor of this shop has a good selection of distinctive Cuban film art posters as well as other original poster prints, paintings and pictures. See also "Clothing, books and music".

Fondo de Bienes Culturales Ave. 1ra e/ 15 y 16. Varadero's best and biggest craft market consists of over 30 stalls around a little roadside square. Here you'll find all the trademark Cuban crafts, textiles and gift items, like wooden statuettes, lace shawls, coral necklaces, cigar boxes and Che T-shirts as well as bags and ceramics.

Fería Los Caneyes Ave. 1ra e/ 51 y 52. Around twenty stalls with a good selection of wooden hand-carved ornaments and all the usual Cuban-market arts and crafts.

Taller de Cerámica Ave. 1ra e/ 59 y 60. You can watch pottery being made in the busy workshop and then buy a piece in the good-quality little shop where everything for sale is an original and not the usual tourist tack. Daily 9am–5pm; July & August daily 9am–7.30pm.

Cigars and rum

Casa del Habano Ave. 1ra e/ 63 y 64. Varadero's outstanding cigar store, which not only has an impressive selection of all the major brands but also all sorts of smoking paraphernalia, a smokers' lounge, a separate section selling rum and coffee and an upstairs bar.

Casa del Habano Ave. Playa esq. 31. A professional little shop located in the same ranch-like building as *La Vega* restaurant (see p.278), not to be confused with the much bigger Casa del Habano (above).

Casa del Ron Ave. 1ra e/ 62 y 63. As well as stocking the best choice of rum in Varadero, this is one of the peninsula's most novel shops. Occupying almost the whole front room is a captivating model of an early twentieth-century Cuban rum factory and in the back there's a 1920s-era bar set up solely for try-before-you-buy purposes.

Casa del Tabaco at Ave. 1ra esq. 27. A small *tabaquería* where you can also watch cigars being made.

Clothing, books and music

Adidas Ave. 1ra esq. 60. The local branch of this world-famous sportswear specialist, which for many years has been the official supplier of kit to various national Cuban sports teams.

La Casa Ave. 1ra esq. 59. The selection of books downstairs is glossier than you'll find in most other places, though the subject matters are limited to revolutionary and political themes or Cuban architecture and gift books. Upstairs is a room full of CDs, in addition to the posters and pictures.

Coral Negro Calle 63 esq. Ave. 2da. A well-stocked branch of the Cuban jewellery specialist whose products tend to be on the showy side. Watches and perfume are sold here, too.

Librería Hanoi Ave. 1ra e/ 43 y 44. Stocks a limited selection of mostly Cuban political literature and fiction that makes up the biggest section of the cramped premises.

Librería Varadero Ave. 1ra e/ 31 y 32. Varadero's best selection of English-language novels and other fiction, all second-hand, in this neat little shop which also stocks all sorts of Cuban journals and periodicals, most with an artistic, academic or political slant.

Peletería Verona Calle 63 e/ Ave. 1ra y Ave. 2da. The widest selection of footwear in Varadero, much of it for women.

Puma Calle 63 e/ Ave. 1ra y Ave. 2da. Sneakers, T-shirts, swimsuits, accessories and other bits and pieces from the local branch of this classic sports brand.

Shopping galleries and malls

Centro Comercial Caimán Ave. 1ra e/ 61 y 62. Home to a small craft market, as well as a couple of the best gift shops in the town, and a good place for cigars, rum and perfume.

Centro Comercial Todo en Uno Calle 54 e/ Ave. 1ra y Autopista del Sur. Another tiny group of shops but a better choice of clothing than at the other *centros comerciales* in the town area.

Galería de Tiendas Palma Real Ave. 3ra esq. Calle 62. A short line of retail outlets along a first-floor balcony where the highlight is a music shop with a plentiful supply of CDs and a surprisingly broad range of instruments, from congas and full drum sets to keyboards and guitars.

Plaza América Autopista del Sur, next to the *Meliá Varadero* hotel. The only mall and by far the best shopping centre in Varadero. This is where you'll find the largest stock of brand names (including Gucci, Bennetton and Mango), clothing boutiques and generally the more upmarket merchandise and souvenirs as well as a cigar shop and a couple of restaurants.

Plaza Caracol Ave. 1ra e/ 53 y 54. A comparatively slick – by Cuban standards – set of just four shops which include a small supermarket, a beach-gear specialist and a store selling toys and children's clothing.

Todo en Uno Calle 54 esq. Autopista del Sur. This leisure complex with restaurants and fast-food outlets also has a number of shops selling clothing, sports gear and holiday items.

Listings

Airlines Aerocaribbean Ave. 1ra esq. 23 ☎ 45/61-1470; Aerotaxi ☎ 45/66-7540 & 61-2929; Air Canada ☎ 45/61-3016 & 61-2010; ; Cubana ☎ 45/61-2133 & 61-3016 (Mon–Fri 8am–4pm); Martinair ☎ 45/25-3624.

Airport information ☎ 45/24-7015, 25-3614 & 61-2133.

Banks and money The Banco Financiero Internacional, Ave. 1ra e/ 32 y 33, entrance on Ave. Playa (Mon–Fri 9am–7pm), is the bank most experienced in foreign currency transactions and the best place for wiring money. The Banco de Crédito y Comercio, Ave. 1ra e/ 35 y 36 (Mon–Fri 9am–1.30pm & 3–7pm), is the cheapest place to change traveller's cheques. There are Cadeca *casas de cambio* for buying pesos at Ave. Playa e/ 41 y 42 (Mon–Sat 8am–5pm, Sun 8am–noon) and Ave. 1ra esq. 59 (Mon–Sat 8am–5pm; Sun 8am–noon). There is an ATM at Plaza América.

Bicycle rental Bikes can be rented from Motoclub at Ave. 1ra esq. 17 and Ave. 1ra e/ 37 y 38 (☎ 45/61-3110), where there are also scooters.

Car rental Cubacar at Ave. 1ra esq. 21 (☎ 45/66-7332; 24hrs), Ave. 1ra e/ 54 y 55 (☎ 45/61-1875), Ave. de las Américas next to *Hotel Las Morlas* (☎ 45/66-7230 & 61-3913) and Juan Gualberto Gómez Airport (☎ 45/25-3621); Havanautos at Ave. 1ra esq. 31 (☎ 45/61-4409) and Juan Gualberto Gómez Airport (☎ 45/25-3630); Micar at Calle 20 e/ Ave. 1ra y Ave. 2da (☎ 45/61-1808; 24hrs); Rex at Calle 36 opposite the bus station (☎ 45/66-2121).

Consulates Canadian Consulate, Casa 223, Villa Tortuga ☎ 45/66-7395.

Immigration and legal The Immigration office, for visa extensions and passport matters, is at Calle 39 y Ave. 1ra (Mon–Fri 9am–4pm). Tourist cards can also be extended through hotels and information centres. For a more extensive set of services

– including legal advice and assistance as well as help with passports, visas and tourist cards – go to the Consultoría Jurídica Internacional at Ave. 1ra y 21 (Mon–Fri 9am–noon & 2–5pm; ☎45/66-7082). Asistur at Calle 31 y Ave. 1ra (☎45/66-7277 & 61-2164) provide travel and medical insurance services and can deal with lost luggage problems and financial difficulties.

Internet The ETECSA Centro de Llamadas at Ave. 1ra y 30 (24hr) has Internet facilities. Sala de Telecomunicaciones (daily 8.30am–7.30pm) at the Plaza América shopping mall has telephone booths and three PCs for Internet use. Cibercafé at Ave. 1ra e/ 39 y 40 (Mon–Sat 9am–6pm).

Left luggage Terminal de Omnibus, Calle 36 esq. Autopista del Sur ($2CUC per item).

Library Biblioteca José Smith Comas, Calle 33 e/ Ave. 1ra y Ave. 3ra (Mon–Fri 9am–6pm, Sat 9am–5pm). Small and friendly with a great selection of English literature, including a surprisingly good selection of Penguins. You can take books out by leaving your hotel and passport details.

Medical Clínica Internacional de Varadero at Ave. 1ra y 61 (☎45/66-7710 & 66-7711, ✉clinica@clinica.var.cyt.cu), which includes the best-stocked pharmacy in Varadero, is open 24hr. At the other end of town is another reasonable pharmacy at Ave. Kawama e/ 2 y 3 (daily 9am–7pm). The nearest major hospital is in Matanzas (see p.299). For an ambulance call ☎45/61-2950.

Petrol stations There are three Servi-Cupet convertible-peso petrol stations at the Todo en uno complex on Calle 54 y Autopista del Sur, Autopista del Sur y 17 and on the Vía Blanca 1km from the Varadero bridge.

Photography Photoservice at Calle 63 esq. Ave. 2da or Photoclub at Ave. 1ra esq. 42 and in Plaza América, Autopista del Sur, next to the *Meliá Varadero* hotel.

Police ☎116. Police station at Calle 39 y Ave. 1ra.

Post office Branches at Ave. 1ra y 36, and Calle 64 e/ Ave. 1ra y Ave. 2da (both Mon–Sat 8am–6pm). Many hotels also have their own post office service. DHL has an office at Ave. 1ra no.3903 e/ 39 y 40 (☎45/66-7330).

Radio stations As well as the national Cuban stations (see p.73) you can pick up Florida Keys-based stations on a normal FM radio. These include WAIL FM (99.5; mostly rock) and WEOW FM (92.5; pop and R&B).

Scooter rental Palmares Moto Club at Ave. 1ra esq. 38 has the biggest number of scooters for rent. There are also rentals at the side of the road every fifteen blocks or so on Ave. 1ra, as well as in a number of hotels.

Taxis Taxis OK ☎45/61-4444 & 61-1616; Transgaviota ☎45/61-9761 or 62; Transtur Taxi ☎45/61-3415 & 61-3728.

Telephone The ETECSA Centro de Llamadas and head office is at Ave. 1ra y 30 (24hr). There are also ETECSA phone cabins at Ave. 1ra esq. 15, Ave. 1ra e/ 46 y 47 and Ave. Kawama e/ 5 y 6. See also Internet.

Around Varadero

The small town of **Cárdenas**, just 10km southeast of Varadero, is ideally placed for a day-trip from the beach resort. Spending more than a day there would be pushing it, since what was once one of Cuba's most prestigious towns has, like the provincial capital Matanzas, had little attention paid to its upkeep in recent years. Following the road in the other direction from the Varadero bridge, towards Matanzas, will take you past the side road for the airport. Hiding in the bushes near the start of this side road, the **Cueva de Saturno** provides a neatly packaged detour on a journey out this way and offers just enough to make parking your car worth it. The cave can, however, occupy a more substantial outing if you visit it on a diving trip.

Cárdenas

A ten-kilometre drive southeast from the bridge that joins the Península de Hicacos to the mainland, **CÁRDENAS** is the nearest place to Varadero where you can get a glimpse of Cuban life untainted by tourism. Normally, its greatest natural asset would be its location, hugging the shoreline of the **Bay of Cárdenas**, but unfortunately most of the coastal area is an industrial zone. If you've travelled around in Cuba there'll be very little here that you haven't seen before and the town's near-perfect grid plan adds a touch of mundane familiarity. Cárdenas is far from a waste of time, however, especially if you're passing this way, and its **Catedral de la Inmaculada Concepción** is of greater architectural merit than anything in Varadero.

Known as the **Ciudad Bandera** (Flag City), it was here in 1850 that what became the national flag was first raised by the Venezuelan General Narciso López and his troops, who had disembarked at Cárdenas in a US-backed attempt to spark a revolt against Spanish rule and clear the way for annexation.

The attempt failed, but the flag's design was later adopted by the independence movement. This history, though, has more recently been overshadowed by Cárdenas' position of prestige as the birthplace of **Elian González**, the young boy who came to symbolize the ideological conflict between the US and Cuba during a 1999 custody battle of unusual geopolitical significance. The government wasted no time in setting up a **museum** here to commemorate their perceived triumph when Elian was returned to his home town.

Day-trips to Cárdenas are available through the travel agents in Varadero. Cubanacán charge $21CUC for their five-hour tour.

Arrival and accommodation

The interprovincial **bus terminal** at Ave. Céspedes esq. Calle 22 (℡45/52-1214) serves buses arriving from everywhere except Varadero. Travelling to and from Varadero, buses run every hour right up to (theoretically) 7pm, from the smaller terminal on Calle 13 esq. Ave. 13 (℡45/52-4958). From either terminal it's a straightforward ten-minute walk into the centre. Arriving by car or scooter couldn't be easier as the main road from Varadero cuts directly into the centre of town. In the unlikely event that you arrive by **train** from Colón, you'll pull in at the station on Ave. 8 y Calle 5 (℡45/52-1362 & 52-2562), a few blocks from the centre.

There are a few *casas particulares* in Cárdenas currently providing the only available **accommodation** in town since the hotel *La Dominica* (℡45/52-2140) closed for lengthy renovations. The best is the *Casa de Ricardo Domínguez* at Palma no.520 e/ Coronel Verdugo y Industria (cell phone ℡528 944 31; ❶) with two large and neatly kept rooms, one with a first-rate bathroom, and a superb backyard patio.

Orientation and getting around

Cárdenas revolves around **Avenida Céspedes**, running right down the centre of town towards the port. Anything running parallel with it is also an *avenida*, while the *calles* run perpendicular to it, with Calle 13 crossing Avenida Céspedes bang in the centre of town. The *calles* number from 1, at the port, to 27 at the other end of town. Locals have stuck to using the original street names, before they were changed to numbers following the Revolution, few of which are still in evidence. Almost everything you are likely to want to see in town is concentrated within four or five blocks of the crossroads at Calle 13 and Ave. Céspedes.

Getting around and travelling between the three plazas around which much of the life in the centre revolves can easily be done on foot. Should you decide to explore beyond them, the best way to go is on one of the numerous horse-drawn carriages plying the streets, particularly along Avenida Céspedes. The charge will often depend on the driver and whether or not he realizes you are a foreign visitor, but Cubans pay 1 peso for any journey.

The Town

Picking out the highlights in Cárdenas is a relatively quick and easy process. The only really prestigious building, the **cathedral**, is at **Parque Colón** and all the museums, including the **Museo a la Batalla de Ideas** with its fantastic **views** of the town, are on or right next to the **Parque José Antonio Echevarría**. There are, however, one or two other pockets of slight interest, such as the bustling market at **Plaza Malacoff**.

Parque Colón

Cárdenas's main square, **Parque Colón**, at Ave. Céspedes between calles 8 and 9, is only a square in name, bisected down the middle by the main street and conducive to neither a sit-down nor a stroll around. The abandoned and dilapidated *Hotel Europa*, closed down before Cuba's current era of tourism, occupies the southeastern side. Opposite is the noble but withered **Catedral de la Inmaculada Concepción**, dating from 1846 and bordered by healthy-looking bushy gardens. Featuring two stone lighthouse-like columns flanking the entrance, with portholes running the length of the stout building and a straight-edged dome poking its head above the treetops from the rear, it's the best photo opportunity in the city and certainly the grandest building, though it's almost always closed. Further reason to whip out the camera is the elevated **statue** of a romantic-looking Columbus with a globe at his feet, directly in front of the cathedral. Sculpted in 1862, it's said to be the oldest statue of the explorer in the whole of the Americas.

Parque José Antonio Echevarría

If you head three blocks south from Parque Colón on Avenida Céspedes and take a left on Calle 12, after two blocks you'll come to the northeastern border of plain but tranquil **Parque José Antonio Echevarría**, the archetypal town square that Parque Colón fails to be, dotted with trees and benches and enclosed by buildings on all sides. The real reason to visit, though, is for the museums that comprise two of its borders.

Founded in 1900 and one of the oldest museums in the country, the **Museo Oscar María de Rojas** (☎45/52-2417; Tues–Sat 10am–5pm, Sun 8am–noon; $1CUC), occupying the square's entire southwestern side, houses an eclectic set of collections, from currency and medals to bugs and butterflies and, as is customary in Cuban museums, a selection of firearms that includes, more unusually, reproductions of pre-Columbian weapons. Looming in the entrance hall is a remarkably ornate nineteenth-century funeral carriage, looking appropriately morbid. The most substantive part of the museum are the last two rooms on the clockwise tour of the building. The first of these is the Room of Aboriginal Cuban Culture, which features human skeletal remains almost 5800 years old; next door, in the Room of American Archeology, are some fascinating artefacts of pre-Columbian cultures elsewhere in Latin America. There's also a bizarre shrunken head from southern Ecuador and some stone idols discovered in Mexico, as well as jewellery and various examples of Mayan art.

Across Ave. 4 on the square's northwestern side is the **Museo José Antonio Echevarría** (Tues–Sat 10am–6pm, Sun 10am–1pm; free), birthplace of the anti-Batista student leader, a statue of whom stands casually, hand in pocket, in the square outside. Less engaging than its neighbour but more consistent in its content, the museum's exhibits relate to the nineteenth- and twentieth-century independence and revolutionary struggles, with the usual overemphasis on political history and undercutting of the social background so characteristic of Cuban history museums. More uniquely, on the first floor is a space given over to Echevarría himself. Actively involved in the popular struggle against Batista, Echevarría and several of his comrades were shot and killed by Batista's police during the March 13, 1957 attack on the Presidential Palace in Havana.

Museo a la Batalla de Ideas

At Ave. 6 and Calle 12, touching the corner of the Parque José Antonio Echevarría, is the propagandist **Museo a la Batalla de Ideas** (Tues–Sat 9am–5pm & Sun 9am–1pm; entrance $2CUC, guided tour $2CUC). As much a symbol of victory as a museum, it's housed in a cheery yellow edifice featuring a central tower flanked by two smaller turret-style blocks with white trim portholes and ramparted rooftops. This cartoon-like fortress is actually a nineteenth-century fire station with a twenty-first-century paintjob. Opened in June 2001 the museum represents the triumph claimed by Fidel Castro over the US when Elian González, the six-year-old boy who came to personify the political and theoretical conflict between the US and Cuba, returned from Florida to Cuba (see p.603).

The contents of the museum boldly demonstrate the Cuban government's continuing fervour in upholding its ideological principles. There are specific exhibits like the statue of José Martí holding a small child in the entrance hall, but much of the space is occupied by two rooms loaded with posterboards detailing a written history of US interest in Cuba and a photographic look at the whole Elian episode. On the other side of the bright and colourful central courtyard, lined with busts of political and military Cuban heroes, is a third room themed around the Cuban education system. There are examples of schoolbooks found across the country such as *El Diario del Che en Bolivia*. As in so many areas of Cuban life, Che Guevara is revered in classrooms as the model which pupils should strive to emulate, demonstrated on one posterboard here depicting a group of school kids with an inscription of their daily motto "*Seremos como el Che*", "We will be like Che".

The whole museum takes up only the ground floor of this four-storey building, but make sure to venture upstairs to the rooftop **viewing platform** looking over the whole city and beyond – well worth the extra charge. There is usually a museum staff member on hand to point out the various sights, including a rarely seen perspective, on the distant horizon, of the Varadero peninsula.

Plaza Malacoff

More of a curiosity than a tourist attraction is **Plaza Malacoff**, in between avenidas 3 and 5 at Calle 12. An old market square, its centre is occupied by a fifteen-metre-high, cross-shaped commerce building consisting of little more than four two-storey hallways and a large iron and zinc dome in the centre which gives it the appearance of a run-down Islamic temple. The building still operates as it has done since since its inception in 1859, as host to the trading stalls and booths that make up the food market here. While the square has seen better days, it is still full of life and perhaps the best place to go in town for some genuine local flavour.

Eating, drinking and nightlife

In keeping with its role as a quick-stop destination for tourists, there are a disproportionate number of **fast-food** places in Cárdenas, including three branches of hot dog and pizza pusher *El Rápido*, one of these on Plaza Malacoff. The nearest thing to a formal restaurant is *Café Espriu* on the Parque José Antonio Echevarría, which compensates for a lack of character by offering the most reliable stock of traditional Cuban dishes. The only peso establishment worth a look is *Las Palmas* at Ave. Céspedes esq. Calle 16. Avoid the gloomy hall and enjoy a quiet drink on the shady garden terrace of this half-Japanese half-Spanish-style villa, where food is also occasionally served. Also worth stopping at for a drink is *El Fuerte*, a nineteenth-century fortress-turret offering modest views from the far end of town, in between calles 26 and 27.

Besides a few of the peso bars playing loud music, **nightlife** in Cárdenas is almost exclusively restricted to *La Cachamba* (Wed–Sun; 3 pesos) in the same grounds as *Las Palmas*, behind the villa. A young crowd packs out the large courtyard at weekends, when they are treated to pure pop and glossy dance routines performed by local talent. Otherwise, you're left with the **cinema** (☎45/52-2639) at Ave. Céspedes esq. Calle 14 or, during the day, the *sala de video* in the Museo a la Batalla de Ideas. You may also be able to play some pool at the Casa del Educador ($1CUC), a scrappy local hangout on Ave. Céspedes e/ Calle 17 y 18.

Cueva de Saturno

Just by the road connecting Juan Gualberto Gómez Airport to the Vía Blanca, a few hundred metres south from the Vía Blanca itself, is the **Cueva de Saturno** (☎45/25-3272; daily 8am–6pm; $5CUC), a flooded cave where you can snorkel and scuba dive. Modest in comparison to the Cuevas de Bellamar nearer Matanzas, the cave isn't worth going out of your way for unless you intend to scuba dive – in which case you'll need to pre-book a visit with one of Varadero's dive clubs (see p.281). However, it makes a good stopoff between Varadero and Matanzas. You can take in the cave, walk down through the impressive gaping mouth of the cave to the pool at the bottom and take a swim. A snack bar has been built near the steps down into the cave, mostly to serve the organized visits that regularly come here from Matanzas and Varadero.

Matanzas and around

One of the closest and most accessible day-trip destinations from Varadero is **MATANZAS**, the biggest city in the province of the same name and just 25km west along the coast from the resort. Clustered on the hillsides around a large bay and endowed with several small beaches, the city's natural setting is perhaps its greatest asset, though as with much else about the place, this remains largely unexploited and few foreign visitors stay for more than a day.

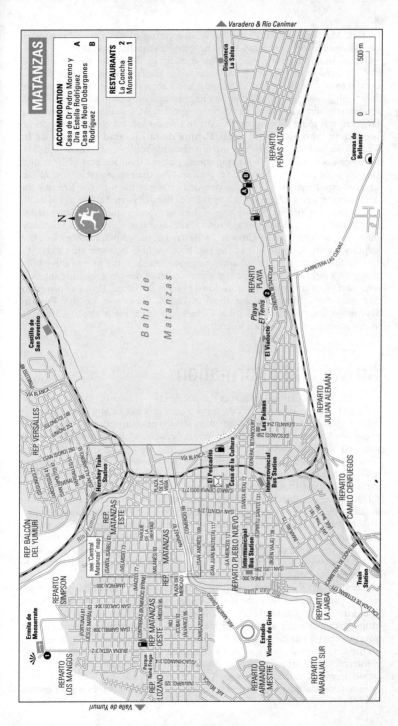

▲ Varadero & Río Canímar

MATANZAS

ACCOMMODATION
Casa de Dr Pedro Moreno y
Dra Estella Rodríguez   A
Casa de Noel Dobarganes
Rodríguez   B

RESTAURANTS
La Concha   2
Monserrate   1

0   500 m

Bahía de
Matanzas

Castillo de
San Severino

REP VERSALLES

REP BALCÓN
DEL YUMURÍ

Hershey Train
Station

REP
MATANZAS
ESTE

REPARTO
SIMPSON

Ermita de
Monserrate

REPARTO
LOS MANGOS

see 'Central
Matanzas' map

REP MATANZAS
OESTE

Estadio
Victoria de Girón

REPARTO
ARMANDO
MESTRE

REPARTO
NARANJAL SUR

Train
Station

REPARTO
LA JAIBA

REPARTO
CAMILO CIENFUEGOS

REPARTO
JULIAN ALEMÁN

Intermunicipal
Bus Station

Interprovincial
Bus Station

REPARTO
PUEBLO NUEVO

Casa de la Cultura

El Pescadito

Las Palmas

El Viaducto

Playa
El Tenis

REPARTO
PLAYA

REPARTO
PEÑAS ALTAS

Discoteca
La Salsa

Cuevas de
Bellamar

CARRETERA LAS CUEVAS

N

▲ Valle de Yumurí

289

In fact, Matanzas is one of the most uninspiring of the Cuban provincial capitals, much less interesting than the specific attractions nearby.

Having briefly become more visitor-friendly in the recent past, when the city appeared to be on the up, Matanzas has in the last couple of years slipped back into a state of neglect. The only hotel accepting tourists is no longer functioning, and numerous other buildings around the centre have been closed for renovations, with work on them progressing at a snail's pace. There are, however, still some sites worth checking out, most located conveniently on or between the two main town plazas, **Parque de la Libertad** and **Plaza de la Vigía**. Beyond the plazas the slightly claustrophobic town centre quickly becomes a series of similar-looking streets plagued by drainage problems, and tangible focal points are few and far between. For the best available view of the bay and city head away from the crowded centre of town to the **Ermita de Monserrate**, a recently restored quaint little church. Located at the top of a hill, from where the **Yumurí Valley**, one of the more picturesque nearby attractions, springs into view. The valley is as good a reason as any to visit this area, but many more people come for the **Cuevas de Bellamar**, the caves tunnelling into the hillsides on the opposite side of the city. If you're here for more than a day it's best to base yourself in the suburban neighbourhoods at the foot of these hills, along the southern shore of the bay, where much of the city's nightlife, most *casas particulares* and some tiny run-down beaches are found. If you've driven to Matanzas from Havana along the Vía Blanca, look out for the **Puente Bacunayagua**, the tallest bridge in Cuba and near to one of the best available views available of the Yumurí Valley.

Arrival and information

National network **trains** pull in at the nondescript station (℡ 45/29-2409) on the southern outskirts of the city, from where nothing of any convenience is within walking distance. The other train service into the city is on the picturesque but leisurely **Hershey line**, running between Matanzas and Havana and carrying the only electric trains in Cuba. The station (℡ 45/24-4805 is in Versalles, the neighbourhood north of the Río Yumurí, and a fifteen-minute walk northeast of the Parque de la Libertad. It costs $2.80CUC to travel between Matanzas and Havana on this line.

During the day there are usually private **taxis** waiting outside the train station to take you into town for between $2CUC and $4CUC, depending on how willing you are to negotiate. If you arrive at night, however, you will have to ring for a taxi (℡ 45/24-4350). There is a **local bus service** leaving from the train station at highly irregular intervals and if you're lucky enough to coincide with it, it'll take you to the Plaza del Mercado, within a few blocks of the Parque de la Libertad, for less than a peso. More likely to be waiting when you arrive are the *bicitaxis* and the *coches*, horse-drawn carriages which should charge in pesos to take you at least as far as the market square. A local bus, the Omnibus Yumurí, leaves from the Parque de la Libertad roughly every hour, between 9am and 6pm daily, linking the city centre with the Cuevas de Bellamar, the most popular tourist attraction in the area, and the Ermita de Monserrate on the opposite side of the city, where there are a couple of eateries and views of the Yumurí Valley.

Interprovincial **buses** arrive at the Estación de Omnibus (℡ 45/29-1473), across from the junction between Calle 272 and Calle 171. There are often private taxis waiting in the car park, but there's no other obvious way of getting into the centre, although walking isn't out of the question – you should be able to get to the Plaza de la Libertad within twenty minutes. As elsewhere in Cuba, streets in Matanzas have both old and new names (see box, below).

If you **drive** to Matanzas from Varadero, be ready for the $2CUC charge at the Matanzas–Varadero tollgate a few kilometres after the bridge linking the beach resort to the mainland. **Parking** in the city can be a bit of a problem with no official car parks, though there are parking spaces at Plaza de la Vigía where there is usually an unofficial attendant who will watch over the vehicle for a tip. This is also the best place to leave your car overnight, though if you're staying in a *casa particular* the chances are your hosts will make sure a safe spot is found for it.

Since its Infotur office has closed, the only readily available source of **information** in Matanzas are the *jineteros*, who congregate around the Parque de la Libertad in search of lost-looking foreigners.

Accommodation

Since the *Hotel Louvre* on the Parque de la Libertad has closed for renovations, there are currently no hotels in the city. There are, however, plenty of *casas particulares* providing a **place to stay** in Matanzas, particularly in the southern suburb of Reparto Playa. Finding them, though, is relatively difficult as very few advertise their existence with signs, thanks to the extra tax burden that this incurs. Expect to pay a minimum of $20CUC a night anywhere in Matanzas.

Casa de Enriqueta Cantero Contreras no.29016 e/ 290 y Zaragoza ☏ 45/24-5151. They don't come much more central than this place, just half a block from the Parque de la Libertad. The room for rent here is comfortable enough and features a/c and a refrigerator. ❷

Casa de Dr Pedro Moreno y Dra Estella Rodríguez Calle 127 no.20807 e/ 208 y 210, Reparto Playa ☏ 45/26-1260. The spacious double room in this distinctive bungalow, with its central patio-cum-conservatory, has a fridge, a/c and private bathroom. The highlight is the well-kept, attractive back garden, with a door opening out onto low cliffs, sea breezes and the lapping water of the bay down below. ❷

Casa de Noel Dobarganes Rodríguez General Betancourt no.20615 e/ 206 y 208 ☏ 45/26-1446. A separate, well-equipped apartment attached to the owners' bungalow, 50m from the edge of the bay, and offering complete privacy and independence. With access via the back garden and their own key, guests here can come and go as they please. ❷

Hostal de Roberto y Margarita Contreras no.27608 e/ 280 y 272 ☏ 45/24-2577. One of the largest houses renting rooms in the centre of the city, this nineteenth-century residence has two airy rooms, one triple and one double, and a garage. Almost everything here seems to be on a large scale, including the bedroom furniture and the open-air central patio. ❷

Old and new names of principal streets in Matanzas	
Old name	**New Name**
Ayuntamiento	Calle 288
Calzada de Esteban	Calle 171
Contreras	Calle 79 or Bonifacio Byrne
Daoiz	Calle 75
Jovellanos	Calle 282
Maceo	Calle 77
Medio	Calle 85
Milanés	Calle 83
Santa Teresita	Calle 290

The City

The best place to get your bearings, but also where you are most likely to be pestered by *jineteros*, is the more central of Matanzas' two plazas, the **Parque de la Libertad**. Here you'll find the fantastically well-preserved **Museo Farmacéutico Matanzas**, which qualifies as one of the few essential places to visit on any city tour. A couple of blocks towards the bay is the **Catedral de San Carlos Borromeo**, old as the city itself and worth a brief look on the way down to the other main square, the **Plaza de la Vigía**. While the plaza itself is less inviting than Libertad, there is more here to occupy your interest, including the historical collection in the **Museo Provincial** and the stately (and still functioning) **Teatro Sauto**. Once you get out of the centre and a little higher up, it's more pleasant, with great views from the recreational **Parque René Fraga**, and the recently developed area around the **Ermita de Monserrate** beyond it to the north.

Parque de la Libertad

A traditional Spanish-style plaza, the **Parque de la Libertad** is a welcome open space amidst the city's claustrophobic streets and provides one of the few central opportunities to sit down and relax outside in pleasant surroundings. The mostly colonial and neocolonial buildings around the square demand only a passing perusal, such as the Provincial Government headquarters from 1853, which occupies the entire east side, and the old casino building, built in 1835 and now housing a library.

More deserving of your time is the **Museo Farmacéutico Matanzas**, in the southwestern corner of the square (Mon–Sat 10am–5pm, Sun 10am–2pm; $3CUC). Founded in 1882 by two doctors, Juan Fermín de Figueroa and Ernesto Triolet, it functioned as a pharmacy right up until May 1964, when it was converted into a museum. Claimed to be the only pharmacy of its kind preserved in its entirety, it represents one of the most complete historical collections on the island – it's hard to believe that business has stopped. All the hundreds of French porcelain jars lining the shelves and cabinets, along with the many medicine bottles, and even the medicines still inside them, are originals. While some of the medicines would have been imported, principally from Spain, France, Germany and the United States, many were made in the laboratory at the back of the building, using formulae listed in one of the 55 recipe books kept in the compact but comprehensive library. You can't fail to spot the fabulous old cash till, which looks as though it should have been driven by a steam engine.

Catedral de San Carlos Borromeo

A block east towards the bay from Parque de la Libertad is the often-closed **Catedral de San Carlos Borromeo**, whose heavy frame, with its detailed Neoclassical exterior, is squeezed in between the two busiest streets in the centre. One of the city's first buildings, it was founded in 1693 and originally made of wood which, unsurprisingly, didn't last. Rebuilt in 1755, it has not survived the last two and a half centuries entirely intact. A quick look inside reveals the neglect which so much of the city's historic architecture has suffered, though there is still much left of historic and artistic value, including the original altar. The patchwork interior is a mixture of the chipped and faded original paintwork with sporadic areas of restoration, mostly on the high arches. Slightly at odds with the existing decor are the more modern-style paintings hung about the church.

Plaza de la Vigía and around

From the cathedral walk two blocks towards the bay along Calle 85 to get to the humble **Plaza de la Vigía**, struggling for space with the heavy traffic running along one side. The plaza is little more than a trumped-up road island with a swashbuckling statue of a rebel from the Wars of Independence in the centre.

On the plaza itself there are a number of simple places worth a brief peek inside. In the corner nearest the river, facing the back of the statue in the middle, is the **Taller Editorial Ediciones Vigía** (Mon–Fri 8.30am–5pm; free). This small, environmentally friendly cooperative-style publisher produces books made entirely from "*materiales rústicos*". There's actually very little to see in the small workshop besides the small display of endearing handmade books, all signed by their authors, who range from local poets to nationally known writers. Looking like sophisticated scrapbooks, the delightfully designed covers may tempt you into buying one of these unique publications, especially as prices begin at only $3CUC.

Next door is the **Galeria de Arte** (June–Sept Mon–Sat 10am–5pm; Oct–May Mon–Sat 1–7pm), where all the pieces, ranging from masks and plates to paintings and pottery, are done by local artists. Less ambiguous about its financial aspirations but still in the business of *artesanía* is **La Vigía**, a couple of doors down at the end of the row, whose stock is made up mostly of jewellery and small wooden carvings. The opposite side of the plaza is occupied by a still functioning ornate but austere Neoclassical fire station. It's worth peering inside to see the old fire engine from 1888, which is still in perfect working order.

Slavery on the sugar plantations in the nineteenth century

The **sugar industry** in Cuba, and indeed all over the Caribbean, was up until the end of the nineteenth century inextricably linked to the slave trade and **slavery** itself. It's been estimated that at least a third of the slaves in Cuba during the nineteenth century worked on sugar plantations, and the fact that slaves were the largest single investment made by all plantation owners is testament to the vital role slave labour played in Cuba's biggest industry. Although never very good, working conditions were considerably worse on the massive sugar estates than for slaves on the smaller tobacco or coffee plantations. Death from overwork was not uncommon as, unlike tobacco and coffee, levels of production were directly linked to the intensity of the labour, and plantation owners demanded the maximum possible output from their workforce. The six months of harvest were by far the most gruelling period of the year, when plantation slaves often slept for no more than four hours a day, rising as early as 2am. They were divided into gangs and those sent to cut cane in the fields might be working there for sixteen hours before they could take a significant break. A small proportion would work in the mill grinding the cane and boiling the sugar-cane juice. Accidents in the mills were frequent and punishments were harsh; it was not unknown for slaves to be left in the stocks – which took various forms but usually involved the head, hands and feet locked into the same flat wooden board – for days at a time.

Slaves were most often housed in communal barrack buildings, which replaced the collections of huts used in the eighteenth century, subdivided into cramped cells, with the men, who made up about two-thirds of the slave workforce, separated off from the women. This was considered a safer way of containing them as there were fewer doors through which it was possible to escape.

Teatro Sauto

On the north side of Calle 85, and facing the ceremonious-looking pink 1826 court building known as the Palacio de Justicia, is the august **Teatro Sauto** (℡45/24-2721), one of the city's best-preserved historic monuments and the country's most prestigious theatre buildings. Its Neoclassical architecture has lost none of its grandeur, but the absence of detail and ornamentation on the dignified exterior means that it falls short of real magnificence, from the outside at least. The highly decorative interior, however, features a painted ceiling depicting the muses of Greek mythology in the main hall and a three-tier auditorium that's atmospheric enough to make an attendance at one of its performances a priority while in Matanzas. The monthly programmes are usually quite varied as the theatre hosts everything from ballet to comedy acts. It's worth making enquiries a few days in advance, as shows often play no more than two or three times. You can also tour the theatre outside of performance times, but to do so you must either join an organized excursion from Varadero or speak to the staff at the Infotur information office on Parque de la Libertad who can make arrangements for you.

Museo Provincial

Facing the plaza just north from the Teatro Sauto is the orderly **Museo Provincial** (℡45/24-2193 & 24-3464; Tues–Sat 9.30am–noon & 1–5pm, Sun 9.30am–noon; $2CUC), with a varied collection that charts the political and social history of the province. Its chronological layout – a rarity in Cuban history museums – helps to create a succinct overview of the last two hundred years in Matanzas. The ground floor features early plans and pictures of the city, including a fantastic, large-scale drawing dating from 1848. Alongside these are a number of displays depicting the living and working conditions of slaves on the sugar plantations and in the mills (see box, opposite). The centrepiece is a large wooden *cepo*, the leg clamps employed in the punishment of slaves. On the second floor, highlights include a 1934 copy of *Bandera Roja*, one of the Cuban Communist Party's original newspapers, and the mangled remains of a piece of *La Coubre*, a Franco-Belgian ship carrying arms for the revolutionary government that was blown up in Havana harbour by the United States in March 1960.

The Ermita de Monserrate and Parque René Fraga

Tucked away atop a hill emerging from the residential neighbourhood in the northwestern corner of the city is the **Ermita de Monserrate**, a recently renovated church and a peaceful spot where you can enjoy some of the best views in town, with the city and bay on one side and a fantastic perspective on the magnificent Yumurí Valley on the other. Perched on a large flat platform at the top of a steep slope, the humble and diminutive Ermita was brought back from disrepair and abandonment in 2006, having been originally built between 1872 and 1875 by colonists from Catalonia and the Balearic Islands. The renovations are part of a larger project to create a more tangible visitor attraction out of the hilltop, with a snack bar and cliff-edge café, great views of the valley and the older *Restaurante Monserrate* (see p.297) given a makeover.

On the western edge of the city centre is the **Parque René Fraga**, a concrete dominated city park with a baseball diamond, basketball court and dusty running track. Lively in the evenings the park is not particularly picturesque but there are good views back down to the bay and it's a nice escape from the narrow streets of the centre.

Versalles

Over the Puente de la Concordia, which spans the Río Yumurí about three blocks north from the Plaza de la Vigía, is the almost exclusively residential **Versalles** district – though technically the name refers only to the most central of the neighbourhoods on the north side of the river. There's very little of any interest, but if you're absolutely determined to see all there is to see, a visit to the abandoned **Iglesia de San Pedro Apóstol**, a short way up the hill at calles 266 and 57, provides a break in the suburban landscape. The shrubs growing from one of the bell towers are testament to its ruined state, the locked gates preventing any closer inspection. It's a pity, as the architecture rivals that of the cathedral, the Islamic-style tower in the centre making it look more prestigious than its location would suggest. Walk a little further up the hill for some good views across the bay and into the city centre.

Castillo de San Severino

The only attraction north of the Río Yumurí worth a look is the **Castillo de San Severino**, a mid-eighteenth-century fort in an industrial zone on the north face of the bay. To get there from the centre, take the Vía Blanca along the coastline through Versalles and look for the right-hand turn once the road starts heading away from the bay; the fort is several hundred metres beyond this turn-off. It houses an unfinished museum, the **Museo de la Ruta de los Esclavos** (☎45/28-3259; Tues–Sat 9am–4pm, Sun 9am–1pm;

△ View from the Ermita de Monserrate

$2CUC or $3CUC with a guide), but the main draw is the fort itself, in considerable disrepair but still impressively intact. The original construction was completed in 1734 and is based around a wide open central square and surrounded by a now-empty moat. Its imposing, thick stone walls and broad ramparts, where three cannon still stand, actually occupy an area larger than that of the Castillo de la Real Fuerza in Havana. The principal structure in the city's colonial defence system, the fort once guarded Matanzas from pirates intent on plundering the substantial wealth of the city. It functioned as a prison in the latter part of the nineteenth century but stood derelict thereafter, though hearsay has it that right up until the late 1970s political prisoners of the revolutionary regime were locked up inside.

The central theme of the **museum**, the slave trade, reflects the fort's one-time use as a storage unit for slaves unloaded from boats on the coast below, many of them destined for nearby sugar plantations. The somewhat cobbled-together exhibits, which include handmade figures representing some of the Afro-Cuban *orishas*, or deities, currently do little justice to this big subject.

Eating

The lack of decent options for **eating out** in Matanzas is another reflection of its long fall from grace. While the state-run establishments are almost all either fast-food joints for passing tourists or run-down and outdated peso restaurants, the threat of local enterprise steering trade away from these uninspiring eateries has been stamped out by the government's banning of *paladares*. Local law does, however, allow privately run eateries as long as there are no tables and chairs, effectively forcing would-be *paladar* owners to run takeaway services. For ice cream, the local branch of Coppelia is at Calle 272 esq. 131, over the road from the bus station. Self-caterers would do well to visit the **Plaza del Mercado** next to the river at the Puente Sanchez Figueras. As well as a source of fruit, vegetables and meat this is a good place for peso-priced snacks. Saturdays are always very lively.

Café Atenas Calle 272 e/ 83 y 85, Plaza de la Vigía. It's a sad reflection on a city when a soulless *cafétería* like this is the most polished eatery around. Offers rudimentary pizzas and pasta and slightly better Cuban food, with nothing priced higher than $5CUC. One of the few places where you can eat after 10pm (it's open until midnight).

La Concha Playa El Tenis. A down-to-earth, open-air, lunchtime-only peso restaurant right near the city's unimpressive main beach where you can wipe out your hunger for no more than 25 pesos. There are just three main dishes: ham, fried chicken or smoked pork loin.

En Familia 2 de Mayo esq. 91 (Río). A fast-food station, on a patio in the shell of a semi-ruined building, serving pizza, burgers, fried chicken and ice cream, Daily 10am–11.30pm.

Monserrate next to the Ermita de Monserrate. Standard creole cooking in the best-located restaurant in the city: it's located in an open-sided building with great views of the bay. Prices are in national pesos, making it good value. Daily noon–10.45pm.

Ruinas de Matasiete Vía Blanca, a block south of the Río San Juan. A touristy snack bar in the ruins of a colonial sugar warehouse where you can have a cheap meal based on pork, chicken or fish, or something lighter such as a tortilla or a sandwich.

Venecia Calle 85 e/ 286 y 288. One of the town's few functioning and well-kept restaurants, serving fairly crude pizzas and pastas. Prices are in national pesos. Daily noon–10pm.

La Vigía Calle 272 esq. 85, Plaza de la Vigía. This burger joint, with its wooden floor, high ceiling fans and gallery of pictures, has more character but fewer choices than its neighbour, *Café Atenas*. Offers ten different burgers for less than $2CUC each. Daily 10am–10pm.

Drinking, nightlife and entertainment

The centre of Matanzas, especially during the week, is remarkably lifeless at night, and the only place where there is any sense of anything going on is at the Parque de la Libertad, where locals come out every evening to shoot the breeze. Outside the centre there are some isolated pockets of action, but you could pass most of the venues without knowing it since they are predominantly small, low-key affairs. The *Cafetería Velasco*, at Contreras no.28803 on the Parque de la

Libertad, is your best bet in Matanzas for a **drink** (being the one most likely to be open late), while *Café Atenas* and the *Ruinas de Matasiete* are as much drinking as they are eating venues.

Just a short bus or taxi ride beyond the Matanzas city limits is the most spectacular night-time venue in the province: the *Tropicana* cabaret (see p.301). In the city itself most of the **nightlife** is in the southern part of town, on or within sight of the Vía Blanca, but the venues are few and far between.

Having earned the moniker "Athens of Cuba" for the many renowned artists and intellectuals it has produced, particularly during the nineteenth century, present-day Matanzas seems to lag behind its reputation somewhat. A reminder of its past glory, and the centrepiece in the city's contemporary cultural life, is the **Teatro Sauto** (see p.294), which features a performance of some kind almost every night. National theatre groups and ballet companies play here, though local productions are just as prevalent. Contact the theatre directly for information on its matinee and evening performances; the entrance fee for non-Cubans is usually $5CUC. When it finally reopens, the Sala de Conciertos José White (☎45/26-0153), on the Contreras side of the Parque de la Libertad, will host live music

A few doors away, on the corner of Contreras and Calle 288, the Teatro Velasco (☎45/29-3125) shows Cuban and American **films**. National-league **baseball games** are played weekly from October to April at the Estadio Victoria de Girón (☎45/24-3881), twenty minutes' walk from Parque de la Libertad.

Live music venues and nightspots

Bar El Jaguey *Ruinas de Matasiete*. Amid humble ruins is a tiny little bar, a bunch of plastic tables and chairs and a small stage where live musical performances take place on an irregular basis. Mon–Fri 9pm–1am, Sat & Sun 10pm–2am.

Casa de la Cultura Calle 272 no.11916 esq. 121 (Mercedes) ☎45/29-2709. Rarely visited by foreigners, this is more a local community centre than anything else. At weekends there is sometimes live music and dance or a disco. Free. Closed Mon.

Discoteca La Salsa Vía Blanca A popular venue in this part of town and one of the marginally more spruced-up venues.

Discoteca Libertad Parque de la Libertad. A cheesy but very popular budget nightclub aimed at

couples. Tues–Sun 9pm–2am; $45CUP.

Las Palmas Calle 254 esq. General Betancourt ☎45/25-3252. Live Cuban music is performed under the stars, in the courtyard of a large mansion. This is the most professionally packaged night out in Matanzas, aimed predominantly at tourists. No shorts or sleeveless tops. Sun & Mon 10am–10pm, Tues–Thurs noon–midnight, Fri & Sat noon–2am; $1CUC.

El Pescadito Calle 272 e/ 115 y 117 ☎45/29-2258. This unpretentious venue, which stages small-scale cabarets, is a local favourite. Wed–Sun 9pm–2am.

Viaducto between Vía Blanca and General Betancourt. A wide-open space with a *cafétería* and a stage, which attracts a large crowd most weekends when it becomes the liveliest spot in the city. For details of performances, visit the venue during the day and speak to the *cafétería* staff.

Listings

Banks and money For foreign currency and credit-card transactions, go to Banco Financiero Internacional at Medio esq. 2 de Mayo or Banco de Crédito y Comercio e/ 288 y 282.
Internet See Telephone.
Left luggage At the interprovincial bus station ($2CUC per day).

Legal There is a branch of the Consultoría Juridica Internacional at Calle 282 e/ Medio y Río.
Library Biblioteca Gener y Del Monte, on the Parque de la Libertad, carries few recent titles likely to be of much interest to foreign visitors, but has one or two old English-language novels.

Medical The relatively new and well-equipped hospital Comandante Faustino Pérez Hernández is located on the Carretera Central about 1km from the city (☎ 52/25-3426 & 25-3427, ✉ hospital@atenas.inf.cu).

Photography Photoservice, Medio no.28614 esq. 288.

Post office Main branch at Medio e/ 288 y 290. Next door there's a DHL and EMS centre.

Shopping Artex has shops in its Complejo Cultural on General Betancourt and at Medio e/ 288 y 290, selling maps of the city, CDs and various artistic and touristic bits and pieces. The best-stocked supermarkets are in the Atenas de Cuba department store at Calle 286 esq. 83 and at the Mercado San Luis, out from the centre on Calle 298 e/ 119 y 121. La Vigía on the Plaza de la Vigía is the best place for cigars, rum and T-shirts.

Taxis Ring ☎ 45/24-4350. Alternatively, should there be no local taxis available, you can call a taxi to come from the Juan Gualberto Gómez Airport on ☎ 45/61-2133 & 61-3066.

Telephone There is an ETECSA Telepunto in Matanzas at Calle 282 esq. Milanes (daily 8.30am–9.30pm) with ten phone cabins and several Internet terminals. For after-hours calls, there's a payphone in *Cafetería Velasco*, open around the clock.

Travel agents Campismo Popular, Medio e/ 290 y 292 ☎ 45/24-3951.

Around Matanzas

The sights around Matanzas are more appealing than the city itself and reason enough to spend a few days in the area. Getting from the centre of Matanzas to any of the sights covered below shouldn't take more than twenty minutes in a car, while public transport is also a viable option. The **Cuevas de Bellamar** make for the quickest day-trip and have become a classic tour for groups visiting the area from Varadero. Not as visitor-friendly but arguably more stunning is the **Yumurí Valley**, a fantastic showcase of Cuban plantlife in a sublime and peaceful landscape. Last and probably least in the day-trip pecking order is the **Río Canímar**, where you can combine a boat trip with spending the night or just having a meal at the nearby *Hotel Canimao*. There is a very good reason, however, to come here after dark: the prodigious **Tropicana** cabaret, located right next to the hotel and grander than any other nightlife venue in Varadero.

Las Cuevas de Bellamar

In 1897 Samuel Hazard, an American writer and traveller, declared that anybody who hasn't seen **Las Cuevas de Bellamar** hasn't seen Cuba. Though the cave system to which he referred, just beyond the southeastern outskirts of Matanzas, does not really live up to such billing, if you're in the area for a day or two you should make time for it. The easiest way to get up here, if you don't have your own transport, is to catch the local Omnibus Yumurí from the Parque de la Libertad in the city (see p.292). You can also catch a private taxi from the bus station in Matanzas, which shouldn't cost more than $3CUC. Alternatively, you can book a day-trip from Varadero through any of the travel agents there (see p.263); Cubanacán, for example, offer a four-hour trip which takes in the caves and a tour of Matanzas for $25CUC. Guided tours (daily 9am–6pm; ☎ 45/25-3538 & 25-3551; $5CUC, $2CUC to take pictures) of the caves set off once every hour, usually timed to begin with the arrival of tour groups. While it's possible to simply turn up and join a party, that gives you no guarantee of an English-speaking guide.

One of Cuba's longest-standing tourist attractions, the caves were first happened upon in 1861 – although there is some dispute over whether credit should go to a slave working in a limestone pit or a shepherd looking for his lost sheep – and today they attract coachloads of holidaymakers from Varadero.

A small complex called Finca La Alcancía, which includes a **restaurant** serving basic traditional chicken and pork dishes (daily noon–8.30pm), as well as a shop and children's playground, has been built around the entrance to the caves. The most awe-inspiring sight is the first, huge gallery, abundant in stalagmites and stalactites. However, this does nothing to spoil the excitement of descending over 30m along 750m of narrowing and widening underground corridors and caverns lined with crystal formations on the walls and ceiling. Your attention is directed to images which have formed naturally in the rock and you're invited to drink at the unimpressive-looking Fountain of Youth and the Fountain of Love, which are supposed to improve your chances of lasting longer in both. Almost inevitably, the tour turns back on itself sooner than expected.

The Yumurí Valley

Hidden from view directly behind the hills that skirt the northern edges of Matanzas, the **Yumurí Valley** is the provincial capital's giant back garden, stretching westwards from the city into Havana province. Out of sight until you reach the edge of the valley itself, it's one of the most spectacular landscapes in the country, and it comes as quite a surprise to find it so close to the grimy city streets. There's a new scene around every corner, as the landscape changes from rolling pastures to fields of palm trees, and small forests merge into cultivated plots of banana, maize, tobacco and other crops.

The valley has remained relatively untouched by tourism, with its tiny villages few and far between. Though Yumurí Valley draws much of its appeal from being so unspoilt, this also means that there's no obvious way to explore it independently. Several minor roads allow you to cut through the centre of the landscape but you may as well just get off at any one of the stations on the Hershey train line and wander about.

For a more structured approach, head for the **Rancho Gaviota**, the only tourist-oriented stop in the valley, where you can eat a hearty Cuban meal and go horse riding. For the most breathtaking views of the valley, however, make your way to the bridge marking the Havana–Matanzas provincial border, the **Puente Bacunayagua**, 20km northwest along the Vía Blanca from Matanzas. At 112m high, this is the tallest bridge in Cuba, spanning the border between Havana and Matanzas province. Up the hill from here is the viewpoint, **Mirador de Bacunayagua**, where a snack bar looks out to the coastline and from where a trail leads down to the sea, a thirty-minute walk away by the side of a river.

If you're driving from Matanzas, head for the Parque René Fraga, from where the road heading west out of town will take you directly into the valley. To get to the heart of the valley by public transport, take any train from the Hershey station in Matanzas (4 trains daily) and get off at Mena, the first stop on the line and no more than ten minutes from the city.

Río Canímar and around

Snaking its way around fields and woodlands on its journey to the coast, the **Río Canímar** meets the Bay of Matanzas 4km east of the city. Resembling the Amazon in stretches, with thick, jungle-like vegetation clasping its banks and swaying bends twisting out of sight, a trip up the Canímar is an easily accessible way to delve a little deeper inland and one of the most relaxing ways of experiencing the Cuban countryside around these parts. An impromptu visit will most likely leave you restricted to the shore, but a short stay at the *Hotel Canimao* (see opposite) combines well with one of the boat trips that leave from the nearby tourist centre, where you can head directly for information, though there is no tourist literature other than the odd promotional leaflet. A night or two spent at the hotel also puts you just a few steps away from the *Tropicana*, sister venue of the internationally renowned cabaret in Havana and one of the most stunning entertainment centres in the country. Alternatively, an organized excursion to the river from Varadero can be booked through Cubatur for around $50CUC per person, or you can visit on the action-packed Discover Tour (see box on p.262).

Centro Turístico Canímar and Hotel Canimao

The Cubamar-operated tourist centre, **Centro Turístico Canímar** (☎45/26-1516 & 25-3582, ⓦwww.cubamarviajes.cu), which also rents out snorkelling equipment and motor boats besides running the boat trips up the river, is located below the bridge that carries the Vía Blanca road over the Canímar. Expect to pay around $25CUC per person for the one-and-a-half-hour excursion, which usually leaves before midday and includes lunch and musical entertainment. The schedule is dependent on demand, however, and there are often days when the excursion doesn't run. There are various flooded **caves** along the river's borders and the opportunity to swim in one is generally on the itinerary. With the chance to explore beyond the riverbanks on horseback also included in most tours, the Río Canímar, along with the Yumurí Valley, is one of the only places on the northern side of the province where you can retreat from the man-made landscapes of the Varadero catchment area.

On the Matanzas side of the bridge which looms over the tourist centre, a few metres from the bridge itself, is the turn-off for the *Hotel Canimao* (☎45/26-1014, ⓕ25-3429, ⓔcomercial@canimao.co.cu; ❸). The hotel roosts high above the river, which coils itself halfway around the foot of the steep, tree-lined slopes dropping down from the borders of the hotel grounds. It's a relatively well-equipped complex with views of the river – the hotel organizes at least one upriver boat trip every week – and includes a cabaret building also used for discos at the weekends, when it attracts plenty of young Matanceros. Only twenty minutes by bus from Matanzas, it's a convenient alternative to staying in the city and a bargain compared to hotels of similar standard in Varadero, a twenty-minute drive in the other direction. Buses #16 and #17 run from the city to the bridge and back, every hour or so on a daily basis. You can pick up either bus outside the cathedral on Calle 83 and you should stay on until the end of the route just over the bridge. To drive here, simply follow the Vía Blanca from either Varadero or Matanzas and take the turn-off next to the bridge.

The spartan *El Marino* **restaurant** (daily noon–10pm; ☎45/26-1014 & 26-1483), at the entrance to the road leading up to the hotel, is less sophisticated than its bow-tied waiters would suggest but still offers a better choice of food than any Matanzas restaurants, with its fish, shrimp and lobster menu. Most main dishes are priced between $6CUC and $15CUC.

The Tropicana

Right next to the hotel is the Matanzas version of Havana's world-famous **cabaret nightclub**, *Tropicana* (switchboard ☎45/26-5380, reservations 26-5555; show nights are Thurs–Sat 8.30pm–2.30am, showtime 10pm). The huge outdoor auditorium is no less spectacular than the original, with lasers shot into the night sky during showtime, attracting partygoers from Varadero. The shows themselves are everything you would expect from such a renowned outfit, with troops of glittering and gaudy dancers and a stream of histrionic singers (the full cast consists of over one hundred singers and dancers) working through back-to-back sets of ballads, ear-busters and routines that include a number of classic Cuban musical styles, from romantic *bolero* to energetic *salsa* and the more traditional *son*. After the show there is a disco. Ticket prices range between $40CUC and $70CUC, depending on whether you choose to have a meal while you watch the show, whether you opt for transfers to and from your hotel and how close your table is to the stage, with only a complimentary drink included in the cheapest entrance price. To enjoy a full restaurant meal with the show itself, which usually lasts about an hour and a half, you'll need to ring and book it in advance.

Museo El Morrillo

Directly opposite the turning for the *Hotel Canimao* is a road sloping down to an isolated, simple two-storey building near the mouth of the river. This is the home of the **Museo El Morrillo** (Tues–Sun 9am–5pm; entrance $1CUC, guided tour $1CUC), which exhibits pre-Columbian and colonial-era artefacts as well as bits and pieces commemorating the life and death of Antonio Guiteras Holmes, a political activist in 1930s Cuba. Originally an eighteenth-century Spanish fort, the Castillo del Morrillo (as it is sometimes referred to in tourist literature) looks more like a villa, with its terracotta-tiled roof, beige paintwork and wooden shuttered windows. Only the two cannon facing out to sea suggest this place was once used to defend the settlement at Matanzas from pirates and other invaders.

The museum itself is somewhat threadbare, its pre-colonial collection consisting of little more than a miscellany of basic tools and fragments of clay pots as used by the Ciboney and Taíno peoples, while the colonial pieces amount to even less. The most interesting set of exhibits are those relating to Guiteras, who was killed in this very building, thus lending the place national monument status. Guiteras, plotting with his companion Carlos Aponte and a small group of revolutionaries to overthrow the Mendieta regime, had chosen El Morrillo as a hideout and point of departure by boat to Mexico, where they would plan their insurrection. They were intercepted by military troops before they could leave, however, and were shot down on May 8, 1935. The rowboat that transported the corpses of Guiteras and Aponte is on show, as well as the tomb containing their remains.

San Miguel de los Baños and Colón

The **provincial interior** of Matanzas, stuck between the two touristic poles of Varadero and the Zapata peninsula, is dominated by agriculture, with islands of banana and vegetable crops dotting the sugar-cane fields that flow south to the edge of the forest and swampland dominating the province's southern third. Dotted around this sparsely populated territory is the occasional stopoff that won't offer much besides the opportunity to rest for an hour or two.

Heading south from Varadero and the small town of Cárdenas leads into sugar-cane country, the land plastered with green forests of reedy grass pretty much all the way down to the Península de Zapata at the other end of the province. About 20km into this journey you'll hit the **Carretera Central**, the main road bisecting the province. Most people head right across and make a beeline for the peninsula, but there are a couple of worthwhile diversions off this national highway if you get the exploring itch: the towns of **San Miguel de los Baños** and **Colón**. Closer to Varadero and considerably more picturesque, San Miguel de los Baños was once famous for its *balneario*, which is now in a state of semi-ruin; the real appeal of the place is its natural setting, closely surrounded by forested hills and offering some fantastic views. Colón, on the other hand, is like any other small Cuban town, where the pace of life is soothingly slow and tourists are still something of a curiosity. With the Carretera Central running through its centre, Colón makes a handy place to take a roadtrip break and a taste of untainted Cuban life.

San Miguel de los Baños

Off the official tourist track and reachable only by car, **SAN MIGUEL DE LOS BAÑOS** is one of the province's lesser known treats, a cross between an Alpine village and a Wild West ghost town. Hidden away in its own cosy valley 25km southwest of Cárdenas, it's easy to miss; to get there, head east on the Carretera Central from Matanzas and take a right turn just before entering the small town of Coliseo. Situated 8km from the Carretera Central turn-off, this once opulent village has lost most of its wealth, with the wooden-panelled ranch-style houses and villas on the hillside amongst the few reminders of what San Miguel de los Baños once was.

However, these faded signs of success are part of the enchantment of a place which made its fortune during the first half of the twentieth century through the popularity of its health spa and hotel, the **Balneario San Miguel de los Baños**. Located near the centre of the village, this turreted, mansion-like hotel is now completely derelict, but you can still wander through its entrancingly overgrown gardens. At the rear of the building and spread around the garden, the redbrick wells and Romanesque baths built to accommodate the sulphurous springs are still more or less intact. The three wells are themselves only about 3m deep, with inset stone steps that would have allowed guests to descend into them to scoop up the medicinal waters. Each well was supplied from a different source and the supposed healing properties of the waters differed accordingly. However, drinking today from the shallow pools that you see slushing around in the wells would be more likely to make you vomit than cure you of any ailments. With the stone benches encircling the centre of the garden and the wall of shade provided by the old trees this is a pleasant spot for a picnic, the silence broken only by the sound of running water.

Five minutes' walk from the hotel through the centre of the village is a magnificently set public **swimming pool**, raised up on a small mound of land. Even if there's no water in the pool, which is quite possible given its sporadic maintenance, it's still worth stopping by just for the view of the fir-covered and

A history of sugar in Cuba

Despite the old Cuban saying that "*sin azúcar no hay país*" – without sugar there's no country – the crop is not native to the island, having been introduced by colonial leader Diego Velázquez in 1511. Also, though its humid tropical climate and fertile soils make the island ideal for the cultivation of sugar cane, which requires plenty of sun, wind and rain, sugar production in Cuba got off to a slow start. Within a couple of decades of Cuban colonization, Spain turned its attention instead to the vast quantities of gold and silver found in mainland South America, and the island was relegated to a stepping stone between the mother country and her vast American empire.

Following decades of declining population in Cuba, during which time sugar was produced almost entirely for local consumption, the construction of sugar refineries was authorized by Spain's king Philip II in 1595 as Europe began to develop its sweet tooth. However, while the English and French invested heavily and developed new techniques in sugar production elsewhere in the Caribbean, the Spanish failed to take notice and, during the next century and a half, the industry in Cuba remained relatively stagnant. While water-driven mills were increasing efficiency on islands like Jamaica and Santo Domingo, output in Cuba, where the mills were driven by plodding oxen or horses, remained comparatively low. Furthermore, Spain was slow to stake a claim in the African slave trade which, by the early eighteenth century, was dominated by the English. In the labour-intensive world of sugar production, the lack of a substantial and regular supply of slaves in Cuba was the single most important impediment to the development of the sugar trade up until 1762.

A combination of events coincided in the second half of the eighteenth century to make Cuba one of the world's three biggest sugar producers. Until 1762 Cuba had been forced to trade only with Spain, which imposed strict and stifling regulations on the export and import of goods to Cuban ports. However, in that year the English took control of Havana and during their short occupation opened up trade channels with the rest of the world, which at the same time opened the industry to the techno-logical advances being made in sugar production elsewhere. Subsequently, the number of slaves imported to Cuba almost doubled in the last two decades of the eighteenth century. Prior to 1791, neighbouring French-controlled Santo Domingo had been the dominant force in world sugar, producing an average of over 70,000 tons annually, compared to Cuba's 10,000 tons. Then, in that year, a slave revolt all but wiped out Santo Domingo's sugar industry, simultaneously causing sugar prices and the demand for Cuban sugar to rise, while many French sugar plantation owners relocated to Cuba. At the same time, economic growth and increasing population size in Europe, as well as a newly independent United States after 1783, meant an increase in the global demand for sugar. In the space of a few decades, the industry had been turned on its head.

As the nineteenth century got underway, sugar production increased dramatically after the refining process was mechanized, which included the introduction of steam engines, used to squeeze the juice from the cane, and, in the 1830s, the establish-ment of the first railways in Latin America and the Caribbean. Technological advances throughout the century saw Cuba's share of the world market more than double as

palm-dotted hills enclosing the village. There are a few tables and chairs overlooking the pool and a poorly stocked outdoor bar selling mostly rum for pesos, but it's enough to just take a seat and digest the captivating scenery.

Loma de Jacán

One of the more prominent sights near to town is **Loma de Jacán**, the highest peak in the province yet one of the most straightforward to reach,

sugar became the focus of the entire Cuban economy. Cattle ranches and tobacco plantations were converted to cane fields, while all the largest sugar mills were linked by rail to Havana. It was during this century that sugar profoundly affected Cuban society in general and, to a certain extent, helped shape the island's modern identity. With hundreds of thousands of slaves being shipped into Cuba, the island's racial mix came to resemble something like it is today. Equally significant, the economic and structural imbalances between east and west, which were to influence the outbreak of the Ten Years' War in 1868 and its successor in 1895, emerged as a result of the concentration of more and larger sugar mills in the west, closer to Havana. These Wars of Independence, which ended in 1898 after the US intervened in what became the Spanish-American War, weakened the Cuban sugar industry to the point of vulnerability, thus clearing the way for a foreign takeover, which is effectively what happened when the US established a stranglehold over the island.

Cuba began the twentieth century under indirect North American control, thanks to the Platt Amendment (see p.591), with the successful sugar industry amongst the major reasons why the US so desired a controlling stake in the island. The North Americans further modernized the production process, with huge factories known as *centrales* processing cane for a large number of different plantations. By 1959 there were 161 mills on the island, over half of them under foreign ownership, a fact that had not escaped the notice of Fidel Castro and his nationalist revolutionary followers. It was no surprise then that one of the first acts of the revolutionary government was, in 1960, to nationalize the entire sugar industry, and the *zafra* – sugar harvest – became the measuring stick by which the success of the revolutionary economy was measured. Trying to prove just what could be achieved under such a system, Castro declared that in 1970 the nation would harvest ten million tons of sugar. This desperately unrealistic aim was not met, and in the late 1970s the government made the first relatively successful attempt to diversify the economy and move away from the dependency on sugar. By the 1980s, the economy seemed to have shaken off the negative impact of its previous reliance on sugar production – it helped, of course, that Russia was paying artificially high prices for Cuban sugar all the while. Cuba's reliance on what was in effect a subsidy became apparent after the Soviet Bloc collapsed in 1989, taking with it over eighty percent of Cuba's trade and plunging the country into one of its worst economic crises of the century. The government sought once again to diversify the economy, as it had tried and failed to do in the past, and this time turned to tourism to put the country back on its feet, an industry which, with the Revolution, they had vehemently rejected.

Since the mid-1990s the Cuban tourist market has seen steady growth, but this has coincided with a sharp decline in the productivity of sugar. In 2002 a government plan to make sugar production more efficient meant almost half of Cuba's sugar mills were closed while the output of those that remained would, in theory, increase. It remains to be seen whether this, the biggest revamping of the sugar industry for decades, will be successful, but, with production targets set at just over 50 tonnes per hectare by 2007 and current levels hovering around 35 tonnes per hectare, it certainly looks like an uphill struggle.

thanks to a large set of concrete steps leading up it. From the swimming pool in the village you should be able to see the route to the foot of the steps, a short drive from the northern edge of town up a steep and potholed road. The 448 steps up the peak are marked by murals depicting the **Stations of the Cross**, and at the top is a shrine, whose concrete dome houses a spooky representation of the Crucifixion, the untouched overgrowth and the airy atmosphere contributing to the appropriate mood of contemplation. For years the shrine has attracted local pilgrims who leave flowers and coins at its base, though the real attraction here is the all-encompassing **view** of the valley and beyond.

Colón

Back on the Carretera Central, heading east through central Matanzas and its endless miles of sugar-cane fields, you'll pass through **Jovellanos**, one of the biggest towns hereabouts but with little to recommend it. Another 30km or so along, the road cuts straight through the centre of **COLÓN**, a classic colonial town and a better place to stop for some refreshment. There's nothing essential to see here, but the town's appeal is that it remains virtually untouched by tourism. A quick wander around the relatively wide streets, lined almost entirely by modest neocolonial columned houses, gives a sense of the subdued pace of Cuban life away from the big cities.

The only street of any interest besides the main street, Máximo Gómez, is Martí, where most of the shops and services are located. Martí leads south directly to the town square, the inviting **Parque Colón**, with a big, faded pink **cinema**, which is still functioning but mostly operates as a *sala de video*. In the centre of the square, guarded by four rather malnourished bronze lions, is a statue of the town's namesake Christopher Columbus (Cristóbal Colón), pointing eastwards to the route out of town.

Practicalities

There are two very basic and ugly **hotels** in town, both on Máximo Gómez and within three blocks of one another. The *Santiago Habana* does not accept foreigners, so the only option is the run-down *Gran Hotel Caridad* (ⓣ45/3-2959; ❶).

At the far eastern end of the town's main street, Máximo Gómez (what the Carretera Central is named in Colón), is *Cafeteria Piropo*. Although it's no more than a **bar** in the shade with a few tables and chairs, this forgettable roadside stopoff is, to be honest, more likely than anything else here to stop travellers from just driving straight through Colón.

Península de Zapata

The whole southern section of the province is taken up by the **Península de Zapata**, also known as the Ciénaga de Zapata, a large, flat **national park** covered by vast tracts of open swampland and contrastingly dense forests. The largest but the least populated of all Cuba's municipalities, the peninsula is predominantly wild and unspoilt, making it an ideal location for getting first-hand experience of Cuban animal life, including boars, mongoose and iguana. Its proximity to the migratory routes between the Americas makes it a birdwatcher's paradise as well, as do the endemic species that live here, amongst them the Zapata Rail and the Cuban Pygmy Owl. The peninsula also holds

some appeal as a sun-and-sand holiday destination, with over 30km of accessible Caribbean coastline and crystal-clear waters to rival Varadero, though the beaches here are quite poor.

As one of the most popular day-trips from Havana and Varadero, the peninsula has built up a set of relatively slick and conveniently packaged diversions. Just off the *autopista* on the peninsula's northern verge, the **Finca Fiesta Campesina** is a somewhat contrived but nonetheless delightful cross between a farm and a small zoo, with some of the region's most memorable native wildlife kept in captivity here. Further in, about halfway down to the coast, **Boca de Guamá** draws the largest number of bus parties with its **crocodile farm**, restaurants and pottery workshop. This is also the point of departure for the boat trip to **Guamá**, a convincingly reconstructed Taíno Indian village on the edge of a huge lake, much of it built over the water on stilts, and now a hotel resort. Further south, the **beaches** at the **Playa Girón** and **Playa Larga** resorts are nowhere near as spectacular as their northern counterpart, but the superior scuba diving on this side of the province helps to redress the balance. One dimension to the area unmatched by Varadero is its historical relevance, as it was here that the famous **Bay of Pigs** invasion took place in 1961. The invasion is commemorated in a museum at Playa Girón and along the roadside in a series of identical-looking grave-like monuments, each one representing a Cuban casualty of the conflict. There are a large number of *casas particulares* on the peninsula, predominantly in the tiny village of **Australia**, near to the Finca

Fiesta Campesina, and in the small crops of houses dispersed around Playa Larga and Playa Girón. Often unfriendly rivals, sun-and-sea holidays and ecotourism exist comfortably side by side here, with large hotel complexes offering all the usual beach-based holiday ingredients while also providing a base for treks into muddy forests and bird-spotting river trips. While there are enough ready-made tourist attractions to effortlessly fill a few days, you'll only make the most of a stay on the peninsula by combining these with the more active business of birdwatching, diving or trekking. In order to do so, you'll need to hire a **guide** and rent a car, as entrance is restricted to most of the protected wildlife zones, which are widespread and not explorable on foot. Although this does mean losing a degree of independence, the English-speaking guides, available through Cubanacán (see p.310), are specialists in the local flora and fauna, making the whole experience all the more rewarding.

Arrival, information and getting around

Whether arriving by car or bus, your point of entry is the **Entronque de Jagüey**, a junction where the *autopista*, which runs more or less along the

The Bay of Pigs

The triumph of the Cuban revolution was initially treated with caution rather than hostility by the US government, but tensions between the two countries developed quickly. As Castro's reforms became more radical, the US tried harder to thwart the process and in particular refused to accept the terms of the agrarian reform law, which dispossessed a number of American landowners. Castro attacked the US in his speeches, became increasingly friendly with the Soviet Union and in the latter half of 1960 expropriated all US property in Cuba. The Americans responded by cancelling Cuba's sugar quota and secretly authorizing the CIA to organize the training of Cuban exiles, who had fled the country following the rebel triumph, for a future invasion of Cuba.

On April 15, 1961, US planes disguised with Cuban markings and piloted by exiles bombed Cuban airfields but caused more panic than actual damage, although seven people were killed. The intention had been to incapacitate the small Cuban air force so that the invading troops would be free from aerial bombardment, but Castro had cannily moved most of the Cuban bombers away from the airfields and camouflaged them. Two days later Brigade 2506, as the exile invasion force was known, landed at Playa Girón. The brigade had been led to believe that the air attacks had been successful and were not prepared for what was in store. As soon as Castro learned of the precise location of the invasion he moved his base of operations to the sugar refinery of Central Australia (see p.311) and ordered both his air force and land militias to repel the advancing invaders.

The unexpected aerial attacks caused much damage and confusion; two freighters were destroyed and the rest of the fleet fled, leaving 1300 troops trapped on Playa Larga and Playa Girón. During the night of April 17–18 the Cuban government forces, which had been reinforced with armoured cars and tanks, renewed attacks on the brigade. The battle continued into the next day as the brigade became increasingly outnumbered by the advancing revolutionary army. Several B-26 bombers, two manned by US pilots, flew over to the Bay of Pigs from Nicaragua the next morning in an attempt to weaken the Cuban army and clear the way for the landing of supplies needed by the stranded brigade. Most of the bombers were shot down and the supplies never arrived. Castro's army was victorious, having captured 1180 prisoners who were eventually traded for medical and other supplies from the US. Other ways would have to be found to topple the Cuban leader (see box, p.310).

△ Cueva de los Peces, Península de Zapata

entire northern border of the peninsula, meets the **Carretera de la Ciénaga**, the only reliable road leading south into the park. This junction is marked by *La Finquita*, the snack bar and information centre, and is where you will be dropped off if arriving by Víazul bus. The only accommodation within walking distance of the junction is the *Batey Don Pedro* or the *casas particulares* in nearby Jaguey Grande, so you should be prepared to call a **taxi**: try Turistaxi on ☏45/91-4147 & 91-7219.

American assassination attempts on Fidel Castro

Even before the dramatic failure of the military offensive at the Bay of Pigs, the US had been planning less overt methods for removing Fidel Castro from power. Fabián Escalante, the former head of Cuban State Security, claims that between 1959 and 1963 over six hundred plots were hatched to kill the Cuban president. The plots became more devious and ludicrous as the US grew increasingly desperate to take out the communist leader. In 1960, during a visit which Castro was making to the UN, it was planned that he be given a cigar which would explode in his face. Back in Cuba, in 1963, Rolando Cubela, who had been a commander in the rebel army, was given a syringe disguised as a pen to be used in assassinating Castro. The Mafia also took a stab at killing Castro with their poison pill plot but got no further than their CIA counterparts did. Some of the more outlandish plots have included poisoning a diving suit, poisoning a cigar, leaving an explosive shell on a beach frequented by Castro and spraying LSD in a television studio in the hope of inducing an attack of uncontrollable laughter.

The best place to go for **information** when visiting the Península de Zapata is *La Finquita* (daily 8am–8pm; ☎45/91-3224, ⒺCUcomercial @peninsula.co.cu), a snack bar-cum-information centre by the side of the *autopista* at the junction with the main road into Zapata. It's run by Cubanacán (ⓌWwww.cubanacan.cu), the travel agent and tour operator responsible for most of the attractions and organized excursions on the peninsula; they also have *buros de turismo* in the lobbies of the *Hotel Playa Larga* (☎45/98-7294 & 98-7206) and *Hotel Playa Girón* (☎45/98-4110). The organization in charge of the more workmanlike function of protecting this national park is the Unidad de Area Protegidas, which works in conjunction with the Empresa Municipal de la Agricultura (EMA) who supply most of the guides used by Cubanacán for trekking, birdwatching and fishing trips. For information and arrangements relating specifically to these activities, ask at the EMA park office (☎45/98-7249), located in a pink-and-beige bungalow just before the fork in the main road at Playa Larga.

Public transport in this area is virtually nonexistent, and unless you're content to stick around one of the beach resorts, you'll need to rent a car or scooter. Both Havanautos (☎45/98-4123) and Transautos (☎45/98-4126) rent **cars**, starting at around $50CUC per day for a week, from Playa Girón, where you can also rent out bicycles. Both of the beachfront hotels rent out scooters, at an average rate of $15CUC for three hours. The hotels also run various excursions, which if utilized can reduce the need for transport of your own.

Driving into and around the peninsula is pretty simple, the Carretera de la Ciénaga offering very few opportunities for wrong turns as it cuts more or less straight down from the *autopista* to the top of the Bahía de Cochinos, the Bay of Pigs. Almost all the land west of the Carretera de la Ciénaga, well over half the peninsula, is officially protected territory and is open only to those with a guide in tow.

Finca Fiesta Campesina and around

After turning onto the Carretera de la Ciénaga from the *autopista*, almost immediately on the right you'll see the **Finca Fiesta Campesina** (daily 9am–6pm; $1CUC). Set up as a showcase of the Cuban countryside, this delightfully laid-out little ranch presents an idealized picture of rural life in Cuba but is no less worthwhile for it. It's best approached as a light-hearted introduction to traditional Cuban food, drink and crafts, and there's a good spread of activities and things to see. You can watch cigars being made by hand, sample a Cuban coffee or take a swig of raw-tasting *guarapo*, pure sugar-cane juice. Dotted around the beautifully landscaped gardens are small cages and enclosures containing various species of **local wildlife**, all of which can be found living wild on the peninsula. One of the most fascinating of these is the *manjuari*, an eerie-looking stick-like fish that's been around since the Jurassic period. There's an English-speaking guide available for no extra cost and for a peso you can take a short horse ride or even ride the ranch's own bull. A good viewpoint for admiring the whole complex is the stone-pillared *El Canelo*, a suitably laid-back patio **restaurant** serving reasonably priced fish, pork, chicken and beef dishes under a low roof in the shade. Note, though, that since the place is really organized around tourist groups, some of the organized activities, such as cockfighting, are unlikely to take place unless you happen to coincide with a group visit. This is most likely during July and August, when coachloads of tourists arrive from Havana and Varadero every two or three hours.

Less than a kilometre south of the *finca* is the pocket-sized village of **AUSTRALIA**, where a right turn onto the Carretera de la Ciénaga takes you into the peninsula. Continuing straight on about 100m past the turning, however, brings you to **Central Australia**. This is not, as you might expect, the heart of the village, but in fact a sugar refinery used by Fidel Castro in 1961 as a base of operations during the Bay of Pigs invasion. Despite its name, the **Museo de la Comandancia** (Mon–Sat 8am–5pm, Sun 8am–noon; $1CUC), in the building which Castro and his men occupied, is less a tribute to its purpose in the famous Cuban victory over the United States and more a survey of the whole area's broader history. Although the collection is a bit dated, there are some interesting photographs and documentation of life in Australia and the nearby town of Jaguey Grande in the early twentieth century, but it's disappointing to find so little information on the base itself. Natural history is also touched upon with a few stuffed local animals. Outside is an indistinguishable piece of an aircraft that was shot down during the invasion.

Practicalities

Billed as a chance to experience the lifestyle of a typical peasant family, 🍴 *Batey Don Pedro* (☎45/91-2825, or book through *La Finquita* ☎45/91-3224; ❷), next door to Finca Fiesta Campesina, is thankfully a far cry from the basic, sometimes squalid conditions in which a large number of Cuba's rural population actually live. That aside, this immaculately kept little cabin complex is the best bargain on the whole of the peninsula, consisting of ten simply and thoughtfully furnished, spacious wooden cabins joined by stone pathways running through closely cropped lawns. There are ceiling fans instead of full air conditioning, but this is in keeping with the overall homespun appeal. There's an on-site **restaurant**, but it only opens when there are large groups staying. However, in addition to *El Canelo* at Finca Fiesta Campesina, reasonable meals are served within walking distance at *La Finquita*, the snack bar and information centre at the turn-off for the peninsula; or, if you have a car, you can try *Pío Cuá* (daily noon–11.45pm; ☎45/91-3343 & 91-2377), a roadside restaurant serving traditional Cuban food 10km down the peninsula road.

Boca de Guamá and Guamá

Eighteen kilometres down the Carretera de la Ciénaga from the *autopista*, **Boca de Guamá** is a heavily visited roadside stop. Most people make straight for its headline attraction, the crocodile farm, but there is also a pottery workshop and, a short boat ride away, a replica Taíno village. Busloads of day-trippers spend an hour or two at this most touristy of the peninsula's attractions, to eat at one of the restaurants, make the brief tour of the complex and purchase mementoes from the ample supply of souvenir shops. Though it can seem rather fake, this efficiently run attraction does make a refreshing change from the half-hearted and underfunded museums and galleries that are all too often the norm in Cuba.

Boca, as it's referred to locally, is most famous for the **Criadero de Cocodrilos** (daily 9am–5pm; $5CUC), a crocodile-breeding farm that forms the centrepiece of the complex. The setting is pleasant enough, with a short path leading from the car park, over a pond, to the small swamp where the beasts are fenced in. The crocodiles themselves are more or less left alone and you may even have trouble spotting one on the short circuit around the swamp. However, if you keep your eyes peeled you should be able to catch the sinister glare of one or two gliding through the water. For a more dramatic encounter, it's best to visit during one of the twice-weekly feeding times, though unfortunately there is no regular timetable. To get an idea of when the next feeding session is scheduled, call the administration office on ☎45/91-5562 or 91-5662.

Established shortly after the 1959 revolution, the farm was set up as a conservation project in the interests of saving the then-endangered Cuban crocodile (*cocodrilo rhombifer*) and American crocodile (*cocodrilo acutus*) from extinction. Since then, these ideals seem to have become a little blurred: before arriving at the edge of the swamp, you are invited to first witness a mock capture of an exhausted-looking baby crocodile and then to eat one. At the *Croco Bar* crocodile meat – a delicacy rare enough for the government to pass laws declaring only tourists may eat it – is served in whole and half portions for $10CUC and $5CUC respectively, although chicken and fish also feature on the short menu.

The **Taller de Cerámica Guamá** (no fixed timetable, usually open daily 10am–2pm; free) is Boca's more run-of-the-mill attraction, a kind of pottery warehouse-cum-production line. A walk around the several workshops here offers a chance to witness the production process, which includes setting the moulds and baking them in large furnaces, behind the hundreds of pieces of pottery shelved throughout the building. As well as the tacky ornamental pieces there are replicas of Taíno cooking pots and the like. Disappointingly, there is nothing to show how the Taínos themselves would have gone about producing their pottery; staff are kept busy churning out five thousand pieces every month, all of which are for sale.

The largest **restaurant** at the complex, *La Boca*, is for pre-booked tour groups only, but the *Colibri* (daily noon–4pm) is basically a smaller version of the same and offers a good choice of moderately priced main dishes. If you arrive after 4pm food can still be ordered from the bar.

Guamá

Boca is the departure point for boats travelling to **Guamá**, the second part of the package usually offered to day-trippers stopping here, and an

Coastal Cuba

On an island blessed with kilometre upon kilometre of beckoning shoreline, you'll want to spend at least part of your trip soaking up rays on one or more of Cuba's three hundred beaches. Whether you're dipping your toes in the warm currents of the Atlantic, zoning out under the shade of an umbrella or hopping aboard a glass-bottom boat in the Florida Straits, it won't be long before you realize why Cuba's white-sand beaches and crystalline waters make it one of the top destinations in the Caribbean.

Beaches

From the rocky but picturesque coastline of Caleta Buena to the high sand dunes and wild grasses at Playa Prohibida, Cuba has everything a sun-and-sand worshipper could want.

In Havana province, on the island's northern rim, lively **Playas del Este** – comprising Playa Santa María del Mar, Playa Boca Ciega and Playa Guanabo – offers a quintessentially Cuban beach-going experience. Hugging the Atlantic coast, these three fine-sand beaches form a long, twisting ochre ribbon which vanishes in the summer beneath the crush of weekending Habaneros and tourists.

Unashamed luxury can be found in the resorts of Ciego de Ávila province. On **Cayo Coco**, shallow crystal waters lap the continuous

▲ The Varadero coastline

strips of silvery sand beaches at **Playa Larga** and **Playa Las Conchas**, while tangerine-coloured starfish make for good snorkelling at the golden-swathed **Playa Los Flamencos**. On the western tip of **Cayo Guillermo**, gorgeous **Playa Pilar** is a must for its limpid clear shallows and squeaky-clean beaches.

▶ Playa Santa María del Mar

Despite being part of a thriving tourist resort, the lively **Playa Guardalavaca**, on the island's northern coast, retains a charmingly homespun air. A shady boulevard of palms, tamarind and sea grape trees runs along the centre of the beach, the branches strung with hammocks and T-shirts for sale creating a youthful, vibrant feel. On the southern coast of Cuba, the **Playa de Ancón**, a narrow, five-kilometre finger of land, curls like a twisted root out into the placid waters of the Caribbean against a backdrop of rugged green mountains. The beach has a natural feel, with shrubs and trees creeping down to the shoreline, while there is more than enough fine-grained golden-beige sand to keep a small army of holidaymakers happy. And while it probably won't be your first choice for a beach excursion, the fruit-field-filled **Isla de la Juventud**, with its beautiful white-sand beach, is one of Cuba's best-kept secrets.

Vacationing in Varadero

Deservedly the most famous beach in Cuba, **Varadero** – which faces the Florida Straits and runs for 25km from one end of the Península de Hicacos almost to the other – is a golden carpet of fine sand bathed by placid emerald-green waters. With its postcard-perfect scenery, Varadero has come to represent Cuban tourism at its most developed – though some would point out that, despite its increasing number of four- and five-star hotels, the poor nightlife, entertainment and restaurant options outside of the hotels keep it from being a truly world-class holiday resort. Before the Revolution, this was one of the most renowned, thoroughly modern and hedonistic vacation spots in the Caribbean. Castro's hostility to tourism changed much of that, but things have been on the upswing since the government embraced tourism in the 1990s.

Because the peninsula rarely exceeds half a kilometre in width, the beach at Varadero is never more than a ten-minute walk away. What's more, Varadero is the best place in Cuba for watersports, with three marinas on the peninsula and several diving clubs set up to take advantage of the calm seas.

Watersports at resorts

In addition to diving and snorkelling, there are numerous other popular **watersports** to take part in here — Cuba's major resorts are well-equipped with facilities for everything from water-skiing and kayaking to parasailing and jet-skiing. Not every beachfront hotel is well catered for in this respect, however, and generally there is less chance of finding motorized equipment at resorts totalling just two or three hotels. If you're aching to go surfing, you might be in for a disappointment: while surfboards are rented out at a number of resorts, you're more likely to catch a cold than a wave at most of them.

Diving and snorkelling

With 5745km of coastline, an average water temperature of 24°C and a thirty-year break from the potentially damaging effects of the international tourist market, Cuba is a **scuba diving** paradise. There is a fantastic variety of dive sites all over the island; in addition to reefs there are numerous underwater caves and tunnels, and explorable wrecks are also common.

◀ Diving in the Caribbean Sea

The beach resort of Varadero boasts over thirty rewarding **dive sites** – including a 40-metre-long boat sunk during World War II that now provides shelter for a variety of fish. About 5km from Varadero, heading southwest along the Matanzas coastline, is a two-kilometre stretch of **coral reef** inhabited by a busy population of parrotfish, trumpetfish and basslets amongst many others. West of there, Caleta Buena is one of the best places in the area for **snorkelling** – you needn't go more than 150m out from the beach to enjoy a rich, coral-coated sea bed.

In Pinar del Río, on the island's western coast, the virgin, bay-protected waters of **María La Gorda** are optimal for diving — spectacularly calm and clear, and enhanced by a quick drop in depth. Sites feature an abundance of black coral remains from sunken Spanish galleons along with underwater caves and tunnels. Among the spectacular fish life you may encounter are barracuda, moray eels, snappers, lobsters and even whale sharks.

inventively designed resort covering a number of small islands that is intended to re-create the living conditions of the Taíno. A perfectly straight, fir tree-lined canal leads east from Boca to the **Laguna de Tesoro**, the largest natural lake in Cuba and named for the treasures thrown to its bottom by the local Taínos to prevent the Spanish getting them. During the crossing the thatched roofs of the *bohio* huts which make up the resort emerge into view. The first of Guamá's neatly spaced islets, where you'll be dropped off, is occupied by life-sized Taíno statues in photogenic poses, each representing an aspect of their culture. Cross the footbridge to reach the diminutive museum detailing Taíno life and featuring a few genuine artefacts. If the 45 minutes or so allotted here by tours isn't enough, you could stay the night in one of the 44 **cabins** of *Villa Guamá* (☎45/91-5551, ✉minturcienaga @enet.cu; ❹). Dotted around eleven of the twelve islets and joined by a network of bridges and paths, the resort combines the Taíno theme with a disco and swimming pool, neither of which adds up to much, as well as a restaurant in the largest of the huts. If you do stay the night, bear in mind there's not much to do, and besides taking small boats out on the lake ($2CUC per hour) there's a good chance you'll end up spending a lot of your time watching TV and swatting mosquitoes.

Passenger **boats** seating 35 people leave Boca for the village at 10am and noon every day; alternatively, you can cross in a five- or six-seat **motor boat** any time between 9am and 6.30pm. In either case, English-speaking guides are available and the round trip costs $10CUC per person.

Playa Larga, Playa Girón and around

Many visitors, once they reach the peninsula's coastline, rarely stray more than a stone's throw from the sea, and there is actually no need to go any further as virtually all the worthwhile stopoffs and distractions hereabouts line the seafront. The Carretera de la Ciénaga splits at the point where it reaches the Bay of Pigs. Unless accompanied by an official guide, you'll have to make your way down the east side of the bay where the hotel and beach resorts of **Playa Larga** and **Playa Girón** provide the focal points, based as they are around the only sandy sections of the otherwise rocky shore. There are, however, other places worth pulling up for. You can combine lunch with either a visit to a sunken cave, dense with fish, at the **Cueva de los Peces**, or a spot of sunbathing, albeit on grass or sunloungers, at **Punta Perdíz** or **Caleta Buena**. On the western side of the bay, in the protected **nature reserve** which occupies the most untouched part of this national park, are **Las Salinas** and **Santo Tomás** (see box, overleaf), two of the peninsula's best areas for birdwatching. To get to them you must take the right-hand fork at the top of the bay and pass a checkpoint just beyond the tiny village of Caletón, which you will only be able to do with a guide.

Information

As with the rest of the peninsula, the best place to go here for **information** on getting around and visiting both the protected wildlife zones and the man-made attractions around the coastal areas is Cubanacán-run *La Finquita* (☎45/91-3224) at the junction where the *autopista* meets the Carretera de la Ciénaga (see p.310). There are Cubanacán *buros de turismo* in the hotels *Playa Larga* and *Playa Girón*, but the staff at these tend to be more keyed into

Besides managing most of the attractions on the peninsula, Cubanacán (Ⓦ www.cubanacan.cu) also organizes less touristy trips into the heart of the nature reserve, offering tailor-made packages which can be spread over a number of days or weeks, or ready-made day-trips to specific areas of natural interest. They can supply specialist guides, some of whom speak English, for fishing, diving and especially birdwatching. The three excursions described below are to UNESCO-protected areas of the peninsula that can only be visited with a guide and which together provide a varied experience of what the area has to offer. The best place to arrange a trip is at *La Finquita*, at the entrance to the peninsula, though the *buros de turismo* in the hotels can also sometimes help. Alternatively, go directly to where the guides are based at EMA's Playa Larga office (☎ 45/98-7249). You will need your own car for these excursions, as Cubanacán cannot always supply transport. Havanautos and Transautos both have rental offices at Playa Girón.

The Río Hatiguanico

Hidden away in the woods on the northwestern edge of Zapata is the base camp for boat trips on the peninsula's widest river, the Hatiguanico. As the slow motorboats make their way down the tree-lined canal to the river, the abundance of birdlife becomes obvious as Zapata sparrows swoop across the water, Cuban green woodpeckers stare through the branches and a whole host of other birds flock over the untouched landscape. Before reaching the widest part of the river, the canal flows into a narrow, twisting corridor of water where you're brushed by leaning branches as the outboard motor churns up the river grass. After the river opens out into an Amazonian-style waterscape, it curves gracefully through the densely packed woodland. Trips last between one and two hours, cost $19CUC per person and usually include a packed lunch, a short hike into the woods, and a swim in one of the river alcoves. Fishing is also an option; $50CUC per person pays for a total of six hours including equipment.

Santo Tomás

Thirty kilometres west from the small village just before Playa Larga, along a dirt road through dense forest, Santo Tomás sits at the heart of the reserve. Beyond the scattered huts which make up the tiny community that lives here is a small, two-metre-wide tributary of the Hatiguanico. In winter it's dry enough to walk but during the wet season groups of four to six are punted quietly a few hundred metres down the hidden little waterway, brushing past the overhanging reeds. This is real swamp land and will suit the dedicated birdwatcher who doesn't mind getting dirty in the interests of listening and looking out in the perfect tranquillity for, amongst many others, the three endemic species in this part of the peninsula: the Zapata wren, Zapata sparrow and the Zapata rail. Trips cost $10CUC per person and vary considerably in length depending on your preferences.

Las Salinas

In stark contrast to the dense woodlands of Santo Tomás are the open saltwater wetlands around Las Salinas, the best place on the peninsula for observing migratory and aquatic birds. From the observation towers dotted along the track that cuts through the shallow waters you can see huge flocks of flamingoes socializing in the distance and solitary blue heron gliding over the shallow water, while blue-wing duck and many other species pop in and out of view from behind the scattered islets. Trips to Las Salinas cost $10CUC per person and usually last several hours but can go on longer if you arrange it with your guides.

touristy excursions and less well informed about the possibilities of exploring the nature reserve and the other dirty-shoes activities. You'll get more expert knowledge and information at the Empresa Municipal de la Agricultura (EMA) office (☎45/98-7249) right next to the hotel *Playa Larga*. This is the organization in charge of most of the expert guides used by Cubanacán for all the nature reserve expeditions.

Accommodation

This part of the peninsula is dominated by the two large **hotels**, which offer postal and money services as well as most of the restaurants around. There are also a decent number of *casas particulares* in this area, mostly concentrated in the small neighbourhood just down the road from Playa Girón and within walking distance of the beach. The houses at Playa Larga are even closer to the coast, one or two of them on the water's edge itself. The tax on renting rooms here is even higher than in Havana, and is reflected in the higher-than-average costs, currently $25CUC per room.

Hotels

Hotel Playa Girón ☎45/98-4110, ℱ98-4117, ℮recepcion@hpgiron.co.cu. The largest tourist complex on the peninsula, with most of its family-sized, fully furnished bungalows facing out to sea. There's a buffet restaurant serving unexciting food, a diving centre, a pool, tennis court, disco, car rental and all the usual services you'd expect from an international hotel, though the grounds are a little scrappy. ❻

Hotel Playa Larga ☎ & ℱ45/98-7294, 98-7206 & 98-7241, ℮recepcion@hplargac.co.cu. A reasonably comprehensive resort with comfortable, well-equipped bungalows stretching for a few hundred metres along the coastline and featuring a poor-quality restaurant, a swimming pool, tennis court and even a small soccer pitch. ❹

Casas particulares

Casa de Osnedy González Pita Caletón, Playa Larga ☎45/98-7133. Backing onto the seafront, this is one of the more presentable houses amongst a grouping of shacks off an inlet at the top of the bay. The bedroom, with two double beds, en-suite bathroom and a/c, looks out onto the water, just five metres away, and you're usually given the run of the house as the owners like to stay out of the way. Owner Osnedy is a qualified diving instructor. ❷

Hostal Osorio Playa Girón ☎45/98-4341. There are two clean and spacious rooms for rent in this compact bungalow on the main road just before the turning for the *Hotel Playa Girón*. The rooms share a bathroom and meals are served on the backyard patio. ❷

K S Abella Carretera de Cienfuegos, Playa Girón ☎45/98-4383 & 98-4260. The English-speaking owner of this proudly kept-up house, on the road at the eastern edge of the village at Playa Girón, used to work as a chef at the nearby hotel and offers buffet breakfasts and dinners. There are two single beds in the attractive little room-for-rent and a pleasant backyard with a grass lawn. ❷

Villa Morena Barrio Mario López, Playa Larga ☎45/99-7131. The twin room with a/c is pleasant enough and the house is full of sculpted wooden furniture; the lower rates make up for its back-street location. Driving down to the bay on the Carretera de la Ciénaga, 50m beyond the sign announcing Playa Larga, a right-hand turn leads down to a dirt track where another right turn leads up to the house. ❷

Playa Larga

Taking the main road east from the junction at the top of the bay will bring you almost immediately to **Playa Larga**, a resort area right on the beach with little more to offer than the facilities of the complex itself. The beach itself is about 100m long, with traces of seaweed on the shore and the grass encroaching onto the sand from behind. Nearby **diving** points can be explored by arrangement with the hotel's own *Club Octopus* diving centre (☎45/98-3224 & 98-7225), on a jut of land at the opposite end of the beach, beyond the large car park just before the hotel. There's a snack bar here, too.

Cueva de los Peces and Punta Perdíz

More or less midway between Playa Larga and Playa Girón, the roadside attraction of **Cueva de los Peces** (daily 9am–4pm; $1CUC, free if you eat at the restaurant), also known as **El Cenote**, beckons you to leave your car and investigate. At the bottom of a short track leading down from the road, a glassy-smooth natural saltwater pool emerges, oasis-like, against the backdrop of almost impenetrable woodlands. Enclosed by the scrub and no bigger than a family-sized swimming pool, it's the kind of place you wish you'd discovered solo and kept secret from the rest of the world. Despite the pool's proximity to the road it's perfectly tranquil and you're free to dive in and swim with the numerous species of fish living in the pool, many of which have been introduced since the natural population died out. The pool leads to a flooded cave system of mostly unexplored underwater halls and corridors, more than 70m deep and ideal for scuba diving, which can be arranged through the dive centres at either of the hotels. There's a restaurant here, one of the best in the area, with the mostly seafood main dishes at between $5CUC and $10CUC, split in two with a section right by the pool's edge and a more formal section set further back.

Another few kilometres further down towards Playa Girón, **Punta Perdíz** (entrance $1CUC) is another excuse for taking a roadside break, as obvious a place as any to stop, enjoy the sunbaked coastline and clamber down the rocky shore into the emerald window of water. Basically a scrap of grassy land jutting out into the sea, this spot has been altered very little from its natural, relatively featureless state. The glaringly man-made addition is the boat-themed **restaurant** where the menu includes seafood and crocodile and is quite pricey by Cuban standards. This place suffers a little because of

Scuba diving and fishing

The Península de Zapata is one of the best places in Cuba for cave **diving**, the waters here generally calmer than those around Varadero, from where most of the dive trips are organized – contact Cubanacán (☎45/91-3224, ⓔminturcienega@enet.cu). Scorpion fish, moray eels, groupers and barracuda are among the species you might see, while the coral life is extremely healthy, with an abundance of brightly coloured sponges, some giant gorgonians and a proliferation of sea fans. There are at least ten good dive sites spread along the eastern coast of the bay and beyond, right down to the more exposed waters around the *Hotel Playa Girón*. Most of the coral walls are no more than 40m offshore so dives take place from the shore itself, while there are also a number of easily accessible shipwrecks to explore. The principal cave dive on the peninsula is at El Cenote, known in tourist literature as the Cueva de los Peces. The limestone cave here, with its entrance surrounded by forest, is linked to the sea through an underground channel and is home to numerous tropical fish.

Once on the peninsula, the points of contact for ad hoc dives are one of the dive centres found at Playa Larga, Playa Girón or Caleta Buena. Club Octopus (☎45/98-3224 & 98-7225) at Playa Larga charges $25CUC for a single dive or $30CUC for a night dive, with an initiation class only $10CUC, while tank rental is $5CUC. Prices are similar at the other centres.

The marshes and rivers of Zapata are good areas for fly **fishing**. Las Salinas (see box p.314) is home to bonefish, permit and barracuda, while tarpon and snook can be found in the Río Hatiguanico. Fishing holidays can be arranged from abroad through specialist foreign travel agents that have secured fishing rights on the peninsula as well as elsewhere in Cuba (see "Basics", p.81).

its tour-group focus, with the attention mostly on getting coach parties fed and watered rather than serving quality food. Closer to the shore there are individual wooden sun shelters, and you can also rent **snorkelling** equipment ($3CUC/hr). The snorkelling isn't bad, but it's better down the road at Caleta Buena. There are also, a little bizarrely, board games for rent here, namely chess, chequers and dominoes.

Playa Girón and around

Following the coastal road, it's roughly another 10km from Punta Perdíz to **Playa Girón**, where the course of Cuba's destiny was battled out over 72 hours in April 1961 (see box, p.308). The **beach** here is more exposed than Playa Larga, and though it's blessed with the same transparent green waters, there is an unsightly three-hundred-metre-long concrete wave breaker which creates a huge pool of calm seawater but ruins the view out to sea. Although the hotel complex hogs the seafront here, non-guests are free to use the facilities as well as wander down through it to the beach. This is also the only place on the peninsula with a **car rental office**, with both Transautos (☎45/98-4114) and Havanautos (☎45/98-4123) represented.

The other main reason for stopping here is the **Museo Girón** (daily 9am–noon & 1–5pm; $2CUC), a two-room museum right next to the hotel that documents the events prior to and during the US-backed invasion. Outside the building is one of the fighter planes used to attack the advancing American ships. Inside, the era is successfully evoked through depictions of pre-revolution life, along with dramatic photographs of US sabotage and terrorism in Cuba leading up to the Bay of Pigs. The second room goes on to document the invasion itself, with papers outlining Castro's battle instructions and some incredible photography taken in the heat of battle. Various personal belongings and military equipment are laid out in front of the photographs along with, most poignantly, photographs of each of the Cuban casualties. To bring it all to life it's worth asking the staff if you can watch the museum's ten-minute documentary film, shot during the fighting.

Caleta Buena

Eight kilometres east from Playa Girón, the last stop along this side of the bay is **Caleta Buena** (entrance $3CUC; with buffet lunch $12CUC), a rocky but very picturesque stretch of coastline and one of the best places on the peninsula for snorkelling, appropriately equipped with its own **diving centre**. Based around the calm waters of a large sheltered inlet with flat rocky platforms jutting out into the sea, the unspoilt serenity here befits this most secluded of Zapata's coastal havens. It's a perfect place for lazing about on the beach, with red-tile-roof shelters on wooden stilts providing protection from the midday sun. The best way to spend time here is to go snorkelling or diving and take advantage of the fact that you needn't go more than 150m out from the beach to enjoy a coral-coated sea bed. A single dive costs $25CUC and renting snorkelling equipment a mere $3CUC. Diving initiation courses are available for $10 and should be arranged in advance through Cubanacán. There is also a **volleyball** net and **row boats** for rent ($3CUC per hour). There's generally nothing happening at Caleta Buena in the evenings – you're likely to find the place deserted after 5pm.

Of the two modest **eateries** here, *Rancho Benito* (daily 9am–4pm; ☎45/98-3224), a rustic open-air grill tucked away in the corner of the complex, is the better located and looks over a crystal-clear pool full of lively fish, but the decent food is all prepared in the same kitchen. Lobster, shrimp, frogs' legs and fish cocktail can be ordered at the tiny restaurant set further back from the shore.

Travel details

Astro buses

Cárdenas to: Jagüey Grande (1 daily; 2hr); Jovellanos (1 daily; 1hr); Matanzas (1 daily; 1hr 15min); Santa Clara (1 daily; 3hr).
Matanzas to: Camagüey (3 weekly; 9hr); Cienfuegos (1 daily; 5hr 30min); Havana (3 daily; 2hr 10min); Santa Clara (1 daily; 4hr); Santiago (1 daily; 15hr).
Varadero to: Havana (1 daily; 2hr 40min); Santa Clara (1 daily; 4hr); Santiago (1 daily; 13hr).

Víazul buses

Entronque de Jagüey, Península de Zapata to: Havana (2 daily; 2hr); Varadero (daily; 1hr 30min).
Varadero to: Entronque de Jagüey, Península de Zapata (daily; 1hr 30min); Havana (3 daily; 2hr 45min); Matanzas (1 daily; 45min); Trinidad (1 daily; 5hr 50min).
Matanzas to: Havana (3 daily; 2hr); Varadero (3 daily; 45min).

Trains

Cárdenas to: Colón (1 daily; 1hr 30min); Jovellanos (runs according to availability of fuel; 1hr).
Colón to: Cárdenas (1 daily; 1hr 30min); Havana (3 daily; 3hr); Holguín (1 daily; 12hr); Matanzas (1 daily; 1hr 30min); Sancti Spíritus (1 daily; 4hr).
Matanzas to: Colón (1 daily; 1hr 30min); Havana (1–3 daily; 2hr); Holguín (3 weekly); Jovellanos (1 daily; 50min); Sancti Spíritus (3 weekly; 6hr); Santiago (1 daily; 12hr).

Hershey trains

Matanzas to: Havana Casablanca (4 daily; 3hr).

4

Cienfuegos and Villa Clara

CHAPTER 4

Highlights

✳ **Casas particulares on La Punta** The exclusive housing on the narrow La Punta peninsula in Cienfuegos – one of the best locations for a night's stay on the island – includes several classy *casas particulares*. See p.326

✳ **Jardín Botánico de Cienfuegos** These flourishing botanical gardens have one of the country's most complete collections of tropical plants. See p.337

✳ **The Jagua ferry** The chug across the Jagua Bay in Cienfuegos is a great way to enjoy the slow, laid-back pace of local life whilst taking in views of the city and the far-off mountains. See p.338

✳ **Parque Vidal** The main square in Santa Clara is amongst the most vibrant in Cuba, particularly in the evenings at weekends when young and old converge on it. See p.345

✳ **Museo Memorial al Che** Santa Clara's most popular museum, devoted to its adopted son and revolutionary hero. See p.346

✳ **Las Parrandas** On Christmas Eve, the townsfolk of Remedios take to the streets for a festive, anarchic celebration. See p.357

✳ **The northern cays** The drive to these secluded islets alone, along a fifty-kilometre-long causeway skimming above clear waters, makes a trip here worthwhile. See p.359

△ Playa Santa María

Cienfuegos and Villa Clara

D
espite attracting an increasing number of tourists, the neighbouring provinces of Cienfuegos and Villa Clara still offer a taste of undiluted Cuban life, albeit at the subdued pace which characterizes so much of the country away from Havana. Capital of the eponymous province, **Cienfuegos** is one of Cuba's more attractive big cities, situated alongside a large enclosed bay and within easy day-trip distance of the province's other destinations. The nearby beach at **Rancho Luna** is a pleasant enough base for longer stays, while the most memorable of Cienfuegos's attractions is the **botanical gardens**, roughly a fifteen-kilometre drive from the city.

The province of **Villa Clara** sits at the top of Cienfuegos, along its northern border. Its capital city, **Santa Clara**, is dominated by more Cubans than tourists and enjoys status as the region's liveliest cultural hot-spot. You'll find an excellent range of accommodation here, a large student population and some of the best nightlife in provincial Cuba.

In the northeastern reaches of the province, almost 50km out to sea, are **Cayo Las Brujas** and **Cayo Santa María**, where a fantastically secluded yet fully equipped beach resort is beginning to rival the longer-established Cayo Coco resort, across the provincial border in Ciego de Ávila. In between the tourist centres of Santa Clara and here, about 10km inland from the northern coastline, **Remedios** is a tranquil, welcoming little town steeped in history and filled with *casas particulares*, while nearby **Caibarién** is a larger, more run-of-the-mill coastal town providing some pleasant accommodation for a fraction of the price you'd pay on the cays. More out of the way, **Lago Hanabanilla**, halfway between Santa Clara and Trinidad, provides relatively straightforward access into the Sierra del Escambray. Like Remedios, the lake is a magnet for tourists looking for a more low-key experience: less developed than other nature-based resorts in Cuba, it's nonetheless equipped with facilities for fishing, hiking and simple boat trips.

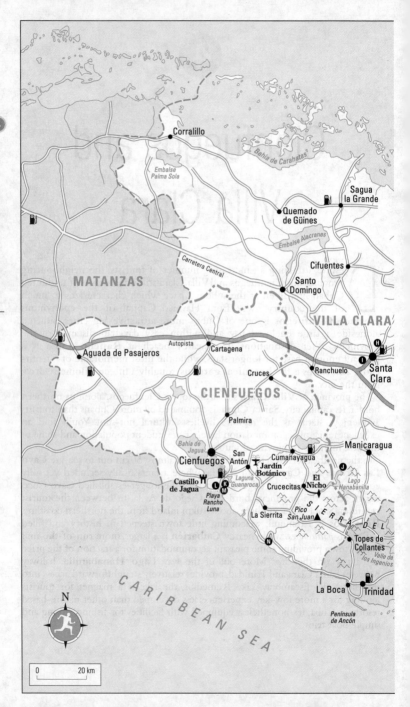

0   20 km

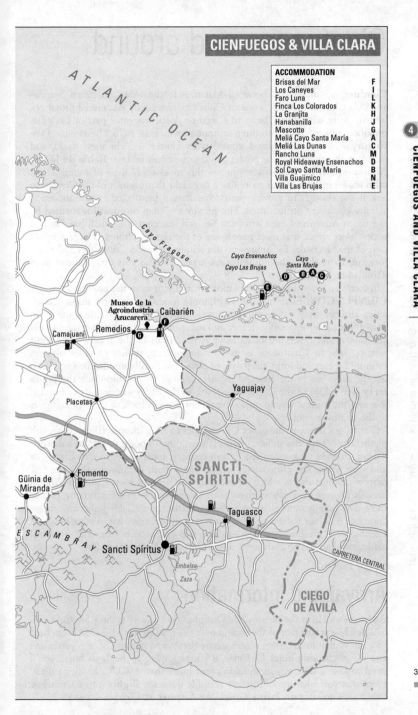

ACCOMMODATION

Brisas del Mar	F
Los Caneyes	I
Faro Luna	L
Finca Los Colorados	K
La Granjita	H
Hanabanilla	J
Mascotte	G
Meliá Cayo Santa María	A
Meliá Las Dunas	C
Rancho Luna	M
Royal Hideaway Ensenachos	D
Sol Cayo Santa María	B
Villa Guajimico	N
Villa Las Brujas	E

ATLANTIC OCEAN

Cayo Fragoso

Cayo Ensenachos
Cayo Las Brujas
Cayo
Santa María

Museo de la
Agroindustria
Azucarera

Caibarién

Camajuani
Remedios

Yaguajay

Placetas

SANCTI
SPÍRITUS

Güinia de
Miranda
Fomento

Taguasco

ESCAMBRAY

Sancti Spíritus

CARRETERA CENTRAL

Embalse
Zaza

CIEGO
DE ÁVILA

Cienfuegos and around

Cienfuegos, sandwiched between Matanzas to the west, and Sancti Spíritus and Villa Clara to the east, is one of Cuba's more recently established provinces, which, along with Villa Clara and Ciego de Ávila, was once part of Las Villas province, broken down into three separate provinces in 1975. This is one of the country's most industrialized zones, with clusters of chimney stacks and factories, and even a nuclear power plant, gathered around the **Bahía de Jagua**. Also known as the Bay of Cienfuegos, this rock-steady mass of water, whose calm waters make it appear more like a large lake than an inlet of the Caribbean Sea, is big enough to provide waterfront havens unaffected by the industrial activity elsewhere on its shores. The province's 70km of **coastline**, bathed by the warm currents of the Caribbean Sea and scattered with small beaches and rocky inlets, are all that most people see of the region. Though a large proportion of the Sierra del Escambray nestles within its borders, these forested peaks form no more than a backdrop for most people, who visit them instead from Trinidad or Santa Clara.

In fact, you are unlikely to stray more than 25km from the provincial capital, **CIENFUEGOS**. Established in 1819, more recently than most major Cuban cities, and the only city in the country founded by French settlers, this is an easy-going place, noticeably cleaner and more spacious than the average provincial capital and deserving of its label as the "Pearl of the South". The most alluring side to Cienfuegos is its bayside location, which provides pleasant offshore breezes and some sleepy views across the usually undisturbed water. To get the most out of the city and its surroundings you should catch the **Jagua ferry** (see p.338) to the fort at the mouth of the bay, a wonderfully unhurried journey and a great way to enjoy the fantastic views back to the city and over to the nearby mountains.

Cienfuegos is one of the easier Cuban cities to relax in, especially in the south of the city where the stylish, open-plan neighbourhoods, similar to suburban Miami, provide wide-open spaces and uninterrupted views to the south, east and west across the calm waters of the bay, a stark contrast to the crowded, narrow colonial streets which characterize the heart of most Cuban provincial capitals. Despite the city's relatively comprehensive tourist infrastructure, two or three days here is more than enough to exhaust the available sights and entertainment. As a base for seeing what the rest of the province has to offer, however, Cienfuegos is ideal, with several easy day-trip destinations – beaches, botanical gardens and an old Spanish fortress – within a 25-kilometre radius.

Arrival and information

All **buses** pull in at the Terminal de Omnibus on Calle 49 e/ 56 y 58 (☎43/51-5720), while **trains** stop at the station over the road (☎43/52-5495). From here you can walk into the town centre where there are a number of *casas particulares* and the enchanting hotel *La Unión*; if you're staying at the *Jagua* hotel, you'll need to take a **taxi**, which shouldn't cost more than $4CUC. In the unlikely event that you take one of the few available domestic **flights** into Cienfuegos, they touch down at the **Jaime González Airport** (☎43/55-1328 & 55-2267), several kilometres to the east, from where you'll have little choice but to call for a taxi (see below) to get into the city. Arriving by **car** from Trinidad, you'll enter the city on Ave. 5 de Septiembre, which connects up with the city grid four blocks east of Prado, Cienfuegos's main street, also known as Calle 37, and the road on which you'll arrive if you've driven from Havana or Varadero.

For **information**, head for one of the city's travel agents. The Cubatur office is at Prado no.5399 e/ Ave. 54 y Ave. 56 (Mon–Fri 9am–noon & 1–6pm, Sat 9am–noon; ☎43/55-1242, ⓔcubaturcfg@enet.cu), which organizes city tours and excursions into the mountains and to other attractions both within the province and beyond. Alternatively, Havanatur at Ave. 54 no.2906 e/ 29 y 31 (Mon–Fri 8.30am–noon & 1–4.30pm, Sat 8.30am–noon; ☎43/55-1393, ⓔhavanatur.cienfuegos@cimex.co.cu) also organizes trips, as does Cubanacán across the road at no.2903 (Mon–Fri 8.30am–5.30pm, Sat 8.30am–noon; ☎43/55-1680, ⓔcuba@viajes.cfg.cyt.cu), where the helpful staff supply maps and local information and can arrange scuba diving down at Rancho Luna (see p.337). All three agents can also sell you Víazul bus tickets.

For information on the cultural goings-on in the city, such as films, theatre performances and live music, an excellent resource is the state-sponsored website ⓦwww.azurina.cult.cu. With local listings in newspapers and travel agencies so low on the ground, this is by far the best source for such things.

Orientation and city transport

Finding your way around Cienfuegos couldn't be easier as the entire city is mapped out on a spacious grid system. Roads running north–south are known as *calles* and have odd numbers, while those running east–west are even-numbered *avenidas*. Almost everything of interest is located not far from the city's main road, the **Prado** (officially known as the Paseo del Prado or Calle 37), either in **Pueblo Nuevo**, the northern main town area, or in **Punta Gorda**, the city's southern section, jutting out towards the coast. If you stick to the area between the Prado and **Parque José Martí**, then you can conceivably get around exclusively on foot.

If you do decide to venture beyond this area, there are **buses** and **horse-drawn carriages** operating up and down the Prado all day. You shouldn't have to wait long for the latter which are supposed to take you anywhere along the line for a peso, but are as likely to ask for a convertible peso. Apart from the occasional bus from the station down to the beach at Playa Rancho Luna, travelling further afield, even within the city, means calling for a **taxi** – Turistaxi (☎43/55-1172 & 55-1700) have cars hanging around the *Jagua* hotel car park. At the foot of Calle 25 in Pueblo Nuevo is the waiting area for the **ferry** across the bay to the Castillo de Jagua (see p.338).

Accommodation

Unusually for a provincial town in Cuba, Cienfuegos has two excellent **hotels** right in the city centre that are aimed exclusively at the international market. There are also a number of cheaper **casas particulares**, mostly in between the bus station and Parque José Martí and along the length of the Prado, with some particularly comfortable options as you get down into Punta Gorda. There are also a few houses for rent along La Punta, the town's southernmost point, a narrow peninsula extending into the bay from Punta Gorda. Although it's a bit of a hike from the centre, this is the place to head for peace, quiet and beautiful surroundings.

Hotels

Jagua Prado no.1 e/ Ave. 0 y Ave. 2, Punta Gorda ℡ 43/55-1003, Ⓔ reservas@jagua.co.cu. This block building's interior is considerably more graceful than its exterior, but it nevertheless lacks any distinct character. Fortunately, it has a picturesque location at the foot of Punta Gorda, with views into town and across the bay, and all the amenities you'd expect from a large hotel, including two restaurants, a shop, a games room and a swimming pool. ❼

Palacio Azul Prado e/ Ave. 12 y Ave. 14, Punta Gorda ℡ 43/55-5828 & 29, Ⓦ www.Cubanacán.cu. This stately, well-presented mansion on the edge of the bay is the best-value hotel in the city. All rooms are large (some are huge) and well equipped, and a few have views of the bay. Its convenient location next to *Club Cienfuegos* means that nights here can be a bit noisy, however. The restaurant serves breakfast only. ❹

La Unión Calle 31 esq. 54 ℡ 43/55-1020, Ⓦ www.Cubanacán.cu. Easily the most appealing and stylish accommodation in Cienfuegos, this charming and luxurious 1869 hotel has patios done in glorious Spanish tiles, a sauna, a gym, a hot tub, an art gallery and a small, sparkling swimming pool ($5CUC for non-guests). The 49 rooms are equipped with satellite TV and spotless bathrooms and there's a roof-terrace bar overlooking the bay. ❼

Casas particulares

Casa Angel y Isabel Calle 35 no.24 e/ 0 y Litoral, La Punta ℡ 43/51-1519, Ⓔ atorralba@jagua.cfg .sld.cu. Magnificent but crumbling neocolonial house on the water's edge, complete with a colonnaded porch and fairy-tale turrets. The two double rooms, in a separate modern block out at the back with its own waterside patio and roof terrace, are fresh and clean, with a/c, fridge and private bathrooms. ❸

Casa de Isabel Martínez Cordero Ave. 52 no.4318 e/ 43 y 45 ℡ 43/51-8276, Ⓔ isapepe @cfg.rimed.cu. A neocolonial house about four blocks east of the Prado that has two large and smart bedrooms for rent, each with its own fridge and refurbished bathroom. The lovely terraced back garden features a functioning well, and the talkative and likeable owners have installed their own generator so that the house never suffers from blackouts. ❷

Casa de Jorge A. Piñeiro Vázquez Calle 41

no.1402 e/ 14 y 16, Punta Gorda ℡ 43/51-3808, Ⓔ casapineiro@cubanonet.com. Luxurious by Cuban standards, this airy bungalow is one of the most comfortable and spacious *casas particulares* in Cienfuegos. The two available bedrooms, both with a/c, have their own private bathrooms; the best room is in its own block upstairs and costs a justifiable $5CUC extra. There's a pleasant patio where meals are eaten, and an attractive garden. ❷

Casa de la Amistad Ave. 56 no.2927 e/ 29 y 31 ℡ 43/51-6143, Ⓔ casamistad @correosdecuba.cu. Though this first-floor flat is conveniently located just off the Parque José Martí and full of genuine colonial hallmarks, the best thing about a stay here is the chatty, lively, gregarious elderly owners. Armando will gladly talk revolutionary politics for hours whilst Leonor excels at playing the host, fixing cocktails at the bar or cooking her house speciality, chicken in cola. (Vegetarian meals are also a speciality.) The two rooms for rent are light and airy and a roof terrace has great views. ❷

Casa de Mery Ave. 6 no.3511 e/ 35 y Prado, Punta Gorda ℡ 43/51-8880, Ⓔ mery3509@yahoo .com. A top-notch, bright and orderly *casa particular* where guests can enjoy complete independence thanks to the private entrance to the separate block where the spacious rooms are situated. Room facilities, including TV, CD player, fridge and well-appointed en-suite bathroom, are excellent, whilst communal spaces include a lovely, leafy central patio and a great little roof terrace with views of the bay. ❷

Pension Bosch Ave. 54 no.3917 e/ 39 y 41 ℡ 43/52-5528, Ⓔ obeltrand@cementoscfg.com. A colonial building with a lamp-lit passageway that leads to two comfortable double rooms featuring a/ c and simple, attractive furnishings. The hosts are very friendly and sociable, and the bus station is nearby, ❷

Villa Lagarto Calle 35 no.4b e/ 0 y Litoral, La Punta ℡ /℻ 43/51-9966, Ⓔ villalagarto_16@yahoo.com. At the very end of La Punta, just at the entrance to the park, this top-notch, fantastically situated house is right on the water's edge and has its own tiny pier. There are two decent double rooms on the upstairs veranda, each with its own fridge, that benefit from plenty of natural light and the fresh breezes blowing in across the bay, and there's a small, saltwater swimming pool too. ❸

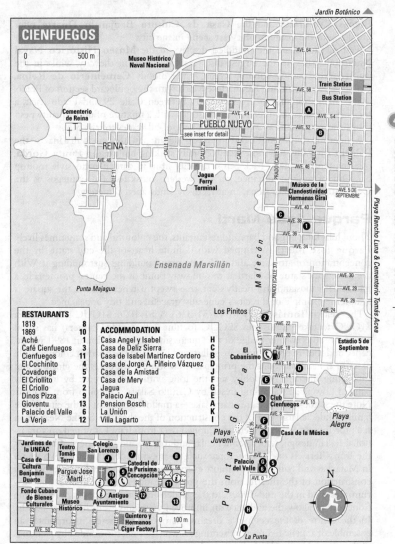

CIENFUEGOS

0   500 m

Museo Histórico
Naval Nacional

Jardín Botánico ▲

AVE. 64

Train Station

AVE. 58

Bus Station

AVE. 54

Ⓐ   AVE. 54

PUEBLO NUEVO
see inset for detail

AVE. 52

Ⓑ

Cementerio
de Reina

REINA

AVE. 46

AVE. 11

CALLE 19

CALLE 31

PRADO (CALLE 37)

CALLE 43

CALLE 49

AVE. 46

Jagua
Ferry
Terminal

Museo de la
Clandestinidad
Hermanas Giral

AVE. 5 DE
SEPTIEMBRE

AVE. 40

Ⓒ

AVE. 38   Ⓘ

AVE. 36

AVE. 34

Ensenada Marsillán

Malecón

AVE. 30

AVE. 28

AVE. 26

Punta Majagua

Los Pinitos

AVE. 24

Estadio 5 de
Septiembre

Ⓩ

AVE. 22

AVE. 20

AVE. 18

RESTAURANTS

1819	8
1869	10
Aché	1
Café Cienfuegos	3
Cienfuegos	11
El Cochinito	5
Covadonga	5
El Criollito	7
El Criollo	2
Dinos Pizza	9
Gioventu	13
Palacio del Valle	6
La Verja	12

ACCOMMODATION

Casa Angel y Isabel	H
Casa de Deliz Sierra	C
Casa de Isabel Martínez Cordero	B
Casa de Jorge A. Piñeiro Vázquez	D
Casa de la Amistad	J
Casa de Mery	F
Jagua	G
Palacio Azul	E
Pension Bosch	A
La Unión	K
Villa Lagarto	I

El
Cubanísimo

Calle 35

AVE. 16

AVE. 14

Ⓔ

AVE. 12

AVE. 10

Ⓒ

Club
Cienfuegos

Ⓕ

AVE. 8

AVE. 6

Ⓕ

Playa
Juvenil

Calle 35

AVE. 4

Casa de la Música

Playa
Alegre

Palacio
del Valle

Ⓖ Ⓔ

AVE. 2

AVE. 0

Ⓗ

Ⓘ

La Punta

N

Playa Rancho Luna & Cementerio Tomás Acea

Ⓐ

CIENFUEGOS AND VILLA CLARA | The City

4

Jardines de
la UNEAC

Teatro
Tomás
Terry

Colegio
San Lorenzo

AVE. 58

Ⓙ

Casa de
Cultura
Benjamin
Duarte

Parque Jose
Martí

Ⓖ

Catedral de
la Purísima
Concepción

Ⓗ

AVE. 56

Ⓘ

Ⓚ

CALLE 35

CALLE 37

Fondo Cubano
de Bienes
Culturales

Museo
Histórico

Ⓘ

Antiguo
Ayuntamiento

AVE. 54

Ⓘ

CALLE 33

Ⓛ

AVE. 52

Ⓜ

Quintero y
Hermanos
Cigar Factory

CALLE 25

CALLE 27

CALLE 29

CALLE 31

0   100 m

AVE. 50

The City

Sightseeing in Cienfuegos focuses on the picturesque **Parque José Martí**, the main square in the more built-up northern section of the city, **Pueblo Nuevo**. The illustrious interior of the **Teatro Tomás Terry**, a nineteenth-century theatre, is the most appealing place on the square, followed by the more modest **cathedral**. Elsewhere on the square, the pleasant but scanty **Museo Provincial** consists mostly of paintings and old furniture, while the **Fondo Cubano de**

Bienes Culturales and the Casa de Cultura Benjamín Duarte offer insights into the contemporary art scene in the city.

West of the square the muddled displays in the **Museo Histórico Naval Nacional** make up the largest historical collection in the city, while in the isolated, westernmost suburb, Reina, is the moody **Cementerio de Reina**. Going eastwards, linking Parque José Martí with the boulevard section of Prado, is the main shopping area, Avenida 54 between Calle 29 and Prado itself, a sociable pedestrianized section of the street with a mixture of poor-quality peso shops and restaurants as well as several jack-of-all-trades tourist shops.

Wandering south on Prado takes you down past the city's marina to the **Palacio de Valle**, the most architecturally striking building in **Punta Gorda**, offering pleasing views back across the city from its garden-patio-style rooftop bar. Out of walking distance, on the western outskirts of Cienfuegos, is the **Cementerio Tomás Acea**, an attractively landscaped cemetery.

Parque José Martí

Though lacking in good bars and restaurants, the colourful and sometimes lively **Parque José Martí** is stamped with definite heart-of-the-city status by the concentration of attractive and strikingly grand buildings surrounding it. With the trademark statue of Martí at the midway point of the central promenade, a traditional bandstand and neatly kept, tree-swept patches of lawn, the square is a supreme example of the city's generally graceful and tidy appearance.

The **Teatro Tomás Terry** (☎43/51-3361 & 51-1026; $1CUC plus an extra $1CUC to take photos and $2CUC to film with a video camera) has stood proudly on the northern edge of the square since its foundation in 1890. Music, dance and theatre productions are still staged here, and the Spanish colonial-style exterior is handsome, but the principal attraction for visitors is the glorious and captivating interior. The lobby sets the tone with walls covered by intricately painted flowers and a ceiling fresco by Camilo Salaya, a Filipino from Madrid. Note the statue of the theatre's namesake – a millionaire patron of the city, whose family funded a large part of the construction of the theatre – by the Neapolitan sculptor Tomaso Solari, which was shipped over from Italy. Fashioned on a traditional Italian design, with a semicircular auditorium and three tiers of balconies, the Tomás Terry is one of only three such theatres in Cuba, the other two found in Matanzas and Santa Clara. Almost everything here dates back to the original construction of the theatre, from the predominantly wooden 950-seat auditorium (restored in the mid-1960s), to the golden-framed stage sloping towards the front row to allow the audience an improved view, and even the ticket booths. In the centre of the ceiling, a dreamy Baroque-style fresco incorporates an ensemble of angelic figures representing Dawn (Aurora), surrounded by paintings of flowers and birds. **Guided tours** (daily 9am–6pm) of the theatre are included in the entrance charge, unless rehearsals are taking place, and can be arranged through the adjoining shop. For details of performances either call or check the blackboards at the entrance (see also p.334).

To the right of the theatre at Ave. 56 no.2505 e/ 25 y 27 is the **Centro Provincial de las Artes Plásticas** (Tues–Sat 8am–6pm, Sun 8am–noon; free) where the work of local artists, some of which is for sale, is nicely exhibited in three light, white rooms. Next door to the theatre, the **Colegio San Lorenzo**, the most classically Greco-Roman structure on the square, is now host to a high school. Across from the school on the square's northeastern corner, the stained glass and various fetching altars of the **Catedral de la Purísima Concepción** merit a look inside (Mon–Fri 7am–3pm,

Sat 7am–noon & 2–4pm, Sun 7am–noon; Mass daily 7.15am, Sun also 10am). Built in 1833, it had the bell tower added thirteen years later, and in 1903 cathedral status was granted. It retains much of its original spirit as a local church and receives as many resident worshippers as it does tourists, not something that can be said of all Cuban cathedrals. The only sign of ostentation in the elegantly simple structure is at the main altar where a statue of the Virgin Mary, with snakes at her feet, shelters under an ornately decorated blue-and-gold half-dome.

Opposite the Colegio San Lorenzo you will see an example of the square's more recent architecture, in the form of the dome-topped provincial government headquarters, the **Antiguo Ayuntamiento**. Though you won't get further than the lobby, this is nonetheless one of the few buildings in the city that's made it onto the front of a postcard. With four nine-metre-high columns flanking the grand entrance and the Neoclassical dome sitting centrally on a wide, balustraded block base, this 1929 construction, painted an upbeat light blue with the dome capped in burgundy, is a distinctly Caribbean variation on classical government architecture. Next door to the west is the **Museo Provincial** (Tues–Sat 10am–6pm, Sun 9am–1pm; $2CUC), housed in a blue balconied building founded in 1892 as a casino. Downstairs there are dry collections of rocks, shells and bones found throughout the province, as well as a couple of slightly more substantial displays of colonial-era furniture. A room for temporary art exhibitions, showcasing works by local, national and occasionally international artists, is the most engaging section on the ground floor. Upstairs there is another mishmash of exhibits, from firearms used in the revolutionary wars and a nineteenth-century iron to a bullet-making machine and a model of the square outside. More coherent is the room consisting of nineteenth- and early twentieth-century furniture, paintings and memorabilia which once belonged to the relatively rich and famous in Cienfuegos.

Also on this southern side of the square, a block west between calles 27 and 25, the **Fondo Cubano de Bienes Culturales** (Mon–Sat 9am–6.30pm, Sun 9am–1pm) sells paintings ranging from rather tacky cityscapes to finely executed abstracts, as well as carvings and a good set of poster prints; even if you don't intend to buy anything, this is the best place in town to see local arts and crafts. More absorbing than the artwork are the two rooms of antiques taken from houses in and around the city: most of the items date from the early part of the twentieth century, and everything is for sale. This makes for an enthrallingly motley collection, encompassing old cameras, lamps, ornaments, china sets, clocks and various other personal artefacts.

On the southwest corner of the square where Avenida 54 crosses Calle 25, the **Casa de Cultura Benjamín Duarte** (☎43/51-6584; daily 9am–6pm; $1CUC) feels a bit lifeless for a cultural centre but takes on a more interesting character after a guided tour, though these are generally done for tour groups only and requests for impromptu tours are sometimes met with blank looks. The tour sheds light on the history of the building itself and on Duarte, an artist, writer and political activist born in Cienfuegos in 1900. The centre's highpoint, both literally and figuratively, is at the top of the winding staircase in the attractive six-columned **watchtower** on the roof. From here you can survey the bay and the harbour, as well as getting a fantastic perspective on the square and Punta Gorda.

Just south of the square, at Calle 31 no.5006 e/ Ave. 50 y Ave. 52, is the diminutive **Quintero y Hermanos cigar factory**. The only way to visit it is on an organized excursion (see p.335).

Museo Histórico Naval Nacional and Cementerio de Reina

A few blocks northwest of Parque José Martí, in a pleasant grassy setting on a small peninsula on the edge of Pueblo Nuevo, the **Museo Histórico Naval Nacional** (Tues–Sat 10am–6pm, Sun 10am–1pm; $1CUC) contains a more eclectic mix of exhibits than its name suggests. The first section is devoted to the uprising of September 1957 (known as the Levantamiento de 5 de Septiembre), in which local rebels joined forces with Fidel Castro's M-26-7 Movement in a revolt that instigated an insurrectionary coup at the naval barracks, now the museum's buildings and grounds. The revolutionaries held the city for only a few hours before the dictator General Batista sent in some two thousand soldiers and crushed the rebellion in a battle that ended with a shoot-out at the Colegio San Lorenzo on Parque José Martí. As well as various humdrum military possessions, the displays include the bloodstained shirt of one of the rebel marines and a neat little model of the naval base. Rather than the expected rundown of Cuba's nautical past that you might expect, the rest of the museum is a sketchy collection of items related to sea travel and naval warfare, dispersed throughout various displays pertaining to a more general picture of life on the island since pre-Columbian times. These include a small section on natural history and a cabinet full of some fantastic old compasses.

Six blocks south of the museum, following Avenida 48 westwards to its conclusion then walking a block north – a twenty-minute walk in total from the naval museum – lies the rather unspectacular Cementerio Municipal del Paseo de la Reina de Cienfuegos, better known as the **Cementerio de Reina** (daily 8am–6pm). Crossing the railway tracks on the way, you enter a distinctly residential section of town with a more rural feel, which makes for a somewhat surreal atmosphere as you step through the heavy gates. Established as the city's first cemetery in 1839 and often flagged in Cuban tourist literature, the site is stuffed full of marble statues and gravestones – even the walls are lined with tombs. The ruined ramparts at the back are the remains of what was once a covered tomb, where the first priest of Cienfuegos was buried in 1862.

Museo de la Clandestinidad Hermanas Giral

Heading a few blocks south on the Prado from Pueblo Nuevo towards Punta Gorda, you'll find the **Museo de la Clandestinidad Hermanas Giral** at Ave. 42 no.3709 e/ 37 y 39 (Tues–Sat 10am–6pm, Sun 9am–noon; free). The museum, which contains little more than a preserved bedroom, a few personal effects and revolutionary miscellanea, is dedicated to Cristina and Lourdes Giral y Andreu, the two sisters who lived here in this house and became involved in the 1950s civil resistance movement in Havana. Assassinated without trial by Batista's henchmen in revenge for the attempted murder of the government secretary, which they were not involved in, the sisters have subsequently been heralded as local martyrs. Serving mainly as a reminder of the rough justice that ruled before the Revolution, this museum is only worth visiting, however, if you have a specialist interest.

Punta Gorda

The southern part of the city, **Punta Gorda**, has a distinctly different flavour to the rest of Cienfuegos, and it's here that the city's relatively recent founding is most keenly felt. Open streets and colourful bungalow housing – unmistakably influenced by the United States of the 1940s and 50s – project an image of affluence and suburban harmony. Although this image would have been more

accurate prior to the Revolution, there are still some very comfortable homes here, many of them renting rooms to visitors. Though there are no museums and few historic monuments in Punta Gorda, the most notable exception being the magnificent **Palacio de Valle**, it's the best area in the city to spend time outside, whether for an evening stroll down the Prado, or a drink sitting on the wall of the *malecón* – the bayside promenade.

One of the primary focal points in this part of town, **Club Cienfuegos** (daily 10am–1am; free during the day, $3CUC to $5CUC in the evening), is a commercial entertainment centre at Prado e/ Ave. 8 y Ave. 12 and a much newer addition to the area, though the palatial main building does date back to 1918. The centre, by far the most comprehensive leisure facility in the city, features a snack bar and restaurant (daily noon–9pm), a shop (daily 10am–6pm), a few indoor games including pool tables, a small collection of very low-key amusement park installations (see p.335) and a car rental office. More impressively it also has its own marina, from where you can tour the bay by boat, and even its own tiny man-made **beach**. The centre also hosts programmes of night-time entertainment (see p.335) on the large, covered terrace which looks out over the marina.

Right next to Club Cienfuegos is **Marina Cienfuegos** (☏43/55-6120 & 55-1699, ⓔreserva@nautica.cfg.cyt.cu), at Calle 35 e/ Ave. 6 y Ave. 8, from where you can rent boats, arrange fishing trips and go on organized excursions. Sandwiched between the marina and the shell of an old building is Playa Juvenil Ruben Martínez Villena, a fifty-metre scrap of **beach** with a few wooden parasols and a little refreshments kiosk. There's another, even scrappier beach in Punta Gorda, which you can get to if you follow Avenida 16 six blocks east of Prado and then turn right. It's popular with locals at weekends despite the murky water and pebbly sand. Before swimming at any of these beaches, bear in mind that the waste water from the city is emptied directly into the bay.

Palacio de Valle and La Punta

The best reason to come down this way, however, is the **Palacio de Valle** (daily 10am–10pm; free). It has a striking appearance, with two dissimilar turrets, chiselled arches and carved windows, looking like a cross between a medieval fortress, an Indian temple and a Moorish palace. Just as striking is the interior, where tiled mosaic floors, lavishly decorated walls and ceiling, marble staircase, and painstakingly detailed arches and adornments scattered throughout are as captivating as the building as a whole as intriguing. Built as a home between 1913 and 1917, the decidedly Islamic-influenced interior is a curiosity for a city founded by Frenchmen. An Italian architect, Alfredo Collí, was responsible for the overall design, but structural contributions were made by a team of artisans, who included Frenchmen, Cubans, Italians and Arabs. Nowadays it functions principally as a restaurant, but if you're not eating there's nothing to stop you wandering up the spiral staircase to the **rooftop bar**, the best spot for a drink in Cienfuegos. The views are better than you might anticipate given the unremarkable height of the building.

Beyond the Palacio de Valle, the land narrows to a two-hundred-metre peninsula, where the most opulent residential architecture in the city, some of it now converted for administrative use, is to be found. Wooden and concrete mansions and maisonettes lead the way down to **La Punta**, where there is a pretty little park right at the water's edge. A great place to chill out during the week, the park springs into life at the weekends when the town's teenagers converge to listen to music, drink rum, flirt, show off their swimming gear and cool down in the murky water.

Cementerio Tomás Acea

A five-minute taxi ride from the centre, on the Avenida 5 de Septiembre, is the much larger, more picturesque of the city's two cemeteries, the **Cementerio Tomás Acea** (daily 6am–5pm; free). Completed in 1926, the overly grand Parthenon-styled entrance building, at the end of a long driveway with gardens on either side, leads into the gentle slopes of the cemetery grounds. This is the nearest thing to a landscaped city park in Cienfuegos, its rolling, sweeping lawns punctuated by the odd tree and, from the highest point, pleasant views of the distant bay. There are some interesting tombs to look out for, the most striking being the monument to the Martyrs of September 5, 1957, local rebels who were killed in the uprising commemorated by the Museo Histórico Naval Nacional (see p.330). Occasionally there is a guide on hand offering informal tours, with a tip the only payment expected.

Eating

In theory, there are plenty of dining options in Cienfuegos, and while wandering around the city centre you will inevitably notice state-run **restaurants** dotted about the place. The reality, however, is that the vast majority are severely limited in what they offer, and are appealing only to those on a strict budget. Most of these poorer national-peso establishments are in Pueblo Nuevo. Almost all the restaurants in Punta Gorda are aimed at the tourist market and therefore tend to be more reliable but also often overpriced. There are two legal **paladares** in Cienfuegos: *El Criollito* and *Aché*. Prices at both are quite reasonable, but remember you will pay extra if you are escorted to either of them by a *jinetero*, who will charge the owner a commission. The best **fast food** in town is served up at *Carlos III* on Prado esq. Ave. 54, and the best ice cream is at the local *Coppelia* at Prado esq. Ave. 52. There are also a number of fast-food restaurants and *caféterias* dotted along the *malecón* section of Prado.

Pueblo Nuevo and around

1819 Prado e/ 56 y 58 ☏ 43/51-5514. Set in the front room of a colonial mansion, whose modest nineteenth-century architecture does little to imprint a sense of history on the bare interior. Offers a reasonable selection for a peso restaurant; the no-frills chicken, pork and fish dishes are extremely cheap, even though you'll be asked to pay in convertible pesos. Closed Mon.

1869 in *La Unión*, Calle 31 esq. 54 ☏ 43/55-1020. An almost-elegant restaurant with a broad selection of meat and seafood dishes, including the chicken and mayonnaise-based "Omar" salad, a seafood broth starter and the house-special Caribbean fillet – a beefsteak crowned with grilled shrimp and cheese. Unfortunately, the chef never quite meets the expectations set by the menu, though most meals are still better than the average local offerings. Daily 7–9.45am, noon–2.45pm & 7–9.45pm.

Aché Ave. 38 no.4106 e/ 41 y 43 ☏ 43/52-6173. The *paladar* locals most frequently recommend, *Aché* serves wholesome, well-prepared Cuban dishes, including excellent seafood, in the backyard of a pretty bungalow surrounded by gardens. Meals cost around $10CUC. Mon–Fri noon–10pm.

Cienfuegos Ave. 54 no.3503 e/ 35 y 37. Simple, unpretentious peso restaurant with a central courtyard for smokers. The menu includes pork and (unusually) a couple of tofu options In addition to the house special, roast chicken. Main dishes are between $14CUP and $32CUP. Has a good bar too (see p.334).

El Criollito Calle 33 no.5603 e/ 56 y 58 ☏ 43/52-5540. Located in a high-ceilinged front room, *El Criollito* is less homely and inviting than the city's other *paladar*, but it's also the one more likely to be open. The satisfying but unremarkable three main dishes – chicken, pork and fish – are served with mountainous side orders and will cost $8CUC if you arrive without a *jinetero*.

Dinos Pizza Calle 31 e/ 54 y 56 ☏ 43/55-1121. Inexpensive and uninspiring Italian restaurant serving pasta and delicious pizzas as well as a few Cuban staples; it's the best place in the city for an uncomplicated lunch. Add any combination of the eleven pizza toppings for between 50c and $4CUC a pop.

Gioventu Prado e/ 52 y 54. Basic pizzas and pastas are served on an equally basic open-air patio terrace, but it's less dingy than most and unbelievably cheap.

La Verja Ave. 54 no.3306 e/ 33 y 35 ☏ 43/51-7452. An imposing colonial residence with European-style bronze statues dotted around and arched, stained-glass windows. The menu changes daily but unfortunately the peso-standard Cuban food, served to foreigners at inflated convertible pesos prices, doesn't quite match up to the surroundings. Closed Tues.

Punta Gorda

Café Cienfuegos *Club Cienfuegos*, Prado e/ Ave. 8 y Ave. 12 ☏ 43/51-2891 ext. 112. There are over 15 simple seafood dishes at this polished and fairly elegant first-floor Cuban-cuisine restaurant with a classic saloon bar. A meal here is particularly appealing during daylight hours, when you can enjoy views of Punta Gorda and the bay from the tables on the small balcony. Avoid the one or two non-Cuban dishes, like the tomato-flavoured rice masquerading as vegetarian *paella*. Most main dishes are priced between $5CUC and $10CUC.

El Cochinito Prado e/ 4 y 6 ☏ 43/51-8611. Escalope of pork and fried chicken make up the entire menu, but the food is better quality than at any of the state-run restaurants in Pueblo Nuevo, and cheaper than most of its classier counterparts down here. Set in a dimly lit, rustic, lord-of-the-manor-type hall with dark brick walls and a fireplace, it's most atmospheric in the evenings; there's an outdoor grill as well.

Covadonga Prado e/ 0 y 2 ☏ 43/51-6949. Rice and meat scraps in gravy, referred to as *paella*, is the unmerited speciality on an otherwise seafood-based menu, but the below average and admittedly cheap food ultimately comes a poor second to the great location on the edge of the bay, which, along with the far-off mountains, is visible through the wall-to-wall windows.

El Criollo Los Pinitos, Prado esq. Ave. 22. Reasonable roast and fried pork and chicken dishes at the open-air national peso-charging restaurant within the Los Pinitos complex. You may have to eat to the sounds of reggaeton, but at least it won't cost you more than the equivalent of a couple of convertible pesos. Daily noon–11pm.

Palacio del Valle Prado esq. Ave. 0, next door to the *Hotel Jagua* ☏ 43/55-1226. A wide choice of seafood – such as Mexican-style shrimp and lobster or fish in béchamel sauce – with chicken, beef or *paella* dishes as alternatives. The excellent pianist and elegant arched interior provide a sense of occasion and outshine the unspectacular but nevertheless better-than-average food.

Drinking

Cienfuegos has several non-tourist **bars** with cheap rum and plenty of undiluted local flavour. However, the touristy bars, including some of the hotel ones, are not to be sniffed at, as they offer by far the best selection of drinks and some character of their own.

Bars and cafés

Café Teatro Terry between Teatro Tomás Terry and Colegio San Lorenzo, Parque José Martí. Ice-cream treats, sumptuously decorated with wafers, cocktail umbrellas and frilly paper pineapples, served in a bijou courtyard under a roof of exuberant hanging vines and flowers. Occasional live music. Tues–Sun 9am–midnight.

Caféteria San Carlos Prado esq. Ave. 56. A colourless place, but it's sealed off from the street behind tinted windows and has a/c, making it a convenient spot to take a break and cool off. Serves coffee, tea, cold drinks, sandwiches and one or two cheap meals.

Cienfuegos Ave. 54 e/ 35 y 37, One of the best drinking spots for experiencing local flavour. Has a mixture of convertible and national peso drinks, including excellent *mojitos*.

Don Luis Calle 31 e/ 54 y 56, A tiny but atmospheric saloon opposite the *Unión* hotel where you can prop up the bar with the locals.

El Embajador Ave. 54 esq. 33. This cigar shop is ideal for a good-quality coffee or rum during the afternoon, accompanied by the aroma of tobacco. Has a stylishly simple but inviting little bar at the back and a more comfortable upstairs gallery, with easy chairs around a coffee table.

La Fernandina Prado no.5202 esq. 52. This dim, neon-lit bar on the main drag is not as divey as it looks and is one of the easier-to-find, straight-up drinking joints.

Palacio de Valle Prado esq. Ave. 0. The views over the bay and the city from the rooftop bar here makes it hands-down the best place in the city for a laid-back drink. Daily 10am–10pm.

El Palatino Ave. 54 esq. Calle 27, Parque José Martí. A pleasant bar off the main square with one of the town's better selections of drinks bar; it's a popular spot with tour groups Daily 9am–11pm.

El Polinesio Calle 29 no.5410 e/ Ave. 54 y Ave. 56, Parque José Martí. Dark and a bit dingy inside, with a slightly bizarre bohemian vibe, this is the only non-touristy drinking joint on the main square. There is a more welcoming street-side terrace.

El Ranchón Los Pinitos, Prado esq. Ave. 22. An outdoor bar and café sheltered under a high wooden roof in the bayside gardens of the Los Pinitos complex. This would be a really pleasant spot but for the reggaeton and pop reverberating around the place. Daily noon–midnight.

La Venus Negra *Hotel Unión*, Calle 31 esq. 54. The fourth-floor rooftop patio bar in this excellent hotel has fabulous 360-degree views of the city and is a great place to hide out and chill. There is a pool table here too.

Nightlife and entertainment

During the week, **nightlife** is subdued, especially outside of July and August, with venues often relatively empty. At the weekends, however, Punta Gorda really comes alive, with locals out in force and modern pop and *salsa* echoing in the streets. There are several outdoor venues which particularly benefit from this injection of life, most notably *Los Pinitos*, set in gardens jutting out from the end of the *malecón*.

More sedate evening **entertainment** can be enjoyed on and around the Parque José Martí, with excellent-value musical and theatrical shows occasionally put on at the Casa de la Cultura (☏43/51-6584); there's a much fuller programme at the Teatro Tomás Terry (☏43/51-3361 & 51-1026, ✉terry@azurina.cult.cu; $5CUC, box $40CUC; shorts and sleeveless tops not permitted). Performances at the latter usually start at 9pm during the week and on Saturdays, whilst on Sundays there is only a matinee performance, usually starting at 5pm. A monthly programme is posted on the noticeboards out front. On Saturdays, from around 8pm, some brilliant local musicians grace the bandstand in the square, attracting an older but buoyant and sociable crowd. **Films** are shown at the Teatro Luisa, Prado esq. Ave. 50, and Cine Prado, Prado esq. Ave. 54, as well as on smaller screens at the Sala de Video Tomás Gutierrez *Alea*, in the Jardines de la UNEAC on the main square (see below).

There's a **bowling alley** and small **games arcade** at Prado e/ Ave. 48 y Ave. 50 (daily noon–midnight; entrance $1CUC); on top of the entrance fee, which includes a drink, there are additional charges for bowling ($1CUC per game), pool ($2CUC per game) and air hockey ($0.50CUC per game). Down at *Club Cienfuegos* there's a small set of **leisure facilities**, including a minute go-cart track ($1CUC), bumper cars ($1CUC) and crazy golf ($1CUC). For national-league **baseball** check out the Estadio 5 de Septiembre, Ave. 20 y 47 (☎43/51-3644); game days are Tuesday to Thursday, Saturday and Sunday.

You can also enjoy a number of **organized excursions** within the city, which can be arranged at the local travel agencies (see p.325). Cubanacán offer a two-hour trip from the city all the way to the mouth of the bay and back for $16CUC; the price includes two drinks on board. Organized excursions are also the only way you can visit the **Quintero y Hermanos cigar factory** near the Parque José Martí. Cubanacán currently charge $10CUC for a two-hour jaunt, which includes a tour of the factory and a stop in the local cigar shop, El Embajador.

Live music venues, cabarets and nightclubs

Cabaret Guanaroca *Hotel Jagua*, Prado no.1 e/ Ave. 0 y Ave. 2, Punta Gorda. There's a varied weekly programme at this cabaret spot, featuring a different theme every night. Expect all the usual camp glamour and glitz. Wed–Mon 10pm–3am; $5CUC.

Casa de la Música Calle 37 e/ 4 y 6, Punta Gorda ☎43/51-1720. The biggest, most prestigious live concert venue in the city, where top Cuban musical groups – like Isaac Delgado, Bamboleo and La Charanga Habanera – have been performing since it opened in 2001. The venue's open-air section, which holds several thousand people, is used for famous performers, who almost always play on Frid and Sat. Less high-profile acts use the smaller indoor *caféteria* section, where drinks and light meals are available at the pontoon-style bar that juts out into the water and which, along with the adjoining disco, is open nightly ($1–3CUC), Live acts aren't always playing, so sometimes you'll have to make do with just drinks and dancing. Daily 10am–2am; performances usually start at 10pm. Entrance costs for big concerts vary and start at around $5CUC.

Club Cienfuegos Prado e/ Ave. 8 y Ave. 12 ☎43/51-2891. The most reliable live music venue, with varied programming and something on almost

every night; Cuban music predominates, but local rock and rap acts perform here too. You can enjoy waiter service from one of the tables on the wide terrace looking over the marina, where the acts perform. The entrance charge entitles you to $2CUC consumption. Sun–Fri 10pm–1am, $3CUC, Sat 10pm–2am, $5CUC.

El Cubanísimo Calle 35 e/ Ave. 16 y Ave. 18. Just over the road from the bay's edge, this open-air venue hosts contemporary and traditional live music on its sheltered stage, surrounded by tables. Attracting a good mix of locals and tourists, this is one of the more unvarnished live music spots. Mon–Thurs & Sun 9.30pm–midnight, Fri 9.30pm–2am, Sat 9.30pm–3am; $2CUC.

Discoteca El Benny Ave. 54 e/ 29 y 31 ☎43/55-1105. Unusually slick and polished for a Cuban nightclub, especially one in the provinces. Don't expect any action before 11pm. The cover charge is $6CUC per couple, and entrance is generally restricted to couples only. The music is dominated by pop and *salsa*. Daily 10pm–1am.

Jardines de la UNEAC Calle 25 e/ Ave. 54 y Ave. 56, Parque José Martí ☎43/51-6117. This semi-open-air patio has a basic bar and is one of the most congenial and intimate venues for live music. A great place to enjoy some local bands and soloists playing Cuban musical styles such as *bolero*, *trova* and *son*. $3CUC.

Listings

Banks and exchange The bank best prepared to deal with foreign currency is the Banco Financiero Internacional, Ave. 54 esq. 29 (Mon–Fri 8am–3pm). To buy pesos, head for the Cadeca *casa de cambio* at Ave. 56 no.3314 e/ 33 y 35 (Mon–Sat 8.30am–6pm, Sun 8.30am–noon) where you can also change traveller's cheques and withdraw money with a credit card.

Car rental Micar at Calle 39 e/ Ave. 12 y Ave. 14, Punta Gorda (☎43/55-1605; Mon–Sat 8am–8pm) is the best bet, but there is also Havanautos at Prado esq. 18 (☎43/55-1211 & 55-1154; daily 8am–8pm); Cubacar opposite the *Hotel Unión* at Calle 31 e/ 54 y 56 (daily 8am–7pm; ☎43/55-1172 & 55-1700).

Immigration and legal To extend tourist visas, visit the Department of Immigration at Ave. 46 esq. 29 (Mon–Thurs 8am–3pm; ☎43/55-1283). Consultoría Jurídica Internacional at Calle 54 no.2904 e/ 29 y 31 (Mon–Fri 8.30am–noon & 1.30–5.30pm; ☎43/55-1572) offer legal advice and assistance. In cases of theft or money problems go to Asistur.

Internet There is an ETECSA Telepunto Calle 31 e/ 54 y 56 (daily 8.30am–9.30pm) with several Internet terminals and six phone booths. See also "Telephones" below.

Marina Marina Cienfuegos, Calle 35 e/ 6 y 8, Punta Gorda (☎43/55-6120 & 55-1699).

Medical There's a small but well-stocked convertible peso pharmacy in the *La Unión* hotel (Mon–Fri 8am–4.30pm, Sat 8am–noon), or try the Clínica Internacional, Prado no.202 e/ 2 y 4, in Punta Gorda, which is open 24 hrs. There's also a doctor on duty here and this is the place to call for an ambulance (☎43/55-1622 & 23).

Photography Photoservice has a branch in the town centre at Ave. 54 no.3118 e/ 31 y 33 and a marginally better one in Punta Gorda on the Prado opposite the *Hotel Jagua*. Alternatively, there's Photoclub in Salón Juvenil at Ave. 54 e/ 31 y 33.

Police Call ☎116.

Post office The main branch is at Calle 35 esq. Ave. 56 (Mon–Sat 8am–8pm, Sun 8am–noon).

Scooter rental Shopping The best supermarket is the Mercado Habana, Ave. 58 esq. 31. El Embajador, Ave. 54 esq. 33, has a good selection of cigars, rum and coffee. El Fundador on Parque José Martí at Calle 29 esq. Ave. 54 sells cigars, CDs, T-shirts, maps and souvenirs. The shop in *La Unión* hotel stocks CDs, postcards and a few books, and El Topcacío at Calle 54 no.3508 e/ 35 y Prado has postcards, a reasonable selection of CDs, books (some in English) and some fairly dire souvenirs.

Taxis Cubataxi (☎43/51-9145) & Turistaxi (☎43/55-1172 & 55-1700).

Telephones International phone-card calls can be made at the 24hr ETECSA cabin at Calle 31 e/ Ave. 54 y Ave. 56, which also has an Internet connection. There are several ETECSA cabins (phones only) dotted around town including opposite the *Hotel Jagua* in Punta Gorda. See also "Internet" above.

Around Cienfuegos

From Cienfuegos there are several manageable day- or half-day trips offering the chance to enjoy some satisfyingly uncontrived but still tourist-friendly diversions. Fifteen kilometres or so from the city are the flourishing grounds of the **Jardín Botánico**, whose compact size allows you to fit a tour easily into a couple of hours, while the huge variety of different species can keep you there for a day.

Next to the mouth of the bay, a 45-minute drive from Cienfuegos, is **Playa Rancho Luna**, a pleasant beach, though second-rate by Cuban standards, and the most obvious alternative to the city for a longer stay in the province. On the other side of the narrow channel linking the bay to the sea, only two minutes away by ferry, the **Castillo de Jagua** stands guard over the entrance to the bay. A plain but atmospheric eighteenth-century Spanish fortress, today it contains a small history collection. Though conveniently close to Playa Rancho Luna, it's well worth taking the boat to the fortress from the city and enjoying the full serenity of the bay. Further afield is **El Nicho**, a beautiful set of waterfalls in the mountains and a great trekking destination.

Jardín Botánico de Cienfuegos

About 15km east of the city limits, the **Jardín Botánico de Cienfuegos** (daily 9am–5pm; $2CUC; ☏43/54-5115) has one of the most complete collections of tropical plant species in the country. The one-square-kilometre site is home to over two thousand different species, divided up into various different groups, most of them merging seamlessly into one another so that in places this feels more like a natural forest than an artificially created garden. A road runs around the outside of the park and cuts into it in places, but the best way to explore is on foot. **Guides** are available, at no extra cost, and are invaluable if you want to know what you're looking at; ask at the lodge at the end of the main road along the northern border of the enclosure. There's a definite appeal to just wandering around on your own, though, following the roughly marked tracks through the varied terrain and past a series of pools and waterways. The most defined sections of the park include the cactus and fern houses, and the palm collection, which is the most popular amongst visitors with some 325 different species of palm from five continents. If you don't have your own transport the only way to get to the gardens, other than on an organized excursion, is by **taxi** from the centre of Cienfuegos (about $20CUC round-trip). **Organized excursions** to the Jardín Botánico can be arranged through either Havanatur or Cubanacán in Cienfuegos (see p.325). Trips last between two and four hours and currently cost $10CUC per person.

Refugio de Fauna Guanaroca-Gavilanes

Around 12km from the city, on the way to the nearby beaches on the south coast, is the **Laguna Guanaroca**, a lake joined to the Bahía de Cienfuegos by a narrow channel and set up as a nature reserve, the **Refugio de Fauna Guanaroca-Gavilanes** (☏43/52-1213 & 52-3573), in 1995. Only recently established as a tourist attraction, the cost of visiting here has yet to be finalized; the main draws are boating on the lake, two- to three-hour guided walks around its borders and birdwatching, for which some lookout towers have been erected. Keep your eyes open for pink flamingoes, Florida cormorants, wood ducks, Cuban todies, Cuban Emeralds and Great Lizard cuckoos. The entrance to the reserve is marked by a small building at the side of the road and a sign.

Playa Rancho Luna and around

Less than 20km south of the city is the province's most developed section of coastline, an unspoilt but relatively unimpressive stretch of beach called **Playa Rancho Luna**. Two hotels provide the focus for the area, spread out along 4km of mostly rocky, tree-lined shores that reach round to the mouth of the Jagua Bay. This is a good place for **scuba diving** with over thirty dive sites along the coral reef stretching the length of the local coastline and two of the hotels closely linked to diving centres. Though there is no reliable timetable, **buses** leave the main station in Cienfuegos several times a day for the beach and, at a peso each way, will save you the $9CUC taxi fare, if you have the patience to wait around for them.

There are only a few hundred metres of actual **beach** in all, and the *Rancho Luna* **hotel** (☏43/54-8012, ✉rpublicas@ranluna.cfg.cyt.cu; ●) has by far the best of it, a wide curve of soft beige sand, falling under the occasional shadow of a bushy tree, and sinking into the warm, slightly murky waters. The all-inclusive hotel features a buffet and Italian restaurants, a beach grill, games room, mini-golf, tennis courts and swimming pool. Attached to the hotel, the Whale Shark Scuba Center (☏43/55-1275 & 54-8087, ✉buceocom@nautica.cfg.cyt.cu), actually no more than two small concrete cabins down on the beach, usually conducts two dives a day at 9.15 and 11.15am. A single dive costs $30CUC, with various packages of dives such as $139CUC for five or $242CUC for nine dives. The centre also offers ACUC-and-SNSI certificated diving courses, the open water courses starting at $300CUC. The centre, like the one at *Faro Luna* (see below), is run by Marlin (ⓦwww.nauticamarlin.com).

Faro Luna and west to the mouth of the bay

To escape from this more populated section of the beach, you'll have to sacrifice some quality and walk the five minutes or so west along the shore to the scrappier section near the *Faro Luna* (ⓣ43/54-8030 & 54-8040, Ⓕ54-8062, Ⓔrpublicas@ranluna.cfg.cyt.cu; ⓞ), run by the same chain as the *Rancho Luna*, Cubanacán (ⓦwww.hotelesCubanacán.com). Smaller and considerably more subdued than its neighbour, this hotel has less of a family-vibe than the *Rancho Luna* and is better suited to couples. Its modest but neatly kept grounds roost just above the rocky water's edge, with views spreading out to the horizon. There's a diminutive pool and scooter rental facilities. This is also a good place to stay if you're planning to do any scuba diving, which is handled by the adjacent Faro Luna Diving Centre (ⓣ43/54-8040, Ⓔdcfluna@acuc.cfg.cyt.cu & buceocom@nautica.cfg.cyt.cu). Offers include single dives for $30CUC and ten for $265CUC, as well as ACUC courses starting at $60CUC. All dives take place within a couple of hundred metres of the shore, where a varied stretch of coral is punctuated by a number of wrecked ships. With sheer vertical coral walls and numerous caves and tunnels, there are pretty good chances of coming across some big fish such as nurse sharks, barracuda and tarpon. The centre also rents out sets containing a snorkel, flippers and mask for $10CUC per day.

Neighbouring the hotel, a couple of hundred metres along the coast, are the stands of an attractive **dolphinarium** (Thurs–Tues 9.30am–4pm; shows $10CUC adults, $6CUC children, $1CUC to take photos). Two shows are held daily in a natural pool, a sea inlet with submerged fences preventing the animals from escaping, surrounded on three sides by trees and bushes. The morning show, at 10am, features dolphins and sea lions whilst the afternoon show, at 2pm, is sea lions only. Shows last about 30 minutes but are extended by 20 minutes for anyone willing to pay an extra $50CUC ($33CUC for children) to swim with the dolphins.

If you would rather stay in a **casa particular** there is one good option 2km west along the coastal road from the *Faro Luna*. The *Finca Los Colorados* (ⓣ43/54-8044, Ⓔfincaloscolorados@casapineiro.com; ⓞ), opposite the lighthouse which gives the *Faro Luna* its name, is an old, ranch house with two double rooms for rent. This delightful place features stylish rustic furniture, sturdy iron beds and swings and seesaws on a sandy patio where meals are served. Although situated right next to the sea, the rocks lining the shore make swimming impossible.

About 3km further up the road, perched above the channel linking the bay to the Caribbean, is ugly *Hotel Pasacaballo*, currently being used as lodging for hospital patients. At the foot of the slopes leading up to the hotel you can catch a **ferry** to the other side of the channel and visit the Castillo de Jagua, but it's much more of an event to take the ferry all the way from the city.

Castillo de Jagua and the ferry from Cienfuegos

Half the fun of a visit to the seventeenth-century Spanish fortress at the mouth of the Jagua Bay, known as the **Castillo de Jagua** (daily 8am–4pm; $1CUC), is getting there. A local passenger **ferry** leaves Cienfuegos five times a day, approximately every two and a half hours from 8am onwards, from a wharf next to the junction between Calle 25 and Avenida 46, where it'll cost you 50¢ to climb on board or $1CUC with a bike. There's a small outdoor waiting area with benches and a noticeboard with the ferry timetable, though this is not always up to date. A rusty old vessel looking vaguely like a tugboat, the ferry chugs across the placid waters at a pace slow enough to allow a relaxed contemplation of the bay, including the tiny, barely inhabited cays where the ferry makes a brief call to pick up passengers. The deck is lined with benches but the metal roof is the best place to sit, allowing unobscured views in all directions.

After a little less than an hour, the ferry docks just below the fortress, on the opposite side of the channel to Playa Rancho Luna, from where a dusty track leads up to the cannon guarding the castle drawbridge. Overlooking a rustic little collection of bayfront shacks and patched-up villas, the fortress isn't particularly engaging once you get inside. It contains a small museum detailing the history of the fort, originally built to defend against pirate attacks; a couple of tables in a sunken courtyard where you can get something to eat and drink; and steps winding up to the top of the single turret from where there are modest views. Before heading back, take a peek at the cramped and dingy prison cell and the chapel on the courtyard level.

Parque El Nicho

Near the eastern border of the province, in the lush green Sierra del Escambray mountains, is **El Nicho**, a captivating set of waterfalls and natural pools. Falling within the Topes de Collantes nature reserve, which spans the Cienfuegos–Sancti Spíritus border (most of which is usually visited from the Trinidad side; see p.387), this area has recently been declared the **Parque El Nicho** (daily 8.30am–6.30pm; $5CUC). The entrance to the park, marked by a stone gateway, leads into an official trail known as Reino de las Aguas, which cuts through the dense woodlands and crosses over rivers and streams, taking in numerous waterfalls, mountain vistas and abundant birdlife (much of it endemic to the region). At their most spectacular, the waterfalls, emerging from thick vegetation in the shadows of overhanging branches, drop some 25 metres. There are several pools ideal for bathing, all of them fed by cascading water and some providing opportunities for diving. There is also a restaurant within the park, but it is set up to cater predominantly to groups.

Most visitors to El Nicho arrive on **organized excursions** and, given the precarious and rough nature of the roads leading up to it, this is a good idea. Havanatur (☎43/55-1393) and Cubanacán (☎43/55-1680), in the provincial capital, both offer day-trips which include lunch, a guided trek and bathing in the

---

Villa Guajimico

If you're into **diving**, an excellent base is the *Villa Guajimico* hotel at Carretera de Cienfuegos, Km 42 (☎432/54-0947 to 48), located exactly halfway along the coastal road that runs between Trinidad and Cienfuegos. The resident dive centre organizes trips to twelve nearby sites, including the wreck of the ship *La Arabela* ($40CUC per dive with equipment), while catamarans ferry those more interested in snorkelling out to sea. Land-based activities include forest trails and nearby caves to explore. With tasteful, multicoloured modern brick-and-concrete bungalows set around a natural lagoon and enclosed by woodland, a restaurant, bar, games room and swimming pool with a view of the sea, *Villa Guajimico* is a good place for active people to relax.

pools for $30CUC per person; it's worth booking in advance, as a minimum number of up to eight people is usually required. If you do make your own way here, note that there are around sixty kilometres of road between the park and the centre of Cienfuegos, so renting a four-wheel-drive vehicle is recommended.

Villa Clara

The province of **Villa Clara** combines visitor-friendly towns and postcard-perfect beach resorts with unadulterated Cuban culture. Over the last few years investment dollars have been pumped into the area, with the most intensive changes being made on the isolated network of cays off the north coast. Development elsewhere has progressed at a steadier pace, ensuring that everyday life in the towns and sole major city has not been spoilt. The vibrant provincial capital, **Santa Clara**, has one of Cuba's most dynamic cultural scenes, and has so far retained a sense that what goes on here is predominantly for the benefit of the locals rather than visitors. That said, busloads of tourists arrive every day to visit the city's monuments, and it has long been a place of pilgrimage for **Che Guevara** worshippers, being home to the hero's ashes and the scene of his most famous victory during the revolutionary conflict.

Forty kilometres or so northeast of Santa Clara, the small town of **Remedios** – a principal day-trip destination for holidaymakers staying at the ever-expanding resort just 60km away on the northern cays – has a splendid church and a couple of engaging museums to offer. Its greatest appeal, however, lies in the fact that, despite a steady increase in the number of visitors, this is a place where, so far, history continues to evolve mostly undisturbed by commercialism.

Without doubt the major tourist centre in the province is on the dozens of small cays, dotted around the shallow waters about 40km off the northern coastline. On **Cayo Las Brujas** there is an attractive cabin complex, next to an empty virgin beach, while on larger **Cayo Santa María** and **Cayo Ensenachos** there are four massive hotel complexes and work on more is currently in progess.

One of the few mountain resorts in this region, on the other side of the province, is located on the shores of the man-made **Lago Hanabanilla**, one of the largest reservoirs on the island. Tucked into the bright green slopes of the Sierra del Escambray, and offering good fishing and other excursions arranged through its solitary hotel, the resort attracts Cubans and foreigners alike.

Santa Clara

One of the largest and most happening cities in Cuba, **SANTA CLARA**, landlocked near the centre of the province, is a must for anyone looking to experience Cuban provincial life at its most pure. Home to the country's third-biggest university, Santa Clara owes little of its vitality to the significant number of visitors it receives. Local life revolves instead around the vibrant Parque Vidal, at the very heart of the town, where tourist activity is also centred, though there are several more isolated venues also attracting large numbers of visitors, most especially the Memorial al Che, in the southeastern reaches of the city.

Arrival and information

Astro and Víazul **buses** drop off passengers at the Terminal de Omnibus Nacionales (☎42/29-2113 and 29-2114), on the corner of Carretera Central and Oquendo, in the western limits of the city, from where a taxi to the Parque Vidal will cost between $2CUC and $3CUC. Buses serving provincial destinations, such as Remedios, depart from the Terminal de Omnibus Intermunicipal on the Carretera Central e/ Pichardo y Amparo near the Memorial al Che. Walking to Parque Vidal from the **train station** (☎42/20-2895 or 96), on the Parque de los Mártires, shouldn't take more than ten minutes, or you can jump in one of the horse-drawn carriages or taxis that wait outside. Arriving by **car** from the west or east, the Carretera Central, which becomes an extension of a street named Marta Abreu, takes you within a few blocks of the Parque Vidal at the very heart of Santa Clara. To drive into the centre, if arriving from the east you should turn off the Carretera Central at Colón, and from the west at Rafael Tristá.

The best places for tourist **information** are the offices of the three major national travel agents based in the city. Havanatur is at Máximo Gómez no.13 e/ Boulevard y Alfredo Barreras (Mon–Fri 8.30am–noon & 1–5pm, Sat 8.30am–12.30pm; ☎42/20-4001 & 02). They organize day-trips to Lago Hanabanilla and the northern cays, as do Cubatur at Marta Abreu no.10 e/ Máximo Gómez y Enrique Villuendas (daily 8am–9pm; ☎42/20-8980, @operaciones@cubaturvc.co.cu) and Cubanacán at Colón no.101 esq. Candelaria (Mon–Fri 8.30am–5.30pm & Sat 8.30am–12.30pm; ☎42/20-5189, @coordinaciones@viajes.vcl.cyt.cu). All three agencies also sell interprovincial bus tickets and offer **tours** of the city, visiting all the major attractions by minibus for around $10CUC per person, usually with a minimum number of three people.

City transport and orientation

Much of what the town has to offer is within walking distance of the Parque Vidal. The main shopping street is within a block of the square, while many of the notable buildings and museums are on the square itself. Almost everything else you'll need or that's worth visiting is less than a ten-minute walk, the obvious exceptions being both bus stations and the Memorial al Che. To get between the Parque Vidal and two of the three major Santa Clara hotels, however, a **taxi** will be necessary and the best place to find one is at the taxi rank on Máximo Gómez between Parque Vidal and Boulevard. For the longer distances within the town, principally between the Plaza de la Revolución and the main square, there are a large number of **bicitaxis** and **horse-drawn carriages** on the street. There's a *bicitaxi* rank on Marta Abreu e/ Villuendas y J.B. Zayas, while the horse-drawn and motorcycle-carriages operate one-way on Marta Abreu (towards the bus terminal) and Rafael Tristá (towards Parque Vidal), as well as running on Cuba (away from Parque Vidal) and Colón (towards Parque Vidal) and up and down Maceo. In theory a ride should cost you no more than two pesos.

The bustling, pedestrianized stretch of Independencia between J.B. Zayas and Maceo changes its name to Boulevard. As with most Cuban towns and cities, Santa Clara is laid out on the block system, though there are no handily numbered or lettered streets so you'll need to remember at least a few street names. The most important arteries are Marta Abreu, a straight road

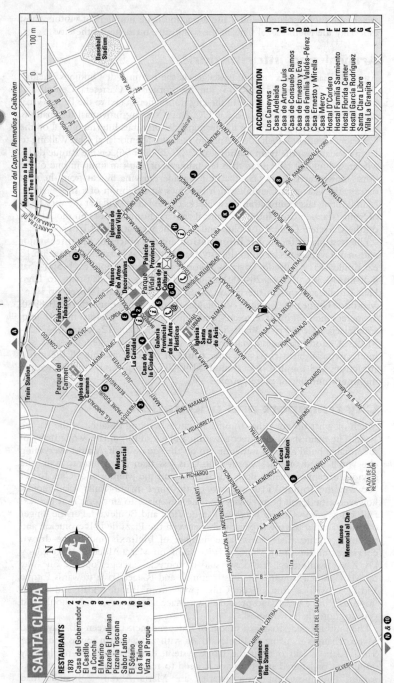

SANTA CLARA

RESTAURANTS

1878	2
Casa del Gobernador	4
El Castillo	9
La Concha	7
El Marino	8
Pizzeria El Pullman	1
Pizzeria Toscana	5
Sabor Latino	3
El Sótano	6
Los Tainos	10
Vista al Parque	6

ACCOMMODATION

Los Caneyes	N
Casa Adelaida	J
Casa de Arturo Luis	M
Casa de Consuelo Ramos	C
Casa de Ernesto y Eva	D
Casa de Familia Valdés-Pérez	B
Casa Ernesto y Mirella	I
Casa Mercy	F
Hostal D'Cordero	E
Hostal Familia Sarmiento	H
Hostal Florida Center	K
Hostal García Rodríguez	G
Santa Clara Libre	A
Villa La Granjita	N

connecting Parque Vidal with the Memorial al Che, and Independencia, linking the centre of town with the north and the Monumento a la Toma del Tren Blindado. Though it's less widespread here than in some cities, there are some streets here with both pre- and post-revolutionary names; where applicable, the old names have been given in brackets. For journeys beyond the city limits, go to the Terminal de Autos de Alquiler, opposite the Terminal de Omnibus Inter-municipal, where private taxis collect passengers travelling within the province. For details of taxi and car rental firms, see p.353.

Accommodation

There's a reasonable variety of **accommodation** in Santa Clara, and an especially large number of **casas particulares**. Most are clustered around the centre, with the greatest concentration found to the east and south of Parque Vidal; Maceo and Colón have particularly good selections. As in most major Cuban cities, tourists who arrive at the bus station are met by an enthusiastic crowd of touts offering you a place to stay. Don't assume that they're telling the truth if they warn you that your house of choice is full or no longer exists, and remember that if a tout accompanies you to a house, you'll end up paying their commission. Rates for rooms are generally $20CUC in July, August, December and at Easter and $15CUC for most of the rest of the year.

The only centrally located hotel available to foreigners is the *Santa Clara Libre*, as the *Modelo* at Maceo no.210 is exclusively for Cubans. For the greatest comfort and the best facilities, *Los Caneyes* and *La Granjita*, beyond the town's outskirts, win hands down, but they are only convenient if you've got a car or are prepared to take taxis.

Hotels

Los Caneyes Ave. de los Eucaliptos y Circunvalación ☎ 42/ 20-4512, switchboard 21-8140, ✉ reservas@caneyes.hor.tur.cu. Tucked away in the low grassy hills just beyond the southwestern outskirts of the city, about 1km from the Plaza de la Revolución and a $3CUC taxi ride from Parque Vidal, this neatly laid-out complex on the edge of a small wood features Amerindian-style accommodation huts, thoughtfully furnished and with good facilities. There's a restaurant, small pool and a hot tub. ⑥

Santa Clara Libre Parque Vidal no.6 e/ Tristá y Padre Chao ☎ 42/20-7548 to 50. A lime-green, eleven-storey tower with superb views and an unbeatable location. Though cramped and slightly decrepit, this hotel is still quite lively and attracts a refreshing mixture of Cuban and foreign guests. Some rooms are a little dim and confined, but many have good views and all are sufficiently equipped, including cable TV. There's a reasonable, inexpensive restaurant, a basement *caféteria* and a rooftop nightclub. ③

Villa La Granjita Carretera de Maleza Km 2 ☎ 42/21-8190 & 91, ✉ reserva@granjita.vcl.cyt.cu. Sizeable and simply furnished rooms in concrete cabins, scattered throughout a spacious site with its own woodlands and a stream; there's a

restaurant, a pool and a hot tub as well. Slightly further out of town, with plenty of palms and pines, the site looks more natural than landscaped and is somewhat less contrived than *Los Caneyes*. ⑤

Casas particulares

Casa Adelaida Maceo no.355a e/ Serafín García (Nazareno) y E.P. Morales (Síndico) ☎ 42/20-6725 & 29-3678. One comfortable double room, with a/c and bathroom, in a simple house with a first-floor terrace. The whole place is kept in tip-top condition and made all the more inviting by the warmth and friendliness of the hosts, one of whom speaks good English. ②

Casa de Arturo Luis Sterling no.108 e/ J.B. Zayas y Alemán ☎ 42/21-4118. The whole of the upstairs is for rent to guests, making this a great option for anyone wanting privacy, independence and some peace and quiet. There's a kitchen-diner, a double bedroom, a bathroom and access to a roof terrace. ②

Casa de Consuelo Ramos Calle Independencia no.265, apto. 1 e/ Unión (Pedro Estevez) y San Isidro ☎ 42/20-2064, ✉ marielatram@yahoo.es. A surprisingly cavernous apartment with some interesting features (like an interior wall of plants) within a humdrum-looking block of flats. Also unexpected is the large, tree-filled garden patio where benches are shaded underneath a leafy canopy. Each of the spacious double rooms has a bathroom, a fridge and a/c. Run by an old couple, one of whom speaks some English. ❷

Casa de Ernesto y Eva J.B. Zayas no.253a e/ Berenguer y Padre Tuduri ☎ 42/20-4076, ✉ nestyhostal@yahoo.es. Cushy apartment, great for self-caterers, with an open-plan kitchenette-living room and a balcony. Located in the upstairs part of a house that's full of original touches, such as a window that's been converted into a wardrobe and a broad, twisting staircase. Also upstairs is an intimate, reposeful terrace with benches and an additional room for rent. ❷

Casa de Familia Valdés-Pérez Berenguer no.106 e/ Maceo y Luis Estévez ☎ 42/20-3657. On the first floor, at the back of this pristine house, is an area set aside exclusively for guests that will suit anyone looking for a bit of privacy. The pleasingly airy room, with en-suite bathroom, a/c, two fans and a fridge, has its own dinky, leafy, partially covered terrace. There are two additional communal terraces, one on the roof with views of the city. ❷

Casa Ernesto y Mirella Cuba no.227 altos e/ Sterling (Pastora) y E.P. Morales (Síndico) ☎ 42/27-3501, ✉ ernesto_tama@yahoo.com. One plainly furnished but good-sized room with a/c, TV, fridge and en-suite bathroom, plus a balcony and a living room with hi-fi. ❷

Casa Mercy Eduardo Machado (San Cristóbal) no.4 e/ Cuba y Colón ☎ 42/21-6941, ✉ omeliomoreno@yahoo.com & isel@uclv.edu.cu. Two clean, spacious, first-floor, double rooms, both with a/c, a private bathroom and a fridge stocked with beers and soft drinks; they share a cosy terrace area for guests' exclusive use. The charming hosts, who speak English, Italian and French, provide a laundry service plus excellent meals (including vegetarian ones), are full of local knowledge and are generally extremely warm and helpful. ❷

Hostal D'Cordero Rolando Pardo no.16 e/ Parque Vidal y Maceo ☎ 42/20-6456, ✉ o_cordero2003 @yahoo.com. Two large and well-maintained bedrooms – both with a/c, TV, two beds and en-suite bathroom, one with a fridge – in a very clean, airy house that's less than a block from the main square. Meals are served on an upstairs terrace. ❷

Hostal Familia Sarmiento Lorda no.61, apto 1 e/ Boulevard y Martí ☎ 42/20-3510, ✉ lorda61 @yahoo.com. Don't be put off by the peeling paintwork on the outside: this smart, open-plan, ground-floor flat – seemingly a cross between a modern, big-city apartment and an old aristocratic country villa – has bags of character. Kitsch little touches include a tiger rug and plush drapes over arched doorways, and the furnishings are a mixture of colonial and retro styles from the 1950s and 70s. There are two comfy double rooms, each with its own bathroom, and meals are served on a small patio. The owners are a welcoming young couple. ❷

Hostal Florida Center Maestra Nicolasa (Candelaria) no.56 e/ Colón y Maceo ☎ 42/20-8161. Based around a fantastic, tropical-rainforest-like courtyard, this large, authentic colonial residence crammed with nineteenth-century furnishings has two superbly distinguished rooms for rent: one with a fantastic Art Deco bed and wardrobe, the other with colonial-era beds; both have TV, a minibar, a/c and a spotless private bathroom. Breakfast and dinner are served on tables that nestle amongst the fronds and ferns. English, French and Italian spoken. ❷

Hostal García Rodríguez Cuba no.209, apartment 1 e/ Serafín García (Nazareno) y E.P. Morales (Síndico) ☎ 42/20-2329, ✉ garcrodz@yahoo.com. One double and one triple room are available in this well-looked-after apartment. Though a little low on natural light, the rooms are spacious and have a/c and en-suite bathrooms. The owners are extremely helpful, offering a stash of leaflets on local services. ❷

The Town

Nowhere is the town's vitality more apparent than in the main square, **Parque Vidal**, as sociable a plaza as you'll find in Cuba. The square is definitely one of Santa Clara's highlights, but there are plenty of other places worth visiting. Some, like the **Museo de Artes Decorativas**, with its accurate reconstructions of colonial aristocratic living conditions, are on the square itself, while within walking distance is one of the city's most famous national memorial sites, **Monumento a la Toma del Tren Blindado**. A derailed train here marks one of the most dramatic events of the Battle of Santa Clara, a decisive event in the revolutionary war of the late 1950s. Linking this with Santa Clara's other most visited attraction, the **Plaza de la Revolución** and the **Memorial al Che**, is the city's adopted native son, **Ernesto Che Guevara**.

Parque Vidal

Declared a national monument in 1996, **Parque Vidal** is the geographical, social and commercial nucleus of Santa Clara. A spacious, traditional, pedestrianized and always crowded town square, it exudes a bustling, vivacious atmosphere. Weekends are particularly animated, with live music performances on the central bandstand in the evenings, and on the porch of the ornate Casa de la Cultura (see p.352).

The square's attractive core, a paved circular **promenade** laced with its own diverse plantlife, from towering palms to small, shrub-peppered lawns, is traversed by shoppers and workers throughout the day and, in the evenings, fills up with young and old alike; kids hide behind trees and race around the promenade, while their elders stick to the benches, and the park hums with chatter. The scene is elegantly framed by a mixture of predominantly colonial and neocolonial buildings, the more modern *Santa Clara Libre* hotel being the most obvious exception. The grandest of the lot is the **Palacio Provincial**, once the seat of the local government and now home to the **Biblioteca José Martí** (Mon–Fri 8am–10pm, Sat 8am–4pm, Sun 8am–noon), on the northeastern face of the square. Built between 1904 and 1912, its wide facade, featuring two bold porticoes, stands out as the square's most classically Greek architecture. Ask at reception and a guide will take you round and explain the history of the building for a small tip. There are occasional live musical performances in the fabulous concert room – check the board at the entrance for details.

On the northwest side of Parque Vidal is the **Museo de Artes Decorativas** (☎ 42/20-5368; Mon, Wed & Thurs 9am–6pm, Fri & Sat 1–10pm, Sun 6–10pm; $2CUC plus $2CUC extra if you want to take photos), featuring furniture and *objets d'art* spanning four centuries of style, from Renaissance to Art Deco. Each of the eleven rooms is opulently furnished, with most of the exhibits collected from houses around Santa Clara; some of them appear as they might have been when the building – older than most of its neighbours but of no particular architectural merit in itself – was home to a string of aristocratic families during the colonial period. In addition to the front room, with its marvellous crystal chandelier, there is a dining room with a fully laid table, a bedroom with an ostentatiously designed wardrobe and a room furnished almost entirely in wicker. Individual pieces to look out for include a stunning seventeenth-century bureau with ivory details and a fantastic Art Nouveau iron coat holder, with a mirror in its centre and full of artistic flourishes. A central courtyard is occasionally used for small concerts and fashion shows.

A few doors down on the same northwestern side of the square is the **Teatro La Caridad** (☎ 42/20-5548), with a fabulous, ornate interior, sold short by the building's relatively sober exterior. It was built in 1885 with money donated by Marta Abreu Estevez, a bronze statue of whom stands on the opposite side of the square. Estevez was a civic-minded nineteenth-century native of Santa Clara with an inherited fortune of more than four million pesos. As part of her wider quest to help the poor and contribute to the city's civil, cultural and academic institutions, a portion of the box office receipts were set aside to improve living conditions for the impoverished, thus spawning the theatre's name ("Charity"). Restored for a second time in the early 1980s, the theatre is in fantastic condition, with a semicircular three-tiered balcony enveloping the central seating area and a stunning painted **ceiling**. Three central angelic figures, representing Genius, History and Fame, are stationed in the clouds above a map of Cuba, while around the outside are painted portraits of eight Spanish playwrights. The creation of Camilo Salaya, who was also responsible for the interior decoration of the Teatro Tomás Terry in Cienfuegos (see p.328), this huge fresco is the theatre's crowning glory. You can get closer to it on a twenty-minute **guided tour** in English, which takes you up into the balcony (Tues–Sun 8am–5pm; $1CUC; $1CUC extra to take photos). For details of performances at the theatre see p.351.

Just off the square, at Máximo Gómez no.3 e/ Martha Abreu y Barreras, is the **Galería Provincial de las Artes Plásticas** (Tues–Sat 10am–6pm, Sun 9am–1pm; free), hosting temporary exhibitions on roughly a monthly basis showcasing predominantly the work of Cuban painters and other artists.

Casa de la Ciudad

A couple of blocks west of the square, the **Casa de la Ciudad** at Boulevard esq. J.B. Zayas (☎42/20-5593; Tues–Sat 8am–9pm, Sun 8am–6pm; $1CUC) has a rather pedestrian collection of antiquities, including colonial-era furniture, as well as a more interesting small art collection that covers a mishmash of styles ranging from simple pencil drawings to abstract oils and rather tacky landscapes. The museum's permanent and temporary exhibitions feature pieces by well-known Cuban artists, such as Wilfredo Lam and Carlos Enríquez, as well as international ones. Built in the late 1840s by a wealthy Barcelona-born businessman, the grand family house in which the museum is located has clearly seen better days, but still retains a strong sense of its former glory with its marble floors, stained-glass windows and tranquil porticoed courtyard.

Museo Memorial al Che and Plaza de la Revolución

On the southwestern outskirts of the city, about fifteen blocks along Rafael Tristá from Parque Vidal, Santa Clara pays tribute to its adopted son and hero, **Ernesto Che Guevara**. The monument commemorating the man and his vital part in the armed struggle against General Batista's dictatorship is in classic Cuban revolutionary style: simple, bold and made of concrete. On a thick, table-top base stand four concrete slabs; towering down from the tallest one is a burly-looking **statue of Guevara**, on the move and dressed in his usual military garb, rifle in hand. Inscribed on the concrete podium are the words "Hasta La Victoria Siempre" ("Ever onwards to victory"), one of the catch phrases of the Revolution. The slab next to the statue depicts, in a huge, somewhat jumbled mural, Guevara's march from the Sierra Maestra to Santa Clara and the decisive victory over Batista's troops.

Spreading out before the monument, the **Plaza de la Revolución**, like its counterpart in Havana, is little more than an open space. From the monument, head down towards the Carretera Central for the **shop** on the edge of the road junction for a selection of memorabilia and books on Che, as well as more general books, CDs, T-shirts and postcards. The shop, and the small café next door, are open daily from 9am to 5.30pm.

The statue of Guevara and the mural are classic photo opportunities, but for a more emotive experience and some detailed insights into the revolutionary's life, the best place to spend time here is in the **Museo Memorial al Che**, underneath the monument (☎42/20-8846 & 20-5878; Tues–Sat 8am–9pm, Sun 8am–5pm; free).

You'll be ushered first through a door marked "Memorial", which leads into a softly lit chamber where the mood of reverence and respect is quite affecting. Resembling a kind of tomb with an eternally flickering flame, this is a dedication to the Peruvians, Bolivians and Cubans who died with Guevara in Bolivia, each of whom is commemorated by a simple stone portrait set into the wall. The mood lightens in the museum opposite the memorial door, where

No one embodies the romanticism of the Cuban Revolution more than **Ernesto "Che" Guevara**, the handsome, brave and principled guerrilla who fought alongside Fidel Castro in the Sierra Maestra during the revolutionary war of 1956–59. He was born to middle-class, strongly left-wing parents in Rosario, Argentina on June 14, 1928. The young Ernesto Guevara – later nicknamed "Che", a popular term of affectionate address in Argentina – suffered from severe asthma attacks as a child. Despite this life-long affliction, he became a keen soccer and rugby player while at the University of Buenos Aires, where, in 1948, he began studying medicine.

By the time he graduated in 1953, finishing a six-year course in half the time, Che had made an epic journey around South America on a motorbike (which he chronicled later in *The Motorcycle Diaries*, ravishingly filmed in 2004 by Walter Salles), with his doctor friend Alberto Granado. These travels, which he continued after graduation, were instrumental in the formation of Guevara's political character, instilling in him a strong sense of Latin American identity and opening his eyes to the widespread suffering and social injustice throughout the continent. He was in Guatemala in 1954 when the government was overthrown by a US-backed right-wing military coup, and had to escape to Mexico.

It was there, in November 1955, that Guevara met the exiled Fidel Castro and, learning of his intentions to return to Cuba and ignite a popular revolution, decided to join Castro's small rebel army, the **M-26-7 Movement**. The Argentinian was among the 82 who set sail for Cuba in the yacht *Granma* on November 24, 1956, and, following the disastrous landing, one of the few who made it safely into the Sierra Maestra. As both a guerrilla and a doctor, Guevara played a vital role for the rebels as they set about drumming up support for their cause amongst the local peasants while fighting Batista's troops. His most prominent role in the conflict, however, came in 1958 when he led a rebel column west to the then province of Las Villas, where he was to cut all means of communication between the two ends of the island and thus cement Castro's control over the east. This he did in great style, exemplified in his manoeuvres during the Battle of Santa Clara (see p.349).

Unlike Castro, Guevara endured the same harsh conditions as the other rebels and refused to grant himself any comforts that his higher status might have allowed. It was this spirit of sacrifice and brotherhood that he brought to the philosophies which he developed and instituted after the triumph of the Revolution in 1959, during his role as Minister for Industry. The cornerstone of his theories was the concept of **El Hombre Nuevo** – the New Man – and this became his most enduring contribution to Cuban communist theory. Guevara believed that in order to build communism a new man must be created, and the key to this was to alter the popular consciousness. The emphasis was on motivation: new attitudes would have to be instilled in people, devoid of selfish sentiment and with a goal of moral rather than material reward, gained through the pursuit of the aims of the Revolution.

Despite working out these abstract theories, Guevara remained at heart a man of action and, after serving four years as a roaming ambassador for Cuba to the rest of the world, he left for Africa to play a more direct role in the spread of communism, becoming involved in a revolutionary conflict in the Congo. In 1966 he travelled to Bolivia where he once again fought as a guerrilla against the Bolivian army. There, on October 8, 1967, Guevara was captured and shot. Referred to in Cuba today simply as "El Che", he is probably the most universally liked and respected of the Revolution's heroes, his early death allowing him to remain untarnished by the souring of attitudes over time, and his willingness to fight so energetically for his principles viewed as evidence of his indefatigable spirit.

Guevara's life is succinctly told through neatly presented photos, maps, quotes and other paraphernalia, including his beret, jacket and camera. There are some memorable photographs, and it's these that hold the interest in the face of the usual technical information and array of weapons. Besides those of his early childhood, there are pictures of him alongside his rugby team-mates, on his contraption of a motorbike about to set off on a tour of his native Argentina in January 1950, and on a raft on the Amazon. Some of the now classic photographs taken during the Sierra Maestra campaign, depicting Guevara, Castro and their rebel companions in the thick forests of the eastern mountains, are also on display. Near the end, you will find the most famous photograph of them all, taken on March 5, 1960, at the burial of a group of sabotage victims; this portrait of Guevara, complete with beret, staring sternly beyond the camera, is arguably one of the most iconic images of the twentieth century.

Fábrica de Tabacos Constantino Pérez Carrodegua

Less than a five-minute walk from Parque Vidal along Maceo, on the corner of Berenguer, is the local cigar factory, the **Fábrica de Tabacos Constantino Pérez Carrodegua** (☏42/20-2211 & 20-6385; Mon–Fri 7am–noon & 1–4pm; $3CUC). With more than four hundred employees, the factory produces some 30 million cigars annually for a number of brands, including Romeo y Julieta, Partagás, Punch and Montecristo, all of which are on sale in La Veguita (☏42/20-8952), the excellent little **cigar shop** across the road at no.176. For a guided tour of the factory it's a good idea to ring in advance or inquire at reception, from where visits are organized on a very ad hoc basis. More reliably, contact Havanatur (☏42/20-4001 & 02), based just off the Parque Vidal, who regularly organize visits. Tours usually last about 45 minutes. Alternatively, you can often see quite a lot of what's going on from the street through the shutters running the length of the main room.

El Carmen and the Museo Provincial

From the cigar factory turn left along Berenguer and then right along Máximo Gómez to find the pleasant little **El Carmen** park, which houses the **Iglesia de Carmen**, a simple church with an altar almost as large as the back wall it sits up against. Built in 1774 to commemorate the foundation of the city, it stands on the site where, on July 15, 1689, the Spanish founders of Santa Clara held their first Mass; during the 1868–78 First War of Independence, the building served as a prison for women. Despite this interesting history, the church doesn't really warrant a visit for its own sake. In the northwestern corner of the park stands a bizarre-looking monument – a circular concrete girder, held aloft by a set of concrete columns, enclosing a tree in the centre – that was built in 1952 to mark the city's beginnings.

From the park, follow Padre Tuduri westwards and turn right on Pons y Naranjo to get to the **Museo Provincial** (Mon–Fri 9am–4.30pm, Sat 9am–1pm; $1CUC), situated on a hill at the top of a piece of empty land. Despite its large size and number of exhibits, attempts to convey a sense of history are lost due to the revolutionary overkill and muddled layout. Look for a few interesting photos, including some of the Battle of Santa Clara. There are natural history displays downstairs, supposedly representing Cuba's fauna, but actually featuring a distinctly foreign zebra, baboon and anteater.

Monumento a la Toma del Tren Blindado

A block behind the Museo de Artes Decorativas, Luis Estévez meets Independencia, Santa Clara's main shopping street, where a right turn and a five-minute walk leads to the **Monumento a la Toma del Tren Blindado** (☏42/20-2758), which honours one of the city's most significant events. The derailed carriages of an armoured train which make up most of the site have lain here since they were toppled from the tracks to the north during the Battle of Santa Clara, in 1958. This clash – between the dictator Batista's forces and a small detachment of about three hundred rebels, led by Che Guevara – was to be one of the last military encounters of the Revolutionary War. By December 1958, over ten thousand government troops had been sent by Batista to the centre of the island to prevent the rebels from advancing further west towards Havana, and one of the principal components of this defensive manoeuvre was an armoured train. However, Guevara, with only a fraction of his total number of troops, took the upper hand when, using tractors to raise the rails, they crashed the armoured train and ambushed the 408 officers and soldiers within, who soon surrendered. The train was later used by the rebels as a base for further attacks.

Few visitors leave Santa Clara without a snapshot of the derailed train, but don't expect to be occupied by it for more than a few minutes. Though the Cuban historians responsible for churning out government-approved books and texts on the Revolution never tire of telling the tale of the against-the-odds military victory which the monument commemorates, there is surprisingly little fuss made of the story here. The five derailed carriages lie strewn at the side of the road, in between the river and the train track, with plenty of local traffic passing by, giving the sense that they're as much a part of the local landscape as the trees and the buildings around them. Rather more drama is evoked by the large concrete monoliths shooting out from the wreck, while the bulldozer which helped do the damage sits atop a large concrete star looking over the scene. You can step inside the carriages (Mon–Sat 9am–5.30pm; $1CUC, photos $1CUC), where there are exhibits relating to the event and some dramatic photos of the scene just after the derailment.

Three blocks further along the main road here, the Carretera de Camajuaní, brings you to the Cuban Communist Party provincial headquarters where, out front, is an unusual, slightly bizarre bronze **statue** of Che Guevara, by the Spanish sculptor Casto Solano Marroyo. Known locally as the **Che de los Niños** and easy to miss if you're not looking out for it (it's slightly set back from the road), the life-sized figure is striding forward purposefully, head held high and looking every inch the revolutionary. At first sight this appears to be a fairly straightforward representation of the man; however, a closer inspection reveals symbols that represent elements of Che's life. On his right shoulder is a tiny child riding a goat, a reference to Che the child as he rode away from the security of his family in Argentina, while a crowd of tiny figures emerging from his belt buckle celebrates his achievements and represent the movement from pre-revolutionary darkness into the light.

Loma del Capiro

Beyond the Che statue, on the northeastern outskirts of the city, a couple of kilometres from the centre, is the surprisingly inconspicuous **Loma del Capiro**, a large mound of a hill rising abruptly from the comparatively flat surroundings, and providing splendid views over the city and the flatlands to the north and east. This is a peaceful, unspoilt spot for a picnic, where you're more likely to encounter a few kids flying kites than other tourists. There's a small car park near the summit from where a concrete staircase climbs gently 150m up to the top, and a steel monument commemorating the taking of the hill by Che Guevara in 1958, during the Battle of Santa Clara.

To get to the hill, a good half-hour's walk from Parque Vidal, take the fifth right turn off the Carretera de Camajuaní after the Monumento a la Toma del Tren Blindado, onto Ana Pegudo, then the second left onto Felix Huergo, which you should follow to its conclusion, and then turn right for the car park. Alternatively, you can take a taxi from the centre for around $2CUC.

Eating

There are a number of **paladares** in the city, but only one that can be considered a bona fide restaurant. Some time ago, laws in Santa Clara decreed that any new *paladares* were forbidden to provide their customers with tables and chairs, and could only offer a limited range of food and drink, excluding alcohol, seafood and dairy products. As a result, there are several standing-only *paladares* around the city. On the whole, the **state restaurants** fail to combine good food with an agreeable atmosphere and usually lack either one or the other, although almost all of them charge in national pesos, making Santa Clara a cheap place to eat out. However, you're generally better off eating at a *casa particular* or one of the hotels on the outskirts of the city, namely *Los Caneyes* and *Villa La Granjita*. For ice cream head to *Coppelia* at Colón e/ Eduardo Machado y Domingo Mujica or *Cafétería Piropo* at Boulevard esq. Lorda. **Self-caterers** should check out the Agromercado Sandino, a farmers' market in the northeast part of Santa Clara that has the widest variety of fresh food and charges in national pesos. It's about a kilometre from the centre in the shadow of the Estadio Sandino baseball stadium. To walk there, follow Colón for a few blocks south of the centre, then turn left onto the Avenida 9 de Abril which will take you over the river and to within sight of the stadium.

Restaurants and paladares

1878 Máximo Gómez e/ Parque Vidal y Boulevard ☎42/20-2428. The best national peso restaurant in town, serving reasonable *comida criolla* to the soothing sounds of live piano music. Though the finish is decidedly unpolished, it lends a certain authenticity to this nineteenth-century building. Main meals cost around $30CUP. Daily 8.30–10.30am, noon–2.45pm & 7–10.45pm.

Casa del Gobernador Boulevard esq. J.B. Zayas ☎42/20-2273. Typical *criolla* fare, but served to a higher standard than usual in a beautiful colonial building. You can choose to eat on a sunny, plant-filled patio, or in the stately dining room.

El Castillo 9 de Abril (San Miguel) no.9 e/ Cuba y Villuendas. If you don't mind standing up at a bar while eating, you won't get better value than at this *paladar*, in a neocolonial fort-like residence. Decent helpings of reliable pork, chicken or liver dishes are around a dollar each. Daily noon–3pm & 6–9pm, closed Tues.

La Concha Carretera Central esq. Danielito ☎42/21-8124. A host of classic Cuban dishes, like *ropa vieja* and grilled lobster, as well as extremely cheap pizza and good-value pork and chicken meals are on the large menu here. For choice and variety, this is the most reliable restaurant in the

city centre but, situated right next to the main road, it feels a bit like a motorway café. Charges only in convertible pesos, but still inexpensive.

El Marino Carretera Central esq. Ave. Ramon González Coro ☎42/20-5594. Extremely cheap chicken, pork and fish dishes, plus a solitary spaghetti option, served in a canteenish concrete bungalow. Given the prices (as low as $4.90CUP for a main dish), the quality isn't bad. Priced in national pesos, but you can pay in convertibles. Daily noon–2.45pm & 7–10.45pm.

Pizzería El Pullman Boulevard e/ Lorda y Máximo Gómez. Stodgy but very cheap pizzas at this fast-food peso *cafétería* with a street-side terrace. It's big enough to practically guarantee you'll get a seat.

Pizzería Toscana Máximo Gómez esq. Parque Vidal. Pizza, pasta and *comida criolla* are served up for national pesos in this attractive if rough around the edges restaurant, with a pleasant bar and some tables outside on a garden terrace. Daily 8–10am, noon–2.45pm & 7–10.45pm.

Sabor Latino Esquerra no.157 e/ Julio Jover y Berenguer ☎42/20-6539. Food is taken very seriously here, with the best selection and quality of Cuban cuisine in the city. Everything is cooked *al momento*, and any off-menu request is catered to (providing they have the ingredients for it). The house special, *Zarzuela Caribeña*, is a hot pot of lobster, shrimp and snapper, and there are numerous tasty chicken, pork and seafood dishes as well. Service is attentive, the decor is attractively restrained and this is simply the best place to eat out in the city. Expect to pay $10CUC or $15CUC for a main dish.

El Sótano *Santa Clara Libre*, Parque Vidal no.6. Cheap sandwiches and fried chicken in a dark and moody basement *cafétería* with a certain clandestine air about it. Open in the daytime only.

Los Tainos *Los Caneyes*, Ave. de los Eucaliptos y Circunvalación ☎ 42/21-8140. The buffet restaurant at this hotel serves up some of the best-quality food in the city, usually laying out a

couple of different meats, plenty of vegetables, and a decent pasta; additionally, this is the only place in Santa Clara you will find a salad counter. Evening meals are accompanied by live music, and the restaurant itself is housed in a faithfully designed if slightly phoney-feeling Taíno-style circular lodge. The all-you-can-eat buffet costs $12CUC. Daily 7.30–10am, noon–3.30pm & 7–10pm.

Vista al Parque *Santa Clara Libre*, Parque Vidal no.6. Although somewhat lacking in character, this clean, modern and extremely popular 24hr café, conveniently located on the ground floor of the *Santa Clara Libre*, serves a good selection of snacks, juices, coffees and beers.

Drinking

Santa Clara is endowed with several atmospheric places for a **drink**, including the saloon-style bar in *1878* (see p.350) and a number of down-at-heel but characterful joints. Boulevard is lined with *cafeterías* open till late, some of which have simple little bars attached but most with a strictly limited selection of drinks.

Bars and cafés

La Cuevita de Ultra Boulevard e/ Lorda y Luis Estévez. Concealed behind a smoked-glass door, this charming grotto-like bar has a snug atmosphere and walls imaginatively painted with swirling skies and fluffy clouds.

Europa Boulevard esq. Luis Estévez. Redeems its otherwise soulless character by its location on a sociable corner of the pedestrianized section of Independencia. Open 24 hours.

La Marquesina Parque Vidal esq. Máximo Gómez. In the corner of the theatre building, has beer, rum, soft drinks, a couple of cocktails and is the liveliest bar after dark when there's live music almost every night.

Pullman Máximo Gómez esq. Boulevard. A cosy, wood-panelled bar with old-fashioned, humming ceiling fans and a good range of beers, rums and liqueurs.

La Terraza *Santa Clara Libre*. A dark, intimate rooftop bar with great views and a small dance floor.

Nightlife and entertainment

Nightlife focuses predominantly on pedestrianized Boulevard and lively Parque Vidal, where there are plenty of people, both young and old, buzzing around until the early hours of the morning at weekends. You could conceivably spend the whole night hanging out on the square, especially if there is live music from the bandstand, but there are several venues on or within a few blocks of Parque Vidal that can provide something different.

Santa Clara's busy cultural calendar, the fullest in the region, includes a seven-day theatre **festival** at *El Mejunje* (see p.352) during the last week of January, and a city-wide **film festival** that runs for about five days towards the end of November. Most of the highest-profile cultural events take place at the **Teatro La Caridad** on Parque Vidal, which hosts **plays**, **orchestral performances** and **ballet**, though it doesn't follow a strict programme of events. Past performers here have included Alicia Alonso and the Cuban National Ballet as well as Chucho Valdés, one of the greatest Cuban pianists of all time and band leader of internationally renowned jazz outfit Irakere. Show nights are generally Wednesday, Friday and Saturday from 8.30pm onwards and on Sunday from 5pm. Theatre tickets vary in price but should rarely exceed $10CUC. **Films** are screened at the *Cine Cubanacán*, at Boulevard no.60 e/ Villuendas y J.B. Zayas, and the Cine Camilo Cienfuegos (☎ 42/20-3005), in the *Santa Clara Libre*. The noticeboard outside the latter has details of films showing at *salas de video* at these two cinemas and around the city.

National-league **baseball** games are held at the Estadio Sandino, entrance on Calle 2 (☎ 42/20-6461 & 20-3838), on Tuesdays, Wednesdays, Thursdays, Saturdays and Sundays during the season; as at all live sport venues in Cuba, it'll cost you a peso to get in. The **swimming pool** at the *Los Caneyes* hotel on the southern outskirts of the city is open to the public for $5CUC.

Cabarets, nightclubs and live music venues

El Bosque Calle 1 esq. Carretera Central, next to the bridge over the Río Cubanicay ☎ 42/20-4444. For the full-on cabaret experience, with its slick comedians and professional singers and dancers, this is generally regarded as being the best show in town. The entrance charge of $5CUC covers groups of up to four and includes a free bottle of rum. Wed–Sun at 10pm.

Casa de la Ciudad Boulevard esq. J.B. Zayas ☎ 42/20-5593. Monthly programmes of traditional Cuban music, such as *trova* and *danzón*, performed on the central patio of this delightful colonial residence. There are afternoon and evening shows. Entrance costs vary but rarely exceed $1CUC and are often charged in pesos.

Casa de la Cultura Parque Vidal ☎ 42/21-7181. Hosts mainly local but also national dance and music groups. There is a fairly diverse monthly programme (posted in the foyer) which usually includes *trova* and *danzón* nights as well as nights for kids. The most reliable times to catch live music here are Sat between 4 and 6pm (when there are performances out front in the street) and on Sat and Sun at 9pm. Open Wed–Sat 10am–10pm. Entrance is free.

Club Boulevard Independencia 225 e/ Maceo y Union ☎ 42/21-6236. The only place in town that

can call itself a true nightclub, albeit a very small one. Slightly more sophisticated and image-conscious than other spots. Daily 10pm–2am, closed Mon; $3CUC Tues–Thurs, $5CUC Fri–Sun.

El Dorado Luis Estévez e/ Independencia y Céspedes. A cross between a school disco and an underground jazz club, this usually buzzing "piano bar" attracting predominantly local couples is full of 1980s cheesiness, but it's still authentic contemporary Cuban nightlife. You may have to tap on the door to get in. Daily 9pm–1am; $1CUC.

El Mejunje Marta Abreu no.12 e/ J.B. Zayas y Rafael Lubián ☎ 42/28-2572. The city's most varied programme of live shows, dances and music, attracting a bohemian crowd and popular with the local gay community. Staged in an Arcadian open-air courtyard under the shade of a capacious flamboyan tree, the entertainment ranges from rock nights to live jazz and *salsa*. As well as traditional Cuban music, at the weekends there's either a disco or a transvestite show. Check for notices on the door or a board just inside for details of the week's programme. $1–2CUC.

La Terraza *Santa Clara Libre*, Parque Vidal. On the cramped U-shaped roof terrace of the hotel there's an unglamorous small-scale cabaret that's probably best for taking in views of the city accompanied by music. Daily 9pm–2am; $1CUC.

Listings

Banks and exchange The best bank for foreign currency transactions is the Banco Financiero Internacional, Cuba e/ Rafael Tristá y Eduardo Machado (San Cristóbal) (Mon–Fri 8am–3pm). Credit card withdrawals and traveller's cheques are also handled at the Banco de Crédito y Comercio, Parque Vidal esq. Rafael Tristá y Cuba (Mon–Fri 8am–3pm), and the Banco Popular de Ahorro, Cuba esq. Maestra Nicolasa (Candelaria) (Mon–Fri 8am–3.30pm). For changing dollars to pesos, go to the Cadeca *casa de cambio*, Rafael Tristá esq. Cuba (Mon–Sat 8.30am–6pm, Sun 8.30am–12.30pm), where there's also an ATM; there's an ATM at Banco Popular de Ahorro, Máximo Gómez esq. Alfredo Barrero, as well.

Bookshop Pepe Medina on Parque Vidal esq. Colón has some international titles, all in Spanish. Librería Vietnam, Boulevard e/ Luis Estévez y Plácido, sells predominantly Cuban books.

Car rental For the best cars go to Rex at Marta Abreu no.162 e/ Alemán y J.B. Zayas ☎ 42/22-2244, where Havanautos (☎ 42/20-9117) also has an office. Cubacar operate from the third floor of the *Santa Clara Libre* hotel (☎ 42/21-8177); Micar are at Independencia esq. Virtudes near the local bus station (☎ 42/20-4570).

Immigration and legal To extend your tourist card go to the Department of Immigration office near the Estadio Sandino at Reparto Sandino no.9

e/ Carretera Central y Avenida Sandino (Mon–Thurs 8am–noon & 1–3pm). For all other legal matters visit the Consultoría Jurídica Internacional at Rafael Tristá no.5 e/ Villuendas y Cuba (Mon–Fri 8.30am–noon & 1.30–5.30pm).

Internet Telepunto, Marta Abreu no.51 esq. Enrique Villuendas (daily 8.30am–9.30pm); InfoInternet, Marta Abreu no.57 e/ Parque Vidal y Villuendas (Mon–Sat 8am–5pm); Salón Juvenil Palmares, Marta Abreu esq. Enrique Villuendas (daily 9am–6pm). See also "Telephones" below.

Medical The Clínico Quirúrgico Arnaldo Milián Castro is the most comprehensively equipped hospital in the area. For information call ☎42/27-2016. For an ambulance call ☎42/27-1008.

Money transfer Western Union in Praga department store, Boulevard esq. Máximo Gómez (Mon–Sat 9am–5pm & Sun 9am–noon).

Pharmacy The only so-called international pharmacy is in the *Los Caneyes* hotel; of the peso pharmacies the one at Luis Estévez y Boulevard is as good as any.

Photography Photoservice has a branch at Máximo Gómez no.17 e/ Boulevard y Parque Vidal, and there's a Photo Club at Marta Abreu e/ Máximo Gómez y Enrique Villuendas.

Police In an emergency call ☎116. The central police station is at Colón no.222 e/ Serafín Garcia (Nazareno) y E.P. Morales (Síndico) (☎42/21-2623).

Post office Main branch is at Colón no.10 e/ Parque Vidal y Eduardo Machado (San Cristóbal) (Mon–Sat 8am–6pm, Sun 8am–2pm); DHL and EMS services are available.

Shopping The best place for groceries and rum is the Supermercado Praga, Boulevard esq. Villuendas. For tapes and CDs, try Video Centro, Parque Vidal esq. Leoncio Vidal or Mi Ilusión, which also stocks toiletries, at Colón no.16 e/ Parque Vidal y Eduardo Machado (San Cristóbal). You can buy cigars, rum and coffee from La Veguita over the road from the Fábrica de Tabacos on Maceo e/ Berenguer y Julio Jover. The best variety and quality of arts and crafts are at the Fondo de Bienes Culturales at Luis Estévez e/ Parque Vidal y Boulevard. For something more novel have a look through the bric-a-brac at the *casa comisionista* (a Cuban-style pawn shop) at Boulevard e/ Luis Estévez y Plácido.

Taxis Transtur, on the third floor of the *Santa Clara Libre* hotel (☎42/21-8177); Cubataxi (☎42/20-6903); Taxi OK (☎42/20-2040 & 20-0905).

Telephones Telepunto, Marta Abreu no.51 esq. Enrique Villuendas (daily 8.30am–9.30pm); ETECSA Cabina de Llamadas at Eduardo Machado (San Cristóbal) esq. Cuba (daily 7.30am–10.30pm).

Remedios and around

Just over 40km northeast of Santa Clara and less than 10km from the coast, the town of **REMEDIOS** sits unobtrusively near the developing resort area on the northern cays. One of the earliest Spanish towns in Cuba, founded shortly after the establishment of the seven *villas*, Remedios has a history longer than Santa Clara's, going back as far as the 1520s. Today's provincial capital was, in fact, founded by citizens of Remedios who, following a series of pirate attacks towards the end of the sixteenth century, transplanted the settlement further inland. However, the local populace was far from united in its desire to desert Remedios and in an attempt to force the issue, those who wanted to leave burnt the town to the ground. Rebuilt from the ashes, by 1696 the town had its own civic council and went on to produce not only one of Cuba's most renowned composers, Alejandro García Caturla, but also a Spanish president, Dámaso Berenguer Fuste, who governed Spain in the 1930s.

With a history rivalling that of Trinidad, Remedios remains relatively unexploited in comparison, albeit less elegant. The faded paintwork and terra-cotta roofs of the generally modest, still-lived-in colonial homes and the notice-able absence of motorized transport around the centre reflect a town unchanged by the advent of the market economy, although with the general development of tourism in the region, Remedios has now established its place on the visitor's map. Part of the town's fame comes from its status as the birthplace of **Las Parrandas**, the festivals celebrated every Christmas when the town divides in two and fights a mock war using carnival floats. Though the modest number of sights in Remedios will provide no more than half a day of sightseeing, its superb and reasonably priced hotel, the *Mascotte*, and the town's friendly, relaxed atmosphere make it well worth stopping over for a night.

There are organized excursions to Remedios from Santa Clara, some of which stop off here on their way to or from the cays off the north coast. Cubanacán offer an eight-hour day-trip taking in all the museums and lunch in the *Mascotte* hotel for $29CUC per person, whilst Havanatur include a stop here on their day-trip to Cayo Las Brujas for $40CUC.

Arrival, information and practicalities

To get to Remedios from Santa Clara, you can catch an intermunicipal **bus** from the terminal on the Carretera Central e/ Pichardo y Amparo (2 daily) or an interprovincial Astro bus from the Terminal de Omnibus Nacionales, on the corner of Carretera Central and Oquendo (1 daily). Alternatively, you can make the ninety-minute journey in a private **taxi**, which you can find opposite either bus terminal. If you **arrive** at the **bus station** on the outskirts of the more urbanized centre of the town, there are no straightforward alternatives other than to walk the eight blocks north along Independencia which lead directly to Plaza Martí.

For general **information** or **guides** (see opposite), call in at the reception desk of the *Hotel Mascotte*, where they are used to helping tourists, whether or not they are guests of the hotel. While there's nowhere in town to exchange foreign currency (the nearest place to do that is Caibarién; see p.358), Remedios does have a **post office**, at José Antonio Peña esq. Antonio Romero (Mon–Sat 8am–6pm). Uniquely, the town has its own **valet parking service**, based at Avenida Marcelo Salado no.62. Ring ☎42/39-5130 to have your car picked up from anywhere in town and brought back at 8.30am the next day, all for a charge of $2CUC.

Accommodation

For its size, Remedios has a disproportionately large selection of **accommodation** with around twenty *casas particulares*, many quite basic, and one excellent hotel. There is a particular concentration of houses renting rooms on José A Peña, the road off the main square on the church side. Expect to pay between $15CUC and $25CUC per night for a *casa particular*.

Hostal Barcelona de Haydee y Juan K José Antonio Peña no.75 e/ Maceo y La Pastora ☎42/39-5062. A spick-and-span compact house, run by a friendly couple. The subtly decorated, fresh-looking rooms with a/c and en-suite bathrooms are based around a gorgeous little central patio, where Haydee serves great food. (Don't miss her *frituritas* with honey.) Juan loves to talk politics, so this is a good option for anyone with an interest in the Revolution. ❷

Hostal El Chalet Brigadier González no.29 e/ Independencia y José Antonio Peña ☎42/39-6301. A spacious, modern, bright-blue house that's luxurious by local standards, with a garden and parking for two cars. There are two double rooms based around a fantastic roof terrace, and guests have the run of this upstairs floor. The biggest room, more like a mini apartment, is particularly impressive; it basks in a wonderful natural light, has a comfortable reception area and affords views over the treetops to the church on the main square. ❷

Hostal Gladys Aponte Brigadier González no.32 altos e/ Independencia y Pi y Margall ☎42/39-5398. One huge room with two double beds in an apartment which has seen better days. Nevertheless, it has a wonderful tiled floor and a roof terrace, complete with a pigeon coop and views of the town's red-tiled rooftops. ❸

Hostal La Casona Cueto Alejandro del Río no.72 ☎42/39-5350, ✉amarelys@capiro.vcl.sld.cu. This late eighteenth-century house just behind the Plaza Martí has two basic double rooms, a central courtyard with steps to a roof terrace and a spacious indoor communal area with an authentic colonial look. ❷

Mascotte On the Máximo Gómez side of Plaza Martí ☎ 42/39-5144, 39-5145 & 39-5467, ℱ 39-5327, ⒺÓ reservas@mascotte.vcl.cyt.cu. The town's only hotel has a courteous staff, a charming down-to-earth character and an elegant yet simple interior. Booking is advisable as there are only ten rooms, all well furnished and most of them located around an open-air balcony overlooking the delightful patio bar. Excellent value. ❹

The Town

Easily manageable on foot, Remedios is an inviting place to stroll around without having to think too much about what you choose to visit, as all the museums are either on or within shouting distance of the central **Plaza Martí**, the unremarkable main square. English- and French-speaking **guides** based at the *Mascotte* hotel on Plaza Martí conduct three-hour-long tours of the town centre, setting off at 9.30am daily, although you can always ask if a tour would be possible later in the day ($3CUC per person).

Iglesia de San Juan Bautista

By far the most stunning sight in Remedios is the main altar of the **Iglesia de San Juan Bautista**, the town's principal church, occupying the southern face of the Plaza Martí, with more to offer than the similar-looking Iglesia del Buen Viaje, set back from the plaza on the opposite side. Entry is usually via the back door but don't let the fact that you may have to knock deter you, as the friendly staff are well used to receiving foreign visitors. Once inside, the magnificence of the main altar seems all the more shocking in comparison with the attractive but simple and rather withered exterior. Made from gilded precious wood, not a single square inch of the surface has escaped the illustriously detailed design of this impressively large shrine. It was commissioned by a Cuban millionaire named Eutimio Falla Bonet, who funded the restoration of the whole church between 1944 and 1954 following his discovery that he had family roots in Remedios. Though the current building dates back only to the late eighteenth century, a church has stood on this site since the sixteenth. However, it was only after Bonet's revamping that the church acquired its most notable features, such as the splendid timber ceiling and the set of golden altars lining the walls, collected from around Cuba and beyond, which have transformed the place into a kind of religious trophy cabinet.

Museo de la Música Alejandro García Caturla

Also on the Plaza Martí, at Camilo Cienfuegos no.5, opposite the hotel, the simple **Museo de la Música Alejandro García Caturla** (☎42/39-6851; Tues–Sat 9am–noon & 1–6pm, Sun 9am–1pm; $1CUC) is dedicated to the town's most successful musician, who lived and worked in the building for the last twenty years of his life. A lawyer with a passion for music, especially the piano and violin, Caturla reached the lofty heights of performing with the Havana Philharmonic Orchestra as well as laying some of the foundations of modern Cuban music with his boundary-breaking combinations of traditional symphonic styles and African rhythms. Sadly, he was murdered in December 1940 by a man whom he was due to prosecute the following day. Caturla's study has been preserved and still contains all its original furniture and books, while photographs charting the various stages of his life, including some of his many trips overseas, help bring a personal touch to the overwhelming number of documents and photocopies on display. The museum has a small concert room where you can sometimes catch live musical performances in the afternoon or evening.

Museo de las Parrandas Remedianas

One and a half blocks north of the *Mascotte* on Máximo Gómez, the **Museo de las Parrandas Remedianas** (Tues–Sat 9am–noon & 1–6pm, Sun 9am–1pm; $1CUC) is the nearest you're likely to get to experiencing *Las Parrandas*, the annual festival on December 24 for which Remedios is renowned throughout Cuba (see box, opposite). The scene in the town every Christmas Eve is portrayed downstairs with a scale model of the main square and two opposing floats, which form the centrepieces of the event. Upstairs, photographs dating back to 1899 provide a more vivid picture of what goes on, showing some of the spectacular floats, known as *carrozas*, and the stationary *trabajos de plaza*, which have graced the event over the years. There are also examples of the torches, instruments, colourful costumes and flags, which form such an integral part of the raucous celebrations.

Museo de Historia Local

Slightly deeper into the local neighbourhood, a few minutes' walk away from the Plaza Martí, at Maceo no.56, the **Museo de Historia Local** (Mon 8am–noon, Tues–Sat 8am–noon & 1–5pm; $1CUC) charts the history of the town and surrounding region from aboriginal times to the Revolution. There are two rooms containing some fine examples of nineteenth-century Cuban baroque furniture – easier to appreciate than most of the other displays in the museum, which skim the surface of themes like geology and wildlife and look more closely at local history, from the Wars of Independence to the "pseudo" republic to the Revolution. It's a good idea to opt for a guided tour, when everything is placed in its historical context and the museum attendant is relieved from her boredom.

Eating, drinking and nightlife

The *Mascotte's* **restaurant**, *Las Arcadas* (daily 7.30–10.30am, noon–3pm & 7–10pm), should be your first choice for a meal, with reasonably priced seafood and meat dishes. Alternatively, the *Colonial* (daily 11am–10pm) at Independencia no.25 e/ Brigadier González y Antonio Romero serves up smoked pork, chicken, ham and rice for pesos in an elegant old mansion house with a black-and-white marble floor and an enormous chandelier. The balcony of the upstairs bar has great views and makes a good spot for a sundowner. When it comes to getting a **drink**, other than the bar in the *Mascotte* hotel, El Louvre (Mon–Fri 8am–midnight, Sat & Sun 8am–1am), on the same side of the plaza, has twice as much choice and style as the one or two basic alternatives around the town.

Nightlife in Remedios takes place almost exclusively at weekends. Next door to *El Louvre* is *Las Leyendas* (T 42/39-6264; Wed–Sun 10am–2am; $1CUC), a pleasant patio with a bar and stage hosting small-scale cabarets and live music. The *Casa de la Cultura*, facing the plaza on the same side as the Iglesia de San Juan Bautista, usually hosts live bands on Friday, Saturday and Sunday nights at 9pm. A recently constructed outdoor venue enclosed by black railings is *El Guije*, at Maceo esq. Independencia, where live music and dance feature amongst the weekly shows. The other focus for musical and social activity is the Parque de la Trova, an extension of the Plaza Martí where outdoor discos and concerts by the Remedios brass band take place on alternate nights of the week. One of the liveliest times to be here is in the first week of March, when **La Semana de la Cultura** (Culture Week) sees concerts and cultural activities taking place day and night.

Las Parrandas

Once a year, on the night of December 24th, the usually sedate citizens of Remedios let themselves go in a grand occasion of organized anarchy: **Las Parrandas**, a 200-year-old tradition which originated in the town and has spread throughout the province and beyond. Since the end of the nineteenth century there have been annual *parrandas* in neighbouring towns like Camajuani, Zulueta and Caibarién, but the one in Remedios remains the biggest and the best. During the festival, the town divides into northern and southern halves, with the frontier running through the centre of Plaza Martí: north is the San Salvador neighbourhood, whose emblem is an eagle on a blue background, and south is the Carmen neighbourhood, represented by a rooster on a red background. The opposing sides mark their territory with huge static constructions (which look like floats but are in fact stationary), known as *trabajos de plaza*, whose extravagant designs change annually, each one built to be more spectacular than the last. The celebrations kick off at around 4pm when the whole town gathers in the plaza to drink, dance, shout and sing. *Artilleros*, the fireworks experts, set off hundreds of eardrum-popping **firecrackers** until the square is shrouded in an acrid pall of black smoke and people can hardly see. Following that, the revellers form huge, pulsing **congas** and traipse around the square for hours, cheering their own team and chanting insult songs at their rivals. The neighbourhoods' avian symbols appear on a sea of waving banners, flags, staffs, placards and bandanas tied around their citizens' necks.

As night falls, the two large **floats**, the *carrozas*, which along with the *trabajos de plaza* form the focus of the celebrations, do a ceremonial round of the plaza. Built to represent their respective halves of the town, the floats are fantastical creations with multicoloured decorations and flashing lights forming intricate patterns. Contructed by the town's resident population of *parrandas* fanatics, who devote the majority of their free time throughout the year to designing and creating them, the floats are judged by the rest of the town on looks and originality. As everyone makes up their minds, a massive fireworks display illuminates the sky and further heightens the tension. Finally, in the early morning hours, the church bell is ceremoniously rung and the winner announced. The president of the winning neighbourhood is then triumphantly paraded around on his jubilant team's shoulders before everyone heads home to recover, enjoy Christmas and start planning the next year's festivities.

Museo de la Agroindustria Azucarera

A few kilometres outside Remedios, on the road to the coast and Caibarién, is a large sign for the **Museo de la Agroindustria Azucarera** (☎42/36-3636; Mon–Sat 8am–6.30pm; $1CUC; $3CUC photos), sometimes known as the **Museo de Vapor**, a sugar factory half-converted into a museum of the Cuban sugar industry. Shortly after the sign is a left turn leading straight down to the museum itself. The museum is more accustomed to receiving tour groups, but you can still visit independently, although this sometimes means missing out on the full tour for groups, which includes a visit by steam train to a restaurant at nearby Finca Curujey. Visit the *Hotel Mascotte* in Remedios to book a place with a tour group which costs $15CUC per person and requires a minimum of ten people, making it advisable to book in advance.

Set in the spacious, dilapidated grounds of the old Marcelo Salado sugar refinery, founded in 1891, the factory seems frozen as it stood when it finally ground to a halt in 1999, as part of a wave of closures affecting the most inefficient branches of the industry. Opened as a museum in 2002, the place is laid out almost exactly as it was left, with a vacant, airport-hangar-sized warehouse dominating one side, and at its core a large train shed and dormant factory floor under a metal roof. There are also a few bits and pieces imported to give a fuller picture of the colonial and twentieth-century Cuban sugar industry. Though it's a little disjointed and the layout a bit messy, the functioning steam trains (the highlight here) and the real-life setting make this an engaging place to visit.

The guided **tours** start with a short, fairly pointless video in the reception building about steam engines in Cuba. The first tangible section of the museum is in a corner of the factory where most of the machinery used in the sugar production process was and still is housed. A small area in front of the machinery has been cleared to exhibit reconstructed scenes and preserved artefacts from the age before steam, when sugar was produced by machinery driven predominantly by slaves and animals. Amongst the primitive equipment on display is a *trapiche*, invented at the end of the eighteenth century to press sugar cane, as well as some large brick ovens. Beyond these exhibits is the factory machinery itself, most of it functioning right up until the whole placed closed. In a completely separate, much smaller building the steam-powered train theme is taken up again with pictures of the earliest steam engines in Cuba, including a train named *La Junta*, dating from 1843 and the oldest preserved steam train in Cuba, currently kept in Havana. The most interesting part of the museum is in the nearby train shed, where there are six fabulous working steam trains, built in the US between 1904 and 1920 by the famous Baldwin Locomotive Works. A seventh engine is on display with its shell removed, revealing all the working parts.

Caibarién and the northern cays

From Remedios it's about 10km further to the run-down but pleasant port town of **Caibarién**, a good base for exploring the cays if you prefer to stay on the mainland, where the accommodation is significantly less expensive. The town's streets are lined by rows of wooden sugar warehouses, painted in a faded rainbow of colours, which testify to this sleepy backwater's nineteenth-century heyday. Largely unaffected by tourism and enjoying a leisurely speed of life, Caibarién provides a marked contrast to the development on the cays.

Local **buses** from Remedios (3 daily; 30min) stop just outside Caibarién's train station. From here, it's a short walk along Calle 8, past the statue of José Martí, to the town's quiet central square, **Parque de la Libertad**, bordered by stone benches, shaded by elegant trees and with a distinctive, pale yellow, domed and colonnaded gazebo in the middle. The pretty ochre- and cream-coloured church, La Iglesia de la Inmaculada Concepción, on the southern side of the square is worth a peek. Though there are no formal opening hours, if someone's around to open the door you can climb the bell tower for a breathtaking view over the rooftops to the sea. There is a branch of the travel agents Havanatur (☎42/35-1171 & 35-1173; Mon–Fri 8.30am–noon & 1.30–4.30pm, Sat 8.30am–noon) on the square which you can use as an **information** centre, but its principal function is booking organized excursions.

The only other main centre of activity in town is the *malecón*, the fairly desolate seafront promenade. To get to it, stay on the same road from Remedios and Santa Clara as it takes you straight into town, all the way down to the end where a right turn leads over to the newly renovated section of the *malecón*: a three-hundred-metre stretch of pavement flanked on one side by a dinky seawall and on the other by a line of low palms. This is a good place for a midday break by the sea and you can get a drink and a bite to eat here at the *Cafeteria Piropo*, a fast-food joint serving hot dogs, fried chicken and sandwiches, or you can try one of the small kiosks set up over the road from the seafront, but there's very little else to do.

There is a newly built hotel and a reasonable selection of *casas particulares* in town providing **accommodation**, though they are difficult to find. The hotel, the *Brisas del Mar* (☎42/35-1699; ❹) is located beyond the *malecón*, from where the coastal road runs along the edge of a small natural harbour full of fishing boats onto a small peninsula. The simple but handsome hotel sits just above a tuft of beach with its rooms facing out to sea; guests have use of a pool just over the road, which non-guests can use for $5CUC. Amongst the *casas particulares*, *Villa Virginia*, at Ciudad Pesquera no.73 (☎42/36-3303; ❷), is 1.5km west of the centre along the seafront in a convivial housing estate that's also home to a fishing community. The friendly hosts offer good food and two decent double rooms which lack natural light but have air conditioning, tiled bathrooms and shared TV and fridge. There's also *Pension de Eladio*, no.1016b Ave. 35 e/ 10 y 12 (☎42/36-4253; ❷), on the opposite side of town half a block from the seafront near the new section of the *malecón*. There are two pleasant and adequately equipped rooms in this upstairs flat, with views of the town from the roof terrace, rocking chairs on the front-of-house balcony and a magnificent fortress-shaped fish tank in the living room. The price includes breakfast and dinner.

You'll find a couple of basic cafés on the main square, as well as the Villa Blanca dollar supermarket for picnic supplies, but the best place in town to **eat**, outside of the *casas particulares*, is the *Cafetería Villa Blanca* (☎42/36-3305), four blocks away from the square along Avenida 9, where seafood, chicken and steaks are served at tables dotted around a small garden. They also rent out scooters and have a telephone that accepts international phone cards. Nearer the *malecón* is *La Ruina*, where the fish, pork and fried chicken dishes are no more than $4CUC each.

Nightlife is limited to a stroll down the *malecón* or the live music and karaoke supposedly put on at *Cafeteria Piropo*, but this will depend principally on whether there is a visiting tour group from the cays. There is also a **cinema** at Calle 14 no.1709.

The northern cays

From Caibarién, the second and only other road into town besides the one from Remedios heads south, roughly parallel with the coastline, until just before a bridge over the road 4km from the town. Here there is a left turn leading down to the 24-hour checkpoint that marks the start of the causeway linking the mainland to the **northern cays** – one of Cuba's newest major tourist resorts, set on a network of dozens of mostly very small islets leading up to Cayo Santa María, a much larger cay almost 20km in length. Only one of these small islands, Cayo Las Brujas, is suitable for day-trippers; the others are either inaccessible or the exclusive domain of the hotel guests, though you can pay a fee (usually around $40CUC) for a one-day hotel pass which entitles you to full use of all the facilities. To pass the checkpoint you'll be asked to produce your passport and pay $2CUC per vehicle; keep the receipt as you will need to show it, and pay another $2CUC, on your return. If you haven't rented a car, taxis from Caibarién to the cays can be organized through Transgaviota who have an office in the town (☎42/35-1353) and another in the hotel *Sol Cayo Santa María*. The trip costs $25CUC each way.

The drive down the 48-kilometre-long causeway to the outcrop of miniature islands is quite spectacular and half the fun of a visit. The dark, deeper waters nearer the land give way to shallow turquoise around the cays and then become almost clear as the network of cays increases in number and complexity. It's worth stopping your car along the side of the road to appreciate the phenomenon of being miles from land but surrounded by water just a few inches deep, the absolute silence broken only by the occasional vehicle on the near-empty causeway. The sea is dotted with mangrove colonies, while herons and cormorants swoop overhead and the occasional iguana basks in the sun on the hot tarmac. The solid rock causeway is broken up by small bridges allowing the sea currents to flow through and providing drivers with distance markers, there being around fifty bridges in all, each of them visibly numbered. The development on the cays begins just after bridge 36.

Cayo Las Brujas

Turning left at the pocket-sized airport terminal on arriving at the first of the developed cays, **Cayo Las Brujas**, a road cuts through the green brush that covers most of the islet and skirts around the edge of the small **airport** that serves the cays with three flights a week to Havana and Cayo Coco (☎42/35-0009 & 35-0011). At the end of the road is a minuscule car park where you will have to show your passport to the attendant and from where a short wooden gangway leads to the carefully hidden **beach** and the *Villa Las Brujas* (see below). At the reception building you may be asked for what appears to be an unofficial fee to use the beach, usually $1CUC, or $3CUC if you intend to use the restaurant, though this does supposedly entitle you to a sandwich. Sitting snugly at the end of the craggy platform along which the hotel cabins are lined up is *Restaurant El Farallón*, the only option for **food**. Serving a few moderately priced meat and seafood dishes, it has been appropriately designed and fitted with wooden furniture, floors and walls, in keeping with the overall natural feel. A spiral staircase leads up to the lookout tower and a modest view of the ocean on one side and a sea of green scrub on the other. Dividing the two is the narrow, curving sandy **beach**, dotted with palm thatch umbrellas, which arches round enough to form an open bay of usually placid bluey-green waters.

At the far end of the boardwalk is **Marina Las Brujas** (☎42/35-0013), offering catamaran excursions, diving and fishing. The catamaran excursions include sunset cruises and day-long trips to snorkel at the wreck of the *Barco San Pasqual* – an American ship that sits weighed down by its heavy cargo of molasses on the shallow sea floor – lunch, an open bar and beach time ($57CUC per person, minimum 10 people). Diving costs $35CUC for the first immersion and $20CUC for subsequent dives, while yacht fishing for tarpon, marlin and snapper is $50CUC per person for four hours, with equipment included in all cases.

Back at the main road, just beyond the airport terminal, on the opposite side of the road, is the only **gas station** on the cays and a **car rental** office. Continuing from Cayo Las Brujas, the causeway links up with the next significant cay, **Cayo Ensenachos**, where the beach is now the property of the hotel established here in 2005. About 15km beyond Cayo Las Brujas, the causeway concludes at **Cayo Santa María**, boasting a stunning twenty-kilometre-long beach, which Fidel Castro is said to have described as superior to Varadero.

There are **organized excursions** from Santa Clara to Cayo Las Brujas available through the three main travel agencies there. Havanatur, for example, offer a day-trip for $40CUC per person, for a minimum of four people, which includes lunch on the cay and a stopoff in Remedios.

Accommodation

There is only one hotel on the cays accustomed to regularly receiving guests on spec: *Villa Las Brujas*. However, there is nothing to stop you from booking a

△ Cayo Las Brujas

room at one of the other, much more upmarket hotels – though it's a good idea to ring well in advance. The prices for these all-inclusive hotels, where most guests are on package holidays, are given here as the rack rates, but there are usually considerable savings for holidaymakers who book through a travel agent back home. They all have car, scooter and bicycle rental, as well as evening entertainment in the form of live music or cabaret.

Meliá Cayo Santa María Cayo Santa María
☎ 42/35-0500, ⊛ www.solmeliacuba.com. Offers a wide range of facilities, including four restaurants, three swimming pools, basketball and tennis courts, a sauna, Jacuzzi, gymnasium, reading room, scuba-diving centre and an amphitheatre. The rooms are quite homely, decorated in pastel colours and furnished with simple yet elegant metal-frame couches and beds and wicker chairs. Trees and plantlife blanket the grounds, and the whole place is in balance with the natural setting it was carved out of. ❾

Meliá Las Dunas Cayo Santa María ☎ 42/35-0100, ⊛ www.solmeliacuba.com. A hotel of truly staggering proportions, with 925 rooms, seven restaurants, a beer garden, an ice cream café, a gargantuan pool area, a small climbing wall, tennis courts, a central square and a palatial lobby skirted by waterways. The smart rooms are in balconied mansion-esque blocks, with wooden gangways leading down through the bushy scrub to the beach, while tacky Romanesque touches

(like classical-looking statues) are found throughout. ❾

Royal Hideaway Ensenachos Cayo Ensenachos ☎ 42/35-0300, ⊛ www .royalhideawayensenachos.com. The classiest hotel on these cays takes exclusivity to another level. Accommodation is split into three sections; one set, the Royal Suite section, is housed on its own peninsula, where there is a concierge and butler service, an exclusive swimming pool and private golf carts for guests' personal transport. The cost of staying in the Royal Spa section includes treatments at the state-of-the-art spa, which has a thermal pool, sauna, Jacuzzi and fitness room. ❾

Sol Cayo Santa María Cayo Santa María ☎ 42/35-0200, ⊛ www.solmeliacuba.com. This luxurious hotel is aimed at families, with children staying for free. The rooms, grouped into small villas, are arranged around a landscaped area of lawns, flowerbeds and waterways and are decorated in an attractive faux-rustic style with painted wooden

361

furniture and terracotta floor tiles. The nicest decorative touches are in the bathrooms, where one wall consists entirely of window, usually with a sea view. Has several restaurants, a dive centre, a children's play area, a gym, tennis courts and an enormous serpentine pool that snakes its way around the central area. ❾

Villa Las Brujas Cayo Las Brujas ☎ 42/35-0199, ℱ 35-0099, ℗ brujagav@enet.cu. This complex is simple, picturesque and peaceful, with a line of wooden cabins connected by a boardwalk, raised just above sea level on a natural platform along the rocky shore. The rustically comfortable cabins, decorated in earthy tones, have a/c, cable TV and balconies facing out across the water. ❻

Lago Hanabanilla

Closer to Trinidad but actually easier to access from Santa Clara, a fifty-kilometre drive away, **Lago Hanabanilla** twists, turns and stretches around the hills on the northern edges of the Sierra del Escambray. Tucked away behind the steep slopes marking the border between the countryside south of Santa Clara and the more mountainous terrain it merges into, the elongated 36-square-kilometre lake, technically a reservoir, looks more like a wide river that has spilled its banks. On arrival, views of the lake reveal no more than a small section as it slinks out of sight behind the steep, hilly slopes which come right down to the water's edge, but the valley in which it rests provides a beautiful backdrop unlikely to disappoint from any angle. Along with its unforgettable setting the lake's claim to fame is as host to the biggest number of largemouth bass in the world, as well as an abundance of trout, and is one of the prime locations for freshwater **fishing** in Cuba.

Almost all visits to the lake are channelled through the *Hanabanilla* **hotel** (☎ 42/20-8550 & 20-2399; ❸). Thankfully the dull, unimaginative architecture of the hotel, which stands right on the edge of the lake near the northern tip, is balanced out by the location. Less commercial than many tourist hotels in Cuba, the place is also appealing because, unlike some places on the island, there are Cubans as well as foreigners renting rooms here.

A day-trip to the hotel from Santa Clara is a viable option, with rowboats for rent, most of which come with an outboard motor. The boats are usually rented as part of a **fishing session** that includes a guide and four hours of fishing, for $45CUC per person, though no equipment is supplied. With no commercial fishing here for decades, waters thick with nutrients and the ideal temperature for their reproduction, the bass in Lago Hanabanilla reach record sizes, many weighing in at over 7kg, and the fishing here attracts an ever-growing number of enthusiasts. Peak season for fishing is from November until the end of March.

On the whole, the banks of the lake are difficult to access but they are well worth exploring, in some places covered in thick forest, in others idyllic grassy hillocks peppered with palms. There are attractive views from all sides of the lake and getting out along its banks, out of sight of the hotel, is a great way to appreciate this peaceful and secluded location up in the hills. The best and easiest way around the accessibility problem, and the most rewarding way to spend your time here if you're not fishing, is to take one of the four or five **boat excursions** offered by the hotel. They each cost between $20CUC and $50CUC for two people, last two or three hours and feature a **meal** at the *Río Negro Restaurant*, an excursion in itself and, if you're here for the day only, probably the best single option. It's $15CUC if you rent your own two-person motorboat, or $3CUC, excluding the cost of the food, if you join a group trip on one of the larger boats, usually taking place daily. The outdoor *Río Negro*, 7km from the hotel and perched on one of the forested slopes at the top of a stone staircase, is an assemblage of tiled platforms under matted *bohío* roofs and feels a little like an elaborate Tarzan camp. It's set up to cater specifically for excursion groups, so there's usually no choice: you take what they've got, which will invariably be roast pork or fish accompanied by vegetables, rice and *viandas*.

Of the other two worthwhile excursion destinations around the lake, each of them starting out in a boat across the lake from the hotel, there is the **Casa del Campesino**, a *guajiro* family house in a clearing in the woods where you can sample and buy the cigars manufactured here or the locally grown coffee or honey. Other than that, you can visit a **waterfall**, a 1.5-kilometre walk from where the boat will leave you, with opportunities for bathing. The lush forests around the waterfall are home to myriad birds, including trogons and Cuban todies.

To get to the lake from Santa Clara, take a right turn at the crossroads in the centre of the small town of Manicaragua and take the left turn marked by the faded sign for the lake about 15km beyond this. **Pre-booked excursions** to the lake can be arranged through Havanatur and Cubanacán in Santa Clara and are currently priced at $33CUC per person, with a minimum of three people required.

Travel details

Astro and intermunicipal buses

Cienfuegos to: Camagüey (1 daily; 6hr); Havana (5 daily; 4hr 30min); Sancti Spíritus (1 daily; 2hr 45min); Santa Clara (2 daily; 1hr 45min); Santiago de Cuba (1 daily; 14hr); Trinidad (2 daily; 2hr); Varadero (1 daily; 6hr).

Santa Clara to: Caibarién (1 daily; 1hr 30min); Cienfuegos (2 daily; 1hr 45min); Havana (1 daily; 4hr 30min); Sancti Spíritus (2 daily; 1hr 45min); Trinidad (1 daily; 3hr); Varadero (1 daily; 4hr); Remedios (3 daily; 1hr 30min); Varadero (1 daily; 4hr).

Víazul buses

Cienfuegos to: Havana (2 daily; 4hr); Trinidad (2 daily; 1hr 30min).

Santa Clara to: Havana (3 daily; 3hr 45min); Sancti Spíritus (4 daily; 1hr 30min); Trinidad (1 daily; 3hr); Varadero (1 daily; 3hr 30min).

Trains

Cienfuegos to: Havana (2 daily; 10hr); Sancti Spíritus (1 daily; 5hr 40min); Santa Clara (1 daily; 2hr 30min).

Santa Clara to: Caibarién (1 daily; 2hr); Cienfuegos (1 daily; 2hr 30min); Havana (daily; 6hr); Sancti Spíritus (1 every other day; 2hr 30min).

5

Trinidad and Sancti Spíritus

CHAPTER 5

Highlights

* **Museo Romántico** Beautifully preserved nineteenth-century furniture and architecture offer an inside look at how aristocratic Trinidadians lived in colonial times.
See p.375

* **Iberostar Grand Hotel Trinidad** A great place to visit, whether you fork out for one of the elegant rooms, eat in the plush restaurant, chill in the smokers' lounge or sip cocktails at the bar.
See p.380

* **Casa de la Música** The standout live music venue in Trinidad, offering traditional Cuban sounds and more

modern *salsa* most nights.
See p.382

* **Steam train to Manaca-Iznaga ride** Enjoy a half-hour ride from Trinidad in a charming old wooden carriage.
See p.386

* **Topes de Collantes** Excellent hiking trails are found at this beautiful national park in the steep, forested slopes of the Sierra del Escambray.
See p.387

* **Hostal del Rijo** Occupying a finely restored colonial mansion, this Sancti Spíritus hotel offers up loads of charm at reasonable prices.
See p.392

△ Plaza Mayor

5

Trinidad and Sancti Spíritus

W ith its location so close to both the beach and the mountains, and its status as the country's most perfectly preserved colonial city, **Trinidad** is justifiably the single most visited destination in central Cuba. This fantastically restored sixteenth-century town in the southwestern corner of **Sancti Spíritus** province has a time-frozen quality rivalled only by Habana Vieja, and, as a well-established point on the tourist trail, is well set up to receive visitors, with numerous excellent *casas particulares* and a reasonable variety of places to eat. Most of the flashier hotels are a fifteen-kilometre drive away on the **Península de Ancón**, which has the best beach on this part of the southern coast. In the opposite direction, **Topes de Collantes**, a mountain resort, makes an excellent base for exploring the steep, lavishly forested slopes of the **Sierra del Escambray**. East of Trinidad, the provincial capital of **Sancti Spíritus** attracts fewer visitors but is not without appeal. Best treated as a one-night stopoff, the city is as much a time capsule of the 1980s – since which time very little has changed– as it is of the last four centuries.

Trinidad and around

The vast majority of visitors to the province of **Sancti Spíritus** head directly for **TRINIDAD**, one of the island's foremost tourist attractions. While Trinidad draws more tourists than many of Cuba's larger cities, its status as a UNESCO-declared World Heritage Site has ensured that its marvellous architecture has remained unspoiled. Plenty of other Cuban towns evoke a similar sense of the past, but there is a completeness about central Trinidad's cobbled traffic-free streets, red-tiled rooftops and jumble of colonial mansions that sets it apart. Walking the streets of the colonial district

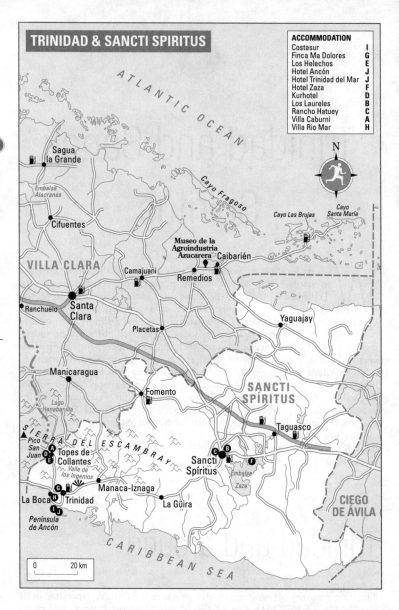

TRINIDAD & SANCTI SPIRITUS

ATLANTIC OCEAN

N

Sagua la Grande

Embalsa Alacranes

Cayo Fragoso

Cayo Las Brujas

Cayo Santa María

Cifuentes

Museo de la Agroindustria Azucarera

Caibarién

VILLA CLARA

Camajuani

Remedios

Ranchuelo

Santa Clara

Placetas

Yaguajay

Manicaragua

Fomento

SANCTI SPÍRITUS

Taguasco

Lago Hanabanilla

S I E R R A   D E L   E S C A M B R A Y

Pico San Juan

A
D E
Topes de Collantes

Valle de los Ingenios

C B
Sancti Spíritus
F

Embalse Zaza

G
La Boca
H
Trinidad
I J

Manaca-Iznaga

La Güira

CIEGO DE ÁVILA

Península de Ancón

C A R I B B E A N   S E A

0   20 km

in particular, there is something of a village feel about the place – albeit a large and prosperous village – where horses are as common a sight as cars. With tourism continuously on the rise in this town of 70,000, however, there is a stronger sense of being amongst visitors here than in most other provincial towns and cities. On walks around the colonial centre you are as likely to see a foreign face as a local one – though there are still plenty of streets seemingly unaffected by these changes. Beyond the cobbled-street centre, there are fewer specific sights, but a wander into the more recently constructed neighbourhoods is a good way of tapping into local life.

From Trinidad, most of the province's highlights are within easy reach. In fact, the city's proximity to the **Valle de los Ingenios**, site of most of the sugar estates on which the city built its fortune, the **Península de Ancón** and its Caribbean beaches, and the lush mountain slopes around the **Topes de Collantes** hiking resort, makes it one of the best bases on the island for discovering the different facets of Cuba's landscape.

Some history

Though the chronicles of one of Columbus's seamen suggest that Europeans first spotted the coast around Trinidad in 1494, it wasn't until December 1513 that a Spanish settlement was established here. By 1518 there were some sixty or seventy Spanish families living alongside the native population, making their living from gold, small-scale agriculture or cattle farming. The gold ran out that year and interest in the area began to wane, particularly as news spread of the riches to be found in Central America. It was in Trinidad that the young, ambitious **Hernan Cortés** rallied troops and mounted the expedition that conquered Mexico, creating a steady flow of emigration that left the town all but empty by 1544. By this time, however, the indigenous population had adjusted to the settlers' ways of life and it was they who kept the economy alive, farming the land and raising cattle, so that when Spanish interest in the area was reawakened in the 1580s they simply took over the reins from the Amerindians.

Approachable only by sea, with no roads to the capital, it was impossible for the authorities in Havana to control the town, and by the end of the sixteenth century corruption flourished. Easily manoeuvring around the debilitating trading and production restrictions imposed by the Spanish crown, Trinitarios built up illicit trading links with nearby Jamaica and with English, Dutch and French traders. The export of meats, hides and tobacco, in exchange for manufactured products and clothing, increased the wealth of the territory enough to attract numerous **pirates**, who ransacked the city three times during the seventeenth century. Despite these setbacks, by the 1750s the region possessed over a hundred tobacco plantations, at least as many farms, numerous cattle and sheep ranches, sugar mills and textile workshops, and a population of almost six thousand.

The mid-eighteenth century marked the start of the **sugar boom** (see p.585), a roughly hundred-year period during which Trinidad become one of the country's most prosperous cities, acquiring a host of splendid colonial mansions, many of which are still standing today. Despite the technological advances in sugar production, in Trinidad it remained a labour-intensive activity and thousands of **African slaves** were imported to cope with the increasing demands of the local industry. Population ranks were also swelled in the nineteenth century by **European** immigrants (including French refugees fleeing a slave uprising in nearby Haiti) attracted by the city's affluence, enhancing Trinidad's standing as one of Cuba's most cosmopolitan cities of the era. As much as anything, it was the huge wealth of the local elite that graced the city with its artistic flavour. Furniture and jewellery as well as luxury foods were imported from Europe and the United States by sugar barons like Brunet, Iznaga and Borrell.

Trinidad's prosperity peaked when the economic tide began to turn in the 1830s and 1840s. **Slave revolts** on the sugar plantations in 1838 and 1839 began a series of disruptions to the industry on which the region had come to depend. All the cultivable land had been exhausted by the middle of the century, while the clearing of the forests in order to plant sugar meant that one of the region's principal sources of fuel had also been exhausted and wood now had to be imported at increased cost. At the same time, Trinidad's economic foundations were being eroded by outside forces, with European sugar-beet production challenging the dominance of Caribbean cane. The downward spiral accelerated with the Wars of Independence, beginning in 1868. A large number of local sugar and tobacco plantations were destroyed as the rebels fought the Spanish for control of the city and the surrounding land, gaining the upper hand by 1897 but only after the backbone of the local economy had been broken.

The second War of Independence ended in 1898, by which time the US had become involved. As the twentieth century got under way, **US dominance of Trinidad's economy** meant foreign ownership of the vast majority of local land and the concentration of all sugar production in a single mill. Unemployment shot up and many workers left the area altogether, as only a small proportion of the potential farmland was under production. Trinidad's fortunes didn't improve until the 1950s, when major roads linked it to the provincial capitals of Sancti Spíritus and Cienfuegos, which increased tourism and encouraged the construction of a small airport and the *Hotel Las Cuevas*, both still standing today.

This brief period of prosperity was cut short by the revolutionary war that ended in January 1959. It was in the Sierra del Escambray around Trinidad that, for five years following the rebel triumph, US-backed counter-revolutionaries based some of their most concerted efforts to topple the new regime. The guerrilla conflict that ensued saw significant numbers of local men killed before the region was pacified in 1965, after which followed a two-decade-long process of rebuilding the infrastructure. Trinidad began the rise to its current prominence as one of the most important cities in Cuba after its historic centre and the nearby Valle de los Ingenios were declared World Heritage Sites by UNESCO in 1988, and its picture-perfect attractions have made it a core attraction on the visitor itinerary.

Arrival and information

Interprovincial buses navigate their way slowly into Trinidad's **bus terminal** (℡41/99-4448) at Piro Guinart e/ Maceo e Izquierdo, just inside the colonial centre of the town and within easy walking distance of a number of *casas particulares*. Arriving on the coastal road by **car** from Cienfuegos or further west will bring you into town on Piro Guinart, which leads directly up to the two main roads cutting through the centre of the city, Martí and Maceo. From Sancti Spíritus and points east, the Circuito Sur takes cars closer to *Las Cuevas* hotel, but a left turn at Lino Pérez will take you into *casa particular* territory.

On the southwestern edge of town, the **train station** (℡41/99-3348) serves only local destinations, including El Valle de los Ingenios, and a few kilometres further in the same direction is Trinidad's small **airport** (℡41/99-6393), predominantly serving chartered flights. From here the only way to get into town is to take a taxi for a few convertible pesos; you'll pay at least twice as much to get to the hotels on the Península de Ancón.

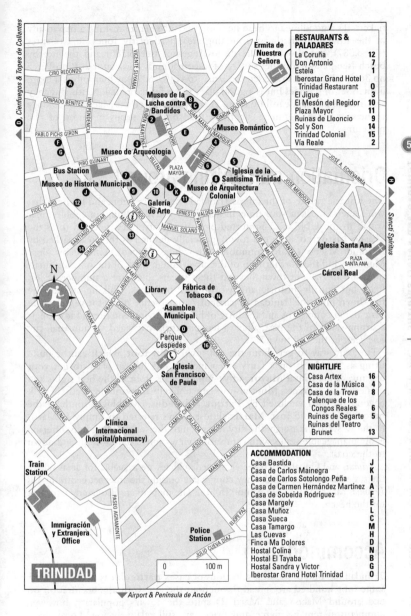

RESTAURANTS & PALADARES

La Coruña	12
Don Antonio	7
Estela	1
Iberostar Grand Hotel Trinidad Restaurant	0
El Jigue	3
El Mesón del Regidor	10
Plaza Mayor	11
Ruinas de Lleoncio	9
Sol y Son	14
Trinidad Colonial	15
Vía Reale	2

Ermita de Nuestra Señora

Museo de la Lucha contra Bandidos

Museo Romántico

Museo de Arqueología

Bus Station

Museo de Historia Municipal

Iglesia de la Santisima Trinidad

Museo de Arquitectura Colonial

Galería de Arte

Iglesia Santa Ana

Cárcel Real

Library

Fábrica de Tobacos

Asamblea Municipal

Parque Céspedes

Iglesia San Francisco de Paula

Clínica Internacional (hospital/pharmacy)

Train Station

Immigración y Extranjera Office

Police Station

NIGHTLIFE

Casa Artex	16
Casa de la Música	4
Casa de la Trova	8
Palenque de los Congos Reales	6
Ruinas de Segarte	5
Ruinas del Teatro Brunet	13

ACCOMMODATION

Casa Bastida	J
Casa de Carlos Mainegra	K
Casa de Carlos Sotolongo Peña	I
Casa de Carmen Hernández Martínez	A
Casa de Sobeida Rodríguez	F
Casa Margely	E
Casa Muñoz	L
Casa Sueca	C
Casa Tamargo	M
Las Cuevas	H
Finca Ma Dolores	D
Hostal Colina	N
Hostal El Tayaba	B
Hostal Sandra y Victor	G
Iberostar Grand Hotel Trinidad	0

TRINIDAD

0   100 m

Airport & Península de Ancón

For **information**, the best place is Cubatur, either at Maceo no.129 esq. Francisco Javier Zerquera (daily 9am–7pm; ☎/⒡41/99-6314 & 99-6315, ⒠operaciones@cubaturss.co.cu), or their other office at Simón Bolívar no.352 e/Maceo y Izquierdo (daily 9am–7pm; ☎41/99-6368). In addition to offering general advice on sightseeing in Trinidad, they can assist with organized excursions, book you a taxi or a rental car and sell you Víazul bus tickets. It's a good idea to head here for guidance before making a trip to any of the attractions in the surrounding area, particularly Topes de Collantes (see p.387), but also the Valle de los Ingenios (see p.386) and the nearby beach (see p.384). Another source of information is Havanatur at Lino Pérez no.366 e/ Maceo y Francisco Codania (☎41/99-6390), which offers a more limited set of services but is a good place to go for car rental. Neither agency sells **maps**, but you can buy those at the **post office** on Maceo e/Colón y Francisco Javier Zerquera or from the souvenir shops at most of the museums.

Orientation and getting around

The historic centre of the city is Trinidad's main attraction, and it's here that you'll spend most of your time. In general, if you're walking on cobblestones you're in the UNESCO-protected part of the city, often referred to as the "**casco histórico**" (the old town), generally defined as the area marked by Antonio Maceo (more commonly known as Maceo), Lino Pérez, José Mendoza and the northern tip of the city. Though most of the official tourist spots are in the old town, beyond these streets there are a number of less fêted but equally historic and worthwhile buildings. Walking around the **northern** limits of Trinidad in particular, the absence of motor vehicles, the basic living conditions and the buzz of human activity lend the muddy streets a strong sense of the past, albeit a less pristinely packaged version than the one seen in the old town.

The only way to get about the old town is **on foot**, which can be quite tiring as it is built on a fairly steep incline. The logical place to get your bearings is the **Plaza Mayor**, a five-minute walk from all the best sights and numerous restaurants. Most visitors are unlikely to want or need to walk beyond the area enclosed by **Parque Céspedes**, two blocks south of the historic centre, and **José Martí** (almost always referred to as simply as Martí) to the west. To the north, the city merges into the surrounding hills, offering easily manageable walks with captivating views across the rooftops and down to the coast.

Bicitaxis and Cubatur two-seater moped vehicles are available for areas where the streets are not cobbled. They congregate outside the Internet centre in *Las Begonias* café at Maceo esq. Simón Bolívar. The mopeds are also handy transport for the beach.

Accommodation

Trinidad has one of the best selections of **casas particulares** in the country: some four hundred are spread throughout the city, with a concentration on and around Maceo and Martí. Despite the town's popularity, however, competition remains fierce and prices are still relatively low. Locals have taken to holding up picture boards of their houses, in the hope of being noticed in the scrum that forms at the bus station every time a Víazul coach arrives; touts may offer you illegal rooms for as little as $10CUC, while legal rooms usually cost $15–25CUC. If you have a house in mind, the touts may claim that it is full or has closed down, but it's always best to confirm that information for yourself. It's also worth booking ahead and asking your hosts

Trinidad's new and old street names

The confusion arising from old and new **street names** encountered in many Cuban towns is particularly acute in Trinidad. Most names were changed after the revolution, but new maps and tourist literature are reverting to the old names in the interests of the town's historical heritage. However, street signs still carry the revolutionary names, and the addresses appearing in this book follow suit. Note also that the full name of a street often does not appear on street signs, most notably the major thoroughfares of Antonio Maceo and José Martí, which usually appear simply as Maceo and Martí, and are always referred to as such.

New name	Old name
Abel Santamaría	Lirio Blanco
Antonio Maceo	Gutiérrez
Camilo Cienfuegos	Santo Domingo
Colón	Colón
Eliope Paz	Vigía
Ernesto Valdés Muñoz	Media Luna
F.H. Echerrí	Cristo
Fidel Claro	Angarilla
Francisco Gómez Toro	Peña
Francisco Javier Zerquera	Rosario
Francisco Pettersen	Coco
Frank País	Carmen
General Lino Peréz	San Procopio
Gustavo Izquierdo	Gloria
José Martí	Jesús María
José Mendoza	Santa Ana
Jesús Menéndez	Alameda
Juan Manuel Márquez	Amargura
Julio A. Mella	Las Guasimas
Piro Guinart	Boca
Rubén Martínez Villena	Real
Santiago Escobar	Olvido
Simón Bolívar	Desengaño

to meet you at the bus stop with your name on a sign. The only hotel in town is the *Iberostar Grand Hotel Trinidad*, which opened in February 2006.

Hotels

Las Cuevas Finca Santa Ana ⊤41/99-6133 & 99-6434, Ⓕ6161, Ⓔreservas@cuevas.co.cu. A large, spacious complex of simple but sufficiently equipped concrete cabins, superbly located on a hillside overlooking the town and the coast. It's only a twenty-minute walk from the Plaza Mayor but perfectly secluded. There's access to the cave network over which the site was built, a nightly musical show, a tennis court and a pool. ❺

Finca Ma Dolores Carretera de Cienfuegos Km 1.5 ⊤41/99-6394 & 99-6395, Ⓕ6481, Ⓔalojamiento@dolores.co.cu. Popular with tour groups, this 40-room hotel's 26 modern cabins

might lack character but are well equipped, with TVs, fridges and kitchenettes. Located 3km out of town on the scenic banks of the moss-green Guaurabo River, boat trips are available downstream to the river's mouth at La Boca. Other activities include horse riding and Cuban country-music evenings, and there's a swimming pool, a restaurant and a bar as well. ❻

Iberostar Grand Hotel Trinidad José Martí no.262 e/ Lino Pérez y Colón ⊤41/99-6073, 99-6074 & 99-6075, Ⓔrecepcion@iberostar.trinidad.co.cu. This fabulously plush hotel on Parque Céspedes is full of understated luxury, with just one or two ostentatious touches. There's a delightfully reposeful central patio dotted with plants and a fountain, a cushy yet dignified smokers' lounge, a large buffet restaurant and forty fantastically furnished rooms, each with either a balcony or a terrace. ❾

Casas particulares

Casa Sueca Juan Manuel Márquez no.70a e/ Piro Guinart y Ciro Redondo ☎ 41/99-3462, ✉ balioni@centromed.ssp.sld.cu. Two huge, simply styled rooms, one with three double beds and one with two, in a beautiful, tranquil, colonial-era house at the top of town. Communal areas include a delightful and intimate central split-level patio. Run by a mother and her two daughters, who create a warm family atmosphere; all three are accomplished cooks as well. ❶–❷

Casa Bastida Maceo no.537 e/ Simón Bolívar y Piro Guinart ☎/℺ 41/99-6686, ✉ julio_cecilia @yahoo.es. Two en-suite rooms, one a very spacious triple with a street-side balcony and roof access, in an excellent *casa particular* run by bright owners who have produced their own little guide to the town. This was once also a *paladar*, and the meals are still of excellent quality. ❷

Casa de Carlos Mainegra Rubén Martínez Villena no.21 e/ Simón Bolívar y Francisco Javier Zerquera; no phone, ✉ yohan.mendez@gmail.com. A modest colonial house very conveniently located just off the Plaza Mayor, with one double bedroom to rent. The house isn't in great nick, but this makes it one of the easier places to negotiate a cheaper price. The owner speaks some English. ❶–❷

Casa de Carlos Sotolongo Peña Rubén Martínez Villena no.33 e/ Simón Bolívar y Francisco Javier Zerquera ☎ 41/99-4169. Built in 1825, and occupied by sixth-generation Trinitarios, this spacious house right on the Plaza Mayor has a large colonial-era room inside as well as a modern one in an extension out back. Both rooms have en-suite bathrooms and look onto a large courtyard. ❷

Casa de Carmen Hernández Martínez Maceo no.718 e/ Conrado Benítez y Ciro Redondo ☎ 41/99-6330. There are two double bedrooms at this basic bungalow and the pleasant, down-to-earth owners are prepared to rent out the whole house if you want complete self-sufficiency. It's on a bumpy track in a more run-down part of town, away from the noise and the action. ❶

Casa de Sobeida Rodríguez Maceo no.619 e/ Piro Guinart y Pablo Pichs Girón ☎ 41/99-4162, ✉ zobeidarguez@yahoo.es. One of the best-appointed homes in the city, the comfortable, modern and thoughtfully designed interior is

luxurious by Cuban standards. The two bedrooms are in their own independent block upstairs and the whole place is in pristine condition. Just around the corner from the bus station. ❷

Casa Margely Piro Guinart no.360a e/ F.H. Echerrí y Juan Manuel Márquez ☎ 41/99-6525. Guests have considerable privacy in their own section of the house, behind a pretty garden gate at the back of a central patio, where there's an open-air, roof-covered dining room in addition to two double rooms. The house itself is a graceful, fairly opulent colonial residence. ❷

Casa Muñoz José Martí no.401 e/ Fidel Claro y Stgo. Escobar ☎/℺ 41/99-3673, ⓦ www.casa.trinidadphoto.com. One of the most fantastically furnished and best-equipped colonial residences in Trinidad, this house is a museum piece in itself. Crammed with original nineteenth-century furniture and a wonderful display of photographs taken by the owner, it also features two large bedrooms (each with its own clean bathroom), a spacious rooftop terrace and room to park three cars. An added benefit is that the hosts speak English. Expect to pay about $5CUC more than average. ❷

Casa Tamargo Francisco Javier Zerquera no. 266 e/ Martí y Maceo ☎ 41/99-6669, ✉ felixmatilde@yahoo.com. A very professionally and proudly run *casa particular* where menus are kept in the two spotless bedrooms for rent so you can mull over your meal choices at your leisure. A smart dining room opens up onto a lovely patio, full of hanging plants and shrubs, around which the rooms are based. There's also a neat roof terrace. ❷

Hostal Colina Maceo no.374 e/ Lino Pérez y Colón ☎ 41/99-2319, ✉ zulenaa @yahoo.com.es. A highly impressive *casa particular* with an immaculate, sweeping, split-level central patio where a hotel-standard bar has been installed and countless plants create a park-like feel. The perfectly restored 1830 colonial section of the house, authentically furnished and decorated, contrasts the rest of the otherwise modern mini-complex. Both fantastic, pristine pastel-painted bedrooms have excellent en-suite bathrooms. ❷

Hostal El Tayaba Juan M Márquez no.70 e/Piro Guinart y Ciro Redondo ☎ 41/99-4197, ✉ eltayaba@yahoo.es. Two beautifully appointed rooms in a *casa particular* par excellence. The house is dotted with colonial *objets d'art* and there is a central patio perfect for leisurely breakfasts. A rooftop patio with views over the nearby church is an added bonus, as are the helpful and friendly owners who can arrange tours to local sites. ❷

5

TRINIDAD AND SANCTI SPÍRITUS | Accommodation

Hostal Sandra y Victor Maceo no.613a e/ Pablo Pichs Girón y Piro Guinart ☎/℻ 41/99-2216. ✉ hostalsandra@yahoo.com. Two large bedrooms, each with two double beds and its own bathroom, in a fabulously airy and spotlessly clean modern house. The upstairs is exclusively for guests; there's a balcony at the front and a wide-open terrace at the back plus two communal rooms indoors. The food is excellent. ❷

The Town

Trinidad boasts the highest number of **museums** per capita in the country, and with most of them within a few blocks of one another you can enjoy a full day of sightseeing without breaking a sweat. However, it's worth saving the time and energy to simply wander around the old town's narrow streets shadowed by colonial houses whose shuttered porticoes form a patchwork of blues, greens, pinks and yellows; this is one of the highlights of any tour of Trinidad, and worth missing some museums for if your time is limited. Three of the museums are on the central **Plaza Mayor**, including the memorable **Museo Romántico**, with another two only a few minutes' walk away. If you walk a little further, north of the Plaza Mayor there are wide-reaching views from the hillside overlooking Trinidad, marked at its base by the ruined **Ermita de Nuestra Señora** church.

Heading downhill from Plaza Mayor will lead you south out of the historic centre towards **Parque Céspedes**, the hub of local activity, where people come to while away the afternoons, chatting under the shade of the square's canopied walkway or meeting up at weekends for a street party. To the east, a more subdued section of town where visitors are more conspicuous, is Trinidad's main commercial centre, centred around **Plaza Santa Ana**, and the **El Alfarero** ceramics factory.

Plaza Mayor

At the heart of the UNESCO-protected colonial section of Trinidad is the beautiful **Plaza Mayor**. The steeply sloping streets of Simón Bolívar and Francisco Javier Zerquera form its northeastern and southwestern borders, joined at the top and bottom by Fernando Echerrí and Rubén Martínez Villena respectively. This is the old town's focal point, comprising four simple fenced-in gardens, each with a palm tree or two and dotted with various statuettes and other ornamental touches, all of it surrounded by colourfully painted colonial mansions which are adorned with arches and balconies and now house museums and art galleries. Though principally crowded with camera-wielding tourists, there is nevertheless something quite captivating about this vibrant, compact and trim little plaza.

Museo Romántico

Overlooking the plaza on the corner of Fernando Echerrí and Simón Bolívar is the fabulous **Museo Romántico** (Tues–Sun 9am–5pm; $2CUC, extra $1CUC to take photos), an essential part of the reliving-the-past experience of visiting Trinidad. With one of the country's finest and most valuable collections of **furniture** packed into its fourteen rooms, there is no better place to go for a picture of aristocratic lifestyle and tastes in colonial times. Dating from 1808, the house itself – built for the very wealthy **Brunet family** – is a magnificent example of elegantly unadorned nineteenth-century domestic Cuban architecture. Though the museum's contents have been gathered together from

375

various buildings all over town, there is a wonderful consistency and completeness to the collection, befitting the perfectly preserved and restored rooms. Not a single piece looks out of place, from the precious eighteenth-century Viennese bureau, intricately decorated with pictures from Greek mythology, to the one-and-a-quarter-ton plain marble bathtub – although the armchair toilet stranded in the middle of a large and otherwise empty room does look somewhat comical. All the rooms are fantastically furnished, with two of the standouts being the exquisite dining room with its Italian marble floor and the master bedroom featuring a four-poster bed and French wardrobe, miraculously constructed without nails or screws.

Iglesia de la Santísima Trinidad

On the other side of Simón Bolívar, occupying the other half of the square's highest border, is the city's main church, **Iglesia de la Santísima Trinidad** (also known as the Parroquial Mayor). Though there has been a church on this site since 1620, the original building was destroyed in a storm that swept through town in 1812. The structure now standing was officially finished in 1892, the first brick having been laid in 1817, but much of what you'll see inside dates from the twentieth century.

Beyond its unremarkable facade, there's plenty to look at within the church's three naves. Amongst the pictures and paintings, it's the disproportionate number of **altars** that grabs most people's attention. The majority were created by Amadeo Fiogere, a Dominican friar assigned to the church in 1912, who set about livening up the interior, drawing on his own personal fortune to donate many of the images on display today. Whatever you ultimately think about the fourteen wooden altars here, there's a distinct mix of elaborate artificiality and genuinely impressive craftsmanship that won't fail to make you stop and stare. This is especially true of the main one in the central nave, a mass of pointed spires and detailed etchings, looking like a miniature facade of a Gothic cathedral. The **best time to visit** the church is from Monday to Saturday between 11am and 12.30pm when there is no Mass.

Plaza Mayor's other museums

Working your way clockwise around the square from Fernando Echerrí, following the church is the **Museo de Arquitectura Colonial** (Sat–Thurs 9am–5pm; $1CUC), a sky-blue and white building with a courtyard vibrantly bedecked with plants. This is the former residence of the Sánchez-Iznaga family, Trinidad aristocrats who made their fortune from sugar. Constructed in 1738, the building was actually built in two separate stages, with its southern half added in 1782. The museum's central theme is the development of domestic architectural styles in Trinidad during the eighteenth and nineteenth centuries. Though the cut-aways of walls, examples of doorways and rooftops along with various other fixtures and fittings are worth taking some time looking over, this isn't a place for lingering; you'll do better to experience the city's architecture firsthand than inside the museum doors. In fact, two of the most captivating exhibits do not entirely tally with the museum's theme: a reproduction of a painting of Trinidad from 1850 and, in a block out the back, a US-made Art Noveau shower, complete with thermometer and three shower heads, dating from 1912.

Similarly, it won't take long to look round the **Galería de Arte** (daily 9am–5pm; free), at the bottom end of the square, whose displays comprise a mixture of soulless paintings, all for sale, and temporary exhibitions with a more original slant. Most of the exhibitions are housed in the six rooms upstairs, with anything from lacework, ceramics, sculpture and paintings likely to be on display. From the first floor you can also catch a perfectly framed view of the plaza through the open shutters.

On the plaza's northwestern side, at the corner of Simón Bolívar and Rubén Martínez, is the **Museo de Arqueología** (Sun–Fri 9am–5pm; $1CUC), housing a modest collection of pre-Columbian and colonial-era artefacts. Its most substantial single exhibit is the original and fully intact nineteenth-century kitchen, the last of the rooms and the only one relating to the eighteenth-century house that the museum occupies. Overall, the findings displayed here, such as rudimentary aboriginal-Cuban tools and items relating to slavery, lack coherence. There are some attempts to explain aboriginal Cuba and one or two more substantial exhibits, notably skeletal remains dating back around a thousand years, but the collection is too limited to be particularly illuminating.

Museo de Historia Municipal and Museo de la Lucha Contra Bandidos

The other highlights of the colonial centre lie a few blocks from the Plaza Mayor. On Simón Bolívar, one block southwest from the plaza, is the **Museo de Historia Municipal** (Sat–Thurs 9am–5pm; $2CUC), another converted colonial residence. The first part of the museum follows the same format as the Museo Romántico, with various superb examples of nineteenth-century furniture conveying the everyday surroundings and living conditions of a wealthy colonial-era Trinidad family, in this case the **Canteros**. Born here in 1815, Justo German Cantero made his fortune in the sugar industry, more specifically as owner of the Buena Vista sugar mill; his portrait, along with that of his wife, can be found in the third room on the counter-clockwise tour of the downstairs. The first three rooms, with their well-presented colonial exhibits, make up the most well-rounded part of the museum; from here on the collection moves abruptly into a rundown of the area's history. Though there are some interesting objects scattered about, like a gramophone from the early twentieth century, the museum never really gets going and runs out of exhibits too quickly. Don't leave, however, without heading upstairs, where a spiral staircase leads up into a tower providing some great **views**, including a classic snapshot of the plaza.

A block north of Plaza Mayor, where Fernando Echerrí meets Piro Guinart, the building housing the **Museo de la Lucha Contra Bandidos** (Tues–Sun 9am–5pm; $1CUC) is also host to the dome-topped yellow- and white-trimmed **bell tower** that's become Trinidad's trademark image. The tower is part of the eighteenth-century church and convent, known respectively as the Iglesia and Convento de San Francisco de Asís, which previously stood on this site. Even if the museum's contents don't appeal to you, it's well worth paying the entrance fee to climb up the rickety wooden staircase to the top of the tower, which has a panoramic view over the city and across to the hills and coastline. Down in the museum itself, displays initially cover the Revolution, in particular the struggles and battles that took place locally between 1956 and 1958 in what was then Las Villas province. A larger part of the museum is concentrated on the counter-revolutionary groups – the **bandidos**, or bandits – that fought Castro's army during the years immediately following his seizure of power in 1959. The most striking exhibit is in the central courtyard, where a military truck and a motorboat mounted with machine guns stand as examples of the hardware employed by and against the *bandidos* in their struggle to overthrow the revolutionary government. There's no shortage of detail when it comes to charting the conflict between the two sides, much of which took place in the nearby Sierra del Escambray, but the maps, military equipment and endless mug shots become a little repetitive. It's better to spend more time in the first few rooms, containing dramatic and compelling photographs of the rebel war – including shots of fatigue-clad Fidel and Che – and the student struggle between 1952 and 1959.

Ermita de Nuestra Señora

As it heads up and away from Plaza Mayor, Simón Bolívar leads out of Trinidad's historic centre and through a less pristine part of town; soon the road becomes a dirt track heading steeply up to a dilapidated **church** marking the last line of buildings before the town dissolves into the countryside. The church's ponderous full name, **Ermita de Nuestra Señora de la Candelaría de la Popa del Barco**, pays homage to a Colombian legend about a statue of the Virgin that miraculously broke free from a sinking ship that was transporting it, floating to the surface afterwards. There's nothing to see of the church itself but a ruined framework, but it's worth making the easy fifteen-minute walk up the hill for the **views** alone. At the summit the lush landscape on the other side of the hill is revealed, as well as views back across the town and down to the coast. Just beyond the ruined church you can easily cut across to the *Las Cuevas* hotel complex, on the adjoining hillside, where non-guests can use the hillside **swimming pool** ($5CUC) and other facilities.

Parque Céspedes and around

Plaza Mayor may be the city centre for sightseers, but as far as the town's population is concerned, **Parque Céspedes** is Trinidad's main square. South of the cobbled streets that define the protected part of the town, a ten-minute walk from Plaza Mayor down Simón Bolívar and left onto Martí, Parque Céspedes may not have Plaza Mayor's enchanting surroundings but it's markedly more lively, particularly in the evenings. Schoolchildren run out onto the square in the afternoon, while older locals head here at the end of the day to chat on the benches lining the three walkways. In the square's centre, a distinctive dome-shaped leafy canopy provides plenty of shade, while flower-frilled bushes encase the simple gardens, which are marked in each corner by a handsome royal palm. On the southeastern side, local hustlers hang around outside the cigar shop on Lino Pérez, while town councillors walk to and fro past the stately yellow-columned entrance of the Asamblea Municipal building, which occupies the square's entire northwestern side. Set back from the southwestern edge of the square, next to the school, are a **cinema** and a modest tiled-roof church.

A few blocks north of Parque Céspedes, on the corner of Maceo and Colón, is the **Fábrica de Tobacos**, Trinidad's tiny cigar factory. There's no entrance fee, as visitors are allowed no further than the first small room. However, you can see most of the activity from here: workers sitting at desks sorting leaves or hand-rolling cigars, including the well-known Romeo y Julieta brand. Despite the inevitable brevity of a visit, this window on one of the country's oldest industries is fascinating. There are no fixed opening hours, but it's advisable to turn up before 4pm and to leave a tip.

A couple of blocks back towards the historic centre, a **street market** operates on Ernesto Valdés Muñoz (daily 9am–5pm). Aimed squarely at tourists, the mainly wooden *artesanía* on sale range from models of 1950s cars to tortoises with nodding heads and buxom female figurines with gravity-defying breasts.

East of the old town

From Parque Céspedes, a ten-minute walk east along Lino Pérez brings you to the only other tangible tourist attraction outside of the colonial centre, **Plaza Santa Ana**. The plaza itself is little more than an open space, its neglected status emphasized by the derelict shell of a church, the Iglesia Santa Ana, which stands on one side. It's the shops, bar and restaurant around the courtyard of the converted **Cárcel Real**, the old Royal Prison on the plaza's southeastern side, that coachloads of tour groups stop here for. Disappointingly, the 1844 building's commercial aspect is the main draw and very little is made of its history as a military jail. Clustered around a large cobbled courtyard, the **shops** stock *artesanía*, books about Cuba in Spanish, English and German, a few cigars and various other bits and bobs. Behind the old prison railings you'll find a nicely furnished **bar** and a **restaurant** (daily 9am–10pm) whose speciality, *Bistec Santa Ana* – pork filled with ham and cheese and coated in breadcrumbs – is for some reason heavily touted in the local tourist literature.

El Alfarero

Well beyond the historic centre of town, five blocks southeast along Rubén Batista from Plaza Santa Ana and then a right turn onto Andrés Berro Macias, is **El Alfarero**, a timeworn little **ceramics factory**, decidedly off the beaten track – a fact to which it owes much of its appeal. No provision has been made for receiving visitors, but no one will object to you wandering in and taking a look around during working hours (usually Mon–Fri 7am–noon & 1.30–5pm). The warehouse-style workshop, in existence since 1892, is filled with shelves of pots of differing shapes and sizes destined for shops, hotels and workplaces all over the country. The workshop turns out an average of around 1500 pieces a day, and the production process is on full display with potters' wheels in amongst the mess and the brick kilns out in the back. Characteristic of the Cuban workplace, the scrawled slogans all over the walls encourage workers to keep going in the face of adversity.

If getting completely away from the touristy part of town appeals to you, then the walk here, through one of the least-visited parts of town but usually bustling with locals, will be as good a reason for coming as the workshop itself. The most straightforward route from the centre is southeast all the way along Maceo which, after it curves around to the left, meets Andrés Berro Macias at its southern end.

Eating

With so many of its colonial mansions converted into **restaurants**, eating out is one of the easiest ways to soak up Trinidad's gracefully dignified interiors. Though the choice of food is almost exclusively restricted to *comida criolla*, the quality is, as a rule, far higher than in many of Cuba's larger cities. As well as a good selection of state-run restaurants, there are three *paladares* in the city, two of them serving top-notch cuisine. Despite these options, a large number of visitors eat at the house they are staying in and restaurants are often surprisingly empty, especially at night in low season. Dinner usually costs $6–10CUC in both *paladares* and state restaurants. The most convenient place for a **snack** is *Las Begonias* (daily 9am–10pm) at Maceo esq. Simón Bolívar, which has become a traditional first stop for recently arrived backpackers.

State restaurants and paladares

La Coruña José Martí no.430 e/ Piro Guinart y Stgo Escobar. Family-run *paladar* with tables squeezed into an intimate backyard patio where there is a stronger sense than normal of intruding on someone's home. The menu of *comida criolla* is limited but tasty, though the food here is slightly poorer than at either of the other two *paladares* in town. Meals are charged at $8CUC. Daily noon–10pm.

Don Antonio Izquierdo no.112 e/ Simón Bolívar y Piro Guinart ☏ 41/99-6548. Though only serving food at lunchtimes, there's typically a fair selection of meals to choose from here, from meat dishes to salmon, or lighter items such as tuna salad or vegetable omelettes. The atmosphere is elegant but subdued, with both a canopied courtyard and a comfortable interior. Daily 10am–8pm.

Estela Simón Bolívar no.557 e/ Juan Manuel Márquez y José Mendoza ☏ 41/99-4329. Not only do the pork, chicken and fish dishes at this peaceful backyard *paladar* represent the best in Cuban home-cooking, but a feast of extras like fried green bananas and yucca is laid on. The two-tier patio surrounded by high walls and trees makes this one of the most relaxing spots in town.

🏃 **Iberostar Grand Hotel Trinidad Restaurant** José Martí no.262 e/ Lino Pérez y Colón ☏ 41/99-6073, 99-6074 & 99-6075. Untouchable in Trinidad for the quality and variety of its food; the grand dining room of this hotel restaurant provides an appropriately fancy setting for the comparative luxuries on offer here, such as smoked salmon, serrano ham, beef carpaccio and, unheard of in Cuba, a selection of cheese. Main dishes include candied tenderloin steak in red wine and pork fillet with vegetable risotto. Set-menu three-course lunches are $20CUC and buffet dinners are $35CUC.

El Jigue Rubén Martínez Villena no.69 esq. Piro Guinart ☏ 41/99-6476. Subtly decorated restaurant in the large front room of a rustic colonial residence. The beef, chicken and pork set-meals come with random side orders (such as carrots, spaghetti or rice), a dessert and coffee for less than $8CUC. Alternatives include a mixed seafood platter and a couple of lobster dishes. There's usually live music in the eve.

El Mesón del Regidor Simón Bolívar no.424 e/ Muñoz y Rubén Martínez Villena ☏ 41/99-6572. Standard *comida criolla*, where the lobster costs only $15CUC and the meat dishes are just above the $5CUC mark; overall the menu lacks variety. The unpolished, unfussy decor features a brick and terracotta-tiled floor with pastel-pink and blue walls.

Plaza Mayor Rubén Martínez Villena no.15 esq. Francisco Javier Zerquera ☏ 41/99-6470. Large, slickly restored colonial mansion invaded every lunchtime by tour groups. The small set of attractive terraces in and around the crumbling brick arches and walls out the back provide one of the nicest outdoor lunch spots in the city and a mellower dining environment when the interior is busy. Choose from the seafood, pork and chicken dishes on the menu or, between midday and 3pm daily, opt for the good-value buffet ($8CUC), which offers rarely seen but unremarkable options like pasta and salads.

Ruinas de Lleoncio Izquierdo no.112 e/ Simón Bolívar y Piro Guinart. A set of open-air ruins with plastic chairs and tables and a lack of atmosphere, this is more a *cafétéria* than a restaurant, though it does have a decent list of sandwiches and Cuban staples at cheap prices. Good for an uncomplicated budget lunch. Daily 10am–9pm.

🏃 **Sol y Son** Simón Bolívar no.283 e/ Frank País y José Martí. Choose from a wide selection of spaghetti dishes, fish dinners and chicken and pork entrees. Everything is carefully prepared, full of flavour and served in a romantically lit courtyard brimming with plantlife, making this *paladar* one of the best places to eat in the city.

Trinidad Colonial Maceo no.402 esq. Colón ☏ 41/99-6473. Fish, shrimp, lobster and pork – served with all the trimmings and cooked in a wider variety of styles than elsewhere – feature on one of the most extensive menus in the city. Housed in a large, prestigious-looking, restored nineteenth-century mansion, with chandeliers, ornately framed portraits and antique dressers dotted about the place.

Vía Reale Rubén Martínez Villena no.74 e/ Piro Guinart y Ciro Redondo ☏ 41/99-6476. A lunchtime stopoff joint dishing up $5CUC pizzas and very basic pastas as well as a couple of seafood and meat dishes on a diminutive, canopy-covered patio in a colonial building. Daily 9.30am–5pm.

Drinking

For **drinking**, the restaurants and hotels account for a high proportion of the bars with only a few places existing solely as drinking venues. The *Iberostar Grand Hotel Trinidad* has a plush bar with an excellent selection of spirits, a good wine list and, hidden away behind a closed door, a cosy little smokers' lounge. Most of the live music venues (see p.382) also double up as *caféterias* or bars, and you can usually get a drink whether or not a band is playing.

Bars and cafés

Bar Daiquiri Lino Pérez no.313 e/ José Martí y Francisco Codania. With tables and chairs out on the street as well as inside, this café-bar is a sociable little spot and one of the few places catering exclusively to drinkers.

Bar Escalinata Well-situated halfway up the stairs to the lively *Casa de la Música* (see p.382), there are plenty of chairs and tables and a band plays here most nights from 9pm. Serves rum, beer and an impressive range of Cuban cocktails,

Bar La Ruina Ruinas del Teatro Brunet, Maceo e/ Francisco Javier Zerquera y Simón Bolívar. Before and after the live music performances staged here this place functions as a *caféteria* and bar.

La Bodeguita del Trinitario Colón no.91 e/ José Martí y Maceo. A tiny but welcoming bar popular with both locals and visitors, located just around the corner from Parque Céspedes.

La Canchánchara Rubén Martínez Villena e/ Piro Guinart y Ciro Redondo. A small bar, relaxed and sociable, gives onto a long thin shady courtyard, the covered half of which is lined with squat little benches. The house special is a cocktail of rum, honey, lemon, water and ice.

Mesón de Regidor Simón Bolívar no.424 e/ Muñoz y Rubén Martínez Villena A simple, straightforward daytime bar attached to the rustic restaurant right near the Plaza Mayor. A convenient place to cool off with a *mojito*.

Plaza Mayor Rubén Martínez Villena no.15 esq. Francisco Javier Zerquera. The decent terrace bar tucked into a corner of the series of terraces that back onto the Plaza Mayor restaurant makes a very pleasant spot for a lazy outdoor drink during the day.

Trinidad Colonial In its own separate section and with one of the only authentic colonial-style bar counters in Trinidad, this is the best restaurant-bar in town for straight-up drinking. A spiral staircase leads up to a roof terrace, where there are great views.

Nightlife and entertainment

Given the number of visitors this small town receives, **nightlife** in Trinidad is relatively low-key, and most of the town lies dormant at night, creating a sense even on some of the main streets that there is nothing going on at all. However, there are some pockets of activity and a few hidden gems waiting to be discovered, particularly if you're looking for live music.

By far the liveliest place at weekends is Parque Céspedes, which has an **open-air disco** most Fridays and Saturdays; the modern *salsa* and pop music is geared to the large crowd of young locals who provide the atmosphere and numbers so lacking in some of the town's more tourist-oriented venues. There's only one **nightclub** here, *La Ayala* (daily 10.30pm–3am; $10CUC, including unlimited drinks), up at the *Las Cuevas* hotel, where the fantastic location in a hillside cave network is let down by a frequent lack of guests.

The Casa de la Cultura at Francisco Javier Zerquera no.406 (☎41/99-4308) is not a live music venue as such, but it's worth dropping by to check out the weekly programme which often includes some sort of musical entertainment. There is a **cinema**, the Cine Romelio Cornelio, on Antonio Guiteras at Parque Céspedes, open Tuesday to Sunday.

Dance and percussion lessons are available at the Ruinas del Teatro Brunet and through Paradiso (see p.383).

Live music and dance venues

Casa Artex Lino Pérez e/ Francisco Codania y José Martí ($1CUC). One of the less reliable music venues, in an old colonial mansion near Parque Céspedes. Puts on Cuban dance and music shows on its spacious central courtyard; when there's no live music *Casa Artex* (also known as *Casa Fischer*) functions as a bar and pumps out modern *salsa* and reggaeton. Daily 9am–5pm & 9pm–midnight.

Casa de la Música Francisco Javier Zerquera no.3 (☎41/99-3414; $1CUC). The headline spot for live music, located up the broad flight of stairs to the right of the Iglesia de la Santísima Trinidad. There's a garden and a large terrace, surrounded by high stone walls and iron grilles, where traditional Cuban bands as well as more modern *salsa* outfits play most nights. The music usually starts at around 9pm; sometimes the bands set up outside the venue itself, in the middle of the spacious staircase next to *Bar Escalinata*. Daily 10–2am.

Casa de la Trova F.H. Echerrí no.29 e/ Patricio Lumumba y Jesús Menéndez, Plazuela Segarte (☎41/99-6445 & 99-6484; $1CUC). Trinidad's other renowned live music spot has a constantly changing cast of excellent musicians playing *salsa*, *bolero* or *son* every night. It's a tightly packed little place, and though it doesn't have the capacity or the party atmosphere of the open-air *Casa de la Música*, its intimate covered backyard terrace provides an up-close appreciation of the musicians and more of an after-hours bar-type vibe. Expect to see several groups in one night. Daily 9–2am

Finca Ma Dolores Carretera a Cienfuegos Km 1.5 ☎41/99-6394 & 99-6395 ($5CUC). Traditional rural Cuban shindigs – *fiestas campesinas* – are held regularly at this hotel ranch. These folk dances and musical performances are aimed predominantly at tour groups but are no worse for it. Usually 9.30pm–midnight.

Hotel Las Cuevas Finca Santa Ana ☎41/99-6133 & 99-6434. Free hour-long live shows covering different aspects of Cuban music and dance are staged on a nightly basis on the terrace outside the hotel's main restaurant. Although the performances' themes – ranging from Afro-Cuban to acoustic-guitar-based *campesino* music – can seem a little contrived, they're performed with enough energy to compensate.

Palenque de los Congos Reales F.H. Echerrí no.33 e/ Francisco Javier Zerquera y Patricio Lumumba ($1CUC). A simple open-air venue where one-hour-long traditional, energetic Afro-Cuban dance shows are staged nightly, usually starting at around 10pm. The Ballet Folklórico de la Ciudad are the resident outfit.

Ruinas de Segarte Jesús Menéndez e/ Galdos y Juan Manuel Márquez, Plazuela Segarte ($1CUC). Outdoor, cosy and atmospheric little enclosure in the old town which tends to attract people whether or not there is live music, which most nights there is. Expect traditional Cuban sounds. Daily noon–10pm.

Ruinas del Teatro Brunet Maceo e/ Francisco Javier Zerquera y Simón Bolívar ☎41/99-6547 ($1CUC). A weekly schedule of highly theatrical song-and-dance performances in an enchanting courtyard under the ruined arches of Trinidad's first theatre. Built in 1840 but closed in 1901 when the roof caved in, the space now features moody red lighting and excellent acoustics. Currently Afro-Cuban nights are Tues–Fri, with less specialist shows (the Noches de Variedades and Noches Cubanas), at weekends. Shows start around 10pm. Daily 9pm–2am.

Listings

Banks and exchange The Banco de Crédito y Comercio (Mon–Fri 8am–3pm & Sat 8–11am) is at José Martí no.264 e/ Colón y Francisco Javier Zerquera. You can change traveller's cheques and withdraw money with a credit card here, or head to the Cadeca *casa de cambio* (Mon–Sat 8.30am–5.30pm, Sun 8.30am–noon), at Martí no.166 e/ Lino Pérez y Camilo Cienfuegos, where you can also buy pesos.

Bike rental Ruinas del Teatro Brunet, Maceo e/ Francisco Javier Zerquera y Simón Bolívar (☎41/99-6547; daily 9am–5pm). You can rent a bike for $3CUC a day.

Bus station Piro Guinart e/ Maceo y Izquierdo ☎41/99-4448

Car rental Havanautos is in the Centro Comercial Trinidad on the road to the airport (☎41/99-6301); Transautos is in the Cubatur office on Maceo (☎41/99-6110); Cubacar is at Lino Pérez no.366 e/ Maceo y Francisco Codanía (☎41/99-6317 or 99-6633).

Horse riding Contact Elvis Valmaseda at Muñoz

no.1a e/ Martí y Carlos Ribero (☎ 41/99-3907) or Rodolfo Bravo Pediraja, at Piro Guinart no.174 e/ Martí y Maceo (☎ 41/99-3560), who hires well-looked-after horses and organizes day-trips for around $20CUC per person.

Immigration For tourist cards go to the Immigración y Extranjera office (Tues & Thurs 9am–noon; ☎ 41/99-6650 & 99-3595) next to the police station on Julio Cueva Díaz.

Internet *Las Begonias* café at Maceo esq. Simón Bolívar has a bank of computers with Internet connections (daily until 10pm; $6CUC per hour), or try the ETECSA Telepunto centre on Lino Pérez no.274 at Parque Céspedes e/ José Martí y Miguel Calzada ($6CUC per hour).

Library Biblioteca Gustavo Izquierdo, Martí no.265 e/ Colón y Francisco Javier Zerquera (Mon–Fri 8am–10pm, Sat 8am–5pm). Tourists are not permitted to remove books from the building.

Medical Clínica Internacional at Lino Pérez no.103 esq. Anastasio Cárdenas (☎ 41/99-6492 & 99-6240), which has a 24hr pharmacy, should cover most medical needs. For an ambulance call ☎ 41/99-2362. Serious cases may be referred to the Clínico Quirúrgico Camilo Cienfuegos (☎ 41/2-4017 & 2-6017), the provincial hospital in Sancti Spíritus.

Percussion lessons Ruinas del Teatro Brunet (☎ 41/99-6547; Mon–Sat 9–11am), at Maceo e/ Francisco Javier Zerquera y Simón Bolívar; $10CUC for a two-hour class; or contact Paradiso in the *Casa de la Trova*, F.H. Echerrí no.29 e/ Patricio Lumumba y Jesús Menéndez, Plazuela Segarte (daily 9.30am–5pm) for classes at the Palenque de los Congos Reales for $5CUC an hour.

Photography Photoservice, Martí s/n e/ Lino Pérez y Camilo Cienfuegos, develops film and sells very basic equipment. Julio Muñoz, the owner of *Casa Muñoz* (☎/℡ 41/99-3773, ⓦ www.trinidadphoto .com), offers photography workshops and advice to beginners.

Police Call ☎ 116 in emergencies. The main station is on Julio Cueva Díaz to the south of town ☎ 41/99-3901 & 99-6330.

Post office The only branch providing international services is at Maceo no.416 e/ Colón y Francisco Javier Zerquera (Mon–Sat 8am–6pm).

Salsa lessons Contact Mireya Medina Rodríguez at Maceo 472 e/ Simón Bolívar y Francisco Javier Zerquera (☎ 41/99-3994; $5CUC/hr). Try also the Ruinas del Teatro Brunet over the road or Paradiso

in *Casa Artex*, Lino Pérez e/ Francisco Codania y Martí (☎ 41/99-6485 & 99-6308) where there are evening classes also for $5CUC/hr.

Scooter rental Motoclub at the Cárcel Real, Plaza Santa Ana (☎ 41/99-6423) rents scooters at $10CUC for 2 hours or $20CUC for a day. There is also scooter rental at the Ruinas del Teatro Brunet (daily 9am–5pm; ☎ 41/99-6547), at Maceo e/ Francisco Javier Zerquera y Simón Bolívar, where charges are $5CUC for an hour or $30CUC per day.

Shopping Casa del Tobaco y el Ron, Maceo esq. Francisco Javier Zerquera, and the Casa del Tobaco, Lino Pérez esq. Martí, have the best selection of rum and cigars. The best places for music are the shops in the *Casa de la Música* and *Casa de la Trova*, both near Plaza Mayor. Bazar Trinidad on Maceo esq. Francisco Javier Zerquera sells poster prints, T-shirts and humdrum *artesanía*. Tienda de Arte Amelia Pelaez (Fondo de Bienes Culturales) on Simón Bolívar esq. Muñoz sells a large selection of handmade crafts. Galería Comercio Universo is a tiny commercial complex at Martí no.281 e/ Francisco Javier Zerquera y Colón, where there is a basic supermarket, a shoe shop, a clothes shop, a perfume specialist and a photography store.

Swimming pool The only pool in Trinidad is at the *Las Cuevas* hotel and is available to non-guests for $5CUC per day.

Taxis Cubataxi ☎ 41/99-2214; Taxi OK ☎ 41/99-6454 & 99-6633; Transtur, in the Cubatur office on Maceo, is available 24hr ☎ 41/99-5314 & 5317; Transgaviota ☎ 41/99-6236.

Telephones International calls can be made at the ETECSA Telepunto, Lino Pérez no.274 e/ Martí y Miguel Calzada (daily 6.30–midnight) on Parque Céspedes.

Train station General Lino Pérez y final ☎ 41/99-3348.

Travel Agents Cubatur, Maceo no.129 esq. Francisco Javier Zerquera (daily 9am–7pm; ☎ 41/99-6314) and Simón Bolívar e/ Maceo y Izquierdo no.352 (daily 9am–7pm; ☎ 41/99-6368); Havanatur Lino Pérez no.366 e/ Maceo y Francisco Codania (daily 10am–6pm; ☎ 41/99-6390); Paradiso in the Casa de la Trova, F.H. Echerrí no.29 e/ Patricio Lumumba y Jesús Menéndez, Plazuela Segarte (daily 9.30am–5pm) and in *Casa Artex*, Lino Pérez e/ Francisco Codania y José Martí (☎ 41/99-6485 & 99-6308).

Around Trinidad

Some of the province's foremost attractions are within easy reach of Trinidad, whether you're driving or using public transport. Probably the least taxing option is the twenty-minute drive down to the **Península de Ancón**, one of the south coast's biggest beach resorts, though still tiny by international standards, having recently upgraded from two to three hotels. A half-hour train ride north from Trinidad is the **Valle de los Ingenios**, home to the sugar estates that made Trinidad's elite so wealthy. About 4km west of the city along the coast road, Carretera de Cienfuegos, a right turn inland takes you onto the mountain road that crosses the **Sierra del Escambray**, whose borders creep down to the outskirts of Trinidad. Some 14km into the mountains from the turn-off you'll come to the **Topes de Collantes**, a rather run-down resort that offers excellent hikes in the surrounding national park of the same name.

There are plenty of **private taxis** near the Trinidad bus station on Piro Guinart looking for tourists travelling to any of these destinations. A day-trip to the mountains can be negotiated for $20–30CUC depending on the car and the driver, while a trip to the beach should only cost half as much. The **train**, a cheaper option, is by far the most enjoyable way to get to the valley.

Península de Ancón

A narrow five-kilometre finger of land curling like a twisted root out into the placid waters of the Caribbean, set against a backdrop of rugged green mountains, the **Península de Ancón** enjoys a truly fantastic setting. Covered predominantly in scrub, the peninsula itself is not terribly impressive but does boast about 1.5km of sandy **beach** and an idyllic stretch of mostly undisturbed coastline. The beach has an encouragingly natural feel, with shrubs and trees creeping down to the shoreline, while there is more than enough fine-grained golden-beige sand (the best of it around the three hotels) to keep a small army of holidaymakers happy. In fact, other than hotel staff, holidaymakers are usually the only people on the peninsula, where the hotel resorts exist very much in isolation, and you need only wander a few hundred metres from their grounds to find yourself completely alone.

To **get there** from Trinidad, follow Paseo Agramonte out of town and head due south for 4km to the quiet village of Casilda. Continue for another 4km west along the northern edge of the Ensenada de Casilda, the bay clasped between the mainland and the peninsula, and you will hit the only road leading into Ancón. Whether staying in Trinidad and visiting the peninsula as a day-trip or vice versa, the taxi fare is around $6CUC one way.

The hotels and around

There's little point in spending your time here anywhere except **Playa Ancón**, the beach at the far end of the peninsula that has put the area on the tourist map. Although inexorable hotel construction has made finding a private patch of sand more difficult than it used to be in the resort's infancy, you're still unlikely to be disappointed with the boomerang-shaped beach at Playa Ancón, the longest stretch on the peninsula. Non-guests can access the entire length of the beach.

Heading out from the mainland, the first of the three hotels you'll come to is *Costasur* (T 41/99-6174, F 6173, E reservas@costasur.hor.co.cu; G), which has its own private but small section of beach featuring simple, attractive seafront bungalows. A little further along is the *Brisas Trinidad del Mar* (☎41/99-6500 to 07, ⓔreservas@brisastdad.co.cu; ⓪), the most modern and luxurious of the three hotels here. Smaller and quieter than most resort hotels, and popular with Europeans and Canadians, it has smart if unremarkable rooms. The overall design supposedly resembles Trinidad, complete with a miniature Plaza Mayor, but with the town itself just up the road, the imitation is both disappointing and pointless. Two restaurants, bars, a couple of swimming pools, a gym and non-motorized watersports are all included in the price. Approaching the tip of the peninsula you reach the much older all-inclusive *Hotel Ancón* (☎41/99-6120 & 99-6123 to 29, ⓔreservas@ancon.co.cu; ⓪), right on the seafront. Despite the Soviet-influenced architecture, the hotel has a welcoming atmosphere and is where most activity on the peninsula is focused. There are a number of bars and places to eat around the lobby and on the beachfront, as well as a large swimming pool, two tennis courts, a basketball hoop, volleyball net and pool tables. The hotel rents bicycles for $7CUC per day and scooters for $10CUC an hour, with reduced rates for longer periods.

On the beach, the International Diving Centre (daily 9am–5pm) rents out *pedalos*, kayaks and surfboards, and also organizes **diving** and **snorkelling** trips with the **Marina Trinidad** (☎419/6205, ⓔmarinastdad@ip.etecsa.cu), opposite the *Hotel Ancón*, on the other side of the peninsula. Diving excursions cost $30CUC for a single dive, $59CUC for two dives and $87CUC for three dives. Equipment is rented separately and goes for $15CUC for the full set. Diving courses, beginning at $60CUC, are also available. **Fishing trips** can be arranged as well, and cost either $30CUC per person for deep-sea fishing (requiring a minimum of six people) or $200CUC to rent a whole boat and go fly fishing.

One of the most popular snorkelling excursions is to Cayo Blanco, a narrow islet 8km from the peninsula with its own coral reef where the waters teem with parrotfish, trumpetfish and moray eels. Trips cost from $40CUC per person and usually include a lobster lunch. The area is known for its easy diving with good visibility, minimal currents and an abundance of vertical coral walls.

La Boca and around

Away from the hotels, the signs of package tourism die out almost immediately, leaving the rest of the peninsula and the adjoining coastline almost unaffected by the nearby developments. Continuing west from the hotels, the relatively quiet coastal road runs 7km along the mostly rocky shore to **LA BOCA**, a waterfront fishing village due west of Trinidad. About halfway along, the road passes by a pleasant stopoff point, the *Grill Caribe*, an outdoor **restaurant** on a platform above a tiny strip of beach and the only spot on the peninsula, outside of the hotels, where you can eat. They serve freshly caught seafood up until 10pm, and, ideally, you should aim to stop by at sunset when the atmosphere is tantalizingly calm.

Since La Boca itself has remained almost untouched by the hordes of tourists settling upon the main attractions nearby, and also features a high proportion of *casas particulares*, it's a good alternative place to stay at during visits to the peninsula, giving a taste of how Cubans like to spend their holidays. You'll need your own transport to get around; ask at a *casa particular* about hiring a private taxi or renting bikes. The short distance between the village and the hotel strip is a glorious ride along the coast with the turquoise blue of the Caribbean just a few metres away and the lofty mountains of the Sierra del Escambray never out of sight. La Boca's own small, scruffy and rather stony beaches are not particularly tempting, but still come alive at the weekends when they throng with Trinitarios enjoying themselves.

One of the best **casas particulares** in La Boca is *Hospedaje Vista El Mar* at Real no.47 (☎41/99-3716 & 99-4134; $25CUC), right on the seafront. There are two double rooms, both with air conditioning, in this well-kept house, and a lovely veranda wraps around the back, offering views of the sea. Another good option is the *Villa Rio Mar*, at San José no.65 e/ Real y rio (☎41/99-3108; $25CUC), a few metres from the beach and the local Guarabo River; both of the smart bedrooms have colonial-style shuttered windows, and there's a delightful, shady terrace.

The village's main drag is lined with stalls serving tasty cheese pizzas for Cuban pesos. You'll find a reasonable seafood menu at the only **restaurant**, *El Ranchón*, but if you eat here be wary of the staff short-changing you – something they have made a bit of a habit of doing. You're better off eating at your *casa particular*.

Valle de los Ingenios

A two-carriage train leaves Trinidad twice daily for the **Valle de los Ingenios**, a large, open valley that was once one of the country's most productive agricultural areas, dotted with dozens of the sugar refineries on which Trinidad built its wealth during the eighteenth and nineteenth centuries. Today just one refinery remains, but the valley's main draw is actually one of the old colonial estates, located at Manaca-Iznaga, the train's seventh stop, half an hour from Trinidad. From here, the **train** continues on to a few more stops in the valley and then makes the return journey to Trinidad, usually passing back through Manaca-Iznaga about 45 minutes after it stopped on the outgoing journey. You can also make the half-hour journey direct in a 1919 **steam train** with lovely old wooden carriages that leaves Trinidad daily at 9.30am and returns from the estate at 2.30pm. Tickets (currently $10CUC but set to go up to $20CUC) can be bought in advance from either Cubatur or Paradiso in Trinidad, or on the day at the station. Organized excursions are also available by road: Paradiso currently offer a day-trip for $9CUC per person or $21CUC with lunch included but requiring a minimum of four people.

If you're **driving** here, follow the main road to Sancti Spíritus, the Circuito Sur, from the east of Trinidad for around 15 kilometres. An essential stop is located about halfway between Trinidad and the estate, where there is a lookout point, the **Mirador de La Loma del Puerto**, up on a hill to the left, with a bar and fantastic views of the emerald green valley below.

Manaca-Iznaga estate

Whichever train you take to the old **Manaca-Iznaga estate** (daily 9am–4pm; $1CUC), the journey leads through a lush landscape with the ruffled peaks of the Sierra del Escambray visible to the north and stops at a tiny station platform that's two minutes' walk from the old house and tower, the main attractions here. Most people can't resist heading straight for the 45-metre **tower**, vaguely resembling a concrete rocket with its pointed, spired roof and slender body. It was built in the eighteenth century by one of the most successful sugar planters in Cuba, Alejo María del Carmen e Iznaga, supposedly due to a wager between Alejo and his brother Pedro. Legend has it that when Alejo promised to build the tower, his brother Pedro declared that he would dig a well whose depth would match the tower's height. No well has ever been found, however, and it seems more likely that the tower's bird's-eye view of the surrounding area was used by plantation overseers for surveillance of their slaves working in the fields below. The huge bell that once hung in the tower, which used to ring out the start and finish of the working day, now sits near the front of the house where there are also some rusty old nineteenth-century sugar cauldrons and a few stalls with small wooden sculptures, home-made clothing and other arts and crafts for sale. A small fee lets you climb the precarious wooden staircase to the top of the tower for views of the entire valley, a sea of sugar cane interrupted by the odd crop of houses.

Next to the tower is the **Casa Hacienda**, the colonial mansion where the Iznaga family would have stayed, though they spent more of their time at their residences in Trinidad and Sancti Spíritus. Despite one or two touches of the original decoration, for now the building's predominant function is as a **restaurant**, where run-of-the-mill pork and chicken dishes are served up on the terrace, overlooking a small garden. Over the road are the scattered dwellings of the old slave barracks, now converted into family homes.

Sierra del Escambray and Topes de Collantes

Rising up to the northwest of Trinidad, the steep, pine-coated slopes of the Guamuhaya mountain range are more popularly known as the **Sierra del Escambray**. These make for some of the most spectacularly scenic – and dangerous – drives in Cuba, whether you're cutting through between Trinidad and Santa Clara, or over to Cienfuegos, where most of the range, including its highest peak, the 1140-metre Pico San Juan, lies.

Four kilometres from central Trinidad along the Trinidad–Cienfuegos coast road, a right-hand turn takes you north into the mountains. About 5km along you'll find the *Campismo Manacal* (☏41/99-2168; ❶), a good option for those looking to spend a night or two getting away from it all. Nestled in a valley, with simple concrete *cabañas*, the *campismo* has a rough-and-ready rustic charm. You

△ Topes de Collantes

If you want to go hiking around Topes de Collantes, the best way to do so is to book an organized excursion in Trinidad, at Cubatur, Paradiso or Havanatur. If you arrive independently, the place to head first is the Centro de Información (daily 8am–6pm; ☏42/54-0219, ⓕ54-0117, ⓔcomercial@topescom.co.cu), the park's **information centre**, marked by a huge sundial right at the heart of the resort, a couple of minutes' walk from most of the hotels. This is where you pay if you want to follow any of the official trails (highlighted below), which are the only permitted hiking routes through this national park. Charges are between $3CUC and $6.50CUC per person, depending on the length of the trail. The English-speaking guides at the centre can advise you on the various trails around the area, but if you want a guide to accompany you, you will need to have booked an organized excursion in advance.

Excursions from Trinidad vary considerably in cost and content. For example, Cubatur offer their Trinitope tour for $29CUC per person, which includes the transfer up into the mountains from where you follow the trail down to the Salto del Caburní. Alternatively, their longer day-trip sets out from Trinidad in a minibus, transfers to a customized truck at Topes de Collantes and continues on to the Parque Guanayara, where the hike itself takes place, for $55CUC per person. Paradiso offer their own Salto del Caburní and Parque Guanayara hikes, for $29CUC and $43CUC respectively. Most excursions include a lunch and there is normally a minimum of at least three people required.

If it's pouring rain, which it often is up here, you may need sturdy hiking boots; otherwise trainers should prove adequate footwear for all of the hikes. Typically, trails are well marked and shady, cutting through dense woodlands, smothered in every kind of vegetation – from needle-straight conifers to bushy fern and grassy matted floors – opening out here and there for breathtaking views of the landscape. Also bear in mind that the air is a few degrees cooler than in the city or on the beach, and you may need more than just a T-shirt, even during summer.

Salto del Caburní

The most popular target for hikers in Topes de Collantes is this sight, a fantastically situated **waterfall** surrounded by pines and eucalyptus trees at the end of one of the park's more challenging trails. The 2.5-kilometre trek begins at the northernmost point of the resort complex and takes you on a clearly marked trail down steep inclines through the dense forest to the rocky falls. In the shadow of an impressive

can go horse riding, walk endless mountain trails, explore caves and swim in the jade-green, crystal-clear river that runs right through the middle of the site. A little further up the road there's a viewpoint off to the left; it's well worth climbing up its steep steps for the stunning views back across the Sierra's undulating foothills to the Península Ancón, which extends its long, sand-bordered finger out into the azure water.

A further 8km along the road are the scattered houses of El Chorrito village; immediately beyond here is the resort of **Topes de Collantes**. The resort is a kind of hotel village with roads linking its heavy-handed, box-like buildings together. Don't expect too much in the way of eating, entertainment or nightlife, but as a base for **hiking** this is the only obvious starting point for visiting the much larger area encompassed by the 175-square-kilometre Topes de Collantes National Park. A taxi from Trinidad shouldn't cost more than $25CUC round trip and, given the lack of public transport and the dangerous roads, is the best way of getting here unless you are on an organized excursion.

expanse of red rock, the 62-metre waterfall crashes down vertically for only a short stretch before changing gear and cascading more gently around a corner of chiselled rock and pouring into the small **pool** at the bottom. You can take a swim in the pool before summoning up the energy to make the fairly strenuous uphill return journey. The round trip usually takes about three hours, though you should add on at least half an hour's swimming time. $6.50CUC.

Guanayara

Fifteen kilometres north of the resort is an area known as the **Parque Guanayara**, host to one of the most scenic hiking routes. The gentler hike here follows the Guanayara River for a couple of kilometres up to the **Salto El Rocío**, a beautiful waterfall, and the **Poza del Venado**, a natural pool; along the way it incorporates some memorable views of Pico San Juan. Lunch is at the **Casa de la Gallega**, a simple cabin restaurant nestling in the trees. You will need your own four-wheel-drive vehicle to get to Guanayara if you are not here on an organized excursion. $6.50CUC.

La Batata

There are several trails leading to **La Batata**, a subterranean river at the foot of a lush green valley where you can bathe in the cool waters of the cave, which lies about 3km west (as the crow flies) of the heart of Topes de Collantes. Some of these trails are considerably longer than 3km, but the easiest route starts at the southwestern corner of the resort. The other focal point here is **Hacienda Codina**, an old Spanish coffee-growing ranch where you can stop for a drink. From the ranch there are easily manageable walks, some no more than a kilometre, into the forest, alive with a stunning variety of different plant species; these can be combined with circuits around a bamboo garden and an orchid farm. $3CUC.

El Cubano

Just 5km from Trinidad, but within the boundaries of the protected national park, this is the most popular location for horseback riding and is one of the most popular organized excursions from the city. The route here, which can also be done on foot, takes in a *campesino* house and the remains of a colonial sugar ranch, as well as rivers, brooks and waterfalls. Costs $5CUC or $15CUC from Trinidad on an organized excursion.

There are no taxis actually based at Topes de Collantes, so you should arrange for your driver to wait for you at the resort.

The best way to take advantage of what's on offer in the park is to follow one of the designated **trails**, which you can organize as an excursion from Trinidad or at the park's information centre (see box, above). Though the resort, with its style completely out of keeping with the beauty of its surroundings, is unlikely to lure you unexpectedly into staying the night, you may have to stay if you want to make the most of the trails. Conditions, however, are fairly good, with the three hotels available to international tourists as comfortable and well equipped as you could realistically hope for, given the obvious lack of investment in this once popular resort.

This mountainous area has its own **microclimate** and is always a couple of degrees cooler than Trinidad. It is far more likely to rain here than down by the coast, and for much of the year it rains almost every afternoon, making it a good idea to get up here early if you are visiting on a day-trip.

Resort practicalities

There are four **hotels** within the resort (Ⓦ www.gaviota-grupo.com), three of which are permitted to rent rooms to non-Cubans. Best of the lot is the *Villa Caburní* (Ⓣ 42/54-0330 & 54-0194; ❹) at the start of the trail to the eponymous waterfall, which has 29 dinky, ice-cream-coloured bungalows, each with its own little lawn and parking space, spread around a grassy area like a model 1950s American village. Most have two double rooms, bathroom and kitchenette, and all feature wonderful views of the mountains. If that's full, try the dated-looking *Los Helechos* (Ⓣ 42/54-0330 to 35, Ⓕ 54-0117; ❹), whose rooms with balconies are surprisingly light and airy. There's a disco and a restaurant in a separate, marginally more run-down building, as well as a bowling alley and a large indoor pool.

The only reason to opt instead for the massive *Kurhotel* (Ⓣ 42/54-0180 to 89; ❹) is to make use of its programmes of **therapeutic treatments**. Coming here feels a bit like stumbling on the secret hideout of a religious cult, what with hotel guests kitted out in identical tracksuits and, wandering around this monstrous building which resembles a huge inner-city institution. Treatment programmes, from massage to hydrotherapy, start at around $80CUC per day, including accommodation and food. Many of the treatments are administered in the Complejo de Cultura Física (Mon–Sat 8am–5pm), a fitness and therapy centre behind the hotel that's also open to non-guests. The facilities at *Kurhotel*, which include outdoor squash and tennis courts, an indoor swimming pool and a gymnasium, aren't exactly top-notch, but neither are the prices.

The only place in the park to **eat**, other than on the trails and outside of the hotels, is *Restaurante Mi Retiro*, 3km along the road back to Trinidad, where you can choose from roast pork ($5.95CUC), ham steak ($4.40CUC) or omelettes ($2–2.75CUC), served on a veranda on top of a small hill in a scenic valley enclosed by two big hills shaped like camels' humps.

Sancti Spíritus and around

East from Trinidad and its immediate environs, the rest of the **province of Sancti Spíritus** offers only one or two interesting ports of call. The provincial capital, also called **Sancti Spíritus**, is located about halfway between Santa Clara and Ciego de Ávila on the Carretera Central (which runs right through the town). Most often viewed as a transit town, but as one of Cuba's original seven *villas* founded by Diego Velázquez in the early 1500s, it offers ample reason to stop by for a day or two. A ten-kilometre drive southeast of the city, the huge **Zaza Reservoir** is ideal for fishing and hunting, with some appealing aspects for the non-specialist also.

As it's situated in the dead centre of the island, this is a good place to stop for the night if you're making the journey between Havana and Santiago. Though Sancti Spíritus has kept pace with similarly sized Cuban cities in commercial terms and boasts a relatively high standard of accommodation, culturally speaking the city lags some way behind its provincial neighbours, particularly

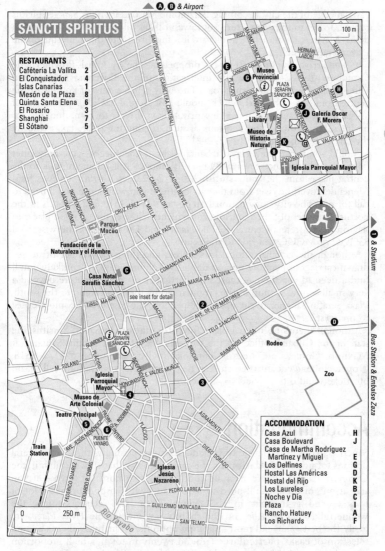

SANCTI SPÍRITUS

RESTAURANTS
Cafétería La Vallita	2
El Conquistador	4
Islas Canarias	1
Mesón de la Plaza	8
Quinta Santa Elena	6
El Rosario	3
Shanghai	7
El Sótano	5

ACCOMMODATION
Casa Azul	H
Casa Boulevard	J
Casa de Martha Rodríguez Martínez y Miguel	E
Los Delfines	G
Hostal Las Américas	D
Hostal del Rijo	K
Los Laureles	B
Noche y Día	C
Plaza	I
Rancho Hatuey	A
Los Richards	F

Santa Clara and Trinidad. Keep it short and sweet in Sancti Spíritus and you'll leave satisfied.

Arrival, information and getting around

Arriving by **car**, whether from Trinidad, Santa Clara, the west or the east, you'll enter Sancti Spíritus on the Carretera Central, which cuts along the eastern edge of the city, becoming Bartolomé Masó as it enters Sancti Spíritus proper. To get to the centre, turn southwest off Bartolomé Masó onto Avenida de los Mártires, an attractive boulevard leading directly to the main square, the Plaza Serafín Sánchez.

If you arrive by **bus**, you'll be dropped at the Terminal Provincial de Omnibus (☎41/2-4142), at the intersection of the Carretera Central and Circunvalación, the outer ring road. The only reliable way of getting to the centre from here is by **taxi**, which should cost around $2CUC. The arrival of a Víazul bus usually prompts a few private taxi drivers to come looking for business, but as there is no taxi rank as such, ringing for a state taxi is usually the safest option; Cubataxi (☎41/2-2133).

Should you arrive from Havana, Santa Clara or Cienfuegos – the only cities linked directly to Sancti Spíritus by rail – it's about a half-kilometre walk to the central plaza from the **train station** (☎41/2-4228 & 2-4790), on Ave. Jesús Menéndez, over the river from the city centre; if you want a taxi you'll need to call for one. The city's tiny national **airport** (☎41/2-4316 & 2-3104) is in the northern reaches of Sancti Spíritus, conveniently close to the two best places to stay on the Carretera Central, *Rancho Hatuey* and *Los Laureles*. Otherwise, it's a $3CUC or $4CUC taxi ride to the centre.

Although the city has a local **bus** system and there's a number of horse-drawn carriages operating up and down Bartolomé Masó, it's unlikely you'll find a need to use them – there's no particular reason to venture beyond a very small central section of the city, marked by the Río Yayabo to the south, Plaza Serafín Sánchez to the north, Céspedes to the east and Máximo Gómez to the west.

Although there's no official place for **information** in Sancti Spíritus, the staff in the Cubatur office on the western side of Plaza Serafín Sánchez at Máximo Gómez no.7 esq. Guardiola (daily 9am–6pm ☎41/2-8518, ⓔoperaciones@cubaturss.co.cu) can help with hotel reservations, sell Víazul bus tickets and offer advice.

Accommodation

Sancti Spíritus is a transit town, and so, unsurprisingly, there are several options for **accommodation** on the main highway that runs through it, the Carretera Central. There are four good hotels; two north of town – if you stay at one of these you'll need to have your own transport or take a lot of taxis – and two right in the centre. These two central hotels, the wonderful *Hostal del Rijo* and the slightly less memorable *Hotel Plaza*, are easily the best value and most appealing options. Alternatively there's a good selection of **casas particulares** (around twenty in total), a high proportion located on or within a few blocks of Plaza Serafín Sánchez in the centre of town with several others on the Carretera Central. A room in a house here is unlikely to cost any less than $15CUC in low season or any more than $25CUC in high season, with many charging a maximum of $20CUC.

Hotels

🏃 **Hostal del Rijo** Honorato del Castillo no.12 ☎ 41/2-8588, 2-7102 & 2-7168, ⓔdamaris@hostalrijo.co.cu. This exquisite little hotel occupies a fine colonial mansion built in

1818, and its careful renovation highlights original features like the impressive bronze-studded doors and crumbly terracotta-and-wood staircase. The spacious rooms, arranged around a charming patio, strike a perfect balance between comfort and simplicity, with stained-wood furnishings, marble washbasins, iron-base lamps, minibar and satellite TV. One of the most pleasant and reasonably priced hotels in the country. ④

Los Laureles Carretera Central Km 383 ☎41/2-7016, ⑤41/2-3913, ⑥recepcion@loslaureles.co.cu. A sociable roadside complex of concrete bungalows with a swimming pool, a restaurant serving Cuban staples and pizza, and occasional entertainment in the form of an open-air cabaret and karaoke. Rooms are large and cheery, with cable TV. ③

Plaza Independencia esq. Ave de los Mártires ☎41/2-7102. This characterful and compact city hotel on Plaza Serafín Sánchez is in good nick, having been refurbished in 2006; the reception area is smart yet homely, the rooms are reasonably equipped, although slightly poky – ask for one of the four larger ones – and there's a pleasant terrace bar and shady central patio. ④

Rancho Hatuey Carretera Central Km 384 ☎41/2-8315, ⑤2-8830, ⑥reserva@rhatuey.co.cu. This picturesque complex, set back some 400m from the road, is mostly used by tour groups stopping over for a night or two. The grassy site is larger than it needs to be, leaving the box-like villas a little stranded, but there's a nice pool area and facilities are relatively good. ⑤

Casas particulares

Casa Azul Maceo no.4 (sur) e/ Avenida de los Mártires y Doll ☎41/2-4336, ⑩www.la-casa-azul.3a2.com. Two inviting, well-equipped double rooms in a modern, homely apartment. One room has a pair of fetching hand-crafted, colonial-style mahogany beds and the other (up on the roof garden) with plenty of natural light. ①

Casa Boulevard Independencia no.17 altos e/ Avenida de los Mártires y Ernesto Valdes Muñoz ☎41/2-3029. Huge and impressive first-floor apartment whose front half is for the exclusive use of guests. Smartly and comfortably furnished, one of the highlights is a rooftop *ranchón*, a

rustic restaurant. The owner, Ricardo Rodríguez, is also the proprietor of nearby *Los Richards* (see below). ①

Casa de Martha Rodríguez Martínez y Miguel Plácido no.69 e/ Calderón y Tirso Marín ☎41/2-3556. The landlady here takes her business very seriously, insisting the freshly furnished rooms are cleaned daily, offering a menu (in Spanish and English) for meals and generally providing excellent service to her guests. There's a neat little dining room just outside the two rooms which leads onto a cosy terrace; a second, rooftop terrace can be used for sunbathing. ①

Los Delfines Quintín Bandera no.7 e/ Agusto Guardiola y Cándido Calderón ☎41/2-3408. The upstairs, self-contained apartment for rent here has its own dining room, a small set of terraces and even a tiny open-air bar with three stools and views of the far-off hills. The whole place has a spruce and orderly feel. ①

Hostal Las Américas Bartolomé Masó no.157 (sur) e/ Cuba y Cuartel ☎41/2-2984. This pink 1950s house is the best option for those that like their home comforts. Each of the two cool, airy rooms has its own bathroom, TV, safety deposit box, fridge and mosquito-proof windows, plus you can feast on the bananas and mangoes that grow in the back garden. Parking is available and the bus station is a five-minute walk away. ①

Noche y Día Martí no.111 e/ Comandante Fajardo y Frank País ☎41/2-7553. Relaxed, friendly and roomy colonial house with a pleasant open patio (partly occupied by the owner's 1958 Rambler), around which two different guestrooms are based; both have en-suite bathroom and a/c. ①

Los Richards Independencia no.28 (altos), Plaza Serafín Sánchez ☎41/2-3029 & 2-6745. Both of the rooms in this spacious, unpolished, family-run apartment have a small balcony overlooking the central plaza, a/c, a private bathroom and a living-room area. A large roof terrace provides good views of the city and, surprisingly, there's a ranch-style dining area out the back. ①

The Town

The logical place to begin exploring Sancti Spíritus is the central square, **Plaza Serafín Sánchez**, one of the city's few communal spaces with a sense of purpose. All the best sights are south of here; the most animated route for getting to them is along the main shopping street, Independencia, whose newly paved pedestrianized section, known as **Boulevard**, begins at the southeast corner of the square. A daily street market occupies a small stretch of Independencia just after the Boulevard section, and beyond this a small but confusing jumble of roads links up to the **Museo de Arte Colonial**, by far the most absorbing sight in the city. It's worth taking your time in the impressively well-furnished rooms, as none of the other museums will keep you longer than ten or fifteen minutes. Best of the rest are the modest **Museo Provincial** and the mixture of paintings at the **Galería Oscar F. Morera**, both on Céspedes. If you stay for the evening there are one or two nightspots around town, but expect at most a quiet drink, or if you're lucky some live music, rather than a five-course meal and a raucous night on the dance floor.

Plaza Serafín Sánchez and around

Though certainly one of the more pleasant and lively spaces in the centre of town, the **Plaza Serafín Sánchez** lacks the laid-back, sociable feel character-istic of other town squares. Nevertheless, it does attract an enthusiastic young crowd on weekend nights and though it's disturbed by the traffic passing through on all sides during the day, there are plenty of rickety metal seats around the simple bandstand for a sit in the shade. It's symbolic of Sancti Spíritus that two of the most striking and best-maintained buildings around the square, standing out amongst the otherwise vacant-looking two- and three-storey colonial buildings, are a bank and a fast-food joint. The third is the majestic **Biblioteca Provincial Rubén Martínez Villena**, on the corner of Máximo Gómez and Solano. Built between 1927 and 1929, this provincial library was renovated in 1999 and looks more like a colonial theatre with its balustraded balconies, Corinthian columns and arched entrance.

Right next to the library to the north, the easily manageable **Museo Provincial** (Mon–Thurs & Sat 9am–5pm, Sun 8am–noon; $1CUC) showcases a hotchpotch of historical objects dating mostly from the nineteenth and the twentieth centuries. Refreshingly, the common temptation to tie as much as possible in with the Revolution has been avoided here, and there are even displays from the 1950s unrelated to the dictatorship which Castro and his followers overthrew. That said, photos of Castro and his band of merry men entering Sancti Spíritus on January 6, 1959, on their victory march to Havana, are as engaging as anything else in here.

Occupying the square's southwest corner is the **Museo de Historia Natural** (Mon–Wed 8.30am–5pm, Fri & Sat 2–10pm, Sun 8.30am–noon; $1CUC) at Máximo Gómez no.2. Though there are some attractively displayed birds, this small, poorly stocked museum could do with a makeover and is unlikely to hold your attention for more than a few minutes. It's much more fun to visit, or at least look in the window of, the nearby **El Cañonazo**, about a block south of the plaza at Independencia no.6 e/ Plaza Serafín Sánchez y Honorato (daily 8am–3pm). Known as a *casa de comisiones* (the Cuban equivalent of a **pawnshop**), this is an absolute treasure trove of retro style, packed with miscellaneous bric-a-brac that includes 1950s pocket watches, 1970s radios, clothes, furniture, jewellery, crockery, cameras and just about any old thing you can pin a price tag on. Everything is priced in pesos, and although you should expect to pay at least a few hundred for anything decent, most items work out relatively cheap.

From the Iglesia Parroquial Mayor to the river

From the plaza it's a short walk on Independencia, or more directly on Máximo Gómez, to Sancti Spíritus's main church and oldest building, the **Iglesia**

Parroquial Mayor on Agramonte Oeste (Tues–Fri 9–11am & 2–4pm), which was built in 1680. Were it not so close to the city's finest museum it wouldn't necessarily warrant a visit, the chipped and faded yellow exterior being an accurate reflection of what to expect inside, but you may as well take a peek inside if passing by during opening hours. With the dramatic exception of an unusual blue-and-gold arch spanning the top section of the nave, however, the interior is simple and slightly bedraggled.

Museo de Arte Colonial and around

The best museum in Sancti Spíritus is unquestionably the **Museo de Arte Colonial** (☎41/2-5455; Tues–Sat 9am–6pm, Sun 8am–noon; $2CUC plus an incredible $1CUC for every photo you take inside) at Plácido no.74 esq. Ave. Jesús Menéndez, one block towards the river from the church. Built for the wealthy sugar-plantation Valle-Iznaga family, who spent most of their time in and around Trinidad, the museum has been restored to resemble a typical home of the nineteenth-century Cuban aristocracy. Over half its pieces were already in the house when the museum was started, with many others donated or bought from local families. There's a great selection of precious furniture and household objects, many of them imported from Europe; amongst the oldest pieces on display are the opulent French Baroque mirrors in the front room, which date back to the eighteenth century. Be sure to check out the American piano that forms the centrepiece to the music room. It was commissioned in 1900 and shipped to Casilda, a port just south of Trinidad, at the behest of the family's youngest daughter who wished to learn to play. An unfortunate group of slaves was commandeered, in the absence of roads, to carry it cross-country, on their shoulders, all the way to Sancti Spíritus. By the time the piano arrived, the girl had lost all interest, and she never once played it. The museum's collection is seamlessly

△ Puente Yayabo

authentic, and, its mood becomes more functional at the back of the building, where you'll find the kitchen, with its built-in cooking surface, and the courtyard – the living and working area for the slaves and servants.

On the other side of Jesús Menéndez from the museum, an area of cobblestone streets extends down to the river. Surprisingly, this clearly historic part of the city has not been refurbished for tourism and is a welter of ignored backstreets and local neighbourhood activity. This does, however, create a sense of stumbling on something undiscovered, and a quick wander around can be fascinating. Walk down A. Rodríguez to the river for a good view of the fairy-tale **Puente Yayabo**, the five-arch humpbacked stone bridge, built in 1825 and said to be amongst the oldest of its kind in Cuba. The Sancti Spíritus train station is located just a short distance from the far side of the bridge.

Along Céspedes

Running parallel with Plaza Serafín Sánchez and Independencia, a block over to the east, is **Céspedes**, along which you'll find the rest of Sancti Spíritus's worthwhile sights. At no.26 is the **Galería Oscar F. Morera** (Tues–Sat 8.30am–noon & 1–5pm, Sun 8.30am–noon; free), with another entrance on Independencia. The museum is housed in the former residence of the city's first well-known painter, who died in 1946, and the number and variety of works on display here make for an appealing wander around. As well as the purely representational art of Morera – which occupies several of the rooms and includes portraits, landscapes, still lifes and paintings of Sancti Spíritus – there are reproductions of internationally famous paintings as well as two rooms dedicated to temporary exhibitions, usually displaying the work of local artists.

Three blocks north on Céspedes, at no.112 e/ Comandante Fajardo y Frank País, the **Casa Natal Serafín Sánchez** (Tues–Sat 8.30am–5pm, Sun 8am–noon; 50¢) commemorates one of the city's heroes of the two Wars of Independence, killed in combat on November 18, 1896. Consisting mostly of Sánchez's personal effects and photographs of him and his family, along with a colourful portrait of the man on his horse, it's a bit bare and not terribly interesting.

Fundación de la Naturaleza y el Hombre

Two blocks further north along Céspedes, on the southern side of Parque Maceo, the **Fundación de la Naturaleza y el Hombre** (Mon & Sat 9am–noon, Tues–Fri 9am–4pm; 40¢) is one of Sancti Spíritus's quirkier sights. The tiny museum tells the story of an expedition organized by the late, well-known Cuban writer Antonio Nuñez Jimenez who, in 1987, led a team rowing down the Amazon in five one-ton, 13-metre-long canoes, each one carved from the trunk of a single Amazonian Suncho tree by the Quichua Indians of Ecuador. The expedition travelled east through Brazil, north up the Orinoco River into Venezuela and across the Caribbean, stopping off at San Salvador in western Cuba before finally arriving at their destination in the Bahamas, a journey of 17,422km. The aim of the trip, which took a year to complete, was to learn and appreciate what the first colonizers of Cuba, the Guanahatabey, who arrived there from South America around 3000 BC, might have experienced. Nuñez later published a book about his experiences, *En Canoa del Amazonas al Caribe* (1987), several copies of which, in the original Spanish, are held by the museum, along with one of the monolithic canoes, route maps, newspaper clippings and some yellowing photographs that the writer took of the indigenous Amazonian tribes he met on his journey.

Eating

Sancti Spíritus has two standout **restaurants**, the *Mesón de la Plaza* and *Quinta Santa Elena*, both centrally located and favourite dining spots of tourists. All the other state-run restaurants are much poorer (but cheaper) national peso-charging establishments, many of which keep short and sometimes unreliable opening hours. Also operating on unreliable timetables are the five legal **paladares** in the city, most of them difficult to find, all frequented predominantly by locals and none of them presenting particularly inviting dining environments. For **fast-food** there's a 24-hour branch of *El Rápido*, on the south side of the main square, and Cremería Kikiri at Independencia no.32, just round the corner from the square, where you can get basic sandwiches, hamburgers and ice cream.

State restaurants and paladares

Cafétéria La Vallita Ave. de los Mártires esq. Julio A Mella. Though essentially characterless, this shady, outdoor roadside café (on one of the city's most attractive avenues) is as reliable as anywhere for an inexpensive lunch. The choice is limited to sandwiches, burgers or ham steak, but almost everything is less than $1CUC and there is a good supply of beer and soda. Mon–Fri 9am–10pm, Sat & Sun 9am–midnight.

El Conquistador Agramonte no.52 e/ A. Rodríquez y Ave. Jesús Menéndez ☎ 41/2-6803. Cheap Cuban cuisine in a dignified yet lustreless colonial house in the centre of town. An inviting little patio is out the back.

Hostal del Rijo Restaurant Honorato del Castillo no.12 ☎ 41/2-8588. Decent fish and meat dishes, such as slices of pork with honey, served on the hotel's attractive central patio, where there's a fountain and views out to the small plaza.

Islas Canarias Ave. de los Mártires e/ Cuartel y Circunvalación ☎ 41/2-5241. It's a pleasant fifteen-minute walk from the centre to this faded but dignified peso restaurant, on the twelfth floor of a residential apartment building. The beef and pork dishes are basic but very cheap, and there's a bar with an outdoor roof terrace and fantastic views of the city.

Mesón de la Plaza Máximo Gómez no.34 near the Iglesia Parroquial Mayor ☎ 41/2-8546. This rustic tavern-restaurant with earthenware plates, heavy wooden tables and wrought-iron lamps hanging from the ceiling rafters offers an eclectic menu that includes beef stewed with corn, *ropa vieja* with raisins and red wine and an excellent, rich chickpea stew amongst the specials. Unusually, they also serve two types of sangria. Daily 11.30am–9pm.

Quinta Santa Elena Padre Quintero s/n e/ Llano y Manolico Día ☎ 41/2-8167. Offers a range of fish as well as the usual chicken- and pork-based dishes, and has a bar and a long cocktail list as well. The dining room in the handsome colonial-era building is fairly standard, while the best tables are those on the large terrace shaded by trees, overlooking the Puente Yayabo and the river.

Rancho Hatuey Buffet Restaurant Carretera Central Km 384 ☎ 41/2-8315. Dinner at the Rancho Hatuey hotel complex (see p.393) consists of a modest comida criolla buffet served in a comfortable canteen-style room

El Rosario F.E. Broche no.111 e/ Raimundo de Pisa y Adolfo del Castillo. East of the centre, and lost in the local neighbourhood, is this simple but excellent-value front-room *paladar*, serving large, inexpensive chicken- and pork-based meals for 50 Cuban pesos each; the speciality of the house is *Lonjas de Cerdo Asado* (slices of roast pork). Has tiny built-in bar as well. Daily 10am–10pm.

Shanghai Independencia no.9 e/ Plaza Serafín Sánchez y E. Valdes Muñoz. This Chinese restaurant offers one of the few alternatives to *comida criolla* when eating out in the city and is slightly more formal than most of the other national-peso joints. The food is quite heavy. Daily noon–2pm & 7–9.45pm.

El Sótano Eduardo R. Chibas 18c e/ 26 de Julio y Jesús Menéndez (☎ 41/2-5654). Tables and chairs at this *paladar*, located down a short alleyway and some stairs, look out over the river from just above its banks. Serves pork, chicken and lamb for 30 to 45 Cuban pesos per meal.

Drinking, nightlife and entertainment

Weekend **nightlife** for locals consists mainly of hanging out around the Plaza Serafín Sánchez. Some find their way into *Café Artex*, in between the bank and *El Rápido*, for the straightforward karaoke and **disco**, helped along by the very up-for-it crowd. Also on the south side of the plaza, on the corner with Máximo Gómez, the *Casa de la Cultura* hosts occasional *boleros* but has no regular programme of events. Around the corner at Máximo Gómez sur no.26 e/ Solano y Honorato are the more cultured surroundings of the *Casa de la Trova* (☎41/2-6802), which has a busier, more reliable schedule consisting predominantly of traditional **live music shows** from around 9pm onwards each Friday, Saturday and Sunday night. Entrance is free and there's a bar that makes for the best place in town for a drink. There's plenty of local flavour at *Café Central*, on Independencia just off the plaza, where the music and singing flow with the rum. Heading south, the *Casa de la Música* at San Miguel no.6, on the right-hand side of the Puente Yayabo, hosts live music on Friday, Saturday and Sunday nights in its dinky courtyard with balconies that overlook the river. The music kicks off at 10pm and is followed by a cabaret (☎41/2-4963; $5CUP).

If you're looking for other ways to while away the evenings, there are two **cinemas** on the Plaza Serafín Sánchez, Cine Conrado Benítez (☎41/2-5327) and Cine Serafín Sánchez (☎41/2-3839), and a *sala de video* in the basement of the library. The city's primary venue for **theatre** and **dance** is the diminutive Teatro Principal (☎41/2-5755) at Jesús Menéndez esq. Padre Quintero near the Puente Yayabo. The main local event to draw in the crowds is the **rodeo**, held once or twice a month at the weekend, in the Feria Agropecuaria on Bartolomé Masó to the east of the centre; entrance is one peso. The pathetic **zoo** next door is an exercise in cruelty to animals and, frankly, should be shut down. National-league **baseball** games are played at the Estadio José A. Huelga (☎41/2-2504 & 2-2770) just beyond Circunvalación on Ave. de los Mártires.

Listings

Banks and exchange The best bank for foreign currency transactions is the Banco Financiero Internacional, Independencia no.2 e/ Plaza Serafín Sánchez y Honorato (Mon–Fri 8am–3pm). The Cadeca *casa de cambio* is at Independencia no.31 e/ Ave. de los Mártires (Plaza Serafín Sánchez) y E. Valdes Muñoz (Mon–Sat 8.30am–6pm, Sun 8.30am–noon).

Bookshop Julio Antonio Mella Bookshop, at Independencia 29 sur e/ Plaza Serafín Sánchez y Ernesto Valdes Muñoz, has a small selection of mainly Cuban books and some magazines.

Car rental Micar, Honorato no.60 esq. Q. Banderas (☎41/2-8257). Also Transtur (☎41/2-8533) has a booth on the northern side of Plaza Serafín Sánchez and an office in *Los Laureles*.

Immigration To extend your tourist visa, visit the immigration office at Independencia no.107 norte e/ Frank Pais y Cruz Pérez, one block south of Parque Maceo (Mon–Thurs 7am–3pm, Fri 7am–noon).

Internet Telepunto, Independencia no.14 e/ Plaza Serafín Sánchez y E. Valdes Muñoz (daily 8.30am–9.30pm) has several Internet terminals and a line of phone cabins.

Library Biblioteca Provincial, Rubén Martínez Villena, on the Plaza Serafín Sánchez.

Market The Mercado Agropecuario just off Boulevard is a great little fresh-food market.

Medical The main hospital is the Clínico Quirurgíco Camilo Cienfuegos (☎41/2-4017 or 2-6017) halfway down Bartolomé Masó. For an ambulance call ☎41/2-4462.

Pharmacy There's a peso pharmacy at Comandante Fajardo no.53 e/ Céspedes y Martí.

Police Emergency number ☎116. There is a police station right on the Plaza Serafín Sánchez at Independencia sur no.3.

Post office Independencia no.8 e/ Plaza Serafín Sánchez y Honorato (Mon–Sat 8am–8pm, Sun 8am–noon). There are also DHL and EMS services.

Shopping There's a small convertible-peso supermarket with a good selection of rum upstairs at Independencia no.50 e/ Comandante Fajardo y Hernan Laborí. For arts and crafts the best places are the two local branches of the Fondo de Bienes Culturales at Cervantes no.11 esq. Máximo Gómez on Plaza Serafín Sánchez and Independencia no.55.

Telephones You can buy international calling cards in the ETECSA phone cabin at the southern end of the Plaza Serafín Sánchez. See also "Internet", opposite.

Taxis Cubataxi (☎41/2-2133); Taxi OK at the Rancho Hatuey (☎41/2-8315) or call Orlando (☎41/2-3744).

Train station ☎41/2-4790.

The Zaza Reservoir

Ten kilometres or so east from the city is Cuba's largest artificial lake, the **Zaza Reservoir**, a hunting and fishing centre and another option for a night's stopover on your journey across the island. There's no public transport there, but a taxi from Sancti Spíritus usually costs $8–10CUC one way. However, unless you are interested in either hunting or fishing, it's most likely not worth your time to come all the way out here unless you have your own car.

Most activity on the reservoir revolves around the **hotel**, sited on the network of inlets at the lake's northern edge. The *Hotel Zaza* (☎41/2-7015 & 2-5490, ℮director@hzaza.co.cu; ❸) is popular with Italian **hunting** enthusiasts who come here to shoot duck, quail and pigeon; they have exclusive rights to the hotel's hunting facilities and packages. This, however, does not detract from the utter tranquillity of the location, where everybody not hunting is concentrating on taking it easy.

In terms of non-hunting activities, a **motorboat** which takes a guide and up to three guests around the lake for up to an hour costs $15CUC for half an hour. You can also combine your boating with **fishing** sessions, though these are usually part of a package that includes full board at the hotel for around $90CUC a night. Otherwise, you will be limited to entertaining yourself within the hotel and its grounds, from where the reservoir looks bleak and unimpressive, its vastness impossible to gauge. The hotel itself is an adapted 1970s Soviet-style building, and though the conversion has mostly been a successful one, the rooms (which all have a/c and satellite TV) still look a little tired. The grounds feature a reasonably sized **swimming pool**, however, and spread right down to the water's edge. There's also a restaurant, coffee shop and bar on site.

Travel details

Astro and intermunicipal buses

Sancti Spíritus to: Camagüey (3 weekly; 3hr 30min); Ciego de Ávila (3 weekly; 1hr 15min);

Cienfuegos (1 daily; 2hr 45min); Havana (1 daily; 5hr); Santa Clara (2 daily; 1hr 45min); Trinidad (4 daily; 2hr).

Trinidad to: Cienfuegos (2 daily; 2hr); Havana

(3 weekly; 5hr 30min); Sancti Spíritus (4 daily; 2hr);
Santa Clara (1 daily; 3hr).

Víazul buses

Sancti Spíritus to: Ciego de Ávila (3 daily; 1hr);
Havana (3 daily; 5hr); Santa Clara (4 daily; 1hr
30min); Trinidad (2 daily; 1hr 30min); Varadero
(1 daily; 3hr 30min).

Trinidad to: Havana (2 daily; 5hr 30min); Cienfuegos (2 daily; 1hr 30min); Sancti Spíritus (2 daily;
1hr 30min); Santa Clara (1 daily; 3hr); Varadero
(1 daily; 5hr 30min).

Trains

Sancti Spíritus to: Cienfuegos (1 daily; 5hr
40min); Havana (1 daily; 10hr); Santa Clara
(1 every other day; 2hr 30min).

6

Ciego de Ávila and Camagüey

CHAPTER 6

Highlights

* **Laguna la Redonda** Located just outside Morón and tailor-made for an idle afternoon of boating or fishing. See p.415

* **Loma de Cunagua** This 364-metre tall hill, the lone high ground in an area of unremittingly flat farmland, is a favourite with birdwatchers. See p.416

* **Boquerón campsite** Hidden in the depths of the Ciego de Ávila countryside, this rustic retreat is hard to reach independently but well worth the hassle. See p.417

* **Diving on the northern cays** There are at least five excellent dive sites close to the northern cays, home to one of the world's longest coral reefs. See p.421

* **Playa Pilar** A gorgeous beach on Cayo Guillermo's western tip, named after Ernest Hemingway's yacht, *The Pilar*. See p.426

* **Hotel Colón** Almost a museum in itself, this beautiful 1927 hotel in the heart of Camagüey has been artfully renovated, preserving its eclectic mix of styles. See p.430

* **Plaza de San Juan de Dios** Camagüey's most photogenic square is lined by well-kept lemon-yellow and dusty-pink buildings, their windows hemmed with twists of sky-blue balustrades. See p.437

△ Playa Las coloradas

Ciego de Ávila and Camagüey

S panning the trunk of the island some 450km east of Havana, the provinces of **Ciego de Ávila** and **Camagüey** form the farming heart of Cuba, their handsome lowland plains given over to swathes of sugar cane, fruit trees and cattle pasture. The westernmost of the two, sleepy **Ciego de Ávila** is sparsely populated, with only two medium-sized towns often bypassed by visitors keen to reach the province's star attraction: the line of cays stretching west from **Cayo Coco** to **Cayo Guillermo**, home to some of the country's most dazzling white-sand beaches and most flamboyant birdlife, with one of the Caribbean's biggest barrier reefs creating a superb offshore diving zone. Home to a hard-working agricultural community, the low-key provincial capital, **Ciego de Ávila**, doesn't particularly pander to tourists, though its couple of attractive buildings and unaffected air make it an agreeable place for a pit stop. Further north, smaller but more picturesque and appealing **Morón** is a moderately popular day-trip centre and can easily be incorporated into a visit to the cays – it's also a handy budget alternative to the luxury accommodation there. Also in the town's favour is its proximity to the nearby lakes, **Laguna de la Leche** and **Laguna la Redonda**, the nucleus of a hunting and fishing centre popular with enthusiasts from Europe and Canada. As most of the province's sights are focused in the north, much of what remains is verdant farmland with comparatively little to offer the visitor. Heading south, the countryside becomes a generous expanse of cane fields and citrus groves that continue unabated to Camagüey.

Livelier than its neighbour, **Camagüey** province has several sights worthy of a visit, including provincial capital **Camagüey city**, one of the original seven *villas* founded by Diego Velázquez in 1515. Nurtured by sugar wealth that dates to the late sixteenth century, Camagüey has grown into a large and stalwart city with many of the architectural hallmarks of a Spanish colonial town, and is deservedly beginning to compete as a tourist centre. While the government pushes the plush northern beach resort of **Santa Lucía** as the province's chief attraction, the region's least spoilt beach is just west of the resort at **Cayo Sabinal**, which offers 33km of undisturbed beaches, their peace thus far preserved by a treacherous access road that deters the casual visitor. Away from the capital and tourist attractions, Camagüey province is

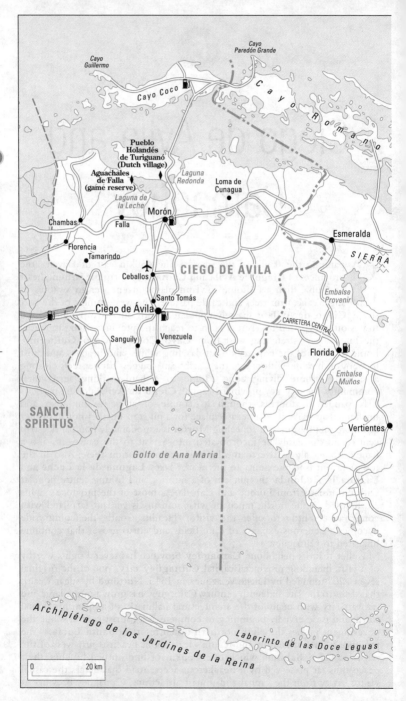

Cayo
Guillermo

Cayo
Paredón Grande

C a y o   P a r e d ó n

Cayo Coco

C a y o   R o m a n o

**Pueblo
Holandés
de Turiguanó
(Dutch village)**

*Laguna
Redonda*

**Aguachales
de Falla
(game reserve)**

Loma de
Cunagua

*Laguna de
la Leche*

Morón

Chambas

Falla

Esmeralda

SIERRA

Florencia

Tamarindo

CIEGO DE ÁVILA

Ceballos

*Embalse
Provenir*

Santo Tomás

Ciego de Ávila

CARRETERA CENTRAL

Sanguily

Venezuela

Florida

*Embalse
Muños*

Júcaro

SANCTI
SPÍRITUS

Vertientes

Golfo de Ana Maria

Archipiélago de los Jardines de la Reina

Laberinto de las Doce Leguas

0   20 km

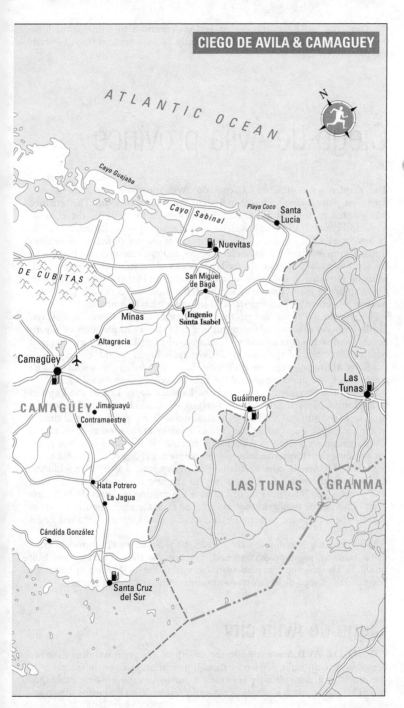

ATLANTIC OCEAN

Cayo Guajaba

Cayo Sabinal

Playa Coco

Santa Lucia

Nuevitas

San Miguel
de Bagá

DE CUBITAS

Minas

Ingenio
Santa Isabel

Altagracia

Camagüey

Las
Tunas

CAMAGÜEY   Jimaguayú

Contramaestre

Guáimero

LAS TUNAS   GRANMA

Hata Potrero

La Jagua

Cándida González

Santa Cruz
del Sur

the country's cattle-farming centre, and it's common to come across lone bullocks wandering or being herded skilfully by *vaqueros* (cowboys) beneath the palm trees.

Ciego de Ávila province

The slender waist of Cuba, **Ciego de Ávila** province forms the island's narrowest point, spanning less than 100km from north to south. The territory was granted to the Spanish conquistador Jacomée de Ávila by the colonial municipal council in Puerto Príncipe – now Camagüey – as a hacienda in 1538. "Ciego" means flat savannah, a fair description of the low plains and marshland that make up much of this somnolent region, and even the provincial capital to the south, also called **Ciego de Ávila**, is a quiet place, its main attraction lying in its remote charm and the insight it offers into traditional provincial living. More attractive than Ciego de Ávila itself, the province's second-largest town, **Morón**, features eye-catching architecture and a friendly ambience.

The province's main draws, the paradisiacal **Cayo Coco** and **Cayo Guillermo**, lie offshore to the north and offer the twin pleasures of superb beaches and virgin countryside – a Caribbean Shangri-la perfect for an escapist holiday. With one of the longest offshore reefs in the world, the cays have excellent **diving** sites and are themselves home to a variety of wildlife, which is why the government designated the cays an ecological protected zone.

South of the cays, on the mainland, the **Laguna de la Leche** and **Laguna la Redonda**, bordering the **Isla de Turiguanó** peninsula, are popular spots for hunting and shooting. Those not bent on slaughter can enjoy the natural charms of the area, as well as visiting the curious **Pueblo Holandes**, a reconstructed Dutch village set among swaying palms. In contrast, the caves and cool rivers surrounding the **Boquerón** campsite, on the western edge of the province near the town of Florencia, offer a refreshing and scenic natural alternative, while the far south of the province is given over to farming countryside flecked with one-street towns. The area's biggest draw is the pristine **Jardínes de la Reina** cays, 77km off the southern coast and reached from the undistinguished port of Júcaro, where there are numerous excellent dive sites, superb fishing and virgin cays to explore.

Aside from the blossoming tourist trade, the province makes its money from cattle farming, sugar production and, primarily, as the country's main fruit producer. The pineapple, in particular, is so vital to the local economy that it has been used as Ciego de Ávila's town motif since the eighteenth century.

Ciego de Ávila city

CIEGO DE ÁVILA is more like the suburb of a larger town than an urban centre in its own right. A friendly though pedestrian place set in the plains of the province, it is surprisingly young for a provincial capital – only established in 1849 – and its youth is its sole newsworthy feature. With no tourist attractions,

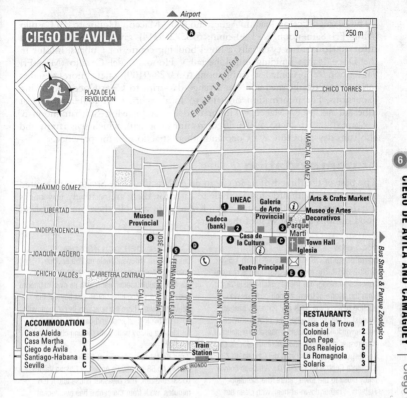

and precious little nightlife, Ciego de Ávila is often bypassed by visitors en route to the northern cays, but the town is not without charm and a stopoff here, on your way to the showier parts of the province, will reveal Cuba at its most modest and unaffected. Encounters with tourists are not everyday occurrences for the locals, but you will generally be warmly, if curiously, received; refreshingly, Ciego de Ávila has much less of a problem with hustlers and *jineteros* than bigger towns like Havana or Santiago de Cuba.

Arrival and information

Domestic **flights** from Havana arrive once a week at the Máximo Gómez airport at Ceballos, 24km north of town (☏33/26-6003); to get to the centre, the waiting metered **taxis** will charge about $5CUC, there are *colectivos* you can share (as a foreigner you may be charged a couple of convertible pesos), or you can take the **bus**, except for when there are petrol shortages. International flights also arrive here from Europe and Canada, but these are almost exclusively for package-tour holidaymakers en route to the cays, in which case onward transport is included.

All **buses** pull into the terminal on the Carretera Central Extremo Oeste (☏33/22-5105), about 3km from the town centre. You can share a horse-drawn carriage into the centre for a handful of pesos or catch a *bicitaxi* for a couple of convertible pesos. The **train station** (☏33/2-3313) is six blocks from the centre on Avenida Iriondo; *bicitaxis* can ferry you into town if you're not up to walking.

The Islazul office on Joaquín Agüero no.85 e/ Maceo y Honorato del Castillo (Mon–Fri 8am–noon & 1.30–5pm; ☎33/2-5314) gives out some **tourist information** but is essentially a hotel booking centre for Cubans. Infotur in the Doce Planta building esq. Libertad y Honorato del Castillo (Mon–Fri 9am–noon & 1–6pm, Sat 8am–noon; ☎33/20-9109) offers more rounded information on the area and can arrange day-trips to Cayo Coco and diving excursions. For information on trips to local sights, head to Havanaturs at Libertad no. 54 e/ Maceo y Honorato del Castillo (Mon–Sat 8am–noon & 1–6pm; ☎/🖷33/26-6339, 🖃palfredo@cimex.com.cu), which sells **maps** and also runs day-trips to Cayo Coco and other attractions in the province.

Accommodation

The best of the three **hotels** in Ciego de Ávila is the *Hotel Sevilla*, well located in the centre. With little tourist trade to cater for, there are relatively few **casas particulares**, and although their standard is quite variable, there are a couple of good options slightly west of the centre.

Hotels

Ciego de Ávila Carretera a Ceballos Km 1.5 ☎33/2-8013. The town's largest hotel is reasonably good looking, has friendly staff and is 2km from the centre of town, though *bicitaxis* wait outside to ferry you back and forth. It's best and liveliest at weekends when the pool is crowded with townsfolk, and boasts a passable restaurant, hairdresser, disco, bar and car rental offices. ❺

Santiago-Habana Honorato del Castillo no.73 esq. Carretera Central ☎33/2-5703. Although conveniently close to the town centre, the *Santiago-Habana* is rather down-at-heel, with clean but dingy rooms, some with balconies, and a restaurant that's functional but no more. ❷

Sevilla Independencia no.57 e/ Maceo y Honorato del Castillo ☎33/2503 or 2-5647. The 25-room *Sevilla* is by far the best hotel in town, with an airy reception full of squawking caged parakeets and budgerigars, a richly tiled balcony overlooking Parque Martí, and small, well-maintained rooms. The third floor plays host to the *Macarena Cabaret* (Tues–Sun 9.30pm–1am; $2CUC), while the small ground-floor restaurant serves tasty pork and chicken dishes. ❸

Casas particulares

Casa Aleida Independencia no.259 e/ José Antonio Echevarría y Calle 1 ☎33/20-0162. Two sizeable double rooms, each with its own bathroom and a/c, in a welcoming house just beyond the railway tracks. There's a spacious living room with an attractively tiled floor and carved wooden furniture, a shady patio with rocking chairs and available meals. ❷

Casa de Miriam Marzabal Gómez Marcial Gómez no.58 e/Joaquín Agüero y Chicho Valdés ☎33/20-3295. This pleasant house about ten minutes' walk from the centre has two decent-sized rooms, both with TV and a/c. The sun-filled patio is an added bonus. ❶

Casa Martha José M. Agramonte no.19 e/ Independencia y Joaquín Agüero ☎33/20-1327. This warm, cosy, centrally located house, run by a friendly young couple, is tastefully decorated in a different style to the Cuban norm. There are two double bedrooms with TVs and spotless bathrooms, and a comfortable roof terrace with tables and chairs. ❶

The City

Much of Ciego de Ávila has a close-knit, suburban feel, and on a swift tour around its residential streets lined with squat, whitewashed, modern houses you can see families on their verandas, old men in rocking chairs, and entrepreneurs selling corn fritters and fruit juice from peso stalls. The pace of Ávilean life flows slowly, its roads dominated by bicycles rather than cars, while horse-drawn *coches* weighed down with passengers sweat and strain their way across town.

At the heart of town, the small but pleasant **Parque Martí** is fringed with sturdy trees and with a central 1920s bust of the ubiquitous José Martí in reflective pose that makes him appear more poet than warrior. In the daytime older folk line the benches, shooting the breeze with the *bicitaxi* men while they wait to pick up fares or watching children playing marbles. The park is bordered by the town's four main streets, and any essentials you are likely to need, including shops, Internet facilities and places to eat, can be found around here. On the park's south side stands the central **cathederal**, San Eugenio de la Palma, a bland modern structure with a gigantic concrete saint tacked to the outside, next to which stands the stately **town hall**. On the same side of the square, on Independencia, the **Galería de Arte Provincial** contains a collection of glossy oil landscapes painted by local artists.

The prettiest building in the centre is the **Teatro Principal** on the corner of Joaquín Agüero and Honorato del Castillo. It was built between 1924 and 1927 by wealthy society widow Angela Hernández Vda de Jiménez in an attempt to make the town more cosmopolitan. Its decadently regal columned exterior, a riot of clashing Baroque, Renaissance and Imperial styles, gives way to a sumptuous interior, where Adonic marble figures nestle into alcoves and elaborate bronze chandeliers hang from an ornate stucco ceiling. There is no official guide, but you are free to enter and look around in the daytime.

Set in a beautiful colonial building on the east side of the square, the **Museo de Artes Decorativos** (Tues–Sat 8am–noon & 4–10pm, Sun 8am–noon & 6–10pm; $1CUC) is the new jewel in Ciego's crown. Built in the late 1920s as housing for visiting students from Spain, it was opened as a museum in 2003. Leading off from the elegant hallway, adorned with fabulous tall-necked Art Nouveau vases in gold and claret glass, is a nursery fitted out with white *pajilla* cane furniture, including a rocking nursing chair with a Cuban family crest. The room opposite is a mishmash of bedroom and dining furniture, while upstairs a Chinese red lacquer screen steals the show. Though few of the exhibits are of Cuban origin, as a whole they provide an illuminating insight into the level of luxury enjoyed by colonial Creoles.

Facing the park on Honorato del Castillo is a small arts and crafts market where a clutch of stalls selling homespun jewellery and the like are worth a swift browse. A block further north, at the corner of Honorato del Castillo and Máximo Gómez is the freshly relocated **Museo Provincial de Ciego de Ávila** (Tues–Sat 8am–noon & 1–5pm, Sun 8am–noon; $1CUC), with a room devoted to relics from local Taíno communities and a scale model of La Trocha Jucaro (see p.427). West of here, parallel to the tracks on Chicho Valdes and Fernando Callejas, a vibrant **farmers' market** (Tues–Sun 8am–4.30pm) sells fresh produce.

Eating, drinking and entertainment

State **restaurants** are thin on the ground in Ciego de Ávila, but the ones that are here are popular at weekends; you'll have to call early in the morning to reserve a table in the evening. Alternatively, you can snack well at the peso stalls along and around Independencia, while the *Hotel Sevilla* has a pleasant restaurant serving tasty chicken and pork, as well as a small **cabaret bar** on the third floor. Your best bet for a full meal is to ask a taxi driver for the whereabouts of the town *paladares*. In a small town like Ciego de Ávila these are unlicensed and therefore can't advertise; even though you will be charged in convertible pesos as a visitor, the bill should still be considerably less than in the bigger towns.

There are a couple of options for **live music**, although on weeknights, when nothing much happens, you may choose to catch a **film** at Cine Carmen at Maceo esq. Libertad, which also has a *sala de video*. On Saturday nights the town rouses itself from its habitual torpor for the weekly Fiesta

Ávileña, when the town's younger population gathers near the centre to dance to booming sound systems and feast on huge joints of pork roasting aromatically on sidewalk barbecues.

Restaurants

Colonial Independencia no.110 e/ Maceo y Simón Reyes, ☎ 33/2-3595. A Spanish restaurant hung with bullfight posters, with some outdoor seating in a dainty courtyard complete with a well. The menu includes pottage, *fabada* (bean stew) and tortilla, making it a change from the usual Cuban fare. A meal with drinks costs about $8CUC. Open eve only, with three seating times: 6pm, 8pm and 10pm. Reservations advised.

Don Pepe Independencia no.303 e/ Maceo y Simón Reyes, ☎ 33/2-3713 An atmospheric little eatery serving good pork dishes with rice and peas for pesos, and the unique Don Pepe cocktail (a house speciality made from rum and orange with a sprig of mint), with live music and dancing most nights. Along the walls are caricatures of local characters, some of whom regularly prop up the bar. Reservations advised.

Dos Realejos Joaquín Aguilero e/ Fernando Calleja y M Agramonte. Chunky fittings and a dusky interior give this restaurant/bar the feel of a Spanish taverna. All prices are in pesos so it's much patronized by locals and does very reasonable food. Dishes are the typical pork and beans run of things but well prepared and served with a smile.

La Romagnola Carretera Central esq. Marcial Gómez ☎ 33/22-5989. Billed as an Italian restaurant, this taverna-style spot with redbrick walls is really more of an upmarket pizza joint, although there are a couple of pasta options. The peso prices make this one of the best-value options in town. Open eve only and reservations are advisable.

Solaris Doce Plantas, 12th floor, Honorato del Castillo e/ Libertad y Independencia ☎ 33/2-2156. Standard meat-based dishes for mid-range prices, served in an original setting on the top floor of Parque Martí's tallest building. To get there, walk under the building through the alley next to the

telephone office. Turn left at the back and the lift there will whisk you skywards. A dress code – no sandals, men must wear a formal shirt – is strictly enforced. Closed Mon.

La Vicaria Carretera Central opposite the bus station ☎ 33/26-6477. Clean, bright and open until midnight, this is a welcome pit stop for anyone just getting off a bus. Expect fries, chicken, pork and rice at a couple of convertible pesos apiece.

Yisan Carretera Central e/ Calle 8 y 13 de Marzo. Salty fried rice and pork chow mein (adapted to use local vegetables) are served in this pleasant restaurant decorated in faded *chinoiserie*. Main dishes range from $4–9CUC. Closed Tues.

Nightlife

Batanga Disco in *Hotel Ciego de Ávila*, Carretera a Ceballos Km 1.5. Ciego de Ávila's teenage trendies and older swingers converge nightly on this disco, where, despite the age differences, everyone has a laugh together dancing to *salsa* and reggaeton in near-total darkness; passports required at the door. Tues–Sun 9.30pm–2.30am; $5CUC.

🏃 **Casa de la Cultura** Independencia no.76 e/ Maceo y Honorato del Castillo. A range of bands encompassing everything from *bolero* to Mexican country music play on Fri, Sat and Sun nights, kicking off at 9pm.

Casa de la Trova Libertad no.130 e/ Maceo y Simón Reyes. The best bet for a night out – the bar sometimes serves locally brewed beer and always has good Cuban rum and your choice of 25 cocktails, while local music groups play traditional *boleros*, *son* and *guarachas* to an older crowd when there's a full house. Closed Mon.

🏃 **UNEAC** Libertad no.105 e/ Maceo y Simón Reyes ☎ 33/20-4511. A romantic building with pale tiled floors and high ceilings that suit the *bolero* and choral concerts that are held here. Programmes usually start around 8.30pm and finish at midnight. Closed Mon.

Listings

Airlines The Cubana office is on Carretera Central e/ Honorato del Castillo y Maceo ☎ 33/26-6627.

Airport Information ☎ 33/30-9165.

Banks You can change traveller's cheques and get cash advances on credit cards at the Banco Financiero Internacional on Honorato del Castillo, at the edge of the square (Mon–Fri 8am–3pm,

last working day of month 8am–noon) and at the Cadeca *casa de cambio*, Independencia no.118 e/ Maceo y Simón Reyes (Mon–Sat 8.30am–6pm, Sun 8.30am–12.30pm), where you can also buy pesos.

Car rental Micar has an office at Fernando Callejas esq. Libertad (☎ 33/26-6157) and a desk at the *Hotel Santiago-Habana* (☎33/26-6169). Cubacar has a desk in the *Hotel Ciego de Ávila* (☎33/2-8013 or 22-5105) and at the *Hotel Morón* in Morón (☎335/22-30).

Internet The ETECSA centre on Honorato de Castillo y Maceo (daily 9am–9pm) supplies Internet usage at $3CUC for half an hour. The shared email address is ✉telepunto@av.tel.etecsa.cu.

Medical Try the 24-hour surgery on República no. 52 esq. A. Delgado ☎33/2-2611. For an ambulance call ☎185.

Pharmacy There is a 24hr pharmacy at Independencia no.163.

Photography Photoservice at Maceo no.9 e/ Independencia y Libertad.

Police Call ☎116.

Post office You can buy peso stamps, send telegrams and use DHL and EMS services at the main 24hr post office on Máximo Gómez esq. Carretera Central.

Shopping Supermarket Libertad at Libertad no.68 e/ Maceo y Honorato del Castillo is the best place for picnic supplies and rum.

Taxis Cubataxi ☎33/26-6666 or Taxis Ávila ☎33/22-3582.

Telephones ETECSA have an international call centre opposite the square in the Doce Plantas building (daily 9.15am–9.15pm) and a phone cabin on Independencia e/ Simón Reyes y José M. Agramonte where you can buy phonecards. There is also a centre on Honorato de Castillo y Maceo (daily 9am–9pm).

Viazúl (Terminal de Omnibus Interprovincial) ☎33/22-5105.

Morón and around

Lying 36km north of Ciego de Ávila on the road to the cays, surrounded by flat farming countryside replete with glistening palm trees, banks of sugar cane and citrus trees, picturesque **Morón** is a popular stopoff on the tourist itinerary. Fanning out from a cosy downtown nucleus, its few gaily painted colonial buildings and proximity to Cayo Guillermo and Cayo Coco ensure its popularity with day-trippers from the cays, and it's certainly the best place to stay if you want to visit the cays but can't afford to stay in a luxury hotel. For now, though, the area's main tourist revenue comes from hunting and fishing, as enthusiasts from around the world converge on **Laguna de la Leche** and **Laguna la Redonda** 15km north of town, where several species of fish and flocks of migrating ducks are sitting targets.

Morón makes a great base for exploring the sights en route to the cays, most of which can be squeezed into a day-trip. Chief among them is the peninsula **Isla de Turiguanó**, whose peak, Loma de Turiguanó, you can see throughout the flatlands, and the **Pueblo Holandés**, an incongruous mock Dutch village built in the 1960s. To the east, the densely wooded slopes of the **Cunagua Hill** are home to myriad birds, while on the western edge of the province, between the two small farming villages of Florencia and Chambas, the **Boquerón campsite**, beside a clearwater river overhung with deep-grooved cliffs pocked with caves, is a rustic retreat that's a perfect alternative to the beaches.

Arrival and information

Three daily **trains** from Ciego de Ávila release their passengers at the elegant station in the hub of the town; this also serves as the drop-off and collection point for *colectivos*, *camiones* and **buses**. Although all the sights and accommodation are within walking distance, the private **taxis** waiting under the trees in front of the station are useful for forays into the countryside. For state taxis, the only reliable transport option to the northern cays for those without a rental car, try Cubataxi (☎335/3290) or Cubacar in the *Hotel Morón* (☎335/2230) which, in the absence of a tourist office, has some **information** about local excursions and sells **maps**.

The main street, Martí, boasts most of the town's services, including the **post office** (Mon–Sat 8am–6pm) and **telecommunications centre** (daily 8am–9.45pm), both housed in the blue-and-white 1920s period building, Colonial Española. A couple of blocks south, the Cadeca *casa de cambio* handles all types of foreign currency transactions and sells pesos (Mon–Sat 8.30am–5.30pm, Sun 8.30am–noon).

Accommodation

Most visitors are en route to the cays and stay at the concrete-block *Hotel Morón* lurking on the edge of town. However, a clutch of very reasonable **casas particulares** has recently sprung up in response to the growing number of visitors to the region. Otherwise, your best choice is the small, amicable *La Casona de Morón*.

Hotels

La Casona de Morón Cristóbal Colón no.41 ☏ 335/2236. A pretty, friendly sunshine-yellow villa with a lot more personality than the region's bigger hotels, hidden behind a mass of trees east of the train station. It has seven rooms, all with marble floors and high ceilings, and usually caters to the hunting and fishing crowd, with organized tours of Laguna de la Leche and Laguna la Redonda and boat and tackle rental. You can cook your spoils yourself on the open grill by the tiny swimming pool. Reservations are advisable. ❹

Hotel Morón Ave. Tarafa s/n ☏ 335/2230 to 32, ✉ hhmm@hmoron.cav.cyt.cu. As the only big hotel in the region, the *Morón* draws the crowds of visitors heading to and from the cays, despite being rather run-down, ugly and anonymous. Rooms are spacious though colourless, with the hotel's real saving grace being the large, warm and clean swimming pool. ❹

Casas particulares

Belkys y Oscar Quintero Cristobel Colón e/ Carreterra de Patria y Ferrocaril ☏ 335/50-5763. Two large and airy rooms in a colonial house near the train station. Ample parking space is a bonus. ❷

Casa Carmen General Peraza no.38 e/ Felipe Poey y Carlos Manuel de Céspedes ☏ 335/4181. This handsome, spacious house near the train station is filled with elegant antique furniture and ornate mirrors. Run by a friendly all-female family, it has two rooms with a/c. Take the opportunity to eat here, as the delicious dishes are prepared with care and originality. ❶–❷

Juan Carlos Espinoza Cristóbal Colón no.39 e/ Carretera de Patria y Linea de Ferrocarril ☏ 335/4177. Two plain and simple rooms in a regal, 1920s, double-fronted mansion house just yards from the train station with, surprisingly, a sizeable swimming pool and a thatch-roofed bar in the back garden. ❷

Juan C. Peréz Oquendo Belgica Silva Castillo no.189 e/ San José y Serafín Sánchez ☏ 335/3823 Very friendly owners and comfortable a/c rooms at this *casa particular*, a short walk from the centre of town. ❶–❷

Onaida Ruíz Fumero Calle 5 no.46 e/ 6 y 8 ☏ 335/3409. Pleasant a/c rooms, one double and one triple, with parking and meals in a quiet residential street near the *Hotel Morón*. ❷

The Town

The first thing to strike you about clean, compact Morón is the shining **bronze cockerel**, symbolizing the town's turbulent Spanish heritage (see box, opposite) as well as its charming and slightly quirky character, and perched at the foot of a clock tower on an oval green in front of the *Hotel Morón* just inside the southern entrance to the town. Morón is sliced in two by train tracks that aren't separated from the road by any barriers – it is quite common to see trains impatiently honking horns as bicycles bearing two or three passengers lazily roll over the rails – and slice through the town's main street, **Martí** (its southern reaches also known as Avenida Tarafa). At the mouth of the tracks, roughly in the centre of town, is the **train station**. Built in the 1920s and one of the oldest in Cuba, it remains largely unchanged, and inside, amidst the elegant archways

The cock of Morón

Named by Spanish settlers after their Andalucían home town, **Morón de la Frontera**, the Cuban town has also appropriated one of its founders' legends. In the sixteenth century, the townsfolk of Spanish Morón found themselves the victims of a corrupt judiciary that continually levied high taxes and confiscated their land without explanation. Having suffered these oppressive conditions for several years, the people set upon and expelled the main offender, an official nicknamed "**the cock of Morón**". The gamble paid off, as the remaining officials, fearing a more serious rebellion, promptly lessened the taxes. The incident was quickly immortalized in an Andalucían ballad that proclaimed that "the cock of the walk has been left plucked and crowing" (a saying still used throughout Cuba today to mean that somebody has had their plans scuppered), and has ensured Morón's slim slice of fame in the annals of Cuban history.

The first **rooster monument** was erected here in the 1950s, under Batista's rule, but was torn down after the Revolution by officials who saw it as a symbol of the previous regime. Fond of their town mascot, locals complained and in 1981 the present bronze statue was erected at the foot of the clock tower. As a dubious stroke of genius the clock tower was fitted with a crackling amplifier, enabling everyone to hear the mechanical cock manfully crowing twice daily at 6am and 6pm.

and fine wrought-iron awnings, you can still buy tickets at original ticket booths and check destinations on a hand-painted blackboard, while high above the rows of worn wooden benches and the original stained-glass *vitrales*, birds nest under the eaves.

From the station, a five-minute walk north along Martí will take you to the **Museo Municipal**, Martí no.374 (Tues–Fri 8am–noon & 1.30–5.30pm, Sat 8am–noon, Sun 8–10am; $1CUC), newly opened in one of the town's eye-catching colonial buildings, fronted by simple columns and wide steps. It houses an assortment of small pre-Columbian Cuban artefacts, mainly fragments of clay bowls and shards of bone necklace. By far the most impressive exhibit is the *Idolillo de Barro*, a clay idol shaped into a fierce snarling head, found outside the city in 1947. Further north along Martí the **Galería del Arte**, at no.151 (Tues–Sat 8am–noon & 1–5.30pm, Sun 8am–noon), exhibits and sells an array of locally painted landscapes, colourful abstracts, lovingly executed sculptures of female nudes and mawkish religious figures. If you're planning to buy a sculpture in the area, this is the place to do it as they're a lot cheaper here than at the resorts.

Eating, drinking and entertainment

Morón is a town of modest means where the locals' idea of a good night's entertainment is to cluster around a neighbour's television (or even peer through their window) to catch up with the latest soap opera. Your options, all rather tame, are to enjoy a gentle night-time promenade around the star-lit streets, catch a film at the Apolo **cinema** (next door to the *Jardín del Apolo*), or, if you are driving, to head out in the early evening to one of the lakeside **restaurants** (see p.415).

Alondra Martí no.298, e/ Serafín Sánchez y Callejas. Slick, shiny glass-and-tile ice-cream parlour, charging around $1CUC for a very kitsch candy-coated sundae complete with spangly cocktail stick. Daily 10am–11pm.

Casa de la Trova Libertad e/ Narciso López y Martí. A small but pleasantly unassuming local watering hole where the town's minstrels serenade drinkers with traditional *guajiras* and *son* amid basic decor that's remained unchanged for years. An authentic Cuban experience. Closed Tues.

Doña Neli Serafín Sánchez no.86 e/ Narciso López y Martí. A bakery serving an excellent selection of fresh breads, flaky pastries and cakes elaborately coated in meringue. Arrive early in the morning to avoid being stuck with the bullet-like bread rolls. Daily 8am–8pm.

Las Fuentes Martí no.169 e/ Libertad y Agramonte. Creamy soups and pastas enliven the standard selection of chicken and pork dishes in this warm, rustic-style restaurant where you eat to the sound of water trickling down the eponymous fountains, surrounded by jungly ferns. Main courses cost around $5CUC.

Jardín del Apolo Martí e/ Carlos Manuel de Céspedes y Resedad. Fried chicken and beer served in a courtyard to the accompaniment of charmless soft rock music. Open 24hr.

Morón Martí no.219 e/ Callejas y Serafín Sánchez. Although not exactly a gastronomic experience, the meat-based meals served in this large, canteen-style dining room are more imaginative than most peso restaurants and the large menu changes daily. Expect dishes like fried pork, *ropa vieja*, and chicken cooked with tomatoes. Prices start at $6CUC. Closed Tues.

Around Morón

Set in lush countryside dappled by lakes and low hills, the area surrounding Morón offers a welcome contrast to the unrelentingly flat land to the south, and holds a few surprises well worth venturing beyond the town limits to explore. Ten kilometres north of town, the large **Laguna de la Leche** is fringed by reeds and woodland that hide the **Aguachales de Falla** game reserve, while 7km further northeast the tranquil **Laguna la Redonda** is an idyllic spot for drifting about in a boat. Just north of the lakes is the peninsula **La Isla de Turiguanó**, home to the mock-Dutch village **Pueblo Holandés de Turiguanó**, its faux-timbered, red-roofed houses looking completely out of place beneath tropical palms. Towards the east, rising from the plains like the shell of a tortoise, is the gently rounded **Cunagua Hill**, its dense tangle of woodland full of bright parakeets and parrots, and a favourite spot for day-trekkers and birdwatchers. West from Morón, in an area straddled by the tiny villages of Chambas and Florencia, are the **Boquerón caves** and **campsite**, its riding, river-swimming and rock-climbing opportunities an irresistible draw for nature enthusiasts.

Unless you are driving, the only way to **get around** the Morón area is to negotiate a day rate with one of the Moronero taxi drivers (see p.411). The bigger your group the more they'll want to charge you, but for two people you should count on around $25CUC.

Laguna de la Leche

With a circumference of 66km, **Laguna de la Leche** (Milk Lake), 10km north of Morón, is the largest lake in Cuba and, decked out with palm trees and a pint-sized lighthouse, looks like a tiny seafront. The opacity of its water comes from gypsum and limestone deposits beneath the surface, but despite the evocative name it looks nothing like Cleopatra's bath: rather, the lake fans out from a cloudy centre to disperse into smudgy pools of green and blue around the edges. Despite its murky appearance there are always a few local children splashing in the shallows, and anglers regularly plumb its depths for the wealth of bass, tilapia and carp within. The lake's wooded north and west shores, soupy with rushes and overhung branches, are great for exploring but accessible only by boat. Boat rental should be pre-arranged through *La Casona de Morón* (☎335/2236).

This lake's peaceful calm is only mildly disturbed by the distant gunshots of eager sportsmen firing at the hapless ducks, white-crowned pigeons and doves that swoop through the **Aguachales de Falla hunting reserve** on the west shore. The government's promotion of blood sports here may seem at odds with the ecotourism touted on the northern cays just a few kilometres north (see p.418), but firearms are entrenched in Cuban culture and familiarity with them is seen as an essential skill in a country still intermittently defending its sovereignty. As the popular motto goes, "Every Cuban should know how to shoot and shoot well".

Set back slightly from the southern shore is *La Cueva de la Laguna de la Leche* (Tues–Sun 8am–7pm), a palm-shaded open-air **bar and restaurant** which serves fresh catches from the lake. Around the back of the bar is a gloomy man-made cave with a dimly lit dance floor where, on Fridays and Saturdays (10pm–2am), there's a free cabaret featuring scantily clad women lip-synching and dancing as professionally as their elaborate fruit turbans will allow.

No buses go to the lake, but a private taxi from Morón should cost no more than $5CUC. If driving, take Martí north out of town, turn left and head for the cays until the signposted turning.

Laguna la Redonda

The smaller of the region's two lakes, measuring only 3km at its widest point, **Laguna la Redonda** (Circle Lake), 7km further north and reached by a canalside turning off the main road to the cays, has five mangrove canals that radiate out from the central body of water like the spokes on a bicycle wheel. Quieter and altogether more intimate than Laguna de la Leche, it's perfect for an idle afternoon's boating or trout fishing or just drifting over to the uncharted territory on the far side of the lake and wandering through the undergrowth.

The serene *La Redonda* **restaurant** (9am–8pm) which overhangs the lake serves freshly caught tilapia and carp as well as pasta, steaks, chicken and omelettes and rents out boats ($3CUC each for a maximum of 6 people with a guide, or you can hire a boat for two and take off on your own), while *San Fernando*, Carretera Ciego de Ávila Rotonda, is a pleasant villa off the lakeside road, converted into an upmarket restaurant serving good Cuban cuisine and dire spaghetti for around $7CUC to $10CUC a head. It has an attractive

△ Laguna la Redonda

outside bar which should be avoided on Saturday nights when a tawdry cabaret show takes over.

Tours to the lake and boat rental are organized by *La Casona de Morón* in Morón (☎335/2236; see p.412); fishing costs $35CUC per person for four hours, including equipment.

Pueblo Holandés de Turiguanó

Sitting in the middle of a frill of palms and purple bougainvillea, 6km north of Laguna la Redonda and 26km from Morón, at the foot of the causeway to the cays, the Dutch-timbered houses of the **Pueblo Holandés de Turiguanó** are nothing if not anomalous. Before the Revolution, this was a US-owned cattle farm, virtually inaccessible because of widespread marshland; in the early 1960s, with the Americans long gone, the land was expropriated and drained and the present mock-European village built to house the Cuban cattle hands who had previously lived here under poor conditions. The Dutch styling was the whim of Celia Sánchez, a core revolutionary, secretary and special friend of Fidel Castro, who had developed a penchant for Dutch architecture while spending time in Holland in the 1950s. Still serving its original function today, the village raises Santa Gertrudis cattle, one of the island's best breeds, much of whose meat goes to feed the tourists in the cays. Ducks waddle around the village green and across the neat lawns that separate the whitewashed gabled houses. The red-tiled roofs are actually painted corrugated iron, but this discovery doesn't really spoil the illusion. No buses come here, but a taxi from Morón will cost between $8CUC and $10CUC each way should you feel it is worth the time.

Criadero Cocodrilo and Loma de Cunagua

Heading 9km east out of Morón on the Carretera de Bolivia, the **Criadero Cocodrilo** (daily 7am–7pm; $1CUC) makes the highly spurious claim to be a conservation centre, but is really nothing more than a glorified zoo. The luckless crocodiles are housed in a filthy concrete pool at one end of which sits a bar-restaurant on stilts. For a small fee, the waiters will dangle a piece of fish through a large hole in the floor, provoking the powerful reptiles to leap up with a businesslike snap of the jaws. The centre makes a further mockery of its ecological pretensions by housing a small community of fighting cocks, their talons filed to razor-sharp points and each highly strung male confined to his own cage.

Far more enticing is the **Loma de Cunagua**, 9km further up the road. Standing 364m tall and the lone high ground in an area of unremittingly flat farmland stretching all the way to the coast, the hill can be seen for miles around. Just past the hill is a gate (daily 9am–4pm) where you must stop and pay the $1CUC entrance fee. From here a gravelly road weaves and winds its way up through the dense tangle of spindly trees clinging precariously to the steep slopes. A favourite with **birdwatchers**, the hill's forests, crisscrossed by a network of trails, are home to dazzlingly coloured parrots, as well as the *tojosa* (a small endemic dove), the *zunzún* (Cuban emerald hummingbird), and the *tocororo* which was chosen as the country's national bird due to its startling red, white and blue plumage, the same colour scheme as the Cuban flag. If you're lucky, you might also catch a glimpse of an enormous Cuban tree rat, known locally as *jutía*. Racoon-sized, with wiry grey coats, long tails and snouty rodent faces, they root around in the undergrowth and claw their way up trees to eat succulent young leaves.

The hill's summit offers panoramic views over the surrounding countryside and out to sea, and there's a rustic **restaurant** where you can eat a mountain of pork, yucca and potatoes with fruit, dessert, a drink and coffee, all for $10CUC.

Those wishing to explore at dusk or dawn can choose **to stay** the night; there are three basic but comfortable rooms, each with two single beds, in a simple wooden house (●). The nights here are incomparably tranquil, with no sound except for the humming of cicadas and chattering of crickets. Horse riding is also available; trips cost $2CUC per hour and include a biologist guide. There's no public transport to the area, but a taxi here from Morón should charge about $15 for the round trip.

Florencia, Chambas and around

The undulating terrain around the tiny towns of **Florencia** and **Chambas**, 30km west of Morón, is prime farming country, pocketed with dazzling sugar fields, corrals of slow-moving cattle and tobacco meadows. Dotted around the area are several sugar mills and villages, which, despite their unassuming appearance as just clusters of concrete houses, bear witness to the changes that revolution brought to rural Cuba. Before 1959, this region was crippled by grinding poverty, illiteracy, unemployment and inadequate health care. Work in the privately owned fields was seasonal and there was no welfare structure to tide people over from one year to the next. The 1959 Agrarian Reform, one of the revolutionary government's first acts, ensured that provisions were made for peasant health, housing and education.

The glorious countryside can be explored on guided **horse treks**, run daily by Rumbos in Florencia (☎33/6-9294), through the coconut groves and banana fields. One excursion takes you past local farms to a rodeo show, where local cowboys wow the crowd with demonstrations of their animal-handling prowess, before the day culminates in a pig roast. During the **tobacco** harvest the tour also includes a bus trip to a tobacco-curing house near Florencia. Alternatively, you can ride to the shores of the Liberacíon de Florencia **lake** to the east of the town. From here you'll be whisked by motorboat to the restaurant on the island in the middle. Keep a lookout for the majestic ceiba tree near the lake. Identifiable by its gigantic stature and webbed roots overlaying the tree base, it's believed by followers of the Afro-Cuban religion Santería to have magical powers.

There's no better place to stay in the area than the superb **Campismo Boquerón** (bookings through Rumbos on ☎33/6-9294; ●), 5km west of Florencia. Tucked away down a series of twisted lanes which at times become waterlogged dirt tracks, it's not the easiest place to reach independently, but really is worth the hassle. Veiled behind the folds of the Jatibonico Sierra (the rugged tail of the Sierra de Meneses chain stealing into the province from Sancti Spíritus to the west) and framed by a halo of royal palms, the campsite occupies a hidden paradise of banana groves, fruit trees and flitting humming-birds. It offers an area to pitch tents, as well as triangular **huts**, each lined with four basic but clean single bunks for which you should bring your own sheets. The Jatibonico River twists through the hills and makes an excellent spot nearby for shady **swimming**, while a phalanx of skinny horses waits to take you **cross-country trekking**, and the cavernous crags jutting out above the site are ripe for **mountaineering**. The campsite promises **food**, but you're better off taking your own provisions and cooking on the communal barbecue.

Another place to stay if you are touring around here is the *Hotel Colón* in Chambas at Martí no. 56 (☎33/6-7540; ●), which has clean if characterless rooms (each with its own bathroom, TV and fridge), a small balcony bar overlooking the town and car rental facilities. Failing that, your only other option is the *Motel Las Pojas* (☎33/6-4129; ●) just off the road from Morón, 10km before Florencia, with sixteen concrete cabins scattered around a garden, the glorious scenery almost compensating for the basic, rather institutional accommodation.

Trips to the area can be arranged through Havanaturs in Ciego de Ávila (℡/₣ 33/26-6339), while Chambas and Florencia are served by a **train** from Morón three times a week.

The northern cays

Christened "The King's Garden" by Diego Velázquez in 1514 in honour of King Ferdinand of Spain, the **northern cays**, lying 30km off Ciego de Ávila's coast and hemmed in by 400km of coral reef, are indisputably the dazzling jewels in the province's crown – a rich tangle of mangroves, mahogany trees and lagoons iced by sugar sands and thick with pink flamingos, and a top **diving** location with an infrastructure to match.

Despite their auspicious naming in the sixteenth century, the numerous islets spanning the coastline from Ciego de Ávila to Camagüey remained uninhabited and relatively unexplored until as recently as the late 1980s. Until then, the cays had only been visited by colonial-era pirates and corsairs seeking a bolthole to stash their spoils; Ernest Hemingway, who sailed around them in the 1930s and 40s; and former dictator Fulgencio Batista, who had a secret hideaway on tiny Cayo Media Luna, a mere pinprick on the map and now a favourite haunt for sunbathers and snorkellers.

The exclusivity of the northern cays was breached in 1988 by the construction of a 29-kilometre stone **causeway** or *pedraplén* across the Bahía de los Perros, connecting the Isla de Turiguanó peninsula to Cayo Coco. The narrow road, barely raised above water level and offering untrammelled views over the tranquil Caribbean Sea, was lauded in several state publications as a revolutionary triumph over the hardships of the Special Period, exemplary of the Cuban people's selfless devotion to the common good. The delighted state began to create a tourist haven destined to be as sumptuous as Varadero, and so far two of the islands – **Cayo Coco**, very popular with European and Canadian holidaymakers, and smaller **Cayo Guillermo** – have been primed for luxury tourism, with all-inclusive hotels planted along their northern shores. Ironically, Cubans are currently banned from visiting the cays, except on allocated holidays and honeymoons, casual access being prohibited by the state in a bid to prevent an influx of *jineteros*. The building of the causeway has also had a negative environmental impact on the cays themselves, disrupting the natural flow of water and impoverishing conditions for local wildlife.

The two cays are connected by a causeway, with an offshoot running east to the breakaway **Cayo Paredón Grande**, uninhabited but providing another option for beaches should you exhaust those on the main cays.

Arrival, information and getting around

What with Cubans being banned from the cays, **getting there** independently without the umbrella of a tour guide, state taxi or rental car can be a bit of a mission. Your best bet, ultimately, is to use a rental car. Don't try to go in a private taxi, as your driver will just be hassled by the authorities before being routed back home, leaving you dumped at the barrier. One or two travellers are generally able to sneak onto one of the worker buses that leave for the cays from the bronze cockerel in Morón between 5 and 8am – it may help to offer to contribute a convertible peso or two – but many more are turned away. Alternatively, you can hitch a lift with the **tour bus** that departs from the *Hotel Morón* (see p.412) if there's space. If you go for the state taxi option, the

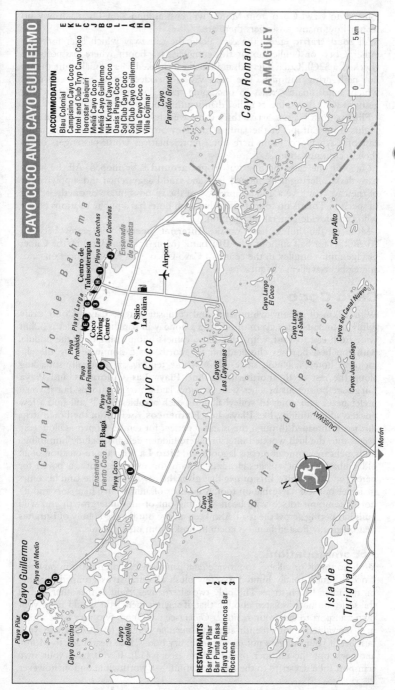

journey to Cayo Coco from Morón will cost around $25CUC each way, no matter how many passengers there are.

All **road traffic** enters the cays along the causeway which later forks for either Coco or Guillermo; at the entrance is a booth where passports are checked, a $2CUC fee is levied, and rental cars looked over to make sure they're not harbouring nationals. The causeway is speckled with large green crabs which, unfortunately, react to oncoming traffic by making bold threatening gestures with their pincers rather than scuttling out of harm's way.

Flights from Havana arrive three times weekly, as well as some international flights from Europe, at the Jardines del Rey airport (☎33/30-8228) on the east of Cayo Coco. From here hotel representatives whisk passengers off to their accommodation.

Once on the cays, the best way to **get around** is by moped. All the hotels have desks offering taxis, moped, jeep and sand buggy rental and supply **maps** of the cays that give a good impression of the islands but are distinctly lacking in specifics. There's no tourist office, but each hotel has a public relations officer who can provide general information.

Most of the hotels have on-site **Internet access** with rates between $3–5CUC for half an hour. The **BFI bank** (Mon–Fri 9am–3pm) by the Cupet Garage mini-complex in the centre of Cayo Coco gives cash advances on cards and cashes traveller's cheques.

Cayo Coco

With 22km of creamy-white sands and cerulean waters, **Cayo Coco** easily fulfils its tourist-blurb claim of offering a holiday in paradise. The islet is 32km wide from east to west, with a hill like a camel's hump rising from the middle, with the best beaches clustered on the north coast, dominated by the all-inclusive hotels (all built since 1992) whose tendrils are gradually spreading along the rest of the northern coastline. **Playa Las Coloradas** and **Playa Larga** are boisterous beaches with activities laid on by the hotels, but if you'd prefer peace and quiet to volleyball and beach aerobics, you'll still find a few pockets of tranquillity, like **Playa Los Flamencos**. Away from the beach strip, dirt roads threaded through the island – perfect for rented moped – allow easy access into the lush wooded interior where hidden delights include humming-birds, pelicans, some gorgeous lagoons and **Sitio La Güira**, a re-creation of an old Cuban peasant village. Heading toward the extreme south, a haven for herons and the **white ibis** or *coco* that gives the cay its name, the land becomes marshier but still navigable on foot. A number of animals live here, too, and it's not uncommon to see wild boars scooting out of the undergrowth and wild bulls lumbering across the road. Also keep an eye out for the colony of **iguanas** that originally floated here on coconut husks from other islands.

Accommodation

With no towns or villages to provide *casas particulares*, accommodation on Cayo Coco is almost totally limited to a few plush **all-inclusives** grouped together on the main beach strips. The only two alternatives, right at the other end of the scale, are both isolated enough that, if staying there, you would need your own transport to get around. *Sitio la Güira* (see p.423) has two very basic rooms in a reproduction nineteenth-century *campisino* cottage (❷). Otherwise, your best bet, if your budget's not up to the luxury hotels, is to head back to Morón and seek out the cheaper options there (see p.412). If you have your own transport then day-trips to the cays are definitely a worthwhile option; however,

Boat trips, diving and excursions

While many head to the cays to bask in the Caribbean sun, there are many opportunities for those up for more energetic pastimes. **Diving** is a prime activity here, as is exploring on foot or horseback through the lush interior that spreads south of the hotel strip through Cayo Coco. Further pursuits include fishing expeditions and organized boat trips.

Diving

Encrusted in the waters of the Atlantic Ocean on the northeast coast of the Cayo Coco is one of the world's longest coral reefs, with shoals of angel fish, butterfly fish, nurse sharks and surgeon fish weaving through forests of colourful sponges and alarmingly large barracudas bucking below the water line. There are at least five excellent **dive sites** spread between Cayo Paredón and Cayo La Jaula (east of Cayo Coco), where you can reach depths of 35m, and all the hotels organize dive trips and give free induction classes to guests. The Coco Diving Centre (☏33/30-1323), just west of the *Hotel and Club Tryp Cayo Coco* on Playa Larga, offers dives for $40CUC, including all equipment and transport to the dive site, as well as PADI open-water courses that take four days and cost $300CUC. It also provides **"seafari" trips** in a pleasure yacht that cruises around the coast and to the cay's celebrated flamingo community, and catamaran excursions for offshore swimming and snorkelling ($35 per person for half a day, including lunch and an open bar). A more professional, better-equipped dive school is the Cuban-Italian-owned Blue Diving (☏33/30-8180, ⓦwww.bluediving.com), on Playa Las Coloradas in front of the *Meliá Cayo Coco*, which has single dives for $40CUC, including equipment, and charges $365 CUC for the PADI open-water course.

Fishing and boat trips

Coco Diving Centre also runs **fishing expeditions** around Cayo Media Luna, where the plentiful billfish, snapper and bass make rich pickings; four hours at sea costs $290CUC for up to six people including all the tackle and an open bar. Jungle Tours (☏33/30-1515), based on Cayo Guillermo but with representatives in all the hotels, offer the chance to captain your own two-person **motorboat** on tours into the narrow canals between the dense mangrove thickets that fringe the cays, while Cubatur (desks are in all the hotels) organize glass-bottomed boat trips and a range of snorkelling excursions.

Excursions

Though you can strike off on your own – ask at the hotels' public relations desks about hiring horses or arranging horse-drawn carriage tours – **Cubatur** (see p.38) organizes land-based day-trips to various locations throughout the cays and day-trips to Morón. If you've always wanted to gallop through the shallows on a tropical beach, Catec (☏33/30-1404 or ask at the hotels) offer **horse-trekking** on Playa Piedra, during the day and at sunset.

those relying on public transport will find getting there fairly troublesome. It's a good idea to phone the hotels directly to enquire about cheaper rates, as some of the all-inclusives will offer rooms at a reduced cost when they are not full.

All-inclusive hotels

Blau Colonial Playa Larga ☏33/30-1311. This luxury hotel is built in the style of a colonial village, and though somewhat twee, its red-tiled roofs, wooden balconies and cobbled pathways are quite attractive and help create a friendly and warm atmosphere. The pool is expansive, while the six restaurants on site provide endless choice. ❾

Hotel and Club Tryp Cayo Coco Playa Larga ☏33/30-1300 and 30-1311,

@ventas2.tcc@solmeliacuba.com. The strip's oldest hotel is actually two hotels combined; the *El Club* part has modern, ochre-coloured buildings shaded by healthy palms, while the more convivial colonial village-style *El Colonial* is painted in muted blues, greens and pinks. Guests can eat at the range of restaurants in either section and are ferried between the two by a toy-train bus. Although reminiscent of a theme park, and equipped with all the usual mod cons including nursery, fitness centre and beach activities, it actually feels more Cuban than the other all-inclusives on the strip because the buildings bear a passing resemblance to authentic Cuban architecture. ⑧

Meliá Cayo Coco Playa Las Coloradas ☏ 33/30-1180, @ jefe.reservas.mcc@solmeliacuba.com. This opulent hotel is aimed squarely at the romance market, with deluxe chalet-style accommodation set around a lagoon, a large pool and a full range of amenities, including sauna, gym and watersports. The lack of a disco makes it peaceful and quiet, there are special deals for honeymooners and you can even get married here. ⑨

Oasis Playa Coco Carretera a Cayo Guillermo ☏ 33/30-2550, ⓦ www.globalia-hotels.com. This good-looking hotel has a couple of features to set it apart from the herd. Pluses include pastel-coloured blocks in tangerine, lemon and cobalt blue, evenly spaced over a well-tended lawn; a long adults' pool; a separate kids' pool; a shallow stretch of

sea; and a soft-sand beach well peppered with parasols. A Japanese restaurant adds an unusually cosmopolitan touch. ⑧

NH Krystal Cayo Coco Playa Las Coloradas ☏ 33/30-1470, ⓦ www.nh-hotels.com. A fairly anonymous, modern hotel with accommodation in rather featureless mustard-yellow blocks that benefit from big windows but lack balconies; there are also some pricier, but far more attractive, rustically luxurious villas spread around a lagoon and connected by a boardwalk. The facilities are excellent, with international and Chinese buffets, a variety of à la carte restaurants, four swimming pools and a state-of-the-art gym. ⑧

Sol Club Cayo Coco Playa Las Coloradas ☏ 33/30-1280, @ jefe.reservas.scc@solmeliacuba.com. This popular family-oriented hotel painted in bright tropical colours has a mini-club for kids, free non-motorized watersports, a buffet, snack bar and beach grill and a lively atmosphere with excited children running around causing mayhem. ⑧

Villa Cayo Coco Cayo Coco Playa Las Conchas ☏ 33/30-2180, @ carpeta@villagaviota.co.cu. While this is not the splashiest all-inclusive on the cay, it still has its good points, like two-storey blocks laid out in spacious surroundings with sea views. A jetty leads down to a small private beach with golden sand. An on-site fitness centre provides a sauna and massage centre, though this is not all-inclusive. ⑦

The beaches

Cayo Coco's big three beaches, home to the all-inclusives, hog the narrow easternmost peninsula jutting out of the cay's north coast. Spanning the tip and home to the *Sol Club Cayo Coco*, *Meliá Cayo Coco* and *NH Krystal Cayo Coco*, **Playa Las Coloradas**, though filled with crowds of beach chairs, is exceptionally picturesque, with fine sand and calm waters. It's a good place for watersports, busy with cruising **catamarans and pedalos** – all-inclusive **day-passes**, sold by all the hotels for $40–50CUC, which include all meals and drinks, will let you join in. Three kilometres west, **Playa Larga** and **Playa Las Conchas**, divided by name only, form a continuous strip of pure sand beach. With shallow crystal waters lapping silvery beaches, they are arguably the best beaches on the island, although very crowded during the organized activities laid on by the *Hotel and Club Tryp Cayo Coco*. Non-guests are welcome to use the beaches during the day – access is through the hotel – though to use any facilities you must pay $40CUC for an all-inclusive day-pass; access is restricted at night.

For solitude, head west along the main dirt road to **Playa Los Flamencos**, demarcated by a stout stucco flamingo, which has 3km of clean golden sands and clear waters where tangerine-coloured starfish float through the shallows and there is good **snorkelling** out to sea. It gets busy in the daytime, but wandering down the beach away from the lively, expensive **bar** should guarantee some privacy. Finally, hidden behind a sand dune 1km east off the same road is **Playa Prohibida**. Although parts of this beach are narrower than Los Flamencos and strewn with seaweed, it's usually deserted and a high dune seeded with wild grasses makes for a pleasing backdrop. There's a tiny **beach bar** serving tasty barbecue chicken, fish, lobster and soft drinks.

Centro de Talasoterapia

Perched on a rocky outcrop near Playa Larga, **Centro de Talasoterapia** (daily 9am–7pm; ☎33/3205) is the cays' first and only health and beauty centre. A perfect location and excellent facilities bode well for this ambitious attempt to tap into the lucrative international market for wellbeing and pampering. The spa has been designed with style and taste: treatment rooms lead off a central atrium set around a fountain and planted with trees alive with hummingbirds. The centre also has a "fit farm" and offers anti-cellulite and anti-ageing treatments as well as programmes for those suffering from respiratory and skin conditions. Facilities are very expansive with four hot pools, a swimming pool, gym and various water massage chambers. The tranquil outdoor seawater pool has an unmarred view over cobalt waters, while there is a smaller indoor pool for swimming lengths. Other treatments include algae and mud treatments, aromatherapy, water therapy, massages, manicures and hair styling. Five-day treatment programmes start from $260CUC, but individual treatments are also available.

Sitio La Güira

In the centre of the cay, 6km from the north coast, is **Sitio La Güira** (☎33/30-1208), a mocked-up early twentieth-century peasant community built in 1994 to impart some idea of traditional Cuban farming culture to visitors who might never venture further than the beach. Though it's something of a novelty theme park, a number of interesting exhibits rescues it from complete tackiness, and if you don't feel like going to Morón and beyond for some more authentic sights, this is a reasonable substitute. The main features are a typical country cottage made entirely from palms with a thatched roof, a ranch where charcoal is made, and a *bohío*, a triangular palm hut in which tobacco leaves are dried. Less appealing are the animal shows, put on several times a day, featuring buffalo, dogs and bulls performing tricks, as well as cockfights (see box, p.424).

Surrounded by lush greenery, Sitio La Güira also offers **walking and riding tours** ($5CUC an hour for the horse; guide rates negotiable) through the mangrove outback filled with woodpeckers and nightingales and on to the lakes in the interior where waterfowl and wild ducks nest. The ranch also has a couple of rooms for rent (❷) and a **restaurant** (see p.424).

El Bagá Nature Reserve

Given their exceptional natural beauty, the cays are the ideal site for the **El Bagá Nature Reserve** (Mon–Sat 8.30am–5pm). While the reserve tries to be all things to all visitors, with Indo-Cuban cultural shows, a children's fairground and a re-created Taíno village all within the grounds, its real strength lies in the radiant countryside where it's situated. The park is speckled with lakes and crisscrossed by several trails, enlivened by various well-tended animal enclosures where iguanas, crocodiles and *jutías* are all on display. The easiest – albeit most pedestrian – way to see the park is on one of the **guided walks** leaving from the Visitors' Centre at the reserve's entrance (on the hour from 9am–noon and then at half past from 1.30–3.30pm). More adventurous types may prefer to explore on horseback, by bike or on a boat trip, all of which can be arranged through the Visitors' Centre.

Eating, drinking and entertainment

With **all food and drinks included** in your hotel bill, you probably won't need to look elsewhere for meals while staying on the cays, although there are

Cock fighting

Cock fighting has been the sport of Cuban farmers since the eighteenth century, with sizeable sums of money changing hands on bets, and thefts of prized specimens and allegations of rooster nobbling common. There is a particular breed of rooster indigenous to Cuba that exercises considerable cunning in defeating its opponent, parrying attacks and throwing false moves, and the bloodlines of these birds are protected and nurtured as carefully as those of any racehorse.

Since the **ban on gambling** introduced by the Revolution, the practice has been pushed underground – although the sport itself is still legal. Nowadays cock fighting is a clandestine affair, taking place on smallholdings deep in the country at the break of dawn when the fowl are in vicious ill-humour and at their fighting best. Unlike the shows laid on for tourists, where the cocks are eventually separated, the spurred cocks here will slug it out to the death.

a few places that cater for day-trippers. If you've paid for a **day-pass** at one of the hotels, you can dine there and go on to the hotel disco afterwards.

The best **night out** on the cays is to be found at the *Sol Club Cayo Coco* on Tuesdays and Thursdays at midnight. With live *salsa* bands playing at top volume, glitter balls and a dance floor of illuminated tiles, it's raucous, glitzy and lots of fun without being too tacky. Guests from all Solmeliá-owned hotels are invited for free, while those from other chains pay $5CUC, which includes an open bar. *Hotel and Club Tryp Cayo Coco* has a central disco with live *salsa* and tacky floorshows. For a different kind of nightlife, there's a glittery, loud cabaret followed by a disco (Tues–Sat 9pm; $5CUC) at the **Cueva del Jabalí**, a natural cave 5km inland from the hotel strip which takes its name from the wild boar evicted to make way for the venue, now housing a community of bats as well as disco dancers.

Playa Los Flamencos Bar A friendly, though pricey, beach-bar with ample trestle tables under a palm wattle roof, serving Cuban cuisine and occasionally lobster to the strains of a *mariachi* band.

Playa Prohibida Bar A tiny beach-bar serving tasty barbecued chicken and fish.

Rocarena Playa Las Coloradas (☎33/30-1431). *Comida criolla* is served in a charmless concrete construction which has a great location on a headland with views over Playa Larga. There's a well-stocked bar, a pool table and live *salsa* and *son* on Mon, Wed and Fri nights.

Sitio la Güira A ranch restaurant in the midst of the theme park, serving moderately priced spaghetti and steaks and expensive seafood, and holding a *Guateque*, "a farm party with animation activities and lessons on typical dances". Daily 9am–10pm.

Cayo Guillermo

Bordered by pearl-white sand melting into opal waters, **Cayo Guillermo**, the sleepy cay west of Cayo Coco, to which it's joined by a fifteen-kilometre causeway, is a quieter, more serene retreat than its neighbour, a place to fish, dive and simply relax. It is here that the cays' colony of twelve thousand **flamingos** (celebrated in all Cuban tourist literature) gathers, and although they are wary of the noise of passing traffic, as you cross the causeway you can glimpse them swaying in the shallows and feeding on the sandbanks. As the presence of the birds testifies, there is a wealth of fish, notably marlin, in the waters, and the cay's marina offers a range of deep-sea fishing expeditions.

At only thirteen square kilometres the cay is tiny, but its 4km of deserted beaches seem infinite nonetheless. It's quite a trek from the mainland if you are not staying overnight, but arriving early and spending a day lounging on the

Ernest Hemingway's hunt for submarines

The affection that **Ernest Hemingway** had for Cuba sprang from his love of fishing, and numerous photographs of him brandishing dripping marlin and swordfish testify to his success around the clear waters of the northern cays. He came to know the waters well and, when the United States entered World War II, Hemingway, already having seen action in World War I and the Spanish Civil War, was more than ready to do his bit.

With the full support of the US ambassador to Cuba, Spruille Braden, he began to spy on Nazi sympathizers living in Cuba, calling his organization – colleagues from the Spanish Civil War and staff from the US Embassy – the "Crook Factory". He gathered enough information to have his twelve-metre fishing boat **The Pilar** commissioned and equipped by the Chief of Naval Intelligence for Central America as a kind of Q-ship (an armed and disguised merchant ship used as a decoy or to destroy submarines); the crew, all men devoted to Hemingway, were even armed with grenades for lobbing down the periscope towers. His search-and-destroy missions for Nazi submarines off the cays continued until 1944 and he was commended by the ambassador, although according to some critics – notably his wife Martha Gellhorn – the whole thing was mainly a ruse for Hemingway to obtain rationed petrol for his fishing trips. Although he never engaged in combat with submarines, Hemingway's boys' own fantasies found their way into print in the novel *Islands in the Stream*.

heavenly beaches and exploring the beautiful offshore coral reef definitely merits the effort.

Accommodation

Development on Cayo Guillermo has been steadily growing, and although still considerably quieter than its rowdier neighbour, it's no longer the peaceful haven it once was. However, all the **hotels** are fairly close together on Playa El Medio and Playa El Paso while the rest of the cay's stunning beaches remain largely untouched – with so much space, you'll never have a problem finding solitude. **Day-passes** to enter any of the hotels (inclusive of meals and drinks) will set you back $40–50CUC, but there are plenty of other places to access the beach if that's all you want. All the hotels have car and moped rental facilities and agency desks, whose staff provide local information and organize tours.

Iberostar Daiquiri Playa El Paso ☎ 33/30-1650, Ⓔ comercia@ibsdaiq.gca.tur.cu. Despite the palatial reception area, this hotel lacks the charm of its neighbours. Rooms are pleasant enough, strung along corridors in rather austere accommodation blocks done out in earthy tones and topped with princely crenellations. There are four restaurants to choose from, and there's a nightly show and disco. ❽

Meliá Cayo Guillermo Playa El Paso ☎ 33/30-1680, Ⓔ jefe.rrpp.mcg @solmeliacuba.com. Popular with divers on account of its in-house diving centre, this swish luxury hotel is stylishly and imaginatively decorated in cool aquamarines. Entering the rooms, with stencils of fishes and shells around the walls, feels a bit like plunging into an aquarium, albeit a luxury one. There's a high-tech gym and the long rickety wooden pier on the beach in front is perfect for sunset strolls. ❾

Sol Club Cayo Guillermo Playa El Medio ☎ 33/30-1760, Ⓔ ventas1.scg@solmeliacuba.com. Small, friendly, painted in pretty pastels and patronized largely by couples and honeymooners, this hotel has a very Spanish feel with its immaculately tiled reception area full of tinkling fountains; attractive, sunny rooms with pleasing wooden furniture and balconies; and all the standard facilities. ❻

Villa Cojímar Playa El Paso ☎ 33/30-1712, Ⓔ alojamiento@cojimar.gca.tur.cu. Set apart from the others, this calm and quiet hotel offers all mod cons with its snazzy blue-and-yellow bungalows spread around spacious, manicured gardens, a large free-form pool, four restaurants and ample sports facilities. ❼

The beaches

The two main beaches on Guillermo are **Playa El Medio** and **Playa El Paso** on the north coast, where all the hotels are located. Popular with package-tour holidaymakers, both are suitably idyllic with shallow swimming areas and lengthy beaches, though El Medio also has towering sand dunes celebrated as the highest in the Caribbean, and in low tides sand bars allow you to wade out to sea.

Gorgeous **Playa Pilar** on the western tip of the cay is named after Ernest Hemingway's yacht, *The Pilar*, and was the author's favourite hideaway in Cuba. Every year as the swordfish swarmed to cross the coral reef in the Gulf Stream, Hemingway would sail from Cojímar to pursue them off the coasts of Cayo Guillermo. So enchanted was he by the cay that he immortalized it in his novel *Islands in the Stream*, in which his protagonist Thomas Hudson eulogizes, "See how green she is and full of promise?" (see box, p.425). With limpid clear shallows and squeaky-clean beaches, Playa Pilar is without doubt the top beach choice on Guillermo, if not in the entire cays; however, there are no facilities here other than a small beach-bar.

From Playa Pilar, speedboats ferry sunbathers and snorkellers the short distance to **Cayo Media Luna**, a tiny crescent cay just across the water, with nothing other than a small, simple café. The return journey costs $25CUC, and for a few more convertible pesos you can stop off to go snorkelling at a nearby reef.

Dive trips to the best sites around Cayo Media Luna are organized by the German-owned Cuba Divers, at the entrance to the cay near the *Villa Cojímar* (℡33/30-1704, ⊛www.cuba-divers.com). Each dive costs $49CUC including equipment, while PADI open-water courses take five days and cost $350CUC. For deep-sea **fishing** excursions and yacht "seafaris", with time set aside for offshore swimming and snorkelling, head to the Marina Puerto Sol (℡33/30-1637, ⊛www.cayoguillermofishingclub.com) on Playa El Paso, home to the Cayo Guillermo Fishing Club.

Eating, drinking and entertainment

Options for eating, drinking and entertainment outside the hotels are severely limited. **Cuba Libre**, a tiny beach-bar between the *Iberostar Daiquiri* and *Meliá Cayo Guillermo* on Playa El Paso, serves seafood and drinks during the daytime. Halfway along the unpaved road to Playa Pilar, a turning to the right leads to the 24-hour **Punta Rasa** bar, a small wooden pavilion on the beach of the same name, which offers cheap chicken, costly seafood, beer, cocktails and soft drinks. Every night the tables are pushed back to make space for post-dinner dancing. On Playa Pilar there's a simple wooden lean-to where you can eat excellent but pricey barbecued fish and lobster as skinny cats twirl around your ankles; opening times fluctuate depending on the whims of the chef, but you are usually guaranteed service around lunchtime. A few hundred metres out to sea, the wooden bar on Cayo Media Luna mirrors the one on Playa Pilar with the same menu and prices.

Cayo Paredón Grande

Connected to Cayo Coco by a small causeway starting around 6km east of Playa Las Coloradas, **Cayo Paredón Grande** is a thumbnail of a cay 12km to the northeast. With a couple of clean, pleasant beaches, it makes an ideal retreat if you can get there, particularly as the view over the sea as you cross the causeway is glorious. The islet's focal point is the elegant nineteenth-century **lighthouse** (no entry) on the rocky headland of the northern tip, built by Chinese immigrant workers to guide ships through the coral-filled waters. If you are taking a day-trip to the island, take provisions as there are no facilities. The causeway leads through the uninhabited **Cayo Romano**, which is technically in Camagüey province though usually treated as an extension of the major cays.

Southern Ciego de Ávila

Back on the mainland, the area below Ciego de Ávila is made up of agricultural farming areas and small one-street towns like **Venezuela** and **Silveira**, each a clutch of humble concrete houses (built since the Revolution to house workers who previously lived in shacks), a central *bodega* and a doctor. Even in the smallest community, however, you can see electricity lines, another of the Revolution's achievements, and despite severe shortages rural households have electricity for at least part of the day.

As you journey south on the road to the coast you will pass the remnants of an old Spanish garrison which at one time divided the province from north to south (see box, below). The countryside is snaked with narrow rail tracks that indicate the extensive infrastructure that serves the sugar industry, conveying the crop from the fields to the towns and ports; parts of the railways are still in use, with working stations at Morón and Ciego de Ávila.

Júcaro and the Archipiélago de los Jardines de la Reina

Thirty-two kilometres south of Ciego de Ávila is the barren fishing village of **Júcaro**, a miserable collection of wooden shacks and half-finished cement constructions set around a derelict-looking Parque Martí, a malodorous fishing port and a fly-blown soft-drinks stand. There's absolutely no reason to venture down here, unless you plan to visit the **Archipiélago de los Jardines de la Reina**, a cluster of over 600 tiny virgin cays, most of which are scrubby and piled with driftwood and all of which are completely deserted except for **Cayo Caguamas**, 120km offshore from Júcaro, home to a restaurant as well as a decent beach where members of the fearless iguana community will eat from your hand. Staying until nightfall will reward you with the sight of **turtles** venturing out onto the sand in the moonlight. More than fifty **dive sites** around the archipelago boast caves, canyons, and wall, spur and groove coral

---

Fortifications between La Trocha Júcaro and Morón

Driving through the province on the road running from Júcaro to Morón via Ciego de Ávila, the tumbledown stubby structures you'll see are the remains of a **fortification line** built by the Spanish between April 1871 and 1873. Increasingly worried by the Mambises (the rebel army fighting for independence) and their plans to move west through the island, the Spanish General Blas Villate de la Hera planned a 67km-long row of fortifications to block the advance. The forts were made of concrete with solid walls of stone, brick and wood and built at intervals of 3–4km. Each was manned by a single sentry, who had to enter by a removable wooden staircase, and each had two cannon. It was supposedly an impassable chain of defence, but the ineffectiveness of the whole idea was immediately apparent in 1874 when the Cuban General Manuel Suárez triumphantly breezed through with his cavalry. Most of the forts today are in a poor state of repair, though the odd one still gives an impression of their original appearance. Plans to restore them have been under way for some time.

formations, while divers have a high chance of encountering silky and Caribbean reef sharks and the aptly named, enormous, Goliath groupers. This is also one of the country's richest **fishing** regions, with shoals of bonefish, tarpon and relatively rare mutton snappers beckoning keen anglers. Mercifully, if you want to sleep over, you don't have to bed down in town; instead you can be ferried from Júcaro port to the Italian-run *La Tortuga* (⑤), an air-conditioned, double-decker, fourteen-berth floating **hotel** moored offshore in a protected canal. Information on the hotel and diving opportunities is available directly from the owners, Press Tours in the *Habana Libre* hotel in Havana (☎7/033-3222, ⓦwww.avalons.net), or you can also book through the **Júcaro Marina**, whose office is on the seafront opposite the square (☎33/9819), or via Sergio Alonso at the *Hotel Morón* in Morón (☎335/2230).

Camagüey province

Sandwiched between Ciego de Ávila to the west and Las Tunas to the east, **Camagüey** is Cuba's largest province, a half-moon of sweeping savanna, with a central ripple of high land, curving into the Caribbean Sea. Most of the province is given over to cattle farming and what little tourism there is tends to be low-key: perfect if you fancy exploring a pocket of Cuba largely unswamped by crowds. Most visitors head straight for the **beaches** rimming the northern cays, bypassing completely the centre of the province and the colonial charms of **Camagüey city**. One of the seven original settlements founded by Diego Velázquez in 1514–15, birthplace of one of the country's most renowned poets, Nicolas Guillén, and former home of the celebrated revolutionary Ignacio Agramonte, this one-time pirate haunt is brimming with history, its handful of sights, museums and buildings – particularly its enigmatically decaying **churches** – infused with legend.

North of the city, tourism has blossomed along the cay-fringed coast, with lively **Santa Lucía**, famous for its well-kept golden beaches, the region's main resort. For real desert-island appeal, head for the sands of **Cayo Sabinal**, at the northernmost point of the province, where empty beaches and rustic accommodation make the perfect retreat for solitude-seekers. South of the provincial capital, much of the land is dominated by tracts of panoramic pasture, and there is little to tempt you out this far.

Camagüey city

Nestled in the heart of the province 30km from the north coast, **Camagüey** is aptly called the city of legends, its winding streets and wizened buildings weaving an atmosphere of intrigue. On first view it is a bewildering city to negotiate, with a seemingly incomprehensible labyrinth of roads that were deliberately laid out thus in a futile attempt to confuse marauding pirates (see box, p.430). So long as you're not in a hurry to get anywhere this needn't matter too much, and an aimless wander along the narrow cobbled streets overhung by delicate balustrades and Rococo balconies is the best way to explore, as you round corners onto handsome parks and happen upon crumbling churches. Several museums and fine buildings offer further sightseeing.

Despite its quaint appearance, Camagüey is by no means a sleepy colonial town. Every Saturday, people cram onto Independencia for the weekly "Camagüeyan night" shindig (see p.440), and pull out all the stops for the annual June **carnival**, the highlight of the Camagüeyan calendar.

Some history

One of the seven original settlements in Cuba, Camagüey was established between 1514 and 1515 on the site of a sizeable Amerindian village, and although the original inhabitants were swiftly eradicated, traces of burial sites and ceramics have been found in the area. Now the only legacy of the indigenous people remains in the city's name, thought to originate from the word *Camagua*, a wild shrub common to the lowlands and believed to have magical properties.

Initially known as **Santa María del Puerto del Príncipe**, the fledgling city started life as a port town on the north coast, where modern-day Nuevitas lies. Just a year later, when farmers from Seville arrived in 1516, it was moved to the fertile lands of modern-day Caonao on the northwestern edge of the province, until, according to some sources, a rebel band of Amerindians forced the settlers out, and the town moved once more, to its present site, in 1528. Straddling the Tínima and Hatibonico rivers, so as to be in the middle of the trade route between Sancti Spíritus and Bayamo, the newly settled town began to consolidate itself. During the 1600s its economy developed around sugar plantations and cattle farms, generating enough income to build the distinguished churches and civil buildings in the following century. Despite intermittent ransacking by pirates, Puerto Príncipe grew into a sophisticated and elegant city, one its townsfolk fought hard to win from the Spanish during the Wars of Independence. Eventually, in 1903, following the end of Spanish rule, the city dropped its lengthy moniker and adopted the name by which it is now known.

Arrival and information

Daily flights from Havana arrive at the Ignacio Agramonte **airport** (℡32/26-1010), 7km north of the city, from where you can catch a bus or unmetered taxi ($4CUC) into town. Two daily **buses** from Havana pull in at the Astro bus station (℡32/27-1668) on the Carretera Central, 3km south of the town centre; an unmetered taxi or horse-drawn carriage into town should cost around $6CUC. **Trains** from Havana and the neighbouring provinces arrive at the frenetic train station (℡32/29-2633) on the northern edge of town, next door to the local bus station. A ride to the centre in a *bicitaxi* should cost no more than fifteen pesos, an unmetered taxi $1CUC. If you feel up to negotiating the imbroglio of town planning, it's a fifteen-minute walk along Van Horne to República, the straight road leading directly into the centre.

There are a number of sources of **information** in the city. One of the best is Cubanacán, in either the *Gran Hotel* (daily 8.30–11am, 2–5pm; ℡32/29-2093) or the *Hotel Plaza* (daily 11am–1pm; ℡32/29-7374), which sells **maps**, phone cards and flight, bus and train tickets; it also organizes day-trips to Playa Santa Lucía, the Sierra de Cubitas – nearby hills whose steep, forested slopes are studded with limestone caves – and the Jardines de la Reina. The Islazul **tourism bureau**, no.448 Ignacio Agramonte e/ López Recio y Independencia (Mon–Fri 1–5pm, Sat 8am–noon; ℡32/29-8947), also sells maps and has a car rental and taxi desk, but it's far surpassed for helpfulness by Cubatur, at Ignacio

Pirates in Camagüey

Although not the only city to suffer constant attack from **pirates**, irresistibly wealthy Camagüey was one of those consistently plagued, and buccaneers regularly rampaged through the city before retiring to the northern cays or the Isla de la Juventud to hide their spoils. To confound pirates, the heart of the city was built as a web of narrow and twisted streets rather than following the usual colonial city plan with roads laid out in a regular grid pattern; however, the design did not deter the invaders, who left many legends in their wake. The first pirate to arrive was the singularly unpleasant Frenchman **Jacques de Sores** in 1555, who roamed the farms on the north coast stealing cows, cheeses and women. (These last he would abandon violated in Cayo Coco to the mercy of the elements.) In 1668, English buccaneer **Henry Morgan** – the terror of the Caribbean seas – and his men managed to occupy the city for several days before making off with a hefty booty of gold and jewels belonging to the Spanish bourgeoisie. With a dashing show of irreverence, he is also reputed to have locked the town elders into the Catedral de Santa Iglesia to starve them into revealing the whereabouts of their riches. Struggling to reassert itself eleven years later, in 1679 the city fell prey to the wiles of another Frenchman, **François de Granmont**. Nicknamed *El Caballero* (the gentleman), he sacked the city and captured fourteen women. After nearly a month of occupying the town he marched to the coast and released all the women unharmed, thus earning his nickname.

Agramonte no.421 (Mon–Sat 9am–5pm; ☎322/25-4785, ✉cubatur@cmg.colombus.cu). The services offered here include booking Víazul bus tickets, selling accommodation in Santa Lucía, and assisting with visa extensions. A third Cubanacán branch, at no.1 Calle Van Horne e/Avellaneda y República (daily Mon–Fri 9am–noon, 1–5pm, Sat 9am–noon; ☎32/28-3551), can book hotels and air tickets. When dialling Camagüey from another province you will need to prefix the number with either 032 or 32. The only way to distinguish which is by trial and error.

Accommodation

In comparison to the towns in Ciego de Ávila, Camagüey has a decent variety of reasonably priced **hotels**, most of them charming hideaways rather than fancy tourist palaces. There are also a number of excellent, centrally located **casas particulares** to choose from. Be aware that some touts in Camagüey are particularly wily and will stoop to various underhand tricks in an attempt to guide you to a house that will pay them commission. (For more information see p.56).

Hotels

Colón República no.472 e/ San José y San Martín ☎32/25-4878, ✉rrppcolonn2001@yahoo.es. This beautiful hotel in the heart of the city is almost a museum piece. Built in 1927, it has been artfully renovated, preserving its eclectic mix of styles with Baroque balconies, exquisite tiling, a cracked marble staircase and corridors bathed in greenish light. The comfortable rooms, furnished with reproduction 1920s furniture, are small and lack natural light, but this is more than compensated for by the building's class and character; the best rooms are arranged around a pretty patio housing a bar and a veranda where breakfast is served. ❹

Gran Hotel Maceo no.67 e/ Ignacio Agramonte y General Gómez ☎32/29-2093 and 94, ℉29-3933. Graciously faded eighteenth-century building that became a hotel in the 1930s, with well-maintained rooms, some with balconies overlooking the busy street below. A small pool, an elegant marble dining room with panoramic views, and a dark and sultry piano bar are pluses. ➍

Plaza Van Horne no.1 e/ República y Avellaneda ☎32/28-2413. Basic accommodation at a reasonable rate, in a friendly hotel opposite the train station. The size of the rooms differs greatly, so check beforehand to ensure you get one of the larger ones with a balcony. ➌

Casas particulares

Alfredo y Milagros Cisneros no.124 esq. Raúl Lamar ☎32/29-7436. Ⓔ allan.carnot@gmail.com. Very professionally run outfit, with both English and French spoken. Both of the rooms are well appointed, with fridges, fans, a/c, private bathrooms and desks. A pretty patio tiled in pink and green marble and a tropical fish tank complete the picture. Garage parking available. ➋

Casa Caridad Oscar Primelles no.310a e/ Bartolomé Masó y Padre Olallo ☎32/29-1554. Two rooms with new mattresses, private bathrooms, a/c and fully stocked minibar-style fridges ($1CUC per item) arranged along a sunny passageway in a spacious house whose best feature is a pretty garden complete with a large *tinajon* (see p.439) and a swinging love seat under a flowery bower. Garage parking available. ➋

Casa de Eliza Baez Astillero no.24 e/ San Ramón y Lugareño ☎32/29-2054. Double rooms and huge, tasty home-cooked meals in this comfortable, clean and very friendly spot close to the centre. Call to make a reservation. ➋

Casa Lucy Alegría no.23 e/ Ignacio Agramonte y Montera ☎32/28-3701. A roomy, spotlessly clean house run by a charming family. The two big bedrooms have private bathrooms and minibars, while the beautiful garden boasts a fountain, a pond filled with carp and terrapins, caged songbirds, rocking chairs and its very own bar. ➋

Manolo Banegas Misa Independencia no.251 (altos) esq. Plaza Maceo ☎32/29-4606. This fabulous apartment overlooking Plaza Maceo is decorated with antique furniture, colourful floor tiles and glittery chandeliers. The four large double rooms on offer have curly wrought-iron and brass bedsteads (though no en-suite bathrooms), and there's a balcony from which you can watch life go by on the square below. ➋

La Terraza República no.358A (altos) e/ Francisquito y Van Horne ☎32/29-4687, Ⓔ laterrazajc@yahoo.es. Well located at the top of an apartment block in the centre of the main drag, the highlight here is the fantastic redbrick patio with views of the city's spires. Both rooms are neat, one has a big bathroom, and the owner is extremely friendly. ➋

Los Vitrales Avalleneda no.3 e/ General Gómez y Martí ☎32/29-5866. This beautiful former convent is chock-full of antiquities and stained-glass panels, from which it takes its name. The three bedrooms are big, the hosts are friendly, and the food is excellent. Parking is available. ➋

The Town

Sprinkled with churches and colonial squares, Camagüey will take a couple of days to explore fully, although those breezing through can do the main sights in a half day or so. Since the pope's visit during his three-day trip to Cuba in January 1998, church attendance in the city has risen, as it has throughout Cuba, and accordingly money has been poured into repairing the romantically crumbling facades and maintaining church interiors.

Although the city's irregular town plan makes it difficult to get your bearings, most of the main sights are clustered together in easy walking distance of the main shopping drag, **Calle Maceo**, including **La Iglesia de la Soledad**, one of the city's oldest churches. Very close to hand is the **Plaza de los Trabajadores**, a prosaic little square much enhanced by the **Iglesia Nuestra Señora de la Merced**, the most impressive of Camagüey's churches, and the **Casa Natal de Ignacio Agramonte**, birthplace of the city's most revered son, a martyr of the struggle for independence. A couple of streets away the **Casa Natal de Nicolás Guillén** honours the life and times of one of Cuba's premier poets.

Heading south of here, past the **Plaza de Antonio Maceo**, a useful landmark at the southern end of Maceo, takes you to the congenial **Parque Agramonte**, the city's main park and a popular gathering spot for locals, home to the important but rather dull **Catedral de Santa Iglesia**, while a few blocks east is the more picturesque **Sagrado Corazón de Jesús**. Further south is the **Plaza**

de San Juan de Dios which, blessed with the **Iglesia San Juan de Dios** and **Museo de San Juan de Dios**, is Camagüey's most attractive colonial square.

Although the northern end of town has fewer sights, it's still worth venturing up for a breeze around the **Museo Ignacio Agramonte**, the provincial museum that has several interesting exhibits and a quietly impressive collection of paintings.

La Iglesia de la Soledad and Centro Provincial de las Artes Plasticas

The hub of town centres on the two streets of **Maceo** and **República**, where the most picturesque hotels are clustered, hard currency shops and peso markets are strung along the roads and the streets are thronged with window-shoppers and gaggles of people queuing to buy the same pair of trainers, CD players, secondhand books and, quaint handmade children's toys, including classic cars fashioned from clay. Presiding over the intersection of the two streets is **La Iglesia de la Soledad** (daily 8am–noon), the church where Ignacio Agramonte (see box, p.436) was baptized and married, tiered like a wedding cake and with a lofty tower that can be seen from all over the city. There has been a church on this site since 1697, the original built from wood and guano, the present structure dating from 1758; although the exterior is in disrepair, the interior, its domed roof painted with Baroque frescoes, merits a look. Like others in the town, the church has its very own creation myth. Apparently one rainy morning an animal carrier became stuck in the mud in the road in front of the site now occupied by the church. Everyone gathered around to push the wagon free and in the process a box bounced off the back and smashed open to reveal a statue of the Virgin. As the cart-driver could lay no claim to it, it was taken as a sign that the Virgin wanted a chapel built on this spot.

Close by, about halfway along República at no.289, you'll find the **Centro Provincial de las Artes Plasticas** (daily 10am–6pm). This art gallery has a mixed bag of temporary exhibitions that is well worth dipping into – if only for the cool, airy space flanked by wrought-iron gates. The work featured is predominantly painting which comes from Camagüey as well as other provinces and is of a generally high standard. A look around here gives an insight into visual arts in Cuba away from the tourist trail.

La Iglesia Nuestra Señora de la Merced

One block west of Maceo is the **Plaza de los Trabajadores**, a disappointingly modern polygon of tarmac beautified by a border of attractive colonial buildings and **La Iglesia Nuestra Señora de la Merced** (Mon 3.30–6pm, Tues–Sat 9.30–11.30am & 3.30–6pm), Camagüey's most impressive building. A recent slick of paint has taken the edge off its whimsical appeal, though the romance of its whispered origins endures undiminished. The story goes that one day in the seventeenth century, when the plaza was still allegedly submerged beneath a lake, the townsfolk heard shouts and screams from the thickets on the banks. Terrified to approach, they kept watch from a distance over several days until, to their amazement, a shimmering white church emerged from the water. Beckoning from the portal was a priest with a cross clasped in his hand: the Merced church had arrived. A more prosaic history tells that the church was built as a convent in 1747, and the rooms to the left of the chapel, set around a central patio, still serve as such today. Inside the grounds, shadows of mango leaves dapple the patio and large, well-kept *tinajones* (see p.439) perch on the cloisters. Art Deco frescoes swirl across the corridor ceiling in muted shades of grey and yellow, while doors open onto classrooms, reading rooms and an ample library where you can browse through weighty religious tomes.

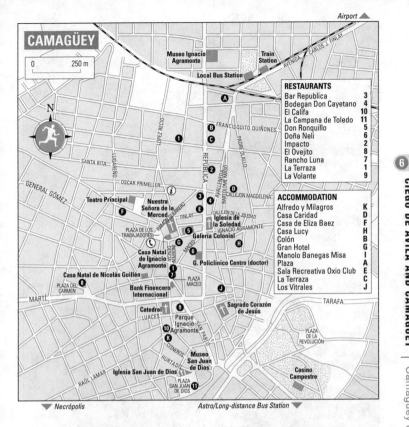

The adjoining church is a confection of styles. Built on the side of the seventeenth-century chapel, the first church was constructed in 1748, rebuilt a hundred years later, and again between 1906 and 1909 following a fire that destroyed the altar. Now it boasts a richly ornate neo-Gothic wood and gilt altar imported from Spain, a contrast to the delicate eighteenth-century Baroque balconies swooping above. The most intriguing item, however, is the **Santo Sepulcro**, an ornate silver coffin, thickly coated with intertwined hand-beaten bells and flowers, made in 1762 from 25,000 molten silver coins by Mexican silversmith Juan de Benítez, and commissioned by an ill-fated merchant (see box, p.435).

Hidden beneath the church, accessible by a tiny flight of stairs behind the main altar, is a fascinatingly macabre little crypt. Formerly an underground cemetery that ran all the way to López Recio 500m away, much of it was bricked up following the fire and only a claustrophobic sliver remains. Among the musty relics, several life-sized statues gleam in the half-light, while embedded in the walls are the skeletal remains of a woman and her child: look carefully and you will see that live cockroaches play across their surfaces. For a guided tour of the church and convent, ask at the convent (daily 8.30am–5pm); there's no charge but contributions towards the upkeep of the church are much appreciated.

Half a block away, the **Galería Colonial** at Ignacio Agramonte no.406 e/ República y López Recio has been designed as a sort of one-stop shop for

△ La Iglesia Nuestra Señora de la Merced

visitors to the city. This carefully restored mansion houses an information desk, a restaurant, bar, shops and nightly entertainment (see p.440).

Casa Natal de Ignacio Agramonte

Facing the church and convent, on the other side of Plaza de los Trabajadores, is the **Casa Natal de Ignacio Agramonte** (Tues–Sat 10am–6pm, Sun 8am–noon; $2CUC), an attractive colonial house with dark wood balustrades

In eighteenth-century Puerto Príncipe (as Camagüey was then known), a wealthy merchant, **Manuel de Agüero**, and his family employed a widowed housekeeper, **Señora Moya**. Master and servant each had a son of the same age, and it seemed natural for the boys to play and grow up together. Agüero paid for both to go to Havana to study at the university, and they seemed assured of bright futures. Tragedy struck when both young men met and fell in love with the same woman, and in a fit of pique Moya challenged Agüero to a duel and killed him.

Distraught, Agüero Senior promptly banished the murderous boy and his mother from his sight, lest his remaining sons avenge their brother's death. However, his woes were not over, as his wife, sick with a broken heart, wasted away and died soon after. Torn apart by grief, Agüero decided to become a friar, and, with his surviving sons' approval, poured their inheritance into jewels and treasures for the church. The most splendid of all his tributes was the **Santo Sepulcro**, the silver coffin that he commissioned in readiness of his own death. Long seen as a hero who rose above personal disaster to overcome bitterness, his is a puzzling tale of uneasy colonial values.

and a fine, heavy wooden door, birthplace of the local hero of the first War of Independence. All Agramonte's possessions were confiscated when he took up arms against the colonial powers and, although never returned to him while he was alive, they now form part of the museum's collection. After his death the Spanish authorities converted his home into a market and then later, adding insult to injury, a bar. It opened as a museum in 1973. The standard of life enjoyed by wealthy sugar plantation owners like the Agramontes is well highlighted in their impressive furniture on display, including a well-crafted piano and oversized *tinajones* out in the central patio. Rather more mundane are the personal papers, pocket watch and other ephemera belonging to Agramonte himself. Free piano recitals are held in the central patio every Saturday night at 8.30pm.

Teatro Principal

Tucked two blocks northeast of Plaza de los Trabajadores along San Ramón is Camagüey's **Teatro Principal**. Its splendour dulled with a thick mat coat of ochre paint, the theatre is not the jewel that many townsfolk enthusiastically claim it to be, but is nevertheless quietly stylish, with yellow and red *vitrales*. Inside, a marble staircase sweeps up to the spacious first floor where a central oval balcony gazes down on a splendid chandelier. The theatre keeps erratic opening hours, but there's usually someone around to let you in; if there's no one in the main hall, take the alleyway on the left-hand side to the back and ask for an impromptu tour.

Casa Natal de Nicolás Guillén

One block south of Plaza de los Trabajadores is the **Casa Natal de Nicolás Guillén** (Mon–Fri 8am–noon & 1–4.30pm, Sat 8am–noon; $1CUC). An Afro-Cuban born in 1902, Guillén was one of Cuba's foremost poets and is renowned throughout Latin America, particularly for his eloquent pieces on the condition of black people in Cuba, whose profile he raised and cause he championed in his writing. A founding member of the National Union of Writers and Artists (UNEAC), an organization responsible for much of the promotion of the arts in Cuba, and recipient of the Lenin Peace Prize, he died in 1989. The small house has relics of his life, but despite a half-hearted attempt at a reconstruction of his kitchen nothing really gives you much of an insight into his days there.

Ignacio Agramonte – Daredevil of the Wars of Independence

The son of wealthy Camagüeyan cattle farmers, **Ignacio Agramonte** (1841–73) studied law in Havana and then in Spain before returning in 1868 to become a revolutionary leader in the first War of Independence against Spain. Back in his homeland, he incited the men of Camagüey to take up arms against the Spanish, taking the town at the end of that year and forming a small unorthodox republic with some of the local farm owners. He was known as the **Daredevil of the Wars of Independence** for his often misguided valour – on one occasion, when one of his fighters was captured by the Spanish, he dashed off to rescue his unfortunate compatriot from the 120-strong enemy column, armed only with a machete and 34 of his most trusted men – and actually lived to tell the tale. Killed aged 32 on the battlefields of Jimaguayú, Agramonte's youth as well as his passion for his province guaranteed him a revered place as one of Camagüey's martyrs who lost their lives in the Wars of Independence.

There are, however, many of his poems in poster form on the walls, and a good selection of photographs to peruse. In an adjoining building is the Centro Nicolás Guillén, a socio-cultural study centre.

Parque Agramonte and the Catedral de Santa Iglesia

A few blocks south of the Casa Natal de Nicolás Guillén is the bijou **Plaza de Antonio Maceo**, from where it's one block south through narrow streets to **Parque Ignacio Agramonte**, the town's social centre. The small square is filled with shady tamarind trees, *tinajones* (see box, p.439) and marble benches, where parents watch their offspring whizz about on makeshift skateboards and clamber all over the central statue of Ignacio Agramonte.

Each corner of the square is pegged by a royal palm to symbolize the deaths of four independence fighters – leader Joaquín Agüero, Tomás Betancourt y Zayas, Fernando de Zayas and Miguel Benavides – shot for treason here by the Spanish in the early struggles for independence. The men were immediately hailed as martyrs and the townsfolk planted the four palms as a secret tribute, the Spanish authorities ignorant of their significance. Local women also sheared off their long hair, claiming that it was unseemly to be beautiful in times of hardship. By such subversive means the people of Camagüey kept the memories of the heroes alive; now, in front of each palm, is an explanatory plaque.

Dominating the *parque*'s south side is the **Catedral de Santa Iglesia** (daily 9am–noon), built in the seventeenth century to be the largest church in the Puerto Príncipe parish. It was rebuilt in the nineteenth century when it took its present form, but despite its auspicious heritage it is one of Camagüey's least impressive churches, with a large but empty interior and a faded exterior.

La Iglesia de Sagrado Corazón de Jesús

A ten-minute walk east from Parque Agramonte along Luaces is one of the city's only twentieth-century churches, **La Iglesia de Sagrado Corazón de Jesús** on Plaza de la Juventud (daily 9am–noon). Built in 1920, it is quaint rather than awesome, but nevertheless worth a look if you are passing. After passing through the forbidding mahogany doorway, you'll find yourself under a neo-Gothic crossed roof, while lining the walls are four wooden altars skilfully painted in a *trompe l'oeil* to look like marble, typical of the era. Birds nest behind the marble main altar, while light trickling through cracked stained glass gives this rather faded church a pleasing air of serenity.

△ Parque Ignacio Agramonte

Plaza de San Juan de Dios

Head six blocks south of the Sagrado Corazón to reach the eighteenth-century **Plaza de San Juan de Dios**, the city's most photogenic square. A neat cobbled plaza with red-tiled pavements and little traffic, it's bordered with well-kept lemon-yellow and dusty-pink buildings, their windows hemmed with twists of sky-blue balustrades.

On the northern corner sits **La Iglesia San Juan de Dios** (daily 8am–noon), built in 1728. A single squat bell tower rises like a turret from a simple symmetrical facade saved from austerity by soft hues of green and cream. The dark interior is richly Baroque, typical of Cuban colonial style, with rows of chocolatey wood pews and a gilded altar. Notice the original brick floor, the only one remaining in any church in Camagüey.

Fitted snugly to the side of the building is the old **Hospital de San Juan de Dios**. It was to this hospital that the body of Ignacio Agramonte was brought after he was slain on the battlefield; the Spanish hid his body from the Cubans without allowing them to pay their last respects and burned him as an example to other would-be dissidents. It now houses the **Museo de San Juan de Dios** (Mon–Sat 8.30am–5pm, Sun 8am–4pm; $1CUC including Spanish-speaking guide), with some early maps and photographs of the town in bygone years. The display only takes up a small corner of the hospital, and the real pleasure lies in looking around the well-preserved building, admiring the original heavy wood staircase, cracked *vitrales*, courtyard filled with *tinajones* and palms and the view over the church tower from the second floor.

Necrópolis

About a ten-minute walk southwest of Plaza San Juan de Dios is the older part of town, but although the streets are narrower and the curled iron grilles framing the windows more eroded, there's not much to distinguish it from the rest of colonial Camagüey. It's home to the **Necrópolis** (daily 6am–6pm; free) next to the nondescript Iglesia Santo Cristo del Buen Viaje. Buried here are Camagüeyan martyrs Fernando Zayas y Cisneros and Tomás Betancourt y Zayas, assassinated by the Spanish. Lime-green lizards skitter over the extravagant Gothic mausoleums, while marble Christ figures gleam in the sunlight. More modern graves are brightly tiled and quietly tended by mourners, while at the back of the cemetery the tombs are tightly packed, morgue-like, into cupboard-style rows to make the most of the remaining space. Although the Necrópolis is in constant use, you are free to wander quietly around.

Casino Campestre and around

Continuing southeast from Plaza de San Juan de Dios will eventually bring you to the main road through the town, Avenida Tarafa, which runs parallel to the murky Río Hatibonico. On the other side of this is the vast **Casino Campestre**, the biggest city park in Cuba. Spliced by the Hatibonico and Juan del Toro rivers and dappled by royal palms, it has a beer tent, children's area and a bandstand, while amongst the shady trees are monuments to local martyr Salvador Cisneros Betancourt and former mayor Manuel Ramón Silva.

To the west of the park is the huge concrete **Rafael Fortún Chacón Sports Centre** (daily 6am–7pm; ℡32/28-8893), the biggest of its kind in any provincial town. Named after Camagüey's 100-metre athletics champion of the 1950s, it boasts a swimming pool and large arena with activities as varied as tae kwon do, basketball and trampolining, as well as a beauty centre offering mud wraps, honey treatments and the chance to bake in the sauna for a nominal fee. Amateur sports competitions, including judo and basketball, and *salsa* concerts are often held here: ask for details at reception.

Museo Ignacio Agramonte

While the north end of town has less to see, you should still make the effort to check out the **Museo Ignacio Agramonte**, on Avenida de los Mártires at the top end of República (Tues–Thurs & Sat 10am–5.45pm, Fri noon–7.45pm, Sun 10am–2pm; $2CUC plus $1CUC to take photos). Also known as the Museo Provincial, it has an elegant Art Deco exterior, the unassuming white

Tinajones

Tucked beneath the trees in Parque Agramonte are the large bulbous clay jars known as **tinajones**. Seen throughout Camagüey, they were originally storage jars used to transport wine, oil and grain and were introduced by the Spanish as the solution to the city's water shortage, placed beneath gutters so that they could fill with water. Slightly tapered at one end, they were half-buried in earth, keeping the water cool and fresh. They soon came to be produced in the town, and every house had one outside; inevitably, they became a status symbol, and a family's wealth could be assessed by the style and quantity of their *tinajones*. They also came in handy during the Wars of Independence when soldiers escaping the Spanish would hide in them. Indeed, so proud are the Camagüeyans of their *tinajones* that a local saying has it that all who drink the water from one fall in love and never leave town.

facade masking its sleek lines and geometric lettering. While there's nothing within to suggest a connection with its namesake, the museum's engaging array of exhibits includes some quality nineteenth-century furniture, most notably a *tinajero* washstand with a stone basin inset and some fine Sèvres china. Most impressive is the fine art collection, which includes a Victor Manuel García original, *Muchacha*, and a good example of the Cuban vanguard movement, which introduced modern art in Cuba between 1920 and 1960. You may wish to avoid the dusty cages of stuffed birds and beasts in the natural history room and head instead for the garden where original *tinajones* sit at the base of the breadfruit trees.

Eating

For a provincial capital, Camagüey has a good selection of **restaurants**, and there are a couple of **local specialities** that will come as a welcome break after the gastronomic wastelands of other parts of the island. At carnival time steaming pots of meat and vegetable broth called *ajiaco* scent the air, cooked in the street over wood fires. All the neighbours pile out of the houses and chuck in their own ingredients while an elected chef, often a hapless child, stirs the concoction to perfection. You can occasionally sample this delicacy in local eateries throughout the year; it's particularly delectable washed down with the locally brewed Tinima, a thirst-quenching malty beer. Camagüey also boasts a couple of excellent *paladares* whose popularity has prevented them from going the way of many of their counterparts in other cities. As with elsewhere in Cuba, watch out for overcharging and always ask for a menu where the prices are clearly stated.

Bodegan Don Cayetano República no.79 e/ Callejon de la Soledad y Callejon Magdelena. Immense wooden doors, tiled floor and dark-stained wooden beams all give this atmospheric restaurant a taverna feel in keeping with the tapas menu. *Chorizo*, prawns, tuna and *frituras* are all tasty and good value. Bench tables seating four either side mean this is a good place to hang out with groups of friends; there's a pleasant cobbled outdoor area as well.

Cafeteria El Ferro República esq. Van Horne. Snacks and drinks on a big patio close to the train station.

El Califa San Clemente no.49 esq. Cisneros. This cosy *paladar*, in a small, a/c dining room hung with red drapes, serves huge tasty portions of chicken and steak, accompanied by rice, fried plantains and salad, for $8CUC.

La Campana de Toledo Plaza de San Juan de Dios. This state restaurant is set in a leafy courtyard inside a pretty blue-and-yellow building with a redbrick roof and a quaint tradition of tolling the bell when anyone enters or leaves. It serves the usual quasi-international and Cuban cuisine, but the tranquil setting makes this a top choice for a mellow, moderately priced meal. Dishes are from $7CUC.

Don Ronquillo Galería Colonial, Ignacio Agramonte no.406 e/ República y López Recio. Cuban cuisine cooked to a quasi-gourmet standard, with high prices to match, in a shaded patio at the back of the Galería Colonial.

Doña Neli Maceo e/ Ignacio Agramonte y General Gómez. This bakery, directly opposite the *Gran Hotel*, serves freshly baked bread, biscuits, delicious pastries and other sticky treats.

Impacto República no.366 e/ Santa Rita y Oscar Primelles. Extravagant sundaes with sauces and foamy whipped cream and cakes with neon-coloured icing served in a spotlessly clean ice-cream parlour.

Mesón República e/ San Martín y Callejón de Correa. A good little spot for lunchtime Cuban cuisine which also serves local beer. The pirate-conquistador mural adds a nice touch of unintentional humour.

El Ovejito Hermanos Agüeros no.280 e/ Plaza del Carmen y Honda. As its name suggests, this smart restaurant specializes in lamb dishes. If you eat here, it's worth walking a little way further towards the square to check out the lifelike bronze street sculptures of local characters. Open 10am–9pm. Closed Tues.

Rancho Luna no.2 Plaze Maceo. For an authentic Cuban experience, join the queue at this spick-and-span peso restaurant and enjoy a veritable smorgasbord of pork dishes. Wait to be seated and bossed about by gloriously irreverent waitresses. Daily noon–10pm.

La Terraza Santa Rosa no.8 e/ San Martín y Santa Rita. This atmospheric, wood-panelled *paladar* is identifiable by a string of lights over the door. Head north along República and then one and half blocks west along Santa Rosa – if you can't spot it, ask a local, who will definitely know. Like most places it specializes in pork, but cooks it in ten different ways, all costing about $7CUC. Other options include a range of chicken plates and omelettes. Daily noon–midnight.

La Volante Parque Agramonte ☎ 32/29-1974. An old colonial house with tall windows overlooking the park, serving basic food that bears little relation to what's on the menu, to the cheesy strains of a Hammond organ. The appetizing *ropa vieja* (meat stew) and lamb dishes are the best bets. It caters mainly for Cubans and you may get away with paying in pesos. Closed Mon.

Drinking, nightlife and entertainment

An excellent weekend **nightlife** makes Camagüey a lively town. Every Saturday night, revellers stream onto Maceo for the free weekly knees-up "**Camagüeyan night**", when *salsa* queens get down to the sound of live groups while shyer souls, usually tourists, pin themselves to the walls and watch wistfully. Although some Camagüeyans consider the event rowdy and lowbrow, for the visitor it's lively and friendly and an excellent opportunity to meet locals, although you should keep an eye out for pickpockets. During the rest of the week, Camagüey has a quiet, understated nightlife based around a handful of central **rum bars**.

Camagüey is particularly vibrant during its week-long **carnival** in late June. An exuberant parade takes place on the main streets and musicians dressed in multicoloured, frilled costumes twirl huge batons adorned with silver glitz and shaped like prisms or bang drums and clap cymbals while others dance, swig beer and quarrel with the parade officials. Floats with disco lights, bouncing speakers and unsmiling girls in home-made costumes dancing energetically bring up the rear, while running in between the different trucks are *diablitos*, men disguised head to foot in raffia, who dart into the crowd with the sole purpose of terrorizing the assembled children. Stages are set up at various points around the town centre, and local *salsa* singers, acrobats and other performers entertain the gathered throngs while stalls selling gut-rot beer in vast paper cups (hang on to your empties – supplies often run out) and roast suckling pig provide refreshment.

The two local **cinemas**, Cine Casablanca and Cine Encanto, right next door to each other on Ignacio Agramonte e/ República y López Recio, show a selection of Cuban, Spanish and North American films and charge two pesos. The Teatro Principal (☎ 32/29-3048) has regular theatre and ballet performances, usually thoroughly entertaining.

The **Sala Recreativa Oxio Club**, República no.278 e/San Esteban y Finlay (daily 8am–10pm), is a games and sports arcade likely to appal die-hard Cuba traditionalists but delight bored teenagers. Big and brash, it sports a bowling alley ($2CUC a lane), a pleasant but smallish outdoor pool (daily 9am–5pm; $5CUC including $3CUC-worth of snacks and drinks), a billiards table ($3CUC an hour) and various noisy arcade games.

Bar Republica República no.293 e/ San Esteban y Finlay. Pleasant little local drinking bar where you can get an ice-cold local Tinima beer for a handful of Cuban pesos. Open from midday to midnight,

Bar Siboney San Rafael esq. Lugareño. Much cleaner, lighter and friendlier than most – and less intimidating for lone women – this excellent rum bar sells a couple of local specialities.

El Cambio Parque Agramonte. A friendly 24hr rum bar opening onto the park, with an old-fashioned though silent jukebox. A great place to slowly sip an afternoon away.

Casa de la Trova Salvador Cisneros no.171 e/ Martí y Cristo. The town's *Casa de la Trova* is a good place to catch live music all day long. The fun really kicks off at the weekends, when excellent local bands play in the palm-tree-fringed courtyard and get audiences (a good mix of locals and visitors) on their feet and dancing. Mon–Sat

noon–7pm, 9pm–1am, Sun 11am–6pm, 9pm–2am. $3CUC.

Galería Colonial Ignacio Agramonte no.406 e/ República y López Recio. Attracting tourists and *nouveau riche* Cubans who can afford the $7CUC entrance fee, the *Galería* hosts slick cabaret shows on weekend nights that feature a mix of professional dancers, international singers and touring Cuban bands (10pm–3am). Attractions earlier in the week range from stand-up comedians to fashion shows.

Gran Hotel Maceo no.67 e/ Ignacio Agramonte y General Gómez. Though all the big hotels have their own bars, the only one worth lingering in is this dark, atmospheric piano bar, which sometimes has live music.

Oasis Independencia esq. General M Gómez. An attractive, open-sided street-corner bar where vaguely chilled local Tinima beer is served with a smile. Open 24 hours.

Shopping

Although most of what's for sale in Camagüey is a collection of home-grown cosmetics and Cuba T-shirts, a few gems make **shopping** here a worthwhile pursuit. Chief among them is a nameless little emporium, tucked away at Cisneros no.208 e/ Hermanos Agüeros y Martí, which sells a fast-moving collection of original screen-printed Cuban film posters. Wooden carvings are available all over the place, worth considering if you have room in your luggage for a weighty piece of mahogany; the best bet is to buy direct from one of the town's best sculptors, Julain Besú Ruíz, at Avenida Betancourt no.2, Reparto Puerto Príncipe. Galería Colonial at Ignacio Agramonte no.406 has a smart cigar shop selling all the major brands and a smoking room, furnished with big squashy chairs, where you can watch TV and sample one of your purchases, and another separate outlet in the same grounds specializing in coffee and rum. Fonorama on Ignacio Agramonte has a good selection of CDs, tapes, postcards and kitsch souvenirs along the lines of jolly Cuban crocodiles waving cigars. On Cisneros, the town art gallery (Mon–Sat 8am–7pm) has a range of visual arts by local notables.

Listings

Airlines Cubana, República no.400 esq. Correa ☏ 32/29-2156. (Mon–Fri 8.15am–4pm).

Banks and money You can draw cash advances on credit cards, change traveller's cheques and buy pesos at the Cadeca *casa de cambio* at República no.353 e/ Oscar Primelles y Santa Rita (Mon–Sat 8.30am–6pm, Sun 8.30am–noon), or El

Banco Financiero Internacional, Independencia no.221 on Plaza Maceo (Mon–Fri 8am–3pm), where there's usually less of a queue.

Car rental Cubacar in Islazul at Ignacio Agramonte no.448 e/ López Recio y Independencia ☏ 32/28-5327 and 29-2550; Transtur in the Hotel Plaza ☏ 32/28-2413;

Havanautos at Independencia no.210 (Mon–Sat 9am–5pm; ☎ 32/29-6270).

Immigration Cubatur at Ignacio Agramonte no. 421 (Mon–Sat 9am–5pm; ☎ 32/25-4785, ⓔ cubatur@cmg.colombus.cu) can assist with extending tourist visas.

Internet There's a 24hr Internet service in Islazul at Ignacio Agramonte no.448 e/ López Recio y Independencia ($3CUC/30min, $5CUC/hr) and an Internet café in the *Hotel Colón* at República no.472 e/ San José y San Martín (daily 9am–10pm; $2CUC/30min, $3CUC/hr), but there is usually a long queue.

Medical The 24hr Policlínico Centro is on República no.211 e/ Grl. Gómez y Castellano (☎ 32/29-7810). For an ambulance call ☎ 32/28-1248 or 28-1257.

Pharmacy There's a convertible-peso pharmacy at Ignacio Agramonte no.449, near the post office (Mon–Sat 9am–5pm).

Photography Photo Service is on General Gómez e/ Maceo y Independencia.

Police Call ☎ 116 in an emergency.

Post office The main post office is at Ignacio Agramonte no.461 (daily 7am–10pm).

Taxis Cubacar ☎ 32/28-5327 and 29-2550; Transtur ☎ 32/27-1015.

Telephones The Telepunto República esq. San Martí y San José (daily 8.30am–9.30pm) has Internet access and phones and sells phone cards.

Víazul bus station ☎ 32/27-0396.

Around Camagüey

Although it's the country's largest province, aside from its capital and northern beaches (see p.418) there ultimately isn't that much to see in Camagüey. The small villages dotted around the city are quiet and rural, more concerned with the day-to-day management of their cattle and sugar farms than entertaining tourists. If you have your own transport you can roam around the essentially flat countryside east and west of the provincial capital, admiring the swathes of shimmering sugar cane and breezing through some of the larger one-horse towns. A possible diversion is tiny **Guáimaro**, 65km east of Camagüey, almost on the border with Las Tunas province. The town centres on a careworn square with a statue commemorating Guáimaro's moment of fame: it was here in April 1869 that the first Cuban constitution was drafted by such luminary revolutionaries as Ignacio Agramonte and Carlos Manuel de Céspedes.

North of Camagüey, the flat scenery begins to bulge gently into the low hills of the Sierra de Cubitas, although the near-straight road to the coast, off which lie a couple of minor sights, is as even as anywhere else in the province. The musically minded might like to stop off in **Minas**, about 40km northeast from Camagüey, for a tour around Cuba's only string instrument factory, the **Fábrica de Instrumentos Músicales** (Mon–Fri 7–11am & 1–5pm, Sat 7–11am; free, but tip the guide), in order to view, and possibly buy, the violins, guitars and *laudes* (Cuban twelve-string guitars) being lovingly hand-crafted. Also worth a look in the area is the **Ingenio Santa Isabel**, just east off the road roughly 17km from Minas. An intriguing tumbledown tower, standing alone by the side of the Río Saramaguacán, this is all that remains of an early sugar mill built at the end of the eighteenth century by local merchant Francisco de Quesada y Agüero and named after his daughter.

Sparsely populated northern Camagüey province is centred around **Nuevitas**, 77km northeast of the provincial capital. Though an industrial centre with several factories and a thermoelectric plant, its sea view and wooden pastel-coloured houses help it retain an air of an out-of-the-way provincial village. Even with the clouds of smoke and electrical wires crisscrossing the sky, you can still see vestiges of a colonial past in the colonnades outside the older buildings. There's not much to see and nothing to do but it's an agreeable enough spot to stop and refuel at one of the food stands in the main street.

Made up of low-lying farmland dappled with a few rural villages, the area south of Camagüey holds little of interest; offshore, however, the waters around the virgin cays of the **Archipiélago de los Jardínes de la Reina** (see p.427) offer magnificent diving and fishing opportunities. Access from Camagüey's south coast is very limited: you could try heading to the tiny fishing town of Santa Cruz del Sur, where you may find an opportunist fisherman willing to take you the 40km out to sea, but the only reliable way is from Júcaro in Ciego de Ávila (see p.427) or through the Camagüey Cubanacán representative (☎32/29-7374 or 32/29-2093), offering day-trips by bus and boat to Cayo Caguama.

Practicalities

Although exploring Camagüey province is easier by car, **buses** to Minas and Nuevitas leave twice a day from the provincial capital's intermunicipal bus station, next to the train station. Although you're unlikely to want to make an overnight stop in the region, should you need a **bed** your best option is the rather run-down *Hotel Caonaba* (☎32/4-4803; ❸) in Nuevitas, while should you find yourself stranded in Guáimaro, head for the passable *Hotel Guáimaro* (☎32/8-2102; ❷).

The north coast

Cut off from the mainland by the Bahía de Nuevitas, 10km north of Nuevitas town, are Camagüey's north-coast **beaches**. The remote resorts of **Santa Lucía**, and **Cayo Sabinal** to the west, both make perfect retreats for those seeking sun and sea holidays. While Santa Lucía derives an infrastructure of sorts from the knot of all-inclusive hotels arrayed along the beachfront, Cayo Sabinal is castaway country. With only the most basic accommodation, it virtually guarantees solitude. Those wishing to explore completely virgin territory should head for **Cayo Romano** in the far western reaches of the province.

Santa Lucía and around

Hemmed in by salt flats on the northern coast, 128km from Camagüey, **Santa Lucía** is one of Cuba's smaller beach resorts. Much more low-key than the hectic resorts on the northern cays, it's perfect if you want to park yourself on the sand for a fortnight, soak up some rays and indulge in a few watersports, but those looking for a more well-rounded destination may find it lacking. The road up here from Camagüey passes through the idyllically pastoral countryside that typifies this region, with lush grazing meadows, cowboys herding their cattle and meandering goats impeding the traffic, the air thick with clouds of multi-coloured butterflies that flutter about like confetti.

If you're not driving to Santa Lucía, you can catch an unmetered **taxi** ($35CUC) from outside the train station. It's worth noting that Cubatur (see p.429) can organize transfers and day-trips for groups of ten or more people for $20CUC. For general **information** you can speak to the public relations officer at your hotel.

Accommodation

Except for the cheapest hotel, *Escuela Santa Lucía*, which operates independently, the Santa Lucía resort revolves around its four good all-inclusive **hotels**, which between them carve up almost the entire beach strip. Residency at one entitles you to use the beaches, though not the facilities, of the others. All hotels offer a range of watersports, including windsurfing, snorkelling and catamarans.

There's no legal accommodation outside of the hotels but there are plenty of people offering **rooms** in Santa Lucía village and in La Boca, a fishing community that's basically just a string of wooden shacks at the entrance to Playa Coco.

Prices quoted are those you would pay at the hotels' receptions, but it's worth checking with Cubanacán in Camagüey before setting off, as they are often able to offer discount rates (☎32/29-4905), as are Cubatur (☎32/25-4785).

Amigo Mayanabo ☎32/36-5168 to 70, ✆services@mayanabo.stl.cyt.cu. The shabbiest all-inclusive on the strip, with old-style breeze-block architecture but helpful, friendly staff and facilities that include a gym, a large pool and tennis courts. **❼**

Brisas Santa Lucia ☎32/36-5120 to 23, ✆comerc@cvientos.stl.cyt.cu. A friendly and unpretentious family-oriented hotel with excellent rooms, a pool with a swim-up bar, a gym, billiards, darts, archery, watersports and activities for children. **❼**

Club Amigo Caracol ☎32/36-5158, ✆sales@caracol.stl.cyt.cu. The emphasis here is on activity, with beach volleyball, table tennis, windsurfing, catamarans, kayaks, mountain biking and tennis offered. The cabin-style layout gives the hotel a more personalized and less institutional feel than the others. **❼**

Gran Club Santa Lucía, ☎32/33-6109, ✆aloja@clubst.stl.cyt.cu. This part-Italian-owned complex, geared to Italian guests, enjoys a spacious layout of bungalows and two-storey apartment blocks, with palatial rooms, ample shops, a good pool, a gym, three restaurants and a pier-end bar that's perfect for sunset-watching. **❼**

The town and its beaches

The **resort**, such as it is, consists of little more than a beach strip lined by a few hotels, set well back from the coastal road and heavily guarded, while the surrounding vicinity is restricted by marshland. The town, which you pass en route to the hotel strip, has nothing to offer tourists, and you will quickly get the impression that you are out in the middle of nowhere with nothing to see or do away from the sun and sea. Meeting townsfolk themselves is near impossible, as they are refused entrance to the hotels and the beaches

The **beaches** are wide expanses of soft, fine sand bordered by turquoise waters, if a little sullied by seaweed drifting in from the barrier reef. There are five excellent **dive sites** catered to by a competent dive centre (see box, opposite). As with many nascent resorts in Cuba, the scene revolves around the all-inclusive hotels, most of them set in attractive properties and all with friendly staff.

Eating, drinking and entertainment

Outside of the hotel restaurants, there's little in the way of independent **eating** and **drinking** in the area. *Luna Mar*, near the beach between the **Gran** *Club Santa Lucía* and *Club Amigo Caracol*, is a relatively authentic Italian restaurant that provides a welcome respite from the hotel eateries and offers pizzas, pastas and lobster, served, unusually, with a choice of orange and coffee sauces. Also, the main road behind the beach strip has a couple of Rumbos cafés selling chicken and fries.

Similarly, at Santa Lucía you are limited to the hotels for evening **entertainment**, an endless diet of jovial staff roping drunken guests into bawdy Benny Hill-type pantomimes. The resort's only disco, *La Jungla*, has air hockey and billiards but other than that is swanky, soulless and given to playing uninspiring mainstream Cuban and international disco music at deafening volumes. It's part of the Gran *Club Santa Lucía* complex but all comers are welcome (daily 11pm–3am; $5CUC with open bar).

Playa Coco

Offering a change of scene 8km west from Santa Lucía's main beach drag is the idyllic **Playa Coco**. The local claim that it's a beach to rival the best in Cuba

Diving at Santa Lucía

Blessed with five good sites, Santa Lucía offers some excellent **diving** possibilities, although most will suit skilled divers more than complete beginners. All sites are accessible by boat and have sharp drop-offs. Highlights include the lobsters, giant eels, stingrays, eagle rays and mantas at **Las Mantas**; the shimmering orange sponges and black coral at **El Canyon**; and the Spanish wreck **Mortera**, sunk in 1896, which is coated with soft corals, gorgonian corals and sponges, and home to myriad snooks, snappers and bull sharks – arguably the most fascinating site of all, though beware of the strong currents. At **Las Amforas**, a collection of nineteenth-century earthenware jars, discarded by sailors on Spanish galleons, lies scattered on the sea bed, providing refuge for innumerable iridescent tropical fishes, while the inquisitive tarpon and groupers at **Poseidon 1** are perfect subjects for underwater photography.

The optimistically named **Shark's Friends Diving Centre** (☏032/36-5182, ✉sharks_friends@sunnet.stl.cyt.cu), on the stretch of beach nearest to *Hotel Cuatro Vientos*, runs two daytime dive trips at 9am and 1pm ($30CUC per dive including equipment); night dives, when the sea glitters with starry phosphorescence ($45CUC), and dives at *La Mortera* during which the instructor fearlessly hand-feeds 3-metre-long bull sharks ($50CUC). It also offers ACUC (American Canadian Underwater Certification) registered courses (around $310CUC), excursions to fish for sea bream, barracuda, reef sharks and snapper starting at $200CUC, and also trips to Cayo Sabinal.

is stretching it a bit, but it certainly makes a welcome break from Santa Lucía, as it's open to Cubans and has a less touristy feel. On the way there, you pass salt flats swarming with flamingos and the egrets (*cocos*) that give the beach its name.

There are a couple of excellent **restaurants** right on the beach and it's definitely worth stopping for a meal here. Chicken, fish, lobster and spaghetti are served up for reasonable prices 24 hours a day at *La Bocana*, a wooden hut at the far end of the beach with tables on the sand where curious crabs dance around your feet but never come too close. Otherwise, *Bucanero*, at the Santa Lucía end of the beach, is smarter, with a more formal dining room and nautical decor. There's a massive range of sumptuous seafood dishes as well as brochettes and the house speciality, roast beef, on offer. A meal will set you back $10–15CUC.

To **get here**, a minibus picks up from the Santa Lucía hotels at 10am and drops you back at 3pm, or you can hire one of the horse-drawn carriages that wait outside the hotels.

Cayo Sabinal and Cayo Romano

Twenty-five kilometres west along the north coast from Santa Lucía, **Cayo Sabinal** could not be more different – a deserted white-sand beach cay that's almost eerie it's so paradisiacal. The reason it's yet to be discovered by the masses is its geographical isolation, hidden away at the end of a seven-kilometre stretch of notoriously bumpy dirt-track road, part of which forms a causeway across the bay, flanked by foaming salt marshes; there's no public transport, and very little general traffic makes it this far. Peppered with rocks and cavernous potholes, the road is sometimes impassable without a 4WD, especially during the rainy season, so check conditions before you set off. This resort is **for tourists only**, with passports examined and Cubans allowed no further than the entry checkpoint, something to bear in mind if travelling in an unmetered taxi. A metered taxi from Camagüey will set you back around $45CUC.

All the **beaches** are on the north side, accessible by signposted turnings off the single main road, bordered by thick vegetation. The longest beach is pearl-white **Playa Los Pinos**, where the sea is a clear, calm turquoise and wild deer and horses roam through the woodland that backs onto the sand. Occasionally a group of holidaymakers arrives by boat from Santa Lucía, but otherwise it's a top choice for a couple of days' total tranquillity. Just 2km further west, smaller **Playa Brava** has similar soft white sands. **Playa Bonita** another 3km west has a lengthy stretch of coral reef perfect for snorkelling, as well as 3km of pure white sand.

The beaches' sole **accommodation** option is a simple hut with a palm-rush roof and cold running water on Playa Los Pinos (❷ you can turn up on spec, but you're better off booking through Cubatur offices in Camagüey (☎32/29-4807).

On the west side of the coastline is **Cayo Romano**, an undeveloped ninety-kilometre-long mass of fragmented cays covered with marshes and woodland. With no accommodation or restaurants, it is an archetypal untamed wilderness worth exploring if you have the time and your own transport. A causeway runs from Playa Jigüey on the north coast into the centre of the cay, although you can also reach the western tip from Cayo Coco.

Travel details

Víazul buses

Camagüey to: Ciego de Ávila (2 daily; 1hr 30min); Havana (2 daily; 8hr); Santa Clara (2 daily; 4 hr); Santiago de Cuba (3 daily; 6hr); Sancti Spíritus (2 daily; 2hr 30min); Trinidad (1 daily; 5hr).
Ciego de Ávila to: Camagüey (2 daily; 1hr 30min); Havana (2 daily; 6hr); Holguín (2 daily; 6hr); Las Tunas (2 daily; 4hr); Santa Clara (2 daily; 3hr).

Astro buses

Camagüey to: Ciego de Ávila (3 daily; 2hr); Havana (2 daily; 8hr); Las Tunas (1 daily; 2hr 30min); Manzanillo (1 daily; 7hr); Matanzas (1 daily; 8hr); Minas (2 daily; 40min); Nuevitas (2 daily; 1hr 20min); Santa Lucía (1 daily; 2hr 30min).
Ciego de Ávila to: Camagüey (3 daily; 2hr); Cienfuegos (3 weekly; 4hr 30min); Havana (1 daily; 6hr); Holguín (3 weekly; 6hr); Las Tunas (3 weekly; 4hr); Matanzas (3 weekly; 8hr); Morón (10 daily; 45 min); Santa Clara (3 weekly; 3hr).

Morón to: Ciego de Ávila (10 daily; 45min).

Trains

Camagüey to: Bayamo (1 daily; 6hr); Ciego de Ávila (1 daily; 2hr); Havana (3 daily; 8hr); Holguín (1 daily; 3hr); Matanzas (3 daily; 6hr); Las Tunas (1 daily; 2hr); Morón (1 daily; 3hr); Santiago de Cuba (1 daily; 6hr).
Ciego de Ávila to: Camagüey (1 daily; 2hr); Havana (3 daily; 7hr); Holguín (1 daily; 5hr); Matanzas (3 daily; 6hr); Morón (5 daily; 1hr).
Morón to: Camagüey (1 daily; 3hr); Ciego de Ávila (5 daily; 1hr); Júcaro (1 daily; 40min); Santa Clara (1 daily; 4hr).

Domestic flights

Camagüey to: Havana (9 weekly; 1hr 35min).
Cayo Coco to: Havana (3 weekly; 2hr).
Ciego de Ávila to: Havana (2 weekly; 1hr 25min).

Northern Oriente

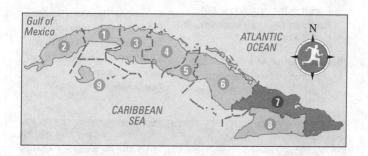

CHAPTER 7 **Highlights**

✻ **Holguín** Smart parks, a cosmopolitan air, and one of the finest restaurants outside of Havana make Holguín worth a visit. See p.455

✻ **Gibara** This picture-perfect town is the base for travelling to the geologically rich Cavernas de Panadernos, one of the region's treasures. See p.464

✻ **Playa Guardalavaca** With over a kilometre and a half of sugar-white sand, this beach is the crown jewel of Northern Oriente's coastline. See p.470

✻ **Aldea Taína** An inventive and imaginative reconstruction of a Taíno village that offers an insight into a long-extinguished culture. See p.472

✻ **Villa Pinares de Mayarí** Waterfalls, lakes and pine forests create an idyllic haven of calm at this hotel, cupped by mountains and the centre of the ultimate nature retreat. See p.475

✻ **Baracoa** This vibrant small town set on Cuba's southeast tip is surrounded by some of the country's most breathtaking mountains and countryside. See p.481

✻ **El Yunque** The easily scaled El Yunque is as famous for its mention in the 1492 log of Christopher Columbus as its rare orchids and ferns. See p.490

△ Playa Guardalavaca

Northern Oriente

Traditionally, the whole of the country east of Camagüey is known simply as the "Oriente", a region that in many ways represents the soul of Cuba, awash with historic sites and political passions. Running the length of the area's north coast, the three provinces that make up the **northern Oriente** – Las Tunas, Holguín and Guantánamo – form a landscape of panoramic mountains fringed by flatlands, with some of the country's most breathtaking peaks and striking white-sand beaches.

The smallest and most westerly of the three provinces is **Las Tunas**, given over mainly to farming. Possibly the quietest and least dynamic province in Cuba, it is often overlooked by visitors, though the unassuming and friendly provincial capital, **Victoria de las Tunas**, is not without charm. Nearby, the picturesque coastal town of **Puerto Padre** is another of the province's modest highlights, with a couple of congenial beaches close by.

By contrast, larger and livelier **Holguín** province has a variety of attractions. It was here that Christopher Columbus first came ashore, the stunning country-side and beautiful beaches prompting his famous utterance that "the island is the most beautiful eyes have ever seen". Chequered with parks, the busy and crowded provincial capital, **San Isidoro de Holguín**, manages to be modern and cosmopolitan while still retaining the feel of its colonial past, with several handsome old buildings, museums and antique churches.

The once-mighty nineteenth-century port of **Gibara**, presiding over the north coast, also has vestiges of its former glory visible in a few fine buildings and an old fort, while the gently undulating hills honeycombed with under-ground caves surrounding the town are perfect for independent exploration. Holguín's biggest attraction is the **Guardalavaca** resort, where dazzling white beaches and a lively atmosphere draw hundreds of holidaymakers. Nearby, the province's ancient historical pedigree can be seen in the remnants of pre-Columbian Taíno culture in and around the little village of **Banes**. Further east, the exclusive beach resort of **Cayo Saetía** is a well-guarded paradise of white sands and glistening seas, with exotic animals to be seen in its lush woodland – an altogether idyllic place to relax.

Inland, where rugged terrain dominates the landscape, the cool pine forests, waterfalls and lakes of **Mayarí** are unmatched for isolated serenity. Further south in Holguín, buried in the heart of sugar-farm country, Fidel Castro's prosaic birthplace at **Biran** fascinates many who take the revolutionary pilgrimage across Cuba.

Of the three provinces the best known is undoubtedly **Guantánamo**, with the notorious US naval base at **Caimanera**. Although the town of Guantánamo is largely unspectacular, it forms a useful jumping-off point for

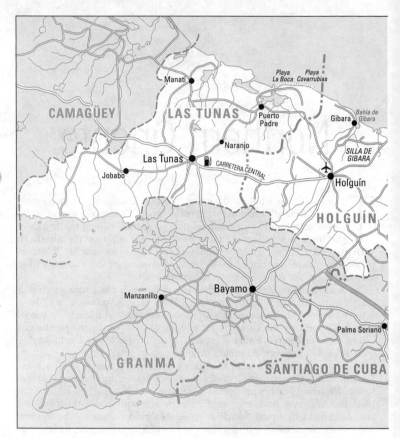

the seaside settlement of **Baracoa**, one of Cuba's most enjoyable destinations. Sealed off from the rest of the island by a truly awe-inspiring range of rainforested mountains – which are fantastic for trekking – Baracoa's small-town charm is immensely welcoming and a visit here is the highlight of many trips to Cuba.

Las Tunas

With no bright lights, glistening beaches or beautiful colonial buildings, the little province of **Las Tunas**, studded with the flat-leafed prickly pear *tunas* cactus that gives it its name, is often side-stepped by visitors heading to more

glamorous regions. But while it's not somewhere you're likely to want to linger, the province is pleasant and attractive enough and has enough modest attractions to merit a brief stopover.

With a refreshing absence of hustlers, amiable **Victoria de las Tunas** – or, more usually, just Las Tunas – feels more like a village than the provincial capital. On the north coast, near the old colonial town of **Puerto Padre**, the small resort at **Playa Covarrubias** and the undeveloped beach at **Playa La Boca** are worth visiting for their pretty pale sands. The rest of the province is mostly agricultural, the main industry being **sugar** production, as evidenced by the fields of emerald-green cane.

Victoria de Las Tunas

VICTORIA DE LAS TUNAS seems to have been built to a traditional Cuban recipe for a quiet town: take one central plaza, a small main hotel, a Revolution square and a thriving market, add a pinch of culture and bake in the sun for two hundred years. The result is a pleasant but slow-moving town where the faster pace of life elsewhere in the world seems but a rumour.

The town's hub is **Parque Vicente García**, a small but comfortable central plaza hemmed by trees. It's an appealing spot to watch the town's comings and goings, with horse-and-cart taxis clip-clopping through the streets and fleets of kerbside manicurists sharpening their files for a day's business. On the east side of the park, the **Museo Provincial Mayor General Vicente García** (Tues–Fri 9am–5pm, Sat 1–9pm, Sun 8am–noon; $1CUC) is housed in a distinguished sky-blue and white colonial building adorned with an elegant clock face. The city history detailed within includes a worthy, though brief, record of slavery, featuring some horrific chains and shackles, while upstairs a natural history room displays a motley collection of stuffed sea creatures. On the park's southern corner is the **Plaza Martiana de Las Tunas**, a modern art monument to José Martí made up of six white man-sized spikes, one of which is embossed with a bust of Martí. The whole sculpture forms an ingenious gigantic sundial that illuminates the bust each May 19 to commemorate the hero's death on the battlefield.

If you have time to kill, you could breeze round the **Museo Memorial Vicente García** (Mon–Fri 9am–5pm, Sat 11am–7pm, Sun 8am–noon; $1CUC), five minutes' walk west of the square. The museum is built on the birthplace of one Major General Vicente García, who led the people of Las Tunas into battle against the Spanish in September 1876. In 1897, facing the town's imminent recapture, he rashly declared that Las Tunas would rather be burnt to the ground than become enslaved to the Spanish, and promptly torched the city. Consisting of a few antique ceremonial swords and photographs of the hero and his family, the museum is set around an attractive central courtyard filled with spiky *tunas* cacti.

The most arresting museum in Las Tunas is the small but poignant **Museo Memorial Martires de Barbados**, about half a kilometre further west from

the square at Lucas Ortíz no.344 (Mon–Fri 11am–7pm; free); it commemorates the horrific October 6, 1976 plane crash which wiped out the national junior fencing team. Minutes after the plane took off from Barbados, en route to Cuba, there was a massive double explosion and the plane plunged into the sea, killing all 73 passengers, including the team. When it was revealed several months later that an anti-Castro terrorist linked to the CIA had planted the bomb, the incident was popularly seen as a direct attack on Cuban youth and achievement, all part of the ongoing campaign to undermine the Revolution. The terrorist, part of a Cuban exile group called CORU, had planted the bomb beneath his seat before disembarking at the plane's stopover in Barbados.

The museum itself is located in the tiny former home of one of the three team members from Las Tunas, and is an evocative tribute. Unsmiling photographs of the victims and of weeping crowds in Havana, old fencing gear and trophies, and a script of the pilot's final pleas for help skilfully tug at the heartstrings. Outside in the grounds is a part-time fencing school for local students, opened in the 1980s as a tribute.

Across the street is a lively local **market** (6am–6pm; closed Mon) which sells fresh milkshakes, fruit, vegetables and assorted ephemera.

Practicalities

Interprovincial **buses** plying the Carretera Central between Holguín and Camagüey pull in at the terminal located just under a kilometre south of the centre on Francisco Varona (T31/4-3060), from where you can get a *bicitaxi* into town. The provincial bus station is about 2.5km northeast of town on Avenida Cienfuegos, with the **train station** in an adjacent building. Again, *bicitaxis* and horse-drawn carriages wait here to whisk you into the centre ($2CUC), or you can hire unmetered **taxis** for excursions around the province.

There's no real reason to stay overnight in Las Tunas, but there are several **accommodation** options should you find yourself so inclined – or stranded. The top choices include the friendly *Casa de Yolanda Rodríguez Torres*, Lucas Ortíz no.101 e/ Villalón y Coronel Fonseca (T31/4-3461; ❶–❷), which offers two spacious double bedrooms, each with private bathroom, and the cosy *Casa de Carlos Alberto Patiño*, directly opposite at Lucas Ortíz no.120 (T31/4-2288; ❶–❷). Also excellent is *Casa de Roberto Tamayo*, Velasquez no.13 e/ Frank Pais y Lucas Ortiz (T31/34-0132; ❶–❷), where tasty, hefty meals put it head-and-shoulders above the competition. If no vacancies can be found, there's the rather grim state tourist hotel, *Hotel Las Tunas*, on the outskirts of town at Ave. 2 de Diciembre esq. Carlos J. Finlay (T31/4-5014; ❷).

When it comes to grabbing a bite to **eat** in town, your best bet is *Las Rocas paladar*, no.108 Lucas Ortiz e/ Villalon y Gonzales de Quezada, for tender lamb stew and other well-prepared dishes. Also worth considering is *Taberna Don Juan*, Francisco Varona no.225, near Parque Vicente García, where you can enjoy decent Cuban food and excellent local beer in pesos. The main divisa option is the twee, 24-hour *La Bodeguita*, Francisco Varona no.296, selling fried chicken and some pasta dishes. *Doña Neli*, opposite the bus terminal on Francisco Varona, sells pastries and cakes, and also has a small pizzeria to one side.

The best time to show up in Las Tunas is on a Saturday night when a regular **street party**, complete with pig roasts, sound systems and dancing, comes to life around Parque Vicente García and Francisco Varona. Outside of this weekly event, there's not much nightlife or entertainment to speak of except during the summer, when the annual **El Cucalambé music festival** is held over three days each June or July. Based in the grounds of the otherwise unremarkable *Hotel El Cornito* (☏31/4-5015), about 7km out of town, the festival features live folk and *salsa* in a lively atmosphere awash with beer and food stalls.

All the main convertible-peso shops in Las Tunas are strung along Vicente García and Francisco Varona, and it's around here that you'll also find the **bank**, **telephone centre** and main **post office**. The telephone centre is at Francisco Vegas no.237 e/ Lucas Ortiz y Vincente García and is open daily 8.30am–9pm.

Puerto Padre and the north coast

Although Las Tunas has just 70km of coastline, a small stretch compared to neighbouring provinces, there are still some pleasant spots. The attractive little seaside town of **PUERTO PADRE**, 56km northeast of Las Tunas, is a worthwhile diversion on the coastal road through the province. Here, a clutch of colonial buildings, including a church with a handsome spire, spreads along a spacious boulevard that heads down to a *malecón*. The chief attraction here is a small, crumbling and quietly impressive stone **fort**, built by the Spanish at the turn of the nineteenth century, with a circular tower on two of its four corners linking its once-solid walls. It's best viewed from the outside, as the interior is a mass of overgrown weeds and graffiti.

Buses from Las Tunas (Avenida Cienfuegos terminal) arrive in town twice daily. The *Hotel Villa Azul*, General Rabí no.27 e/ S. Cisnero y Playa Girón (☏31/5-2017; ❷), has an open-air restaurant and is nice enough if you find yourself stranded for a night.

Playa La Boca

Playa La Boca, 19km northeast of Puerto Padre, is a wide sweep of clean golden sand spread around a clear blue-green bay, backed by palms and shrubs and dotted at intervals by mushroom-shaped concrete shades. Despite its obvious charms, it's often fairly deserted – no public transport comes out this far, making it one of the few beaches in northern Oriente not overrun with sun-worshippers, windsurfers, snorkellers and the like.

There's nowhere to stay at Playa La Boca and the only place to **eat** on the beach is a peso stall selling pizza and lukewarm soft drinks.

Playa Covarrubias

About 30km east along the coastal road from Puerto Padre is **Playa Covarrubias**, a small, white-sand beach with shallow, crystal-clear waters, wide sandbanks and an offshore coral reef, all in the lee of a large, perplexingly located all-inclusive hotel. It's a pleasant beach, thronging with beachcombers and watersports enthusiasts, but it's by no means spectacular, and a long haul for a day-trip. **Buses** from Las Tunas only run as far as Puerto Padre, so you're better off taking one of the unmetered taxis ($30CUC) from outside Las Tunas' train station. The only **place to stay** is the deluxe and all-inclusive *Hotel Villas Las Covarrubias* (☏31/4-6230; ❻), which offers comfortable rooms with all mod cons, a large pool and nightly entertainment.

Holguín

Wedged between Las Tunas to the west, Granma and Santiago de Cuba to the south and Guantánamo to the east, **Holguín** is one of Cuba's most varied provinces, a mix of lush farmland, sublime mountains, historical sites and appealing rural towns, as well as the beaches that constitute its main attraction.

The capital, **San Isidoro de Holguín**, is a well-ordered town in the centre of the province and a developing tourist destination. Known throughout Cuba as the "City of Parks" and replete with museums, it has an almost European feel and enjoys a quirky fame as the country's sole manufacturer of mechanical organs – their music can be heard around the town. Close by, the secluded coastal fishing village of **Gibara** boasts a wealth of history and is one of the most captivating corners of the province.

On the coast further east, the dazzling beaches at **Guardalavaca**, **Esmeralda** and **Pesquero** together form the third-largest resort in the country, a lively destination for throngs of dedicated fun-seekers. However, those in search of solitude and natural beauty are more likely to find what they are looking for just inland, in the cool, pine-forested mountains around **Mayarí**, dotted with lakes, caves and waterfalls. In addition to its many natural attractions, Holguín also boasts more Taíno sites than any other province, particularly near **Banes**, where a museum pays tribute to the region's pre-Columbian heritage.

The province's industrial core is betrayed by the nickel mines and factories that taint the air around **Moa**, in the far east, and **Nicaro**, on the coast near Mayarí; ugly as they are, they provide much-needed revenue for the region.

San Isidoro de Holguín

Nestled in a valley surrounded by hills, 72km east of Las Tunas, **SAN ISIDORO DE HOLGUÍN** – or Holguín for short – is a thriving industrial town balancing quieter backstreets with a busier central district of handsome colonial buildings, where the streets are crowded with bicycles and horn-blasting cars. Despite having the bustling air of a large metropolis, Holguín's centre is compact enough to explore on foot and has a couple of fine eighteenth-century **churches** and some small-scale **museums** which will keep you quietly absorbed for a day or so. The city is also spotted with numerous elegant **plazas**; these open spaces, ideal for people-watching, are central to the Holguín lifestyle, and in the evenings it seems that the whole city turns out just to sit, chat and watch their children play in one or other of them.

On Holguín's northwest edge, a hearty climb up to the summit of **La Loma de la Cruz** affords a panoramic view over the city. Named for the cross that sits at the top, this hill is the site of the fervent **Romería de Mayo** pilgrimage held every May 3, when a Mass at the summit is followed by a week-long celebration down in town.

Some history

The area around Holguín was once densely populated by indigenous Taíno, but the Spanish had wiped them out by 1545, after Captain García Holguín, early

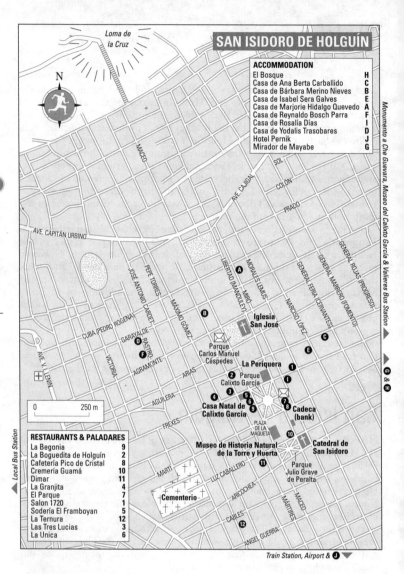

SAN ISIDORO DE HOLGUÍN

Loma de
la Cruz

N

Monumento a Che Guevara, Museo del Calixto García & Valieres Bus Station

ACCOMMODATION

El Bosque	H
Casa de Ana Berta Carballido	C
Casa de Bárbara Merino Nieves	B
Casa de Isabel Sera Galves	E
Casa de Marjorie Hidalgo Quevedo	A
Casa de Reynaldo Bosch Parra	F
Casa de Rosalía Días	I
Casa de Yodalis Trasobares	D
Hotel Pernik	J
Mirador de Mayabe	G

Iglesia
San José

Parque
Carlos Manuel
Céspedes

La Periquera

Parque
Calixto García

Casa Natal de
Calixto García

Cadeca
(bank)

PLAZA
DE LA
MAQUETA

Museo de Historia Natural
de la Torre y Huerta

Catedral de
San Isidoro

Parque
Julio Grave
de Peralta

Cementerio

RESTAURANTS & PALADARES

La Begonia	9
La Boguedita de Holguín	2
Cafetería Pico de Cristal	8
Cremería Guamá	10
Dimar	11
La Granjita	4
El Parque	7
Salon 1720	1
Sodería El Framboyan	5
La Ternura	12
Las Tres Lucias	3
La Unica	6

Train Station, Airport & J

colonizer and veteran of the conquest of Mexico, established his cattle ranch around La Loma de la Cruz. Although a small settlement remained after his death, a town wasn't fully established here for 150 years, and it was only officially named on April 4, 1720 – San Isidoro's Day – with a commemorative Mass held in the cathedral.

Being an inland town with no port, Holguín was destined to be overshadowed in importance by coastal Gibara. In spite of its rather grand blueprint, laid out in accordance with Spanish colonial city planning laws, it developed slowly. However, by the nineteenth century an economy based on sugar production and fruit-growing, as well as a little tobacco cultivation, had been established and the town grew accordingly.

As with other parts of Oriente, Holguín province saw plenty of action during the Wars of Independence. Shortly after the start of the Ten Years' War, on October 30, 1868, the city was captured by General Julio Grave de Peralta's force of Mambises, who lost Holguín to the Spanish on December 6. The tides turned again four years later on December 19, 1872, when the city was recaptured by General Máximo Gómez and Holguín's own son, General Calixto García.

After independence, the province was largely dominated by US corporations and Holguín chugged along much the same as it always had. Since the Revolution, however, it has become more of an industrial city with several factories and engineering plants, and was designated provincial capital when the province was created in 1975.

Arrival and information

International and domestic **flights** land at the Aeropuerto Frank País (℡24/46-2512), about 4km out of town, from where metered taxis will run you to the centre for about $8CUC.

Local buses and interprovincial **colectivos** pull into the Valiares Terminal de Omnibus in front of the Calixto García stadium car park on Avenida de los Liberatadores to the east of the centre. **Interprovincial buses** arrive at the Astro Estación José María, Carretera Central e/ Independencia y 20 de Mayo (℡24/42-2111), about 1km west from the centre where horse-drawn carriages, *bicitaxis* and taxis wait to ferry you into town. **Trains** arrive at Terminal de Ferrocaril Vidal Pita no.3 e/ Libertad y Maceo (℡24/42-2331), 1km south of the town centre, also served by taxis and *bicitaxis*.

There's no real centre for tourist **information**, although in a pinch the rather charmless staff at the Islazul reservations office, Libertad no.199 esq. Martí, by Parque Calixto García, may be able to give advice. The central **post office**, by the Parque Calixto García at Libertad no.183 e/ Frexes y Martí, and the Pedro Rojena shop, Libertad no.193 e/ Frexes y Martí (Mon–Fri 9am–5.30pm, Sat 9am–3pm), sell **maps**, which become harder to find the further east you go.

Accommodation

While the three state **hotels** catering for tourists are sound options, they're all slightly out of town, which is a drag if you don't have your own transport. A more central option is any one of the well-appointed *casas particulares*, most of which rent rooms for $20–30CUC, with a possible reduction for longer stays. If the ones listed here have no vacancies, the *bicitaxi* drivers who congregate around Parque Calixto García are good people to ask, though they are likely to charge a $5CUC daily commission that will be added to your accommodation bill. It's also worth remembering that the taxi drivers who pick up from the bus station are fairly mercenary, and even if you direct them to your chosen *casa particular* they may still try to charge you a proprietor's commission – the more unscrupulous will attempt to drive you to a *casa particular* of their own choosing. A good way of avoiding this is to ask the owners to come and collect you.

Hotels
Hotel El Bosque Ave. Jorge Dimitrov Reparto Pedro Díaz Coello ℡24/48-1012,

ⓔbosque@bosque.holguin.info.cu. The best convertible-peso hotel in Holguín, located on the outskirts of town, 2km east of the centre. Although

Braying for beer

The *Mirador de Mayabe* hotel's resident celebrity is Pancho, a beleaguered donkey whose star turn is consuming vast quantities of Mayabe beer bought for him by well-meaning guests. Rumour has it that the original donkey died some years ago and his successor is a pale imitation who can't hold his drink and has been seen staggering after one too many. If you do make it out this far, you'll find Pancho, or his impersonator, in a stable conveniently located next to the hotel's open-air bar.

not very modern, the individual self-contained blocks, with two or three rooms apiece, are well maintained and set in leafy grounds. Some rooms have refrigerators and all are super-clean, with spotless bathrooms, and hibiscus flowers strewn on the bed. Two restaurants, a bar and a pool flesh out the attractive package. ❹

Hotel Pernik Ave. Jorge Dimitrov ☏ 24/48-1667, Ⓦwww.hotelpernik.cu. A bulky, imposing hotel located near the Plaza de la Revolución, a good half-hour's walk from the town centre, although taxis wait outside to ferry you in. It's a bit grim and overpriced, with half-hearted service and an erratic hot-water supply, but there are usually rooms available which are clean and good-sized, with satellite television. ❹

Mirador de Mayabe Alturas de Mayabe ☏ 24/42-3485. This recently refurbished hotel, 8km south of town, is Holguín's most picturesque. The clean and comfortable rooms are grouped in graceful, red-tile-roofed, pale yellow chalets that are connected by flowerbeds tangled with verdant vines and creepers. There's a gorgeous lobby bar with panoramic views over the valley and swinging wooden love seats (not to mention a drunk donkey nearby; see box, above), two restaurants, and an invitingly large pool. ❹

Casas particulares

Casa de Ana Berta Carballido Aguilera 163 e/ Narciso López y G. Feria ☏ 24/46-1375. One double room with a bathroom, fridge, pleasant patio and private entrance in a bright, airy house. English, Portuguese and Italian are spoken. ❷

🏃 **Casa de Bárbara Merino Nieves** Martires no.31 e/ Agramonte y Garayalde

☏ 24/42-3805. Two excellent, double rooms, each with its own bathroom and one with private kitchen. TV, a/c, use of a sunny terrace and very friendly and helpful owners make this one of the best *casas particulares* in town. ❷

Casa de Isabel Sera Galves Narciso López no.142 e/ Aguilera y Frexes ☏ 24/42-2529. Two sizeable double rooms with fridges in a handsome, high-ceilinged house with a pretty garden shaded by coconut palms. The disadvantage here is that both rooms share a single bathroom. ❶

Casa de Marjorie Hidalgo Quevedo Libertad no.79 e/ Cuba y Garayalde ☏ 24/42-8499. This friendly household offers a double room with bathroom and a pleasant apartment with a kitchen/dining room and a roof terrace affording views over the Loma de la Cruz. There's a garage, making it an ideal option for drivers, and meals are available. ❷

Casa de Reynaldo Bosch Parra Rastro no.41 e/ Agramonte y Garayalde ☏ 24/42-4651. Two rooms in a friendly household. This is a fine choice for a travelling group, with one twin room and one double, patio, leafy roof terrace, kitchen and washing area. ❷

Casa de Rosalía Días Frexes 176 e/ Miró y Morales Lemus ☏ 24/42-3395. One large room in a friendly, centrally located household with bathroom and a/c. ❷

Casa de Yodalis Trasobares Rastro no.37 e/ Agramonte y Garayalde ☏ 24/42-5229. Somewhat kitsch choice offering two rooms, each with en-suite bathroom, a/c and large wooden wardrobes, and both decorated with crazy-haired dolls and novelty lamps. ❷

The Town

The centre of town is easy to negotiate, with most of the sights spreading out from the central **Parque Calixto García**, an oval expanse of ornamental pink marble and Cuban jade-green marble. In the park's centre, a square marble column is topped by a statue of war hero Calixto García leaning upon his sword. A bushy rim of trees lines the park's outer edge and the benches beneath are packed with old men relaxing in the shade, the more garrulous of whom will gladly fill you in on the entire history of the province.

△ Holguín

It was often part of the original Spanish plans for colonial towns to build a square, presided over by a church, every four blocks, and an overview of the city shows that in Holguín this was well executed. The squares were used for public meetings, markets and fairs – and to allow the church authorities to keep a beady eye on their parishioners. Of particular note is the **Plaza de la Maqueta**, a beautiful testimony to colonial architecture one block southwest of Calixto García which is currently being restored. Most of the town's museums, such as the **Museo Provincial de Holguín** and the **Museo de Historia Natural de la Torre y Huerta**, are located near the centre, while the most worthwhile sight in the outskirts is the imposing **Monumento al Guerrillero Heróico Ernesto Che Guevara**. Also, Holguín's several churches are all handsome enough to warrant closer inspection, especially the **Iglesia San José** and the **Catedral de San Isidoro de Holguín**. Finally, a climb up **La Loma de la Cruz** is a literally breathtaking way to admire the city from on high.

Museo Provincial de Holguín

Presiding over the northeastern side of Parque Calixto García is the **Museo Provincial de Holguín** (Mon–Fri 8am–9pm, Sat & Sun 9am–5pm; $1CUC entrance, $1CUC to use a camera), where a number of worthwhile exhibits are displayed in one of the town's most impressive buildings. The handsome ochre edifice, lined with simple columns, delicate iron balconies and an elegant rooftop balustrade, was built between 1860 and 1868 as both the private house and business premises of Francisco Roldán y Rodríguez, a wealthy Spanish merchant. He devoted much time and effort to the project, even ferrying the head carpenter and mason over from Spain, but never managed to move in. While the great house awaited the finishing touches, the first War of Independence broke out and, with Rodríguez's blessing, the Spanish army in Holguín hastily holed up here, capitalizing on its fortress-like proportions. The measure paid off and throughout the siege of the city the Mambises, unable to capture the building, had to content themselves with yelling "Parrots, parrots, climb out of your cage" at the yellow-and-red-clad Spanish soldiers as they peeked from the windows. The house has since been known as **La Periquera** or "the parrot cage".

The building's indomitability – proved once more in a further attack by Mambises in 1872 – earned it a long life of public service, and it functioned variously as governor's residence and town hall until being converted into a museum in 1978. It retains some beautiful features, most noticeably the iron door knocker cast in the form of a woman's head, representing the spirit of friendship and the symbol of the city.

The primary reason to come here is actually the building, as the museum occupying the ground floor is none too impressive. The collection of historical flotsam and jetsam on display is rather sparse, with independence fighter José Martí's sword in prime position in a glass case, while the modern revolutionaries are represented by a grisly selection of bloodstained shirts accompanied by solemn, staring photographs of their unfortunate owners. The best section is the small set of pre-Columbian artefacts found in and around Holguín, including bone fragments of necklaces and pieces of clay pots. Most impressive of the artefacts here is a polished, olive-coloured Taíno axe, known as the Axe of Holguín, which was discovered in 1860 in the hills surrounding the city. Carved with a grimacing, crowned male figure, it was most likely used for religious ceremonies.

Museo de Historia Natural and Casa Natal de Calixto García

A block south of the park, at Maceo no.129, is the **Museo de Historia Natural de la Torre y Huerta** (Tues–Sat 9am–10pm, Sun 9am–9pm; $1CUC). Once again, the building itself is the real reason to come here, a fanciful nineteenth-century confection with a pillared portico and an entrance portal exquisitely tiled in bright ceramic squares of lacquered aqua and rose, complementing the richly patterned floor inside. The decor, in addition to the light raining down through stained-glass windows, completely outshines the museum's lacklustre exhibits of *polimitas* snail shells, stuffed animals and dead fish.

Also disappointing in its holdings is the **Casa Natal de Calixto García**, an austere, faded white-and-blue structure a block west of the plaza at Miró no.147 (Tues–Sat 9am–9pm; $1CUC), where General Calixto García was born on August 4, 1839. Although he won several battles during the Ten Years' War, the general is not a particularly significant figure in the history of Cuba and is highly honoured in Holguín mainly because he was born here. Inside, the bland glass cabinets filled with disjointed trivia and the dry histories related on placards tell little of the man himself, and you are left feeling that his rust-spotted swords, his mother's black lace mantilla and his wire-rimmed spectacles would be better off incorporated into a larger collection elsewhere.

Iglesia San José

Three blocks north of Parque Calixto García, fronting the shady, cobbled Plaza Carlos Manuel de Céspedes, is the **Iglesia San José**. With its single weather-beaten clock tower rising above stone arches and topped with a domed turret, the church is easily the most attractive spot in town. If you are around on a Saturday, be sure to pay a visit around 8pm, when a mechanical organ player fills the interior with romantic tunes. There's been a church on this site since 1815, though various overhauls over the years have rendered the original building unrecognizable. The Neoclassical tower was the town's tallest structure for a while, after being added in 1841, and was used as a lookout point by the Mambises during the siege of the city in 1868. Contrasting with many Cuban churches, the ornate Baroque interior is vibrant and welcoming, with sturdy central pillars appealingly decorated in pink-and-white candy-like spirals above a faded black-and-white marble-flagged floor. The rest of the church leans towards more traditional Catholic decor, with life-sized effigies of saints huddled above altars and sentimental paintings of the life of Christ on the walls. While the church's opening hours are irregular, mornings are usually a safe bet for a look around.

Catedral de San Isidoro

The **Catedral de San Isidoro de Holguín** on Libertad (daily 8am–noon & 4–6pm; free), named for the city's patron saint, lords it over the stately Parque Julio Grave de Peralta (also known as Parque de los Flores and originally called the Parque San Isidoro), a couple of blocks south of Parque Calixto García. Surrounded by a walled patio, the stalwart but simple cathedral, with two turrets and a red-tiled roof, glows in the Caribbean sun. A slick of magnolia paint has added a certain debonair austerity to the cathedral's crumbling romanticism.

The original church on this site, completed in 1720, was one of the first buildings in Holguín; a humble affair built from palm trees, it lasted ten years until a sturdier structure with a tiled roof and stone floor was erected in 1730. When this started to deteriorate, in the late 1790s, the church elders exerted gentle pressure on the wealthier Holguíneros, and the current building was finished in 1815. The small Jesús de Nazareth chapel to the back of the building, now an office cum inner sanctum for church officials, was added in 1862, and the twin towers in 1910. Built as a parish church, and also used as the city crypt, it was only elevated to cathedral status in 1979, which accounts for its straightforward design and small size.

A spicy, warm smell of wood drifts through the simple interior, where balustrades over the windows, celestial blue altars and graceful high ceilings, lined with unadorned wooden rafters, add to the church's dignified air. On your way out, have a look at the heavy, wooden main door, pockmarked by bullets fired during the Wars of Independence.

Museo Calixto García and Monumento al Ernesto Che Guevara

Away from the sights clustered around Holguín's centre are two attractions worth visiting. Housed in the Calixto García stadium, 1km east of town, the minute **Museo del Estadio Calixto García** (Mon–Fri noon–8pm, Sat & Sun 8am–noon; $1CUC) is entertaining enough, although essentially a space-filler for the stadium foyer. It combines trophies and medals from various local sports stars with some quaint photographs of such revolutionaries as Camilio Cienfuegos and Raúl Castro playing baseball. Check out the one of a youthful and lithe Fidel Castro, baseball bat poised, and another of Che Guevara enjoying a more sedentary game of chess.

From here you can stroll further east for roughly 1km along Avenida de los Libertadores for a look at the **Monumento al Guerrillero Heróico Ernesto Che Guevara**, an impressive three-part sculpture with panels showing a silhouette of Guevara approaching, striding forward and receding. Executed in sombre stone, it's an eye-catching and accomplished piece of work, its triptych of images said to allude to, respectively, his revolutionary influence, presence and lasting legacy.

La Loma de la Cruz

Rising above Holguín, **La Loma de la Cruz**, or Hill of the Cross, is the largest of the hills that form a natural border to the north of the city. The steep, 458-step stairway starts from the northern end of Maceo, to the summit, where you'll find a faithful replica of the hefty wooden cross erected on May 3, 1790, by Friar Antonio de Algerías, following the Spanish tradition of the *Romería de la Cruz* (Pilgrimage of the Cross). This custom commemorates the day that, according to legend, St Elena, mother of Constantine the Great, rediscovered the original cross of Christ's crucifixion. Every May 3, a Mass is held for the faithful – who until the construction of the staircase in 1950 had to toil up the hill the long way round – along with a low-key week-long festival in town, where locals gather nightly around beer stalls and food stands set up around the centre. Note that if you'd rather not hike up, a metered taxi will run you to the summit from downtown for around $5–6CUC.

The hill was also used by the Spanish as a lookout during the Wars of Independence, and a bijou **fort** on the plateau set back from the cross remains as evidence. You can appreciate why the Spanish chose this point when you gaze down at the town's rigid grid below and the panorama of lush green land on one side and dry countryside on the other, with parched and dusty hillocks visible in the distance. The fort now houses a small gallery, with a selection of local artwork and original gifts like handmade notebooks for sale. Also taking advantage of the magnificent views is a **restaurant**, the *Mirador de Holguín* (see below), strategically placed at the summit.

Eating and drinking

In common with much of the rest of Cuba, Holguín lost most of its *paladares* to high taxes some time ago. However it is still possible to **eat** well, and cheaply, in Holguín. There are a number of good-quality state restaurants, while peso snack stalls are plentiful around the central streets. Ice-cream fans will find a wealth of tasty choices at many establishments with which to satisfy their sweet cravings. **Bars** are thin on the ground, though, and those looking for somewhere to drink are better off in one of the restaurants or cafés listed below.

State restaurants

La Begonia Maceo s/n e/ Frexes y Martí. A reasonably priced, 24hr open-air café overlooking Parque Calixto García beneath a canopy of begonias. Ordering a chicken salad sandwich off menu is far better than braving the greasy fried chicken, fries and pizza. Also good are the huge pots of creamy ice cream. This is a popular *jineteros* hangout.

La Boguedita de Holguín Aguilera no.249 esq. Martires. A pleasant restaurant specializing in grilled pork with a bar area where *trovadores* play in the evenings. The cheap prices and friendly atmosphere more than compensate for the fact that most of the menu options are usually unavailable.

Cafetería Pico de Cristal Martí s/n esq. Libertad. Although somewhat lacking in character, this mid-range, centrally located café, specializing in the usual fried chicken, spaghetti, pizzas and sandwiches, is popular with locals.

Cremería Guamá Luz Caballero y Libertad. Join the queue for the best peso ice cream in Holguín. Standard flavours on offer are strawberry and chocolate.

Dimar Martíres 133 esq. Luz Caballero. An attractive, intimate gem of a restaurant featuring tasty, sophisticated fish and shrimp dishes. Charming waiters in sailor suits complement the ocean-going theme.

La Granjita Máximo Gómez no.264 e/ Frexes y Aguilera. No-frills peso restaurant doling out basic, inexpensive Cuban meals.

Mirador de Holguín La Loma de la Cruz. Good-value restaurant at the top of the hill (to the left of the summit), featuring chargrilled dishes and superb views over the city. Friendly and unpretentious.

El Parque Libertad e/Frexes y Martí. Standard snack bar dishing up flaccid pizzas, good toasted sandwiches, omelettes and fried chicken.

Salon 1720 Calle Frexes 190 e/ Miró y Holguín ☎24/46-8150. With its splendid decor and attentive service, this may be one of the best dining experiences you have in Cuba. By European standards the food is good, by Cuban standards it's excellent. Try the delicate onion soup garnished with oregano followed by beef medallions or lamb chops with tamarind sauce. Another surprise is that everything on the menu actually appears to be available, though the Cuban wine is best avoided. Expect to pay $5–10CUC for a main course, $22CUC for lobster.

Sodería El Framboyan Maceo esq. Frexes. With a mind-boggling list of sundaes and other delicious icy confections, this ice-cream stall offers a range of exotic flavours including orange-pineapple, almond and hazelnut alongside the standard strawberry and chocolate.

Las Tres Lucías Martíres e/ Frexes y Aguilera. Appealing little café with a cinematic theme. Film posters and black-and-white stills hang on the walls, and the name itself is a reference to the Humberto Solas film. Movies are shown on some evenings. Open daily 7am–3pm & 5pm–1am.

La Unica Maceo e/ Frexes y Martí. A petite soda fountain that does a swift trade in good-quality ice cream and cakes.

Paladares

La Ternura José Antonio Cardet no.293 altos e/ Cables y Angel Guerra ☎24/42-1223. Small, cosy *paladar* serving chicken and pork prepared in a variety of styles. Main courses cost $5–7CUC.

Nightlife and entertainment

Although Holguín doesn't boast much in the way of **nightlife**, there are a few places that offer a cheap (entrance fees shouldn't exceed $5CUC) and lively evening out. If you're in the mood for other kinds of **entertainment**, the small and intimate Cine Martí, beside Parque Calixto García, shows Cuban and international **films**, as does the Cine Baría, four blocks east on Libertad. The Teatro Eddy Suñol, on the north side of Parque Calixto García, puts on **plays** and musical entertainment. One of the busiest daytime hangouts in Holguín is La Bolera, a **bowling alley** on Calle Habana e/ Maceo y Libertad (10am–4pm; $1CUC a game), 10 minutes' walk from the centre. **Baseball** games are often played during the national league's season between October and April, and less often throughout the rest of the year at the Estadio Calixto García, Avenida 20 Aniversario esq. Avenida de los Libertadores (☎24/46-2014), about 1km east of town. Tickets are on sale at the entrance and cost a few Cuban pesos.

Café Cantante Libertad esq. Frexes. A spacious pub-style bar which hosts a song-and-dance show each night at 9pm ($1CUC).

Cafetería Pico de Cristal Martí s/n esq. Libertad. This buzzing bar/café, right on Parque Calixto García, attracts a sophisticated older crowd for evening drinks. On the third floor, the *Pico Cristal* is a brash disco which keeps going until the early hours.

Casa de la Trova Maceo no.174 e/ Frexes y Martí. A mixed crowd of cross-generational foreigners and Cubans fills the big wooden dance floor for exuberant *salsa* and traditional *trova* sessions, with live bands playing every night from 10pm ($1CUC). The club offers *bolero* and *salsa* classes and also hosts occasional conferences on Cuban music and folklore.

Club 80 Martíres esq. Frexes. Night owls in search of more mellow entertainment should head to this sultry late-night piano bar (with an original 1950s counter) that's open until 4am.

Mona Lisa Centro Cultural, Callejon Marcado II, Plaza de la Maqueta. Various musical, cabaret and, occasionally, fashion shows are held in the pretty courtyard of this cultural centre. Usually *bolero* is played from Mon to Wed, and traditional music is performed on Fri. Daily 9am–6pm & 9pm–1am.

Salon 1720 Calle Frexes 190 e/ Miró y Holguín. The restaurant's well-stocked bar, on a romantic lantern-lit roof terrace, is the top choice for moonlight cocktails.

Shopping

Most of Holguín's **shopping** opportunities are clustered around the central area, in particular **Parque Calixto García**, where you'll find the Pedro Rojena shop, Libertad no.193, selling a selection of T-shirts, tapes, CDs, postcards, stationery and socialist-themed books in English, French and Spanish. On the same block is the peso department store Casa Azul, a good place to browse. Although you're unlikely to find any recognizable labels, it's a good source of quirky and eclectic pieces – anything from cotton nightdresses to pink marble ashtrays – all of them at rock-bottom prices. Across the park on Maceo, the Centro de Arte displays the works of contemporary Cuban artists from Holguín and further afield. Further around the park on Calle Frexes, the Fondo de Bienes Culturales sells rustic furniture, colourful landscapes, guitars and gimcrack souvenirs, of the lighter-keyring ilk.

Also worth checking out is the **Plaza de la Maqueta**, a boulevard of shops and bars next to a large but dilapidated colonial building that's currently being restored. The predominantly upmarket shops are aimed at the tourist buck – the ones most worth checking out are Egrem, selling CDs, drums, claves and other musical instruments; Tienda Mona Lisa, with music as well as books in Spanish and English, T-shirts, posters and some well-made souvenirs; and La Cohoba, offering a fine selection of those Cuban stalwarts, rum, cigars and coffee.

Listings

Airlines Cubana, Martí esq. Manduley (☎ 24/46-2512, 46-2534).

Airport ☎ 24/47-4525.

Banks and exchange CADECA, Libertad no.205 e/ Martí y Luz Caballero (Mon–Sat 8.30am–5.30pm, Sun 8am–noon), can change traveller's cheques, give cash advances on Visa cards and change convertible pesos into Cuban pesos.

Car and scooter rental Havanautos (☎ 24/48-815717) has a desk at the airport and another at *Hotel El Bosque*. Micar (☎ 24/46-8559) is located in the central Edificio Pico de Cristal, Libertad esq. Martí. There is a scooter rental point by Parque Calixto García, next to the cinema. It's worth dropping by to make reservations a day or two in advance, as the scooters are in short supply.

Immigration and legal The immigration office, where you can renew standard tourist visas, is at Fromento s/n esq. Peralejos Repto Peralta (Mon, Wed & Thurs 8am–5pm, Fri 8am–noon ☎ 24/40-2322). Arrive early to avoid long queues.

Internet ETESCA (daily 9am–6pm), facing Parque Calixto García on Martí, has Internet access and sells phone and Internet cards.

Medical The *Hotel Pernik* and the *Hotel El Bosque* both have medical services, while the main hospital, Hospital Lenin, is on Avenida Lenin (☎ 24/42-5302). Call ☎ 104 for an ambulance.

Photography Photo Services, Libertad no.132 e/ Frexes y Aquilera.

Police Call ☎ 106.

Post office The most central post office is at Libertad no.83 e/ Frexes y Martí (Mon–Fri 9am–6pm, Sat 9am–5pm), with a DHL service, pay phones for international calls. There is also a 24hr office at Maceo 114 e/ Aria y Agramonte on Parque San José.

Taxis Transtur can be reached on ☎ 24/42-4187, Cubataxi Miro e/ Frexes y Aguilera ☎ 24/42-3290.

Telephones The ETECSA international call centre is on República 9 Rastro esq. Frexes (Mon–Fri 6am–9pm, Sat & Sun 8am–9pm), with convertible-peso phone cards sold for international calls.

Víazul bus terminal ☎ 24/42-2111.

Gibara

After travelling 35km north from Holguín, through a buxom set of mountains that locals compare to a woman's breasts, you reach the pleasingly somnolent fishing port of **GIBARA**, which spreads from a calm and sparkling bay into the surrounding rugged hillside. This little-visited gem is just the place to spend a few hours – or even days – enjoying the tranquil views, historical ambience, away-from-it-all atmosphere and lush scenery. Gibara is also an ideal base from which to explore the countryside and nearby pockets of interest like the **Cavernas de Panadernos** caves.

Some history

The name "Gibara" comes from the word *giba*, or hump, and refers to the **Silla de Gibara**, a hill which, seen from the sea, looks like a horse's saddle. Gibarans swear this is the one Christopher Columbus mentioned in his log when approaching Cuban shores, but although he did first land in Holguín province the hill he wrote about is generally taken to be El Yunque in Baracoa. The spot where **Columbus** first disembarked in Cuba on October 28, 1492 is Playa Don Lino, about 20km east of Gibara, in the Bahía de Bariay; it is marked today by a small monument on the hillside near the pretty pale sand beach.

Founded in 1827, Gibara became the main north-coast port in Oriente due to its wide, natural bay. During the nineteenth century the town enjoyed valuable trade links with Spain, the rest of Europe and the United States and was considered important enough to justify a construction of a small fortification on the Los Caneyes hilltop, the ruins of which remain. Though small, Gibara was a fashionable and wealthy town, home to several aristocratic families and famed for its elegant edifices. Its beauty prompted several pseudonyms: "Encanto Eden" (Enchanted Eden), "Perla del Oriente" (Pearl of the Orient), and, from sailors who were dazzled by its whitewashed houses, "La Villa Blanca".

The glory days were not to last, however, and Gibara's importance began to slip away with the introduction of the railway, which could more easily transport freight around the country. The decrease in trade left the town floundering, and during the 1920s and 1930s many townsfolk moved elsewhere in search of work, leaving Gibara to shrink into today's pleasant village whose main industries are farming and fishing. Vestiges of the town's halcyon era are still evident, though, in the ornate tiles adorning several buildings and the elegant sweep of the municipal buildings.

Arrival and information

Buses to Gibara leave the Valiares depot in Holguín around 7am daily and take an hour to reach Gibara; you can catch a private *camión* truck from the same place for about 10 Cuban pesos. A metered **taxi** will take you there and back for $25–30CUC, depending on how many passengers there are and how hard you bargain. There's no tourist office in town; however, the helpful staff in the Oficina de Historia, no.1 Plaza del a Fortaleza (☎24/3-4588), housed in an old fort accessed by a drawbridge, go some way towards compensating for this, and can give information on local sights and some historical background to Spanish speakers. The bank and post office are both on Independencia within a block of the Plaza de la Iglesia.

Accommodation

Since there are no state hotels in Gibara, *casas particulares* comprise all **accommodation** options. There are currently 27 houses, the majority of which are centrally located and of an extremely high standard, often housed in an old colonial home; the best options are listed below. An added bonus is that many will provide tasty, simple meals for a few extra convertible pesos.

Casa Colonial Independencia no.20 e/ Luz Caballero y Peralta ☎24/3-4383. Two available rooms in a comfortable, rambling house. The helpful, English-speaking owners partially compensate for the somewhat ascetic conditions. ❷

La Casa de la Fortuna Martí no.22 e/ Sartorío y Independencia ☎24/3-5453. A friendly household in an attractive nineteenth-century house offering two decent rooms, each with its own bathroom. ❷

🏃 **Hostal Vitral** Calle Independencia no.36 ☎24/3-4469. A tranquil and beautiful colonial house offering two rooms with private bathrooms. One of the best *casas particulares* in the region, featuring a large rooftop terrace with hammocks from which to enjoy views over the Silla de Gibara. ❷

La Terraza Calle Donato Marmol no.51a ☎24/3-4619. One large room in a third-floor apartment with its own bathroom and sitting room. Bonuses include a terrace with hill views, a lovely host, and cheap rates. ❶

Los Hermanos Calle Céspedes no.13 e/ Luz Caballero y Peralta ☎24/3-4542. Three rooms set alongside a sunny courtyard in a pleasant household. All rooms have their own bath. ❶

The Town

An enjoyable place for a wander, Gibara's streets fan out from the dainty **Plaza de la Iglesia**. Rimmed with large Inbondeiro African oak trees imported from Angola in the 1970s, the plaza is dominated by the Iglesia de San Fulgencio, a late nineteenth-century church built in a medley of styles. In the centre of the square is the marble **Statue of Liberty**, erected to commemorate the rebel army's triumphant entrance into town on July 25, 1898, during the second War of Independence. Sculpted in Italy, the statue is smaller and less austere than her North American counterpart and bears the winsome face of Aurora Peréz Desdín, a local woman considered so captivating that the town supplied the sculptor with her photograph so that he might preserve her beauty forever. The aubergine-and-yellow building on the c/ Independencia side of the square is a cigar factory, where a peek inside reveals workers industriously rolling away.

Even the smallest Cuban town has a moth-eaten collection of stuffed animals, and Gibara is no exception, although at least their **Museo Historia Natural** (Tues & Wed 8am–noon & 1–5pm, Thurs–Sun 8am–noon, 1–5pm & 8–10pm; $1CUC), which borders the plaza, is worth a peek, not least for its *pièce de résistance* of Cuban grotesque: a long-dead hermaphrodite chicken which was once both rooster and hen. The rest of the exhibits include a collection of *polimitas* shells and a sad old humpback whale killed by mistake in 1978.

The best museum in town is the **Museo del Arte Colonial** (Tues & Wed 8am–noon & 1–5pm, Thurs–Sun 8am–noon, 1–5pm & 8–10pm; $2CUC), one block away at Independencia no.19. The sumptuous building, beautifully lined with yellow-and-blue tiles, was built in the nineteenth century as the private residence of José Beola, a wealthy local merchant. Its interior is quietly splendid, with a narrow staircase sweeping upstairs to the fine, though small, collection of paintings. Among them is a meticulous depiction of the town in its glory days, with ships approaching a wide sweep of harbour, and majestic houses crowding the hillside beyond. Amongst the collection of colonial furniture is a spectacular bedroom suite, with a huge mirror studded with pineapples – a showy display of the family's wealth. The delicately coloured, pale pink-and-blue stained-glass windows are original to the house and the biggest in the province.

Next door, at no.20, the **Museo Municipal** (Tues & Wed 8am–noon & 1–5pm, Thurs–Sun 8am–noon, 1–5pm & 8–10pm; $1CUC) is not as captivating but still worth a glance. Along with some general colonial ephemera are odds and ends from Cubans who fought and died in Angola during the 1970s. A torn flag and discarded asthma inhaler stand out as poignant reminders of both the war and the fragility of its warriors.

Gibara is at its prettiest along the seafront, where **Playacita Ballado** and **Playa La Concha** are both tiny, scenic scoops of yellow sand enjoyed by local kids and good places for a dip after meandering through the town. Finally, one sight not to be missed is the old naval **fort** overlooking the town up on Los Caneyes hill – a forty-minute walk from sea level. Although the small fort is little more than a broken-down shell, the view it provides over the bay and town below easily compensates.

Cavernas de Panadernos

Gibara's most rewarding feature, the **Cavernas de Panadernos**, is located on the outskirts of town, about 2km from the centre. To reach this series of under-ground limestone caves, take Calle Bargas east, passing the cemetery on your left, then take the overgrown path on the right continuing on past the abandoned military post on the left to reach a clearing. From here, bearing round to the left for about half a kilometre will take you to the caves' entrance. Taking a guide is the best way to visit the caves; nature specialist José Corella knows the caves inside out and has buckets of information to boot. He works at the Oficina de Historia, no.1 Plaza de la Fortaleza (⊕24/3-4588).

Formed from glacial movement during the ice age, the caves have gradually flooded and drained over the Quaternary period to form a labyrinth of **mineral galleries**. You are strongly advised not to stray into the pitch-black depths of the catacombs without a torch and a professional guide. The caves are home to a sizeable colony of bats that scurry above you as you pass from gallery to gallery and whose presence adds to the generally eerie air. In the gallery nearest to the cave mouth take a good look at the walls where genera-tions of visitors have cut their names into the rock, with some even dating back to the early 1900s. Surprisingly, the caves are not cool, but hot and damp while the walls and floor are slick with moisture and slippery – be sure to wear sturdy footwear.

In all, there are nineteen interconnected galleries stretching 11km under the Gibara hillside, though you probably won't go the whole distance. There's much to be seen, however, in the most accessible chambers, including a glittering myriad of sculptural stalactites and a huge elephantine bulge nicknamed "the mammoth". Heading further underground, you're rewarded with a magnificent lake glinting in the Tolkienesque gloom.

Eating, drinking and entertainment

As you might expect in a spot so far off the beaten track, there are few **restaurants** and **bars** in Gibara. In addition to those highlighted below, some of the *casas particulares* may offer meals if asked. As far as the nightlife scene, there is very little going on, and your best bet is to head to the El Colonial Centro Cultural by Luz Caballero square for live music (**Open** Tues–Sun 10am–midnight) in a pleasant courtyard with palm trees and a fountain. Cine Jiba on Plaza de la Iglesia has a large screen, as well as a *sala de vídeo*, and shows a mixture of Cuban and international films. The annual Festival de Cine Pobre, which translates roughly as the Festival of Fringe Cinema, takes place every April and is a draw for those interested in Cuban cinema.

Casa Colonial Independencia no.20. Housed in the eponymous *casa particular* (see p.465), this *paladar* is well placed in front of the Museo Colonial and serves up good portions of pork, chicken and shrimp with rice, beans and salad.

El Faro Parque de las Madres. Also known as *La Concha*, this state restaurant is the town's only convertible-peso establishment. Although there's not much to recommend in the rather substandard

fried chicken and fries-style fare, the restaurant boasts a sea view, crackling sound system and pool table.

Los Hermanos Calle Céspedes no.13 e/ Luz Caballero y Peralta. A *paladar* doubling as a *casa particular*, with a couple of tables set around a sunny, attractive courtyard. Service and food are both excellent, with satisfying portions of *comida criolla* and some seafood, all served with imagination and flair.

whilst they accept convertible pesos for beer, rum and soft drinks, it's best to bring national pesos as well, as they are unlikely to have much change.

Guardalavaca and around

Despite being the province's main tourist resort, **GUARDALAVACA**, on the north coast 72km northeast from Holguín, retains a charmingly homespun air. The area's name pays tribute to a buccaneer past – Guardalavaca meaning "keep the cow safe", which is thought to refer to the need to protect livestock and valuables from marauding pirates who once used the area as a refuge point. Surrounded by hilly countryside and shining fields of sugar cane, the resort combines small-scale intimacy with a vibrant energy lent by its youthful clientele. The lively **Playa Guardalavaca** and **Playa Las Brisas** have one plush hotel complex each, while the two exclusive satellite resorts to the west, **Playa Esmeralda** and **Playa Pesquero**, which incorporates the nearby Playa Turquesa, are popular with those seeking luxury and solitude. The **town of Guardalavaca**, which backs onto its namesake resort, is little more than a clutch of houses.

Should you tire of sunning yourself on the beach, the surrounding area has enough excellent sights to keep you busy for a few days. All the hotels arrange excursions to the fascinating Taíno burial ground, about 3km away in the Maniabon hills, which incorporates the **Museo de Chorro de Maita** and **Aldea Taína**, a re-creation of a Taíno village that really brings the lost culture to life. Close to Playa Esmeralda, at the Bahía de Naranjo, an offshore **aquarium** offers an entertaining day out, also arranged via the hotels. Alternatively, one of the most rewarding pastimes in Guardalavaca is to **rent a bicycle or moped** and head off into the dazzling countryside to enjoy stunning views over hills and sea; you can also make the trip on horseback with a guide.

Arrival, information and transport

Flights for visitors on package holidays land at Holguín's Aeropuerto Frank País and visitors are ferried to the resort by special buses. There's no public transport from Holguín to Guardalavaca, but a metered **taxi** will take you there for $25CUC and bring you back for the same amount. Alternatively, *colectivo* shared taxis also run this route and leave throughout the day until about 5pm.

Each hotel has its own **excursions** officer who arranges trips to the local sights (see box, opposite) and can supply some information in the absence of formal tourist offices. You can cash traveller's cheques at all the hotels and at the Banco Financiero Internacional, opposite *Club Amigo Atlántico*, where you can also get advances on credit cards.

All the hotels have **car rental** desks or you can visit the central offices of Cubacar, Playa Guardalavaca (☎24/3-0243), or Havanautos, at the Cupet Cimex garage, Playa Guardalavaca (☎24/3-0223). **Mopeds** can be rented from roadside stands outside *Las Brisas* at Playa Guardalavaca, *Paradisus Rio de Oro* at Playa Esmeralda and the *Maritím* at Playa Pesquero ($8CUC for the first hour, $6CUC for the second, $4CUC for the third), while Transtur (☎24/3-0134) at Playa Guardalavaca rents **motorbikes**. All the hotels rent **bicycles**, an excellent way to get around. **Taxis** usually loiter outside hotels, or you can call Transtur or Transgaviota (☎24/3-0166).

While you can get to most sites independently, it is usually easier to go on a tour. All excursions from Guardalavaca are organized by Cubatur (☏ 24/3-0171), which has a representative in each hotel.

Banes Although Banes itself is a bit of a backwater, this trip takes you to the Museo Indocubano with its small but worthy collection of pre-Columbian artefacts (see p.473), and also takes in local sites including the Museo de Chorro de Maita, Aldea Taína and a visit to a *campesino* house. $51CUC.

Cayo Saetía A day-trip to one of the most unusual resorts in the country. Enjoy the charms of the white-sand beach and take a safari through the surrounding woodland and savannahs to see zebras, ostriches and the like roaming freely. $69CUC. Those wishing to make the trip by helicopter can do so for $129CUC.

Havana You are flown to Havana for a whistle-stop tour of Habana Vieja and Vedado, with some free time for shopping. Lunch at one of the better Havana restaurants is included. $189CUC.

Holguín A half-day jaunt to the provincial capital, including a visit to a cigar factory where you can see cigars being handmade in the classic Cuban way, a trip up the Loma de la Cruz hill, lunch and free time to explore the town centre. Although you could just as easily rent a car to get to Holguín, the only way to visit the cigar factory is as part of an organized tour. $44CUC.

Santiago de Cuba A full day-trip to Cuba's second biggest city. The bus ride there and back takes you through some of the region's most scenic countryside, while Santiago itself is a handsome colonial city bursting with historical sites. The trip includes visits to the Santa Ifigenia cemetery, the Castillo el Morro and a cigar factory. $69CUC.

Accommodation

As a prime resort, Guardalavaca's **accommodation** consists of all-inclusive hotels at the top end of the price range, and while most deliver the standards you would expect for the price, a couple are slightly lacking. As the region has grown up with the tourist industry, there are no peso hotels nor any registered *casas particulares*, and although you might be able to find unregistered accommodation in the houses near the beach they are subject to frequent police checks and should be avoided. Playa Guardalavaca and Las Brisas, 1.5km to the east, are dominated by one resort complex apiece, each of which is replete with restaurants and luxury facilities, not to mention free watersports. Of the two, Playa Guardalavaca is the older and more worn around the edges. The hotels at Playa Esmeralda and Playa Pesquero are all decidedly fabulous and offer a full complement of facilities in a beautiful, if isolated, setting.

Playa Guardalavaca and Playa Las Brisas

Las Brisas ☏ 24/3-0218, ✉ reserva@brisas.gvc .cyt.cu, 🖳 www.brisasguardalavaca.com. The plusher of the two hotels, *Las Brisas* boasts four restaurants, two snack bars, a beauty salon, massage parlour, kids' camp and watersports, as well as mercifully restrained variety-show-style entertainment. There's a choice between rooms and suites within the hotel block or more privacy in newer bungalow-style rooms, although all are

equally luxurious (suites have hot tubs). Non-guests can wallow in luxury by buying a $25CUC day-pass which covers meals and use of facilities. **⑥**

Club Amigo Atlántico Guardalavaca ☏ 24/3-01-80, ✉ booking@clubamigo.gvc.cyt.cu. The *Atlántico* is a friendly and unpretentious resort that feels more Cuban than the others and attracts a varied clientele. It's a free-form complex (compiled from three previously independent hotels) with blocks of guestrooms, pools, bars and restaurants dotted around in a seemingly random layout and connected by meandering pathways. There's a variety of accommodation options catering for a range of needs and budgets but also varying in quality: the "Villa" section is easily the most appealing, with cool, airy houses painted in soothing pastels boasting balconies and simple but attractive furnishings; the "Tropical" and "Standard" areas offer plain but decent rooms – some with a sea view – strung along shadowy corridors, while the best-avoided "Bungalow" section seems stuck in a 1970s time warp. ❼

Playa Esmeralda

Paradisus Río de Oro ☎ 24/3-0090, ⓔ paradisus .ro@solmeliacuba.com. Undoubtedly one of the best in Cuba, this hotel is aimed at those seeking top-of-the-line Caribbean-style luxury. The accommodation blocks, attractive two-storey villas in muted yellow, orange and rose, are set amongst gorgeous gardens brimming with fragrant tropical plantlife, home to clouds of butterflies. The hotel boasts four excellent à la carte restaurants, including, unusually, a Japanese one serving a range of sushi delights, as well as an airy buffet restaurant where tiny, fearless birds will share your meal if you are not careful. There's a new spa with a sauna as well. ❾

Sol Club Río de Luna y Mares ☎ 24/3-0030 or 24/3-0060. This complex comprises two hotels that have been joined together to operate as one. The "Luna" section is more attractive and offers spacious, light accommodation in three-storey blocks arranged around a central pool, while the "Mares" section features well-appointed rooms grouped in a single block. Altogether there are two buffet restaurants, four à la carte restaurants and eight bars. Facilities include tennis, sauna and gym, as well as excursions into the surrounding countryside. ❾

Playa Pesquero and Playa Turquesa

Breezes Costa Verde ☎ 24/3-0520, ⓔ reservationsmanager@breezescostaverde.cu.

Popular with Canadian scuba enthusiasts, *Breezes* offers smart, if slightly sterile, rooms in small blocks painted cheerful yellow, orange and apple green. There's quite a sociable atmosphere, partially due to the range of entertainment, including outdoor Jacuzzis, pool tables, table football, ping pong and a disco. The beach is a few minutes' walk away over a wooden bridge spanning a mangrove lagoon populated by schools of shimmering fish and the long-legged wading birds that feed on them. Unusually, diving is included, although the number of free dives you can have depends on availability. ❾

Grand Playa Turquesa ☎ 24/3-0540, ⓔ jef_reservas@occidentaltuequesa.cu. The only hotel situated on the exquisite Playa Turquesa, *Grand Playa* features extensive gardens in which the original forest habitat has been preserved and indigenous tree species flourish. Attractions include elegant rooms, a range of restaurants, and circular swimming pools arranged in a descending series and fed by a cascade of water. ❾

Maritim ☎ 24/3-0510, ⓔ asistente.ventas.hog @maritim.co.cu. The hotel, with well-appointed rooms in high-rise blocks grouped around the reception area, feels more compact than its neighbours. All the well-appointed rooms, done in rather overwhelming primary colours, have views over the rather sparse gardens to the sea and all the usual facilities are on offer. ❾

Playa Pesquero ☎ 24/3-0530, ⓔ jefe.ventas @ppesquero.tur.cu. This huge complex offering the ultimate in get-away-from-it-all luxury is the biggest hotel in Cuba. With a large selection of restaurants, including one specializing in vegetarian fare, a vast swimming pool, its own mini shopping mall, sports facilities and activities for babies, children and teenagers, this is a good option for families. The cool, stylish rooms, furnished with natural materials, are set in two-storey blocks painted in white and pretty pastels; each has its own balcony with flower-filled window boxes and wicker furniture. ❾

Playa Guardalavaca and Playa Las Brisas

A 1500-metre-long stretch of sugar-white sand dappled with light streaming through abundant foliage, **Playa Guardalavaca** is simply a delight. A shady boulevard of palms, tamarind and sea grape trees runs along the centre of the beach, the branches strung with hammocks and T-shirts for sale. One of the most refreshing aspects of Playa Guardalavaca is that, unlike many resort beaches, it's open to Cubans as well as tourists, giving it a certain vitality with a marked lack of hustle. Groups of friends hang out chatting or resting in the shade while children play in the water. Those seeking solitude should head to the eastern end, where the beach breaks out of its leafy cover and is usually fairly deserted.

△ Playing volleyball on Playa Guardalavaca

Midway along, a **restaurant** serves simple snacks and drinks, and there are stands renting out **snorkelling equipment** ($8CUC for 3 hours) so you can explore the coral reef offshore.

A chain of large natural boulders divides the public beach from the relatively small **Playa Las Brisas**, which lies to the east of Playa Guardalavaca and fronts *Las Brisas*. Non-guests are not permitted to access the beach via the hotel unless they purchase a day-pass.

Playa Esmeralda

A five-kilometre trip from Guardalavaca west along the Holguín road, picture-perfect **Playa Esmeralda** – also known as Estero Ciego – boasts clear blue water, powdery sand speckled with thatched sunshades, and two luxury hotels hidden from view by thoughtfully planted bushes and shrubs. If you want unashamed hassle-free luxury where the intrusion of local culture is kept to a bare minimum, this is the place for you. The beach is owned by the hotels but open to non-guests, who have to pay for a day-pass (around $40CUC) that covers facilities, meals and drinks.

Opposite the *Sol Río de Luna y Mares* complex is the Rancho Naranjo **horseriding centre**, with negotiable rates for treks into the countryside depending on group size and excursion length. The hotel's **dive centre**, Delphis, on the beach near the *Luna* part of the complex, offers regular dives for $35CUC, night dives for $45CUC and courses for between $350CUC and $800CUC. Local marine attractions include parrotfish and barracuda as well as black coral.

Playa Pesquero and Playa Turquesa

Fifteen kilometres west of Playa Guardalavaca, this is the resort's most recent development with three state-of-the-art hotels on **Playa Pesquero** and one on the exquisite **Playa Turquesa**, 3km away. Playa Pesquero, lined with gnarled and twisted sea grape trees and thatch umbrellas providing much-needed shade, is a 1.2-kilometre-long horseshoe-shaped bay of sparkling sand. The quieter

Playa Turquesa (also known as Playa Yuraguanal) is one of the most beautiful in the region. The shallow bay, bordered by mangrove forest at its eastern boundary, boasts its own small coral reef a short swim offshore, while a strip of dense forest between *Grand Playa Turquesa* and the beach makes it feel like an undiscovered paradise.

The Blue World **diving centre** in front of the *Maritím* on Playa Pesquero offers dives for $45CUC and ACUC courses. Both beaches can be accessed from the road but those wishing to use any of the hotels' facilities will have to purchase day-passes (around $40CUC). There are no facilities outside the hotels.

Museo de Chorro de Maita and the Aldea Taína

The fascinating **Museo de Chorro de Maita** (daily 9am–5pm; $2CUC), 6km east of the Playa Guardalavaca hotel strip in a somewhat isolated spot in the Maniabon hills, is a must-see for anyone interested in pre-Columbian history. A shallow pit in the middle of the museum holds 108 Taíno skeletons (mostly original, some reproductions) buried on this site between the 1490s and the 1540s, and uncovered in 1986. You can walk around the viewing gallery above the pit and to inspect the skeletons, still folded into the traditional foetal position in which the Taíno buried their dead. Tests have revealed that all the deaths were natural, although, perplexingly, half the number are children.

The most interesting aspect of the burial pit is that one of the skeletons was found to be a young male European buried in a Christian position with his arms folded across his chest. While no records exist to support this theory, it's thought that the European had been living in harmony with the Taíno community, possibly as a friar, and other pieces of evidence on display, like the Spanish-designed ceramic fragments, also point to European contact. Interestingly, some of the later Taíno skeletons are also buried in a Christian manner, suggesting that the mystery European managed to convert at least some members of the community.

In cabinets around the walls of the museum are fragments of earthenware pots along with shell and ceramic jewellery, while arrows positioned in the grave indicate where these were found. The area around the museum has more indigenous remains than any other part of Cuba, with villagers still unearthing artefacts and remnants of jewellery today.

Aldea Taína

Just across the road from the Museo de Chorro de Maita is the **Aldea Taína** (daily 9am–5pm; $3CUC), an excellent and evocative reconstruction of a Taíno village, offering valuable insight into an extinguished culture and bringing to life many of the artefacts seen in museums around the country. The painstakingly authentic little settlement features houses made from royal palm trees populated by life-sized models of Taínos posed cooking and preparing food or attending to community rituals. Of particular note is the group inside one of the houses watching the medicine man attempt to cure a patient, and another group outside depicted in a ceremonial dance. Details like the colourful *eanáhuas* skirts that each woman began to wear after her first menstruation have been carefully reproduced, with lifelike model dogs – the Taínos trained them never to bark – further adding to the atmosphere.

The village's **restaurant**, decorated with designs found on the wall of Taíno caves, continues the theme, serving Taíno foods including herb teas, sweet potato and cassava bread. The recommended dish is the *ajiaco*, a tasty potato, maize and meat stew.

Acuario Cayo Naranjo

The only real reason to take a boat out to the Bahía de Naranjo, 6km west of Guardalavaca beach, is the **Acuario Cayo Naranjo** (daily 7am–4pm, marine show noon–1pm; ℡ 24/3-0132), a complex built on stilts in the shallows of the bay about 250m offshore. Although calling itself an aquarium, it's really more of a tourist centre cum marine zoo, its smattering of sea creatures in tanks overshadowed by giddier attractions: yacht and speedboat "seafari" excursions around the bay, a saccharine sea-lion show and, most thrillingly, the chance to swim with a few frisky dolphins. Though undoubtedly more commercial than educational, it's a pleasant enough day out, and there's also a good restaurant on site dishing up lobster dinners while hosting an interesting but rather incongruous Afro-Cuban dance and music show.

The aquarium has a range of offers, of which the cheapest and most basic covers boat passage, entrance fee and dolphin and sea-lion show ($40CUC). It costs $50CUC extra to swim with the dolphins. All local hotels offer these deals and can arrange transport.

Eating, drinking and nightlife

As most visitors here are staying in an all-inclusive, you'll probably **eat** most of your meals in your hotel. Most have buffet-style restaurants and while the standard is better than those experienced outside the resort, the emphasis is generally on quantity rather than quality. Should you tire of your hotel, there are a few places to turn to; *paladares* are not permitted in the area so all restaurants are state-owned. The top choice is *Pizza Nova* near the *Atlántico* complex, which serves very good thin-crust pizzas. For seafood try *El Ancla*, opposite the complex, and for tasty lobster check out *El Cayuelo*, a short walk east along the beach from *Las Brisas*.

Similarly, **bars** and **nightlife** options are largely confined to the hotels where entertainment teams host nightly stage shows in which they urge guests to take part in boisterous slapstick sketches and dances. To escape ignominy, head for lively *Disco Club La Roca* (nightly 9.30pm–3am; $1CUC) on the beachfront five minutes' walk west of the main strip.

Banes

There are two reasons to stop off at the sleepy town of **BANES**, a mix of characterful wooden houses and rather more anonymous concrete ones, 31km east of Guardalavaca. The first is to gawp at the **Iglesia de Nuestra Señora de la Caridad**, on the edge of a central park with a neat domed bandstand. This is where, on October 10, 1948, **Fidel Castro** married his first wife, Mirta Diaz-Balart, sister of a university friend and daughter of the mayor of Banes. The couple divorced in 1954, the bride's conservative family allegedly disapproving of the young Castro, already known as a firebrand at the university. Although the church is fairly prosaic in itself, it's mildly interesting for the historical connection.

The second, rather more substantial, attraction is the **Museo Indocubano**, on Avenida General Marreo no.305 (Tues–Sat 9am–5pm, Sun 8am–noon, 2–5pm & 7–9pm; $1CUC, $2CUC includes a guided tour in Spanish or English), one of only two museums in Cuba exclusively devoted to pre-Columbian Cuban history; the other is located in Baracoa (see p.486). Whilst many of the fragments of ceramic pots and utensils and the representational sketches of indigenous communities are similar to exhibits in larger museums in the country, there is a unique and absorbing gathering of jewellery gleaned from the Holguín region, its centrepiece a tiny but stunning gold idol.

If you have time, take a look at the **Casa de la Cultura** on the opposite side of General Marreo, at no.327 (daily 9am–5pm). With a black-and-white marble tiled floor, pale pink and gold walls and a sunny courtyard at the back, this elegant building is one of Banes's most outstanding. As the town's theatre and music hall it has regular performances of traditional music and dance, and players are generally unfazed if you pass by to admire the building and catch snippets of their rehearsals during the daytime.

Practicalities

You can see Banes in a couple of hours at most, but should you decide to **stay**, the best option is the friendly *Casa Las Delicias* at Augusto Blanca no.1107 e/ Bruno Meriño y Bayamo (℡24/8-3718; ❷), which offers a spotless room with its own bathroom and air conditioning. Other good options include the *Casa de Jose Alberto Peréz Vicente*, Calle H no.103 e/ Coco y Victoria (no phone; ❷), a down-to-earth, no-frills *casa particular*, or *Casa de Odalis Pérez Bacallao*, Calle H no.77 e/ Avenida de Cardenas y Pizonero (℡24/8-3243; ❷) a clean and simple wooden house with basic facilities. Unfortunately, there is only one place **to eat** in town; *Caféteria Vicaria* at General Marreo 730 dishes up indifferent pizzas, spaghettis and the ubiquitous fried chicken 24 hours a day. *Las 400 Rosas* is a popular **bar** next to the museum on General Marreo serving drinks under a small marquee.

Eastern Holguín

In the east, Holguín province becomes at once astonishingly beautiful and increasingly industrial, with several opencast nickel mines and their processing plants scarring the hillsides. Cuba is one of the world's largest producers of nickel, all of it mined in this region.

Among the most significant features for visitors is **Cayo Saetía**, a magnificent island near the crescent-shaped **Bahía de Nipe**, the largest bay in the country. Once the exclusive reserve of state officials, it is now a holiday resort combining a safari park of imported wildlife with a fabulous white-sand beach and excellent diving. Its beauty, oddly, is not diminished by the pale orange smog drifting across the bay from grimy **Nicaro**, a distinctly uneventful town wreathed in plumes of factory smoke. South of here, the ground swells and erupts into livid green mountains, with the peaceful **Pinares de Mayarí** a perfect base for exploring the waterfalls, lakes and ancient caves hidden throughout this clear, cool highland region.

Much of the lowland countryside ripples with sugar cane, and there's a particularly notable plantation near **Biran**, which is less famous for its produce than for being Castro's birthplace – an interesting diversion for the obsessive. The far eastern corner of the province ends in the small manufacturing town of **Moa**, a useful jumping-off point for Baracoa in Guantánamo province.

Cayo Saetía

Hidden away on the east side of the Bahía de Nipe near the village of Felton, and connected to the mainland by a narrow strip of land, picture-postcard, isolated **Cayo Saetía** is the most bizarre – and exclusive – resort in the country. A one-time private game reserve and paradisiacal beach catering to government party officials, it opened to the public during the 1990s, yet still retains its air of exclusivity and is only open to guests of the hotel. It's run by Gaviota, the army-owned tourist group, which may explain the vaguely military aura, present in the ranks of Soviet helicopters waiting to ferry guests to and from the resort.

The perfect place to escape from the outside world, Cayo Saetía has two quite distinct faces. On the one hand are the scoops of practically deserted soft white **beach** along its northern coast, hemmed in by buttery yellow rockface and sliding into the bay's sparkling turquoise waters. Close to shore, the island's shelf makes for perfect **snorkelling**, with a wealth of brightly coloured sea life to explore, while further out to sea a coral reef offers good rather than spectacular **diving** possibilities.

Inland, Cayo Saetía's 42 square kilometres of woodland and meadows are home to the most exotic collection of animals in the country – a menagerie of imported zebras and antelopes, deer, wild boars and even ostriches, all freely galloping about. It's as close as Cuba gets to a **safari park** and guests are presented – totally without irony – with the choice of taking a jeep safari through the lush grounds, to admire and photograph the creatures, or blasting the hell out of them with rented rifles.

Practicalities

Most guests arrive at Cayo Saetía by **helicopter** from Nicaro airport (call Gaviota in Havana ☎7/203-0686), rather than chancing the ten-kilometre-long bumpy dirt track from the mainland. There's no way to visit without staying, and you're better off checking availability rather than turning up on spec as **accommodation** is limited to a central lodge house with nine comfortable double cabins and three suites (☎24/9-6900; ❸), catered to by a **restaurant** well stocked with exotic meats like antelope. You are not encour-aged to roam about on your own – in case someone takes a pot shot at you. Instead, there are **jeep safari tours** ($9CUC) to take you through the grounds, and the lodge house also provides transport ($4CUC) to the beach, 8km away. The hotel also offers reasonably priced horse riding, snorkelling expeditions and day-trips around the cay by speedboat.

The Pinares de Mayarí

High in the mountains of the Sierra de Nipe, 45km south of Cayo Saetía, the isolated and beautiful **Pinares de Mayarí** pine forest, surrounding the *Villa Pinares de Mayarí*, is a great place to trek through or just chill out in. The forest is reached from the nondescript little town of **Mayarí**, 26km to the north. From Mayarí, head south towards the Carretera Pinares and take the right-hand track where the road forks, past tiny Las Coloradas. Be aware that the road, though passable in a rental car, is both steep and poorly maintained so requires masterful driving. The route affords crisp views over the Bahía de Nipe and the terracotta opencast nickel mines to the east, near Nicaro. This lofty region is also Cuba's main producer of **coffee**, with stretches of coffee plants visible along the way.

On your drive up the hill, look out for a turning on the left that leads to **La Planca**, a scenic little flower garden (24 hours; free) with a bench overlooking the placid La Prescita lake. At the top of the hill the sharp incline evens out into a plateau, where the lush green grass, low hills and cool air form a scene that's more alpine than Caribbean. Perched up here is the alpine-themed *Villa Pinares de Mayarí* (☎24/5-3308; ❸). Comprising two chalet-style villas with quaint rooms richly inlaid with wood, the **hotel** makes a perfect base for exploring the nearby wilds and is decidedly picturesque in itself, with a small pool and a central dining room boasting a beamed ceiling, like some giant's cabin. The friendly staff are extremely accommodating, but nevertheless call ahead to make sure the hotel is open as it sometimes closes in slow periods.

Near the hotel is the wide and tranquil **La Presa lake**, though there's more exhilarating swimming to be had at the foot of the majestic **Saltón de Guayabo waterfall,** a definite must-see if you are in the area. If you drive for about ten minutes back down the hill towards Mayarí, a steep and narrow dirt track on the left will get you to a viewpoint (daily 8am–4pm; $3CUC), which provides a splendid vista over a mountainside coated with a thick mist of shaggy pine trees parted by two turbulent cascades, which collectively comprise the Saltón de Guayabo, thundering down to a pool below. At 104m, the larger of the two is the highest waterfall in Cuba. Guided treks along the nature trail to the foot of the falls can also be arranged here at the viewpoint and last 1–2 hours ($5CUC).

Also within comfortable reach of the hotel are the intriguing **Farallones de Seboruco caves**, tucked away through a tangle of countryside roughly 2km to the west, with faint but still perceptible traces of pre-Columbian line sketches on the walls – bring a torch. The wide-mouthed caves, overhung by gnarled cliffs and spattered with delicately ringed snails' shells, have an aura of mystery which is helped along by rumours that this deserted spot is the site of illegal cow killings by black-market profiteers – many locals refuse to come here even after dark. Given the nickname "the sacred cow", all cattle in Cuba come under state jurisdiction and their private slaughter is strictly prohibited, part of the government drive to maximize milk yields in the face of shortages and to control profit from the sale of beef and dairy products. In remote areas such as this, the sight of discarded cow horns with tattered meat still clinging to the edges gives this illegal activity a grisly reality.

Biran and the Finca Las Manacas

The whole swathe of land southwest from Bahía de Nipe and west of the Pinares de Mayarí – a vast area of swaying cane and working plantations – is given over to sugar. There's nothing here for the casual visitor, though true Castro devotees may wish to make a pilgrimage to the tiny community of **BIRAN**, 44km southwest of Mayarí, near which, at the **Finca Las Manacas** plantation, **Fidel Castro** was born on August 13, 1926. He spent part of his youth here, until sent to school in Santiago, and he still owns the farm and visits regularly. The tidy and well-maintained farm has recently been opened as the **Sitio Historico de Birán museum** (Tues–Sat 9am–noon & 1.30–4pm, Sun 9am–noon; $10CUC, $20CUC with camera $40CUC with camcorder), where you'll find a collection of photographs, clothes and Fidel's childhood bed. Near the entrance are the well-tended graves of Fidel's father Angel Castro and mother Lina Ruz. It's a challenge to find the place: from Holguín follow the road to Mayarí then turn west onto the road to Marcané; take a left at the sign to Biran and carry on.

Moa

On the northern coast, close to the border with Guantánamo province and dominated by the nickel-smelting plant on the east side of town, is desolate, industrial **MOA**. The town is bereft of attractions but is a handy jumping-off point for Baracoa in Guantánamo province, accessible from here by the coastal road. It's small wonder that there are **no buses** on this route as this is one of the worst roads in the whole of the country: potholes 2m wide on steep roads will push your driving skills to their utmost limit. Moa also has an airport with a weekly flight to and from Havana (tickets are sold at the Cubana office on Avenida del Puerto Rolo Monterrey; ☏24/6-6889). A morning **bus** to Holguín leaves from the Terminal de Omnibus, near the town centre, which is also served by *colectivo* shared taxis. In the unlikely event that you'll want to **stay**, head for the *Miraflores* hotel, on Avenida Amistad on the hilltop west of the city (☏24/6-6103; ❹), which is also the best place in town for **food**.

Guantánamo

Synonymous with the beleaguered history of the US naval base, **Guantánamo** province is an enduring legacy of the struggle between the US and Cuba. In name at least, it's one of the best-known places in Cuba: many a Cuban and a fair few visitors can sing the first bars of the immortal song *Guantanamera* – written by Joseito Fernández in the 1940s as a tribute to the women of Guantánamo. Made internationally famous by North American folk singer Pete Seeger during the 1970s, it has become something of a Cuban anthem and a firm – if somewhat hackneyed – favourite of tourist-bar troubadours the country over, a fitting fate for the song which includes words from José Martí's most famous work, *Versos Sencillos*.

For many visitors, the **base** is the main reason to come to Cuba's easternmost province, and it's undeniably a fascinating piece of the Cuban-American relations jigsaw, although you cannot actually enter – and can barely see it – from Cuban territory. But the province of Guantánamo has a lot more to offer than its most notorious attraction, with a sweeping, deeply varied landscape of desert and thick rainforest and a uniquely mixed population. Many Cubans living in this region are of Haitian and Jamaican origin – the result of late nineteenth- and early twentieth-century immigration – while an indigenous heritage is still visible in the far east.

The provincial capital, small and quiet **Guantánamo**, is a very ordinary place, but it makes a useful starting point for excursions into the fine surrounding countryside, as well as to **Mirador Malones** and **Caimanera**, from where you get a long-distance view of the naval base. The province's real charms lie to the east, where splendidly isolated **Baracoa**, one of the most enchanting towns in the country, clings to the north coast by the last tip of the island as it trails off into the mixed waters of the Atlantic Ocean and the Caribbean Sea.

Guantánamo town and around

Even though the town of **GUANTÁNAMO** is only on the tourist map because of its proximity to the US Guantánamo naval station, 22km southeast, the base plays a very small part in the everyday life of the town itself. For the most part, this is a slow-paced provincial capital marked by a few ornate

The US naval base at Guantánamo

Described by Fidel Castro as the dagger in the side of Cuban sovereignty, the **US naval base at Guantánamo** is approximately 118 square kilometres of North American territory planted on the southeast coast of Cuban soil. Seemingly ever poised for attack, with more than 3000 permanent military personnel, two airstrips and anchorage for 42 ships (enough for an entire war fleet, as Cubans often point out), it seems ludicrously over-equipped for its official functions as a refuelling stop and marine training base.

The history of the naval base dates back to Cuba's nominal victory in the Wars of Independence with Spain, whereupon the US government immediately began to erode Cuba's autonomy. Under the terms of the **1901 Platt Amendment**, the US ordered Cuba to sell or lease land necessary for a naval station, declaring without irony that it was "to enable the United States to maintain the independence of Cuba". Its primary aim, however, was to protect the nascent Panama Canal from any naval attacks. An annual rent was set at 2000 gold coins (which today works out at US$4085, or less than a cent per square metre of land) and the base was born. In 1934 the Treaty of Reciprocity, born of the Good Neighbour Policy, repealed the Platt Amendment but did not alter the conditions surrounding the leasing of the base. As it is stipulated that the lease cannot be terminated without the consent of both parties, it seems unlikely that Cuba will regain sovereignty of the land under its present regime. Famously, Fidel Castro has not cashed a single rent cheque from the US government, preferring to preserve them for posterity in a locked desk drawer.

Although the US quickly broke off all relations with the Cuban government after the Revolution, they were less speedy to give up their territory. Communications soon broke down between base and host country, and acts of provocation ensued on both sides. The whole area bristles with animosity, with the base now surrounded by a dense minefield and rimmed with sentry posts brandishing the

buildings, attractive but largely featureless streets and an easy-going populace. Most visitors bypass it altogether, and those who don't tend to use it simply as a stepping stone to the naval base and attractions further afield.

The small town fans out around the central **Parque Martí**, a small concrete square neatly bordered by intricately trimmed evergreens with hooped gateways. On its north side is the **Parroquía Santa Catalina de Riccis**, a pretty ochre church built in 1863. Running parallel to the park is Pedro A. Pérez, where the town's most beautiful building towers over the road. Constructed between 1918 and 1920, though looking older than its years, the **Palacio de Salcines**, once home to local architect Leticio Salcines, is an eclectic neo-Rococo building with shuttered windows, cherubs over the door and, on its high spire, an outstretched figure with bugle in hand which has become the symbol of the city. It now houses the small **Museo de Artes Decorativas** (Tues–Thurs 8.30am–noon & 2.30–5.30pm, Fri 8.30am–noon & 5–9pm, Sat 5–9pm; $1CUC), with a sparse collection of antique furniture and a downstairs **art gallery** (Mon–Fri 9am–7pm, Sat 5–7pm) displaying work by local artists. A rickety spiral staircase leads to the cupola at the base of the statue, from which there are sweeping views over the city to the hills beyond.

One block behind the park, at Martí no.804, is the humble **Museo Provincial** (Mon 2–6pm, Tues–Sat 8am–noon & 2–6pm; $1CUC). Built on an old prison site, it displays the remains of some fearsome padlocks and bolts, though more interesting are the photos of US antics at the naval base, including one of a

Cuban star-and-stripes flag, an atmosphere that prompted one writer to describe the perimeter as "the cactus curtain".

Known as **"Gitmo"** by US servicemen, Guantánamo base is like an American theme park inside, with stateside cars zooming along perfectly paved roads bordered by shops and suburban houses. There are softball and soccer fields, a drive-in movie theatre, even a *McDonald's*, all imported to cater for the 7000 or so personnel and their attendant families. From the 1970s until the mid-1990s, such material riches gave the base an El Dorado lustre that lured many a dissident Cuban to brave the heavily mined perimeter or chance the choppy surrounding waters to reach this ersatz chunk of North America in the hope of gaining US citizenship as a political asylum seeker.

The base's history took another twist in December 2001 with the US decision to detain Islamic militants captured as part of the "War on Terror". Prisoners were initially kept in the makeshift Camp X-Ray but were transferred to a larger, permanent site, **Camp Delta**, in April 2002. Over 600 people, representing 40 different nationalities, have been held there without charge or access to any court, legal counsel or family visits. Since then, images of orange-jumpsuited, shackled detainees, along with reports of numerous suicide attempts and persistent allegations of abuse from the few prisoners to have been released, have provoked international condemnation. The US government was able to avoid clarification of the inmates' legal status because they are foreign nationals held outside US sovereign territory – the "legal equivalent of outer space" according to one US government official. However, a June 2004 decision by the US Supreme Court ruled that the detainees should come under the jurisdiction of US courts and that the policy of holding prisoners indefinitely without the right to judicial review was unlawful.

The base cannot be visited from within Cuba, but two **viewpoints** have been created as popular tourist attractions, from which visitors can content themselves with whatever they can glimpse through binoculars.

delinquent marine baring his bottom at the Cuban guards. Finally, one of the most intriguing buildings in town is the quite fantastical **agricultural marketplace**, at Los Maceos esq. Prado a couple of blocks northeast from the park, with its big pink dome and crown-like roof bearing statues of regal long-necked geese at each corner. By morning the market is a scene of intense activity, with housewives scrutinizing the piles of fresh fruit and vegetables, farmers hawking their wares and scavenging dogs slinking underfoot.

Practicalities

Buses from Santiago, Bayamo, Havana and Holguín arrive at the Astro Terminal de Omnibus, Carretera Santiago (☎21/32-5588), 2.5km out of town, from where you can walk or catch a *bicitaxi* into the centre. Daily trains from Santiago, Havana and Las Tunas pull in at the central **train station**, housed in a squat Art Deco folly on Pedro A. Pérez.

Accommodation is limited to one hotel, the *Guantánamo* at Ahogados esq. 13 Norte, Reparto Caribe (☎21/38-1015; ❸), a hulking, fading monolith 5km north from town, and a number of decent *casas particulares* clustered near the centre. *Casa de Lissett Foster Lara*, Pedro A. Pérez 761 altos e/ Jesús del Sol y Prado (☎21/32-5970; ❷), offers two clean and comfortable double rooms with air conditioning and private bathrooms in a large, airy, modern apartment with a roof terrace. Two other good *casas particulares* are the friendly *Casa de Elsy Castillo Osoria*, Calixto García no.766 e/ Prado y Jesús del Sol (☎21/32-3787; ❶) which boasts a sunny courtyard, and, nearby, the welcoming and attractive

Casa de Campos y Tatika, Calixto Garcia, no.718 e/ Jesús del Sol y N López (no phone; ①).

There are several **restaurants** in the centre, though only a few have a decent selection of food. The best option is the vegetarian restaurant on Pedro A. Pérez esq. Colombe, where inventive and tasty dishes include okra and vegetable stew, with sides of *malanga,* green beans and rice. *La Cubanita,* a *paladar* on Martí esq. Crombet serves enormous portions of pork, chicken or shrimp with rice, beans, salad and fried bananas for around $6–7CUC, while the *Guantánamo* hotel restaurant, *Guaso,* boasts a more interesting menu than most, with a house speciality of chicken "Gordon Blue" – stuffed with ham. The tastiest food in town, including fritters, milkshakes and hot rolls, comes from the street stands clustered at the south end of Pedro A. Pérez, while *Coppelia,* at Pedro A. Pérez esq. Varona, sells bargain bowls of ice cream for a couple of pesos.

Around Guantánamo

Many visitors come to see the US base (see box, p.478) – although you can get to the two lookout points, **Mirador Malones** and **Caimanera**, with a little groundwork, there really isn't a lot to see, as you cannot enter the base itself. Venturing into the **countryside** is more rewarding, with bizarre contrasts between lush valleys and the weird desert scenery of sun-bleached barren trees. Just north of town is the offbeat **Zoológico de Piedras**, a "zoo" entirely populated by sculpted stone animals.

Mirador Malones

The more accessible of the two naval-base lookouts, **Mirador Malones**, 38km from town on the east of the bay near Boquerón, also affords the (relatively) better view. At the top of a steep hill of dusty cacti and grey scrubs, a purpose-built platform is equipped with a restaurant and high-powered binoculars. The view of the base, some 6km away, is rather indistinct, but you can make out a few buildings and see the odd car whizzing past. It's quite a distance to come for the dubious pleasure of the not-so-great view. The real wonder here is the view of the whole bay area, with its dramatically barren countryside, luminous sea and unforgiving desert mottled with hovering vultures. You can arrange authorization for the trip here through the *Guantánamo* hotel (see p.479; $5CUC per person, plus roughly $30CUC for an unmetered taxi, plus $10CUC if you choose to take a guide), or *Villa Santiago* in Santiago (℡22/64-1598).

Caimanera

Bordered by salt flats that score the ground with deep cracks and lend a haunting wildness, **CAIMANERA**, 23km south of Guantánamo, takes its name from the giant caiman lizards that used to roam here, although today it's far more notable as the closest point in Cuba to the US naval base. The village is a restricted area, with the ground between it and the base one of the most heavily mined areas in the world, although this hasn't stopped many Cubans from braving it in the slim hope of reaching foreign soil and escaping to America. The village is entered via a checkpoint at which guards scrutinize your passport before waving you through.

The **lookout** is in the grounds of the *Caimanera* (℡21/9-1414; ③), the village's only **hotel** and **restaurant**, which has a view over the bay and mountains to the base – though even with binoculars you only see a sliver of it. At the time of writing, only groups of seven or more people were being admitted, both as guests of the hotel or visitors to the viewpoint, but this may change in the future. A taxi from town costs $25CUC, and you will need a guide, which you can arrange through the *Guantánamo* hotel (see p.479). On the seafront is a small museum ($1CUC), with a history of the base and yet more photos of US marines mooning at cameras and waving their weapons at Cuban soldiers.

Prior to the Revolution the town was the site of carousing between the naval-base officers and the townswomen, its main streets were lined with bars, and rampant prostitution, gambling and drugs were the order of the day. Little evidence of that remains today, however, with modern Caimanera a sleepy and parochial town.

Zoológico de Piedras

Roughly 20km north of Guantánamo, in the foothills of the Sierra Cristal, is an altogether more whimsical attraction. Set in a private coffee farm, the slightly surreal sculpture park known as the **Zoológico de Piedras** (daily 9am–6pm; $1CUC) was created in 1977 by local artist Angel Iñigo Blanco, who carved the stone in situ. Cool and fresh, dotted with lime and breadfruit trees, hanging vines and coffee plants, the park centres on a path that weaves around the mountainside, with stone animals peeking out from the undergrowth at every turn. Slightly cartoonish in form, the creatures bear little relationship to their real-life counterparts: a giant tortoise towers over a hippo the size of a modest guinea pig. You can wander round on your own or take a guided tour with the sculptor's father. Needless to say, it's a hit with children. Before you leave, venture up the path on the right-hand side of the car park for a superb view over the lopsided farmland of Guantánamo.

Baracoa

In the eyes of many visitors, **BARACOA** is quite simply the most beautiful place in Cuba. Set on the coast on Cuba's southeast tip and protected by a deep curve of mountains, its isolation has so far managed to protect it from some of the more pernicious effects of tourism which have crept into other areas of the island. Self-contained and secluded, the tiny town vibrates with an energy that is surprising for such a small place.

Baracoa was the first town to be established in Cuba, founded by Diego de Velázquez in 1511 on a spot christened Porto Santo in 1492 by Christopher Columbus who, as legend has it, planted a cross in the soil. The early conquistadors never quite succeeded in exterminating the indigenous population, and today Baracoa is the only place in Cuba where direct descendants of the Taíno can still be found. Their legacy is also present in several myths and legends habitually told to visitors.

Surrounded by awe-inspiring countryside – whose abundance of cacao trees makes it the nation's leading **chocolate** manufacturer, with local brand Peter's widely available – Baracoa has become an absolute must on the traveller's circuit. Although many will be happy enough to wander through town, enjoying its easy charm, there are also several tangible attractions including an excellent **archeological museum** with one of Cuba's best collections of pre-Columbian artefacts. Another of Baracoa's notable exhibits is **La Cruz de la Parra**, the celebrated cross reputed to have been erected by Christopher Columbus himself. It is housed in the picturesque **Catedral de Nuestra**

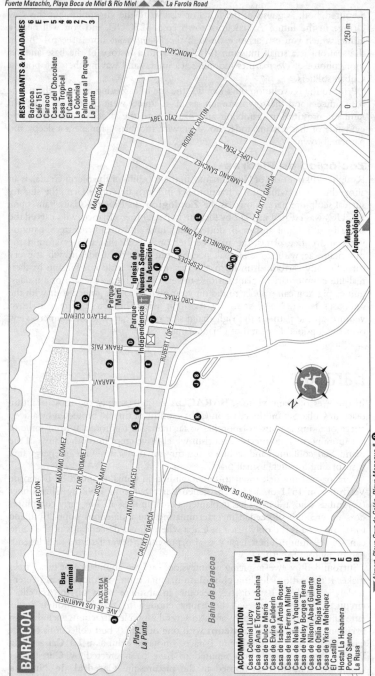

Fuerte Matachín, Playa Boca de Miel & Río Miel ▲▲ ▲ La Farola Road

BARACOA

RESTAURANTS & PALADARES

Baracoa	6
Café 1511	1
Caracol	5
Casa del Chocolate	4
Casa Tropical	8
El Castillo	2
La Colonial	7
Palmares al Parque	3
La Punta	

ACCOMMODATION

Casa Colonial Lucy	H
Casa de Ana E Torres Lobaina	M
Casa de Dulce María	A
Casa de Elvira Calderín	D
Casa de Isabel Artola Rosell	I
Casa de Ilsa Ferran Milhet	N
Casa de Nelia y Yaquelin	K
Casa de Nelsy Borges Teran	F
Casa de Nilson Abad Guilarte	C
Casa de Otilia Rojas Montero	L
Casa de Ykira Mahiquez	G
El Castillo	J
Hostal La Habanera	E
Porto Santo	O
La Rusa	B

Iglesia de Nuestra Señora de la Asunción

Parque Martí

Parque Independencia

Museo Arqueológico

Bus Terminal

Plaza de la Revolución

Bahía de Baracoa

Playa La Punta

▶ Airport, Playa Cruz de Colón, Playa Managua & ○

0   250 m

Señora de la Asunción, on the edge of leafy **Parque Independencia**, a local gathering point.

On the east side of town you'll find the **Fuerte Matachín**, one of a trio of forts built to protect colonial Baracoa, and now the site of the town **museum**. Further east is the town's main beach, **Playa Boca de Miel**, a lively summer-time hangout shingled in jade, grey and deep crimson stones. Converted from the second of the town's fortifications, which overlook the town from the northern hills, the **Hotel El Castillo** is a beautiful and peaceful retreat, and an appealing place for a refreshing cocktail. On the western side of town, the third fort, **Fuerte La Punta**, is now a restaurant and overlooks the smaller of the two town beaches, **Playa La Punta** – the better bet for solitude seekers.

Arrival, information and transport

Although Baracoa is perhaps one of the most trying places to reach in all of Cuba, with only two routes into the town, you shouldn't let this put you off. If you're coming from Santiago by **bus**, it's definitely worth making advance bookings – the same goes for your departure – as the Víazul bus to Santiago via Guantánamo theoretically runs once a day from Baracoa, but the service is often disrupted. If you don't book in advance you could find yourself, especially in high season, queuing early in the morning for a first-come-first-served distribution of remaining spaces and may end up waiting several days to leave.

Driving is an infinitely preferable manner of arrival, since half the fun of a visit to Baracoa is getting there. Before the Revolution, the town was actually only accessible by sea, but the opening of the **La Farola** road through the mountains changed all that by providing a direct link with Guantánamo 120km away, and a flood of cars poured into the previously little-visited town. Considered one of the triumphs of the Revolution, the road was actually started by Batista's regime but temporarily abandoned when he refused to pay a fair wage to the workers, and work was only resumed in the 1960s. Today, La Farola makes for an amazing trip through the knife-sharp peaks of the Cuchillas de Baracoa mountains.

A second but less preferable route is the **coastal road** from Moa which, although beautiful, makes for treacherous driving even in good conditions and becomes impassable in places in the rainy season. Either route should only be attempted in daylight as the steep banks bordering the road in places, combined with a cracked and broken road surface, make it extremely dangerous in the dark.

The **airport**, Aeropuerto Gustavo Rizo (☎64/5375), is near the *Porto Santo* hotel, on the west side of the bay 4km from the centre. With two weekly flights to Havana, flying is a direct route out of Baracoa, should you choose to brave the Cuban airlines; taxis wait to take you into town for $2–3CUC. **Buses** pull up at the Astro bus terminal (☎64/3880), west on the Malecón; it's a short walk down Maceo to the centre, or you can take a *bicitaxi* for ten pesos. The private peso trucks that arrive from over the mountains via La Farola drop off on Maceo.

There's no official **information** bureau in town, but the staff at both the Rumbos office in *Hostal la Habanera* (☎64/5155), and the Cubatur office at Martí no.181 (☎64/5306), are extremely helpful and can book bus and plane tickets.

The best way to **get around** Baracoa is on foot, as most of the places you'll want to see are within easy reach of the centre. If travelling further afield, you can catch a *bicitaxi* or unmetered taxi from outside the tobacco factory at Calle

Martí no.214 or rent a moped from the stand at *El Castillo*. There's little point relying on public transport – buses are scarce and always jam-packed.

Accommodation

In *El Castillo* and *La Habanera*, Baracoa has two of the most characterful **hotels** on the island, though the sheer volume of visitors means that these and the two other hotels are often full at peak times. Until new hotels are built – there are longstanding plans for two on Maguana beach – the taxes on private accommodation remain low, and you'll find a number of superb **casas particulares**, all within a few streets of one another.

Further afield, there are a couple of possible **campismo** options for those wanting to explore the surrounding rainforests and countryside; *Campismo El Yunque* at the foot of El Yunque and *Campismo Bahía de Taco*, 40km northwest of Baracoa on the road to Moa near the the Alejandro de Humboldt National Park (see box, p.489). Both are often closed to foreign visitors, but if you want to stay it is worth enquiring at the *campismo* office at Baracoa on Martí no.225 (☎64/2776).

Hotels

El Castillo Calixto García ☎64/5165. Perched high on a hill overlooking the town, this former military post, one of a trio of forts built to protect Baracoa, was built between 1739 and 1742 and is now an intimate, comfortable and very welcoming hotel. Glossy tiles and wood finishes give the rooms a unique charm, while the handsome pool patio ($2CUC for non-guests) is the best place in town to sip *mojitos*. Very popular and often fully booked, making reservations essential. ❺

Hostal La Habanera Maceo 68 esq. Frank País ☎64/5273 and 5274. Baracoa's newest hotel, with its pretty pink exterior and airy reception filled with comfy sofas, is a treat. The 10 rooms, arranged around a courtyard, are clean and comfortable with TV, a/c and private bathrooms. ❹

Maguana Playa Maguana (no tel). The only beach accommodation in the area, with four comfortable double rooms and plenty of privacy; make reservations through *Porto Santo*. ❻

Porto Santo Carretera Aeroporto ☎64/5106. Set on diminutive Cruz de Colón beach, where Columbus is said to have planted the first cross in Cuba, this old-style hotel on the outskirts of town is convenient for the airport but not much else. The rooms are well maintained but dark, and there's a bijou swimming pool with views over the bay. ❻

La Rusa Máximo Gómez no.161 ☎64/3011. Named after its much-esteemed Russian former owner, Magdelana Robiskiai, who settled in Baracoa before the Revolution, small and squat *La Rusa* sits on the Malecón. The charming rooms are modest but cosy and complemented by a friendly atmosphere. ❸

Casas particulares

Casa Colonial Lucy Céspedes 29 e/ Maceo y Rubert López ☎664/3548. Two spacious, comfortable rooms with a/c, fridges and private bathroom, one with two double beds and one with a double and a single. The attractive house and its friendly owner (who offers excellent meals) make this an top choice. ❷

Casa de Ana E Torres Lobaina Calixto García no.162 ☎64/2754. One clean, comfortable a/c room in a colonial house with a pretty front porch. The friendly owners also provide meals. ❷

Casa de Dulce Maria Máximo Gómez no.140 e/ Pelayo Cuervo y Ciro Frías ☎64/2214. A characterful little room with one double bed and one single, as well as a private bathroom and a kitchen with fridge. Good for a longer stay. ❷

Casa de Elvira Calderin Frank País no.19 e/ Martí y Maceo ☎64/3580. This ample, central property has two pleasant, airy rooms, both with a/c and private bathroom, and a courtyard out back. Meals are available. ❷

Casa de Ilsa Ferran Milhet Calixto García no.64 e/ Céspedes y Coroneles Galano ☎64/2754. One spacious a/c rooftop room with twin beds, accessed by a rickety spiral staircase, with its own sun patio and a small verdant garden, furnished with deckchairs and a thatched umbrella. The sister house of that owned by Ana E Torres Lobaina, above. ❷

Casa de Isabel Artola Rosell Rubert López no.39 e/ Ciro Frías y Céspedes ☎64/5236, ✉olambert @infomed.sld.cu. A very hospitable, pretty little house with two rooms, near the town centre. One bedroom has twin beds, making it a good choice for friends sharing. The owners also provide meals and a laundry service. ❷

Casa de Nelia y Yaquelin Mariana Grajales no.11 altos e/ Calixto García y Julio Mella ☏6/2412. Two smallish a/c rooms in a friendly house. Although this house is a short walk from the centre, the standard is fine and makes a good standby when others closer to the centre are fully booked. ❷

Casa de Nelsy Borges Teran Maceo no.171 e/ Ciro Frías y Céspedes ☏6/3569. Two ample a/c rooms, with the exclusive use of the top floor, which has a beautiful terrace overlooking the sea and mountains. ❷

Casa de Nilson Abad Guilarte Flor Crombet no.143 e/ Ciro Frías y Pelayo Cuervo ☏64/3123 Fantastic, spacious apartment close to the centre of town, with two beds (one double, one single) and its own kitchen. The sun-trap roof terrace, where the amicable owners serve up gourmet versions of traditional Baracoan meals, makes this one of the best houses in town. ❷

Casa de Otilia Rojas Montero Rúbert López no.69 e/ Robert Reyes y Coroneles Galano ☏64/3254. One clean, pleasant (though small) room with a/c and private bathroom in an airy colonial house. ❷

Casa de Ykira Mahiquez Maceo 168A e/ Céspedes y Ciro Frías; ☏64/2466. Excellent accommodation, with a terrace overhung with begonias, on a friendly street one block from the main square. The owner knows almost everyone in town with a room to let, so if her place is full she'll be able to point you elsewhere. ❷

The Town

Just walking around Baracoa is one of the town's greatest pleasures. Its quaint and friendly central streets are lined with tiny, pastel-coloured colonial houses with wedding-cake trim, and modern development is confined to the outskirts, where new apartment blocks were built after the Revolution. All the sites of interest are within easy walking distance of one another, radiating out from the **Parque Independencia** on Antonio Maceo, where, under the shade of the wide laurel trees, generations of Baracoans gather around rickety tables to play chess and dominoes. From the hillsides of the town you can see across the bay to the Sleeping Beauty mountains, so called because they look uncannily like a generously endowed woman lying on her back.

On the plaza's east side, opposite a bust of Taíno hero Hatuey), stands the **Catedral Nuestra Señora de la Asunción** (Tues–Fri 8am–noon & 2–5pm, Sat 8am–noon, Sun mass at 9am), built in 1805 on the site of a sixteenth-century church. This unobtrusive structure houses one of the most important religious relics in the whole of Latin America, the antique **La Cruz de la Parra**, supposedly the antique cross brought from Spain and planted in the sands of the harbour beach by Christopher Columbus. It's undeniably of the period, having been carbon-dated at 500 years old, but as the wood is from the *Cocoloba Diversifolia* tree, indigenous to Cuba, the truth of the legend is doubtful. It was in front of this cross that the celebrated defender of the Indians, Fray Bartolomé de Las Casas, gave his first Mass in 1510. Originally 2m tall, the cross was gradually worn down by time and souvenir hunters to its present modest height of 1m, at which point it was encased in silver for its protection. The cross now stands in a glass case to the left of the altar, on an ornate silver base donated by a French marquis at the beginning of the twentieth century. When Pope John Paul II arrived on his Cuban visit in 1998, it was the first thing he asked to see.

Parque Martí and Fuerte Matachín

A block north of Parque Independencia towards the sea, **Parque Martí**, more a collection of benches and trees than a park, is the town's busiest square, crowded with shops and stalls selling snacks and drinks, notably Prú, the local speciality (see p.487). East of here, along Martí past the shops and the triangular Parque Maceo – complete with bust – is the **Fuerte Matachín** (daily

Baracoa art

Baracoa has a strong tradition of **local art**, with reasonably priced originals sold at La Casa Yara, Maceo no.120 (Mon–Fri 8am–noon & 2–6pm, Sat & Sun 8am–noon), along with coconut-wood jewellery, handmade boxes and other trinkets. Artwork is also available from the Casa de la Cultura, on Maceo no.124 – look out for paintings by Luís Eliades Rodríguez – and at the Galería del Arte, Maceo no.145 (Tues–Fri 9am–noon & 4–9pm, Sat & Sun 4–10pm), which offers good-quality woodcarvings and some rather head-spinning oil paintings.

8am–noon & 2–6pm; $1CUC), one of a trio of forts that protected Baracoa from marauding pirates in the nineteenth century. Built in 1802, the fort is well preserved to this day, and you can see the original cannons ranged along the fort walls. Its cool interior now houses the town **museum**, with a good collection of delicately striped *polimitas* snail shells, some Amerindian relics and a history of the town's most celebrated characters.

Museo Arqueológico

A steep climb up the thickly forested Loma Paraíso brings you to Las Cuevas del Paraíso, a series of caves once used by the Taíno for ceremonies and funeral chambers that are now home to Baracoa's fascinating new **archeological museum** (daily 8am–6pm; $2CUC including a guide, English and Spanish spoken). Archeologists have unearthed a treasure trove of pre-Columbian artefacts, in the caves themselves and the surrounding countryside, that pertain to the successive indigenous groups who made the region their home: the Guanahatabey occupied the area from about 3000 to 1000 BC, the Siboney from approximately 1000 BC until 1100 AD, and the Taíno who supplanted them until arrival of the Spanish in the fifteenth century. Cave 1 contains an impressive collection of petroglyphs – stone sculptures depicting animal and human forms, and some ancient maps showing networks of local pathways. From here a spiral staircase leads down to Cave 2, which houses a wealth of Taíno artefacts: look out for the rock and coral phalluses, symbols that were used to encourage fecundity in humans and animals; the spatulas that were used to induce vomiting, purging the body to facilitate communication with the gods; and the skull of *Megalonus*, a giant tree sloth which the Taíno hunted to extinction.

The most interesting exhibits are undoubtedly the human remains in the funerary chamber, a little further up the hill. The skeletons are displayed as they were found, in the traditional foetal position, and all the specimens' skulls are badly misshapen. It is thought likely that the Taíno tied heavy weights to babies' heads, flattening the forehead by pushing the bone down horizontally and extending the back of the skull. The malformed bodies were buried with *esferolitas*, small round stones used to indicate the person's age and social standing – the *esferolitas* found here indicate that this was the resting place for important and wealthy people.

The Malecón and Playa Boca de Miel

A walk along the **Malecón**, a ragged collection of the backsides of houses and ugly apartment blocks, is something of a disappointment. To the west is the town's **Plaza de la Revolución**, surely the smallest in Cuba, decorated only with a couple of revolutionary posters. On its westernmost point, the Malecón is sealed by the third of the town's forts, **La Punta**, built in 1803 and now converted into an elegant restaurant (see p.488). A door built into the western wall leads down a flight of stairs to the tiny **Playa La Punta**, a good spot for a quiet dip (daily 9am–5pm).

At the eastern end of the Malecón, accessed by the stone stairs to the right of an imposing stone statue of Christopher Columbus, is the main town beach, **Playa Boca de Miel**, a boisterous hangout mobbed in summer by vacationing schoolchildren. People walk their dogs along the multicoloured shingle near town, but the brilliant stones fade into sand a little further along, making for a decent swimming spot. The best spot for a paddle, however, lies beyond the clump of trees at the far eastern end of the beach, in the gentle **Río Miel**, which has its own legend. Many years ago, a Taíno maiden with honey-coloured hair used to bathe daily in the waters. One day a young sailor steered his ship down the river and spotted her. Captivated by her beauty, he instantly fell in love and for a while the happy couple frolicked daily in the river. However, as the day of the sailor's departure approached, the young girl became increasingly depressed and would sit in the river crying until her tears swelled its banks. Impressed by this demonstration of her love, the sailor decided to stay in Baracoa and marry her, from which grew the saying that if you swim in the Río Miel, you will never leave Baracoa, or that if you do you will always return.

Boca de Miel and Playa Blanca

Venturing beyond the reaches of Playa Boca de Miel you are rewarded with an unaffected and intimate view of Baracoan life in the hamlet of **Boca de Miel**, comprising little more than a handful of simple, single-storey homes and, further on, the bijou pale sand beach at Playa Blanca. While the beach is not the finest in Cuba (never mind what the locals say), the walk to reach it is a pleasant ramble. At the easternmost edge of Playa Boca de Miel where the river reaches the sea ("boca de miel" means "river mouth"), turn towards the river and follow the path down to the picturesque though rickety wooden bridge. Children play outside the houses lining the path while pigs and chickens root through the undergrowth. Take the path to the left of the bridge and head up the hill. Turning right at the pink house once clear of the hamlet, follow the dust track until you pass the concrete bunkers. Turn left past the next field and follow the narrow path to where it forks. Take the right-hand route through the thigh-high grass, passing some odd breeze-block structures and you'll find **Playa Blanca** on the other side of a little grove of trees. The tiny hoop of coarse, blondish sand makes a good spot to relax for an afternoon, though you should be very mindful of the vigorous undertow if you go swimming. There are no facilities here, so be sure to take a supply of water; locals will offer to prepare you fried fish and water coconuts.

Eating and drinking

After the monotonous cuisine in much of the rest of Cuba, **food** in Baracoa is ambrosial in comparison, drawing on a rich local heritage and the region's plentiful supply of coconuts. Tuna, red snapper and swordfish fried in coconut oil are all favourite dishes, and there is an abundance of clandestine lobster, as well as a few vegetarian specials. Look out for *cucurucho*, a deceptively filling concoction of coconut, orange, guava and lots of sugar sold in a palm-leaf wrap. Other treats for the sweet-toothed include locally produced chocolate and the soft drink *Prú*, widely available from *oferta* stands, a fermented blend of sugar and secret spices that's something of an acquired taste.

State restaurants

Baracoa Maceo no.129 A sparsely furnished, high-ceilinged restaurant dishing up cheap, reasonable Cuban staples.

Café 1511 Maceo 68 esq. Frank País. The extensive morning menu (until 10am) in *Hostal La Habanera*'s breezy restaurant makes it the best place in town for breakfast. In the afternoons and evenings a reasonably priced menu offers a range of fish and meat dishes and tasty snacks.

Caracol halfway down the Malecón. A peso restaurant serving cheap, filling fried pork with rice and beans and occasionally fresh fish. Check beforehand, as they've been known to charge foreign visitors in convertible pesos.

Casa del Chocolate Maceo no.121. This barren little chocolate café, furnished with just the minimum of chairs and tables, sells hot and cold drinking chocolate subject to availability. Be warned that the chocolate here is an acquired taste, a cross between a mousse and a cold milkshake.

El Castillo Calixto García ☏ 64/2125. The Sat-night buffet at this hotel restaurant offers possibly the best meal you will have in town: a feast of Baracoan dishes featuring coconut, maize, local vegetables and herbs, all for $10CUC. During the rest of the week a varied menu offers a selection of international dishes and local specialities. Their shrimp à la Santa Barbara – cooked with coconut and sweet pepper – is highly recommended.

La Punta Ave. de los Martires, at the west end of the Malecón. An elegant restaurant in the grounds of La Punta fort, serving traditional Cuban and Baracoan food, some spaghetti dishes and the house speciality, *bacan*, a delicious baked dish with meat, green bananas and coconut milk. There's a cabaret show from 9pm to midnight, Thurs to Sun, so arrive early if you want a peaceful meal.

Palmares al Parque Maceo esq. Rafael Trejo. A fairly charmless 24hr café serving spaghetti, sandwiches and fried chicken under a flowering trellis.

Paladares

Casa Tropical Martí no.175 e/ Céspedes y Ciro Frias. A very central *paladar* with a cool interior and a friendly atmosphere offering meals to non-guests. Excellent swordfish cooked in coconut milk and generous helpings of shellfish are served in a courtyard beside an ailing papaya tree.

La Colonial Martí no.123 e/ Maravi y Frank País ☏ 64/5391. A homely place offering standard, though very well-prepared, Cuban dishes in a lovely nineteenth-century house complete with whirring fans and colourful tiled floor. It gets very busy, so reservations are recommended – and make sure to arrive early so you can get the day's speciality before the rush. Daily 10am–midnight; $6–8CUC per person.

Entertainment and nightlife

Baracoa has quite an active **nightlife**, perhaps surprisingly so for such a small town, though it's essentially centred on two small but boisterous venues near Parque Independencia, and things are much quieter further afield. Most entrances will only set you back $1CUC. The most sophisticated option is twilight cocktails at the *Hotel El Castillo* rooftop bar. Baracoa's small **cinema**, Cine-Teatro Encanto, Maceo no.148, screens Cuban and North American films every evening.

Casa de la Cultura Maceo e/ Frank País y Maravi. ☏ 64/2364. A haven of jaded charm, with live music and dancing on the patio nightly plus regular *rumba* shows. Things tend to get going around 9pm and the place is open until 1am.

Casa de la Trova Victorino Rodríguez no.149B e/ Ciro Frias y Pelayo Cuevo. Concerts take place in a tiny room opposite Parque Independencia, after which the chairs are pushed back to the wall and exuberant dancers spill onto the pavement. A lively, unaffected atmosphere makes for one of the most vibrant and authentic nights out in town. Daily 9pm–midnight.

El Patio Maceo esq. Maravi. The live traditional music every night at 9pm draws a crowd while the bar does a fine trade in expertly prepared *mojitos*.

El Ranchon Loma Paraíso. Take the steep stone staircase cut into the hillside to the east of *El Castillo* on Calixto García to reach this open-air nightspot on the hilltop. The quality of an evening is patchy here, sometimes the pitch-black dance floor and loud music can be a laugh, while on other occasions the ranks of loved-up *jineteras* and attendant foreigners are something of a trial. There's live music from 10pm until midnight, followed by a booming disco specializing in a slightly jarring combination of *salsa* and reggaeton.

With an abundance of verdant countryside, exploring the surrounding area is one of the pleasures of a visit to the Baracoa region. Without your own car, the only option is to take a guided tour, which can be arranged at the Rumbos office in *Hostal La Habanera* (☎64/5155) or the Cubatur office at Maceo no.147 (daily 8am–9pm ☎64/5306), both of which offer the same packages for the same prices. The prices quoted below are for guide and transport only, and you should arrange your own supplies for the trips, which run daily during high season and alternate days at other times.

Boca de Yumarí Though its tranquil nature has been damaged somewhat by tourism, Boca de Yumurí still offers splendid views and swimming spots. This excursion includes a boat ride and a tour of the local cocoa plantation, which cannot be visited any other way. $32CUC.

Parque Nacional Alejandro de Humboldt The lush rainforests, curving and swelling into hills above coastline tangled with mangroves, cover some 100km of land and were designated a UNESCO biosphere and national park in 2000. It is definitely worthy of the accolade. Views are fantastic and access to secluded beaches and surrounding countryside easy. Although you cannot roam freely deep into the park without a guide, the tour takes you through some of the most beautiful scenery on hillside hikes or boat trips around the coast. $36CUC.

Playa Duaba Only 6km outside of Baracoa, Playa Duaba is set on an estuary. The beach itself is a scrubby grey, but is pleasant enough for a swim. The tour includes a short guided walk, while lunch at the *Finca Duaba* is an optional extra. $8CUC. This tour is offered with the Río Toa tour as a full-day excursion. $17CUC.

Río Toa Reached through some gently undulating rainforest filled with a cornucopia of cocoa trees and air plants, one of the country's longest rivers lies 10km northwest of Baracoa. Wide and deep, the Río Toa is one of the most pleasant places to swim in, although you should choose your spot carefully and watch out for a fairly brisk current. Return is by boat. $18CUC.

Saltadero A visit to the picturesque waterfall at Saltadero 10km west of the town makes for a relaxing day-trip. Secluded by a rugged rock face, the 35-metre waterfall cascades down into a natural swimming pool. The route down to the pool is fairly slippery, so wear shoes with some grip. $16CUC.

El Yunque Nestling in lush rainforest is the hallmark of Baracoa's landscape, El Yunque. The area is rich with banana and coconut trees, while the views are astounding. If you are striking out alone, start your climb at the *Campismo El Yunque*. Entrance costs $13CUC and includes an obligatory guide. $16CUC.

La Terraza Calle Maceo no.120. This appealing rooftop terrace is a good spot for a quiet early-evening drink, while later in the evening it heats up as crowds of Baracoans and foreigners alike pile in for the comedy or magic floor shows followed by disco dancing. The club runs a gay night on Wed. Entry $1CUC. Nightly 8pm to 2 or 3am.

Listings

Airlines Cubana, Maceo no.181 ☎64/5374 (Mon, Wed, Fri 8am–noon & 2–4pm).
Bicycles Palmeras al Parque, Maceo esq. Rafael Trejo, has an office where you can rent a bicycle for $3–4CUC per day.
Car rental Cubacar (☎64/5212) has an office in *Rumbos al Parque*, Maceo esq. Rafael Trejo;

Havanautos are at the airport (☎64/5344); Víacar are based at *Hotel Porto Santo* (☎64/5137).
Internet You can get Internet access at the Centro de Llamadas (daily 8.30ama–7.30pm; $6CUC. per hour) on Maceo next door to the post office.
Medical There's an international pharmacy in *Hostal La Habanera* (daily 8am–5pm) and a 24hr

peso pharmacy at Maceo no.132 (☎64/2271). The 24hr *policlinico* is on Martí no 427 (☎64/2162). Call ☎64/2472 for a public ambulance.

Photography For film and batteries, head to Photoservice on Martí no.204 (24hr).

Police The police station is on Martí towards the Malecón, near the bus station (☎64/2479). In an emergency call ☎116.

Post office Maceo no.136 (Mon–Sat 8am–8pm).

Shopping The Yumurí Convenience Store, Maceo no.149 (Mon–Sat 8.30am–noon & 1.30–5pm, Sun 8.30am–noon), is a small supermarket useful for everyday supplies. Identifiable by the swarms of people outside, La Primada convertible-peso store is on Martí opposite the park, selling food, clothes, toiletries and small electrics.

Taxis Cubataxi (☎64/3737); Transgaviota are based at *El Castillo* (☎64/5165).

Telephones Next door to the post office is an ETECSA phone booth (daily 7am–10.30pm), where you can buy phonecards. International calls can also be made at *El Castillo* hotel.

Around Baracoa

Cradled by verdant mountains smothered in palm and cacao trees, and threaded with swimmable rivers, the Baracoan countryside has much to offer. **El Yunque**, the hallmark of Baracoa's landscape, can easily be climbed in a day, while if you have a car and a little time to spare you could take a drive east along the coast and seek out some quintessentially Cuban fishing villages, including **Boca de Yumurí**. Alternatively, just head for the **beach** – there are a couple of good options northwest of town.

El Yunque

As square as a slab of butter, **El Yunque**, 10km west of Baracoa, is an easy climb. At 575m, streaked in mist, it seems to float above the other mountains in the Grupo Sagua Baracoa range. Christopher Columbus noted its conspicuousness: his journal entry of November 27, 1492 mentions a "high square mountain which seemed to be an island" seen on his approach to shore – no other mountain fits the description as well. El Yunque is the remnant of a huge plateau that dominated the region in its primordial past. Isolated for millions of years, its square summit has evolved unique species of ferns and palms, and much of the forest is still virgin, a haven for rare plants including orchids and bright red epiphytes.

△ El Yunque

The polimitas snail

Along the beach you may spot the brightly coloured shell of the **polimitas snail**. According to local Amerindian legend, there was once a man who wanted to give his beloved a gift. As he had nothing of his own to give, he set out to capture the colours of the universe: he took the green of the mountains, the pink of the flowers, the white of the foam of the sea and the yellow of the sun. When he went to claim the blue from the sky it vanished as the sun went down and he had to content himself with the black of the night. He then set all the colours into the shells of the snails and presented them to his love. Each snail is unique, ornately decorated in delicate stripes and consequently quite sought after – the Duchess of Windsor in the 1950s, for instance, had a pair encrusted with gold studs and made into earrings. Such caprices have severely depleted the snails' numbers, and although locals still sell them, buying is not recommended. With luck and a little searching, however, you may find an empty shell or two lying on the beach.

The energetic, though not unduly strenuous, hike to the summit should take about two hours, starting near *Campismo El Yunque* ($9CUC for entrance to El Yungue), 3km off the Moa road. Guided excursions are a good way to see the mountain and can be arranged by *El Castillo* hotel and the Cubatur office.

Playa Maguana and Playa Nava

The two main **beaches** near Baracoa are close to each other on the right-hand side of the Moa road, 25km northwest of town. Partly lined with the spindly though leafy *Coco thrinas* palm, indigenous to the area, **Playa Maguana** is an attractive, narrow beach with golden sand, plenty of shade and a reef for snorkelling. It's also near an archeological zone where fragments of Taíno ceramics have been found. Popular with locals as well as visitors, the beach is less exclusive than many in Cuba, although plans to build new hotels close by may change this. Along the beach fishermen hang freshly caught iridescent **fish** from the trees, which they will offer to cook with rice and banana, washed down with coconut milk. At the far end of the beach is the *Maguana* (no phone; ➒), a secluded **hotel** with comfortable rooms and plenty of privacy; book through *El Castillo* or *Porto Santo* in Baracoa (see p.484). Take care of valuables whilst swimming here, as there have been reports of bags being taken.

Six kilometres further on is tiny **Playa Nava**. There are no facilities and the yellow sand is often smothered in seaweed and sea debris, but, on the bright side, it's almost always deserted, making it one of the few places in Cuba that's virtually guaranteed to be a complete retreat.

Boca de Yumurí

Thirty kilometres east of Baracoa, past the Bahía de Mata – a tranquil bay with a slim, shingled beach and a splendid view of the mountains – is the little fishing village of **BOCA DE YUMURÍ**, standing at the mouth of the eponymous river. Known as a place to find the highly prized *polimitas* snails (see box, above), the rather bland, brown-sand beach is also lined with houses whose owners will offer to cook you inexpensive and wholesome **meals** of fish, rice and bananas: a particularly good bet is Neris Acosta Cardesuñer's wooden house, about halfway down the beach – locals will point it out to you. The village has suffered somewhat from the more pernicious effects of tourism and it's more than likely that you'll be besieged with *jineteros* trying to steer you towards their restaurant of choice and flog you shells from your moment of arrival. Avoid all but the most insistent and head to the end of the beach and a wooden jetty from where you can catch a **raft taxi** ($2CUC) further upstream, where the river is clearer and better for swimming and banked by a high rock face.

Travel details

As with everywhere in Cuba, public transport is a haphazard affair, prey to last-minute cancellations and delays. You should always check to see if buses and trains are still running the route required before setting off.

Trains

Guantánamo to: Havana (1 every other day; 16hr); Holguín (1 every other day; 6hr); Las Tunas (1 every other day; 5hr); Matanzas (1 every other day; 14hr); Santa Clara (1 every other day; 11hr 30min).
Holguín to: Guantánamo (1 every other day; 6hr); Havana (1 every other day; 14hr); Las Tunas (1 daily; 2hr 30min).
Las Tunas to: Camagüey (1 daily; 12hr 45min); Ciego de Ávila (2 weekly; 4hr); Guantánamo (1 every other day; 6hr); Havana (1 daily; 12hr); Holguín (1 daily; 1hr 40min); Santiago (1 daily; 8hr).

(1 daily; 14 hr); Holguín (1 every other day; 5hr); Las Tunas (1 every other day; 5hr); Santiago de Cuba (1 daily; 1 hr 30min).
Holguín to: Banes (1 daily; 2hr 30min); Gibara (2 daily; 1hr); Guantánamo (1 every other day; 5hr); Havana (5 daily; 12hr); Mayarí (1 every other day; 2hr); Moa (1 every other day; 4hr); Santa Clara (4 daily; 5hr); Santiago de Cuba (4 daily; 3hr 20min); Trinidad (1 daily; 9hr).
Las Tunas to: Bayamo (5 daily; 2hr); Guantánamo (1 every other day; 5hr); Havana (5 daily; 11hr); Puerto Padre (1 every other day; 1hr); Santiago (4 daily; 5hr 30min).

Buses

Baracoa to: Guantánamo (10–11 weekly; 3hr 30min); Havana (1 every other day; 19hr); Santiago (10–11 weekly; 6hr).
Guantánamo to: Baracoa (10–11 weekly; 3hr 30min); Camagüey (1 every other day; 8hr); Havana

Flights

Baracoa to: Havana (2 weekly; 2hr 30min).
Guantánamo to: Havana (2 weekly; 2hr 10min).
Holguín to: Havana (2 daily; 1hr 45min).
Las Tunas to: Havana (4 weekly; 1hr).
Moa to: Havana (1 weekly; 2hr 30min).

Santiago de Cuba and Granma

CHAPTER 8

Highlights

* **Hotel Casa Granda** Presiding over Santiago's prettiest park, this elegant hotel with rooftop bar makes a perfect spot to soak up the city's atmosphere. See p.502

* **Museo de la Lucha Clandestina** A fascinating look at the history of the Revolution, housed in a reproduction eighteenth-century house. See p.510

* **Carnival in Santiago** The country's best *salsa and trova* bands, along with outré floats, take over the streets during this July event. See p.512

* **El Castillo del Morro San Pedro de la Roca** An impressive seventeenth-century stone fortress, built on a cliff outside of Santiago to ward off pirates. See p.521

* **Santiago's Casa de la Trova** There may be no better place to hear authentic Cuban music. See p.524

* **Sierra Maestra mountains** Trekking in the country's highest peaks makes for exhilarating exploration. See p.536

* **Playas Las Coloradas** The site where the *Granma* yacht deposited Fidel, Che and the other revolutionaries at the inception of the struggle. See p.544

* **El Guafe** Take the nature trail into this idyllic woodland park to see ancient petroglyphs and spot all manner of trees, birds and butterflies. See p.544

△ El Castillo del Morro San Pedro de la Roca

Santiago de Cuba and Granma

The southern part of Oriente – the island's easternmost third – is defined by the **Sierra Maestra**, Cuba's largest mountain range, which binds together the provinces of **Santiago de Cuba** and **Granma**. Rising directly from the shores of the Caribbean along the southern coast, the mountains make much of the region largely inaccessible, a quality appreciated by the rebels who spent years waging war here.

At the eastern end of the sierra, the roiling, romantic **city of Santiago de Cuba**, capital of the eponymous province and Cuba's most important urban area outside of Havana, draws visitors mainly for its **music**. Brewed from the legions of bands that have grown up here, the regional scene is always strong, but it boils over in July when **carnival** drenches the town in *rumba* beats, fabulous costumes, excitement and song. This talent for making merry has placed Cuba's second city firmly on the tourist map, but there's much more to the place than carnival. Briefly the island's first capital, Santiago maintains a rich colonial heritage, evident throughout its historical core and in the splendid coastal fortification of **El Morro**. The city played an equally distinguished role in more recent history, as recorded in the **Moncada barracks** museum, where Fidel Castro and his small band of rebels fired the opening shots of the Revolution, and the **Museo de la Lucha Clandestina**, a reproduction of the old police station burnt down during the troubles.

Spread along the coastline **around Santiago**, the attractions of the **Gran Parque Natural Baconao** – and especially its **beaches**, of which **Playa Siboney** is the outstanding favourite – form the perfect antidote to the hectic pace of city life. A day-trip to the east offers gentle **trekking** into the **Sierra de la Gran Piedra**, where one of the highest points in the province, Gran Piedra itself, offers far-reaching vistas. In the lush, cool mountains west of the city, the town of **El Cobre** features one of the country's most important churches, housing the much-revered relic of the Virgen de la Caridad del Cobre. Still further west, bordering Granma province, the heights of the **Sierra Maestra** vanish into awe-inspiring cloudforests, and although access to the **Parque Nacional Turquino** – around Pico Turquino, Cuba's highest peak – is often restricted, you can still admire from afar.

Unlike Santiago de Cuba, which revolves around its main city, the province of **Granma** has no definite focus and is much more low-key than its neighbour. The small black-sand beach resort at **Marea del Portillo** on the south coast

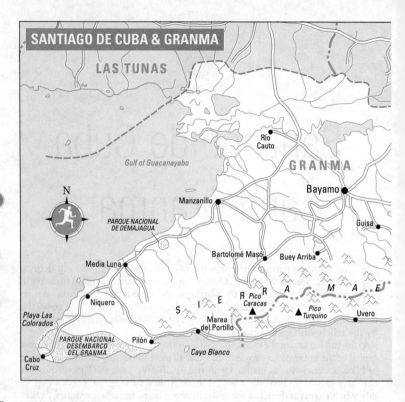

gives Granma some sort of tourist centre, but the highlight of the province, missed out on by many, is the **Parque Nacional Desembarco del Granma**. Lying in wooded countryside at the foot of the Sierra Maestra, this idyllic park, home to an assortment of intriguing stone petroglyphs, can be easily explored from the beach of **Las Coloradas**. Further north, along the Gulf of Guacanayabo, the museum at **Parque Nacional La Demajagua**, formerly the sugar estate and home of Carlos Manuel de Céspedes, celebrates the War of Independence amidst tranquil, park-like grounds.

Granma's two main towns are underrated and often ignored, but the fantastic Moorish architecture in the coastal town of **Manzanillo** is reason enough to drop by, while **Bayamo**, the provincial capital, with its quiet atmosphere and pleasant scenery, appeals to discerning visitors looking for an easy-going spot to stay.

Santiago de Cuba city

Beautiful, heady **SANTIAGO DE CUBA** is the crown jewel of Oriente. Nowhere outside of Havana is there a city with such definite character or such

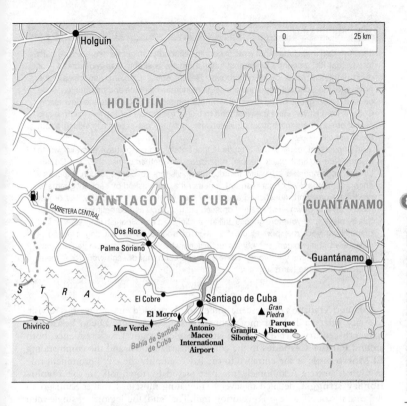

determination to have a good time. Spanning out from the base of a deep-water bay and cradled by mountains, the city is credited with being the most Caribbean part of Cuba, a claim borne out by its laid-back lifestyle and rich mix of inhabitants. It was here that the first slaves arrived from West Africa, and today Santiago boasts a larger percentage of black people than anywhere else in Cuba. Afro-Cuban **culture**, with its music, myths and rituals, has its roots here, with later additions brought by the French coffee-planters fleeing revolution in Haiti in the eighteenth century. Santiago's proximity to Jamaica has encouraged a natural crossover of ideas, and it is one of the few places in Cuba to have a strong Rastafari following, albeit a hybrid one – devout Jamaican Rastas are teetotal vegetarians who don't wolf down huge plates of fried pork with lashings of beer, as their Cuban counterparts tend to do.

The leisurely pace of life doesn't make for a quiet city, however, with the higgledy-piggledy net of narrow streets around the colonial quarter ringing night and day with the beat of drums and the toot of horns. **Music** is a vital element of Santiaguero life, whether heard at the country's most famous **Casa de la Trova** and the city's various other venues, or the numerous impromptu gatherings that tend to reach a crescendo around **carnival** in July, attended by rucksacked visitors seeking *rumba* and rum. As well as being the liveliest, the summer months are also the hottest – the mountains surrounding the city act as a windbreak and the lack of cooling breezes means that Santiago is often several degrees hotter than Havana and almost unbearably humid.

⑧

Racism and harassment

It's often said that Cuba is not a racist country, although it might be nearer to the truth to say that it's a country where institutional racism is simply less widespread – or overt – than in some of its neighbours. Recent social problems, specifically the poverty of the Special Period and consequent increasing crime and prostitution, have caused a resurgence of the **racial discrimination** that existed before the Revolution. Cubans from Havana and the west tend to blame easterners for the rise in crime and cast them as the perpetrators of *jineterismo*, but they are essentially talking about black people.

An unpleasant result of this attitude is that hotels and shops have been known to discriminate against black people, regardless of whether or not they are Cuban. Unless accompanied by white friends, black visitors to Santiago can expect to encounter some level of **harassment**, whether it's being asked by security guards to produce a passport, questioned about why they want to enter a hotel or bar or just looked up and down – especially if dressed casually. You can sometimes circumvent this by playing up your foreignness, talking audibly in a non-Spanish language, or just brandishing your passport at the first sign of trouble. While causing a scene is obviously to be avoided, sometimes just asking why you have been singled out may mean that next time you are left alone – an approach that doesn't work for Cubans suffering the same harassment.

Although Santiago's music scene and carnival are good enough reasons to visit, the city offers a host of more concrete attractions, too. Diego Velázquez's sixteenth-century merchant house and the elegant governor's residence, both around **Parque Céspedes** in the colonial heart of town, and the commanding **El Morro** castle at the entrance to the bay exemplify the city's prominent role in Cuban history. Additionally, the part played by townsfolk in the **revolutionary struggle**, detailed in several fascinating museums, makes Santiago an important stopoff on the Revolution trail. That said, the legions of single men who visit the city, armed with pretty frocks and fat wallets, have an altogether different agenda, involving the local *jineteras*.

Despite what many Cubans say, **street hustle** – begging, bag-snatching and being propositioned – is no more of a problem in Santiago than in other tourist areas, although that's not to say that it doesn't happen, particularly around Parque Céspedes.

Some history

Established by **Diego Velázquez de Cuéllar** in 1515 and moved the following year to its present location from its original site on the banks of the Río Paradas, the port of Santiago de Cuba was one of the original seven *villas* founded in Cuba. Velázquez, pleased to find so excellent a natural port near to reported sources of **gold** (which were quickly exhausted) and satisfied by its proximity to Jamaica, Española and Castilla del Oro, named the port Santiago (St James) after the patron saint of Spain. With the construction of the central trading house shortly afterwards, the settlement of Santiago became the island's capital.

After this auspicious start – boosted by the discovery of a rich vein of **copper** in the foothills in nearby El Cobre – the city's importance dwindled somewhat. Buffeted by severe earthquakes and **pirate attacks** – notably by Frenchman Jacques de Sores in 1554 and Henry Morgan in 1662 – Santiago developed more slowly than its western rival and in 1553 was effectively ousted as capital when the governor of Cuba, Gonzalo Pérez de Angulo, moved his office to Havana. In 1558, when the governor decreed that only Havana's port could engage in commerce, its future as Cuba's second city was confirmed, though it remained the major centre in what was then the province of **Oriente**, comprising modern-day Las Tunas, Holguín, Guantánamo, Santiago and Granma.

However, Santiago's physical bounty led to a new boom in the eighteenth century, when Creoles from other areas of the country, keen to exploit the lush land and make their fortune, poured **sugar** wealth into the area. The cool mountain slopes around Santiago proved ideal for growing **coffee** and French planters, accompanied by their slaves, emigrated here after the 1791 revolution in Haiti, bringing with them a cosmopolitan air and continental elegance, as well as a culturally complex slave culture.

Relations with Havana had always been frosty, especially as culturally distinct Santiago had fewer Spanish-born *peninsulares*. The Cuban-born Creoles, who predominated in Santiago, were not keen to cede their fortunes to Spain, and minor power struggles erupted sporadically between the two centres. This rivalry boiled over during the **Wars of Independence**, which were led by the people of Oriente, much of the fighting between 1868 and 1898 taking place around Santiago, led in part by the city's most celebrated son, **Antonio Maceo**.

The Cuban army had almost gained control of Santiago when in 1898 the United States intervened, no longer content to shout instructions from the sidelines. Eager to gain control of the imminent republic, they usurped victory from the Cubans by securing Santiago and subsequently forcing Spanish surrender after a dramatic battle on **Loma de San Juan**, a hill in the east of the city, between Roosevelt's army of six thousand "Rough Riders" and the Spanish army of seven hundred. The Cubans were not even signatories to the resultant Paris peace settlement between the North Americans and the Spanish, and all residents of Santiago province were made subject to the protection and authority of the United States. As an added insult, the rebel army that had fought for independence for thirty years was not even allowed to enter Santiago city.

Over the following decades, this betrayal nourished local anger and resentment, and by the 1950s Santiago's citizens were playing a prime role in the civil uprisings against the US-backed president Fulgencio Batista. Assured of general support, **Fidel Castro** chose Santiago for his debut battle in 1953, when he and a small band of rebels attacked the **Moncada barracks**. Further support for their rebel army was later given by the M-26-7 underground movement that was spearheaded in Santiago by **Frank and Josue País**. It was in Santiago's courtrooms that Fidel Castro and the other rebels were subsequently tried and imprisoned.

When the victorious Castro swept down from the mountains, it was in Santiago that he chose to deliver his maiden speech, on the night of January 1, 1959. The city, which now carries the title "Hero City of the Republic of Cuba", is still seen – especially in Havana – as home to the most zealous revolutionaries, and support for the Revolution is certainly stronger here than in the west. The rift between east and west still manifests itself today in various prejudices, with Habaneros viewing their eastern neighbours as trouble-making criminals, and considered as solipsistic and unfriendly by Santiagueros in return.

Arrival and information

International and domestic **flights** arrive at the **Aeropuerto Internacional Antonio Maceo** (☎22/69-1052), near the southern coast, 8km from the city.

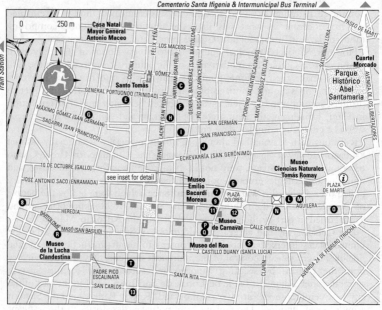

Metered and unmetered **taxis** wait outside and charge around \$15–18CUC to take you to the centre, though there is sometimes a **bus** that meets flights from Havana, only charging around \$5CUP for the same journey. You can arrange **car rental** at the Havanautos desk at the airport (☏22/68-6161) or at agencies in town (see p.527).

Interprovincial **buses** pull in to Santiago at the **Astro bus terminal** on Avenida de los Libertadores (☏22/62-3050), 2km north of the town centre. Next door, tourist buses arrive at the **Víazul bus depot** (☏22/62-8484). Taxis descend on tourists arriving on the Víazul like locusts on ears of corn; the journey to the centre from either terminal is around \$5–6CUC. Provincial buses pull in at the **Terminal de Omnibus Intermunicipal**, on Paseo de Martí, north of Parque Céspedes (☏22/62-4325).

Arriving by **train**, you'll alight at the attractive, modern station near the port, on Paseo de Martí esq. Jesús Menéndez (☏22/62-2836). From here, horse-drawn buggies and **bicitaxis** can take you the short jaunt to the centre for around \$3CUC, while a taxi will cost about \$5CUC.

Information

Santiago does not have an official tourist **information** bureau, but the staff at the two Cubatur offices – one on Parque Céspedes at Heredia 701 esq. San Pedro, the other, shared with a couple of other tour companies, at the *Hotel Santiago de Cuba* – can help with general enquiries. You can buy **maps** in the Librería Internacional on Parque Céspedes under the cathedral and at the shop in the *Hotel Casa Granda*'s basement.

Santiago's weekly newspaper, the *Sierra Maestra* (20c), is available from street vendors and occasionally from the bigger hotels, and has a brief **listings** section detailing cinema, theatre and other cultural activities.

City transport and tours

Although a large city, Santiago is easy to negotiate, as much of what you'll want to see is compactly fitted into the historic core around Parque Céspedes. Even the furthest sights are no more than approximately 4km from Parque Céspedes, making Santiago an excellent city for exploring on foot. Taxis are the best way to reach outlying sights as the buses are overcrowded and irregular.

Metered taxis wait on the cathedral side of Parque Céspedes or around Plaza Marte and charge 40–80¢/km with a $1CUC surcharge, while the **unmetered taxis** parked up on San Pedro negotiate a rate for the whole journey – expect to pay about $3–4CUC to cross town. Touts skulk around the main streets but you will strike a slightly cheaper deal if you negotiate with drivers themselves. For state-registered taxis try Veracuba at *Hotel Santiago de Cuba* (☏22/68-7070), Cubataxi (☏22/65-1038) or Transtur (☏22/68-7000).

Renting a car can be handy for out-of-the-way places, and the city itself is easy to drive around in. There are Havanautos **car rental** offices at the airport (☏22/68-6161) and at *Hotel Las Américas* (☏22/68-7160). Transtur (☏22/62-3884) have desks in the basement of the *Hotel Casa Granda*, *Hotel Libertad* and *Hotel Las Américas*; Veracuba has a desk at *Hotel Santiago de Cuba* (☏22/68-7070) and Micar are situated in the Cubatur office at Heredia 701 esq. San Pedro (☏22/62-9194).

Tours

In the *Hotel Santiago de Cuba* (daily 8am–12.30pm & 1.30–5pm; ☏22/68-7040) representatives of Havanatur and Cubatur share an office and offer **city tours**, excursions and tickets for flights and Víazul buses. Rumbos also have an office

Many streets in Santiago have two names, one from before the Revolution and one from after. Theoretically, street signs show the post-revolutionary name, but as these signs are few and far between, and locals tend to use the original name in conversation, we follow suit in the text. Cuban maps, however, usually show both names, with the original in brackets; in our maps we've followed their example. The most important roads are listed below.

Old name	New name	Old name	New name
Calvario	Porfirio Valiente	Sagarra	San Francisco
Carnicería	Pío Rosado	San Basilio	Bartolomé Masó
Clarín	Padre Quiroga	San Félix	Hartmann
Enramada	José A. Saco	San Gerónimo	Echevarría
Máximo Gómez	San Germán	San Pedro	General Lacret
Reloj	Mayía Rodríguez		

in the centre at Heredia 701 esq. San Pedro, near the *Hotel Casa Granda*. All agencies offer similarly priced **excursions** throughout the province. Prices decrease slightly according to the number of people attending each excursion but prices listed are based on one person going alone. Options include an eight-hour trip to Baracoa (minimum four people; $60CUC including breakfast and lunch), with more leisurely excursions to the Gran Piedra (minimum two people; $62CUC), El Castillo del Morro San Pedro de la Roca ($20CUC), El Cobre ($17CUC) and the somewhat pedestrian "Tour of the City" including the Cathedral and Museo de Ambiente Cubano ($19CUC).

Accommodation

Accommodation in Santiago is plentiful and varied. Except during carnival in July, when rooms are snapped up well in advance, you can usually turn up on spec, though making a reservation will save you having to trudge around looking, especially as the city's accommodation is spread over a wide area. There are a handful of **state hotels**, from the luxurious *Hotel Santiago de Cuba* through the characterful smaller city hotels, like *Casa Granda*, to various places set in suburban greenery. **Casas particulares** are abundant, many conveniently central and most offering reduced rates for stays longer than a couple of nights. Look out for the state-issued stickers – a blue triangle on a white background – which let you know they are open for business. Touts for these are everywhere; avoid them and their $5CUC-a-night surcharge by booking directly. (For more information on handling touts, see p.58.) *Casas particulares* are a little more expensive here than in smaller towns and you should expect to pay around $20–25CUC a night, although those further from the centre are more likely to negotiate a lower price.

Hotels

Las Américas Ave. de Las Américas y General Cebreco ☎ 22/64-2011, ℗ 68-7075. While not the ritziest in town, this pleasantly low-key hotel combines a comfortable, friendly atmosphere and good facilities – including a taxi rank, car rental

office and pool – with clean, bright and functional rooms equipped with cable TV and refrigerator. A short taxi ride from the main sights. ⑥

Casa Granda Heredia no.201 e/ San Pedro y San Félix ☎ 22/68-6600, ℗ comercia@casagran.gca .tur.cu. A tourist attraction in itself on account of its beauty, the regal *Casa Granda* is a sensitively restored 1920s hotel overlooking Parque Céspedes. From the elegant, airy lobby to its two atmospheric bars, it has a stately, colonial air matched in its tasteful rooms. ❼

Gran Hotel Enramada esq. San Félix ☎22/65-30-20, @ana@ehtsc.co.cu. A very central, friendly hotel operating in convertible pesos for visitors and pesos for Cubans. While it no longer merits the "grand" of its title, the vaguely colonial exterior and faded charm of the rooms are very appealing if you don't mind roughing it a bit – the somewhat grubby bathrooms don't look their best in the harsh fluorescent lights. Singles, doubles and triples all come with a/c and many with a tiny balcony overlooking the busy shopping street. ❸

Islazul San Juan Carretera de Siboney, km 1 ☎22/68-7200, @hotel@sanjuan.scu.cyt.cu. Close to historic Loma de San Juan (see p.519), *Villa San Juan* has the most congenial location of all the Santiago hotels, set amid tropical trees and lush plants. The hotel itself is tasteful though a bit bland, with smart, attractive rooms and clean communal areas. An inviting pool area and friendly staff complete the pleasant atmosphere. Roughly 4km from the centre, this is well located for those driving. ❺

Libertad Aguilera s/n e/ Serafín Sánchez y Pérez Carbo ☎22/62-7710. This cosy, mid-range hotel offers unexciting but decent rooms with cable TV spread along corridors lined with bold Spanish tiles. Those at the back are quieter. ❸

Meliá Santiago de Cuba Ave. de las Américas y Calle M ☎22/68-7070, @reservas.1.msc @solmeliacuba.com. Santiago's biggest, brashest hotel caters for business types and luxury-seekers. The blocky red, white and blue exterior is ultra-modern and fits well with the shiny green marble interior, while facilities include a beauty parlour, boutiques, a gym, conference rooms and the best pool in town ($10CUC for non-guests), as well as bars and restaurants galore. The rooms are tastefully decorated, some with original paintings by local artists, and fully equipped with all mod cons. ❼

San Basilio San Basilio 403 e/ Calvario y Carnicería ☎22/65-1702, @68-7069. This gorgeous little hotel, with a blue-and-white exterior that makes it look like a frosted cake, offers excellent value for the money. Its eight tastefully furnished rooms, arranged around a bright, plant-filled patio, come with cable TV, fridge and a/c. ❹

Casas particulares

Casa Colonial Maruchi San Félix no.357 e/ San Germán y Trinidad ☎22/62-0767,

@maruchi@ciges.inf.cu, ⓦwww .casasantiagodecubacolonial.sitio.net. Two rooms are available in this magnificent colonial house. Vintage brass beds, exposed brickwork and wooden beams add romance, while a well-tended patio filled with lush plants and a menagerie of birds and other pets is the perfect spot for the alfresco breakfast, included in the price. ❷

Casa de Arlex Rojas Cruz San Francisco no.303 e/ San Félix y San Bartolome ☎22/62-2517. Although there isn't much natural light in either of the two a/c rooms, this colonial house is still a very viable option. It boasts a tranquil patio furnished with rocking chairs and is home to two docile dogs and entertaining owners. Parking available. ❷

Casa de Bernardino Alvarez Moraguez Calle 8 no.60 e/ 1ra y 3ra Reparto Viste Alegre ☎22/64-1150. Two spacious a/c rooms, one with television, in a pleasant house in Viste Alegre. While this is some way from the centre, it will suit those looking for a quieter, more suburban house and perhaps those with a car. ❷

Casa de Caridad Roque Carnicería 408 e/ San Geronimo y San Francisco ☎22/65-4732. The small, plain, self-contained double bedroom is located in splendidly quiet isolation up on the roof, although the stairs, in the rainy season, can be quite treacherous. ❷

Casa de Dulce M Soulry Mora Trinidad no.503 e/ San Felix y San Bartolome ☎22/65-4727. @jcsoulary67@yahoo.com. Two rooms set around a central, tranquil, red-tiled courtyard. Clean and functional, with modern fittings, both the rooms have a/c, TV and a fridge. ❷

Casa de Leonard y Rosa Clarín no.9 e/ Aguilera y Heredia ☎22/62-3574. Two-room mini-apartment with two beds, a bathroom, a fridge and a small patio in a wonderful eighteenth-century house featuring period ironwork, wooden walls, high ceilings and red-and-blue stained-glass windows. ❷

Casa de Mabel Martínez Torrez Corona no.753 e/ Santa Rita y Santa Lucía ☎22/69-5926. Offering two unremarkable but clean rooms with bathroom, a/c and fridge. A good fall-back if other options are full. ❷

Casa de Mary and Felix San Germán no.165 e/ Rastro y Gallo ☎22/65-3720. Two nicely furnished, comfortable a/c rooms, both with a second bed for a child, are available for rent in this exceptionally friendly household. An enchanting lantern-lit garden out back and a roof terrace with swings are a real bonus. A little far from the centre but very good value, this is a top choice. ❷

Casa de Migdalia Gámez Rodrígues Trova Corona 371 Altos e/ San Germán y Trinidad

⊕ 22/62-4569. Two good-sized a/c double rooms with private bath are on offer in this welcoming household, as well as a self-contained apartment with a double bedroom, kitchen/dining room, laundry facilities and TV that would suit someone on a longer stay. There's also a communal roof terrace with lovely views, and meals are available. ❷

Casa de Nolvis Rivaflecha San Basilio no.122 e/ Padre Pico y Teniente Rey ⊕ 22/62-2972. Two clean, a/c rooms, each with two beds and its own hot-water bathroom, in a sociable house with a lively communal area. Close to the Padre Pico steps, in a quiet area of town with off-road parking; a good selection for those with a car. ❷

Casa de Raimundo Ocaña y Bertha Peña Heredia no.308 e/ Carnicería y Calvario ⊕ 22/62-4097, ⓔ co8kz@yahoo.es. A charming, very central household with an attractive, sunny patio, unfortunately bedevilled by noisy passing traffic. Two rooms, both with a/c, and private bathrooms with hot water. ❷

Casa de Ylia Deas Díaz San Félix no.362 e/ San Germán y Trinidad ⊕ 22/65-4138. A pleasant house owned by a big welcoming family offering one spacious, high-ceilinged, comfortable room with a/c and TV. The bathroom is shared and you have to walk through the house to get to it. ❷

The City

While many of Santiago's sights are gathered in the colonial quarter to the west side of town – and you will need at least a day to do this area justice – you'll also want to take a half-day or so to explore the newer suburbs out to the east and north. The city's other sights are dotted randomly on the outskirts and can be squeezed into the tail end of a visit to other areas.

The colonial district's must-see sights are clustered around the picturesque **Parque Céspedes**, among them some of the most eye-catching buildings in the city: the **Cathedral**, the sixteenth-century governor's house (now the **Ayuntamiento**, or town hall), the grand **Museo de Ambiente Histórico Cubano**, once the home of Diego Velázquez, and, close by, the **Balcón de Velázquez**, site of an early fortification, offering a splendid view west over the red rooftops to the bay.

A couple of blocks southwest of Parque Céspedes, in the **El Tivolí** district, is the **Museo de la Lucha Clandestina**, which details Santiago's pre-revolutionary underground movement. It adjoins the towering **Padre Pico escalinata** on Calle Padre Pico, a staircase built to straddle one of Santiago's steepest hills.

Heading east from Parque Céspedes lands you on the liveliest section of **Calle Heredia**, with its craft stalls, music venues and museums, amongst them the quirky **Museo de Carnaval**. On the street parallel to Heredia to the north, the superb **Museo Emilio Bacardí Moreau** houses one of the country's prime collections of fine art, artefacts and absorbing curios. In the parallel street to the south, the **Museo del Ron** provides a diverting introduction to Cuba's most popular liquor.

East of the historic centre, Avenida de los Libertadores, the town's main artery, holds the **Moncada barracks**, where Santiago's much-touted **Museo Histórico 26 de Julio** fills you in on Fidel Castro's celebrated – though futile – attack. Nearby, the **Parque Abel Santamaría** boasts an impressive concrete sculpture set on top of a gushing fountain. Further east still, the once-wealthy suburb of **Reparto Vista Alegre** shows off some of the city's finest and most fantastical mansions, particularly along **Avenida Manduley** where several have been converted into restaurants. South of here, on the edge of the city, is the **Loma de San Juan**, the hill where Teddy Roosevelt and his Rough Riders swept to victory during the Spanish–American War in 1898.

Scattered through the lattice of streets and beyond to the north are a few secondary sights, some of which are worth going out of your way to see. Most notable among these are the massive, modernist **monument to Antonio Maceo** which presides over the Plaza de la Revolución – much more memorable than the rather feeble museum to him beneath the plaza – and, out on the city limits, the **Cementerio Santa Ifigenia**, burial site of José Martí and various other luminaries.

Presiding over the bay 8km south of the city is Santiago's most magnificent sight, the **Castillo del Morro San Pedro de la Roca**, a statuesque seventeenth-century Spanish fortress. Just a kilometre from here, tiny **Cayo Granma** with its handful of houses and restaurants makes a good venue for a leisurely meal.

Parque Céspedes and around

The spiritual centre of Santiago is without a doubt charismatic **Parque Céspedes**. Originally the Plaza de Armas, the first square laid out by the conquistadors, it is more of a plaza than a park, its plants and shrubs neatly hemmed into small flowerbeds, and wrought-iron benches evenly spaced along smart red and grey flagstones. There's a gentle ebb and flow of activity as sightseers wander through the park between museum visits, and old folk sit enjoying the expansive shade of the weeping fig trees and watching the hustlers size up the tourists. Often, there will be a brass and percussion band playing, which draws a crowd irrespective of the time of day. Unfortunately, the engaging nineteenth-century tradition of the evening promenade, which saw gentlemen perambulating the park in one direction, ladies in the other, coquettishly flirting as they passed, has been replaced in recent years by a less attractive influx of Western men on the prowl for *jineteras*. The park is known as a favourite pick-up point, although legislation has kept the trade underground.

The rooftop bar at the picturesque *Hotel Casa Granda* on the park's east side provides a fantastic place to admire the sunset as well as the surrounding sights, while the hotel's balcony bar is a great place to people-watch over a tall glass of fresh lemonade. Next door to the hotel is the **Casa de Cultura** (daily 9am–6pm), housed in an exquisite nineteenth-century building that begs a visit if only to admire the romantic decay inside.

On the south side, a small **monument** celebrates the park's namesake, **Carlos Manuel de Céspedes**, one of the first Cubans to take up arms against the Spanish, issuing the *Grito de Yara* (cry of Yara) and urging his slaves and his comrades to arm themselves (see p.540). Splendid buildings surround the park on all sides.

Catedral de Nuestra Señora de la Asunción

On the south side of the square is the handsome **Catedral de Nuestra Señora de la Asunción** (Tues–Fri 8am–noon & 5–6.30pm, Sat 8am–noon & 4–5pm; Mass Tues–Fri at 6.30pm, plus Sat at 5pm and Sun at 9am & 6.30pm). Painted white and primrose-yellow, it is ornate without being extravagant and has a pleasing symmetry that blends well with the other buildings on the square. The first cathedral in Cuba was built on this site in 1522, but repeated run-ins with earthquakes and pirates – in 1662 English privateer Christopher Mygns even snaffled the church bells after blowing the roof off – made their mark, and Santiagueros started work on a second cathedral on the site in 1670. They finished in 1675, only to see the building demolished by an earthquake just three years later. Reconstruction began again, and in 1680 another cathedral was up and running, this one holding out for over a hundred years, though debilitated by earthquakes in 1766 and 1800, before being finally damaged beyond repair by a tremor in 1803.

△ Catedral de Nuestra Señora de la Asunción

The present cathedral, completed in 1818, has fared better, having been built with a fortified roof and walls in order to withstand natural disasters. Raised above ground level, it's reached by flights of stairs on its east and west fronts, with the cavernous space below, once the cathedral crypt, now housing convertible-peso shops. The cathedral features a Baroque-style edifice, its twin towers gleaming in the sunshine and its doorway topped by an imposing herald angel, statues of **Christopher Columbus** and **Bartolomé de las Casas**, defender of the Indians, erected in the 1920s, and four Neoclassical columns.

The cathedral interior is no less ornate, with an arched Rococo ceiling rising above the first rows of pews into a celestial blue dome painted with a cloud of cherubs. Cherubs and angels are something of a theme, in fact, being strewn across the ceiling and up the walls. Facing the congregation is a modest marble altar framed by rich dark-wood choir stalls, while to the right a more ornate altar honours the Virgen de la Caridad, patron saint of Cuba. Since the visit of Pope John Paul II in January 1998, the state has relaxed its hitherto censorial stance on the Catholic Church, once seen to be in league with capitalism, and the cathedral, like other churches throughout Cuba, now has a daily procession of devotees supplicating the Virgen de la Caridad for favours, as well as a few *jineteros* keen to take advantage of the tourists. The prize piece of the cathedral, though almost hidden on the left-hand side, is the tremendous **organ**, no longer used but still replete with tall gilded pipes. Lining the wall is a noteworthy frieze detailing the history of St James, the eponymous patron saint of Santiago.

In an upstairs room on the cathedral's east side is the tiny **Museo Arquidi-ocesano** (Mon–Sat 9.30am–5.30pm; $1CUC), which exhibits a small collection of beautifully penned calligraphic correspondence between various cardinals and bishops, portraits of all the past bishops of the cathedral and not much else. Although it's the only museum of its kind in Cuba, the subject matter is probably of limited interest to most.

Museo de Ambiente Cubano
Built in 1515 for Diego Velázquez, one of the first conquistadors of Cuba, the magnificent stone edifice on the west side of the park is the oldest residential building in Cuba. It now houses the **Museo de Ambiente Cubano** (Sept–April daily 9am–4.45pm; May–Aug Mon–Fri 9am–5.45pm, Sat 9am–5pm, Sun 9am–12.45pm; $2CUC, $1CUC extra for each photo taken), a wonderful collection of early- and late-colonial furniture, curios, weapons and fripperies which offers one of the country's best insights into colonial lifestyles, and is so large that it spills over into the house next door.

Start your tour on the first floor, in the family's living quarters, where you'll find some unusual **sixteenth-century** pieces. All the windows have heavy wooden lattice balconies and shutters – intended to hide the women, keep the sun out and protect against attack – which lend the house a surprising coolness, as well as the look of an indomitable fortress. The original ceilings, now restored, are lavishly timbered in heavy cedar wood and detailed with crests, while the hallway walls are chased with magnificent Moorish swirls and blocks of muted primary colour in place of wallpaper.

The house was strategically built facing west so that the first-floor windows looked out over the bay, and a **cannon** is still trained out of the bedroom window. The next two adjoining rooms represent the mid- and late **seventeenth century**. The first holds a chunky, carved mahogany chest, a wooden plaque painted with a portrait of Velázquez and a delicate Spanish ceramic inkwell that has survived intact through three centuries. Reflecting the refinement and European cultural influence that had infiltrated Cuban society by the end of the seventeenth century, the second room houses an exquisite Spanish *secretaire*, its twelve mahogany drawers inlaid with bone mythological figures.

The final rooms on this floor take you into the **eighteenth century**, and the furnishings seem incongruously grand, set against the plain white walls and cool tiled floors of the house. Especially notable are the luxurious Cuban mahogany four-poster bed, the cedar wardrobe inlaid with large pansies, the English desk and the profusion of dainty French porcelain. Also in this room, cut into the inner wall, there's the very peculiar and bizarrely named **Pollo de la Ventana** (Window Chicken), a tightly latticed spy window overlooking the hallway, which allowed inhabitants to check on the movements of other people in the house.

Out in the cool, dark-wood upstairs **hallway** you can fully appreciate the cleverness of its design in its stark contrast with the dazzling, sunny central courtyard visible below, where there's an elegant central fountain and a huge *tinajón* water jar from Camagüey. Before you venture downstairs, walk to the end of the hallway to see the remains of the stone **furnace** that Velázquez built into the corner of the house so that he could smelt his own gold.

The rooms on the **ground floor**, where Velázquez had his offices, are now laid out with more extravagant eighteenth-century furniture and artefacts – among them a particularly curvaceous French chest of drawers and a beautiful French clock representing the world's first air-balloon journey. More impressive, perhaps, are the details of the house itself, such as the wide entrance made to accommodate a carriage and the expansive trading rooms with a stone central arch, marble flagged floor and window seats.

The collection overflows into the **house next door**, which has a similar decor but dates from the nineteenth century. Again, much of what's on display is imported from Europe and shows off the good life enjoyed by Santiago's bourgeoisie, but the most interesting items are native to Cuba. These include chairs with latticework back and seat, a style developed in Cuba to combat the heat, and the tobacco-drying machine in the kitchen. Possibly the most quintessentially Cuban item on display is the reclining *pajilla* smoking chair with an ornate ashtray attached to the arm, made for the proper enjoyment of a fine cigar.

Ayuntamiento

On the north side of the park is the brilliant-white **Ayuntamiento**, or town hall. During colonial times, the building on this site was the Casa del Gobierno, the governor's house, though the first two structures were reduced to rubble by earthquakes and the present building, erected in the 1940s, is a copy of a copy. It's not open to the public, but you can still admire the front cloister covered in shiny red tiles and fronted by crisply precise arches, with snowflake-shaped peepholes cut into the gleaming walls and shell-shaped ornamentation below the windows. The balcony overlooking the park was the site of Fidel Castro's triumphant speech on New Year's Day, 1959.

Balcón de Velázquez

From the Ayuntamiento, head west two blocks down Aguilera to the fortification known as the **Balcón de Velázquez** (Tues–Sat 9am–6pm, Sun 9am–noon; free), on Heredia esq. Corona. Built between 1539 and 1550, it was a lookout point for incoming ships, and originally equipped with a semicircle of cannons facing out over the bay. When it later fell into disrepair, a house was built on the site, and it wasn't until 1950 that the city council decided to rebuild the fortress in honour of Velázquez. It was completed in 1953, sadly without its most intriguing feature, a tunnel entered from beneath the circular platform in the centre of the patio and running for less than a kilometre down to the seafront. This was presumably used by the early townsfolk for making a swift exit when under siege. The modern covered entrance is lined with a history of Santiago (in Spanish) and honorary plaques to influential dignitaries. Despite these worthy efforts, however, by far the best part of the fortification is its **view** over the ramshackle, red-tiled rooftops down towards the bay and the ring of mountains beyond.

△ Museo de Ambiente Cubano

El Tivolí

Occupying the hills about four blocks south of the Balcón de Velázquez is the **El Tivolí** neighbourhood, named by the French plantation owners who settled there after fleeing the Haitian slave revolution at the end of the eighteenth century. With no real boundaries – it lies loosely between Avenida Trocha to the south and Calle Padre Pico in the north – there's not much to distinguish it from the rest of the old quarter, save for its intensely hilly narrow streets writhing down towards the bay. The immigrant French made this the most fashionable area of town, and for a while its bars and music venues were *the* place for well-to-do Santiagueros to be seen. While the *Casa de las Tradiciones* (see p.524) is still good for a knees-up, the area has definitely lost its former glory. The main attractions in El Tivolí now are the **Museo de la Lucha Clandestina** and the **Padre Pico escalinata**, a towering staircase of over fifty steps, built to accommodate the almost sheer hill that rises from the lower end of Calle Padre Pico.

Museo de la Lucha Clandestina

Just west of Padre Pico, perched on the Loma del Intendente, the **Museo de la Lucha Clandestina** (Tues–Sat 9am–7pm, Sun 9am–5pm; $1CUC; English, Italian and Spanish guides available; no photographs) is a tribute to the pre-revolutionary struggle. Spread over two floors, the museum comprises a photographic and journalistic history of the final years of the Batista regime and is a must for anyone struggling to understand the intricacies of the events leading up to the Revolution.

The immaculate building is a reproduction of an eighteenth-century house built on the site as the residence of the quartermaster general under Spanish rule. In the 1950s it served as the Santiago police headquarters until burnt to the ground during an assault orchestrated by schoolteacher-cum-underground leader **Frank País** on November 30, 1956. The three-pronged attack also took in the customs house and the harbour headquarters in an attempt to divert the authorities' attention from the arrival of Fidel Castro and other dissidents at Las Coloradas beach on the southwest coast. The attack is well documented here, with part of the museum focusing on the lives of Frank País and his brother and co-collaborator Josue, both subsequently murdered by Batista's henchmen in 1957. However, as in so many museums in Cuba, there's little discrimination in the exhibits, so that photographs of País's massively attended funeral procession share space with a red jumper he once wore, making the experience by turns moving and slightly comical.

The best exhibits are those that give an idea of the turbulent climate of fear, unrest and excitement that existed in the 1950s in the lead-up to the Revolution. Most memorable is a clutch of **Molotov cocktails** made from old-fashioned Pepsi Cola bottles, a hysterical newspaper cutting announcing Fidel Castro's death and another published by the rebels themselves refuting the claim. Also noteworthy are the evocative images of a young Castro and comrades in Mexico, Castro's Revolution manifesto written in exile, and a photograph of the triumphant gang on the town-hall balcony on the day of Castro's victory speech.

Calle Heredia

A couple of blocks east of Parque Céspedes is the lively patch of **Calle Heredia** where the catcalls of street vendors hawking hand-carved necklaces, wood sculptures and gimcrack souvenirs combine with the drums emanating from the *Casa de la Trova* music hall (see p.524) to create one of the hippest, friendliest areas in the city. Santiagueros often comment that you haven't really been to the city until you've been to Calle Heredia, and indeed you can spend hours checking out the sights – namely the mildly interesting **Casa Natal de José María Heredia** and the excellent **Museo de Carnaval** – and just drinking in the atmosphere and enjoying idiosyncrasies like Librería La Escalera, a tiny secondhand bookshop at no.265 (see p.526) where a *trovador* trio plays requests all day long.

Casa Natal de José María Heredia

The handsome colonial house at Heredia no.260 is the **Casa Natal de José María Heredia** (Tues–Sat 9am–5pm, $1CUC), the birthplace of one of the greatest Latin American poets. While not the most dynamic museum in the world, it's worth a quick breeze through the spartan rooms to see the luxurious French *bateau* bed, the family photos and the various first editions. A good time to visit is on Tuesdays and Thursdays (5–9pm; free), when local poets meet for discussions and recitals on the sunny patio at the back of the house.

Although Heredia (1803–39) only lived in the house for two and a half years before his family moved to the US in 1806, he is considered a son of Santiago and honoured accordingly, with the street itself named after him. After the death of his father in 1820 he returned to Cuba, settling in Matanzas. Heredia practised law there until denounced as a supporter of independence by colleagues at the prestigious law firm where he worked, whereupon he went into exile in the United States in 1824. His poetry combined romanticism and nationalism, and was forbidden in Cuba until the end of Spanish rule. The best-remembered poem by Heredia is *Himno del Desterrado* (Hymn of the Outcast), which he wrote when he sailed close to Matanzas en route to Mexico from New York.

Museo del Carnaval

Much more enjoyable than Heredia's birthplace is the **Museo del Carnaval**, at Heredia no.301 (Tues–Sat 9am–8pm, Sun 9am–5pm; $1CUC, plus $1CUC for a camera, $5CUC for a camcorder), a must if you can't make it for the real thing in July. Thoughtfully laid out on the ground floor of a dimly lit colonial house, the museum is a bright and colourful collection of psychedelic costumes, atmospheric photographs and carnival memorabilia.

Beginning with scene-setting **photographs** of Santiago in the early twentieth century, showing roads laced with tram tracks and well-dressed people promenading through the parks, the exhibition moves on to photographs, newspaper cuttings and **costumes** belonging to the pre-revolutionary carnivals of the 1940s and 1950s. Pictures of extravagant **floats** – including one bearing the logo of now-exiled sponsors Bacardí – are jumbled together with minutely embroidered satin capes garlanded with flowers, harlequin outfits and giant, head-shaped, papier-mâché masks.

In a separate room are photographs of some of the musicians who have played at carnival accompanied by their **instruments**, displayed in glass cases. A final room shows off costumes made for post-Revolution carnivals, often rather less glamorous than their predecessors. The most recent prize-winning costume is kept in the centre of the room, along with some of the immensely intricate prototypes of floats that are constructed in miniature months before the final models are made.

When the museum closes, its flamboyant carnival atmosphere is brought to life with a free, open-air, hour-long **dance recital** (Mon–Sat 4–5pm,) called the *Tardes de Folklórico* (folklore afternoon), in which the dances and music of various *orishas* (deities) are performed.

Museo Emilio Bacardí Moreau and around

Of all the museums in Santiago, by far the most essential is the stately **Museo Emilio Bacardí Moreau**, on the corner of Aguilera and Pío Rosado (Tues–Sat

The ten-day extravaganza that is **Santiago's carnival** has its origins in the festival of Santiago (St James), which is held annually on July 25. While the Spanish colonists venerated the saint, patron of Spain and Santiago city, their African slaves celebrated their own religions, predominantly Yoruba. A religious procession would wend its way around the town towards the cathedral, with the Spanish taking the lead and slaves bringing up the rear. Once the Spanish had entered the cathedral the slaves took their own celebration onto the streets, with dancers, singers and musicians creating a ritual that had little to do with the solemn religion of the Spanish – the frenzied gaiety of the festival even earned it the rather derisive name **Los Mamarrachos** (The Mad Ones).

Music was a key element right from the start, and slaves of similar ethnic groups would form *comparsas* (carnival bands) to make music with home-made bells, drums and chants. Often accompanying the *comparsas* on the procession were *diablitos* (little devils) – male dancers masked from head to toe in raffia costumes. This tradition is still upheld today and you can see the rather unnerving, jester-like figures running through the crowds and scaring children. Carnival's popularity grew, and in the seventeenth century the festival was gradually extended to cover July 24, the festival of Santa Cristina, and July 26, Santa Ana's day.

When the French colonials arrived with their African slaves, following the 1791 slave revolution in Haiti, they brought significant contributions to Los Mamarrachos. The *comparsas* began to incorporate elements of French dance genres, most notably the *contredanse*, with its highly choreographed, ballroom-style steps, and as a result the parades became more stylized and structured. Although the festival was still essentially a black celebration, it was watched by bourgeois Cubans from their windows and balconies, from where they would often throw money at the feet of performers as they passed through the streets.

The festival underwent its biggest change in 1902 with the birth of the new republic, when politics and advertising began to muscle in on the action. It was during this era that the festival's name was changed to the more conventional "carnaval", as the

9.15am–8.15pm, Sun 9am–12.15pm, Mon 2–8.15pm; $2CUC, $1CUC extra for cameras, although photography of most displays is prohibited). Its colonial antiquities, excellent collection of Cuban fine art and archeological curios – including an Egyptian mummy – make it one of the most comprehensive hoards in the country.

Styled along the lines of a traditional European city museum, it was founded in 1899 by Emilio Bacardí Moreau, then mayor of Santiago and patriarch of the Bacardí rum dynasty (see box, p.514), to house his vast private collection of artefacts, amassed over the previous decades. The original museum occupied a more modest venue on Enramada, but Bacardí felt that his tremendous collection deserved better and the present structure was purpose-built to his instructions. Photographs on the first floor recall the man, his project and his wife Elvira Cape, who saw the construction through to fruition when Bacardí died.

The exhibits are arranged over three floors. The ground floor is devoted to the **Sala de Conquista y Colonización**, full of elaborate weaponry like sixteenth-century helmets, cannons and spurs, and a heavy mace like a twist of silver candy, although copper cooking pots and the like add a suggestion of social history. Much more sinister here are the whips, heavy iron chains and the *Palo Mata Negro* (or Kill-the-Black stick), all used to whip and beat slaves. The chopping board on display was used to slice off insubordinate slaves' arms, hands

middle classes sought to distance the celebrations from their Afro-Cuban roots. With the introduction of the annually selected *Reina de Carnaval* (Carnival Queen) – usually a white, middle-class girl – and carnival floats sponsored by big-name companies like Hatuey beer and Bacardí rum, the celebration was transformed from marginal black community event to populist extravaganza. With sponsorship deals abundant, the *carrozas* (floats) flourished, using extravagant and grandiose designs.

After the Revolution, the new regime poured money into all areas of carnival entertainment, which in the absence of big-name sponsors became reliant on public funding. Following a hiatus during the Special Period – which saw carnival cancelled for several years in the 1990s – the festival regained its egalitarianism and every neighbourhood now has its own *comparsa* made up of adults and children, all wearing home-made costumes. Bands practise extensively, often rehearsing in the parks and local streets in the run-up to the main parade. Everything and anything is used to make music, including metal tyre rims and frying pans for percussion, as well as the more conventional trumpets and drums. An essential part of the Santiago carnival sound is formed by the *corneta china* (Chinese horn), a double-reeded horn with a plaintive, wailing sound that was introduced by Chinese indentured labourers in the late nineteenth century.

Perhaps the most distinctive element of modern-day carnival in Santiago is the **conga parade** that takes place in each neighbourhood on the first day of the celebrations. Led by the *comparsas*, seemingly everyone in the neighbourhood, many still dressed in hair curlers and house slippers, leaves their houses as the performers lead them around the streets in a vigorous parade. Children join in with home-made rattles and drums, while the adults dance in what has become the unofficial signal of the start of carnival.

The carnival takes place every year from July 18–27, with the main parades scheduled for the last three days. The best place to watch the processions is Ave. Garzón, where there are seats for viewing ($2CUC after 9pm); to buy a ticket, visit the temporary booth near the seating stands earlier in the evening.

or feet, a punishment which took place in public, on Calle Carnicería ("Carnage Street"). Also displayed on the ground floor are drums, a crown and a chair used as a throne by the Congo Juan de Góngora *cabildo*, one of the secret slave chapters that used to practise their own religion in defiance of colonial Catholicism.

A separate room at the back houses the **Sala de Arqueología**, where a substantial selection of Egyptian artefacts includes some fine jade and bluestone eagle-head idols, as well as the only **Egyptian mummy** in Cuba. Thought to be a young woman from the Thebes dynasty, the mummy was brought over from Luxor by Bacardí himself; her well-preserved casket is on display nearby, covered in hieroglyphs and pictures. Other relics include two Peruvian mummies from the Paracas culture, believed to be over a thousand years old, and artefacts from the Tsantsa people of the Amazon region, including an arm shield, a bow decorated with clumps of hair from victims' scalps, and some small but perfectly formed shrunken heads. There is little in the Sala de Arqueología from Cuba, other than a few tenth- and eleventh-century stone and quartz idols from Oriente, depicting pregnant women with hollowed-out eyes and gaping mouths.

On the first floor the theme turns to the history of the fight for **independence**, exhibiting the printing press where Carlos Manuel de Céspedes's independence manifesto newspaper *El Cubano Libre* was produced. Representing

The Bacardí dynasty

Don Facundo Bacardí Massó emigrated to Santiago de Cuba from Spanish Catalonia in 1829, and eventually established what is today the fourth largest spirits company in the world. A wine merchant back home, it was a natural progression for Bacardí to turn his attentions to Cuba's abundant liquor. At the time, **rum** was a rasping drink favoured by pirates and slaves – hardly the type of tipple served to the Cuban aristocracy. However, Bacardí was swift to see the drink's potential and set to work refining it. Several attempts later he discovered that filtering the rum through charcoal removed impurities, while ageing it in oak barrels provided a depth that made it eminently more drinkable.

Buoyed by his successful discovery, Facundo and his brother Jos opened their first distillery on February 4, 1862. Company legend relates that when Don Facundo's wife Dona Amalia glimpsed the colony of fruit bats living in the building's rafters, she suggested they adopt the insignia of a **bat**, symbolizing good luck in Taíno folklore, as the company logo. This proved a shrewd marketing tool as many more illiterate Cubans could recognize the trademark bat than could read the name "Bacardí".

The company went from strength to strength, quickly becoming the major producer of quality rum, and their involvement in **Cuban politics** grew in tandem with their business interests. As major traders they were quick to see the benefits of independence from Spain to whom high trade taxes were paid. The family became instrumental in the push for independence and subsequent alliance with the US. Emilio Bacardí, Don Facundo's eldest son, was exiled from Cuba for anti-colonial activities but later returned as a Mambises liberation fighter in the rebel army during the Second War of Independence. The Bacardís' loyalty to the cause was rewarded in 1899 when American General Leonard Wood appointed Emilio Bacardí mayor of Santiago de Cuba. While Faucudito – Facundo senior's younger son – ran the company and supervised research into further refining the rum, Emilio Bacardí concentrated on public life. The **Emilio Bacardí Moreau Municipal Museum** opened the year he became mayor, its future star attraction a mummy, still on display today, which he procured himself on an expedition to Egypt in 1912.

Meanwhile, business was booming back at the distillery. The widespread popularity of two new rum-based cocktails – the **Cuba Libre**, concocted by the US Signal Corps in

the actual fighting is an assortment of the Mambises' ingenious bullet belts, cups, sandals and trousers, all handmade from natural products while on the warpath. The generals' gallery is less exciting, with an unenlightening array of artefacts from the key players, like Antonio Maceo's drinking cup, top hat and saddle, and José Martí's fountain pen. Better, although unrelated, is the armaments gallery over to one side, with more pistols, machetes, daggers and engraved samurai swords than you can shake a stick at.

The museum really comes into its own on the second floor, with an excellent display of **paintings** and **sculpture**, including some fascinating nineteenth-century portraits of colonial Cubans, amongst them Frederico Martínez Matos's insightful society studies and Manuel Vicens's 1864 family portrait, *Interior de la Casa de Juan Bautista Sagarra*. A surprise is the delicately executed series of watercolours – including a rather camp cavalryman and an enigmatic picador – by the multitalented Emilio Bacardí himself.

The second floor also features a strong collection of **contemporary** painting and sculpture, with several of the country's most prominent artists represented. Highlights include the iridescent *Paisaje* by Víctor Manuel García, who died in the late 1960s, and Fauvist Adigio Benitez's captivating *Punto de Control*, in which a steely yet sensual daughter of the Revolution operates machinery. The

Havana, and the **Daiquirí**, invented by American mining engineer Jennings S Cox – helped swell the family coffers. Facundito's brother-in-law Henri Schueg supervised company expansion with the opening of new bottling plants in Barcelona and New York. Though the New York plant was closed during the **Prohibition** years, Bacardí still did well during the twenties and thirties. As Cuba became the smart place for holidaying North Americans to drink and make the sort of whoopee outlawed at home, the island's biggest purveyors of alcohol were ready both to serve them and to join in the fun.

Testimony to the family bounty stands in the fabulous 1930 Art Deco **Edifico Bacardí** on Havana's Neptuno, which combined a company headquarters with an elegant and well-appointed bar. During World War II, the company was led by Schueg's son-in-law José Pepin Bosch, who also founded Bacardí Imports in New York City. Also a political mover and shaker, he was appointed Cuba's Minister of the Treasury in 1949 during Carlos Prío's government.

The **Revolution**, with its core aim of redistributing the country's wealth to the benefit of the underprivileged peasant classes, completely altered the course of the Bacardí family's history. Enraged by the 1960 nationalization of their main distillery in Santiago, the company spurned the Cuban government's offers of compensation and shipped out of Cuba, relocating their headquarters to the Bahamas where sugar cane – and cheap labour – were in plentiful supply.

Though no longer based in Cuba, the Bacardí family have not relinquished their desire to shape the country's destiny. While keen to make much of their Cuban heritage and tap into the image of Cuba's *joie de vivre* "Latin Quarter" in an international marketing campaign, the company has done little to assist Cuba since their departure and not surprisingly have done what they could to undermine the Revolution. Author Hernando Calvo Ospina, in his 2002 book *Bacardí, The Hidden War*, claims that Bacardí financed 1960s counter-revolutionary groups (including the attack on the Bay of Pigs), helped found the ultra-right-wing Cuban American National Foundation (CANF) and were so intimately involved with drafting the Helm-Burton Act of 1996 that opposing US senators dubbed it the "Helms-Bacardí Act". The Bacardís have denied most of these allegations but have made no secret of the fact that there is no love lost between them and the Cuban government.

simple but powerful *Maternidad*, by Pedro Arrate, is a perfect composition, with a young mother kneeling on a bare wooden floor nursing her newborn child.

Museo del Ron

One block south of Calle Heredia, at San Basilio no.358 esq Carnicería, the **Museo del Ron** (Mon–Sat 9am–5pm; $2CUC, entrance includes a Spanish-English- or German-speaking guide) explores the history and production of Cuba's most popular liquor. The collection includes a number of antique machines used in the various stages of rum production, from the extraction of molasses from sugar cane to the ageing and bottling of the rum. Occupying the fine nineteenth-century home of Mariano Gómez, who was in charge of managing the Bacardí family's enormous wealth (see box, above), the museum is replete with Carrera marble floors, glittering chandeliers and red-and-green *vitrales*. There is a rather dingy on-site bar, but you get a free shot with admission.

Museo Ciencias Naturales Tomás Romay and Plaza Marté

At the east end of Enramada, about a ten-minute walk east from the Museo Emilio Bacardí Moreau, taxidermy enthusiasts will thrill to the moth-eaten

Summing up his goals with the words "a small engine is needed to help start the big engine", Fidel Castro decided in 1953 to lead an attack to capture the weapons his guerrilla organization needed and hopefully also spark a national uprising against the Batista regime. Santiago's **Moncada Barracks** seemed perfect: not only was it the second largest in the country, with some thousand-odd troops, but it was also based in Oriente, where support for the clandestine movement against the government was already strongest.

The attack was organized from Havana in such secrecy that only two members of the group, besides Castro himself, even knew of the plan – some of the supporters thought they were being taken to Santiago carnival as a reward for hard work. Castro shrewdly chose July 26, reckoning that many soldiers would be unfit to fight in the early hours of the morning after carousing at carnival the night before. He rented a farm at Siboney, about 14km from the city, and the attackers mustered here. With limited funds and only a few secondhand weapons, it was an ambitious military debut for the small cell of 135 men and two women who would stage the attack.

A three-pronged assault was planned, with the main body of men, led by Fidel Castro, attacking the barracks themselves, while Raúl Castro, Fidel's brother, would attack the nearby Palace of Justice, overlooking the barracks, with ten men to form a covering crossfire. At the same time, Abel Santamaría, Castro's second-in-command, was to take the civil hospital opposite the Palace of Justice with 22 men; the two women, his sister Haydee Santamaría and his girlfriend Melba Hernández, were to treat the wounded.

The attack was an unqualified fiasco. At 5.30am on July 26, the rebels' motorcade of 26 cars set off from Siboney headed for Santiago. Somewhere between the farm and the city limits, several cars headed off in the wrong direction and never made it to the barracks. The remaining cars reached the barracks, calling on the sentries to make way for the general, a ruse which allowed the attackers to seize the sentries' weapons and force their way into the barracks.

Outside, things were going less well. Castro, who was in the second car, stopped after an unexpected encounter with patrolling soldiers and the subsequent gunfire alerted the troops throughout the barracks. Following their previous orders, once they saw that Castro's car had stopped, the men in the other cars streamed out to attack other buildings in the barracks before Castro had a chance to re-evaluate the

---

stuffed animals at the **Museo Ciencias Naturales Tomás Romay** (Mon 2.30–5.30pm, Tues–Fri 8am–5.30pm, Sat 8am–3pm; $1CUC). Everyone else should instead wander through the lively **Plaza Marté**, one block east, where gaggles of game-playing schoolchildren, loudspeakers transmitting radio broadcasts and plenty of benches beneath shady trees would make this an enjoyable place to sit down were it not for the attendant *jiniteros*. The tall column, a **monument** to local veterans of the Wars of Independence, has a particular significance as the plaza was formerly the execution ground for prisoners held by the Spanish. The Smurf-like cap at its summit is the *gorro frigio*, given to slaves in ancient Rome when they were granted their freedom, and a traditional symbol of Cuban independence.

The Cuartel Moncada and Parque Abel Santamaría

Several blocks north from Plaza Marté and just off the Avenida de los Libertadores, the **Cuartel Moncada**, futilely stormed by Fidel Castro and his band of

situation. The rebels inside the first building found themselves cut off amid the general confusion and as free-for-all gunfire ensued, the attackers were reduced to fleeing and cowering behind cars. Castro gave the order to withdraw, leaving behind two dead and one wounded.

By contrast, the unprotected Palace of Justice had been captured successfully, although Raúl Castro's group were also forced to withdraw once their role was rendered useless. Similarly, the attack on the hospital had also been successful, although the attackers did not receive the order to retreat and had to hide in the hospital itself, disguised as patients.

The aftermath

The real bloodshed was yet to come, however, as within 48 hours of the attack somewhere between 55 and 70 of the original rebels had been captured, tortured and executed by Batista's officers after an extensive operation in which thousands were detained. The casualties included Abel Santamaría, whose eyes were gouged out, while his sister, Haydee, was forced to watch. Her boyfriend, Boris Santa Coloma, was castrated and other prisoners were beaten with rifle butts before being shot. The soldiers then attempted to pass the bodies off as casualties of the attack two days before.

Thirty-two rebels survived to be brought to trial, including Fidel Castro himself. Others managed to escape altogether and returned to Havana. Although a disaster in military terms, the attack was a political triumph: the army's brutality towards the rebels sent many previously indifferent people into the arms of the clandestine movement and elevated Fidel Castro – previously seen as just a maverick young lawyer – to hero status throughout Cuba.

The rebels were tried in October, and despite efforts to prevent Castro appearing in court – an attempt was apparently made to poison him – he gave an erudite and impassioned speech in his own defence. Speaking for five hours, he charted the plight of the Cuban people, using an arsenal of statistics to assault the regime and charging Batista with being the worst dictator in Cuban history. A reprise of the speech was later published as a manifesto for revolution, known as "history will absolve me". Although the declamation did little to help Castro at the time – he was sentenced to fifteen years' imprisonment – the whole episode set him on the path to the leadership of the Revolution.

revolutionaries on July 26, 1953 (see box, above), is a must-see, if only for the place it has in Cuban history. With a commanding view over the mountains, the ochre-and-white building, topped with a fat row of castellations, is still peppered with bullet holes from the attack. These were plastered over on Fulgencio Batista's orders, only to be hollowed out again rather obsessively by Fidel Castro when he came to power, with photographs used to make sure the positions were as authentic as possible.

Castro closed the barracks altogether in 1960, turning part of the building into a school, while the one-time parade grounds outside are now occasionally used for state speeches. Also inside is the **Museo 26 de Julio** (Tues–Sat 9am–7.30pm, Sun 9am–1pm; $2CUC, $1CUC for a camera, $5CUC for a video camera), which is not without flashes of brilliance when it comes to telling the story of the attack, but is otherwise rather dry. Note that English-, Spanish- and Italian-speaking **guides** will take you round the museum at no extra charge.

After learning that it was built by the Spanish in 1850, occupied by the North American army in 1898 during the Wars of Independence, accidentally burnt down in 1937 and rebuilt in 1938, you can bypass the pedantic history of the garrison. The museum gets properly under way with its coverage of the 1953 attack. A meticulous **scale model** details the barracks, the now-demolished hospital and the Palacio de Justicia, and gives the events a welcome clarity – the model is even marked with the positions where rebel bullets landed. The museum pulls no punches on the subject of the **atrocities** visited upon the captured rebels by the Regimental Intelligence Service, Batista's henchmen: a huge collage, blotted with crimson paint, has been created from photographs of the dead rebels lying in their own gore. There are short biographies of some of the unfortunates, along with gruesome bloodstained uniforms and some sobering sketches of the type of weapons used.

Thankfully, the last room has a less oppressive theme, with **photographs** of the surviving rebels leaving the Isla de Pinos (now Isla de la Juventud), where they had been imprisoned following the attack, and in exile in Mexico. There's also a scale model of the celebrated yacht *Granma* that carried them back to Cuba. If you can tear yourself away from the lovingly preserved burgundy jumper and US-issue backpack that Castro wore in the Sierra Maestra, have a look at the **guns** used in the war, in particular the one in the middle of the display, carved with the national flag and the inscription "*Vale más morir de pies a vivir de rodillas*" (It's better to die on your feet than to live on your knees).

The exhibits peter out after this and you're left with a cluster of cuttings from early editions of Revolution newspapers, full of promises about the forth-coming utopia, some of which have actually been fulfilled; a dinner jacket belonging to José Martí; and an incomprehensible diagram showing how the different levels of assemblies, committees and local bodies mesh together to form the Cuban government. The museum ends with a big **mural** lauding Santiago's achievements in health, education and culture.

Parque Abel Santamaría

A couple of blocks west of the barracks, on the site of the Civil Hospital which Santamaría captured during the Moncada attack, **Parque Histórico Abel Santamaría** is less of a park and more like a small field of concrete centred on a monument to Abel Santamaría. Set above a gushing fountain, a gigantic cube of concrete is carved with the faces of Santamaría and fellow martyr José Martí and the epigram "*Morir por la patria es vivir*" (To die for your country is to live). Seemingly buoyed up by the jet of water, the floating cube is rather impressive and worth a look while you're in the area.

Reparto Vista Alegre and Loma de San Juan

East of town is the residential suburb of **Reparto Vista Alegre**, which was established at the beginning of the twentieth century as an exclusive neighbour-hood for Santiago's middle classes. Today its lingering air of wealth is confined to a few top-notch **restaurants** dotted around wide and regal Avenida Manduley, which are most people's reason for visiting (see p.522), although a clutch of interesting museums also makes a trip up to this part of town worth-while. Some of the handsome Neoclassical buildings lining the main road – best seen in springtime under a cloud of pink blossoms – are still private residences, while others are government offices. Although most of the buildings are a bit worn around the edges, they make for pleasant sightseeing, especially the madly ornate peach-coloured palace – one-time Bacardí family residence – that's now the headquarters of the children's *Pionero* youth movement.

Should you be in the area, a place well worth your time is the small and quirky **Museo de la Imagen**, Calle 8 no.106 (Mon–Sat 9am–5pm; $1CUC). This museum presents a brief history of photography told through antique Leicas, Polaroids and Kodaks, and some brilliant (and odd) one-off photographs, such as the one showing Fidel Castro, in Native American feathered headdress, accepting a peace pipe from the leader of the White Bird tribe.

About a block north stands the **Centro Cultural Africano Fernando Ortiz** at Ave. Manduley no.106 esq. Calle 5ta (Mon–Fri 9am–5pm; $1CUC), a worthwhile institution dedicated to the study and promotion of African culture in Cuba. Named after Cuba's most important ethnologist and anthropologist, the centre holds a small collection of African art and artefacts including paintings, masks, beautifully sculpted woodcarvings and an enormous elephant's tusk, and a library of books about the African experience in Cuba and the Caribbean.

Casa de las Religiones Populares

Anyone interested in Cuba's idiosyncratic home-grown religions should head four blocks east to the fascinating **Casa de las Religiones Populares** at Calle 13 no.206 esq. 10 (Mon–Sat 9am–6pm; $2CUC with guide). The collection spans the different belief systems, including Santería and voodoo, which developed in different parts of the country, each local variation shaped by the traditions of the homelands of the African slaves and all influenced by the Catholicism of the Spanish settlers. It's striking to see how Christian iconography has been fused with some of the African culture-based paraphernalia, with the animal bones, dried leaves and rag dolls presented alongside church candles, crucifixes and images of the Virgin and Child. The Christian influence is most evident in the altars bedecked with candles, flowers and photos which grieving families construct to honour their dead relatives.

Loma de San Juan and Parque Zoológico

The **Loma de San Juan**, the hill where Teddy Roosevelt rode his army to victory against the Spanish, is about 250m south from Avenida Manduley, which runs through the centre of Reparto Vista Alegre. The neatly mowed lawns framing a bijou fountain, the dainty flowerbeds and the sweeping vista of mountain peaks beyond the city make it all look more suited to a tea party than a battle, but the numerous plaques and monuments erected by the North Americans to honour their soldiers are evidence enough. The sole monument to the Cuban sacrifice is squeezed into a corner; erected in 1934 by Emilio Bacardí to the unknown Mambí soldier, it's a tribute to all liberation soldiers whose deaths went unrecorded. The park would be a peaceful retreat were it not for the persistent attentions of the attendant crowd of hustlers.

On Avenida Raúl Pujol, 250m west of Loma de San Juan, is Santiago's **Parque Zoológico** (Tues–Sun 10am–5pm; $1CUC). Covering 19 hectares, it is larger than most zoos in Cuba, but still a rather miserable place where a menagerie of mournful creatures lies, for the most part, cramped and listless in rather squalid cages. The most celebrated animals include a chimpanzee who smokes cigarettes – given the chance – a pair of lions which cower when approached, and some apathetic hyenas. With more space to move about, the numerous species of birds – including parrots, flamingos and Cuba's national bird, the tocororo – fare slightly better, with the exception of the ill-fated white ducks which are bred exclusively to feed the torpid pythons caged nearby. The wide range of animals also includes horses which you can ride ($2CUC an hour), but it's really not the place for animal lovers.

Monumento Antonio Maceo

Two kilometres north of the centre, on Avenida de los Américas, by the busy junction with Avenida de los Libertadores, is the **Plaza de la Revolución**, an empty space backed by a park in which stands the gargantuan **Monumento Antonio Maceo**. The sixteen-metre steel effigy, on a wide plateau at the top of a jade marble staircase, shows Maceo, the "Bronze Titan" – so named because he was of mixed race – on his rearing horse, backed by a forest of gigantic steel machetes representing his rebellion and courage. On the other side of the marble plateau, wide steps lead down behind an eternal flame dedicated to the general, to the **Museo Antonio Maceo** (Mon–Sat 9am–5pm, Sun 9am–1pm; $1CUC), housed in the plateau basement. Inside you'll find a somewhat lifeless collection of sketches representing key events and some fuzzy holograms showing Maceo's watch, ring and pen in three-dimensional detail.

Cementerio Santa Ifigenia

Most visitors who trek out to the **Cementerio Santa Ifigenia** (daily 7am–6pm; $1CUC), about 3km northwest of Parque Céspedes, do so to visit **José Martí's mausoleum**, a grandiose affair of heavy white stone with the inevitable statue located near the cemetery entrance at the end of a private walkway. Every half an hour there's a five-minute changing of the guard ceremony in which the soldiers goose-step down the walkway in time to thunderous revolutionary marching music. The soldiers are carefully selected to be less than 1.75 metres in height so that they do not need to bow their heads to pass under the ledge at the entrance of the tomb.

A relatively recent arrival at the cemetery is **Compay Segundo**, a native Santiaguero, legendary singer and guitarist, member of the Buena Vista Social Club and author of the ubiquitous *Chan Chan*. Segundo, who died in 2003 at the age of 95, was buried with full military honours in recognition of his achievements during the Revolution, long before he became famous as a musician.

The burial site of **Frank and Josue País** is flanked by the flags of Cuba and the M-26-7 movement. Frank País, a former schoolteacher and much-loved revolutionary, led the movement in the Oriente until his assassination, on Batista's orders, at the age of 22. Among other luminaries buried here are Carlos Manuel de Céspedes and Antonio Maceo's widow, but some of the lesser-known structures, like the Naser family's mosque-like domed tomb, and the replica of El Morro fort honouring Spanish and Cuban war veterans, are the most eye-catching. Once you've paid your respects, you can wander undisturbed through the cemetery's palm trees, admiring the magnificent tombs and trying to ignore the unfortunate smell of sewage wafting over from the town's nearby treatment plant. Guides are available to show you around in return for a small tip.

Out from the city

Just 8km south of the city is one of Santiago's most dramatic and popular sights, the **Castillo del Morro San Pedro de la Roca**, a fortress poised on the high cliffs that flank the entrance to the Bahía de Santiago to Cuba, and home to the Museo de la Piratería. A half-day trip out here by taxi from the centre can also easily take in the diminutive **Cayo Granma**, 2km away, where a peaceful rural village offers an excellent spot for a meal. You can expect to pay around $10–12CUC, with an extra $3CUC to reach the ferry point.

El Castillo del Morro San Pedro de la Roca

One of Santiago's most essential sights, **El Castillo del Morro San Pedro de la Roca** (daily 8am–7pm; $4CUC, $1CUC extra for a camera, $5CUC for a camcorder), is a giant stone fortress designed by the Italian military engineer Juan Bautista Antonelli, also responsible for the similar fortification in Havana. Named after Santiago's then-governor, though usually shortened to "El Morro", it was built between 1633 and 1639 to ward off pirates. However, despite an indomitable appearance – including a heavy drawbridge spanning a deep moat, thick stone walls angled sharply to one another and, inside, expansive parade grounds stippled with cannons trained out to sea – it turned out to be nothing of the sort. In 1662 the English pirate Christopher Myngs captured El Morro after discovering, to his surprise, that it had been left unguarded.

Ramps and steps cut precise angles through the heart of the fortress, which is spread over three levels, and it's only as you wander deeper into the labyrinth of rooms that you get a sense of how awesomely huge it is. Even when the fortress is completely overrun by busloads of visitors, you can move through the prison cells, chapel and dormitories – with accommodation for the 150 soldiers once billeted there – without feeling too crowded. The small, square *tinajones* water carriers and the twisted, blue balustrades in front of the windows add a note of distinction, while the room stacked with cannonballs and fitted with the heavy shaft that would roll them to the cannon illustrates the seriousness of the castle's business.

El Morro also houses the **Museo de Piratería**, which details the pirate raids on Santiago during the sixteenth century by the infamous Frenchman Jacques de Sores and Englishman Henry Morgan. Detailed explanations in Spanish are complemented by weapons used in the era, now rusted by the passing years. It's an interesting addition, but the real splendour of the castle is the magnificent scale, the sheer cliff-edge drop and superb views out to sea.

Cayo Granma

Take the road that turns off the main road to Santiago by El Morro and follow the signs for "Embarcadero" for 2km, until you reach the ferry point for tiny **Cayo Granma**, a grassy, beachless dune just offshore, with red-tiled homes and a scattering of restaurants clustered around the coast. There's no sign for the actual ferry point, but it's roughly opposite the cay and there are usually a few people queuing. The ferry crosses to the island at half past each hour from 5am to midnight ($1CUC) and takes about fifteen minutes – ask for the return times on your outward journey.

You can work up an appetite walking round the cay – it only takes twenty minutes – and taking in the near-panoramic view of the mountains from the top of its one hill, before relaxing at one of the **restaurants**. *Restaurant El Cayo* (T22/69-0109) does fancy seafood, including lobster, paella and shrimp, with prices starting at $6CUC, while *Restaurant Paraíso* does basic meals very cheaply. You can also ask around for a *paladar*, which are theoretically not allowed here, but that doesn't stop a few from operating below the radar.

Eating

As with most other regions in the country, the majority of **restaurants** in Santiago fall back on the old favourites of pork or chicken accompanied by rice and beans, although there are a few original dishes and most state restaurants, especially the higher-end ones, usually have a tasty seafood dish. You won't be stuck for places to try, with plenty of restaurants and cafés around the **centre** all serving decent meals at affordable prices.

The best area for daytime **snacks** is by the bus station on Avenida de los Américas, where there's an abundance of stands selling maize fritters and fried pork sandwiches, with a few more stands dotted around closer to the centre. Around Avenida Manduley, in **Reparto Vista Alegre**, the restaurants are more upmarket and it's here that you can dine out in some style. High taxes and tight controls on what food can be served have pushed most of the **paladares** in town out of business, which limits choices somewhat, but some *casas particulares* make tasty meals for their guests.

Avoid drinking **unsterilized or unboiled water** (remember that this includes ice cubes in drinks), especially during the summer months, when reports of parasites in Santiago's water supply are common.

State restaurants

Boulevard Dolores Plaza de Dolores. This trio of Palmares-run restaurants comprises a vaguely upmarket restaurant complex. The *Don Antonio* is the best choice for good but expensive lobster amongst its *comida criolla* dishes; the mediocre *La Perla del Dragón* has a variety of Chinese dishes with a Cuban twist; and *Teressina* dishes up the ubiquitous spaghetti with tomato sauce and decent pizza. All three eateries are serviceable but not outstanding.

Cafetería La Isabelica Calvario esq. Aguilera. Atmospheric little 24hr coffeeshop with wooden fittings and whirling ceiling fans offering a variety of coffees; the most popular come with a shot of rum.

Coppelia Ave. de los Libertadores esq. Garzón. Freshly made ice cream at unbeatable peso prices in an outdoor café that looks like a mini-golf course. Very popular with locals, so arrive early before the best flavours of the day sell out. Tues–Sun 9am–11pm.

La Casona Meliá Santiago de Cuba Ave. de las Américas y Calle M ✆ 22/68-7070. If you can't face another piece of fried pork, head to the *Hotel Santiago*, where thin-crust pizza, fresh salads and overcooked broccoli are part of an all-you-can-eat buffet ($20CUC a head, excluding drinks).

La Corona Félix Pena no.807 esq. San Carlos. Excellent bakery with an indoor café serving up a wide variety of breads and sweets, as well as pastries filled with custard or smothered in super-sticky meringue.

Dolores San Basilio e/ Carnicería y San Félix. A gem of a restaurant, with seating in an open-air courtyard that makes for a pleasant place to linger for after-dinner drinks. The good-quality, inexpensive *comida criolla* is complemented by live music and efficient service.

Libertad *Hotel Libertad*, Aguilera s/n e/ Serafin Sánchez y Pérez Carbo. Within its cheery yellow walls, this decent, unpretentious restaurant serves up fruit salad, French toast and much more on a widely ranging breakfast menu. Its reasonably priced lunch and evening menu also offers more variety than most, with dishes like Uruguayan steaks and crème caramel enlivening the standard fare.

La Maison Ave. Manduley esq. 1 no.52, Reparto Vista Alegre ✆ 22/64-1117. A swanky restaurant in La Maison (a small complex of fashion boutiques) serving good steaks, red snapper and seafood specialities including paella and surf 'n' turf grill. Prices start at $8CUC.

Mar Init Calvario e/ Aguilera y Enramadas. Although purporting to be a seafood specialist, more often than not there's just pork in stock and the only fish you'll see are those decorating the walls. Still, the pork's fairly good, the prices are cheap, the service is friendly and you can eat to the strummings of an electric guitar.

Matamoros Calvario esq Aguilera. An agreeable restaurant on this popular square serving up the usual chicken and pork dishes. It's reasonably priced and a musical trio plays while you eat.

El Morro Perched next to the fortress in a lovely, breezy spot overlooking the bay, this relatively pricey restaurant boasts a generous array of choices and serves good-quality cuisine including soups, fish, seafood, chicken and pork dishes. Main courses start at $7CUC, lobster will set you back $25CUC.

Pizza Nova *Hotel Santiago de Cuba*, Ave. de las Américas y Calle M. This outdoor café is the best place in town for thin-crust pizza with a range of toppings, and great spaghetti at sensible prices. There's also a takeaway service.

San Basilio San Basilio 403 e/ Calvario y Carnicería. The hotel's mid-range restaurant has only five tables but it's worth trying to get one of them as the varied menu includes some unusual dishes such as fish with coconut sauce and "dreaded" beef – fried with breadcrumbs.

Sodería Alondra Garzón esq. Calle C. It's a bit of a trek to this ice-cream parlour but worth it for the excellent ice cream and the thick frozen yogurt, all served neat or under a layer of sugar sprinkles with a fabulous variety of decorations ranging from cocktail umbrellas to frilly paper tomatoes.

La Taberna de Dolores Aguilera no.468 esq. Reloj ☎22/62-3913. A lively restaurant, serving reasonable *comida criolla*, popular with older Cuban men who while away the afternoon with a bottle of rum on the sunny patio. Musicians play in the evenings. Book to reserve a seat on the balcony overlooking the patio or street.

El Zunzun Ave. Manduley no.159 esq. Calle 7 ☎22/64-1528. Arguably the classiest restaurant in town, with a series of private dining rooms for an intimate dinner. Choose from an imaginative menu including pork in citrus sauce, and seafood stir-fried in garlic butter and flaming rum. Main courses start at $7CUC, there's an international wine list and injudicious use of reggaeton music.

Paladares

Las Gallegas San Basilio no.305. Excellent *paladar* close to the centre with a range of typical, well-prepared Cuban food. There's a tiny balcony that's perfect for a pre-dinner drink.

Salon Tropical Fernando Markane Rpto Sta Barbara e/ 9 y 11 ☎22/64-1161. A brisk *paladar* with a pleasant terrace for pre-dinner drinks. Tasty though salty chicken fricassee and grilled fish served with *tamales* are good choices here. Round the meal off with crème caramel and coffee. As this is really on the outskirts of town, you'll want to arrange a taxi to and fro. Reservations advised.

Drinking and nightlife

As much of the action in Santiago revolves around music, there are few places that cater specifically for **drinkers**, although the *Hotel Casa Granda* has two excellent bars (see p.525). **Musical** entertainment in Santiago is hard to beat, with several excellent live *trova* venues – all a giddy whirl of rum and high spirits with soulful *boleros* and *son* banged out by wizened old men who share the tunes and the talent of the likes of Ibrahim Ferrer and Compay Segundo, if not their fame. Oriente is the birthplace of the *trova* (or ballad) and it really does seem as though every second resident of Santiago can whip out a guitar and sing like a nightingale. Keep an eye out for the superb *trova* group Estudiantina Invasora, who often play at the *Casa de la Trova*. You don't have to exert too

△ Hotel Casa Granda

much effort to enjoy the best of the town's music scene; the music often spills onto the streets at weekends and around carnival time (see p.512) when bands set up just about everywhere. Sometimes the best way to organize your night out is to follow the beat you like the most. The best nights are often the cheapest, and it's rare to find a venue charging more than $5CUC.

Music played in **discos** tends to be as loud as the sound system will permit, sometimes louder, and anything goes, from Cuban and imported *salsa*, through reggae and rock to very cheesy house. They tend to draw a young, sometimes edgy and high-spirited crowd, including many of the *jinetero* and *jinetera* types who hang out in Parque Céspedes trying to win your attention. Both male and female visitors should be prepared for lots more of this behaviour, and taken in the right vein it can be amusing and even make you some friends, but it's a situation that attracts a lot of police interest, and trouble spots are often closed without warning in a bid to stem the flesh trade. At those discos still open, you can expect to pay between $1CUC and $5CUC entrance.

Artex Heredia no.304, e/ Calvario y Carniceria. Bypass the inside bar (which smells of fried chicken) and head to the outside patio for live *bolero*, *rumba*, *son* and lively *salsa*. It's a good place to warm up before heading on to the *Casa de la Trova* further down the same road. Daily 9am–midnight.

Bar Claqueta Santo Tomás e/ San Basilio y Heredia. A small, welcoming open-air club with excellent, energetic live music from the two resident bands, Los Amantes del Son and Sonora Huracán.

El Baturro Aguilera esq. San Félix. This pub-style bar, decorated with Spanish bullfighting memorabilia, hosts live bands playing Santana covers and other crowd-pleasers until 1am. Serving peso cocktails and dollar convertible-peso beers, this is a rough-and-ready venue which on some nights can feel a bit edgy.

Casa de la Cultura San Pedro, on Parque Céspedes. Formerly a high-society club, this gracefully decaying venue is perfect for classic sounds. There's often a band playing on Sat, a fairly regular *rumba* night, occasional classical music performances and, on the first and third Sun of every month, a daytime show featuring a *trova* group.

Casa de la Música Corona no.564, e/ Aguilera y Enramadas. Santiago's newest music venue, with the country's most popular bands regularly headlining. There's live music every night, with dancing and high-spirited *jiniteras* much in evidence. Daily 10pm–2.30am, $5CUC.

Casa de los Estudiantes Heredia e/ San Pedro y San Félix. This appealing building with a long balcony forms a centre for a hotchpotch of exuberant activity and entertainment. There are traditional music shows on Mon, Wed and Fri mornings (9am–1pm) and occasional performances by Ballet Folklórico Cutumba, one of Cuba's most renowned traditional dance companies, and in residence here. Bands also play in the evening to a lively crowd – an even mix of Cubans and visitors, and there's a bar as well. It's an excellent venue to drink, dance and socialize. Cover $1CUC.

Casa de Té Felix Peña esq Aguilera. Pleasant teahouse overlooking the park. Serves a variety of brews, from camomile tea to hot chocolate.

Casa de las Tradiciones Rabí no.154 e/ Princesa y San Fernando. A different *trova* band plays into the small hours every night, in a tiny, atmospheric house with walls lined with photographs and album sleeves.

Casa de la Trova Heredia no.208 e/ San Pedro y San Félix. A visit to the famous, pocket-sized *Casa de la Trova* is the highlight of a trip to Santiago, with musicians playing day and night to an audience packed into the tiny downstairs room or hanging in through the window. Upstairs is more expansive but just as atmospheric, and excellent bands play every evening. Although this venue attracts much tourist attention, it is still the top choice in town for hearing excellent music and a definite must-see on the Santiago circuit. Entrance costs $2–5CUC depending on who's playing.

Casa del Caribe Calle 13 no.154 esq. 8, Reparto Vista Alegre. ℡22/64-3609. This Afro-Cuban cultural centre hosts ballet, Afro-Americano dance, *folklorico*, and traditional music every night at 8pm on a lovely patio. An informal atmosphere and enthusiastic performances make this worthy of the trip to the town outskirts.

Club 300 Aguilera no.300 e/ San Pedro y San Félix. Slick and sultry, *Club 300* is a dark little hideaway with leather seats and is open to 3am, serving cheap cocktails, quality rum and single malt whiskies. It's busier when bands play – ask inside for details.

Coro Madrigalista Carnicería no.555 e/ Aguilera y Heredia. This homely venue, which feels much like a village hall, is home to Santiago's oldest choir whose repertoire includes classical, sacred and traditional Cuban music. You're welcome to pop in and listen to the daily practice session (9am–noon); a nightly *peña*, featuring an assortment of local *son* and *trova* bands, takes place at 9pm.

Discoteca La Irís Aguilera no.617 e/ Barnada y Plácido. Pitch-black and packed, this club plays a mix of *merengue*, soul, reggae, rock and *salsa*, all of it at top volume. The cover charge of $3CUC includes a free cocktail. Closed Tues.

Los Dos Abuelos Pérez Carbo 5, Plaza Marte. A variety of local groups play *son* and *guaracha* on this bar's pretty patio, shaded by fruit trees, at 10pm every night. There's an extensive range of rums and snacks available.

Folklorico Ikaché San Felix no.552 e/ Callejon de Carmen y Enramades. A small music group, run by a flamboyant woman called Zenalda, give *salsa* classes ($7CUC an hour), have daily *folklorico* shows (between 4 and 7pm) and also perform Santería ceremonies in this small studio space.

Hotel Casa Granda Heredia no.201 e/ San Pedro y San Félix. Benefiting from a cool breeze, the hotel's balcony bar is the best central spot to soak up the local atmosphere, and somewhere to linger given the comfortable seating and the troubadour trio that sometimes plays. Later on you should retire to the open-air rooftop bar, which has views over the bay and the surrounding countryside and is the best place from which to watch the sun slide down behind the mountains. Both bars are open all day, though the rooftop bar charges $2CUC in the evenings.

Patio de la Trova Heredia no.304 e/ Calvario y Carnicería. Local groups play live traditional music every night in an attractive red-brick patio. You can relax and watch the show from the balcony above.

Pista Bailable Teatro Heredia, Ave. de las Américas s/n ☎ 22/64-3190. Pumped-up *salsa*, *son*, *bolero* and *merengue* tunes all get the crowd dancing at this unpretentious local club, with live music some nights.

Sala de Conciertos Esteban Salas Plaza Dolores. Take a break from the *salsa* and *son* drums and refresh your soul with a choral or classical concert at this concert hall set in the former church on the corner of Plaza Dolores. Daytime concerts are given daily; ask inside for performance details.

UNEAC Heredia no.266 e/ San Felix y Carnecería. Traditional and contemporary music *peñas* play here most nights. Check the door for the weekly programme. Open Tues–Sat 6pm–midnight.

Theatres, cabaret and cinemas

Santiago's obsession with music means that there's not much in the way of straight **theatre**. Teatro Heredia, beside the Plaza de la Revolución (☎22/64-3190), is the only large venue for plays, musicals and children's drama. Also in the complex is the *Café Cantante* club, hosting a Cuban variety-show evening (Fri–Sun; $5CUC) which pulls acts from a mixed bag of musicians, magicians, poets and comedians.

Cabaret fares better, with twice-weekly open-air spectaculars of bespangled dancers and variety acts at the *Santiago Tropicana* (☎22/6-8700), just over 1km northeast of the centre on the *autopista*, and tamer versions of the same thing at *Cabaret San Pedro del Mar*, near El Castillo del Morro (☎22/69-2373). Shows at both venues will set you back around $40–50CUC.

Of the several **cinemas** in town, Cine Rialto, at San Tomás near the cathedral, is the most central, while the one in the Teatro Heredia complex is usually guaranteed to show the latest Cuban releases. There's also a **video room** at Santo Tomás no.755 that screens mainly US imports.

Shopping and galleries

Although Santiago is no shoppers' paradise, there are still several places you can go to sniff out an authentic bargain or curiosity, while the town's art galleries occasionally have some worthy paintings and sculptures.

The **peso shops** in Enramada, one street north of Parque Céspedes – still bedecked with original, though non-functioning, neon signs – hold some surprising treasures if you're prepared to root, and there are also several dollar convertible-peso shops and supermarkets. The one shop here not to be missed is the peso department store near the corner of San Pedro, with two floors of goodies ranging from small tropical fish in plastic bags to cotton dresses.

For all things **musical**, try the shop in the *Casa de la Trova*, Heredia no.208 e/ San Pedro y San Félix, which has an excellent range of CDs, including a large selection of *son*, *bolero*, *salsa* and more by Santiago musicians, as well as books about Cuban music and musical instruments such as guitars, *guiros*, maracas and drums. If you're looking for **books**, try Librería La Escalera, at Heredia no.265 e/ San Félix y Carnicería, an extraordinary little den filled with all manner of secondhand titles for sale as well as the eccentric owner's display of business cards and liquor bottles from around the world; there's also a small selection of foreign-language titles available on an exchange basis ($1CUC). Alternatively, the Librería Internacional on Parque Céspedes, in the former crypt of the cathedral, has a decent selection of novels, history and natural history books, some in English. At Tienda la Catedral, around the corner, it's worth trawling through their stock of tacky handmade dolls, woven boxes and woodcuts for occasional finds like handmade leather belts and sandals.

Nearby, Heredia boasts a wealth of little trinket shops – including Tienda la Minerva on the corner of Carnicería which sells brightly coloured papier-mâché masks, pots and 1950s cars, handmade leather sandals, jewellery, wooden sculptures and other knick-knacks – as well as a thriving **street market** (daily 9am–6pm) selling bone and shell jewellery, bootleg tapes, maracas and drums, as well as general souvenirs. Another great place for high-quality souvenirs is Fondo Cubano de Bienes Culturales, on Heredia esq. San Pedro, with a diverse collection of paintings by local artists, cloth wall hangings, trinket boxes, leather bags and silver jewellery set with semiprecious local stones, as well as some big and beautiful – though not very portable – precious-wood sculptures.

The best place for women's **clothes** is ♣ Quitrín, on San Geronimo (Mon–Sat 9am–5pm; ☎22/62-2528). Although somewhat off the beaten track, it's worth the walk as all the exquisitely made, 100-percent white cotton dresses, skirts and shirts are fashioned on the premises. If you can't find your size, ask about their bespoke service; the seamstresses can make up clothes within five or six days. The highlights include traditional *guayabera* shirts, dresses and sun tops with hand-worked lace insets and contemporary crochet work. A second pleasure is the space itself: an eighteenth-century house which belonged to Raúl Castro's wife Vilma but was donated to the revolutionary cause and converted into a workshop where former prostitutes could retrain as seamstresses. With crystal chandeliers and chequered flagstones, the house is an oasis where white clothes flutter on rails. The **café** in the courtyard is an excellent place to relax and admire your purchases.

Of several commercial **galleries** dotted around the centre, the best are Galería Oriente, San Pedro no.163 (Tues–Sun 9am–9pm), with some excellent revolutionary and carnival posters and a few colourful surrealist oil paintings by local artists, and the small but notable Galería El Zaguan, Heredia e/ San Félix y San Pedro (Mon–Sat 9am–5pm), which sells a real mixture of paintings, from delicate landscape miniatures to thick oil portraits and rather ugly abstracts.

Rum aficionados will adore Barrita Ron Caney at Ave. Jesús Menéndez s/n San Ricardo y San Antonio, near the train station (Mon–Sat 9am–6pm, Sun 9am–noon), which has friendly staff and a huge selection, including a wicked, silky-smooth fifteen-year-old Havana Club ($85CUC). The shop is furnished with tables and chairs so you can indulge in your purchases straight away.

Listings

Airlines Cubana, Enramada esq. San Pedro (Mon–Fri 8.15am–1pm; ☎22/65-1577); Aerocaribbean, San Pedro 601A e/ Heredia y San Basilio (Mon–Fri 9am–noon & 1–4.30pm, Sat 9am–noon; ☎22/68-7255, ⓔaerocaribbeanscu@enet.cu).

Banks and exchange There are several banks near Parque Céspedes, including the Banco de Crédito y Comercio at Aguilera esq. San Pedro (Mon–Fri 9am–5pm) and the Banco Popular de Ahorro at Aguilera no.458 e/ Reloj y Calvario (Mon–Fri 8am–3.30pm); you can change traveller's cheques and get an advance on a credit card at both, while the latter also has an ATM. The Cadeca at Aguilera 508 e/ Reloj y Rabí (Mon–Sat 8.30am–6pm, Sun 8.30am–noon) offers the same services and also exchanges convertible pesos for Cuban pesos.

Car rental Havanautos are at *Hotel Las Américas* (☎22/68-7160) and at the airport (☎22/68-6161); Veracuba are at *Hotel Santiago de Cuba* (☎22/68-7070); Transtur (☎22/62-3884) have desks in *Hotel Casa Granda*, *Hotel Libertad* and *Hotel Las Américas*; Micar are situated in the Rumbos office at Heredia 701 esq. San Pedro (☎22/62-9194).

Immigration You can renew visas at the immigration office, Calle 13 no.6 e/ 4 y Carreterra del Caney, Reparto Viste Alegre (Mon, Wed, Fri 8am–noon, 2–5pm ☎22/64-1983).

Internet Try *Hotel Libertad* on Plaza Marte ($4CUC/hr); the business centre at the *Hotel Santiago* ($5CUC/hr); or the Centro de Llamadas Internacionales (daily 8.30am–7.30pm; $6CUC/hr), on Parque Céspedes.

Medical Call ☎185 for a public ambulance or, for a private ambulance, the Clinica Internacional (☎22/64-2589) at Ave. Raúl Pujol esq. Calle 10 which also offers general medical services to foreigners. The most central state hospital is the Hospital Provincial Clinico Quirúgico Docente, Ave. de los Libertadores (☎22/62-6571 to 9). Policlinico Camilio Torres is a 24hr doctors' surgery at Heredia no.358 e/ Reloj y Calvario. There are pharmacies at Enramada no.402, *Hotel Santiago* and the Clinica Internacional. The latter also has a dental surgery.

Newspapers Some US publications and Italian and Spanish newspapers can be found at the gift shop in the *Hotel Santiago de Cuba*.

Photography Photoservice are at San Pedro esq. San Basilio (daily 9am–9pm).

Police The main station is at Corona y San Gerónimo. In an emergency call ☎116. The tourist support group Asistur offers 24hr assistance in emergency situations (☎7/867-1315). The local headquarters (Mon–Fri 8am–5.30pm, Sat 8.30am–12.30pm; ☎22/68-6128) are in the offices beneath the *Hotel Casa Granda*, though service can be a bit flustered due to chronic staff shortages.

Post office The main post office is at Aguilera y Clarín. Stamps can also be bought from the *Hotel Casa Granda* and *Hotel Santiago de Cuba*. The most central agent for DHL is at Aguilera no.310, esq. San Félix (Mon–Sat 8am–4pm).

Sports Baseball games are played at the Estadio Guillermon Moncada (☎22/64-2640) on Ave. las Américas from Dec to April.

Taxis The metered state taxis include Veracuba, *Hotel Santiago de Cuba* (☎22/68-7070), Cubataxi (☎22/65-1038 and 39) and Transtur/Transgaviota (☎22/68-7173).

Telephones The Centro de Llamadas Internacionales (daily 7am–11pm) at Heredia esq. Félix Pena on Parque Céspedes sells phone cards and allows international calls. Phone cards are also available from *Hotel Casa Granda* and *Hotel Santiago de Cuba*, which both have international pay phones.

Santiago de Cuba province

The urbanity and powerful personality of the capital city dominates the otherwise rural **province of Santiago de Cuba**, but to see only the city would be to miss out on much of the region's character. The **mountains** to the east, with their rich wildlife, simply beg to be explored, with a day-trip from the capital easily taking in the **Sierra de la Gran Piedra**, as well as the rare blooms at the nearby **Jardín Botánico** and the old coffee plantation at **La Isabelica**. Along the coast, the **Gran Parque Natural de Baconao** is most often visited for its **beaches**, notably Playa Siboney and Playa Cazonal.

West of the city, the **Iglesia de la Caridad del Cobre**, or "El Cobre" for short, is one of the country's most revered churches and worth a visit. Frankly, even a simple drive west along the magnificent **coastal road**, with the clear sea on one side and the sensual mountain curves on the other, comes highly recommended.

East of Santiago

Many of the attractions you'll want to see outside Santiago lie to the east and you'll need at least a couple of days to properly see all of them. Cool and fresh, the mountains of the **Sierra de la Gran Piedra** make an excellent break from the harsh city heat, and the giant Gran Piedra is a fine lookout point. Nearby is the atmospheric, little-visited **Museo Isabelica**, set on one of several colonial coffee plantations in the mountains, and the often-overlooked **Jardín Botánico**, with an excellent display of tropical flowers.

Spanning the east coast is the **Gran Parque Natural Baconao**, not so much a park as a vast collection of beaches and other tourist attractions, among them a vintage **car collection** and the **Comunidad Artística Verraco**, home, gallery and workplace for several local artists. Although none of the province's **beaches** is spectacular, all are attractive, and if you wish to stay there are a number of hotels to choose from.

If you've got your own **transport**, head east out of the city towards the Loma de San Juan, then turn off south down Avenida Raúl Pujol, from where the road runs straight towards the coast and the turn-off for the Sierra de la Gran Piedra.

Sierra de la Gran Piedra

Just east of Santiago, the **Sierra de la Gran Piedra** is one of the most easily accessed ranges in the country. Eleven kilometres along the coastal road from town, a turn-off inland leads you up a steep, curving mountain road. As the route ascends, temperate vegetation such as fir and pine trees gradually replaces the more tropical palms and vines of the lower levels.

Jardín Botánico

After about 13km you come to the **Jardín Botánico** (daily 8am–4pm; $1CUC), which is more of a nursery than a botanical garden, as it grows flowers for weddings and other ceremonies. Its tidy beds of heavy-scented white gardenias and Cuban forget-me-nots share space with orange and pine trees and the flame-coloured rainfire bush. Several types of fruit flourish here, including apples which can grow only in the cooler mountains. The prize of the collection is the blue-and-orange bird of paradise flower, each bloom resembling a bunch of spiky fireworks.

La Gran Piedra

Two kilometres further along, a purpose-built staircase leads up from the road to the mountains' highest peak, **La Gran Piedra** (daily 24hr; $1CUC), or "The

Big Rock", sculpted by ancient geological movement from surrounding bedrock and now forming a convenient viewing plateau 1234m above the city. It's an easy, though still invigorating, climb to the top, through woodland rich in animal and plant life, including over two hundred species of fern. When the thick fug of cloud that often hangs over the area melts away there's a panoramic view over the province and beyond to the sea. Locals say that at night you can even see the lights of Haiti. Although there's no public transport to get you there, an unmetered taxi from Parque Céspedes will charge you $10–15CUC to take you to the foot of the staircase.

Museo Isabelica

Continuing on a kilometre or so along the same mountain road, a left turn leads to the **Museo Isabelica** (daily 8am–4pm; $1CUC), set in the grounds of the Cafetal Isabelica, a coffee plantation established by an immigrant French grower who fled the Haitian slave revolution of 1791. Housed in a small, two-storey estate house covered in red lichen and surrounded by ferns, the museum's collection is unfortunately fairly dull, with axes, picks and bits of old machinery downstairs and the owner's living quarters above, furnished with a collection of nineteenth-century pieces. The main reason to come here is the atmosphere, with the mountains' unearthly, mist-shrouded hush broken only by birdsong and the tapping of sheep crossing the stone coffee-bean drying area. You can explore the overgrown paths leading off round the house into the derelict plantation and inspect what is left of the disused mill – now just a stone wheel and a few wooden poles.

Heading back past La Gran Piedra and towards the coastal road is the **Prado de las Esculturas** (daily 8am–4.30pm; $1CUC), a drive-through sculpture park that you can explore in just a couple of minutes. Most of the twenty exhibits, all by international artists, are rather ugly hulks of metal, though Japanese sculptor Issei Amemiya's wooden, temple-like *Meditation II* is quietly impressive.

Gran Parque Natural Baconao

An attractive stretch of countryside interspersed with several tourist attractions and some of the province's best beaches, the **Gran Parque Natural Baconao**, 25km southeast of Santiago, makes for a good day out but is hardly the rugged wilderness suggested by its name. With no public transport serving the area, your best bet – unless you're driving – is to take a taxi from the city, which will cost upwards of $25CUC. A cheaper way to get there is with one of the motorbike taxis that congregate around Parque Céspedes, though not all will go this far out of town.

To Playa Siboney

The first diversion en route to the coast, two kilometres past the La Gran Piedra turn-off, is the **Granjita Siboney** (daily 9am–5pm; $1CUC), the farm which Fidel Castro and his rebel group used as their base for the Moncada attack (see p.516). The pretty little red-and-white house, pockmarked by bullet holes (perhaps from target practice, as no fighting actually took place here), now holds a museum that largely reproduces information found in bigger museums in the city. Inside is the usual round of newspaper cuttings, guns and bloodstained uniforms, presented in glass cabinets.

From here it's just a little further to **Playa Siboney**, 19km from Santiago. This is the nearest and biggest beach to the city and the best if you want to join in with the crowd rather than bask in solitude. The brown sands, overlooked by a towering cliff, are lively with crowds of Cubans and visitors, while the small but ebullient seaside is dappled with palm trees and jaunty wooden houses. There is a **restaurant** on the road behind the beach, *La Rueda Carretera Siboney*, offering inexpensive fried chicken, tasty fish and good lobster, as well as sandwiches and pizza. The best place to stay is the excellent *Casa de Ovídio Gonález Sabaldo* (☎22/3-9340; ❷), a *casa particular* with a sea view on Avenida Serrano Alto de Farmacia. Although you can catch the #214 bus to here from the terminal on Avenue de los Libertadores, a taxi is a more reliable option and shouldn't cost more than $10CUC or $15CUC.

To Playa Daiquirí

A further 4km east on the main road, **El Oasis Rodeo** (Sun 9am & 2pm; $3CUC) is tailor-made for the tourist industry, a chance to see Cuban cowboys ride, lasso, and generally show off their impressive acrobatic skills with a series of long-suffering bulls. The rodeo also offers **horse riding** in the surrounding countryside (Tues–Sun 9am–5pm; $5CUC for the first hour, $3CUC per hour thereafter).

One kilometre further on, a signposted turn down a potholed track leads to Finca el Porvenir (☎22/62-9064; daily 9am–5pm; $1CUC), a nice spot for **lunch**. A stone staircase descends the hillside to a bar-restaurant with tables shaded by mango and palm trees and sunloungers surrounding an inviting **swimming pool**. The restaurant's menu offers reasonably priced grilled fish, shrimp, pork and fried chicken.

Along the same road, 1km from the Finca, you'll come across one of the area's more unusual attractions, the **Valle de la Prehistoria** (daily 8am–4.45pm; $1CUC, $1CUC extra to take photos), populated by practically life-sized stone models of dinosaurs and Stone Age men. Stegosauruses graze on the Caribbean plain, while a herd of Tyrannosauruses moves in for the attack. While essentially a bit kitsch, it's worth a look for those with kids or those in search of the ultimate photo opportunity: astride a brontosaurus.

One of Baconao's biggest attractions, the **Museo Nacional de Transporte Terrestre por Carretera** (daily 8am–5pm; $1CUC, $1CUC extra to take photos), which has an excellent collection of vintage cars and a formidable display of 2500 toy cars, is located about 4km further to the east. Outside in the car park sit the 1929 Ford Roadster belonging to Alina Ruz, Fidel Castro's mother; Benny Moré's ostentatious golden Cadillac; and the 1951 Chevrolet that Raúl Castro drove to the attack on the Moncada barracks (see p.516). While you can see many similar models still limping around the country, it's quite heart-warming to see those here looking so scrubbed up and shiny.

More or less opposite the museum is the turning for **Playa Daiquirí**, the beach where the US army landed when they intervened in the War of Independence in 1898 and which gave its name to the famous cocktail. Home to a holiday camp for military personnel, the beach is closed to foreign visitors.

To Playa Cazonal

Ten kilometres east from the museum on the main road, in an attractive clearing beneath tall trees, is the unique **Comunidad Artística Verraco**, a small artists' community that's home to nine sculptors, painters and potters. At the far end of the clearing, a central gallery sells a selection of the artists' works – particularly good are the wildly psychedelic depictions of musicians by local painter Renilde. However, you get a better sense of the place by wandering around the houses-cum-workshops, where you can check out pieces in progress and buy additional exhibits, while sculptors quietly shape wood, painters ponder their next brush stroke and musicians strum guitars.

Continuing east for 8km you'll come to the **Acuario Baconao** (Tues–Sun 9am–5pm; $5CUC), an aquarium with a selection of marine animals, including turtles and sharks, housed in rather small tanks. Faring a little better, with a reasonably sized pool, are the dolphins – the big stars – performing their party pieces twice a day (shows at 10.30am & 3pm); there's also the chance to hop into the pool with them yourself ($39CUC).

Playa Cazonal, less than a kilometre from Acuario Baconao, is the most attractive beach east of Santiago. Backed by two congenial all-inclusive hotels, *Los Corales* (☎22/35-6122; ◉) and *Carisol* (☎22/35-6115; ◉), a wide curve of cream-coloured sand nestles against a dazzling green hillside from which the palms spill onto the beach's edge. Pretty as it is, this beach is no secluded paradise, and is instead awash with windsurfers, Western sun-worshippers and snorkellers exploring the nearby coral reef. Non-guests can buy a day-pass at *Los Corales* ($15CUC) which includes a buffet meal and drinks.

The last attraction in the province to the east, roughly 3km from Playa Cazonal, **Laguna Baconao** is a serene spot from which to enjoy the unaffected beauty of the surrounding mountains. There's little wildlife, but you can hire a boat ($2CUC) to row on the lake. Unless you're driving, however, there's no point heading out this far as there's no public transport nor any facilities.

West of Santiago

Although there are fewer sights to see west of Santiago, those that exist are interesting enough to warrant a visit if you have a spare day. The **Iglesia de la Caridad del Cobre**, presiding over the town of El Cobre in the hills to the northwest, houses the icon of Nuestra Señora de la Caridad, Cuba's patron, and is one of the most important – and most visited – churches in the country. The **beaches** west of the city are mostly smaller than those on the eastern side, and correspondingly less developed and more intimate, the playgrounds of Cubans rather than foreign visitors. In contrast, the resort of **Chivirico** is dedicated to international tourism, with two palatial hotels dominating its fine-sand beach. Again there is no reliable public transport to this area so you'll need to hire a taxi or take your own transport.

Iglesia de la Caridad del Cobre

The imposing and lovely **Iglesia de la Caridad del Cobre** (daily 8am–6pm), 18km northwest of Santiago, is one of the holiest sanctuaries in the country, home to the statue of the Virgen de la Caridad. In 1606 the icon was found floating in the Bahía de Nipe, off Cuba's northern coast, by three sailors from El Cobre town on the verge of being shipwrecked. They claimed not only that the the icon – a mother and child figurine – was completely dry when drawn from the water but also that the sea was instantly becalmed. Inscribed with the words "I am the Virgin of Charity", the icon became the most important image in Cuban Catholicism, gaining significance by becoming intertwined and twinned with Ochún, the Santería goddess of love, whose colour, yellow, mirrors the Virgin's golden robe. In 1916 the Virgen de la Caridad became the patron saint of Cuba, following a decree by Pope Benedict XV.

8

Pleasingly symmetrical, its three towers capped in red domes, the present church was constructed in 1927, on the site of a previous shrine to the icon. Inside, coloured light rains down from the portholes of stained glass set into the ceiling, and a huge, ornate altar throws the surprisingly plain walls into relief. The icon has pride of place high up in the altar and during **Mass** (Tues–Sat 8am, Thurs 8pm, Sun 10am & 4.30pm) looks down over the congregation; at other times she is rotated to face into an inner sanctum reached by stairs at the back of the church, where another altar is always liberally garlanded with floral tributes left by worshippers.

Soon after her discovery, local mythology endowed the Virgin with the power to grant wishes and heal the sick, and a steady flow of believers visits the church to solicit her help. A downstairs chamber holds an eclectic display of the many relics left by grateful recipients of the Virgin's benevolence, including a rosette and team shirt from Ana Fidelia Quirot Moret, the Olympic 800m gold medallist, college diplomas, countless photographs and, most bizarrely, an asthmatic's ventilator. The most famous relic is the small, golden guerrilla figure pledged by Lina Ruz, the mother of Fidel, in return for her son's safe deliverance from the fighting in the Sierra Maestra. The other celebrated holding, the Nobel Prize medal won in 1954 by Ernest Hemingway for his novel *The Old Man and the Sea*, can no longer be seen after being stolen by a visitor in 1986. Although later recovered, the medal is now kept safely in a vault.

The western beaches and Chivirico

The drive along the coast west towards Chivirico, with the seemingly endless curve of vivid mountains on one side and a ribbon of sparkling shallow sea on the other, is one of the most fantastic in the country. However damage caused by Hurricane Dennis means the road requires careful negotiation and should be avoided after dark. Don't be put off by **Playa Mar Verde**, a small, rather grubby hoop of roadside shingle-sand about 15km from the city, but carry on along the coastal road for another couple of kilometres to **Playa Bueycabón**. Here, an orderly lawn of grass dotted with short palms stretches almost to the sea, and with its calm, shallow waters and narrow belt of sand it is altogether an excellent little spot to pass the day. There are no facilities so you should bring your own provisions.

Chivirico

Nearly 70km from Santiago, **CHIVIRICO** is a quiet coastal village and an interchange point for buses and trucks running between Pilón and Santiago. Other than that, the main action, such as it is, centres around a micro-resort of three hotels capitalizing on good brown-sand beaches and impressive mountain views. This is a better place to stay rather than visit on a day-trip, as the best beaches are now the domain of two large all-inclusive resort hotels which charge non-guests for the privilege of using them.

Access to **Playa Sevilla** (daily 9am–5pm; $35CUC per day, inclusive of meals and drinks), the easternmost beach of the three, is controlled by the palatial beachfront *Brisas Sierra Mar* (T22/2-9110, E reservat@smar.scu.cyt.cu; ●), which has a full complement of watersports, five bars and several restaurants. It's almost worth the price tag to spend a luxurious day in this beautiful setting, with its wide, soft sands and superb mountain views, though you'll be jostling with crowds of holidaymakers from the expansive hotel.

The central beach, **Playa Virginia**, is narrower but free to enter. Tiny mangrove-coated cays lie not far offshore, though there can be dangerous undertow currents. It's here you'll find the rather appealing *Motel Guáma* (T22/2-6124; ●), the strip's sole budget accommodation option, though the only café is often closed.

Finally, **Playa Chivirico** is the private preserve of the attractive hilltop *Hotel Los Galeones* (☎22/2-6160; ②), which boasts magnificent views over the rolling mountains and the sea. The small swathe of brown sand is speckled with palms and couples from the hotel. There is a $10CUC day charge to use the beach.

Granma and the Sierra Maestra

Protruding west from the main body of Cuba, cupping the Bahía de Guaca-nayabo, **Granma** is a tranquil, slow-paced province, where the closest things get to bustling is in its appealingly low-key capital **Bayamo**, birthplace of the father of Cuban independence, Carlos Manuel de Céspedes. Granma is nonetheless growing in popularity; the peaceful black-sand resort on the southern coast at **Marea del Portillo** is already a firm favourite with Canadian retirees, and you could do worse than spend a couple of days here, sampling some of the day **excursions** into the surrounding mountains of the Sierra Maestra or the numerous **diving** opportunities. A visit to the small and simple rural town of **Pilón**, just a few kilometres away, is a marked contrast to the all-inclusive world.

On the southwestern tip of Granma's coastline is **Playa Las Coloradas**, where Fidel Castro and his revolutionaries came ashore on the *Granma* – visiting the site is the highlight of any Revolution pilgrimage – while nearby, the **Parque Nacional Desembarco del Granma** has several excellent guided nature trails, including **El Guafe** with its three pre-Columbian petroglyphs. Up along the western coast, sleepy **Manzanillo**, though not somewhere you're likely to spend a lot of time, is worth visiting for the flashes of brilliant Moorish architecture that light up the town centre. There is little to draw you to the Llanura del Cauto Guacanayabo plains north of Manzanillo, mostly character-ized by swampland and a few one-street towns.

The **Sierra Maestra**, Cuba's highest and most extensive mountain range, stretches along the southern coast of the island, running the length of both Santiago and Granma provinces. The unruly beauty of the landscape – a vision of churning seas, undulating green-gold mountains and remote sugar fields – will take your breath away. That said, once you're done admiring the country-side there's not an awful lot to do: national park status notwithstanding, much of the Sierra Maestra is periodically declared out of bounds by the authorities, sometimes supposedly because of an epidemic in the coffee crops but more often for no given reason. Should you get the opportunity to go **trekking** here, though, seize it.

There are some excellent trails, most notably through the stunning cloud forest of the **Parque Nacional Turquino** to the island's highest point, Pico Turquino, at 1974m. Although a considerable part of the Sierra Maestra falls in

△ The Sierra Maestra

Santiago province, Parque Nacional Turquino included, the best chance you have to do any trekking is to base yourself in Bayamo, where you can arrange a guide and suitable transport; see the box on p.536 for more information.

Bayamo

On the northern edge of the Sierra Maestra mountains in the centre of Granma, provincial capital **BAYAMO** is one of the most peaceful towns in Cuba. Its spotless centre is based around a pleasant park filled with playing children; there are near-zero levels of hassle on the streets; and, with the streets pedestrianized, even the cars are silenced.

Although a fire destroyed most of Bayamo's colonial buildings in 1869, it left the heart of town untouched, and the splendid **Iglesia de Santísimo Salvador** still presides over the cobbled **Plaza del Himno**. Elsewhere, neat rows of modern candy-coloured houses, dotted with pretty tree-lined parks, stand testament to a well-maintained town. There are a couple of engaging museums, notably the **Casa Natal de Carlos Manuel de Céspedes**, which celebrates the town's most famous son, a key figure in the Wars of Independence. Bayamo is smaller than you'd expect a provincial capital to be, and you could cram its few sights into one day, but if you've no agenda, it's better to do some gentle sightseeing, eat well and match the town's unhurried pace.

Some history

The second of the original seven Cuban towns or *villas* founded by Diego Velázquez de Cuéllar in November 1513, Bayamo flourished during the seventeenth and eighteenth centuries when, along with its neighbour Manzanillo, it was heavily involved in dealing in contraband goods. Here, European smugglers exchanged slaves, leather, precious woods and luxury goods like the Dutch ceramic tiles still visible on the roof of the town's Iglesia de Santísimo Salvador.

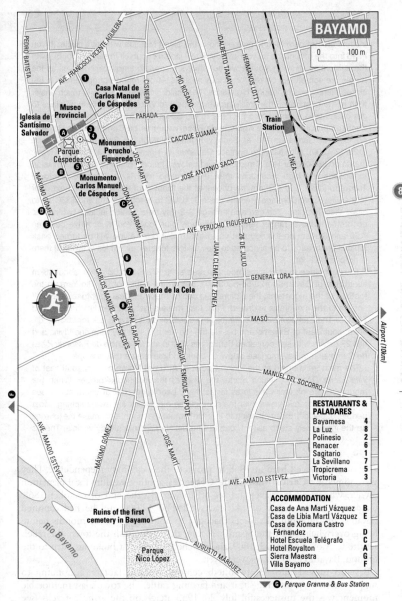

BAYAMO

0   100 m

Casa Natal de
Carlos Manuel
de Céspedes

Museo
Provincial

Iglesia de
Santísimo
Salvador

Train
Station

Parque
Céspedes

Monumento
Perucho
Figueredo

Monumento
Carlos Manuel
de Céspedes

AVE. PERUCHO FIGUEREDO

Galería de la Cela

N

Ruins of the first
cemetery in Bayamo

Río Bayamo

Parque
Nico López

Airport (10km)

**RESTAURANTS &
PALADARES**

Bayamesa	4
La Luz	8
Polinesio	2
Renacer	6
Sagitario	1
La Sevillano	7
Tropicrema	5
Victoria	3

ACCOMMODATION

Casa de Ana Martí Vázquez	B
Casa de Libia Martí Vázquez	E
Casa de Xiomara Castro Férnandez	D
Hotel Escuela Telégrafo	C
Hotel Royalton	A
Sierra Maestra	G
Villa Bayamo	F

Parque Granma & Bus Station

Bayamo became one of the most prosperous towns in the country and by the nineteenth century had capitalized on the fertile plains to the west of the city, becoming an important sugar-growing and cattle-rearing area.

Bayamo's cosmopolitan and literary-minded sons were often educated abroad, and they returned home with progressive views. Influential figures like wealthy landowner Francisco Vicente Aguilera and composer Pedro Figueredo established

Visitors are not permitted to go trekking in the Sierra Maestra without a guide. (If you head into the mountains on your own, you risk landing yourself in serious trouble with the authorities.) Having a guide will not always guarantee entrance, however, as the routes are sometimes closed for various reasons – from reports of epidemics in the coffee plantations to visiting dignitaries. That said, access is currently much easier than in the past, given the area's growing appeal to visitors. The only local place to get guaranteed information on access to the Sierra Maestra, including the areas in Santiago province, is at the **Agéncia de Reservaciónes de Campísmo**, in Bayamo on General García no.112 e/ Saco y Figueredo (Mon–Fri 8am–noon & 2–5pm; ⊤23/42-4200). Alternatively, contact Cubamar in Havana (⊤7/831-3151, ⓦwww.cubamarviajes.cu) or *Villa Santo Domingo* below. The only place to grant permission to **access** the high mountains from the Bayamo side is the **Parque Nacional Turquino** (daily 7.30–8.30am; no phone) at the foothills of the mountains next door to the *Villa Santo Domingo*. Permits costs $11CUC to reach La Plata and $33CUC to scale Pico Turquino. You can also arrange 2–3 day treks, which include two nights' accommodation at ranger huts along the way plus food. You must arrive between 7.30 and 8.30am on the day that you want to visit or else you will be turned back (guides arrive early to be allocated to their visitors for the day but leave swiftly if there is no one waiting).

The best **place to stay** in the mountain area is the *Villa Santo Domingo*, about 68km southwest of Bayamo (⊤23/56-5368; ③). Set on the banks of the Río Yara, in the foothills of the mountains, the picturesque cabins make an ideal spot to relax even if access to the mountains is denied. Plus, they make a tasty packed lunch for around $3CUC. The *Campismo La Sierrita* (call the operator on ⊤00 and ask for LD326; ②), 50km southeast of Bayamo and beside the Río Yara, is similarly rural and idyllic and has 27 cabins with self-contained bathrooms. Call in at the Agéncia de Reservaciónes de Campísmo in Bayamo (see below) to book and make sure they are open.

The main trails begin at the lookout point of **Alto del Naranjo**, 5km southeast of *Villa Santo Domingo*, which marks the start of the mountains proper. When the mountains are off limits this is as far as many people get, but at 950m above sea level, the panoramic views over the surrounding mountains are awe-inspiring. Most people, especially those planning to trek further into the mountains, make the journey up the immensely steep ascent road to Alto del Naranjo in a sturdy vehicle. There's

a revolutionary cell here in 1868 to promote their call for independence. They were joined by **Carlos Manuel de Céspedes**, another wealthy local plantation owner, who freed his slaves and set off to war. By the end of October 1868, Céspedes's modest army of 147 had swelled to 12,000 and he had captured Bayamo and Holguín. His forces managed to hold out for three months before being overwhelmed by the Spanish. Rather than relinquish the town, the rebels set fire to it on January 12, 1869, and watched the elegant buildings burn to the ground. Bayamo's glory days were over.

Bayamo moved into the twentieth century without fanfare, continuing to support itself by producing sugar and farming cattle. The town's last memorable moment was the unsuccessful July 26, 1953 attack on the army barracks (see p.540), timed to coincide with Castro's attack in Santiago – though this happened over half a century ago, it still keeps several old-timers gossiping today.

Arrival and information

Domestic **flights** arrive from Havana at the Aeropuerto Carlos M. de Céspedes (⊤23/42-7514), 10km northeast of the centre on the Holguín road,

Cuban music and dance

It's an unwritten rule in Cuba that, regardless of what you're into – from jazz to hip-hop to thrash metal – all Cubans can dance *salsa*. And while *salsa* is the island's best-known musical genre, Cuba's rich and hugely influential musical heritage is about so much more – this is, after all, the home of everything from *rumba* and *son* to *trova* and *chachachá*. Visitors will find the cliché that you can hear music on every street corner to be closer to truth than to myth – meals are often accompanied by strumming guitarists and maraca-shaking vocalists while impromptu street gigs are seemingly unavoidable. What's more, the country's wealth of fine musicians stretches far beyond well-known recording artists: from hotel lobbies to the ubiquitous *Casas de la Trova*, top-class players are everywhere, not just in the large-scale venues of Havana and Santiago.

Music in daily life

Live music in Cuba is not so much easy to catch as it is difficult to avoid. **Restaurants** in particular are musical hot spots, and places like *Café Taberna* in Habana Vieja, with its seven-piece Beny Moré tribute band, and *El Gato Tuerto* in Vedado, where renowned *filin* and *bolero* artists have been performing since the 1950s, are standouts. Wherever you dine, however, if the music is live it will almost certainly be of high quality.

Equally unavoidable, particularly if you travel beyond Havana into the provinces, are the weekly musical performances held in the **town plazas**. Any decent-size town or city has a central square, and many of them, particularly those in provincial capitals like Santa Clara and Cienfuegos, are graced with bandstands where, at weekends, local orchestras play to throngs of people. Also worth checking out are the **Casas de Cultura**. These humble community centres, established by the revolutionary government to promote Cuban cultural identity, usually have at least one free concert a week.

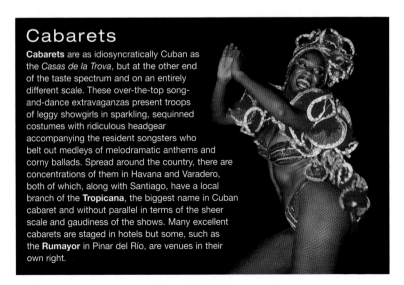

Cabarets

Cabarets are as idiosyncratically Cuban as the *Casas de la Trova*, but at the other end of the taste spectrum and on an entirely different scale. These over-the-top song-and-dance extravaganzas present troops of leggy showgirls in sparkling, sequinned costumes with ridiculous headgear accompanying the resident songsters who belt out medleys of melodramatic anthems and corny ballads. Spread around the country, there are concentrations of them in Havana and Varadero, both of which, along with Santiago, have a local branch of the **Tropicana**, the biggest name in Cuban cabaret and without parallel in terms of the sheer scale and gaudiness of the shows. Many excellent cabarets are staged in hotels but some, such as the **Rumayor** in Pinar del Río, are venues in their own right.

Casas de la Trova and Casas de la Música

▶ Casa de la Trova, Trinidad

The best places in the country to see and hear the top players of traditional Cuban musical styles, like *son* and *bolero*, are the **Casas de la Trova**, basically informal social clubs, sometimes with bars, where musicians gather to play and people gather to listen, socialize and dance. Often in relatively modest and intimate surroundings – usually a rustic colonial residence, though sometimes housed in grand old buildings – they are a great way of getting up close to some of the country's best musicians. Most cities have at least one of these institutions, but the most renowned is in **Santiago**, where music is performed every day and night.

Less widespread but packing more of a punch are the **Casas de la Música**. These comparatively slick concert venues are larger and more commercial than the Casas de la Trova and attract a younger, more energetic crowd. Doubling up as nightclubs, they are usually the hottest spot in town and pull in the biggest names in modern Cuban music, particularly *salsa* bands but reggaeton and pop acts too, as well as legends like Los Van Van and Irakere. Currently there are two *Casas de la Música* in Havana, with four others around the country, in Varadero, Cienfuegos, Trinidad and Santiago.

Musicians to look out for

Telmary The queen of Cuban hip-hop is widely acclaimed for fusing Cuban styles with traditional hip-hop.

Adalberto Alvarez A pianist, composer and bandleader whose work is said to be covered more than any other contemporary Cuban *sonero*.

Roberto Fonseca Hugely talented pianist and musical arranger and leader of the new generation of Cuban jazz artists.

Jovenes Clasicos del Son This seven-piece band are regarded as both modernizers and traditionalists of the classic Cuban *son* sound.

Diego Gutierrez One of the most respected contemporary exponents of the Cuban *trovador* tradition.

Gerardo Alfonso An outstanding singer-songwriter who's toured all over the world and been winning awards for more than three decades.

Clave y Guaguancó The latest incarnation of this legendary *rumba* outfit, formed in the 1960s.

Eddy K At the forefront of the explosion in Cuban reggaeton that has taken place in recent years.

Rumba and Afro-Cuban dance

▼ Dancing at UNEAC, Havana

Rumba is inextricably linked with Afro-Cuban religious worship, the most popular form being Santería, during which participants' bodies, believed to be possessed by spirits, twist and flex to the rhythms produced by the *rumba* drummers. These acts of worship are usually private affairs, although a number of venues around the country hold staged performances. The **Callejón de Hamel**, a shrine-filled backstreet in Centro Habana, offers the most authentic exhibition of Afro-Cuban religious musical expression with its Sunday ceremonies, while the Museo de los Orishas in Habana Vieja and the Bazar de los Orishas in Guanabacoa are other intriguing options. The small town of **Trinidad** has two prominent Afro-Cuban dance venues – the Ruinas de Segarte and the Palenque de los Congos Reales – while in **Viñales** you can catch daily Afro-Cuban dance and music shows at the Palenque de los Cimarrones.

no public transport, but trips can be arranged through the Agéncia de Reservaciónes de Campísmo.

Pico Turquino trail

At 1974m above sea level, **Pico Turquino** stands proud as the highest point in Cuba. From Alto de Naranjo it's approximately 12km to the summit, and while it's possible to ascend and return in a day, you are better off arranging with your guide to stay overnight at the very rudimentary *Campamento de Joaquín* mountain hut (see above) and stretching the trek over a day and a half. This is not a trek for the faint-hearted: the final kilometre is a very steep slog, though not dangerous. Take something warm to wear, as temperatures plummet after nightfall and even the days are cool in the high cloud forest.

The Pico Turquino is overhung with plants and ancient tree ferns, the forest air exuding an earthy dampness and the ground oozing with thick red mud. Through the breaks in the dense foliage you can occasionally see blue-green mountain peaks and birds circling lazily above the gullies. Just before the final ascent, a short ladder to the left of the path gives a panoramic view over the surrounding landscape; it's worth grabbing the opportunity at this stage in your trek as the summit itself is often shrouded in thick clouds.

La Plata trail

A less taxing trek is **to La Plata**, 3km west of Alto de Naranjo, where Fidel Castro based his rebel headquarters during the Revolution. The trail is well marked and you can complete the reasonably strenuous climb in around two hours. The headquarters are spread over two or three sites, the first of which is the very basic hospital (it's little more than a wooden hut) that Che Guevara founded and ran. The second site comprises a small but worthy museum which was originally the rebels' workshop, a modern-day helicopter pad and graves of revolutionaries who fell in battle. Most evocative are the wooden huts where the rebels lived and ate, which were covered with branches to protect them from enemy air strikes. Castro's small quarters consist of a rudimentary bedroom with a simple camp bed, a kitchen, a study and a secret trap door to escape through if he was under attack.

where unmetered taxis wait to bring you into town for around $3–5CUC. Bayamo is well served by three main roads from Las Tunas, Holguín and Santiago de Cuba; interprovincial **buses** pull in at the Astro terminal (☎23/42-4036) in the western outskirts of town, on the Carretera Central towards Santiago de Cuba. From here horse-drawn coaches will take you into the centre for about five pesos. **Colectivos** also use the Astro terminal as their unofficial base. The **train** station is on Calle Linea e/ Prada y Figueredo (☎23/42-3012), and from here you can catch a horse-drawn coach into the centre, about 1km away.

While there are no official tourist offices, the Cubatur office located in the *Hotel Royalton* (daily 8am–noon & 1–6pm; ☎23/42-2224) sells **maps** of the town and province along with tickets for flights and Víazul buses, while the Agencia de Reservaciones de Campísmo, General García no.112 e/ Saco y Figueredo (☎23/42-4200), has information on **campsites** and **excursions** into the mountains. You can also get general information about excursions at the tourist bureau in the *Hotel Sierra Maestra* (☎23/42-7970).

Accommodation

Unless you're driving, you'll want **to stay** in the centre where you can choose from two good-value hotels, the *Royalton* and *Escuela Telégrafo*, and a number of attractive *casas particulares* – with little passing tourist trade, there are only a handful registered in the town but the standard is generally excellent.

Hotels

Hotel Escuela Telégrafo Saco no.108 e/ General García y Donato Mármol ☎23/42-5510, ⬤www .ehtgr.co.cu. Recently renovated and painted mint-green, this small hotel offers comfortable rooms with a/c, TV and fridge and is very good value for the money. While the service is not the best, the staff more than compensate with charm and enthusiasm. ❸

Hotel Royalton Maceo no.53 ☎23/42-2224, ⓔhroyalton@islazul.grm.tur.cu. The pretty, white exterior blends into this picturesque hotel's elegant surroundings right on Parque Céspedes. Rooms are decent and tasteful, all with a/c and clean bathrooms. ❸

Villa Bayamo Carretera Central (vía Manzanillo) km 5.5 ☎23/42-3102. This hotel, on the outskirts of town in a quiet, flower-filled area, is quite run-down but extremely cheap. There's a selection of singles, doubles and cabin-style suites which sleep up to four. With a large and busy swimming pool, and restaurant and bars in the grounds, this is a good choice for larger groups with their own transport. ❷

Casas particulares

Céspedes 4 e/ Maceo y Canducha, Plaza del Himno ☎23/42-5323, ⓔmarti@net.cu. Two a/c rooms with TV, stereo, fan, fridge and private bathrooms in a beautiful baroque house bedecked with chandeliers, tiled floors and pink armchairs. Slightly more expensive than most but worth it if you like your creature comforts. Breakfast and dinner are available. ❷

Casa de Libia Marti Vázquez Máximo Gómez, 56 Int e/ Saco y León ☎23/42-5671, ⓔimartivazquez@yahoo.es. Don't be deterred by the long gloomy corridor from the street to the front door – once inside you'll find a pastel-pink room with a/c, a bathroom, a fan and a fridge. A private balcony overlooking the river and meals cooked by the owner and his wife are bonuses. ❶

Casa de Xiomara Castro Férnandez Máximo Gómez 44 e/ Léon y Saco ☎23/42-2644. Although the two double, self-contained bedrooms here are a little gloomy, the hosts are extremely friendly and the price includes use of the living room, kitchen and laundry facilities. ❶

The Town

Most of the sights in Bayamo are within view or easy walking distance of the central **Parque Céspedes** – also known as Plaza de la Revolución – a shiny expanse of marble fringed with palm trees where children play outside their *Pioneros* clubhouse or queue for rides in the goat-pulled pony cart. On opposite sides of the plaza are two monuments honouring the town's most famous sons. At the northern end is a small three-panel tribute to **Perucho Figueredo**, a local independence fighter principally remembered for writing the patriotic poem *La Bayamesa* in 1868, which later became the Cuban national anthem, still sung today. The elegant black-and-white marble monument features a solemn bust of the hero accompanied on one side by the words of his poem and by the anthem's musical score, finely detailed in gold, on the other. The monument to **Carlos Manuel de Céspedes** (see box, p.540), at the southern end of the plaza, is rather more grandiose: a statue of the man himself, dignified and sombre in tailcoat, on top of a podium with four bas-relief panels depicting his struggle for independence, including the shooting of his son, Oscar.

La Iglesia de Santísimo Salvador, survivor of the great fire of 1869, is a good landmark, situated just west of the park. The **Casa Natal de Carlos Manuel de Céspedes**, next to the *Hotel Royalton* on the north side of the plaza, is stuffed full of exhibits, some more relevant than others, while the **Museo Provinical** next door is worth a quick visit. General García, the main shopping street, is a pleasant place to stroll and catch the flavour of the town; pedestrianized, its muted marble walkway makes a good foil for the fun sculptures of giant tubes of paint and the sinuous benches. The **Galería de la Cera**, a waxworks gallery (Mon–Fri 9am–1pm & 2–5pm, Sat 6–10pm; free) is worth a quick look. All the models, which include indigenous birds and personalities like Compay Segundo and Benny Moré, are made by a local man and his sons. A short walk south along General García, are the old barracks, site of the July 26 attack, now named the **Parque Ñico López** in honour of one of the men involved.

The only sight that you'll need transport for is pleasant **Parque Granma**, out east on the Carretera Central towards Santiago. Rambling over two square kilometres and with a central lake, it's a great place to relax.

La Iglesia de Santísimo Salvador

The showpiece of Bayamo architecture, the sixteenth-century **La Iglesia de Santísimo Salvador** (daily 9am–noon & 3–5pm), which dominates the small Plaza del Himno, was one of the few buildings to survive the great fire of 1869. Although further damaged over subsequent decades, it is slowly being restored to its former glory, its biscuit-brown exterior rising to an elegant domed pinnacle. Inside, oval portraits of the Stations of the Cross line the walls, while winged cherubs swoop across the celestial blue ceiling. The impressive mural over the main altar depicts an incident on November 8, 1868, when Diego José Baptista, the parish priest, blessed the rebel army's newly created flag before a mixed congregation of Cuban rebels, including Vicente Aguilera, an early Bayamo independence fighter, and Perucho Figueredo. Hovering above the congregation is an image of the Virgen de la Caridad (see p.531), painted in 1919 by the Dominican artist Luis Desangles. This piece is unique in Latin America as an ecclesiastical painting with political content – the imagery indicates that the new republic received the approbation of the Church.

Casa Natal de Carlos Manuel de Céspedes and Museo Provincial

The **Casa Natal de Carlos Manuel de Céspedes**, on the north side of Parque Céspedes (Tues–Fri 9am–5pm, Sat 9am–2pm & 8–10pm, Sun 10am–1pm; $1CUC), is another survivor of the fire of 1869, and contains a hotchpotch of exhibits relating to the nineteenth century in general and the life of Carlos Manuel de Céspedes, born here in 1819, in particular.

On the ground floor, the walls are plastered with fulsome quotes about the man, many relating to the death of his son, Oscar, while various cabinets hold some staid personal effects, among them his ceremonial sword, as well as more characterful pieces like an ingenious table bell in the shape of a nodding tortoise.

Upstairs, efforts have been made to furnish the rooms in an authentic nineteenth-century manner, and the stuffy tapestry chairs, marble floors and European and North American china and furniture all successfully create an image of sterile opulence. In the bedroom is the *pièce de résistance*: a magnificent bronze bed with ornate oval panels, inlaid with mother-of-pearl and depicting a fantastic coastline, at the foot.

The **Museo Provincial** next door (Mon, Wed–Fri 9am–noon & 1–5pm, Sat & Sun 9am–noon & 5–10pm; free) contains a rather sparse collection of miscellany pertaining to important historical figures (Che Guevara's multi-tool penknife) alongside some archeological remnants. Look out for the imposing sculpture of Antonio Maceo, hero of the Wars of Independence.

Parque Ñico López

Bayamo's spacious walled garden, **Parque Ñico López**, landscaped with swaying palms and intersected with layers of marble steps, was arranged in the

Carlos Manuel de Céspedes

A key figure in the fight for independence, **Carlos Manuel de Céspedes** is much lauded in Cuba as a liberator. A wealthy plantation owner, he freed his slaves on October 10, 1868, and called for the abolition of slavery – albeit in terms least likely to alienate the wealthy landowners upon whose support he depended. Giving forth his battle cry, the *Grito de Yara*, which summoned Cubans, whether slaves or Creoles, to take arms and fight for a future free of Spain, he marched in support of the independence movement. Céspedes summed up the dissatisfaction that many Cubans felt in a long declaration which became known as the **October 10th manifesto**, nationally credited as the inception of Cuban independence because it was the first time that Cubans had been talked about in terms of a nation of people.

The newly formed army set out with the intention of capturing the nearby town of Yara, but were overtaken by a column of the Spanish army and utterly trounced, reduced to a fragment of the original 150-strong force. Undefeated, Céspedes proclaimed, "There are still twelve of us left, we are enough to achieve the independence of Cuba."

Céspedes is most remembered for the death of his son, Oscar, captured by the Spanish and subsequently shot when Céspedes refused to negotiate for peace under Spanish conditions. This act earned him the title "Padre de la Patria" (Father of the Homeland): as he famously replied to the letter requesting his surrender, "Oscar is not my only son. I am father to all the Cubans who have died to liberate their homeland."

grounds of the Bayamo barracks as a tribute to Ñico López, one of the 28 men who tried to storm and capture the building on July 26, 1953.

The attack was synchronized with the assault on the Moncada barracks in Santiago, partly to secure weapons for the rebel cause but primarily to prevent more of General Batista's troops being drafted in from Bayamo to Santiago. The attempt failed when the whinnying of the cavalry horses, alarmed at the sound of the rebels scrambling over the wall, aroused the sleeping soldiers, and though López escaped, later meeting up with fellow rebels in exile in Mexico, several other men died in the attack. López returned to Cuba aboard the yacht *Granma* in 1958, only to be killed a few days later in an early skirmish. The garden honours both his contribution to the cause, and, probably more crucially, his status as the man who introduced Che Guevara to Fidel Castro in 1955. López himself is commemorated by a sculpture in the grounds.

Inside the barracks is a rather poor **museum** (Tues–Fri 9am–5pm, Sat noon–8pm, Sun 8am–noon; 50¢) giving a scanty account of events accompanied by photographs of the men involved and a cutting from the following day's newspaper. You'd be better off giving it a miss and instead striking up a conversation with the old men who sometimes sit in the park, several of whom remember the attack.

Parque Granma

Parque Granma (Tues–Sun 8am–7pm; free), south of the centre, is one of Bayamo's highlights, purely for its serene lakeside setting complete with a tumbledown pagoda reached by a boardwalk, in a great expanse of countryside. Wild cotton and tamarind trees loom out of the long grasses, and it's one of the few places in the town where you can enjoy an unrestricted view of the mountains. At the southern end of the park is a children's fun park, filled with rickety swings and roundabouts reminiscent of tin clockwork toys, while close by is a **microzoo** (Wed–Sun 9am–4pm; 20¢), housing a set of rather pedestrian animals, including a herd of bulls and a caged and disgruntled tabby cat. To reach

Parque Granma, head out of town on the Carretera Central (vía Santiago) and take the first right after the Cupet garage, just before the *Hotel Sierra Maestra*. The ten-minute return taxi ride will cost around $8–10CUC.

Eating

Surprisingly for such a small town, Bayamo boasts several **restaurants**, though many are cheap and somewhat run-down peso-only establishments – the better ones are listed below. Around the park end of General García are several stalls selling snacks, some of them, like the corn pretzel-style cracker, unique to Bayamo.

State restaurants

Bayamesa Parque Céspedes, esq. General García. Large portions of chicken, pork, duck or turkey with rice, salad and fried green banana at rock-bottom prices. Excellent value but rather grubby, it's a good option if you are practically penniless.

Hotel Escuela Telégrafo Saco no.108 e/ General García y Donato Mármol. Although the menu is limited, the chicken and pork dishes are good quality and the restaurant is located in the hotel's airy, attractive lobby.

La Luz General García e/ Maso y Lora. Popular ice-cream parlour which also stocks cakes and creamy natural and fruit-flavoured yogurts.

Renacer General García e/ Lora y Figueredo. Basic, decent Cuban peso restaurant dishing up reliable pork, rice and beans.

La Sevillana General García e/ Figuero y Lora ✆23/42-1472. Decent Cuban fare masquerading as Spanish cuisine. Best dishes are paella, *bistec de cerdo*, (pork chops), and *pescado a la Gallega*, (Galician fish stew).

Tropicrema Figueredo e/ Libertad y Céspedes. Pleasant, open-air peso ice-cream parlour, sometimes serving up cake, too. Tables are shared with the next person in the queue and everyone waits for everyone else to finish before leaving the table. Oddly, if they run out of ice-cream, they'll occasionally substitute Spam rolls.

Victoria Parque Céspedes, esq. General García. Cosy, wood-panelled restaurant dishing up Cuban staples for pesos. Closed Mon.

Paladares

Polinesio Parada no.125 e/ Pío Rosado y Capotico. An unpretentious place – basically four tables in a living room – serving good food at reasonable prices.

Sagitario Marmol no.107 e/ Ave. Castro y Maceo. Long-established *paladar* serving well-priced, generous portions of pork, chicken and fish in a pleasant courtyard with a thatched roof.

Drinking and nightlife

Bayamo is a relaxed place to go out – the choice isn't huge, but what's there is good value and most places are within a couple of streets of each other. The best place to sink a few **cocktails** is the outdoor bar-cum-restaurant on the veranda of the *Hotel Royalton*, while for something a bit livelier head to the peso bar *La Bodega* on Plaza del Himno behind the church, where there's beer and dancing until 3am in an intimate courtyard overlooking the Río Bayamo.

Everyone in town who can sing or play the guitar does so at the *Casa de la Trova*, Maceo no.111 (Tues–Sun 9am–6pm & 9pm–2am, Mon 9am–6pm), easily Bayamo's best **live music** venue. The strict dress code at *La Luz*, on General García, marks it out as the town's most exclusive venue, with a live show every night and cheap cocktails. If you're looking for something different, the *Casa de la Cultura*, on General García (✆23/42-5917), has occasional evening **theatre** and **dance** performances – check the board outside for weekly listings, while Cine Céspedes, next to the post office, shows a mix of Cuban and international films. On the western fringes of town, outside the *Sierra Maestra*, on the Carretera Central, a raucous informal **disco** draws hordes of local youths at weekends.

Listings

Airlines Cubana, Martí no.52 esq. Parada (Tues & Thurs 2–4pm; ☎ 23/42-7514).

Banks and exchange The Banco de Crédito y Comercio at General García 101 esq. Saco (Mon–Fri 8am–3pm) and the Cadeca at Saco no.109 e/ General García y Marmol (Mon–Sat 8.30am–noon & 2.30–5.30pm, Sun 8.30am–noon) change traveller's cheques and give cash advances on Visa and Mastercard.

Car rental Havanautos is based at the Cupet Cimex service station on the Carretera Central (vía Santiago) ☎ 23/42-7375.

Internet Idict, General García no.60 Altos e/ Saco y Figueredo (Mon–Fri 8am–8pm, Sat 8am–noon; $6CUC/hr).

Medical Call ☎ 185 for a public ambulance. Bayamo's general hospital is Carlos Manuel de Céspedes, Carretera Central (vía Santiago) ☎ 23/42-5012 or 42-6598. The most central 24hr *policlinico* doctors' surgery is on Pío Rosado, and there's a 24hr pharmacy, Piloto, at General García no.53.

Police In an emergency, call ☎ 116.

Post office The post office on Parque Céspedes (Mon–Sat 8am–8pm) has a DHL service and sells phone cards.

Taxis Cubataxi, Martí no.480 esq. Armando Estévez ☎ 23/42-4313.

Telephones You can buy international calling cards in the post office or *Hotel Royalton* and use the public phones in the hotel or on Parque Céspedes.

Marea del Portillo and around

Smack in the middle of Granma's southern coast, backed by a sweeping wave of mountains, is the resort of **Marea del Portillo**. Accessible from Granma's west coast and 150km southwest from Bayamo, the resort is set on a black-sand beach which looks impressive from a distance, but like a muddy field close up. It won't be most people's first choice for a beach holiday, although the white sands of tiny **Cayo Blanco** just offshore go some way to making up for this.

Appealing largely to older Canadians and Germans, as well as a few families, Marea del Portillo doesn't have the universal appeal of some resorts, especially as there is little infrastructure – just two hotels on the beach and another nearby, and a dive shop. The surrounding countryside is beautiful, however, including the picturesque **El Salton waterfall**, and there are eighteen **dive sites**, including the *El Real* Spanish galleon sunk in 1846, to keep keen divers busy.

Practicalities

The newer and better of Marea del Portillo's two beach **hotels** is the all-inclusive *Hotel Farallón del Caribe* (☎23/59-7081; ❼), with two restaurants, five bars, a handsome pool area and a resident iguana, while next door the rather down-at-heel *Club Amigo Marea del Portillo* (☎23/59-7102; ❼) offers a similar package, though in less congenial grounds. Away from the all-inclusive resorts, the best place to stay, and **eat**, is the *Motel Mirador de Pilón* (☎23/59-4365; ❷) on the road towards Pilón, with four cabins high up on the hillside overlooking the sea. A further 2km along the same road, *Villa Turística Punta Piedra* (☎23/59-4421; ❸) has basic rooms, including triples, and a restaurant.

The resort's Marlin **dive centre** (☎ 23/59-7034) rents out equipment and offers dives from $30CUC, as well as deep-sea fishing and trips to Cayo Blanco. Land-based **excursions** from the resort include horse riding to the El Salton waterfall ($35CUC for a four-hour trip), organized by Cubatur at the *Hotel Farallón del Caribe*, and hiking along the El Guafe nature trail to see the pre-Columbian petroglyphs ($35CUC; see p.544).

Transport links to and from Marea del Portillo are diabolical – if you can rent a car before you arrive, do so and make sure you have sufficient cash before you arrive as the only banks in the province are in Bayamo.

Pilón

Tiny sugar town **PILÓN**, 8km west of Marea del Portillo, is like a remnant of past times with open-backed carts laden with sugar cane zigzagging across the roads and the smell of boiling molasses enveloping the town in its thick scent. The small but engaging **Casa Museo Celia Sánchez Manduley** (Mon–Sat 9am–5pm, Sun 9am–1pm; $1CUC), erstwhile home of revolutionary Celia Sánchez, offers a ragbag of exhibits, from Taíno ceramics

The Granma

Under constant surveillance and threat from the Batista regime following his release from prison, Fidel Castro left Havana for exile in Mexico in the summer of 1955. Along with other exiled Cubans sympathetic to his ideas, he formed the **26 July Movement** in exile – the Cuban counterpart was run by Frank País – and began to gather weapons and funds to facilitate the return to Cuba. It was during his time in Mexico that many of the significant players of the Revolution were drawn together, most notably Ernesto "Che" Guevara, who was introduced to Castro in November 1955 by Ñico López, veteran of the attack on the Bayamo army barracks.

Castro was anxious to return to Cuba as soon as possible. Leaks within the organization had already resulted in the confiscation of arms by the Mexican government and there was an ever-present threat of assassination by Batista's contacts in Mexico. By October the following year Castro had gathered enough support and money and declared himself ready to return. He bought a 58-foot yacht with the winsome name of *Granma* from a North American couple for $15,000, and hatched a plan to sail it from Tuxpan, on the east coast of Veracruz in Mexico, to Oriente, following the tracks of José Martí who had made a similar journey sixty years before. A cache of weapons was found by the Mexican police following a tip-off, and escalating events led the rebels to leave sooner than they planned. On November 21 the Mexican authorities gave Castro three days to leave Mexico City and the rebels left from Veracruz so quickly that several received no military training.

At around 1.30am on November 25, 1956, with 82 men crammed into the eight-berth yacht, the *Granma* set off for Cuba. Due to the stormy weather all shipping was kept in port and the yacht had to slip past the Mexican coastguard to escape. Foul weather, cramped conditions and a malfunctioning engine meant that the journey that was supposed to take five days took eight. The plan had been to come ashore at Niquero, where Celia Sánchez, a key revolutionary, was waiting to ferry them to safety, but on December 2 they ran out of petrol just 35m from the coast, and at 6am the *Granma* capsized just off Playa Las Coloradas. As Che later commented: "It wasn't a landing, it was a shipwreck."

Exhausted, sick and hungry, the 82 young men waded ashore only to find themselves faced with a kilometre of virtually impenetrable mangroves and sharp saw grass. They eventually made camp at Alegría de Pío, a sugar-cane zone near the coast, with the intention of resting for a few hours. It was to be their baptism by fire as Batista troops, who had been tipped off about their arrival and had been strafing the area for several hours, came across the men and attacked. Completely unprepared, the rebels ran for their lives, scattering in all directions. Thanks to the efforts of Celia Sánchez, who had left messages at the houses of peasants sympathetic to the rebels' cause, the rebels were able to regroup two weeks later. It was hardly a glorious beginning, but the opening shots of the Revolution had been fired.

through shrapnel from the Wars of Independence to a photographic history of the town.

There's little else to see here and even less to do, but the two beaches, **Playa Media Luna**, with beautiful views over the Sierra Maestra and a rocky coastline good for snorkelling, and the narrow white-sand **Playa Punta**, have an unruliness that's refreshingly different from the smarter resort beaches.

There's nowhere to stay or eat, though the local service station on the Marea del Portillo road sells sweets, snacks and cold drinks.

Parque Nacional Desembarco del Granma

West of Pilón, the province's southwestern tip is commandeered by the **Parque Nacional Desembarco del Granma**, which starts at the tranquil holiday haven of **Campismo Las Coloradas**, 47km from Pilón, and stretches some 20km south to the tiny fishing village of **Cabo Cruz**. The forested interior of the park is littered with trails, but the most famous feature is **Playa Las Coloradas** on the western coastline, where the *Granma* yacht deposited Fidel Castro on December 2, 1956 (see box, p.543).

The only **place to stay** in the park, *Campismo Las Coloradas*, has excellently simple and clean chalets with air conditioning and hot water, along with a **restaurant** and **bar**. Bookings should be made via **Cubamar** in Havana (☎7/831-2891; ❷) and are essential at weekends, when this is a favourite target for Cubans. Cubamar can also arrange **group excursions** (for ten or more) to visit the other trails.

Playa Las Coloradas

Named after the murky red colour that the mangrove jungle gives to the water, **Playa Las Coloradas** – in reality little more than a shoreline – is situated 2km south of *Campismo Las Coloradas*. It's completely hidden and you can't see or even hear the sea from the start of the path on the right-hand side that leads down to the **Monumento Portada de la Libertad** (Tues–Sat 8am–6pm, Sun 8am–noon; $1CUC, including guide), which marks the spot of the landing. Flanked on either side by mangrove forest hedged with jagged saw grass, the kilometre-long path makes a pleasant walk even for those indifferent to the Revolution, although even the most jaded cynics will find it hard to resist the guides' enthusiasm for the subject, their compelling narrative (in Spanish) bringing to life the rebels' journey through murky undergrowth and razor-sharp thicket.

The tour also takes in a life-size replica of the **yacht**, which the guide can sometimes be persuaded to let you clamber aboard, and a rather spartan **museum** with photographs, maps and an emotive quotation from Castro on the eve of the crossing that neatly sums up his determination to succeed: "*Si salimos, llegamos. Si llegamos, entramos, y si entramos, triumfamos*" (If we leave, we'll get there. If we get there we'll get in, and if we get in we will win).

El Guafe and other trails

The park's interior is made up of idyllic woodland that skirts the western verge of the Sierra Maestra. From Las Coloradas you can walk to the start of **El Guafe** (Mon–Fri 8.30am–5pm, Sat & Sun 8am–2pm; $3CUC entrance plus $5CUC for a guide), one of the four trails in the park, celebrated for the intriguing stone petroglyphs found in the vicinity, the remnants of Indian culture. It's an easy and reasonably well-signposted walk – roughly a three-kilometre circuit – which you can do on your own, although the guides have extensive knowledge of both the history of the area and the cornucopia of birds and butterflies, trees and plants you'll see along the way. Look out for the ancient cactus nicknamed "Viejo Testigo" (the Old Witness), thought to be five-hundred years old and now so thick and twisted it has formed a robust, tree-like trunk.

The small, human-form **petroglyphs**, sculpted with haunting, hollowed-out eyes, are in a low-roofed cave musty with the smell of bats, believed to have been used as a crypt by the aboriginal Indians, who carved the idols as guardians. Fragments of ceramics and a large clay jar decorated with allegorical characters were also found, supporting the theory. A second cave close to the exit of the trail houses another petroglyph known as the **Idolo del Agua** (the water idol), thought to have been carved into the rock to bless and protect the sweet water of the cave – a rarity in the area. Along the walk, look out for the tiny, iridescent green, red and blue Cartacuba bird, which looks like a pom-pom and has a gruff call like a grunting pig.

The **other trails** run along the southern coastline twenty to thirty kilometres east of El Guafe. Highlights include the Agua Fina cave, roughly 20km from El Guafe, and, some 7km further east, the Morlotte and El Furstete caves and Las Terrazas, a natural coastline shelf sculpted by geographic formations to look like man-made terraces. To visit any of these places you'll need to contact **Cubamar** (see p.38).

Manzanillo and around

Though run-down and ramshackle, **MANZANILLO**, 75km up the coast from Playa Las Coloradas, still possesses some charm. Now a fairly pedestrian coastal fishing village, it was established around the harbour at the end of the eighteenth century and for a time enjoyed a brisk trade in contraband goods. Sugar trade replaced smuggling as the primary business hereabouts in the nineteenth century, but the town's heyday had passed and it never grew much bigger.

Manzanillo's sole attraction these days is its fantastic **Moorish architecture**, dating from the 1910s and 1920s. The sensual buildings, all crescents, curves and brilliant tiles, are best seen in the town's central **Parque Céspedes**. Most eye-catching is the richly decorated gazebo presiding over the park, giving an air of bohemian elegance well suited to the sphinx statues in each corner and the melee of benches, palm trees, and faux-nineteenth-century streetlamps.

Opposite the park, the pink **Edificio Quirch** is no less splendid,

EL GUAFE NATURE TRAIL

although its crescent arches and tight lattice design are rather wasted on the couple of convertible-peso shops it houses. If you have time, it's fascinating just to wander around the surrounding streets looking at the building's various spires, domes and peaks. Don't miss the roof of an unnamed apartment block, one block east of Parque Céspedes, attractively coated in brown-and-cream tiles like discs of milk chocolate.

Trains from Bayamo arrive at the train station on the eastern edge of town, around 1km from the centre. **Buses** from Bayamo and Pilón pull in at the bus station 2km east of town, but the service is irregular and if coming from Bayamo you're better off catching one of the *colectivo* **taxis**. If you need to change **money**, head to the Cadeca at Martí no.184 (Mon–Sat 8.30am–6pm, Sun 8am–1pm). There's no real reason to **stay** in Manzanillo, but should you need to, *César y Blanca* at Sariol no.245 e/ Doctor Codina y Saco (☎23/5-3131; ❷) is an excellent *casa particular* offering two comfortable double rooms and tasty meals, while the state hotel, the *Guacanayabo*, on Avenida Camilio Cienfuegos (☎23/5-4012; ❷), is rather grim and has a mediocre **restaurant**.

Parque Nacional de Demajagua

Twenty kilometres south of Manzanillo, the **Parque Nacional de Demajagua** (Mon–Sat 8am–5pm, Sun 8am–noon; $1CUC, $1CUC extra for a camera, $5CUC for a camcorder) is a pleasant place to while away an hour or two. It was from here that Carlos Manuel de Céspedes set out to win Cuban independence from Spain (see box, p.540), and with splendid views over the bay and the cane fields, the one-time sugar plantation is a picture of serenity. The small building housing the **museum** was built in 1968, the centenary of the uprising, the original plantation having been completely destroyed by shells from a Spanish gunboat on October 17 1868.

The museum itself is depressingly sparse, with a brief history of the plantation detailing its ownership by Céspedes' older brother forming the main part. Glass cases display various metal keys and broken plate fragments, as well as a moth-eaten square of red, white and blue cloth, the highlight of the museum, which turns out to be the first Cuban flag ever made, hand-sewn by Céspedes' mistress. The grounds, while not extensive, are a nice spot to relax – look out for the two big tubs just beyond the museum's entrance, which were originally used to boil the sugar cane. The most significant sight, however, is the Demajagua bell, built into a dry-stone wall on the far side of the lawn, with which Céspedes summoned his slaves to freedom.

Travel details

Domestic flights

Bayamo to: Havana (2 weekly; 2hr).
Manzanillo to: Havana (3 weekly; 2hr 30min).
Santiago de Cuba to: Havana (4–6 weekly; 2hr 15min).

Trains

Bayamo to: Camagüey (1 every other day; 5hr 30min); Havana (1 every other day; 13hr); Manzanillo (2 daily; 3hr); Santiago de Cuba (1 daily; 4hr 15min).
Manzanillo to: Bayamo (2 daily; 3hr); Havana (1 every other day; 15hr); Santiago de Cuba (1 daily; 6hr).
Santiago de Cuba to: Bayamo (1 daily; 4hr 15min); Havana (1 dailly; 12–14hr); Manzanillo (1 daily; 6hr).

Buses

Note that problems relating to petrol shortages are particularly severe in this region; although Víazul buses usually run on time, there are often delays on other services.

Bayamo to: Camagüey (1 every other day; 4hr); Havana (4 daily; 12hr); Manzanillo (1 every other day; 1hr 45min); Niquero (1 every other day; 3hr 15min); Pilón (1 every other day; 3hr 30min); Santiago de Cuba (7 daily; 2hr 45min); Trinidad (1 daily; 8hr 30min).
Manzanillo to: Bayamo (1 every other day; 1hr 45min); Havana (1 daily; 12hr); Pilón (1 every other day; 2hr 30min).
Pilón to: Bayamo (1 every other day; 3hr 30min); Chivirico (3 weekly; 4hr); Manzanillo (1 every other day; 2hr 30min).
Santiago de Cuba to: Baracoa (1–2 daily; 6hr); Bayamo (7 daily; 2hr 45min); Camagüey (3 daily; 6hr); Havana (3 daily; 15hr 30min); Mar Verde (5 daily; 1hr); Santa Clara (3 daily; 12hr); Trinidad (1 daily; 12hr).

Isla de la Juventud
and Cayo Largo

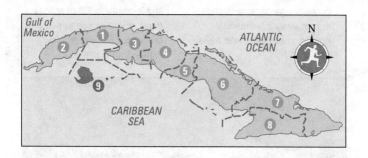

CHAPTER 9   # Highlights

* **Museo Provincial** The oldest building in Nueva Gerona houses the island's heirlooms, with an emphasis on the maritime exploits that have shaped local history. See p.559

* **Museo de Presidio Modelo** A walk around the huge ruined cell blocks of this "Model Prison", with its forbidding atmosphere and grim history, is unforgettable. See p.564

* **La Jungla de Jones** Take a stroll around these verdant botanical gardens, with their impressively international collection of plants and trees. See p.567

* **Cuevas de Punta del Este** These atmospheric caves, once home to the Siboney people, hold significant examples of early pre-Columbian art. See p.569

* **Punta Francés** On a remote, upturned hook of land, silver sands and limpid waters make this paradisiacal beach the best on Isla de la Juventud. See p.571

* **Coral gardens** Cayo Largo is one of Cuba's most rewarding diving areas, its clear and shallow waters full of stunning coral, primeval sea turtles and brilliantly coloured tropical fishes. See p.576

△ Cayo Largo

Isla de la Juventud
and Cayo Largo

About 100km south of the mainland, the little-visited Isla de la Juventud (Island of Youth) is the largest of over three hundred scattered emerald islets that make up the **Archipiélago de los Canarreos**. Most visitors to the archipelago, however, are destined for the comparatively tiny Cayo Largo to the east, arguably Cuba's most exclusive holiday resort.

Extending from the personable island capital of Nueva Gerona, in the north, to the superb diving region of Punta Francés, 70km to the southwest, the comma-shaped **Isla de la Juventud** is bisected by a military checkpoint designed to limit access to ecologically vulnerable areas. The island's northern region is mostly farmland, characterized by citrus orchards and mango groves, while the restricted southern swampland is rich in wildlife. Although it has an air of timeless somnolence, the island was actually once a pirate haunt, ruled over for three centuries by French and English buccaneers and adventurers. Development here has been unhurried, and even today there are as many horse-drawn coaches on the roads as there are cars or trucks.

It probably won't be your first choice for a beach holiday, although it's a good place to unwind once you've visited the more flamboyant – and hectic – sights elsewhere in Cuba. With little tourist trade, its charm is anchored to its unaffected pace of life and pleasant beaches, and the lack of traffic and predominantly flat terrain make **cycling** an excellent way to explore. The island's single real town, **Nueva Gerona**, has few of the architectural crowd-pullers that exist in colonial towns, and so is a refreshingly low-key and relaxing place to visit, easily explored over a weekend. For those keen to explore further, there are some intriguing pre-Columbian **cave paintings** in the south and, close to the capital, the museum at the abandoned **Presidio Modelo**, a prison whose most famous inmate was Fidel Castro. With a couple more small but worthy museums, some of the country's best offshore **dive sites** and one beautiful white-sand beach, Isla de la Juventud is one of Cuba's best-kept secrets.

A necklace of islets streaming 150km east, the Archipiélago de los Canarreos is a fantasy paradise of pearl-white sand and translucent, coral-lined shallows. While most are still desert cays too small to sustain a complex tourist structure, **Cayo Largo**, the archipelago's second-largest landmass after La Isla, is beaten only by Varadero in terms of package tourist pulling power. Unlike its mainland counterpart, however, this resort operates exclusively for foreign visitors and

ISLA DE LA JUVENTUD & CAYO LARGO

ACCOMMODATION
Los Codornices **B**
Colony **C**
Villa Isla de
la Juventud **A**

ISLA DE LA JUVENTUD

Cubans are officially banned. Created in 1977 to serve the sun-worshipping Canadians and Europeans who flock here in high season, the resort capitalizes on its flawless, 22-kilometre-long ribbon of white sand and features a marina, dive shop and a growing clique of all-inclusive hotels. The building boom suffered a setback in 2001 when the island received a severe battering at the hands of Hurricane Michelle, but the damage has since been repaired and there are plans afoot for further construction.

Getting to the islands

There are three daily **flights** from Havana to the **Isla de la Juventud** (40min). The most economical way to reach the island had for a long time been to take the daily **ferry** from Batabanó on the mainland coast; the trip takes between two and five hours depending on which boat is available. However, a massive price hike has seen the cost of a combined bus and ferry ticket soar from $13 CUC to $50CUC each way. There is talk of lowering the cost in the near future, so check before you make your travel plans. Buying tickets from the Oficina Naviera booth at Havana's Astro bus terminal (daily 8am–12.30pm; ☏7/878-1841) is probably the best option, since the direct bus to the ferry terminal at Batabanó (daily at noon; 1hr 30min) is included in the price and, as most visitors set off from Havana, you may find on reaching Batabanó that all the convertible-peso seats on the ferry have already been sold. If possible you should buy tickets in advance, as demand often outstrips seat capacity. A passport is needed to buy all tickets to the island. See "Travel details", p.577, for information on leaving the island by ferry.

The only way to reach **Cayo Largo** is by **plane**, and its airport sees numerous international arrivals, as well as domestic planes from Havana (2 daily; 40min). Although only 140km apart, short of swimming, there is no way to get here from Isla de la Juventud unless you're sailing your own yacht. Note that you'll be required to book accommodation along with your flight.

Isla de la Juventud

A vision of fruit fields and soft beaches, it is little wonder that the **Isla de la Juventud**, or "La Isla", as it's known locally, allegedly captured Robert Louis Stevenson's imagination as the original desert island of *Treasure Island*. Although Christopher Columbus chanced upon the island in 1494, the Spanish had scant use for it until the nineteenth century, mostly because the shallow, coral-lined waters surrounding the island had repeatedly scuppered their ships. Instead it was left to swarms of pirates to discover the lush, pine-forested land, hidden caves and the impenetrable swampy interior in the south. They soon realized that the island's proximity to the mainland was not only convenient for raiding Havana – the most lucrative port in the Caribbean – but also that it was ideally placed for attacks on the trade routes; a conspicuous lack of governors cemented its appeal.

Development of the island unfolded at an unhurried pace and even today the quiet, underpopulated countryside and placid towns have the air of a land waiting to awaken. The main focus of the island is in the **north**, where you'll find many of the sights and most of the population. Nestling up against the Sierra de Casa, the island capital of **Nueva Gerona** is small and satisfyingly self-contained, ambling along a couple of decades behind developments on the mainland. Spread around the town is a wide skirt of low-lying fields, lined with orderly citrus orchards and fruit farms and peppered with most of the island's modest tourist attractions. Two of these sights are former prison buildings, a testament to the island's longstanding underpopulation and relative isolation: **El Abra**, a hacienda briefly converted in 1869 into a holding pen for the Cuban independence suffragist José Martí pending his exile to Spain, and the **Presidio Modelo**, set up in 1926 to contain more than six thousand criminals, most famously Fidel Castro. Deserted, but still a dominating presence on the island's landscape, the formidable prison and its museum make for a fascinating excursion. There are also a couple of brown-sand beaches, **Playa Bibijagua** and **Playa Paraíso**, within easy reach of Nueva Gerona.

South from the capital are several sights that can be explored in easy day-trips. Beyond the island's second biggest town, the rather mundane **La Fe**, known for its medicinal mineral waters, is a **crocodile farm** offering an excellent opportunity to study the creatures at close range. Just south of here is the **military checkpoint** at Cayo Piedra, in place to conserve the marshy region to the southeast that forms the **Siguanea Nature Reserve**, much of which is off-limits to visitors. Off to the west of here are verdant botanical gardens, **La Jungla de Jones**, that are well worth a visit.

South of the checkpoint on the east coast is one of the island's most intriguing attractions, the **pre-Columbian paintings** in the Punta del Este caves. On the west side is the tiny hamlet of **Cocodrilo**, set on a picturesque curve of coastline and an ideal spot for swimming, while close to hand is the picture-perfect white-sand beach, **Playa El Francés**, from where you can enjoy the island's celebrated dive sites, including underwater caves and a wall of black coral.

Some history

The island's earliest known inhabitants were the **Siboney** people who, some 1100 years ago, sailed in dugout canoes from island to island through the Caribbean, settling in the most favourable places. Living a simple life, they stayed close to the island's shores where they could fish and hunt, eschewing its pine-forested interior. Tools and utensils made from conch shell and bone have been found at Punta del Este, suggesting that the Siboney based themselves around the eastern caves, although some remains at Caleta Grande, in the north, indicate the presence of another, smaller group.

By the time **Christopher Columbus** landed here in June 1494, on his second trip to the Americas, Indians no longer lived on the island. Although Columbus named the island "Juan La Evangelista" and claimed it for Spain, the Spanish Crown had little interest in the island over the next four centuries. Neither the northern coastline, webbed with mangroves, nor the excessively shallow southern bays afforded a natural harbour to match the likes of Havana, and the Golfo de Batabanó, separating the island from mainland Cuba, was too shallow for the overblown Spanish galleons to navigate.

Left outside the bounds of Spanish law enforcement, the island attracted scores of **pirates** between the sixteenth and eighteenth centuries, most famously John Hawkins, Henry Morgan, John Rackham, better known as Calico Jack, and the Frenchman Latrobe. It came to be known as **La Isla de Pinos** – after its plentiful pine trees, ideal for making masts and repairing ships – and, informally, as the Isla de las Cotorras, for its endemic green parrot population. Lurid stories of a Bacchanalian commune fuelled by wine, women and warmongering were enough to keep all but the most determined settlers away from the island, and so the pirates ruled the roost for nigh on three hundred years. Their success was in part due to a barter system set up with the incipient cattle-farming community, with whom they would exchange their booty of alcohol, bolts of cloth and African slaves for leather, sugar and other basic commodities.

The pirates' glory days drew to a close in the early nineteenth century when Spanish interest was renewed in the island. Visiting priests had expressed dismay at the pirates' moral laxity and the conspicuous absence of a church, and in 1821 the United States, which had been slowly growing in influence in the region since its independence, established an anti-pirate naval squadron. Supported by

Spain and England, who were eager to protect their own commercial interests, trouncing the enemy turned out to be a relatively simple task. Many of the pirates even proved compliant, leaping at the chance to become pillars of the community by accepting prestigious governor positions and knighthoods, or simply retiring with their wealth.

Rather belatedly, the Spanish set about staking their claim and in 1827 Colonel Clemente Delgado y España was despatched, along with **Dr José Labadía**, by the Capitán General of Cuba to assess the island's potential. On the basis of Labadía's report, it was decided that the island should be fortified against illegal trading, and in 1830 it was rechristened "Colonia de la Reina Amalia", though it continued to be popularly known as Isla de Pinos. España named the island's newly appropriated township Nueva Gerona in honour of the Capitán General of Cuba's victorious battle in Gerona in Spain – an act of sheer obsequiousness which shortly paid off when España was put in military command of the island.

Despite a massive push by royal decree for whites to populate the island, there was comparatively little response, and even by the turn of the twentieth century, the population still stood at under four thousand. The Spanish authorities then capitalized on the island's isolation, using it as a convenient **offshore prison** during the Wars of Independence, but still failed to exploit its full potential. By the early twentieth century, they were ruing their indifference, as much of the property had fallen into the hands of shrewd North American businessmen and farmers who had waited in the wings during the troubled years.

When Cuba won its independence from Spain in 1901, the island's small population allowed the North Americans to muscle in and start development unimpeded, and by the time the Spanish deigned – in 1926 – to ratify the 1902 treaty which ensured that the Isla de Pinos was Cuban territory, a US-funded infrastructure of banks, hotels and even prisons – namely the vast Model Prison – was already in place. By the time of the Revolution the island had become a popular North American holiday resort.

The North Americans promptly departed following the Revolution, and the history of the island took another turn when the state's drive to create arable land established it as one of the country's major producers of fruit for export. In 1966 it became a centre for experimental agriculture to which a flood of students came to work the fields and study. In 1976 the government extended this free education to **foreign students** from countries with a socialist overview, and, until the Special Period curtailed the flow, thousands of students arrived from countries like Angola, Nicaragua and South Yemen. When Cuba hosted the eleventh World Youth and Student Festival in 1978, the government changed the island's name from Isle of Pines to **Isle of Youth**, shedding the final trace of the island's rebellious past, although islanders still refer to themselves – and their national-league baseball team – as Pineros.

Nueva Gerona

The island's only sizeable town, **NUEVA GERONA** lies in the lee of the Sierra de Casa, on the bank of the Río Las Casas. Whether you are coming by plane or boat, this is where you will arrive and where you're likely to be based. According to an 1819 census, the population stood at just under two hundred and it boasted just "four guano huts and a church of the same". While the town has certainly moved on since then, it's still a small and quirky place, with a cosiness more suited

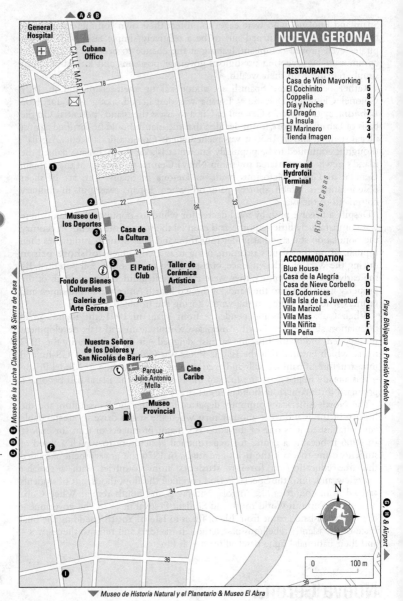

G, E, Museo de la Lucha Clandestina & Sierra de Casa

NUEVA GERONA

RESTAURANTS

Casa de Vino Mayorking	1
El Cochinito	5
Coppelia	8
Día y Noche	6
El Dragón	7
La Insula	2
El Marinero	3
Tienda Imagen	4

ACCOMMODATION

Blue House	C
Casa de la Alegría	I
Casa de Nieve Corbello	D
Los Codornices	H
Villa Isla de La Juventud	G
Villa Marizol	E
Villa Mas	B
Villa Niñita	F
Villa Peña	A

General Hospital

Cubana Office

CALLE MARTÍ

Museo de los Deportes

Casa de la Cultura

El Patio Club

Taller de Cerámica Artística

Fondo de Bienes Culturales

Galería de Arte Gerona

Ferry and Hydrofoil Terminal

Río Las Casas

Playa Bibijagua & Presidio Modelo

Nuestra Señora de los Dolores y San Nicolás de Barí

Parque Julio Antonio Mella

Cine Caribe

Museo Provincial

G, H & Airport

N

0   100 m

Museo de Historia Natural y el Planetario & Museo El Abra

to a village than an island capital, and a sleepy peacefulness well offset by the hub of action around the central streets. Even half a day here breeds a sense of familiarity, and much of the town's attraction lies in wandering its streets, chatting with locals, a few of whom speak English, and visiting the low-key museums.

Architecturally, Nueva Gerona floats in a no-man's-land between old-style colonial buildings and modern urbanity. When the town was brought under

Spanish control in the 1830s there were only thirty-odd private houses, and life centred around the military garrison, the commander's house and a prison galley (since removed) by the dock. Today, it's a pretty town, with many of its concrete, one- and two-storey buildings painted into cubes of pastel colour, and its few older buildings, complete with stately colonnades and red-tiled roofs, adding a colonial touch.

You'll find most of the town's attractions on and just off the main street, cheerful **Calle Martí**. Starting off at the **Museo de los Deportes**, with its somewhat scanty display of sporting trophies and medals, Martí runs south past the **Fondo de Bienes Culturales**, which offers souvenirs, some locally produced, and the **Galería de Arte Gerona**, home to regularly changing displays of local artwork. A block further south, the handsome **Iglesia Nuestra Señora de los Dolores y San Nicolás de Barí** brightens up the rather bland **Parque Julio Antonio Mella**, while opposite, the **Museo Provincial**, the town's best museum, shows off the island's heirlooms. One block east of Martí, the **Taller de Cerámica Artística** makes a passable enough diversion for those interested in ceramics production, while three blocks west, the fascinating **Museo de Jesús Montané Oropesa** displays memorabilia relating to the underground revolutionary movement of the 1950s. The town's most far-flung attraction, the rather sparse **Museo de Historia Natural y el Planetario**, stands ten minutes' walk southwest of the centre; it boasts a large rock collection and a scaled-down reproduction of the pre-Columbian cave paintings found in the south of the island.

Arrival and information

Flights from Havana arrive at Rafael Cabrera Mustelier airport (℡46/32-2300), 10km south from the town centre. Have some small change in pesos ready for the buses that meet the planes and run to the town centre, or take a taxi for about $7CUC. The **ferry** from Batabanó docks at the terminal on the Río Las Casas in Nueva Gerona (Mon–Fri 8am–noon & 2–5pm; ℡46/32-4415). From here it's a ten-minute walk to the centre or you can jump on one of the *bicitaxis* or numerous horse-drawn carriages that wait to pick up passengers, although it's hard not to notice that the horses here are underfed and overworked, even by Cuban standards.

The only place for **information** in the centre of town is the Ecotur office at Calle Martí e/ 24 y 26 (Mon–Sat 7.30am–5.30pm; ℡46/32-7101, ✉ecoturpineroij@yahoo.es), which sells fairly uninformative maps. Ecotur also sells permits and excursions to the southern part of the island, as well as tours to La Fe, La Jungla de Jones, Punta Francés and (somewhat bizarrely, given their green-sounding name) hunting trips to the interior. The *Villa Isla de la Juventud* hotel on the town outskirts (see p.558) also provides information, especially on diving activities, or you could ring the *Hotel Colony*, on the island's southwest coast (see p.572).

Getting around

Compact Nueva Gerona is easily seen on foot but the best way to explore the rest of the island is by renting a car or jeep here since the bus network is skeletal and often suspended anyway due to petrol shortages. **Taxis** are an alternative option with two state taxi companies, Transtur at Calle 37 s/n e/ 20 y 22 (℡46/32-6666) and Islatran at Calle 39 esq. 47 (℡46/32-2222). You'll find fewer unmetered taxis than in other towns; a good place to look is outside the convertible-peso supermarket on Calle 32 e/ 35 y 37, or ask in a *casa particular*.

The best way to see the north end of the island is by **bike**; there are no rental outlets, but *casas particulares* are often willing to loan you the family bicycle for a few convertible pesos a day.

Accommodation

Unless you've come for the diving, in which case you'll be based in the western Ensenada de la Siguanea, Nueva Gerona is the only base for a stay on the island. The three state **hotels** on the town outskirts have the advantage of cool swimming pools and pretty countryside, but to really enjoy the centre of town you're probably best off in one of the excellent *casas particulares*. To stem what was in reality a minor (though, as everywhere, politically sensitive) *jinetera* problem, *casas particulares* on Isla de la Juventud cannot be self-contained and the landlord must sleep on the premises. In the unlikely event that all are fully booked you can try the state *Hotel La Cubana* (❸), next to the Cubana office, which occasionally accepts foreigners.

Hotels

Los Codornices Carretera Aeropuerto Km 4.5 ☎46/32-4981. Serviceable, if slightly gloomy, rooms in a chalet-like motel 5km southeast of town, with a swimming pool and good views over the surrounding countryside – rather inconvenient for everything but the airport. Heading along the road from the airport, take the right fork after the bridge then turn right at the open-air peso café. ❸

Villa Isla de La Juventud Autopista La Fe Km 1.5 ☎46/32-3290. Rather plain state hotel whose highlight is a pool with sun terrace to which much of the town flocks at the weekends (10am–6pm; $2CUC for non-guests). The decent single, double and triple rooms, all with bathrooms, are arranged around the pool in two-storey beach-hut-style blocks that are gaily painted but have rather plain interiors. ❸

Casas particulares

Blue House Calle 45 no.2411 e/ 24 y 26 ☎46/32-2606. ✉larisa34@web.correosdecuba.cu. A spotless room with a rooftop terrace and its own entrance. Has a fridge, a TV, a radio, a well-appointed bathroom and both a fan and a/c. ❷

Casa de la Alegría Calle 43 no.3602 e/ 36 y 38 ☎46/32-3664. Two pleasantly furnished double rooms close to the centre, with a/c, private bathrooms and a living room exclusively for guests. Offers meals and provides laundry service as well. ❶

Casa de Nieve Corbello Calle 24 no.5108 e/ 51 y 53 ☎46/32-4437. This welcoming, second-storey *casa particular*, accessed by a spiral staircase, has two a/c double rooms, each with a TV and private bathroom, and a bright sitting room complete with rocking chairs. ❶

Villa Marizol Calle 24 no.5107 e/ 51 y 53 ☎46/32-2502. Airy, homely *casa particular* with a relaxing shady terrace and two a/c rooms with a pink satiny bed cover on each bed. Six blocks from the centre on a quiet, pretty street with hill views. ❷

Villa Mas Calle 41 no.4108 e/ 8 y 10, apto. 7 ☎46/32-3544. This apartment, situated behind the hospital, offers two spotlessly clean, stylishly decorated, self-contained rooms with TV and fridge. There's also a fabulous roof terrace with a tinkling fountain, chirping songbirds, views over the city and an owner who's also a professional chef and will provide meals. Although a little hard to find, this is well worth the effort. ❶

Villa Niñita Calle 32 no.4110 e/ 41 y 43 ☎46/32-1255. One room, run by very kind owners, with a kitchen, terrace and private bath. The attractive tiled floor and gorgeous hill views from the front and back terraces are pluses. ❷

Villa Peña Calle 10 no.3710 e/ 37 y 39 ☎46/32-2345. Big, friendly household offering two rooms, each of which has its own bathroom with an electric hot-water shower. Food is available and, unusually, vegetarian meals are a speciality; a fridge is shared between the two guestrooms. Around 300m out of town but a good choice, nonetheless. ❶

The Town

The best place to start any walking tour of Nueva Gerona is Calle Martí, the hub of the town, where you'll find the main shops as well as the town gallery and a local museum. At the street's southern end, set around the plaza of Parque

Julio Antonio Mella, you'll find the Iglesia Nuestra Señora de los Dolores and the provincial museum, while the Museo de Jesús Montané Oropesa, dedicated to the activities of locals during the Revolution, lies a few blocks off to the west. The only draw beyond the town centre is the Museo de Historia Natural y el Planeterio.

Calle Martí

Nueva Gerona's heart lies on **Calle Martí**, the amiable central street, also known as Calle 39, that gives the town its defining character and which is where the majority of shops, restaurants and attractions are located. It's a good-looking strip, with the running verandas of the low buildings offering welcome respite from the sun. At the northern end of its main drag is a small and rather ordinary park. A couple of blocks south, the tiny **Museo de los Deportes**, between calles 22 and 24 (Tues–Sat 8am–noon & 1–5pm; free), serves as a modest tribute to local sports heroes who have gained national recognition. The tiny one-room museum displays sweatshirts worn by record breakers, photos of athletes and baseball players in action and a timeworn collection of trophies, all proudly laid out as if in a grandmother's parlour.

The **Fondo de Bienes Culturales**, a little further down, on the opposite side of the street at no.2418 between Calles 24 and 26 (Mon–Fri 8am–noon & 1–5pm, Sat 9am–noon), has an eclectic range of souvenirs, from finely detailed ornamental plates and good-quality Cuban art posters to Che Guevara lighters and guinea pigs sculpted from hairy coconuts. More thought-provoking is the **Galería de Arte Gerona**, close by at no.2424 (Tues–Fri 9am–10pm, Sat & Sun 8am–8pm), which has a small collection of local art, some of it for sale. The gallery's regularly changing selection of ceramics (for which the island enjoys a quiet fame), big splashy abstracts, obscure watercolour collages and even underwater photography definitely merits a quick stop.

Parque Julio Antonio Mella

At the southern end of the central strip, past the pedestrianized centre lined with kiosks selling everything from soap to frilly knickers, and a couple of more upmarket convertible-peso stores, is the **Parque Julio Antonio Mella**. Although unspectacular in itself – it's basically a wide slab of plaza sweltering in the sun – it's bordered by some picturesque buildings. On the western side, for example, is a handsome, pastel-yellow villa, now converted into a school, with elegant, unadorned arches and wonderful stained-glass windows.

Presiding over the plaza's northeast corner is the grandiose, ochre-coloured church of **Nuestra Señora de los Dolores y San Nicolás de Barí** (Mon–Fri 8.30am–noon), boasting a curvaceous red-tiled roof and a sturdy bell tower with two delicate rounded balconies painted with snailshell rings. The stalwart design is intended to ensure that the church does not suffer the same fate as its predecessor, built in 1853, which collapsed in the face of a hurricane in 1926. The present building was completed in 1929 and, though reminiscent of a colonial Mexican church, is actually a copy of the San Lorenzo de Lucina church in Rome. The interior is disappointing: a sparsely decorated sky-blue shell houses a huddle of pews. It's only worth entering for a swift glance at the altar to the Virgen de la Caridad, the patron saint of Cuba, backed by the national flag.

Across the square from the church is the **Museo Provincial** (Tues–Sat 9am–10pm, Sun 9am–1pm; $1CUC), housed in the old town hall, a stately cream-and-white colonial building with simple pillars lining the facade and a small clock tower. Dating to 1830, this is the oldest building in Nueva Gerona.

The carefully put together exhibits inside use an impressive collection of artefacts to portray the island's rich history.

Most of the post-Columbian displays focus on the maritime exploits that played a central role in the island's development. Portraits, weapons and naval relics illustrate the lives of the pirates whose activities dominated the region for over 200 years. Moving on in time, some rather mundane exhibits about more contemporary shipping and the usual mismatch of revolutionary memorabilia are countered by displays of compelling photographs from the early years of the twentieth century and a wonderfully retro collection of pamphlets and advertisements dating from the island's heyday as a tourist destination in the 1940s and 50s. Be sure to also look for the intricate model of *El Pinero*, the boat that ferried passengers and supplies to and from the mainland throughout the first half of the twentieth century, and which carried Fidel Castro following his release from the Presidio Modelo in 1955.

Taller de Cerámica Artística

Lined with trestle tables at which potters and ceramicists work silently on vases, plant pots, over-elaborate ornaments and surreal plates – some featuring disembodied eyes and breasts – the **Taller de Cerámica Artística**, Calle 26 esq. 37 (Mon–Fri 8am–5pm; free), is a rather transparent attempt to cash in on passing tourist trade. Despite the eye-catching red-brick entrance, built to resemble a giant chimney, there's not a lot to do inside; even wandering the aisles feels intrusive, like spying on artists at work. The island's rich red earth – mounds of which are crushed in a vast tub on the premises, with demonstrations freely available – is ideally suited to ceramics, and the workshop supplies many of the country's tourist shops as well as selling pieces at the Fondo de Bienes Culturales on Calle Martí (see p.559).

Museo de Jesús Montané Oropesa

A few blocks west from Calle Martí, on Calle 24 e/ 43 y 45, the **Museo de Jesús Montané Oropesa** (Tues–Fri 9am–5pm, Sat 9am–4pm, Sun 8am–noon; $1CUC) packs into a modest wooden house a surprising number of items relating to the islanders' part in the revolutionary struggle. While Cuba is stuffed with such museums, there are a couple of exhibits that actually make this one special.

Even if your Spanish is up to it, you probably won't want to linger too long on the anthology of letters sent from the Presidio Modelo by the Moncada rebels, including Fidel Castro. The same goes for the rather staid personal effects of eponymous underground member Montané Oropesa who opened his house, at great personal risk, to family and friends who came to visit the rebels during their imprisonment. Instead, head for the second room, where you can see an original copy of *Sierra Maestra*, the official organ of the M-26-7 movement, published in Miami and smuggled back to Cuba by the core cell of revolutionaries exiled to Mexico. Filled with progress reports on the revolutionary struggle, this exemplary piece of propaganda has an unaffected feel, particularly in the arresting shot of Castro, flanked by rebels, reclining on a grassy verge in trainee beard and full camouflage regalia.

Other exhibits include the black-and-red M-26-7 armbands worn by supporters and a copy of the commemorative photo album compiled after the Revolution to celebrate the original band that arrived on the yacht *Granma*. Each page of the album features photographs of two revolutionaries, most of them still in their twenties, framed by a dramatic line drawing depicting their struggles, making them look like comic-book heroes. Also noteworthy are the

1960s photos of excited crowds celebrating nationalization outside banks and factories, and, best of all, an ingenious fake cigar used by the rebels to smuggle messages.

Museo de Historia Natural y el Planetario

Located fifteen minutes' walk southwest of the town centre, on Calle 41 esq. 52, the **Museo de Historia Natural y el Planetario** (Mon–Sat 9am–noon & 1–5pm, Sun 9am–noon; $1CUC) essentially consists of a motley menagerie of stuffed animals, a rock collection, and a scaled-down model of the pre-Columbian cave paintings in the south of the island that doesn't do them justice. Despite the inclusion of a grotesque, but strangely compelling, deformed and pickled pig, the museum is a bit of a sorry affair, even as stuffed animal collections go. The small domed **planetarium** is housed in a separate building next door and whimsically decorated with zodiac symbols and a 1970s-style row of flying ducks on the wall. At the time of writing its star attraction, a powerful telescope, was broken and not available to the public.

Eating

Though Nueva Gerona is hardly a gastronomic capital, and many **restaurants** rely on the tried-and-tested formula of pork with rice and beans, you can always find homely establishments dishing up cheap and filling meals. Higher taxes have squeezed out *paladares*, but almost all the *casas particulares* have a licence to prepare food. For **snacks**, stock up at the Universo convertible-peso supermarket on Calle Martí e/ 22 y 24 (Mon–Sat 10am–7pm, Sun 9am–1.30pm) or buy filled rolls at one of the roast-pork stands in the pedestrianized centre of Calle Martí. Prú, the ginger beer-like spicy soft drink common to Oriente, can also be bought here, and is a better choice for a cold drink than a peso *refresco*, as the water in it has been boiled – the island's **water supply** can be affected by parasites when there hasn't been much rain. Whether you apply the same logic and avoid the delicious ice creams on sale at *Coppelia* and the home-made ones (also made with non-boiled water) from a stall on Calle 24, half a block from Calle Martí, is up to you.

El Abra Carretera Siguanea Km 1 ☏46/32-4927. A backdrop of mountains, a lake and a field scattered with large abstract stone sculptures carved by local artists make this a better-than-average setting for standard, inexpensive Cuban cuisine of turkey, pork and tortillas.

El Cochinito Calle Martí esq. 24. Dig into ample portions of sautéed pork with yucca, rice and beans at this somewhat dingy looking, standard peso restaurant. To eat alfresco, pass through to the patio at the back or eat on the side terrace overlooking the street, at the front.

Coppelia Calle 32 esq. 37. Excellent ice cream up to the usual *Coppelia* standard, sometimes served with sauces and wafers. Particularly good sprinkled with a handful of the warm roasted peanuts sold by numerous mobile street vendors.

Día y Noche Calle Martí s/n e/ 24 y 26. This breezy, spacious 24hr café serves steaks and other meat dishes at rock-bottom convertible-peso prices.

El Dragón Calle Martí esq. 26 ☏46/32-4479. Mid-range Chinese food served with a Cuban twist. The house speciality is fried rice with chicken, pork and vegetables.

La Insula Calle Martí esq. 22. Nueva Gerona's swankiest convertible-peso establishment boasts a variety of chicken and pork dishes, a well-stocked bar and a friendly atmosphere.

El Marinero Calle Martí s/n e/ 22 y 24. Part general store and part bakery, which conjures up flaky chocolate *señorita* pastries and extravagant, foamy meringue cakes.

Tienda Imagen Calle Martí s/n e/ 24 y 26. A gem of a peso restaurant serving delicious *chorizo* sandwiches, chicken and chips and sticky sweet *refrescos*. A snack meal will cost just 20 pesos. There's also a bakery counter selling fresh bread and sugary pastries.

Drinking and entertainment

While some visitors with new-found islander friends may be swept away to wild private parties, left to your own devices you're more likely to find low-key entertainment, notable for a refreshing absence of tacky foreigner-only discos. The standard night out is to take some beers or a bottle of rum along to the open-air street **bar** halfway along Calle Martí, where the crowds gather at night to dance to booming reggaeton and watch the town's fashion queens prowl past on improbably high platform heels. If you're feeling experimental, head for the ᛘ *Casa de Vino Mayorking* at Calle 41 e/20 y 22, an unusual bar specializing in **wines** made from tropical fruits like grapefruit, orange, banana and raisin. Light meals are also served, or you can sample a range of cheeses to complement the wines.

For a more active night out, the lively ᛘ *Casa de la Cultura*, Calle 24 e/ 37 y 39, is well worth a visit, with entertainment most nights ranging from singing troupes and Afro-Cuban **dancing** to burlesque pantomimes and daytime children's shows. Check out Thursday's *trova* night, kicking off at 8.30pm, when accomplished local artists play a selection of classic *boleros* and *son*. Off Calle Martí on Calle 24, *El Patio* (Tues–Sun evenings; $3CUC per couple) hosts a fabulously camp **cabaret**, with girls in fluffy bras and fishnets gyrating with lissom young men, and a crooner thrown in for the ladies. Directly opposite, the *Disco Rumbos*, with its strident ultraviolet and strobe lighting, is where Nueva Gerona's youth strut their funky stuff to a mixture of disco, hip-hop and *salsa* beats (closed Mon). *El Dragón*, Calle Martí esq. 26, offers a less elaborate version of *El Patio*'s cabaret, with a nightly variety show plus regular singers and occasional guest performances by magicians and comedians. Those who wish to do the singing themselves should head to *La Insula* restaurant at Calle Martí esq. 22 which transforms into a **karaoke** bar ($3CUC) every night at 10pm. La Carpa, on Calle 37 esq. 28, is a noisy plastic shack selling beers by the park – its blaring reggaeton has made it the current weekend destination of choice for the island's young and glamorous.

Cine Caribe, on the east side of Parque Julio Antonio Mella, shows Cuban and international **films**, while a *sala de video* at Calle 39 y Calle 26 offers similar fare on the small screen.

On **weekend afternoons** the place to see and be seen is the swimming pool at the *Villa Isla de la Juventud* ($2CUC). The entire town seems to migrate here en masse to sit in the shallow end, drink beer on the sun terrace, relax on poolside chairs and do just about everything else save for actually swimming.

Listings

Airlines Cubana, Calle Martí no.1415 e/ 16 y 18 (Mon–Fri 8am–noon and 1.30–5pm; ☏46/32-4259).
Banks and exchange Banco de Crédito y Comercio, Calle Martí esq. 18 (Mon–Fri 8am–3pm), gives cash advances on Mastercard and Visa and changes traveller's cheques, as does the Cadeca *casa de cambio* at Calle Martí esq. 20, which also converts convertible pesos to national pesos (Mon–Sat 8.30am–6pm, Sun 8.30am–noon). There are two ATMs, one at the Banco de Crédito y Comercio and one at the Banco Popular de Ahorro at Calle Martí esq. 26. Both accept only Visa cards and dispense convertible pesos.

Bookshop The nameless bookshop at Calle Martí esq. 22 has a range of books in Spanish and the occasional English title (Mon–Sat 8am–10pm).
Car rental The Havanautos office is at Calle Martí esq. 32 ☏46/32-4432, Transtur are at Calle 37 s/n e/ 20 y 22 ☏46/32-6666.
Internet There is Internet access at the Telepunto office at Calle 41 esq. 28 near Parque Julio Antonio Mella (daily 8.30am–9.30pm; $6CUC/hr).
Medical The only hospital on the island is the Héroes del Baire, on Calle 41 e/ 16 y 18. For an ambulance call ☏46/32-4170. The state hotels

have medical posts, while the most accessible pharmacy is in the hospital grounds, facing the entrance.

Photography Photoservice, Calle Martí e/ 30 y 32 (9am–noon & 1–5.30pm), sells and develops film.

Police Call ☎116.

Post office The main post office, from where you can send telegrams, is on Calle Martí e/ 18 y 20 (Mon–Sat 8am–6pm). There's a DHL desk in the

stationery shop at Calle Martí s/n e/ 22 y 24 (Mon–Fri 8am–noon & 1–5pm, Sat 8am–noon).

Taxis For unmetered taxis, see p.557. Transtur are on ☎46/32-6666, Islatran are on ☎46/32-2222.

Telephone You can buy phone cards and make international collect calls at the ETECSA booth at Calle 39 esq. 28 on the corner of Parque Julio Antonio Mella (daily 7am–11pm).

Around Nueva Gerona

The hillsides, beaches and museums around Nueva Gerona can easily keep you occupied for a couple of days. West of town, the gently undulating **Sierra de Casa** hills make for a pleasant and energetic climb, with the additional attraction of a lagoon in the caves beneath.

Heading southwest out of town, down Calle 41, the road passes through farmland and orchards dotted with small settlements. The picturesque **Museo El Abra** is housed at the farm where José Martí was imprisoned in 1869, and while the exhibits lack flavour, the high bank of mountains behind the farm and the pretty grounds dappled with flowers and shady trees make it worth the trip.

East of Nueva Gerona is the **Presidio Modelo**, where Fidel Castro and his Moncada renegades were incarcerated following the attack in Santiago. Walking through the now abandoned prison is an eerie experience that's not to be missed. Two kilometres further east are the nearest beaches to town, the small and rather insignificant **Playa Paraíso** and the larger and more attractive **Playa Bibijagua**.

Sierra de Casa and Cueva del Agua

The best way to appreciate Nueva Gerona's diminutive scale is to take the short but exhilarating climb up the hills of the **Sierra de Casa** range just to the west for a bird's-eye view over the town and the surrounding countryside. To get there, head half a kilometre west from the town centre down Calle 24 past the swell of banana plants and rustling breadfruit trees peeking out of back gardens; take the first left turn and carry on another few hundred metres along a well-trodden path until you reach the foot of the first hill, oddly marked by two lone concrete poles poking out of the ground. It's under an hour's easy climb up to the summit, beneath which are spread the town's orderly rows of streets, curtailed by the stretch of blue beyond. To the east, below the cliff edge, the flat landscape of the island is occasionally relieved by a sparse sweep of hills; to the south, you can see the gleaming quarry which yields the stone for so many of Cuba's marble artefacts.

Before heading back to town, make time to explore the underground **Cueva del Agua**, whose entrance (24hr; free) is at the foot of the hill. The steep, narrow staircase cut from the rock bed can be slippery, so take care descending and bring a torch. Of the numerous caves dotted around the island, this one's natural lagoon and captivating rock formations make it worth visiting. Although locals sometimes swim in the large, rather stagnant lagoon, it's probably better for your health just to wade out a little way. The real treat here, though, lies along a narrow tunnel on the right-hand side just before the mouth of the pool, where intricate, glittery stalactites and stalagmites are slowly growing into elaborate natural sculptures.

Museo El Abra

Two kilometres southwest of town, on the Carretera Siguanea, the continuation of Calle 41 which heads towards *Hotel Colony* (see p.572), a signposted turning leads to the **Museo El Abra** (Tues–Sat 9am–5pm; $1CUC), the Spanish-style hacienda where José Martí spent three months in 1869. Although just sixteen years old at the time, Martí had already founded the magazine *La Patria Libre*, and his editorials contesting Spanish rule had him swiftly pegged as a dissident. Arrested after the discovery of a letter he'd written to a friend accusing him of supporting Spain, Martí was sentenced to six years' hard labour in a chain gang working the San Lázaro stone quarry in Havana.

Thanks to the small amount of influence his father, a Havanan policeman, was able to use, Martí's sentence was mitigated and the now ailing teenager was exiled to El Abra, where he was permitted to serve out his sentence under the custody of family friend and farm owner José María Sardá. Martí only spent three months there before the Spanish governor expelled him from Cuba altogether, but it was long enough for the family to record that he was melancholic and quiet, and prone to wandering through the handsome estate reading poetry. It was here that he wrote the essay *El Presidio Político en Cuba* ("The Political Prison in Cuba"), which became the seminal text of the independence struggle.

Nestling at the foot of the marble Sierra de Caballo, and edged with spiky mother-in-law's tongue, the whitewashed farmhouse – with Spanish-style red-tiled roof, Caribbean-blue balustrade windows and a charming stone sundial from Barcelona – has rather more style than substance. Inside is a strained collection of inconsequential artefacts from Martí's life, or at least those that could be spared by larger museums in Havana. Letters and documents vie for attention with his old bed and with a replica of the manacles from which Martí was freed on his arrival.

If you've got time to spare, consider heading a further 5km south along the Carretera Siguanea to the lakeside **restaurant** *El Abra*, whose basic *comida criolla* is offset by the panoramic views.

Museo de Presidio Modelo

The looming bulk of the **Museo de Presidio Modelo** (Mon–Sat 8am–4pm, Sun 8am–noon; $2CUC, photography $3CUC extra) lies 2km east of Nueva Gerona – turn off the road to Playa Bibijagua at the small housing scheme of Reparto Chachol. Although this massive former prison has housed a fascinating museum for over thirty years and is now one of the most visited sights on the island, its forbidding atmosphere has been preserved. Surrounded by guard towers, the classically proportioned governor's mansion and phalanx of wardens' villas mask the four circular cell buildings which rise like witches' cauldrons from the centre of the complex.

Commissioned by the dictator Machado, the "Model Prison" was built in 1926 by its future inmates as an exact copy of the equally notorious Joliet Prison in the US. At one time, it was considered the definitive example of efficient design, as up to six thousand prisoners could be controlled with a minimum of staff, but it soon became infamous for unprecedented levels of corruption and cruelty. The original plan for six wings was amended to four but even so, the capacity in the circular blocks alone was for 3720 men. The last prisoner was released in 1967; since then the buildings have slid into decay, although the magnificent governor's mansion has been converted into an extra-curricular centre for children, run by the *Pioneros* organization (similar to the Scouts and Guides movement).

The cell blocks

Unmanned by museum staff and falling into disrepair, the four huge cylin-drical **cell blocks** still feel as oppressive as they must have been when crammed with inmates. As you wander past row after row of vacant cells, and listen to the eerie echo, it's easy to imagine the desperation and injustice in which the prison's history is steeped. The prisoners, housed two or more to a cell, were afforded no privacy, with every moment of their lives on view through the iron bars. Note the gun slits cut into the grim tower in the dead centre of each block, allowing one guard and his rifle to control nearly a thousand inmates from a position of total safety. To really appreciate the creepy magnitude of the cell blocks, you can take the narrow marble staircase to the top floor, although with all the iron bars and railings long since removed, it's not a trip for vertigo sufferers.

The prison museum

Less disturbing than the cell blocks, the **prison museum** is located in the hospital block at the back of the grounds. Knowledgeable, Spanish-speaking guides take you around and will expect a small tip. While the exhibits include scores of original blueprints, faded ledgers of prison admissions and other unexceptional artefacts like giant soup pots – painstakingly hoarded for the best part of seventy years – the captivating showpieces like the impressive portfolio of 1930s stills of prisoners breaking rock and the aerial photos of the massive complex more than compensate.

The most impressive part of the museum, however, is the dormitory where **Fidel Castro** and the rebels of the Moncada attack were sequestered on the orders of Batista, for fear of them inflaming the other prisoners with their firebrand ideas. Above each of the 26 beds is the erstwhile occupant's mug shot and a brief biography, while a piece of black cloth on each sheet symbolizes the rags the men tore from their trouser legs to cover their eyes at night, when lights were shone on them constantly as torture.

On February 13, 1954, Batista made a state visit to the prison. As he and his entourage passed their window, the rebels broke into a revolutionary anthem. As a result, Castro was confined alone in the room that now opens off the main entrance but was at the time next to the morgue, within full view of the corpses. For the early part of his forty-week sentence he was forbidden any light – prompting the wry joke that he now metes out the same to his own people in the form of frequent blackouts. Despite the prohibition, a crafty home-made lamp enabled Castro to read from his small library and to perfect the speech he had made at his defence, which was later published by the underground press as *La Historia me Absolverá* and became the manifesto of the cause.

The northern beaches

East of the Presidio Modelo, a couple of beaches lie an easy bike ride away from town. Take the signposted turning off the main road from the prison, from where it's a pleasant 2km further to **Playa Paraíso**. Popular with locals, who call it "El Mini", this small hoop of rather grubby, seaweed-strewn sand is somewhat redeemed by its friendly atmosphere and a striking hill behind, whose shadow lengthens over the beach in the afternoon. The odd hump of land visible about 60m out to sea, **Cayo los Monos**, used to be a monkey zoo but is now deserted.

Rather better is **Playa Bibijagua**, another 4km along the road, which has an attractive and well-maintained grassy approach through the remains of an old hotel. Billed as a black-sand beach, it's actually a mottled brownish colour, the result of marble deposits in the sand. Although not the prettiest beach on the island, it has a charming view over a curve of coastline enveloped with pine trees, and a lively atmosphere, with local families watching their children play and men fishing patiently on the pier. Make sure you bring plenty of insect repellent witih you to ward off the vicious sand flies.

On the western side of the beach, *El Tiburón* peso restaurant serves up the usual Cuban staples, while the bar next door specializes in fresh coconut milk spiced up with rum, sugar, ice and lemon. Alternatively, locals will offer to cook up delicious fresh fish and fries for a few convertible pesos. A little further east along the road that runs past the beach, the shoreside *Campismo Arenas Negras* (☏46/32-5266; ❶) has attractive pink-and-yellow concrete **cabañas** dotted around a picturesque park, with graceful palms providing much-needed shade. Popular with holidaying Cubans, the campsite has a friendly ambience and a couple of rooms reserved for foreign visitors.

South of Nueva Gerona

Travelling south from Nueva Gerona along the sole main road, the land looks like a tamed and well-run estate, with row upon row of orderly fields and orchards. It is sparsely inhabited, with only a few bunches of neat houses clustered into the occasional modest roadside hamlet.

At **La Fe**, site of some mineral springs, a right-hand turn leads you to La Jungla de Jones **botanical gardens**, home to myriad trees and plants and the stunning Bamboo Cathedral. Continuing on south past La Fe, the road dissolves into a potholed track. At the point where the fecund farmland begins to metamorphose into swampland is an open-plan **crocodile farm**, where several hundred reptiles are bred every year for release into the southern marsh, and, just beyond, the military checkpoint at **Cayo Piedra** (see box, p.568).

La Fe and La Jungla de Jones

The island's one motorway – such as it is – heads south from Nueva Gerona through orchards and pine forests towards the southern marshes. About 27km along, you can take a marked turning to detour through **LA FE**, or Santa Fe as it's sometimes called, the island's second-largest town – although it's not much more than a handful of streets lined with utilitarian housing blocks built after the Revolution.

The town lives out a modest existence, with little to attract visitors other than the **Manantial de Santa Rita** (daily 24hr), a natural underground spring which surfaces at the northeast end of town. Join the queue of locals filling up their water bottles from three free-flowing taps, each producing a different mineral water: Magnesio, reputed to be good for the digestive system; Santa Lucia, which is thought to improve eyesight; and Ferroso, which, with its rich iron content, is beneficial for pregnant women and anaemics. You can also visit the town's nearby **baths** (Mon–Sat 8am–4pm; $3CUC) where men and women relax separately in small, indoor, pleasantly cooling 26°C pools fed by the spring.

The spring's reputation dates back to the mid-1880s, when La Fe became quietly popular with well-to-do Creoles who came to bathe and take the waters, reputed to cure a multitude of complaints from tuberculosis, laryngitis and kidney problems to arthritis, epilepsy and even elephantiasis. Although it remained popular in the twentieth century with visiting North Americans, the spring fell into disrepair in the 1960s, and was gradually submerged by floods and land movement until being restored in 2003.

La Jungla de Jones

Six kilometres west from La Fe, along the road that bisects the island, **La Jungla de Jones** botanical garden (T46/39-6246; daily 24hr; $6CUC) is home to an impressive collection of trees from all over the world. Relatively wild and unkempt, the gardens are crisscrossed by a web of leaf-littered trails. Over eighty species of trees and plants flourish in the rich soil, including ten species of bamboo, twenty types of mango and two trees that are endemic to Cuba and grow nowhere else: the Ayúa, studded with vicious spines like a giant cactus, and the Yamagüa, whose leaves are traditionally used to heal wounds. However, the one unmissable attraction here is the **Bamboo Cathedral**, a vast, magical, enclosed space illuminated by shafts of light that pour in between soaring bamboo poles, the ethereal silence disturbed only by the eerie creaking of the bamboo in the wind.

The arboretum's beauty masks a tragic history. It was set up in 1902 by two passionate American botanists, Helen Rowan Jones and her husband Harris, with the aim of cultivating and studying plants and trees from all corners of the globe. The couple dedicated their lives to the gardens, which became immensely popular with the American health tourists who flocked to the area. When Harris died in an accident at the age of 38, Helen decided to carry on alone, but in 1960 her life was also cut short when she was murdered by four escaped prisoners from the Presidio Modelo in a bungled robbery. The convicts burnt down her house in an attempt to hide the evidence but were later captured and returned to the prison. The gardens lay abandoned until 1998 when restoration work brought them back to their present state.

Criadero Cocodrilo

Continuing south from La Fe, a subtle change begins to come over the terrain as the road opens up, the potholes increase and the prolific fruit groves gradually become marshy thicket. Just past the settlement of Julio Antonio Mella, 12km on, you'll come to a left turn heading to the **Criadero Cocodrilo** (daily 7am–5pm; $3CUC, bring small bills as keepers rarely have change, and repellent as the mosquitoes are ravenous). Looking more like a swampy wilderness than a conventional farm, this crocodile nursery is actually, on closer inspection, teeming with reptiles. The large white basins near the entrance form the nursery for a seething mass of four-month-old, 25cm-long snappers, surprisingly warm and soft to the touch – ask to pick one up. Nearby, what at first looks like a seed bed reveals itself to be planted with a crop of crocodile eggs which are removed from the female adults once laid, and incubated for around eighty days before hatching. Larger specimens cruise down enclosed waterways choked with lily pads and teeming with birds and butterflies.

The crocodiles are endemic to the area, but were in danger of extinction until the farm's creation. It keeps five hundred crocodiles at any one time, and periodically releases herds of them into the southern wilds when they reach seven years of age, at which point they measure about 1m in length. The prize of the collection is a 30-year-old monster kept as a showpiece: over 3m long and weighing 186kg, the irascible male eats once every three days and conserves his energy by lying motionless most of the time, although the keeper will obligingly throw him a couple of titbits so you can watch his head whip round at an astonishing speed.

To visit anywhere beyond the crocodile farm means crossing the military border, for which you'll need a pass and a guide (for full details, see box, below).

The southern military zone

Rumours abound concerning the purpose of the **military zone**, but the primary function seems to be to conserve and restrict access to the **Siguanea nature reserve**. Parts of the reserve are completely closed to the public, as the luxuriant vegetation of the area shelters such **wildlife** as the tocororo, Cuba's national bird, wild deer and green parrots. However, it has been rumoured that the military are here in force because of the rogue parcels of narcotics from other Latin American countries that wash up on its southern shores. Another theory claims that it has been seen as an ideal invasion point for counter-revolutionaries based in Miami and so needs to be well guarded.

As flat as the north, if not more so, the land south of the checkpoint conforms to the storybook ideal of a desert island, with caves and sinuous beaches fringing a swampy interior of mangroves and thick shrubs teeming with wild deer, gigantic crabs and the green parrots that are endemic to the island. It's also home to one of the most impressive sights on the island: the **pre-Columbian paintings** in the caves of the Punta del Este, believed to date back some 1100 years, making them among the oldest in the Caribbean. The white-sand beaches of nearby **Playa Punta del Este** and **Playa Larga**, further along the coast, are clean and soft, though a bit narrow.

Further along the southern coast near the island's western hook is **Cocodrilo**, a tiny hamlet cupped by the sea that's a pocket of English speakers, largely descended from the Cayman Islanders who came over in the early part of the twentieth century. Its pleasant charms are increased by a rugged granite-rock coastline that forms natural pools and is ideal for snorkelling. An additional attraction here is the **Sea Turtle Breeding Centre**, which allows you to view several species at close range. Close by, **Playa El Francés**, named after the French pirate Latrobe who spent time there, is easily the island's most pleasant white-sand beach and accordingly is

Crossing the military border

To cross into the military zone at Cayo Piedra you will need to buy a one-day **pass** and engage the services of a **registered guide** before you set off. The only place to organize this is the Ecotur office in Nueva Gerona (see p.557 for details). A permit and Spanish- Italian- French- German- or English-speaking guide costs $12CUC per person. As you'll have to make the trip from Nueva Gerona in a rental jeep (the cavernous potholes and long stretches of unpaved road necessitate a 4WD), it's a good idea to find some other people with whom to split the cost. You shouldn't encounter any difficulties at the checkpoint as long as you avail yourself of the necessary documentation – there are usually only one or two guards there to wave you past the checkpoint hut; however, should you arrive at the checkpoint without a guide and pass you will be unceremoniously turned back.

often reserved for private use by the cruise ships that dock nearby once a week – check when you apply for your southern permit.

Most visitors to Playa Francés do not approach it from the southern coast but from the **Hotel Colony**, situated just north of the military border at the end of the Carretera Siguanea and the only place to stay outside Nueva Gerona. Although the hotel has seen better days, it still attracts scores of underwater enthusiasts because the **diving** off the western point is superb, with over fifty sites to explore, among them two wrecks sunk in the 1970s and a wall of black coral.

Cuevas de Punta del Este

Within walking distance of the southeast coast, 25km down a dirt track leading east from the checkpoint at Cayo Piedra, the **Punta del Este** caves, half-buried amid overgrown herbs and greenery, contain significant examples of early pre-Columbian art, pointing to an established culture on the island as early as 900 AD. These paintings are among the few remaining traces of the Siboney – the first inhabitants of Cuba – who arrived from South America via other Caribbean islands between three and four thousand years ago and are thought to have died out shortly after the paintings were made. There are no signposts to the caves, but your guide will know exactly where to go.

The six Punta del Este caves were discovered by accident at the turn of the twentieth century by one Freeman P. Lane, who disembarked on the beach and sought shelter in one of them. The discovery made archeologists reconsider their assumption that Siboney culture was primitive, as the paintings are thought to represent a solar calendar, which would indicate that the Siboney had a sophisticated cosmology. Annually, on March 22, the sun streams through a natural hole in the roof of **Cave One**, the largest of the group, illuminating the pictographs in a beam of sunlight. Being linked to the vernal equinox, the effect is thought to celebrate fertility and the cycle of life and death. When bones were excavated here in 1939, it became apparent that the caves' function was not only ceremonial, but that they had also been used for habitation and burial.

Of the 230 pictographs, the most prominent are the tight rows of concentric red and black circles overlapping one another on the low ceiling of Cave One. Despite creeping erosion by a virulent algae, the fading images are still very visible. Major excavation work got under way in the 1940s, when five more caves were discovered, though the paintings within are in a far worse state of repair and you'll need a keen eye to spot them. Even so, you should take a look at **Cave Two**, 500m away, where more fragments of circles are outshone by the fragile remains of a painted fish.

Further along the path, tufts of undergrowth give way to beach after a surprisingly short distance. The small white-sand strand of **Playa Punta del Este**, sown with sea grass and rimmed by mangroves, is a good spot for a refreshing dip, though it can't compare to the beauty of the beaches to the south.

Playa Larga and the Carapachibey lighthouse

Following the road 20km south from the checkpoint all the way to the coast, you come to the narrow wedge of sand that comprises **Playa Larga**. Though not really the best spot for a swim, it's a popular place with local fishermen from Cocodrilo, to the west, and the pretty pine-backed stretch is littered with golden-pink conch shells emptied of their flesh and discarded by fishermen. The beach was the landing site for several Camagüean *balseros* (rafters) intent on emigrating to the United States, who arrived here in 1994 after a turbulent journey from the mainland, jubilantly believing themselves to be on North American soil, only to discover that they had not left Cuban territory.

About 5km west of Playa Larga you can take a quick detour down a pine-lined drive to the **Carapachibey lighthouse**. Although Art Deco-like in its straight-lined simplicity, it wasn't built until 1983 and only enjoyed thirteen trouble-free years before being damaged by Hurricane Lili in 1996. It has since been repaired, and a wall surrounding the base shows typical Cuban resourcefulness, being made of rubble salvaged from the hurricane's destruction. It's worth asking the keeper if you can make the steep climb up 280 stairs to enjoy the views over the rocky coastline and turquoise sea.

Cocodrilo and around

A few kilometres north of Playa Larga, the main highway from Nueva Gerona branches west to run along the southern coast of the island, petering out just beyond **COCODRILO**. This peaceful haven boasts just a few palm-wood houses and a school in front of a village green that backs onto the sea. Isolated from the north of the island by poor transport and the military checkpoint, it's a fairly rustic community seemingly unaffected by the developments of the twentieth century, albeit healthy and well educated thanks to the Revolution. Originally named Jacksonville, after one of its first families, the hamlet was founded at the beginning of the twentieth century by Cayman Islanders who came here to hunt the large numbers of turtles – now depleted – that once populated the waters and nested along the southern beaches. Some of the village's older residents still speak the English of their forefathers.

At the north end of the hamlet, cupped by a semicircle of rocky cliff, the electric-blue water of a natural **rock pool** is an excellent place to spend a few hours. It's about a two-metre drop to the water below, but take care if jumping, as the pool is shallow. If you've brought equipment, it's also worth heading offshore to snorkel among the myriad tiny, darting fish.

The Sea Turtle Breeding Centre

One kilometre west from the village, past breaks in the coastline where spume shoots through gaps in the rocks, is the frequently unstaffed **Experimental Sea Turtle Breeding Centre** (daily 8am–6pm; $1CUC). Swimming in rows of tanks, livid-green with algae, the turtles range in size from hand-sized tiddlers to impressively huge adults. The centre is not a tourist attraction per se, but rather an attempt to boost the turtle population, which is depleted every year by hunting. Though the farm is a worthy attempt to redress the problem, some of its pens do seem rather overcrowded and several of the turtles have battered and beaten fins where others have taken a chunk out of them.

Despite the efforts of conservationists, turtle meat is still considered a delicacy in Cuba, and turtleshell products, including mounted heads, are widely available. Officially, turtle hunting is limited, and banned outright during the breeding season, but poachers continue to flout the law. Refusing to buy turtle products is one way of helping conservation efforts.

△ Punta Francés

Punta Francés and the Hotel Colony

From Cocodrilo a ten-kilometre track heads northwest to the island's most remote upturned hook of land, **Punta Francés**, where you'll find the silver sands and limpid water that make **Playa Francés** the island's top beach. Equally attractive is the excellent **diving** offshore (see box, p.572). Punta Francés is not the easiest place to visit independently, as it is often closed to allow cruise-ship passengers to enjoy the beach without the hoi polloi; ask if

Diving off the west coast

There are two places on the island where you can organize diving: the *Hotel Colony* and the Marina Siguanea. A five-day CMAS course with either costs $365CUC and gives you a training day in the swimming pool, plus three dives. If you already have a diving certificate, a single dive costs $35CUC, two dives in a day $60CUC, and a night dive $40CUC.

There are over fifty sites close to Punta Francés, running from north to south, parallel to the west coast, while Los Indios Wall and two shipwrecks are all close to Cayos Los Indios, about 30km out from the *Hotel Colony*. The best sites are listed here.

El Arco de los Sábalos 2km northwest of Punta Francés. At a depth of just 13m, this is a straightforward dive for initiates, teeming with inquisitive yellowtail snappers, tarpon and bright sponges.

El Cabezo de las Isabelitas 5km west of Playa El Francés. This shallow site has plenty of natural light and a cornucopia of fishes, including goatfish, trumpetfish and parrotfish. An uncomplicated dive, ideal for beginners.

Cueva Azul 2km west of Playa El Francés. Reaching depths of 42m, this site takes its name ("the blue cave") from the intensely coloured water. Although there are several notable types of fish to be seen, the principal thrill of this dive is ducking and twisting through the cave's crevices.

Cueva Misteriosa 4km west of Playa El Francés. You'll be provided with a lamp to explore this dark, atmospheric cave where Christmas tree worms, tarpon and a wealth of other fish species take refuge.

Los Indios Wall 5km from Cayos Los Indios. A host of stunning corals, including brain, star, fire and black coral, cling to a sheer wall that drops to the sea bed, while you can see stingrays on the bottom, some as long as 2m. There's a $10CUC supplement for this dive and you need a minimum of five people.

Pared de Coral Negro 4km northwest of Punta Francés. The black coral that gives this dive its name is found at 35m down, while the rest of the wall is alive with colourful sponges and brain corals as well as several species of fish and green moray eels.

the beach is open when you buy your permit for the military zone. The *El Ranchón* restaurant, the only facility at the beach, serves up tasty seafood for around $12CUC at lunchtime. The best way to get to the beach, with guaranteed access, is to take a **diving trip** with the *Hotel Colony* ($15–25CUC, buy tickets from Ecotur in Nueva Gerona;see p.557), around the bay from Punta Francés, just north of the military zone and reachable by two early-morning daily buses from Nueva Gerona.

Built in the 1950s by the Batista regime as a casino hangout for American sophisticates, **Hotel Colony** (℡46/39-8181, ℮reservas@colony.co.cu) was abandoned just weeks after its opening when Batista fled the Revolution. The only place to stay with access to Punta Francés, the hotel, with its old-fashioned decor, feels as if it has seen better days, but is very reasonably priced. The rooms are basic and all benefit from large windows and sea views (❸), while the *cabañas* are also built in a dull concrete but are more attractive (❻). There's a shop selling snacks, toiletries and souvenirs, a pool, a restaurant, a pleasant strip of beach and a *mojito* bar that hovers above the cool blue water at the end of a long wooden pier.

Two kilometres south of *Hotel Colony*, the **Marina Siguanea** (daily 9am–4.30pm) offers the same variety of dives and courses and has a decompression chamber. Small and strictly functional, the marina is not somewhere to pass the time: there are no services other than the dive facilities and a medical post.

Cayo Largo

Separated from the Isla de la Juventud by 140km, **Cayo Largo**, a narrow, low-lying spit of land fringed with powdery beaches, is totally geared to package-holiday makers. The tiny islet, measuring just 20km from tip to beachy tip, caters to the quickening flow of European and Canadian tourists who swarm here to enjoy its excellent watersports, diving and Club Med-style hotels. For a holiday cut adrift from responsibilities and the outside world, this is as good a choice as any, though some may find it a tad manufactured.

Development of the cay began in 1977 when the state, capitalizing on its extensive white sands and offshore coral reefs, built the first of seven hotels that currently line the western and southern shores. Construction suffered a setback in November 2001 when Hurricane Michelle blew in, wreaking havoc on the cay and necessitating large-scale evacuations. All the damage has since been repaired and plans are under way for even more hotels. Although the cay is being relentlessly developed, it has a long way to go before being spoilt; indeed, the infrastructure away from the hotels is so sparse that at times hanging out in the resort can seem rather monotonous. The artificiality which works well in the hotels fails somewhat in the small "village" on the west of the island, which has a distinctly spurious air, consisting of just a shop, restaurants, a museum and a bank and, behind the tourist facade, blocks of workers' accommodation.

Arrival, information and transport

All national and international **flights** to Cayo Largo arrive at the tiny Vilo Acuña airport, 1km from the main belt of hotels; courtesy buses meet every flight and whisk passengers off to their hotels. All domestic flights are from Havana, on a rickety Russian forty-seater plane; note that if you come independently, you will need to book accommodation when you arrange your flight. A quicker option is to take a day-trip **from Havana** with Cubatur (℡7/33-3569), departing at 5.30am and leaving the island at 5pm. The trip costs around $140CUC and includes a boat trip to Cayo Iguana, snorkelling,

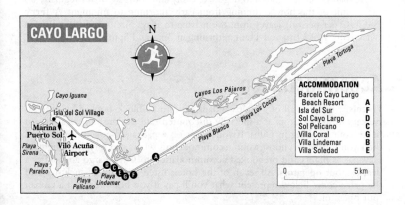

CAYO LARGO

N

ACCOMMODATION	
Barceló Cayo Largo	
Beach Resort	A
Isla del Sur	F
Sol Cayo Largo	D
Sol Pelícano	C
Villa Coral	G
Villa Lindemar	B
Villa Soledad	E

0   5 km

△ Strolling along Cayo Largo

lunch and time on the beach. As there is no boat service between the islands, only **yacht** owners – for whom the clear shallow seas, excellent fishing and serviceable marinas make it a favourite destination – can breeze in by water to the main Marina Puerto Sol on the village coastline.

Though there is no main **tourist office** on the cay, the desk at the *Sol Cayo Largo* is staffed by representatives from various tour companies who offer information and arrange diving and excursions (daily 9.30–11am & 6–7pm). There are also two informative websites, ⓦwww.cayolargo.net and www.cayolargodelsur.cu. You can buy **maps** at the hotel shops and at the post office (daily 8am–7pm), in front of the *Isla del Sur* hotel, which also sells postcards, telephone cards and has a fax service. There's a **bank** (Mon–Fri 8.30am–noon & 2–3.30pm, Sat–Sun 9am–noon) on the corner of the village pláza. Although the cay's hotels promote themselves as all-inclusive, diving, motor sports and excursions usually cost extra.

The island is small enough to negotiate easily and courtesy **buses** regularly do the circuit of the hotels, running from early morning to midnight. A **ferry** ($4CUC per person) leaves from the marina to Playa Sirena and Playa Paraíso twice daily at 9.30am and 11am, returning at 3pm and 5pm.

Accommodation

Hotels, which are all of a high standard, tend to be block-booked by overseas package-tour operators at a specially discounted rate, but are not cheap if you make your booking in Cuba. If you're not on a package booked from abroad then you'll have to choose your accommodation when you buy your flight in Havana, as flights and prebooked accommodation to Cayo Largo are sold as a deal by tour operators. All seven of the hotels listed here are all-inclusive and the price codes below represent what you'll pay if you book through a Cuban tour operator.

The *Villa Coral, Isla del Sur, Villa Lindamar* and *Villa Soledad* hotels form something of a cooperative. They all share a phone and fax number (☎45/24-8111 to 18, ⒻŒ24-8160) and guests from each hotel are welcome to eat and use the facilities at any of the others, including the tennis and squash courts at the *Isla del Sur*, and the Nautical Centre on the beach in front of the *Lindamar* that provides free *pedalos*, kayaks and snorkelling equipment.

Barceló Cayo Largo Beach Resort ☎45/24-8080, ⓦwww.barcelocayolargo.com. A large, squat, rather old-fashioned accommodation block dominates the cay's newest hotel. Situated some distance from the main cluster of hotels, to the west along Playa Blanca, it suits those seeking a quieter beach. You can choose between comfortable but very plain rooms strung along gloomy corridors in the monolithic central structure and cheerier, more attractively furnished villas dotted around the grounds. The enormous buffet restaurant is reminiscent of a school cafeteria but there are a couple of appealing à la carte options. ⑧

Isla del Sur Though its reception is sunny and pleasant, this is a slightly dowdy hotel, patronized by an almost exclusively Italian clientele, with old-style shadowy, lurid-green corridors. The rooms are simple but comfortable, almost all with sea views, and there's a buffet restaurant, snack bar and lively 24hr lobby bar. ⑦

Sol Cayo Largo ☎45/24-8260, ⒺŒjefe.reservas.scl@solmeliacuba.com. An appealing, buzzy, Caribbean-themed hotel with airy rooms painted in tropical colours in smart blocks set around palm trees and rather parched lawns. With an all-inclusive buffet, beach grill and à la carte restaurants, two swimming pools, free non-motorized watersports, a health centre, tennis courts and a football field, this is the biggest and plushest place on the cay, with a clientele of twenty-something couples, families and retirees all mingling happily. ⑧

Sol Pelícano ☎45/24-8333, ⒺŒjefe.reservas.spl@solmeliacuba.com. A family-friendly luxury hotel with dedicated play area and children's entertainment, four all-inclusive restaurants, two swimming pools and bold blue-and-yellow two- and three-storey villas with cheerful sun-and-sea inspired decor complete with hand-painted motifs of shells and seahorses. ⑧

Villa Coral This family-oriented hotel offers rather gaudy pink-and-green blocks with red-tiled roofs, divided by neat beds of sea shrubs and palms to ensure a sense of privacy. Rooms have spacious balconies and smart sun terraces, with shaded seating surrounding a sparkling circular pool. ⑦

Villa Lindamar A stylish complex that backs onto an ample stretch of beach lined with sunshades and loungers. These thatched cabins, each with its own porch and hammock, are perched on stilts, overlooking a garden of sea grass and hibiscus bushes, and feel self-contained and private – a definite plus. ⑧

Villa Soledad A poor relation to the other hotels. Although it has comfortable, well-kept rooms, some with a sea view, this resort is let down by the absence of pool, restaurant and snack bar, which makes it rather odd that it costs the same as its sister properties *Isla del Sur* and *Villa Coral*. ⑦

The Cay

While Cayo Largo is undoubtedly the stuff of exotic holiday fantasy, it's not a place to meet actual Cubans. There are no born-and-bred locals, and while the hotel staff hail from Isla de la Juventud, Havana, or further afield, they only live on the island in shifts, so while people are as easy-going and friendly as elsewhere in Cuba, the atmosphere is more than a little contrived.

Isla del Sol village

Built on the southwestern coast – to optimize the pleasant view over cay-speckled waters – the artificial **Isla del Sol village** doesn't offer much of a reason to leave the resorts. Among the prettified, red-roofed ochre buildings ranged around the small but attractive Plaza del Pirata you'll find the obligatory tourist trappings: a shop selling cigars, postcards and sunscreen, a bank, museum, restaurant and bar. The village's main focal point is the **Marina Puerto Sol**,

With over thirty **dive sites** in the clear and shallow waters around the cay, Cayo Largo is deservedly well known as one of Cuba's best diving areas. Particularly outstanding are the coral gardens to be found in the shallow waters around the islet, while other highlights include underwater encounters with hawksbill and sea-green turtles. The cay's **dive centre** (☏45/24-8214) at the Marina Puerta Sol offers dives for $50CUC, including all equipment and transfer to the site; prices per dive decrease with subsequent dives. Open-water SSI courses take five days and cost $395CUC.

The marina also runs a variety of day-long **snorkelling expeditions** which usually include a visit to the coral gardens, tiny Cayo Iguana (the nearest cay to Cayo Largo where the eponymous reptiles can be fed by hand) and a "natural swimming pool" where the water is only 1m deep, along with a lobster lunch and an open bar for $69–73CUC. Half-day trips to the coral gardens and Cayo Iguana cost $39CUC but do not include lunch. The waters around the cays also harbour excellent **fishing**, and the marina offers high-sea expeditions for $220CUC for four hours inclusive of equipment and $290CUC for eight hours (minimum two people). Also on offer is a day-trip in a catamaran, which includes snorkelling and a lobster lunch ($69CUC for the day).

west of the plaza, an area that bustles with activity when motorboats dock to collect or release the sunbathers, snorkellers and divers en route to and from dive sites and beaches. For the rest of the day the village sinks into a slightly unnerving somnolence, from which the attractions of the **Casa Museo** and **Turtle Farm** can offer a brief diversion. The museum (daily 9am–noon, 2–6pm & 8–10pm; $1CUC) aims to bring Cayo Largo's one-thousand-year-long history to life, but like the village itself comes across as a rather forced attempt to present a broader context for a place that, these days at least, exists solely for the pleasure of foreign visitors. Its small collection includes paintings of flags used to adorn pirate ships of bygone eras, some native plants, a huge stuffed iguana and, possibly most interesting, a series of photographs showing the flooding and devastation caused by Hurricane Michelle in 2001. The farm (daily 7am–noon & 1–6pm; $1CUC), just off the plaza, houses a restless collection of the wild turtles that populate the waters around the archipelago. Although they look healthy enough, their small pens seem a poor exchange for the open sea.

The beaches

There's rather more activity around the beaches to the south and along the hotel strip, where warm shallow waters lap the narrow ribbon of pale downy sand. Protected from harsh winds and rough waves by the offshore coral reef, and with over 2km of white sands, **Playa Sirena** enjoys a deserved reputation as the most beautiful of all the beaches on Cayo Largo and is consequently the busiest. There's a road to there from the *Sol Pelícano*, but as it's frequently covered by rifts of sand you're better off catching one of the ferries or speedboats from the marina. A café on Playa Sirena serves drinks, sandwiches and snacks. Further south along the same strand, **Playa Paraíso** is almost as attractive and popular as Sirena, with the added advantage that its shallow waters are ideal for children. Heading east, **Playa Lindamar** is a serviceable five-kilometre curve of sand in front of the *Lindamar, Pelícano, Soledad* and *Coral* hotels and is the only one where you can play volleyball and windsurf.

For real solitude, though, you need to head off up the central road that runs the length of the island to the southeastern beaches. **Playa Blanca**, occupied only at its western extremity by the *Barceló Cayo Largo Beach Resort*, boasts over 6km of deserted, soft beach, backed by sand dunes, and staking out your own patch shouldn't be a problem, though you'll need to bring your own refreshments as there's not an ice-cream stand in sight. Further east still, the lovely **Playa los Cocos** is seemingly endless, and it's the only nudist beach on the cay. The far-flung **Playa Tortuga** is similarly deserted, while the interior is largely a mass of pine trees with not much to see.

Eating, drinking and entertainment

Although all the hotels' packages include free meals, guests can choose to pay for meals in other hotels and there are a couple of eateries in the village operating outside the deals altogether. Within the packages, menus are fairly standard, with all the buffets offering a range of international dishes. The à la carte options tend to be of a higher standard and it's worth remembering that all the hotels will provide a free picnic lunch for those who wish to spend the day at the beach. While many of the restaurants lack atmosphere, the hotel bars tend to have more character, allowing you to sip your free cocktails in something approaching style.

Of the buffet **restaurants**, the *Sol Pelícano* has the largest selection and the cheeriest atmosphere. *Villa Coral* has a pleasant and airy snack bar in a pink-tiled pool area, serving small pizzas, sandwiches and ice cream. Also at the *Villa Coral* is an à la carte restaurant, *La Piazzoletta*, which serves authentic Italian food, while the *Ranchón Espigon* at the *Villa Lindamar* specializes in *comida criolla*. The *Coral*, *Lindamar*, *Soleded* and *Isla del Sur* buffets all offer seafood, including lobster, for an additional charge.

Down in the quiet of the village, the *El Criollo* restaurant has a distinctive Wild West flavour with classic Cuban chicken, pork and seafood concoctions served in a wooden-ceilinged, saloon-style dining room complete with cow-hide chairs and ornamental saddles. Large groups can pre-order a hog roast, with prices ranging from $150CUC to $380CUC depending on the size of the pig. The thatched *Taberna del Pirata* bar, on the plaza overlooking the picturesque harbour, is a good spot to enjoy the cooling sea breezes while the sun sets.

Sol Cayo Largo is the best spot on the island for **drinking**, with a friendly palm-thatched bar in the middle of a fish pond that's mercifully set back from the stage where an entertainment team puts on nightly cabaret shows with enforced hilarity, including Miss Cayo Largo competitions (non-guests pay $15CUC entrance, which includes an open bar). Should you feel like doing the entertaining yourself, the hotel also has a karaoke bar.

Travel details

There is little public transport on the Isla de la Juventud – only a few bus routes, which are often cancelled. Journeys south of the checkpoint will require renting a car and guide (see box, p.565). Cayo Largo has no public transport. Leaving the Isla de la Juventud by ferry can be problematic. There is no advance booking service, and all those wishing to leave are required to turn up at 6am on the day they plan to travel, take a number and queue for the chance to buy a ticket on the two daily ferries. Bear in mind that there is no guarantee you will be able to travel on the day you want if the ferry is particularly busy and you may end up having to spend an extra night on the island before your turn comes up.

Buses

La Fe to: Nueva Gerona (15 daily; 45min).
Nueva Gerona to: *Hotel Colony* (2 daily; 2hr); La Fe (15 daily; 45min); Reparto Chachol (12 daily; 20min).
Reparto Chachol to: Nueva Gerona (12 daily; 20min).

Flights

Cayo Largo to: Havana (2 daily; 40min).
Nueva Gerona to: Havana (3 daily; 40min).

Ferry

Nueva Gerona to: Batabanó (2 daily; around 2 hours 30min).

Contexts

Contexts

History

The strategic and geographical importance of Cuba to the shifting global powers of the last five centuries has dictated much of the Caribbean island's history. Having served principally as a stepping stone between Spain and its vast American empire for 250 years, Cuba has been struggling to achieve a real and lasting independence ever since, passing from Spanish colony to US satellite and, despite the nationalist Revolution of 1959, relying on economic support from the Soviet Union until 1989. At the start of the twenty-first century Cuba is at a crossroads, having finally reached a stage in its history when it can claim genuine self-sufficiency, with the ideals and achievements of one of the world's last remaining communist countries set firmly against survival in a capitalist global economy.

Pre-Columbian Cuba

Unlike Central America with its great Maya and Aztec civilizations, no advanced societies had emerged in Cuba by the time Columbus arrived in 1492. Although ancient cultures – Amerindians who had worked their way up through the Antilles from the South American mainland – had inhabited the island for thousands of years, they lived in simple dwellings and produced comparatively few artefacts and tools for future archeologists to discover. There are thought to have been at least 100,000 Amerindians living in Cuba on the eve of the European discovery of the Americas, but piecing together the history of the island prior to the arrival of the Spanish relies heavily on guesswork.

The **Guanahatabey** were the first to arrive and were almost certainly living in Cuba by 3000 BC. These primitive hunter-gatherers were based in what is now Pinar del Río, often living in cave systems, such as the one in Viñales. The **Ciboney** arrived later and lived as fishermen and farmers, but it wasn't until the arrival of the **Taíno**, the last of the Amerindian groups to settle in Cuba, that the cultural make-up of the islanders reached a level of significant sophistication. Most historians agree that the Taíno found their way to Cuban shores around 1100 AD, and certainly by the time Columbus got there they were the dominant cultural group. Settling predominantly in the eastern and central regions, they lived in small villages of circular thatched-roof huts known as *bohíos*, an architectural style replicated in hotel accommodation throughout the island today; grew tobacco, cassava, yucca and cotton; produced pottery; and practised religion. Though there is some evidence to suggest that the Taíno enslaved some of the Ciboney or drove them from their home territory, they were a mostly peaceful people, largely unprepared for the conflict they were to face once the Spanish arrived.

The conquest

On October 27, 1492, having already touched down in the Bahamas, **Christopher Columbus** landed on the northeastern coast of Cuba, probably in the natural harbour around which the town of **Baracoa** was later to emerge, though the exact spot where he first dropped anchor is hotly disputed. This first short expedition lasted only seven days, during which time Columbus marvelled at the Cuban landscape, briefly encountered the locals (who fled on sighting the new arrivals), and left a wooden cross now preserved in the Catedral Nuestra Señora de la Asunción in Baracoa.

On their second voyage of discovery in 1494, Columbus and his men worked their way along the southern coast of the island, landing also at the **Isla de la Juventud**. One of the principal aims of this expedition was to establish whether Cuba was an island or, as Columbus himself suspected, part of the mainland. After a number of weeks spent exploring, he concluded that the width of the coastline meant it was too large to be an island, and made every man in the fleet swear an oath that Cuba was part of the mainland of Cathay, or China. On his later voyages to the Caribbean, Columbus paid little attention to Cuba, but his insistence that he had discovered a western route to Asia left the Spanish unconvinced, and by the time King Ferdinand sent an expedition for a more thorough exploration of the island, the belief had been dismissed.

The first colonial expedition did not begin until late 1509, when **Diego Velázquez**, a rich settler from neighbouring Hispaniola, and the man charged with the mission by the Spanish Crown, landed near Guantánamo Bay with three hundred men. By this time the Amerindians were wary of the possibility of an invasion, word having spread via refugees from already occupied Caribbean islands. The most legendary of these forced immigrants was **Hatuey**, a bold Taíno from Hispaniola, who led the most concerted resistance effort against the advancing colonists. The Indians fought fiercely but their initial success was cut short by the Spanish capture of Hatuey. Before burning him at the stake the Spaniards offered him salvation if he would convert to Christianity, an offer met with a flat refusal as Hatuey declared that heaven would be the last place he'd want to spend eternity if it was full of Christians.

The rest of the indigenous population did not last much longer and were either slaughtered or enslaved as the conquistadors worked their way west across the island, driving them eventually into the furthest reaches of Pinar del Río where, on the Península de Guanahacabibes, the last settlements of Cuban Amerindians lived out their final years. Those who were not killed died from either diseases brought over from Europe or the harsh living and working conditions forced upon them through the *encomienda* system (see opposite), while some even committed suicide rather than face enslavement. By the end of the sixteenth century, there was almost no trace of the original Cuban population left.

Meanwhile, the colonizers had exhausted the small reserves of gold on the island and interest in Cuba quickly died out as Spain expanded its territories in Central and South America, where there was far greater mineral wealth. However, as Spain consolidated its American empire, Cuba gained importance thanks to its location on the main route to and from Europe, with ports like **Havana** becoming the principal stopping-off points for ships carrying vast quantities of gold, silver and other riches across the Atlantic.

Colonization and slavery

By 1515 Velázquez had founded the first towns in Cuba, known as the **seven villas**: Baracoa, Santiago de Cuba, Bayamo, Puerto Príncipe (now Camagüey), Sancti Spíritus, Trinidad and San Cristóbal de la Habana. The population grew slowly, consisting mostly of Spanish immigrants, many from the Canary Islands, but also Italians and Portuguese. Numbers were also increased as early as the 1520s by the importation of African **slaves**, brought in to replace the dwindling indigenous population. Still, by the seventeenth century, Havana, the largest city, had only a few hundred inhabitants.

Early colonial society was based on the **encomienda** system, whereby land and slaves, both African and Amerindian, were distributed to settlers by the authorities. The conditions of slavery in Cuba during the sixteenth and much of the seventeenth centuries, though dehumanizing, were, in some ways, less oppressive than those experienced elsewhere, in the British colonies of North America, for example. This is not to suggest that the Spanish colonizers were any more compassionate than their European counterparts, but merely reflected the comparative underdevelopment of the Cuban economy. The more advanced industries on islands such as Saint-Domingue (modern-day Haiti) and Jamaica meant not only a higher demand for slaves, but more gruelling living and working conditions for the slaves themselves.

The proportion of slaves in Cuba up until the British occupation of 1762 was lower than almost anywhere else in the Caribbean, the larger number of them working as servants in the cities, and the smaller scale of plantations translating to a less impersonal relationship between slave and master. And whereas the English allowed their colonies to develop their own independent codes of practice, the detailed laws governing slavery in Spain were applied equally to their territories overseas. Though this would not necessarily have meant that the Spanish master would have fed his slaves any better or punished them less brutally, it did grant slaves a degree of legal status unheard of in other European colonies. Slaves in the Spanish Empire could marry, own property and even buy their freedom. Known as the right of *coartación*, this possibility of freedom meant that by the eighteenth century there was a higher proportion of **free blacks** in Cuba than in any other major Caribbean island. Slaves would often earn money through extra work in the cities or by way of growing and selling their own produce, made possible by their right to own small plots of land (rights far from guaranteed, with the Spanish lawmakers thousands of miles away).

However, the priorities of the Spanish Crown obviously lay in the wealth its colonies could create, with the rights of slaves incidental at best, and Spanish ordinances did as much to perpetuate slavery as they did to allow individual slaves their freedom. Laws were passed banning slaves from riding horses or from travelling long distances without their masters' permission and preventing women slaves from keeping their children. The life of a slave, particularly in the countryside, was a miserable existence, characterized by constant beatings, chains and shackles, overwork and suicides. The worst was yet to come, however, as the sugar boom of the late eighteenth and nineteenth centuries was to usher in the most intense period of slave importation in Cuban history (see p.586).

Many of the early settlers created huge cattle ranches, trading with the hides and meat, but the economy came to be based heavily on more profitable **agricultural farming**. Cassava, tropical fruits, coffee and increasingly tobacco and sugar were among the chief Cuban export products on which the colony's trade with Spain depended. **Sugar** production got off to a slow start, and the crop was initially produced principally for local consumption. However, as Europe developed its sweet tooth and the Spanish Crown saw its potential selling power, by the early seventeenth century the sugar industry was given preferential treatment, subsidized and exempted from duties, and an estimated fifty sugar mills were constructed.

The commercial value of **tobacco**, on the other hand, was more immediate and needed no artificial stimulus. In fact, following its increased popularity in Europe in the late sixteenth century, it became the object of increasing government regulation and taxation as the monarchy in Spain sought to commandeer the large profits being made through the tobacco trade. As tobacco farming expanded across the island it served to disperse the population further inland, in part because farmers sought to escape the fiscal grip of the colonial government, whose relatively scarce resources were concentrated in the towns and whose jurisdiction did not, effectively, apply to the Cuban interior.

Despite these developments the economic and political structure of Cuba remained relatively unchanged throughout the late sixteenth and seventeenth centuries. The island continued to be peripheral to the Spanish Empire and life evolved somewhat haphazardly, with contraband an integral part of the economy, removed from the attentions and concerns of the monarchy in Spain.

When, at the beginning of the eighteenth century, the Bourbon Dynasty took over the throne in Spain, it sought to regain control of Spanish assets overseas, particularly in the Caribbean. Through improved colonial administration and closer, more direct links between the empire and home, it began to direct more of the revenue from the colonies into royal purses. This was particularly true of Cuba, which had quietly and slowly become a source of potentially significant wealth. The Bourbons stepped up their monopoly on trade, and in 1717 ordered that all tobacco be sold to commercial agents of the Crown. Resentment from the tobacco farmers, by this time drawn predominantly from the Cuban-born population, increased as these Spanish agents paid them artificially low prices and, in the same year, growers in Havana revolted, surrounding the residence of the colonial governor. The uprising, and two subsequent ones in 1721 and 1723, were easily repressed by the colonial authorities and had no effect on the restrictive measures employed by the ruling elite. In fact these measures became even more institutionalized when in 1740 a trading company, the **Real Compañia de Comercio de la Habana**, was set up by a group of wealthy merchants in Havana. With direct links to Madrid, the Spanish merchants in charge of the company sought to control all trade entering and leaving Cuba, fixing artificially high prices on imported products from Europe and slaves from Africa while paying well below the odds for Cuban-produced items. Discontent increased as profits for Cuban producers dropped, and the lines drawn between the *criollos*, those of Spanish descent but born in Cuba, who tended to be small-scale farmers or members of the emerging educated urban class, and the *peninsulares*, those born in Spain who made up the ruling elite, became more pronounced.

This division was exacerbated further when the Spanish monarch, King Philip V, reacting to the growing discontent in the colony, introduced dictatorial measures affecting the way in which Cuba was governed. Almost all political power was taken away from the local town authorities, known as *cabildos*, who up until then had worked in conjunction with the governor and shared the responsibility for the leasing of land, enforcement of the law and all general administrative duties. Power was now vested more exclusively in the governor, enabling him to implement Spanish wishes without opposition. The military presence on the island, already considerable, especially in Havana, was stepped up as Cubans were frozen out of holding positions of any civil or military authority. These divisions between *criollos* and *peninsulares*, in other words between the interests of Cuba and Spain, were to widen during the course of the next century.

The first half of the eighteenth century saw Cuban society become more sophisticated, as wealth on the island slowly increased. Advancements in the **cultural** character of Cuba are particularly notable during this era, partly as a result of encouragement from the Bourbons but also as a consequence of an emerging Cuban identity, unique from that of Spain. By the end of the century the colony had established its first printing press, newspaper, theatre and university.

The British occupation of Havana

Economic progress had been severely held back by the restrictive way in which Cuba, and indeed the whole Spanish Empire, was run by the Crown, forcing the colony to trade exclusively with Spain and draining the best part of the wealth away from the island into the hands of the colonial masters. This was to change in 1762 with the **British seizure of Havana**. Engaged in the Seven Years' War against Spain and France, the British sought to weaken the Spanish position by attacking Spain's possessions overseas. With Spanish attention focused in Europe, the British navy prepared a strike on the Cuban capital, control of which would strengthen their own position in the Caribbean and disrupt trade between Spain and its empire.

With a force of 200 ships and 22,000 men, the English landed at Cojímar, just outside the city, and attacked El Morro fortress. Militias from Havana and neighbouring Guanabacoa, made up largely of peasants and less than half the size of the British forces, managed to withstand a siege for two months under the leadership of José Antonio Gómez, better known as Pepe Antonio, a councilman from Guanabacoa. Despite this brave effort, on August 12, 1762, the British took control of Havana. They immediately lifted the disabling trade restrictions and opened up new markets in North America and Europe.

Within eleven months Cuba was back in Spanish hands, exchanged with the British for Florida, but the impact of their short stay was enormous. A number of hitherto unobtainable and rarely seen products, including new sugar machinery as well as consumer goods, flowed into Cuba, brought by traders and merchants, who were able for the first time to do business on the island. Cubans were able to sell their own produce to a wider market and at a greater profit and, even in such a short space of time, standards of living rose, particularly in the west where much of the increased commercial activity was focused. So much had changed by the time the Spanish regained control that to revert back to the previous system of tight controls would, the Bourbons realized, provoke fierce discontent among large and powerful sections of the population. Moreover, the new Spanish king, Charles III, was more disposed to progressive reforms than was his predecessor, and the increased output and efficiency of the colony did not pass him by. Free trade was therefore allowed to continue, albeit not completely unchecked, transforming the Cuban economy beyond recognition.

Sugar and slavery

After 1762, with the expansion of trade, sugar's profitability increased, causing the industry to begin operating on a much larger scale and marking a significant development in Cuban society. In 1776 the newly independent United States was able to start trading directly with Cuban merchants at the same time that the demand for sugar in Europe and the US increased. The plantations and mills grew in number and size, and Cuban landowners began modernizing, leading to a considerable increase in output. However, none of this would have been possible without stepping up the size of the workforce, and as a consequence slaves were imported in unprecedented numbers. The racial make-up of the island changed, shaping itself into something closer to the mix seen on the island today.

In 1791 **revolution in Haiti** destroyed the sugar industry there and ended French control of one of its most valuable Caribbean possessions. Cuba soon became the largest producer of sugar in the region. Fleeing Haiti, thousands of French sugar plantation owners and coffee growers settled in Cuba, bringing with them their superior knowledge of sugar production. These developments, combined with scientific advances in the sugar industry and improved transportation routes on the island during the first four decades of the nineteenth century, transformed the face of Cuban society. The introduction of steam power to Cuban mills in 1817, the construction of the first Cuban railroad, completed in 1838, and the destruction of forests to clear the way for sugar plantations, all contributed to the sugar boom that has characterized the history of the island. With ever-increasing portions of the land being taken over for the planting of sugar cane and the number of mills rising from just over 500 in 1792 to more than 1400 in 1850, labour, still the most important component in the production of sugar, was needed on a vast scale. In the 1820s some 60,000 slaves were brought to the island and total numbers during the first half of the nineteenth century reached over 350,000.

As the size of the **slave population** swelled so the conditions of slavery, particularly in the sugar industry, worsened, fuelled by the plantation owners' insatiable appetites for profit. The seemingly endless demand for sugar, increasingly from the United States, and the capacity to meet these demands meant slaves were worked harder than ever before. Those who worked in the cities, as domestic servants, coachmen, gardeners, carpenters and even musicians, were afforded higher status than rural slaves, with greater opportunities to earn extra cash, closer relationships with their white masters, and sexual relations between black and white all features of urban life. The story was quite different in the countryside, where the vast majority of slaves lived and worked. Some worked on coffee and tobacco farms, but most were involved in sugar production, where conditions were at their worst. On the vast sugar estates, the kind of personal relationships between master and slaves found in the towns, cities and the more intimate tobacco and coffee plantations were nonexistent. Where before, in the seventeenth and eighteenth centuries, slaves had lived in collections of small huts and even been allowed to work their own small plots of land, now they were crowded into barrack buildings and all available land was turned over to sugar cane. Floggings, beatings and the use of stocks were common forms of **punishment** for even minor insubordinations and were often used as an incentive to work harder. The whip was in constant use, employed to keep the slaves on the job and to prevent them from falling asleep, most likely during the harvest season when they could be made to work for eighteen hours of every day for months at a time.

Unsurprisingly, such harsh treatment met with resistance and **slave rebellions** became more common from the 1840s to the 1860s. A large proportion of the slaves in Cuba during this period were West African Yoruba, a people with a strong military tradition, who launched frequent and fierce revolts against their oppressors. Uprisings were usually spontaneous, and frequently very violent, often involving the burning and breaking of machinery and the killing of whites. Not all sugar estates experienced rebellion, but those owned by particularly ruthless sugar barons, or run by especially cruel overseers, suffered recurring disturbances. A minority of slave rebellions were highly organized and even involved whites and free blacks.

Two such revolts occurred in Matanzas province, where sugar production, and therefore slavery, was most intensely concentrated, followed by the other three main sugar provinces, Colón, Santiago de Cuba and Sagua la Grande. In 1825, a slave uprising there resulted in the destruction of 25 sugar estates; another in 1843 at the Triunvirato estate, also in Matanzas, involving several hundred slaves, was afterwards declared to have been part of a conspiracy to overthrow the government. Such scaremongering was commonly used by the colonial authorities as justification for the executions that always followed uprisings and the continued use of brutally repressive measures to prevent similar rebellions in the future.

Reform versus independence

In the final decade of the eighteenth century and the first few decades of the nineteenth, a number of new cultural and political institutions emerged, alongside new scientific developments, all aimed specifically at improving the lives of Cubans. Though most of these changes affected only a small proportion of Cubans, they formed the roots of a **national identity**, a conception of Cuba as a country with its own culture, its own people and its own needs, separate from those of the Spanish, who formed a minority of the population but held all the highest political and administrative positions.

In 1791 the **Sociedad Económica de Amigos del País** was established, counting many big *criollo* landowners among its founder members. This organization was set up to promote business interests in all areas of industry, agriculture and commerce, acting as an avenue through which scientific, economic and political information could be shared, for the mutual benefit of the island's businesses. As time passed its role expanded and it began actively encouraging educational programmes, opening the first public library in Cuba and providing financial support to schools. The founder of the society, a leading sugar-mill owner named **Francisco de Arango y Parreño**, sought to enhance production techniques within the industry while favouring the abolition of internal restrictions on trade, such as the tobacco monopoly and restrictions on buying and selling land, which, despite the improvements since the British occupation of Havana, still existed. In the same year as the founding of the Sociedad Económica de Amigos del País, 1791, the *Papel Periódico de la Habana*, Cuba's first **newspaper**, was published, written with solely Cuban interests in mind. There were scientific developments during the 1790s also, including the introduction of the first steam engine for use on sugar plantations and the use of water mills for the first time in Cuba.

The slave rebellions, which tended to increase in number and frequency as each decade of the nineteenth century passed, were symptomatic of an increasingly divided society, one which pitted *criollos* against *peninsulares*, black against white, and the less developed eastern half of the country against the more economically and politically powerful west. However, further lines of division were drawn between each of these opposing groups so that, for example, a wealthy *criollo* sugar baron in the west had closer ties to the Spanish administrators controlling trading laws than with a small-scale *criollo* farmer from the east. The sugar boom had caused Cuban society to become more stratified, creating sharper lines between the landed elite, who had benefited most from the sugar revolution, and the smaller landowners, petit bourgeoisie and free blacks who had become increasingly marginalized by the dominance of large-scale sugar production.

The American Revolution of 1776 proved to be a precursor to the **Wars of Independence** that swept across mainland Spanish America during the initial decades of the nineteenth century, prompted by Napoleon's invasion of Spain in 1808 which cut the colonial master off from its subjects, leaving Spain with just Puerto Rico and Cuba by 1826. Though these events inspired ideas of independence and freedom among Cuban traders, merchants and farmers who desired greater autonomy and more political power, there were forces against independence not found on the mainland that delayed the arrival of Cuba's own bid for self-rule. Not least of these was the period of economic prosperity, which had come late to Cuba compared to other Spanish colonies and went some way to appeasing sections of the wealthier classes that had, up until the sugar boom, desired self-government as a way to greater profit. Furthermore, most *criollos* identified more closely with the Spanish than with the black slave population, who, by the start of the nineteenth century, formed a larger part of the total population than in any other colony, and *criollo* calls for reform were tempered by a fear of the slaves gaining any influence or power. The economy in Cuba relied more heavily on slavery than any of the South American states, with the livelihood of *criollos* and *peninsulares* alike dependent upon its continued existence.

Nevertheless, a **reformist movement** did emerge, but though there were a number of dissatisfied groups, they were unable to present a united front as their various grievances did not form a compatible set of demands. There were calls, predominantly from big businessmen and well-to-do trade merchants, for fiscal reform within Spanish rule; separatists who wanted total independence; and another group still that formed an **annexationist movement** whose goal was to become part of the United States. As the US was the biggest single market for Cuban sugar, many of the largest plantation owners supported the idea; there was growing support within the US, too, where it was felt that Cuba held tremendous strategic importance, especially since the 1803 Louisiana Purchase, which had made the Mississippi a vital trading route for the central states. Annexation was attempted by force when **Narcisco López** led an invasion at Bahía Honda in 1851, with an army recruited in the US, but failed miserably, in part because López, a former officer in the Spanish army, spoke as little English as his troops spoke Spanish.

With the wealthier *criollos* and the *peninsulares* unwilling to push for all-out independence, the separatist cause was taken up most fervently by *criollos* of modest social origins and free blacks. Their agenda, unlike that of their wealthier counterparts, became not just independence but social justice and, most importantly, the abolition of slavery. As the reformist movement became more radical, Spanish fear of revolution intensified and, following the slave rebellions in Matanzas and elsewhere in the country in the early 1840s, the colonial government reacted with a brutal campaign of repression known as **La Escalera** (the ladder), taking its name from a punishment employed by the Spanish, which involved tying the victim to a ladder and whipping him. In an atmosphere of hysteria fuelled by the fear that a nationwide slave uprising was imminent, the Spanish authorities killed hundreds of enslaved and free black suspects and arrested thousands more. At the same time, the military presence on the island grew as soldiers were sent over from Spain, and the governor's power was increased to allow repression of even the slightest sign of rebellion. The reform movement and the abolition of slavery became inextricably linked, and this fusion of ideas was increasingly embraced by reformers themselves. In 1865 the **Partido Reformista** (Reformist Party) was founded by a group of *criollo* planters, providing the most coherent expression yet of the desire for change. Among their demands were a call for Cuban representation in the Spanish parliament and equal legal status for *criollos* and *peninsulares*.

The Wars of Independence

The life of the Reformist Party proved to be a short one. In 1865 an official review of the demands of the party had been set up by the liberal O'Donnell administration in Spain. However, two years later the Junta de Información, the board that had been elected to carry out the review, was dismissed by a new, reactionary Spanish government. Having failed to obtain a single concession, the Reformist Party soon dissolved, while the reform movement as a whole suffered further blows as the new Spanish government issued a wave of repressive measures, including the banning of political meetings and censorship of the press. Meanwhile, pro-independence groups were gaining momentum in the east, where the proportion of *criollos* to *peninsulares* was twice that in the west and where the interests of smaller planters had become increasingly overlooked, isolated by the huge sugar-estate owners whose land was concentrated in the west.

Since 1866, a group of landowners, headed by **Carlos Manuel de Céspedes**, had been plotting a revolution; but it had got no further than the planning stage when the colonial authorities learned of it and sent troops to arrest the conspirators. Pre-empting his own arrest on October 10, 1868, Céspedes freed the slaves working at his sugar mill, La Demajagua, near Manzanillo, effectively instigating the **Ten Years' War**, the first Cuban War of Independence. The size of the revolutionary force grew quickly as other landowners freed their slaves, and soon numbered around 1500 men. Bayamo was the first city to fall to the rebels and briefly became the headquarters of a revolutionary government. Their manifesto included promises of free trade, universal male suffrage, though this meant whites only, and the "gradual" abolition of slavery. Though there were disturbances elsewhere, the war itself was mostly confined to the east and the rebels initially took the upper hand. Supported by the peasants, they were able to master the local terrain, adopting guerrilla tactics to outmanoeuvre the visiting Spanish troops. During the course of the war Spain sent over to Cuba one hundred thousand soldiers.

Support for the cause spread quickly across eastern and central parts of the country as two of the great heroes of the Wars of Independence, the mulatto **Antonio Maceo** and the Dominican **Máximo Gómez**, emerged as military leaders. The most revered name of all in Cuban history books, **José Martí**, first came to prominence in the west of the country, where a much smaller insurgency movement, concentrated in Havana, had taken its cue from the events in the east, but was soon arrested and exiled. On the whole, however, the landowners in the west of the country remained on the side of the colonial authorities. Attempts were made to pull the western third of Cuba into the war, but an invading force from the east, led by Gómez, got only as far as Colón in Matanzas. Then, in 1874, Céspedes was killed in battle and the revolutionary movement began to flounder, losing a number of future leaders either in battle or through exile, and becoming increasingly fragmented as many *criollos* did not trust the peasants and ex-slaves who fought on the same side.

Seizing on this instability, the Spanish offered what appeared to be a compromise, which was accepted by most of the military revolutionary leaders as the best they could hope for, given their own loss of momentum. The **Pact of Zanjón** was signed on February 10, 1878, and included a number of concessions on the part of the Spanish, such as increased political representation for the *criollos*. There remained, however, sections of the rebel army, led by Maceo, that refused to accept the Pact of Zanjón, asserting that none of the original demands of the rebels had been met. In 1879 this small group of rebels reignited the conflict in what became known as the **Guerra Chiquita**, the Small War. It petered out by 1880, and Maceo, along with José Martí and others, was forced into exile.

Over the course of the next fifteen years reformists, among them ex-rebels, became increasingly dismayed by the Spanish government's failure to fulfil the promises made at Zanjón. Though in 1880 the first phase in the **abolition of slavery** seemed to suggest that genuine changes had been achieved, this development proved to be something of a false dawn. Slavery was replaced with the apprentice system whereby ex-slaves were forced to work for their former owners, albeit for a small wage. It was not until 1886 that slavery was entirely abolished, while in 1890, when universal suffrage was declared in Spain, Cuba was excluded.

These years saw the independence movement build strength from outside Cuba, particularly in the US where many of the rebels had moved and where there was already a sizeable Cuban émigré community. No one did more to stimulate support and interest in Cuban independence than **Martí**. From his base in New York, he worked tirelessly, visiting various Latin American countries trying to gain momentum for the idea of an independent Cuba, appealing to notions of Latin American solidarity. In 1892 he founded the **Partido Revolucionario Cubano**, or Cuban Revolutionary Party (PRC), aiming to unite the disjointed exile community and the divided factions on the island in pursuit of a common goal: a free and fully independent Cuba. Martí did more than any single individual to unify the separatist cause and inspire ideals of nationhood. He believed in complete racial equality and wrote passionately on social justice while warning of the imperialist intentions of the US. The PRC began to coordinate with groups inside Cuba as preparations were laid for a **Second War of Independence**.

On February 24, 1895, small groups, in contact with the PRC, mounted armed insurrections in Havana, Matanzas, Las Villas, Camagüey and Oriente. Then, on April 1, Maceo landed in Oriente, followed a fortnight later by Martí and Gómez, who then mobilized a liberation force of around six thousand Cubans. The uprisings in the west had been easily dealt with by the Spanish army and the fighting was once again based in the east.

In May of the same year, in his first battle, at Dos Ríos, Martí was killed. The revolutionaries were not deterred and they fought their way across the country until, on January 1, 1896, they reached Havana province. Intense fighting took place here, where the Spanish forces were at their strongest. Meanwhile, the newly appointed governor of Cuba, Valeriano Weyler, instituted a measure known as the **reconcentración**, a forced relocation of the country's rural poor to the cities designed to freeze production, remove popular support for the rebels and cut off food supplies. Thousands died but the rebels fought on and by 1897 almost the entire country, besides a few heavily garrisoned towns and cities, was under their control.

Riots in Havana gave the US the excuse they had been waiting for to send in the warship **Maine**, ostensibly to protect US citizens in the Cuban capital. On February 15, 1898, the *Maine* blew up in Havana harbour, killing 258 people; the US accused the Spanish of sabotage and so began the **Spanish-American War**. To this day the Cuban government remains adamant that the US blew up its own ship in order to justify its intervention in the War of Independence, but evidence is inconclusive. Whatever the true cause of the explosion, it was the pretext the US needed to enter the war, though its support was far from welcomed by many Cubans, who believed victory was already in their grasp. Furthermore, they were not oblivious to US intentions and rightfully feared an imperial-style takeover from their powerful neighbour. In an attempt to allay these fears, the US prepared the **Teller Amendment**, declaring that they did not intend to exercise any political power in Cuba once the war was over, their sole aim being to free the country from the colonial grip of Spain. Yet despite Cuban involvement in battles fought at El Caney and San Juan in Santiago, Cuban troops were either forced into the background or their efforts ignored. When the **Spanish surrendered** on July 17, 1898, Cuban troops were prevented by US forces from entering Santiago, where the victory ceremony took place.

The pseudo-republic

On December 10, 1898, the Spanish signed the **Treaty of Paris**, thereby handing control of Cuba, as well as Puerto Rico and the Philippines, to the US. Political power on the island lay in the hands of **General John Brooke**, who maintained a strong military force in Cuba while the US government decided what to do with the island they had coveted for so long. The voices of protest in Cuba were loud and numerous enough to convince them that annexation would be a mistake, so they opted for the next best alternative. In 1901 Cuba adopted a new constitution, devised in Washington without any Cuban consultation, which included the **Platt Amendment**, declaring that the US had the right to intervene in Cuban affairs should the independence of the country come under threat – an eventuality open to endless interpretation. The intention to keep Cuba on a short leash was made even clearer when, at the same time, a US naval base was established at Guantánamo Bay. On May 20, 1902, under these terms, Cuba was declared a **republic** and Tomás Estrada Palma, the first elected Cuban president, headed a long line of US puppets.

With the economy in ruins following the war, **US investors** were able to buy up large stakes of land and business relatively cheaply. Soon three-quarters of the sugar industry was controlled by US interests and few branches of the economy lay exclusively in Cuban hands as the North Americans invested in cigar factories, railroads, the telephone system, electricity, tourism and anything else that made money. **Tourism** was particularly lucrative; with millions of Americans just over ninety miles away and, during the second decade of the century, the Cuban economy beginning to prosper, conditions were perfect for attracting visitors to this holiday paradise. Places like Havana and Varadero became flooded with casinos, strip clubs, fancy hotels and exclusive sports clubs, as the island gained a name as an anything-goes destination, a reputation enhanced during the years of Prohibition in the US.

The Machado era and the Depression

The first two decades of the pseudo-republic saw four corrupt Cuban presidents come and go and the US intervene on a number of occasions, temporarily installing a governor in 1906 after a rebellion against Palma's government and sending in troops in 1912 following an uprising in protest against racial discrimination under the presidency of José Miguel Gómez. In 1925 **Gerardo Machado** was elected on the back of a series of promises he had made to clean up government. Though initially successful – he was particularly popular for his defiance of US involvement in Cuban politics – his refusal to tolerate any opposition wrecked any legitimate efforts he may have made to improve the running of the country. Strikes by sugar mill and railroad workers, led by **Julio Antonio Mella**, founder of the **Partido Comunista Cubano** (Cuban Communist Party) in 1925, led to the assassinations of a host of political leaders. In 1928 Machado changed the constitution, extending his term in office to six years and effectively establishing a dictatorship.

The **global economic crisis** that followed the Wall Street Crash in 1929 caused more widespread discontent, and opposition became increasingly radical. Machado ruthlessly set about trying to wipe out all opposition in a bloody and repressive campaign involving assassinations of anyone deemed to be of any threat, from students to journalists. Fearing a loss of influence, the US sent in an ambassador, **Sumner Welles**, with instructions to get rid of Machado and prevent a popular uprising. As Welles set about negotiating a withdrawal of the Machado administration, a general strike across the country in late 1933, together with the loss of the army's support, which had long played an active role in informal Cuban politics, convinced the dictator that remaining in power was futile and he fled the country. Amid the chaos that followed emerged a man who was to profoundly shape the destiny of Cuba over the following decades.

The rise of Fulgencio Batista

A provisional government led by Carlos Manuel de Céspedes y Quesada filled the political vacuum left by Machado but lasted only a few weeks. Meanwhile, a young sergeant, **Fulgencio Batista**, staged a coup within the army and replaced most of the officers with men loyal to him. Using his powerful military position he installed **Ramón Grau San Martín** as president, who went on to attempt to nationalize electricity, which was owned by a US company, and introduce progressive reforms for workers. This was too much for US President Franklin Roosevelt, who accused Grau of being a communist and refused to recognize his regime. Not wanting to antagonize the US, Batista deposed Grau and replaced him in January 1934 with **Carlos Mendieta**. Batista then continued to prop up a series of Cuban presidents until in 1940 he was himself elected.

Demonized more than any other pre-Revolution leader by the current regime, Batista was not, at least during these early years, the hated man that communist Cuba would have people believe. Some of his policies were met with widespread support and, despite the backing he received from the US, he was no puppet. In 1934 he presided over the dissolution of the Platt Amendment, which was replaced with a new agreement endowing Cuba with an unprecedented degree of real independence. In a move designed to harmonize some of the political groupings in Cuba and appease past opponents, in 1937 Batista released all political prisoners, while using the army to institute health and education programmes in the countryside and among the urban poor. By the time he lost power in 1944, ironically to Ramón Grau, Cuba was a more independent and socially just country than it had been at any other time during the pseudo-republic.

Grau showed none of the reformist tendencies that he had demonstrated during his previous short term in office and was replaced in 1948, after proving himself no less corrupt than any of his predecessors. **Carlos Prío Socarrás**, under whom very little changed, led the country until 1952 when Batista, who had left the country after his defeat in 1944, returned to fight another election. Two days before the election was to take place, Batista, fearing failure, staged a **military coup** on March 10 and seized control of the country. He subsequently abolished the constitution and went on to establish a dictatorship bearing little if any resemblance to his previous term as Cuban leader. Fronting a regime characterized principally by violent repression, corruption and self-indulgent decadence, Batista seemed to have lost any zeal he once had for social change and improvement. Organized crime became ingrained in Cuban life, particularly in Havana, where notorious American gangster Meyer Lansky controlled much of the gambling industry. During these years living conditions for the average Cuban worsened as investment in social welfare decreased.

Fidel Castro and the revolutionary movement

Among the candidates for congress in the 1952 election was **Fidel Castro**, a young lawyer who saw his political ambitions dashed when Batista seized power for himself. Effectively frozen out of constitutional politics by Batista's intolerance of organized opposition, Castro sought to challenge the authority of the new regime and make a mark for his own movement, aimed at restoring democracy and implementing social reform. A year after the military coup, on July 26, 1953, Castro and around 125 others attacked an army barracks at **Moncada** in Santiago de Cuba. Castro regarded the attack "as a gesture which will set an example for the people of Cuba". The attack failed miserably and those who weren't shot fled into the mountains where they were soon caught. Castro would certainly have been shot had his captors taken him back to the barracks, but a sympathetic police sergeant kept him in the relative safety of the police jail. A trial followed in which Castro defended himself and gave what has become one of his most famous speeches. In his summing-up, he uttered the now immortal words, "Condemn me if you will. History will absolve me." He was sentenced to fifteen years' imprisonment but had served less than three when, under popular pressure, he, along with the other rebels, was released and sent into exile.

Now based in Mexico, Castro set about organizing a revolutionary force to take back to Cuba; among his recruits was an Argentinian doctor named **Ernesto "Che" Guevara**. They called themselves the **Movimiento 26 de Julio**, the 26th of July Movement, often shortened to **M-26-7**, after the date of the attack at Moncada. In late November 1956 Castro, Guevara and around eighty other revolutionaries set sail for Cuba in a large yacht called the *Granma*. Landing in the east at Playas Coloradas, in what is today Granma province, they were immediately attacked and suffered massive casualties, but the dozen or so who survived headed directly for the Sierra Maestra, where they wasted no time in building up support for the cause among the local peasantry and enlisting new recruits into their army. Waging a war based on guerrilla tactics, the rebels were able to gain the upper hand against Batista's larger and better-equipped forces.

△ Fidel Castro

As the war was being fought out in the countryside, an insurrectionary movement in the cities began a campaign of sabotage aimed at disabling the state apparatus, as the base of support for the Revolution grew wider and wider. By the end of 1958, the majority of Cubans had sided with the rebels and the ranks of the revolutionary army had swelled. The US, sensing they were backing a lost cause, had withdrawn military support for Batista, and there were **revolts within the army** – not only had hundreds of troops been killed but large numbers of those captured by the revolutionaries had been humiliatingly returned to Batista, many of them refusing to continue fighting. Realizing that he no longer exercised any authority, on January 1, 1959, Batista escaped on a plane bound for the Dominican Republic. The army almost immediately surrendered to the rebels, and Fidel Castro, who had been fighting in the east, began a **victory march** across the country, arriving in Havana seven days later on January 8, 1959.

On the eve of the Revolution, Cuba was a prosperous country, the United States' favoured Latin American state. With good relations between the countries, Cuba enjoyed an imported culture through public services and manufactured goods including cars, clothes and electrical equipment – even the telephone system was North American – while the US benefited from cheap sugar, the reward for massive investment in the agricultural industry. The flip side of the picture was that the US used Cuba as its playpen and showed scant regard for its citizens, with the Mafia, crime and prostitution all operating behind the scenes, while Cuba's opulent hotels, cabarets and casinos glittered for the world. Meanwhile, outside of the cities the rural population lived in abject poverty, with no running water, electricity, health care, education or even at times enough food. Peasant wages were desperately low and those working on sugar farms would only draw a wage for a few months of seasonal work a year.

The Cuban Revolution: the first decade

Though the Revolutionary War ended in 1959, this date marks only the beginning of what in Cuba is referred to as the Revolution. The new government appointed as its president Manuel Urrutia, but there was no doubt that the real power lay in the hands of Fidel Castro, who, within a few months of the revolutionary triumph, took over as prime minister. The **1960s** were both trying and exciting times for Cuba, as the government, with Fidel Castro at its head, and Che Guevara soon in charge of the economy, to a large extent felt its way through the decade. It wasted no time in instituting its programme of social and political transformation, passing more than 1500 laws in its first year.

Early reforms

One of the most radical of the new laws was the first **Agrarian Reform Law** of May 1959, by which the land, much of it foreign-owned until now, was either nationalized or redistributed among the rural population. Under the new law, individual ownership could not exceed 400 hectares – just under 1000 acres – and any land in excess of this limit was put under direct state control. Much of it remained in state hands, to be farmed by cooperatives set up for the purpose, but some was given to peasant farmers at a minimum of 27 hectares – almost 70 acres – per individual holding. By 1961 over forty percent of Cuba's farmland had been expropriated and reorganized along these lines. The 1959 law also established the **Agrarian Reform Institute** (INRA), which soon became a kind of government for the countryside, administering most of the rural reform programmes, including new health and educational facilities, housing developments and road construction. The push to eradicate **illiteracy**, initiated in 1961, when Fidel Castro sent more than 250,000 teachers, volunteers and schoolchildren into the countryside to teach reading and writing, affected the peasants more than anyone else. The programme was so successful that illiteracy was slashed from 23.6 percent to 3.9 by the end of 1962. Empowering the peasants both financially and intellectually was seen as key to correcting existing inequalities, and by addressing the imbalance in the distribution of resources between town and country, the revolutionaries changed the social landscape of Cuba beyond recognition.

Health and **education** (see box, p.596) in particular became the focus for the reshaping of the country and the conditions in which its citizens lived. Free education for all was one of the core dicta of revolutionary objectives, as private schools were nationalized and education until the sixth grade made compulsory. Universities proliferated, as numbers of teachers and schools multiplied. By 1968 there were almost 60,000 schoolteachers across the country, compared to just under 20,000 ten years earlier, while the number of schools had doubled. Today it is clear that, just as in the early days of power, the state uses education to put its message across as early as possible (Che Guevara once called youth the "anchor of the revolution".)

Health, too, saw great gains in the early years of the Revolution and is an area that continues to elicit praise for Cuba. Although the country did have good medical care before the Revolution, with a sophisticated, albeit exclusive, health service, staffed by 6300 doctors, there was no national health service and half the doctors worked in Havana. Outside the cities hospitals, where they existed,

Education in the Revolution

In Cuba, children are educated to believe in the Revolution wholeheartedly, and no opportunity to debunk the ideals of capitalist society, specifically the United States, is lost, as can be seen by a glance at any Cuban textbook, be it geography, history or Spanish. Following the dictum that education should go beyond academia, in the Revolution's early years Che Guevara developed schemes to make rural farm work a part of every child's experience, in order to break down the barriers and prejudices dividing rural labourers and white-collar urban workers. Countryside **boarding schools** were set up where work and study were combined and were considered very successful during the 1970s and 1980s, although the Special Period of the 1990s saw them affected by massive shortages. Even today schoolchildren annually spend several weeks of their summer at **camp**, harvesting crops and learning how to shoot weapons and fight in combat. Further to their formal education, from the age of six to thirteen, children are expected to be part of the **Pioneros**, the José Martí Pioneers Organization, similar to the Boy Scouts or the Girl Guides, in which socialism replaces religion. As well as sporting, cultural and recreational activities children learn the core values of the Revolution. Not for nothing is the motto of the Young Cuban Communists (UJC) "Trabajo, Estudio, Fusil" – Work, Study, Gunmanship; being ever ready to defend your country is a cornerstone of revolutionary ideology.

were badly managed and medicines expensive. New hospitals and health care centres were built and a new emphasis put on preventive medicine and care in the community, thus alleviating some of the hospitals' burden. There was also investment in medical research in an attempt not just to provide a domestic source of medical products but also to develop medical technologies for export. There was, however, a rise in infant mortality in these early years and, though by the 1990s the rate had dropped to a level comparing favourably with some of the most highly developed countries in the world, in 1967 rates had gone up by ten percent compared to ten years earlier, with just under 45 deaths per 1000 live births.

Sport was another area targeted for reform in the early 1960s, as Cuba laid the foundations of a system that has gone on to produce some of the world's finest athletes and make Cuba one of the most successful sporting nations on the planet. In 1961, the National Institute of Sport, Physical Education and Recreation (INDER) was set up to administer a programme of mass participation in physical activity, which the revolutionaries regarded as a vital proponent of social development. Specialist sport schools were established and exercise routines were introduced into the workplace, ensuring that everybody became engaged in some kind of regular physical activity.

Opposition and emigration

While these very real gains for large sections of the Cuban population ensured continued popular support for the new regime, not everyone was happy, and the Revolution was not without its victims in these early years. Many of those who had served under Batista, from government officials to army officers, were tried, and – with little regard for their legal rights – convicted for sometimes purely ideological crimes, and executed. Moderates and liberals became increasingly isolated from the political process and disillusioned, both with the nature of revolutionary change and the way it was carried out. Under Castro, the government had little sympathy for the constitutional framework in which the liberals felt it must operate and, appealing to what it regarded as the higher ideals of social justice and the interests of the collective over the individual, swept much of the legal machinery aside in its drive to eliminate opponents of the Revolution and carry out reforms. Among those deemed too liberal was the president, Manuel Urrutia, who, despite his defence of the government against some of its opponents, was forced out of office in July 1959. As the decade wore on, the regime became more intolerant of dissenting voices, declaring all those who challenged government policy to be counter-revolutionaries, and by the end of the 1960s there are estimated to have been over 20,000 **political prisoners** in Cuban jails.

Those in Cuba who, in material terms, stood to gain least and, especially in the case of landowners or big-business moguls, were actually more likely to lose both money and capital, were the upper-middle and upper classes, among them doctors, lawyers and a whole host of other professionals. During the first few years of the Revolution, as Cuban–US relations soured (see below) and the Revolution seemed to be swinging further to the left, these groups sought refuge overseas, predominantly in the US. Between 1960 and 1962 around 200,000 **emigrants**, most of them white, left Cuba, forming large exile communities, especially in **Miami**, and setting up powerful anti-Castro organizations, intent on returning to Cuba as soon as possible, even if it meant another war.

Cuban-Soviet-US relations

As huge sectors of Cuban industry were **nationalized** and foreign businesses, most of them US-owned, found themselves dispossessed, the US government retaliated by freezing all purchases of Cuban sugar, restricting exports to the island and then, in 1961, breaking off diplomatic relations. Seeking to overthrow the new regime, the US now backed counter-revolutionary forces within Cuba as well as terrorist campaigns in the cities aimed at sabotaging the state apparatus, but finally, under President John F. Kennedy, opted for all-out invasion. On April 17, 1961, a military force of Cuban exiles, trained and equipped in the US, landed at the **Bay of Pigs** in southern Matanzas. The revolutionaries were ready for them and the whole operation ended in failure within 72 hours.

In December of that year, in the face of complete economic and political isolation from the US – the country Castro had hoped would support the Revolution and which he had visited as early as April 1959, seeking diplomatic ties – the Cuban leader declared himself a **Marxist–Leninist**. The debate continues to this day as to whether this was considered opportunism on the part of Castro or whether, as he himself declared, he had always held these beliefs but chosen up until then not to make them public for fear of scaring off potential support for the Revolution. Sincere or not, there was no doubt whose support he coveted at the time of his declaration, and the **Soviet Union** was only too happy to enter a pact with a close neighbour of its bitter Cold War adversary.

The benefits for Cuba were immediate as the Soviets agreed to buy Cuban sugar at artificially high prices while selling them petroleum at well below its market value. Then, in 1962, on Castro's request, the Soviets installed over forty **missiles** on the island. Angered by this belligerent move, Kennedy declared an embargo on any military weapons entering Cuba. Soviet Premier **Nikita Khrushchev** ignored it, and Soviet ships loaded with more weapons made their way across the Atlantic. Neither side appeared to be backing down and nuclear

△ Che Guevara

weapons were prepared for launch in the US. A six-day stalemate followed, after which a deal was finally struck and the world breathed a collective sigh of relief – the **Cuban Missile Crisis** had passed. Khrushchev agreed to withdraw Soviet weapons from Cuba on the condition that the US would not invade the island. This triggered the tightening of the trade embargo by the US.

Economic policy in the 1960s

The government, attempting to diversify the economy and institute massive social change, occasionally allowed revolutionary ideals to outweigh realistic policy and planning. Nowhere was this more apparent than in the new **economic policies**. The basic aim, initially, was to reduce Cuba's dependence

Cuban revolutionary ideology

Initially, the Cuban Revolution was an expression of **nationalism**. In Fidel Castro's earliest speeches, following the attack on Moncada in 1953, for example, he made numerous references to self-determination, social justice and equality, but there was little indication of the Marxist-Leninist ideologies with which the Cuban state has become associated. Despite Castro's claims that he had always been a communist, it is more likely, considering the text of his speeches, that his beliefs and those of many of his fellow revolutionaries evolved into the system that now characterizes the Revolution. Castro and his followers arrived at what is now established Cuban ideology partly through opportunism and circumstance – specifically the break with the US and the alliance with the Soviet Union – and partly through a need to intellectualize the revolutionary process, thereby providing a theoretical guide to what they hoped and intended to achieve.

A milestone in Cuban revolutionary theory – and now a core text of the official ideological framework on which the Cuban state is based – is Che Guevara's *Man and Socialism in Cuba*, published in 1965. This immediately became one of the key theoretical bases informing the programmes of development and reform in Cuba. At its essence is the concept of what Guevara called **El Hombre Nuevo** – The New Man – a state of mind to which all Cubans should aspire. Fundamental to achieving an egalitarian and just society, Guevara believed, was not just what people did, but also what they thought. Capitalism, he argued, encouraged the individual to pursue only selfish ends and material gain, and to change that would require an entirely new political culture. The Revolution would have to transform the motivations that determine behaviour – people would have to be taught to be motivated by the interests of the collective.

This idea – that the values of *El Hombre Nuevo* would not simply be acquired but would have to be taught – effectively legitimized the process of **indoctrination** through schools, the workplace, the media and sloganeering that still exists. It was believed that there was a kind of ideological hangover from the previous regime, that market forces had affected the social conscience and that what was required was a kind of rehabilitation of the individual. Once this transformation was complete, there would be no need for material incentives in the workplace, as people would be satisfied by moral rewards and the knowledge that they had served the wider objectives of the Revolution.

C

on sugar production, through industrialization and expansion in both the output and the variety of agricultural products and consumer goods manufactured. In their enthusiasm for the principles of what they were doing, and spurred on by the knowledge of how much they had already achieved, a number of factors were overlooked.

The **mass exodus of professionals** during the early years of the decade, though eliminating a large part of the potential opposition, made the transition from an essentially monocultural capitalist economy to a more diverse, industrialized yet highly centralized one extremely problematic. There were simply not enough workers with the kinds of skills and experience necessary to realize such ambitious plans. Furthermore, the **impact of the US embargo** had been severely underestimated: the Americans had supplied machinery, raw materials and manufactured goods easily, quickly and inexpensively and, despite subsidies from the Soviet Union, the greater distances involved and less sophisticated economy of Cuba's new suppliers could not match up. Agricultural output actually dropped significantly and in 1962 **rationing** had to be introduced. The revolutionaries had aimed too high and in doing so had placed extra stresses and strains on an economy simply not prepared for such rapid change. After the failure of initial attempts at producing the type of industrial goods and machinery that had been imported until now, and following Castro's visit to the Soviet Union in 1964, during which the Russians promised to purchase 24 million tons of sugar over the next five years, it was decided that the economy should focus once again on **sugar**. Ambitious targets were set for each harvest, none more so than in 1970, when Castro declared that Cuba would produce, ten million tons of sugar. This blind optimism was to prove disastrous as not only were the impossible production targets not met, but other areas of the economy suffered from neglect and under-investment, leaving Cuba even more dependent on sugar than it had been prior to the Revolution.

The 1970s and 1980s

The 1960s had been a period of experimentation and discovery for the Cuban revolutionaries. In the following decades, with an established ideological framework and the foundations of genuine social gains for large parts of the population, despite the hardships caused by failed economic policies, the government sought to consolidate its objectives. Having already encouraged and, in cases like that of Bolivia, participated in popular uprisings against what they saw (usually correctly) as oppressive regimes, in the 1970s Cuba expanded its policy of assisting sympathetic ideologies in countries beyond Latin America, becoming engaged in a fifteen-year conflict in Angola and a shorter war in Ethiopia, among others.

Economic policy and performance

Following the disastrous economic experiments of the 1960s, Cuba began the next decade with a complete reappraisal of economic policy and planning. Much had been learned, and the wild optimism that inspired previous policy was rejected in favour of a more realistic programme. A balance was struck, with the state still in control of heavy industry and the essential components of the economy, while the private sector was expanded and given greater freedom. In a clear compromise of revolutionary ideology, **material incentives** were introduced, while wage policies were also adjusted to bring them into line with the needs of the economy.

In 1975 the government adopted its **first Five Year Plan**, setting relatively realistic targets for growth and production, not all of which were met. With rises in the price of sugar on the world market in the first half of the decade and increased Soviet assistance, there were tangible improvements in the country's economic performance. The policy changes were carried on into the next decade as the economy continued to make modest improvements, though the mass exodus of some 125,000 Cubans in the **Mariel boatlift** of 1980 (many of them criminals whom the government released to be freed of the burden of housing them) demonstrated that, for many, times were still hard.

As more private enterprise was permitted, however, Castro became alarmed at the number of people giving up their state jobs and concluded that he had made a mistake. In 1986, he issued his **Rectification of Errors** and the economy returned to centralization. With increasing sums being ploughed into defence, the economy survived only through heavy Soviet support.

The politics of a one-party state

The government, having declared itself the **Partido Comunista Cubano**, or Cuban Communist Party (PCC), in 1965, did not hold its first Congress until 1975. The following year a new constitution was drawn up and approved. Castro's position as head of state became constitutionalized, thus doing away with the last vestiges of democracy and openly declaring his power and authority as unchallengeable. Attempts were made, on the other hand, to decentralize power by introducing an extensive system of **local government**. However, as agents of central government these local assemblies had little or no real independence.

Countless **mass organizations** had, by this time, been established, among them the Committees for the Defence of the Revolution (CDR), the Union of Young Communists (UJC) and the Federation of Cuban Women (FMC). In theory, membership of these organizations was the popular expression of support for the Revolution and its ideals, but in reality they were – and are – closer to being the watchdogs of the regime, ensuring that at every level people are behaving as good citizens.

The 1990s and beyond

In 1989 the bubble burst. The **collapse of the Soviet bloc** and subsequently the Soviet Union itself led to a loss of over eighty percent of Cuba's trade. In 1990, as the country stumbled into an era of extreme shortages, the government declared the beginning of the **Special Period** (Periodo Especial) to combat the problems, a euphemism that essentially meant compromise and sacrifice for all Cubans in all areas of life. Public transport deteriorated dramatically as the country lost almost all of its fuel imports, strict rationing

---

Race relations in Cuba

At the onset of the Revolution in 1959, Fidel Castro declared that he would erase racial discrimination, establishing the unacceptability of racism as one of the core tenets of the Revolution. He carried through his promise with legislation that threw open doors to previously white-only country clubs, beaches, hotels and universities and, more importantly, established equality in the workplace.

However, the question of race in Cuba is still a problematic issue. Official statistics put the **racial mix** at 66 percent white (of Hispanic descent), 12 percent black, 21.9 percent mulatto (mixed race between black and Hispanic) and 0.1 percent Asian. There is, however, an obvious disparity between figures and facts and the claims by some that as much as 70 percent of the population have some trace of black heritage seem to be closer to the truth. Some critics of the official figures claim they are a way of downplaying the importance of the black heritage.

Although institutional racism has been somewhat lessened, its existence is still apparent in the lack of black people holding the highest positions across the professional spectrum. A more recent dimension in the race question has arisen from the tourist trade. *Jineteros* and *jineteras* (hustlers, escort girls and prostitutes) are nationally perceived as exclusively Afro-Cuban, and this in turn has led to the stereotype of wealthy Afro-Cubans as prostitutes, pimps and touts, while white Cubans with money are generally assumed to be supported by relatives in Miami.

of food was introduced, and timed power cuts became frequent as even electricity had to be rationed.

The US government, in 1992, took advantage of Cuba's crisis to tighten up the trade embargo even further as, not for the first time since 1959, thousands of Cubans risked their lives trying to escape the country across the Florida Straits. Obsessed with toppling the regime, the Cuban exile community in Miami, by now consisting of a number of well-organized and powerful political groups, rubbed its hands with glee at the prospect of the Revolution crumbling, as reports in the US press regularly predicted the fall of Fidel Castro. Forced to make huge ideological readjustments and drastic changes to the way the country was run, the government embarked on one of its most ideologically risky journeys when, in August 1993, the **US dollar** was declared legal tender (though it no longer is), and with this came other reforms as the Cubans sought to rebuild the economy by opening the floodgates to the worldwide tourist trade. To wrest back control of the economy the state was forced to make all but the most basic products and services chargeable in dollars, opening dollar stores, restaurants and hotels, ensuring that the money made its way back into the state coffers. However, until the new tourism industry began to boost the beleaguered economy, people were scrabbling to survive: sugar and water were at times all that some had to live on.

Tales of survival from the era are by turns grotesque, comic and heroic. While stories of vendors replacing cheese with melted condoms on pizzas and CDR meetings called with the express purpose of ordering people to stop dining on the neighbourhood cats and dogs are urban myths, their very existence highlights the desperate living conditions during those times. Hard-currency **black markets** prospered as those who could used dollars to buy products that were not available in the empty peso stores. Small-scale **private enterprise** was also legalized as the face of modern-day Cuba began to take shape. Private farmers' markets became the norm, industrious cooks took to selling their culinary creations from the front windows of their houses, and house owners began renting out their bedrooms to tourists. The risk to both revolutionary ideology and its control of the economy that the government has taken by allowing even this limited degree of capitalism may prove to be the start of the end of the Cuban Revolution. Possibly as a preventative measure, the Cuban government announced in October 2004 that the dollar would no longer be accepted as currency.

Cuba in the twenty-first century

While the country has survived, the Special Period left deep scars on society. Shortages still prevail, particularly of medicines, which has tarnished the state's excellent health record, and for those without direct access to money brought in by tourism life can be extremely difficult. The advent of private enterprise has ended up creating distinct class-based divisions in society. Revolutionary ideology has been severely undermined, with Cubans blatantly pursuing personal rather than collective gain, through all kinds of activity. While the rural community, which has benefited most from improvements in health care, housing and education, remains overwhelmingly loyal to the Revolution, in the cities, where the influence of capitalist culture is greater, there is a distinct restlessness.

The economic hardships following the collapse of the Soviet bloc and the measures taken by the government to deal with them have made Cuba's **lack of social and political freedoms** more apparent than at any time since the

Perhaps one of the single most symbolic events in Cuba-US relations to have taken place in recent years was the saga of the young Cuban boy, **Elián González**. In November, 1999, the five-year-old was rescued by fishermen who found him floating on an inner tube off the coast of Fort Lauderdale. Having fled Cuba and their home town of Cárdenas with his mother aboard a small motorboat, into which were crammed another twelve would-be refugees, Elián was one of several survivors after the boat sank in heavy seas and he was taken into the care of his Miami relatives.

A battle for **custody of the boy** immediately sprang up between his new-found family on one side and on the other his four grandparents and father, who claimed Elián's mother had kidnapped the child, back in Cuba. Inevitably the politicians and political activists wasted no time in getting involved. The more extreme elements of the Miami-based, anti-Castro collective adopted the image of Elián to illustrate their campaign for the continued economic blockading of Cuba in the determination that neither Castro nor his government should be given any recognition or legitimacy. In the words of Ninoska Pérez-Castellon, spokeswoman of the **Cuban-American National Foundation** (CANF), "Elián's mother lost her life to give him a future". At the same time, Fidel Castro led the calls for "justice" and for the boy to be returned to his father. A highly charged legal battle raged for seven months, during which time the father was reportedly offered $1 million by the Miami-Cuban faction to claim political asylum in the US, until finally in June 2000 the US Supreme Court ruled that Elián should be returned to his homeland. In the final act of this drama, Elián had to be snatched from his relatives by Federal agents, who stormed the house in Miami where he had been staying.

After its resolution, it seemed that the whole Elián drama had highlighted the growing isolation from the American political mainstream of the anti-Castro Cuban-American community's more hardline fringe. However, any increased hopes for reconciliation between the two countries have not come to any fruition since then, especially since during his two terms in office, US President George W. Bush's aggressively anti-Castro rhetoric and the tightening of travel restrictions has only continued to exacerbate the war of words on both sides.

C

1960s. Cubans speak wistfully of how much better things were "*antes*" – before – and while many foreigners have taken this to mean before the Revolution, often people just mean before the Special Period began.

Without the right to demonstrate, organize political opposition or vote for a change of government, widespread feelings of powerlessness and frustration, numbed in the past by economic security, have developed. And while most recognize and laud the improvements made since 1959 – not just in health and education but in sport and social attitudes, with race relations hugely improved and the advances in sexual equality – many Cubans, in private, voice the opinion that worthwhile though the gains have been, enough material sacrifice has been made and now it's time for some new improvements and changes, most especially to individual freedoms.

Denouncing as an enemy of the state anyone who publicly criticizes the Revolution or gives negative accounts to the foreign press, Fidel Castro has always externalized the country's problems, laying the blame at the feet of capitalist powers and their conspirators. It must be remembered that the constant aggression visited against the country by the US has definitely assisted, if not entirely created, the rationale for this paranoid point of view. Although the regime has witnessed a degree of liberalization in terms of its handling of dissidents since the 1960s and 1970s, open opposition to the government and even the principles of the Revolution are still all but illegal. Moreover, according to sources which include Amnesty International, there are still **political prisoners** in Cuba; most notable recently are the 75 Varela Project dissidents jailed in March 2002 and charged with disrespect for authority after pushing for, among other things, free elections and freedom of worship, speech and the press. Even considering these factors, and given all the trials and tribulations suffered by the country, especially since the Special Period, the imminent internal collapse gleefully predicted by right-wing pundits still looks like wishful thinking.

Arguably Cuba is in a stronger position economically and politically than at any time since the fall of the Soviet Bloc. In Venezuela, under Chavez, Cuba and Castro have acquired a staunch ally, and their position and influence in the region looks set to gain strength within the context of a general shift to the left throughout much of Latin America. A number of governments, such as those in Bolivia, Ecuador and Nicaragua, are now much closer to Castro and Cuba, both in their policies and diplomatic relations, than they are to the US administration. Initiatives such as Misión Milagro, an exchange of medical resources and expertise established between Cuba and Venezuela in 2004, are expanding to other Latin American countries, increasing and solidifying mutual dependencies and ties with Cuba within the region. Furthermore, in 2006 the UN voted in favour of a motion, raised annually, calling for an end to the US blockade and a change of policy towards Cuba by a record 183 countries to 4. Meanwhile, the Cuban economy continues to show encouraging signs of growth. The special relationship with Venezuela has brought increased investment and aid, crucially in the supply of oil to the island. France, Spain and Canada, amongst others, continue to invest significantly in Cuba, whilst economic relations with China and India have improved quite dramatically. China is now Cuba's third largest trading partner and has invested over $1 billion in Cuba's nickel industry, as well as in tourism and other sectors.

Despite these recent changes in Cuban fortunes, the million-dollar question remains: what will happen in a post-Castro Cuba? For now, the whole country is holding its breath whilst the rest of the world watches on.

Wildlife and the environment

Over the last five million years, the island of Cuba has been shaped by a combination of violent volcanic activity, erosion and continental plate movement. Odd-shaped, often flat-topped mountains fall away to swamps, plains and pouch-shaped bays, an unusually varied geography that provides a diversity of habitats and some unique wildlife species. The vast majority of Cuba's animal life is invertebrate: mammals are scarce, and even reptiles and amphibians are few when compared with the Central American region. Birdlife, however, is abundant; marine life is mesmerizing; and there are some spectacular types of insect. While many species are common to southern Florida, Mexico and neighbouring islands, Cuba is also graced with a large number of specialized local species.

Unfortunately, the predictable consequences of human habitation have driven many of these endemic species to extinction. Over the last two hundred years, uncultivated land cover has dropped from ninety percent to a paltry nineteen percent and it is only in designated national parks, or inhospitable landscapes, that you will come across wildlife. Where they do exist, mangrove forests, pine forests, and tropical rainforests are largely unspoiled with sparse facilities.

Fauna

The main characteristics of Cuban **fauna** are large numbers of highly localized groups, an unusually high quantity of small-sized animals, and a great deal of interspecies variety. In practice, this means that the delicate and strange takes precedence over the massive and magnificent.

Marine life

Running underneath the island is a flat, silty ledge that extends out to a chain of clear, coral-fringed cays. This is one of the most biologically productive ecosystems on earth, although none of the species found here is endemic to Cuba.

On the sea bed grow large "fields" of monotonous **turtle grass**, home to myriad molluscs, sea urchins, sea stars, sponges, fish, and even the occasional **manatee**, also known as a **sea cow**. This implausible creature can be seen grazing on the underwater grass beds with the same inscrutable ease as its landbound namesake. Although carrying an inflated head of wrinkled grey rubber, these two-metre-long beasts were once thought to be beautiful mermaids tempting sailors to suicide.

The **hawksbill** and **loggerhead turtles** from which the underground savannah gets its name are all but gone now. A more frequent visitor is the **common octopus**, which subsists on the **queen conch**, a huge mollusc that scrapes microscopic algae from the ocean floor. Vicious-looking **barracuda** and the charming **bottle-nosed dolphin** also make appearances, although these fish tend to congregate around outcrops of rock and their consequent forests of coral and sponge. Here many smaller fish, such as **snappers**, **hogfish**, the repulsive **toadfish** and the glorious **parrot fish**, feed on the oasis of microscopic life the rocks provide. The same fish can also be found further out from shore, towards the cays, where wide coral reefs host thousands of species. Taking a boat trip or diving from one of the coastal resorts are the easiest ways to get out to the reefs.

Typically for an island, **freshwater** fauna is sparse. There are some curiosities, like the **Cuban blind fish**, and various species of delicate **shrimp**, but most impressive are the **Cuban garfish** and the **manjuarí**, both species that have been around since the dinosaurs. Sometimes described as a "living fossil", the bizarre looking *manjuarí* came close to extinction in recent times and is still very rare, though its numbers have increased thanks to the Cuban law preventing its capture and, to a lesser extent, the extremely hard scales that cover its body and protect it from most predators. Its elongated snout-like jaws, which contain three sets of sharp teeth, are attached to an equally drawn-out body with the dorsal fin set right back near the rounded tail. The diet of this ferocious, reptilian-looking fish has been known to include frogs, chicks of small aquatic birds and even its own young. Found predominantly in the lakes and rivers of the Península de Zapata, it generally inhabits shallow waters and, like the crocodile, also a native of this region, is able to go for long periods of time without feeding, thanks to its slow digestive system.

Insects, spiders and molluscs

With over 17,000 described species, **insect life** on Cuba is varied and abundant. Among the usual bewildering array of tiny oddities, there are some impressively large spiders and scorpions. None is dangerous, although this is hard to believe when you see the **giant Cuban millipede**. Also known as "the dog maimer", these repulsive creatures cause swelling and great discomfort when stepped on. Less commonly found are Cuba's huge-headed **harvester ants**.

Land **snails** are, if anything, what Cuba is famous for, as a look around any of the country's natural history museums will confirm. Among species of all sizes and hues, the most extraordinary is the spectacular **painted snail** (*polymita*), some of which are striped with all the colours of the rainbow. Such intense pigmentation would appear to be counter-productive, but being multicoloured they are difficult for predators to fix on. Human beings have no problem, of course, and have reduced their numbers to dangerously low levels.

Cuba is not as magnificently well endowed with **butterflies** as neighbouring regions, but it is home to the unusual **Cuban clearwing**, distinguished, as the name suggests, by large but completely transparent wings. Some of the most eye-pleasing colours can be found on the **avellaneda**, a large yellow insect named after the Cuban poet Gertrude Avellaneda that inhabits the Sierra Mestra.

Mammals

Mammals other than humans and dogs are rarely seen in Cuba. There are now only 32 species of mammal on the island, the majority of which are **bats**. Although some bats live in deserted buildings, most make their homes in the innumerable caves of the limestone regions. Most eat fruit and vegetable matter, although Cuba's largest bat feeds on small fish. The second smallest bat in the world, the **butterfly bat**, is native to Cuba, though it is unlikely to be seen as it lives in caves and hunts by night in woody areas.

The **Cuban hot caves bat** is a little more sociable, feeding as it does on the pollen of the ubiquitous royal palm.

The largest indigenous land mammals are the gentle **tree rats** (*jutías*), of which there are three species. More like a beaver than a rat, the timid, vegetarian *jutías* are rarely seen. Even more difficult to spot is the dishevelled **almiquí**, the only insectivore common exclusively to Cuba. This odd nocturnal rat-like creature, another of Cuba's "living fossils", faces an uncertain future as its habitat, the Bayamo region, continues to be developed for human use.

Reptiles and amphibians

The **Cuban boa** is the largest snake in the Greater Antilles. Brown, with flashes of iridescent green, this ground dweller feeds mainly on birds. Some eat bats and rats, but unfortunately they have a particular taste for poultry, and have thus been largely exterminated by irate peasants. Even more highly endangered is the **Cuban crocodile**, now restricted to the Península de Zapata and Lanier swamps, where food is becoming more difficult to come by.

The inoffensive but disconcertingly fast **jubo** snake may be encountered, as may the long and thin blue **correcosta** lizard, both of which are quite common, and, like other Cuban reptiles, harmless. Of these, most widespread are the **anole** family of lizards. The **bearded anole**, a miracle of camouflage, blends impressively with lichen-coloured trees and stones. Its bright cousin, the small **blue anole**, is commonly seen in many of Cuba's parks and gardens. Other common varieties include the pale brown **stream anole** and the large green **knight anole**.

In Cuba's lakes and rivers you might be lucky enough to find a **Cuban turtle**, although numbers are dwindling. More common are various types of frog and toad.

Birds

Over 300 varieties of **bird** can be seen in Cuba, about seventy of which are indigenous. Cuba is a popular resting place for migrating birds, which mingle with the wide range of local teals, sparrows, warblers, owls, hawks, cranes, herons and parrots. Keen birdwatchers usually head for the Baracoan mountains and the Sierra Maestra, where **peregrine falcons**, **blue-winged teals**, **great blue herons** and **mourning doves** can all be spotted. The Península de Guanahacabibes and the Sabana-Camagüey cays are home to a wide range of colourful **spoonbills**, **flamingos** and **black hawks** – all, alas, in danger of extinction.

The three endemic bird species which seem most to have endeared themselves to Cubans are as colourful as the flamingo but at the other end of the spectrum in size. The **tocororo** or Cuban trogon is the national bird, sharing the red, white and blue of the Cuban flag. It is still abundant in forest areas, where it perches in an almost vertical position, nests in holes made by woodpeckers, and feeds on fruits, flowers and insects which it catches in flight. Other features are its distinctively shaped tail and the call that gives it its name.

The *cartacuba* or **Cuban tody** is only 12cm high, with a brilliant green back and a bright red patch under its bill. Though never abundant, it can be found in forested areas throughout Cuba. It feeds on insects for which it is constantly searching among the foliage. It lays its eggs at the end of a tunnel which it digs in a bank or in a tree trunk, and its chicks seem to be the best-fed in the world; it is reckoned that a pair of parents will bring each chick up to 140 insects a day.

Cuba is also home to the smallest bird in the world, the **zunzuncito** or bee hummingbird, 6.5cm in length. The female is slightly larger than the male, but the male boasts more brilliant colours. Like other hummingbirds, the *zunzuncito* hovers on rapidly beating wings to extract the nectar from flowers. It can be found in forested areas such as Cienaga de Zapata and Sierra del Rosario, and in mountainous areas like Escambray and the Sierra Maestra.

Another beautiful bird is the **blue-headed quail dove**. Although its main form of locomotion is walking, the unique clacking of its wings is as close as many get to seeing its fine plumage, as it too is becoming rare. More common and equally fantastic is the fierce-looking light-brown **Cuban pygmy owl**, which emits a fifteen-note piercing shrill. Also frequently seen, and more frequently heard, are the many species of woodpecker that inhabit the island. Most attractive is the **Cuban red-bellied woodpecker** with its elegant yellow headgear and fine red breast, although the **Cuban green woodpecker** is also pretty.

Flora

Cuba, it is said, looks all ways of the world, and nowhere is this more evident than in Cuba's diverse flora, of which over 6000 species, more than any other island in the Antilles, grow even today.

The principal zones of remaining forest are the mountains of Pinar del Río, the Sierra del Escambray, the Sierra Maestra and the highlands of Baracoa. Those arboreal species still surviving in the heavily deforested plains are few. One is the dignified silver-stalked **royal palm**. Adorning the country's coat of arms, it is known for its majesty – heights of over 30m are not uncommon – and its utility: from roots to leaves, every portion serves some useful purpose. There are more than thirty other species of palm, including the common **coconut palm**, a rare and ancient species of **cork palm** and the bulbous **big belly palm**. The oddly shaped, lichen-painted **sabal palm**, now threatened by parrot poaching and charcoal production, is the cornerstone of the Península de Zapata's ecosystem, housing and feeding many species of bird, lizard and small mammal.

Another tree left on the plains is the strange **ceiba** tree. These silk-cotton trees, frequently reaching an immense 45m, are sacred to all Cuban cultures, aboriginal and colonial alike. The most famous in the country can be found at the Plaza de Armas in Havana, marking the spot where the city was founded.

Other commonly found trees include the **sea grape** (*uva caleta*), found along stretches of coast and bearing grape-like fruit; the great **jaguey** fig tree with its peculiar aerial roots; and a far eastern import, the bright red- and orange-flowered **royal poinciana**.

Orchids and cacti are represented by hundreds of varieties. Cuba's national flower, the delicate white **butterfly jasmine**, is common.

Threats to the environment

Columbus remarked on his initial survey of Cuba that he had "never seen anything so beautiful. The country around the river is full of trees, beautiful and green and different from ours, each with flowers and its own kind of fruit. There are many birds of all sizes that sing very sweetly, and there are many palms different from those in Guinea or Spain." Since then, Cuba's natural fortunes have declined tragically.

Cuba lost most of its **primary forests** (which once covered about 95 percent of the territory) in the early years of European occupation. Calculations suggest that by 1774 the forested area of Cuba had been reduced to 83 percent. The Spanish settlers enthusiastically began clearing virgin forests for sugar-cane plantations. This intensive log-farming, along with the introduction of foreign dogs, rats, monkeys and goats, did little for the fortunes of local fauna. Insects thrived, of course, and sea life was yet to be affected, but the giant walking owls, Cuban monkeys and colossal sloth soon disappeared.

The new arrivals, in their defence, unwittingly brought with them viruses and bacteria against which local wildlife had no defences, and much colonial rapacity was due to simple ignorance. Nevertheless, with Cuba's breathtaking wilderness now huddled in a few isolated pockets it is hard not to see conscious human policy as the main environmental threat.

Destruction reached its peak in the **nineteenth century**, with 320-square-kilometres a year being destroyed. By 1900 the forested area had been reduced to 41 percent, by 1926 to 21 percent and by 1958 to just 16 percent. After the 1959 Revolution serious attempts at reforestation were made for the first time, but mistakes were made, such as inappropriate selection of species and inadequate care of plantations, and replanting went side by side with continued deforestation for the construction of dams, roads and further clearing for sugar production. In recent years the tide has turned, with forested areas increasing to 19 percent coverage by 1990. But even today, among the vast majority of local people ignorance and economic necessity prevail.

There is hope, however. The last decade has seen a discernible increase in **ecological awareness** and acknowledgement of the need for urgent measures to conserve animal and plant species. There have been serious attempts to identify and count endemic species, and the work of the National Enterprise for Conservation of Flora and Fauna has included a census of parrots, cranes and parakeets and a conservation programme for the pink flamingo which has led to a significant increase in the population. **Ecotourism** has taken hold, and though it brings its own problems it has provided an added incentive for the conservation of wildlife in general and endangered species in particular. How far these measures are successful in reversing the mortal tide of human activity remains to be seen.

Darren Bills

Cuban music

Cuba is beyond question the most important source of music in Latin America. Its root rhythms – *rumba* and *son* – created the pan-Latin music of *salsa*, as developed in New York, Miami and across Latin America, and in their older forms they continue to provide abundant riches, now globally recognized in the success of the Buena Vista Social Club projects. But Cuban musical success and influence is by no means new. Its *danzón* groups helped to shape jazz in the early decades of the twentieth century and continued at the forefront of the music through to the 1950s, unleashing *mambo* and *chachachá* crazes throughout Europe and the US, and providing the template for much modern African music, in particular Congolese *soukous*. And even after the non-Latin West backed away from post-revolutionary Cuba, the island continued to produce a wealth of jazz, *salsa* and *son*, as well as the influential *nueva trova* or "new song".

Son and Afro-Cuban music

"¡Qué rico bailo yo!" – "How well I dance!" The title of a classic song by Orquesta Ritmo Oriental epitomizes the confidence and spirit of Cuban music. For this is the island that has given the world the *habanera*, *rumba*, the *mambo*, the *danzón*, the *chachachá* – dance music that has travelled all over the new world, the old world, and gone back to its roots in Africa. And at home it is a music that feels inseparable from Cuba's daily life and history, whether drawing on African rituals, commenting on topical issues, or just celebrating rhythm and sensuality.

African roots

African slaves were imported to Cuba from the 1520s until well into the nineteenth century. Little surprise, then, that Cuban music has deep and evident roots in **African ritual and rhythm**, even when its forms are essentially developments of the European dances brought by the Spanish colonists. By contrast, there is almost no detectable influence from the pre-Hispanic tribes, beyond the use of *maracas* (shakers); Cuba's indigenous culture was effectively obliterated by colonization.

Cuba's slaves were brought mostly from the West African coast – Nigeria, Ghana, Togo, Cameroon, Benin and Congo – and by the 1840s they constituted nearly half of the population. They preserved their identity in mutual aid associations called *cabildos*, from which emerged the four main Afro-Cuban religions of Lucumi, Abakua, Congo and Arara, and their cults, each of which developed its own music, rhythms and rituals. **Santería**, the dominant Afro-Cuban religion, drew on a spread of cults, and revered a panoply of African deities or **orishas**, later paired with Catholic saints.

In Cuba today a fair section of the population maintains a faith based on Santería, and you can see dances and music performed in honour of the various *orishas*. Each *orisha* has its own colour; Changó, the spirit of war and fire (twinned with Santa Barbara), is red and white, while Oshún, the flirtatious goddess of love and water (twinned with the Virgen de la Caridad del Cobre,

Cuba's patron saint), has gold. As well as a colour and an element, each deity has its own characteristic set of **toques** – rhythms played by the hourglass-shaped **batá drums** and **chekere** (rattles), which provide the sounds and ambience for religious rituals.

These complex rhythms are the heartbeat of Cuban popular music, working away beneath the Latin layers on top. The *batás* and *chekere* of the ceremonies crop up regularly in contemporary bands, and the physical and emotional intensity of Cuban music derives in part from the power of African ritual and its participatory nature. Celina González, for example, Cuba's "Queen of Country Music", pays homage to Changó in her wonderful song "Santa Barbara" (a classic, immortalized by Cuban exile Celia Cruz). The links between Afro-Cuban religions and music-making remain significantly close.

Afro-Cuban rumba

Forget the glitzy ballroom-dancing image of **rumba**. The genuine article is informal and spontaneous – a pure Afro-Cuban music for voices and percussion. Performed in neighbourhood bars, tenement patios or on street corners, it becomes the collective expression of all who take part.

Rumba has roots in Afro-Cuban religion but it consolidated as a form in the docks of Havana and Matanzas, with workers in their spare moments singing and dancing and playing rhythms on cargo boxes. Its modern repertoire divides into three main dances: the *guaguancó*, *yambú* and *columbia*. The **guaguancó** is a dance for a couple in which a symbolic game of sexual flirtation is initiated; at its climax the man executes a pelvic thrust or *vacunao*, which the woman may, through her own dance, accept or reject. The **yambú** is also a couple dance, with slower, more stately steps (and no *vacunao*), popular with older people. In contrast, the **columbia** is a fast, furious and highly acrobatic solo male dance.

The music of *rumba* consists of percussion and vocal parts. The typical percussion includes one or two **tumbadores** (low-pitched conga drums), a high-pitched conga drum called a **quinto** (which is usually the "lead" drum) and a pair of **palitos** – sticks beaten against the wooden body of one of the drums. The vocal sections involve a leader (solo voice and *quinto*) and responder (chorus, low congas and *palitos*). *Guaguancó* and *yambú* also include a short defining, vocal introduction called the *diana*.

As interlocking cross-rhythms are created, the *claves* – a pair of sticks struck against one another – join in and establish the pattern called the **clave**, meaning "key", in the sense of a key to a code, to which all the other rhythms relate. Further percussion might include the *cata* or *guagua* (a wooden tube played with sticks); the *maruga* (an iron shaker); and often a *cajón* (wooden packing-case). For religious occasions, *batá* drums might be added.

The basic **pattern of rumba** informs much Afro-Cuban music. A long lyrical vocal melody unfolds above the muttering drums, allowing the lead singer an opportunity to express emotions and show mastery of improvisation. Then on a cue from the band leader, the rhythm tightens up, the chorus joins in, and the call-and-response section steams off, the *quinto* improvising wildly under the singer's *inspiraciones*. This section, when the band really gets going and the dancing starts to heat up, is known as the *montuno*. Fused with the rhythms of *son*, it created **son montuno** – which was in turn transformed into *salsa*.

Rumba texts deal with a wide variety of concerns – sad, humorous or everyday topics – and are generally sung in Spanish, although the *columbia* often interjects chants from Santería and other Afro-Cuban cults. *Rumbas* may be improvised through repetition of just a few phrases.

Roots-style *rumba* can be heard easily enough around the island. Good events and places to check out in **Havana** are the *Sabados de Rumba* (*Rumba* Saturdays), organized by the Conjunto Folklórico Nacional, and the Callejon Hamel, in Centro Habana, which painter Salvador González has set up with the spirited young group Claves y Guaguanco. In the town of **Matanzas**, you should visit the local Casa de la Trova where the stunning **Los Muñequitos de Matanzas** (Little Dolls of Matanzas) perform. The group has been going for nearly fifty years, its members now embracing three generations.

Danzón, charanga and the chachachá

While the *rumba* represents the essential Afro-Cuban tradition, **danzón** is the basic musical strain of Cuba's European settlers. Played by an *orquesta típica*, these (mostly) sedate and dignified dances were Cuba's original dance music exports.

The **orquesta típica** developed partly as a recreational version of the military marching band, its sound coming from the lead of violins and brass, with a pair of *timpani* (round-bottomed marching drums) playing melodies descended from European dance traditions. Originally played in the ballrooms of the big colonial houses, these were gradually Africanized as they were adopted by domestic servants and urban Cubans, until they took shape as the **habanera** (see opposite). Their petty-bourgeois flavour is about as "respectable" as Cuban music gets – not that there are any associations of class. Most of today's *danzón* aficionados are black and creole, and, on the whole, elderly, meeting up in atmospheric dancehalls on a Saturday night.

Cuban band leader **Miguel Failde** is allegedly responsible for the first *danzón*, when he slowed down the country dance form in the late 1880s, dividing it into sections and adding a provocative pause and syncopated rhythm. The country dance originated in the *contredanse* brought in during the 1800s by the French who had fled to the Santiago area from nearby Saint-Domingue (today's Haiti) after the Haitian slave revolution. Listen carefully to *danzón* and you'll hear those insistent Afro-Cuban percussion rhythms, reminding you where you are.

Other *danzón* pioneers, who developed the music at a similar time and along a similar course to New Orleans jazz, include **Antonio María Romeu**, **José Urfe** and **Enrique Jorrín**, all of whom were active in Havana in the early decades of the twentieth century. Later, in the 1930s, a key contribution was made by the orchestra **Arcaño y sus Maravillos**, who introduced a final montuno section to the *danzón*. They also incorporated *congas*, a new style, close to *son*, which caught on like wildfire, consolidating the pre-eminence of *son* over *danzón* as the leading Cuban dance music.

In the early twentieth century, the *orquestas típicas* playing *danzón* had also created an offshoot known as **charanga** or *charanga francesa*, in which brass instruments were replaced with violins, flute, double bass and piano. The "francesa" tag had a double source: the absorption of the classic French trio of flute, piano and violin; and the music's popularity with *las francesas*, the madames who ran the high-class brothels in early twentieth-century Havana.

The *charanga* ensemble thrived through the twentieth century, taking many Cuban musical forms and making them a part of its repertoire, particularly in their glory years between the 1930s and 1950s. Great *charangas* of this age included **Orquesta Aragón**, **Orquesta Riverside** and **Orquesta América**. The last, founded by the violinist Enrique Jorrín, are acknowledged as the creators of **chachachá**, the most popular-ever Cuban dance, which swept across

The essential skill of every **sonero** is a total awareness of what every instrument is doing in order to improvise their vocals. The voices of the great *soneros* differ, but in general a high-pitched, somewhat nasal voice has been favoured.

The most popular themes in *son* **lyrics** are love and romance. Cuban musicians are besotted with their island and its women, composing romantic serenades to each, often interlinked and metaphorical. The language, usually very witty, often has a double meaning, which can be both chauvinistic and very funny.

The **bolero**, which evolved in the early twentieth century as a popular slow-dance song with lyrics in European *bel canto* style, unashamedly illustrates this sentimental and romantic tradition. It became popular as a voice and guitar idiom throughout much of Latin America from the 1920s. Although heavily influenced by Italian song, the *bolero* also accommodates subdued Afro-Cuban rhythms.

Europe and, above all, the US in the 1950s. Jorrín apparently composed the first *chachachá*, "La Engañadora", after watching Americans struggle with the complex Cuban dance rhythms. In New York, *chachachá*, with its straightforward 1-2-3 footwork, was popularized by top Cuban-led big bands such as those of **Machito**, **Perez Prado**, **Tito Puente** and **Tito Rodríguez**, until it was pre-empted by the *mambo*, a development that came more from the tradition of *son conjuntos*.

In Havana, several of the leading *charangas* are still going, half a century after their creation, often with musicians who played with the founders. The most notable is Orquesta Aragón, who have flourished for years under the guidance of virtuoso flautist **Richard Egües**. Among younger generation *charangas*, **Candido Fabré y su Banda** and **Charanga Habanera** carry on the tradition of adopting and mutating styles, the latter playing a style forged in the late 1990s called **timba**.

Cuban counterpoint

The thread that links these earlier Cuban styles of *danzón* and *charanga* to *son* and *salsa* is what music writer Peter Manuel has called the "anticipated bass" – a bass line pattern in which the final note of a bar anticipates the harmony of the following bar. This characteristic evolved from the **habanera**, with its suave, romantic melodies and recurring rhythm, and from its offshoot, the **bolero**. Its persistence underpins the flowing sequence and fertile relationship between dance genres that has developed over the decades in Cuba.

The rhythm works through the omission by the bass of the downbeat of the first bar, with an elision into the second bar, so that the music follows a two-bar pattern. The deliberate avoidance of the downbeat – with the rhythm in effect riding over it, with a multitude of polyrhythms released by other instruments – lends the music its unique flow and momentum, making it ideal for the fluid and supple *salsa* dance style. The body can choose to follow various rhythms at any one time, with different unstressed-stressed moments playing, yet all the time the maracas and cowbell underlying the strong tempo. Manuel maintains – and he is almost certainly right – that this Cuban rhythm pattern has influenced the whole basis of modern Latin music, from Colombian *cumbia* to Dominican *merengue*.

The great Cuban folklorist Fernando Ortíz explains the development of the island's music as the interplay between **sugar and tobacco**. Cuba's African slaves were settled on the great sugar estates and created their religious and secular music from African traditions. The Spanish grew tobacco, and they brought with them the tradition of **décima** verse (ten-line verses, with a rhyming scheme established by the first line), and couple dancing. Most popular music forms – and not only in Cuba – have developed from the fusion of these two cultures.

Ortíz wittily calls this "Cuban counterpoint" – and *son*, which stands at the core of Latin music, is its prime example.

The sound of son

Son is the predominant musical force in Cuba and is regarded almost as a symbol of the island, unifying its European and Black culture. These days it takes many forms, from simple, rustic bands to the brassy arrangements of New York *salsa*. It has a common form, however, which as in *rumba* is centred upon a clave rhythm (related to the *rumba* clave). Bongos, maracas and *guiro* (scraper) add an improvisatory rhythmic counterpoint to the clave, while the bass plucks the "anticipated" movement described on p.613. On top comes what is often referred to as the "Latin" layer of harmonic and melodic elements – notably the Cuban guitar known as the **tres** (so-called for its triple sets of double strings), which, with the vocals, provides the classic sound and texture.

Structurally, or at least lyrically, *sones* follow either the traditional Spanish *décima* form or the *verso* form. *Son* begins with a set of opening verses, then moves into a section known as the **montuno** in which the improvising *sonero* sings a repeated phrase, accompanied by the melodies of the *tres*, and is answered by the chorus.

As one of the most famous early *soneros*, Miguel Matamoros, told it: "No one knows exactly where *son* is from. It is from the Oriente countryside, the mountains, but not from any one place. They say it is from Baracoa but anywhere in the mountains there someone would bring a *tres* guitar and right away a song was created. The old *sones* were made of nothing more than two or three words, which when I was young old black men could sing repeatedly for the whole night. Like that *son* which goes 'Alligator, alligator, alligator, where is the alligator?'"

In the late nineteenth century, **Oriente** had a very mixed population that included thousands of refugees – black and white – from Haiti's revolutionary wars. The francophone immigrants brought new elements to Cuba's African and Spanish mix, lending the extra ingredient to *son*, which was being forged in the 1880s by black and mulatto musicians. *Son* reached Havana around 1909, notably via the **Trio Oriental** who during the following decade created the classic sextet format. Renamed the **Sexteto Habanero**, they featured *tres*, guitar, bongo, string bass and a pair of vocalists (who also played claves and maracas).

Son began spreading in all kinds of directions, gathering Afro-Cuban roots in the bongo players' adoption of rhythmic elements from the cults, and at the same time being brought into the repertoire of the society *danzón* orchestras. American companies began recording groups like the Sexteto Habanero and **Sexteto Boloña** as early as 1912, but it was the advent of Cuban radio in 1922 and the regular broadcasting of live bands that consolidated *son*'s success. In 1920 the singer and bandleader Miguel Matamoros copyrighted a *son* for the first time – "El Son de La Loma", one of the most popular ever written.

In the late 1920s, with the addition of a trumpet, the *sexteto* became a **septeto** and the *son* began to swing. One of the most significant *septetos*, **Septeto**

△ Dancing at a disco in Havana

Nacional (another group still going strong), came into being in 1927 under the leadership of the great **Ignacio Piñeiro**. Piñeiro was the composer of the acclaimed and enduring "Echalé salsita" (Throw Some Sauce In It), whose opening theme was adapted by George Gershwin for his *Cuban Overture,* after he had befriended Piñeiro on a trip to Havana. The song is also thought to be one of the sources for the term "*salsa*" in Latin music. During a long career, Piñeiro composed *guajira-son*, *bolero-son* and *guaracha-son*, a fusing of genres typical of Cuban popular music.

Another classic *son*, "El Manicero" (The Peanut Vendor), emerged in 1928. Written by Moises Simon for **Rita Montaner**, it was a huge hit for her in Paris, breaking Cuban music for the first time in Europe. In 1930 Don Aspiazu's Havana Orchestra, with their singer **Antonio Machín**, took the song to New York. Machín sang it to a slow *rumba* rhythm, with dancers performing choreographed *rumbas* on stage, and it became the top-selling record in the US in 1931 – the first Cuban music to chart in America.

Two leading instrumentalists and bandleaders furthered the *son* sound in the middle years of the century: the blind *tres* player **Arsenio Rodríguez** and trumpeter **Félix Chappotín**. Rodríguez is considered the father of modern Afro-Cuban sound. His musical roots lay in the Congolese rituals of his family, instilled in him by his grandfather who was a slave, and he brought many of the *toques* used to address deities into *son*. He was a prodigious composer – his *sones* remain dominant in the repertoire – and his group, which he expanded with first congas and later an extra trumpet, more percussion and piano, became the most influential of the 1940s. Rodríguez also changed the structure of *son*, expanding the *montuno* with a *descarga* section of improvised solos. In 1951 he moved to New York, turning his group over to Chappotín, whose most significant innovation was to add the tight horn arrangements favoured by American swing bands of the period. Buena Vista star Rúben González was just one of the great Cuban musicians who passed through these bands.

A perhaps even more seminal bandleader – and one of Cuba's greatest ever *soneros* – was **Beny Moré**, the "Barbarian of Rhythm". Moré began his career

Casas de la Trova

The best place to hear music in Cuba is in a **Casa de la Trova**. Most towns have at least one of these clubs, which are essentially a Revolution-era update of an old Cuban institution – a place where *trovas* or ballads are sung by *trovadores*. Nowadays the performances are more diverse and often completely spontaneous, with people joining in and getting up to play whenever they feel like it. You can hear anything from a single *trovador* with a guitar to a traditional Cuban sexteto or septeto.

The *casas* range from grand old colonial buildings with courtyards and palm trees to small, impromptu performing spaces with a few chairs off the street. In practice, they are like informal clubs or bars where musicians gather to play, people gather to listen and everybody exchanges opinions and reminiscences.

The most celebrated Casa de la Trova is in **Santiago**, on Heredia, and there is music here afternoons and evenings, every day of the week. It's just one room with wide windows and doors open onto the street and a small platform at the end for the performers. Further up Heredia are other venues like the *Peña del Tango* and the *Museo de Carnival*, which often have more organized musical performances. At the weekends there are likely to be bands on the street as well.

In **Havana** there are two Casas de la Trova, the *Cerro* (Panchito Gómez 265 e/ Perfecto Lacoste y Néstor Sardiñas) and the *10 de Octubre* (Calzada de Luyanó e/ Reforma y Guanabacoa). The latter is a little out of the way, in the Lujana area, but worth finding: a small local hall in a line of severely peeling colonial terraces, it possesses all the charm of old Havana, and appropriately enough features regular performances by the historic Sexteto Habanero.

There are other good Casas de la Trova in **Baracoa**, **Sancti Spíritus**, **Matanzas**, **Trinidad**, **Pinar del Río** and **Guanabacoa**. See the relevant chapters for more information.

Also worth checking out for concerts are the **Casas de Cultura** around the island, another revolutionary Cuban institution.

singing with Miguel Matamoros and then with the highly influential jazz-oriented band of Cuban expat Pérez Prado, in Mexico City. When he returned to Cuba in 1953, he formed a trailblazing band that he led with characteristic showmanship, singing, dancing and conducting. He was a brilliant arranger, too, drawing on a whole spectrum of styles, including *son* and *guaracha* rhythms, slower, romantic *boleros*, and the *mambo* that he had evolved with Prado. After the Revolution, he stayed in Cuba and kept the party going until his death, hastened by alcohol, in 1963. Just 43, he was already a legend: 100,000 Cubans attended his funeral, and he continues to be cited by modern *son* musicians as the greatest of them all.

Cuban *son*, in the broader sense, was very much a part of mainstream popular music in the 1940s and 1950s, in North and South America as well as the Caribbean. The big US crazes were for *chachachá* and up-tempo *mambo*, while all other variants tended to be termed *rumba* (or *rhumba*), which came to be a catch-all for anything Latin. In New York, the mix of *mambo* with the Latin rhythms of Puerto Rico, Colombia and Dominican Republic – added to an injection of hi-tech instrumentation and rhythm – was eventually to transmute *son* into **salsa**.

Music and the Revolution

It is impossible to understand developments in Cuban music without taking into account the **politics of the island**. Havana, during the 1920s and 1930s, became the favourite nightclub playground for American tourists evading the prohibition laws, and, postwar, developed as a major centre for gambling and prostitution. While this gained Havana Mafia connections and an undesirable reputation as the "whorehouse of the Caribbean", it did mean good money for entertainment and music – even though the population at large remained desperately poor. In addition, the close links with New York gave rise to stylish, inventive and cutting-edge big bands.

After 1959 and the **Revolution**, the island's music business was, like everything else, transformed. Radio stations and record companies became state institutions. The mob pulled out with dictator Batista, and US-owned property was appropriated for workers. As hotels and nightclubs remained empty, many musicians joined those Cubans leaving the country for exile in Miami or New York. Among their number were **Celia Cruz** and her band **Sonoro Matancera**, who applied for US residency after securing a series of gigs at the Hollywood Palladium. In the decades since, Cruz has become the unrivalled "Queen of Salsa", while identifying herself strongly with the anti-Castro/Cuban boycott movement.

For Cubans who remained, the US boycott meant a desperate struggle for economic survival amid chronic shortages of basic goods. For musicians, at least until the liberalizing of the economy in the late 1990s, opportunities to record and sell records, or to tour, were severely limited. It is only in the past few years that Cuban music, as played in Cuba, has re-entered the international mainstream.

On the island, the post-Revolution music scene soon shifted from the glamour of nightclubs and big orchestras to more local music-making centred on **Casas de la Trova** (see box, opposite) and to a system of state-employed musicians. From the 1960s onwards, promising young players were given a Conservatoire training – a university musical education drawing on both classical and popular island traditions. When they graduated, they joined the ranks of full-time musicians categorized as *profesionales*, and could draw a state salary from the Ministry of Culture – which in turn took ninety percent of their earnings.

With few opportunities to travel, musicians were forced to return to their roots, playing continually to local audiences. This was frustrating, especially for younger musicians who found it tough and often impossible to get equipment to form bands or to make their own records. **Egrem**, Cuba's state-owned recording company, had to function in an economy which had higher priorities than importing vinyl. Popular albums sold out instantly on release and the shortage of vinyl meant no re-pressing.

Artists who managed to tour abroad could record for foreign labels. But life wasn't so easy for them, either, and the defection of Irakere musicians **Arturo Sandoval** and **Paquito D'Rivera**, both at one time ardent supporters of the Revolution, brought into sharp focus the pressures on the music industry under Castro's government. And for musicians who didn't make it onto international tours, the US blockade continued to frustrate any direct contact with the Latin fusions developing in places like New York.

The legalization of the dollar and consequent changes in the economy have been welcomed by musicians. These days they are still nominally organized through Institutes of Music but they can work freely inside and outside the country, contract to a recording company, negotiate their own rates, and pay only a small percentage of hard currency earnings to the government. Some musicians are now among the highest paid professionals in Cuba.

Egrem, meanwhile, has been licensing its priceless archive to a host of companies around the world and renting out its old studio in Havana to

"This is the best thing I was ever involved in," said **Ry Cooder** upon the release of *Buena Vista Social Club*, the album of acoustic Cuban rhythms he recorded in Havana. Since then *Buena Vista* has sold more than two million copies, won a Grammy award and become a live show capable of selling out New York's Carnegie Hall.

Yet Cooder is the first to admit that *Buena Vista* is not really his album at all. He rightly wanted all the glory to go to the legendary Cuban veterans who were rescued from obscurity and retirement and assembled in Havana's Egrem studio to record the album over seven days in March 1996. "These are the greatest musicians alive on the planet today, hot-shot players and classic people," said Cooder. "In my experience Cuban musicians are unique. The organization of the musical group is perfectly understood, there is no ego, no jockeying for position, so they have evolved the perfect ensemble concept."

The role of composer and guitarist **Compay Segundo**, who has since passed away, was central to the project. "As soon as he walked into the studio it all kicked in. He was the leader, the fulcrum, the pivot. He knew the greatest songs and how to do them because he's been doing them since World War One."

Initially a clarinettist, Segundo invented his own seven-stringed guitar, known as the *armonico*, which gives his music its unique resonance. In the late 1920s he played with **Nico Saquito** before moving to Havana where he formed a duo with Lorenzo Hierrezuelo. In 1950 he formed **Compay Segundo y su Grupo**, yet by the following decade he had virtually retired from music, working as a tobacconist for seventeen years.

Rúben González (1919–2003) is described by Cooder as "the greatest piano soloist I have ever heard in my life, a cross between Thelonius Monk and Felix the Cat." Together with Líli Martínez and Peruchín, González forged the style of modern Cuban piano playing in the 1940s. He played with Enrique Jorrín's orchestra for 25 years, travelling widely through Latin America. When invited to play on *Buena Vista*, González did not even own a piano. However, following the release of his first solo album, González toured Europe and recorded his second solo album in London. "Chanchullo" was released in 2000 to wide acclaim, as critics across the board favoured the lusher, more elaborate and rhythmic material.

Other key members of the Buena Vista club included **Omara Portuondo**, the *bolero* singer known as "the Cuban Edith Piaf", **Eliades Ochoa**, the singer and guitarist from Santiago who leads Cuarteto Patria, and the *sonero* **Ibrahim Ferrer**, whose solo album Cooder produced on a return visit to Havana.

Archive footage of Segundo and González can be seen in Wim Wenders' full-length documentary feature *film*, *Buena Vista Social Club*, filmed in Cuba and at the Buena Vista concerts in Amsterdam and New York in 1998.

Nigel Williamson

producers and bands from outside Cuba. They have built a new up-to-date recording studio, as have other private investors, among them the musicians Silvio Rodríguez and Pablo Milanés. Many new **venues** for live music have also been opened, for both tourists and the Cuban public.

Such changes perhaps reflect a belated recognition of Cuba's musical resources by the government. In the 1980s, it was reported that musicians travelling abroad brought in the economy's largest hard currency earnings after sugar, fruit and tobacco. And that figure must have soared in the last few years, spurred by the vastly successful *Buena Vista Social Club* recordings, produced by US guitarist Ry Cooder, Cuban arranger Juan de Marcos González and the London-based World Circuit label (see box, above).

The son goes on

With the exception of the "singer-songwriter" *nueva trova* artists (see p.622), all of the best-known contemporary Cuban bands and musicians – both on the island and abroad – have evolved from the *son* tradition. They include traditionalists, revivalists and a good number of groups re-booting the tradition, or fusing it with other forms.

Among the traditional groups, leaders include **Septeto Nacional**, originally founded by Ignacio Piñeiro and re-established in 1985 to perform classic *son*, and the wonderful, unfeasibly long-established **Orquesta Aragón**, with their even more old-fashioned *charanga*. **Orquesta Ritmo Oriental**, with a traditional flute and violin *charanga* line-up, play a mix of *son*, *charanga* and *música campesina* (country music), while **Orquesta Original de Manzanillo** have also adapted the *charanga* sound.

An excellent revival band, following the classic sexteto traditions, is **Sierra Maestra**. They remain firmly Cuban-based but tour frequently in Latin America and Europe. One of their founders was *tres* player and arranger **Juan de Marcos González**, the mastermind behind Buena Vista Social Club. These projects are, of course, themselves *son* revivals, bringing together old and new generation players – something Cuba has always been good at. Their "old world" sound, harking back to the pre-revolutionary era when many of the players made their names, contrasts with the more urgent, streetwise music coming out of Cuba today.

Two important types of music that have fed into *son* are **música campesina** and **changui**, both of them rural. *Campesina* (country music) is characterized by classic vocal harmonies and upbeat, swingy guitar and percussion. Its top exponent, who has really created her own form with doses of Afro-Cuban *rumba* and *son*, is **Celina González** (see box, p.621). The key player in *changui*, over the past decades, was the late **Elio Revé**, whose **Orquesta Revé** provided opportunities for a string of young players. The potency of Revé's music came from the fusion of its strong regional form with urban *son* and the use of *batá* drums from Santería ceremonies. His lyrics were imaginative, too, reflecting popular opinions on social and political issues. A charismatic personality, his death in a car accident in 1997 was a major loss. His sound lives on, in a rather more *salsa*-driven form, in **Dan Den**, a band formed by his long-time cohort Juan Carlos Alfonso.

An earlier partner in Revé's band – and arguably the most significant figure in late-twentieth-century *son* – was Juan Formell, who in 1969 formed his own group, **Los Van Van**. At root a very tight *charanga* band – flute, violin, piano and percussion – Los Van Van invented new changes in rhythm and timbre, with Formell introducing Afro-Cuban elements and, like band leaders before him, duplicating percussion parts to other instruments, notably strings. Adding a trombone, synthesizer and drum, Van Van developed a variant of *son* called **songo**. They remain at the innovative edge of Cuban dance music, producing infectious hit songs like "Titimani" and "Muevete", whose topical lyrics capture the ironic edge of daily life in the capital.

A more jazz-oriented direction was taken by the group **Irakere**, which was formed in 1973 by composer-pianist Jesús "Chucho" Valdés, Paquito D'Rivera and Arturo Sandoval. Irakere were the first big contemporary Cuban jazz group, combining *son* and Afro-Cuban music with modern jazz. Their name and their music emphasized their African inheritance – Irakere is Yoruba for "forest" – and their arrival heralded a new age in Cuban and Latin jazz. Irakere's line-up has changed often over the years, with members going on to found their own groups, though its most notable transformation came in the late 1980s when D'Rivera and Sandoval both defected from the island.

In the same period, Adalberto Alvarez and his band **Son 14** took *son* further, demonstrating a challenging awareness of *salsa* developments outside the island, and creating a wealth of compositions which have had huge coverage abroad.

As to a new generation, perhaps the future was indicated at the beginning of the 1990s by the band whose name implies just that: **NG La Banda** (New Generation The Band). Founded in 1988 by ex-Van Van and Irakere flautist José Luis Cortés, they set out to "search for the Cuban music of the future", establishing a more aggressive, street-based contact with their public. Their position on the musical map was established with the 1993 hit, "Echale Limon" – literally, "Put a Lemon In It", the Cuban slang for when things go wrong. The lyrics, couched in uncompromising *barrio* slang, caught the mood of the country.

A decade on, NG remain hugely popular and innovative, mixing in elements of hip-hop and jazz, along with complex arrangements by *los metales de terror* (the horns of terror). Their lead in bringing rap into *son* looks set to become a pattern – already Havana has a number of young would-be **hip-hop** stars.

Cuban hip-hop and reggaeton

Until relatively recently, **hip-hop** in Cuba existed solely as live music, with none of the home-grown artists having officially recorded any of their material, but that has been changing over the past few years, with the sound gaining growing local and international followings.

Since its inception in 1995, the biggest event in the Cuban hip-hop scene has been the annual **Festival de Rap**, held in Alamar on the eastern outskirts of Havana. The festival's sole venue, an open-air concrete amphitheatre in the middle of a neighbourhood of high-rise apartment buildings, with its capacity of no more than a few hundred, was representative of Cuban hip-hop in general, underexposed and strictly amateur. The first few groups to gain any kind of reputation – notably Amenaza, members of which went on to form Orishas – did so in the mid-1990s almost exclusively by word of mouth and sporadic performances. In 1997, Primera Base, a Havana-based trio, became the first group to emerge from this scene and record an album. Despite the lack of exposure and sales, the scene continued to grow steadily, boosted by support from both the US and Europe. When Dead Prez and Black Star attended the 1998 Festival de Rap, becoming the first American hip-hop acts to perform in Cuba, it proved somewhat of a turning point, and the several Cuban hip-hop compilations released since then have exhibited increasingly sophisticated production and a style that's less dependent on mimicking US artists. In the years since, the Festival de Rap has expanded to multiple venues around the capital and has been graced by international stars like Common and Erykah Badu.

For years most of the significant Cuban hip-hop albums were recorded by **foreign-based labels**, usually in France or Spain, a trend that began in 1999 with the first Orishas album, *A Lo Cubano*, which sold hundreds of thousands of copies in Europe and was extremely popular in Havana as well. However, a small stable of Cuban rappers are gaining exposure thanks to home-based releases, predominantly on the EGREM and BisCuba labels. Prominent among these are Obsesión, Telmary Díaz, Fres K and Papo Record. Most groups still rely on home-made recordings to get their music heard, and some of the most respected names within the Cuban hip-hop community, such as Los Paisanos, Ogguere and Junior Clan, have yet to officially record and release their own

With its layers of pulsating African percussion, Latin melodies on guitar and *tres* and Afro-Cuban rhythmic patterns, there's no mistaking Cuban country music for its American namesake. **Música campesina** is a kind of roots *salsa* and its undisputed queen is **Celina González**. Her music ranges from a sparse combination of voice, percussion and guitar, to more of a big-band sound with punchy brass and strings. But whatever the line-up, her style is rooted in the music of the Cuban countryside.

In the 1970s, after the death of her husband, their son Reutilio Junior joined Celina as her singing partner, and, with the band **Campo Alegre**, helped update the music by incorporating the trumpet, bass, congas and marimba from the urban septetos of Havana. Although this kind of music was looked down on and discriminated against before the Revolution, these days every single Cuban radio station has at least one daily programme devoted to *música campesina*, while Celina has her own daily programme on Radio Taíno.

In 1998, her fiftieth anniversary as a performer, Celina recorded a new album of her own as well as another with the classic *charanga* group, **Orquesta América**, singing witty *guarachas* in her startlingly bright, swingy tones. She's a huge star in Colombia, Venezuela and beyond, with numerous awards to her name. With new albums recorded in 2001 and 2002, her popularity shows no sign of waning.

music. Having toured extensively around Europe and recorded a third album, Orishas stands alone among Cuban hip-hop acts in terms of commercial success and popularity and remain the only group to have gained international recognition.

Despite the explosion of Cuban hip-hop groups and the increasingly sophisticated lyrics and production of the island's hip-hop artists, the groups gaining the most recognition and radio air-play are moving the sound in a different direction. Groups like Marka Registrada, Eddy K and Punto Cero, whose albums are sold in shops all over the country, have helped to establish pop-rap in Cuba, with a sound fluctuating between early 1990s American R&B and watered-down commercial reggae. This in turn has led to the latest trend in Cuban popular music, reggaeton, and Cuban reggaeton artists have already eclipsed their hip-hop equivalents in terms of popularity and studio time.

Today, despite the establishment of an officially endorsed Cuban hip-hop magazine, *Movimiento*, official recognition from the State of hip-hop has a valid genre of Cuban music and still-increasing public interest, most of the Cuban artists creating a genuine and distinct Cuban sound to the music are lurking in the shadows and waiting in the wings. With so many Cuban groups writing lyrics that ignore all the current trends in US and Western hip-hop of rampant materialism and violence and sticking instead to more creative, honest and meaningful songs reflecting their own thoughts and experiences, you could argue that Cuban hip-hop is just what the rest of hip-hop needs.

Trova and Nueva Trova

Post-Revolution Cuba produced one great musical style that stood outside the mainspring of *son*, and which instead had close links with the pan-Latin American developments of *nueva canción*.

Nueva trova (new ballad) – like *nueva canción* – is associated with the 1960s and 1970s, the years of protest throughout Latin America, when Cuba was seen by many as a beacon against the oppression of the continent's dictators. Cuba's new song, like its Chilean and Argentinian counterparts, miraculously instilled politics into achingly beautiful songs of love and loss and personal exploration, and perfectly suited the times.

Although no longer at the forefront of Cuban music, *trova* remains an active part of the scene, to be heard throughout the island in Casas de la Trova (see p.616). Its key singers – **Silvio Rodríguez** and **Pablo Milanés** – remain hugely respected both on the island and throughout the Spanish-speaking world.

Troubadour roots

Cuba's original **trovadores** were true troubadours, who roved the island in the early decades of the twentieth century, accompanying themselves on guitar while singing country songs, *sones* and *boleros*. Their songs were typically concerned with love and patriotism, often with Cuba personified as a woman.

One of Cuba's most popular singers of all time was the diminutive **Sindo Garay**, from Santiago de Cuba, the creator of the unforgettable *bolero* "La Bayamesa" (Girl from Bayamo), written in 1909 and still a part of the *trova* repertoire. The town of Bayamo was the cradle of the independence movement and the "girl" in question was thus the love of all Cuban patriots. Garay was a leading *trova* singer during the Machado dictatorship in the 1930s and 40s and was a fixture at the *Bodeguita del Medio*, a bar near the cathedral in Habana Vieja which was to play a key role in the run-up to the Revolution as a meeting place of intellectuals and critics of Batista.

Another major figure of the early *canción* world was **Joseíto Fernández**, who wrote the rustic "Guantanamera" (a tribute to the women of Guantánamo, with various versions including lines from Cuba's national poet, José Martí), one of the most covered songs of all time, and regarded as a kind of national hymn. **Nico Saquito** from Santiago de Cuba composed over five hundred songs in the *trova* tradition (and, incidentally, worked with both the young Celina González and Compay Segundo). **Carlos Puebla**'s quartet sang witty songs of the Revolution's achievements, including such classics as "Y en eso llegó Fidel" (And Then Fidel Arrived) and "El son de la alfabetización" (The Son of Literacy).

A regular at the *Bodeguita del Medio*, Carlos Puebla's strength – bolstered by his *cuarteto típico*, the **Tradicionales** – lay in his lilting, poetic subversion of country *guajira* and *guaracha* forms, singing in duo with his right-hand man and with key use of the *marimbula*. Nicknamed "the voice of the Revolution", he was Cuba's only notable political singer until the *nueva trova* movement of the early 1970s. In common with those later singers, however, political songs amounted to only a small portion of his output, and he also performed covers of *sones* by Matamoros and others.

New ballads

The **nueva trova** movement had clear links with the *nueva canción* (new song) composers appearing in this period throughout Latin America, but its emergence was entirely independent. The form was created by those who were reaching adolescence at the time of the Revolution – those for whom Fidel's maxim of "Within the Revolution, everything; outside the Revolution, nothing" seemed

¡Ojalá! – Let's hope! – is the name given to the recording studios **Silvio Rodríguez** built in Havana in the mid-1990s, and seems to epitomize a man who is arguably the most significant singer-songwriter of his generation in the world. One of those responsible for creating *nueva trova*, Rodríguez, like his close friend and fellow singer Pablo Milanés, has been one of the Revolution's major supporters and, for a time, one of its major wage earners. As well as building the studios where the Ojalá label records everything from Cuban rap to new, young *trovadores*, Rodríguez has recently been involved in directing the building of a large complex of state-owned studios in Havana, one of which can accommodate an entire symphony orchestra.

"In the beginning people didn't understand us," Rodríguez recalls. "Our songs were self-critical and there was no tradition of that, but they were songs full of commitment. The 1960s were the hot soup of what was happening – new things – and there was a moment when the *nueva trova* was in the front line of the ideological fight. Now we see clearly that it was and it is a privilege that before us no other generation of *trovadores* could be real protagonists."

While his actions have rarely cast a shadow on his steadfast relationship with the state – which he explores in the classics "Te Doy una Canción" (I Offer You A Song) and "Vamos Andar" (Let's Walk) – Rodríguez's undogmatic, metaphoric songs, many with a broad, international perspective, are very far from being a mouthpiece for the Revolution. Despite his membership of the Cuban parliament since 1992, he states that "I have never tried to be the voice of the Revolution – that is Fidel. It doesn't appeal to me to be something official because there hasn't been anything more anti-official than my songs, which are critical a lot of the time, show contradictions, doubts and reservations. But yes, I am someone who feels for the Revolution, who believes in it, who believes in Fidel. I feel it is necessary to have a sense of unity in terms of feelings for the country and the will to overcome all the problems we have. Even though I think it will always be like this, there will always be things to overcome and we are going to be in disagreement with a whole lot of things because that is life. One does things for human reasons not for ideological ones."

only logical given the experiences of their childhood. Great emphasis was placed on lyrics, replacing the love and nationalism of the old *trova* with an exploration of personal experience and desires, relating the contradictions and anxieties of life from within the context of a revolutionary society.

The new music drew on folk guitar traditions from Cuba and the wider Spanish-speaking world (which in turn were influenced by French *chanson*). Its singers became known as *canto-autores* (singer-songwriters), and while their philosophy and perspective were Cuban, they had something in common with North American and British singer-songwriters, as well as with singers such as Joan Manuel Serrat and Lluis Llach, struggling to maintain their Catalonian identity under Franco's dictatorship, and with the *nueva canción* singers of Chile and Argentina.

A key development in *nueva trova* occurred when a group of young musicians came together at Havana's ICAIC film school and recorded basic sessions with Cuba's leading composer and guitarist, **Leo Brouwer**. Among a group which included Vicente Feliú, Noel Nicola and Sara González were **Pablo Milanés** and **Silvio Rodríguez**, arguably the most influential singers of their generation in the Spanish-speaking world.

Both Milanés and Rodríguez have composed a huge body of work, including bittersweet love songs which captured a mood absent in other Cuban music. The root ingredients are those of the classic troubadour – vocals and solo acoustic guitar – though both have gone on to lead bands of varying size, their music developing in various directions, easily adapting itself to big arrangements.

Hallmarks of their songs are a sense of metaphysical emotion in joy and loss, an existential questioning (particularly of the vicissitudes of personal relationships), a pervasive use of metaphor and indirect subject, a sense of reflection and vulnerability and a non-gendered approach to the complex and uneven experience of love.

The Cuban experience is pre-eminent in the lyrics of both composers. Indeed, in the early 1990s, after a key tour to celebrate the achievements of the Revolution – singing from a huge repertoire of love songs on every aspect of island life – Silvio Rodríguez seemed to have followed in the steps of José Martí and taken on the mantle of national poet in the eyes of his public and the Cuban press. Between 1992 and 1996 he produced a triptych of albums, this time paring down from his big band to solo vocals and guitar. The feel of the records was almost deliberately amateur, with Rodríguez multi-tracking to duet with himself – keeping nuanced stumbles and asides. Each of the albums included a reflective sequence of powerful, sometimes bleak, songs rooted in cameos of individual lives. The whole process was a political statement in itself, a wooing of small audiences back to basics.

In the early 1990s, a new and more critical generation found a voice in the highly articulate songwriter **Carlos Varela**. His songs expressed the troubles of Cuban society and the frustrations of the island's youth, without much recourse to metaphor. His song "Guillermo Tell" (William Tell), for example, had a direct warning to the old generation of politicians: "William Tell, your son has grown up/And now he wants to shoot the arrow/It's his turn now to prove his valour/Using your very own bow!" Musically, Varela fluctuates between the old-style acoustic treatment of Milanés and Rodríguez and a rock (often heavy rock) backing. Recently he has recorded in Spain, producing material with a modern Spanish rock feel.

Jan Fairley

A fuller version of this article appears in The Rough Guide to World Music: Vol. 2 – the Americas, Asia and Pacific.

Discography

Compilations

Ahora Si! Here Comes Changui (Corason, Mexico). A superb set of *changui* from Grupo Changui de Guantánamo, Familia Valera Miranda and Grupo Estrellas de Campesinas.

Cuba Caribe (EMI Hemisphere, UK). A fine 1999 selection of contemporary bands unashamedly oriented around *salsa*. Hot tracks from Adalberto Alvarez, Juan Formell, Tamayo, and a *salsa*-rock creation from José Luis Cortés and NG La Banda.

Cuba Classics 2: Dancing with the Enemy and *Cuba Classics 3: ¡Diablo al Infierno!* (Luaka Bop/Warner, US). Compilations mixing the big names with some truly obscure recordings. Vol 2 covers the Cuban sound of the 1960s and 1970s; Vol 3 delves into the more eclectic 1980s and 1990s.

Cuba: the Essential Album (Union Square Music, UK). If you like the Buena Vista Social Club album and want to dig a bit deeper, this two-disc set released in 2004 is a perfect way in, featuring solo material from Buena Vista members along with plenty of other classic performers of traditional Cuban music.

Cuba, I Am Time (Blue Jackal Entertainment, US). This magnificent 4-CD compilation, released in 1997, features more than fifty artists and includes pretty much the best of each style.

Cuba Música Campesina (Auvidis, France). The best *campesina* anthology – a collection of bands capturing the country style in all its freshness. It even has a decent version of the most popular of Cuban songs, "Guantanamera".

Qué Linda Es Cuba (EGREM, Cuba). Many of the traditional greats, including Ibrahím Ferrer and Omara Portuondo of Buena Vista fame, appear on this CD, released in 2002 and presented as a collection of songs inspired by the island itself, with tributes to towns and cities up and down the land.

Vintage recordings

Various *Hot Cuban Dance Music 1909–37* (Harlequin, UK) and *The Cuban Danzón* 1906–29 (Arhoolie, US). Surprisingly good recordings of *son* in its earliest acoustic form – a transition between formal dance tunes and jazz.

Various *The Roots Of Salsa* and *Sextetos Cubanos* (Arhoolie, US). A pair of discs that move the story on to the 1920s and 1930s, and the developed *son* of the Havana sextetos.

Tracks are rough-and-ready and utterly charming.

Conjunto Chappotín y sus Estrellas *Tres Señores del Son* (Egrem, Cuba). The unfailingly inventive trumpeter Chappotín has a status in Cuban music on a level with Louis Armstrong in American jazz. This fabulous collection showcases some of the great figures of the 1940s and 1950s.

Conjunto Matamoros *Bailaré tu Son* (Tumbao, Spain). An entrancing selection of classic-era *son*, with hugely enjoyable vocals, performed by a typical old-style combo with congo, bongo, piano and trumpet.

Machito and his Afro-Cubans *Cha Cha Cha at the Palladium* (Tio, US). The powerful riffing and layered textures of big swing jazz bands brought to Cuban dance music to majestic effect.

Beny Moré *La Colección Cubana: Beny Moré* (Nascente, UK). A budget introduction to the master, compiled mainly from RCA recordings of the 1950s.

Orquesta Aragón *Riverside Years* (RCA International, US). The seminal *charanga* band, featuring the golden voice of Beny Moré and stunning piano solos from Perez Prado.

Arsenio Rodríguez *Dundunbanza* (Tumbao, Spain). This is irresistible Cuban-era Arsenio, featuring tracks recorded in Havana from 1946 to 1951 with a horn section led by Felix Chappotín.

Modern recordings

Adalberto Alvarez y Su Son *La Salsa Caliente* (Sonido/Vogue, France). This is a good example of pianist, singer and *guiro supremo* Alvarez's highly commercial sound – making the odd nod to *son* – that goes down a storm on his regular festival tours. *El Son de Adalberto suena cubano* (Bis Music, Cuba). An excellent danceable album with a polished delivery that confirms Alvarez' position at the helm of Cuban *salsa*.

Afro-Cuban All Stars *A Todo Cuba Le Gusta* (World Circuit, UK). A second wonderful record from the Buena Vista crew, with irresistible swing, formidable singing and great arrangements. Check also for the subsequent albums *Distinto, Diferente* (World Circuit, UK) and the more recent and more eclectic *Step Forward* (DM Ahora, Cuba).

Asere *Yo Soy El Son* (Label Bleu, France). This seven-piece outfit has created an album of authentically Cuban music, following in the traditions of *son* and more particularly *nueva trova*, while at the same time projecting a thoroughly modern sound and savvy look.

Buena Vista Social Club *Buena Vista Social Club* (World Circuit, UK). Big-band *son* of the old style, with historic songs imaginatively and seductively updated.

Cuarteto Patria *A Una Coqueta* (Corason, Mexico). Cuarteto Patria emerged in 1940 in Santiago de Cuba and is still going strong. Recorded in Cuba and Mexico between 1986 and 1993, this is a delightful selection of well-known *sones* and *boleros* with a gentle country sound.

Cubanismo *Cubanismo!* (Hannibal/ Ryko, UK). Jesús Alemañy has been reworking the classic Cuban trumpet sound over the past few years to stunning effect with his fifteen-piece group, Cubanismo. This was their first album.

Dan Den *Viejo Lazaro y Otros Exitos* (Qbadisc, US). Trombone-heavy dance band Dan Den hit a peak of popularity in the mid-1990s with their funky mix of contemporary Cuban dance grooves.

Estrellas de Areito *Los Heroes* (World Circuit, UK). The "Stars of Areito", a dream band including three generations of musicians, got together for a legendary five-day recording session in 1979. The sound ranges through classic *conjun* to *son*, *danzón* and *chachachá* into more jazz-oriented *descargas*.

Extraño Corazón *No Preguntes* (Unicornio, Cuba). An interesting album from one of Cuba's leading rock groups. Rock ballads interpreted with a Latin twist.

Ibrahim Ferrer *Mi Sueño* (World Circuit, UK). This was the album of achingly romantic *boleros* that Ferrer always wanted to make; though he died during its recording in 2005, there were enough demo tapes to finish the job. With a host of Buena Vista Social Club names involved, the high quality of musicianship is nothing less than guaranteed.

Roberto Fonseca *Zamazu* (Enja, Germany). The hottest name in Cuban jazz, this hugely talented pianist, a graduate of the Cuban School of Art, is assisted on his latest offering by his sax- and clarinet-playing partner, Javier Zalba, and an energetic rhythm section.

Celina González *Fiesta Guajira* (World Circuit, UK). An excellent compilation drawn from Celina's 1980s albums on the Havana-based Egrem label.

Rubén González *Introducing Rubén González* (World Circuit, UK). An utterly wonderful series of *son*/jazz improvisations, with elegant, restrained backing from the Buena Vista crew.

El Indio *Espíritu y Tradición* (Bis Music, Cuba). The first solo outing from one of the finest contemporary Cuban vocalists in the field of traditional *son*.

Irakere and Chucho Valdes *La Colección Cubana* (Nascente, UK). This budget-priced 1998 compilation exhibits the band's tradition of

combining virtuoso musicianship and sophisticated improvisation with a profound appreciation of their African roots.

Jóvenes Clásicos del Son *Tambor en el Alma* (Tumi, UK). This excellent septet continue on their mission to update Cuban *son* on this album released in 2003, full of energy and bringing a truly contemporary Cuban sound to one of the great Cuban musical traditions.

Pucho López *Buscando la Caja Negra* (Bis Music, Cuba). The second album from another much-talked-about jazz pianist, this is very much Cuban jazz, shot through with the kinds of rhythms the island is so famous for.

Juan Formell y Los Van Van *En el Malecón de La Habana* (Unicornio, Cuba). A live recording on a concert performed in 2001, this captures all the rapture and rhythm of one of Cuba's foremost *salsa* groups.

Polo Montañez *Guajiro Natural* (Lusafrica) and *Guitarra Mía* (Lusafrica). Both the debut album released in 2000 and the 2002 follow-up of this traditional *son* artist are rich and soulful, full of inspired vocals; explaining why Polo Montañez has enchanted Cuba and the wider world.

NG La Banda *En la Calle* (Qbadisc, US). The 1992 debut: a disc of flat-out performances and innovative arrangements.

Orquesta América *Cha Cha Cha*; *Bolero*; *Danzón*; *Guaracha-Son* (Tumi Music, UK). This series of four CDs is a helpful and authentic introduction to four of the principal traditional Cuban styles, performed by the latest incarnation of an all-time classic Cuban musical outfit, who are themselves credited as the creators of the cha cha cha. Each CD features collaborations with other Cuban greats such as Omara Portuondo and Chuco Valdés.

Orquesta Revé *La Explosión del Momento* (Real World, UK). Afro-Cuban *changui-son* at its best, played by its creators: quirky, rhythmic and infectious with sassy contemporary lyrics.

Orquesta Ritmo *Oriental Historia de la Ritmo Vol 1 and Vol 2* (Qbadisc, US). Retains the line-up of a traditional *charanga* band, but the arrangements and style of playing reflect the sharper, more punchy sound of modern Cuban dance music.

Omara Portuondo *Flor de Amor* (World Circuit, UK). Her second album since the Buena Vista explosion, this delightful collection of relaxing songs combines elements of Brazilian *bossa nova* with a distinctively Cuban base to compliment Portuondo's enchanting voice.

Elio Revé y su Charangón *Changui Homenaje – 45 años* (Tumi, UK). The second album from Elio Revé Jnr since he took over as band leader of what was Orquesta Revé, keeps the *changui-son* sound alive but updated to make this thoroughly modern *salsa*.

Alejandro Rodríquez Oliva 'Andito' *Por Muchas Razones* (Unicornio, Cuba). A recent offering from one of the greatest Cuban troubadours, working through a repertoire of *bolero* and *guaracha* numbers.

Compay Segundo *Compay Segundo y su Grupo, 1956–57* (Tumbao, Spain). Strong melodies with tight rhythm, perfect harmonies and a killer chorus, this reissue is a winner.

Septeto Nacional *Más Cuba Libres* (World Network, Germany). This celebration of the Septeto's 70th anniversary brought in some very special guests, including Buena Vista star Pío Leyva.

Sierra Maestra *Dundunbanza* (World Circuit, UK). Superb 1994 disc fusing sensual rhythms with witty lyrics and a wonderful, caressing mellowness.

Son 14 *Son 14* with Adalberto Alvarez (Tumi, UK). An unerring, joyously headlong selection of the very best from the group's eleven albums.

Los Van Van *Los Van Van: La Colección Cubana* (Nascente, UK). A budget-priced, sixty-minute selection of Los Van Van's finest 1980s and 1990s tracks.

Vieja Trova Santiaguera *Hotel Asturias* (NubeNegra, Spain). This experienced quintet support rough-voiced harmony vocals with *tres*, guitar, bass and hand percussion. A uniquely Cuban mixture of passion, sweetness and relaxation.

Rumba and Afro-Cuban music

Various *Afro-Cuba: A Musical Anthology* (Rounder, US). A useful selection of field and studio recordings from the main Santería cults.

Various *Tumi Cuba Classics Volume 3: Rumba* (Tumi, UK). Probably the best compilation of *rumba* available, mostly *guaguancó*, but with examples of *columbia*, *yambú* and others.

Clave y Guaguancó *Dejalá en la Puntica* (Egrem, Cuba). Contemporary street-corner *rumba* with an edge. Racing drums underpin richly textured *coros* and dramatic solo singers on this fine record.

Grupo Afrocuba De Matanzas *Rituales Afrocubanos* (Egrem, Cuba). Packed full of ritual music, this recording includes not only the usual songs of praise from the Lucumí religion, but also Arara and Bantu music from alternative African roots.

Los Muñequitos de Matanzas *Rumba Caliente* (Qbadisc, US). One of Cuba's top ensembles plays classic Cuban *rumba* – rich in African elements, using only percussion and vocals, and brilliantly melodic.

Lázaro Ros *Olorun* (Green Linnet/ Xenophile, US). Lázaro Ros is the best-known Cuban singer of religious music. Eleven *toques* for eleven *orishas*, with beautiful singing from Ros and Grupo Olórun, backed only by drumming.

Yoruba Andabo *El Callejón de los Rumberos* (PM, Spain). Accessible and exciting roots *rumba*: passionate singing above well-recorded drumming of startling complexity.

Nueva Trova

Pablo Milanés *Cancionero* (World Pacific, US). A marvellous 1993 anthology. Recommended.

Carlos Puebla *Carlos Puebla y sus Tradicionales* (Egrem-Artex, Canada). Some of Puebla's great songs – political and otherwise – with his classic quartet of guitar, *marimubula*, close harmonies and percussion.

Silvio Rodríguez *Cuban Classics 1: Canciones Urgentes* (Luaka Bop/

Warner). As the Cuban press has said of his songs: "Here we have the great epic poems of our days." This compilation shows the man at his very best – check the live recording of "Unicornio" in particular.

Carlos Varela *Monedas al Aire* (Qbadisc, US). Varela's revelatory first album, rocking up the familiar guitar with less metaphoric, more direct lyrics than *nueva canción*.

Hip-Hop and Reggaeton

Free Hole Negro *Superfinos Negros* (Rhino, UK). Not strictly a hip-hop album, but impossible to place in any one genre. The half-singing, half-rapping three-man outfit blend funk and rock with distinctively Cuban percussion to produce a refreshingly original set of songs.

Obsesión *Un Montón de Cosas* (EGREM, Cuba). Lyrically and musically the most innovative hip-hop album recorded in Cuba to date, the programmed beats are true to the classic hip-hop sound while there are also less familiar-sounding tracks based on live acoustic guitar and piano riffs.

Orishas *A Lo Cubano* (EMI, France). An inspired mix of traditional *son* and *rumba* riffs and instrumentation, over which rap alternates with the soulful voice of a *sonero*.

Orishas *Emigrante* (EMI, France). Orishas' second album sticks to the same formula as the first, though lyrically it's delivered with a little more venom.

Various *Cuban Hip-Hop All-Stars Vol. 1* (Papaya Records, Holland). True to its title, this 2001 recording features the cream of Cuban hip-hop artists, including Obsesión, Anónimo Consejo and Junior Clan. The tracks are all produced by the same man, Pablo Hererra, who sticks to the classic hip-hop formula of heavy beats and bass lines .

Various *Cuban Rap Ligas* (2good, France). Recorded in Havana and Paris, this compilation is a showcase for some of the best MCs in the Cuban capital. The production is polished and melodic,

with a lot of sampled speeches and a few tracks feature live scratching – a first for recorded Cuban hip-hop.

Various *Reggaeton a lo Cubano* (AhiNamá, Cuba). This album features the cream of Cuban reggaeton artists, including Cubanito 2002, Control Cubano and Klan Destino.

C

CONTEXTS | Discography

Cuban sport

Since the 1959 Revolution, Cuba has achieved a level of sporting success that would make any country proud, consistently finishing among the top ten in the Olympic Games' medals tables, the biggest test of a country's sporting prowess. Yet Cuban sportsmen and women keep unusually low profiles, attracting far less media attention than many of their foreign counterparts. Uniquely, this nation of just eleven million people has reached the highest international standards in a great many sports, but has remained outside of the professionalization and commercialization so rampant in the rest of the world.

Cuban sport prior to the Revolution

Before Castro, Cuba had had very few sports stars of truly international calibre. It was, however, one of the first nations to take part in the **Modern Olympic Games**, competing as one of the twenty countries present in Paris in 1900. It was at these games, the second of the modern era, and four years later in St Louis, that twelve of the fourteen Olympic **medals** collected by Cuban competitors before the Revolution were won. All twelve medals were in **fencing**, a sport at which Cubans continue to excel, and the hero was Ramón Fonst. Having won the épée event in Paris, he went on to secure two further victories in St Louis, thereby becoming the first man in Olympic history to win three individual gold medals.

Cuba was also one of the three original founding members of the **Central American and Caribbean Games**, the oldest regional international sporting tournament in the world. In October 1926, 269 sportsmen from Mexico, Cuba and Guatemala took part in the inaugural championships and in 1930 Cuba staged the second of these games, when women participated for the first time.

The majority of the Cuban population, however, were alienated not only from these successes but from organized sport in general, as only the privileged classes had access to athletic facilities. The sporting infrastructure was based predominantly on **private clubs**, from which black Cubans were almost always banned, reflecting the social divisions that marked society as a whole. It's no coincidence that the country's highest Olympic achievement was in fencing, a traditionally aristocratic discipline. Class determined participation in less competitive arenas, too: tennis, golf and sailing were all the exclusive domain of organizations such as the Havana Yacht Club or the Vedado Tennis Club. A large number of clubs belonged to the Unión Atlética Amateur de Cuba, a governing body for which, in order to become a member, applicants were required to supply a photograph confirming their skin colour. Many of the most popular spectator sports, though accessible to a broader swathe of the population, were just as representative of the socio-political situation. The appeal of horse racing, dog racing, cock fighting, billiards and boxing derived mainly from **gambling** and, particularly during the 1940s and 1950s, was inextricably tied up with tourism and corruption. Furthermore, no government during the six decades before the Revolution made any significant investment in sport. There were only 800 physical education teachers in a population of ten million, while just two percent of schoolchildren received any kind of formal physical education at all.

It was in **boxing** and **baseball** that popular sporting culture was most avidly expressed. These were genuinely sports for the masses, but though Cuba had one of the world's first national baseball leagues and hosted its own boxing bouts, the really big names and reputations were made in the US. Indeed, both baseball and boxing were brought to Cuba by Americans and owe much of their popularity to American commerce and organization. With such close links between the two countries during the years of the "pseudo-republic" when a significant number of Americans lived and worked in Cuba, very few talented sportsmen went unnoticed by the fight organizers and league bosses on the other side of the Florida Straits. Almost all the biggest names in these two sports during this period – baseball players like **Tony Pérez**, **José Cardenal** and **Tito Fuentes** and boxers such as **Benny Paret** and **Kid Chocolate** – gained their fame and fortune in the US. Exploitation, particularly of boxers, was common and a significant proportion of them were simply pawns in a corrupt world of fight rigging and bribery.

Sport and the Revolution

With sport prior to 1959 characterized by corruption, social discrimination and a generally poor standing in international competitions, the revolutionary government had more than enough to get its teeth into. Led by Fidel Castro himself, who has always shown a keen interest in sport, under the new regime the entire system of participation was shaken up and restructured.

The new ideology of sport

Like the Russians before them, the Cubans developed a whole new ideology around sport and its role in society. Though borrowing heavily from the Soviet model, this ideology was very much a Cuban creation, influenced as much by the desire to make Cuba a great sporting nation as by the desire to institute social change. Rather than looking to Marx as a guide, the revolutionaries chose the ideas of Baron **Pierre de Coubertin**, the Frenchman responsible for the revival of the Olympic Games in 1896. Coubertin believed that one of the reasons the Ancient Greeks had reached such high levels of social and cultural achievement was the emphasis they placed on physical activity. Rejecting the neo-Marxist argument that the competitive element of sport promotes social division and elitism, the Cubans adopted Coubertin's basic premise that participation in sport was capable of bridging differences in politics, race and religion, thus encouraging feelings of brotherhood and social equality. Believing that it is not the nature of sport but the way in which it is approached and practised that would determine its effect, the Cuban state made sport one of the priorities in the transformation of society.

Sport and physical education were incorporated into the wider revolutionary goals of education in general, and were considered inseparable from the process of development towards Che Guevara's concept of *El Hombre Nuevo* – the New Man (see box, p.599) – one of the cornerstones of Cuban communist theory. The Cubans claim that as well as promoting better health and fitness, organized

Just as few governments have shown the kind of interest and involvement in sport that the Cuban government has demonstrated since 1959, so there are even fewer political leaders who have shown the personal commitment to sport that Fidel Castro has always had. He has made numerous speeches over the years, demanding that Cubans achieve more in international competitions, lauding Cuban performances at major championships, and generally promoting participation in sport and sporting excellence. One such speech, in 1959, pre-empted the creation of INDER, and many of Castro's goals for Cuban sport became the objectives of that organization. He has, on more than one occasion, involved himself in disputes over scandals implicating Cuban sports stars, and rarely misses the chance to greet a winning team's homecoming from an overseas tournament.

This enthusiasm stems from Castro's own sporting prowess, attested to in photographs in museums and restaurants around the country depicting the Cuban leader making cameo appearances at baseball and basketball games, as well as on the football field and in numerous other physical activities. His involvement, however, goes well beyond political gimmickry, and can be traced back to his high-school days at the Belen school in Havana, where he played basketball and baseball and, in 1944, was voted the top high-school athlete in the country. In his early university years he continued to play basketball and baseball, trained as a 400-metre runner, and was even rumoured to have been scouted by American professional baseball teams. It is Castro's belief that his own background in sports had a major influence on his later life, and he has said that had he not been a sportsman he would never have been a revolutionary, asserting that it was his physical training as an athlete that had allowed him to fight as a guerrilla in the Revolutionary War.It is not surprising then that as early as January 1959, within a month of the rebel victory, Castro made a lengthy speech in the Ciudad Deportiva and declared: "I am convinced that sporting activity is necessary for this country. It's embarrassing that there is so little sport … The Cuban results in international competitions up until now have been shameful."

It would be shortsighted to suppose that there has been no political motivation behind Castro's commitment to sport. However, no one in Cuba has been more insistent than Castro that the system should be free of exploitation and that everyone should enjoy the right to participate. He considers the achievements in sport since the Revolution a matter of intense pride, as evidenced in his public outrage at the confiscation of medals from four Cuban athletes at the 1999 Pan American Games. Describing the results of the tests that found traces of steroids in three weightlifters and cocaine in the high jump world record holder, Javier Sotomayor, as "a colossal lie", he personally appeared in a two-day televised hearing, demanding that the medals be returned.

physical activities and games encourage discipline, responsibility, willpower, improved social communication skills, a cooperative spirit, internationalism, and generally contribute to a person's ethical and moral character. Few governments have placed such emphasis on sport, and the right of all Cubans to participate in physical education and organized sports was even included in several clauses of the 1976 Cuban Constitution. This principal commitment – that every Cuban has the right to practise sport and should be guaranteed the necessary conditions to do so – paved the way for the changes made in this sphere from the very start of revolutionary change after 1959.

The transformation of post-revolutionary Cuban sport began in earnest on February 23, 1961, with the creation of **INDER** (National Institute of Sport, Physical Education and Recreation). Still very much an active institution today, this body was directly responsible for carrying out the programmes of *masividad*, or sport for the masses, which formed the foundation of the new system. With the creation of INDER, a campaign was launched aiming to diversify the number of sporting activities available to the public, to eliminate exclusivity and to involve every citizen in some kind of regular physical activity.

The "cradle-to-grave" politics of the Revolution applied as much to sport as anything else, and the Cubans wasted no time in introducing children to the benefits of physical exercise. Under the banner of slogans such as "the home is the gymnasium", INDER has always encouraged parents to actively pursue the physical health of their **children**, with classes in massage and physical manipulation offered for babies as young as 45 days old. Early in the morning during term time, it is still common to see groups of schoolchildren doing exercises in the local parks and city squares with their teachers. These places are also where the so-called **circulos de abuelos** meet, groups of elderly people, usually past retirement age, performing basic stretches together. No section of society was exempted as sport and exercise became ingrained in the Cuban way of life, with many of the most significant changes taking place during INDER's first decade.

In 1966 legislation was passed guaranteeing workers paid leisure time for recreational activities, and in 1967 entrance charges to sport stadiums and arenas were abolished, making not just participation in sport but also spectating a right of all Cuban citizens. (Spectator sport is still easily accessible to the masses today, with entry charges generally only one or two pesos.) In 1971, ten years after the creation of INDER, the success of its campaigns was tangible. The number of students actively involved in one sport or another had risen from under 40,000 to just over a million, while it was estimated in a UNESCO-backed report that a further 1.2 million people were participating in some kind of regular physical exercise.

Making champions

Mass participation in sport was to form the base of the Coubertin-inspired **pyramid** that underpins Cuban sport and accounts, to a large extent, for the tremendous success of Cuban sportsmen and women over the last thirty years. With millions of people involved in sport throughout the country at the base level of the pyramid, the subsequent levels, leading up to the summit, are determined by regional and specialized institutions set up in order to maximize the possibility of discovering potential champions. From primary schools to universities, physical education is a compulsory part of the curriculum and the progress of all pupils is monitored through regular **testing**. Thus, at as early as seven or eight years of age, the most promising young athletes can be selected for the **EIDE** (Escuelas de Iniciación Deportiva Escolar) **sports school**, of which there is one in every province. Here, pupils continue with their academic studies while their sporting progress, usually in a specific discipline, is even more closely watched. Physiological tests, trainers' reports and interprovincial competitions all form a regular part of school life at the EIDE, where pupils remain until they are fifteen or sixteen. The best EIDE pupils are then selected for the **ESPA** (Escuelas Superiores de Perfeccionamiento Atlético) schools, one stage below the Equipo Nacional – the National Team – which sits at the top of the pyramid. Using this structure, the Cubans have demonstrated the reciprocal relationship between the top and the bottom of the pyramid: mass participation produces world champions and, in turn, success in international competitions encourages greater numbers to practise sport.

Ironically, the most American of sports is also the most Cuban, and **baseball** stands out as one of the few aspects of US culture which the revolutionaries continued to embrace after 1959. It was introduced to the island in the late 1800s by American students studying in Cuba and by visiting sailors who would take on the local workers in Cuban dockyards. The first officially organized game took place between the Matanzas Béisbol Club and the Havana Béisbol Club on December 27, 1874. Frowned upon by the Spanish colonial rulers, who even banned the game for a period, baseball really took off following the end of the Spanish-American War in 1898. A national league was established, but the Major League in the US dominated the fortunes of the best players. Cuban and American baseball developed in tandem during the pre-revolutionary era, as the island became a supply line to the US teams with players like Adolfo Luque, Conrado Marrero and Miguel Angel González, who coached the World Series-winning St Louis Cardinals team, among the numerous Cubans to be won over by Major League riches. These were almost exclusively white players, as black Cubans suffered discrimination in both countries and were mostly restricted either to the black leagues or the Cuban league, in which Habana, Almendares, Marianao and Santa Clara were the only teams competing.

Since 1959, Cuban baseball has transformed itself from the stepchild of the US Major League to one of the most potent, independent forces in the game. The **national league** now consists of sixteen teams instead of four and has gone from professional to amateur without losing any of the excitement that characterizes its hottest confrontations. The national team dominates international baseball and has done so since the early 1980s, winning Olympic titles and unbeaten in the **Intercontinental Baseball Cup** – the baseball world championships – since 1983. However, while the national team has made the biennial baseball world championships a celebration of Cuban sporting achievement, the big question that remains is whether Cuba's amateurs can hold their own against the professional players of the US, who up until recently have played no part in international competitions. The 2000 Sydney Olympics changed that, with Cuba losing to the US in the final, but the first test came in 1999 when the Baltimore Orioles made an unprecedented visit to Cuba to take on the national team. In a good-spirited game the visitors stole a 3-2 victory, but perhaps more significant than the result was the visit itself, characterized by a friendly rivalry and a mutual respect in defiance of the two nations' political antagonism.

That Cuban players are among the best in the world is in little doubt, a point sorely proven by a number of Cuban nationals who have escaped Cuba and signed huge contracts with **Major League** clubs. Some of the biggest names in recent years are the Hernández brothers. Having signed a six-million-dollar contract with the Florida Marlins, Liván Hernández took the team to World Series victory and was named MVP (Most Valuable Player), while his brother Orlando, who was denied a place on the Olympic team that went to Atlanta in 1996, followed him by signing with the New York Yankees and helped them win a handful of World Series as well. In October 2003, Cuban stars Maels Rodriguez and Yobal Dueñas defected to the US with the intent of playing professional ball there, and another half-dozen came ashore in the Florida Keys a year later. One of the reasons for the continued defections could be the shortage of equipment engendered by Cuba's poor economy, with some players reporting that they had to nail broken bats together in order to keep playing. By no means all the best Cuban players have left, however, with Omar Linares probably the most famous name to have rejected Major League offers in favour of staying in Cuba.

The nurturing of potentially world-class athletes is taken so seriously in Cuba that each individual sport has to be officially sanctioned before it is recognized as suitable for competition standard. The basic principle behind this is specialization, and since the Revolution the Cubans have made sure each of their major sports is developed to a high international standard before another is introduced, an approach that leaves very little to chance.

Many of the **coaches** in Cuba during the first two decades of the Revolution were supplied by other Communist bloc countries, but as time has worn on INDER has had time to train its own experts, most of them at the Instituto Superior de Cultura Física "Comandante Manuel Fajardo" in Havana. Cuban coaches have had almost as much success as the athletes they have trained, working in over forty countries, particularly Spain and throughout Latin America.

World beaters

In the biggest test of a nation's sporting prowess, the **Olympic Games**, the Cubans have been among the top twelve in the medals tables since 1976, when they ranked eighth at the Montréal Olympics. Despite finishing fourth in the Moscow Games in 1980, Cubans consider their finest performance to have been at the Barcelona Olympics in 1992, when their fourteen gold medals helped to place them fifth in the final rankings, ahead of countless other, far wealthier, countries. The result in Moscow was tarnished by the stigma of not having competed against some of the best sporting nations in the world, notably the US, which chose to boycott the tournament.

It has been at the Olympics that some of the best-known and most successful Cuban sportsmen and women have made their mark on the rest of the world. One of the first was **Alberto Juantorena**, who remains the only man in Olympic history to win both 400-metre and 800-metre events, which he did in Montréal in 1976. It was during the same era that the best Cuban boxer in history reigned supreme, **Teófilo Stevenson**, three times Olympic champion and one-time potential opponent of Muhammad Ali. Stevenson was prevented from fighting the self-proclaimed "greatest of all time" by the governing body of the sport during the 1970s, which ruled it illegal for an amateur to fight a professional. Even Ali himself, in a visit to Havana in 1996, admitted that had the two ever met it would have been a close-run contest. Unable to compete in the professional fight extravaganzas which make all the headlines in boxing, the Olympic Games have been the best opportunity for Cuban boxers to show off to the world, regularly taking home a clutch of medals. In Athens in 2004, Cuban boxers took an impressive eight medals, including five golds, more than any other country. The most famous and successful Cuban boxer since the 1990s has been Félix Savón, whose gold at the Sydney Olympics in 2000 saw him triumph in his category for the third consecutive Games and emulate Stevenson's great achievement.

In the 1990s **Javier Sotomayor**, known as "El Príncipe de las Alturas" – The Prince of Heights – was recognized as the best high jumper in the world, holder of the world record and gold-medal winner in Barcelona. Though the decade finished on a sour note for him, after being charged in the 1999 Pan American Games with having taken cocaine the night before he competed, he rode the storm out and took home a silver medal at Sydney, his final Olympic Games appearance. Among the notable winners in Cuba's ninth-place achievement in

Sydney was Anier García, who stormed to victory in the 110-metre hurdles. Cuban track and field athletes have been among the most respected in the world over the last thirty years, with García and Sotomayor, along with the long jumper **Ivan Pedroso** and the 800-metre specialist **Ana Fidelia**, medal winners since the turn of the millennium.

Countless other athletic disciplines have given Cuba world champions, including volleyball, wrestling and weightlifting, while this small island nation has long made the result of the **Central American and Caribbean Championships** – in which Mexico, Colombia, Venezuela and Puerto Rico, amongst others, compete – a foregone conclusion, having finished first every time since 1966. Perhaps even more impressive is Cuba's habitual second place, beaten only by the US, in the **Pan American Games**, a championship contested by all the countries of the American continent. Whether Cuba's eleventh position in the medals table in the 2004 Athens Olympics (the first time it has dropped out of the top ten in three decades) is a blip, delayed reaction to the problems of the Special Period or the beginning of a decline in standards remains to be seen.

Conspicuous by its absence from Cuban world successes in sport is **football (soccer)**. The Cuban team qualified for the World Cup in 1938 but haven't appeared in the tournament since, though they came reasonably close to going to France in 1998 before being knocked out in the regional qualifiers by Jamaica. Support for the game is generally increasing, with the government well aware of the benefits of improving the national standard at the most popular sport in the world. The popularity of football in Cuba has visibly increased since the France '98 games, with local parks and fields now nearly as often host to football matches as baseball games. Although football still has a long way to go, with the national baseball and basketball leagues attracting far more attention and greater crowds, the game's grassroots have long since been laid down and are finally starting to grow.

Books

There has been more written on Cuba than perhaps any other Latin American country, with numerous titles devoted to unravelling the intricate politics between the US and Cuba. These make compelling – if sometimes heavy-going – reading, while a more palatable introduction to Cuban culture and politics can be gained through the cornucopia of fiction by Cuban writers both contemporary and classic, much of it translated into English and widely available. There are also plenty of novels written in English by exiled Cubans and non-Cubans, most famously Ernest Hemingway and Graham Greene. Travel writing and photography are also well represented – some of the best coffee-table photographic books can be bought in Cuba itself. Secondhand books are also widely available in Havana with a cluster of secondhand bookstands in Habana Vieja and many others throughout the city. You can often find core Cuban texts about the Revolution: transcripts of interviews with Fidel, for example, sometimes translated into English. Sadly, these interesting tomes are often let down by poor translation and proofreading but are worth a browse none the less.

History, politics and biography

Juan M. de Aguila *Cuba: Dilemmas of a Revolution* (Westview Press). A good reference book for students of the Revolution, with well-selected topics and plenty of useful subheadings. While it's concerned more with the questions that the Revolution has raised rather than the story of what actually happened, the pattern of historical events still forms the framework of the intelligent, balanced discussions.

Leslie Bethell (ed) *Cuba: A Short History* (Cambridge University Press). Somewhat incomplete and at times lacking in coherence, this history nevertheless covers some periods well, such as the two decades prior to the 1959 Revolution.

Simon Calder and Emily Hatchwell *Cuba in Focus: A Guide to the People, Politics and Culture* (Latin American Bureau, UK; Interlink Publishing, US). A succinct overview of the country and its history, touching on a lively variety of different subject areas, from race to tourism, all dealt with intelligently and in just enough detail to be informative. Small enough to read from cover to cover on the plane.

CIA Targets Fidel (Ocean Press). A word-for-word reproduction of a CIA report compiled in 1967 and declassified in 1994, detailing the various plots that were hatched in the US, some in coordination with the Mafia, to assassinate or depose Fidel Castro during the early 1960s. Preceding the report is an interview conducted with a former head of Cuban State Security, who reveals that the Cuban Ministry of the Interior's own files list 612 US-backed plots against Castro from 1959 to 1993, also suggesting that the same body of CIA operations was behind the assassination of John F. Kennedy. Unsurprisingly, the report makes rather tedious reading, but the candid way in which Castro's assassination is discussed is quite eye-opening.

Leycester Coltman *The Real Fidel Castro* (Yale University Press, US and UK). Succeeds where so many biographies of the man fail in being both a balanced and highly readable account of Castro's extraordinary life. Refreshing in its political neutrality and its animated, non-academic style, this is also a highly accessible insight into the Cuban Revolution itself.

Dick Cluster and Rafael Harnández *The History of Havana* (Palgrave Macmillan, UK & US). One of the few books in English to cover the history of the Cuban capital specifically, it provides a history of Cuba too. This engaging, people-centred account takes a social and cultural perspective as much as an economic and political one and is peppered with lively personal testimonies helping to make the facts of the past more pertinent and more real.

Clive Foss *Fidel Castro* (Sutton Publishing). Very readable in both length and style, this is a well-balanced mini-biography of the Cuban leader, untainted by political leanings. An engaging mix of anecdotal information, storytelling and basic fact relaying make this a highly accessible introduction to the man for anyone wanting to avoid too much focus on endless academic debate over Castro's *true* political character and philosophies.

Fernando D. García and Oscar Sola (ed) *Che: Images of a Revolutionary* (Pluto Press, UK and US). An easy-going biography of Che Guevara, packed with great photos as well as extracts from Che's own writings. This title goes into just the right amount of depth for anyone with an interest in the man but wanting to avoid the excruciating detail of other Che biographies.

Guillermo Cabrera Infante *Mea Cuba* (Faber and Faber, UK). A collection of writings on Cuba from 1968 to 1993 by a Cuban exile and opponent of the current regime. His vehement criticisms of Fidel Castro are uncompromising and can make for rather heavy reading,

but there are plenty of thoughtful and eyebrow-raising commentaries from a man who is clearly passionate about his subject matter.

Franklin W. Knight *Slave Society in Cuba during the Nineteenth Century* (o/p). A detailed and sensitively handled treatment of all aspects of slavery in Cuba, from the lives of the slaves and race relations, to the broader political and economic context in which slavery evolved. The book is packed with information and the author thankfully refrains from over-intellectualizing the topic.

Geraldine Lievesley *The Cuban Revolution: Past, Present and Future Perspectives* (Palgrave Macmillan, UK). A studious and sympathetic analysis of the Cuban Revolution with some particularly interesting assessments of Cuba in the 1990s and in the new millennium. With extended discussions of some relatively specialist subject matters, this book is more suitable for readers with some prior knowledge of the Revolution wanting to dig a bit deeper.

Peter Marshall *Cuba Libre: Breaking the Chains?* (o/p). Lively and upbeat analysis of the Revolution, highlighting its achievements without ignoring the mistakes. Written in 1987, it is somewhat outdated but excellent chapters on education, the economy and the management of the Revolution make this an above-average study.

Luis Martínez-Fernández *Fighting Slavery in the Caribbean: The Life and Times of a British Family in Nineteenth-Century Havana* (M.E. Sharpe). Using the well-charted experiences of an Englishman working in the foreign office and living in Cuba with his family, this is a vivid social and economic history of Cuba in the mid-nineteenth century. Full of fascinating detail about the niceties of Havanan society, the drive for abolition of slavery and plenty of observations about the city itself.

Professor José Cantón Navarro *History of Cuba* (Cuba Editorial SIMAR S.A.). A political overview of Cuban history through the eyes of a revolutionary historian. A somewhat revisionist and romantic version of events, but interesting nevertheless.

Hernando Calvo Ospina *Bacardí, The Hidden War* (Pluto Press). A revealing account uncovering the secret operations and dealings of the world's most famous rum producer and its attempts to both undermine and overthrow the Castro regime. The author charts the history of the company from its inception and shows it to have been corrupt right from the beginning, but the text does sometimes lapse into a political rant and this may be too much information on this one particular subject for some readers.

Louis A. Pérez, Jr. *Cuba: Between Empires 1878–1902* (University of Pittsburgh Press); *Cuba: Between Reform and Revolution* (Oxford University Press). The first is a scholarly and perspicacious account of how the United States managed to supplant Spanish suzerainty, despite Cuba's struggle for independence. Superbly researched and very readable, the second title tends towards economic issues, though it's still far from one-dimensional.

Louis A. Pérez, Jr. (ed) *Slaves, Sugar and Colonial Society* (Scholarly Resources Inc, US). An extensive collection of accounts written by predominantly US and British travellers to Cuba during the nineteenth century. Divided into eight chapters, each covering a different topic, from religion to crime, as well as sugar and slavery, many of the essays are intriguing not just for their reflection

of Cuban society during the period, but also for the insights into the cultural background of the writers themselves.

Robert E. Quirk *Fidel Castro* (W.W. Norton). An impressively detailed biography of the Cuban president, at times quite critical of its subject matter but without the kind of thoughtless Castro-bashing that other commentators indulge in.

Roger Ricardo *Guantánamo, The Bay of Discord: The Story of the US Military Base in Cuba* (Ocean Press). A brief history of the role of Guantánamo Bay in the ongoing standoff between the US and Cuba.

Julio Le Riverend *Breve Historia de Cuba* (Editorial de Ciencias Sociales, Cuba). Written by one of Cuba's leading historians, and also available in English, at times this history lapses into political rhetoric and revolutionary propaganda, but it does provide some useful insights as well as information often missed by non-Cuban authors of the country's history.

Isaac Saney *Cuba A Revolution in Motion* (Fernwood Publishing). An accessible and intelligent account of the mechanics behind the Revolution written from a Marxist standpoint. This is an essential read for anyone wishing to see how the Revolution estimates itself. It also provides up-to-date information on how Cuba expects to carry the Revolution forward over coming decades.

Rosalie Schwartz *Pleasure Island – Tourism and Temptation in Cuba* (Bison Books, US). A must for anyone bemused by the stark contrast between apparent prostitution and *jineterismo* throughout the island and the upstanding ideals of the Revolution, Schwartz's readable and lively history charts the history of tourism in Cuba during its pre-Revolution days and draws a few comparisons with its modern-day incarnation. The book cuts to the heart of the matter, analysing the political and economic benefits and backhanders as well as giving a fascinating account of the role played by the Mafia. Essential reading for those wishing to be clued-up visitors.

Geoff Simons *Cuba: From Conquistador to Castro* (Macmillan, UK). An incisive and thought-provoking history of Cuba, which aims to convey an understanding of events within their wider context, such as the religious climate in Europe during the Spanish colonization of Cuba. The writing is spiced up by the author's boldness in expressing his anti-imperialist views and his scathing account of US politics and capitalism.

Jaime Suchlicki *Cuba: From Columbus to Castro and Beyond* (Brassey's). Now in its fifth edition,

this is one of the best up-to-date complete histories of the country and should be one of the first books to read for anyone interested in the subject matter. Concise yet comprehensive, extremely well informed yet not too wordy or academic, and refreshingly the author has no political axe to grind.

Hugh Thomas *Cuba or the Pursuit of Freedom* (Da Capo Press). Written with a right-wing slant, this authoritative and exhaustive history of Cuba from 1762 to the present day is meticulously researched, full of fascinating facts and immensely readable despite its epic proportions.

Stephen Williams *Cuba: The Land, the History, the People, the Culture* (Prion). A highly enjoyable and easy-going coffee-table read, decorated with a lively collection of illustrations and photographs.

Culture and society

Roberto González Echevarría *The Pride of Havana: A History of Cuban Baseball* (Oxford University Press, US). Painstakingly detailed, this exhaustive history of Cuba's national sport may prove a little too detailed for the casual reader, but aficionados of the game should appreciate this passionate attempt to record and explain Cuban baseball's role in the history of the game itself as well as its unique evolution on the island.

Stephen Foehr *Waking Up In Cuba* (Sanctuary Publishing, UK). An entertaining and fascinating portrait of contemporary Cuba as reflected in its music and musicians. This lively account is based on the author's own experiences on the island and his encounters with a wide and intriguing range of music makers, from ground-breaking rappers and

reggae artists to pioneers of the *nueva trova* movement and the Buena Vista Social Club.

Jonathan Futrell and Lisa Linder *Up in Smoke* (Conran Octopus, UK). An artistically presented guide to the culture of cigar production and smoking, with a chapter dedicated to Cuba, as well as advice on cigar etiquette, what to look for in a cigar and a selection of recommended smokes.

Guillermo Cabrera Infante *Holy Smoke* (Faber and Faber, UK; Overlook Press, US). A pompous and entertaining tribute to the Havanan cigar, full of painful puns and obscure references.

Ian Lumsden *Machos, Maricones and Gays* (Latin American Bureau, UK;

Temple University Press, US). One of the few available books that discusses homosexuality in Cuba. A thorough and sensitive treatment, covering the history of homophobia in Cuba and such complex issues as the Cuban approach to AIDS.

Robin D. Moore *Nationalizing Blackness: Afrocubanismo and Artistic Revolution in Havana, 1920–1940* (University of Pittsburgh Press). A clear and compelling analysis of the cultural and artistic role of black Cubans during an era of prejudice. A good introduction to black culture in Cuba.

Pepe Navarro *La Voz del Caimán* (Blume, Spain). This engaging collection of short encounters with Cubans from all walks of life aims to portray the lives, opinions and aspirations of a society in all its complexity. This is an ideal book to dip into at any page and the cast really does make up an impressively diverse set of occupations and lifestyles with all kinds of fascinating anecdotes and insights of modern Cuba.

Pedro Peréz Sarduy and Jean Stubbs (eds) *AfroCuba: An Anthology of Cuban Writing on Race, Politics and Culture* (Latin American Bureau, UK; Ocean Press, US). Essays and extracts written by black Cuban writers covering religion, race relations, slavery, plantation culture and a fascinating variety of other topics. This anthology contains a wide variety of writing styles with excerpts from plays, novels, poems and factual pieces, but some of the quality of the texts is lost in the occasionally stilted translations.

C. Peter Ripley *Conversations With Cuba* (The University of Georgia Press). The framework for this illuminating text is the set of seven trips made by the author to Cuba

since 1991. Through his account of these visits Ripley provides a forum for the people he meets and befriends to express views on an array of fascinating subjects. These rare recordings of views from the street offer some everyday Cuban perspectives, rarely heard outside the island, on such issues as the Elián González saga and the US trade embargo.

Daisy Rubiera Castillo *Reyita The life of a Black Cuban Woman in the Twentieth Century* (Ocean Press). Told in the first person to her grand-daughter, *Reyita* is a very personal account of the life of a black woman which spans most of the twentieth century. Told without emphasis, the political and social conditions emerge incidentally as she relates growing up in poverty in the east of the island, the aftermath of slavery and racial prejudice of the 1920s and 1930s as well as life after the Revolution. It is simply told, with many details seeming at first irrelevant, but all go towards creating a rounded picture of a life typical of many others.

Sue Steward *Salsa: Musical Heartbeat of Latin America* (Thames and Hudson, UK). Tracing the roots of *salsa* and examining its place in its various home territories, from Miami to London, with three chapters concentrating specifically on Cuba.

Philip Sweeney *The Rough Guide to Cuban Music* (The Rough Guides). An excellent handbook charting everything you'll need to know about Cuban music including detailed biographies of musical luminaries and a panoramic historical background to the music scene. Particularly useful are the glossary of musical terms and the discographies that will help you wade through the plethora of CDs available.

Travel writing

John Duncan *In The Red Corner: A Journey Into Cuban Boxing* (Yellow Jersey Press, UK). The story of an English journalist's attempt to go to Cuba and arrange the fight of the century, between the great Cuban heavyweight Felix Savón and Mike Tyson. Effectively two books in one, around half the chapters are dedicated to the history of Cuban boxers and can become a little dry, but the observations of contemporary life in Cuba and all its idiosyncrasies are both perceptive and witty and should strike a chord with most Westerners who have visited Cuba.

Carlo Gébler *Driving through Cuba: An East-West Journey* (o/p). Down-to-earth account of the author's journey around the island, covering most of the major tourist destinations, prior to the collapse of trade with the Soviet Union. Straightforward writing and unpretentious observations of Cuban life and customs, sprinkled with historical references.

Che Guevara *The Motorcycle Diaries* (Fourth Estate, UK; Verso, US). Written before he met Fidel Castro, this lively read portrays a side to Che rarely discussed or revealed. The book follows his motorcycle tour of South America with his friend and fellow doctor Alberto Granado. Amusing but rarely gripping, a large part of the book's appeal is the contrast it casts with Che's later life.

🏃 John Jenkins (ed) *Travelers' Tales of Old Cuba* (Ocean Press). A worthy collection of eighteen stories and accounts of Cuba by travellers through the ages. Arranged chronologically, the tales start with Alexander O. Exquemelin's undated account of the pirate Henry Morgan's attempt to sack a city and concludes in 1958 with Frank

Ragano and Selwyn Raab's fun vignette relating life in the Mafia's casinos. What's fun about this book is comparing old Havana with your own modern-day experiences. Although many of the authors may be unheard-of, a smattering of renowned writers make an appearance, with a delicate description of Havana and Santa Clara by Anais Nin and a Hemingway appearance by proxy.

Louis A. Pérez (ed) *Impressions of Cuba in the Nineteenth Century: The Travel Diary of Joseph J. Dimock* (Scholarly Resources, Inc.). An elaborate first-person account of many aspects of Cuba, including the lives of slaves, Spanish and Creoles. At times unwittingly comic, it is as revealing of Cuba as it is of the opinionated stuffed-shirt author.

🏃 Alan Ryan (ed) *The Reader's Companion to Cuba* (Harcourt Brace and Co., US). Twenty-three accounts by foreign visitors to Cuba between 1859 and the 1990s, including trips to Havana and Santiago de Cuba by Graham Greene and fascinating observations on race relations by Langston Hughes. A broad range of writers, from novelists and poets to journalists and naturalists, covers an equally broad range of subject matter, from places and people to slavery and tourism.

Stephen Smith *The Land of Miracles: A Journey Through Modern Cuba* (Little, Brown, and Co). Entertaining accounts of all the important aspects of Cuban culture from classic cars and Santería to love hotels and Guantánamo are surpassed by Smith's ability to pinpoint the foreigner's experience in Cuba.

Wallace and Barbara Smith *Bicycling Cuba* (W.W. Norton, US and UK). This specialist travel guide written specifically for people intending to tour Cuba by bicycle includes some interesting and sensitively written essays as well as specialist sections that feature detailed route descriptions, airline policies on bikes and a glossary of cycling terms in Spanish. The authors have spent a total of over six months pedalling around Cuba.

Photography and architecture

Juliet Barclay and Martin Charles *Havana: Portrait of a City* (o/p). A graceful social history of the city filled with intriguing vignettes complemented by skilful photography.

Alexandra Black and Simon McBride *Living in Cuba* (Scriptum Editions, UK). Essentially a photographic portrait of the interiors of houses and other preserved colonial buildings around Cuba. The book does a fine job of displaying Cuba's vibrant architectural heritage but, despite its title, shows very little of the environment in which everyday life unfolds. A little like a museum handbook, in nonetheless splendid style.

John Comino-James *A Few Streets, A Few People* (Dewi Lewis Publishing, UK). Depicting everyday street scenes and people in the Cayo Hueso district of Havana, this photo collection captures the essence of Centro Habana life, so much of it lived outdoors and on view.

Gianni Costantino *Cuba: Land and People* (Ediciones Gianni Costantino, Italy). Sold in bookstores throughout Cuba, this collection of mostly postcard-style photography is a relatively dispassionate depiction of Cuban society, predominantly covering cities, landscapes and architecture, with the occasional street scene.

Walker Evans *Havana 1933* (Thames & Hudson, UK; Pantheon, US). An exceptional set of photographs taken by Walker Evans, a US photographer commissioned to visit Cuba to supply pictures for a book entitled *The Crime of Cuba* by Carleton Beals. A highly evocative portrayal of 1930s Havana, illustrating, among other facets of the culture, the poverty of the time.

María E. Haya *Cuba La Fotografía de Los Años 60* (Cuba Fototeca de Cuba). A collection of definitive photographs by Raúl Corrales, Ernesto Fernández, Mario García Joya, Alberto Korda and Osvaldo Salas of the revolutionary struggle and the early years after its triumph. Iconic and atmospheric, they are a moving tribute to the era's optimism.

Tania Jovanovic *Cuba ¡Que Bola! a photographic essay* (Ocean Press). Through lucid and evocative black-and-white portraits Jovanovic perfectly captures the exuberance, camaraderie and *joie de vivre* of Cuba.

Christophe Loviny *Cuba by Korda* (Ocean Press). Alberto Korda was the man who photographed the iconic portrait of Che Guevara and unwittingly created the most popular T-shirt image of all time. This collection of his work includes numerous other classic shots, such as those of Castro and his rebels in the Sierra Maestra during the Revolutionary War. There are lesser-known photos here too, from dramatic scenes during the Bay of Pigs invasion and the Cuban Missile Crisis to a picture of Castro and a tiger at the Bronx Zoo.

Fiction

Edmundo Desnoes *Memories of Underdevelopment* (Rutgers University Press). In this novel set in 1961 the jaded narrator takes the reader through early revolutionary Cuba after his family has fled for Miami. Its bleak tone and unflinching observations are in stark contrast to the euphoric portrayal of the era generally offered by the state.

Alejandro Hernández Díaz *La Milla* (Pinos Nuevos, Cuba). A short novel about two men who try to make the ninety-mile journey from Cuba across the Florida Straits to the US. Thought-provoking and relatively accessible to non-native speakers.

James Ferguson (ed) *Traveller's Literary Companion: The Caribbean* (In Print Publishing Ltd, UK; Passport, US). This literary anthology's chapter on Cuba is an erudite introduction, blending the most renowned, respected and revealing writers on Cuba, both national and international. Among the nineteen diverse extracts literary giants Ernest Hemingway and Guillermo Cabrera Infante are represented, alongside lesser-known authors including Edmundo Desnoes and seminal Cuban poet Nicolás Guillén.

Cristina García *Dreaming in Cuban* (Ballantine, US). Shot through with wit, García's moving novel about a Cuban family divided by the Revolution captures the state of mind of the exile in the States and beautifully describes a magical and idiosyncratic Cuba.

Graham Greene *Our Man in Havana* (Penguin). Greene's atmospheric 1958 classic is a satirical romp through the world of espionage and despotic duplicity in the run-up to the Revolution. Unequalled entertainment.

Pedro Juan Gutierrez *Dirty Havana Trilogy* (Faber & Faber, UK). Disturbingly sexy and compelling, this is the story of life under Castro through the eyes of poverty-stricken Gutierrez. Unlikely to ever be acclaimed by the Cuban Tourist Board, this book is as candid as it gets, airing untold stories of vice and poverty in the heart of Cuba. Very, very dirty.

Ernest Hemingway *To Have and Have Not; The Old Man and the Sea* (both Arrow, UK; Scribner, US). The first is a stark novel full of racial tension and undercurrents of violence, with a plot concerning rum-running between Cuba and Key West in the 1930s. The second is the simple, powerful account of an epic battle between an old fisherman and a giant marlin. Set in Cuban waters and the fishing village of Cojímar, this novella won Hemingway the Nobel Prize for literature in 1954.

Pico Iyer *Cuba and the Night* (Quartet Books, UK; Vintage, US). Against a backdrop of the Special Period Iyer's bleak and claustrophobic tale of a jaded Western man's affair with a Cuban woman captures the pessimism, cynicism and ambiguity of such relationships in Cuba.

Ana Menendez *In Cuba I Was a German Shepherd* (Headline Book Publishing, UK). Set in the nether land between Miami and Havana inhabited by displaced Cubans, this collection of short stories comprises sensitive and achingly melancholic accounts of jealous husbands, old dreamers and fading wives. Menendez is skilled in evoking the nostalgia felt by old Cubans pining for a lost homeland and that of a generation of young US Cubans living in the shadow of a never-seen Shangri-la. A promising debut.

Leonardo Padura *Havana Red; Havana Black; Havana Blue* (all Bitter Lemon Press, UK). Published a decade ago but only recently translated into English, these award-winning detective novels broke new ground in Cuba with their gritty and very real depictions of Havana life and their flawed protagonist, Lieutenant Mario Conde, revitalizing a genre characterized previously by party line-towing plots and detectives. Like in all the best crime fiction, the plots in these stories serve as a vehicle for exploring the human condition as much as for creating suspense.

Juana Ponce de León and Esteban Ríos Rivera (eds) *Dream with No Name* (Seven Stories Press). A poignant and revealing collection of contemporary short stories by writers living in Cuba and in exile. Mixing the established talent of Alejo Carpentier, Reinaldo Arenas and Onelio Jorge Cardoso with the younger generation of writers represented by Jacqueline Herranz Brooks and Angel Santiesteban Prats, the anthology covers a diversity of subjects from rural life in the 1930s to lesbian love in modern Cuba.

Language

Language

Language

A fter the collapse of trade with the Soviet Union, English replaced Russian as the second language of Cuba. However, relatively few Cubans speak English fluently, many not at all. This won't stop some people from trying to practise what they know with anyone willing to listen, and shouts of "My friend" or "Where you from, man?" echo incessantly around the streets of Habana Vieja.

Learning a few basic phrases in Spanish will prove invaluable, especially if you use public transport, when asking for information is the only way you'll get any. Cuban Spanish bears a noticeable resemblance to the pronunciation and vernacular of the Canary Islands, one of the principal sources of Cuban immigration during the colonial era. Students of Castilian Spanish may find themselves a little thrown by all the variations in basic vocabulary in Cuba. Though the language is full of Anglicisms and Americanisms, like *carro* instead of *coche* for car, or *queic* instead of *tarta* for cake, the Castilian equivalents are generally recognized and making yourself understood should be easier than understanding other people yourself. Things aren't helped any by the common Cuban habit of dropping the final letters of words and changing the frequently used -ado ending on words to -ao.

Despite these areas of confusion, the rules of pronunciation for all forms of Spanish are straightforward and the basic Latin American model applies in Cuba. Unless there's an accent, all words ending in d, l, r and z are stressed on the last syllable, all others on the second last. All vowels are pure and short.

a somewhere between the A sound in "back" and that in "father".

e as in "get".

i as in "police".

o as in "hot".

u as in "rule".

c is soft before E and I, hard otherwise: *cerca* is pronounced "serka".

g works the same way: a guttural H sound (like the ch in "loch") before E or I, a hard G elsewhere: *gigante* becomes "higante".

h is always silent.

j is the same sound as a guttural G: *jamón* is pronounced "hamon".

ll is pronounced as a Y: *lleno* is therefore pronounced "yeno".

n is as in English, unless it has a tilde (accent) over it, when it becomes NY: *mañana* sounds like "manyana".

qu is pronounced like the English K.

r is, technically speaking, not rolled but you will frequently hear this rule contradicted.

rr is rolled.

v sounds more like B: *vino* becomes "beano".

z is the same as a soft C: *cerveza* is thus "servesa".

Idiom and slang

Cuban Spanish is rich in idiosyncratic words and phrases, many borrowed from English, often misinterpreted and given their own unique slant, with some comic-sounding results for native English-speakers. Far from being a bastardization of English or Castilian Spanish, however, language in Cuba is as heterogeneous as the history and culture that spawned it, with notable influences from the West African languages brought over through the slave trade and, more recently, the involvement of the US in the island. Some of the slang is common to other Latin American countries, particularly Puerto Rico, whilst there are all sorts of *cubanismos* unique to the island.

Basic Cuban vocabulary

A number of everyday Cuban words, particularly for items of clothing, differ completely from their Castilian equivalent. These are not slang words, but equate to the same kind of differences that exist between North American and British English.

el blúmer	knickers	el overol	dungarees
la camiseta	vest	el pitusa	jeans
el carro	car	el pulover	T-shirt
el chubasquero	kagoule	el queik	cake
el chor	shorts	el saco	a suit
la guagua	bus	los tenis	trainers, sneakers
el jonrón	home run in baseball	el yin	jeans
el ómnibus	long-distance bus		

Popular expressions and slang

The following list of words is a cross section of some of the more often heard idiosyncrasies of Cuban Spanish and might be most useful to students and speakers of European Spanish. Some of the terms, such as *barbacoa*, have emerged because of uniquely Cuban practices, while others reflect aspects of Cuban culture, such as the destigmatization of referring to people by their skin colour or racial characteristics.

Asere A commonly heard term, similar to "mate" or "buddy", but often used as an exclamation.

Barbacoa The term given to the popular Cuban practice of creating two rooms from one by building in a floor halfway up the wall.

Bárbaro/a Used both as an adjective and a noun to refer to something or someone as outstanding, but also used as a way of saying "Excellent!" or "That's great!"

Baro Dollar or dollars.

Chance Literally "chance" and often heard in the expression *Dame un chance*, "Give me a chance!"

Chao A common way of saying goodbye.

Chino/a A person with facial characteristics commonly found in Chinese people.

Chivatón A grass, an informer.

Chopin Appropriation of the word "shopping", used to mean a dollar shop. *Voy a la chopin para comprarme un pitusa*, "I'm going to the dollar shop to buy myself some jeans".

Coger lucha To get stressed out or upset.

¿Cómo andas? How's it going?

Compañero/a Very popular expression since the 1959 Revolution, used by both young and old alike, and literally meaning "comrade" but equivalent to "friend", "mate" or "pal" and also acceptable as a formal address to a stranger.

Coño Often shortened to *ño*; equivalent in usage and vulgarity to "shit".

Cursí Roughly equivalent to "corny".

Empatarse To get it together with someone romantically or sexually.

En candela Messed up or useless.

Estar puesto/a To fancy or be attracted to someone. *¿Estás puesto pa' ella?*, "Do you fancy her?"

Fula Dollar or dollars.

Fulano/a So-and-so, what's-his/her-name; used to refer to someone without knowing or specifying their name. *Fulano me dijo …*, "So-and-so told me …".

Guapo A criminal or street hustler-type character.

Gusano/a A hostile term for a Cuban refugee; also denotes a counter-revolutionary.

¿Gusta?, ¿Gustas? Most commonly used to ask someone arriving at a meal, "Would you like some?"

Irse para afuera To go abroad.

Jabáo Describes a person with physical characteristics not usually found on people of that skin colour, eg a blond-haired person with thick, bushy eyebrows.

Maceta A player or hustler; indicates wealth acquired illegally.

Monada A pejorative term for a group of policemen.

Moña A general term for swing and hip-hop music.

Pa' Shortened version of para – *Voy pa' afuera.*

Papaya Tourists should be careful with this word, used as commonly to refer to female genitalia as to the fruit.

Pepe A tourist.

Pila A lot, a load. *Hay una pila de gente aqui*, "There's a load of people here".

Pinga Literally "penis", but commonly heard in the expression *De pinga*, meaning "Fuck off!" or "Shit!". *Está de pinga* can mean either "It's shit" or "It's superb", depending on the way it's used.

Prieto/a Dark-skinned.

¿Qué bolá? "What's up?", "How's it going?"

Socio/a Equivalent to "mate" or "buddy".

¿Te cuadra? "Does that suit you?"

Tonga A lot.

Trigueño/a Light-brown-skinned.

Voy echando "I'm out of here", "I'm off".

Ya Has a number of meanings but is frequently heard as a form of agreement, equivalent to *vale* in Spain.

Yuma Foreigner.

Yunta Close friend.

Spanish language basics

Essentials

Sí	Yes	Con	With
No	No	Sin	Without
Por favor	Please	Buen(o)/a	Good
Gracias	Thank you	Mal(o)/a	Bad
Disculpe	Sorry	Grande	Big
Permiso or Perdón	Excuse me	Pequeño/a, chico/a	Small
Señor	Mr	Más	More
Señora	Mrs	Menos	Less
Señorita	Miss	Los servicios	The toilets
Aquí/acá	Here	Señoras	Ladies
Allí	There	Caballeros	Gentlemen
Esto	This	No entiendo	I don't understand
Eso	That	No hablo español	
Abierto/a	Open	Spanish	I don't speak
Cerrado/a	Closed	No sé	I don't know

Numbers and days

Un/uno/una	1		Setenta	70
Dos	2		Ochenta	80
Tres	3		Noventa	90
Cuatro	4		Cien(to)	100
Cinco	5		Ciento uno	101
Seis	6		Doscientos	200
Siete	7		Doscientos uno	201
Ocho	8		Quinientos	500
Nueve	9		Mil	1000
Diez	10		Dos mil	2000
Once	11		Primero/a	First
Doce	12		Segundo/a	Second
Trece	13		Tercero/a	Third
Catorce	14		Quarto/a	Fourth
Quince	15		Quinto/a	Fifth
Dieciséis	16		Lunes	Monday
Veinte	20		Martes	Tuesday
Veitiuno	21		Miércoles	Wednesday
Treinta	30		Jueves	Thursday
Cuarenta	40		Viernes	Friday
Cincuenta	50		Sábado	Saturday
Sesenta	60		Domingo	Sunday

Greetings and responses

Hola	Hello		Me llamo ...	My name is ...
Buenos dias	Good morning		¿Cómo se llama	What's your name?
Buenas tardes/ noches	Good afternoon/night		usted? or ¿Cómo te llamas? (informal)	
Adios/Chao	Goodbye		Soy inglés(a)	I am English
Hasta luego	See you later		americano(a)	... American
Mucho gusto	Pleased to meet you		australiano(a)	... Australian
¿Cómo está (usted)? or ¿Cómo andas? (informal)	How are you?		canadiense(a)	... Canadian
			irlandés(a)	... Irish
			escosés(a)	... Scottish
De nada/ por nada	Not at all/You're welcome		galés(a)	... Welsh
			neozelandés(a)	...a New Zealander

Asking directions, getting around and driving terms

¿Por dónde se va para llegar a...?	How do I get to...?		¿Está cerca/lejos?	Is it near/far?
¿A dónde nos lleva esta carretera?	Where does this road take us?		¿Qué distancia hay desde aquí hasta...?	How far is it from here to...?
¿Es esta la carretera para...?	Is this the right road to...?		¿Hay un hotel aquí cerca?	Is there a hotel nearby?

Doble a la izquierda/ derecha	Turn left/right
Siga todo derecho/ recto	Carry straight on
Frente/enfrente	Opposite
Al lado de	Next to
¿Dónde está…?	Where is…?
…el terminal de ómnibus	…the bus station
…la estación de ferrocarriles	…the train station
…el aeropuerto	…the airport
…la gasolinera más cercana	…the nearest petrol station
…el próximo pueblo	…the next town
¿De dónde sale la guagua para…?	Where does the bus to… leave from?
¿Cuándo es la próxima guagua para…?	When is the next bus to…?
¿Es está la parada para…?	Is this the stop for…?
¿Dónde hay buen lugar para coger botella?	Where is a good place to hitchhike?
¿Dónde puedo coger un taxi?	Where can I get a taxi?
Llévenos a esta dirección	Take us to this address

¿Es éste el tren para La Habana?	Is this the train for Havana?
Quisiera boleto/ pasaje (de ida y vuelta) para…	I'd like a (return) ticket to…?
¿A qué hora sale (llega a…)?	What time does it leave (arrive in…)?
Quisiera alquilar un carro	I'd like to rent a car
¿Está incluida la gasolina?	Is the petrol/ gasoline included?
Llénelo por favor	Fill it up please
¿Puede usted comprobar…?	Could you check…?
…el aceite	…the oil
…el agua	…the water
…los neumáticos	…tyres
Autopista	Motorway
Carretera principal	Main road
Bache	Pothole
Semáforo	Traffic light
Cruce	Crossroads
Crucero	Railway crossing
Mapa	Map
Carné de conducir	Driver's licence
Ceda el paso	Give way

Needs and asking questions

Quiero	I want
Quisiera	I'd like
¿Sabe…?	Do you know…?
(¿) Hay (?)	There is (is there)?
¿Cuánto cuesta?	How much is it?
¿Aceptan aquí tarjetasde crédito/ cheques de viajero?	Do you accept credit cards/traveller's cheques here?
Deme…	Give me…
(uno así)	(one like that)
¿Tiene …?	Do you have…?
¿Habla usted inglés?	Do you speak English?
Por favor, ¿Puede	Could you speak

usted hablar más despacio?	slower please?
¿Qué quiere decir esto?	What does this mean?
Por favor, ¿Me puede ayudar?	Can you help me please?
¿Dónde…?	Where…?
¿Cuándo…?	When…?
¿Qué…?	What…?
¿Qué es eso?	What's that?
¿Qué hay para comer?	What is there to eat?
¿Como se llama esto en español?	What's this called in Spanish?

Time

¿Qué hora es?	What time is it?
Es la una	It's one o'clock
Son las dos	It's two o'clock
Dos y cuarto	Quarter past two
Dos y media	Half past two
Tres menos cuarto	Quarter to three

Ahora	Now	Esta noche	Tonight
Más tarde or después	Later	Mañana	Tomorrow
La mañana	The morning	Ayer	Yesterday
La tarde	The afternoon	Un día	A day
La noche	The night	Una semana	A week
Hoy	Today	Un mes	A month

Accommodation

¿Tiene una habitación?	Do you have a room?	¿No tiene algo más barato?	Don't you have anything cheaper?
...con dos camas/ cama matrimonial	...with two beds/ double bed	¿Se puede...?	Can one... ?
...con vista al mar	...facing the sea	¿...acampar aqui (cerca)?	...camp (near) here?
...con vista a la calle	...facing the street	No funciona el televisor/el radio	The TV/radio doesn't work
...en la planta baja	...on the ground floor	Carpeta or recepción	Reception
...en el primer piso	...on the first floor	Llave	Key
Hemos reservado una habitación doble	We have booked a double room	Piscina	Swimming pool
es para una persona/ dos personas	It's for one person/ two people	Servicio de habitación	Room service
		Servicio de lavandería	Laundry service
...para una noche	...for one night	Baño	Toilet/bathroom
Está bien, cuánto es?	It's fine, how much is it?	Balcón	Balcony
Es demasiada...	It's too...	Caja de seguridad	Safety deposit box
...cara	...expensive	Aire acondicionado	Air conditioning
...oscura	...dark	Ventilador	Fan
...ruidosa	...noisy	Agua caliente	Hot water

Cuban menu reader

Food and restaurant basics

Aceite	Oil	Desayuno	Breakfast
Ají	Chilli	Ensalada	Salad
Ajo	Garlic	Entrantes	Starters
Almuerzo	Lunch	Entremeses	Starters
Arroz	Rice	Guarnición	Side dishes
Azúcar	Sugar	Huevos	Eggs
Bocadillo/Bocadito	Sandwich	Huevos fritos	Fried eggs
Cena	Dinner	Huevos hervidos	Boiled eggs
Cereal	Cereal	Huevos revoltillos	Scrambled eggs
Combinaciones	Set meals	Mantequilla	Butter or margarine
Comidas ligeras	Light foods	Mermelada	Jam (UK); jelly (US)
Cuenta	Bill	Miel	Honey

Mostaza	Mustard	Sal	Salt
Pan	Bread	Sopa	Soup
Pimienta	Pepper	Tortilla	Omlette
Platos combinados	Set meals	Tostada	Toast
Potaje	Soup	Vinagre	Vinegar
Queso	Cheese		

Table items

Botella	Bottle	Mesa	Table
Carta	Menu	Servieta	Napkin
Cuchara	Spoon	Tenedor	Fork
Cuchillo	Knife	Vaso	Glass

Cooking styles

A la brasa	Braised	Estofado/a	Stewed/braised
A la jardinera	With tomato sauce	Frito/a	Fried
A la parrilla	Grilled	Guisado/a	Stewed
A la plancha	Grilled	Grillé	Grilled
Agridulce	Sweet and sour	Hervido/a	Boiled
Ahumado/a	Smoked	Lonjas	Slices/strips
Al horno	Baked	Poco cocinado/a	Rare (meat)
Asado/a	Roast	Regular	Medium (meat)
Bien cocido/a	Well done (meat)	Revoltillo	Scrambled
Crudo/a	Raw	Tostado/a	Toasted
Empanadilla	Puff pastry/pie		
Enchilado/a	Cooked in tomato sauce		

Cuban dishes

Bistec Uruguayo	Steak covered in cheese and breadcrumbs	Lechón	Roast pork suckling
		Moros y cristianos	Rice and black beans
Chicharrones	Fried pork skin/pork scratchings	Palomilla	Steak fried or grilled with lime and garlic
Congrí	Rice and red beans (mixed)	Ropa vieja	Shredded stewed beef
		Tasajo	Shredded and jerked stewed beef
Langosta enchilada	Lobster in a tomato sauce	Tostones	Fried plantains

Fish (pescados) and seafood (mariscos)

Aguja	Swordfish	Calamares	Squid
Anchoas	Anchovies	Camarones	Prawns, shrimp
Arenque	Herring	Cangrejo	Crab
Atún	Tuna	Langosta	Lobster
Bacalao	Cod	Merluza	Hake

Pargo	Red snapper (tilapia)	Tetí	Small fish, local to
Pulpo	Octopus		Baracoa
Salmón	Salmon	Trucha	Trout

Meat (carne) and poultry (aves)

Albóndigas	Meatballs	Lomo	Loin (of pork)
Bacon	Bacon	Oveja	Mutton
Bistec	Steak	Pavo	Turkey
Brocheta	Kebab	Pato	Duck
Buey	Beef	Pechuga	Breast
Cabra/Chivo	Goat	Picadillo	Mince
Carnero	Mutton	Pierna	Leg
Cerdo	Pork	Pollo	Chicken
Chorizo	Spicy sausage	Rana	Frog's meat
Chuleta	Chop	Res	Beef
Conejo	Rabbit	Ropa vieja	Shredded beef
Cordero	Lamb	Salchichas	Sausages
Costillas	Ribs	Sesos	Brains
Escalope	Escalope	Solomillo	Sirloin
Hamburguesa	Hamburger	Ternera	Veal
Hígado	Liver	Tocino	Bacon
Jamón	Ham	Venado	Venison
Lacón	Smoked pork		

Fruits (frutas)

Albaricoque	Apricot	Mango	Mango
Almendra	Almond	Maní	Peanut
Avellana	Hazelnut	Manzana	Apple
Cereza	Cherry	Melocotón	Peach
Ciruelas	Prunes	Melón	Melon (usually
Coco	Coconut		Watermelon)
Fresa	Strawberry	Naranja	Orange
Fruta bomba	Papaya	Pera	Pear
Guanábana	Soursop	Piña	Pineapple
Guayaba	Guava	Plátano	Banana
Lima	Lime	Toronja	Grapefruit
Limón	Lime/Lemon	Uvas	Grapes
Mamey	Mamey (thick, sweet		
	red fruit with a single		
	stone)		

Vegetables (verduras/vegetales)

Aguacate	Avocado	Cebolla	Onion
Berenjenas	Aubergine/eggplant	Chícaro	Pea (pulse)
Boniato	Sweet potato	Col	Cabbage
Calabaza	Pumpkin	Esparragos	Asparagus

Frijoles	Black beans	Pepino	Cucumber
Garbanzos	Chickpeas	Pimiento	Capsicum pepper
Habichuela	String beans/green beans	Quimbombo	Okra
		Rábano	Radish
Hongos	Mushrooms	Remolacha	Beetroot
Lechuga	Lettuce	Tamale	Local dish made with steamed cornflour
Malanga	Starchy tubular vegetable		
		Tomate	Tomato
Papa	Potato	Yuca	Cassava
Papas fritas	French fries	Zanahoria	Carrot

Sweets (dulces) and desserts (postres)

Arroz con leche	Rice pudding	Jimaguas	Two scoops of ice cream
Churros	Long curls of fried batter similar to doughnuts	Queso	Cheese
		Merengue	Meringue
Cocos	Sweets made from shredded coconut and sugar	Natilla	Custard/Milk pudding
		Pasta de Guayaba	Guava jam
...en almíbar	in syrup	Pay	Pie (fruit)
Galleta	Biscuit/cookie	Pudín	Crème caramel or hard-set flan
Empanada de Guayaba	Guava jam in pastry		
		Tortica	Shortbread-type biscuit
Flan	Crème caramel		
Helado	Ice cream	Tres gracias	Three scoops of ice cream

Rums (rones) and cocktails (cocteles)

Cuba libre	Rum and coke	Presidente	White rum, curaçao, grenadine and sweet white vermouth
Cubanito	White rum, lemon juice, salt, Worcester sauce, hot sauce and crushed ice		
		Ron...	
		...añejo	Dark rum, aged seven years
Daiquirí	White rum, white sugar, lemon juice and crushed ice	...carta blanca (Ron blanco)	White rum, aged three years
Daiquirí Frappé	White rum, maraschino (cherry liqueur), white sugar, lemon juice and crushed ice	...carta oro	Dark rum, aged five years
		...gran reserva	Dark rum, aged fifteen years
Habana Especial	White rum, maraschino, pineapple juice and ice	Ron Collins	White rum, lemon juice, white sugar and soda
Mulata	Dark rum, white sugar, lemon juice and cacao liqueur		

L

LANGUAGE | Cuban menu reader

Other drinks (bebidas)

Agua	Water	Leche	Milk
Agua mineral	Mineral water	Limonada natural	Lemonade (fresh)
...(con gas)	...(sparkling)	Prú	Fermented drink flavoured with spices
...(sin gas)	...(still)		
Batido	Milkshake	Refresco	Pop/Fizzy drink
Café	Coffee	Refresco de lata	Canned pop
Café con leche	Coffee made with hot milk	Té	Tea
		Vino tinto	Red wine
Cerveza	Beer	Vino blanco	White wine
Chocolate caliente	Drinking chocolate	Vino rosado	Rosé wine
Ginebra	Gin	Vodka	Vodka
Jerez	Sherry	Whisky	Whisky
Jugo	Juice		

Glossary

Agromercado A peso market selling fresh produce.

Apagón A blackout.

Artesanía Arts and crafts.

Asere mate/pal.

Autopista Motorway. There is only one motorway in Cuba, running most of the length of the country, referred to as el autopista or marked on maps as Autopista Nacional.

Balneario Health spa.

Barro Dollar or dollars, eg Tres barro.

Bicitaxi Three-wheeled bicycle taxi.

Bodega A peso general store only open to those with a corresponding state-issue ration book.

Bohío Thatched hut as made and lived in by pre-Columbian peoples on the island.

Bolsa Negra Black market.

Buceo Diving.

Cabildo Town council during the colonial era.

Cambio Bureau de change.

Camello Juggernaut-style bus.

Camión Truck. Often *camiones* work interprovincial routes in lieu of state buses when there are petrol shortages.

Campismo Cuban equivalent to a campsite, usually with concrete cabins rather than tents.

Carné de Identidad Identity card.

Carretera Highway; main road.

Carro Car.

Casa comisionista Cuban equivalent to a pawnbrokers.

Casa de Cambio Often "kiosk" but sometimes more like "bank", this is for the express purpose of changing dollars into pesos.

Casa particular House with one or more rooms available to rent to tourists.

CDR (Committee for the Defence of the Revolution) Neighbourhood-watch schemes devised to root out counter-revolutionaries.

Ciclotaxi See Bicitaxi.

Cimarón Escaped slave.

Coger Botella To hitchhike.

Cola Queue.

Comida criolla Traditional Cuban food.

Cordillera Mountain range.

Criollo/a A pre-independence term to describe a Cuban-born Spanish person; also used to describe something as specifically or traditionally Cuban.

Días alternos Every other day (used on bus and train timetables).

Divisa Hard currency or US dollars.

Embalse Reservoir.

En efectivo In cash.

Finca Ranch; country estate.

Guagua Local bus.

Guajiro/a Rural person; sometimes used to express a lack of education or sophistication.

Guardabolso Cloakroom for bags, usually at the entrance to dollar shops.

Guayabera A lightweight shirt, often with four pockets.

Habanero/a A native of Havana.

Habanos Cuban cigars.

Humidor Box for storing and preserving cigars.

Ingenio Sugar refinery.

Jinetera Sometimes used to mean prostitute but generally refers to any woman using tourists for material or financial gain.

Jinetero Male hustler who specifically targets tourists.

Malecón Seaside promenade.

Mambí, Mambíses Member of the nineteenth-century rebel army fighting for independence from Spain.

Mirador Place, usually at the top of a hill or mountain, from where there are good views.

Mogote Boulder-like hills found only in Pinar del Río, particularly in Viñales.

Moneda Nacional National currency (pesos).

Municipio Political division of a city equivalent to a borough or electoral district.

Orisha A deity in Afro-Cuban religions like Santería.

Paladar Restaurant run in the owner's home.

Palenque A hideout or settlement occupied by runaway slaves during the colonial period.

Peninsular/es Spanish-born person living in Cuba prior to independence.

Pizarra Switchboard.

Playa Beach.

Ponchera Puncture repair and bicycle maintenance, usually privately run from a shed or the front room of a house.

Posada Establishment renting rooms for couples to have sex in.

Reparto Neighbourhood or area of a city. Also apartment blocks mainly built since the Revolution.

Sala de video Sometimes a state-run venue but more often a room in a house where films are shown on a video.

Taller Workshop.

Taxi colectivo A shared taxi, often run more like a bus service.

Trapiche Machine used to press sugar cane.

Vega Tobacco farm.

Veguero Tobacco farmer.

Villa Village complex.

Vitrales Arched stained-glass windows, unique to Cuba.

Zafra The sugar harvest.

Travel
store

D Rough Guide
DIRECTIONS for
short breaks

Available from all good bookstores

ROUGH GUIDES

Complete Listing

Small print and
Index

A Rough Guide to Rough Guides

Published in 1982, the first Rough Guide – to Greece – was a student scheme that became a publishing phenomenon. Mark Ellingham, a recent graduate in English from Bristol University, had been travelling in Greece the previous summer and couldn't find the right guidebook. With a small group of friends he wrote his own guide, combining a highly contemporary, journalistic style with a thoroughly practical approach to travellers' needs.

The immediate success of the book spawned a series that rapidly covered dozens of destinations. And, in addition to impecunious backpackers, Rough Guides soon acquired a much broader and older readership that relished the guides' wit and inquisitiveness as much as their enthusiastic, critical approach and value-for-money ethos.

These days, Rough Guides include recommendations from shoestring to luxury and cover more than 200 destinations around the globe, including almost every country in the Americas and Europe, more than half of Africa and most of Asia and Australasia. Our ever-growing team of authors and photographers is spread all over the world, particularly in Europe, the USA and Australia.

In the early 1990s, Rough Guides branched out of travel, with the publication of Rough Guides to World Music, Classical Music and the Internet. All three have become benchmark titles in their fields, spearheading the publication of a wide range of books under the Rough Guide name.

Including the travel series, Rough Guides now number more than 350 titles, covering: phrasebooks, waterproof maps, music guides from Opera to Heavy Metal, reference works as diverse as Conspiracy Theories and Shakespeare, and popular culture books from iPods to Poker. Rough Guides also produce a series of more than 120 World Music CDs in partnership with World Music Network.

Visit www.roughguides.com to see our latest publications.

Rough Guide travel images are available for commercial licensing at www.roughguidespictures.com.

Rough Guide credits

Text editor: Amy Hegarty
Layout: Anita Singh
Cartography: Ashutosh Bharti
Picture editor: Mark Thomas
Production: Aimee Hampson
Proofreader: Karen Parker
Cover design: Chloë Roberts
Photographer: Lydia Evans
Editorial: **London** Kate Berens, Claire
Saunders, Ruth Blackmore, Polly Thomas,
Alison Murchie, Karoline Densley, Andy
Turner, Keith Drew, Edward Aves, Nikki Birrell,
Alice Park, Sarah Eno, Lucy White, Jo Kirby,
Samantha Cook, James Smart, Natasha Foges,
Roísín Cameron, Emma Traynor, Emma Gibbs,
Joe Staines, Duncan Clark, Peter Buckley,
Matthew Milton, Tracy Hopkins, Ruth Tidball;
New York Andrew Rosenberg, Steven Horak,
AnneLise Sorensen, April Isaacs, Ella Steim,
Anna Owens, Joseph Petta, Sean Mahoney;
Delhi Madhavi Singh, Karen D'Souza
Design & Pictures: **London** Scott Stickland,
Dan May, Diana Jarvis, Jj Luck, Chloë Roberts,
Nicole Newman, Sarah Cummins; **Delhi** Umesh
Aggarwal, Ajay Verma, Jessica Subramanian,
Ankur Guha, Pradeep Thapliyal, Sachin Tanwar,
Nikhil Agarwal
Production: Vicky Baldwin
Cartography: **London** Maxine Repath, Ed
Wright, Katie Lloyd-Jones; **Delhi** Jai Prakash
Mishra, Rajesh Chhibber, Rajesh Mishra,
Animesh Pathak, Jasbir Sandhu, Karobi Gogoi,
Amod Singh, Alakananda Bhattacharya, Swati
Handoo
Online: **New York** Jennifer Gold, Kristin
Mingrone; **Delhi** Manik Chauhan, Narender
Kumar, Rakesh Kumar, Amit Verma, Rahul Kumar,
Ganesh Sharma, Debojit Borah
Marketing & Publicity: **London** Liz Statham,
Niki Hanmer, Louise Maher, Jess Carter, Vanessa
Godden, Vivienne Watton, Anna Paynton, Rachel
Sprackett; **New York** Geoff Colquitt, Megan
Kennedy, Katy Ball; **Delhi** Reem Khokhar
Manager India: Punita Singh
Series Editor: Mark Ellingham
Reference Director: Andrew Lockett
Publishing Coordinator: Helen Phillips
Publishing Director: Martin Dunford
Commercial Manager: Gino Magnotta
Managing Director: John Duhigg

Publishing information

This fourth edition published August 2007 by
Rough Guides Ltd,
80 Strand, London WC2R 0RL
345 Hudson St, 4th Floor,
New York, NY 10014, USA
14 Local Shopping Centre, Panchsheel Park,
New Delhi 110017, India
Distributed by the Penguin Group
Penguin Books Ltd,
80 Strand, London WC2R 0RL
Penguin Group (USA)
375 Hudson Street, NY 10014, USA
Penguin Group (Australia)
250 Camberwell Road, Camberwell,
Victoria 3124, Australia
Penguin Books Canada Ltd,
10 Alcorn Avenue, Toronto, Ontario,
Canada M4V 1E4
Penguin Group (NZ)
67 Apollo Drive, Mairangi Bay, Auckland 1310,
New Zealand

Cover concept by Peter Dyer.
Typeset in Bembo and Helvetica to an original
design by Henry Iles.
Printed in Europe
© Fiona McAuslan and Matt Norman 2007

680pp includes index
A catalogue record for this book is available from
the British Library
ISBN: 978-1-84353-811-0

The publishers and authors have done their
best to ensure the accuracy and currency of all
the information in **The Rough Guide to Cuba**,
however, they can accept no responsibility for
any loss, injury or inconvenience sustained by
any traveller as a result of information or advice
contained in the guide.

1 3 5 7 9 8 6 4 2

Help us update

We've gone to a lot of effort to ensure that the
fourth edition of **The Rough Guide to Cuba** is
accurate and up to date. However, things change
– places get "discovered", opening hours are
notoriously fickle, restaurants and rooms raise
prices or lower standards. If you feel we've got it
wrong or left something out, we'd like to know,
and if you can remember the address, the price,
the time, the phone number, so much the better.
We'll credit all contributions, and send a copy
of the next edition (or any other Rough Guide
if you prefer) for the best letters. Everyone who
writes to us and isn't already a subscriber will
receive a copy of our full-colour thrice-yearly
newsletter. Please mark letters: "**Rough Guide
Cuba Update**" and send to: Rough Guides, 80
Strand, London WC2R 0RL, or Rough Guides,
345 Hudson St, 4th Floor, New York, NY 10014.
Or send an email to **mail@roughguides.com**.
    Have your questions answered and tell others
about your trip at
www.roughguides.atinfopop.com.

SMALL PRINT

Acknowledgements

Fiona McAuslan: Thank you to Maruchi and family in Santiago, Barbara and co in Holguin and Yoel in Trinidad for making the job a pleasure not a chore. In Havana, the biggest thanks to Maurisio and family for assistance beyond the call of duty. Finally, love and thanks to Marcus for your contrasting viewpoints. I hope that one day you'll love Cuba as much as I do.

Matt Norman: In Havana, much love and appreciation to the family, Miriam, Sinaí, Ricardo and Hildegard, and a huge thank you to Nimueh for all her hard work; love also to Hector, Etienn (for his help with the sports information) and the rest of *el piquete*; and thanks to Marta for the radio stuff. In Cienfuegos, thanks to Jorge Piñeiro for his generosity and to Armando and Leonor for their warmth and hospitality. In Santa Clara, thanks to Omelio and Mercy for their usual kindness and helpfulness. Thanks also to Lili at Cubatur in Trinidad; to Freddy

Ramirez at Las Terrazas; to Abel Rojas Valdés on the Península de Guanahacabibes; to Igor Caballero at the Cuban Embassy in London and to Annie McDonald and Tim Webb for being great company. Finally, a huge hug and thanks to Cath, my sister, for her help, patience and forgivingness and for being there to laugh with.

The **authors** would also like to thank Andrew Rosenberg, AnneLise Sorensen and in particular Amy Hegarty at Rough Guides for being a great team to work with.

The **editor** would like to thank Matt Norman and Fiona McAuslan for their great work, as well as Anita Singh, Umesh Aggarwal, Mark Thomas, Ashutosh Bharti, Maxine Repath, Katie Lloyd-Jones, Karen Parker, Lydia Evans, Emma Traynor, Diana Jarvis, Chloë Roberts, Aimee Hampson, Seph Petta, AnneLise Sorensen and Andrew Rosenberg.

Readers' letters

Thanks to all the readers who have taken the time to write in with comments and suggestions (and apologies if we've inadvertently omitted or misspelt anyone's name):

Martine Adesioye, Sabine Altendorf, Amanda Ariss, Tero Auralinna, Abena Baffoe, Nicholas Bailey, Sue Barber, Michael Barrett, Eloïse Benecke-Scott, Florence Bernard, Radana Bernatova, Ute Bernet, Christopher Blackman, Ian Blaikie, Josef Bonkamp, Joel Bonnet, Frank Brannigan, Paul Brookes, Elisabeth Brown, Russell Brown, Simon Brown, Juan Carbonell, Martin Carr, Andrew Carver, Ethan Casady, Judith Ciotti, Lynn Clark, Andrew Clarke, Caroline Clarke, Steve Cleary, Elizabeth Cooper, William Cottle, Nicola Crompton, Peter S. Dewar, Michele Di Maio, Peter Drehmanns, Marie Ericsson, Lynda Fleming, Alison Foot, Mike Forrester, Christiane Franz, Ian A. Fraser, Justus Fritsch, Dr Ernesto García, Marisol Garcia, Sabine Gebele, Scott Hahn, Phil Harrison, Tony Harrison, Robert Harvey, Helen Haworth, Nelson Hermilla,

Yamelis Elizalde Hernandez, Victoria Herriott, Peter Hiscock, Frank Horwich, Marie-Claude Horwich, Simon Hurley, Alan Jenkins, Joanna Jones, Patricia Kandelaars, Peter Lawrence, Anna Lee, Federico C. Llanes Regueiro, Yvonne Lloyd, Wilma Lock, Peter Mackridge, Chris Manthorp, Chris Merkel, Felix Michl, Jane Muris, Terry Murphy, Benjamin Nande, Sam Naylor, Sarah Newton, Stefano Nicoletti, Paddy O'Brien, Pascal O'Neill, Gloria Ortiz-Tejonero, Julio Padilla, Jacqueline Phillips, Philip Pool, Consuelo Ramos Rodriguez, Ganapathi Reddy, Robert S. Reid, Mireya Rodriguez, Yvon Rotink, Hans Rysdyk, Tim SanJule, Minna Schendlinger, Ashley Seaman, John Shipton, Marc Struyvelt, Huw Thomas, Chiara Toglia, Alex Tuck, Darren Utting, Gerrit van Essen, Marc Warne, Carolyn Waudby, Roger Wilson, Richard Woolf, Tom Zagon

Photo credits

All photos © Rough Guides except the following:

Introduction
Man with instrument © Angelo Cavalli/Getty Images
Street art © Marcus Ludewig
Café in Havana © Jenny Acheson/Axiom
Fidel Castro © David Hume Kennerly/Getty Images

Things not to miss
02 Baracoa © James Sparshatt/Axiom
08 Street party © Jenny Acheson/Axiom
09 Baseball © Kevin Fletcher/Corbis
10 Carnival in Santiago © John Harden/Robert Harding Picture Library/Alamy
11 Diving © WaterFrame/Alamy
13 Salsa lessons © Lydia Evans
18 Valle de los Ingenios © David Norton/Alamy
20 Che memorial © SAS/Alamy
23 Birdwatching in Zapata © Melba Photo Agency/Alamy
25 *Tropicana* © Ellen Rooney/Alamy

Colour section: Coastal Cuba
Chairs on beach © Anne-Marie Weber/Getty Images
Santa María del Mar beach © Jurgen Vogt/Getty Images
Boat and pelicans © Wilmar Photography/Alamy
Diving © WaterFrame/Alamy

Colour section: Cuban music and dance
Cabaret dancing © Donald Nausbaum/Alamy
Jazz band © Adam Eastland/Alamy

Black and whites
p.212 María la Gorda © isifa Image Services s.r.o/Alamy
p.361 Cayo Las Brujas © Alicia Clarke/Alamy
p.448 Playa Guardalavaca © Eric James/Alamy
p.467 Holguín © Peter Horree/Alamy
p.471 Volleyball on Playa Guardalavaca
p.490 El Yunque © Peter M. Wilson/Alamy
p.534 The Sierra Maestra © Philippe Roy/Alamy
p.550 Cayo Largo beach © F.R./Alamy
p.569 Cave painting in Punta del Este © Melba Photo Agency/Alamy
p.574 People on Cayo Largo beach © Gimmi/ CuboImages srl/Alamy
p.594 Fidel Castro © Dmitri Batlermants/The Dmitri Baltermants Collection/Corbis
p.598 Ernesto "Che" Guevara © Madeleine Repond/Corbis
p.615 Disco © Rolf Brenner/Alamy

SMALL PRINT

Selected images from our guidebooks are available for licensing from:

ROUGHGUIDESPICTURES.COM

Index

Map entries are in colour.

I

J

INDEX

Y

Z

W

INDEX

❶

Map symbols

maps are listed in the full index using coloured text

ˑˑ —	Provincial boundary	◉	Accommodation
– – –	Chapter boundary	◼	Restaurant/*paladar*
▬▬	Motorway	🛢	Fuel station
═══	Road	🅿	Parking
——	Dirt road	ⓘ	Tourist information office
⫿⫿⫿	Steps	☎	Telephone office
- - - -	Footpath	@	Internet
——	Waterway	⊠	Post office
▬▬●	Railway	⊞	Hospital
▲	Peak	♦	Museum
〰	Mountain range	♙	Castle
⌒	Cave	☉	Statue/memorial
⋎	Viewpoint	⅏	Ruins/archeological site
⚘	Turtle nesting site	⬭	Stadium
🗼	Lighthouse	▬	Building
✈	Airport	⊹	Church (town maps)
♦	Point of interest	▦	Park
⛳	Golf course	⬚	Mangrove swamp
⚲	Gardens	▤	Marsh
⛌	Military checkpoint	⬚	Beach
⬠	Shelter/lodge	⊤₊	Cemetery
⛺	Campsite/*campismo*